Joel Whitburn's ROCK TRACKS

**Mainstream Rock
1981-2002**

**Modern Rock
1988-2002**

Bonus Section!

**Classic Rock Tracks
1964-1980**

Billboard.

Compiled from *Billboard's* "Mainstream Rock Tracks" charts 1981-2002
and *Billboard's* "Modern Rock Tracks" charts 1988-2002.

ISBN 0-89820-153-5

Record Research Inc.
P.O. Box 200
Menomonee Falls, Wisconsin 53052-0200   U.S.A.

Phone: (262) 251-5408
Fax: (262) 251-9452
E-Mail: books@recordresearch.com
Web site: www.recordresearch.com

Dedication

In the summer of 1953, Bill Haley With Haley's Comets streaked across the pop charts with "Crazy Man, Crazy." This rockin' and rollin' little number hit position 12 and became the first rock 'n' roll song to make a deep impact on the mainstream pop charts. As the earliest of all "rock tracks," it helped blaze the trail for the imminent rock 'n' roll revolution.

Listen to this historic record at: www.recordresearch.com/haley.htm

The author wishes to extend a special note of thanks to:

The staff of Record Research....

Top: Joel Whitburn, Bill Hathaway, Jeanne Olynick, Kay Wagner; Middle: Frances Whitburn, Sue Hustad, Kim Bloxdorf, Paul Haney; Bottom: Brent Olynick, Nestor Vidotto

From pastime to passion to profitable enterprise, the growth of Record Research has been the outgrowth of Joel Whitburn's hobby. Joel began collecting records as a teenager in the 1950s. As his collection grew, he began to sort, categorize and file each record according to the highest position it reached on *Billboard's* Hot 100 charts. He went on to publish this information in 1970 and a business was born.

Today, Joel leads a team of researchers who delve into all of *Billboard's* music charts to an unmatched degree of depth and detail. Joel is widely recognized as the most authoritative historian on charted music. Joel's own record collection remains unrivaled the world over and includes every charted Hot 100 and pop single (back to 1920), every charted pop album (back to 1945), collections of nearly every charted Country, R&B, Bubbling Under The Hot 100 and Adult Contemporary record. Ever the consummate collector, Joel also owns one of the world's largest picture sleeve collections.

In person, this walking music encyclopedia stands 6'6" — a definite advantage when he played high school, college and semi-pro basketball. An avid sports fan, Joel actively engages in a wide variety of water, winter and motor sports. A native of Wisconsin, Joel has been married for 38 years to Fran, a native of Honduras; their daughter, Kim Bloxdorf, is part of the Record Research team, as are two of Joel's friends and key employees of 30 years, Bill Hathaway and Brent Olynick. Joel's lifelong passion for music, old and new, and his penchant for accurate detail continues into the 21st century.

CONTENTS

MAINSTREAM ROCK TRACKS

An alphabetical listing, by artist, of every track to chart on *Billboard's*
"Mainstream Rock Tracks" chart from March 21, 1981, through October 26, 2002.

A chronological listing, by peak date, of every title to top
Billboard's "Mainstream Rock Tracks" chart.

MODERN ROCK TRACKS

This second edition of **Rock Tracks** surveys the songs and artists played on rock radio over the past two decades. Rock's continual transformation and expanding popularity during those 21 years is chronicled here as it happened on *Billboard's* "Mainstream Rock Tracks" and "Modern Rock Tracks" charts. *Billboard* began charting album rock in 1981, just as the format experienced great growth. The following is a brief history of how album rock radio came to be.

Rock and roll arrived on the popular music scene in the 1950s over AM radio airwaves and on the 45 rpm single. The hit-making pioneers of rock and roll, such as Elvis Presley, Buddy Holly and Chuck Berry, released their hits as singles, initially; their token albums that followed were a hodge podge of hits and unreleased songs. Best-selling albums belonged to comedians, movie soundtracks, Broadway casts and stereo percussion.

In the mid-'60s, The Beatles ushered in the era of album-oriented rock (AOR) in 1967 with their phenomenally successful concept album *Sgt. Pepper's Lonely Heart's Club Band*. They introduced the long-play record as a suitable canvas for artistically themed rock. Rock mushroomed into a myriad of styles — acid, art, folk, glam, psychedelic, etc. — much of it too heavy for Top 40 AM radio. FM stations offered a broadcast outlet for artists such as Jimi Hendrix, Vanilla Fudge, MC5, Grateful Dead, Velvet Underground and The Stooges.

The '70s further cemented AOR's place on the radio dial. Bands like Led Zeppelin, Pink Floyd and Black Sabbath earned huge album sales and tremendous airplay success without following the pop formula of releasing singles and securing airplay on Top 40 stations. At the same time, more and more underground and college stations emerged, exposing cutting-edge rock bands such as the New York Dolls, Television, and The Ramones. These stations at the end of the dial kept pace with the punk revolution in Great Britain (Sex Pistols, the Slits, the Buzzcocks) and in Los Angeles (the Germs, Black Flag, X). (Punk would not sweep America until the 1990's.)

Billboard began monitoring the rising rock radio format now riding rock's "new wave" with the "Album Rock Tracks" chart in 1981, the year of the revolutionary debut of MTV. By the mid-'80s, the marriage of rock and video was evident with the immense popularity of flashy, glam-rock bands like Mötley Crüe and Poison. Bands once relegated to college radio (U2 and R.E.M.) bubbled up from the underground and into the mainstream, paving the way for bands like Sonic Youth, Meat Puppets and Dinosaur Jr.

By the late '80s, rock radio subdivided into classic rock or super rock (Aerosmith, Led Zeppelin, etc.) and alternative or "new" rock (Jane's Addiction and Morrissey). *Billboard* recognized this subformatting with the introduction of the "Modern Rock Tracks" chart in 1988.

In the years since, the power of rock radio has multiplied, making it a format that will likely be around for a long time. The pages to follow explore in great detail the rest of album rock's rousing history.

Kim Bloxdorf
Joel Whitburn

RESEARCHING BILLBOARD'S ROCK TRACKS CHARTS

This is the second edition of **Rock Tracks** which is compiled from *Billboard's* "Mainstream Rock Tracks" and "Modern Rock Tracks" charts. *Billboard* published its first rock tracks chart in 1981 and titled it simply "Top Tracks." It was a weekly Top 60 airplay chart compiled from rock radio as indicated by the nation's leading album-oriented and top track stations.

What is a track? In an article explaining this new chart, *Billboard's* Mike Harrison said "Quite simply, a track is an individual song played on the raw merits of its popularity regardless of its mechanical configuration (meaning regardless of whether it is a 45 rpm single, LP cut or whatever)." *Billboard* continues to regard a track by this same definition, although today's mechanical configuration is generally CD album tracks or CD singles.

Below is a brief history of both rock tracks charts:

MAINSTREAM ROCK TRACKS

DEBUT DATE	CHART TITLE	POSITIONS	NOTES
3/21/81	**TOP TRACKS**	60	Weekly chart; first #1 track: "I Can't Stand It" by Eric Clapton
9/15/84	**TOP ROCK TRACKS**	60	Chart title changed to include Rock
10/20/84	**TOP ROCK TRACKS**	50	Chart reduced to a Top 50
4/12/86	**ALBUM ROCK TRACKS**	50	Chart title changed to include Album
11/23/91	**ALBUM ROCK TRACKS**	50	Began using actual monitored airplay (Broadcast Data Systems*) only to compile the chart
6/27/92	**ALBUM ROCK TRACKS**	40	Chart reduced to a Top 40
4/13/96	**MAINSTREAM ROCK TRACKS**	40	Chart title changed to Mainstream

MODERN ROCK TRACKS

DEBUT DATE	CHART TITLE	POSITIONS	NOTES
9/10/88	**MODERN ROCK TRACKS**	30	Weekly chart; first #1 track: "Peek-A-Boo" by Siouxsie And The Banshees
6/12/93	**MODERN ROCK TRACKS**	30	Began using a combination of actual monitored airplay (Broadcast Data Systems*) and radio station playlists to compile the chart
1/22/94	**MODERN ROCK TRACKS**	30	Began using actual monitored airplay (Broadcast Data Systems*) only to compile the chart
9/10/94	**MODERN ROCK TRACKS**	40	Chart increased to a Top 40.

*BDS is a subsidiary of *Billboard* that electronically monitors actual radio airplay. They have installed monitors throughout the country which track the airplay of songs 24 hours a day, seven days a week. These monitors can identify each song played by an encoded audio "fingerprint."

The focal point of **Rock Tracks** is contained in two thoroughly researched artist sections. These sections contain all of the songs that hit the "Mainstream Rock Tracks" and "Modern Rock Tracks" charts, respectively. Each artist's charted tracks are listed in chronological order, but there are some exceptions. In addition to listing tracks chronologically, all tracks that charted from the same album are grouped together. Listing same-album tracks together takes precedence over chronological order.

EXPLANATION OF COLUMNAR HEADINGS

DEBUT: Date first charted

PEAK: Highest charted position (highlighted in bold type). All #1 tracks are identified by a special #1 symbol (**❶**).

WKS: Total weeks charted

Pop: Peak position achieved on *Billboard's* "Hot 100" or "Bubbling Under The Hot 100" Pop Charts (the weeks at #1 or #2 are shown as a superior number next to the Pop position). Also includes the peak position of non-Hot 100 hits from *Billboard's* "Hot 100 Airplay," "Hot 100 Sales" and "Christmas" singles charts.

Gld: ● RIAA-certified Gold album* (500,000 units sold) — refers to album listed to the right of symbol

       ▲ RIAA-certified Platinum album* (1,000,000 units sold — additional million units sold are indicated by a numeral following the symbol)

ALBUM TITLE: Title of the album from which the track attained its airplay appears in italics. If the track is from an album other than that artist's, then following the title in parentheses is the name of the album's artist or "various artists" for a compilation album by various artists or "soundtrack" for a soundtrack by various artists. Also, keep in mind that many tracks were later available on an artist's greatest hits or compilation album. Such an album is not listed unless, of course, it is the album from which the track attained its airplay.

       "(single only)" indicates the track is from a single release (7" or 12" vinyl, cassette or CD)

ALBUM LABEL & NUMBER: Original label and number of album

*The Recording Industry Association of America (RIAA) began certifying gold albums in 1958, platinum albums in 1976 and multi-platinum albums in 1984. Some record labels have never requested RIAA certifications for albums that would otherwise have qualified for these awards.

EXPLANATION OF SYMBOLS

★21★ Number next to an artist name denotes an artist's ranking among the Top 100 Artists (see ranking explanation on pages 160 and 262)

2³ Superior number to the right of the #1 or #2 peak position is the total weeks the track held that position

+ Indicates that track peaked in the year after it first charted

↑ Indicates the weeks charted data is subject to change since the track was still charted as of the 11/23/02 cut-off date

PEAK POSITIONS ATTAINED ON HOT 100 AIRPLAY, HOT 100 SALES & CHRISTMAS CHARTS

The peak position of a song that hit either the Hot 100 Airplay, Hot 100 Sales or *Billboard's* seasonal Christmas singles charts, but did not hit the Hot 100, is included in the "Pop" column. The following letter designations are shown in superscript next to the peak position attained on these charts:

A: Hot 100 Airplay
S: Hot 100 Sales
X: Christmas

LETTERS IN BRACKETS AFTER TITLES:

[C] - Comedy Recording
[F] - Foreign Language Recording
[I] - Instrumental Recording
[L] - Live Recording

[N] - Novelty Recording
[R] - Re-entry, reissue, remix or re-recording of a previously charted track by that artist
[X] - Christmas Recording

ARTIST BIOGRAPHIES

Below every artist name is a brief biography of that artist. For this book, an extra effort was made to list each band's members, their instruments and where the band was formed. Individual birthdates are also listed for many of the major artists. With the ever-changing lineups of many bands, each band's members are listed at the time of their charted track(s). Mention is made of a band's earlier members if their history is related to or included within this book. The classifications (rock, pop, etc.) of the artists are very broad since musical labels are very subjective and these definitions evolve over time. Also true in many cases, a particular category may not fit a band whose sound changes during its career.

TITLE NOTES

Directly under some track titles are notes indicating backing vocalists, guest instrumentalists, the name of a famous songwriter or producer, etc. Duets and other important name variations are shown in bold capital letters. All movie, TV and album titles, and other major works, are shown in italics. In the title notes "Bubbled Under" refers to *Billboard's Bubbling Under The Hot 100* chart.

ARTISTS CROSS REFERENCED IN BOLD TYPE

Names of artists and groups mentioned in the biographies and title notes of other rock track artists are highlighted in bold type if they have their own track listings elsewhere in this book. For example, **Eddie Vedder** is bold in the Pearl Jam artist biography which indicates that Eddie Vedder has his own track listings in either the "Mainstream Rock" or "Modern Rock" artist sections. A name is only made bold the <u>first</u> time it appears in an artist's biography.

You will find this to be an extremely useful feature in tracing the integral history of many of these artists. For a good example of this, see Whitesnake.

TOP TRACKS AT A GLANCE

The following four features help quickly identify an artist's top charted tracks:

- Every #1 track is identified by a special #1 symbol (❶).
- Every Top 10 track is shaded.
- Artists with 10 or more charted tracks have their highest-charted track identified by a heavy underscore below the track title. Ties among an artist's top tracks are broken based on total weeks at the peak position, total weeks in the Top 10, total weeks in the Top 20 and total weeks charted.
- Listed in bold type right below the artist's biography in rank order are:
    the Top 3 track of every artist with 10 to 19 charted tracks and
    the Top 5 tracks of every artist with 20 or more charted tracks.

PICTURES OF THE TOP 40 ARTISTS

A picture of each of the Top 40 artists is shown next to their listing in the artist sections. Their overall ranking is listed to the right of their name. (The ranking positions of the Top 41-100 artists appear to the left of the artist name.)

WHAT'S NEW WITH THIS EDITION

The following new features are included in this second edition of *Rock Tracks*.

RIAA CERTIFICATION

RIAA Gold (●) and Platinum (▲) album certifications are listed in the "Gld" column to the left of each certified album. A superscript number to the right of the platinum triangle indicates album was awarded multi-platinum status [ex.: ▲³ indicates an album was certified triple platinum (three million units sold)].

HOT 100 AIRPLAY, SALES & CHRISTMAS HITS

The column "Pop" lists the Hot 100 peak position and now also lists the peak position attained on *Billboard's* Hot 100 Airplay and Hot 100 Sales charts, and also *Billboard's* seasonal Christmas singles charts.

BIG HITS HIGHLIGHTED

The biggest hits of each artist are now easier to spot. All #1 tracks are identified by a special #1 symbol (❶). All Top 10 tracks are shaded with a gray background.

NEW TITLE ORDER

Each artist's charted tracks are listed in chronological order as before, but there are now some exceptions. In addition to listing tracks chronologically, all tracks that charted from the same album are grouped together. Listing same-album tracks together takes precedence over chronological order.

CLASSIC ROCK TRACKS SECTION

All those memorable classic rock artists and tracks from The Beatles invasion in 1964 up to the debut of *Billboard's Rock Tracks* chart in 1981 are listed by artist in a special bonus section.

Rock Tracks ™

Top Tracks

This Week	Last Week	Weeks On Chart	ARTIST—Title, Label
1	NEW ENTRY		ERIC CLAPTON—I Can't Stand It, RSO
2	NEW ENTRY		STEVE WINWOOD—While You See A Chance, Island
3	NEW ENTRY		JOURNEY—Party's Over, Columbia
4	NEW ENTRY		.38 SPECIAL—Hold On Loosely, A&M
5	NEW ENTRY		THE WHO—You Better You Bet, Warner Bros.
6	NEW ENTRY		LOVER BOY—Turn Me Loose, Columbia
7	NEW ENTRY		RUSH—Limelight, Mercury
8	NEW ENTRY		STYX—Rocking The Paradise, A&M
9	NEW ENTRY		REO SPEEDWAGON—Keep On Loving You, Epic
10	NEW ENTRY		RUSH—Tom Sawyer, Mercury
11	NEW ENTRY		POLICE—Don't Stand So Close To Me, A&M
12	NEW ENTRY		GARLAND JEFFREYS—96 Tears, Epic
13	NEW ENTRY		REO SPEEDWAGON—Don't Let Him Go, Epic
14	NEW ENTRY		BRUCE SPRINGSTEEN—Fade Away, Columbia
15	NEW ENTRY		MANFRED MANN—For You, Warner Bros.
16	NEW ENTRY		STYX—Best Of Times, A&M
17	NEW ENTRY		REO SPEEDWAGON—Take It On The Run, Epic
18	NEW ENTRY		ERIC CLAPTON—Rita Mae, RSO
19	NEW ENTRY		RANDY MEISNER—Hearts On Fire, Epic
20	NEW ENTRY		DONNIE IRIS—Ah Leah, MCA/Carousel
21	NEW ENTRY		JAMES TAYLOR—Stand Up & Fight, Columbia
22	NEW ENTRY		PRETENDERS—Message Of Love, Sire
23	NEW ENTRY		STEVE WINWOOD—Arc Of A Diver, Island
24	NEW ENTRY		THE CLASH—Police On My Back, Epic
25	NEW ENTRY		REO SPEEDWAGON—Tough Guys, Epic
26	NEW ENTRY		RICK SPRINGFIELD—Jessie's Girl, RCA
27	NEW ENTRY		APRIL WINE—Just Between You and Me, Capitol
28	NEW ENTRY		STYX—Too Much Time On My Hands, A&M
29	NEW ENTRY		THE OUTLAWS—Ghost Riders, Arista
30	NEW ENTRY		JOURNEY—Dixie Highway, Columbia
31	NEW ENTRY		PAT BENATAR—Treat Me Right, Chrysalis
32	NEW ENTRY		APRIL WINE—Sign Of A Gypsy Queen, Capitol
33	NEW ENTRY		GRACE SLICK—Sea Of Love, RCA
34	NEW ENTRY		STYX—Snowblind, A&M
35	NEW ENTRY		BLONDIE—Rapture, Chrysalis
36	NEW ENTRY		ERIC CLAPTON—Catch Me If You Can, RSO
37	NEW ENTRY		JAMES TAYLOR & J. D. SOUTHER—Her Town Too, Columbia
38	NEW ENTRY		PHIL COLLINS—I Missed Again, Atlantic
39	NEW ENTRY		APRIL WINE—All Over Town, Capitol
40	NEW ENTRY		TOTO—Live For Today, Columbia
41	NEW ENTRY		JOHN LENNON—Woman, Geffen
42	NEW ENTRY		BRUCE SPRINGSTEEN—I'm A Rocker, Columbia
43	NEW ENTRY		TED NUGENT—Flying Lip Lock, Epic
44	NEW ENTRY		PHIL COLLINS—In The Air Tonight, Atlantic
45	NEW ENTRY		THE SHERBS—The Skill, Atco
46	NEW ENTRY		ELVIS COSTELLO—From A Whisper To A Scream, Columbia
47	NEW ENTRY		ALAN PARSONS PROJECT—Snake Eyes, Arista
48	NEW ENTRY		TODD RUNDGREN—Compassion, Bearsville
49	NEW ENTRY		STEELY DAN—Time Out Of Mind, MCA
50	NEW ENTRY		JIM CARROLL BAND—People Who Died, Atco
51	NEW ENTRY		JIMMY BUFFET—Its My Job, MCA
52	NEW ENTRY		JOHN COUGAR—Ain't Even Done With The Night, Mercury
53	NEW ENTRY		XTC—Generals and Majors, RSO
54	NEW ENTRY		JOHN LENNON—I'm Losing You, Geffen
55	NEW ENTRY		JOAN JETT—Do You Wanna Touch Me, Boardwalk
56	NEW ENTRY		TED NUGENT—Jail Bait, Epic
57	NEW ENTRY		JUICE NEWTON—Angel Of The Morning, Capitol
58	NEW ENTRY		TODD RUNDGREN—Time Heals, Warner Bros.
59	NEW ENTRY		.38 SPECIAL—Fantasy Girl, A&M
60	NEW ENTRY		DIRE STRAITS—Expresso Love, Warner Bros.

Billboard's first "Rock Tracks" chart - March 21, 1981

MAINSTREAM ROCK TRACKS

Lists, alphabetically by artist name, every track that <u>debuted</u> on *Billboard's* "Mainstream Rock Tracks" charts from March 21, 1981, through October 26, 2002.

KEY

Here's a quick reference guide to our symbols. Refer to *RESEARCHING BILLBOARD'S ROCK TRACKS CHARTS* and *USER'S GUIDE* for complete descriptions. (The artist and titles below are NOT real.)

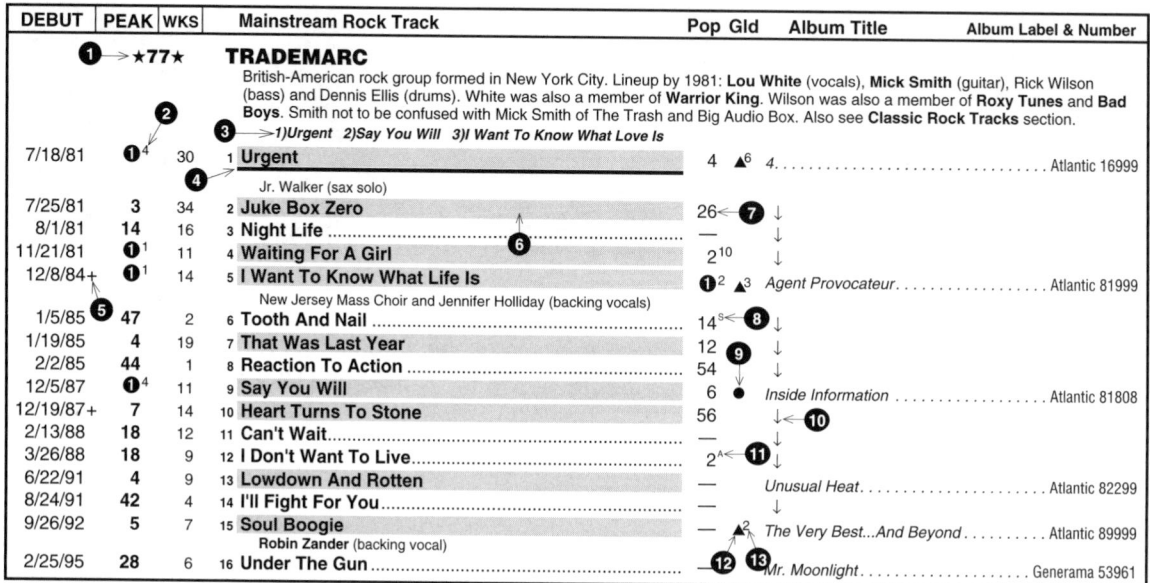

1. artist's ranking within the Top 100 artists
2. peak weeks (#1 & #2 hits only)
3. artist's top 3 or top 5 hits
4. artist's biggest hit (underlined)
5. peaked in the following year
6. Top 10 hit (shaded)
7. peak position attained on Billboard's *Hot 100* or *Bubbling Under The Hot 100* chart

8. peak position is from Hot 100 Sales chart (S)
9. Gold seller (●) [500,000 units sold]
10. track from album listed directly above
11. peak position is from Hot 100 Airplay chart (A)
12. platinum seller (▲) [1,000,000 units sold]
13. multi-platinum (number of million units sold)

DEBUT	PEAK	WKS	Mainstream Rock Track	Pop	Gld	Album Title	Album Label & Number

A

ABC
Electro-pop group from Sheffield, Yorkshire, England: Martin Fry (vocals), Mark White (guitar). Stephen Singleton (sax), Mark Lickley (bass) and David Palmer (drums). Alan Spenner replaced Lickley in 1983.

| 10/16/82 | 32 | 1 | 1 The Look Of Love (Part One) | 18 | ● | the Lexicon of Love | Mercury 4059 |
| 2/4/84 | 35 | 2 | 2 That Was Then But This Is Now | 89 | | Beauty Stab | Mercury 814661 |

ACCEPT
Hard-rock group from Solingen, Germany: Udo Dirkschneider (vocals), Wolf Hoffmann and Hermann Frank (guitars), Peter Baltes (bass) and Stefan Kaufmann (drums).

| 2/25/84 | 21 | 5 | Balls To The Wall | — | ● | Balls To The Wall | Portrait 39241 |

AC/DC ★23★
Hard-rock group formed in Sydney, Australia: brothers Angus (guitar; born on 3/31/55) and Malcolm (guitar; born on 1/6/53) Young, Ron Belford "Bon" Scott (vocals; born on 7/9/46; died of alcohol abuse on 2/19/80, age 33)), Mark Evans (bass; born on 3/2/56) and Phil Rudd (drums; born on 5/19/54). Scott and the Young brothers were born in Scotland. Cliff Williams (born on 12/14/49) replaced Evans in 1977. Brian Johnson (born on 10/5/47) joined as lead singer after Scott's death. Simon Wright (born on 6/19/63) replaced Rudd in 1985. Wright joined **Dio** in 1989; replaced by Chris Slade (born on 10/30/46) of **The Firm**. Rudd returned in 1995, replacing Slade. Group made a cameo concert appearance in the 1997 movie *Private Parts*. Group inducted into the Rock and Roll Hall of Fame in 2003. Also see **Classic Rock Tracks** section.

1)Stiff Upper Lip 2)Hard As A Rock 3)Big Gun 4)Moneytalks 5)Dirty Deeds Done Dirt Cheap

3/28/81	50	1	1 Hells Bells	—	▲19	Back In Black	Atlantic 16018
3/28/81	51	2	2 Back In Black	37	↓		
4/11/81	60	1	3 Shoot To Thrill	—	↓		
4/11/81	4	17	4 Dirty Deeds Done Dirt Cheap	—	▲6	Dirty Deeds Done Dirt Cheap	Atlantic 16033
4/18/81	26	7	5 Big Balls	—	↓		
			above 2 recorded in 1975 (vocals by Bon Scott)				
12/5/81+	4	18	6 For Those About To Rock (We Salute You)	—	▲4	For Those About To Rock We Salute You	Atlantic 11111
12/19/81+	9	15	7 Let's Get It Up	44	↓		
12/19/81+	38	14	8 Put The Finger On You	—	↓		
9/3/83	26	8	9 Flick Of The Switch	—	▲	Flick Of The Switch	Atlantic 80100
9/24/83	37	4	10 Guns For Hire	84	↓		
11/3/84	33	11	11 Jailbreak	—	▲	'74 Jailbreak	Atlantic 80178
			recorded in 1974 (vocals by Bon Scott)				
8/31/85	44	4	12 Sink The Pink	—	▲	Fly On The Wall	Atlantic 81263
5/31/86	23	12	13 Who Made Who	—	▲5	Who Made Who	Atlantic 81650
2/6/88	20	12	14 Heatseeker	—	▲	Blow Up Your Video	Atlantic 81828
4/30/88	28	7	15 That's The Way I Wanna Rock N Roll	—	↓		
9/29/90	5	10	16 Thunderstruck	—	▲4	The Razors Edge	Atco 91413
11/10/90+	3	18	17 Moneytalks	23	↓		
3/9/91	16	10	18 Are You Ready	—	↓		
10/31/92	29	4	19 Highway To Hell [L]	—	▲3	Live	Atco 92215
			studio version was a #47 pop hit in 1979 (vocals by Bon Scott)				
6/5/93	❶2	20	20 Big Gun	65	▲	Last Action Hero (soundtrack)	Columbia 57127
9/23/95	❶3	24	21 Hard As A Rock	—	▲2	Ballbreaker	EastWest 61780
12/2/95+	9	15	22 Cover You In Oil	—	↓		
3/16/96	25	8	23 Ballbreaker	—	↓		
11/1/97	6	15	24 Dirty Eyes	—	▲	Bonfire	EastWest 62119
			recorded in 1977 (vocals by Bon Scott); early version of "Whole Lotta Rosie" which appeared on their 1977 album *Let There Be Rock*				
2/19/00	❶4	23	25 Stiff Upper Lip	115	▲	Stiff Upper Lip	EastWest 62494
6/3/00	7	20	26 Satellite Blues	—	↓		
9/16/00	22	9	27 Meltdown	—	↓		
3/31/01	21	10	28 Safe In New York City	—	↓		

ADAM AND THE ANTS
Pop-rock group formed in London by lead singer **Adam Ant** (born Stuart Goddard on 11/3/54). Early Ants Matthew Ashman (guitar), Lee Gorman (bass) and Dave Barbarossa (drums) left in 1980 to form **Bow Wow Wow**. Replaced by Marco Pirroni (guitar; **Siouxsie And The Banshees**), Terry Miall (percussion), Kevin Mooney (bass) and Chris Hughes (drums). Adam Ant went solo in 1982. Ashman died of diabetes on 11/21/95 (age 35).

3/28/81	15	6	1 Dog Eat Dog	—	●	Kings Of The Wild Frontier	Epic 37033
4/25/81	14	12	2 Antmusic	—	↓		
4/25/81	19	1	3 Physical (You're So)	—	↓		
12/4/82	7	9	4 Goody Two Shoes	12	●	Friend Or Foe	Epic 38370
			ADAM ANT				

DEBUT	PEAK	WKS	Mainstream Rock Track	Pop	Gld	Album Title	Album Label & Number

ADAMS, Bryan ★19★
Born on 11/5/59 in Kingston, Ontario, Canada. Rock singer/songwriter/guitarist. Lead singer of Sweeney Todd in 1976. Teamed with Jim Vallance in 1977 in songwriting partnership. Cameo appearance in the 1989 movie *Pink Cadillac*.

1)Run To You   2)Somebody   3)Can't Stop This Thing We Started   4)Heat Of The Night   5)Lonely Nights

DEBUT	PEAK	WKS	Track	Pop	Gld	Album Title	Album Label & Number
1/23/82	3	16	1 Lonely Nights	84		You Want It, You Got It	A&M 4864
4/3/82	15	11	2 Fits Ya Good	—		↓	
2/12/83	6	24	3 Cuts Like A Knife	15	▲	Cuts Like A Knife	A&M 4919
2/19/83	21	14	4 Take Me Back	—		↓	
2/19/83	44	3	5 The Only One	—		↓	
3/5/83	26	9	6 I'm Ready	—		↓	
6/4/83	32	7	7 Straight From The Heart	10		↓	
8/13/83	21	10	8 This Time	24		↓	
1/28/84	9	9	9 Heaven	—		A Night In Heaven (soundtrack)	A&M 4966
			also see #15 below				
11/3/84	❶4	15	10 Run To You	6	▲5	Reckless	A&M 5013
11/24/84	7	25	11 It's Only Love	15		↓	
			BRYAN ADAMS/TINA TURNER				
12/8/84	40	8	12 Summer Of '69	5		↓	
12/15/84+	42	6	13 Kids Wanna Rock	—		↓	
1/19/85	❶2	16	14 Somebody	11		↓	
4/27/85	27	8	15 Heaven . . . . [R]	❶2		↓	
			same version as #9 above				
8/31/85	7	12	16 One Night Love Affair	13		↓	
7/13/85	21	10	17 Diana	—		(single only)	A&M 256
			only available as a British import single				
12/28/85+	31	3	18 Christmas Time . . . . [X]	4x		(single only)	A&M 8651
3/28/87	2²	11	19 Heat Of The Night	6	▲	Into The Fire	A&M 3907
4/11/87	33	4	20 Another Day	—		↓	
4/18/87	6	16	21 Into The Fire	—		↓	
5/30/87	3	12	22 Hearts On Fire	26		↓	
8/8/87	10	9	23 Victim Of Love	32		↓	
9/8/90	7	9	24 Young Lust [L]	—		The Wall - Live In Berlin (**Roger Waters**)	Mercury 846611
			recorded on 7/21/90 at the Berlin Wall; first recorded by Pink Floyd in 1979				
6/29/91	10	10	25 (Everything I Do) I Do It For You	❶7	▲	Robin Hood: Prince Of Thieves (soundtrack)	Morgan Creek 20004
9/14/91	2²	16	26 Can't Stop This Thing We Started	2¹	▲4	Waking Up The Neighbours	A&M 5367
12/7/91+	6	13	27 There Will Never Be Another Tonight	31		↓	
3/7/92	14	8	28 Thought I'd Died And Gone To Heaven	13		↓	
5/2/92	13	8	29 Touch The Hand	—		↓	
2/7/98	38	2	30 Back To You . . . . [L]	42A		MTV Unplugged	A&M 540831
			recorded on 9/26/97 at the Hammerstein Ballroom in New York City				

ADDICT
Rock group from London: Mark Aston (vocals), Nikolaj Juel (guitar), James Denham (bass) and Luke Bullen (drums).

DEBUT	PEAK	WKS	Track	Pop	Gld	Album Title	Album Label & Number
5/23/98	24	13	1 Monster Side	—		Stones	Big Cat 81845
12/26/98	39	4	2 Nobody Knows	—		↓	

ADEMA
Hard-rock group from Huntington Beach, California: Mark Chavez (vocals), Mike Ransom and Tim Fluckey (guitars), Dave DeRoo (bass) and Kris Kohls (drums).

DEBUT	PEAK	WKS	Track	Pop	Gld	Album Title	Album Label & Number
7/14/01	16	23	1 Giving In	—	●	Adema	Arista 14696
12/15/01+	21	24	2 The Way You Like It	—		↓	
6/8/02	25	10	3 Freaking Out	—		↓	

ADRENALIN
Rock group from Detroit: Marc Gilbert (vocals), brothers Mike (guitar) and Jim (sax) Romeo, brothers Mark (keyboards) and Brian (drums) Pastoria, Mike "Flash" Haggerty (guitar) and Bruce Schafer (bass).

DEBUT	PEAK	WKS	Track	Pop	Gld	Album Title	Album Label & Number
7/28/84	28	5	Faraway Eyes	—		American Heart	Rocshire 9517

ADVENTURES, The
Pop group from Belfast, Ireland: Terry Sharpe (vocals), husband-and-wife Patrick (guitar) and Eileen (vocals) Gribben, Gerard "Spud" Murphy (guitar), Tony Ayre (bass) and Paul Crowder (drums).

DEBUT	PEAK	WKS	Track	Pop	Gld	Album Title	Album Label & Number
4/16/88	39	5	Broken Land	95		The Sea Of Love	Elektra 60772

DEBUT	PEAK	WKS	Mainstream Rock Track	Pop Gld	Album Title	Album Label & Number

AEROSMITH ★3★

Rock group from Boston: Steven Tyler (vocals; born on 3/26/48), Joe Perry (guitar; born on 9/10/50), Brad Whitford (guitar; born on 2/23/52), Tom Hamilton (bass; born on 12/31/51) and Joey Kramer (drums; born on 6/21/50). Perry left for own **Joe Perry Project** in 1979; replaced by Jimmy Crespo. Whitford left in 1981; replaced by Rick Dufay. Original band reunited in April 1984. Tyler is the father of actress/model Liv Tyler. Group appeared in the movies *Sgt. Pepper's Lonely Hearts Club Band* and *Wayne's World 2*. Group inducted into the Rock and Roll Hall of Fame in 2001. Also see **Classic Rock Tracks** section.

1)Livin' On The Edge 2)Cryin' 3)Jaded 4)Falling In Love (Is Hard On The Knees) 5)Deuces Are Wild

DEBUT	PEAK	WKS	#	Mainstream Rock Track	Pop Gld	Album Title	Album Label & Number
10/9/82	21	9	1	Lightning Strikes	— ●	Rock In A Hard Place	Columbia 38061
11/2/85	18	10	2	Let The Music Do The Talking	— ●	Done With Mirrors	Geffen 24091
12/21/85+	20	10	3	Shela	—	↓	
8/29/87	4	10	4	Dude (Looks Like A Lady)	14 ▲5	Permanent Vacation	Geffen 24162
9/12/87	12	18	5	Rag Doll	17	↓	
11/14/87	14	14	6	Hangman Jury	—	↓	
1/30/88	2³	14	7	Angel	3	↓	
5/21/88	42	4	8	Magic Touch	—	↓	
1/23/88	44	2	9	Rocking Pneumonia And The Boogie Woogie Flu	— ●	Less Than Zero (soundtrack)	Def Jam 44042
				#52 Pop hit for Huey Smith & The Clowns in 1957			
11/26/88+	13	12	10	Chip Away The Stone	77 ●	Gems	Columbia 44487
				recorded in 1978			
9/2/89	❶²	11	11	Love In An Elevator	5 ▲7	Pump	Geffen 24254
9/23/89	2¹	18	12	Janie's Got A Gun	4	↓	
11/25/89+	14	9	13	F.I.N.E. (Fucked-up, Insecure, Neurotic, Emotional)	—	↓	
1/13/90	❶¹	19	14	What It Takes	9	↓	
4/14/90	17	9	15	Monkey On My Back	—	↓	
6/16/90	❶²	16	16	The Other Side	22	↓	
8/25/90	27	6	17	Love Me Two Times	—	Air America (soundtrack)	MCA 6467
				#25 Pop hit for The Doors in 1968			
11/16/91	21	4	18	Helter Skelter	— ▲	Pandora's Box	Columbia 46209
				first recorded by The Beatles in 1968			
12/7/91	36	17	19	Sweet Emotion	36	↓	
				above 2 recorded in 1975			
4/10/93	❶⁹	20	20	Livin' On The Edge	18 ▲7	Get A Grip	Geffen 24455
5/1/93	5	18	21	Eat The Rich	—	↓	
6/5/93	❶⁶	20	22	Cryin'	12	↓	
9/4/93	5	10	23	Fever	—	↓	
10/30/93	3	24	24	Amazing	24	↓	
5/21/94	7	14	25	Crazy	17	↓	
1/15/94	❶⁴	26	26	Deuces Are Wild	— ▲²	The Beavis & Butt-Head Experience (various artists)	Geffen 24613
11/5/94	3	16	27	Blind Man	48 ▲⁴	Big Ones	Geffen 24716
1/28/95	16	7	28	Walk On Water	—	↓	
3/1/97	❶⁵	26	29	Falling In Love (Is Hard On The Knees)	35 ▲²	Nine Lives	Columbia 67547
4/19/97	37	1	30	Nine Lives	—	↓	
5/10/97	4	17	31	Hole In My Soul	51	↓	
5/17/97	❶⁴	29	32	Pink	27	↓	
12/13/97+	3	19	33	Taste Of India	—	↓	
5/30/98	4	24	34	I Don't Want To Miss A Thing	❶⁴ ▲⁴	Armageddon (soundtrack)	Columbia 69440
7/25/98	4	22	35	What Kind Of Love Are You On	—	↓	
10/28/00	4	14	36	Angel's Eye	— ▲²	Charlie's Angels (soundtrack)	Columbia 61064
1/27/01	❶⁵	26	37	Jaded	7 ▲	Just Push Play	Columbia 62088
5/5/01	10	15	38	Just Push Play	—	↓	
10/27/01	23	10	39	Sunshine	—	↓	
6/1/02	25	11	40	Girls Of Summer	— ▲	O, Yeah! Ultimate Aerosmith Hits	Columbia 86700

AFTER THE FIRE

Rock group from England: Andy Piercy (vocals, bass), John Russell (guitar), Peter Banks (keyboards) and Pete King (drums). Banks was a member of **Yes**.

3/5/83	4	12		Der Kommissar	5	ATF	Epic 38282
				Kommissar is German for "detective"; also see **Falco**'s original German version			

ALARM, The

Rock group from Rhyl, Wales: Mike Peters (vocals; born on 2/25/59), Dave Sharp (guitar; born on 1/28/59), Eddie MacDonald (bass; born on 11/1/59) and Nigel Twist (drums; born on 7/18/58).

1)Sold Me Down The River 2)Rain In The Summertime 3)Devolution Workin' Man Blues

3/31/84	39	5	1	Sixty Eight Guns	106	Declaration	I.R.S. 70608
11/2/85+	12	15	2	Strength	61	Strength	I.R.S. 5666
2/15/86	29	9	3	Spirit Of '76	—	↓	
10/31/87	6	15	4	Rain In The Summertime	71	Eye Of The Hurricane	I.R.S. 42061
2/20/88	16	11	5	Presence Of Love	77	↓	

DEBUT	PEAK	WKS	Mainstream Rock Track		Pop	Gld	Album Title	Album Label & Number
			ALARM, The — Cont'd					
6/18/88	35	5	6 Rescue Me	[L]	—		Electric Folklore Live	I.R.S. 39108
9/9/89	2²	17	7 Sold Me Down The River		50		Change	I.R.S. 82018
12/2/89+	9	11	8 Devolution Workin' Man Blues		—	↓		
2/10/90	33	7	9 Love Don't Come Easy		—	↓		
11/3/90	16	11	10 The Road		—		Standards	I.R.S. 13056
5/11/91	29	7	11 Raw		—		Raw	I.R.S. 13087

ALIAS
Rock group formed in Los Angeles by former **Sheriff** bandmates Freddy Curci (vocals) and Steve DeMarchi (guitar), with former **Heart** members Roger Fisher (guitar), Steve Fossen (bass) and Mike Derosier (drums).

DEBUT	PEAK	WKS	Mainstream Rock Track		Pop	Gld	Album Title	Album Label & Number
6/30/90	18	9	Haunted Heart		—		Alias	EMI 93908

ALICE IN CHAINS ★31★
Male hard-rock group formed in Seattle: Layne Staley (vocals; born on 8/22/67; died of a drug overdose on 4/5/2002, age 34), **Jerry Cantrell** (guitar; born on 3/18/66), Mike Starr (bass) and Sean Kinney (drums; born on 5/27/66). Mike Inez (born on 5/14/66) replaced Starr by 1994. In 1995, Inez recorded with **Slash's Snakepit** and Staley recorded with **Mad Season** and **Class Of '99**. Scott Olson (guitar) joined in 1996.

1)No Excuses 2)Heaven Beside You 3)Get Born Again 4)Over Now 5)Got Me Wrong

DEBUT	PEAK	WKS	Mainstream Rock Track		Pop	Gld	Album Title	Album Label & Number
4/13/91	18	20	1 Man In The Box also see #20 below		—	▲²	Facelift	Columbia 46075
9/14/91	27	9	2 Sea Of Sorrow		—	↓		
8/8/92	31	8	3 Would? also see #17 below		—	▲	Singles (soundtrack)	Epic 52476
10/17/92	24	9	4 Them Bones		—	▲⁴	Dirt	Columbia 52475
1/30/93	34	5	5 Angry Chair		—	↓		
3/13/93	7	20	6 Rooster		—	↓		
10/2/93	10	21	7 Down In A Hole		—	↓		
7/3/93	19	12	8 What The Hell Have I		—	▲	Last Action Hero (soundtrack)	Columbia 57127
2/12/94	❶²	26	9 No Excuses		48^	▲²	Jar Of Flies	Columbia 57628
5/14/94	10	26	10 I Stay Away		—	↓		
10/29/94	25	7	11 Don't Follow		—	↓		
12/31/94+	7	21	12 Got Me Wrong		—		Clerks (soundtrack)	Columbia 66660
10/21/95	7	16	13 Grind		—	▲²	Alice In Chains	Columbia 67248
12/23/95+	3	26	14 Heaven Beside You		52^	↓		
5/11/96	8	26	15 Again		—	↓		
8/3/96	4	26	16 Over Now	[L]	—	▲	MTV Unplugged	Columbia 67703
11/2/96	19	18	17 Would? live version of #3 above; above 2 recorded on 4/10/96 at the Majestic Theater in New York City	[L-R]	—	↓		
6/12/99	4	19	18 Get Born Again		106	●	Nothing Safe	Columbia 63649
10/30/99	11	14	19 Fear The Voices		—		Music Bank	Columbia 69580
12/30/00	39	2	20 Man In The Box live version of #1 above	[L-R]	—		Live	Columbia 85274

ALIEN ANT FARM
Rock group from Los Angeles: Dryden Mitchell (vocals), Terry Corso (guitar), Tye Zamora (bass) and Mike Cosgrove (drums).

DEBUT	PEAK	WKS	Mainstream Rock Track		Pop	Gld	Album Title	Album Label & Number
8/18/01	18	24	1 Smooth Criminal #7 Pop hit for **Michael Jackson** in 1989		23	▲	ANThology	New Noize 450293
2/9/02	38	3	2 Movies		—	↓		

ALLMAN, Gregg, Band
Born on 12/8/47 in Nashville; raised in Daytona Beach, Florida. Rock singer/organist. Founding member of **The Allman Brothers Band**. Married to Cher from 1975-77. Acted in the movie *Rush*. His band included brothers Dan (guitar) and David (drums) Toler, Tim Heding (keyboards), Chaz Trippy (percussion) and Bruce Waibel (bass). Also see **Classic Rock Tracks** section.

DEBUT	PEAK	WKS	Mainstream Rock Track		Pop	Gld	Album Title	Album Label & Number
2/14/87	❶¹	14	1 I'm No Angel		49	●	I'm No Angel	Epic 40531
4/18/87	3	10	2 Anything Goes		—	↓		
6/20/87	25	8	3 Can't Keep Running		—	↓		
7/9/88	3	12	4 Can't Get Over You		—		Just Before The Bullets Fly	Epic 44033
10/1/88	17	8	5 Slip Away #6 Pop hit for Clarence Carter in 1968		—	↓		

ALLMAN BROTHERS BAND, The
Rock group from Macon, Georgia. Original lineup: brothers **Gregg Allman** (vocals, organ) and Duane Allman (lead guitar), **Dickey Betts** (guitar), Berry Oakley (bass), with Butch Trucks and Jai Johnny Johanson (drums). Duane Allman died in a motorcycle crash on 10/29/71 (age 24). Oakley died in a motorcycle crash on 11/11/72 (age 24). Lineup in 1981: Gregg Allman, Betts, Trucks and Johanson, with David Goldflies (bass) and David Toler (drums). Lineup in 1990: Gregg Allman, Betts, Trucks and Johanson with Warren Hayes (guitar), Allen Woody (bass) and Johnny Neel (keyboards). Neel left in 1991; replaced by Mark Quinones. Hayes and Woody formed **Gov't Mule**. Woody died on 8/26/2000 (age 44). Group inducted into the Rock and Roll Hall of Fame in 1995. Also see **Classic Rock Tracks** section.

DEBUT	PEAK	WKS	Mainstream Rock Track		Pop	Gld	Album Title	Album Label & Number
8/15/81	11	15	1 Straight From The Heart		39		Brothers Of The Road	Arista 9564
6/24/89	26	5	2 Statesboro Blues recorded in 1970		—	●	Dreams	Polydor 839417

DEBUT	PEAK	WKS	Mainstream Rock Track	Pop Gld	Album Title	Album Label & Number

ALLMAN BROTHERS BAND, The — Cont'd

DEBUT	PEAK	WKS	Track	Pop Gld	Album	Label
7/7/90	❶¹	16	3 Good Clean Fun	—	Seven Turns	Epic 46144
9/15/90	12	9	4 Seven Turns	—	↓	
12/22/90+	26	8	5 It Ain't Over Yet	—	↓	
7/6/91	2¹	15	6 End Of The Line	—	Shades Of Two Worlds	Epic 47877
9/28/91	42	8	7 Bad Rain	—	↓	
5/7/94	7	15	8 No One To Run With	— ●	Where It All Begins	Epic 64232
9/3/94	29	6	9 Back Where It All Begins	—	↓	

AMBROSIA
Pop group from Los Angeles: David Pack (vocals, guitar), Joe Puerta (vocals, bass), Christopher North (keyboards) and Burleigh Drummond (drums). Puerta later joined **Bruce Hornsby & The Range**.

5/29/82	44	2	For Openers (Welcome Home)	—	Road Island	Warner 3638

ANDERSON, Jon
Born on 10/25/44 in Lancashire, England. Lead singer of **Yes**. Half of **Jon & Vangelis** duo.

6/19/82	59	1	1 Olympia	—	Animation	Atlantic 19355
8/18/84	16	9	2 Cage Of Freedom	—	Metropolis (soundtrack)	Columbia 39526

ANDERSON, Michael
Born in Grand Rapids, Michigan. Rock singer/songwriter.

6/18/88	17	9	Sound Alarm	—	Sound Alarm	A&M 5203

ANDERSON, BRUFORD, WAKEMAN, HOWE — see YES

ANDREWS, Jake
Born in 1980 in Austin, Texas. Blues-rock singer/guitarist.

5/8/99	32	9	Time To Burn	—	Time To Burn	Jericho 90002

ANGEL CITY
Hard-rock group from Australia: Doc Neeson (vocals), brothers Rick and John Brewster (guitars), Jim Hilbun (bass) and Brent Eccles (drums).

1/26/85	35	5	Underground	—	Two Minute Warning	MCA 5509

ANIMAL BAG
Rock group from Charlotte, North Carolina: Luke Edwards (vocals, guitar), Rich Parris (guitar), Bill "Otis" Hughes (bass) and David "Boo" Duckworth (drums). Duckworth died of a drug overdose on 6/6/2002 (age 35).

4/17/93	29	7	Everybody	—	Animal Bag	Stardog 512885

ANIMALS, The
Rock group from Newcastle, England: Eric Burdon (vocals), Hilton Valentine (guitar), Alan Price (keyboards), Bryan "Chas" Chandler (bass) and John Steel (drums). Chandler died of a heart attack on 7/17/96 (age 57). Group inducted into the Rock and Roll Hall of Fame in 1994. Also see **Classic Rock Tracks** section.

8/27/83	34	17	The Night	48	Ark	I.R.S. 70037

ANT, Adam — see ADAM AND THE ANTS

ANTHRAX
Hard-rock group from New York City: John Bush (vocals), Scott Ian and Dan Spitz (guitars), Frank Bello (bass) and Charlie Benante (drums).

5/22/93	26	9	1 Only	— ●	Sound Of White Noise	Elektra 61430
10/9/93	38	3	2 Black Lodge	—	↓	

APARTMENT 26
Hard-rock group from England: Biff (vocals), Jon Greasley (guitar), A.C. Huckvale (keyboards), Louis Cruden (bass) and Kevin Temple (drums).

6/3/00	33	6	Basic Breakdown	—	Hallucinating	Hollywood 62248

APRIL WINE
Rock group from Montreal: Myles Goodwyn (vocals, guitar), Brian Greenway and Gary Moffet (guitars), Steve Lang (bass) and Jerry Mercer (drums). Lang, Moffet and Mercer replaced by Daniel Barbe (keyboards), Jean Pellerin (bass) and Marty Simon (drums) in 1985. Also see **Classic Rock Tracks** section.

3/21/81	11	10	1 Just Between You And Me	21 ▲	The Nature Of The Beast	Capitol 12125
3/21/81	19	4	2 Sign Of The Gypsy Queen	57	↓	
3/21/81	29	5	3 All Over Town	—	↓	
6/26/82	9	12	4 Enough Is Enough	50	Power Play	Capitol 12218
7/10/82	26	3	5 If You See Kay	—	↓	
2/18/84	23	10	6 This Could Be The Right One	58	Animal Grace	Capitol 12311
11/6/93	35	7	7 That's Love	—	Attitude	F.R.E. 104

ARCADE
Hard-rock group formed in Los Angeles: Stephen Pearcy (vocals; **Ratt**), Frank Wilsex and Donny Syracuse (guitars), Michael Andrews (bass) and Fred Coury (drums; **Cinderella**).

4/17/93	29	6	1 Nothin' To Lose	—	Arcade	Epic 53012
7/31/93	27	6	2 Cry No More	—	↓	

DEBUT	PEAK	WKS	Mainstream Rock Track	Pop	Gld	Album Title	Album Label & Number

ARC ANGELS
Rock group formed in Austin, Texas: **Charlie Sexton** (vocals, guitar), **Doyle Bramhall II** (guitar), Tommy Shanon (bass) and Chris Layton (drums). Shannon, Layton and Bramhall's father were members of **Stevie Ray Vaughan**'s band. ARC: Austin Rehearsal Complex. Also see **Storyville**.

5/2/92	6	20	1 Living In A Dream	—		Arc Angels	DGC 24465
8/15/92	6	16	2 Sent By Angels	—		↓	
11/14/92+	2³	19	3 Too Many Ways To Fall	—		↓	
3/20/93	13	10	4 Shape I'm In	—		↓	

ARMATRADING, Joan
Born on 12/9/50 in St. Kitts, West Indies; raised in Birmingham, England. Black singer/songwriter/guitarist.

| 5/21/83 | 33 | 10 | 1 Drop The Pilot | 78 | | The Key . . . . | A&M 4912 |
| 7/12/86 | 37 | 5 | 2 Kind Words | — | | Sleight Of Hand . . . . | A&M 5130 |

ART IN AMERICA
Pop-rock trio from Detroit: brothers Chris (vocals, guitar) and Dan (drums) Flynn, with sister Shishonee Flynn (vocals, harp).

| 2/26/83 | 23 | 10 | 1 Art In America | — | | Art In America . . . . | Pavillion 38517 |
| 3/5/83 | 33 | 3 | 2 Undercover Lover | — | | ↓ | |

ARTISTS UNITED AGAINST APARTHEID
Benefit group of 49 superstar artists formed to protest the South African apartheid government; proceeds went to political prisoners in South Africa. Organized by **Little Steven** and Arthur Baker. Featuring **Pat Benatar**, Bono (**U2**), **Jackson Browne**, **Bob Dylan**, **Peter Gabriel**, **Bonnie Raitt**, **Lou Reed**, **Bruce Springsteen**, and many others.

| 11/23/85 | 41 | 5 | Sun City | 38 | | Sun City . . . . | Manhattan 53019 |

A's, The
Pop-rock group from Philadelphia: Richard Bush (vocals), Rick DiFonzo (guitar), Rocco Notte (keyboards), Terry Bortman (bass) and Mike Snyder (drums).

| 6/20/81 | 18 | 11 | A Woman's Got The Power | 106 | | A Woman's Got The Power . . . . | Arista 9554 |

★70★ ASIA
All-star rock group from England: John Wetton (vocals, bass; **King Crimson**, **Uriah Heep**), Steve Howe (guitar; **Yes**), Geoff Downes (keyboards; Yes, The Buggles) and Carl Palmer (drums; **Emerson, Lake & Palmer**). Mandy Meyer (**Krokus**) replaced Howe in 1985. Pat Thrall (**Hughes/Thrall**) replaced Meyer in 1990.

1)Heat Of The Moment 2)Don't Cry 3)Days Like These

4/3/82	❶⁶	22	1 Heat Of The Moment	4	▲⁴	Asia	Geffen 2008
4/3/82	10	19	2 Sole Survivor	—		↓	
4/10/82	28	16	3 Wildest Dreams	—		↓	
5/1/82	8	22	4 Only Time Will Tell	17		↓	
7/3/82	40	1	5 Here Comes The Feeling	—		↓	
7/31/82	43	1	6 Time Again	—		↓	
8/6/83	❶¹	14	7 Don't Cry	10	▲	Alpha	Geffen 4008
8/20/83	5	12	8 The Heat Goes On	—		↓	
8/20/83	20	11	9 True Colors	—		↓	
10/29/83	25	12	10 The Smile Has Left Your Eyes	34		↓	
8/27/83	24	3	11 Daylight	—		(single only)	Geffen 29571
11/9/85	7	13	12 Go	46		Astra	Geffen 24072
1/11/86	30	5	13 Too Late	—		↓	
8/18/90	2³	11	14 Days Like These	64	●	Then & Now	Geffen 24298

ASTLEY, Jon
Born in Manchester, England. Noted rock producer (**The Who**, **Eric Clapton** and **Corey Hart**).

| 7/11/87 | 7 | 11 | Jane's Getting Serious | 77 | | Everyone Loves The Pilot (Except The Crew) . . . . | Atlantic 81740 |

ATLANTA RHYTHM SECTION
Rock group formed in Doraville, Georgia: Ronnie Hammond (vocals), Barry Bailey and J.R. Cobb (guitars), Dean Daughtry (keyboards), Paul Goddard (bass) and Roy Yeager (drums). Also see **Classic Rock Tracks** section.

| 9/5/81 | 18 | 13 | Alien | 29 | | Quinella . . . . | Columbia 37550 |

AUDIOSLAVE
Group of former **Rage Against The Machine** members Tom Morello (guitar), Tim Commerford (bass) and Brad Wilk (drums), with **Chris Cornell** (vocals; **Soundgarden**).

| 10/12/02 | 6↑ | 7↑ | Cochise | 77↑ | | Audioslave . . . . | Epic 86968 |

AUDIOVENT
Rock group from Calabasas, California: Jason Boyd (vocals), Ben Einziger (guitar), Paul Fried (bass) and Jamin Wilcox (drums).

| 5/18/02 | 9 | 19 | The Energy | — | | Dirty Sexy Knights In Paris . . . . | Atlantic 83544 |

AUTOGRAPH
Rock group from Los Angeles: Steve Plunkett (vocals, guitar), Steve Lynch (guitar), Steven Isham (keyboards), Randy Rand (bass) and Keni Richards (drums).

| 11/17/84+ | 17 | 20 | 1 Turn Up The Radio | 29 | ● | Sign In Please . . . . | RCA 8040 |
| 10/26/85 | 38 | 5 | 2 Blondes In Black Cars | — | | That's The Stuff . . . . | RCA 7009 |

AXE
Rock group from Gainesville, Florida: Bobby Barth (vocals, guitar), Michael Osborne (guitar), Edgar Riley (keyboards), Wayne Haner (bass) and Ted Mueller (drums). Osborne died in a car crash on 7/21/84 (age 34).

| 6/19/82 | 23 | 9 | 1 Rock 'N' Roll Party In The Streets | 109 | | Offering . . . . | Atco 148 |
| 11/26/83 | 36 | 7 | 2 I Think You'll Remember Tonight | 94 | | Nemesis . . . . | Atco 90099 |

DEBUT	PEAK	WKS	Mainstream Rock Track	Pop Gld	Album Title	Album Label & Number

B

BABY ANIMALS
Rock group from Sydney, Australia: Suze DeMarchi (vocals), Dave Leslie (guitar), Eddie Parise (bass) and Frank Celenza (drums).

DEBUT	PEAK	WKS	Track	Pop Gld	Album Title	Label & Number
1/4/92	29	11	1 Painless	—	Baby Animals	Imago 21002
3/28/92	46	3	2 One Word		↓	

BAD COMPANY ★37★
Rock group from England: **Paul Rodgers** (vocals), Mick Ralphs (guitar), Raymond "Boz" Burrell (bass) and Simon Kirke (drums). Rodgers and Kirk from Free; Ralphs from Mott The Hoople; and Burrell from **King Crimson**. Rodgers, who left group in late 1982, was a member of **The Firm** (1984-86) and **The Law** (in 1991). Vocalist Brian Howe joined in 1986. Burrell left in 1987. Dave "Bucket" Colwell (guitar) and Rick Wills (of **Foreigner**; bass) joined in late 1992. Howe left in early 1995; replaced by Robert Hart. Rodgers returned briefly in 1999. Band named after a 1972 Jeff Bridges movie. Also see **Classic Rock Tracks** section.

1)How About That 2)Holy Water 3)If You Needed Somebody

DEBUT	PEAK	WKS	Track	Pop Gld	Album Title	Label & Number
9/4/82	2²	13	1 Electricland	74	Rough Diamonds	Swan Song 90001
9/25/82	39	7	2 Racetrack	—	↓	
10/4/86	12	7	3 This Love	85	Fame And Fortune	Atlantic 81684
11/22/86	37	4	4 Fame And Fortune	—	↓	
8/20/88	4	14	5 No Smoke Without A Fire	— ●	Dangerous Age	Atlantic 81884
11/5/88+	9	14	6 One Night	—	↓	
2/11/89	9	11	7 Shake It Up	82	↓	
4/29/89	20	7	8 Bad Man	—	↓	
6/2/90	❶²	15	9 Holy Water	89 ▲	Holy Water	Atco 91371
8/11/90	3	12	10 Boys Cry Tough	—	↓	
10/27/90+	2²	20	11 If You Needed Somebody	16	↓	
2/16/91	9	13	12 Stranger Stranger	—	↓	
8/24/91	14	12	13 Walk Through Fire	28	↓	
8/22/92	❶⁶	17	14 How About That	38 ●	Here Comes Trouble	Atco 91759
11/28/92	21	8	15 This Could Be The One	87	↓	
2/13/93	28	5	16 Here Comes Trouble	—	↓	
6/3/95	17	9	17 Down And Dirty	—	Company Of Strangers	EastWest 61808
3/13/99	15	15	18 Hey, Hey	—	The 'Original' Bad Co. Anthology	Elektra 62349
6/12/99	23	11	19 Hammer Of Love	—	↓	

BAD ENGLISH
All-star rock group: **John Waite** (vocals), **Neal Schon** (guitar), Jonathan Cain (keyboards), Ricky Phillips (bass) and Deen Castronovo (drums). Waite, Cain and Phillips were members of The Babys. Schon and Cain were members of **Journey**. Schon and Castronovo with **Hardline** in 1992.

DEBUT	PEAK	WKS	Track	Pop Gld	Album Title	Label & Number
6/24/89	2¹	13	1 Forget Me Not	45 ▲	Bad English	Epic 45083
9/23/89	10	12	2 When I See You Smile	❶²	↓	
12/23/89+	9	12	3 Best Of What I Got	—	↓	
1/27/90	30	8	4 Price Of Love	5	↓	
4/14/90	12	8	5 Heaven Is A 4 Letter Word	66	↓	
8/31/91	9	9	6 Straight To Your Heart	42	Backlash	Epic 46935

BADFINGER
Rock group from Swansea, Wales: Joey Molland (vocals, guitar), Tom Evans (vocals, bass), Glenn Sherba (guitar), Tony Kaye (keyboards; **Yes**) and Richard Bryans (drums). Evans committed suicide on 11/23/83 (age 36). Also see **Classic Rock Tracks** section.

DEBUT	PEAK	WKS	Track	Pop Gld	Album Title	Label & Number
3/28/81	42	2	Hold On	56	Say No More	Radio 16030

BADLANDS
Hard-rock group from England: Ray Gillen (vocals), Jake E. Lee (guitar), Greg Chaisson (bass) and Eric Singer (drums; **Black Sabbath**, **Kiss**). Gillen died of cancer on 12/1/93 (age 33).

DEBUT	PEAK	WKS	Track	Pop Gld	Album Title	Label & Number
7/22/89	38	5	Dreams In The Dark	—	Badlands	Atlantic 81966

BADLEES, The
Rock group from Philadelphia: Pete Palladino (vocals), Bret Alexander and Jeff Feltenberger (guitars), Paul Smith (bass) and Ron Simasek (drums).

DEBUT	PEAK	WKS	Track	Pop Gld	Album Title	Label & Number
12/9/95+	31	9	1 Fear Of Falling	—	River Songs	Atlas 529266
4/27/96	20	9	2 Angeline Is Coming Home	67	↓	

BAD RELIGION
Punk-rock group from Woodland Hills, California: Greg Graffin (vocals), Brett Gurewitz and Greg Hetson (guitars), Jay Bentley (bass) and Bobby Schayer (drums). Brian Baker replaced Gurewitz in 1995. Gurewitz owns the Epitaph record label.

DEBUT	PEAK	WKS	Track	Pop Gld	Album Title	Label & Number
3/25/95	33	6	1 Infected	— ●	Stranger Than Fiction	Atlantic 82658
4/6/96	38	3	2 A Walk	—	The Gray Race	Atlantic 82870

BAERWALD, David
Born on 7/11/60 in Oxford, Ohio. Half of the **David & David** duo.

DEBUT	PEAK	WKS	Track	Pop Gld	Album Title	Label & Number
5/26/90	22	10	1 All For You	—	Bedtime Stories	A&M 5289
9/15/90	42	4	2 Dance	—	↓	

DEBUT	PEAK	WKS	Mainstream Rock Track	Pop	Gld	Album Title	Album Label & Number

BAILEY, Philip
Born on 5/8/51 in Denver. Co-lead singer of Earth, Wind & Fire.

| 12/1/84+ | 5 | 14 | Easy Lover | 2[2] | | Chinese Wall..................... | Columbia 39542 |
| | | | PHILIP BAILEY with Phil Collins | | | | |

BAIRD, Dan
Born on 12/12/53 in San Diego; raised in Atlanta. Former lead singer of the **Georgia Satellites**.

| 10/10/92 | 5 | 13 | 1 I Love You Period. | 26 | | Love Songs For The Hearing | |
| 1/23/93 | 13 | 8 | 2 The One I Am.................... | — | | Impaired................... ↓ | Def American 26999 |

BALAAM & THE ANGEL
Rock trio from Motherwall, Scotland: brothers Mark (vocals), Jim (guitar) and Des (drums) Morris.

| 3/12/88 | 13 | 12 | I Love The Things You Do To Me .... | — | | Live Free Or Die............. | Virgin 90869 |

BALIN, Marty
Born Martyn Buchwald on 1/30/42 in Cincinnati. Lead singer of **Jefferson Airplane/Starship** and **KBC Band**.

| 6/13/81 | 20 | 10 | Hearts.................... | 8 | | Balin............. | EMI America 17054 |

BALLARD, Russ
Born on 10/31/45 in Waltham Cross, Hertfordshire, England. Pop-rock singer/songwriter/producer.

| 5/12/84 | 15 | 13 | 1 Voices .... | 110 | | Russ Ballard............. | EMI America 17108 |
| 6/29/85 | 15 | 9 | 2 The Fire Still Burns .... | 105 | | The Fire Still Burns........... | EMI America 17162 |

BANANARAMA
Female vocal trio from London: Sarah Dallin, Keren Woodward and Siobhan Fahey. Group name is a combination of the children's TV show *The Banana Splits* and the **Roxy Music** song "Pyjamarama." Fahey married David A. Stewart (of **Eurythmics**) on 8/1/87; later formed duo **Shakespear's Sister**.

| 4/30/83 | 26 | 3 | Na Na Hey Hey Kiss Him Goodbye.............. | 101 | | Deep Sea Skiving............. | London 810102 |
| | | | #1 Pop hit for Steam in 1969 | | | | |

BAND AID
A benefit recording to assist famine relief in Ethiopia. Organized by **Bob Geldof** of The Boomtown Rats. All-star group also included **Bananarama**, **Phil Collins**, **Culture Club**, **Duran Duran**, **Frankie Goes To Hollywood**, **Heaven 17**, **Paul McCartney**, **Spandau Ballet**, **Sting**, **The Style Council**, **Ultravox**, **U2** and **Paul Young**.

| 12/22/84+ | 32 | 5 | Do They Know It's Christmas? .... [X] | 13 | ● | (single only)................ | Columbia 04749 |

BANGLES
Female pop-rock group from Los Angeles: Susanna Hoffs (guitar), Michael Steele (bass), sisters Vicki (guitar) and Debbi (drums) Peterson. All share vocals. Originally named The Bangs. Steele was previously in The Runaways.

8/11/84	59	3	1 Hero Takes A Fall..............	—		All Over The Place.............	Columbia 39220
3/8/86	43	5	2 Manic Monday	2[1]	▲[3]	Different Light.............	Columbia 40039
			written by **Prince** under the pseudonym "Christopher"				
11/28/87	41	8	3 Hazy Shade Of Winter.................	2[1]	●	Less Than Zero (soundtrack)........	Def Jam 44042
			#13 Pop hit for Simon & Garfunkel in 1966				

BARBUSTERS, The — see JETT, Joan

BARDENS, Pete
Born on 6/19/45 in London. Died of cancer on 1/22/2002 (age 56). Rock keyboardist. Former member of Them and Camel.

8/29/87	41	6	1 In Dreams..................	—		Seen One Earth.................	Cinema 12555
8/27/88	49	1	2 Gold	—		Speed of Light.............	Cinema 48967
			Neil Lockwood (vocals, above 2)				

BAREFOOT SERVANTS
Rock group from Boston: **Jon Butcher** (vocals, guitar), Ben Schultz (guitar), Leland Sklar (bass) and Ray Brinker (drums).

| 2/5/94 | 13 | 9 | Box Of Miracles................. | — | | Barefoot Servants............. | Epic 57503 |

BARE JR.
Rock group from Nashville: Bobby Bare Jr. (vocals), Michael Grimes (guitar), Tracy Hackney (harmonica), Dean Tomasek (bass) and Keith Brogdon (drums). Bare is the son of veteran country singer Bobby Bare.

| 1/30/99 | 12 | 14 | You Blew Me Off.............. | — | | Boo-Tay.................... | Immortal 69353 |

BARNES, Jimmy
Born on 4/28/56 in Glasgow, Scotland; raised in Australia. Lead singer of **Cold Chisel**.

3/8/86	41	3	1 No Second Prize..............	—		Jimmy Barnes.............	Geffen 24089
4/5/86	22	7	2 Working Class Man.............	74		↓	
6/20/87	3	12	3 Good Times	47	●	The Lost Boys (soundtrack)........	Atlantic 81767
			INXS AND JIMMY BARNES				
5/14/88	3	11	4 Too Much Ain't Enough Love	91		Freight Train Heart.............	Geffen 24146
8/13/88	38	4	5 Driving Wheels..............	—		↓	

BATON ROUGE
Hard-rock group from New Orleans: Kelly Keeling (vocals, guitar), Lance Bulen (guitar), David Cremin (keyboards), Scott Bender (bass) and Corky McClellan (drums).

| 4/14/90 | 22 | 13 | Walks Like A Woman................. | — | | Shake Your Soul............. | Atlantic 82073 |

BBM
All-star rock trio: Ginger Baker (drums), Jack Bruce (vocals, bass) and **Gary Moore** (vocals, guitar). Baker and Bruce were members of Cream. Moore a member of **Thin Lizzy**.

| 9/10/94 | 30 | 6 | Waiting In The Wings.................. | — | | Around The Next Dream............. | Virgin 39728 |

DEBUT	PEAK	WKS	Mainstream Rock Track	Pop	Gld	Album Title	Album Label & Number

BEAT FARMERS, The
Rock group from Los Angeles: Joey Harris (vocals, guitar), Jerry Raney (guitar), Rollie Love (bass) and Country Dick Montana (drums). Montana died of a heart attack on 11/8/95 (age 40).

| 8/8/87 | 27 | 7 | Dark Light .... | — | | *The Pursuit Of Happiness* .... | MCA/Curb 5993 |

BEATLES, The
Rock group from Liverpool, England: **John Lennon**, Paul McCartney, **George Harrison** (guitars) and **Ringo Starr** (drums). All shared vocals. Won the 1964 Best New Artist Grammy Award. Group starred in the movies *A Hard Day's Night*, *Help*, *Magical Mystery Tour* and *Let It Be*; contributed soundtrack to the animated movie *Yellow Submarine*. Own Apple label in 1968. McCartney publicly announced the group's dissolution on 4/10/70. Won the Grammy's Trustees Award in 1972. Lennon was shot to death on 12/8/80 (age 40). Harrison died of cancer on 11/29/2001 (age 58). Widely considered to be the #1 rock group of all-time. Group inducted into the Rock and Roll Hall of Fame in 1988. Also see **Classic Rock Tracks** section.

| 12/9/95 | 8 | 6 | Free As A Bird .... | 6 | ▲8 | *Anthology 1* .... | Apple 34445 |

original demo recorded by **John Lennon** in 1977, with new vocals and instrumentation by the other Beatles; produced by **Jeff Lynne**

BEAUTIFUL CREATURES
Hard-rock group from Los Angeles: Joe LeSte (vocals), DJ Ashba and Anthony Focx (guitars), Kenny Kweens (bass) and Glen Sobel (drums).

| 9/15/01 | 37 | 3 | Wasted .... | — | | *Beautiful Creatures* .... | Warner 47952 |

BECK
Born Beck David Campbell (later changed his last name to his mother's maiden name of Hansen) on 7/8/70 in Los Angeles. Male rock singer/songwriter/guitarist.

| 4/9/94 | 39 | 2 | Loser .... | 10 | ▲ | *Mellow Gold* .... | DGC 24634 |

samples "I Walk On Guilded Splinters" by Dr. John

BECK, Jeff
Born on 6/24/44 in Wallington, Surrey, England. Prolific rock guitarist. With The Yardbirds from 1964-66. **Rod Stewart** and **Ronnie Wood** were members of the Jeff Beck Group from 1967-69. Member of **The Honeydrippers**.

| 6/15/85 | 5 | 13 | 1 People Get Ready .... | 48 | | *Flash* .... | Epic 39483 |

JEFF BECK and ROD STEWART
#14 Pop hit for The Impressions in 1965

| 8/10/85 | 20 | 7 | 2 Gets Us All In The End .... | — | | ↓ | |

Jimmy Hall (of Wet Willie; vocal)

| 5/17/86 | 14 | 7 | 3 I Been Down So Long .... [L] | — | | *Live! For Life* (various artists) .... | I.R.S. 5731 |

STING with **JEFF BECK**
recorded at The Greek Theatre in Los Angeles

| 10/28/89 | 35 | 7 | 4 Stand On It .... [I] | — | | *Jeff Beck's Guitar Shop* .... | Epic 44313 |

JEFF BECK WITH TERRY BOZZIO & TONY HYMAS

| 12/25/93+ | 10 | 11 | 5 Manic Depression .... | — | ● | *Stone Free: A Tribute To Jimi Hendrix* (various artists) .... | Reprise 45438 |

SEAL AND JEFF BECK
first recorded by Jimi Hendrix in 1967

BEGGARS & THIEVES
Rock group from New York City: Louie Merlino (vocals), Ronnie Mancuso (guitar), Phil Soussan (bass) and Bobby Borg (drums).

| 2/2/91 | 38 | 3 | Beggars & Thieves................................. | — | | *Beggars & Thieves* .... | Atlantic 82113 |

BELEW, Adrian
Born Robert Steven Belew on 12/23/49 in Covington, Kentucky. Singer/songwriter/guitarist. Member of **King Crimson** from 1981-84.

| 5/19/90 | 24 | 7 | Pretty Pink Rose .... | — | | *Young Lions* .... | Atlantic 82099 |

ADRIAN BELEW & DAVID BOWIE

BENATAR, Pat ★34★
Born Patricia Andrzejewski on 1/10/53 in Brooklyn, New York; raised in Lindenhurst, Long Island, New York. Rock singer/songwriter. Married to Dennis Benatar from 1971-79 (took his last name). Married her producer/guitarist Neil Giraldo on 2/20/82. Played "Jeanette Florescu" in the 1980 movie *Union City*. Also see **Classic Rock Tracks** section.

1)Love Is A Battlefield 2)Fire And Ice 3)All Fired Up 4)Shadows Of The Night 5)We Belong

3/21/81	31	2	1 Treat Me Right	18	▲4	*Crimes Of Passion*	Chrysalis 1275
7/18/81	2⁴	21	2 Fire And Ice	17	▲2	*Precious Time*	Chrysalis 1346
7/18/81	15	19	3 Just Like Me	—		↓	

#11 Pop hit for Paul Revere & The Raiders in 1966

7/25/81	16	21	4 Promises In The Dark	38		↓	
7/25/81	32	10	5 Take It Anyway You Want It	—		↓	
10/16/82	3	19	6 Shadows Of The Night	13	▲	*Get Nervous*	Chrysalis 1396
12/11/82+	4	17	7 Looking For A Stranger	39		↓	
12/18/82	23	4	8 The Victim.......................................	—		↓	
3/5/83	38	8	9 Little Too Late	20		↓	
10/1/83	❶4	17	10 Love Is A Battlefield	5	▲	*Live From Earth*	Chrysalis 41444
10/27/84	3	15	11 We Belong	5	▲	*Tropico*	Chrysalis 41471
12/8/84	20	10	12 Diamond Field	—		↓	
1/19/85	22	7	13 Ooh Ooh Song...................................	36		↓	

DEBUT	PEAK	WKS	Mainstream Rock Track	Pop	Gld	Album Title	Album Label & Number
			BENATAR, Pat — Cont'd				
6/29/85	4	14	14 Invincible	10	●	*Seven The Hard Way* .... Chrysalis 41507	
			theme from the movie *The Legend of Billie Jean*				
11/23/85	5	11	15 Sex As A Weapon	28		↓	
1/25/86	19	8	16 Le Bel Age	54		↓	
			title is French for "The Best Year"				
7/2/88	2[1]	12	17 All Fired Up	19	●	*Wide Awake In Dreamland* .... Chrysalis 41628	
9/24/88	44	5	18 Don't Walk Away	—		↓	
4/6/91	17	9	19 Payin' The Cost To Be The Boss	—		*True Love* .... Chrysalis 21805	
			#39 Pop hit for **B.B. King** in 1968				
5/29/93	3	11	20 Everybody Lay Down	—		*Gravity's Rainbow* .... Chrysalis 21982	
			BERLIN				
			Electro-pop group from Los Angeles: Terri Nunn (vocals), Rick Olsen (guitar), Matt Reid and David Diamond (keyboards), John Crawford (bass) and Rob Brill (drums).				
3/12/83	10	7	1 Sex (I'm A...)	62	▲	*Pleasure Victim* .... Geffen 2036	
3/31/84	25	11	2 No More Words	23	●	*Love Life* .... Geffen 4025	
			BETTER THAN EZRA				
			Rock trio from New Orleans: Kevin Griffin (vocals, guitar), Tom Drummond (bass) and Cary Bonnecaze (drums). Travis McNabb replaced Bonnecaze by 1996.				
4/15/95	3	26	1 Good	30	▲	*Deluxe* .... Elektra 61784	
7/29/95	6	19	2 In The Blood	48[A]		↓	
8/10/96	7	15	3 King Of New Orleans	62[A]		*Friction, Baby* .... Elektra 61944	
11/30/96+	10	22	4 Desperately Wanting	48		↓	
			BETTS, Dickey, Band				
			Born on 12/12/43 in Sarasota, Florida. Singer/guitarist of **The Allman Brothers Band**. His band: Warren Haynes (guitar), Johnny Neel (piano), Marty Privette (bass) and Matt Abts (drums). Haynes and Neel were also with The Allman Brothers Band.				
10/8/88	11	8	Rock Bottom	—		*Pattern Disruptive* .... Epic 44289	
			BIG AUDIO DYNAMITE II				
			Rock group from England: Mick Jones (vocals, guitar), Nick Hawkins (guitar), Gary Stonadge (bass) and Chris Kavanagh (drums). Jones was co-founder of **The Clash**; not to be confused with Mick Jones of Foreigner.				
9/28/91	40	7	Rush	32	●	*The Globe* .... Columbia 46147	
			samples "Baba O'Riley" by **The Who**				
			BIG BAM BOO				
			Pop-rock duo: Simon Scardanelli (from England) and David Shark Shaw (from Canada).				
4/8/89	21	7	Shooting From My Heart	—		*Fun, Faith, & Fairplay* .... Uni 8	
			BIG BIG SUN				
			Rock group from England: Robin Boult (vocals, guitar), John Jolliffe (keyboards), David Levy (bass) and Gary Ferguson (drums).				
5/27/89	50	2	Stop The World	—		*Stop The World* .... Atlantic 81964	
			BIG COUNTRY				
			Pop-rock group from Dunfermline, Scotland: Stuart Adamson (vocals, guitar), Bruce Watson (guitar), Tony Butler (bass) and Mark Brzezicki (drums). Adamson committed suicide on 12/16/2001 (age 43).				
9/10/83	3	22	1 In A Big Country	17	●	*The Crossing* .... Mercury 812870	
5/19/84	48	3	2 Wonderland	86		*Wonderland* .... Mercury 818835	
6/21/86	5	12	3 Look Away	—		*The Seer* .... Mercury 826844	
9/10/88	20	8	4 King Of Emotion	—		*Peace In Our Time* .... Reprise 25787	
8/28/93	34	6	5 The One I Love	—		*The Buffalo Skinners* .... Fox 66294	
			BIG HEAD TODD & THE MONSTERS				
			Rock trio from Boulder, Colorado: Todd Park Mohr (guitar, keyboards), Rob Squires (bass) and Brian Nevin (drums). All share vocals.				
3/20/93	9	19	1 Broken Hearted Savior	—	▲	*Sister Sweetly* .... Giant 24486	
8/7/93	21	9	2 Circle	—		↓	
11/20/93	14	13	3 Bittersweet	104		↓	
2/8/97	13	13	4 Resignation Superman	—		*Beautiful World* .... Revolution 24661	
4/11/98	29	8	5 Boom Boom	—		↓	
			BIG HEAD TODD & THE MONSTERS WITH JOHN LEE HOOKER				
			#60 Pop hit for John Lee Hooker in 1962				
			BIG WRECK				
			Rock group from Boston: Ian Thornley (vocals), Brian Doherty (guitar), Dave Henning (bass) and Forrest Williams (drums).				
11/29/97+	9	19	1 The Oaf	—		*In Loving Memory Of...* .... Atlantic 83032	
5/23/98	32	9	2 That Song	—		↓	
			BILLY & THE BEATERS — see VERA, Billy				
			BILLY SATELLITE				
			Rock group from Oakland: Monty Byrom (vocals), Danny Chauncey (guitar), Ira Walker (bass) and Tom Falletti (drums). Chauncey later joined **38 Special**.				
6/23/84	30	10	Satisfy Me	64		*Billy Satellite* .... Capitol 12340	

DEBUT	PEAK	WKS	Mainstream Rock Track	Pop Gld	Album Title	Album Label & Number

BLACK CROWES, The ★15★
Rock group from Atlanta: brothers Chris (vocals; born on 12/20/66) and Rich (guitar; born on 5/24/69) Robinson, Jeff Cease (guitar), Johnny Colt (bass) and Steve Gorman (drums). Marc Ford replaced Cease in late 1991. Eddie Harsch (keyboards) joined in late 1992. Ford left in August 1997. Audley Freed replaced Colt in 1998. Chris Robinson married actress Kate Hudson (daughter of Goldie Hawn) on 12/31/2000.

1)Remedy   2)Hotel Illness   3)Thorn In My Pride   4)Hard To Handle   5)Sting Me

2/24/90	5	23	1 Jealous Again	75	▲5 Shake Your Money Maker.	Def American 24278
6/30/90	11	17	2 Twice As Hard	—	↓	
10/6/90	❶2	21	3 Hard To Handle	26	↓	
			#51 Pop hit for Otis Redding in 1968			
1/19/91	❶1	20	4 She Talks To Angels	30	↓	
5/11/91	21	16	5 Seeing Things	—	▲2 The Southern Harmony And Musical	
4/25/92	❶11	20	6 Remedy	48	Companion	Def American 26916
5/30/92	❶4	23	7 Thorn In My Pride	80	↓	
5/30/92	❶2	15	8 Sting Me	—	↓	
10/10/92	❶6	20	9 Hotel Illness	—	↓	
1/23/93	7	10	10 Sometimes Salvation	—	↓	
5/1/93	40	2	11 Bad Luck Blue Eyes Goodbye	—	↓	
10/29/94	5	13	12 A Conspiracy	—	● Amorica.	American 43000
1/28/95	8	12	13 High Head Blues	—	↓	
5/6/95	7	16	14 Wiser Time	—	↓	
7/13/96	3	14	15 Good Friday	—	Three Snakes And One Charm.	American 43082
9/28/96	6	11	16 Blackberry	—	↓	
11/21/98	3	20	17 Kicking My Heart Around	118	By Your Side.	American 69361
2/27/99	7	14	18 Only A Fool	—	↓	
6/12/99	24	9	19 Go Faster	—	↓	
3/18/00	13	13	20 What Is And What Should Never Be . . . . [L]	—	● Live At The Greek	TVT 2140
			first recorded by Led Zeppelin in 1969			
8/5/00	33	7	21 Ten Years Gone . . . . [L]	—	↓	
			JIMMY PAGE & THE BLACK CROWES (above 2)			
			first recorded by Led Zeppelin in 1975			
4/21/01	9	10	22 Lickin'	—	Lions.	V2 27091
6/30/01	12	16	23 Soul Singing	—	↓	

BLACKEYED SUSAN
Hard-rock group from Philadelphia: Dean Davidson (vocals; Britny Fox), Rick Criniti and Tony Santoro (guitars), Erik Levy (bass) and Chris Branco (drums).

6/1/91	44	3	None Of It Matters	—	Electric Rattlebone	Mercury 848575

BLACKFOOT
Rock group from Jacksonville, Florida: Rickey Medlocke (vocals, guitar), Charlie Hargrett (guitar), Greg Walker (bass) and Jakson Spires (drums). Medlocke and Walker were original members of Lynyrd Skynyrd (Medlocke rejoined Lynyrd Skynyrd in 1995). Hargrett left in 1983. Ken Hensley (keyboards; Uriah Heep) joined in early 1984. Also see Classic Rock Tracks section.

7/11/81	9	9	1 Fly Away	42	Marauder.	Atco 107
10/6/84	55	2	2 Morning Dew	—	Vertical Smiles.	Atco 90218
			first recorded by the Grateful Dead in 1967			

BLACK LAB
Rock group from Berkeley, California: Paul Durham (vocals), Michael Belfer (guitar), Geoff Stanfield (bass) and Bryan Head (drums).

11/1/97+	6	22	1 Wash It Away	—	Your Body Above Me	DGC 25127
4/25/98	26	8	2 Time Ago.	75A	↓	

BLACK 'N BLUE
Hard-rock group from Portland, Oregon: Jaime St. James (vocals), Tom Thayer and Jef Warner (guitars), Patrick Young (bass) and Pete Holmes (drums).

9/8/84	50	4	Hold On To 18.	—	Black 'N Blue.	Geffen 24041

BLACK SABBATH
Hard-rock group from Birmingham, England: Ozzy Osbourne (vocals), Tony Iommi (guitar), Terry "Geezer" Butler (bass) and William Ward (drums). Lineup in 1981: Iommi, Butler, Ronnie James Dio (vocals; Rainbow) and Vinnie Appice (drums). Original lineup reunited in 1997. Also see Classic Rock Tracks section.

12/5/81+	24	11	1 Turn Up The Night	—	● Mob Rules	Warner 3605
12/19/81+	46	6	2 Voodoo.	—	↓	
10/17/98	3	21	3 Psycho Man	—	▲ Reunion	Epic 69115
1/30/99	17	8	4 Selling My Soul	—	↓	

BLADES, Jack — see SHAW, Tommy

DEBUT	PEAK	WKS	Mainstream Rock Track	Pop	Gld	Album Title	Album Label & Number

BLIND MELON
Male rock group formed in Los Angeles: Shannon Hoon (vocals), Rogers Stevens and Christopher Thorn (guitars), Brad Smith (bass) and Glen Graham (drums). Hoon died of a drug overdose on 10/21/95 (age 28).

8/7/93	❶²	20	1 No Rain	20	▲⁴	Blind Melon	Capitol 96585
12/11/93+	10	12	2 Tones Of Home	—		↓	
8/19/95	25	8	3 Galaxie	54ᴬ		Soup	Capitol 28732

BLINDSIDE
Rock group from Stockholm, Sweden: Christian Lindskog (vocals), Simon Grenehed (guitar), Tomas Naslund (bass) and Marcus Dahlstrom (drums).

| 8/24/02 | 18 | 14↑ | Pitiful | — | | Silence | Elektra 62675 |

BLINK-182
Rock trio from San Diego: Tom Delonge (vocals, guitar), Mark Hoppus (vocals, bass) and Scott Raynor (drums). Travis Barker replaced Raynor in late 1998. Delonge and Barker also formed **Box Car Racer**.

| 1/24/98 | 26 | 9 | 1 Dammit (Growing Up) | 61ᴬ | ▲ | Dude Ranch | MCA 11624 |
| 5/29/99 | 19 | 19 | 2 What's My Age Again? | 58 | ▲⁵ | Enema Of The State | MCA 11950 |

BLONDIE
Pop-rock group formed in New York City: **Debbie Harry** (vocals), Chris Stein and Frank Infante (guitars), Jimmy Destri (keyboards), Nigel Harrison (bass) and Clem Burke (drums). Group disbanded in 1982; reunited in 1999.

| 3/21/81 | 35 | 2 | Rapture | ❶² | ▲ | Autoamerican | Chrysalis 1290 |

BLOODHOUND GANG
Rock group from Philadelphia: Jimmy Pop Ali (vocals), Lupus (guitar), Q-Ball (DJ), Evil Jared (bass) and Spanky G (drums).

| 1/4/97 | 28 | 6 | Fire Water Burn | — | ● | One Fierce Beer Coaster | Geffen 25124 |

BLOODLINE
Rock group from Florida: Berry Oakley Jr. (vocals), Joe Bonamassa and Waylon Krieger (guitars), Lou Segreti (keyboards) and Erin Davis (drums). Oakley is the son of the late Berry Oakley of **The Allman Brothers Band**. Davis is the son of the late jazz great Miles Davis. Krieger is the son of **Doors** guitarist Robby Krieger.

| 10/1/94 | 32 | 7 | Stone Cold Hearted | — | | Bloodline | EMI 30060 |

BLUE MURDER
Rock trio: John Sykes (vocals, guitar; **Thin Lizzy**, **Whitesnake**), Tony Franklin (bass; **The Firm**) and Carmine Appice (drums; Vanilla Fudge, Cactus, KGB). Sykes fronted a new lineup in 1994: Nik Green (keyboards), Marco Mendoza (bass) and Tommy O'Steen (drums).

| 7/22/89 | 15 | 9 | 1 Jelly Roll | — | | Blue Murder | Geffen 24212 |
| 3/26/94 | 35 | 4 | 2 We All Fall Down | — | | Nothin' But Trouble | Geffen 24419 |

BLUE ÖYSTER CULT
Hard-rock group from Long Island, New York: Eric Bloom (vocals), Donald "Buck Dharma" Roeser (guitar), Allen Lanier (keyboards), and brothers Joe (bass) and Albert (drums) Bouchard. Rick Downey replaced Albert Bouchard in 1982. Downey left in 1984. Tommy Zvoncheck (keyboards) and Jimmy Wilcox (drums) joined in 1985. Original lineup reunited in 1988. Bloom is a cousin of DJ Howard Stern. Also see **Classic Rock Tracks** section.

7/4/81	❶²	23	1 Burnin' For You	40	●	Fire Of Unknown Origin	Columbia 37389
8/8/81	49	6	2 Joan Crawford	—		↓	
5/1/82	24	4	3 Roadhouse Blues [L]	—		Extraterrestrial Live	Columbia 37946

Robby Krieger (guitar; member of **The Doors** on original version in 1970); recorded on 12/15/81 at The Country Club in Reseda, California

11/26/83	11	15	4 Take Me Away	—		The Revolution By Night	Columbia 38947
12/3/83	16	12	5 Shooting Shark	83		↓	
2/15/86	9	10	6 Dancin' In The Ruins	—		Club Ninja	Columbia 39979
7/30/88	12	9	7 Astronomy	—		Imaginos	Columbia 40618

BLUE RODEO
Folk-rock group from Toronto: Jim Cuddy (vocals, guitar), Greg Keelor (guitar), Bob Wiseman (keyboards), Bazil Donovan (bass) and Cleave Anderson (drums). Group appeared as Meryl Streep's backing band in the 1990 movie *Postcards From The Edge*.

| 2/9/91 | 37 | 6 | Til I Am Myself Again | — | | Casino | EastWest 91601 |

BLUES TRAVELER
Blues-rock group from New York City: John Popper (vocals, harmonica), Chan Kinchla (guitar), Bobby Sheehan (bass) and Brendan Hill (drums). Sheehan died of a drug overdose on 8/20/99 (age 31).

5/29/93	34	4	1 Conquer Me	—	●	Save His Soul	A&M 540080
4/22/95	13	26	2 Run-Around	8	▲⁶	four	A&M 540265
9/30/95	15	22	3 Hook	23		↓	
7/20/96	19	11	4 But Anyway [L]	36ᴬ	▲	Live From The Fall	A&M 540515
6/14/97	4	19	5 Carolina Blues	—	▲	Straight On Till Morning	A&M 540750
10/4/97	27	6	6 Most Precarious	74ᴬ		↓	

BLUR
Techno-rock group from London: Damon Albarn (vocals), Graham Coxon (guitar), Alex James (bass) and Dave Rowntree (drums).

| 5/31/97 | 25 | 10 | Song 2 | 55ᴬ | ● | Blur | Food 42876 |

BOBBY & THE MIDNITES
Rock group led by **Grateful Dead** guitarist Bob Weir. Group also included Grateful Dead member Brent Mydland (keyboards), Bobby Cochran (guitar), Matthew Kelly (harmonica), Alphonso Johnson (bass) and Billy Cobham (drums). Mydland died of a drug overdose on 7/26/90 (age 37).

| 12/19/81+ | 48 | 6 | Too Many Losers | — | | Bobby & The Midnites | Arista 9568 |

DEBUT	PEAK	WKS	Mainstream Rock Track	Pop	Gld	Album Title	Album Label & Number

BoDEANS
Folk-rock group from Waukesha, Wisconsin: Kurt Neumann and Sam Llanas (vocals, guitars), Bob Griffin (bass) and Guy Hoffman (drums). In 1989, Hoffman left; Michael Ramos (keyboards) and Danny Gayol (drums) joined.

10/3/87	16	11	1 Only Love	—		Outside Looking In	Slash 25629
2/13/88	32	7	2 Dreams	—		↓	
7/1/89	20	10	3 You Don't Get Much	—		home.	Slash 25876
10/21/89	50	2	4 Good Work	—		↓	
4/13/91	34	6	5 Black, White And Blood Red	—		Black And White	Slash 26487
12/25/93+	34	5	6 Feed The Fire	—		Go Slow Down	Slash 45455

BOLTON, Michael
Born Michael Bolotin on 2/26/53 in New Haven, Connecticut. First recorded for Epic in 1968. Lead singer of Blackjack in the late 1970s. Began recording as Michael Bolton in 1983.

4/23/83	27	8	1 Fools Game	82	●	Michael Bolton	Columbia 38537
3/16/85	38	7	2 Everybody's Crazy	—		Everybody's Crazy	Columbia 39328
12/19/87+	12	13	3 (Sittin' On) The Dock Of The Bay	11	▲²	The Hunger.	Columbia 40473
			#1 Pop hit for Otis Redding in 1968				
5/14/88	40	4	4 Wait On Love	79		↓	

BONDS, Gary U.S.
Born Gary Anderson on 6/6/39 in Jacksonville, Florida. Black rock and roll singer/songwriter. Had several hits in the early 1960s.

5/2/81	5	14	1 This Little Girl	11		Dedication	EMI America 17051
5/9/81	29	12	2 Jole Blon	65		↓	
			#1 Country hit for Red Foley in 1947				
6/19/82	10	9	3 Out Of Work	21		On The Line	EMI America 17068
			Clarence Clemons (saxophone, above 3); above 3 written (except #2) and produced by Bruce Springsteen				

BONHAM
Born Jason Bonham on 7/15/66 in Birmingham, England. Rock drummer. Son of Led Zeppelin drummer John Bonham. His band included Daniel MacMaster (vocals), Ian Hatton (guitar) and John Smithson (keyboards, bass). Charles West and Tony Catania replaced MacMaster and Hatton by 1997.

9/9/89	9	22	1 Wait For You	55	●	The Disregard Of Timekeeping	WTG 45009
1/6/90	29	7	2 Guilty	—		↓	
4/28/90	47	1	3 Bringing Me Down	—		↓	
8/1/92	32	5	4 Change Of A Season	—		Mad Hatter	WTG 46856
11/8/97	33	5	5 Drown In Me	—		When You See The Sun.	MJJ Music 68182
			THE JASON BONHAM BAND				

BONHAM, Tracy
Born on 3/16/67 in Eugene, Oregon. Female singer/songwriter/guitarist.

4/27/96	18	12	Mother Mother	32ᴬ	●	The Burdens Of Being Upright.	Island 524187

BON JOVI ★35★
Rock group from Sayreville, New Jersey: **Jon Bon Jovi** (vocals, born on 3/2/62), **Richie Sambora** (guitar, born on 7/11/59), Dave Bryan (keyboards, born on 2/7/62), Alec John Such (bass, born on 11/14/56) and Tico Torres (drums, born on 10/7/53). Jon acted in the movies *Moonlight and Valentino*, *The Leading Man*, *No Looking Back*, *U-571* and *Pay It Forward*.

1)*Livin' On A Prayer* 2)*Blaze Of Glory* 3)*Keep The Faith* 4)*Bad Medicine* 5)*I'll Be There For You*

2/11/84	5	13	1 Runaway	39	▲²	Bon Jovi	Mercury 814982
5/5/84	44	7	2 She Don't Know Me	48		↓	
5/4/85	28	7	3 Only Lonely	54	▲	7800° Fahrenheit	Mercury 824509
7/6/85	37	7	4 In And Out Of Love	69		↓	
12/28/85+	24	8	5 Silent Night	—		↓	
8/23/86	9	15	6 You Give Love A Bad Name	❶¹	▲¹²	Slippery When Wet.	Mercury 830264
11/1/86	13	17	7 Wanted Dead Or Alive	7		↓	
12/13/86+	❶²	15	8 Livin' On A Prayer	❶⁴		↓	
3/14/87	11	10	9 Never Say Goodbye	28ᴬ		↓	
9/24/88	3	9	10 Bad Medicine	❶²	▲⁷	New Jersey.	Mercury 836345
10/8/88	7	17	11 Born To Be My Baby	3		↓	
1/28/89	5	13	12 I'll Be There For You	❶¹		↓	
5/27/89	20	9	13 Lay Your Hands On Me	7		↓	
10/21/89	37	6	14 Living In Sin	9		↓	
12/16/89	48	4	15 The Boys Are Back In Town . . . . [L]	—		Make A Difference Foundation: Stairway To Heaven/ Highway To Hell (various artists) . . .	Mercury 842093
			recorded on 8/12/89 at the Moscow Music Peace Festival; #12 Pop hit for Thin Lizzy in 1976				
7/21/90	❶¹	12	16 Blaze Of Glory	❶¹	▲²	Blaze Of Glory/Young Guns II	Mercury 846473
10/6/90	20	8	17 Miracle	12		↓	
1/4/92	27	8	18 Levon	64ᴬ	▲	Two Rooms - Celebrating The Songs Of Elton John & Bernie Taupin (various artists)	Polydor 845750
			JON BON JOVI (above 3) #24 Pop hit for Elton John in 1972				

DEBUT	PEAK	WKS	Mainstream Rock Track	Pop	Gld	Album Title	Album Label & Number
			BON JOVI — Cont'd				
10/24/92	**0**[1]	14	19 Keep The Faith	29	▲[2]	*Keep The Faith* . . . . Jambco 514045	
1/30/93	25	7	20 Bed Of Roses	10		↓	
4/17/93	32	6	21 In These Arms	27		↓	
7/10/93	29	6	22 I'll Sleep When I'm Dead	97		↓	
9/28/02	31	6	23 Everyday	118		*Bounce* . . . . Island 063055	
			BOSTON				
			Rock group from Boston: Brad Delp (vocals), Tom Scholz (guitar, keyboards), Barry Goudreau (guitar), Fran Sheehan (bass) and Sib Hashian (drums). Goudreau formed **Orion The Hunter** in 1982. By 1986, reduced to a duo of Scholz and Delp. Delp and Goudreau formed **RTZ**. Scholz's 1994 Boston lineup: Fran Cosmo and Tommy Funderburk (vocals), Gary Pihl (guitar), David Sikes (bass) and Doug Huffman (drums). Scholz is an avid inventor with several patened inventions. Also see **Classic Rock Tracks** section.				
9/27/86	**0**[3]	9	1 Amanda	**0**[2] ▲[4]		*Third Stage* . . . . MCA 6188	
10/11/86	2[1]	17	2 We're Ready	9		↓	
10/18/86	4	19	3 Cool The Engines	—		↓	
1/31/87	7	10	4 Can'tcha Say (You Believe In Me)/Still In Love	20		↓	
6/4/94	4	9	5 I Need Your Love	51	▲	*Walk On* . . . . MCA 10973	
7/30/94	14	8	6 Walk On Medley . . . . Walkin' At Night/Walk On/Get Organ-Ized/Walk On (some more)	—		↓	
			BOTTLE ROCKETS, The				
			Rock group from Festus, Missouri: Brian Henneman (vocals, guitar), Tom Parr (guitar), Tom Ray (bass) and Mark Ortmann (drums).				
11/4/95	27	11	Radar Gun	—		*The Brooklyn Side* . . . . Atlantic 92601	
			BOURGEOIS TAGG				
			Rock group from Los Angeles: Brent Bourgeois (vocals, keyboards), Larry Tagg (vocals, bass), Lyle Workman (guitar), Scott Moon (keyboards) and Michael Urbano (drums).				
10/17/87	8	14	I Don't Mind At All . . . . produced by **Todd Rundgren**	38		*YoYo* . . . . Island 90638	
★46★			**BOWIE, David**				
			Born David Jones on 1/8/47 in London. Pop-rock singer/actor. Joined Lindsay Kemp Mime Troupe in 1967. Adopted new personas (Ziggy Stardust, Alladin Sane, Thin White Duke) to accompany several of his musical phases. Married to Angie Barnett, the subject of **The Rolling Stones'** song "Angie," from 1970-80. Acted in several movies. Starred in *The Elephant Man* on Broadway. Formed **Tin Machine** in 1988. Married Somalian actress/supermodel Iman on 4/24/92. Inducted into the Rock and Roll Hall of Fame in 1996. Also see **Classic Rock Tracks** section. *1)Blue Jean 2)Dancing In The Street 3)China Girl*				
11/7/81	7	18	1 Under Pressure **QUEEN & DAVID BOWIE**	29	▲	*Greatest Hits* (Queen) . . . . Elektra 564	
3/27/82	9	13	2 Cat People (Putting Out Fire) *also see #4 below*	67		*Cat People* (soundtrack) . . . . Backstreet 6107	
3/26/83	8	16	3 Let's Dance	**0**[1] ▲		*Let's Dance* . . . . EMI America 17093	
4/9/83	11	7	4 Cat People (Putting Out Fire) . . . . [R] *new version of #2 above*	—		↓	
5/7/83	6	32	5 Modern Love	14		↓	
5/28/83	3	17	6 China Girl *first recorded by **Iggy Pop** in 1977*	10		↓	
8/20/83	31	5	7 Criminal World . . . . **Stevie Ray Vaughan** (guitar, above 5)	—		↓	
9/15/84	2[2]	12	8 Blue Jean	8	▲	*Tonight* . . . . EMI America 17138	
10/13/84	40	5	9 Neighborhood Threat	—		↓	
12/8/84	32	6	10 Tonight . . . . **Tina Turner** (backing vocal)	53		↓	
2/9/85	7	11	11 This Is Not America **DAVID BOWIE/PAT METHENY GROUP**	32		*The Falcon And The Snowman* (soundtrack) . . . . EMI America 17150	
8/31/85	3	9	12 Dancing In The Street **MICK JAGGER/DAVID BOWIE** *#2 Pop hit for Martha & The Vandellas in 1964*	7		(single only) . . . . EMI America 8288	
3/29/86	9	9	13 Absolute Beginners	53		*Absolute Beginners* (soundtrack) . . . EMI America 17182	
6/7/86	18	8	14 Underground	—		*Labyrinth* (soundtrack) . . . . EMI America 17206	
4/4/87	3	10	15 Day-In Day-Out	21	●	*Never Let Me Down* . . . . EMI America 17267	
5/2/87	7	13	16 Time Will Crawl	—		↓	
5/23/87	38	11	17 Bang Bang	—		↓	
8/8/87	15	9	18 Never Let Me Down	27		↓	
5/19/90	24	7	19 Pretty Pink Rose . . . . **ADRIAN BELEW & DAVID BOWIE**	—		*Young Lions* (Belew) . . . . Atlantic 82099	
			BOW WOW WOW				
			New-wave group assembled in London by Malcom McLaren (former Sex Pistols manager). Consisted of Annabella Lwin (vocals; born Myant Myant Aye in Burma), Matthew Ashman (guitar), Leroy Gorman (bass) and Dave Barbarossa (drums). The latter three were members of **Adam And The Ants** until 1980. Ashman died of diabetes on 11/21/95 (age 35).				
5/15/82	22	12	I Want Candy . . . . *#11 Pop hit for The Strangeloves in 1965*	62		*The Last Of The Mohicans* . . . . RCA 4314	

DEBUG	PEAK	WKS	Mainstream Rock Track	Pop	Gld	Album Title	Album Label & Number
			BOX, The				
			Rock group from Montreal: Jean Marc (vocals), Claude Thibault (guitar), Guido Pisapia (keyboards), Jean-Pierre Brie (bass) and Philippe Bernard (drums).				
3/2/91	49	1	Temptation	—		The Pleasure And The Pain	Capitol 94953
			BOX OF FROGS				
			Rock group from England: John Fiddler (vocals), Chris Dreja (guitar), Paul Samwell-Smith (bass) and Jim McCarty (drums). The latter three were members of The Yardbirds. McCarty also with Renaissance and Illusion.				
6/30/84	14	13	Back Where I Started	—		Box Of Frogs	Epic 39327
			Jeff Beck (guitar)				
			BOZZIO, Terry — see BECK, Jeff				
			BRAMHALL, Doyle II and Smokestack				
			Born on 12/24/68 in Austin, Texas. Blues-rock singer/guitarist. Son of songwriter Doyle Bramhall (collaborated with **Stevie Ray Vaughan**). His group Smokestack: Susannah Melvoin (vocals), Chris Bruce (bass) and J.J. Johnson (drums). Melvoin is the sister of Wendy Melvoin (of **Prince**'s Revolution) and the late Jonathan Melvoin (of **The Smashing Pumpkins**).				
6/9/01	33	9	Green Light Girl	—		Welcome	RCA 69360
			BRANDOS, The				
			Rock group from New York City: Dave Kincaid (vocals), Ed Rupprecht (guitar), Ernie Mendillo (bass) and Larry Mason (drums).				
9/19/87	34	6	Gettysburg	—		Honor Among Thieves	Relativity 8192
			BRANNEN, John				
			Born in Savannah, Georgia; raised in Charleston, South Carolina. Country-rock singer.				
2/6/88	21	10	Desolation Angel	—		Mystery Street	Apache 71650
			BREAKING BENJAMIN				
			Hard-rock group from Wilkes Barre, Pennsylvania: Ben Burnley (vocals, guitar), Aaron Fink (guitar), Mark Klepaski (bass) and Jeremy Hummel (drums).				
7/27/02	19	17	Polyamorous	—		Saturate	Hollywood 62356
			BREAKING POINT				
			Rock group from Memphis: Brett Erickson (vocals, guitar), Justin Rimer (guitar), Greg Edmondson (bass) and Jody Abbott (drums).				
5/11/02	38	3	One Of A Kind	—		Coming Of Age	Wind-Up 642
			BREAKS, The				
			Pop-rock group from Memphis: Susanne Jerome Taylor (vocals), Pat Taylor (guitar), Tom Ward (keyboards), Rob Caudill (bass) and Russ Caudill (drums).				
10/1/83	39	2	✓ She Wants You	—		The Breaks	RCA 4675
			BREEDERS, The				
			Rock group from Dayton, Ohio: twin sisters/guitarists/vocalists Kim and Kelley Deal, bassist Josephine Wiggs (native of Bedfordshire, England) and drummer Jim MacPherson. Kim was a member of the **Pixies**. Tanya Donelly (**Throwing Muses**, **Belly**) was an early member.				
2/5/94	32	5	Cannonball	44	▲	Last Splash	4 A D 61508
			BRICKELL, Edie, & New Bohemians				
			Born on 3/10/66 in Oak Cliff, Texas. Female singer/songwriter. New Bohemians consisted of Kenny Withrow (guitar), Brad Houser (bass) and John Bush (drums). Joining the band by 1990 were Wes Burt-Martin (guitar) and Matt Chamberlain (drums). Brickell married **Paul Simon** on 5/30/92.				
10/15/88	9	18	1 What I Am	7	▲²	Shooting Rubberbands At The Stars	Geffen 24192
2/4/89	38	6	2 Little Miss S.	—	↓		
4/1/89	32	8	3 Circle	48	↓		
1/27/90	28	6	4 A Hard Rain's A Gonna Fall	—		Born On The Fourth Of July (soundtrack)	MCA 6340
			first recorded by **Bob Dylan** in 1963				
11/17/90	26	9	5 Mama Help Me	—		Ghost Of A Dog	Geffen 24304
			BRILEY, Martin				
			Born in England. Rock singer/songwriter/guitarist.				
4/30/83	15	14	1 The Salt In My Tears	36		One Night With A Stranger	Mercury 810332
1/26/85	31	6	2 Dangerous Moments	—		Dangerous Moments	Mercury 822423
			BRITNY FOX				
			Hard-rock group from Philadelphia: "Dizzy" Dean Davidson (vocals), Michael Kelly Smith (guitar), Billy Childs (bass) and Johnny Dee (drums). Davidson later formed **Blackeyed Susan**.				
7/16/88	33	7	1 Long Way To Love	100		Britny Fox	Columbia 44140
2/10/90	34	9	2 Dream On	—		Boys In Heat	Columbia 45300
			BROADCASTERS, The				
			Rock group from New York City: brothers Billy (vocals, guitar) and Steve (guitar) Roues, Blackie Pagano (bass) and Ed Steinberg (drums).				
1/23/88	48	3	Down In The Trenches	—		13 Ghosts	Enigma 73315
	★96★		**BROTHER CANE**				
			Rock group from Birmingham, Alabama: Damon Johnson (vocals, guitar), Roman Glick (guitar), Glenn Maxey (bass) and Scott Collier (drums). David Anderson replaced Maxey by 1995.				
6/5/93	2¹	22	1 Got No Shame	—		Brother Cane	Virgin 87797
10/23/93	6	18	2 That Don't Satisfy Me	—	↓		
2/26/94	12	14	3 Hard Act To Follow	—	↓		
7/1/95	❶⁶	26	4 And Fools Shine On	—		Seeds	Virgin 40564
10/28/95	25	9	5 Breadmaker	—	↓		
2/17/96	30	7	6 Voice Of Eujena	—	↓		

DEBUT	PEAK	WKS	Mainstream Rock Track	Pop	Gld	Album Title	Album Label & Number
			BROTHER CANE — Cont'd				
3/28/98	**❶**⁴	26	7 I Lie In The Bed I Make	—		Wishpool	Virgin 45561
8/8/98	12	14	8 Machete....................	—		↓	

BROWN, Danny Joe, And The Danny Joe Brown Band
Born in 1951 in Jacksonville, Florida. Lead singer of **Molly Hatchet**. His band included: Bobby Ingram, Steve Wheeler and Kenny McVay (guitars), John Galvin (keyboards), Buzzy Meekins (bass) and Jimmy Glenn (drums).

| 6/27/81 | 12 | 13 | Edge Of Sundown . . . . | — | | Danny Joe Brown And The Danny Joe Brown Band . . . . | Epic 37385 |

★97★ BROWNE, Jackson
Born on 10/9/48 on a U.S. Army base in Heidelberg, Germany; raised in Los Angeles. Pop-rock singer/songwriter/guitarist/pianist. Worked with the **Eagles** and **Warren Zevon**. Wife, Phyllis, committed suicide on 3/25/76. A prominent activist against nuclear power. Also see **Classic Rock Tracks** section.

1)For America 2)Lawyers In Love 3)World In Motion

8/7/82	4	13	1 Somebody's Baby	7		Fast Times At Ridgemont High (soundtrack)	Full Moon 60158
7/9/83	4	17	2 Lawyers In Love	13	▲	Lawyers In Love	Asylum 60268
8/27/83	7	12	3 For A Rocker	45		↓	
9/3/83	37	9	4 Cut It Away	—		↓	
10/29/83	18	8	5 Tender Is The Night	25		↓	
11/2/85	16	11	6 You're A Friend Of Mine	18		Hero (Clemons).	Columbia 40010
			CLARENCE CLEMONS And JACKSON BROWNE includes vocals by actress Daryl Hannah (Browne's then-girlfriend)				
3/1/86	3	11	7 For America	30	●	Lives In The Balance	Asylum 60457
3/29/86	33	9	8 Lives In The Balance	—		↓	
5/17/86	15	10	9 In The Shape Of A Heart	70		↓	
6/3/89	4	9	10 World In Motion	—		World In Motion.	Elektra 60830
			Bonnie Raitt (harmony vocal)				
7/22/89	9	10	11 Chasing You Into The Light	—		↓	
10/30/93	18	10	12 I'm Alive	118	●	I'm Alive	Elektra 61524

BRUCE, Jack — see TROWER, Robin

BUCKCHERRY
Rock group from Los Angeles: Joshua Todd (vocals), Keith Nelson and Yogi (guitars), Jon Brightman (bass) and Devon Glenn (drums).

3/27/99	**❶**³	28	1 Lit Up	—	●	Buckcherry.	DreamWorks 50044
8/21/99	25	10	2 For The Movies.	—		↓	
12/4/99	38	3	3 Dead Again	—		↓	
2/19/00	29	6	4 Check Your Head	—		↓	
2/24/01	9	15	5 Ridin'	—		Time Bomb.	DreamWorks 450287

BUCKINGHAM, Lindsey
Born on 10/3/47 in Palo Alto, California. Rock singer/songwriter/guitarist. Formed Buckingham-Nicks duo with then-girlfriend, **Stevie Nicks**. Both joined **Fleetwood Mac** in 1975.

10/24/81	12	18	1 Trouble	9		Law And Order	Asylum 561
7/28/84	4	14	2 Go Insane	23		Go Insane.	Elektra 60363
7/4/92	23	7	3 Wrong.	—		Out Of The Cradle	Reprise 26182
10/3/92	38	2	4 Countdown	—		↓	

BUFFETT, Jimmy
Born on 12/25/46 in Pascagoula, Mississippi; raised in Mobile, Alabama. Singer/songwriter/guitarist. Settled in Key West, Florida, in 1971. Author of several books. Appeared in the movie FM. Faithful fans known as "Parrotheads." Also see **Classic Rock Tracks** section.

| 3/21/81 | 51 | 5 | 1 It's My Job. . . . . | 57 | | Coconut Telegraph . . . . | MCA 5169 |
| 1/30/82 | 32 | 8 | 2 It's Midnight And I'm Not Famous Yet. . . . . | — | | Somewhere Over China . . . . | MCA 5285 |

BULLETBOYS
Hard-rock group from Los Angeles: Marq Torien (vocals), Mick Sweda (guitar), Lonnie Vencent (bass) and Jimmy D'Anda (drums).

2/11/89	30	9	1 For The Love Of Money	78	●	BulletBoys	Warner 25782
			#9 Pop hit for The O'Jays in 1974				
6/17/89	23	9	2 Smooth Up.	71		↓	
5/25/91	22	9	3 Hang On St. Christopher	—		Freakshow	Warner 26168

BUNBURYS, The
All-star group: **Eric Clapton**, The Bee Gees, **Elton John** and **George Harrison**.

| 9/17/88 | 8 | 8 | Fight (No Matter How Long) | — | ● | 1988 Summer Olympics Album/One Moment In Time (various artists) . . . . | Arista 8551 |

BURTNICK, Glen
Born in New Jersey. Pop singer/guitarist. Joined **Styx** in 1990.

| 3/29/86 | 40 | 4 | 1 Little Red House. . . . . | — | | Talking In Code . . . . | A&M 5114 |
| 8/22/87 | 23 | 9 | 2 Follow You . . . . | 65 | | Heroes & Zeros . . . . | A&M 5166 |

DEBUT	PEAK	WKS	Mainstream Rock Track	Pop	Gld	Album Title	Album Label & Number

BUSH ★52★
Rock group from London: **Gavin Rossdale** (vocals, guitar; born on 10/30/67), Nigel Pulsford (guitar; born on 4/11/63), Dave Parsons (bass; born on 7/2/65) and Robin Goodridge (drums; born on 9/10/66). Rossdale married Gwen Stefani (lead singer of **No Doubt**) on 9/14/2002.
1)Swallowed 2)Comedown 3)The Chemicals Between Us

DEBUT	PEAK	WKS	Track	Pop	Gld	Album Title	Label & Number
2/11/95	5	26	1 **Everything Zen**	40[A]	▲6	*Sixteen Stone*	Trauma 92531
5/6/95	6	26	2 **Little Things**	46[A]	↓		
8/12/95	2[1]	26	3 **Comedown**	30	↓		
11/25/95+	4	26	4 **Glycerine**.	28	↓		
2/24/96	4	26	5 **Machinehead**	43	↓		
11/2/96	2[2]	19	6 **Swallowed**	27[A]	▲3	*Razorblade Suitcase*	Trauma 90091
12/28/96+	5	25	7 **Greedy Fly**	41[A]	↓		
4/19/97	18	9	8 **Cold Contagious**	—	↓		
11/29/97+	28	13	9 **Mouth**	63[A]		*An American Werewolf In Paris (soundtrack)*.	Hollywood 62131
9/25/99	3	31	10 **The Chemicals Between Us**	67	▲	*The Science Of Things*	Trauma 490483
1/29/00	26	9	11 **Letting The Cables Sleep**	113	↓		
5/13/00	16	11	12 **Warm Machine**	—	↓		
9/15/01	10	14	13 **The People That We Love**	114		*Golden State*	Atlantic 83488
			originally titled "Speed Kills" (changed due to the 9/11 terrorist attacks)				
12/15/01	34	7	14 **Headful Of Ghosts**	—	↓		

BUSH, Kate
Born on 7/30/58 in Bexleyheath, Kent, England. Singer/songwriter.

| 11/16/85 | 34 | 5 | **Running Up That Hill** . . . . | 30 | | *Hounds Of Love* . . . . | EMI America 17171 |

BUTCHER, Jon, Axis
Born in Boston. Black rock singer/guitarist. The Axis included Chris Martin (bass) and Derek Blevins (drums). Martin left in early 1985. Thom Gimbel (keyboards) and Jimmy Johnson (bass) joined in 1985. Butcher went solo in early 1987.

4/23/83	26	5	1 **Life Takes A Life**	—		*Jon Butcher Axis*	Polydor 810059
3/10/84	24	5	2 **Don't Say Goodnight**	—		*Stare At The Sun*	Polydor 817493
9/21/85	31	6	3 **Stop**	—		*Along The Axis*	Capitol 12425

JON BUTCHER:

3/7/87	7	12	4 **Goodbye Saving Grace**	—		*Wishes*	Capitol 12542
5/30/87	25	5	5 **Holy War**	—	↓		
8/15/87	42	5	6 **Wishes**	—	↓		
1/21/89	7	11	7 **Send Me Somebody**	—		*Pictures From The Front*.	Capitol 90238
4/8/89	38	4	8 **Might As Well Be Free**	—	↓		

BUTTHOLE SURFERS
Rock group from San Antonio, Texas: Gibby Haynes (vocals), Paul Leary (guitar), Jeff Pinkus (bass) and King Coffey (drums).

| 6/29/96 | 19 | 13 | **Pepper** . . . . | 26[A] | ● | *Electriclarryland* . . . . | Capitol 29842 |

BYRDS, The
Folk-rock group formed in Los Angeles: **Roger McGuinn** and **David Crosby** (guitars), Gene Clark (tambourine, guitar), Chris Hillman (bass) and Mike Clarke (drums). All shared vocals. Group had several hits from 1965-67. Numerous personnel changes. McGuinn, Crosby and Hillman reunited in 1990. Gene Clark died on 5/24/91 (age 46). Mike Clarke died on 12/19/93 (age 49). Original group inducted into the Rock and Roll Hall of Fame in 1991. Also see **Classic Rock Tracks** section.

| 11/3/90 | 14 | 11 | **Love That Never Dies** . . . . | — | | *The Byrds* . . . . | Columbia 46773 |

C

CAFFERTY, John, And The Beaver Brown Band
Rock group from Narragansett, Rhode Island: John Cafferty (vocals, guitar), Gary Gramolini (guitar), Robert Cotoia (keyboards), Michael Antunes (sax), Pat Lupo (bass) and Ken Silva (drums). Wrote and recorded the music for the soundtrack *Eddie And The Cruisers*.

9/1/84	❶5	11	1 **On The Dark Side**	7	▲3	*Eddie And The Cruisers*	Scotti Brothers 38929
11/3/84	10	14	2 **Tender Years**	31	↓		
5/11/85	❶2	13	3 **Tough All Over**	22		*Tough All Over*	Scotti Brothers 39405
7/20/85	9	11	4 **C-I-T-Y**	18	↓		
6/4/88	47	1	5 **Song & Dance**.	—		*Roadhouse*	Scotti Brothers 40980

CAKE
Rock group from Sacramento, California: John McCrea (vocals, guitar), Greg Brown (guitar), Vince DiFiore (trumpet), Victor Damiani (bass) and Todd Roper (drums). Brown left in 1997. Gabriel Nelson replaced Damiani in early 1998.

| 12/14/96 | 38 | 5 | 1 **The Distance**. . . . . | 35[A] | ▲ | *Fashion Nugget* . . . . | Capricorn 532867 |
| 2/6/99 | 40 | 1 | 2 **Never There** . . . . | 78 | ▲ | *Prolonging The Magic*. . . . . | Capricorn 538092 |

DEBUT	PEAK	WKS	Mainstream Rock Track	Pop	Gld	Album Title	Album Label & Number

CALL, The
Rock group from California: Michael Been (vocals, guitar), Tom Ferrier (guitar), Greg Freeman (bass) and Scott Musick (drums). Jim Goodwin (keyboards) replaced Freeman in 1984.

DEBUT	PEAK	WKS	Track	Pop		Album Title	Label
4/23/83	17	6	1 The Walls Came Down	74		Modern Romans	Mercury 810307
3/1/86	17	13	2 I Still Believe (Great Design)	—		Reconciled	Elektra 60440
6/28/86	38	7	3 Everywhere I Go	—		↓	
8/1/87	38	3	4 I Don't Wanna	—		Into The Woods	Elektra 60739
6/10/89	❶¹	19	5 Let The Day Begin	51		Let The Day Begin	MCA 6303
10/14/89	29	8	6 You Run	—		↓	
10/13/90	39	4	7 What's Happened To You	—		Red Moon	MCA 10033

Peter Gabriel and Jim Kerr (of Simple Minds; backing vocals)

Bono (of U2; backing vocal)

CALLING, The
Rock group from Los Angeles: Alex Band (vocals), Aaron Kamin and Sean Woolstenhulme (guitars), Billy Mohler (bass) and Nate Wood (drums).

7/14/01	37	8	Wherever You Will Go	5	●	Camino Palmero	RCA 67585

CANDLEBOX
Rock group from Seattle: Kevin Martin (vocals), Peter Klett (guitar), Bardi Martin (bass) and Scott Mercado (drums). Dave Krusen replaced Mercado in 1997.

8/14/93	18	16	1 Change	—	▲³	Candlebox	Maverick 45313
12/4/93+	6	26	2 You	78		↓	
4/23/94	4	35	3 Far Behind	18		↓	
11/5/94	8	18	4 Cover Me	—		↓	
9/16/95	5	12	5 Simple Lessons	60ᴬ	●	Lucy	Maverick 45962
11/25/95	19	11	6 Understanding	—		↓	
6/27/98	2⁶	18	7 It's Alright	—		Happy Pills	Maverick 46975
10/17/98	13	15	8 10,000 Horses	—		↓	
2/13/99	17	10	9 Happy Pills	—		↓	

CANTRELL, Jerry
Born on 3/18/66 in Tacoma, Washington. Lead guitarist of Alice In Chains.

5/25/96	14	13	1 Leave Me Alone	—		The Cable Guy (soundtrack)	Work 67654
2/28/98	5	23	2 Cut You In	—		Boggy Depot	Columbia 68147
5/30/98	6	21	3 My Song	—		↓	
12/12/98	36	2	4 Dickeye	—		↓	
4/27/02	10	18	5 Anger Rising	—		Degradation Trip	Roadrunner 618451

CAPALDI, Jim
Born on 8/24/44 in Evesham, Worcestershire, England. Singer/drummer. Member of Traffic.

10/6/84	58	2	1 I'll Keep Holding On	106		One Man Mission	Atlantic 80182
10/29/88	4	14	2 Something So Strong	—		Some Come Running	Island 91024

Steve Winwood (guitar, keyboards)

CARAMEL
Rock group from Toronto: Andy Curran (vocals, bass), Simon Brierley and Virginia Storey (guitars), and Eddie Zeeman (drums).

5/23/98	35	7	Lucy	—		Caramel	Geffen 25228

CAREY, Tony
Born on 10/16/52 in Watsonville, California. Rock singer/songwriter/keyboardist. Former member of Rainbow and Planet P.

2/19/83	8	16	1 I Won't Be Home Tonight	79		Tony Carey [I Won't Be Home Tonight]	Rocshire 0001
3/10/84	❶¹	12	2 A Fine Fine Day	22		Some Tough City	MCA 5464
6/16/84	21	8	3 The First Day Of Summer	33		↓	

CARNES, Kim
Born on 7/20/45 in Los Angeles. Singer/songwriter/pianist.

5/2/81	5	12	1 Bette Davis Eyes	❶⁹	▲	Mistaken Identity	EMI America 17052
6/27/81	46	3	2 Break The Rules Tonite (Out Of School)	—		↓	

CAROLINE'S SPINE
Rock group from Tulsa, Oklahoma: Jimmy Newquist (vocals), Mark Haugh (guitar), Scott Jones (bass) and Jason Gilardi (drums).

12/27/97+	23	11	1 Sullivan	—		Monsoon	Hollywood 62087
8/28/99	30	8	2 Attention Please	—		Attention Please	Hollywood 62133
4/1/00	23	10	3 Nothing To Prove	—		↓	

CARRACK, Paul
Born on 4/22/51 in Sheffield, Yorkshire, England. Lead singer of Ace, Squeeze and Mike + The Mechanics.

10/16/82	33	3	1 Lesson In Love	—		Suburban Voodoo	Epic 38161
10/23/82	22	4	2 I Need You	37		↓	
10/24/87+	5	18	3 Don't Shed A Tear	9		One Good Reason	Chrysalis 41578
3/12/88	20	9	4 One Good Reason	28		↓	
11/17/90	37	3	5 Hey You [L]	—		The Wall - Live In Berlin (Roger Waters)	Mercury 846611

recorded at the Berlin Wall on 7/21/90; first recorded by Pink Floyd in 1979

DEBUT	PEAK	WKS	Mainstream Rock Track	Pop	Gld	Album Title	Album Label & Number

CARROLL, Jim, Band
Born on 8/1/50 in New York City. Poet/rock singer. His band included Brian Linsley and Terrell Winn (guitars), Steve Linsley (bass) and Wayne Woods (drums). The 1995 movie *The Basketball Diaries* was based on Carroll's autobiographical book.

| 3/21/81 | 50 | 3 | People Who Died.. 103 | | | *Catholic Boy* . . . . Atco 132 |

★49★ **CARS, The**
Pop-rock group from Boston: **Ric Ocasek** (vocals, guitar; born on 3/23/49), **Benjamin Orr** (bass, vocals; born on 8/9/47; died of cancer on 10/3/2000, age 53), **Elliot Easton** (guitar; born on 12/18/53), Greg Hawkes (keyboards; born on 3/15/50) and David Robinson (drums; born on 4/2/53). Also see **Classic Rock Tracks** section.
1)*Tonight She Comes* 2)*You Might Think* 3)*Magic*

11/28/81+	2^2	21	1 Shake It Up	4	▲	*Shake It Up* . . . . Elektra 567
12/26/81+	37	13	2 Cruiser..	—		↓
2/27/82	39	2	3 Victim Of Love	—		↓
4/3/82	24	4	4 Since You're Gone	41		↓
3/10/84	$❶^3$	14	5 You Might Think...	7	▲³	*Heartbeat City*. . . . . Elektra 60296
3/31/84	$❶^1$	20	6 Magic	12		↓
3/31/84	22	24	7 Hello Again	20		↓
6/2/84	3	21	8 Drive	3		↓
6/9/84	31	16	9 It's Not The Night	—		↓
1/26/85	11	14	10 Why Can't I Have You	33		↓
2/9/85	19	8	11 Breakaway	—		(single only) . . . . Elektra 69657
11/2/85	$❶^3$	14	12 Tonight She Comes	7	▲³	*The Cars Greatest Hits* . . . . Elektra 60464
2/22/86	29	5	13 I'm Not The One..	32		↓
8/29/87	2^3	8	14 You Are The Girl	17	●	*Door To Door* . . . . Elektra 60747
9/12/87	4	11	15 Strap Me In	85		↓
11/28/87	42	3	16 Double Trouble	—		↓

CATHERINE WHEEL
Rock group from England: Rob Dickinson (vocals), Brian Futter (guitar), Dave Hawes (bass) and Neil Sims (drums). Dickinson is the cousin of **Bruce Dickinson** (of **Iron Maiden**).

| 6/17/95 | 24 | 8 | Waydown .... | — | | *Happy Days* . . . . Mercury 526850 |

CETERA, Peter
Born on 9/13/44 in Chicago. Lead singer/bass guitarist of **Chicago** from 1967-85.

| 12/19/81+ | 6 | 16 | 1 Livin' In The Limelight .... | — | | *Peter Cetera* . . . . Full Moon 3624 |
| 9/10/88 | 32 | 6 | 2 You Never Listen To Me .... | — | | *One More Story* . . . . Full Moon 25704 |

CHALK FARM
Rock group from Los Angeles: Michael Duff (vocals, guitar), Trace Ritter (guitar), Orlando Sims (bass) and Toby Scarbrough (drums).

| 9/21/96 | 13 | 15 | 1 Lie On Lie... | — | | *Notwithstanding* . . . . Columbia 67613 |
| 4/26/97 | 35 | 4 | 2 Live Tomorrow .... | — | | ↓ |

CHAPMAN, Tracy
Born on 3/20/64 in Cleveland. Folk-R&B singer/songwriter/guitarist. Won the 1988 Best New Artist Grammy Award.

5/21/88	19	13	1 Fast Car	6	▲⁴	*Tracy Chapman* . . . . Elektra 60774
7/30/88	22	10	2 Talkin' Bout A Revolution	75		↓
10/7/89	26	7	3 Crossroads	90	▲	*Crossroads* . . . . Elektra 60888

CHARLATANS UK, The
Rock group from Northwich, England: Tim Burgess (vocals), Jon Baker (guitar), Rob Collins (organ), Martin Blunt (bass) and Jon Brookes (drums). Collins died in a car crash on 7/23/96 (age 32).

| 12/15/90+ | 37 | 7 | The Only One I Know .... | — | | *Some Friendly* . . . . Beggars Banquet 2411 |

CHARLIE
Rock group from England: Terry Slesser (vocals), Terry Thomas and Julian Colbeck (guitars), John Anderson (bass) and Steve Gadd (drums).

| 8/20/83 | 13 | 6 | It's Inevitable .... | 38 | | *Charlie* . . . . Mirage 90098 |

CHEAP TRICK
Rock group from Rockford, Illinois: **Robin Zander** (vocals), Rick Nielsen (guitar), Tom Petersson (bass) and Brad "Bun E. Carlos" Carlson (drums). Petersson replaced by Jon Brant in 1980; returned in 1988, replacing Brant. Also see **Classic Rock Tracks** section.
1)*The Flame* 2)*Can't Stop Fallin' Into Love* 3)*Tonight It's You*

5/29/82	11	10	1 If You Want My Love.....................................	45	●	*One On One*. . . . . Epic 38021
3/31/84	36	2	2 Up The Creek	—		*Up The Creek (soundtrack)* . . . . Pasha 39333
8/3/85	8	13	3 Tonight It's You	44		*Standing On The Edge* . . . . Epic 39592
4/9/88	3	14	4 The Flame	$❶^2$	▲	*Lap Of Luxury*. . . . . Epic 40922
6/25/88	35	6	5 Let Go..	—		↓
8/6/88	8	9	6 Don't Be Cruel	4		↓
			#1 Pop hit for Elvis Presley in 1956			
11/26/88	32	7	7 Ghost Town	33		↓
3/18/89	45	2	8 Never Had A Lot To Lose	75		↓
7/21/90	4	10	9 Can't Stop Fallin' Into Love	12		*Busted* . . . . Epic 46013
9/29/90	32	5	10 Back 'N Blue	—		↓
4/2/94	16	6	11 Woke Up With A Monster	—		*Woke Up With A Monster*. . . . . Warner 45425
4/26/97	39	2	12 Say Goodbye	119		*Cheap Trick* . . . . Red Ant 002

DEBUT	PEAK	WKS	Mainstream Rock Track	Pop	Gld	Album Title	Album Label & Number
			CHECKER, Chubby				
			Born Ernest Evans on 10/3/41 in Andrews, South Carolina; raised in Philadelphia. Best known for popularizing "The Twist" craze in the early 1960s.				
5/15/82	33	5	Harder Than Diamond 104			*The Change Has Come* .... MCA 5291	
			CHEECH & CHONG				
			Duo of comedians Richard "Cheech" Marin (born on 7/13/46 in Watts, California) and Thomas Chong (born on 5/24/38 in Edmonton, Alberta, Canada). Top selling comedy duo of the 1970s. Starred in several movies. Also see **Classic Rock Tracks** section.				
1/10/98	38	1	Santa Claus And His Old Lady .... [X-C] 3ˣ			*Billboard Rock 'N' Roll Christmas (various artists)* .... Rhino 71789	
			recorded in 1971				
			CHEQUERED PAST				
			Hard-rock group: Michael Des Barres (vocals), Tony Sales and Steve Jones (guitars), Nigel Harrison (bass) and Clem Burke (drums). Sales was a member of **Utopia** and **Tin Machine**. Jones was a founding member of the Sex Pistols. Harrison and Burke were members of **Blondie**.				
8/18/84	50	4	How Much Is Too Much? .... —			*Chequered Past* .... EMI America 17123	
			CHEVELLE				
			Rock trio from Chicago: brothers Pete (vocals, guitar), Joe (bass) and Sam (drums) Loeffler.				
2/26/00	40	1	1 Point #1 .... —			*Point #1* .... Squint 5930	
7/20/02	8↑	19↑	2 The Red .... 101↑			*Wonder What's Next* .... Epic 86157	
			CHICAGO				
			Jazz-oriented rock group from Chicago. Lineup in 1984: **Peter Cetera** (vocals, bass), Chris Pinnick (guitar), Robert Lamm and Bill Champlin (keyboards), James Pankow (trombone), Lee Loughnane (trumpet), Walt Parazaider (reeds) and Danny Seraphine (drums). Group had numerous personnel changes. Also see **Classic Rock Tracks** section.				
5/19/84	7	12	1 Stay The Night 16	▲⁶	*Chicago 17* .... Full Moon 25060	
3/9/85	10	10	2 Along Comes A Woman 14	↓		
			CHILLIWACK				
			Rock group from Vancouver: Bill Henderson (vocals, guitar), Brian MacLeod (guitar), Ab Bryant (bass) and Rick Taylor (drums). Bryant and MacLeod later joined Headpins. Bryant was also with **Prism**. MacLeod died of cancer on 4/25/92.				
9/26/81	16	17	1 My Girl (Gone, Gone, Gone) 22		*Wanna Be A Star* .... Millennium 7759	
10/30/82	29	2	2 Whatcha Gonna Do 41		*Opus X* .... Millennium 7766	
12/25/82+	48	4	3 Don't It Make You Feel Good .... —	↓		
			CHOIRBOYS				
			Rock group from Sydney, Australia: Mark Gable (vocals), Brett Williams (guitar), Ian Hulme (bass) and Lindsay Tebbutt (drums).				
3/18/89	33	6	Run To Paradise 80		*Big Bad Noise* .... WTG 45112	
			CHURCH, The				
			Folk-rock group from Canberra, Australia: Steve Kilbey (vocals, bass), Peter Koppes and Marty Willson-Piper (guitars), and Richard Ploog (drums).				
3/5/88	2¹	17	1 Under The Milky Way 24	●	*Starfish* .... Arista 8521	
7/16/88	27	7	2 Reptile .... —	↓		
3/17/90	11	11	3 Metropolis .... —		*Gold Afternoon Fix* .... Arista 8579	
			CINDERELLA				
			Hard-rock group from Philadelphia: Tom Keifer (vocals, guitar), Jeff LaBar (guitar), Eric Brittingham (bass) and Fred Coury (drums; **Arcade**).				
			1)Shelter Me 2)Heartbreak Station 3)Don't Know What You Got (Till It's Gone)				
8/9/86	41	7	1 Shake Me .... —	▲³	*Night Songs* .... Mercury 830076	
1/10/87	25	10	2 Nobody's Fool 13	↓		
3/21/87	37	5	3 Somebody Save Me 66	↓		
7/9/88	20	9	4 Gypsy Road 51	▲³	*Long Cold Winter* .... Mercury 834612	
9/3/88	10	12	5 Don't Know What You Got (Till It's Gone) 12	↓		
1/28/89	18	8	6 The Last Mile 36	↓		
4/1/89	13	13	7 Coming Home 20	↓		
11/17/90	5	15	8 Shelter Me 36	▲	*Heartbreak Station* .... Mercury 848018	
2/16/91	10	16	9 Heartbreak Station 44	↓		
6/8/91	41	6	10 The More Things Change .... —	↓		
3/14/92	45	2	11 Hot And Bothered .... —		*Wayne's World (soundtrack)* .... Reprise 26805	
11/26/94	37	4	12 Bad Attitude Shuffle .... —		*Still Climbing* .... Mercury 522947	
			CLAPTON, Eric ★12★				
			Born Eric Patrick Clapp on 3/30/45 in Ripley, Surrey, England. Prolific rock-blues guitarist/vocalist. Member of The Yardbirds, John Mayall's Bluesbreakers, Cream and Blind Faith. Nicknamed "Slowhand" in 1964 while with The Yardbirds. Inducted into the Rock and Roll Hall of Fame in 2000. Also see **The Bunburys** and **Classic Rock Tracks** section.				
			1)Pretending 2)Bad Love 3)Forever Man 4)I Can't Stand It 5)It's In The Way That You Use It				
3/21/81	❶²	12	1 I Can't Stand It 10	●	*Another Ticket* .... RSO 3095	
3/21/81	18	11	2 Rita Mae .... —	↓		
3/21/81	23	8	3 Catch Me If You Can .... —	↓		
4/11/81	24	1	4 Blow Wind Blow .... —	↓		
			ERIC CLAPTON AND HIS BAND (above 4)				

DEBUT	PEAK	WKS	Mainstream Rock Track	Pop	Gld	Album Title	Album Label & Number
			CLAPTON, Eric — Cont'd				
2/5/83	24	15	5 I've Got A Rock N' Roll Heart	18		Money And Cigarettes	Duck 23773
3/12/83	32	2	6 Ain't Going Down	—		↓	
3/9/85	❶²	12	7 Forever Man	26	▲	Behind The Sun	Duck 25166
3/30/85	11	11	8 She's Waiting	—		↓	
			Phil Collins (drums, producer)				
5/11/85	20	12	9 See What Love Can Do	89		↓	
11/8/86+	❶¹	15	10 It's In The Way That You Use It	—		The Color Of Money (soundtrack)	MCA 6189
12/13/86+	5	15	11 Tearing Us Apart	—	●	August	Duck 25476
			Tina Turner (female vocal)				
1/24/87	9	13	12 Miss You	—		↓	
4/11/87	21	8	13 Run	—		↓	
			above 3 produced by Phil Collins				
4/30/88	4	9	14 After Midnight	—	▲²	Crossroads	Polydor 835261
			new version of his #18 Pop hit in 1970				
11/11/89	❶⁶	14	15 Pretending	55	▲²	Journeyman	Duck 26074
			Chaka Khan (backing vocal)				
11/25/89+	❶³	21	16 Bad Love	88		↓	
			Phil Collins (drums, backing vocal)				
2/24/90	4	16	17 No Alibis	—		↓	
			Daryl Hall (harmony vocal)				
5/5/90	9	16	18 Before You Accuse Me	—		↓	
			Robert Cray (guitar; first recorded by Bo Diddley in 1959				
8/11/90	40	4	19 Run So Far	—		↓	
			George Harrison (guitar, harmony vocal)				
10/19/91	21	12	20 Watch Yourself [L]	—	●	24 Nights	Duck 26420
			Robert Cray (guitar); recorded at The Royal Albert Hall in London				
1/11/92	9	18	21 Tears In Heaven	2⁴	●	Rush (soundtrack)	Reprise 26794
			Clapton wrote this for his son, Conor, who fell to his death on 3/20/91 (age 4) from a New York City apartment window				
2/8/92	6	20	22 Help Me Up	—		↓	
6/13/92	20	5	23 It's Probably Me	—		Lethal Weapon 3 (soundtrack)	Reprise 26989
			STING with Eric Clapton				
8/15/92	10	7	24 Runaway Train	—		↓	
			ELTON JOHN and ERIC CLAPTON				
9/5/92	9	17	25 Layla [L]	12	▲¹⁰	Unplugged	Duck 45024
			live version of his #10 Pop hit in 1972 (as Derek And The Dominos)				
3/6/93	15	13	26 Running On Faith [L]	—		↓	
8/21/93	26	7	27 My Back Pages [L]	—	●	Bob Dylan - The 30th Anniversary Concert (various artists)	Columbia 53230
			BOB DYLAN & FRIENDS: Roger McGuinn, Tom Petty, Neil Young, Eric Clapton & George Harrison				
			recorded on 10/16/92 at Madison Square Garden in New York City; #30 Pop hit for The Byrds in 1967				
11/13/93	4	13	28 Stone Free	—	●	Stone Free: A Tribute To Jimi Hendrix (various artists)	Reprise 45438
			first recorded by Jimi Hendrix in 1969				
9/10/94	5	13	29 I'm Tore Down	—	▲³	From The Cradle	Duck 45735
			#5 R&B hit for Freddy King in 1961				
12/3/94	23	10	30 Motherless Child	114		↓	
2/21/98	26	6	31 My Father's Eyes	16ᴬ	▲	Pilgrim	Duck 46577
4/4/98	19	15	32 She's Gone	—		↓	
6/17/00	26	11	33 Riding With The King	—	▲²	Riding With The King	Reprise 47612
			B.B. KING & ERIC CLAPTON				
			first recorded by John Hiatt in 1983				
3/3/01	21	11	34 Superman Inside	—	●	Reptile	Duck 47966
			CLARKE, Gilby				
			Born on 8/17/62 in Cleveland. Rock guitarist. Member of **Guns N' Roses** from 1991-95.				
8/6/94	15	14	1 Cure Me...Or Kill Me...	—		Pawnshop Guitars	Virgin 39567
12/17/94+	28	8	2 Tijuana Jail	—		↓	
			Slash (lead guitar, above 2)				
			CLASH, The				
			Eclectic new wave rock group from London: John "Joe Strummer" Mellor (vocals), Mick Jones (guitar), Paul Simonon (bass) and Nicky "Topper" Headon (drums). Political activists, who wrote songs protesting racism and oppression. Headon left in May 1983; replaced by Peter Howard. Jones (not to be confused with Mick Jones of Foreigner) left band in 1984 to form **Big Audio Dynamite**. Strummer disbanded The Clash in early 1986, and appeared in the 1987 movie *Straight To Hell*. Simonon formed **Havana 3 A.M.** in 1990. Group inducted into the Rock and Roll Hall of Fame in 2003. Also see **Classic Rock Tracks** section.				
3/21/81	21	4	1 Police On My Back	—	●	Sandinista!	Epic 37037
4/18/81	53	3	2 Hitsville U.K.	—		↓	
12/19/81+	45	5	3 This Is Radio Clash	—		(single only)	CBS 1797
			available only as a British import single				
6/5/82	13	20	4 Should I Stay Or Should I Go	45	▲²	Combat Rock	Epic 37689
7/24/82	6	22	5 Rock The Casbah	8		↓	
			CLASS OF '99				
			All-star rock group: Layne Staley (vocals; **Alice In Chains**), Tom Morello (guitar; **Rage Against The Machine**), Martyn LeNoble (bass; **Porno For Pyros**) and Stephen Perkins (drums; Porno For Pyros).				
12/26/98+	18	9	Another Brick In The Wall (Part 2)	—		The Faculty (soundtrack)	Columbia 69762
			#1 Pop hit for **Pink Floyd** in 1980				

DEBUT	PEAK	WKS	Mainstream Rock Track	Pop	Gld	Album Title	Album Label & Number

CLEMONS, Clarence
Born on 1/11/42 in Norfolk, Virginia. Saxophonist with **Bruce Springsteen**'s E Street Band. Known as the "Big Man."

11/2/85	16	11	You're A Friend Of Mine	18		Hero .... Columbia 40010
			CLARENCE CLEMONS And JACKSON BROWNE			
			includes vocals by actress Daryl Hannah (Browne's then-girlfriend)			

CLOCKS
Rock group from Wichita, Kansas: Jerry Sumner (vocals, bass), Lance Threet (guitar), Gerald Graves (keyboards) and Steve Swaim (drums).

| 8/7/82 | 47 | 1 | She Looks A Lot Like You............................ | 67 | | Clocks .... Boulevard 37981 |

CLUTCH
Rock group from Germantown, Maryland: Neil Fallon (vocals), Tim Sult (guitar), Dan Maines (bass) and Jean Paul Gaster (drums).

| 6/23/01 | 24 | 12 | Careful With That Mic... .... | — | | Pure Rock Fury .... Atlantic 83433 |

COAL CHAMBER
Hard-rock group from Los Angeles: Brad Fafara (vocals), Miquel Rascon (guitar), Rayna Rose (bass) and Mike Cox (drums). Fafara is the nephew of actor Stanley Fafara (played "Whitey Whitney" on TV's *Leave It To Beaver*).

| 10/16/99 | 26 | 7 | Shock The Monkey .... | — | ● | Chamber Music .... Roadrunner 8659 |
| | | | **COAL CHAMBER Featuring Ozzy Osbourne** | | | |

COC — see CORROSION OF CONFORMITY

COCHRANE, Tom/RED RIDER
Born on 5/13/53 in Lynn Lake, Manitoba, Canada. Rock singer/songwriter/guitarist. Red Rider: Ken Greer (guitar), Peter Boynton (keyboards), Jeff Jones (bass) and Rob Baker (drums). Steve Sexton replaced Boynton in 1982; left in early 1984.
1)Life Is A Highway 2)No Regrets 3)Big League

RED RIDER:

9/12/81	11	26	1 Lunatic Fringe	—		As Far As Siam. .... Capitol 12145
1/29/83	13	8	2 Power (Strength In Numbers)...................	—		Neruda .... Capitol 12226
2/12/83	11	15	3 Human Race	↓		
2/19/83	39	3	4 Crack The Sky (Breakaway)	↓		
5/19/84	13	11	5 Young Thing, Wild Dreams (Rock Me)........	71		Breaking Curfew. .... Capitol 12317

TOM COCHRANE AND RED RIDER:

6/28/86	17	11	6 Boy Inside The Man	—		Tom Cochrane and Red Rider .... Capitol 12484
10/4/86	48	2	7 The Untouchable One	↓		
10/8/88	9	10	8 Big League	—		Victory Day .... RCA 8532
1/14/89	42	4	9 Calling America..................................	↓		

TOM COCHRANE:

| 2/29/92 | 6 | 26 | 10 Life Is A Highway .... | 6 | ● | Mad Mad World .... Capitol 97723 |
| 7/25/92 | 7 | 8 | 11 No Regrets .... | — | | ↓ |

COCKBURN, Bruce
Born on 5/27/45 in Ottawa, Canada. Pop-rock singer/songwriter.

| 9/1/84 | 56 | 3 | 1 Lovers In A Dangerous Time .... | — | | Stealing Fire .... Gold Mountain 80012 |
| 12/22/84+ | 16 | 9 | 2 If I Had A Rocket Launcher .... | 88 | | ↓ |

COCKER, Joe
Born John Robert Cocker on 5/20/44 in Sheffield, Yorkshire, England. Pop-rock singer. Notable spastic stage antics were based on Ray Charles's movements at the piano. Also see **Classic Rock Tracks** section.

3/8/86	11	9	1 Shelter Me	91		Cocker .... Capitol 12394
5/31/86	35	4	2 You Can Leave Your Hat On	—		↓
			first recorded by **Randy Newman** in 1972			
10/17/87	11	13	3 Unchain My Heart	—		Unchain My Heart. .... Capitol 48285
			Clarence Clemons (sax solo)			
1/16/88	11	10	4 Two Wrongs	—		↓
8/12/89	6	16	5 When The Night Comes	11		One Night Of Sin .... Capitol 92861
			co-written by **Bryan Adams**			
6/2/90	44	6	6 What Are You Doing With A Fool Like Me ...	96		Joe Cocker Live .... Capitol 93416
6/27/92	7	10	7 Love Is Alive	—		Night Calls .... Capitol 97801
			#2 Pop hit for **Gary Wright** in 1976			

COCK ROBIN
Pop group from Los Angeles: Peter Kingsbery (vocals, bass), Anna LaCazio (vocals, keyboards), Clive Wright (guitars) and Louis Molino (drums).

| 8/24/85 | 28 | 5 | When Your Heart Is Weak .... | 35 | | Cock Robin .... Columbia 39582 |

COHN, Marc
Born on 7/5/59 in Cleveland. Pop-rock singer/songwriter/guitarist. Won the 1991 Best New Artist Grammy Award.

| 4/6/91 | 7 | 16 | 1 Walking In Memphis .... | 13 | ▲ | Marc Cohn....................... Atlantic 82178 |
| 7/6/91 | 22 | 9 | 2 Silver Thunderbird .... | 63 | | ↓ |

COLD
Rock group from Jacksonville, Florida: Scooter Ward (vocals, guitar), Kelley Hayes (guitar), Jeremy Marshall (bass) and Sam McCandless (drums).

9/9/00	25	12	1 Just Got Wicked..................................	—		13 Ways To Bleed On Stage. .... Geffen 490726
2/24/01	17	17	2 No One	—		↓
7/7/01	24	9	3 End Of The World................................	—		↓
4/27/02	28	8	4 Gone Away	—		WWF: Tough Enough 2 (various artists) . . Geffen 493314

DEBUT	PEAK	WKS	Mainstream Rock Track	Pop	Gld	Album Title	Album Label & Number

COLD CHISEL
Rock group from Adelaide, Australia: **Jimmy Barnes** (vocals), Ian Moss (guitar), Don Walker (keyboards), Phil Small (bass) and Steven Prestwich (drums).

DEBUT	PEAK	WKS	Track	Pop		Album	Label
5/23/81	32	7	My Baby	—		East	Elektra 336

COLE, Jude
Born on 6/18/60 in Carbon Cliff, Illinois; raised in East Moline, Illinois. Male singer/guitarist.

3/24/90	3	17	1 Baby, It's Tonight	16		A View From 3rd Street.............	Reprise 26164
7/21/90	33	6	2 Time For Letting Go	32		↓	
9/5/92	6	12	3 Start The Car	71		Start The Car.....................	Reprise 26898
12/19/92+	19	9	4 It Comes Around	—		↓	

COLLECTIVE SOUL ★18★
Rock group from Stockbridge, Georgia: brothers Ed (vocals; born on 8/3/63) and Dean (guitar; born on 10/10/72) Roland with Ross Childress (guitar; born on 9/8/70), Will Turpin (bass; born on 2/8/71) and Shane Evans (drums; born on 4/26/70).

1)Heavy 2)December 3)Shine

3/26/94	❶8	26	1 Shine	11	▲2	Hints Allegations And Things Left Unsaid	Atlantic 82596
8/6/94	12	13	2 Breathe................................	—	↓		
1/28/95	24	26	3 Gel	49A		The Jerky Boys (soundtrack).........	Select 82708
4/22/95	❶9	26	4 December	20	▲3	Collective Soul.....................	Atlantic 82745
8/19/95	8	13	5 Smashing Young Man	—	↓		
11/11/95+	❶4	26	6 The World I Know	19	↓		
3/23/96	❶2	26	7 Where The River Flows	—	↓		
2/15/97	❶4	26	8 Precious Declaration	65	▲	Disciplined Breakdown	Atlantic 82984
5/24/97	❶5	26	9 Listen	72	↓		
9/27/97	11	11	10 Blame	—	↓		
1/3/98	16	12	11 She Said................................	—	●	Scream 2 (soundtrack).............	Capitol 21911
1/23/99	❶15	33	12 Heavy	73	▲	Dosage	Atlantic 83162
6/19/99	10	14	13 No More, No Less	123	↓		
10/9/99	35	5	14 Tremble For My Beloved	—	↓		
9/30/00	27	26	15 Why Pt.2	111	●	Blender	Atlantic 83400
2/10/01	34	5	16 Vent	—		7even Year Itch: Greatest Hits	
11/3/01	39	3	17 Next Homecoming	—		1994-2001	Atlantic 83510

★42★ COLLINS, Phil
Born on 1/31/51 in Chiswick, London, England. Pop singer/songwriter/drummer. Stage actor as a young child; played the "Artful Dodger" in the London production of *Oliver*. With group Flaming Youth in 1969. Joined **Genesis** in 1970, became lead singer in 1975. Also with jazz-rock group Brand X. Starred in the 1988 movie *Buster*. Left Genesis in April 1996.

1)Against All Odds (Take A Look At Me Now) 2)In The Air Tonight 3)I Don't Care Anymore 4)One More Night
5)Easy Lover

3/21/81	22	24	1 In The Air Tonight	19	▲4	Face Value	Atlantic 16029
3/21/81	8	14	2 I Missed Again	19	↓		
4/4/81	58	1	3 Behind The Lines	—	↓		
11/6/82	41	1	4 Do You Know, Do You Care?...........	—	▲3	Hello, I Must Be Going!	Atlantic 80035
11/13/82	24	14	5 You Can't Hurry Love	10	↓		
			#1 Pop hit for The Supremes in 1966				
12/4/82	3	13	6 I Don't Care Anymore	39	↓		
12/4/82	17	11	7 Like China.............................	—	↓		
3/19/83	34	7	8 Thru These Walls	—	↓		
2/25/84	❶1	14	9 Against All Odds (Take A Look At Me Now)	❶3	●	Against All Odds (soundtrack)........	Atlantic 80152
12/1/84+	5	14	10 Easy Lover	22		Chinese Wall (Bailey)	Columbia 39542
			PHILIP BAILEY with Phil Collins				
2/23/85	38	4	11 The Man With The Horn	—		(single only)	Atlantic 89588
2/9/85	4	13	12 One More Night	❶2	▲12	No Jacket Required.................	Atlantic 81240
3/30/85	9	16	13 Inside Out	—	↓		
4/6/85	33	8	14 Don't Lose My Number	4	↓		
4/13/85	42	3	15 I Don't Wanna Know	—	↓		
5/4/85	10	12	16 Sussudio	❶1	↓		
3/15/86	12	10	17 Take Me Home.......................	7	↓		
			Peter Gabriel and Sting (backing vocals)				
11/4/89	7	12	18 Another Day In Paradise	❶4	▲4	...But Seriously	Atlantic 82050
			David Crosby (backing vocal)				
1/6/90	5	14	19 I Wish It Would Rain Down	3	↓		
			Eric Clapton (guitar)				
5/19/90	49	1	20 Do You Remember?...................	4	↓		
8/11/90	34	7	21 Something Happened On The Way To Heaven	4	↓		
11/6/93	24	5	22 Both Sides Of The Story................	25	▲	Both Sides	Atlantic 82550

DEBUT	PEAK	WKS	Mainstream Rock Track	Pop	Gld	Album Title	Album Label & Number

COLOR RED, The
Rock group from California: brothers Jon (vocals) and Marc (bass) Zamora, Billy Meyer and Adrian Verloop (guitars) and Dave Schartoff (drums).

| 8/24/02 | 34 | 7 | Sore Throat | — | | *Clear* | Dirty Martini 68080 |

COMPANY OF WOLVES
Hard-rock group from New Jersey: Kyf Brewer (vocals), Steve Conte (guitar), John Conte (bass) and Frankie Larocka (drums). Brewer was keyboardist of **The Ravyns**.

2/10/90	26	7	1 Call Of The Wild	—		*Company Of Wolves*	Mercury 842184
6/9/90	49	1	2 The Distance	—		↓	
8/18/90	26	8	3 Hangin' By A Thread	—		↓	

CONCRETE BLONDE
Rock group from Los Angeles: Johnette Napolitano (vocals, bass), James Andrew Mankey (guitar) and Harry Rushakoff (drums). Paul Thompson replaced Rushakoff in early 1990; Rushakoff returned in late 1991, replacing Thompson.

2/28/87	42	6	1 True	—		*Concrete Blonde*	I.R.S. 5835
6/17/89	49	1	2 God Is A Bullet	—		*Free*	I.R.S. 82001
6/23/90	20	14	3 Joey	19	●	*Bloodletting*	I.R.S. 82037

CONEY HATCH
Rock group from Toronto: Carl Dixon (vocals), Steve Shelski (guitar), Andy Curran (bass) and Dave Ketchum (drums).

| 10/23/82 | 44 | 2 | 1 Devil's Deck | — | | *Coney Hatch* | Mercury 4056 |
| 9/17/83 | 38 | 3 | 2 First Time For Everything | — | | *Outa Hand* | Mercury 812869 |

CONTRABAND
Hard-rock group: Richard Black (vocals), Tracii Guns (guitar; **L.A. Guns**), **Michael Schenker** (guitar), Share Pedersen (bass; **Vixen**) and Bobby Blotzer (drums; **Ratt**).

| 4/27/91 | 12 | 11 | All The Way From Memphis | — | | *Contraband* | Impact 10247 |

CONWELL, Tommy, And The Young Rumblers
Born in Philadelphia. Rock singer/guitarist. The Young Rumblers: Chris Day (guitar), Rob Miller (keyboards; **Hooters**), Paul Slivka (bass) and Jim Hannum (drums).

8/6/88	❶¹	14	1 I'm Not Your Man	74		*Rumble*	Columbia 44186
11/5/88+	9	15	2 If We Never Meet Again	48		↓	
9/22/90	15	9	3 I'm Seventeen	—		*Guitar Trouble*	Columbia 46235
12/8/90+	21	9	4 Let Me Love You Too	—		↓	

COOL FOR AUGUST
Rock group from Los Angeles: Gordon Vaughn (vocals), Trevor Kustiak (guitar), Andrew Shives (bass) and Shane Hills (drums).

4/26/97	15	13	1 Don't Wanna Be Here	—		*Grand World*	Warner 46105
9/27/97	24	8	2 Trials	—		↓	
2/7/98	16	12	3 Walk Away	—		↓	

COOPER, Alice
Born Vincent Furnier on 2/4/48 in Detroit. Formed rock group in Phoenix in 1965; adopted his stage name in 1966 from a 16th-century witch. To Los Angeles in 1968, then to Detroit in 1969. Known primarily for his bizarre stage antics. Appeared in the movies *Prince Of Darkness* and *Wayne's World*. Also see **Classic Rock Tracks** section.

8/12/89	15	13	1 Poison	7	▲	*Trash*	Epic 45137
1/13/90	39	7	2 House Of Fire	56		↓	
			co-written by **Joan Jett**				
3/31/90	19	8	3 Only My Heart Talkin'	89		↓	
6/29/91	13	8	4 Hey Stoopid	78		*Hey Stoopid*	Epic 46786
			Ozzy Osbourne (backing vocal); **Slash** (guitar)				
10/12/91	31	6	5 Love's A Loaded Gun	—		↓	

COPE, Julian
Born on 10/21/57 in Bargoed, Wales; raised in Tamworth, England. Singer/songwriter/bassist.

| 2/7/87 | 22 | 7 | World Shut Your Mouth | 84 | | *Julian Cope* | Island 90560 |

CORNELL, Chris
Born on 7/20/64 in Seattle. Lead singer of **Soundgarden** and **Audioslave**.

| 1/24/98 | 8 | 17 | 1 Sunshower | | ● | *Great Expectations (soundtrack)* | Atlantic 83058 |
| 8/28/99 | 5 | 15 | 2 Can't Change Me | 102 | | *Euphoria Morning* | A&M 490412 |

CORROSION OF CONFORMITY
Hard-rock group from Raleigh, North Carolina: Pepper Keenan (vocals, guitar), Woody Weatherman (guitar), Mike Dean (bass) and Reed Mullin (drums).

11/19/94+	19	14	1 Albatross	—		*Deliverance*	Columbia 66208
2/25/95	19	14	2 Clean My Wounds	—		↓	
11/16/96	27	10	3 Drowning In A Daydream	—		*Wiseblood*	Columbia 67583
11/4/00	24	14	4 Congratulations Song	—		*America's Volume Dealer*	Sanctuary 84500
			COC				

COSTELLO, Elvis
Born Declan McManus on 8/25/54 in Paddington, London, England. Leading eclectic rock singer. Changed name to Elvis Costello in 1976. Costello is his mother's maiden name. In 1977, formed backing band The Attractions: Steve "Nieve" Nason (keyboards), Bruce Thomas (bass) and Peter Thomas (drums). Married Cait O'Riordan, former bassist with **The Pogues**, on 5/16/86. Appeared in the 1987 movie *Straight To Hell*. Inducted into the Rock and Roll Hall of Fame in 2003. Also see **Classic Rock Tracks** section.

ELVIS COSTELLO AND THE ATTRACTIONS:

| 3/21/81 | 46 | 1 | 1 From A Whisper To A Scream | — | | *Trust* | Columbia 37051 |
| 9/17/83 | 33 | 4 | 2 Everyday I Write The Book | 36 | | *Punch The Clock* | Columbia 38897 |

DEBUT	PEAK	WKS	Mainstream Rock Track	Pop	Gld	Album Title	Album Label & Number
			COSTELLO, Elvis, And The Attractions — Cont'd				
7/28/84	44	6	3 The Only Flame In Town	56		*Goodbye Cruel World*	Columbia 39429
			Daryl Hall (backing vocal)				
			ELVIS COSTELLO:				
3/29/86	38	4	4 Don't Let Me Be Misunderstood	—		*King Of America*	Columbia 40173
			#15 Pop hit for **The Animals** in 1965				
2/4/89	10	15	5 Veronica	19	●	*Spike*	Warner 25848
			Paul McCartney (co-writer, bass)				
5/6/89	41	5	6 ...This Town...	—		↓	
			Roger McGuinn (guitar); Paul McCartney (bass)				
5/25/91	40	4	7 The Other Side Of Summer	—		*Mighty Like A Rose*	Warner 26575
			COTTON, Josie				
			Born in Dallas. Singer/actress. Appeared in the movie *Valley Girl*.				
8/21/82	34	5	He Could Be The One	74		*Convertible Music*	Elektra 60140
			COUGAR, John — see MELLENCAMP				
			COUNTING CROWS				
			Rock group from San Francisco: Adam Duritz (vocals; born on 8/1/64), David Bryson (guitar), Charlie Gillingham (piano), Matt Malley (bass) and Steve Bowman (drums). Ben Mize replaced Bowman in 1994. Dan Vickrey (guitar) joined in 1996.				
1/1/94	2²	26	1 Mr. Jones	5[A]	▲[7]	*August And Everything After*	DGC 24528
5/7/94	11	17	2 Round Here	31[A]		↓	
7/16/94	4	17	3 Rain King	66[A]		↓	
11/19/94+	17	14	4 A Murder Of One	—		↓	
10/12/96	4	16	5 Angels Of The Silences	45[A]	▲[2]	*Recovering The Satellites*	DGC 24975
12/28/96+	9	18	6 A Long December	6[A]		↓	
5/3/97	24	11	7 Daylight Fading	51[A]		↓	
9/6/97	34	4	8 Have You Seen Me Lately?	—		↓	
11/13/99	37	6	9 Hanginaround	28	▲	*This Desert Life*	DGC 490415
			COURSE OF NATURE				
			Rock trio from Enterprise, Alabama: Mark Wilkerson (vocals, guitar), John Milldrum (bass) and Rickey Shelton (drums).				
1/5/02	9	20	1 Caught In The Sun	—		*Superkala*	Lava 83526
6/8/02	37	4	2 Wall Of Shame	—		↓	
			COVERDALE, David				
			Born on 9/21/51 in Saltburn, North Yorkshire, England. Lead singer of **Deep Purple** and **Whitesnake**.				
2/27/93	❶⁶	15	1 Pride And Joy	—	▲	*Coverdale•Page*	Geffen 24487
3/27/93	3	17	2 Shake My Tree	—		↓	
6/19/93	15	9	3 Take Me For A Little While	115		↓	
8/28/93	24	6	4 Over Now	—		↓	
			COVERDALE•PAGE (above 4)				
12/9/00	33	9	5 Slave	—		*Into The Light*	Dragonshead 112251
			COWBOY JUNKIES				
			Country-punk group from Toronto: siblings Margo (vocals), Michael (guitar) and Peter (drums) Timmins, with Alan Anton (bass).				
4/1/89	50	1	Sweet Jane	52[A]	▲	*The Trinity Session*	RCA 8568
			first recorded by Lou Reed in 1974				
			COWBOY MOUTH				
			Rock group from New Orleans: John Thomas Griffith (vocals), Paul Sanchez (guitar), Rob Savoy (bass) and Fred LeBlanc (drums).				
4/26/97	26	7	1 Jenny Says	—		*Are You With Me?*	MCA 11447
10/31/98	39	2	2 Whatcha Gonna Do?	—		*Mercyland*	MCA 11847
			CRACKER				
			Rock trio from Redlands, California: David Lowery (vocals; **Camper Van Beethoven**), John Hickman (guitar) and Dave Faragher (bass). Faragher left in 1995. Bob Rupe (bass) and Charlie Quintana (drums) joined in 1996.				
5/23/92	27	9	1 Teen Angst (What The World Needs Now)	—		*Cracker*	Virgin 91816
11/27/93+	5	28	2 Low	64	●	*Kerosene Hat*	Virgin 39012
5/7/94	18	16	3 Get Off This	102		↓	
4/6/96	24	6	4 I Hate My Generation	67[A]		*The Golden Age*	Virgin 41498
7/27/96	40	2	5 Nothing To Believe In	—		↓	
10/26/96	33	6	6 Sweet Thistle Pie	—		↓	
			CRACK THE SKY				
			Rock group from Steubenville, Ohio: John Palumbo (vocals), Rick Witkowski (guitar), Vince DePaul (keyboards) and Joe D'Amico (drums).				
5/27/89	49	1	From The Greenhouse	—		*From The Greenhouse*	Grudge 4500
			CRANBERRIES, The				
			Pop-rock group from Limerick, Ireland: Dolores O'Riordan (vocals; born on 9/6/71), brothers Noel (guitar; born on 12/25/71) and Mike (bass; born on 4/29/73) Hogan, and Fergal Lawler (drums; born on 3/4/71).				
12/31/94+	32	7	1 Zombie	22[A]	▲[7]	*No Need To Argue*	Island 524050
5/4/96	25	8	2 Salvation	21[A]	▲[2]	*To The Faithful Departed*	Island 524234

DEBUT	PEAK	WKS	Mainstream Rock Track	Pop	Gld	Album Title	Album Label & Number

CRASH TEST DUMMIES
Pop-rock group from Winnipeg, Canada: brothers Brad (vocals) and Dan (bass) Roberts, with Ellen Reid (keyboards), Benjamin Darvill (harmonica) and Mitch Dorge (drums).

| 4/2/94 | 25 | 7 | ✓ Mmm Mmm Mmm Mmm .... | 4 | ▲² | God Shuffled His Feet .... | Arista 16531 |

CRAVING THEO
Rock group from Portland, Oregon: Calvin Baty (vocals, guitar), Bob Capka (guitar), Brian McMillen (bass) and Jason Dunn (drums).

| 9/8/01 | 39 | 2 | Stomp.. | — | | Craving Theo .... | Valley 15146 |

CRAVIN' MELON
Rock group from Clemson, South Carolina: Doug Jones (vocals), Jim Chapman (guitar), JJ Bowers (bass) and Rick Reames (drums).

| 3/29/97 | 37 | 2 | Come Undone.............................. | — | | Red Clay Harvest .... | Mercury 534305 |

CRAY, Robert, Band
Born on 8/1/53 in Columbus, Georgia. Blues-rock singer/guitarist. Played bass with fictional band Otis Day & The Knights in the movie *Animal House*. Band formed in 1974 as backing tour group for Albert Collins. Lineup from 1986-89: Richard Cousins (bass), Peter Boe (keyboards) and David Olson (drums). Lineup in 1990: Cousins, Tim Kaihatsu (guitar), Jim Pugh (keyboards) and Kevin Hayes (drums). Karl Sevareid (bass) joined in 1992.

11/29/86+	2¹	19	1 Smoking Gun	22	▲²	Strong Persuader	Mercury 830568
3/28/87	28	6	2 I Guess I Showed Her	—	↓		
5/9/87	27	6	3 Right Next Door (Because of Me)	80	↓		
7/30/88	4	10	4 Don't Be Afraid Of The Dark	74	●	Don't Be Afraid Of The Dark........	Mercury 834923
10/22/88	49	3	5 Night Patrol	—	↓		
12/24/88+	24	10	6 Acting This Way	—	↓		
9/15/90	11	10	7 The Forecast (Calls For Pain)	—	●	Midnight Stroll....................	Mercury 846652
12/8/90+	32	9	8 Consequences	—	↓		
9/26/92	33	5	9 Just A Loser	—		I Was Warned....................	Mercury 512721

CRAZY TOWN
Rock-rap group from Los Angeles: Seth "Shifty Shellshock" Binzer and Bret "Epic" Mazur (vocals), DJ AM (DJ), Craig Tyler and Anthony Valli (guitars), Doug Miller (bass) and James Bradley (drums).

| 1/27/01 | 21 | 14 | Butterfly .... | ❶² | ▲ | The Gift Of Game .... | Columbia 63654 |
| | | | samples "Pretty Little Ditty" by the **Red Hot Chili Peppers** | | | | |

CREED ★21★
Rock group from Tallahassee, Florida: Scott Stapp (vocals; born on 8/8/73), Mark Tremonti (guitar; born on 2/18/75), Brian Marshall (bass; born on 4/24/73) and Scott Phillips (drums; born on 2/22/73).

1)Higher 2)My Sacrifice 3)What's This Life For

8/30/97	2¹⁰	44	1 My Own Prison	54^A	▲⁶	My Own Prison	Wind-Up 13049
2/21/98	3	28	2 Torn	—	↓		
6/20/98	❶⁶	39	3 What's This Life For	—	↓		
12/19/98+	2⁷	38	4 One	70	↓		
9/11/99	❶¹⁷	51	5 Higher	7	▲¹⁰	Human Clay......................	Wind-Up 13053
1/8/00	3	26	6 What If	102	↓		
4/22/00	❶⁴	31	7 With Arms Wide Open	❶¹	↓		
9/9/00	4	28	8 Are You Ready?	125	↓		
12/16/00+	28	13	9 Riders On The Storm	—		Stoned Immaculate - The Music Of The Doors (various artists)	Elektra 62475
			#14 Pop hit for **The Doors** in 1971				
10/27/01	❶⁹	28	10 My Sacrifice	4	▲⁵	Weathered.......................	Wind-Up 13075
2/2/02	11	12	11 Bullets	—	↓		
4/27/02	5	26	12 One Last Breath	6	↓		

CRENSHAW, Marshall
Born on 11/11/53 in Detroit. Rockabilly singer/guitarist. Played **John Lennon** in the road show of *Beatlemania* in 1976. Appeared in the movie *Peggy Sue Got Married* and portrayed Buddy Holly in the 1987 movie *La Bamba*.

6/12/82	25	1	1 Someday, Someway	36		Marshall Crenshaw	Warner 3673
			#76 Pop hit for Robert Gordon in 1981				
6/11/83	23	10	2 Whenever You're On My Mind	103		Field Day	Warner 23873

CROSBY, David
Born on 8/14/41 in Los Angeles. Singer/guitarist with **The Byrds** from 1964-68 and later **Crosby, Stills & Nash**. Son of cinematographer Floyd Crosby (*High Noon*). Frequent troubles with the law due to drug charges. Movie cameos in *Backdraft*, *Hook* and *Thunderheart*; appeared on TV's *Roseanne*. Underwent a successful liver transplant on 11/19/94. In early 2000, it was announced that he was the biological father (via artificial insemination) of two children for the couple of **Melissa Etheridge** and Julie Cypher.

| 2/4/89 | 3 | 9 | Drive My Car | — | | Oh Yes I Can .... | A&M 5232 |

DEBUT	PEAK	WKS	Mainstream Rock Track	Pop Gld	Album Title	Album Label & Number

CROSBY, STILLS & NASH

Folk-rock trio formed in Laurel Canyon, California. Consisted of **David Crosby** (guitar), **Stephen Stills** (guitar, keyboards, bass) and **Graham Nash** (guitar). Crosby had been in **The Byrds**, Stills had been in Buffalo Springfield, and Nash was with The Hollies. Won the 1969 Best New Artist Grammy Award. **Neil Young** (guitar), formerly with Buffalo Springfield, joined group in 1970, left in 1974. Reunion in 1988. Trio inducted into the Rock and Roll Hall of Fame in 1997. Also see **Classic Rock Tracks** section.

1)Got It Made 2)American Dream 3)Live It Up

CROSBY, STILLS & NASH:

7/3/82	9	13	1 Wasted On The Way	9 ▲	Daylight Again	Atlantic 19360
7/10/82	39	1	2 Southern Cross	18	↓	
7/31/82	46	1	3 Too Much Love To Hide	69	↓	
6/25/83	13	8	4 War Games	45	Allies	Atlantic 80075

CROSBY, STILLS, NASH & YOUNG:

11/12/88	4	10	5 American Dream	— ▲	American Dream	Atlantic 81888
11/26/88+	❶²	15	6 Got It Made	69	↓	
11/26/88	39	7	7 Nighttime For Generals	—	↓	
12/3/88+	25	12	8 That Girl	—	↓	

CROSBY, STILLS & NASH:

6/9/90	7	9	9 Live It Up	—	Live It Up	Atlantic 82107
8/25/90	44	2	10 If Anybody Had A Heart	—	↓	
10/30/99	34	8	11 No Tears Left	—	Looking Forward	Reprise 47436
			CROSBY, STILLS, NASH & YOUNG			

CROSS, Christopher

Born Christopher Geppert on 5/3/51 in San Antonio, Texas. Singer/songwriter/guitarist. Won the 1980 Best New Artist Grammy Award. Also see **Classic Rock Tracks** section.

9/26/81	13	10	Arthur's Theme (Best That You Can Do)	❶³	Arthur (soundtrack)	Warner 3582

CROW, Sheryl

Born on 2/11/62 in Kennett, Missouri. Pop-rock singer/songwriter/guitarist. Worked as backing singer for **Michael Jackson**, **Don Henley**, **George Harrison** and others. Won the 1994 Best New Artist Grammy Award.

10/8/94	35	6	1 All I Wanna Do	2⁶ ▲⁷	Tuesday Night Music Club	A&M 540126
10/19/96	37	2	2 If It Makes You Happy	10 ▲³	Sheryl Crow	A&M 540587
2/15/97	31	6	3 Everyday Is A Winding Road	11	↓	

CROWDED HOUSE

Pop trio from New Zealand: Neil Flynn (vocals, guitar, piano), Nick Seymour (bass) and Paul Hester (drums). Finn and Hester were members of **Split Enz**.

2/14/87	11	12	1 Don't Dream It's Over	2¹ ▲	Crowded House	Capitol 12485
5/2/87	10	12	2 Something So Strong	7	↓	
8/15/87	45	3	3 World Where You Live	65	↓	
7/2/88	18	10	4 Better Be Home Soon	42	Temple Of Low Men	Capitol 48763
10/8/88	45	2	5 Never Be The Same	—	↓	

CRUEL STORY OF YOUTH

Rock group from New York City: John Are (vocals), Michael Gross (guitar), David Penick (bass) and Bobby Siems (drums).

3/25/89	29	7	You're What You Want To Be	—	Cruel Story Of Youth	Columbia 44206

CRUZADOS

Rock group from Los Angeles: Tito Larriva (vocals), Steven Hufsteter (guitar), Tony Marsico (bass) and Chalo Quintana (drums). Marshall Rohner (guitar) replaced Hufsteter in early 1987.

10/5/85	15	10	1 Motorcycle Girl	—	Cruzados	Arista 8383
6/27/87	4	12	2 Bed Of Lies	—	After Dark	Arista 8439
9/26/87	39	3	3 Small Town Love	—	↓	

CRY OF LOVE

Rock group from Raleigh, North Carolina: Kelly Holland (vocals), Audley Freed (guitar), Robert Kearns (bass) and Jason Patterson (drums).

7/10/93	❶⁴	20	1 Peace Pipe	—	Brother	Columbia 53404
10/30/93+	2³	26	2 Bad Thing	—	↓	
2/26/94	13	11	3 Too Cold In The Winter	—	↓	
8/16/97	22	9	4 Sugarcane	—	Diamonds & Debris	Columbia 66881

CRY WOLF

Rock group from San Francisco: Tim Hall (vocals), Steve McKnight (guitar), Phil Deckard (bass) and Paul Cancilla (drums).

2/23/91	46	2	Pretender	—	Crunch	I.R.S. 13050

CULT, The

Rock group from England. Nucleus of evercharging lineup included Ian Astbury (vocals; real name: Ian Lindsay), Billy Duffy (guitar), Jamie Stewart (bass) and Les Warner (drums). Warner left in 1988; replaced by Matt Sorum (of **Guns N' Roses**). Stewart left in 1990.

1)Rise 2)Fire Woman 3)Wild Hearted Son

3/28/87	15	11	1 Love Removal Machine	— ▲	Electric	Sire 25555
6/20/87	34	5	2 Lil' Devil	—	↓	
9/5/87	39	3	3 Wild Flower	—	↓	

DEBUT	PEAK	WKS	Mainstream Rock Track	Pop	Gld	Album Title	Album Label & Number
			CULT, The — Cont'd				
4/8/89	4	16	4 Fire Woman	46	▲	Sonic Temple .... Sire 25871	
6/24/89	18	8	5 Sun King	—		↓	
9/2/89	17	9	6 Edie (Ciao Baby)	93		↓	
1/20/90	14	10	7 Sweet Soul Sister	—		↓	
9/21/91	12	12	8 Wild Hearted Son	—		Ceremony .... Sire 26673	
1/25/92	41	3	9 Heart Of Soul	—		↓	
10/8/94	13	8	10 Coming Down (Drug Tongue)......................	—		The Cult .... Sire 45673	
7/8/00	26	8	11 Painted On My Heart	—		Gone In 60 Seconds (soundtrack)...... Island 542793	
5/12/01	3	22	12 Rise	125		Beyond Good And Evil .... Lava 83440	

CULTURE CLUB
Pop group formed in London: George "Boy George" O'Dowd (vocals), Roy Hay (guitar, keyboards), Michael Craig (bass) and Jon Moss (drums). Won the 1983 Best New Artist Grammy Award.

DEBUT	PEAK	WKS	Mainstream Rock Track	Pop	Gld	Album Title	Album Label & Number
12/25/82+	21	9	1 Do You Really Want To Hurt Me	2^3	▲	Kissing To Be Clever .... Epic 38398	
5/21/83	17	21	2 Church Of The Poison Mind.......................	10	▲[4]	Colour By Numbers .... Epic 39107	

CURE, The
Techno-rock group from England: Robert Smith (vocals, guitar; born on 4/21/59), Porl Thompson (guitar), Laurence "Lol" Tolhurst (keyboards), Simon Gallup (bass) and Boris Williams (drums). Numerous personnel changes with Smith the only constant.

DEBUT	PEAK	WKS	Mainstream Rock Track	Pop	Gld	Album Title	Album Label & Number
5/6/89	24	11	1 Fascination Street	46	▲	Disintegration .... Elektra 60855	
8/19/89	30	10	2 Love Song...	2^1		↓	
9/29/90	33	7	3 Never Enough...	72	▲	Mixed Up.......................... Elektra 60978	
5/2/92	42	4	4 High	42	▲	Wish .... Fiction 61309	
6/6/92	21	10	5 Friday I'm In Love	18		↓	

CURFMAN, Shannon
Born on 7/31/85 in Fargo, North Dakota. Female blues singer/guitarist.

DEBUT	PEAK	WKS	Mainstream Rock Track	Pop	Gld	Album Title	Album Label & Number
11/13/99	27	13	1 True Friends	—		Loud Guitars, Big Suspicions .... Arista 14614	
4/8/00	37	6	2 Playing With Fire	—		↓	

CUSTOM
Born Duane Lavold in New York City. Singer/songwriter.

DEBUT	PEAK	WKS	Mainstream Rock Track	Pop	Gld	Album Title	Album Label & Number
1/5/02	28	12	Hey Mister...	—		Fast....................... Artist Direct 1016	

CUTTING CREW
Pop-rock group formed in England: Nick Van Eede (vocals), Kevin MacMichael (guitar), Colin Farley (bass) and Martin Beedle (drums).

DEBUT	PEAK	WKS	Mainstream Rock Track	Pop	Gld	Album Title	Album Label & Number
2/28/87	4	14	1 (I Just) Died In Your Arms	❶^2	▲	Broadcast........................ Virgin 90573	
6/13/87	29	6	2 One For The Mockingbird	38		↓	
9/19/87	50	1	3 I've Been In Love Before	9		↓	
5/20/89	41	3	4 (Between A) Rock And A Hard Place	77		The Scattering .... Virgin 91239	

CYSTERZ
Hard-rock group from Chicago: Sammie Ray (vocals), Alex Lynne (guitar), Jake Michaels (bass) and Paul E. David (drums).

DEBUT	PEAK	WKS	Mainstream Rock Track	Pop	Gld	Album Title	Album Label & Number
7/26/86	47	1	Drag You Down	—		Cysterz............................ Rush 103	

D

D.A.D.
Hard-rock group from Copenhagen, Denmark: brothers Jesper (vocals) and Jacob (guitar) Binzer, Stig Pedersen (bass) and Peter Jensen (drums). D.A.D. is abbreviation for Disneyland After Dark.

DEBUT	PEAK	WKS	Mainstream Rock Track	Pop	Gld	Album Title	Album Label & Number
9/9/89	23	10	Sleeping My Day Away	—		No Fuel Left For The Pilgrims .... Warner 25999	

dada
Pop trio from Los Angeles: Joie Calio (vocals, bass), Michael Gurley (guitar) and Phil Leavitt (drums).

DEBUT	PEAK	WKS	Mainstream Rock Track	Pop	Gld	Album Title	Album Label & Number
11/28/92	27	5	Dizz Knee Land	102		Puzzle............................ I.R.S. 13141	

DALTREY, Roger
Born on 3/1/44 in Hammersmith, London, England. Lead singer of **The Who**. Starred in the movies *Tommy, Lisztomania, The Legacy* and *McVicar*.

DEBUT	PEAK	WKS	Mainstream Rock Track	Pop	Gld	Album Title	Album Label & Number
4/17/82	38	2	1 Martyrs And Madmen	—		Best Bits .... MCA 5301	
5/1/82	41	3	2 Say It Ain't So, Joe	—		↓	
			above 2 recorded in 1977				
3/3/84	4	7	3 Walking In My Sleep	62		Parting Should Be Painless.......... Atlantic 80128	
9/14/85	3	11	4 After The Fire	48		Under A Raging Moon .... Atlantic 81269	
			written by **Pete Townshend**				
10/5/85	10	12	5 Under A Raging Moon	—		↓	
12/7/85+	11	13	6 Let Me Down Easy	86		↓	
			co-written by **Bryan Adams**				
2/1/86	11	8	7 Quicksilver Lightning	—		Quicksilver (soundtrack) .... Atlantic 81631	
6/27/87	46	3	8 Take Me Home..	—		Can't Wait To See The Movie .... Atlantic 81759	
7/11/92	6	9	9 Days Of Light	—		Rocks In The Head .... Atlantic 82359	

DEBUT	PEAK	WKS	Mainstream Rock Track	Pop Gld	Album Title	Album Label & Number

DAMNED, The
Rock group from England: David Vanian (vocals), Roman Jugg (guitar), Bryn Merrick (bass) and Chris "Rat Scabies" Miller (drums).

| 4/25/87 | 50 | 2 | Alone Again Or.. | — | *Anything* . . . . | MCA 5966 |

#99 Pop hit for Love in 1970

DAMN YANKEES
All-star rock group: **Ted Nugent** (guitar, vocals), **Tommy Shaw** (guitar, vocals), Jack Blades (bass, vocals) and Michael Cartellone (drums). Nugent was with the Amboy Dukes. Shaw was with **Styx**. Blades was with **Night Ranger**.

3/17/90	❶¹	15	1 Coming Of Age	60	▲² *Damn Yankees*	Warner 26159
6/2/90	5	16	2 Come Again	50	↓	
9/8/90	2¹	22	✓3 High Enough	3	↓	
12/8/90+	9	13	4 Runaway	—	↓	
3/2/91	31	7	5 Bad Reputation	—	↓	
8/1/92	3	9	6 Don't Tread On Me	—	● *Don't Tread*	Warner 45025
9/26/92	6	18	7 Where You Goin' Now	20	↓	
12/19/92+	3	18	8 Mister Please	—	↓	
3/27/93	20	8	9 Silence Is Broken	62	↓	

DANDELION
Rock group from Philadelphia: brothers Kevin (vocals, guitar) and Mike (bass) Morpurgo, Carl Hinds (guitar) and Dante Cimino (drums).

| 8/26/95 | 36 | 4 | Weird-Out.. | 74ᴬ | *Dyslexicon* . . . . | Ruffhouse 64194 |

DANGER DANGER
Hard-rock group from Queens, New York: Ted Poley (vocals), Andy Timmons (guitar), Kasey Smith (keyboards), Bruno Ravel (bass) and Steve West (drums).

| 6/16/90 | 39 | 3 | Bang Bang | 49 | *Danger Danger*. . . . . | Epic 44342 |

DANGEROUS TOYS
Hard-rock group from Austin, Texas: Jason McMaster (vocals), Scott Dalhover and Danny Aaron (guitars), Mike Watson (bass) and Mark Geary (drums).

| 11/11/89 | 46 | 2 | Scared .... | — | ● *Dangerous Toys* . . . . | Columbia 45031 |

DANIELS, Charlie, Band
Born on 10/28/36 in Wilmington, North Carolina. Country-rock singer/fiddle player. Also see **Classic Rock Tracks** section.

| 7/25/81 | 52 | 3 | 1 Sweet Home Alabama .... [L] | 110 | *Volunteer Jam VII (various artists)* . . . . | Epic 37178 |

recorded on 1/17/81 at the Nashville Municipal Auditorium;
#8 Pop hit for **Lynyrd Skynyrd** in 1974

| 3/27/82 | 2¹ | 11 | 2 Still In Saigon | 22 | ● *Windows*. | Epic 37694 |
| 7/18/87 | 22 | 7 | 3 Bogged Down In Love With You................................... | — | *Powder Keg* . . . . | Epic 40760 |

DANZIG
Born Glenn Danzig on 6/23/59 in Lodi, New Jersey. Hard-rock singer/songwriter. His group: John Christ (guitar), Eerie Von (bass) and Chuck Biscuits (drums).

| 11/20/93+ | 17 | 26 | Mother .... | 43 | ● *Danzig*. . . . . | Def American 24208 |

DARLAHOOD
Rock trio from New York City: Luke Janklow (vocals, guitar), David Sellar (bass) and Joe Magistra (drums).

| 10/26/96 | 16 | 16 | Grow Your Own .... | — | *Big Fine Thing* . . . . | Reprise 46214 |

DAVID & DAVID
Pop-rock duo from Los Angeles: **David Baerwald** and David Ricketts.

8/16/86	8	14	1 Welcome To The Boomtown	37	● *Boomtown*.	A&M 5134
10/25/86	14	13	2 Swallowed By The Cracks..	—	↓	
1/10/87	17	10	3 Ain't So Easy	51	↓	

DAVIS, Jimmy, & Junction
Born in Memphis. Rock singer/guitarist. His band Junction: Tommy Burroughs (guitar), John Scott (piano) and Chuck Reynolds (drums).

| 10/10/87 | 32 | 8 | Kick The Wall... | 67 | *Kick The Wall* . . . . | MCA 42015 |

DAVIS, Martha
Born on 1/15/51 in Berkely, California. Lead singer of **The Motels**.

| 11/7/87 | 47 | 4 | Just Like You... | — | *Policy* . . . . | Capitol 48054 |

DAYS OF THE NEW
Rock group from Louisville, Kentucky: Travis Meeks (vocals), Todd Whitener (guitar), Jesse Vest (bass) and Matt Taul (drums). Whitener, Vest and Taul left in 1999 to form **Tantric**; Meeks continued group name as a solo project.

	★83★					
7/26/97	❶¹⁶	46	1 Touch, Peel And Stand	57ᴬ	▲ *Days Of The New*	Outpost 30004
1/3/98	3	26	2 Shelf In The Room	—	↓	
6/6/98	❶¹⁰	27	3 The Down Town	—	↓	
8/7/99	2⁴	26	4 Enemy	110	*Days Of The New*	Outpost 30037
1/29/00	10	12	5 Weapon & The Wound	—	↓	
8/25/01	18	11	6 Hang On To This	—	*Days Of The New*	Outpost 490767

DEACON BLUE
Pop group from Glasgow, Scotland: Ricky Ross and Lorraine McIntosh (vocals), Graeme Kelling (guitar), James Prime (keyboards), Ewen Vernal (bass) and Douglas Vipond (drums). Band name taken from **Steely Dan**'s 1978 pop hit "Deacon Blues."

| 4/2/88 | 22 | 9 | Dignity .... | — | *Raintown*. . . . . | Columbia 40915 |

DEBUT	PEAK	WKS	Mainstream Rock Track	Pop	Gld	Album Title	Album Label & Number

DEAN, Paul
Born on 2/19/46 in Canada. Lead guitarist of **Loverboy**.

| 1/28/89 | 27 | 7 | Sword And Stone | — | | Hard Core | Columbia 44462 |

DEAR ENEMY
Rock group from Melbourne, Australia: Ron Martini (vocals), Les Barker and Chris Langford (guitars), Martin Fisher (keyboards), Peter Lesley (bass) and Ian Morrison (drums).

| 3/10/84 | 59 | 1 | Computer One | — | | Ransom Note | Capitol 12295 |

DeBURGH, Chris
Born Christopher Davidson on 10/15/48 of Irish parentage in Buenos Aires, Argentina. Pop-rock singer.

| 3/26/83 | 29 | 11 | 1 Don't Pay The Ferryman | 34 | | The Getaway | A&M 4929 |
| 6/2/84 | 3 | 14 | 2 High On Emotion | 44 | | Man On The Line | A&M 5002 |

DEEP PURPLE
Hard-rock group from England: Ian Gillan (vocals), Ritchie Blackmore (guitar), Jon Lord (keyboards), Roger Glover (bass) and Ian Paice (drums). Blackmore also formed **Rainbow**. Gillan left in 1989; replaced by **Joe Lynn Turner**, then returned to replace Turner in 1992. Also see **Classic Rock Tracks** section.

11/17/84+	7	19	1 Knocking At Your Back Door	61	▲	Perfect Strangers	Mercury 824003
11/17/84	12	17	2 Perfect Strangers	—	↓		
2/23/85	20	9	3 Nobody's Home	—	↓		
1/17/87	14	8	4 Bad Attitude	—		The House Of Blue Light	Mercury 831318
2/21/87	14	10	5 Call Of The Wild	—	↓		
7/9/88	44	4	6 Hush	—		Nobody's Perfect	Mercury 835897
			new version of their #4 Pop hit in 1968				
10/13/90	6	12	7 King Of Dreams	—		Slaves And Masters	RCA 2421
1/5/91	20	7	8 Fire In The Basement	—	↓		
8/14/93	22	6	9 The Battle Rages On	—		The Battle Rages On...	Giant 24517

DEFAULT
Rock group from Vancouver: Dallas Smith (vocals), Jeremy Hora (guitar), Dave Benedict (bass) and Dan Craig (drums).

| 9/22/01+ | 2⁷ | 44 | 1 Wasting My Time | 13 | ● | The Fallout | TVT 2310 |
| 4/13/02 | 7 | 26 | 2 Deny | — | ↓ | | |

DEF LEPPARD ★16★
Hard-rock group from Sheffield, Yorkshire, England: Joe Elliott (vocals; born on 8/1/59), Steve Clark (guitar; born on 4/23/60; died of alcohol-related respiratory failure on 1/8/91, age 30), Pete Willis (guitar; born on 2/16/60), Rick Savage (bass; born on 12/2/60) and Rick Allen (drums; born on 11/1/63). Phil Collen (born on 12/8/57) replaced Willis in late 1982. Allen lost his left arm in a car crash on 12/31/84. Guitarist Vivian Campbell (**Whitesnake**, **Dio**, **Riverdogs**, **Shadow King**) joined in April 1992.

1)Photograph 2)Stand Up (Kick Love Into Motion) 3)Promises 4)Rock Of Ages 5)Let's Get Rocked

8/22/81	34	6	1 Let It Go	—	▲²	High 'n' Dry	Mercury 4021
2/12/83	❶⁶	26	2 Photograph	12	▲⁹	Pyromania	Mercury 810308
4/23/83	❶¹	24	3 Rock Of Ages	16	↓		
5/21/83	9	15	4 Too Late For Love	—	↓		
7/9/83	9	23	5 Foolin'	28	↓		
9/17/83	24	7	6 Comin' Under Fire	—	↓		
10/15/83	33	4	7 Billy's Got A Gun	—	↓		
10/15/83	42	2	8 Action! Not Words	—	↓		
8/1/87	7	7	9 Women	80	▲¹²	Hysteria	Mercury 830675
8/15/87	5	13	10 Animal	19	↓		
9/12/87+	9	25	11 Hysteria	10	↓		
1/30/88	25	11	12 Pour Some Sugar On Me	2¹	↓		
8/13/88	3	13	13 Love Bites	❶¹	↓		
11/5/88	3	15	14 Armageddon It	3	↓		
2/25/89	5	10	15 Rocket	12	↓		
4/4/92	❶¹	13	16 Let's Get Rocked	15	▲³	Adrenalize	Mercury 512185
4/18/92+	❶⁵	20	17 Stand Up (Kick Love Into Motion)	34	↓		
5/23/92	3	12	18 Make Love Like A Man	36	↓		
8/22/92	7	15	19 Have You Ever Needed Someone So Bad	12	↓		
3/13/93	13	12	20 Tonight	62	↓		
11/7/92	22	2	21 Elected	—	[L]	(single only)	Mercury 864136
			#26 Pop hit for Alice Cooper in 1972				
7/24/93	15	14	22 Two Steps Behind	12	▲	Last Action Hero (soundtrack)	Columbia 57127
10/23/93	12	7	23 Desert Song	—	▲	Retro Active	Mercury 518305
5/11/96	6	12	24 Work It Out	—	●	Slang	Mercury 532486
6/5/99	❶³	19	25 Promises	102	●	Euphoria	Mercury 546212
9/11/99	11	17	26 Paper Sun	—			
2/5/00	22	9	27 Day After Day	—	↓		
8/3/02	26	11	28 Now	—		X	Island 063121

DEBUT	PEAK	WKS	Mainstream Rock Track	Pop Gld	Album Title	Album Label & Number

DEFTONES
Rock group from Sacramento, California: Chino Moreno (vocals), Stephen Carpenter (guitar), Chi Cheng (bass) and Abe Cunningham (drums).

5/9/98	29	7	1 Be Quiet And Drive (Far Away)	— ●	Around The Fur	Maverick 46810
6/3/00	9	24	2 Change (In The House Of Flies)	105 ●	White Pony	Maverick 47667
11/11/00	35	5	3 Back To School	— ↓		
2/17/01	38	4	4 Digital Bath	— ↓		

DEL AMITRI
Pop-rock group from Glasgow, Scotland: Justin Currie (vocals, bass), David Cummings and Iain Harvie (guitars), and Brian McDermott (drums).

3/24/90	17	16	1 Kiss This Thing Goodbye	35	Waking Hours	A&M 5287
6/27/92	18	18	2 Always The Last To Know	30	Change Everything	A&M 5385

DEL FUEGOS, The
Rock group from Boston: brothers Dan (vocals, guitar) and Warren (guitar) Zanes, Tom Lloyd (bass) and Woody Giessmann (drums). Warren Zanes and Giessmann left in 1988; replaced by Adam Roth and Joe Donnelly.

11/23/85	46	4	1 Don't Run Wild	—	Boston, Mass.	Slash 25339
3/1/86	33	7	2 I Still Want You	87	↓	
5/16/87	43	2	3 Name Names	—	Stand Up	Slash 25540
10/21/89	32	8	4 Move With Me Sister	—	Smoking In The Fields	RCA 9860

DEVO
Robotic-rock group from Akron, Ohio: brothers Mark (synthesizers) and Bob (vocals, guitar) Mothersbaugh, brothers Jerry (bass) and Bob (guitar) Casale, and Alan Myers (drums). Also see **Classic Rock Tracks**.

8/8/81	53	7	Working In The Coal Mine	43 ●	Heavy Metal (soundtrack)	Asylum 90004

#8 Pop hit for Lee Dorsey in 1966

DEXYS MIDNIGHT RUNNERS
Pop-rock group from Birmingham, England: Kevin Rowland (vocals), Billy Adams (guitar), Brian Maurice (sax), Paul Speare (flute), Jimmy Patterson (trombone), Micky Billingham (piano), Giorgio Kilkenny (bass) and Seb Shelton (drums). Billingham was later with **General Public**.

12/18/82+	6	19	Come On Eileen	❶[1]	Too-Rye-Ay	Mercury 4069

DeYOUNG, Dennis
Born on 2/18/47 in Chicago. Lead singer/keyboardist of **Styx**.

9/8/84	31	8	Desert Moon	10	Desert Moon	A&M 5006

DFX2
Rock group from San Diego: brothers David (vocals, guitar) and Douglas (guitar) Farage, Eric Gotthelf (bass) and Frank Hailey (drums).

8/13/83	22	6	Emotion	—	Emotion	MCA 36000

DICKINSON, Bruce
Born Paul Bruce Dickinson on 8/7/58 in Worksop, England; raised in Sheffield, England. Lead singer of **Iron Maiden** from 1981-1993.

7/7/90	42	5	1 Tattooed Millionaire	—	Tattooed Millionaire	Columbia 46139
9/10/94	36	4	2 Tears Of The Dragon	—	Balls To Picasso	Mercury 522491

DIESEL
Rock group from Holland: Rob Vunderink (vocals, guitar), Mark Boon (guitar), Frank Papendrecht (bass) and Pim Koopman (drums).

7/18/81	27	19	Sausalito Summernight	25	Watts In A Tank	Regency 19315

DIFFUSER
Rock group from Long Island, New York: Tom Costanza (vocals, guitar), Tony Cangelosi (guitar), Larry Sullivan (bass) and Billy Alemaghides (drums).

12/2/00+	20	14	Karma	—	Injury Loves Melody	Hollywood 162246

DIG
Rock group from San Diego: Scott Hackwith (vocals, guitar), Jon Morris and Johnny Cornwell (guitars), Phil Friedmann (bass) and Anthony Smedile (drums).

2/19/94	34	9	Believe	—	Dig	Radioactive 10916

DILLINGER
Rock group from Kansas: Chris Post (vocals), Blake Bachman (guitar), Buck Bowhall (bass) and Greg Tobin (drums).

10/5/91	45	4	Home For Better Days	—	Horses & Hawgs	JRS 35800

DIO
Hard-rock group formed by Ronnie James Dio (born Ronald Padavona on 7/10/49 in Portsmouth, New Hampshire). Former lead singer of **Black Sabbath** and **Rainbow**. Dio consisted of Vivian Campbell (guitar), Jimmy Bain (bass) and Vinny Appice (drums; Black Sabbath). Claude Schnell (keyboards) joined in 1984. Campbell left in 1986; replaced by Craig Goldie. Campbell also with **Whitesnake**, **Riverdogs**, **Shadow King** and **Def Leppard**.

8/27/83	14	16	1 Rainbow In The Dark	— ▲	Holy Diver	Warner 23836
10/8/83	40	2	2 Holy Diver	—	↓	
8/4/84	10	9	3 The Last In Line	— ▲	The Last In Line	Warner 25100
9/1/84	20	9	4 Mystery	—	↓	
3/2/85	30	6	5 Hungry For Heaven	— ●	Sacred Heart	Warner 25292
8/31/85	26	8	6 Rock 'N' Roll Children	—	↓	
8/1/87	33	5	7 I Could Have Been A Dreamer	—	Dream Evil	Warner 25612

DEBUT	PEAK	WKS	Mainstream Rock Track	Pop	Gld	Album Title	Album Label & Number
	★78★		**DIRE STRAITS**				

Rock group formed in London: brothers Mark (vocals, guitar) and David (guitar) Knopfler, with John Illsley (bass) and Pick Withers (drums). David left in mid-1980; replaced by Hal Lindes (left in 1985). Added keyboardist Alan Clark in 1982. Terry Williams replaced drummer Pick Withers in 1983. Guitarist Guy Fletcher added in 1984. Mark and Guy were also members of **The Notting Hillbillies** in 1990. Lineup in 1991: Knopfler, Illsley, Fletcher and Clark, with Chris White (sax), Paul Franklin (pedal steel), Danny Cummings (percussion), Phil Palmer (guitar) and Chris Whitten (drums). Also see **Classic Rock Tracks** section.

1)Money For Nothing 2)Heavy Fuel 3)Calling Elvis

DEBUT	PEAK	WKS	Mainstream Rock Track	Pop	Gld	Album Title	Album Label & Number
3/21/81	39	5	1 Expresso Love	—	▲	Making Movies	Warner 3480
4/4/81	31	1	2 Skateaway	58		↓	
4/4/81	56	1	3 Solid Rock	—		↓	
10/30/82	9	18	4 Industrial Disease	75	●	Love Over Gold	Warner 23728
2/12/83	12	10	5 Twisting By The Pool	105		Twisting By The Pool	Warner 29800
6/1/85	❶³	20	6 Money For Nothing	❶³	▲⁹	Brothers In Arms	Warner 25264

Sting (backing vocal, co-writer)

DEBUT	PEAK	WKS	Mainstream Rock Track	Pop	Gld	Album Title	Album Label & Number
6/1/85	6	28	7 Walk Of Life	7		↓	
8/17/85	29	13	8 So Far Away	19		↓	
8/24/85	8	14	9 One World	—		↓	
1/11/86	21	10	10 Ride Across The River	—		↓	
9/7/91	3	8	11 Calling Elvis	—	▲	On Every Street	Warner 26680
9/21/91	❶¹	34	12 Heavy Fuel	—		↓	
1/11/92	8	12	13 The Bug	—		↓	

#16 Country hit for Mary-Chapin Carpenter in 1993

DISHWALLA

Pop-rock group from Santa Barbara, California: J.R. Richards (vocals), Rodney Browning (guitar), Scot Alexander (bass) and George Pendergast (drums). Jim Wood (keyboards) added in 1997.

DEBUT	PEAK	WKS	Mainstream Rock Track	Pop	Gld	Album Title	Album Label & Number
3/23/96	2⁴	30	1 Counting Blue Cars	15	●	Pet Your Friends	A&M 540319
10/12/96	24	11	2 Charlie Brown's Parents	—		↓	
8/8/98	17	10	3 Once In A While	—		And You Think You Know What Life's About	A&M 540948

DISTURBED

Hard-rock group from Chicago: **David Draiman** (vocals), Dan Donegan (guitar), Steve "Fuzz" Kmak (bass) and Mike Wengren (drums).

DEBUT	PEAK	WKS	Mainstream Rock Track	Pop	Gld	Album Title	Album Label & Number
5/20/00	12	32	1 Stupify	112	▲²	The Sickness	Giant 24738
12/16/00+	16	26	2 Voices	—		↓	
6/16/01	5	46	3 Down With The Sickness	104		↓	
2/2/02	34	7	4 The Game	—		↓	
8/17/02	3	15↑	5 Prayer	58↑		Believe	Reprise 48320

DIVING FOR PEARLS

Pop-rock group from New York City: Danny Malone (vocals), Yul Vazquez (guitar), Jack Moran (keyboards), David Weeks (bass) and Peter Clemente (drums).

DEBUT	PEAK	WKS	Mainstream Rock Track	Pop	Gld	Album Title	Album Label & Number
12/9/89+	21	13	Gimme Your Good Lovin'	84		Diving For Pearls	Epic 45130

DIVINYLS

Rock group from Australia: Christina Amphlett (vocals), Mark McEntee (guitar), Bjarne Olin (keyboards), Richard Grossman (bass) and J.J. Harris (drums). Grossman joined the **Hoodoo Gurus** in 1989. By 1991, group reduced to a duo of Amphlett and McEntee.

DEBUT	PEAK	WKS	Mainstream Rock Track	Pop	Gld	Album Title	Album Label & Number
11/16/85	12	13	1 Pleasure And Pain	76		What A Life!	Chrysalis 41511
3/23/91	35	7	2 I Touch Myself	4	●	Divinyls	Virgin 91397

DIXIE DREGS — see DREGS, The

DLR BAND — see ROTH, David Lee

DOG'S EYE VIEW

Rock group from New York City: Peter Stuart (vocals, guitar), Oren Bloedow (guitar), John Abbey (bass) and Alan Bezozi (drums).

DEBUT	PEAK	WKS	Mainstream Rock Track	Pop	Gld	Album Title	Album Label & Number
2/10/96	18	15	Everything Falls Apart	14ᴬ		Happy Nowhere	Columbia 66882

DOKKEN

Hard-rock group from Los Angeles: Don Dokken (vocals; born on 6/29/53), George Lynch (guitar), Juan Croucier (bass) and Mick Brown (drums). Jeff Pilson replaced Croucier in late 1983. Disbanded in 1988. Lynch and Brown formed **Lynch Mob** in 1990. Dokken, Lynch, Pilson and Brown reunited as Dokken in early 1995.

1)Alone Again 2)Burning Like A Flame 3)Into The Fire

DEBUT	PEAK	WKS	Mainstream Rock Track	Pop	Gld	Album Title	Album Label & Number
10/15/83	32	13	1 Breaking The Chains	—		Breaking The Chains	Elektra 60290
9/22/84	21	11	2 Into The Fire	—	▲	Tooth And Nail	Elektra 60376
1/5/85	27	7	3 Just Got Lucky	105		↓	
4/27/85	20	14	4 Alone Again	64		↓	
12/21/85+	25	9	5 The Hunter	—	▲	Under Lock And Key	Elektra 60458
3/1/86	24	7	6 In My Dreams	77		↓	
3/14/87	22	7	7 Dream Warriors	—	▲	Back For The Attack	Elektra 60735
11/7/87	20	13	8 Burning Like A Flame	72		↓	
2/13/88	37	5	9 Prisoner	—		↓	
2/4/89	48	3	10 Walk Away	—	●	Beast From The East	Elektra 60823
9/1/90	26	8	11 Mirror Mirror	—		Up From The Ashes	Geffen 24301
			DON DOKKEN				
6/3/95	29	8	12 Too High To Fly	—		Dysfunctional	Columbia 67075

DEBUT	PEAK	WKS	Mainstream Rock Track	Pop	Gld	Album Title	Album Label & Number
			DOLBY, Thomas				
			Born Thomas Morgan Robertson on 10/14/58 in Cairo, Egypt (of British parentage). Singer/songwriter/keyboardist.				
9/11/82	37	2	1 **Europa And The Pirate Twins**	67		*The Golden Age Of Wireless* .... Capitol 12271	
2/19/83	17	16	2 **One Of Our Submarines**	—		↓	
3/5/83	6	12	3 **She Blinded Me With Science**	5		↓	
			features brief spoken-word interludes by British scientist/TV personality Magnus Pyke (died on 10/19/92, age 83)				
3/10/84	39	5	4 **Hyperactive**	62		*The Flat Earth* .... Capitol 12309	
			DOOBIE BROTHERS, The				
			Rock group formed in San Jose, California. Original lineup: **Tom Johnston** (vocals, guitar), **Patrick Simmons** (vocals, guitar), Dave Shogren (bass) and John Hartman (drums). **Michael McDonald** joined as lead singer in 1975. Numerous personnel changes. 1989-91 lineup: Johnston and Simmons (vocals, guitars), Tiran Porter (bass), Hartman and Michael Hossack (drums), and Bobby LaKind (percussion). LaKind left in 1990 due to illness; died of cancer on 12/24/92 (age 47). Also see **Classic Rock Tracks** section.				
5/20/89	❶³	9	1 **The Doctor**	9	●	*Cycles.* .... Capitol 90371	
6/3/89	3	15	2 **Need A Little Taste Of Love**	45		↓	
			first recorded by The Isley Brothers in 1974				
6/10/89	30	8	3 **South Of The Border**	—		↓	
4/13/91	2³	11	4 **Dangerous**	—		*Brotherhood* .... Capitol 94623	
7/6/91	12	9	5 **Rollin' On**	—		↓	
			DOORS, The				
			Rock group formed in Los Angeles: Jim Morrison (vocals), Robby Krieger (guitar), Ray Manzarek (keyboards) and John Densmore (drums). Controversial onstage performances by Morrison caused several arrests and cancellations. Group appeared in the 1969 movie *A Feast of Friends*. Morrison left group on 12/12/70; died of heart failure in Paris on 7/3/71 (age 27). Group disbanded in 1973. 1991 movie based on group's career, *The Doors*, starred Val Kilmer as Morrison. Group inducted into the Rock and Roll Hall of Fame in 1993. Also see **Classic Rock Tracks** section.				
11/5/83	18	12	**Gloria**	[L] 71	●	*Alive, She Cried* .... Elektra 60269	
			recorded as a "soundcheck" in 1969; written by Van Morrison; #10 Pop hit for The Shadows Of Knight in 1966				
			DOPE				
			Hard-rock group from Brooklyn, New York: Edsel Dope (vocals), Acey Slade and Virus (guitars), Simon Dope (keyboards), Sloane Jentry (bass) and Sketchy Shay (drums).				
8/26/00	37	3	1 **You Spin Me 'Round (Like A Record)**	—		*Felons And Revolutionaries* .... Flip 61383	
			#11 Pop hit for Dead Or Alive in 1985				
10/27/01	28	12	2 **Now Or Never**	—		*Life* .... Flip 85644	
3/16/02	29	5	3 **Slipping Away**	—		↓	
			DOUBLEDRIVE				
			Rock group from Atlanta: Donnie Hamby (vocals), Troy McLawhorn (guitar), Joshua Sattler (bass) and Mike Froedge (drums).				
9/4/99	32	8	**Tattooed Bruise**..	—		*1000 Yard Stare* .... MCA 11965	
			DOVETAIL JOINT				
			Rock group from Chicago: Chuck Gladfelter (vocals), Robert Byrne (guitar), Jon Kooker (bass) and Joe Dapier (drums).				
4/17/99	38	3	**Level On The Inside**	—		*001* .... Columbia 69451	
			DOWN				
			Hard-rock group: Philip Anselmo (vocals), Pepper Keenan and Kirk Windstein (guitars), Todd Strange (bass), and Jimmy Bower (drums). Anselmo is the lead singer of **Pantera**.				
11/18/95	40	2	**Stone The Crow**..	—		*Nola* .... EastWest 61830	
			DRAIMAN, David				
			Born in Chicago. Lead singer of **Disturbed**.				
3/2/02	25	10	**Forsaken**	—		*Queen Of The Damned* *(soundtrack)* .... Warner Sunset 48285	
			DRAIN S.T.H.				
			Female hard-rock group from Stockholm, Sweden: Maria Sjoholm (vocals), Flavia Canel (guitar), Anna Kjellberg (bass) and Martina Axen (drums).				
4/19/97	33	6	1 **I Don't Mind**..	—		*Horror Wrestling.* .... Enclave 558459	
7/11/98	25	10	2 **Crack The Liar's Smile**...	—		↓	
7/24/99	34	4	3 **Enter My Mind**	—		*Freaks Of Nature* .... Enclave 546262	
11/6/99	24	12	4 **Simon Says**	—		↓	
			DREAM ACADEMY, The				
			Pop-rock trio from England: Nick Laird-Clowes (guitar, vocals), Gilbert Gabriel (keyboards) and Kate St. John (vocals).				
11/30/85+	7	13	1 **Life In A Northern Town**	7		*The Dream Academy* .... Warner 25265	
3/8/86	37	5	2 **The Edge Of Forever**..	—		↓	
			DREAMS SO REAL				
			Rock trio from Athens, Georgia: Barry Marler (vocals, guitar), Trent Allen (bass) and Drew Worsham (drums).				
11/26/88+	28	10	**Rough Night In Jericho**	—		*Rough Night In Jericho* .... Arista 8555	
			DREAM THEATER				
			Hard-rock group from Los Angeles: James LaBrie (vocals), John Petrucci (guitar), Kevin Moore (keyboards), John Myung (bass) and Mike Portnoy (drums). Derek Sherinian replaced Moore in September 1994.				
12/12/92	10	20	1 **Pull Me Under**	—	●	*Images And Words* .... Atco 92148	
3/27/93	29	5	2 **Take The Time**	—		↓	
6/19/93	22	6	3 **Another Day**	—		↓	
10/8/94	38	3	4 **Lie**	—		*Awake* .... EastWest 90126	

DEBUT	PEAK	WKS	Mainstream Rock Track		Pop	Gld	Album Title	Album Label & Number
			DREAM THEATER — Cont'd					
10/25/97	33	6	5 Burning My Soul		—		*Falling Into Infinity*	EastWest 62060
2/7/98	40	2	6 You Not Me		—		↓	
			DREGS, The					
			Instrumental rock group: Steve Morse (guitar), T Lavitz (piano), Allen Sloan (violin), Andy West (bass) and Rod Morgenstein (drums). Mark O'Connor (violin) replaced Sloan in late 1981. Morse joined **Kansas** in 1986. Group first known as the Dixie Dregs.					
5/9/81	46	7	1 Cruise Control.. [I]		—		*Unsung Heroes*	Arista 9548
4/3/82	18	11	2 Crank It Up		110		*Industry Standard*	Arista 9588
			Alex Ligertwood (of **Santana**; vocal)					
			DREW, David					
			Born in Manhattan, New York. Rock singer/songwriter/guitarist.					
7/23/88	29	6	Green-Eyed Lady		—		*Safety Love*	MCA 42171
			#3 Pop hit for Sugarloaf in 1970					
			DRIVIN' N' CRYIN'					
			Rock group from Atlanta: Kevn Kinney (vocals), Buren Fowler (guitar), Tim Nielsen (bass) and Jeff Sullivan (drums).					
2/9/91	19	14	1 Fly Me Courageous		—	●	*Fly Me Courageous*	Island 848000
6/8/91	15	13	2 Build A Fire...		—		↓	
10/19/91	30	12	3 The Innocent		—		↓	
2/20/93	11	8	4 Turn It Up Or Turn It Off		—		*Smoke*	Island 514319
5/1/93	23	7	5 Smoke		—		↓	
			DROGE, Pete					
			Born on 3/11/69 in Portland, Oregon. Rock singer/songwriter/guitarist.					
12/24/94+	28	8	If You Don't Love Me (I'll Kill Myself)		119		*Necktie Second*	American 45620
			DROWNING POOL					
			Hard-rock group from Dallas: Dave Williams (vocals), C.J. Pierce (guitar), Stevie Benton (bass) and Mike Luce (drums). Williams died on a drug overdose on 8/13/2002 (age 30).					
5/26/01	6	26	1 Bodies		119	▲	*Sinner*	Wind-Up 13065
12/1/01	28	10	2 Sinner..		—		↓	
3/9/02	18	19	3 Tear Away		—		↓	
			DUARTE, Chris, Group					
			Born on 2/16/63 in San Antonio, Texas. Singer/songwriter/guitarist. His group: Reese Wynans (keyboards), John Jordan (bass) and Eric Tatuaka (drums). Wynans was a member of **Stevie Ray Vaughan**'s Double Trouble.					
10/11/97	40	2	Cleopatra		—		*Tailspin Headwhack*	Silvertone 41611
			DUDEK, Les					
			Born on 8/2/57 in Rhode Island. Prolific session guitarist.					
6/27/81	52	3	Deja Vu (Da Voodoo's In You)...........................		—		*Gypsy Ride*	Columbia 36798
			DUKE JUPITER					
			Rock group from Rochester, New York: Marshall James Styler (vocals, keyboards), Greg Walker (guitar), George Barajas (bass) and David Corcoran (drums). Barajas died on 8/17/82 (age 33). Rickey Ellis (bass) joined in 1983.					
3/27/82	16	10	1 I'll Drink To You		58		*Duke Jupiter 1*	Coast To Coast 37912
4/28/84	12	13	2 Little Lady		68		*White Knuckle Ride*	Morocco 6097
			DUNNERY, Francis					
			Born on 12/25/62 in England. Male rock singer/guitarist.					
6/25/94	38	2	American Life In The Summertime		—		*Fearless*	Atlantic 82582
			DUPREE, Jesse James					
			Born in Atlanta. Former lead singer of **Jackyl**.					
6/17/00	34	6	Mainline..		—		*Foot Fetish*	V2 27072
			DURAN DURAN					
			Pop-rock group from Birmingham, England: Simon LeBon (vocals), **Andy Taylor** (guitar), Nick Rhodes (keyboards), John Taylor (bass) and Roger Taylor (drums). None of the Taylors are related. Group named after a villain in the Jane Fonda movie *Barbarella*. In 1984, Andy and Roger left the group. In 1985, Andy and John recorded with supergroup **The Power Station**; Simon, Nick and Roger recorded as Arcadia.					
8/14/82+	❶³	26	1 Hungry Like The Wolf		3	▲²	*Rio*	Harvest 12211
2/12/83	5	14	2 Rio		14		↓	
4/9/83	19	13	3 Girls On Film		—	▲	*Duran Duran*	Capitol 12158
5/14/83	3	15	4 Is There Something I Should Know		4		↓	
11/5/83+	2¹	14	5 Union Of The Snake		3	▲²	*Seven And The Ragged Tiger*	Capitol 12310
1/21/84	4	10	6 New Moon On Monday		10		↓	
5/5/84	35	7	7 The Reflex...		❶²		↓	
11/17/84	42	4	8 The Wild Boys		2⁴	▲²	*Arena*	Capitol 12374
6/22/85	42	3	9 A View To A Kill		❶²		*A View To A Kill (soundtrack)*	Capitol 12413
			DURST, Fred — see LEWIS, Aaron					
			DUST FOR LIFE					
			Rock group from Memphis: Chris Gavin (vocals, guitar), Jason Hughes (guitar), David Rhea (bass) and Rick Shelton (drums).					
10/28/00+	16	18	1 Step Into The Light		—		*Dust For Life*	Wind-Up 13060
4/28/01	39	1	2 Seed		—		↓	

DEBUT	PEAK	WKS	Mainstream Rock Track	Pop Gld	Album Title	Album Label & Number

DYLAN, Bob

Born Robert Zimmerman on 5/24/41 in Duluth, Minnesota; raised in Hibbing, Minnesota. Highly influential singer/songwriter/ guitarist/harmonica player. Innovator of folk-rock style. Took stage name from poet Dylan Thomas. To New York City in December 1960. Worked Greenwich Village folk clubs. Signed to Columbia Records in October 1961. Motorcycle crash on 7/29/66 led to short retirement. Subject of documentaries *Don't Look Back* (1965) and *Eat The Document* (1969). Acted in movies *Pat Garrett And Billy The Kid* (1973), *Renaldo And Clara* (1978) and *Hearts Of Fire* (1987). Member of the supergroup **Traveling Wilburys**. His son Jakob is the lead singer of **The Wallflowers**. Inducted into the Rock and Roll Hall of Fame in 1988. Won Grammy's Lifetime Achievement Award in 1991. Also see **Classic Rock Tracks** section.

1)Silvio 2)Everything Is Broken 3)Slow Train

DEBUT	PEAK	WKS	Track	Pop	Gld	Album Title	Album Label & Number
8/29/81	38	6	1 Shot Of Love..	—		Shot Of Love...................	Columbia 37496
12/17/83+	37	7	2 Neighborhood Bully	—	●	Infidels	Columbia 38819
6/15/85	19	9	3 Tight Connection To My Heart (Has Anybody Seen My Love)	103		Empire Burlesque	Columbia 40110
4/19/86	28	6	4 Band Of The Hand (Hell Time, Man!) .... BOB DYLAN with "The Heartbreakers" produced by **Tom Petty**	—		Band Of The Hand (soundtrack)	MCA 6167
8/2/86	23	7	5 Got My Mind Made Up .... **Tom Petty** (guitar)	—		Knocked Out Loaded	Columbia 40439
11/7/87	25	6	6 The Usual .... **Eric Clapton** (guitar)	—		Hearts Of Fire (soundtrack)	Columbia 40870
6/11/88	5	8	7 Silvio	—		Down In The Groove.	Columbia 40957
2/4/89	8	6	8 Slow Train [L] BOB DYLAN & GRATEFUL DEAD	—	●	Dylan & The Dead	Columbia 45056
9/30/89	8	8	9 Everything Is Broken	—		Oh Mercy	Columbia 45281
9/29/90	21	6	10 Unbelievable...............................	—		Under The Red Sky	Columbia 46794
8/21/93	26	7	11 My Back Pages .... [L] BOB DYLAN & FRIENDS: Roger McGuinn, Tom Petty, Neil Young, Eric Clapton & George Harrison recorded on 10/16/92 at Madison Square Garden in New York City; #30 Pop hit for **The Byrds** in 1967	—	●	Bob Dylan - The 30th Anniversary Concert (various artists)................	Columbia 53230

E

EAGLES

Rock-country group formed in Los Angeles. Original lineup: **Glenn Frey** (vocals, guitar), **Bernie Leadon** (guitar), **Randy Meisner** (bass) and **Don Henley** (drums). **Joe Walsh** in 1975. Leadon replaced by **Timothy B. Schmit** in 1977. Group disbanded in 1982. Henley, Frey, Felder, Walsh and Schmit reunited in 1994. Group inducted into the Rock and Roll Hall of Fame in 1998. Also see **Classic Rock Tracks** section.

DEBUT	PEAK	WKS	Track	Pop		Album Title	Album Label & Number
10/22/94	4	14	1 Get Over It	31	▲7	Hell Freezes Over..................	Geffen 24725
1/21/95	33	7	2 Learn To Be Still	61A		↓	

EARLE, Steve

Born on 1/17/55 in Fort Monroe, Virginia; raised in Schertz, Texas. Country-rock singer/songwriter/guitarist.

DEBUT	PEAK	WKS	Track	Pop		Album Title	Album Label & Number
6/27/87	26	8	1 I Ain't Ever Satisfied .... STEVE EARLE AND THE DUKES	—		Exit O	MCA 5998
10/29/88	10	13	2 Copperhead Road	—	●	Copperhead Road	Uni 7
2/4/89	20	8	3 Back To The Wall	—		↓	
7/14/90	37	5	4 The Other Kind .... STEVE EARLE AND THE DUKES	—		The Hard Way.................	MCA 6430

EARSHOT

Rock group from Los Angeles: Will Martin (vocals), Scott Kohler and Mike Callahan (guitars), and Dieter Hartmann (drums).

DEBUT	PEAK	WKS	Track	Pop		Album Title	Album Label & Number
3/16/02	6	28	1 Get Away	—		Letting Go	Warner 47961
9/21/02	24	10↑	2 Not Afraid............................	—		↓	

EARTH TO ANDY

Rock group from New York City: Andy Waldeck (vocals, guitar), Tony Lopacinski (guitar), Chris Reardon (bass) and Kevin Murphy (drums).

DEBUT	PEAK	WKS	Track	Pop		Album Title	Album Label & Number
1/8/00	39	2	Still After You	—		Chronicle Kings.................	Giant 24727

EASTERHOUSE

Rock duo from Manchester, England: brothers Andy (vocals) and Ivor (guitar) Perry.

DEBUT	PEAK	WKS	Track	Pop		Album Title	Album Label & Number
2/11/89	17	10	Come Out Fighting............................	82		Waiting For The Redbird..........	Columbia 44467

EASTON, Elliot

Born Elliot Shapiro on 12/18/53 in Brooklyn, New York. Lead guitarist of **The Cars**.

DEBUT	PEAK	WKS	Track	Pop		Album Title	Album Label & Number
2/23/85	36	6	(Wearing Down) Like A Wheel	—		Change No Change	Elektra 60393

ECONOLINE CRUSH

Rock group from Vancouver: Trevor Hurst (vocals), Robbie Morfitt and Ziggy (guitars), Don Binns (bass) and Nico Quintal (drums).

DEBUT	PEAK	WKS	Track	Pop		Album Title	Album Label & Number
5/23/98	35	4	1 Home	—		The Devil You Know..............	Restless 72960
10/3/98	18	19	2 Surefire (Never Enough)	—		↓	
3/27/99	18	13	3 All That You Are (X3)	—		↓	
4/14/01	21	11	4 Make It Right............................	—		Brand New History	Restless 773727
7/21/01	29	6	5 You Don't Know What It's Like	—		↓	

EDDIE, John

Born in 1959 in Virginia; raised in New Jersey. Rock singer.

DEBUT	PEAK	WKS	Track	Pop		Album Title	Album Label & Number
5/24/86	17	10	Jungle Boy	52		John Eddie	Columbia 40181

DEBUT	PEAK	WKS	Mainstream Rock Track	Pop	Gld	Album Title	Album Label & Number
			EDDIE AND THE TIDE				
			Rock group from Berkeley, California: Eddie Rice (vocals), Johnny Perri (guitar), Cazz McCaslin (keyboards), George Diebold (bass) and Scott Mason (drums).				
8/24/85	22	7	One In A Million	85		*Go Out And Get It*	Atco 90289
			EDMUNDS, Dave				
			Born on 4/15/44 in Cardiff, Wales. Singer/songwriter/guitarist/producer. Formed Love Sculpture in 1967. Formed rockabilly band **Rockpile** in 1976. Produced for Shakin' Stevens, Brinsley Schwarz and **Stray Cats**. Also see **Classic Rock Tracks** section.				
5/2/81	18	11	√1 Almost Saturday Night	54		*Twangin....*	Swan Song 16034
			#78 Pop hit for **John Fogerty** in 1975				
5/1/82	28	7	√2 From Small Things (Big Things One Day Come)	—		*D.E. 7th*	Columbia 37930
			written by **Bruce Springsteen**				
5/8/82	47	3	3 Me And The Boys	—		↓	
5/28/83	7	13	√4 Slipping Away	39		*Information*	Columbia 38651
			written and produced by **Jeff Lynne** (of **ELO**)				
9/15/84	16	7	√5 Something About You	—		*Riff Raff*	Columbia 39273
			#19 Pop hit for the Four Tops in 1965				
1/31/87	35	7	6 The Wanderer .... [L]	—		*I Hear You Rockin'*	Columbia 40603
			THE DAVE EDMUNDS BAND #2 Pop hit for Dion in 1962				
3/10/90	38	5	7 Closer To The Flame	—		*Closer To The Flame*	Capitol 90372
			805				
			Rock group from New York City: Dave Porter (vocals, guitar), Ed Vivenzio (keyboards), Greg Liss (bass) and Frank Briggs (drums).				
8/14/82	37	4	Young Boys	—		*Stand In Line*	RCA 8013
			8STOPS7				
			Rock group from Los Angeles: Evan Sula-Goff (vocals, guitar), Seth Watson (guitar), Adam Powell (bass) and Alex Viveros (drums).				
3/11/00	26	14	1 Satisfied	—		*In Moderation.*	Reprise 47387
7/29/00	16	11	2 Question Everything	—		↓	
			ELASTICA				
			Rock group from London: Justine Frischmann (vocals), Donna Matthews (guitar), Annie Holland (bass) and Justin Welch (drums).				
6/24/95	40	1	Connection	53	●	*Elastica*	DGC 24728
			ELECTRIC BOYS				
			Male rock group from Sweden: Conny Bloom (vocals), Franco Santunione (guitar), Andy Christell (bass) and Niclas Sigevall (drums).				
5/5/90	16	13	1 All Lips N' Hips	76		*Funk-O-Metal Carpet Ride.*	Atco 91337
6/6/92	29	6	2 Mary In The Mystery World	—		*Groovus Maximus*	Atco 92143
			ELECTRIC LIGHT ORCHESTRA				
			Orchestral rock group formed in Birmingham, England. Core members: **Jeff Lynne** (vocals, guitar), Richard Tandy (keyboards), Kelly Groucutt (bass) and Bev Bevan (drums). Lynne was also a prolific producer and a member of the supergroup **Traveling Wilburys**. Also see **Classic Rock Tracks** section.				
8/15/81	2[1]	16	1 Hold On Tight	10	●	*Time.*	Jet 37371
7/9/83	19	9	2 Rock 'N' Roll Is King	19		*Secret Messages*	Jet 38490
			ELO (above 2)				
2/8/86	22	9	3 Calling America	18		*Balance Of Power*	CBS Associated 40048
			ELEVEN				
			Rock trio from Los Angeles: Alain Johannes (guitar, vocals), Natasha Shneider (clavinet, bass, vocals) and Jack Irons (drums). Irons was also a member of **Red Hot Chili Peppers** and **Pearl Jam**.				
5/28/94	40	1	Reach Out	—		*Eleven.*	Third Rail 61516
			ELY, Joe				
			Born on 2/9/47 in Amarillo, Texas; raised in Lubbock. Country-rock singer/songwriter/guitarist.				
4/4/81	40	3	Musta Notta Gotta Lotta	—		*Musta Notta Gotta Lotta*	SouthCoast 5183
			EMERSON, LAKE & PALMER				
			Classical-oriented rock trio from England: Keith Emerson (keyboards), **Greg Lake** (vocals, guitar, bass) and Carl Palmer (drums). Group split up in 1979, with Palmer joining **Asia**. Emerson and Lake re-grouped in 1986 with new drummer Cozy Powell (**Whitesnake**). Palmer returned in 1987, replacing Powell who joined **Black Sabbath** in 1990. Powell died in a car crash on 4/5/98 (age 50). Also see **3** and **Classic Rock Tracks** section.				
5/24/86	2[2]	13	1 Touch & Go	60		*Emerson, Lake & Powell*	Polydor 829297
			EMERSON, LAKE & POWELL				
6/20/92	44	1	2 Black Moon	—		*Black Moon.*	Victory 480003
			EMMETT, Rik				
			Born in 1953 in Toronto. Rock singer/guitarist. Leader of **Triumph** from 1975-88.				
12/15/90+	22	9	1 Big Lie	—		*Absolutely*	Charisma 91606
2/23/91	16	15	2 Saved By Love	—		↓	
			ENTWISTLE, John				
			Born on 10/9/44 in Chiswick, London, England. Died of a heart attack on 6/27/2002 (age 57). Bass guitarist of **The Who**.				
12/12/81+	41	6	Talk Dirty	—		*Too Late The Hero*	Atco 142
			Joe Walsh (guitar)				
			ENUFF Z'NUFF				
			Rock group from Chicago: Chip Z'Nuff (bass), Donnie Vie (vocals), Derek Frigo (guitar) and Vikki Foxx (drums).				
9/2/89	35	9	1 New Thing	67		*Enuff Z'nuff.*	Atco 91262
1/20/90	27	10	2 Fly High Michelle	47		↓	
4/27/91	17	10	3 Mother's Eyes	—		*Strength*	Atco 91638

DEBUT	PEAK	WKS	Mainstream Rock Track	Pop	Gld	Album Title	Album Label & Number
			EPIDEMIC				
			Hard-rock group from San Diego: Boris (vocals), Bruce Allan (guitar), Jim McDaniel (bass) and Tim Ganard (drums).				
7/27/02	34	5	Walk Away	—		*Epidemic*	Elektra 62769
			ESCAPE CLUB, The				
			Rock group formed in London: Trevor Steel (vocals), John Holliday (guitar), Johnnie Christo (bass) and Milan Zekavica (drums).				
9/10/88	45	5	Wild, Wild West	❶¹ ●		*Wild Wild West*	Atlantic 81871
	★95★		**ETHERIDGE, Melissa**				
			Born on 5/29/61 in Leavenworth, Kansas. Singer/songwriter/guitarist.				
			1)Your Little Secret 2)Similar Features 3)No Souvenirs				
7/23/88	10	13	1 Bring Me Some Water	—	▲²	*Melissa Etheridge*	Island 90875
10/29/88	28	12	2 Like The Way I Do	42	↓		
2/18/89	6	13	3 Similar Features	94	↓		
5/13/89	22	7	4 Chrome Plated Heart	—	↓		
9/9/89	9	12	5 No Souvenirs	95	▲	*Brave And Crazy*	Island 91285
11/18/89	13	12	6 Let Me Go	—	↓		
3/3/90	34	7	7 The Angels	—			
3/14/92	10	10	8 Ain't It Heavy	—	▲	*Never Enough*	Island 512120
9/18/93	10	14	9 I'm The Only One	8	▲⁶	*Yes I Am*	Island 848660
1/1/94	22	12	10 Come To My Window	25	↓		
4/16/94	24	8	11 All American Girl	—	↓		
10/28/95	4	14	12 Your Little Secret	47ᴬ	▲²	*Your Little Secret*	Island 524154
2/3/96	22	10	13 I Want To Come Over	22	↓		
			EUROGLIDERS				
			Pop-rock group from Perth, Australia: Grace Knight (vocals), Crispin Akerman (guitar), Amanda Vincent and Bernie Lynch (keyboards), Ron Francois (bass) and John Bennetts (drums).				
11/3/84	21	11	Heaven (Must Be There)	65		*This Island*	Columbia 39588
			EUROPE				
			Hard-rock group from Stockholm, Sweden: Joey Tempest (vocals), Kee Marcello (guitar), John Leven (bass), Mic Michaeli (keyboards) and Ian Haugland (drums). Founding guitarist **John Norum** went solo in 1987.				
12/27/86+	18	13	1 The Final Countdown	8	▲³	*The Final Countdown*	Epic 40241
4/4/87	22	8	2 Rock The Night	30	↓		
8/1/87	35	8	3 Carrie	3	↓		
8/6/88	9	11	4 Superstitious	31	▲	*Out Of This World*	Epic 44185
			EURYTHMICS				
			Pop-rock duo: **Annie Lennox** (vocals, keyboards) and David A. Stewart (guitar). Lennox was born on 12/25/54 in Aberdeen, Scotland. Stewart was born on 9/9/52 in Sunderland, England. Both had been in The Tourists from 1977-80. Stewart married Siobhan Fahey of **Bananarama** on 8/1/87.				
6/11/83	16	15	1 Sweet Dreams (Are Made of This)	❶¹ ●		*Sweet Dreams (Are Made Of This)*	RCA 4681
1/21/84	8	15	2 Here Comes The Rain Again	4	▲	*Touch*	RCA 4917
4/27/85	2¹	14	3 Would I Lie To You?	5	▲	*Be Yourself Tonight*	RCA 5429
7/13/85	36	5	4 I Love You Like A Ball And Chain	—	↓		
7/5/86	❶¹	14	5 Missionary Man	14	●	*Revenge*	RCA 5847
12/19/87+	32	8	6 I Need A Man	46		*Savage*	RCA 6794
			EVERCLEAR				
			Rock trio formed in Portland, Oregon: Art Alexakis (vocals, guitar; born on 4/12/62), Craig Montoya (bass; born on 9/14/70) and Greg Eklund (drums; born on 4/18/70).				
12/23/95+	❶³	31	1 Santa Monica (Watch The World Die)	29ᴬ		*Sparkle And Fade*	Capitol 30929
5/25/96	29	8	2 Heartspark Dollarsign	85	↓		
9/27/97	15	19	3 Everything To Everyone	43ᴬ	▲	*So Much For The Afterglow*	Capitol 36503
2/14/98	20	13	4 I Will Buy You A New Life	33ᴬ	↓		
8/22/98	29	8	5 Father Of Mine	46ᴬ	↓		
8/21/99	40	2	6 The Boys Are Back In Town	—		*Detroit Rock City (soundtrack)*	Mercury 546389
			#12 Pop hit for **Thin Lizzy** in 1976				
6/17/00	28	10	7 Wonderful	11	▲	*Songs From An American Movie Vol. One: Learning How To Smile*	Capitol 97061
11/18/00+	10	13	8 When It All Goes Wrong Again	121		*Songs From An American Movie, Vol. Two: Good Time For A Bad Attitude*	Capitol 95873
			EVERLAST				
			Born Erik Schrody on 8/18/69 in Valley Stream, New York. Singer/songwriter/guitarist/actor. Former member of rap group House Of Pain. Played "Rhodes" in the movie *Judgment Night*.				
11/21/98+	❶¹	30	1 What It's Like	13	▲²	*Whitey Ford Sings The Blues*	Tommy Boy 1236
4/10/99	13	16	2 Ends	109			
9/25/99	8	27	3 Put Your Lights On	118	▲¹⁴	*Supernatural (Santana)*	Arista 19080
			SANTANA Featuring Everlast				
9/30/00	30	12	4 Black Jesus	—	●	*Eat At Whitey's*	Tommy Boy 1411
			EVERY MOTHER'S NIGHTMARE				
			Hard-rock group formed in Nashville: Rick Ruhl (vocals), Steve Malone (guitar), Mark McMurtry (bass) and Jim Phipps (drums).				
10/27/90	22	11	Love Can Make You Blind	—		*Every Mother's Nightmare*	Arista 8633

DEBUT	PEAK	WKS	Mainstream Rock Track	Pop	Gld	Album Title	Album Label & Number

EVE 6
Rock trio from Los Angeles: Jon Siebels (vocals, guitar), Max Collins (bass) and Tony Fagenson (drums).

8/1/98	5	29	1 Inside Out	28	▲	Eve 6 .... RCA 67617
12/19/98+	10	17	2 Leech	—	↓	
7/15/00	25	9	3 Promise	—	●	Horrorscope .... RCA 67713

EXPANDING MAN
Rock group from New York City: Aaron Lippert (vocals), Dave Wanamaker and Bill Guerra (guitars), Pete Armata (bass) and Chris Hancock (drums).

| 9/14/96 | 22 | 10 | Download (I Will)............................... | — | | Head To The Ground .... QDivision 67601 |

EXTREME
Rock group from Boston: Gary Cherone (vocals), Nuno Bettencourt (guitar), Pat Badger (bass) and Paul Geary (drums). Geary replaced by Mike Mangini by 1995. Cherone became lead singer of **Van Halen** in September 1996.

4/8/89	39	6	1 Kid Ego	—		Extreme .... A&M 5238
9/1/90	45	2	2 Decadence Dance	—	▲²	Pornograffitti .... A&M 5313
3/2/91	12	17	3 More Than Words........................	❶¹	↓	
6/22/91	2⁴	18	4 Hole Hearted	4	↓	
10/26/91	34	7	5 Get The Funk Out	—	↓	
9/12/92	❶²	20	6 Rest In Peace	96	●	III Sides To Every Story .... A&M 540006
12/26/92+	9	11	7 Stop The World	95	↓	
4/10/93	10	13	8 Am I Ever Gonna Change	—	↓	
2/4/95	26	7	9 Hip Today........................	—		Waiting For The Punchline .... A&M 540327

F

FABULOUS THUNDERBIRDS, The
Male blues-rock group from Austin, Texas: Kim Wilson (vocals, harmonica), Jimmie Vaughan (guitar; older brother of **Stevie Ray Vaughan**), Keith Ferguson (bass) and Fran Christina (drums). Preston Hubbard replaced Ferguson in late 1981. Vaughan appeared in the 1989 movie *Great Balls Of Fire* and recorded in **The Vaughan Brothers** in 1990. Disbanded in June 1990. Reorganized in 1991 with Wilson, Hubbard, Christina and guitarists Duke Robillard and Kid Bangham. Ferguson died of liver failure on 4/29/97 (age 49).
1)Powerful Stuff 2)Tuff Enuff 3)Twist Of The Knife

4/11/81	44	1	1 Tip On In	—		Butt Rockin'..................... Chrysalis 1319
			#37 R&B hit for Slim Harpo in 1967			
4/18/81	41	2	2 One's Too Many	—	↓	
2/22/86	4	16	3 Tuff Enuff	10	▲	Tuff Enuff .... CBS Associated 40304
5/24/86	8	11	4 Wrap It Up	50	↓	
			#93 Pop hit for Archie Bell & The Drells in 1970			
8/30/86	20	8	5 Look At That, Look At That	—	↓	
6/27/87	8	8	6 Stand Back	76		Hot Number .... CBS Associated 40818
8/15/87	22	8	7 How Do You Spell Love...........	—	↓	
			above 5 produced by **Dave Edmunds**			
7/16/88	3	12	8 Powerful Stuff	65	▲⁴	Cocktail (soundtrack) .... Elektra 60806
4/22/89	10	8	9 Rock This Place	—		Powerful Stuff................ CBS Associated 45094
7/27/91	7	10	10 Twist Of The Knife	—		Walk That Walk, Talk That Walk.. Epic/Associated 47878

FACE TO FACE
Rock group from Boston: Laurie Sargent (vocals), brothers Angelo and Stuart Kimball (guitars), John Ryder (bass) and William Beard (drums).

| 6/9/84 | 55 | 2 | Out Of My Hands .... | — | | Face To Face..................... Epic 38857 |

FAGEN, Donald
Born on 1/10/48 in Passaic, New Jersey. Pop-rock singer/keyboardist. Member of **Steely Dan**.

10/23/82	17	12	1 I.G.Y. (What A Beautiful World)............	26	▲	The Nightfly .... Warner 23696
			I.G.Y.: International Geophysical Year (July 1957-December 1958)			
3/26/88	12	8	2 Century's End........................	83		Bright Lights, Big City (soundtrack) ..... Warner 25688
11/2/91	17	12	3 Pretzel Logic	[L]	—	The New York Rock And Soul Revue - Live
			DONALD FAGEN & MICHAEL McDONALD			At The Beacon (various artists) .... Giant 24423
			recorded at the Beacon Theatre in New York City; #57 Pop hit for **Steely Dan** in 1974			
6/5/93	20	8	4 Tomorrow's Girls	121	●	Kamakiriad....................... Reprise 45230

FAILURE
Rock group from Los Angeles: Ken Andrews (vocals), Troy Van Leeuwen (guitar), Greg Edwards (bass) and Kellii Scott (drums).

| 12/14/96+ | 31 | 9 | Stuck On You .... | — | | Fantastic Planet .... Slash 46269 |

FAITH NO MORE
Rock group from San Francisco: Michael "Vlad Dracula" Patton (vocals), Jim Martin (guitar), Roddy Bottum (keyboards), Billy Gould (bass) and Mike Bordin (drums). Martin left in 1994; replaced by Dean Menta. Menta left by 1995.

7/14/90	25	11	∨1 Epic	9	▲	The Real Thing..................... Slash 25878
10/13/90	40	5	2 Falling To Pieces........................	92	↓	
7/25/92	32	5	3 MidLife Crisis	—	●	Angel Dust .... Slash 26785
6/21/97	14	21	4 Last Cup Of Sorrow	—		Album Of The Year. .... Slash 46629
11/15/97+	23	12	5 Ashes To Ashes	—	↓	

DEBUT	PEAK	WKS	Mainstream Rock Track	Pop Gld	Album Title	Album Label & Number
			FALCO Born Johann Holzel on 2/19/57 in Vienna, Austria. Died in a car crash on 2/6/98 (age 40). Male singer/songwriter.			
3/19/83	22	12	**Der Kommissar** .... [F] —		*Einzelhaft* .... A&M 4951	
			Kommissar is German for "government official"; original German language version; also see English version by **After The Fire**			
			FALCON, Billy Born on 7/13/56 in Valley Stream, New York. Rock singer/songwriter/guitarist.			
7/20/91	19	12	**Power Windows** 35		*Pretty Blue World* .... Jambco 848800	
			co-produced by **Jon Bon Jovi**			
			FAMILIAR 48 Rock group from Philadelphia: Jay Mannon (vocals), Kevin Hug (guitar), Scott Stanley (bass) and Nick DeNofa (drums).			
3/23/02	30	8	**The Question** .... —		*Wonderful Nothing* .... Refugee 112852	
			FARRENHEIT Rock trio from Boston: Charlie Farren (vocals, guitar), David Heit (bass) and Muzz (drums). Farren was lead singer of the **Joe Perry Project**.			
4/25/87	42	4	**Fool In Love** .... —		*Farrenheit*. .... Warner 25564	
			FASTBALL Rock trio from Austin, Texas: Miles Zuniga (vocals, guitar), Tony Scalzo (vocals, bass) and Joey Shuffield (drums).			
5/9/98	25	16	✓1 **The Way**	5[A] ▲	*All The Pain Money Can Buy* .... Hollywood 62130	
9/5/98	25	13	2 **Fire Escape**	86 ↓		
			FASTER PUSSYCAT Hard-rock group from Los Angeles: Taime Downe (vocals), Greg Steele and Brent Muscat (guitars), Eric Stacy (bass) and Mark Michals (drums). Michals was replaced by Brett Bradshaw in early 1992. Group name taken from the 1965 action movie *Faster Pussycat! Kill! Kill!*			
3/31/90	23	10	1 **House Of Pain**	28 ●	*Wake Me When It's Over* .... Elektra 60883	
9/12/92	35	2	2 **Nonstop To Nowhere** .... —		*Whipped!* . ... Elektra 61124	
			FASTWAY Hard-rock group from England: David King (vocals), Fast Eddie Clarke (guitar), Charlie McCracken (bass) and Jerry Shirley (drums). Clarke was with Motorhead. Shirley was with **Humble Pie**.			
5/28/83	32	6	1 **Easy Livin'** .... —		*Fastway* . ... Columbia 38662	
6/11/83	14	11	2 **Say What You Will** .... —		↓	
7/7/84	27	9	3 **Tell Me** .... —		*All Fired Up* . ... Columbia 39373	
			FEAR FACTORY Hard-rock group from Los Angeles: Burton Bell (vocals), Dino Cazares (guitar), Christian Olde Wolbers (bass) and Raymond Herrera (drums).			
4/3/99	38	2	1 **Descent** .... — ●		*Obsolete* . ... Roadrunner 8752	
5/22/99	16	11	2 **Cars** .... —		↓	
			#9 Pop hit for Gary Numan in 1980			
6/9/01	31	7	3 **Linchpin** .... —		*Digimortal* . ... Roadrunner 8487	
			FEEDER Rock trio from England: Grant Nicholas (vocals), Taka Hirose (bass) and Jon Lee (drums).			
3/21/98	31	5	1 **Cement** .... —		*Polythene* . ... Echo/Elektra 62085	
7/18/98	36	4	2 **High** .... —		↓	
			FELDER, Don Born on 9/21/47 in Gainesville, Florida. Singer/songwriter/guitarist. Member of the **Eagles**.			
8/1/81	5	17	1 Heavy Metal (Takin' A Ride)	43 ●	*Heavy Metal (soundtrack)* .... Asylum 90004	
12/10/83	34	8	2 **Bad Girls** 104		*Airborne* . ... Elektra 60295	
			FENN, Rick — see MASON, Nick			
			FERGUSON, Jay Born John Ferguson on 5/10/43 in San Fernando Valley, California. Member of **Spirit**.			
3/13/82	34	8	**White Noise** .... —		*White Noise* . ... Capitol 12196	
			Joe Walsh (guitar)			
			FERRY, Bryan Born on 9/26/45 in County Durham, England. Lead singer of **Roxy Music**.			
6/29/85	19	9	1 **Slave To Love** .... 109 ●		*Boys And Girls* . ... Warner 25082	
2/27/88	40	5	2 **Kiss And Tell** 31		*Bete Noire* . ... Reprise 25598	
			FIGHT Hard-rock group from England: Rob Halford (vocals), Russ Parrish and Brian Tilse (guitars), Jay Jay (bass) and Scott Travis (drums). Halford was lead singer of **Judas Priest**.			
11/27/93+	21	12	**Little Crazy** .... —		*War Of Words* . ... Epic 57372	
			FILTER Industrial rock duo from Cleveland: Richard Patrick (vocals, guitar, bass) and Brian Liesegang (keyboards, drums). Both worked with Trent Reznor in **Nine Inch Nails**.			
5/13/95	19	18	1 Hey Man Nice Shot	76 ▲	*Short Bus*. .... Reprise 45864	
7/31/99	8	14	2 Welcome To The Fold	— ▲	*Title Of Record* . ... Reprise 47388	
11/6/99+	4	25	3 Take A Picture	12 ↓		
4/15/00	31	7	4 **The Best Things** .... —		↓	
7/13/02	12	10	5 **Where Do We Go From Here** 94		*theAmalgamut* . ... Reprise 47963	
10/19/02	40	1	6 **American Cliche** .... —		↓	

DEBUT	PEAK	WKS	Mainstream Rock Track	Pop Gld	Album Title	Album Label & Number

FINE YOUNG CANNIBALS
Pop-rock trio formed in Birmingham, England: Roland Gift (vocals), Andy Cox (guitar) and David Steele (bass). Cox and Steele were with English Beat. Group name taken from the 1960 movie *All The Fine Young Cannibals*. Group appeared in the movie *Tin Men*. Gift acted in the movies *Sammy And Rosie Get Laid* and *Scandal*.

6/3/89	39	4	1 Good Thing	❶¹ ▲²	*The Raw & The Cooked*	I.R.S. 6273
8/19/89	38	8	2 Don't Look Back	11	↓	

FINGER ELEVEN
Rock group from Toronto: brothers Scott (vocals) and Sean (bass) Anderson, Rick Jackett and James Black (guitars) and Rob Gommerman (drums).

9/26/98	28	10	1 Quicksand	—	*Tip*	Wind-Up 13052
4/17/99	34	7	2 Above	—	↓	

FIONA
Born Fiona Flanagan on 9/13/61 in New York City. Co-starred in the 1987 movie *Hearts Of Fire*.

3/23/85	12	12	1 Talk To Me	64	*Fiona*	Atlantic 81242
10/28/89	22	10	2 Everything You Do (You're Sexing Me)	52	*Heart Like A Gun*	Atlantic 81903
			FIONA with Kip Winger			

FIREHOUSE
Pop-rock group from North Carolina: C.J. Snare (vocals), Bill Leverty (guitar), Perry Richardson (bass) and Michael Foster (drums).

1/19/91	16	18	1 Don't Treat Me Bad	19 ▲²	*Firehouse*	Epic 46186
11/16/91+	25	10	2 All She Wrote	58	↓	
6/20/92	27	10	3 Reach For The Sky	83 ●	*Hold Your Fire*	Epic 48615

FIRM, The
All-star rock group from England: **Paul Rodgers** (vocals), **Jimmy Page** (guitar), Tony Franklin (bass) and Chris Slade (drums). Rodgers was with **Bad Company**. Page was with **Led Zeppelin**. Disbanded in 1986. Franklin joined **Blue Murder** in 1989. Slade joined **AC/DC** in 1990. Rodgers joined **The Law** in 1991.

2/2/85	❶¹	15	1 Radioactive	28 ●	*The Firm*	Atlantic 81239
3/9/85	19	10	2 Closer	—	↓	
3/16/85	4	15	3 Satisfaction Guaranteed	73	↓	
2/1/86	❶⁴	12	4 All The Kings Horses	61	*Mean Business*	Atlantic 81628
3/1/86	21	11	5 Live In Peace	—	↓	

FIXX, The ★55★
Techno-pop group formed in London: Cy Curnin (vocals), Jamie West-Oram (guitar), Rupert Greenall (keyboards), Dan Brown (bass) and Adam Woods (drums).
1)Driven Out 2)Secret Separation 3)Are We Ourselves?

9/18/82	7	21	1 Stand Or Fall	76	*Shuttered Room*	MCA 5345
2/19/83	13	11	2 Red Skies	101	↓	
5/28/83	9	18	3 Saved By Zero	20 ▲	*Reach The Beach*	MCA 39001
6/4/83	2¹	26	4 One Thing Leads To Another	4	↓	
1/21/84	20	4	5 The Sign Of Fire	32	↓	
5/12/84	3	14	6 Deeper And Deeper	—	*Streets Of Fire (soundtrack)*	MCA 5492
8/18/84	❶²	13	7 Are We Ourselves?	15 ●	*Phantoms*	MCA 5507
9/8/84	37	13	8 Sunshine In The Shade	69	↓	
5/17/86	❶²	15	9 Secret Separation	19	*Walkabout*	MCA 5705
7/5/86	13	14	10 Built For The Future	—	↓	
7/4/87	32	5	11 Don't Be Scared	—	*React*	MCA 42008
1/21/89	❶⁴	14	12 Driven Out	55	*Calm Animals*	RCA 8566
4/29/89	23	7	13 Precious Stone	—	↓	
2/16/91	11	9	14 How Much Is Enough	35	*Ink*	MCA 10205

FLAW
Rock group from Louisville, Kentucky: Chris Volz (vocals), Lance Arny (guitar), Jason Daunt (keyboards), Ryan Jurhs (bass) and Chris Ballinger (drums).

11/10/01	33	7	1 Payback	—	*Through The Eyes*	Republic 014891
6/1/02	38	2	2 Whole	—	↓	

FLEETWOOD, Mick
Born on 6/24/42 in London. Blues-rock drummer. Co-founder of **Fleetwood Mac**. Played "Mic" in the 1987 movie *The Running Man*.

7/18/81	30	6	Rattlesnake Shake	—	*The Visitor*	RCA 4080

FLEETWOOD MAC ★66★
Pop-rock group formed in England by **Mick Fleetwood** (drums) and John McVie (bass). Group went through several personnel changes. **Bob Welch** was a member from 1971-74. **Christine McVie** (vocals, keyboards) joined in August 1970 (married to John from 1968-77). Americans **Lindsey Buckingham** (guitar, vocals) and **Stevie Nicks** (vocals) joined in January 1975. Buckingham left in July 1987; replaced by Billy Burnette and Rick Vito. The classic lineup of Fleetwood, John and Christine McVie, Buckingham and Nicks reunited in May 1997. Inducted into the Rock and Roll Hall of Fame in 1998. Also see **Classic Rock Tracks** section.
1)Big Love 2)Seven Wonders 3)Hold Me

4/11/81	59	1	1 Fireflies	60 ●	*Fleetwood Mac Live*	Warner 3500
6/19/82	3	16	↳2 Hold Me	4 ▲²	*Mirage*	Warner 23607
7/24/82	4	17	↳3 Gypsy	12	↓	
7/31/82	36	2	4 Straight Back	—	↓	

DEBUT	PEAK	WKS	Mainstream Rock Track	Pop	Gld	Album Title	Album Label & Number
			FLEETWOOD MAC — Cont'd				
3/28/87	2³	10	5 Big Love	5	▲³	Tango In The Night	Warner 25471
4/25/87	2¹	16	6 Seven Wonders	19	↓		
5/2/87	14	17	7 Isn't It Midnight	—	↓		
5/2/87	28	9	8 Tango In The Night	—	↓		
8/22/87	14	11	9 Little Lies	4	↓		
12/5/87+	22	11	10 Everywhere	14	↓		
11/26/88+	15	12	11 As Long As You Follow	43	▲⁸	Greatest Hits	Warner 25801
12/24/88+	37	7	12 No Questions Asked	—	↓		
4/7/90	3	9	13 Save Me	33	●	Behind The Mask	Warner 26111
4/28/90	7	11	14 Love Is Dangerous	—	↓		
7/28/90	40	4	15 Skies The Limit	—	↓		
12/12/92	26	4	16 Paper Doll	108		25 Years-The Chain	Warner 45129
10/25/97	30	6	17 The Chain [L]	—	▲⁵	The Dance	Reprise 46702
			FLIES ON FIRE				
			Rock group from Los Angeles: Tim Paruszkiewicz (vocals), Howard Drossin (guitar), Mess Messal (bass) and Richard D'Albis (drums).				
8/17/91	38	4	Cry To Myself	—		Outside Looking Inside	Atco 91675
			FLOCK OF SEAGULLS, A				
			New-wave group from Liverpool, England: brothers Mike (vocals, keyboards) and Ali (drums) Score, Paul Reynolds (guitar) and Frank Maudsley (bass).				
5/15/82	3	29	1 I Ran (So Far Away)	9	●	A Flock Of Seagulls	Jive 66000
6/19/82	59	2	2 Space Age Love Song	30	↓		
5/14/83	3	14	3 Wishing (If I Had A Photograph Of You)	26		Listen	Jive 8013
8/4/84	10	10	4 The More You Live, The More You Love	56		The Story Of A Young Heart	Jive 8250
			FLYS, The				
			Rock group from Los Angeles: brothers Adam and Joshua Paskowitz (vocals), Peter Perdichizzi (guitar), James Book (bass) and Nick Lucero (drums).				
9/12/98+	8	30	Got You (Where I Want You)	104		Disturbing Behavior (soundtrack)	Trauma 74007
			FOGELBERG, Dan				
			Born on 8/13/51 in Peoria, Illinois. Singer/songwriter/guitarist. Also see **Classic Rock Tracks** section.				
9/5/81	14	14	1 Hard To Say	7	▲²	The Innocent Age	Full Moon 37393
			Glenn Frey (harmony vocal)				
9/19/81	45	9	2 Lost In The Sun	—	↓		
12/11/82	30	2	3 Missing You	23	▲³	Dan Fogelberg/Greatest Hits	Full Moon 38308
2/25/84	8	10	4 The Language Of Love	13	●	Windows And Walls	Full Moon 39004
4/7/84	31	2	5 Gone Too Far	—	↓		
			Timothy B. Schmit (harmony vocal, above 2)				
5/23/87	13	8	6 She Don't Look Back	84		Exiles	Full Moon 40271
			FOGERTY, John				
			Born on 5/28/45 in Berkeley, California. Singer/songwriter/multi-instrumentalist. Leader of Creedence Clearwater Revival. Also see **Classic Rock Tracks** section.				
12/22/84+	❶³	14	1 The Old Man Down The Road	10	▲²	Centerfield	Warner 25203
1/19/85	5	18	2 Rock And Roll Girls	20	↓		
3/30/85	4	13	3 Centerfield	44	↓		
8/30/86	3	9	4 Eye Of The Zombie	81	●	Eye Of The Zombie	Warner 25449
9/27/86	3	13	5 Change In The Weather	—	↓		
10/4/86	27	6	6 Headlines	—	↓		
6/21/97	14	12	7 Walking In A Hurricane	—	●	Blue Moon Swamp	Warner 45426
10/4/97	32	6	8 Blueboy	—	↓		
6/6/98	19	13	9 Premonition [L]	—	●	Premonition	Reprise 46908
			recorded at The Burbank Studio				
			FOGHAT				
			Rock group formed in England: "Lonesome" Dave Peverett (vocals, guitar), Erik Cartwright (guitar), Craig MacGregor (bass) and Roger Earl (drums). Nick Jameson replaced MacGregor in early 1982. Peverett died of pneumonia on 2/7/2000 (age 57). Also see **Classic Rock Tracks** section.				
7/18/81	15	10	1 Live Now-Pay Later	102		Girls To Chat & Boys To Bounce	Bearsville 3578
11/20/82	12	8	2 Slipped, Tripped, Fell In Love	—		In The Mood For Something Rude	Bearsville 23747
			FOLK IMPLOSION				
			Rock duo from San Francisco: Lou Barlow (vocals, bass) and John Davis (guitar, drums).				
1/27/96	20	10	Natural One	29		Kids (soundtrack)	London 828640

DEBUT	PEAK	WKS	Mainstream Rock Track	Pop	Gld	Album Title	Album Label & Number

★80★ FOO FIGHTERS

Rock group formed in Seattle: **Dave Grohl** (vocals, guitar; born on 1/14/69), Pat Smear (guitar; born on 8/5/59), Nate Mendel (bass; born on 12/2/68) and William Goldsmith (drums; born on 7/4/72). Taylor Hawkins (born on 2/10/68) replaced Goldsmith in 1997. Franz Stahl (born on 10/30/61) replaced Smear in 1998. Grohl was drummer for **Nirvana**. Group name taken from the fiery UFO-like apparitions seen by U.S. pilots during World War II.
1)Learn To Fly 2)Everlong 3)This Is A Call

DEBUT	PEAK	WKS	Track	Pop	Gld	Album Title	Album Label & Number
7/8/95	6	16	1 This Is A Call	35[A]	▲	Foo Fighters	Roswell 34027
10/7/95	12	17	2 I'll Stick Around	51[A]		↓	
3/2/96	18	11	3 Big Me	13[A]		↓	
5/10/97	9	20	4 Monkey Wrench	58[A]	▲	The Colour And The Shape	Roswell 55832
8/23/97	4	28	5 Everlong	42[A]		↓	
1/31/98	8	26	6 My Hero	59[A]		↓	
4/18/98	34	5	7 Baker Street	—		Essential Interpretations (various artists)	EMI-Capitol 93335
			#2 Pop hit for Gerry Rafferty in 1978				
10/2/99	2[4]	30	8 Learn To Fly	19	▲	There Is Nothing Left To Lose	Roswell 67892
2/12/00	9	13	9 Stacked Actors	—		↓	
5/13/00	11	12	10 Breakout	—		↓	
12/29/01+	20	11	11 The One	121		Orange County (soundtrack).	Columbia 85933
9/21/02	7↑	10↑	12 All My Life	51↑		One By One	Roswell 68008

FORBERT, Steve

Born in 1955 in Meridian, Mississippi. Singer/songwriter/guitarist. Also see **Classic Rock Tracks** section.

7/31/82	54	1	Ya Ya (Next To Me)	—		Steve Forbert	Nemperor 37434

FORD, Lita

Born on 9/23/59 in London; raised in Los Angeles. Rock singer/guitarist. Member of The Runaways from 1975-79.

8/4/84	51	5	1 Gotta Let Go	—		Dancin' On The Edge	Mercury 818864
2/27/88	40	5	2 Kiss Me Deadly	12	▲	Lita	RCA 6397
7/30/88	22	8	3 Back To The Cave	—		↓	
4/29/89	25	9	4 Close My Eyes Forever	8		↓	
			LITA FORD (with Ozzy Osbourne)				
7/22/89	37	5	5 Falling In And Out Of Love	—		↓	
5/26/90	14	9	6 Hungry	98		Stiletto	RCA 2090
11/2/91	21	10	7 Shot Of Poison	45		Dangerous Curves	RCA 61025

★44★ FOREIGNER

British-American rock group formed in New York City. Lineup by 1981: **Lou Gramm** (vocals), **Mick Jones** (guitar), Rick Wills (bass) and Dennis Elliott (drums). Gramm was also a member of **Shadow King**. Wills was also a member of **Roxy Music** and **Bad Company**. Jones not to be confused with Mick Jones of The Clash and Big Audio Dynamite. Also see **Classic Rock Tracks** section.
1)Urgent 2)Say You Will 3)I Want To Know What Love Is

7/18/81	❶[4]	30	1 Urgent	4	▲[6]	4.	Atlantic 16999
			Jr. Walker (sax solo)				
7/25/81	3	34	2 Juke Box Hero	26		↓	
8/1/81	14	16	3 Night Life	—		↓	
11/21/81	❶[1]	11	4 Waiting For A Girl Like You	2[10]		↓	
12/8/84+	❶[1]	14	5 I Want To Know What Love Is	❶[2]	▲[3]	Agent Provocateur	Atlantic 81999
			New Jersey Mass Choir and Jennifer Holliday (backing vocals)				
1/5/85	47	2	6 Tooth And Nail	—		↓	
1/19/85	4	19	7 That Was Yesterday	12		↓	
2/2/85	44	1	8 Reaction To Action	54		↓	
12/5/87	❶[4]	11	9 Say You Will	6	▲	Inside Information	Atlantic 81808
12/19/87+	7	14	10 Heart Turns To Stone	56		↓	
2/13/88	18	12	11 Can't Wait	—		↓	
3/26/88	18	9	12 I Don't Want To Live Without You	5		↓	
6/22/91	4	9	13 Lowdown And Dirty	—		Unusual Heat	Atlantic 82299
8/24/91	42	4	14 I'll Fight For You	—		↓	
9/26/92	5	7	15 Soul Doctor	—	▲[2]	The Very Best...And Beyond	Atlantic 89999
			Robin Zander (backing vocal)				
2/25/95	28	6	16 Under The Gun	—		Mr. Moonlight	Generama 53961

FOUR HORSEMEN, The

Hard-rock group from Los Angeles: Frank Starr (vocals), Dave Lizmi and Stephen Harris (guitars), Ben Pape (bass) and Ken Montgomery (drums).

8/3/91	16	12	1 Nobody Said It Was Easy	—		Nobody Said It Was Easy	Def Amer. 26561
11/16/91+	38	9	2 Rockin' Is Ma' Business	—		↓	
2/29/92	27	10	3 Tired Wings	—		↓	

4 NON BLONDES

Pop-rock group from San Francisco: Linda Perry (vocals), Roger Rocha (guitar), Christa Hillhouse (bass) and Dawn Richardson (drums).

4/10/93	16	14	1 What's Up	14	▲	Bigger, Better, Faster, More!	Interscope 92112
10/9/93	39	4	2 Spaceman	117		↓	

DEBUT	PEAK	WKS	Mainstream Rock Track	Pop Gld	Album Title	Album Label & Number
			FRAMPTON, Peter			
			Born on 4/22/50 in Beckenham, Kent, England. Rock singer/songwriter/guitarist. Former member of **Humble Pie**. Played "Billy Shears" in the 1978 movie *Sgt. Pepper's Lonely Hearts Club Band*. Also see **Classic Rock Tracks** section.			
6/13/81	12	11	1 Breaking All The Rules	—	Breaking All The Rules	A&M 3722
1/25/86	4	12	2 Lying	74	Premonition	Atlantic 81290
9/30/89	27	6	3 Holding On To You	—	When All The Pieces Fit	Atlantic 82030
1/29/94	9	16	4 Day In The Sun		Peter Frampton	Relativity 1192
			FRANKE & THE KNOCKOUTS			
			Soft-rock group from New Brunswick, New Jersey: Franke Previte (vocals), Billy Elworthy (guitar), Blake Levinsohn (keyboards), Leigh Foxx (bass) and Claude LeHenaff (drums).			
4/4/81	27	11	1 Sweetheart	10	Franke & The Knockouts	Millennium 7755
4/11/81	45	1	2 Come Back	—	↓	
4/10/82	38	7	3 Never Had It Better	—	Below The Belt	Millennium 7763
			FRANKIE GOES TO HOLLYWOOD			
			Dance-rock group from Liverpool, England: William "Holly" Johnson and Paul Rutherford (vocals), Brian Nash (guitar), Mark O'Toole (bass) and Peter Gill (drums). Group's name inspired by publicity recounting Frank Sinatra's move into the movie industry.			
10/27/84	27	9	Two Tribes	43	Welcome To The Pleasuredome	Island 90232
			FRANKLIN, Aretha			
			Born on 3/25/42 in Memphis; raised in Detroit. Legendary R&B singer/songwriter/pianist. Known as "The Queen of Soul." Inducted into the Rock and Roll Hall of Fame in 1987. Won Grammy's Lifetime Achievement Award in 1994.			
10/4/86	36	4	Jumpin' Jack Flash	21 ●	Aretha	Arista 8442
			Keith Richards (guitar, producer); #3 Pop hit for **The Rolling Stones** in 1968			
			FRASER, Andy			
			Born on 8/7/52 in London. Rock bassist. Formerly with John Mayall's Bluesbreakers and Free.			
6/23/84	43	7	Fine, Fine Line	101	Fine Fine Line	Island 90153
			FREDDY JONES BAND, The			
			Rock group formed in South Bend, Indiana: Marty Lloyd and Wayne Healy (vocals, guitars), brothers Rob (guitar) and Jim (bass) Bonaccorsi and Simon Horrocks (drums).			
9/3/94	37	1	In A Daydream	—	The Freddy Jones Band	Capricorn 42029
			FREHLEY, Ace			
			Born Paul Frehley on 4/27/51 in the Bronx, New York. Rock guitarist. Member of **Kiss**. Also see **Classic Rock Tracks** section.			
5/30/87	27	7	Into The Night	—	Frehley's Comet	Megaforce 81749
			FREY, Glenn			
			Born on 11/6/48 in Detroit. Singer/songwriter/guitarist. Founding member of the **Eagles**. Played "Cody McMahon" on the 1993 TV series *South of Sunset*.			
6/19/82	5	15	1 Partytown	— ●	No Fun Aloud	Asylum 60129
7/17/82	57	2	2 I Found Somebody	31	↓	
10/9/82	25	2	3 Don't Give Up	—	↓	
7/28/84+	13	19	4 Smuggler's Blues	12 ●	The Allnighter	MCA 5501
1/5/85	4	12	5 The Heat Is On	2¹ ▲²	Beverly Hills Cop (soundtrack)	MCA 5547
9/21/85	❶³	11	6 You Belong To The City	2² ▲⁴	Miami Vice (soundtrack)	MCA 6150
8/20/88	15	8	7 True Love	13	Soul Searchin'	MCA 6239
4/27/91	9	9	8 Part Of You, Part Of Me	55	Thelma & Louise (soundtrack)	MCA 10239
			FRIDA			
			Born Anni-Frid Lyngstad on 11/15/45 in Narvik, Sweden. Member of Abba.			
10/16/82+	17	17	I Know There's Something Going On	13	Something's Going On	Atlantic 80018
			Phil Collins (drums, producer)			
			FROM ZERO			
			Hard-rock group from Chicago: Paul "Jett" Weiner (vocals), Joe Pettinato and Peter Capizzi (guitars), Rob Ruccia (bass) and John "Kid" Dinu (drums).			
6/9/01	37	1	Check Ya	—	One Nation Under	Arista 14670
			FRONT, The			
			Hard-rock group from Kansas City: brothers Michael (vocals) and Bobby (keyboards) Franano, Mike Greene (guitar), Randy Jordan (bass) and Shane Miller (drums).			
3/3/90	44	3	1 Fire	—	The Front	Columbia 45260
5/5/90	41	4	2 Le Motion	—	↓	
			FROZEN GHOST			
			Pop-rock duo from Canada: Arnold Lanni (vocals, guitar, keyboards) and Wolf Hassel (bass). Both were members of the group **Sheriff**.			
3/14/87	4	14	1 Should I See	69	Frozen Ghost	Atlantic 81736
9/3/88	44	5	2 Round And Round	—	Nice Place To Visit	Atlantic 81875
			FUEL			
			Rock group from Harrisburg, Pennsylvania: Brett Scallions (vocals; born on 12/21/71), Carl Bell (guitar; born on 1/9/68), Jeff Abercrombie (bass; born on 1/8/69) and Kevin Miller (drums; born on 9/6/70).			
4/11/98	11	26	1 Shimmer	42 ▲	Sunburn	550 Music 68554
10/10/98+	15	22	2 Bittersweet	—	↓	
5/15/99	24	9	3 Jesus Or A Gun	—	↓	

DEBUT	PEAK	WKS	Mainstream Rock Track	Pop	Gld	Album Title	Album Label & Number
			FUEL — Cont'd				
8/26/00	2³	56	4 Hemorrhage (In My Hands)	30	▲²	*Something Like Human*	550 Music 69436
2/10/01	10	16	5 Innocent	113	↓		
6/16/01	14	18	6 Bad Day	64	↓		
11/17/01	21	12	7 Last Time	—	↓		
			FULL DEVIL JACKET				
			Rock group from Jackson, Tennessee: Josh Brown (vocals), Mike Reaves and Jon Montoya (guitars), Kevin Bebout (bass) and Keith Foster (drums).				
4/1/00	23	14	1 Now You Know	—		*Full Devil Jacket*	The Enclave 546809
9/2/00	19	12	2 Where Did You Go?	—	↓		
			FU MANCHU				
			Rock group from Los Angeles: Scott Hill (vocals, guitar), Bob Balch (guitar), Brad Davis (bass) and Brant Bjork (drums).				
2/9/02	23	9	Squash That Fly	—		*California Crossing*	Mammoth 165515
			FURY IN THE SLAUGHTERHOUSE				
			Pop-rock group from Hannover, Germany: Kai Uwe Wingenfelder (vocals), Thorsten Wingenfelder and Christof Stein (guitars), Gero Drenk (keyboards), Hannes Schafer (bass) and Rainer Schumann (drums).				
4/2/94	21	9	Every Generation Got Its Own Disease	—		*Mono*	RCA 66352

G

★59★			**GABRIEL, Peter**				
			Born on 2/13/50 in London. Pop-rock singer/songwriter. Lead singer of **Genesis** from 1966-75. Also see **Classic Rock Tracks** section.				
			1)Sledgehammer 2)Shock The Monkey 3)Digging In The Dirt				
10/2/82	❶²	12	1 Shock The Monkey	29	●	*Peter Gabriel (Security)*	Geffen 2011
10/30/82	34	1	2 Kiss Of Life	—	↓		
12/25/82	46	4	3 I Have The Touch	—	↓		
8/6/83	38	4	4 I Go Swimming [L]	—	●	*Peter Gabriel/Plays Live*	Geffen 4012
5/3/86	❶²	15	5 Sledgehammer	❶¹	▲⁵	*So*	Geffen 24088
6/14/86	3	14	6 Red Rain	—	↓		
			also see #14 below				
6/21/86	❶¹	20	7 In Your Eyes	26	↓		
10/18/86	14	8	8 That Voice Again	—	↓		
11/29/86+	3	15	9 Big Time	8	↓		
9/12/92	❶¹	15	10 Digging In The Dirt	52	▲	*Us*	Geffen 24473
11/7/92	2⁴	20	11 Steam	32	↓		
3/6/93	18	9	12 Kiss That Frog	—	↓		
7/17/93	34	4	13 Secret World	—	↓		
10/1/94	33	3	14 Red Rain [L-R]	—	●	*Secret World Live*	Geffen 24722
			live version of #6 above; recorded on 11/16/93 in Modena, Italy				
			GALES, Eric, Band				
			Blues-rock trio from Memphis: brothers Eric (guitar) and Eugene (vocals, bass) Gales, with Hubert Crawford (drums).				
7/13/91	9	11	1 Sign Of The Storm	—		*The Eric Gales Band*	Elektra 61083
8/21/93	31	5	2 Paralyzed	—		*Picture Of A Thousand Faces*	Elektra 61466
			GAMMA				
			Rock group formed in San Francisco: Davey Pattison (vocals), Ronnie Montrose (guitar), Mitchell Froom (keyboards), Glenn Letsch (bass) and Denny Carmassi (drums). Carmassi later joined **Heart**. Froom, also a producer, married **Suzanne Vega** on 3/17/95.				
3/6/82	10	14	Right The First Time	77		*Gamma 3*	Elektra 60034
			GARBAGE				
			Rock group formed in Madison, Wisconsin: Shirley Manson (vocals, guitar; native of Edinburgh, Scotland), Doug Erikson (guitar, bass, keyboards), Steve Marker (guitar, samples) and Butch Vig (drums). Vig produced albums for **Nirvana**, **Soul Asylum** and **Smashing Pumpkins**.				
8/24/96	39	2	Stupid Girl	24	▲²	*Garbage*	Almo Sounds 80004
			GARY O'				
			Born Gary O'Connor in Toronto. Rock singer.				
3/2/85	23	8	Shades Of '45			*Strange Behavior*	RCA 5304
			GEILS, J., Band				
			Rock group from Boston: Jerome Geils (guitar), Peter Wolf (vocals), Magic Dick Salwitz (harmonica), Seth Justman (keyboards, vocals), Danny Klein (bass) and Stephen Jo Bladd (drums). Wolf left for a solo career in the fall of 1983. Also see **Classic Rock Tracks** section.				
11/14/81+	❶³	25	1 Centerfold	❶⁶	▲	*Freeze-Frame*	EMI America 17062
11/21/81+	8	26	2 Freeze-Frame	4	↓		
2/20/82	30	4	3 Flamethrower	—	↓		
11/20/82	5	15	4 I Do [L]	24	●	*Showtime!*	EMI America 17087
			#37 Pop hit for The Marvelows in 1965				
11/3/84	26	9	5 Concealed Weapons	63		*You're Gettin' Even While I'm Gettin' Odd*	EMI America 17137

DEBUT	PEAK	WKS	Mainstream Rock Track	Pop Gld	Album Title	Album Label & Number

GELDOF, Bob
Born on 10/5/54 in Dublin, Ireland. Leader of The Boomtown Rats. Played "Pink" in the **Pink Floyd** movie *The Wall*. Organized British superstar benefit group **Band Aid** and earned a Nobel Peace Prize nomination.

| 11/15/86 | 23 | 10 | This Is The World Calling .... | 82 | *Deep In The Heart Of Nowhere* .... Atlantic 81687 |

GENE LOVES JEZEBEL
Techno-rock group formed in England: Jay Aston (vocals), James Stevenson (guitar), Peter Rizzo (bass) and Chris Bell (drums).

| 7/14/90 | 12 | 15 | Jealous.......................... | 68 | *Kiss Of Life* .... Geffen 24260 |

GENERAL PUBLIC
Pop group from Birmingham, England: Dave Wakeling (vocals, guitar), **Ranking Roger** (vocals, keyboards), Kevin White (guitar), Micky Billingham (keyboards), Horace Panter (bass) and Stoker (drums). Wakeling and Roger had been in English Beat. Billingham was with **Dexys Midnight Runners**.

| 1/19/85 | 39 | 4 | Tenderness.......................... | 27 | *...All The Rage* .... I.R.S. 70046 |

GENESIS ★22★
Pop-rock trio formed in England: **Phil Collins** (vocals, drums), **Mike Rutherford** (guitar, bass) and Tony Banks (keyboards). **Peter Gabriel** was lead singer from 1967-75. Steve Hackett (of **GTR**) was lead guitarist from 1970-77. Regular touring members included Americans Daryl Stuermer (guitar) and Chester Anderson (drums). Collins announced his departure from the group in April 1996; Ray Wilson (of **Stiltskin**) joined as lead singer in June 1997. Also see **Classic Rock Tracks** section.

1)Throwing It All Away 2)Invisible Touch 3)I Can't Dance 4)No Reply At All 5)That's All!

9/26/81	2[2]	17	1 No Reply At All	29	▲[2] *Abacab* .... Atlantic 19313
			features the Earth, Wind & Fire horn section		
10/17/81	4	26	2 Abacab	26	↓
3/27/82	14	8	3 Man On The Corner..........................	40	↓
6/12/82	2[1]	16	4 Paperlate	32	● *Three Sides Live* .... Atlantic 2000
7/3/82	40	7	5 You Might Recall	—	↓
9/17/83	5	12	6 Mama	73	▲[4] *Genesis* .... Atlantic 80116
10/8/83	16	25	7 It's Gonna Get Better	—	↓
10/29/83	10	19	8 Just A Job To Do	—	↓
11/5/83+	2[1]	17	9 That's All!	6	↓
11/5/83+	21	16	10 Illegal Alien	44	↓
11/5/83+	24	10	11 Home By The Sea	—	↓
2/25/84	41	5	12 Taking It All Too Hard	50	↓
5/31/86	❶[3]	11	13 Invisible Touch	❶[1]	▲[6] *Invisible Touch*.................... Atlantic 81641
6/21/86	❶[3]	18	14 Throwing It All Away	4	↓
6/21/86	29	10	15 The Last Domino	—	↓
6/28/86	11	30	16 Land Of Confusion	4	↓
6/28/86	40	4	17 Anything She Does	—	↓
7/5/86	34	12	18 In Too Deep	3	↓
7/26/86	45	5	19 Tonight, Tonight, Tonight	3	↓
11/2/91	3	14	20 No Son Of Mine	12	▲[4] *We Can't Dance*.................... Atlantic 82344
12/7/91+	2[3]	29	21 I Can't Dance	7	↓
12/21/91+	24	19	22 Jesus He Knows Me	23	↓
6/13/92	25	8	23 Driving The Last Spike	—	↓
8/23/97	25	7	24 Congo	—	*Calling All Stations*.................... Atlantic 83037

GEORGE, Robin
Born in Wolverhampton, England. Rock guitarist.

| 2/16/85 | 40 | 9 | Heartline.......................... | 92 | *Dangerous Music* .... Bronze 90244 |

GEORGIA SATELLITES
Rock group from Atlanta: **Dan Baird** (vocals, guitar), Rick Richards (guitar), Rich Price (bass) nad Mauro Magellan (drums). Richards later joined **Izzy Stradlin & The Ju Ju Hounds**.

10/18/86	2[2]	18	1 Keep Your Hands To Yourself	2[1]	▲ *Georgia Satellites* .... Elektra 60496
1/24/87	11	12	2 Battleship Chains	86	↓
4/18/87	34	4	3 Railroad Steel	—	↓
6/11/88	6	9	4 Open All Night	—	*Open All Night*.................... Elektra 60793
9/3/88	33	5	5 Don't Pass Me By	—	↓
10/22/88	13	7	6 Hippy Hippy Shake	45	▲[4] *Cocktail (soundtrack)* .... Elektra 60806
			#24 Pop hit for The Swinging Blue Jeans in 1964		
10/21/89	47	2	7 Another Chance	—	*In The Land Of Salvation And Sin* ...... Elektra 60887
12/16/89+	17	14	8 All Over But The Cryin'	—	↓

GHOST OF AN AMERICAN AIRMAN
Rock group from Belfast, Ireland: Andrew "Dodge" McKay (vocals), Ben Trowell (guitar), Allan Galbraith (bass) and Matt (drums). Band named for legend of an American pilot shot down over Ireland.

| 11/6/93 | 38 | 1 | King Of Nothing .... | — | *Skin* .... Hollywood 61408 |

DEBUT	PEAK	WKS	Mainstream Rock Track	Pop	Gld	Album Title	Album Label & Number

GIANT
Rock group formed in Nashville: brothers Dan (vocals, guitar) and David (drums) Huff, with Alan Pasqua (keyboards) and Mike Brignardello (bass).

9/9/89	13	14	1 I'm A Believer	56		Last Of The Runaways	A&M 5272
12/16/89+	11	11	2 Innocent Days	—		↓	
3/31/90	7	16	3 I'll See You In My Dreams	20		↓	
4/4/92	16	10	4 Chained	—		Time To Burn	Epic 48509

GILLAN, Ian
Born on 8/19/45 in Hounslow, Middlesex, England. Lead singer of **Deep Purple**. Portrayed Jesus in the rock opera *Jesus Christ Superstar*. Joined **Black Sabbath** for *Born Again* album.

10/8/88	15	7	Telephone Box	—		Accidentally On Purpose	Virgin 90953
			IAN GILLAN & ROGER GLOVER				

GILLIS, Brad
Born in San Francisco. Rock guitarist. Member of **Night Ranger**.

5/1/93	20	8	Honest To God	—		Gilrock Ranch	Guitar 99203
			Gregg Allman (vocal)				

GILMOUR, David
Born on 3/6/44 in Cambridge, England. Rock singer/guitarist. Member of **Pink Floyd**.

3/17/84	10	6	1 All Lovers Are Deranged	—	●	About Face	Columbia 39296
3/31/84	13	12	2 Murder	—		↓	
4/14/84	35	4	3 Blue Light	62		↓	

GIN BLOSSOMS
Pop-rock group from Tempe, Arizona: Robin Wilson (vocals), Jesse Valenzuela and Scott Johnson (guitars), Bill Leen (bass) and Phillip Rhodes (drums). Early guitarist Doug Hopkins died of a self-inflicted bullet wound on 12/5/93 (age 32).

4/3/93	36	2	1 Mrs. Rita	—	▲[4]	New Miserable Experience	A&M 5403
7/10/93	4	20	2 Hey Jealousy	25		↓	
11/6/93+	5	26	3 Found Out About You	25		↓	
6/18/94	40	1	4 Until I Fall Away	21[A]		↓	
9/17/94	20	10	5 Allison Road	24[A]		↓	
8/12/95	4	16	6 Til I Hear It From You	11	●	Empire Records (soundtrack)	A&M 540384
2/10/96	6	13	7 Follow You Down	9	▲	Congratulations I'm Sorry	A&M 540469
6/1/96	29	9	8 Day Job	—		↓	

GIRLS AGAINST BOYS
Rock group from Washington DC: Eli Janney (vocals), Scott McCloud (guitar), Johnny Temple (bass) and Alexis Fleisig (drums).

6/20/98	28	10	Park Avenue			Freak*On*Ica	DGC 25156

GIUFFRIA
Rock group from California: Gregg Giuffria (keyboards), David Glen Eisley (vocals), Craig Goldy (guitar), Chuck Wright (bass) and Alan Krigger (drums). Lanny Cordola and David Sikes replaced Goldy and Wright in late 1985. Giuffria, Wright and Cordola joined **House Of Lords** in 1988.

11/17/84+	3	16	1 Call To The Heart	15		Giuffria	MCA 5524
2/16/85	41	4	2 Do Me Right	—		↓	
4/20/85	43	3	3 Lonely In Love	57		↓	
5/10/86	28	7	4 I Must Be Dreaming	52		Silk + Steel	MCA 5742

GLAMOUR CAMP
Pop-rock group from New York City: Christopher Otcasek (vocals), Eddie Martinez and Sid McGinnis (guitars), Mark Egan and Will Lee (bass), Alexander Lasarenko (keyboards) and Andy Newmark (drums). Otcasek is the son of **Ric Ocasek** of **The Cars**. McGinnis and Lee were members of David Letterman's *Late Show* band.

3/18/89	42	6	She Did It	—		Glamour Camp	EMI 48685

GLASS TIGER
Pop-rock group from Canada: Alan Frew (vocals), Al Connelly (guitar), Sam Reid (keyboards), Wayne Parker (bass) and Michael Hanson (drums).

8/2/86	17	9	1 Don't Forget Me (When I'm Gone)	2[1]	●	The Thin Red Line	Manhattan 53032
			Bryan Adams (response vocal)				
3/21/87	21	6	2 I Will Be There	34		↓	
4/16/88	12	9	3 I'm Still Searching	31		Diamond Sun	EMI-Man. 48684

GLOVER, Roger
Born on 11/30/45 in Brecon, Powys, Wales. Rock singer/bassist. Member of **Deep Purple** and **Rainbow**.

6/2/84	20	8	1 The Mask	—		Mask	21 Records 9009
10/8/88	15	7	2 Telephone Box	—		Accidentally On Purpose	Virgin 90953
			IAN GILLAN & ROGER GLOVER				

GOANNA
Rock group from Australia: Shane Howard (vocals), Warrick Harwood and Graham Davidge (guitars), Peter Coughlan (bass) and Robert Ross (drums).

6/11/83	31	9	Solid Rock	71		Spirit Of Place	Atco 90081

GODFATHERS, The
Rock group formed in London: brothers Peter (vocals) and Chris (bass) Coyne, Mike Gibson and Kris Dollimore (guitars), and George Mazur (drums).

2/6/88	38	10	Birth, School, Work, Death	—		Birth, School, Work, Death	Epic 40946

DEBUT	PEAK	WKS	Mainstream Rock Track	Pop Gld	Album Title	Album Label & Number

GODLEY & CREME
Duo from Manchester, England: Kevin Godley (born on 10/7/45) and Lol Creme (born on 9/19/47). Both were members of 10cc.

| 7/27/85 | 6 | 10 | Cry | 16 | *The History Mix Volume 1* . . . . Polydor 825981 |

GODS CHILD
Rock group from New York City: Chris Seefried (vocals, guitar), Gary DeRosa (keyboards), Craig Ruda (bass) and Alex Alexander (drums).

| 8/27/94 | 18 | 10 | Everybodys 1 . . . . | — | *Everybody* . . . . Qwest 45632 |

★67★ **GODSMACK**
Hard-rock group formed in Boston: Salvatore "Sully" Erna (vocals; born on 2/7/68), Tony Rombola (guitar; born on 11/24/64), Robbie Merrill (bass; born on 6/13/63) and Tommy Stewart (drums; born on 5/26/66).

10/24/98+	7	44	1 Whatever	116	▲4	*Godsmack* . . . . Republic 53190
5/8/99	5	48	2 Keep Away	—	↓
11/20/99+	5	37	3 Voodoo	102	↓
6/17/00	8	26	4 Bad Religion	—	↓
10/14/00+	❶1	53	5 Awake	101	▲2	*Awake* . . . . Republic 159688
3/24/01	3	32	6 Greed	123	↓
9/15/01	12	13	7 Bad Magick	—	↓
2/16/02	❶4	41↑	8 I Stand Alone	102	●	*The Scorpion King (soundtrack)* . . . . . Universal 017115

GO-GO'S
Female rock group formed in Los Angeles: Belinda Carlisle (vocals), Jane Wiedlin (guitar), Charlotte Caffey (guitar), Kathy Valentine (bass) and Gina Schock (drums). Disbanded in 1984. Reunions in 1990, 1994 and 2001.

8/15/81	15	32	✓1 Our Lips Are Sealed	20	▲2	*Beauty And The Beat* . . . . I.R.S. 70021
2/13/82	7	13	✓2 We Got The Beat	23	↓
7/10/82	13	13	✓3 Vacation	8	●	*Vacation* . . . . I.R.S. 70031
9/18/82	46	1	4 He's So Strange	—	↓
10/2/82	46	1	5 Get Up And Go	50	↓
3/31/84	33	7	✓6 Head Over Heels	11	*Talk Show* . . . . I.R.S. 70041

GOLDEN EARRING
Rock group formed in Amsterdam, Holland: Barry Hay (vocals), George Kooymans (guitar), Rinus Gerritsen (bass) and Cesar Zuiderwijk (drums). Also see **Classic Rock Tracks** section.

11/20/82+	❶1	26	✓1 Twilight Zone	10	*Cut* . . . . 21 Records 9004
3/31/84	9	2	2 When The Lady Smiles	76	*N.E.W.S.* . . . . 21 Records 9008
5/17/86	31	6	3 Quiet Eyes	—	*The Hole* . . . . 21 Records 90514

GOMM, Ian
Born on 3/17/47 in Ealing, London, England. Pop-rock singer/songwriter/guitarist.

| 3/28/81 | 53 | 2 | Here It Comes Again . . . . | — | *What A Blow* . . . . Stiff 36433 |

★89★ **GOO GOO DOLLS**
Rock trio from Buffalo, New York: Johnny Rzeznik (vocals, guitar; born on 12/5/65), Robby Takac (bass; born on 9/30/64) and Mike Malinin (drums; born on 10/10/67).
1)Name   2)Slide   3)Long Way Down

4/8/95	21	11	✓1 Only One	—	▲2	*A Boy Named Goo* . . . . Warner 45750
8/5/95	38	3	2 Flat Top	—	↓
9/9/95	❶5	26	3 Name	5	↓
1/27/96	8	15	4 Naked	47A	↓
6/1/96	7	17	✓5 Long Way Down	—	▲	*Batman & Robin (soundtrack)* . . . . Warner Sunset 46620
7/26/97	9	14	6 Lazy Eye	—	❶18A ▲5	*City Of Angels (soundtrack)* . . . . . Warner Sunset 46867
5/2/98	8	26	7 Iris	8	▲2	*Dizzy Up The Girl* . . . . Warner 47058
9/26/98	4	26	8 Slide	108	↓
3/6/99	13	14	9 Dizzy	16	↓
7/17/99	28	9	10 Black Balloon	18	●	*Gutterflower* . . . . Warner 48206
4/6/02	29	9	11 Here Is Gone

GORKY PARK
Rock group from Russia: Nikolai Noskov (vocals), Alexei Belov and Jan Ianenkov (guitars), "Big" Sasha Minkov (bass) and "Little" Sasha Lvov (drums). Group named after a famous park in Moscow.

| 9/23/89 | 41 | 4 | Bang . . . . | — | *Gorky Park* . . . . Mercury 838628 |

GOV'T MULE
Rock trio from Macon, Georgia: Warren Haynes (vocals, guitar), Allen Woody (bass) and Matt Abts (drums). Haynes and Woody were both members of **The Allman Brothers Band**. Woody died of a heart attack on 8/26/2000 (age 44).

| 4/15/00 | 40 | 1 | Bad Little Doggie . . . . | — | *Life Before Insanity* . . . . Capricorn 546489 |

GRAMM, Lou
Born Lou Grammatico on 5/2/50 in Rochester, New York. Lead singer of **Foreigner** and **Shadow King**.

1/31/87	❶5	14	1 Midnight Blue	5	*Ready Or Not* . . . . Atlantic 81728
2/28/87	7	16	2 Ready Or Not	54	↓
6/13/87	47	2	3 Heartache	—	↓
10/28/89	4	15	4 Just Between You And Me	6	*Long Hard Look* . . . . Atlantic 81915
2/10/90	23	9	5 True Blue Love	40	↓
5/19/90	42	4	6 Angel With A Dirty Face		↓

DEBUT	PEAK	WKS	Mainstream Rock Track	Pop	Gld	Album Title	Album Label & Number
			GRAND PRIX				
			Rock group from England: Robin McCauley (vocals), Mick O'Donoghue (guitar), Phil Lanzon (keyboards), Ralph Hood (bass) and Andy Bierne (drums). McCauley later formed the **McAuley Schenker Group**.				
10/29/83	43	3	Shout	—		Samurai	Chrysalis 41430
			GRANT, Eddy				
			Born Edmond Grant on 3/5/48 in Plaisance, Guyana; raised in London. Rock-reggae singer. Member of The Equals.				
4/30/83	12	14	1 Electric Avenue	2⁵	●	Killer On The Rampage	Portrait 38554
5/26/84	39	9	2 Romancing The Stone	26		Going For Broke	Portrait 39261
			GRATEFUL DEAD				
			Legendary rock group formed in San Francisco: Jerry Garcia (vocals, guitar), Bob Weir (vocals, guitar), Brent Mydland (keyboards), Phil Lesh (bass) and Mickey Hart & Bill Kreutzmann (drums). Weir also formed **Bobby & The Midnites**. Mydland died of a drug overdose on 7/26/90 (age 37); **Bruce Hornsby** then took over keyboards on tour until **Tubes** keyboardist Vince Welnick joined band. Garcia died of a heart attack on 8/9/95 (age 53). Incessant touring band with faithful followers known as "Deadheads." Weir, Lesh, Hart and Hornsby formed The Other Ones. Inducted into the Rock and Roll Hall of Fame in 1994. Also see **Classic Rock Tracks** section.				
			1)Touch Of Grey 2)Hell In A Bucket 3)Foolish Heart				
4/18/81	50	2	1 Ripple [L]	—		Reckoning	Arista 8604
5/2/81	37	4	2 Dire Wolf [L]	—		↓	
7/4/87	❶³	12	3 Touch Of Grey	9	▲²	In The Dark	Arista 8452
7/25/87	3	13	4 Hell In A Bucket	—		↓	
8/8/87	40	4	5 West L.A. Fadeaway	—		↓	
8/15/87	45	5	6 When Push Comes To Shove	—		↓	
12/5/87+	15	10	7 Throwing Stones	—		↓	
2/4/89	8	6	8 Slow Train [L]	—	●	Dylan & The Dead	Columbia 45056
			BOB DYLAN & GRATEFUL DEAD				
10/28/89	8	10	9 Foolish Heart	—	●	Built To Last	Arista 8575
1/13/90	41	5	10 Just A Little Light	—		↓	
			GRAVITY KILLS				
			Techno-rock group from Jefferson City, Missouri: Jeff Scheel (vocals), Matt Dudenhoeffer (guitar), Douglas Firley (keyboards) and Kurt Kerns (bass, drums).				
6/8/96	39	3	1 Guilty	86		Gravity Kills	TVT 5910
6/27/98	35	6	2 Falling	—		Perversion	TVT 5920
2/23/02	24	10	3 One Thing	—		Superstarved	Sanctuary 84539
			GREAT BUILDINGS				
			Pop-rock group from Los Angeles: **Danny Wilde** (vocals), Phil Solem (guitar), Ian Ainsworth (bass) and Richard Sandford (drums). Wilde and Solem later recorded as **The Rembrandts**.				
4/18/81	48	3	Maybe It's You	—		Apart From The Crowd	Columbia 36920
★90★			**GREAT WHITE**				
			Hard-rock group formed in Los Angeles: Jack Russell (vocals), Mark Kendall (guitar), Lorne Black (bass) and Gary Holland (drums). Audie Desbrow replaced Holland in 1986. Michael Lardie (keyboards) joined in 1987. Tony Montana replaced Black in 1987. Teddy Cook replaced Montana in 1993. Sean McNabb replaced Cook in 1998.				
			1)Call It Rock N' Roll 2)Once Bitten Twice Shy 3)House Of Broken Love				
4/7/84	56	1	1 Stick It	—		Great White	EMI America 17111
7/4/87	9	13	2 Rock Me	60	▲	Once Bitten	Capitol 12565
10/31/87	47	2	3 Lady Red Light	—		↓	
12/19/87+	9	15	4 Save Your Love	57		↓	
4/1/89	6	21	5 Once Bitten Twice Shy	5	▲²	...Twice Shy	Capitol 90640
			first recorded by **Ian Hunter** in 1975				
7/1/89	27	9	6 Mista Bone	—		↓	
9/9/89	18	12	7 The Angel Song	30		↓	
1/6/90	7	16	8 House Of Broken Love	83		↓	
2/23/91	4	11	9 Call It Rock N' Roll	53	●	Hooked	Capitol 95330
5/11/91	16	9	10 Desert Moon	—		↓	
9/19/92	20	8	11 Big Goodbye	—		Psycho City	Capitol 98835
12/19/92+	23	10	12 Old Rose Motel	—		↓	
6/11/94	9	16	13 Sail Away	—		Sail Away	Zoo 11080
7/10/99	8	15	14 Rollin' Stoned	—		Can't Get There From Here	Portrait 69547
			GREBENSHIKOV, Boris				
			Born on 11/27/53 in Leningrad. Rock singer/songwriter/guitarist.				
8/5/89	44	4	Radio Silence	—		Radio Silence	Columbia 44364
			produced by Dave Stewart (of **Eurythmics**)				

DEBUT	PEAK	WKS	Mainstream Rock Track	Pop Gld	Album Title	Album Label & Number

★85★ GREEN DAY
Punk-rock trio formed in Berkeley, California: Billie Joe Armstrong (vocals, guitar; born on 2/17/72), Mike "Dirnt" Pritchard (bass; born on 5/4/72) and Frank "Tre Cool" Wright (drums; born on 12/9/72).
1)When I Come Around 2)Good Riddance (Time Of Your Life) 3)Brain Stew/Jaded

5/21/94	13	18	1 Long View	36^A ▲10	*Dookie*	Reprise 45529
8/27/94	9	22	2 Basket Case	26^A ↓		
12/10/94+	2²	26	3 When I Come Around	6^A ↓		
5/20/95	18	14	4 She	41^A ↓		
8/12/95	17	8	5 J.A.R. (Jason Andrew Relva)...............	22^A ↓	*Angus (soundtrack)*	Reprise 45960
10/7/95	9	12	6 Geek Stink Breath	27^A ▲2	*Insomniac*	Reprise 46046
12/30/95+	8	26	7 Brain Stew/Jaded	35^A ↓		
6/22/96	25	7	8 Walking Contradiction	70^A ↓		
9/20/97	9	15	9 Hitchin' A Ride	59^A ▲2	*Nimrod*	Reprise 46794
12/13/97+	7	22	10 Good Riddance (Time Of Your Life)	11^A ↓		
9/16/00	15	11	11 Minority	101 ●	*Warning:*	Reprise 47613
12/30/00+	24	10	12 Warning	114 ↓		

GREN
Rock trio from Culver City, California: Brett (vocals, guitar), Marcus (guitar) and Possum (drums).

1/27/96	39	2	She Shines	—	*Camp Grenada*	I.R.S. 31722

GROHL, Dave — see IOMMI

GTR
Rock group formed in England: Max Bacon (vocals), Steve Hackett and Steve Howe (guitars), Phil Spalding (bass) and Jonathan Mover (drums). Hackett was with **Genesis**. Howe was with **Yes** and **Asia**. Name is short for guitar.

4/26/86	3	14	1 When The Heart Rules The Mind	14 ●	*GTR*	Arista 8400
7/12/86	14	10	2 The Hunter	85 ↓		

GUANO APES
Rock group from Germany: Sandra Nasic (vocals), Henning Ruemenapp (guitar), Stefan Ude (bass) and Dennis Poschwatta (drums).

12/11/99+	24	15	Open Your Eyes	—	*Proud Like A God*	RCA 67858

GUN
Rock group from Glasgow, Scotland: Mark Rankin (vocals), Giuliano Gizzi and Baby Stafford (guitars), Dante Gizzi (bass) and Scott Shields (drums).

2/17/90	19	12	Better Days	—	*Taking On The World*	A&M 5285

★53★ GUNS N' ROSES
Hard-rock group formed in Los Angeles: William "Axl Rose" Bailey (vocals), Saul "Slash" Hudson and Jeffrey "**Izzy Stradlin'**" Isbell (guitars), Michael "Duff" McKagen (bass) and Steven Adler (drums). Rose married Erin Everly (daughter of Don Everly of The Everly Brothers) briefly in 1990. Matt Sorum replaced Adler in 1990. Keyboardist Dizzy Reed joined in 1990. **Gilby Clarke** replaced Stradlin' in late 1991. Slash married model Renee Surran in November 1992. Clarke left band in January 1995. Slash, Sorum and Clarke recorded in 1995 in **Slash's Snakepit**.
1)Don't Cry 2)You Could Be Mine 3)Civil War

4/2/88	37	11	1 Welcome To The Jungle	7 ▲15	*Appetite For Destruction*	Geffen 24148
6/11/88	7	19	2 Sweet Child O' Mine	❶² ↓		
1/21/89	14	11	3 Paradise City	5 ↓		
7/29/89	26	5	4 Nightrain	93		
12/24/88+	7	21	5 Patience	4 ▲5	*G N' R Lies*	Geffen 24198
7/21/90	18	9	6 Knockin' On Heaven's Door	— ●	*Days Of Thunder (soundtrack)*	DGC 24294
			#12 Pop hit for **Bob Dylan** *in 1973*			
8/4/90	4	11	7 Civil War	—	*Nobody's Child - Romanian Angel Appeal (various artists)*	Warner 26280
9/21/91	3	26	8 Don't Cry	10 ▲7	*Use Your Illusion I*	Geffen 24415
9/28/91+	15	26	9 November Rain	3 ↓		
9/28/91	20	12	10 Live And Let Die	33 ↓		
			#2 Pop hit for **Paul McCartney** *& Wings in 1973*			
6/29/91	3	10	11 You Could Be Mine	29 ▲7	*Use Your Illusion II*	Geffen 24420
3/21/92	35	8	12 Pretty Tied Up	— ↓		
10/17/92	13	14	13 Yesterdays	72 ↓		
12/11/93+	16	10	14 Estranged	— ↓		
11/13/93	8	7	15 Ain't It Fun	— ▲	*The Spaghetti Incident?*	Geffen 24617
			first recorded by The Dead Boys in 1978			
12/11/93+	11	13	16 Hair Of The Dog	— ↓		
			first recorded by **Nazareth** *in 1975*			
11/19/94	10	8	17 Sympathy For The Devil	55	*Interview With The Vampire (soundtrack)* ..	Geffen 24719
			first recorded by **The Rolling Stones** *in 1968*			
10/30/99	26	5	18 Oh My God	— ▲	*End Of Days (soundtrack)*	Geffen 490508

DEBUT	PEAK	WKS	Mainstream Rock Track	Pop	Gld	Album Title	Album Label & Number

H

HAGAR, Sammy ★24★
Born on 10/13/47 in Monterey, California. Rock singer/songwriter/guitarist. Nicknamed "The Red Rocker." Lead singer of Montrose (1973-75) and Van Halen (1985-96). Also see **Hager, Schon, Aaronson, Shrieve**.

1)Little White Lie 2)Give To Live 3)Mas Tequila 4)I'll Fall In Love Again 5)Winner Takes It All

DEBUT	PEAK	WKS	Track	Pop	Gld	Album	Label
1/16/82	2³	17	1 I'll Fall In Love Again	43	▲	Standing Hampton	Geffen 2006
3/13/82	31	6	2 There's Only One Way To Rock	—	↓		
4/3/82	35	4	3 Baby's On Fire	—	↓		
5/1/82	49	2	4 Can't Get Loose	—	↓		
8/21/82	21	10	5 Fast Times At Ridgemont High	—		Fast Times At Ridgemont High (soundtrack)	Full Moon 60158
12/18/82+	3	16	6 Your Love Is Driving Me Crazy	13	●	Three Lock Box	Geffen 2021
1/15/83	6	10	7 Remember The Heroes	—	↓		
			Mike Reno (of Loverboy; guest vocal)				
3/5/83	24	7	8 I Don't Need Love	—	↓		
7/14/84	5	13	9 Two Sides Of Love	38	▲	VOA	Geffen 24043
8/11/84	9	16	10 I Can't Drive 55	26			
2/7/87	3	12	11 Winner Takes It All	54		Over The Top (soundtrack)	Columbia 40655
6/13/87	❶³	11	12 Give To Live	23	●	Sammy Hagar (I Never Said Goodbye)	Capitol 24144
7/25/87	15	7	13 Boys' Night Out	—	↓		
8/29/87	20	7	14 Returning Home	—	↓		
10/10/87	22	8	15 Eagles Fly	82	↓		
3/19/94	4	16	16 High Hopes	—	●	Unboxed	Geffen 24702
7/2/94	36	4	17 Buying My Way Into Heaven	—	↓		
5/10/97	❶⁵	16	18 Little White Lie	—		Marching To Mars	MCA 11627
8/9/97	3	13	19 Marching To Mars	—	↓		
10/25/97	11	20	20 Both Sides Now	—	↓		
3/13/99	2⁶	21	21 Mas Tequila	116		Red Voodoo	MCA 11872
6/26/99	22	9	22 Shag	—	↓		
			SAMMY HAGAR and The Waboritas (above 2)				
9/30/00	10	12	23 Serious JuJu	—		Ten 13	Cabo Wabo 78110
12/16/00+	16	13	24 Let Sally Drive (Ride Sally Ride)	—	↓		
10/26/02	36	5↑	25 Things've Changed	—		Not 4 Sale	33rd Street 3315
			SAMMY HAGAR and The Waboritas				

HAGAR, SCHON, AARONSON, SHRIEVE
All-star rock group: **Sammy Hagar** (vocals), **Neal Schon** (guitar), Kenny Aaronson (bass) and Michael Shrieve (drums).

DEBUT	PEAK	WKS	Track	Pop	Gld	Album	Label
3/31/84	15	6	1 Top Of The Rock	—		Through The Fire	Geffen 4023
4/14/84	37	6	2 Missing You	—	↓		
4/28/84	30	6	3 Whiter Shade Of Pale	94	↓		
			#5 Pop hit for Procol Harum in 1967				

HAIRCUT ONE HUNDRED
Pop-rock group from Beckenham, Kent, England: **Nick Heyward** (vocals), **Graham Jones** (guitar), Phil Smith (sax), Mark Fox (percussion), Les Nemes (bass) and Blair Cunningham (drums).

DEBUT	PEAK	WKS	Track	Pop	Gld	Album	Label
5/8/82	18	9	1 Love Plus One	37		Pelican West	Arista 6600
8/21/82	50	7	2 Favourite Shirts (Boy Meets Girl)	101	↓		

HALL, Daryl
Born Daryl Franklin Hohl on 10/11/48 in Philadelphia. Half of **Hall & Oates** duo.

DEBUT	PEAK	WKS	Track	Pop	Gld	Album	Label
8/2/86	11	10	Dreamtime	5		Three Hearts in the Happy Ending Machine	RCA 7196

HALL, Daryl, & John Oates
Daryl Hall (see previous entry) and John Oates (born on 4/7/49 in New York City) met while students at Temple University in 1967. Hall sang backup for many top soul groups before teaming up with Oates in 1972.

1)Maneater 2)Out Of Touch 3)Say It Isn't So

DEBUT	PEAK	WKS	Track	Pop	Gld	Album	Label
4/11/81	54	3	1 Kiss On My List	❶³	▲	Voices	RCA Victor 3646
7/18/81	35	3	2 You Make My Dreams	5	↓		
10/17/81	33	8	3 Private Eyes	❶²	▲	Private Eyes	RCA Victor 4028
11/28/81+	28	11	4 I Can't Go For That (No Can Do)	❶¹	↓		
10/30/82	18	16	5 Maneater	❶⁴	▲²	H₂O	RCA Victor 4383
11/19/83	18	13	6 Say It Isn't So	2⁴	▲²	Rock 'N Soul, Part 1	RCA Victor 4858
2/18/84	23	9	7 Adult Education	8			
10/6/84	18	11	8 Out Of Touch	❶²	▲²	Big Bam Boom	RCA Victor 5309
2/2/85	42	3	9 Method Of Modern Love	5	↓		
			DARYL HALL JOHN OATES (above 2)				
8/31/85	43	3	10 The Way You Do The Things You Do/My Girl [L]	20	●	Live At The Apollo	RCA Victor 7035
			DARYL HALL JOHN OATES with David Ruffin & Eddie Kendrick recorded at the reopening of New York's Apollo Theatre on 5/23/85; medley of #11/#1 Pop hits for The Temptations in 1964/65				

DEBUT	PEAK	WKS	Mainstream Rock Track	Pop Gld	Album Title	Album Label & Number
			HALL, John, Band Born on 10/25/47 in Baltimore. Rock singer/guitarist. Leader of Orleans. Band includes Bob Leinbach (keyboards), John Troy (bass) and Eric Parker (drums).			
11/14/81+	13	21	1 Crazy (Keep On Falling)	42	All Of The Above	EMI America 17058
2/19/83	41	3	2 Love Me Again	64	Searchparty	EMI America 17082
			HAMM, Stuart Born in 1960 in Los Angeles. Rock singer/bassist. Member of **Joe Satriani**'s touring band.			
8/17/91	39	4	Lone Star	[I] —	The Urge	Relativity 1052
			HAMMER, Jan Born on 4/17/48 in Prague, Czechoslovakia. Male jazz-rock keyboardist.			
2/19/83	42	1	1 No More Lies **NEAL SCHON & JAN HAMMER**	—	Here To Stay	Columbia 38428
9/28/85	29	7	2 Miami Vice Theme	[I] ❶¹ ▲⁴	Miami Vice (soundtrack)	MCA 6150
			HARDLINE Rock group formed in San Francisco: **Neal Schon** (guitar; **Journey**), brothers Johnny (vocals) and Joey (guitar) Gioeli, Todd Jensen (bass) and Deen Castronovo (drums; **Bad English**).			
6/13/92	37	4	1 Takin' Me Down	—	Double Eclipse	MCA 10586
9/12/92	25	14	2 Hot Cherie	—	↓	
			HARRISON, George Born on 2/24/43 in Liverpool, England. Died of cancer on 11/29/2001 (age 58). Singer/songwriter/guitarist. Member of **The Beatles** and the **Traveling Wilburys**. Recipient of *Billboard*'s Century Award in 1992. Also see **The Bunburys** and **Classic Rock Tracks** section. *1)When We Was Fab 2)Devil's Radio 3)Got My Mind Set On You*			
6/13/81	6	7	√1 All Those Years Ago tribute to **John Lennon**	2³	Somewhere In England	Dark Horse 3492
7/4/81	51	3	2 Teardrops	102 ↓		
10/24/87	4	11	√3 Got My Mind Set On You first recorded by James Ray in 1962	❶¹ ▲	Cloud Nine	Dark Horse 25643
11/14/87+	2¹	18	√4 When We Was Fab	23 ↓		
11/14/87	4	13	5 Devil's Radio	— ↓		
11/21/87+	9	10	6 Cloud 9	— ↓		
4/16/88	17	7	7 This Is Love	— ↓		
8/5/89	7	8	√8 Cheer Down above 6 produced by **Jeff Lynne** and Harrison	—	Lethal Weapon 2 (soundtrack)	Warner 25985
10/28/89	21	7	9 Poor Little Girl	—	Best Of Dark Horse 1976-1989	Dark Horse 25726

8/21/93	26	7	10 My Back Pages
			    BOB DYLAN & FRIENDS: Roger McGuinn, Tom Petty,
			    Neil Young, Eric Clapton & George Harrison
			    recorded on 10/16/92 at Madison Square Garden in New York City;
			    #30 Pop hit for **The Byrds** in 1967
				[L] — ●	Bob Dylan - The 30th Anniversary Concert (various artists)	Columbia 53230

			HARRISON, Jerry: Casual Gods Born on 2/21/49 in Milwaukee. Rock keyboardist/producer. Member of **Talking Heads**. The Casual Gods are 13 backing musicians.			
2/6/88	7	16	1 Rev It Up	—	Casual Gods	Sire 25663
6/2/90	42	4	2 Flying Under Radar	—	Walk On Water	Sire 25943
			HART, Corey Born on 5/31/62 in Montreal, Canada; raised in Malaga, Spain and Mexico City. Male singer/songwriter/keyboardist.			
6/23/84	15	13	1 Sunglasses At Night	7 ●	First Offense	EMI America 17117
10/27/84	36	7	2 It Ain't Enough	17 ↓		
6/29/85	8	12	3 Never Surrender	3 ●	Boy In The Box	EMI America 17161
			HARVEY DANGER Rock group from Seattle: Sean Nelson (vocals), Jeff Lin (guitar), Aaron Huffman (bass) and Evan Sult (drums).			
8/22/98	33	5	Flagpole Sitta	38^A ●	Where Have All The Merrymakers Gone?	Slash 556000
			HAVANA BLACK Hard-rock group from Helsinki, Finland: Hannu Leiden (vocals), Markku Heiskanen (guitar), Risto Hankala (bass) and Jussi Tegelman (drums). Group name taken from a box of Cuban cigars.			
2/3/90	17	9	Lone Wolf	—	Indian Warrior	Capitol 90567
			HAWKS Rock group from Otho, Iowa: Dave Hearn (vocals), Kirk Kaufman and Dave Steen (guitars), Frank Wiewel (bass) and Larry Adams (drums).			
4/18/81	32	7	It's All Right, It's O.K.	—	Hawks	Columbia 36922
			HAY, Colin James Born on 6/29/53 in Scotland; rasied in Melbourne, Australia. Lead singer/guitarist of **Men At Work**.			
2/14/87	41	6	Hold Me	99	Looking For Jack	Columbia 40611
			HAZIES, The Rock group from Los Angeles: Ken Logan (vocals), Greg Zink (guitar), Wes Eubanks (keyboards), Dave Walker (bass) and Steven Tanner (drums).			
6/8/96	13	14	1 Skin & Bones	—	Vinnie Smokin' In The Big Room	EMI 37369
12/7/96+	21	10	2 Trip Free Life	— ↓		

DEBUT	PEAK	WKS	Mainstream Rock Track	Pop	Gld	Album Title	Album Label & Number

HEADSTRONG
Rock group from London, Ontario, Canada: Matt Kinna (vocals), Joel Krass (guitar), Jon Cohen (bass) and Brian Mathews (drums).

| 2/9/02 | 15 | 15 | Adriana | — | | Headstrong .... RCA 68004 |

HEALEY, Jeff, Band
Born on 3/25/66 in Toronto. Blues-rock singer/guitarist. Blind since age one. Formed own group with Joe Rockman (bass) and Tom Stephen (drums). Group appeared in the 1989 movie *Road House*.

1)Cruel Little Number 2)I Think I Love You Too Much 3)While My Guitar Gently Weeps

10/1/88	11	12	1 Confidence Man	—		See The Light .... Arista 8553
1/14/89	33	6	2 See The Light	—		↓
4/15/89	24	7	3 Angel Eyes	5		↓
5/27/89	29	6	4 Roadhouse Blues	—		Road House (soundtrack) .... Arista 8576
			first recorded by The Doors in 1970			
5/26/90	5	15	5 I Think I Love You Too Much	—	●	Hell To Pay .... Arista 8632
			Mark Knopfler (of Dire Straits; writer, guitar, backing vocal)			
8/11/90	7	17	6 While My Guitar Gently Weeps	—		↓
			George Harrison (writer, guitar, backing vocal); first recorded by The Beatles in 1968			
11/17/90	16	11	7 Full Circle	—		↓
2/16/91	34	4	8 How Long Can A Man Be Strong	—		↓
11/7/92	2¹	13	9 Cruel Little Number	—		Feel This .... Arista 18706
2/6/93	20	7	10 Heart Of An Angel	—		↓
8/26/95	39	4	11 Stuck In The Middle With You	—		Cover To Cover .... Arista 18770
			#6 Pop hit for Stealers Wheel in 1973			

HEAR 'N AID
Collection of 40 hard-rock artists formed to raise money for famine relief efforts in Africa and around the world.

| 5/10/86 | 39 | 4 | Stars | — | | Hear 'N Aid .... Mercury 826044 |
| | | | co-written, produced and arranged by Ronnie James Dio | | | |

HEART ★36★
Rock group formed in Seattle: sisters Ann (vocals) and Nancy (guitar) Wilson, Howard Leese (guitar), Mark Andes (bass; **Spirit**) and Denny Carmassi (drums; **Gamma**). Andes left by 1993. Carmassi left in 1994 to join **Whitesnake**. Nancy married movie director Cameron Crowe on 7/27/86. Also see **Classic Rock Tracks** section.

1)How Can I Refuse 2)Who Will You Run To 3)These Dreams

5/22/82	16	7	1 This Man Is Mine	33		Private Audition .... Epic 38049
6/5/82	15	7	2 City's Burning	—		↓
8/13/83	❶¹	16	3 How Can I Refuse	44		Passionworks .... Epic 38800
10/8/83	43	6	4 Sleep Alone	—		↓
4/21/84	40	4	5 The Heat	—		Up The Creek (soundtrack) .... Pasha 39333
6/1/85	3	16	6 What About Love?	10	▲⁵	Heart .... Capitol 12410
9/7/85	2²	18	7 Never	4		↓
1/25/86	2³	12	8 These Dreams	❶¹		↓
4/26/86	6	10	9 Nothin' At All	10		↓
5/16/87	3	11	10 Alone	❶³	▲³	Bad Animals .... Capitol 12546
6/6/87	2³	16	11 Who Will You Run To	7		↓
11/21/87+	16	12	12 There's The Girl	12		↓
3/31/90	2¹	8	13 All I Wanna Do Is Make Love To You	2²	▲²	Brigade .... Capitol 91820
4/14/90	3	16	14 Wild Child	—		↓
4/28/90	24	8	15 Tall, Dark Handsome Stranger	—		↓
6/30/90	13	9	16 I Didn't Want To Need You	23		↓
10/20/90	25	8	17 Stranded	13		↓
10/12/91	20	7	18 You're The Voice [L]	—		Rock The House Live! .... Capitol 95797
			recorded on 11/28/90 at The Centrum in Worcester, Massachusetts; #82 Pop hit for John Farnham in 1990			
10/30/93	4	8	19 Black On Black II	—	●	Desire Walks On .... Capitol 99627
			first recorded by Dalbello in 1986			

HEAVEN 17
Electro-pop trio from England: Glenn Gregory (vocals), Martyn Ware and Ian Craig Marsh (synthesizers). Ware and Marsh were founding members of **Human League**.

| 4/23/83 | 32 | 3 | Let Me Go | 74 | | Heaven 17 .... Arista 6606 |

(HED)PLANET EARTH
Rap-rock group from Huntington Beach, California: Jahred Shaine (vocals), DJ Product (DJ), Wesstyle and Chizad (guitars), Mawk (bass) and B.C. (drums).

| 8/26/00 | 23 | 14 | Bartender (I Just Want Your Company) | — | | Broke .... Volcano 41710 |

DEBUT	PEAK	WKS	Mainstream Rock Track	Pop Gld	Album Title	Album Label & Number

HELIX
Hard-rock group from Waterloo, Canada: Brian Vollmer (vocals), Brent Doerner and Paul Hackman (guitars), Mike Uzelac (bass; replaced by Daryl Gray in 1984) and Greg "Fritz" Hinz (drums). Hackman was killed in a car crash on 7/6/92.

DEBUT	PEAK	WKS	Track	Pop	Gld	Album Title	Label
9/17/83	23	17	1 Heavy Metal Love	—		No Rest For The Wicked	Capitol 12281
8/4/84	32	8	2 Rock You	101		Walkin' The Razor's Edge	Capitol 12362
6/22/85	20	9	3 Deep Cuts The Knife	—		Long Way To Heaven	Capitol 12411

HELMET
Rock group from New York: Page Hamilton (vocals, guitar), Peter Mengede (guitar), Henry Bogdan (bass) and John Stanier (drums). Rob Echeverria replaced Mengede in 1993.

11/14/92	32	4	1 Unsung	—	●	Meantime	Interscope 92162
7/16/94	39	2	2 Milquetoast	—		Betty	Interscope 92404
3/29/97	19	9	3 Exactly What You Wanted	—		Aftertaste	Interscope 90073

HENLEY, Don ★25★
Born on 7/22/47 in Gilmer, Texas. Rock singer/songwriter/drummer. Own band, Shiloh, in the early 1970s. Worked with **Glenn Frey** in **Linda Ronstadt**'s backing band. Member of the **Eagles**. Married model Sharon Summerall on 5/20/95.

1)The Boys Of Summer 2)The End Of The Innocence 3)Dirty Laundry 4)All She Wants To Do Is Dance
5)The Heart Of The Matter

11/28/81+	26	12	Leather And Lace	6		Bella Donna (Nicks)	Modern 139
			STEVIE NICKS (with DON HENLEY)				
8/21/82	29	3	2 Johnny Can't Read	42	●	I Can't Stand Still	Asylum 60048
			Andrew Gold (keyboards)				
9/11/82	❶³	21	3 Dirty Laundry	3		↓	
			Joe Walsh and Steve Lukather (Toto) (guitar solos)				
10/2/82	44	3	4 You Better Hang Up	—		↓	
			Timothy B. Schmit and J.D. Souther (harmony vocals)				
11/10/84	❶⁵	17	5 The Boys Of Summer	5	▲³	Building The Perfect Beast	Geffen 24026
12/15/84+	7	15	6 Sunset Grill	22		↓	
			Patty Smyth (harmony vocal)				
1/26/85	❶²	18	7 All She Wants To Do Is Dance	9		↓	
			Martha Davis and Patty Smyth (harmony vocals)				
4/13/85	9	10	8 Drivin' With Your Eyes Closed	—		↓	
6/8/85	17	9	9 Not Enough Love In The World	34		↓	
11/1/86	3	13	10 Who Owns This Place	—		The Color Of Money (soundtrack)	MCA 6189
6/24/89	❶⁴	12	11 The End Of The Innocence	8	▲⁶	The End Of The Innocence	Geffen 24217
			co-written and produced by Bruce Hornsby (also on piano)				
7/8/89	2¹	16	12 I Will Not Go Quietly	—		↓	
			Axl Rose (of Guns N' Roses; harmony vocal)				
8/12/89+	8	14	13 If Dirt Were Dollars	—		↓	
			Sheryl Crow and J.D. Souther (backing vocals)				
9/16/89	4	17	14 The Last Worthless Evening	21		↓	
2/17/90	2²	15	15 The Heart Of The Matter	21		↓	
6/30/90	8	11	16 How Bad Do You Want It?	48		↓	
11/3/90	24	11	17 New York Minute	48		↓	
11/25/95+	16	12	18 The Garden Of Allah	—	▲	Actual Miles - Henley's Greatest Hits	Geffen 24834
2/24/96	22	10	19 You Don't Know Me At All	—		↓	
1/25/97	33	4	20 Through Your Hands	—		Michael (soundtrack)	Revolution 24666
4/8/00	21	11	21 Workin' It	—	▲	Inside Job	Warner 47083

HIATT, John
Born on 8/20/52 in Indianapolis. Singer/songwriter/guitarist. Member of **Little Village**.

6/20/87	27	8	1 Thank You Girl	—		Bring The Family	A&M 5158
9/10/88	8	13	2 Slow Turning	—		Slow Turning	A&M 5206
12/3/88+	18	12	3 Paper Thin	—		↓	
6/23/90	17	13	4 Child Of The Wild Blue Yonder	—		Stolen Moments	A&M 5310
9/25/93	16	9	5 Perfectly Good Guitar	—		Perfectly Good Guitar	A&M 540135
1/1/94	31	7	6 Something Wild	—		↓	

HILL, Rocky
Born on 2/1/46 in Dallas. Blues-rock singer/guitarist. Brother of **ZZ Top** bassist Dusty Hill.

4/23/88	31	5	I Won't Be Your Fool	—		Rocky Hill	Virgin 90862

HIMMELMAN, Peter
Born in St. Louis Park, Minnesota. Singer/songwriter.

12/26/87+	41	6	Waning Moon	—		Gematria	Island 90663

HIVES, The
Rock group from Fagersta, Sweden: brothers Pelle (vocals) and Niklas (guitar) Almqvist, Vigilante Carlstrom (guitar), Dr. Matt Destruction (bass) and Chris Dangerous (drums).

8/17/02	35	2	Hate To Say I Told You So	86		Veni Vidi Vicious	Epitaph 48327

DEBUT	PEAK	WKS	Mainstream Rock Track	Pop	Gld	Album Title	Album Label & Number
			HODGSON, Roger				
			Born on 5/21/50 in London. Lead singer of **Supertramp**.				
10/13/84	5	17	1 **Had A Dream (Sleeping With The Enemy)**	48		*In The Eye Of The Storm* . . . . A&M 5004
1/19/85	30	6	2 **In Jeopardy**	—	↓	
10/10/87	38	4	3 **You Make Me Love You**	—		*Hai Hai* . . . . A&M 5112
			HOEY, Gary				
			Born in Boston. Rock guitarist.				
8/28/93	5	20	1 **Hocus Pocus** [I]	—		*Animal Instinct* . . . . Reprise 45350
			#9 Pop hit for Focus in 1973				
7/2/94	15	11	2 **Low Rider** . . . . [I]	—		*The Endless Summer II (soundtrack)* . . . Reprise 45615
			#7 Pop hit for War in 1975				
			HOG				
			Rock trio from Los Angeles: Kirk Miller (vocals, guitar), Dillinger (bass) and Matt Gillis (drums).				
3/30/96	34	4	**Get A Job**	—		*Nothing Sacred* . . . . DGC 24958
			HOLE				
			Rock group formed in Los Angeles: Courtney Love (vocals, guitar), Eric Erlandson (guitar), Kristen Pfaff (bass) and Patty Schemel (drums). Love acted in several movies; married to Kurt Cobain (of **Nirvana**) from 2/24/92 until his death on 4/8/94. Pfaff was found dead in her bathtub on 6/16/94 (age 27); replaced by Melissa Auf Der Maur.				
9/12/98	4	26	1 **Celebrity Skin**	85	▲	*Celebrity Skin.* . . . . DGC 25164
2/13/99	16	9	2 **Malibu**	81	↓	
			HONEYDRIPPERS, The				
			All-star rock group: **Robert Plant** (vocals), **Jimmy Page** and **Jeff Beck** (guitars), and Nile Rodgers (bass). Plant and Page are from **Led Zeppelin** and Rodgers is from Chic.				
10/13/84	8	18	1 **Rockin' At Midnight**	25	▲	*Volume One* . . . . Es Paranza 90220
			#2 R&B hit for Roy Brown in 1949				
10/27/84	11	12	2 **Sea Of Love**	3	↓	
			#2 Pop hit for Phil Phillips in 1959				
			HONEYMOON SUITE				
			Rock group from Toronto: Johnnie Dee (vocals), Dermot Grehan (guitar), Ray Coburn (keyboards), Garry Lalonde (bass) and Dave Betts (drums). Coburn left in 1987; replaced by Rob Preuss.				
7/28/84	7	15	1 **New Girl Now**	57		*Honeymoon Suite* . . . . Warner 25098
10/20/84	47	6	2 **Burning In Love**	—	↓	
2/22/86	8	16	3 **Feel It Again**	34		*The Big Prize* . . . . Warner 25293
5/10/86	22	8	4 **Bad Attitude**	—	↓	
7/19/86	38	6	5 **What Does It Take**	52	↓	
4/9/88	13	11	6 **Love Changes Everything**	91		*Racing After Midnight.* . . . . Warner 25652
			HONKY TOAST				
			Rock group from New York City: Eric Toast (vocals), Richard Croissant (guitar), E.Z. Bake (bass) and Frank Butter (drums).				
3/20/99	29	9	**Shakin' And A Bakin'**	—		*Whatcha Gonna Do Honky?* . . . . 550 Music 69360
			HOOBASTANK				
			Rock group from Agoura Hills, California: Doug Robb (vocals), Dan Estrin (guitar), Markku Lappalainen (bass) and Chris Hesse (drums).				
11/10/01+	7	27	1 **Crawling In The Dark**	68	▲	*Hoobastank* . . . . Island 586435
5/4/02	9	26	2 **Running Away**	44	↓	
10/12/02	28↑	7↑	3 **Remember Me**	—	↓	
			HOOKER, John Lee — see BIG HEAD TODD & THE MONSTERS				
			HOOTERS				
			Pop-rock group from Philadelphia: Eric Bazilian (vocals, guitar), Rob Hyman (vocals, keyboards), John Lilley (guitar), Andy King (bass) and David Uosikkinen (drums). Fran Smith replaced King in early 1989.				
5/11/85	11	13	1 **All You Zombies**	58	▲²	*Nervous Night* . . . . Columbia 39912
8/3/85	3	17	2 **And We Danced**	21	↓	
12/21/85+	3	12	3 **Day By Day**	18	↓	
4/19/86	34	7	4 **Where Do The Children Go**	38	↓	
			Patty Smyth (backing vocal)				
7/11/87	3	10	5 **Johnny B**	61	●	*One Way Home* . . . . Columbia 40659
8/22/87	13	11	6 **Satellite**	61	↓	
12/26/87+	47	3	7 **Karla With A K**	—	↓	
11/11/89	20	10	8 **500 Miles**	97		*Zig Zag* . . . . Columbia 45058
			Peter, Paul & Mary (harmony vocals)				
1/27/90	37	5	9 **Brother, Don't You Walk Away**	—	↓	
			HOOTIE & THE BLOWFISH				
			Pop-rock group formed in South Carolina: Darius Rucker (vocals), Mark Bryan (guitar), Dean Felber (bass) and Jim Sonefeld (drums). Won the 1995 Best New Artist Grammy Award.				
7/30/94	4	26	1 **Hold My Hand**	10	▲¹⁶	*Cracked Rear View* . . . . Atlantic 82613
12/24/94+	9	26	2 **Let Her Cry**	9	↓	
6/10/95	2²	23	3 **Only Wanna Be With You**	6	↓	
10/14/95	21	8	4 **Drowning**	—	↓	
1/13/96	26	9	5 **Time**	14	↓	

DEBUT	PEAK	WKS	Mainstream Rock Track	Pop Gld	Album Title	Album Label & Number
			HOOTIE & THE BLOWFISH — Cont'd			
4/8/95	15	12	6 Hey Hey What Can I Do	— ●	*Encomium: A Tribute To Led Zeppelin*	
			first recorded by **Led Zeppelin** in 1970		*(various artists)* .... Atlantic 82731	
4/20/96	6	11	7 **Old Man & Me (When I Get To Heaven)**	13 ▲³	*Fairweather Johnson*............. Atlantic 82886	
7/20/96	29	8	8 Tucker's Town	38	↓	
★84★			**HORNSBY, Bruce, And The Range**			
			Born on 11/23/54 in Williamsburg, Virginia. Singer/songwriter/pianist. The Range: George Marinelli and David Mansfield (guitars), Joe Puerta (bass) and John Molo (drums). Puerta was a member of **Ambrosia**. Hornsby later toured as a member of the **Grateful Dead** and The Other Ones. Won the 1986 Best New Artist Grammy Award.			
			1)*The Valley Road* 2)*Across The River* 3)*Mandolin Rain*			
6/21/86	18	11	1 Every Little Kiss	72 ▲³	*The Way It Is* .... RCA Victor 5904	
9/13/86	3	15	2 **The Way It Is**	❶¹	↓	
11/29/86+	6	13	3 **On The Western Skyline**	—	↓	
1/24/87	2²	11	4 **Mandolin Rain**	4	↓	
4/30/88	❶³	11	5 **The Valley Road**	5 ▲	*scenes from the southside*............. RCA 6686	
5/21/88	5	17	6 **Look Out Any Window**	35	↓	
5/28/88	11	10	7 Defenders Of The Flag........................	—	↓	
			Huey Lewis (harmonica)			
6/16/90	❶¹	14	8 **Across The River**	18 ●	*A Night On The Town* .... RCA 2041	
			Jerry Garcia (of the **Grateful Dead**; guitar)			
8/4/90	4	13	9 **A Night On The Town**	—	↓	
10/27/90	50	1	10 Fire On The Cross........................	—	↓	
6/1/91	33	6	11 Set Me In Motion	—	*Backdraft (soundtrack)*............. RCA 3141	
4/17/93	38	5	12 Harbor Lights	— ●	*Harbor Lights* .... RCA 66114	
			BRUCE HORNSBY			
			HOTHOUSE FLOWERS			
			Folk-rock group from Dublin, Ireland: Liam O'Maonlai (vocals), Fiachna O'Braonain (guitar), Peter O'Toole (bass) and Jerry Fehily (drums).			
8/27/88	16	10	1 Don't Go	—	*people* .... London 828101	
11/19/88+	23	11	2 I'm Sorry	—	↓	
6/30/90	29	8	3 Give It Up	—	*Home*........................ London 828197	
3/27/93	32	6	4 Thing Of Beauty	—	*Songs From The Rain* ..... London 828350	
			HOUSE OF LORDS			
			Hard-rock group: James Christian (vocals), Lanny Cordola (guitar), Gregg Giuffria (keyboards), Chuck Wright (bass) and Ken Mary (drums). Cordola was with **Ozzy Osbourne**. Giuffria and Wright were both with **Giuffria**; Wright was also with **Quiet Riot**. Mary was with **Alice Cooper**. Michael Guy replaced Cordola in 1990.			
12/17/88+	43	5	1 I Wanna Be Loved	58	*House Of Lords* .... RCA 8530	
4/29/89	50	1	2 Love Don't Lie	—	↓	
9/8/90	10	19	3 **Can't Find My Way Home**	—	*Sahara* .... RCA 2170	
			written by **Steve Winwood**; first recorded by Blind Faith in 1969			
12/15/90+	20	12	4 Remember My Name	—	↓	
			HOWLIN' MAGGIE			
			Rock group from Columbus, Ohio: Harold "Happy" Chichester (vocals), Andy Harrison (guitar), James Rico (bass) and Jerome Dillon (drums).			
4/27/96	25	7	Alcohol	—	*Honeysuckle Strange* .... Columbia 67421	
			HUGHES/THRALL			
			Rock duo: Glenn Hughes (vocals, bass; **Deep Purple**) and Pat Thrall (guitar; **Asia**).			
11/13/82	28	2	The Look In Your Eye	—	*Hughes/Thrall*................. Boulevard 38116	
			HUM			
			Rock group from Champaign, Illinois: Matt Talbott (vocals), Tim Lash (guitar), Jeff Dimpsey (bass) and Bryan St. Pere (drums).			
7/29/95	28	7	Stars	72ᴬ	*You'd Prefer An Astronaut* .... RCA 66577	
			HUMAN LEAGUE, The			
			Electro-pop trio from Sheffield, Yorkshire, England: lead singer/synthesist Philip Oakey, with female vocalists Joanne Catherall and Susanne Sulley. Early members Martyn Ware and Ian Craig Marsh left to form **Heaven 17**.			
4/3/82	4	16	1 **Don't You Want Me**	❶³	*Dare* .... A&M 4892	
1/22/83	22	9	2 Mirror Man	30	*Fascination!* .... A&M 2501	
5/28/83	14	7	3 (Keep Feeling) Fascination........................	8	↓	
			HUMAN RADIO			
			Rock group from Memphis: Ross Rice (vocals), Kye Kennedy (guitar), Peter Hyrka (mandolin), Steve Arnold (bass) and Steve Ebe (drums).			
6/23/90	32	7	Me & Elvis	—	*Human Radio* .... Columbia 45432	
			HUMBLE PIE			
			Rock group from England: Steve Marriott (vocals, guitar), Bobby Tench (guitar), Anthony Jones (bass) and Jerry Shirley (drums). **Peter Frampton** was lead vocalist until October 1971. Shirley later joined **Fastway**. Marriott died on 4/20/91 (age 44). Also see **Classic Rock Tracks** section.			
5/23/81	58	2	Tin Soldier	—	*Go For The Throat*.................. Atco 131	
			HUNGER, The			
			Rock group from Houston: brothers Jeff (vocals) and Thomas (keyboards) Wilson, Stephen Bogle (guitar), Brian Albritton (bass) and Max Schuldberg (drums).			
5/18/96	10	26	**Vanishing Cream**	—	*Devil Thumbs A Ride* .... Universal 53000	

DEBUT	PEAK	WKS	Mainstream Rock Track	Pop	Gld	Album Title	Album Label & Number
			HUNTER, Ian				
			Born on 6/3/46 in Shrewsbury, England. Rock singer/guitarist. Leader of Mott The Hoople from 1969-74.				
9/12/81	47	10	1 I Need Your Love	—		*Short Back N' Sides*	Chrysalis 1326
7/16/83	25	8	2 All Of The Good Ones Are Taken	—		*All Of The Good Ones Are Taken*	Columbia 38628
10/7/89	24	7	3 American Music	—		*Y U I ORTA*	Mercury 838973
			IAN HUNTER/MICK RONSON				
			HURRICANE				
			Hard-rock group from Los Angeles: Kelly Hansen (vocals), Robert Sarzo (guitar), Tony Cavazo (bass) and Jay Schellen (drums). Sarzo is the brother of **Whitesnake**'s Rudy Sarzo. Cavazo is the brother of **Quiet Riot**'s Carlos Cavazo.				
6/18/88	33	9	I'm On To You	—		*Over The Edge*	Enigma 73320
			HYDE, Paul, And The Payola$				
			Pop-rock group from Canada: Paul Hyde (vocals), Bob Rock (guitar), Lawrence Wilkins (bass) and Chris Taylor (drums). Alex Boynton replaced Wilkins in 1984. Hyde and Rock later recorded as the duo **Rock and Hyde**.				
9/11/82	22	15	1 Eyes Of A Stranger	—		*No Stranger To Danger*	A&M 4908
			PAYOLA$				
6/1/85	37	4	2 You're The Only Love	84		*Here's The World For Ya*	A&M 5025
			HYMAS, Tony — see **BECK, Jeff**				
			HYNDE, Chrissie — see **UB40**				
			HYTS				
			Rock group from San Francisco: Pat Little (vocals, guitar), Tommy Thompson (keyboards), Stan Miller (bass) and Roy Garcia (drums).				
2/11/84	48	1	Backstabber	—		*Hyts*	Gold Mountain 80002

I

DEBUT	PEAK	WKS	Mainstream Rock Track	Pop	Gld	Album Title	Album Label & Number
			ICEHOUSE				
			Rock group formed in Sydney, Australia: Iva Davies (vocals, guitar), Anthony Smith (keyboards), Keith Welsh (bass) and John Lloyd (drums). Numerous personnel changes through the 1980s, with Davies the only constant. Group name is Australian slang for an insane asylum.				
7/11/81	51	3	1 We Can Get Together	62		*Icehouse*	Chrysalis 1350
8/1/81	28	11	2 Icehouse	—		↓	
10/16/82	31	1	3 Hey' Little Girl	—		*Primitive Man*	Chrysalis 1390
5/17/86	9	13	4 No Promises	79		*Measure For Measure*	Chrysalis 41527
8/30/86	19	7	5 Cross The Border	—		↓	
9/26/87	10	17	6 Crazy	14		*Man of Colours*	Chrysalis 41592
1/23/88	10	14	7 Electric Blue	7		↓	
			John Oates (of **Hall & Oates**; co-writer, backing vocal)				
			ICICLE WORKS				
			Rock trio from Liverpool, England: Robert Ian McNabb (vocals, guitar), Chris Layhe (bass) and Chris Sharrock (drums).				
3/31/84	18	12	Whisper To A Scream (Birds Fly)	37		*Icicle Works*	Arista 8202
★71★			**IDOL, Billy**				
			Born William Broad on 11/30/55 in Stanmore, Middlesex, England. Rock singer. Leader of punk group Generation X from 1977-81. Appeared in the movie *The Wedding Singer*.				
			1)Cradle Of Love 2)To Be A Lover 3)White Wedding				
8/28/82	31	1	1 Hot In The City	23	●	*Billy Idol*	Chrysalis 41377
4/2/83	4	15	2 White Wedding	36		↓	
11/26/83+	9	15	3 Rebel Yell	46	▲²	*Rebel Yell*	Chrysalis 41450
5/12/84	5	13	4 Eyes Without A Face	4		↓	
8/18/84	8	11	5 Flesh For Fantasy	29		↓	
11/24/84	24	8	6 Catch My Fall	50		↓	
10/4/86	2⁴	14	7 To Be A Lover	6	▲	*Whiplash Smile*	Chrysalis 41514
			#45 Pop hit for William Bell in 1969				
11/15/86+	10	16	8 Don't Need A Gun	37		↓	
3/28/87	26	8	9 Sweet Sixteen	20		↓	
9/5/87	27	7	10 Mony Mony "Live" [L]	❶¹		*(single only)*	Chrysalis 43161
			#3 Pop hit for Tommy James & The Shondells in 1968				
5/5/90	❶²	14	11 Cradle Of Love	2¹	▲	*Charmed Life*	Chrysalis 21735
7/28/90	18	10	12 L.A. Woman	52		↓	
			first recorded by **The Doors** in 1971				
11/24/90+	35	9	13 Prodigal Blues	—		↓	
6/19/93	7	8	14 Shock To The System	105		*Cyberpunk*	Chrysalis 26000
7/23/94	38	2	15 Speed	—		*Speed (soundtrack)*	Arista 11018
			ILL NIÑO				
			Rock group from New Jersey: Cristian Machado (vocals), Marc Rizzo and Jardel Paisante (guitars), Roger Vasquez (percussion), Lazaro Pina (bass) and Dave Chavarri (drums).				
12/29/01+	28	10	What Comes Around	—		*Revolution Revolución*	Roadrunner 8497

DEBUT	PEAK	WKS	Mainstream Rock Track	Pop Gld	Album Title	Album Label & Number

I MOTHER EARTH
Rock group from Toronto: Edwin (vocals), Jagori Tanna (guitar), Bruce Gordon (bass) and Christian Tanna (drums).

| 8/3/96 | 19 | 10 | One More Astronaut | — | Scenery And Fish | Capitol 32919 |

INCUBUS
Hard-rock group from Calabasas, California: Brandon Boyd (vocals), Mike Einziger (guitar), Chris Kilmore (DJ), Alex Katunich (bass) and Jose Pasillas (drums).

12/4/99+	7	32	1 Pardon Me	102	▲² Make Yourself	Immortal 63652
7/15/00	17	16	2 Stellar	107	↓	
12/9/00+	8	26	3 Drive	9	↓	
9/1/01	4	28	4 Wish You Were Here	60	▲² Morning View	Immortal 85227
12/22/01+	9	26	5 Nice To Know You	105	↓	
5/4/02	27	13	6 Warning	104	↓	
9/7/02	31	6	7 Circles	—	↓	

INDIA.ARIE — see MELLENCAMP, John Cougar

INDIGENOUS
Family group from Marty, South Dakota: Mato (vocals, guitar), Horse (percussion), Pte (bass) and Wanbdi (drums) Nanji.

| 1/2/99 | 22 | 12 | Now That You're Gone | — | Things We Do | Pachyderm 0001 |

INDIGO GIRLS
Folk-rock duo from Decatur, Georgia: singers/songwriters/guitarists Amy Ray (born on 4/12/64) and Emily Sailers (born on 7/22/63).

| 8/5/89 | 48 | 1 | Closer To Fine | 52 | ▲² Indigo Girls | Epic 45044 |

INDIO
Born Gordon Peterson in Toronto. Singer/songwriter/guitarist.

| 7/29/89 | 34 | 7 | Hard Sun | — | Big Harvest | A&M 5257 |

INJECTED
Rock group from Atlanta: Danny Grady (vocals, guitar), Jade Lemons (guitar), Steve Slovisky (bass) and Chris Wojtal (drums).

| 2/2/02 | 19 | 15 | 1 Faithless | — | Burn It Black | Island 548878 |
| 8/3/02 | 32 | 9 | 2 Bullet (What Did You Sell Your Soul For?) | — | ↓ | |

INSIDERS
Rock group from Chicago: John Siegle (vocals), Jay O'Rourke and Gary Yerkins (guitars), Jim DeMonte (bass) and Ed Breckenfeld (drums).

| 8/15/87 | 8 | 10 | Ghost On The Beach | — | Ghost On The Beach | Epic 40630 |

INTO ANOTHER
Rock group from New York City: Richie Birkenhead (vocals), Peter Moses (guitar), Tony Bono (bass) and Drew Thomas (drums).

| 4/20/96 | 39 | 2 | T.A.I.L. | — | Seemless | Hollywood 62008 |

INXS ★29★
Rock group from Sydney, Australia: Michael Hutchence (vocals), Kirk Pengilly (guitar, saxophone), Garry Beers (bass) and brothers Tim (guitar), Andy (keyboards) and Jon (drums) Farriss. Hutchence starred in the movies *Dogs In Space* and *Frankenstein Unbound*; formed the group **Max Q**. Jon Farriss married actress Leslie Bega (TV's *Head Of The Class*) on 2/14/92. Hutchence committed suicide on 11/22/97 (age 37).

1)Suicide Blonde 2)The One Thing 3)Devil Inside 4)What You Need 5)Good Times

3/19/83	2¹	20	1 The One Thing	30	● Shabooh Shoobah	Atco 90072
6/11/83	17	12	2 Don't Change	80	↓	
3/31/84	43	10	3 Original Sin	58	▲ The Swing	Atco 90160
			Daryl Hall (backing vocal)			
7/28/84	41	6	4 I Send A Message	77	↓	
10/19/85	11	14	5 This Time	81	▲² Listen Like Thieves	Atlantic 81277
1/25/86	3	15	6 What You Need	5	↓	
4/26/86	12	11	7 Listen Like Thieves	54	↓	
8/16/86	24	7	8 Kiss The Dirt (Falling Down The Mountain)	—	↓	
6/20/87	3	12	9 Good Times	47	● The Lost Boys (soundtrack)	Atlantic 81767
			INXS AND JIMMY BARNES			
10/24/87	12	15	10 Need You Tonight	●¹	▲⁶ Kick	Atlantic 81796
12/26/87+	2¹	17	11 Devil Inside	2²	↓	
3/19/88	8	14	12 New Sensation	3	↓	
6/18/88	33	6	13 Kick	—	↓	
8/13/88	5	14	14 Never Tear Us Apart	7	↓	
12/17/88+	17	13	15 Mystify	—	↓	
9/8/90	●⁴	10	16 Suicide Blonde	9	▲² X	Atlantic 82140
11/3/90+	6	17	17 Disappear	8	↓	
2/2/91	4	15	18 Bitter Tears	46	↓	
11/9/91	14	6	19 Shining Star	—	▲ Live Baby Live	Atlantic 82294

DEBUT	PEAK	WKS	Mainstream Rock Track	Pop	Gld	Album Title	Album Label & Number
			INXS — Cont'd				
7/11/92	4	8	20 Heaven Sent	—	▲	*Welcome To Wherever You Are*	Atlantic 82394
8/22/92	13	11	21 Not Enough Time	28		↓	
4/19/97	37	3	22 Elegantly Wasted	27ᴬ		*Elegantly Wasted*	Mercury 534531
			IOMMI				
			Born Tony Iommi on 2/19/48 in Birmingham, England. Lead guitarist of **Black Sabbath**.				
10/7/00	10	18	Goodbye Lament	—		*Iommi*	Divine 57857
			IOMMI Featuring Dave Grohl				
			IRIS, Donnie				
			Born Dominic Ierace on 2/28/47 in Beaver Falls, Pennsylvania. Rock singer/songwriter/guitarist. Former member of The Jaggerz.				
3/21/81	19	6	1 Ah! Leah!	29		*Back On The Streets*	MCA 3272
4/4/81	47	1	2 I Can't Hear You	—		↓	
9/19/81	31	13	3 Sweet Merilee	80		*King Cool*	MCA 5237
12/12/81+	9	18	4 Love Is Like A Rock	37		↓	
10/23/82	39	5	5 The High And The Mighty	—		*The High And The Mighty*	MCA 5358
11/6/82	26	6	6 Tough World	57		↓	
7/9/83	20	10	7 Do You Compute?	64		*Fortune 410*	MCA 5427
2/9/85	28	9	8 Injured In The Game Of Love	91		*No Muss...No Fuss*	HME 39949
			IRON MAIDEN				
			Hard-rock group formed in London: Paul Di'anno (vocals), Dave Murray and Adrian Smith (guitars), Steve Harris (bass) and Clive Burr (drums). **Bruce Dickinson** replaced Di'anno in early 1982. Nick McBrain replaced Burr in early 1983. Blaze Bayley replaced Dickinson in September 1993. Janick Gers replaced Smith in 1994. Dickinson returned to replace Bayley in 1999; Adrian Smith returned that same year.				
7/18/81	31	5	1 Wrathchild	—	●	*Killers*	Harvest 12141
4/17/82	50	2	2 Hallowed Be Thy Name	—	▲	*The Number Of The Beast*	Harvest 12202
6/18/83	8	12	3 Flight Of Icarus	—		*Piece Of Mind*	Capitol 12274
7/30/83	28	6	4 The Trooper	—		↓	
9/22/84	25	6	5 2 Minutes To Midnight	—	▲	*Powerslave*	Capitol 12321
5/14/88	47	3	6 Can I Play With Madness	—	●	*Seventh Son Of A Seventh Son*	Capitol 90258
6/10/00	19	13	7 The Wicker Man	—		*Brave New World*	Portrait 62208
			ISAAK, Chris				
			Born on 6/26/56 in Stockton, California. Singer/songwriter/guitarist/actor. Acted in several movies; starred in own TV show.				
1/26/91	10	12	1 Wicked Game	6	▲²	*Heart Shaped World*	Reprise 25837
4/20/91	39	6	2 Don't Make Me Dream About You	—		↓	
			ISLE OF Q				
			Rock group from Philadelphia: David Ringler (vocals), Doug Kennedy (guitar), Beau Bodine (bass) and Josh Cedar (drums).				
8/5/00	29	8	1 Little Scene	—		*Isle Of Q*	Universal 157885
12/9/00+	29	10	2 Bag Of Tricks	—		↓	
			ISLEY, Ernie				
			Born on 3/7/52 in Cincinnati. Member of The Isley Brothers and Isley, Jasper, Isley.				
6/9/90	31	6	Back To Square One	—		*High Wire*	Elektra 60902

J

DEBUT	PEAK	WKS	Mainstream Rock Track	Pop	Gld	Album Title	Album Label & Number
			JACKSON, Joe				
			Born on 8/11/55 in Burton-on-Trent, Staffordshire, England. Singer/songwriter/pianist. Also see **Classic Rock Tracks** section.				
9/25/82	7	18	1 Steppin' Out	6	●	*Night And Day*	A&M 4906
3/31/84	12	14	2 You Can't Get What You Want (Till You Know What You Want)	15		*Body And Soul*	A&M 5000
4/12/86	11	11	3 Right And Wrong . . . . [L]	—		*Big World*	A&M 6021
4/22/89	16	8	4 Nineteen Forever	—		*Blaze Of Glory*	A&M 5249
5/4/91	28	6	5 Obvious Song	—		*Laughter & Lust*	Virgin 91628
6/15/91	25	7	6 Oh Well	—		↓	
			#55 Pop hit for **Fleetwood Mac** in 1970				
			JACKSON, Michael				
			Born on 8/29/58 in Gary, Indiana. Self-proclaimed "King of Pop." Lead singer of **The Jacksons**. Played "The Scarecrow" in the 1978 movie musical *The Wiz*. Married to Elvis Presley's daughter, Lisa Marie, from 1994-96. Inducted into the Rock and Roll Hall of Fame in 2001.				
4/30/83	14	5	1 Beat It	❶³ ▲²⁶		*Thriller*	Epic 38112
			Eddie **Van Halen** (lead guitar)				
2/4/84	42	2	2 Thriller	4		↓	
			Vincent Price (rap)				
10/29/83	24	12	3 Say Say Say	❶⁶ ▲		*Pipes Of Peace*	Columbia 39149
			PAUL McCARTNEY AND MICHAEL JACKSON				
			JACKSONS, The				
			Group of brothers from Gary, Indiana: Jackie, Tito, Jermaine, Marlon, Randy and lead singer **Michael Jackson**. Known as The Jackson 5 from 1968-75. Group inducted into the Rock and Roll Hall of Fame in 1997.				
7/14/84	42	2	State Of Shock	3	▲²	*Victory*	Epic 38946
			Mick Jagger (guest vocal)				

DEBUT	PEAK	WKS	Mainstream Rock Track	Pop	Gld	Album Title	Album Label & Number

JACKYL
Hard-rock group from Atlanta: **Jesse James Dupree** (vocals), Jimmy Stiff and Jeff Worley (guitars), Tom Bettini (bass) and Chris Worley (drums).

DEBUT	PEAK	WKS	Track	Pop	Gld	Album Title	Label
9/19/92	32	3	1 I Stand Alone	—	▲	Jackyl	Geffen 24489
11/14/92	24	11	2 The Lumberjack	—	↓		
2/13/93	10	20	3 Down On Me	—	↓		
5/29/93	11	18	4 When Will It Rain	—	↓		
9/4/93	35	5	5 Dirty Little Mind	—	↓		
7/30/94	7	14	6 Push Comes To Shove	—	●	Push Comes To Shove	Geffen 24710
11/12/94	35	4	7 Headed For Destruction	—	↓		
7/19/97	15	11	8 Locked & Loaded	—		Cut The Crap	Epic 67948
10/10/98	31	7	9 We're An American Band	—		Choice Cuts	Geffen 25302

#1 Pop hit for Grand Funk in 1973

★86★ JAGGER, Mick
Born Michael Phillip Jagger on 7/26/43 in Dartford, Kent, England. Lead singer of **The Rolling Stones**. Appeared in the movies *Ned Kelly* and *Freejack*. Married to model Bianca Jagger from 1971-80. Married to actress/model Jerry Hall from 1990-99. Also see "State Of Shock" by **The Jacksons**.
1)*Just Another Night* 2)*Don't Tear Me Up* 3)*Dancing In The Street*

DEBUT	PEAK	WKS	Track	Pop	Gld	Album Title	Label
2/9/85	❶²	13	1 Just Another Night	12	▲	She's The Boss	Columbia 39940
3/9/85	9	12	2 Lonely At The Top	—	↓		
			Pete Townshend (guitar)				
4/27/85	5	12	3 Lucky In Love	38	↓		
			Jeff Beck (guitar, above 3)				
8/31/85	3	9	4 Dancing In The Street	7		(single only)	EMI America 8288
			MICK JAGGER/DAVID BOWIE				
			#2 Pop hit for Martha & The Vandellas in 1964				
6/28/86	14	10	5 Ruthless People	51	●	Ruthless People (soundtrack)	Epic 40398
9/12/87	7	6	6 Let's Work	39		Primitive Cool	Columbia 40919
9/26/87	7	11	7 Throwaway	67	↓		
12/5/87	39	1	8 Say You Will	—	↓		
1/30/93	❶¹	18	9 Don't Tear Me Up	—	●	Wandering Spirit	Atlantic 82436
1/30/93	34	2	10 Sweet Thing	84	↓		
3/13/93	3	15	11 Wired All Night	—	↓		
10/27/01	24	16	12 God Gave Me Everything			Goddess In The Doorway	Virgin 11288

JAM, The
New-wave trio from England: **Paul Weller** (vocals, bass), Bruce Foxton (guitar) and Rick Buckler (drums). Disbanded in 1982. Weller formed **The Style Council**.

4/24/82	31	9	Town Called Malice	—		The Gift	Polydor 6349

JAMES, Colin
Born Colin Munn on 8/17/64 in Regina, Saskatchewan, Canada. Singer/songwriter/guitarist.

9/3/88	30	7	1 Voodoo Thing	—		Colin James	Virgin 90931
6/30/90	7	14	2 Just Came Back	—		Sudden Stop	Virgin 91376
10/20/90	21	11	3 Keep On Loving Me Baby	—	↓		

JAMES, Melvin
Born in Des Moines, Iowa. Rock singer/songwriter/guitarist.

8/29/87	17	10	Why Won't You Stay (Come In, Come Out Of The Rain)	—		The Passenger	MCA 5663

JAMES, Vinnie
Born in Newark, New Jersey. Black rock singer/songwriter/guitarist.

4/27/91	13	10	Black Money	—		All American Boy	RCA 2387

JANE'S ADDICTION
Rock group from Los Angeles: Perry Farrell (vocals), **Dave Navarro** (guitar), Eric Avery (bass) and Stephen Perkins (drums). Farrell and Perkins later formed **Porno For Pyros**. Navarro later joined **Red Hot Chili Peppers**.

10/20/90	29	17	✓1 Been Caught Stealing	—	▲²	Ritual de lo Habitual	Warner 25993
12/6/97	37	1	2 So What!	—	●	Kettle Whistle	Warner 46752
1/24/98	37	2	3 Jane Says [L]	—	↓		

JANUS STARK
Rock trio from England: Gizz Butt (vocals, guitar), Shop (bass) and Pinch (drums).

12/5/98	32	8	Every Little Thing Counts	—		Great Adventure Cigar	Trauma 74008

JARS OF CLAY
Christian pop group formed in Illinois: Dan Haseltine (vocals), Steve Mason and Matt Odmark (guitars), and Charlie Lowell (keyboards).

5/11/96	16	14	✓ Flood	37	▲²	Jars Of Clay	Essential 41580

JASON & THE SCORCHERS
Rock group from Nashville: Jason Ringenberg (vocals), Warner Hodges (guitar), Jeff Johnson (bass) and Perry Baggs (drums).

4/20/85	34	4	1 White Lies	—		Lost & Found	EMI America 17153
11/29/86+	16	11	2 Golden Ball And Chain	—		Still Standing	EMI America 17219

JAYHAWKS, The
Rock group from Minneapolis: Mark Olson (vocals), Gary Louris (guitar), Marc Perlman (bass) and Ken Callahan (drums).

1/9/93	20	10	Waiting For The Sun	—		Hollywood Town Hall	Def American 26829

DEBUT	PEAK	WKS	Mainstream Rock Track	Pop	Gld	Album Title	Album Label & Number

★60★ JEFFERSON AIRPLANE/STARSHIP

Rock group formed as **Jefferson Airplane** in San Francisco: **Marty Balin** and **Grace Slick** (vocals), Paul Kantner (vocals, guitar), Jorma Kaukonen (guitar), Jack Casady (bass) and Spencer Dryden (drums). Numerous personnel changes. Group name changed to **Jefferson Starship** in 1974. Lineup in 1981: **Mickey Thomas** and Slick (vocals), Kantner (guitar, vocals), Craig Chaquico (guitar), David Freiberg (keyboards), Pete Sears (bass) and Aynsley Dunbar (drums). Dunbar was replaced by Don Baldwin in August 1982. Kantner (**KBC Band**) and Freiberg left in 1984. Due to legal difficulties, band name shortened to **Starship**. Sears left in late 1986. Slick left in early 1988; Mark Morgan (keyboards) and Brett Bloomfield (bass) joined. In 1989, the original 1966 lineup reunited as Jefferson Airplane with Kenny Aronoff (from **John Cougar Mellencamp**'s band) replacing Dryden. Jefferson Airplane inducted into the Rock and Roll Hall of Fame in 1996. Also see **Classic Rock Tracks** section.

1)No Way Out 2)We Built This City 3)Find Your Way Back

JEFFERSON STARSHIP:

DEBUT	PEAK	WKS	Mainstream Rock Track	Pop	Gld	Album Title	Album Label & Number
4/11/81	3	15	✓1 Find Your Way Back	29	●	Modern Times	Grunt 3848
5/2/81	17	18	2 Stranger	48	↓		
6/27/81	49	7	3 Save Your Love	104	↓		
10/30/82	16	15	4 Can't Find Love	—	●	Winds Of Change	Grunt 4372
11/6/82	18	15	5 Winds Of Change	38	↓		
11/6/82	33	4	6 Be My Lady	28	↓		
5/12/84	❶[1]	14	✓7 No Way Out	23	●	Nuclear Furniture	Grunt 4921
6/16/84	6	17	✓8 Layin' It On The Line	66	↓		
9/1/84	50	3	9 Sorry Me, Sorry You	—	↓		

STARSHIP:

DEBUT	PEAK	WKS	Mainstream Rock Track	Pop	Gld	Album Title	Album Label & Number
9/7/85	❶[1]	13	✓10 We Built This City	❶[2]	▲	Knee Deep In The Hoopla	Grunt 5488
12/14/85+	12	13	✓11 Sara	❶[1]	↓		
4/26/86	25	7	12 Tomorrow Doesn't Matter Tonight	26	↓		
2/7/87	16	8	✓13 Nothing's Gonna Stop Us Now	❶[2]	●	No Protection	Grunt 6413
6/27/87	9	9	✓14 It's Not Over ('Til It's Over)	9	↓		
12/17/88+	30	7	15 Wild Again	73	▲[4]	Cocktail (soundtrack)	Elektra 60806
8/5/89	10	11	✓16 It's Not Enough	12		Love Among The Cannibals	RCA 9693

JEFFERSON AIRPLANE:

DEBUT	PEAK	WKS	Mainstream Rock Track	Pop	Gld	Album Title	Album Label & Number
9/2/89	24	6	17 Planes	—		Jefferson Airplane	Epic 45271

JEFFREYS, Garland

Born on 6/29/43 in Brooklyn, New York. Black rock singer.

DEBUT	PEAK	WKS	Mainstream Rock Track	Pop	Gld	Album Title	Album Label & Number
3/21/81	5	10	1 96 Tears	66		Escape Artist	Epic 36983
			#1 Pop hit for ? (Question Mark) & The Mysterians in 1966				
3/28/81	25	9	2 R.O.C.K.	—		↓	

JEREMIAH FREED

Rock group from Portland, Maine: Joe Smith (vocals), Nick Goodale and Jake Roche (guitars), Matt Cosby (bass) and Kerry Ryan (drums).

DEBUT	PEAK	WKS	Mainstream Rock Track	Pop	Gld	Album Title	Album Label & Number
3/30/02	36	6	Again	—		Jeremiah Freed	Republic 017057

JESUS & MARY CHAIN, The

Pop-rock group from Glasgow, Scotland: brothers William and Jim Reid (vocals, guitars), Douglas Hart (bass) and Murray Dalgish (drums). Numerous personnel changes with the Reid brothers the only constants.

DEBUT	PEAK	WKS	Mainstream Rock Track	Pop	Gld	Album Title	Album Label & Number
3/10/90	45	4	Head On	—		Automatic	Warner 26015

JESUS JONES

Pop-rock group formed in London: Mike Edwards (vocals, guitar), Jerry DeBorg (guitar), Iain Baker (keyboards), Al Jaworski (bass) and Simon Matthews (drums).

DEBUT	PEAK	WKS	Mainstream Rock Track	Pop	Gld	Album Title	Album Label & Number
4/6/91	7	20	✓ Right Here, Right Now	2[1]	▲	Doubt	Food 95715

JETHRO TULL

Progressive-rock group formed in Blackpool, England: Ian Anderson (vocals, flute), Martin Barre (guitar), Peter Vettese (keyboards), David Pegg (bass) and Gerry Conway (drums). Conway left in 1983. Vettese left in 1986. Doane Perry (drums) joined in 1989. Group named after 18th-century agriculturist/inventor of seed drill. Also see **Classic Rock Tracks** section.

DEBUT	PEAK	WKS	Mainstream Rock Track	Pop	Gld	Album Title	Album Label & Number
5/8/82	20	7	1 Fallen On Hard Times	108		The Broadsword And The Beast	Chrysalis 1380
5/15/82	50	4	2 Beastie	—		↓	
10/13/84	30	6	3 Lap Of Luxury	—		Under Wraps	Chrysalis 41461
9/26/87	10	8	4 Steel Monkey	—	●	Crest Of A Knave	Chrysalis 41590
10/10/87	7	16	5 Farm On The Freeway	—		↓	
12/26/87+	12	10	6 Jump Start	—		↓	
6/11/88	10	10	7 Part Of The Machine	—		20 Years Of Jethro Tull	Chrysalis 41653
9/9/89	6	10	8 Kissing Willie	—		Rock Island	Chrysalis 21708
8/31/91	14	7	9 This Is Not Love	—		Catfish Rising	Chrysalis 21863

★99★ JETT, Joan, & The Blackhearts

Born Joan Larkin on 9/22/60 in Philadelphia. Rock singer/guitarist. Member of The Runaways from 1975-78. The Blackhearts: Ricky Byrd (guitar), Gary Ryan (bass) and Lee Crystal (drums). Kasim Sulton and Thommy Price replaced Ryan and Crystal in 1987. Jett starred in the 1987 movie *Light Of Day* as the leader of a rock band called **The Barbusters**.

1)I Love Rock 'N Roll 2)Crimson And Clover 3)Little Liar

DEBUT	PEAK	WKS	Mainstream Rock Track	Pop	Gld	Album Title	Album Label & Number
3/21/81+	21	9	✓1 Do You Wanna Touch Me (Oh Yeah)	20		Bad Reputation	Boardwalk 37065
			first recorded by Gary Glitter in 1972				
4/4/81	48	1	✓2 Bad Reputation	—		↓	

DEBUT	PEAK	WKS	Mainstream Rock Track	Pop	Gld	Album Title	Album Label & Number

JETT, Joan, & The Blackhearts — Cont'd

DEBUT	PEAK	WKS	Mainstream Rock Track	Pop	Gld	Album Title	Album Label & Number
12/12/81+	❶⁵	26	3 I Love Rock 'N Roll	❶⁷	▲	I Love Rock-N-Roll	Boardwalk 33243
2/6/82	6	23	4 Crimson And Clover	7	↓		
			#1 Pop hit for Tommy James & The Shondells in 1969				
7/17/82	24	9	5 Summertime Blues	—	↓		
			#8 Pop hit for Eddie Cochran in 1958				
7/9/83	18	10	6 Fake Friends	35	●	Album	Blackheart 5437
8/6/83	30	8	7 The French Song	—	↓		
1/17/87	46	4	8 Roadrunner	—		Good Music	Blackheart 40544
2/21/87	13	8	9 Light Of Day	33		Light Of Day (soundtrack)	Blackheart 40654
			THE BARBUSTERS (JOAN JETT AND THE BLACKHEARTS)				
			written by Bruce Springsteen				
5/7/88	20	11	10 I Hate Myself For Loving You	8	▲	Up Your Alley	Blackheart 44146
11/5/88	13	14	11 Little Liar	19	↓		
1/20/90	23	7	12 Dirty Deeds	36		The Hit List	Blackheart 45473
			JOAN JETT				
9/21/91	40	4	13 Backlash	—		Notorious	Blackheart 47488

JIMMIE'S CHICKEN SHACK
Rock group from Bowie, Maryland: James Davies (vocals), David Dowling (guitar), Che Lemon (bass) and Mike Sipple (drums).

DEBUT	PEAK	WKS	Mainstream Rock Track	Pop	Gld	Album Title	Album Label & Number
8/23/97	20	15	1 High			Pushing The Salmanilla Envelope	Rocket 540724
3/28/98	33	8	2 Dropping Anchor	—	↓		

JIMMY EAT WORLD
Rock group from Mesa, Arizona: Jim Adkins (vocals), Tom Linton (guitar), Rick Burch (bass) and Zach Lind (drums).

DEBUT	PEAK	WKS	Mainstream Rock Track	Pop	Gld	Album Title	Album Label & Number
4/13/02	39	3	The Middle	5	▲	Bleed American	DreamWorks 450334

★88★ JOEL, Billy
Born William Martin Joel on 5/9/49 in the Bronx, New York; raised in Hicksville, Long Island, New York. Member of The Hassles in the late 1960s. Involved in a serious motorcycle accident in Long Island in 1982. Married to supermodel Christie Brinkley from 1985-94. Toured and recorded in Russia in 1987. Recipient of *Billboard's* Century Award in 1994. Inducted into the Rock and Roll Hall of Fame in 1999. Also see **Classic Rock Tracks** section.
1)We Didn't Start The Fire 2)Pressure 3)I Go To Extremes

DEBUT	PEAK	WKS	Mainstream Rock Track	Pop	Gld	Album Title	Album Label & Number
10/3/81	11	10	1 Say Goodbye To Hollywood [L]	17	▲³	Songs In The Attic	Columbia 37461
			recorded at the Milwaukee Arena				
10/2/82	8	18	2 Pressure	20	▲²	The Nylon Curtain	Columbia 38200
10/9/82	38	2	3 Scandinavian Skies	—	↓		
11/13/82	27	5	4 A Room Of Our Own	—	↓		
12/18/82	28	15	5 Allentown	17	↓		
8/6/83	17	13	6 Tell Her About It	❶¹	▲⁷	An Innocent Man	Columbia 38837
10/1/83	22	8	7 Uptown Girl	3	↓		
7/27/85	26	7	8 You're Only Human (Second Wind)	9	▲²¹	Greatest Hits, Volume I & Volume II	Columbia 40121
6/14/86	34	5	9 Modern Woman	10	●	Ruthless People (soundtrack)	Epic 40398
8/16/86	14	12	10 A Matter Of Trust	10	▲²	The Bridge	Columbia 40402
12/13/86+	32	7	11 This Is The Time	18	↓		
10/31/87	45	2	12 Back In The U.S.S.R. [L]	—	▲	Kohu,ept	Columbia 40996
			recorded in Leningrad, Russia; first recorded by **The Beatles** in 1968				
10/14/89	6	8	13 We Didn't Start The Fire	❶²	▲⁴	Storm Front	Columbia 44366
12/2/89+	18	10	14 That's Not Her Style	77	↓		
1/20/90	10	10	15 I Go To Extremes	6	↓		
4/14/90	33	8	16 The Downeaster "Alexa"	57	↓		
8/7/93	18	6	17 No Man's Land	—	▲⁵	River Of Dreams	Columbia 53003

JOHANSEN, David
Born on 1/9/50 in Staten Island, New York. Rock singer/actor. Leader of the New York Dolls from 1971-75. Recorded jazz-pop as Buster Poindexter. Acted in several movies.

DEBUT	PEAK	WKS	Mainstream Rock Track	Pop	Gld	Album Title	Album Label & Number
7/3/82	28	12	We Gotta Get Out Of This Place/Don't Bring Me Down/It's My Life [L]	—		Live It Up	Blue Sky 38004
			medley of hits by **The Animals**: #13 Pop hit in 1965/#12 in 1966/#23 in 1966				

JOHN, Elton
Born Reginald Kenneth Dwight on 3/25/47 in Pinner, Middlesex, England. Pop-rock singer/songwriter/pianist. Formed his first group Bluesology. Took the name of Elton John from the first names of Bluesology members Elton Dean and Long John Baldry. Teamed up with lyricist Bernie Taupin beginning in 1969. Formed Rocket Records in 1973. Played the "Pinball Wizard" in the movie version of *Tommy* in 1994. Inducted into the Rock and Roll Hall of Fame in 1994. Also see **The Bunburys** and **Classic Rock Tracks** section.
1)Runaway Train 2)I Don't Wanna Go On With You Like That 3)Ball & Chain

DEBUT	PEAK	WKS	Mainstream Rock Track	Pop	Gld	Album Title	Album Label & Number
6/20/81	36	4	1 Breaking Down Barriers	—		The Fox	Geffen 2002
5/22/82	14	4	2 Ball & Chain	—	●	Jump Up!	Geffen 2013
6/4/83	34	7	3 I'm Still Standing	12	●	Too Low For Zero	Geffen 4006
1/28/84	22	3	4 I Guess That's Why They Call It The Blues	4	↓		
			Stevie Wonder (harmonica solo)				
6/16/84	24	9	5 Sad Songs (Say So Much)	5	▲	Breaking Hearts	Geffen 24031
7/28/84	16	8	6 Restless	—	↓		
9/15/84	18	8	7 Who Wears These Shoes?	16	↓		

DEBUT	PEAK	WKS	Mainstream Rock Track	Pop	Gld	Album Title	Album Label & Number
			JOHN, Elton — Cont'd				
6/18/88	13	11	8 I Don't Wanna Go On With You Like That	2¹	●	Reg Strikes Back	MCA 6240
8/20/88	22	7	9 Goodbye Marlon Brando	—		↓	
10/22/88	42	3	10 A Word In Spanish	19		↓	
8/26/89	23	8	11 Healing Hands	13	▲	Sleeping With The Past	MCA 6321
8/15/92	10	7	12 Runaway Train	—		Lethal Weapon 3 (soundtrack)	Reprise 26989
			ELTON JOHN and ERIC CLAPTON				
			JOHNNY & THE DISTRACTIONS				
			Rock group from Portland, Oregon: Johnny Koonce (vocals), Mark Spangler (guitar), Gregg Perry (keyboards), Laure Todd (bass) and Kevin Jarvis (drums).				
2/20/82	42	4	1 Shoulder Of The Road	—		Let It Rock	A&M 4884
3/13/82	25	7	2 Complicated Now	—		↓	
			JOHNSON, Don				
			Born on 12/15/49 in Flatt Creek, Missouri. Actor/singer. Played "Sonny Crockett" on TV's *Miami Vice* and title role on TV's *Nash Bridges*. Starred in several movies. Twice married to and divorced from actress Melanie Griffith.				
8/23/86	26	8	Heartbeat	5	●	Heartbeat	Epic 40366
			JOHNSON, Eric				
			Born on 8/17/54 in Austin, Texas. Rock guitarist.				
4/21/90	31	8	1 High Landrons	—	●	Ah Via Musicom	Capitol 90517
8/4/90	5	24	2 Cliffs Of Dover [I]	—		↓	
11/24/90+	8	23	3 Righteous [I]	—		↓	
3/16/91	7	15	4 Trademark [I]	—		↓	
9/7/96	33	7	5 Pavilion	—		Venus Isle	Capitol 98331
			JOHNSTON, Tom				
			Born in Visalia, California. Lead singer/guitarist of **The Doobie Brothers**. Also see **Classic Rock Tracks** section.				
6/13/81	54	4	Madman	—		Still Feels Good	Warner 3527
			JON & VANGELIS				
			Duo of **Jon Anderson** (lead singer of **Yes**; born on 10/25/44 in Lancashire, England) and **Vangelis** (born on 3/29/43 in Valos, Greece).				
8/22/81	33	11	The Friends Of Mr. Cairo	—		The Friends Of Mr. Cairo	Polydor 6326
			JONES, Freddy, Band — see FREDDY				
			JONES, Howard				
			Born on 2/23/55 in Southampton, Hampshire, England. Pop singer/songwriter/keyboardist.				
3/31/84	20	14	1 What Is Love?	33		Human's Lib	Elektra 60346
3/31/84	58	1	2 New Song	27		↓	
4/6/85	21	13	3 Things Can Only Get Better	5	▲	Dream Into Action	Elektra 60390
7/13/85	36	8	4 Life In One Day	19		↓	
4/26/86	20	10	5 No One Is To Blame	4		Action Replay	Elektra 60466
			Phil Collins (drums, backing vocal)				
11/8/86	46	5	6 You Know I Love You...Don't You?	17		One To One	Elektra 60499
4/29/89	49	1	7 Everlasting Love	12		Cross That Line	Elektra 60794
			JONES, Jesus — see JESUS				
			JONES, Mick				
			Born on 12/27/44 in London. Rock guitarist. Member of **Foreigner**. Not to be confused with Mick Jones of The Clash.				
8/12/89	16	8	Just Wanna Hold	—		Mick Jones	Atlantic 81991
			written by Jones, **Ian Hunter** and **Mick Jagger**				
			JONES, Rickie Lee				
			Born on 11/8/54 in Chicago. Female singer/songwriter. Won the 1979 Best New Artist Grammy Award. Also see **Classic Rock Tracks** section.				
8/8/81	31	11	1 Woody And Dutch On The Slow Train To Peking	—	●	Pirates	Warner 3432
8/22/81	40	8	2 Pirates (So Long Lonely Avenue)	—		↓	
			JOPLIN, Janis				
			Born on 1/19/43 in Port Arthur, Texas. Died of a heroin overdose on 10/4/70 (age 27). White blues-rock singer. Nicknamed "Pearl." To San Francisco in 1966, joined Big Brother & The Holding Company. Left band to go solo in 1968. The Bette Midler movie *The Rose* was inspired by Joplin's life. Inducted into the Rock and Roll Hall of Fame in 1995. Also see **Classic Rock Tracks** section.				
1/30/82	35	9	One Night Stand	—		Farewell Song	Columbia 37569
			recorded on 3/28/70				
			JORDAN, Sass				
			Born in 1962 in Montreal. Female rock singer.				
4/25/92	11	16	1 Make You A Believer	—		Racine	Impact 10524
8/1/92	12	12	2 You Don't Have To Remind Me	—		↓	
11/21/92	17	11	3 If You're Gonna Love Me	—		↓	
2/19/94	6	11	4 High Road Easy	—		Rats	Impact/MCA 10980

DEBUT	PEAK	WKS	Mainstream Rock Track	Pop Gld	Album Title	Album Label & Number

JOURNEY ★39★

Rock group formed in San Francisco: **Steve Perry** (vocals), **Neal Schon** (guitar), Jonathan Cain (keyboards), Ross Valory (bass) and Steve Smith (drums). Schon had been in **Santana**. Cain was with The Babys. In 1986 group pared down to a three-man core: Perry, Schon and Cain. The latter two hooked up with **Bad English** in 1989. Smith, Valory and Rolie joined **The Storm** in 1991. Schon with **Hardline** in 1992. Reunion in 1996 of Perry, Schon, Cain, Valory and Smith. Steve Augeri (of **Tall Stories**) replaced Perry in 2001. Also see **Classic Rock Tracks** section.

> 1)Separate Ways (Worlds Apart) 2)Be Good To Yourself 3)The Party's Over (Hopelessly In Love) 4)Only The Young
> 5)Ask The Lonely

3/21/81	2¹	10	1 **The Party's Over** (Hopelessly In Love)	34 ▲²	Captured	Columbia 37016
3/21/81	30	1	2 Dixie Highway [L]	—	↓	
8/1/81	4	20	3 Who's Crying Now	4 ▲⁹	Escape	Columbia 37408
8/1/81	13	20	4 Stone In Love	—	↓	
8/15/81	8	26	5 **Don't Stop Believin'**	9	↓	
1/16/82	35	10	6 Open Arms	2⁶	↓	
7/3/82	47	2	7 Still They Ride	19	↓	
8/14/82	22	5	8 Only Solutions	—	Tron (soundtrack)	CBS 37782
2/5/83	❶⁴	25	9 **Separate Ways** (Worlds Apart)	8 ▲⁶	Frontiers	Columbia 38504
2/26/83	30	4	10 After The Fall	23	↓	
12/3/83+	3	12	11 **Ask The Lonely**	—	▲ Two Of A Kind (soundtrack)	MCA 6127
1/26/85	3	12	12 **Only The Young**	9	▲ Vision Quest (soundtrack)	Geffen 24063
4/12/86	2²	10	13 **Be Good To Yourself**	9 ▲²	Raised On Radio	Columbia 39936
5/10/86	9	18	14 Girl Can't Help It	17	↓	
5/10/86	27	5	15 Raised On Radio	—	↓	
6/14/86	11	10	16 Suzanne	17	↓	
1/10/87	26	6	17 I'll Be Alright Without You	14	↓	
1/2/93	32	5	18 Natural Thing	—	● Time³	Columbia 48937
			recorded in 1979			
10/5/96	18	12	19 Message Of Love	—	▲ Trial By Fire	Columbia 67514
2/8/97	33	5	20 Can't Tame The Lion	—	↓	

JUDAS PRIEST

Hard-rock group formed in Birmingham, England: Rob Halford (vocals), K.K. Downing and Glenn Tipton (guitars), Ian Hill (bass) and Dave Holland (drums). Scott Travis replaced Holland in 1990. Halford later formed **Fight** and **Two**. Also see **Classic Rock Tracks** section.

4/18/81	10	9	1 **Heading Out To The Highway**	—	● Point Of Entry	Columbia 37052
7/31/82	4	37	2 **You've Got Another Thing Comin'**	67	▲ Screaming For Vengeance	Columbia 38160
11/13/82	38	2	3 Electric Eye	—	↓	
3/3/84	42	5	4 Some Heads Are Gonna Roll	—	▲ Defenders Of The Faith	Columbia 39219
3/29/86	25	9	5 Locked In	—	▲ Turbo	Columbia 40158
6/7/86	44	4	6 Turbo Lover	—	↓	
4/23/88	47	1	7 Johnny B. Goode	—	Johnny Be Good (soundtrack)	Atlantic 81837
			#8 Pop hit for Chuck Berry in 1958			
11/10/90	29	8	8 A Touch Of Evil	—	● Painkiller	Columbia 46891

JUNGKLAS, Rob

Born in Boston. Rock singer/songwriter/guitarist.

5/31/86	41	4	1 Boystown	—	Closer To The Flame	Manhattan 53017
1/31/87	41	5	2 Make It Mean Something	86	↓	

JUNKYARD

Hard-rock group formed in Los Angeles: David Roach (vocals), Chris Gates and Brian Baker (guitars), Clay Anthony (bass) and Pat Muzingo (drums).

12/16/89	47	4	1 Simple Man	—	Junkyard	Geffen 24227
6/8/91	24	9	2 All The Time In The World	—	Sixes, Sevens & Nines	Geffen 24372

K

KAJAGOOGOO

Pop group formed in London: Chris "Limahl" Hamill (vocals), Steve Askew (guitar), Stuart Neale (keyboards), Nick Beggs (bass) and Jez Strode (drums).

6/4/83	23	5	Too Shy	5	White Feathers	EMI America 17094

KANSAS

Pop-rock group from Topeka, Kansas: Steve Walsh (vocals, keyboards), Kerry Livgren (guitar, keyboards), Rich Williams (guitar), Robby Steinhart (violin), Dave Hope (bass) and Phil Ehart (drums). John Elefante replaced Walsh in 1981. Revised lineup in 1986: Walsh, Ehart, Williams, Steve Morse (guitar; **The Dregs**) and Billy Greer (bass). Also see **Classic Rock Tracks** section.

5/8/82	4	18	1 Play The Game Tonight	17	Vinyl Confessions	Kirshner 38002
6/19/82	54	2	2 Chasing Shadows	—	↓	
7/10/82	33	6	3 Right Away	73	↓	
8/13/83	3	13	4 Fight Fire With Fire	58	Drastic Measures	CBS Associated 38733
10/22/83	34	3	5 Everybody's My Friend	—	↓	

DEBUT	PEAK	WKS	Mainstream Rock Track	Pop	Gld	Album Title	Album Label & Number
			KANSAS — Cont'd				
9/1/84	54	2	6 Perfect Lover	—	▲³	The Best of Kansas	CBS Associated 39283
11/8/86	10	12	7 All I Wanted	19		Power	MCA 5838
1/24/87	38	7	8 Power	84	↓		
10/8/88	13	8	9 Stand Beside Me	—		In The Spirit Of Things	MCA 6254
			KATRINA AND THE WAVES				
			Pop-rock group formed in London: Katrina Leskanich (vocals; born in Topeka, Kansas), Kimberley Rew (guitar), Vince Dela Cruz (bass) and Alex Cooper (drums).				
4/20/85	21	9	Walking On Sunshine	9		Katrina And The Waves	Capitol 12400
			KAY, John — see STEPPENWOLF				
			KBC BAND				
			Rock trio of former **Jefferson Airplane** bandmates: Paul Kantner (guitar), **Marty Balin** (vocals) and Jack Casady (bass).				
10/11/86	6	13	1 It's Not You, It's Not Me	89		KBC Band	Arista 8440
12/13/86+	8	13	2 America	—	↓		
			KELLY, Paul, and The Messengers				
			Born on 1/12/55 in Adelaide, Australia. Rock singer/songwriter/guitarist. The Messengers: Steve Connolly (guitar), Peter Bull (keyboards), Jon Schofield (bass) and Michael Barclay (drums).				
8/8/87	19	8	1 Darling It Hurts	—		Gossip	A&M 5157
8/13/88	49	3	2 Dumb Things	—		Under The Sun	A&M 5207
			KENDRICK, Eddie — see HALL & OATES				
			KERSHAW, Nik				
			Born on 3/1/58 in Bristol, Somerset, England. Pop singer/songwriter/guitarist.				
5/26/84	58	4	Wouldn't It Be Good	46		Human Racing	MCA 39020
			KID ROCK				
			Born Robert Ritchie on 1/17/71 in Dearborn, Michigan. Hip-hop/rock singer.				
12/5/98+	31	10	1 I Am The Bullgod	—	▲¹⁰	Devil Without A Cause	Lava 83119
4/3/99	11	26	2 Bawitdaba	104	↓		
8/28/99	10	18	3 Cowboy	82	↓		
12/25/99+	5	26	4 Only God Knows Why	19	↓		
9/2/00	35	4	5 Wasting Time	—	↓		
5/13/00	20	13	6 American Bad Ass	—	▲²	The History Of Rock	Lava 83314
11/3/01	18	13	7 Forever	—	▲	Cocky	Lava 83482
2/2/02	15	12	8 Lonely Road Of Faith	—	↓		
5/25/02	32	7	9 You Never Met A Motherf**ker Quite Like Me	—	↓		
			KIHN, Greg, Band				
			Born on 7/10/50 in Baltimore. Rock singer/songwriter/guitarist. His band consisted of Dave Carpender (guitar), Gary Phillips (keyboards), Steve Wright (bass) and Larry Lynch (drums). Greg Douglass replaced Carpender in late 1982. Kihn went solo in late 1984.				
4/11/81	39	4	1 Sheila	102		Rockihnroll	Beserkley 10069
			#1 Pop hit for Tommy Roe in 1962				
4/11/81	57	1	2 The Girl Most Likely	104	↓		
5/2/81	5	21	3 The Breakup Song (They Don't Write 'Em)	15			
4/10/82	5	13	4 Testify	—		Kihntinued	Beserkley 60101
5/15/82	30	5	5 Happy Man	62	↓		
2/5/83	5	16	6 Jeopardy	2¹		Kihnspiracy	Beserkley 60224
5/19/84	9	10	7 Reunited	101		Kihntagious	Beserkley 60354
			GREG KIHN:				
3/2/85	24	7	8 Lucky	30		Citizen Kihn	EMI America 17152
4/19/86	50	2	9 Love And Rock And Roll	92		Love And Rock And Roll	EMI America 17180
			Joe Satriani (lead guitar)				
			KIK TRACEE				
			Hard-rock group formed in Los Angeles: Stephen Shareaux (vocals), Mike Marquis and Gregory Hex (guitars), Rob Grad (bass) and Johnny Douglas (drums).				
9/28/91	47	1	You're So Strange	—		No Rules	RCA 2189
			KILZER, John				
			Born on 4/10/63 in Jackson, Tennessee; raised in Memphis. Rock singer/songwriter/guitarist.				
5/7/88	12	12	1 Red Blue Jeans	—		Memory In The Making	Geffen 24190
8/20/88	36	5	2 Green, Yellow And Red	—	↓		
			KIMMEL, Tom				
			Born in Memphis. Rock singer/songwriter.				
6/20/87	17	8	That's Freedom	64		5 To 1	Mercury 832248
			KIND, The				
			Rock group from Chicago: Frank Capek (vocals, guitar), Frank Jalovec (guitar), Mike Gardner (bass) and Frank Sberno (drums).				
2/25/84	43	3	I've Got You	—		Pain And Pleasure	Three-Sixty 334

DEBUT	PEAK	WKS	Mainstream Rock Track	Pop	Gld	Album Title	Album Label & Number

KING, B.B.
Born Riley King on 9/16/25 in Itta Bena, Mississippi. Legendary blues singer/guitarist. His guitar named "Lucille." Inducted into the Rock and Roll Hall of Fame in 1987. Won Grammy's Lifetime Achievement Award in 1987.

| 10/22/88+ | 2¹ | 20 | 1 When Love Comes To Town | 68 | ▲5 | Rattle And Hum (U2) | Island 91003 |

U2 WITH B.B. KING

| 6/17/00 | 26 | 11 | 2 Riding With The King | — | ▲2 | Riding With The King | Reprise 47612 |

B.B. KING & ERIC CLAPTON
first recorded by **John Hiatt** in 1983

KING CRIMSON
Progressive-rock group formed in England: **Adrian Belew** (vocals, guitar), Robert Fripp (guitar), Tony Levin (bass) and Bill Bruford (drums; **Yes**). Also see **Classic Rock Tracks** section.

| 7/31/82 | 57 | 1 | 1 Heartbeat | — | | Beat | Warner 23692 |
| 4/14/84 | 51 | 3 | 2 Sleepless | — | | Three of a Perfect Pair | Warner 25071 |

KINGDOM COME
Hard-rock group formed in America: Lenny Wolf (vocals; from Hamburg, Germany), Danny Stag and Rick Steier (guitars), Johnny Frank (bass), and James Kottak (drums). In 1984, Wolf formed and fronted **Stone Fury**.

2/13/88	4	12	1 Get It On	69	●	Kingdom Come	Polydor 835368
4/9/88	27	7	2 Living Out Of Touch	—		↓	
6/4/88	26	8	3 What Love Can Be	—		↓	
4/22/89	21	7	4 Do You Like It	—		In Your Face	Polydor 839192
7/8/89	37	4	5 Who Do You Love	—		↓	

KINGOFTHEHILL
Rock-funk group from St. Louis: Frankie (vocals), Jimmy Griffin (guitar), George Potsos (bass) and Vito Bono (drums).

| 3/2/91 | 39 | 8 | 1 I Do U | — | | Kingofthehill | SBK 95827 |
| 8/3/91 | 37 | 4 | 2 If I Say | 63 | | ↓ | |

KINGS OF THE SUN
Hard-rock group from Sydney, Australia: brothers Jeffrey (vocals) and Clifford (drums) Hoad, Glen Morris (guitar) and Anthony Ragg (bass).

| 4/9/88 | 19 | 9 | 1 Serpentine | — | | Kings Of The Sun | RCA 6826 |
| 5/5/90 | 30 | 10 | 2 Drop The Gun | — | | Full Frontal Attack | RCA 9889 |

KING SWAMP
Rock group formed in London: Walter Wray (vocals), Steve Halliwell and Dominic Miller (guitars), Dave Allen (bass) and Martin Barker (drums). Halliwell, Allen and Barker were members of **Shriekback**. Miller, who was replaced by Nick Lashley in 1989, was a member of **World Party**.

| 5/6/89 | 21 | 12 | Is This Love? | — | | King Swamp | Virgin 91069 |

KING'S X
Rock trio from Houston: Douglas Pinnick (vocals, bass), Ty Tabor (guitar) and Jerry Gaskill (drums).

11/10/90+	6	18	1 Its Love	—		Faith Hope Love By King's X	Megaforce 82145
3/28/92	17	11	2 Black Flag	—		King's X	Atlantic 82372
1/29/94	20	9	3 Dogman	—		Dogman	Atlantic 82558

KINISON, Sam
Born on 12/8/53 in Peoria, Illinois. Died in a car crash on 4/10/92 (age 38). Shock comedian/actor. Acted in the movie *Back To School* and the TV show *Charlie Hoover*.

| 11/19/88 | 18 | 8 | Wild Thing | — | ● | Have You Seen Me Lately? | Warner 25748 |

#1 Pop hit for The Troggs in 1966

| | ★100★ | | **KINKS, The** | | | | |

Rock group formed in London: brothers Ray (vocals, guitar) and Dave (guitar, vocals) Davies, Ian Gibbons (keyboards), Jim Rodford (bass) and Mick Avory (drums). Inducted into the Rock and Roll Hall of Fame in 1990. Also see **Classic Rock Tracks** section.

1)Destroyer 2)Do It Again 3)Better Things

8/22/81	12	17	1 Better Things	92	●	Give The People What They Want	Arista 9567
10/3/81	3	16	2 Destroyer	85		↓	
1/15/83	17	17	3 Come Dancing	6		State Of Confusion	Arista 8018
7/9/83	26	10	4 State Of Confusion	—		↓	
10/1/83	16	5	5 Don't Forget To Dance	29		↓	
11/17/84	4	14	6 Do It Again	41		Word Of Mouth	Arista 8264
2/9/85	24	9	7 Living On A Thin Line	—		↓	
12/6/86	37	6	8 Rock 'N' Roll Cities	—		Think Visual	MCA 5822
12/20/86+	16	10	9 Working At The Factory	—		↓	
2/28/87	37	5	10 Lost And Found	—		↓	
1/16/88	14	7	11 The Road	—		The Road	MCA 42107
11/4/89	21	7	12 How Do I Get Close	—		UK Jive	MCA 6337
12/21/91	48	2	13 Did Ya	—		Did Ya	Columbia 74050
4/24/93	19	7	14 Hatred (A Duet)	—		Phobia	Columbia 48724

DEBUT	PEAK	WKS	Mainstream Rock Track	Pop	Gld	Album Title	Album Label & Number
	★87★		**KISS**				

Hard-rock group formed in New York City: Paul Stanley (vocals, guitar), Gene Simmons (vocals, bass), **Ace Frehley** (guitar) and Peter Criss (drums). Noted for elaborate makeup and highly theatrical stage shows; Simmons was made up as "The Bat Lizard," Stanley as "Star Child," Frehley as "Space Man" and Criss as "The Cat." Criss replaced by Eric Carr in 1981. Frehley replaced by Vinnie Vincent in 1984. Group appeared without makeup for the first time in 1983 on *Lick It Up* album cover. Mark St. John replaced Vincent in 1984. Bruce Kulick replaced St. John in 1985. Carr died of cancer on 11/25/91 (age 41); replaced by Eric Singer. The original group reunited in 1996. Also see **Classic Rock Tracks** section.

1)Psycho Circus 2)Jungle 3)Heaven's On Fire

DEBUT	PEAK	WKS	Mainstream Rock Track	Pop	Gld	Album Title	Album Label & Number
10/22/83	19	15	1 Lick It Up	66	▲	Lick It Up	Mercury 814297
9/22/84	11	11	2 Heaven's On Fire	49	▲	Animalize	Mercury 822495
9/28/85	20	9	3 Tears Are Falling	51	●	Asylum	Mercury 826099
9/19/87	37	6	4 Crazy Crazy Nights	65	▲	Crazy Nights	Mercury 832626
11/28/87	34	10	5 Reason To Live	64	↓		
11/4/89	22	11	6 Hide Your Heart	66	●	Hot In The Shade	Mercury 838913
2/10/90	17	11	7 Forever	8	↓		
6/16/90	40	4	8 Rise To It	81	↓		
8/3/91	21	8	9 God Gave Rock And Roll To You II	—		Bill & Ted's Bogus Journey (soundtrack)	Interscope 91725
6/20/92	34	5	10 I Just Wanna	—	●	Revenge	Mercury 848037
8/29/92	26	8	11 Domino	—	↓		
5/29/93	22	6	12 I Love It Loud [L]	—	●	Alive III	Mercury 514777
			studio version was a #102 Pop hit in 1983				
3/30/96	13	10	13 Rock And Roll All Nite [L]	—	●	MTV Unplugged	Mercury 528950
			previous live version was a #12 Pop hit in 1976				
10/18/97	8	14	14 Jungle	—		Carnival Of Souls - The Final Sessions	Mercury 536323
9/5/98	❶¹	21	15 Psycho Circus	—	●	Psycho Circus	Mercury 558992
12/19/98+	22	8	16 You Wanted The Best	—	↓		

KIX

Hard-rock group from Hagerstown, Maryland: Steve Whiteman (vocals), Ronnie Younkins and Brian Forsythe (guitars), Donnie Purnell (bass) and Jimmy Chalfant (drums).

DEBUT	PEAK	WKS	Mainstream Rock Track	Pop	Gld	Album Title	Album Label & Number
10/14/89	16	12	1 Don't Close Your Eyes	11	▲	Blow My Fuse	Atlantic 81877
7/20/91	26	8	2 Girl Money	—		Hot Wire	EastWest 91714
2/22/92	42	5	3 Tear Down The Walls	—	↓		

KNACK, The

Rock group formed in Los Angeles: Doug Fieger (vocals, guitar), Berton Averre (guitar), Prescott Niles (bass) and Billy Ward (drums). Also see **Classic Rock Tracks** section.

DEBUT	PEAK	WKS	Mainstream Rock Track	Pop	Gld	Album Title	Album Label & Number
1/26/91	9	10	Rocket O' Love	—		Serious Fun	Charisma 91607

KORN

Techno-rock group from Huntington Beach, California: Jonathan Davis (vocals), Brian Welch and James Munkey (guitars), Reggie Fieldy Arvizu (bass) and David Silveria (drums).

DEBUT	PEAK	WKS	Mainstream Rock Track	Pop	Gld	Album Title	Album Label & Number
8/22/98	15	26	1 Got The Life	—	▲⁵	Follow The Leader	Immortal 69001
2/20/99	10	26	2 Freak On A Leash	106	↓		
11/13/99+	7	26	3 Falling Away From Me	108	▲²	Issues	Immortal 63710
2/19/00	9	26	4 Make Me Bad	114	↓		
7/29/00	23	9	5 Somebody Someone	—	↓		
3/30/02	4	26	6 Here To Stay	72	▲	Untouchables	Immortal 61488
6/29/02	6	22↑	7 Thoughtless	108	↓		

| | ★75★ | | **KRAVITZ, Lenny** | | | | |

Born on 5/26/64 in New York City. Singer/songwriter/guitarist. Married to actress Lisa Bonet (played "Denise Huxtable" on TV's *The Cosby Show*) from 1989-91. Son of actress Roxie Roker (played "Helen Willis" on TV's *The Jeffersons*).

1)Fly Away 2)Are You Gonna Go My Way 3)American Woman

DEBUT	PEAK	WKS	Mainstream Rock Track	Pop	Gld	Album Title	Album Label & Number
11/25/89+	23	13	1 Let Love Rule	89	●	Let Love Rule	Virgin 91290
5/12/90	50	1	2 Mr. Cab Driver	—	↓		
5/4/91	40	4	3 Always On The Run	—	▲	Mama Said	Virgin 91610
3/20/93	❶²	28	4 Are You Gonna Go My Way	—	▲²	Are You Gonna Go My Way	Virgin 86984
7/3/93	15	11	5 Believe	60	↓		
10/9/93	19	9	6 Is There Any Love In Your Heart	—	↓		
2/19/94	37	4	7 Spinning Around Over You	flip	▲²	Reality Bites (soundtrack)	RCA 66364
6/25/94	15	8	8 Deuce	—	●	Kiss My Ass: Classic Kiss Regrooved (various artists)	Mercury 522123
			Stevie Wonder (harmonica); first recorded by **Kiss** in 1974				
9/2/95	4	10	9 Rock And Roll Is Dead	75	●	Circus	Virgin 40696
7/18/98	❶³	47	10 Fly Away	12	▲²	5	Virgin 45605
5/22/99	3	26	11 American Woman	49	▲	Austin Powers - The Spy Who Shagged Me (soundtrack)	Maverick 47348
			#1 Pop hit for The Guess Who in 1970				
9/29/01	11	19	12 Dig In	31	▲	Lenny	Virgin 11233

DEBUT	PEAK	WKS	Mainstream Rock Track	Pop	Gld	Album Title	Album Label & Number

KROEGER, Chad
Born on 11/15/74 in Hanna, Alberta, Canada. Lead singer of **Nickelback**.

5/4/02	**❶**2	24	**Hero**	3	▲	*Spider-Man* (soundtrack)	Columbia 86402
			CHAD KROEGER Featuring Josey Scott				

KROKUS
Hard-rock group from Zurich, Switzerland: Marc Storace (vocals), Fernando Von Arb and Tommy Kiefer (guitars), Chris Von Rohr (bass) and Freddy Steady (drums). Kiefer was replaced by Mark Kohler in late 1981. Steady was replaced by Steve Pace in late 1982. Pace was replaced by Jeff Klaven in 1984. Von Rohr left in 1984.

4/4/81	46	1	1 **Burning Bones**	—		*Hardware*	Ariola 1508
4/11/81	26	6	2 **Winning Man**	—		↓	
5/1/82	22	5	3 **Long Stick Goes Boom**	—		*One Vice At A Time*	Arista 9591
5/29/82	53	2	4 **American Woman**	—		↓	
			#1 Pop hit for The Guess Who in 1970				
5/28/83	33	1	5 **Eat The Rich**	—	●	*Headhunter*	Arista 9623
6/4/83	21	12	6 **Screaming In The Night**	—		↓	
11/19/83	31	9	7 **Stayed Awake All Night**	—		↓	
8/18/84	10	12	8 **Midnite Maniac**	71	●	*The Blitz*	Arista 8243
11/17/84+	22	11	9 **Our Love**	—		↓	

KULA SHAKER
Rock group from London: Crispian Mills (vocals, guitar), Jay Darlington (keyboards), Alonza Bevan (bass) and Paul Winter-Hart (drums). Mills is the son of actress/singer Hayley Mills.

10/18/97	19	14	**Hush**	—		*I Know What You Did Last Summer* (soundtrack)	Columbia 68696

L

L.A. GUNS
Hard-rock group from Los Angeles: Philip Lewis (vocals), Tracii Guns and Mick Cripps (guitar), Kelly Nickels (bass), and Steve Riley (drums). Guns was also a member of **Contraband** in 1991.

10/21/89	47	3	1 **Rip And Tear**	—	●	*Cocked & Loaded*	Vertigo 838592
4/14/90	25	12	2 **The Ballad of Jayne**	33		↓	
7/6/91	16	11	3 **Kiss My Love Goodbye**	—		*Hollywood Vampires*	Polydor 849485
11/30/91	48	1	4 **Some Lie 4 Love**	—		↓	
2/22/92	25	10	5 **It's Over Now**	62		↓	

LAJON
Born Lajon Witherspoon in Atlanta. Lead singer of **Sevendust**.

11/25/00+	11	18	**Angel's Son**	—		*Strait Up* (various artists)	Immortal 50365

LAKE, Greg
Born on 11/10/48 in Bournemouth, Dorset, England. Guitarist/bassist with **King Crimson** and **Emerson, Lake & Palmer**.

12/5/81+	34	8	**Nuclear Attack**	—		*Greg Lake*	Chrysalis 1357

LANE, Robin, & The Chartbusters
Rock group formed in Boston by female vocalist Lane, with Asa Brebner (guitar), Leroy Radcliffe (keyboards), Scott Baerenwald (bass) and Tim Jackson (drums). Lane is the daughter of Dean Martin's pianist, Ken Lane.

5/9/81	53	1	**Send Me An Angel**	—		*Imitation Life*	Warner 3537

LANG, Jonny
Born Jon Langseth on 1/29/81 in Minneapolis. Blues-rock singer/guitarist.

3/8/97	12	22	1 **Lie To Me**	—	▲	*Lie To Me*	A&M 540640
8/30/97	28	7	2 **Hit The Ground Running**	—		↓	
10/3/98	8	26	3 **Still Rainin'**	—	▲	*Wander This World*	A&M 540984
3/13/99	23	12	4 **Wander This World**	—		↓	

LAUPER, Cyndi
Born on 6/20/53 in Queens, New York. Pop-rock singer. Won the 1984 Best New Artist Grammy Award. In the movies *Vibes* and *Life With Mikey*. Married actor David Thornton on 11/24/91.

12/17/83+	10	18	1 **Time After Time**	**❶**2	▲6	*She's So Unusual*	Portrait 38930
1/21/84	16	10	2 **Girls Just Want To Have Fun**	22		↓	
8/4/84	27	9	3 **She Bop**	3		↓	
10/20/84	38	6	4 **All Through The Night**	5		↓	
1/5/85	37	5	5 **Money Changes Everything**	27		↓	

LAW, The
Rock duo from England: vocalist **Paul Rodgers** (Bad Company) and drummer Kenney Jones (**The Who**).

3/16/91	2¹	16	1 **Laying Down The Law**	—		*The Law*	Atlantic 82195
6/8/91	38	7	2 **Miss You In A Heartbeat**	—		↓	
			#39 Pop hit for **Def Leppard** in 1994				

DEBUT	PEAK	WKS	Mainstream Rock Track	Pop Gld	Album Title	Album Label & Number

LED ZEPPELIN

Hard-rock group formed in England: **Robert Plant** (vocals), **Jimmy Page** (guitar), John Paul Jones (bass, keyboards) and John Bonham (drums). First known as the New Yardbirds. Page had been in The Yardbirds from 1966-68. Plant and Bonham had been in a group called Band Of Joy. Group formed own Swan Song label in 1974. In concert movie *The Song Remains The Same* in 1976. Bonham died of asphyxiation on 9/25/80 (age 33). Group disbanded in December 1980. Plant and Page formed **The Honeydrippers** in 1984. Page also with **The Firm** (1984-86). "**Bonham**" is the name of group formed by Jason Bonham, John's son, in 1989. Group inducted into the Rock and Roll Hall of Fame in 1995. Also see **Classic Rock Tracks** section.

DEBUT	PEAK	WKS	Mainstream Rock Track	Pop Gld	Album Title	Album Label & Number
12/11/82	4	11	1 **Darlene** recorded on 11/16/78	— ▲	*Coda*	Swan Song 90051
12/11/82	14	11	2 **Ozone Baby** recorded on 11/14/78	— ↓		
12/18/82	18	7	3 **Poor Tom** recorded on 6/5/70	— ↓		
10/20/90	7	8	4 **Travelling Riverside Blues** [L] recorded on 6/23/69	— ▲10	*Led Zeppelin (Boxed Set)*	Atlantic 82144
9/25/93	4	7	5 **Baby Come On Home** recorded on 10/10/68	— ▲2	*Boxed Set 2*	Atlantic 82477
11/15/97	4	22	6 **The Girl I Love She Got Long Black Wavy Hair** [L] recorded on 6/16/69	— ▲2	*BBC Sessions*	Atlantic 83061

LEE, Alvin

Born on 12/19/44 in Nottingham, England. Rock singer/guitarist. Leader of **Ten Years After**.

| 7/26/86 | 24 | 8 | **Detroit Diesel** | — | *Detroit Diesel* | 21 Records 90517 |

LEE, Geddy

Born Gary Lee Weinrib on 7/29/53 in Toronto. Lead singer/bassist of **Rush**.

| 11/4/00 | 20 | 12 | 1 **My Favorite Headache** | — | *My Favorite Headache* | Anthem 83384 |
| 2/3/01 | 28 | 6 | 2 **Grace To Grace** | ↓ | | |

LEE, Tommy

Born Thomas Lee Bass on 10/3/62 in Athens, Greece; raised in West Covina, California. Rock singer/drummer. Former member of **Mötley Crüe**. Married to actress Heather Locklear from 1986-93. Married to actress Pamela Anderson from 1995-98.

| 3/30/02 | 5 | 26 | **Hold Me Down** | — | *Never A Dull Moment* | MCA 112856 |

LENNON, John

Born on 10/9/40 in Liverpool, England. Shot to death in New York City on 12/8/80 (age 40). Founding member of **The Beatles**. Married to Cynthia Powell from 1962-68; their son is **Julian** Lennon. Met Yoko Ono in 1966; married her on 3/20/69. Formed Plastic Ono Band in 1969. To New York City in 1971. Fought deportation from the U.S., 1972-76, until he was granted a permanent visa. Won Grammy's Lifetime Achievement Award in 1991. Inducted into the Rock and Roll Hall of Fame in 1994. Also see **Classic Rock Tracks** section.

3/21/81	26	3	1 **Woman**	2³ ▲³	*Double Fantasy*	Geffen 2001
3/21/81	54	3	2 **I'm Losing You**	— ↓		
3/28/81	25	9	3 **Watching The Wheels**	10 ↓		
1/21/84	2¹	10	4 **Nobody Told Me**	5 ●	*Milk and Honey*	Polydor 817160
2/11/84	34	7	5 **I'm Stepping Out**	55 ↓		
9/29/84	52	3	6 **Every Man Has A Woman Who Loves Him** first recorded by Yoko Ono in 1980; all of above recorded in 1980 (shortly before Lennon's death)	—	*Every Man Has A Woman* (various artists)	Polydor 823490
2/8/86	25	7	7 **Come Together** [L] #1 Pop hit for **The Beatles** in 1969	— ●	*Live In New York City*	Capitol 12451
2/15/86	20	6	8 **Imagine** studio version was a #3 Pop hit in 1971; above 2 recorded on 8/30/72 at Madison Square Garden	— ↓		
10/8/88	12	6	9 **Jealous Guy** **JOHN LENNON AND THE PLASTIC ONO BAND (with The Flux Fiddlers)** first released on the 1971 album *Imagine*	80 ●	*Imagine: John Lennon*	Capitol 90803

LENNON, Julian

Born on 4/8/63 in Liverpool, England. Singer/songwriter/keyboardist. Son of Cynthia and **John Lennon**.

10/20/84	2¹	14	✓ 1 **Valotte**	9 ●	*Valotte*	Atlantic 80184
12/8/84+	11	18	2 **Too Late For Goodbyes**	5 ↓		
4/20/85	3	10	3 **Say You're Wrong**	21 ↓		
3/22/86	❶³	13	✓ 4 **Stick Around**	32 ●	*The Secret Value of DayDreaming*	Atlantic 81640
3/18/89	❶¹	10	✓ 5 **Now You're In Heaven**	93	*Mr. Jordan*	Atlantic 81928
8/24/91	31	6	✓ 6 **Listen**	—	*Help Yourself*	Atlantic 82280

LE ROUX

Rock group from Louisiana: Jeff Pollard (vocals), Tony Haselden (guitar), Rod Roddy (keyboards), Bobby Campo (horns), Leon Medica (bass) and David Peters (drums).

| 2/13/82 | 7 | 11 | **Addicted** | — | *Last Safe Place* | RCA Victor 4195 |

LEVEL 42

Pop-rock group formed in Manchester, England: Mark King (vocals, bass), brothers Boon (guitar) and Phil (drums) Gould, and Mike Lindup (keyboards).

| 4/12/86 | 45 | 4 | **Something About You** | 7 | *World Machine* | Polydor 827487 |

LEWIS, Aaron

Born on 4/13/72 in Boston. Rock singer. Lead singer of **Staind**.

| 12/16/00+ | ❶² | 26 | **Outside** [L]
 AARON LEWIS from Staid (with Fred Durst) | 56 | *The Family Values Tour 1999*
 (various artists) | Flawless 490641 |

DEBUT	PEAK	WKS	Mainstream Rock Track	Pop	Gld	Album Title	Album Label & Number

LEWIS, Huey, and The News ★27★

Born Hugh Cregg III on 7/5/50 in New York City. Pop-rock singer/songwriter. Formed the News in San Francisco: Chris Hayes (guitar), Sean Hopper (keyboards), Johnny Colla (sax), Mario Cipollina (bass) and Bill Gibson (drums). Lewis acted in the movies *Back To The Future* and *Short Cuts*.

1)The Power Of Love 2)Heart And Soul 3)Hip To Be Square 4)Stuck With You 5)Back In Time

DEBUT	PEAK	WKS	Track	Pop	Gld	Album Title	Label & Number
2/27/82	12	10	1 Do You Believe In Love	7	●	*Picture This*	Chrysalis 1340
3/20/82	20	13	2 Workin' For A Livin'	41		↓	
10/8/83	❶¹	17	3 Heart And Soul	8	▲⁷	*Sports*	Chrysalis 41412
10/22/83	7	23	4 I Want A New Drug	6		↓	
2/18/84	16	15	5 Walking On A Thin Line	18		↓	
3/17/84	5	19	6 The Heart Of Rock & Roll	6		↓	
7/28/84	3	12	7 If This Is It	6		↓	
9/15/84	41	5	8 Finally Found A Home	—		↓	
4/20/85	11	10	9 Trouble In Paradise [L]		▲³	*We Are The World* (USA For Africa)	Columbia 40043
			recorded on 2/21/85 in San Francisco				
6/29/85	❶²	14	10 The Power Of Love	❶²	●	*Back To The Future* (soundtrack)	MCA 6144
7/27/85	3	14	11 Back In Time			↓	
8/2/86	2²	8	12 Stuck With You	❶³	▲³	*Fore!*	Chrysalis 41534
9/6/86	❶¹	13	13 Hip To Be Square	3		↓	
9/6/86	10	23	14 Jacob's Ladder	❶¹		↓	
			co-written by **Bruce Hornsby**				
9/6/86	25	10	15 I Know What I Like	9		↓	
9/13/86	38	6	16 Whole Lotta Lovin'	—		↓	
7/16/88	5	8	17 Perfect World	3	▲	*Small World*	Chrysalis 41622
8/20/88	47	3	18 Walking With The Kid	—		↓	
8/27/88	28	8	19 Small World	25		↓	
4/27/91	3	10	20 Couple Days Off	11	●	*Hard At Play*	EMI 93355
7/6/91	27	7	21 Build Me Up	—		↓	

LIFEHOUSE

Rock trio from Malibu, California: Jason Wade (vocals, guitar), Sergio Andrade (bass) and Rick Woolstenhulme (drums).

11/25/00+	7	28	1 Hanging By A Moment	2⁴	▲²	*No Name Face*	DreamWorks 50231
6/30/01	38	1	2 Sick Cycle Carousel	—		↓	
8/17/02	34	4	3 Spin	84↑		*Stanley Climbfall*	DreamWorks 50377

LIFE OF AGONY

Rock group from Brooklyn, New York: Keith Caputo (vocals), Joey Z (guitar), Alan Robert (bass) and Dan Richardson (drums). Joey Z and Richardson later joined **Stereomud**.

11/8/97	27	13	1 Weeds	—		*Soul Searching Sun*	Roadrunner 8816
4/11/98	37	3	2 Tangerine	—		↓	

LIMP BIZKIT

Hard-rock/hip-hop group from Jacksonville, Florida: **Fred Durst** (vocals; born on 8/20/71), Wes Borland (guitar; born on 2/8/75), Sam Rivers (bass; born in 1979) and John Otto (drums; born in 1978). Also see **Aaron Lewis**.

1/2/99	33	11	1 Faith	—	▲²	*Three Dollar Bill, Y'all$*	Flip 90124
			#1 Pop hit for George Michael in 1987				
6/19/99	6	26	2 Nookie	80	▲⁷	*Significant Other*	Flip 90335
10/16/99	8	26	3 Re-Arranged	88		↓	
3/4/00	19	26	4 Break Stuff	123		↓	
5/27/00	15	17	5 Take A Look Around	115	▲	*Mission: Impossible 2* (soundtrack)	Hollywood 62244
9/23/00	10	26	6 Rollin' (Urban Assault Vehicle)	65	▲⁵	*Chocolate Starfish And The Hot Dog Flavored Water*	Flip 490759
9/23/00	33	7	7 My Generation	—		↓	
3/3/01	4	26	8 My Way	75		↓	
7/28/01	30	8	9 Boiler	—		↓	

LINDLEY, David

Born in 1944 in San Marino, California. Rock session guitarist.

5/9/81	34	13	Mercury Blues	—		*El Rayo-X*	Asylum 524
			#2 Country hit for Alan Jackson in 1993				

LINKIN PARK

Rap-rock group from Los Angeles: Chester Bennington (vocals), Mike Shinoda (rap vocals), Joseph Hahn (DJ), Brad Delson (guitar), Darren "Phoenix" Farrell (bass) and Rob Bourdon (drums).

9/16/00+	4	42	1 One Step Closer	75	▲⁸	*Hybrid Theory*	Warner 47755
4/21/01	3	34	2 Crawling	79		↓	
9/22/01	3	41	3 In The End	2¹		↓	
5/25/02	37	9	4 Runaway	—		↓	

Mainstream Rock

DEBUT	PEAK	WKS	Mainstream Rock Track	Pop	Gld	Album Title	Album Label & Number
			LIT Rock group from Los Angeles: brothers A.J. (vocals) and Jeremy (bass) Popoff, Kevin Blades (bass) and Allen Shellenberger (drums).				
3/27/99	6	26	✓1 My Own Worst Enemy	51	▲	A Place In The Sun	RCA 67775
9/25/99	34	6	2 Zip-Lock	—		↓	
3/4/00	29	10	3 Miserable	117		↓	
9/15/01	28	9	4 Lipstick And Bruises	—		Atomic	RCA 68086
			LITTLE AMERICA Rock group formed in Los Angeles: Mike Magrisi (vocals, bass), Andy Logan and John Hussey (guitars), and Custer (drums).				
4/11/87	10	12	1 Walk On Fire	—		Little America	Geffen 24113
2/18/89	17	11	2 Where Were You	—		Fairgrounds	Geffen 24200
			LITTLE CAESAR Hard-rock group formed in Los Angeles: Ron Young (vocals), Apache and Louren Molinare (guitars), Fidel Paniagua (bass), and Tom Morris (drums). Group named after a 1930 gangster movie.				
5/19/90	17	10	1 Chain Of Fools	88		Little Caesar	DGC 24288
			#2 Pop hit for **Aretha Franklin** in 1968				
2/23/91	35	7	2 In Your Arms	79		↓	
			LITTLE FEAT Rock group formed in Los Angeles: Lowell George (vocals), Paul Barrere (guitar), Bill Payne (keyboards), Kenny Gradney (bass), Sam Clayton (percussion) and Richard Hayward (drums). Disbanded in April 1979. George died of drug-related heart failure on 6/29/79 (age 34). Regrouped in 1988, adding Craig Fuller (vocals, guitar) and Fred Tackett (guitar).				
8/22/81	34	10	1 Rock And Roll Doctor	—		Hoy-Hoy!	Warner 3538
			recorded in 1976				
7/30/88	❶⁴	11	2 Hate To Lose Your Lovin'	—	●	Let It Roll	Warner 25750
8/20/88	3	13	3 Let It Roll	—		↓	
10/29/88	19	11	4 Long Time Till I Get Over You	—		↓	
1/21/89	10	11	5 One Clear Moment	—		↓	
7/22/89	23	7	6 Rad Gumbo	—		Road House (soundtrack)	Arista 8576
4/7/90	❶¹	12	7 Texas Twister	—		Representing The Mambo	Warner 26163
6/23/90	21	8	8 Woman In Love	—		↓	
9/7/91	14	10	9 Shake Me Up	—		Shake Me Up	Morgan Creek 20005
			LITTLE RIVER BAND Pop-rock group formed in Australia: Glenn Shorrock (vocals), Graham Goble, Beeb Birtles and David Briggs (guitars), Wayne Nelson (bass), and Derek Pellicci (drums). Lineup in 1985: John Farnham (vocals), Goble and Stephen Housden (guitars), David Hirschfelder (keyboards), Nelson (bass) and Steven Prestwich (drums).				
9/5/81	9	16	1 The Night Owls	6	●	Time Exposure	Capitol 12163
1/26/85	15	11	2 Playing To Win	60		Playing To Win	Capitol 12365
			LRB				
			LITTLE STEVEN AND THE DISCIPLES OF SOUL Born Steven Van Zandt on 11/22/50 in Boston; raised in New Jersey. Rock singer/guitarist/actor. Member of **Bruce Springsteen**'s E Street Band. Organized **Artists United Against Apartheid**. Plays "Silvio Dante" on TV's The Sopranos.				
11/6/82	30	5	1 Lyin' In A Bed Of Fire	—		Men Without Women	EMI America 17086
1/29/83	39	3	2 Forever	63		↓	
6/9/84	27	8	3 Los Desaparecidos (The Disappeared Ones)	—		Voice Of America	EMI America 17120
5/16/87	29	6	4 Trail Of Broken Treaties	—		Freedom No Compromise	Manhattan 53048
3/4/00	40	2	5 Salvation	—		Born Again Savage	Renegade Nation 6
			LITTLE STEVEN				
			LITTLE VILLAGE All-star group: **John Hiatt** (vocals), Ry Cooder (guitar), **Nick Lowe** (bass) and Jim Keltner (drums).				
2/29/92	17	9	1 She Runs Hot	—		Little Village	Reprise 26713
5/16/92	35	7	2 Solar Sex Panel	—		↓	
	★41★		**LIVE** Rock group formed in York, Pennsylvania: Edward Kowalczyk (vocals; born on 7/16/71), Chad Taylor (guitar; born on 11/24/70), Patrick Dahlheimer (bass; born on 5/30/71) and Chad Gracey (drums; born on 7/23/71).				
			1)Lightning Crashes 2)The Dolphin's Cry 3)Lakini's Juice				
6/4/94	4	25	1 Selling The Drama	43	▲⁸	Throwing Copper	Radioactive 10997
9/24/94	6	26	2 I Alone	38ᴬ		↓	
2/11/95	❶¹⁰	26	3 Lightning Crashes	12ᴬ		↓	
6/3/95	2¹	26	4 All Over You	33ᴬ		↓	
8/5/95	12	12	5 White, Discussion	71ᴬ		↓	
2/1/97	2⁴	26	6 Lakini's Juice	35ᴬ	▲	Secret Samadhi	Radioactive 11590
4/26/97	5	14	7 Freaks	73ᴬ		↓	
7/12/97	3	15	8 Turn My Head	45ᴬ		↓	
10/25/97	15	14	9 Rattlesnake	—		↓	
9/4/99	2⁶	26	10 The Dolphin's Cry	78	▲	The Distance To Here	Radioactive 11966
2/12/00	17	12	11 Run To The Water	—		↓	
8/5/00	24	8	12 They Stood Up For Love	—		↓	
8/11/01	11	11	13 Simple Creed	—		V.	Radioactive 12485
			LIVE Featuring Tricky				

DEBUT	PEAK	WKS	Mainstream Rock Track	Pop Gld	Album Title	Album Label & Number
			LIVING COLOUR			
			Black rock group from New York City: Corey Glover (vocals), Vernon Reid (guitar), Muzz Skillings (bass) and William Calhoun (drums). Doug Wimbish replaced Skillings in early 1992. Glover played "Francis" in the movie *Platoon*.			
12/17/88+	9	20	1 Cult Of Personality	13 ▲²	*Vivid*	Epic 44099
4/15/89	11	10	2 Open Letter (To A Landlord)	82	↓	
9/23/89	26	7	3 Glamour Boys	31	↓	
			Mick Jagger (producer, backing vocal)			
9/8/90	5	9	4 Type	— ●	*Time's Up*	Epic 46202
11/24/90	42	4	5 Pride	—	↓	
2/2/91	28	10	6 Love Rears Its Ugly Head	—	↓	
3/6/93	14	10	7 Leave It Alone	—	*Stain*	Epic 52780
			LOCAL H			
			Rock duo from Zion, Illinois: Scott Lucas (vocals, guitar, bass) and Joe Daniels (drums).			
9/28/96	10	26	1 Bound For The Floor	46ᴬ	*As Good As Dead*	Island 524202
4/5/97	36	3	2 Fritz's Corner	—	↓	
8/29/98	19	12	3 All The Kids Are Right	—	*Pack Up The Cats*	Island 524549
3/23/02	40	1	4 Half Life	—	*Here Comes The Zoo*	Palm 2072
			LOFGREN, Nils			
			Born on 6/21/51 in Chicago; raised in Maryland. Pop-rock singer/guitarist/pianist. Member of **Bruce Springsteen**'s E Street Band from 1984-85.			
3/2/91	37	8	Valentine	—	*Silver Lining*	Rykodisc 10170
			Bruce Springsteen (harmony vocal)			
			LOGGINS, Kenny			
			Born on 1/7/47 in Everett, Washington; raised in Alhambra, California. Pop-rock singer/songwriter/guitarist.			
9/4/82	4	16	1 Don't Fight It	17 ●	*High Adventure*	Columbia 38127
			KENNY LOGGINS with Steve Perry			
2/4/84	2²	14	2 Footloose	❶³ ▲⁹	*Footloose* (soundtrack)	Columbia 39242
5/5/84	42	9	3 I'm Free (Heaven Helps The Man)	22	↓	
3/30/85	18	8	4 Vox Humana	29 ●	*Vox Humana*	Columbia 39174
5/24/86	7	11	5 Danger Zone	2¹ ▲⁹	*Top Gun* (soundtrack)	Columbia 40323
7/23/88	30	6	6 Nobody's Fool	8	*Caddyshack II* (soundtrack)	Columbia 44317
			LONDON QUIREBOYS, The			
			Hard-rock group formed in London: Spike (vocals), Guy Bailey and Guy Griffin (guitars), Chris Johnstone (keyboards), Nigel Mogg (bass) and Ian Wallace (drums).			
3/24/90	15	13	7 O'Clock	—	*A Bit Of What You Fancy*	Capitol 93177
			LONE JUSTICE			
			Country-rock group from Los Angeles: Maria McKee (vocals), Ryan Hedgecock (guitar), Marvin Etzioni (bass) and Don Heffington (drums). Etzioni and Heffington left in early 1986; Shane Fontayne (guitar), Bruce Brody (keyboards), Gregg Sutton (bass) and Rudy Richman (drums) joined.			
5/18/85	29	7	1 Ways To Be Wicked	71	*Lone Justice*	Geffen 24060
			co-written by **Tom Petty**			
11/15/86	26	10	2 Shelter	47	*Shelter*	Geffen 24122
			LORDAN, Bill — see TROWER, Robin			
			LORDS OF THE NEW CHURCH, The			
			Rock group formed in England: Cleveland native Stiv Bator (vocals), Brian James (guitar), Dave Tregunna (bass) and Nicky Turner (drums). Bator died after being struck by a car on 6/4/90 (age 40).			
7/31/82	27	7	Open Your Eyes	—	*The Lords Of The New Church*	I.R.S. 70029
			LORD TRACY			
			Rock group from Texas: Terrence Lee Glaze (vocals), Jimmy Rusidoff (guitar), Kinley Wolfe (bass) and Chris Craig (drums).			
12/9/89+	40	6	Out With The Boys	—	*Deaf Gods Of Babylon*	Uni 606
			LOS LOBOS			
			Latin rock group formed in East Los Angeles: David Hildago (vocals), Cesar Rosas (guitar), Steve Berlin (sax), Conrad Lozano (bass) and Louie Perez (drums).			
12/8/84+	28	9	1 Don't Worry Baby	—	*How Will The Wolf Survive?*	Slash 25177
3/16/85	26	7	2 Will The Wolf Survive?	78	↓	
1/17/87	4	13	3 Shakin' Shakin' Shakes	—	*By The Light Of The Moon*	Slash 25523
4/4/87	21	8	4 Set Me Free (Rosa Lee)	—	↓	
7/11/87	11	9	5 La Bamba [F]	❶³ ▲²	*La Bamba* (soundtrack)	Slash 25605
			#22 Pop hit for Ritchie Valens in 1959			
9/12/87	33	7	6 Come On, Let's Go	21	↓	
			#42 Pop hit for Ritchie Valens in 1958			
9/15/90	33	6	7 Down On The Riverbed	—	*The Neighborhood*	Slash 26131
5/18/91	37	5	8 Bertha	—	*Deadicated* (various artists)	Arista 8669
			first recorded by the **Grateful Dead** in 1971			

DEBUT	PEAK	WKS	Mainstream Rock Track	Pop Gld	Album Title	Album Label & Number
			LOUD LUCY			
			Rock trio from Chicago: Christian Lane (vocals, guitar), Tom Furar (bass) and Mark Doyle (drums).			
2/10/96	**38**	2	**Ticking**	—	*Breathe*	DGC 24733
			LOUDMOUTH			
			Rock group from Chicago: Bob Feddersen (vocals), Tony McQuaid (guitar), Mike Flaherty (bass) and John Sullivan (drums).			
3/20/99	**11**	18	**Fly**	—	*Loudmouth*	Hollywood 62181
			LOVE AND ROCKETS			
			Pop-rock trio formed in England: **Daniel Ash** (vocals, guitar), **David J** (bass) and Kevin Haskins (drums).			
1/17/87	**49**	4	1 **All In My Mind**..	—	*Express*	Big Time 6011
12/5/87+	**18**	13	2 **No New Tale To Tell**	—	*Earth.Sun.Moon.*	Big Time 6058
5/13/89	**9**	16	3 **So Alive**	3 ●	*Love And Rockets*	Beggars Banquet 9715
			LOVE/HATE			
			Rock group from Los Angeles: Jizzy Pearl (vocal), Jon Love (guitar), Skid Rose (bass) and Joey Gold (drums).			
9/22/90	**46**	4	**Why Do You Think They Call It Dope?**	—	*Blackout In The Red Room.*	Columbia 45263
	★77★		**LOVERBOY**			
			Rock group formed in Canada: Mike Reno (vocals), **Paul Dean** (guitar), Doug Johnson (keyboards), Scott Smith (bass) and Matt Frenette (drums). Smith drowned on 11/30/2000 (age 45).			
			1)Hot Girls In Love 2)Working For The Weekend 3)Lovin' Every Minute Of It			
3/21/81	**6**	15	1 **Turn Me Loose**	35 ▲²	*Loverboy*..........................	Columbia 36762
6/6/81	**42**	8	2 **The Kid Is Hot Tonite**	55 ↓		
11/21/81+	**2**¹	22	3 **Working For The Weekend**	29 ▲⁴	*Get Lucky*	Columbia 37638
1/23/82	**21**	22	4 **When It's Over**..	26 ↓		
			Nancy Nash (backing vocal)			
2/20/82	**36**	9	5 **Lucky Ones**..	— ↓		
4/10/82	**23**	10	6 **Take Me To The Top**	— ↓		
6/11/83	**2**³	14	7 **Hot Girls In Love**	11 ▲²	*Keep It Up.*	Columbia 38703
7/16/83	**23**	14	8 **Strike Zone**	— ↓		
7/30/83	**11**	15	9 **Queen Of The Broken Hearts**	34 ↓		
8/24/85	**3**	13	10 **Lovin' Every Minute Of It**	9 ▲²	*Lovin' Every Minute Of It.*	Columbia 39953
11/16/85	**23**	10	11 **Dangerous**	65 ↓		
2/1/86	**9**	9	12 **This Could Be The Night**	10 ↓		
8/22/87	**8**	7	13 **Notorious**	38 ●	*Wildside*	Columbia 40893
			co-written by **Jon Bon Jovi**			
12/2/89+	**27**	8	14 **Too Hot**	84	*Big Ones*	Columbia 45411
			LOVETT, Lyle			
			Born on 11/1/56 in Houston; raised in Klein, Texas. Country singer/songwriter/guitarist. Acted in several movies. Married to actress Julia Roberts from 1993-95.			
9/19/92	**36**	2	**You've Been So Good Up To Now**	— ●	*Joshua Judges Ruth*	Curb 10475
			LOVICH, Lene			
			Born Lili Marlene Premilovich on 3/30/49 in Detroit; raised in England. Singer/actress. Acted in the movies *Cha-Cha* and *Mata Hari.*			
12/25/82	**51**	4	**It's You, Only You (Mein Schmerz)**..........................	—	*No-Man's-Land.*	Stiff 38399
			LOWE, Nick			
			Born on 3/25/49 in Walton, Surrey, England. Pop-rock singer/songwriter/guitarist. Member of **Rockpile** and **Little Village**. Married to country singer Carlene Carter from 1979-90. Also see **Classic Rock Tracks** section.			
3/6/82	**43**	8	1 **Stick It Where The Sun Don't Shine**	—	*Nick The Knife.*	Columbia 37932
9/14/85	**27**	9	2 **I Knew The Bride (When She Use To Rock And Roll)**	77	*The Rose Of England*	Columbia 39958
			NICK LOWE AND HIS COWBOY OUTFIT			
			produced by Huey Lewis			
			LRB — see LITTLE RIVER BAND			
			LYNCH MOB			
			Hard-rock group formed in Los Angeles: George Lynch (guitar), Oni Logan (vocals), Anthony Esposito (bass) and Mick Brown (drums). Lynch and Brown were members of **Dokken**. Esposito was a member of **Beggars & Thieves**.			
11/17/90	**31**	9	1 **Wicked Sensation**	—	*Wicked Sensation.*	Elektra 60954
2/2/91	**19**	9	2 **River Of Love**	— ↓		
5/9/92	**13**	13	3 **Tangled In The Web**	—	*Lynch Mob*	Elektra 61322
8/29/92	**23**	11	4 **Dream Until Tomorrow**	— ↓		
			LYNNE, Jeff			
			Born on 12/30/47 in Birmingham, England. Leader of **Electric Light Orchestra**. Member of the **Traveling Wilburys**. Production work for **George Harrison**, **Roy Orbison** and **Tom Petty**.			
6/2/90	**9**	10	**Every Little Thing**	—	*Armchair Theatre.*	Reprise 26184
			George Harrison (guitar, backing vocal)			

DEBUT	PEAK	WKS	Mainstream Rock Track	Pop Gld	Album Title	Album Label & Number

LYNYRD SKYNYRD
Rock group formed in Jacksonville, Florida: Ronnie Van Zant (vocals), Gary Rossington, Allen Collins and Steve Gaines (guitars), Billy Powell (keyboards), Leon Wilkeson (bass) and Artimus Pyle (drums). Plane crash on 10/20/77 in Gillsburg, Mississippi, killed Ronnie Van Zant and Steve Gaines. Gary and Allen formed the **Rossington Collins Band**. Rossington and vocalist **Johnny Van Zant** (the younger brother of Ronnie and **38 Special** lead singer Donnie Van Zant) regrouped with old and new band members for the 1987 Lynyrd Skynyrd Tribute Tour. Collins (paralyzed in a car accident in 1986) died of pneumonia on 1/23/90 (age 37). Surviving members regrouped in 1991. Original drummer Ricky Medlocke (of **Blackfoot**) joined as a guitarist in 1995. Guitarist Hughie Thomasson (of **The Outlaws**) joined in 1996. Wilkeson died on 7/27/2001 (age 49). Also see **Classic Rock Tracks** section.
1)Smokestack Lightning 2)Good Lovin's Hard To Find 3)Keeping The Faith

DEBUT	PEAK	WKS	Track		Album	Label
9/26/87	12	7	1 Truck Drivin' Man .... [L]	— ●	Legend .... MCA 42084
			previously unreleased song (vocals by Ronnie Van Zant)		
3/26/88	16	7	2 Swamp Music.. [L]	—	Southern By The Grace Of God/Lynyrd Skynyrd
			recorded on 10/23/87 at the Starwood Ampitheatre in Nashville		Tribute Tour - 1987.................. MCA 8027
6/8/91	2[1]	12	3 Smokestack Lightning	—	Lynyrd Skynyrd 1991............... Atlantic 82258
8/10/91	10	9	4 Keeping The Faith	—	↓
2/27/93	6	9	5 Good Lovin's Hard To Find	—	The Last Rebel .... Atlantic 82447
5/22/93	37	2	6 Born To Run	—	↓
5/10/97	22	8	7 Travelin' Man	—	Twenty .... CMC International 86211
8/16/97	33	5	8 Bring It On	—	↓
7/31/99	13	15	9 Workin'	—	Edge Of Forever........... CMC International 86272
11/27/99	26	12	10 Preacher Man	—	↓

M

MAD AT GRAVITY
Rock group from Anaheim, California: J. Lynn Johnston (vocals), James Lee Barlow and Anthony Boscarini (guitars), Ben Froehlich (bass) and Jake Fowler (drums).

| 9/14/02 | 38 | 2 | Walk Away .... | — | Resonance .... Artist Direct 1034 |

MADNESS
Ska-rock group formed in London: Graham McPherson (vocals), Chris Foreman (guitar), Mike Barson (keyboards), Carl Smyth (trumpet), Lee Thompson (sax), Mark Bedford (bass) and Dan Woodgate (drums; later with **Voice Of The Beehive**).

| 5/14/83 | 9 | 17 | Our House | 7 | Madness...................... Geffen 4003 |

MAD SEASON
All-star rock project: Layne Staley (vocals, guitar; **Alice In Chains**), Mike McCready (guitar; **Pearl Jam**), John Baker Saunders (bass) and Barrett Martin (drums; **Screaming Trees**). Band name is an English term for the time of year when psilocybin mushrooms are in full bloom. Staley died of a drug overdose on 4/5/2002 (age 34).

| 4/1/95 | 2[1] | 24 | 1 River Of Deceit | — ● | Above .... Columbia 67057 |
| 7/29/95 | 20 | 8 | 2 I Don't Know Anything.................................... | — | ↓ |

MAGNIFICENT BASTARDS, The
All-star rock project: **Scott Weiland** (vocals; **Stone Temple Pilots**), Zander Schloss (**Thelonious Monster, Red Hot Chili Peppers**) and Jeff Nolan (guitars), and Bob Thomson (bass).

| 6/10/95 | 27 | 6 | Mockingbird Girl | 66[A] | Tank Girl (soundtrack) .... Elektra 61760 |

MAIDS OF GRAVITY
Rock trio from Los Angeles: Ed Ruscha (vocals, bass), Jim Putnam (guitar, piano) and Craig "Irwin" Levitz (drums).

| 8/26/95 | 40 | 1 | Only Dreaming .... | — | Maids Of Gravity.............. Vernon Yard 40178 |

MALLOY, Mitch
Born in Dickinson, North Dakota. Rock singer/songwriter.

| 3/21/92 | 43 | 6 | Anything At All .... | 49 | Mitch Malloy........................ RCA 61044 |

MALMSTEEN('S), Yngwie J., Rising Force
Born on 6/30/63 in Stockholm, Sweden. Rock guitarist. Rising Force: **Joe Lynn Turner** (vocals) and Jens Johansson (keyboards) and Anders Johansson (drums).

| 4/16/88 | 19 | 11 | Heaven Tonight .... | — | Odyssey .... Polydor 835451 |

MANBREAK
Rock group from Liverpool, England: Steve Swindelli (vocals), Snaykee and Mr. Blonde (guitars), Roy Van Der Kerkoff (bass) and Stu Boy Stu (drums).

| 7/12/97 | 37 | 2 | Ready Or Not .... | — | Come And See .... Almo Sounds 80013 |

MANFRED MANN'S EARTH BAND
Born Michael Lubowitz on 10/21/40 in Johannesburg, South Africa. Formed pop-rock group in England: Mann (keyboards), Chris Thompson (vocals, guitar), Steve Waller (guitar), Matt Irving (bass) and Geoff Britton (drums). Also see **Classic Rock Tracks** section.

3/21/81	15	5	1 For You	106	Chance .... Warner 3498
			first recorded by Bruce Springsteen in 1973		
2/4/84	3	13	2 Runner	22	Somewhere In Afrika .... Arista 8194
5/19/84	34	5	3 Rebel	—	↓

MANITOBA'S WILD KINGDOM
Hard-rock group from New York City: Dick Manitoba (vocals), Ross Funicello (guitar), Adny Shernoff (bass) and J.P. Patterson (drums).

| 6/16/90 | 48 | 1 | The Party Starts Now!! .... | — | ...And You? .... MCA 6367 |

DEBUT	PEAK	WKS	Mainstream Rock Track	Pop	Gld	Album Title	Album Label & Number

MANSON, Marilyn
Born Brian Warner on 1/5/69 in Canton, Ohio. Hard-rock singer/songwriter. Noted for his controversial stage performances. His band includes: Scott "Daisy Berkowitz" Putesky (guitar), Steve "Madonna Wayne Gacy" Bier (keyboards), Jeordi "Twiggy Ramirez" White (bass) and Ken "Ginger Fish" Wilson (drums).

DEBUT	PEAK	WKS	Mainstream Rock Track	Pop	Gld	Album Title	Album Label & Number
4/27/96	31	7	1 Sweet Dreams (Are Made Of This)	—	▲	Smells Like Children	Nothing 92641
10/12/96	29	15	2 The Beautiful People	—	▲	Antichrist Superstar	Nothing 90086
2/8/97	30	7	3 Tourniquet	—	↓		
8/29/98	12	21	4 The Dope Show	122	▲	Mechanical Animals	Nothing 90273
1/16/99	25	10	5 I Don't Like The Drugs (But The Drugs Like Me)	—	↓		
4/10/99	28	7	6 Rock Is Dead	—	↓		
11/4/00	22	9	7 Disposable Teens	—		Holy Wood (In The Shadow Of The Valley Of Death)	Nothing 490790
12/8/01+	30	8	8 Tainted Love	—		Not Another Teen Movie (soundtrack)	Maverick 48250

MARCHELLO
Hard-rock group from New York City: Gene Marchello (vocals, guitar), Gary Bivona (keyboards), Nick DiMichino (bass) and John Miceli (drums).

DEBUT	PEAK	WKS	Mainstream Rock Track	Pop	Gld	Album Title	Album Label & Number
4/15/89	46	3	First Love	—		Destiny	CBS Associated 45096

MARCY PLAYGROUND
Rock trio from New York City: John Wozniak (vocals, guitar), Dylan Keefe (bass) and Dan Reiser (drums).

DEBUT	PEAK	WKS	Mainstream Rock Track	Pop	Gld	Album Title	Album Label & Number
12/20/97+	4	27	1 Sex and Candy	8	▲	Marcy Playground	Capitol 53569
6/27/98	30	8	2 Saint Joe On The School Bus	—	↓		

MARILLION
Rock group from Aylesbury, England: Derek "Fish" Dick (vocals), Steve Rothery (guitar), Mark Kelly (keyboards), Pete Trewavas (bass) and Mick Pointer (drums). Ian Mosley replaced Pointer in 1984. Steve Hogarth replaced Fish in late 1988.

DEBUT	PEAK	WKS	Mainstream Rock Track	Pop	Gld	Album Title	Album Label & Number
6/11/83	21	4	1 He Knows, You Know	—		Script For A Jester's Tear	Capitol 12269
8/17/85	14	14	2 Kayleigh	74		Misplaced Childhood	Capitol 12431
3/29/86	30	4	3 Lady Nina	—		Brief Encounter	Capitol 15023
7/4/87	24	6	4 Incommunicado	—		Clutching At Straws	Capitol 12539
11/18/89	49	2	5 Hooks In You	—		Seasons End	Capitol 12877

MARINO, Frank
Born on 8/22/54 in Montreal. Rock singer/guitarist. Leader of Mahogany Rush.

DEBUT	PEAK	WKS	Mainstream Rock Track	Pop	Gld	Album Title	Album Label & Number
12/18/82+	9	18	Strange Dreams	—		Juggernaut	Columbia 38023

MARLEY, Ziggy, And The Melody Makers
Family reggae group from Kingston, Jamaica. Children of **Bob Marley**: David "Ziggy" (vocals, guitar), Stephen, Sharon and Cedella Marley.

DEBUT	PEAK	WKS	Mainstream Rock Track	Pop	Gld	Album Title	Album Label & Number
5/7/88	16	9	1 Tomorrow People	39	▲	Conscious Party	Virgin 90878
8/13/88	43	4	2 Tumblin' Down	—	↓		

MARSHALL TUCKER BAND, The
Rock group from South Carolina: Doug Gray (vocals), Toy Caldwell and George McCorkle (guitar), Jerry Eubanks (sax, flute) and Paul Riddle (drums). Caldwell died of respiratory failure on 2/25/93 (age 45). Marshall Tucker was the owner of the band's rehearsal hall. Also see **Classic Rock Tracks** section.

DEBUT	PEAK	WKS	Mainstream Rock Track	Pop	Gld	Album Title	Album Label & Number
6/27/81	60	1	Silverado	—		Dedicated	Warner 3525

MARTIN, Eric, Band
Born on 10/10/60 in San Francisco. His band included John Nyman and Mark Ross (guitars), David Jacobson (keyboards), Tom Duke (bass) and Troy Luccketta (drums; **Tesla**). Martin formed **Mr. Big** in 1988.

DEBUT	PEAK	WKS	Mainstream Rock Track	Pop	Gld	Album Title	Album Label & Number
10/1/83	42	2	Sucker For A Pretty Face	—		Sucker For A Pretty Face	Elektra 60238

MARTIN, Marilyn
Born in Louisville, Kentucky. Former session singer.

DEBUT	PEAK	WKS	Mainstream Rock Track	Pop	Gld	Album Title	Album Label & Number
2/8/86	18	9	Night Moves	28		Marilyn Martin	Atlantic 81292

MARVELOUS 3
Rock trio from Atlanta: Butch Walker (vocals, guitar), Jayce Fincher (bass) and Slug (drums).

DEBUT	PEAK	WKS	Mainstream Rock Track	Pop	Gld	Album Title	Album Label & Number
2/27/99	23	11	Freak Of The Week	112		Hey! Album	HiFi 62375

MARX, Richard
Born on 9/16/63 in Chicago. Pop-rock singer/songwriter.

DEBUT	PEAK	WKS	Mainstream Rock Track	Pop	Gld	Album Title	Album Label & Number
5/23/87	❶[1]	14	1 Don't Mean Nothing	3	▲[3]	Richard Marx	EMI-Manhattan 53049
8/8/87	7	10	2 Should've Known Better	3	↓		
11/14/87	17	11	3 Have Mercy	—	↓		
2/13/88	41	4	4 Endless Summer Nights	2[2]	↓		
5/6/89	5	11	5 Satisfied	❶[1]	▲[4]	Repeat Offender	EMI 90380
7/22/89	12	9	6 Nothin' You Can Do About It	—	↓		
1/20/90	17	8	7 Too Late To Say Goodbye	12	↓		

MASON, Dave
Born on 5/10/46 in Worcester, England. Singer/songwriter/guitarist. Original member of **Traffic**. Also see **Classic Rock Tracks** section.

DEBUT	PEAK	WKS	Mainstream Rock Track	Pop	Gld	Album Title	Album Label & Number
11/7/87	24	6	Something In The Heart	—		Two Hearts	MCA 42086
			Steve Winwood (synthesizer)				

MASON, Nick, & Rick Fenn
Mason was born on 1/27/45 in Birmingham, England. Drummer of **Pink Floyd**. Fenn was a guitarist with 10cc.

DEBUT	PEAK	WKS	Mainstream Rock Track	Pop	Gld	Album Title	Album Label & Number
8/3/85	21	7	Lie For A Lie	—		Profiles	Columbia 40142

DEBUT	PEAK	WKS	Mainstream Rock Track	Pop Gld	Album Title	Album Label & Number

MASTERS OF REALITY
Rock trio formed in Syracuse, New York: Chris Goss (vocals) and Googe (bass) with legendary British drummer Ginger Baker (Cream, **BBM**). Group name derived from a 1971 **Black Sabbath** album.

| 2/20/93 | 8 | 12 | She Got Me (When She Got Her Dress On) | — | Sunrise On The Sufferbus . . . . Chrysalis 21976 |

MATCHBOX 20
Pop-rock group from Orlando, Florida: **Rob Thomas** (vocals), Kyle Cook and Adam Gaynor (guitars), Brian Yale (bass) and Paul Doucette (drums). Also see "Smooth" by **Santana**.

10/19/96+	8	22	1 Long Day	—	▲12 Yourself Or Someone Like You . . . . Lava 92721
3/15/97	4	35	2 Push	5A	↓
11/1/97+	2²	26	3 3 AM	3A	↓
4/11/98	17	21	4 Real World	38	↓
5/6/00	24	11	5 Bent	❶¹ ▲⁴ Mad Season . . . . Lava 83339
			MATCHBOX TWENTY		

MATTHEWS, Dave, Band
Born on 1/9/67 in Johannesburg, South Africa; raised in New York City. Singer/songwriter/guitarist. His band: Leroi Moore (sax), Boyd Tinsley (violin), Stefan Lessard (bass) and Carter Beauford (drums).

2/25/95	5	26	1 What Would You Say	22A ▲⁶ Under The Table And Dreaming . . . . RCA 66449
7/22/95	18	17	2 Ants Marching	21A	↓
1/20/96	36	4	3 Satellite	55A	↓
4/13/96	9	16	4 Too Much	39A ▲⁷ Crash . . . . RCA 66904
8/3/96	20	10	5 So Much To Say	48A	↓
4/18/98	19	13	6 Don't Drink The Water	50A ▲³ Before These Crowded Streets . . . . RCA 67660
8/15/98	35	5	7 Stay (Wasting Time)	44A	↓
1/27/01	23	13	8 I Did It	71 ▲³ Everyday . . . . RCA 67988

MAY, Brian
Born on 7/19/47 in Twickenham, Middlesex, England. Lead guitarist of **Queen**.

| 2/27/93 | 9 | 9 | Driven By You | — | Back To The Light . . . . Hollywood 61404 |

MAYFIELD FOUR, The
Rock group from Spokane, Washington: Myles Kennedy (vocals), Craig Johnson (guitar), Marty Meisner (bass) and Zia Uddin (drums).

| 7/7/01 | 37 | 4 | Eden (Turn The Page) . . . . | — | Second Skin . . . . Epic 61080 |

McAULEY SCHENKER GROUP
Hard-rock group led by Irish vocalist Robin McAuley (former member of **Grand Prix**) and West German-born guitarist Michael Schenker (brother Rudolf is a member of **Scorpions**). Schenker was also a member of **Contraband**.

3/17/84	55	2	1 Rock My Nights Away	—	Built To Destroy . . . . Chrysalis 41441
			THE MICHAEL SCHENKER GROUP		
10/24/87	40	7	2 Gimme Your Love	—	Perfect Timing . . . . Capitol 46985
1/23/88	49	2	3 Love Is Not A Game	—	↓
12/2/89+	5	17	4 Anytime	69	Save Yourself . . . . Capitol 92752
3/7/92	16	11	5 When I'm Gone	—	MSG . . . . Impact 10385
			SCHENKER/McAULEY		

McCAIN, Edwin
Born on 1/20/70 in Greenville, South Carolina. Singer/songwriter/guitarist.

| 9/9/95 | 25 | 11 | Solitude . . . . | 72 | Honor Among Thieves . . . . Lava 92597 |

McCARTNEY, Paul
Born James Paul McCartney on 6/18/42 in Liverpool, England. Founding member/bass guitarist of **The Beatles**. Married Linda Eastman on 3/12/69 (she died of cancer on 4/17/98, age 55). Formed group Wings in 1971; disbanded in 1981. Starred in own movie *Give My Regards To Broad Street*. Won Grammy's Lifetime Achievement Award in 1990. Knighted by Queen Elizabeth II in 1997. Inducted into the Rock and Roll Hall of Fame in 1999. Also see **Classic Rock Tracks** section.
1)Figure Of Eight 2)My Brave Face 3)No More Lonely Nights

4/24/82	34	2	1 Ebony And Ivory	❶⁷ ▲ Tug Of War . . . . Columbia 37462
			PAUL McCARTNEY (with Stevie Wonder)		
5/15/82	22	8	2 Ballroom Dancing	—	↓
5/22/82	39	7	3 Take It Away	10	↓
5/29/82	44	5	4 The Pound Is Sinking	—	↓
6/12/82	46	1	5 Here Today	—	↓
10/29/83	24	12	6 Say Say Say	❶⁶ ▲ Pipes Of Peace . . . . Columbia 39149
			PAUL McCARTNEY AND MICHAEL JACKSON		
10/20/84	16	9	7 No More Lonely Nights	6 ● Give my regards to Broad Street . . . . . Columbia 39613
11/30/85	31	8	8 Spies Like Us	7	Spies Like Us (soundtrack) . . . . Capitol 5537
9/13/86	44	3	9 Angry	—	Press To Play . . . . Capitol 12475
5/27/89	12	8	10 My Brave Face	25 ● Flowers In The Dirt . . . . Capitol 91653
			co-written by **Elvis Costello**		
12/16/89+	8	11	11 Figure Of Eight	92	↓
3/17/90	43	3	12 We Got Married	—	↓
8/25/90	41	3	13 Hey Jude . . . . [L]	—	Knebworth - The Album (various artists) . Polydor 84702
			#1 Pop hit for **The Beatles** in 1968		
10/27/90	35	7	14 Birthday . . . . [L]	—	Tripping The Live Fantastic . . . . Capitol 94778
			first recorded by **The Beatles** in 1968		
5/24/97	23	12	15 The World Tonight	64 ● Flaming Pie . . . . Capitol

DEBUT	PEAK	WKS	Mainstream Rock Track	Pop	Gld	Album Title	Album Label & Number
			McCLINTON, Delbert				
			Born on 11/4/40 in Lubbock, Texas. Rock singer/harmonica player. Also see **Classic Rock Tracks** section.				
5/16/92	13	14	Every Time I Roll The Dice	—		*Never Been Rocked Enough*	Curb 77521
			Melissa Etheridge (backing vocal); **Bonnie Raitt** (guitar)				
			McDERMOTT, Michael				
			Born in Chicago. Rock singer/songwriter/guitarist.				
8/3/91	34	7	A Wall I Must Climb	—		*620 W. Surf*	Giant 24416
			McDONALD, Michael				
			Born on 2/12/52 in St. Louis. Pop-rock singer/songwriter/keyboardist. Former lead singer of **The Doobie Brothers**.				
8/3/85	4	11	1 No Lookin' Back	34		*No Lookin' Back*	Warner 25291
9/21/85	38	6	2 Bad Times	—		↓	
			Joe Walsh (guitar)				
11/2/91	17	12	3 Pretzel Logic .... [L]	—		*The New York Rock And Soul Revue - Live At The Beacon* (various artists)	Giant 24423
			DONALD FAGEN & MICHAEL McDONALD recorded at the Beacon Theatre in New York City; #57 Pop hit for **Steely Dan** in 1974				
			McGUINN, Roger				
			Born James McGuinn on 7/13/42 in Chicago. Lead singer/guitarist of **The Byrds**. Changed name to Roger in 1968.				
1/19/91	2²	13	1 King Of The Hill	—		*Back From Rio*	Arista 8648
			Tom Petty (co-writer, guest vocal)				
3/30/91	12	10	2 Someone To Love	—		↓	
8/21/93	26	7	3 My Back Pages .... [L]	—	●	*Bob Dylan - The 30th Anniversary Concert* (various artists)	Columbia 53230
			BOB DYLAN & FRIENDS: Roger McGuinn, Tom Petty, Neil Young, Eric Clapton & George Harrison recorded on 10/16/92 at Madison Square Garden in New York City; #30 Pop hit for **The Byrds** in 1967				
			McKENZIE, Bob & Doug				
			The McKenzie brothers are actually Canadian comedians Rick "Bob" Moranis (born on 4/18/54) and Dave "Doug" Thomas (born on 5/20/49) of *SCTV*. Both featured (as the McKenzie brothers) in the movie *Strange Brew*.				
1/23/82	7	11	Take Off [N]	16	●	*Great White North*	Mercury 4034
			Geddy Lee (of **Rush**; vocal)				
			McMURTRY, James				
			Born on 3/18/62 in Fort Worth, Texas. Folk-rock guitarist. Son of novelist Larry McMurtry.				
9/2/89	33	7	Painting By Numbers	—		*Too Long In The Wasteland*	Columbia 45229
			McQUEEN STREET				
			Hard-rock group from Montgomery, Alabama: brothers Derek (vocals) and Chris (drums) Welsh, Michael Powers (guitar) and Richard Hatcher (bass).				
11/23/91+	32	7	In Heaven	—		*McQueen Street*	SBK 96428
			McVIE, Christine				
			Born Christine Perfect on 7/12/43 in Birmingham, England. Singer/keyboardist with **Fleetwood Mac** since 1970. Married to Fleetwood Mac bassist John McVie (1968-77).				
2/4/84	❶²	11	1 Got A Hold On Me	10		*Christine McVie*	Warner 25059
2/25/84	27	5	2 One In A Million	—		↓	
4/7/84	24	10	3 Love Will Show Us How	30		↓	
			MEAT LOAF				
			Born Marvin Lee Aday on 9/27/47 in Dallas. Pop-rock singer. Sang lead vocals on **Ted Nugent**'s 1976 *Free-For-All* album. Played "Eddie" in the Los Angeles production and movie of *The Rocky Horror Picture Show*. Appeared several other movies. Also see **Classic Rock Tracks** section.				
5/18/85	41	3	1 Modern Girl	—		*Bad Attitude*	RCA Victor 5451
9/11/93	10	12	2 I'd Do Anything For Love (But I Won't Do That)	❶⁵	▲⁵	*Bat Out Of Hell II: Back Into Hell*	MCA 10699
12/11/93	17	7	3 Life Is A Lemon And I Want My Money Back	—		↓	
2/5/94	25	7	4 Rock And Roll Dreams Come Through	13		↓	
			MEAT PUPPETS				
			Rock trio from Phoenix: brothers Curt (vocals, guitar) and Cris (bass) Kirkwood with Derrick Bostrom (drums).				
3/5/94	2³	26	1 Backwater	47	●	*Too High To Die*	London 828484
8/13/94	28	7	2 We Don't Exist	—		↓	
9/30/95	20	7	3 Scum	—		*No Joke!*	London 828665
	★74★		**MEGADETH**				
			Hard-rock group formed in Los Angeles: Dave Mustaine (vocals, guitar), Marty Friedman (guitar), Dave Ellefson (bass) and Nick Menza (drums). Jimmy DeGrasso replaced Menza in 1998. Al Pitrelli replaced Friedman in 2000. Mustaine was an early guitarist with **Metallica**.				
			1)Trust 2)Breadline 3)Crush 'Em				
9/5/92	29	7	1 Symphony Of Destruction	71	▲²	*Countdown To Extinction*	Capitol 98531
12/5/92	30	8	2 Foreclosure Of A Dream	—		↓	
2/27/93	27	9	3 Sweating Bullets	—		↓	
6/26/93	18	9	4 Angry Again	—	▲	*Last Action Hero* (soundtrack)	Columbia 57127
11/27/93	23	10	5 99 Ways To Die	—	▲²	*The Beavis & Butt-head Experience* (various artists)	Geffen 24613
11/26/94	29	11	6 Train Of Consequences	—	▲	*Youthanasia*	Capitol 29004
3/18/95	31	7	7 A Tout Le Monde	—		↓	

DEBUT	PEAK	WKS	Mainstream Rock Track	Pop Gld	Album Title	Album Label & Number
			MEGADETH — Cont'd			
5/31/97	5	26	8 Trust	— ●	Cryptic Writings	Capitol 38262
10/11/97	8	26	9 Almost Honest	—	↓	
2/21/98	15	20	10 Use The Man	—	↓	
7/11/98	19	12	11 A Secret Place	—	↓	
7/10/99	6	12	12 Crush 'Em	—	Risk	Capitol 99134
9/25/99	26	8	13 Insomnia	—	↓	
12/4/99+	6	17	14 Breadline	—	↓	
9/30/00	21	11	15 Kill The King	—	Capitol Punishment	Capitol 25916
4/21/01	22	11	16 Moto Psycho	—	The World Needs A Hero	Sanctuary 684503

MEISNER, Randy
Born on 3/8/46 in Scottsbluff, Nebraska. Pop-rock singer/bassist. Member of **Poco** (1968-69), Rick Nelson's Stone Canyon Band (1969-71) and the **Eagles** (1971-77). Also see **Classic Rock Tracks** section.

DEBUT	PEAK	WKS		Pop Gld	Album Title	Album Label & Number
3/21/81	14	3	Hearts On Fire	19	One More Song	Epic 36748

MELLENCAMP, John Cougar ★5★
Born on 10/7/51 in Seymour, Indiana. Rock singer/songwriter/guitarist. Given name Johnny Cougar by **David Bowie**'s manager, Tony DeFries. First recorded for MCA in 1976. Directed and starred in the 1992 movie *Falling From Grace*. Married model Elaine Irwin on 9/5/92. Recipient of *Billboard*'s Century Award in 2001. Also see **Classic Rock Tracks** section.

1)Lonely Ol' Night 2)Paper In Fire 3)Get A Leg Up 4)Again Tonight 5)What If I Came Knocking

DEBUT	PEAK	WKS	Mainstream Rock Track	Pop Gld	Album Title	Album Label & Number
			JOHN COUGAR:			
3/21/81	44	2	1 Ain't Even Done With The Night	17 ▲	Nothin' Matters And What If It Did	Riva 7403
5/1/82	●[1]	26	2 Hurts So Good	2[4] ▲[5]	American Fool	Riva 7501
6/26/82	3	10	3 Jack & Diane	●[4]	↓	
9/25/82	36	7	4 Thundering Hearts	—	↓	
			JOHN COUGAR MELLENCAMP:			
10/15/83	2[1]	19	5 Crumblin' Down	9 ▲[3]	Uh-Huh	Riva 7504
10/29/83+	3	19	6 Pink Houses	8	↓	
1/28/84	34	4	7 Serious Business	—	↓	
2/4/84	28	5	8 Play Guitar	—	↓	
2/18/84	15	11	9 Authority Song	15	↓	
8/17/85	●[5]	14	10 Lonely Ol' Night	6 ▲[5]	Scarecrow	Riva 824865
9/14/85	2[2]	20	11 Small Town	6	↓	
9/14/85	6	22	12 R.O.C.K. In The U.S.A. (A Salute To 60's Rock)	2[1]	↓	
9/21/85+	16	27	13 Rain On The Scarecrow	21	↓	
11/30/85+	28	13	14 Justice And Independence '85	—	↓	
1/18/86	14	11	15 Minutes To Memories	—	↓	
7/5/86	4	10	16 Rumbleseat	28	↓	
2/15/86	19	8	17 Under The Boardwalk	—	(single only)	Riva 884455
			#4 Pop hit for The Drifters in 1964			
8/15/87	●[5]	11	18 Paper In Fire	9 ▲[3]	The Lonesome Jubilee	Mercury 832465
9/5/87	●[1]	20	19 Cherry Bomb	8	↓	
9/5/87	10	13	20 Hard Times For An Honest Man	—	↓	
9/12/87+	3	11	21 The Real Life	—	↓	
2/6/88	3	12	22 Check It Out	14	↓	
5/7/88	7	9	23 Rooty Toot Toot	61	↓	
9/10/88	17	7	24 Rave On	— ▲[4]	Cocktail (soundtrack)	Elektra 60806
			#37 Pop hit for Buddy Holly in 1958			
4/29/89	2[3]	8	25 Pop Singer	15 ▲	Big Daddy	Mercury 838220
5/20/89	8	11	26 Martha Say	—	↓	
6/3/89	42	8	27 Let It All Hang Out	—	↓	
			#12 Pop hit for The Hombres in 1967			
7/8/89	20	8	28 Jackie Brown	48	↓	
			JOHN MELLENCAMP:			
10/5/91	●[3]	25	29 Get A Leg Up	14 ▲	Whenever We Wanted	Mercury 510151
11/2/91+	5	21	30 Love And Happiness	—	↓	
1/25/92	●[2]	20	31 Again Tonight	36	↓	
4/4/92	3	20	32 Now More Than Ever	—	↓	
7/4/92	12	11	33 Last Chance	—	↓	
7/24/93	●[2]	14	34 What If I Came Knocking	— ▲	Human Wheels	Mercury 518088
9/18/93	2[1]	20	35 Human Wheels	48	↓	
12/18/93	35	4	36 When Jesus Left Birmingham	—	↓	
2/5/94	35	4	37 Junior	—	↓	

Mainstream Rock

DEBUT	PEAK	WKS	Mainstream Rock Track	Pop	Gld	Album Title	Album Label & Number
			MELLENCAMP, John — Cont'd				
5/28/94	17	20	38 Wild Night	3	▲	Dance Naked	Mercury 522428
			JOHN MELLENCAMP ME'SHELL NDEGEOCELLO				
			#28 Pop hit for **Van Morrison** in 1971				
10/15/94	21	9	39 Dance Naked	41	↓		
8/17/96	10	14	40 Key West Intermezzo (I Saw You First)	14	▲	Mr. Happy Go Lucky	Mercury 532896
11/30/96+	13	22	41 Just Another Day	46	↓		
11/29/97+	25	13	42 Without Expression	—	▲3	The Best That I Could Do 1978-1988	Mercury 536738
9/19/98	15	14	43 Your Life Is Now	62A	●	John Mellencamp	Columbia 69602
2/13/99	37	4	44 I'm Not Running Anymore	—	↓		
10/6/01	38	3	45 Peaceful World	104	●	Cuttin' Heads	Columbia 85098
			JOHN MELLENCAMP Featuring India.Arie				
			MEMBERS, The				
			Pop-rock group from Surrey, England: Nicky Tesco (vocals), Jean-Marie Carroll and Nigel Bennett (guitars), Simon Lloyd and Steve Thompson (horns), Chris Payne (bass) and Adrian Lillywhite (drums).				
3/5/83	34	2	Working Girl	—		Uprhythm, Downbeat	Arista 6605
			MEN, The				
			Rock group from Santa Monica, California: Jef Scott (vocals, guitar), sisters Lore Wilhelm (guitar) and Nancy Hathorn (bass), and David Botkin (drums).				
5/16/92	8	16	Church Of Logic, Sin, & Love	—		The Men	Polydor 511987
			MEN AT WORK				
			Pop-rock group from Melbourne, Australia: **Colin James Hay** (vocals, guitar), Ron Strykert (lead guitar), Greg Ham (sax, keyboards), John Rees (bass) and Jerry Speiser (drums). Won the 1982 Best New Artist Grammy Award. Speiser and Rees left in 1984.				
7/10/82	46	1	1 Who Can It Be Now?	❶1	▲6	Business As Usual	Columbia 37978
10/23/82	❶5	17	2 Down Under	❶4	↓		
1/22/83	3	9	3 Be Good Johnny	—	↓		
3/5/83	20	4	4 Underground	—	↓		
4/9/83	3	14	5 Overkill	3	▲3	Cargo	Columbia 38660
4/30/83	12	13	6 Dr. Heckyll & Mr. Jive	28	↓		
5/28/83	23	8	7 High Wire	—	↓		
6/11/83	27	11	8 It's A Mistake	6	↓		
6/15/85	28	6	9 Everything I Need	47	●	Two Hearts	Columbia 40078
			MEN WITHOUT HATS				
			Techno-rock group from Montreal: brothers Ivan (vocals), Stefan (guitar) and Colin (keyboards) Doroschuk, with Alan McCarthy (drums).				
8/27/83	21	8	The Safety Dance	3	●	Rhythm Of Youth	Backstreet 39002
			MESH STL				
			Rock group from St. Louis: Scott Gertken (vocals), Matt Arana and Scott Davis (guitars), Rich Criebaum (bass) and Brian Pearia (drums).				
9/29/01	26	15	1 Maybe Tomorrow	—		Lowercase	The Label 45030
3/23/02	39	1	2 Believe Me	—	↓		
			METALLICA ★14★				
			Hard-rock group formed in Los Angeles: James Hetfield (vocals, guitar; born on 8/3/63), Kirk Hammett (guitar; born on 11/18/62), Cliff Burton (bass; born on 2/10/62; died in a bus crash on 9/27/86, age 24) and Lars Ulrich (drums; born on 12/26/63). Original guitarist Dave Mustaine left in 1982 to form **Megadeth**. Jason Newsted (born on 3/4/63) replaced Burton.				
			1)Turn The Page 2)Until It Sleeps 3)I Disappear 4)No Leaf Clover 5)Hero Of The Day				
3/11/89	46	3	1 One	35	▲7	...And Justice For All	Elektra 60812
8/17/91	10	20	2 Enter Sandman	16	▲12	Metallica	Elektra 61113
11/2/91+	10	34	3 The Unforgiven	35	↓		
3/14/92	11	20	4 Nothing Else Matters	34	↓		
7/11/92	25	16	5 Wherever I May Roam	82	↓		
12/5/92+	15	19	6 Sad But True	98	↓		
6/1/96	❶8	26	7 Until It Sleeps	10	▲4	Load	Elektra 61923
7/6/96	15	18	8 Ain't My Bitch	—	↓		
9/21/96	❶3	33	9 Hero Of The Day	60	↓		
1/18/97	6	27	10 King Nothing	90	↓		
6/14/97	6	24	11 Bleeding Me	—	↓		
11/22/97	3	22	12 The Memory Remains	28	▲3	Reload	Elektra 62126
			Marianne Faithfull (female vocal)				
12/6/97+	23	26	13 The Unforgiven II	59	↓		
12/20/97+	6	26	14 Fuel	—	↓		
8/1/98	7	17	15 Better Than You	—	↓		

DEBUT	PEAK	WKS	Mainstream Rock Track	Pop	Gld	Album Title	Album Label & Number
			METALLICA — Cont'd				
11/21/98	❶¹¹	26	16 Turn The Page	102	▲⁵	Garage Inc.	Elektra 62299
			first recorded by **Bob Seger** in 1973				
1/23/99	4	26	17 Whiskey In The Jar	124	↓		
			first recorded by **Thin Lizzy** in 1972				
6/5/99	26	12	18 Die, Die My Darling	—	↓		
12/4/99+	❶⁷	34	19 No Leaf Clover [L]	74	▲⁴	S&M	Elektra 62504
			with the San Francisco Symphony Orchestra; recorded on 4/21/99 at the Berkeley Community Theater				
5/6/00	❶⁷	43	20 I Disappear	76	▲	Mission: Impossible 2 (soundtrack)	Hollywood 62244
			METHENY, Pat, Group — see BOWIE, David				
			MIDNIGHT OIL				
			Rock group formed in Sydney, Australia: Peter Garrett (vocals), Martin Rotsey (guitar), James Moginie (keyboards), Dwayne Hillman (bass) and Rob Hirst (drums).				
2/20/88	6	19	1 Beds Are Burning	17	▲	Diesel And Dust	Columbia 40967
6/4/88	11	14	2 The Dead Heart	53	↓		
10/15/88	37	4	3 Dreamworld	—			
2/17/90	❶¹	14	4 Blue Sky Mine	47	●	Blue Sky Mining	Columbia 45398
4/21/90	11	12	5 Forgotten Years	—	↓		
7/21/90	20	8	6 King Of The Mountain	—	↓		
4/24/93	10	11	7 Truganini	—		Earth And Sun And Moon	Columbia 53793
			MIGHTY JOE PLUM				
			Rock group from Tampa, Florida: Brett Williams (vocals), Marlin Clark (guitar), Davey Mason (bass) and Mark Mercado (drums).				
7/26/97	6	26	Live Through This (Fifteen Stories)	—		The Happiest Dogs	Atlantic 83023
			MIKE + THE MECHANICS				
			Rock group formed in England: **Mike Rutherford** (bass; **Genesis**), **Paul Carrack** and Paul Young (vocals), Adrian Lee (keyboards) and Peter Van Hooke (drums). Young, not to be confused with the same-named solo singer, died of a heart attack on 7/17/2000 (age 53).				
11/9/85	❶⁵	17	1 Silent Running (On Dangerous Ground)	6	●	Mike + The Mechanics	Atlantic 81287
2/1/86	6	14	2 All I Need Is A Miracle	5			
11/5/88	3	11	3 Nobody's Perfect	63	●	Living Years	Atlantic 81923
1/21/89	5	11	4 The Living Years	❶¹	↓		
4/8/89	18	8	5 Seeing Is Believing	62	↓		
3/30/91	30	5	6 Word Of Mouth	78		Word Of Mouth	Atlantic 82233
			MILLER, Steve, Band				
			Born on 10/5/43 in Milwaukee; raised in Dallas. Singer/songwriter/guitarist. Formed band in high school, The Marksmen, which included **Boz Scaggs**. Moved to San Francisco in 1966; formed the Steve Miller Band, which featured a fluctuating lineup. Also see **Classic Rock Tracks** section.				
11/14/81	17	12	1 Heart Like A Wheel	24	●	Circle Of Love	Capitol 12121
6/5/82	4	17	2 Abracadabra	❶²	▲	Abracadabra	Capitol 12216
11/1/86	❶⁶	14	3 I Want To Make The World Turn Around	97		Living In The 20th Century	Capitol 12445
			Kenny G (sax solo)				
12/27/86+	9	12	4 Nobody But You Baby	—	↓		
9/10/88	10	6	5 Ya Ya	—		Born 2B Blue	Capitol 48303
			STEVE MILLER #7 Pop hit for Lee Dorsey in 1961				
6/19/93	7	10	6 Wide River	64		Wide River	Polydor 519441
9/18/93	39	2	7 Blue Eyes	—	↓		
7/9/94	24	7	8 Rock It	—		Steve Miller Band Box Set	Capitol 12263
			MI-SEX				
			Rock group from New Zealand: Steve Gilpin (vocals), Kevin Stanton and Colin Bayley (guitars), Murray Burns (keyboards), Don Martin (bass) and Paul Dunningham (drums). Gilpin died in a car crash on 11/25/92 (age 41).				
3/31/84	31	4	Castaway	—		Where Do They Go?	Epic 39263
			MISSING PERSONS				
			Rock group formed in Los Angeles: Dale Bozzio (vocals), her then-husband Terry Bozzio (drums), Warren Cuccurullo (guitar), Patrick O'Hearn (bass, synthesizer) and Chuck Wild (keyboards). All but Wild were with **Frank Zappa**'s band. Disbanded in 1986. Terry Bozzio worked with **Jeff Beck** in 1989. Cuccurullo joined **Duran Duran** in 1990.				
6/26/82	60	1	1 Words	42		Missing Persons	Capitol 15001
11/6/82	24	14	2 Destination Unknown	42	●	Spring Session M	Capitol 12228
11/13/82+	12	23	3 Walking In L.A.	70	↓		
2/5/83	22	5	4 Windows	63			
3/31/84	29	5	5 Give	67		Rhyme & Reason	Capitol 12315
			MISSION U.K., The				
			Rock group formed in Leeds, England: Wayne Hussey (vocals, guitar), Simon Hinkler (guitar), Craig Adams (bass) and Mick Brown (drums). Hussey and Adams were members of **The Sisters Of Mercy**.				
4/7/90	27	8	Deliverance	—		Carved In Sand	Mercury 842251

DEBUT	PEAK	WKS	Mainstream Rock Track	Pop	Gld	Album Title	Album Label & Number

MR. BIG
Rock group from San Francisco: **Eric Martin** (vocals), Paul Gilbert (guitar), Billy Sheehan (bass) and Pat Torpey (drums).

7/29/89	39	6	1 Addicted To That Rush............................	—		Mr. Big	Atlantic 81990
4/20/91	33	7	2 Green-Tinted Sixties Mind..	—	▲	Lean Into It.................	Atlantic 82209
10/12/91	19	26	3 To Be With You	❶³		↓	
4/25/92	18	9	4 Just Take My Heart	16		↓	
10/9/93	33	4	5 Wild World	27		Bump Ahead	Atlantic 82495

#11 Pop hit for Cat Stevens in 1971

MR. MISTER
Pop-rock group formed in Los Angeles: Richard Page (vocals, bass), Steve Farris (guitar), Steve George (keyboards) and Pat Mastelotto (drums).

4/7/84	36	3	1 Hunters Of The Night................	57		I Wear The Face..............	RCA Victor 4864
8/24/85	4	17	2 Broken Wings	❶²	▲	Welcome To The Real World	RCA Victor 8045
12/14/85+	❶¹	13	3 Kyrie	❶²		↓	
3/22/86	17	11	4 Is It Love	8		↓	
8/22/87	27	8	5 Something Real (Inside Me/Inside You)	29		Go On...	RCA Victor 6276

MITCHELL, Joni
Born Roberta Joan Anderson on 11/7/43 in Fort McLeod, Alberta, Canada; raised in Saskatoon, Saskatchewan. Singer/songwriter/guitarist/pianist. Married to her producer/bassist, Larry Klein, from 1982-94. Recipient of *Billboard*'s Century Award in 1995. Inducted into the Rock and Roll Hall of Fame in 1997. Won Grammy's Lifetime Achievement Award in 2002. Also see **Classic Rock Tracks** section.

11/23/85	28	8	1 Good Friends	85		Dog Eat Dog	Geffen 24074
			Michael McDonald (harmony vocal)				
3/19/88	32	8	2 Snakes And Ladders	—		Chalk Mark In A Rain Storm	Geffen 24172
			Don Henley (harmony vocal)				

MITCHELL, Kim
Born on 7/10/52 in Sarnia, Ontario, Canada. Male rock singer/guitarist.

5/4/85	12	12	1 Go For Soda	86		Akimbo Alogo	Bronze 90257
7/26/86	36	6	2 Patio Lanterns	—		Shakin' Like A Human Being	Atlantic 81664

MODELS
Pop-rock group formed in Melbourne, Australia: Sean Kelly (vocals, guitar), Roger Mason (keyboards), James Valentine (sax), James Freud (bass) and Barton Price (drums).

4/26/86	22	9	1 Out Of Mind Out Of Sight	37		Out Of Mind Out Of Sight	Geffen 24100
7/19/86	29	6	2 Cold Fever	—		↓	

MODERN ENGLISH
New-wave group formed in Colchester, England: Robbie Grey (vocals), Gary McDowell (guitar), Stephen Walker (keyboards), Michael Conroy (bass) and Richard Brown (drums).

3/26/83	7	11	1 I Melt With You	78	●	After The Snow..............	Sire 23821
3/31/84	47	5	2 Hands Across The Sea	91		Ricochet Days	Sire 25066

MOIST
Rock group from Vancouver: David Usher (vocals), Mark Makowy (guitar), Kevin Young (keyboards), Jeff Pearce (bass) and Paul Wilcox (drums).

11/26/94	37	4	Push	—		Silver.	Chrysalis/EMI 29608

MOLLY HATCHET
Rock group formed in Jacksonville, Florida: **Danny Joe Brown** (vocals), Dave Hlubek, Duane Roland and Steve Holland (guitars), Banner Thomas (bass) and Bruce Crump (drums). Jimmy Farrar replaced Brown in 1980; Brown returned and replaced Farrar in 1983. Holland and Thomas left in 1983; John Galvin (keyboards) and Riff West (bass) joined. Bobby Ingram replaced Hlubek in 1988. Also see **Classic Rock Tracks** section.

12/5/81+	31	9	1 Bloody Reunion	—		Take No Prisoners	Epic 37480
12/19/81+	46	5	2 Lady Luck	—		↓	
10/13/84	13	12	3 Satisfied Man	81		The Deed Is Done	Epic 39621
12/15/84+	26	9	4 Stone In Your Heart	—		↓	
9/16/89	26	6	5 There Goes The Neighborhood	—		Lightning Strikes Twice.............	Capitol 92114

MONDO ROCK
Rock group formed in Australia: Ross Wilson (vocals), Eric McCusker (guitar), Duncan Veall (keyboards), Andrew Ross (sax), James Gillard (bass) and J.J. Hackett (drums).

5/9/87	31	6	Primitive Love Rites....................	71		Boom Baby Boom...............	Columbia 40470

MONEY, Eddie ★45★
Born Edward Mahoney on 3/2/49 in Brooklyn, New York. Pop-rock singer. Discovered and subsequently managed by the late West Coast promoter Bill Graham. Formerly an officer with the New York City Police Department. Also see **Classic Rock Tracks** section.

1)Think I'm In Love 2)Take Me Home Tonight 3)The Love In Your Eyes

7/3/82	❶³	14	1 Think I'm In Love	16	▲	No Control.	Columbia 37960
7/24/82	9	27	2 Shakin'	63		↓	
8/7/82	60	1	3 No Control	—		↓	
11/26/83	17	11	4 The Big Crash.........................	54		Where's The Party?	Columbia 38862
9/29/84	25	7	5 I'm Moving On	—		Every Man Has A Woman (various artists)	Polydor 823490

first recorded by Yoko Ono in 1980

DEBUT	PEAK	WKS	Mainstream Rock Track	Pop	Gld	Album Title	Album Label & Number
			MONEY, Eddie — Cont'd				
8/9/86	❶²	15	6 **Take Me Home Tonight**	4	▲	Can't Hold Back	Columbia 40096
			Ronnie Spector (female vocal)				
10/25/86	18	12	7 **We Should Be Sleeping**	90		↓	
12/20/86+	3	15	8 **I Wanna Go Back**	14		↓	
3/21/87	10	11	9 **Endless Nights**	21		↓	
10/1/88	2⁵	12	10 **Walk On Water**	9		Nothing To Lose	Columbia 44302
12/10/88+	❶¹	15	11 **The Love In Your Eyes**	24		↓	
2/18/89	36	5	12 **Forget About Love**	—		↓	
4/29/89	30	5	13 **Let Me In**	60		↓	
12/2/89+	2²	11	14 **Peace In Our Time**	11	●	Greatest Hits Sound Of Money	Columbia 45381
9/14/91	6	8	15 **Heaven In The Back Seat**	58		Right Here	Columbia 46756
11/16/91+	5	12	16 **She Takes My Breath Away**	—		↓	
			MONROES, The				
			Pop-rock group from San Diego: Jesus Ortiz (vocals), Rusty Jones (guitar), Eric Denton (keyboards), Bob Monroe (bass) and Jonnie Gilstrap (drums).				
6/5/82	20	6	**What Do All The People Know**	59		The Monroes	Alfa 15015
			MONSTER MAGNET				
			Hard-rock group from Red Bank, New Jersey: David Wyndorf (vocals), Ed Mundell (guitar), Joe Calandra (bass) and Joe Kleiman (drums). Phil Caivano (guitar) joined in 2000.				
4/29/95	19	15	1 **Negasonic Teenage Warhead**	—		Dopes To Infinity	A&M 540315
5/30/98	3	27	2 **Space Lord**	—	●	Powertrip	A&M 540908
10/31/98	20	24	3 **Powertrip**	—		↓	
4/3/99	25	12	4 **Temple Of Your Dreams**	—		↓	
4/1/00	15	14	5 **Silver Future**	—		Heavy Metal 2000 (soundtrack)	Restless 73717
3/17/01	26	11	6 **Heads Explode**	—		God Says No	A&M 490749
	★93★		**MOODY BLUES, The**				
			Rock group formed in Birmingham, England: Justin Hayward (vocals, guitar), John Lodge (vocals, bass), Patrick Moraz (keyboards) and Graeme Edge (drums). Moraz was a former member of **Yes**. Also see **Classic Rock Tracks** section.				
			1)The Voice 2)I Know You're Out There Somewhere 3)Your Wildest Dreams				
6/6/81	❶⁴	27	1 **The Voice**	15	▲	Long Distance Voyager	Threshold 2901
6/6/81	13	13	2 **Gemini Dream**	12		↓	
7/4/81	38	6	3 **22,000 Days**	—		↓	
8/22/81	11	15	4 **Meanwhile**	—		↓	
9/3/83	3	14	5 **Sitting At The Wheel**	27		The Present	Threshold 2902
10/22/83	32	7	6 **Blue World**	62		↓	
4/19/86	2¹	15	7 **Your Wildest Dreams**	9	▲	The Other Side Of Life	Threshold 829179
6/7/86	11	16	8 **The Other Side Of Life**	58		↓	
6/4/88	2²	10	9 **I Know You're Out There Somewhere**	30		Sur la mer	Polydor 835756
9/3/88	50	1	10 **Here Comes The Weekend**	—		↓	
6/22/91	22	8	11 **Say It With Love**	—		Keys Of The Kingdom	Polydor 849433
			MOON DOG MANE				
			Rock group formed in California: Broadie Stewart (vocals), Frank Hannon (**Tesla**) and Kevin Hampton (guitars), Chris Martinez (keyboards), Joel Krueger (bass) and Cortney Daugustine (drums).				
12/26/98+	36	3	1 **Turn It Up**	—		Turn It Up	Eureka 02262
5/1/99	38	2	2 **I Believe**	—		↓	
			MOORE, Gary				
			Born on 4/4/52 in Belfast, Ireland. Guitarist with **Thin Lizzy** (1974, 1978-79) and **BBM**.				
5/28/83	31	2	1 **Don't Take Me For A Loser**	—		Corridors Of Power	Mirage 90077
4/25/87	24	7	2 **Over The Hills And Far Away**	—		Wild Frontier	Virgin 90588
3/4/89	13	11	3 **Ready For Love**	—		After The War	Virgin 91066
6/2/90	15	12	4 **Oh Pretty Woman**	—	●	Still Got The Blues	Charisma 91369
9/15/90	9	22	5 **Still Got The Blues**	97		↓	
2/16/91	30	6	6 **Moving On**	—		↓	
3/7/92	22	11	7 **Cold Day In Hell**	—		After Hours	Charisma 91825
7/4/92	37	1	8 **Story Of The Blues**	—		↓	
			MOORE, Ian				
			Born on 8/8/68 in Berkeley, California; raised in Austin, Texas. White blues singer/guitarist.				
8/21/93	15	12	1 **How Does It Feel**	—		Ian Moore	Capricorn 42018
12/18/93+	23	10	2 **Nothing**	—		↓	
7/8/95	18	12	3 **Muddy Jesus**	—		Modernday Folklore	Capricorn 42038
			MORISSETTE, Alanis				
			Born on 6/1/74 in Ottawa, Canada. Female singer/songwriter. At age 12, acted on the Nickelodeon cable-TV kids series *You Can't Do That On Television*.				
8/5/95	3	19	1 **You Oughta Know**	13ᴬ	▲¹⁶	Jagged Little Pill	Maverick 45901
10/7/95	8	16	2 **Hand In My Pocket**	15ᴬ		↓	
3/2/96	18	12	3 **Ironic**	4		↓	
7/6/96	40	1	4 **You Learn**	6		↓	

DEBUT	PEAK	WKS	Mainstream Rock Track	Pop	Gld	Album Title	Album Label & Number
			MORRISON, Van				
			Born George Ivan Morrison on 8/31/45 in Belfast, Ireland. Pop-rock singer/songwriter. Leader of Them. Inducted into the Rock and Roll Hall of Fame in 1993. Also see **Classic Rock Tracks** section.				
3/23/85	19	8	1 Tore Down A La Rimbaud	101		A Sense Of Wonder	Mercury 822895
8/2/86	21	6	2 Ivory Tower..	—		No Guru, no Method, no Teacher.....	Mercury 830077
12/1/90	18	13	3 Real Real Gone	—		Enlightenment.	Mercury 847100
10/26/91	43	11	4 Why Must I Always Explain	—	●	Hymns To The Silence	Polydor 849026
6/19/93	36	5	5 Gloria..	—		Too Long In Exile	Polydor 519219
			John Lee Hooker (additional vocal); #10 Pop hit for The Shadows Of Knight in 1966				
			MOTELS, The				
			Pop-rock group formed in Los Angeles: **Martha Davis** (vocals), Guy Perry (guitar), Marty Jourard (keyboards), Michael Goodroe (bass) and Brian Glascock (drums). Guitarist Scott Thurston joined in 1983. Group disbanded in 1987.				
5/1/82	6	22	1 Only The Lonely	9	●	All Four One	Capitol 12177
5/1/82	36	4	2 Take The L.	52		↓	
5/29/82	23	15	3 Mission Of Mercy	—		↓	
9/10/83	❶²	19	4 Suddenly Last Summer	9	●	Little Robbers	Capitol 12288
10/22/83	18	13	5 Little Robbers	—		↓	
1/21/84	12	5	6 Remember The Nights	36		↓	
7/27/85	10	11	7 Shame	21		Shock	Capitol 12378
			MOTHER STATION, The				
			Blues-rock group from Memphis: Susan Marshall (vocals), Gwin Spencer (guitar), Paul Brown (keyboards), Michael Jaques (bass) and Rick Shelton (drums).				
6/11/94	34	6	Put The Blame On Me	—		Brand New Bag.................	EastWest 92366
★63★			**MÖTLEY CRÜE**				
			Hard-rock group from Los Angeles: **Vince Neil** (vocals), Mick Mars (guitar), Nikki Sixx (bass) and **Tommy Lee** (drums). John Corabi replaced Neil from 1992-96. Sixx married actress Donna D'Errico on 12/23/96. Lee was married to actress Heather Locklear from 1986-93; married to actress Pamela Anderson from 1995-98. Lee left group in April 1999. Drummer Randy Castillo joined in early 2000. Castillo died of cancer on 3/26/2002 (age 51).				
			1)Smokin' In The Boys Room 2)Dr. Feelgood 3)Afraid 4)Hooligan's Holiday 5)Without You				
11/12/83+	12	17	1 Looks That Kill	54	▲⁴	Shout At The Devil	Elektra 60289
11/12/83	30	3	2 Shout At The Devil	—		↓	
5/12/84	17	12	3 Too Young To Fall In Love	90		↓	
7/6/85	7	13	4 Smokin' In The Boys Room	16	▲⁴	Theatre Of Pain	Elektra 60418
			#3 Pop hit for Brownsville Station in 1974				
10/5/85	38	6	5 Home Sweet Home	89		↓	
			also see #13 below				
5/30/87	20	9	6 Girls, Girls, Girls	12	▲⁴	Girls, Girls, Girls	Elektra 60725
9/2/89	7	10	7 Dr. Feelgood	6	▲⁶	Dr. Feelgood..................	Elektra 60829
11/4/89	18	15	8 Kickstart My Heart	27		↓	
2/17/90	11	11	9 Without You	8		↓	
5/12/90	13	14	10 Don't Go Away Mad (Just Go Away)	19		↓	
8/18/90	34	8	11 Same Ol' Situation (S.O.S.)	78		↓	
9/7/91	21	10	12 Primal Scream	63	▲²	Decade Of Decadence - '81-'91 .	Elektra 61204
12/14/91+	41	8	13 Home Sweet Home '91 .... [R]	37		↓	
			remix of #5 above				
2/26/94	10	10	14 Hooligan's Holiday	—	●	Mötley Crüe	Elektra 61534
5/7/94	24	7	15 Misunderstood	—		↓	
5/31/97	10	12	16 Afraid	—	●	Generation Swine.............	Elektra 61901
9/20/97	37	3	17 Beauty	—		↓	
10/17/98	22	10	18 Bitter Pill	—	●	Greatest Hits	Beyond 78002
8/14/99	35	4	19 Teaser	—		Supersonic And Demonic Relics	Mötley 78031
7/1/00	13	12	20 Hell On High Heels	—		New Tattoo	Mötley 78120
			MUDVAYNE				
			Hard-rock group from Peoria, Illinois: Chad Gray (vocals), Greg Tribbett (guitar), Ryan Martinie (bass) and Matt McDonough (drums).				
4/21/01	33	9	1 Dig	—	●	L.D. 50........................	No Name 63821
7/28/01	32	8	2 Death Blooms	—		↓	
10/26/02	21↑	5↑	3 Not Falling	—		The End Of All Things To Come	Epic 86487
			MURPHY, Peter				
			Born on 7/11/57 in Northampton, England. Singer/songwriter.				
2/17/90	10	13	Cuts You Up	55		Deep	Beggars Banquet 9877
			MUST				
			Rock trio formed in London: Dave Ireland (vocals, guitar), Kai Lemke (bass) and Reuben Alexander (drums).				
8/24/02	38	4	Freechild	—		Androgynous Jesus	Wind-Up
			MYLES, Alannah				
			Born on 12/25/55 in Toronto; raised in Buckhorn, Ontario, Canada. Female singer.				
12/9/89+	❶²	18	1 Black Velvet	❶²		Alannah Myles...............	Atlantic 81956
5/12/90	19	7	2 Love Is...	36		↓	

DEBUT	PEAK	WKS	Mainstream Rock Track	Pop Gld	Album Title	Album Label & Number

N

NAKED
Rock group from New Jersey: Jonathan Sheldon (vocals, guitar), Jeremy Ireland (guitar), Damon Martin (bass) and Petur Smith (drums).

| 4/5/97 | **13** | 14 | Mann's Chinese .... | — | *Naked.* .... Gasoline Alley 005 |

NAKED EYES
Pop duo from England: Pete Byrne (vocals) and Rob Fisher (keyboards, synthesizer). Fisher later formed Climie Fisher. Fisher died on 8/25/99 (age 39).

| 4/16/83 | **20** | 10 | Always Something There To Remind Me.................. | 8 | *Naked Eyes* .... EMI America 17089 |

#27 Pop hit for R.B. Greaves in 1970

NASH, Graham
Born on 2/2/42 in Blackpool, Lancashire, England. Singer/songwriter/guitarist. Former member of The Hollies. Formed **Crosby, Stills & Nash** in 1968. Also see **Classic Rock Tracks** section.

| 4/5/86 | **14** | 7 | Innocent Eyes.. | 84 | *Innocent Eyes* .... Atlantic 81633 |

Kenny Loggins (backing vocal)

NAVARRO, Dave
Born on 6/6/67 in Santa Monica, California. Rock singer/guitarist. Former member of **Jane's Addiction** and **Red Hot Chili Peppers**.

| 6/2/01 | **9** | 12 | 1 Rexall .... | — | *Trust No One* .... Capitol 32802 |
| 10/20/01 | **38** | 3 | 2 Hungry .... | — | ↓ |

NAZARETH
Hard-rock group formed in Dunfermline, Fife, Scotland: Dan McCafferty (vocals), **Billy Rankin** and Manny Charlton (guitars), John Locke (keyboards), Pete Agnew (bass) and Darrell Sweet (drums). Sweet died of a heart attack on 4/30/99 (age 51). Also see **Classic Rock Tracks** section.

| 7/17/82 | **19** | 12 | Love Leads To Madness .... | 105 | *2XS* .... A&M 4901 |

NDEGÉOCELLO, Me'Shell — see MELLENCAMP, John

NEIL, Vince
Born Vincent Neil Wharton on 2/8/61 in Hollywood. Lead singer of **Mötley Crüe**.

5/23/92	**17**	9	1 You're Invited But Your Friend Can't Come	—	*Encino Man (soundtrack)* .... Hollywood 61330
5/1/93	**12**	10	2 Sister Of Pain	—	*Exposed*....................... Warner 45260
7/24/93	**34**	4	3 Can't Have Your Cake	—	↓

NELSON
Pop-rock duo from Los Angeles: Gunnar (vocals, bass) and Matthew (vocals, guitar) Nelson. The identical twin sons (born on 9/20/67) of Ricky Nelson.

7/21/90	**20**	13	1 (Can't Live Without Your) Love And Affection	❶¹ ▲²	*After The Rain* .... DGC 24290
11/24/90	**39**	8	2 After The Rain	6	↓
4/6/91	**44**	3	3 More Than Ever	14	↓

NENA
Rock group formed in Berlin, Germany: Gabriele "Nena" Kerner (vocals), Carlo Karges (guitar), Uwe Fahrenkrog-Petersen (keyboards), Jurgen Demel (bass) and Rolf Brendel (drums). Karges died of liver failure on 1/30/2002 (age 50).

| 1/28/84 | **23** | 9 | 99 Luftballons.. [F] | 2¹ | *99 Luftballons* .... Epic 39294 |

nuclear protest song

NEUROTIC OUTSIDERS
All-star rock group: Steve Jones (vocals, guitar), John Taylor (vocals, bass), Duff McKagan (guitar) and Matt Sorum (drums). Jones was with the Sex Pistols. Taylor was with **Duran Duran**. McKagen and Sorum were with **Guns N' Roses**.

| 8/31/96 | **31** | 6 | Jerk... | — | *Neurotic Outsiders*.............. Maverick 46290 |

NEVERLAND
Rock group formed in Los Angeles: Dean Ortega (vocals), Patrick Sugg (guitar), Gary Lee (bass) and Scott Garrett (drums).

| 7/27/91 | **41** | 4 | Drinking Again .... | — | *Neverland* .... Interscope 91713 |

NEVILLE, Ivan
Born on 7/23/65 in New Orleans. Rock singer/bassist. Son of Aaron Neville.

| 10/22/88 | **6** | 15 | Not Just Another Girl | 26 | *If My Ancestors Could See Me Now* . . . Polydor 834896 |

NEW AMERICAN SHAME
Rock group from Seattle: Johnny Reidt (vocals), Jimmy Paulson and Terry Bratsch (guitars), Kelly Wheeler (bass) and Geoff Reading (drums).

| 7/3/99 | **35** | 5 | Under It All.. | — | *New American Shame* .... Will 83204 |

NEWMAN, Randy
Born on 11/28/43 in New Orleans. Singer/songwriter/pianist. Nephew of composers Alfred, Emil and Lionel Newman. Scored several movies. Recipient of Billboard's Century Award in 2000. Also see **Classic Rock Tracks** section.

| 10/1/88 | **❶²** | 12 | It's Money That Matters | 60 | *Land Of Dreams* .... Reprise 25773 |

Mark Knopfler (of **Dire Straits**; guitar)

NEWTON, Juice
Born Judy Kay Cohen on 2/18/52 in Lakehurst, New Jersey. Pop-country singer/guitarist.

| 3/21/81 | **57** | 1 | Angel Of The Morning .... | 4 ▲ | *Juice* .... Capitol 12136 |

#7 Pop hit for Merrilee Rush in 1968

DEBUT	PEAK	WKS	Mainstream Rock Track	Pop Gld	Album Title	Album Label & Number

★92★ NICKELBACK

Rock group from Vancouver: brothers **Chad Kroeger** (vocals) and Mike Kroeger (bass), with Ryan Peake (guitar) and Ryan Vikedal (drums).

DEBUT	PEAK	WKS	Track	Pop Gld	Album Title	Label & Number
3/4/00	8	25	1 Leader Of Men	— ●	The State	Roadrunner 8586
8/12/00	10	17	2 Breathe	— ↓		
12/23/00+	24	10	3 Old Enough	— ↓		
7/28/01	❶13	48	4 How You Remind Me	❶4 ▲4	Silver Side Up	Roadrunner 618485
12/15/01+	❶3	32	5 Too Bad	42 ↓		
7/20/02	❶3	19↑	6 Never Again	124 ↓		

★43★ NICKS, Stevie

Born Stephanie Nicks on 5/26/48 in Phoenix; raised in San Francisco. Pop-rock singer/songwriter. Teamed up with **Lindsey Buckingham** in 1973. Both joined **Fleetwood Mac** in 1975.

1)Talk To Me   2)Rooms On Fire   3)Stand Back

DEBUT	PEAK	WKS	Track	Pop Gld	Album Title	Label & Number
8/1/81	2¹	24	1 Stop Draggin' My Heart Around STEVIE NICKS (with Tom Petty and The Heartbreakers)	3 ▲4	Bella Donna	Modern 139
8/8/81	4	25	2 Edge Of Seventeen (Just Like The White Winged Dove) also see #4 below	11 ↓		
11/28/81+	26	12	3 Leather And Lace STEVIE NICKS (with DON HENLEY)	6 ↓		
2/27/82	26	9	4 Edge Of Seventeen (Just Like The White Winged Dove) [L-R] live version of #2 above	—	(single only)	Modern 7401
6/4/83	2³	18	5 Stand Back	5 ▲2	The Wild Heart	Modern 90084
7/16/83	12	12	6 Enchanted	↓		
7/23/83	35	4	7 I Will Run To You STEVIE NICKS (With Tom Petty and the Heartbreakers)	— ↓		
7/30/83	19	9	8 Nothing Ever Changes	— ↓		
9/24/83	8	11	9 If Anyone Falls	14 ↓		
2/11/84	32	2	10 Nightbird STEVIE NICKS (with Sandy Stewart)	33 ↓		
3/31/84	19	8	11 Violet And Blue	— ●	Against All Odds (soundtrack)	Atlantic 80152
11/16/85	❶2	13	12 Talk To Me	4 ▲	Rock A Little	Modern 90479
11/30/85+	6	18	13 I Can't Wait	16 ↓		
12/28/85+	17	11	14 Needles And Pins [L] TOM PETTY and the HEARTBREAKERS with STEVIE NICKS #13 Pop hit for The Searchers in 1964; recorded at the Wiltern Theater in Los Angeles	37	Pack Up The Plantation - Live! (Petty)	MCA 8021
5/6/89	❶1	14	15 Rooms On Fire	16 ▲	The Other Side Of The Mirror	Modern 91245
7/1/89	11	12	16 Long Way To Go	— ↓		
8/31/91	7	9	17 Sometimes It's A Bitch written by Billy Falcon and Jon Bon Jovi (also on guitar)	56 ▲	TimeSpace - The Best Of Stevie Nicks . .	Modern 91711
6/25/94	36	3	18 Maybe Love Will Change Your Mind	57 ●	Street Angel	Modern 92246

NIGHT RANGER

Rock group formed in San Francisco: Jack Blades (vocals, bass), Kelly Keagy (vocals, drums), Jeff Watson and **Brad Gillis** (guitars), and Alan Fitzgerald (keyboards). Blades later joined **Damn Yankees** and formed duo with **Tommy Shaw**.

1)Sister Christian   2)Sentimental Street   3)Don't Tell Me You Love Me

DEBUT	PEAK	WKS	Track	Pop Gld	Album Title	Label & Number
12/11/82+	4	18	1 Don't Tell Me You Love Me	40	Dawn Patrol	Boardwalk 33259
3/19/83	39	2	2 Sing Me Away	54 ↓		
11/19/83	15	19	3 (You Can Still) Rock In America	51 ▲	Midnight Madness	MCA/Camel 5456
2/25/84	26	5	4 Rumours In The Air	— ↓		
3/31/84	2¹	14	5 Sister Christian	5 ↓		
7/7/84	7	15	6 When You Close Your Eyes	14 ↓		
5/25/85	3	13	7 Sentimental Street	8 ▲	7 Wishes	MCA/Camel 5593
8/17/85	13	12	8 Four In The Morning (I Can't Take Any More)	19 ↓		
11/30/85+	16	12	9 Goodbye	17 ↓		
3/21/87	12	10	10 The Secret Of My Success	64	The Secret Of My Success (soundtrack)	MCA 6205
9/24/88	16	8	11 I Did It For Love	75	Man In Motion	MCA/Camel 6238
1/14/89	48	1	12 Reason To Be	— ↓		

NILE, Willie

Born Robert Noonan in 1949 in Buffalo, New York. Rock singer/songwriter.

DEBUT	PEAK	WKS	Track	Pop Gld	Album Title	Label & Number
5/9/81	55	2	1 Golden Down	—	Golden Down	Arista 4284
4/13/91	16	12	2 Heaven Help The Lonely	—	Places I Have Never Been	Columbia 44434

NINE INCH NAILS

Group is actually industrial rock musician Trent Reznor (born on 5/17/65 in Mercer, Pennsylvania).

DEBUT	PEAK	WKS	Track	Pop Gld	Album Title	Label & Number
9/24/94	35	4	1 Closer	41 ▲4	The Downward Spiral	Nothing 92346
2/8/97	21	10	2 The Perfect Drug	46 ●	Lost Highway (soundtrack)	Nothing 90090
9/18/99	21	13	3 We're In This Together	— ▲2	The Fragile	Nothing 490473
1/1/00	27	9	4 Into The Void	— ↓		
6/23/01	37	4	5 Deep	— ●	Lara Croft: Tomb Raider (soundtrack) . . .	Elektra 62665

DEBUT	PEAK	WKS	Mainstream Rock Track	Pop	Gld	Album Title	Album Label & Number

★72★

NIRVANA
Grunge-rock trio from Aberdeen, Washington: Kurt Cobain (vocals, guitar; born on 2/20/67), Krist Novoselic (bass; born on 5/16/65) and Dave Grohl (drums; born on 1/14/69). Cobain married Courtney Love (lead singer of Hole) on 2/24/92. Cobain died of a self-inflicted gunshot wound on 4/8/94 (age 27). Grohl formed Foo Fighters in 1995.

1)You Know You're Right 2)Come As You Are 3)About A Girl

DEBUT	PEAK	WKS	Track	Pop	Gld	Album	Label
11/2/91+	7	24	1 Smells Like Teen Spirit	6	▲10	Nevermind	DGC 24425
1/25/92	3	25	2 Come As You Are	32	↓		
6/20/92	16	16	3 Lithium	64	↓		
12/26/92+	5	17	4 In Bloom	—	↓		
9/18/93	4	21	5 Heart-Shaped Box	—	▲5	In Utero	DGC 24607
12/18/93+	4	26	6 All Apologies	45A	↓		
10/15/94	3	26	7 About A Girl [L]	22A	▲5	MTV Unplugged In New York	DGC 24727
			studio version on their 1989 album *Bleach*				
1/28/95	12	12	8 The Man Who Sold The World [L]	39A	↓		
			first recorded by David Bowie in 1970				
5/27/95	22	9	9 Lake Of Fire [L]	—	↓		
			above 3 recorded on 11/18/93				
9/28/96	11	9	10 Aneurysm [L]	63A		From The Muddy Banks Of The Wishkah	DGC 25105
			recorded on 12/28/91 at Del Mar Fairgrounds in California				
10/12/02	❶4↑	7↑	11 You Know You're Right	45↑		Nirvana	DGC 493507
			recorded on 1/30/94				

NIXONS, The
Rock group from Dallas: Zac Maloy (vocals, guitar), Jesse Davis (guitar), Ricky Brooks (bass) and John Humphrey (drums).

DEBUT	PEAK	WKS	Track	Pop	Gld	Album	Label
1/20/96	6	26	1 Sister	48A		Foma	MCA 11209
7/20/96	27	9	2 Wire	—	↓		
6/7/97	9	17	3 Baton Rouge	—		The Nixons	MCA 11644
9/20/97	22	8	4 The Fall	—	↓		
5/27/00	32	6	5 First Trip To The Moon	—		Latest Thing	Koch 8085

NONPOINT
Rock group from New York City: Elias Soriano (vocals), Andrew Goldman (guitar), KB (bass) and Robb Rivera (drums).

DEBUT	PEAK	WKS	Track	Pop	Gld	Album	Label
3/3/01	24	15	1 What A Day	—		Statement	MCA 112364
6/29/02	36	7	2 Your Signs	—		Development	MCA 112920

NORTHERN PIKES, The
Rock group from Canada: Jay Semko (vocals, bass), Merl Bryck (vocals, guitar), Bryan Potvin (guitar) and Don Schmid (drums).

DEBUT	PEAK	WKS	Track	Pop	Gld	Album	Label
10/10/87	37	6	Things I Do For Money	—		Big Blue Sky	Virgin 90635

NORUM, John
Born in Norway; raised in Stockholm, Sweden. Lead guitarist of Europe from 1982-87.

DEBUT	PEAK	WKS	Track	Pop	Gld	Album	Label
7/9/88	34	6	Back On The Streets	—		Total Control	Epic 44220

NOTHINGFACE
Hard-rock group from Washington DC: Matt Holt (vocals), Tom Maxwell (guitar), Bill Gaal (bass) and Chris Houck (drums).

DEBUT	PEAK	WKS	Track	Pop	Gld	Album	Label
2/10/01	32	9	Bleeder	—		Violence	TVT 5880

NOTTING HILLBILLIES, The
Gorup of rock guitarists: Mark Knopfler and Guy Fletcher (both of Dire Straits), with Brendan Croker and Steve Phillips. Recorded at Knopfler's studio in London's Notting Hill Gate.

DEBUT	PEAK	WKS	Track	Pop	Gld	Album	Label
3/10/90	20	8	Your Own Sweet Way	—		Missing...Presumed Having A Good Time	Warner 26147

NOVA, Aldo
Born Aldo Scarporuscio in Montreal. Rock singer/songwriter/guitarist.

DEBUT	PEAK	WKS	Track	Pop	Gld	Album	Label
2/13/82	3	22	1 Fantasy	23	▲2	Aldo Nova	Portrait 37498
10/8/83	12	16	2 Monkey On Your Back	—	●	Subject: Aldo Nova	Portrait 38721
5/18/91	14	9	3 Blood On The Bricks	—		Blood On The Bricks	Jambco 848513
8/24/91	43	4	4 Medicine Man	—	↓		
			Jon Bon Jovi (backing vocal, above 2)				

NOVO COMBO
Rock group formed in New York City: Pete Hewlett (vocals), Jack Griffith (guitar), Stephen Dees (bass) and Michael Shrieve (drums; Santana).

DEBUT	PEAK	WKS	Track	Pop	Gld	Album	Label
10/17/81+	43	13	1 Up Periscope	—		Novo Combo	Polydor 6331
2/20/82	42	8	2 Tattoo	103	↓		

NUGENT, Ted
Born on 12/13/48 in Detroit. Hard-rock singer/guitarist. Leader of The Amboy Dukes. Later joined Damn Yankees. An avid game hunter and an active supporter of the National Rifle Association. Also see Classic Rock Tracks section.

DEBUT	PEAK	WKS	Track	Pop	Gld	Album	Label
3/21/81	36	3	1 The Flying Lip Lock [L]	—		Intensities In 10 Cities	Epic 37084
3/21/81	56	1	2 Jailbait [L]	—	↓		
3/28/81	47	1	3 Land Of A Thousand Dances [L]	—	↓		
			#6 Pop hit for Wilson Pickett in 1966				
3/3/84	41	2	4 Tied Up In Love	107		Penetrator	Atlantic 80125
3/15/86	22	9	5 Little Miss Dangerous	—		Little Miss Dangerous	Atlantic 81632

DEBUT	PEAK	WKS	Mainstream Rock Track	Pop	Gld	Album Title	Album Label & Number

O

OASIS
Rock group from Manchester, England: brothers Liam (vocals; born on 9/12/72) and Noel (guitar; born on 5/29/67) Gallagher, Paul Arthurs (guitar), Paul McGuigan (bass) and Tony McCarroll (drums). Alan White replaced McCarroll in 1995.

DEBUT	PEAK	WKS	Track	Pop	Gld	Album Title	Album Label & Number
12/24/94	38	2	1 Supersonic	—	▲	Definitely Maybe	Epic 66431
2/25/95	10	14	2 Live Forever	39ᴬ		↓	
12/30/95+	9	17	3 Wonderwall	8	▲⁴	(What's The Story) Morning Glory?	Epic 67351
4/13/96	8	15	4 Champagne Supernova	20ᴬ		↓	
8/16/97	36	5	5 D' You Know What I Mean?	49ᴬ	▲	Be Here Now	Epic 68530
11/15/97	36	4	6 Don't Go Away	35ᴬ		↓	

OCASEK, Ric
Born Richard Otcasek on 3/23/49 in Baltimore. Lead singer/guitarist/songwriter of **The Cars**. Appeared in the 1987 movie *Made In Heaven*. Married supermodel/actress Paulina Porizkova on 8/23/89. His son Christopher Otcasek is leader of **Glamour Camp**.

DEBUT	PEAK	WKS	Track	Pop	Gld	Album Title	Album Label & Number
1/29/83	5	17	1 Something To Grab For	47		Beatitude	Geffen 2022
2/5/83	25	1	2 Jimmy Jimmy			↓	
9/6/86	❶¹	12	3 Emotion In Motion	15		This Side Of Paradise	Geffen 24098
10/11/86	9	17	4 True To You	75		↓	
6/29/91	11	8	5 Rockaway	—		Fireball Zone	Reprise 26552

O'CONNOR, Sinéad
Born on 12/12/66 in Glenageary, Ireland. Female singer/songwriter.

DEBUT	PEAK	WKS	Track	Pop	Gld	Album Title	Album Label & Number
3/31/90	23	7	1 Nothing Compares 2 U	❶⁴	▲²	I Do Not Want What I Haven't Got	Ensign 21759
			written by **Prince**				
5/26/90	40	3	2 The Emperor's New Clothes	60		↓	

★54★ OFFSPRING, The
Punk-rock group from Anaheim, California: Brian "Dexter" Holland (vocals; born on 12/29/66), Kevin "Noodles" Wasserman (guitar; born on 2/14/63), Greg Kriesel (bass; born on 1/20/65) and Ron Welty (drums; born on 1/1/71).
1)Gone Away 2)Pretty Fly (For A White Guy) 3)I Choose

DEBUT	PEAK	WKS	Track	Pop	Gld	Album Title	Album Label & Number
7/16/94	10	26	1 Come Out And Play	38ᴬ	▲⁶	Smash	Epitaph 86432
10/1/94	7	26	2 Self Esteem	45ᴬ		↓	
1/28/95	15	23	3 Gotta Get Away	58ᴬ		↓	
1/18/97	18	7	4 All I Want	65ᴬ	▲	Ixnay On The Hombre	Columbia 67810
3/1/97	❶²	34	5 Gone Away	50ᴬ		↓	
8/2/97	5	22	6 I Choose	—		↓	
10/17/98+	5	25	7 Pretty Fly (For A White Guy)	53	▲⁴	Americana	Columbia 69661
			intro samples "Rock Of Ages" by **Def Leppard**				
2/13/99	10	20	8 Why Don't You Get A Job?	74		↓	
6/12/99	11	26	9 The Kids Aren't Alright	105		↓	
10/23/99	19	16	10 She's Got Issues	—		↓	
6/10/00	36	1	11 Totalimmortal	—		Me, Myself & Irene (soundtrack)	Elektra 62512
10/21/00+	7	18	12 Original Prankster	70	▲	Conspiracy Of One	Columbia 61419
2/10/01	23	10	13 Want You Bad	—		↓	
12/8/01+	8	21	14 Defy You	77		Orange County (soundtrack)	Columbia 85933

OLDFIELD, Mike
Born on 5/15/53 in Reading, England. Classical-rock, multi-instrumentalist/composer.

DEBUT	PEAK	WKS	Track	Pop	Gld	Album Title	Album Label & Number
1/30/88	10	9	Magic Touch	—		Islands	Virgin 90645
			Max Bacon (of **GTR**; vocal)				

OLEANDER
Pop-rock group from Sacramento, California: Thomas Flowers (vocals), Ric Ivanisevich (guitar), Doug Eldridge (bass) and Fred Nelson (drums).

DEBUT	PEAK	WKS	Track	Pop	Gld	Album Title	Album Label & Number
2/20/99	3	33	1 Why I'm Here	107	●	February Son	Republic 53242
9/11/99	24	11	2 I Walk Alone	—		↓	
2/17/01	6	17	3 Are You There?	—		Unwind	Republic 013377

OMAR & THE HOWLERS
Rock group from Austin, Texas: Kent "Omar" Dykes (vocals, guitar), Bruce Jones (bass) and Gene Brandon (drums). Eric Scortia (keyboards) joined in late 1987.

DEBUT	PEAK	WKS	Track	Pop	Gld	Album Title	Album Label & Number
6/6/87	19	10	1 Hard Times In The Land Of Plenty	—		Hard Times In The Land Of Plenty	Columbia 40815
9/24/88	36	5	2 Rattlesnake Shake	—		Wall Of Pride	Columbia 44102

ONE MINUTE SILENCE
Rock group from England: Brian Barry (vocals), Massimo Fiocco (guitar), Glen Diani (bass) and Eddie Stratton (drums).

DEBUT	PEAK	WKS	Track	Pop	Gld	Album Title	Album Label & Number
5/27/00	39	1	Holy Man	—		Buy Now...Saved Later	V2 27069

ONE WAY RIDE
Rock group from Los Angeles: Leldon (vocals, guitar), Chris Scott (guitar), Tim Lunsford (bass) and Brian Carhart (drums).

DEBUT	PEAK	WKS	Track	Pop	Gld	Album Title	Album Label & Number
7/15/00	16	11	Painted Perfect	—		Straight Up!	Refuge 112347

OPEN SKYZ
Rock group from New York City: Hugo (vocals), Adam Holland (guitar), Craig Pullman (keyboards) and Gerard Zappa (bass).

DEBUT	PEAK	WKS	Track	Pop	Gld	Album Title	Album Label & Number
1/8/94	25	7	Every Day Of My Life	—		Open Skyz	Zito 66343

DEBUT	PEAK	WKS	Mainstream Rock Track	Pop	Gld	Album Title	Album Label & Number

ORBISON, Roy
Born on 4/23/36 in Vernon, Texas. Died of a heart attack on 12/6/88 (age 52). Pop-rock singer/songwriter/guitarist. Inducted into the Rock and Roll Hall of Fame in 1987. Won Grammy's Lifetime Achievement Award in 1998. Member of the **Traveling Wilburys**.

1/21/89	2²	13	〰 You Got It	9	▲	Mystery Girl	Virgin 91058
			written by Orbison, **Jeff Lynne** and **Tom Petty**				
3/11/89	26	9	〰 2 She's A Mystery To Me	—		↓	
			written by Bono and The Edge (both of **U2**)				

ORBIT
Rock trio from Boston: Jeff Lowe Robbins (vocals, guitar), Wally Gagel (bass) and Paul Buckley (drums).

| 4/19/97 | 29 | 4 | Medicine . . . . | — | | Libido Speedway . . . . | A&M 540652 |

ORCHESTRAL MANOEUVRES IN THE DARK
Electro-pop group formed in England: keyboardist/vocalists Andrew McCluskey and Paul Humphreys, multi-instrumentalist Martin Cooper and drummer Malcolm Holmes. Humphreys left in 1989.

| 3/26/83 | 32 | 8 | 1 Telegraph . . . . | — | | Dazzle Ships . . . . | Epic 38543 |
| 4/2/83 | 32 | 9 | 2 Genetic Engineering . . . . | — | | ↓ | |

ORGY
Electronic rock group from Los Angeles: Jay Gordon (vocals), Ryan Shuck (guitar), Amir Derakh (keyboards), Paige Haley (bass) and Bobby Hewitt (drums).

1/23/99	18	24	1 Blue Monday	56	▲	Candyass	Elementree 46923
			#68 Pop hit for **New Order** in 1988				
7/24/99	38	4	2 Stitches	—		↓	
9/16/00	38	4	3 Fiction (Dreams In Digital)	—	●	Vapor Transmission	Elementree 47832

ORION THE HUNTER
Rock group formed in Boston: Fran Cosmo (vocals), Barry Goudreau (guitar), Bruce Smith (bass) and Michael DeRosier (drums). Goudreau was a member of **Boston** and **RTZ**. Cosmo joined **Boston** in 1994.

| 4/21/84 | 7 | 12 | So You Ran | 58 | | Orion The Hunter . . . . | Portrait 39239 |

ORR, Benjamin
Born Benjamin Orzechowski on 8/9/47 in Cleveland. Died of cancer on 10/3/2000 (age 53). Bassist/vocalist of **The Cars**.

| 10/25/86 | 6 | 14 | 1 Stay The Night | 24 | | The Lace . . . . | Elektra 60460 |
| 1/31/87 | 25 | 8 | 2 Too Hot To Stop . . . . | — | | ↓ | |

OSBORNE, Joan
Born on 7/8/62 in Anchorage, Kentucky. Singer/songwriter/guitarist.

| 11/11/95+ | 26 | 10 | One Of Us . . . . | 4 | ▲³ | Relish . . . . | Blue Gorilla 526699 |

OSBOURNE, Ozzy ★20★
Born John Osbourne on 12/3/48 in Birmingham, England. Lead singer of **Black Sabbath**. Controversial in his concert antics. Married his manager Sharon Arden on 7/4/82. Appeared in the 1986 movie *Trick Or Treat*. MTV began airing *The Osbournes*, a reality show based on his family's home life, in 2002.

1)Gets Me Through 2)Mama, I'm Coming Home 3)Flying High Again 4)Back On Earth 5)Road To Nowhere

4/18/81	9	21	1 Crazy Train	106	▲⁴	Blizzard Of Ozz	Jet 36812
11/14/81+	2¹	25	2 Flying High Again	—	▲³	Diary Of A Madman	Jet 37492
1/23/82	41	13	3 You Can't Kill Rock And Roll	—		↓	
2/6/82	38	8	4 Over The Mountain	—		↓	
12/25/82+	25	7	5 Paranoid . . . . [L]	—	▲	Speak Of The Devil	Jet 38350
			#61 Pop hit for **Black Sabbath** in 1970				
12/25/82+	32	8	6 Iron Man/Children Of The Grave . . . . . . [L]	—		↓	
			medley of **Black Sabbath** tunes; "Iron Man" was a #52 Pop hit in 1972; "Children Of The Grave" first recorded on their 1971 album *Master Of Reality*; above 2 recorded on 9/26/82 at The Ritz in New York City				
12/10/83+	12	13	7 Bark At The Moon	109	▲³	Bark At The Moon	CBS Associated 38987
2/11/84	40	4	8 Rock 'N' Roll Rebel	—		↓	
2/8/86	10	13	9 Shot In The Dark	68	▲²	The Ultimate Sin	CBS Associated 40026
4/29/89	25	9	10 Close My Eyes Forever	8	▲	Lita (Ford)	RCA 6397
			LITA FORD (with Ozzy Osbourne)				
9/21/91	10	24	11 No More Tears	71	▲⁴	No More Tears	Epic/Associated 46795
12/14/91+	2³	29	12 Mama, I'm Coming Home	28		↓	
5/9/92	3	20	13 Road To Nowhere	—		↓	
9/19/92	34	3	14 Mr. Tinkertrain	—		↓	
10/10/92	6	19	15 Time After Time	—		↓	
6/5/93	9	12	16 Changes . . . . [L]	—	▲	Live & Loud	Epic/Associated 48973
			first recorded by **Black Sabbath** in 1972				
10/14/95	3	23	17 Perry Mason	—	▲²	Ozzmosis	Epic 67091
12/23/95+	5	19	18 See You On The Other Side	—		↓	
5/18/96	24	7	19 I Just Want You	—	●	Beavis And Butt-Head Do America	
11/23/96	28	8	20 Walk On Water	—		(soundtrack)	Geffen 25002
11/1/97	3	26	21 Back On Earth	—	▲²	The Ozzman Cometh	Epic 67980
10/16/99	26	7	22 Shock The Monkey	—	●	Chamber Music	Roadrunner 8659
			COAL CHAMBER Featuring Ozzy Osbourne				

DEBUT	PEAK	WKS	Mainstream Rock Track	Pop Gld	Album Title	Album Label & Number
			OSBOURNE, Ozzy — Cont'd			
7/15/00	2²	41	23 N.I.B.	—	Nativity In Black II: A Tribute To Black Sabbath	
			PRIMUS with Ozzy Osbourne first recorded by **Black Sabbath** in 1970		(various artists)	Divine 26095
9/15/01	2⁶	26	24 Gets Me Through	118 ●	Down To Earth	Epic 63580
12/8/01+	10	23	25 Dreamer	— ↓		
			OTHER ONES, The			
			Rock group consisting of Australian siblings Jayney (vocals), Alf (vocals) and Johnny (bass) Klimek, and Germans Andreas Schwarz-Ruszczynski (guitar), Stephen Gottwald (keyboards) and Uwe Hoffmann (drums).			
5/9/87	38	4	We Are What We Are	53	The Other Ones	Virgin 90576
			OUR LADY PEACE			
			Rock group from Toronto: Raine Maida (vocals), Mike Turner (guitar), Chris Eacrett (bass) and Jeremy Taggart (drums). Duncan Coutts replaced Eacrett in 1996.			
3/25/95	7	16	1 Starseed	—	Naveed	Relativity 1507
6/28/97	14	19	2 Superman's Dead	74ᴬ ●	Clumsy	Columbia 67940
12/13/97+	13	20	3 Clumsy	59ᴬ ↓		
7/4/98	38	2	4 4 AM	— ↓		
9/18/99	16	11	5 One Man Army	—	Happiness...Is Not A Fish That You Can Catch	Columbia 63707
2/12/00	27	9	6 Is Anybody Home?	— ↓		
5/11/02	26	14	7 Somewhere Out There	44 ●	Gravity	Columbia 86585
10/19/02	35	5	8 Innocent	— ↓		
			OUTFIELD, The			
			Pop-rock trio formed in London: Tony Lewis (vocals, bass), John Spinks (guitar) and Alan Jackman (drums). Jackman left by 1990; Lewis and Spinks continued as a duo.			
			1)Voices Of Babylon 2)Your Love 3)Since You've Been Gone			
8/31/85	18	13	1 Say It Isn't So	— ▲²	Play Deep	Columbia 40027
1/18/86	7	15	2 Your Love	6 ↓		
5/24/86	14	11	3 All The Love In The World	19 ↓		
9/27/86	20	8	4 Everytime You Cry	66 ↓		
6/6/87	11	12	5 Since You've Been Gone	31 ●	Bangin'	Columbia 40619
9/19/87	40	3	6 Bangin' On My Heart	— ↓		
3/25/89	2²	12	7 Voices Of Babylon	25	Voices Of Babylon	Columbia 44449
6/17/89	34	6	8 My Paradise	72 ↓		
11/3/90	13	13	9 For You	21	Diamond Days	MCA 10111
6/6/92	46	1	10 Closer To Me	43	Rockeye	MCA 10476
			OUTHOUSE			
			Rock trio from Kansas City: Bill Latas (vocals, guitar), Brad Gaddy (bass) and Shawn Poores (drums).			
4/12/97	30	9	Welcome	—	Welcome	Mercury 534399
			OUTLAWS			
			Rock group formed in Tampa, Florida: **Henry Paul** (vocals, guitar), Hughie Thomasson and Billy Jones (guitars), Frank O'Keefe (bass) and Monte Yoho (drums). By 1981, Freddie Salem, Rick Cua and David Dix had replaced Paul, O'Keefe and Yoho. Thomasson joined **Lynyrd Skynyrd** in 1996. Jones died on 2/7/95 (age 45). O'Keefe died of a drug overdose on 2/26/95 (age 44). Also see **Classic Rock Tracks** section.			
3/21/81	15	4	(Ghost) Riders In The Sky	31 ●	Ghost Riders	Arista 9542
			#1 Pop hit for Vaughn Monroe in 1949			

P

DEBUT	PEAK	WKS	Mainstream Rock Track	Pop Gld	Album Title	Album Label & Number
			PABLO CRUISE			
			Pop-rock group from San Francisco: Dave Jenkins (vocals, guitar), Angelo Rossi (guitar), Cory Lerios (keyboards), John Pierce (bass) and Stephen Price (drums).			
7/25/81	23	16	Cool Love	13	Reflector	A&M 3726
	★68★		**PAGE, Jimmy**			
			Born on 1/9/44 in Heston, Middlesex, England. Rock guitarist. Member of **Led Zeppelin**, **The Honeydrippers** and **The Firm**.			
			1)Pride And Joy 2)Most High 3)Gallows Pole			
6/25/88	4	8	1 Wasting My Time	— ●	Outrider	Geffen 24188
			John Miles (vocal)			
7/2/88	13	10	2 The Only One	— ↓		
			Robert Plant (vocal)			
9/10/88	26	8	3 Prison Blues	— ↓		
			Chris Farlow (vocal)			
2/27/93	❶⁶	15	4 Pride And Joy	— ▲	Coverdale•Page	Geffen 24487
3/27/93	3	17	5 Shake My Tree	— ↓		
6/19/93	15	9	6 Take Me For A Little While	115 ↓		
8/28/93	24	6	7 Over Now	— ↓		
			COVERDALE•PAGE (above 4)			

DEBUT	PEAK	WKS	Mainstream Rock Track	Pop	Gld	Album Title	Album Label & Number
			PAGE, Jimmy — Cont'd				
10/22/94	**2**³	14	8 Gallows Pole	—	▲	No Quarter	Atlantic 82706
			first recorded by **Led Zeppelin** in 1970				
12/17/94+	**8**	14	9 Thank You	—	↓		
			first recorded by **Led Zeppelin** in 1969				
4/18/98	**❶**²	13	10 Most High	—	●	Walking Into Clarksdale	Atlantic 83092
5/30/98	**6**	18	11 Shining In The Light	—	↓		
			JIMMY PAGE & ROBERT PLANT (above 4)				
3/18/00	**13**	13	12 What Is And What Should Never Be .... [L]	—	●	Live At The Greek	TVT 2140
8/5/00	**33**	7	13 Ten Years Gone .... [L]	—	↓		
			JIMMY PAGE & THE BLACK CROWES (above 2)				
			PALMER, Robert				
			Born Alan Palmer on 1/19/49 in Batley, Yorkshire, England; raised on the Mediterranean island of Malta. Lead singer of **The Power Station**. Also see **Classic Rock Tracks** section.				
5/22/82	**59**	2	✓1 Some Guys Have All The Luck	—		Maybe It's Live	Island 9665
			#39 Pop hit for The Persuaders in 1973				
6/18/83	**33**	4	✓2 You Are In My System	78		Pride	Island 90065
			#64 Pop hit for The System in 1983				
2/15/86	**❶**²	14	✓3 Addicted To Love	**❶**¹	▲²	Riptide	Island 90471
5/3/86	**21**	11	✓4 Hyperactive	33	↓		
9/27/86	**41**	4	✓5 I Didn't Mean To Turn You On	2¹	↓		
			#79 Pop hit for Cherrelle in 1984				
7/2/88	**❶**³	12	6 Simply Irresistible	2²	▲	Heavy Nova	EMI-Manhattan 48057
9/3/88	**40**	7	7 Early In The Morning	19	↓		
			#24 Pop hit for The Gap Band in 1982				
3/10/90	**7**	9	8 Life In Detail	—	▲³	Pretty Woman (soundtrack)	EMI 93492
11/17/90	**5**	10	9 You're Amazing	28		Don't Explain	EMI 93935
			PANTERA				
			Hard-rock group formed in Texas: Philip Anselmo (vocals), Diamond Darrell (guitar), Rex Brown (bass) and Vinnie Paul (drums). Darrell and Paul are brothers. Diamond changed his first name to Dimebag in 1994. Group name is Spanish for Panther. Anselmo also with **Down** in 1995.				
9/3/94	**21**	12	1 Planet Caravan	—	▲	Far Beyond Driven	EastWest 92302
			first recorded by **Black Sabbath** in 1971				
9/18/99	**40**	1	2 Cat Scratch Fever	—		Detroit Rock City (soundtrack)	Mercury 546389
			#30 Pop hit for **Ted Nugent** in 1977				
3/25/00	**28**	11	3 Revolution Is My Name	—	●	Reinventing The Steel	EastWest 62451
			PAPA ROACH				
			Rock group from Vacaville, California: Coby Dick (vocals), Jerry Horton (guitar), Tobin Esperance (bass) and Dave Buckner (drums).				
5/6/00	**4**	44	1 Last Resort	57	▲³	Infest	DreamWorks 50223
9/30/00	**18**	20	2 Broken Home	—	↓		
3/3/01	**27**	8	3 Between Angels And Insects	—	↓		
5/18/02	**3**	25	4 She Loves Me Not	76	●	Lovehatetragedy	DreamWorks 50381
10/5/02	**26**	8↑	5 Time And Time Again	—	↓		
			PARKER, Graham				
			Born on 11/18/50 in London. Pop-rock singer/songwriter/guitarist.				
4/17/82	**52**	3	1 Temporary Beauty	—		Another Grey Area	Arista 9589
5/1/82	**42**	4	2 You Hit The Spot	—	↓		
5/11/85	**19**	10	3 Wake Up (Next To You)	39		Steady Nerves	Elektra 60388
			GRAHAM PARKER AND THE SHOT				
5/28/88	**23**	10	4 Get Started, Start A Fire	—		The Mona Lisa's Sister	RCA 8316
			PARKER, Ray Jr.				
			Born on 5/1/54 in Detroit. R&B singer/songwriter/guitarist. Leader of group Raydio from 1977-82.				
7/14/84	**38**	5	Ghostbusters	**❶**³	▲	Ghostbusters (soundtrack)	Arista 8246
			PARR, John				
			Born on 11/18/54 in Nottingham, England. Pop-rock singer/songwriter.				
11/10/84+	**6**	19	1 Naughty Naughty	23		John Parr	Atlantic 80180
3/16/85	**28**	6	2 Magical	73	↓		
6/29/85	**2**³	13	3 St. Elmo's Fire (Man In Motion)	**❶**²	●	St. Elmo's Fire (soundtrack)	Atlantic 81261

DEBUT	PEAK	WKS	Mainstream Rock Track	Pop	Gld	Album Title	Album Label & Number

PARSONS, Alan, Project
Born on 12/20/49 in London. Guitarist/keyboardist/producer. Engineered *Abbey Road* by **The Beatles** and *Dark Side Of The Moon* by **Pink Floyd**. Project features various musicians and vocalists. Eric Woolfson (vocals, keyboards) contributes most of the lyrics. Also see **Classic Rock Tracks** section.

1)Standing On Higher Ground 2)Prime Time 3)Stereotomy

DEBUT	PEAK	WKS	Mainstream Rock Track	Pop	Gld	Album Title	Album Label & Number
3/21/81	47	1	1 Snake Eyes Chris Rainbow (vocal)	67	▲	*The Turn Of A Friendly Card*	Arista 9518
6/26/82	22	11	2 You're Gonna Get Your Fingers Burned Lenny Zakatek (vocal)	—	▲	*Eye In The Sky*	Arista 9599
7/10/82	54	2	3 Psychobabble Elmer Gantry (vocal)	57	↓		
7/17/82	11	14	4 Eye In The Sky Eric Woolfson (vocal)	3	↓		
12/3/83	12	17	5 You Don't Believe Lenny Zakatek (vocal)	54	●	*The Best Of The Alan Parsons Project*	Arista 8193
3/31/84	3	7	6 Prime Time	34	●	*Ammonia Avenue*	Arista 8204
3/31/84	15	8	7 Don't Answer Me Eric Woolfson (vocal, above 2)	15	↓		
2/9/85	10	11	8 Let's Talk About Me David Paton (vocal)	56		*Vulture Culture*	Arista 8263
4/27/85	30	7	9 Days Are Numbers (The Traveller) Chris Rainbow (vocal)	71	↓		
1/18/86	5	11	10 Stereotomy John Miles (vocal)	82		*Stereotomy*	Arista 8384
1/24/87	3	12	11 Standing On Higher Ground Geoff Barradale (vocal)	—		*Gaudi*	Arista 8448

PAUL, Henry, Band
Born on 8/25/49 in Kingston, New York. Rock singer/guitarist. Member of **The Outlaws**. His band: Dave Fiester and Billy Crain (guitars), Wally Dentz (bass) and Bill Hoffman (drums).

| 12/5/81+ | 23 | 12 | Keeping Our Love Alive | 50 | | *Anytime* . . . . | Atlantic 19325 |

PAYOLA$ — see HYDE, Paul

PEARL JAM ★9★
Rock group formed in Seattle: **Eddie Vedder** (vocals; born on 12/23/64), Stone Gossard (guitar; born on 7/20/66), Mike McCready (guitar; born on 4/5/66), Jeff Ament (bass; born on 3/10/63) and Dave Krusen (drums; born on 3/10/66). Dave Abbruzzese (born on 5/17/68) replaced Krusen in 1993. Gossard and Ament were members of Mother Love Bone. All except Krusen played with **Temple Of The Dog**. Band acted in the movie *Singles* as Matt Dillon's band, Citizen Dick. Abbruzzese left band in August 1994. Drummer Jack Irons (of the **Red Hot Chili Peppers**; born on 7/18/62) joined in late 1994. McCready also put together **Mad Season** in 1994. Matt Cameron (born on 11/28/62) replaced Irons in 1999.

1)Better Man 2)Daughter 3)Given To Fly 4)I Got Id 5)Even Flow

DEBUT	PEAK	WKS	Mainstream Rock Track	Pop	Gld	Album Title	Album Label & Number
1/4/92	16	25	1 Alive	107	▲[11]	*Ten.*	Epic/Associated 47857
5/2/92	3	24	2 Even Flow	108	↓		
8/22/92	5	20	3 Jeremy	79	↓		
12/26/92+	3	25	4 Black	—	↓		
9/18/93	26	5	5 Crazy Mary	—		*Sweet Relief: A Benefit For Victoria Williams* (various artists)	Thirsty Ear 57134
10/16/93	3	8	6 Go	—	▲[7]	*Vs.*	Epic/Associated 53136
10/30/93	❶[8]	26	7 Daughter	97	↓		
10/30/93+	21	13	8 Animal	—	↓		
3/12/94	3	23	9 Dissident	118	↓		
6/11/94	23	12	10 Elderly Woman Behind The Counter In A Small Town . also see #29 below	—	↓		
7/2/94	39	1	11 Glorified G	—	↓		
9/3/94	21	19	12 Yellow Ledbetter	flip		*(single only)*	Epic 77935
11/19/94	16	6	13 Tremor Christ	18	▲[5]	*Vitalogy*	Epic 66900
11/19/94	16	3	14 Spin The Black Circle	58	↓		
12/10/94+	❶[8]	26	15 Better Man	13[A]	↓		
1/21/95	22	22	16 Corduroy	53[A]	↓		
4/1/95	12	11	17 Not For You	102	↓		
7/8/95	10	17	18 Immortality	102	↓		
12/9/95+	2[4]	26	19 I Got Id	7	●	*(single only)*	Epic 78199
3/9/96	24	7	20 Leaving Here #76 Pop hit for Eddie Holland in 1964	—		*Home Alive - The Art Of Self Defense* (various artists)	Epic 67486
8/10/96	5	10	21 Who You Are	31	▲	*No Code*	Epic 67500
9/14/96	9	16	22 Hail, Hail	69[A]	↓		
9/14/96	37	4	23 Red Mosquito	—	↓		
1/25/97	34	2	24 Off He Goes	—	↓		
1/3/98	❶[6]	23	25 Given To Fly	21	▲	*Yield*	Epic 68164
2/21/98	14	22	26 In Hiding	—	↓		
4/25/98	6	16	27 Wishlist	47	↓		
10/10/98	40	2	28 Do The Evolution	—	↓		

DEBUT	PEAK	WKS	Mainstream Rock Track	Pop Gld	Album Title	Album Label & Number
			PEARL JAM — Cont'd			
11/28/98	21	11	29 **Elderly Woman Behind The Counter In A Small Town** .... [L-R]	— ●	Live On Two Legs	Epic 69752
			live version of #10 above			
5/29/99	5	18	30 **Last Kiss**	2¹	No Boundaries - A Benefit For The Kosovar Refugees (various artists)	Epic 63653
			#2 Pop hit for J. Frank Wilson and The Cavaliers in 1964			
4/29/00	3	11	31 **Nothing As It Seems**	49 ●	Binaural	Epic 63665
7/1/00	17	9	32 **Light Years**	42ˢ ↓		
10/5/02	7	8↑	33 **I Am Mine**	43	Riot Act......................	Epic 86825
			PENN, Michael			
			Born on 8/1/58 in New York City. Pop-rock singer/songwriter. Brother of actors Sean and Christopher Penn. Son of actor/director Leo Penn and actress Eileen Ryan. Married **Aimee Mann** on 12/29/97.			
12/16/89+	5	16	1 **No Myth**	13	March..........................	RCA 9692
3/31/90	16	12	2 **This & That**	53 ↓		
7/28/90	26	8	3 **Brave New World**	— ↓		
10/31/92	33	4	4 **Seen The Doctor**	—	Free-For-All	RCA 61113
			PERFECT CIRCLE, A			
			Rock duo from Hollywood: Maynard James Keenan (vocals) and Billy Howerdel (guitar). Keenan is also lead singer of **Tool**.			
4/29/00	4	27	1 **Judith**	105 ▲	Mer De Noms.	Virgin 49253
9/16/00	12	23	2 **3 Libras**	— ↓		
2/17/01	14	14	3 **The Hollow**	— ↓		
			PERRY, Joe, Project			
			Born on 9/10/50 in Lawrence, Massachusetts. Lead guitarist of **Aerosmith**. The Project included Charlie Farren (vocals, guitar; **Farrenheit**), David Hull (bass) and Ronnie Stewart (drums).			
7/11/81	48	3	**Listen To The Rock**......................	—	I've Got The Rock 'N' Rolls Again.....	Columbia 37364
			PERRY, Steve			
			Born on 1/22/49 in Hanford, California. Lead singer of **Journey**.			
9/4/82	4	16	1 **Don't Fight It**	17 ●	High Adventure..................	Columbia 38127
			KENNY LOGGINS with Steve Perry			
4/7/84	❶²	13	2 **Oh Sherrie**	3 ▲²	Street Talk	Columbia 39334
5/5/84	43	1	3 **I Believe**	— ↓		
5/12/84	15	16	4 **She's Mine**	21 ↓		
9/22/84	17	8	5 **Strung Out**	40 ↓		
7/16/94	6	11	6 **You Better Wait**	29 ●	For The Love Of Strange Medicine....	Columbia 44287
			PETE.			
			Rock group from Newark, New Jersey: David Terrana (vocals), Rich Andruska (guitar), Lars Alverson (bass) and Scott Anderson (drums).			
6/30/01	17	13	**Sweet Daze**	—	Pete.	Warner 47939
			PET SHOP BOYS			
			Pop duo formed in England: Neil Tennant (vocals) and Chris Lowe (keyboards).			
4/12/86	37	5	**West End Girls**	❶¹ ▲	Please	EMI America 17193

PETTY, Tom, And The Heartbreakers ★2★

Born on 10/20/50 in Gainesville, Florida. Singer/songwriter/guitarist. Formed The Heartbreakers in Los Angeles: Mike Campbell (guitar; born on 2/1/54), Benmont Tench (keyboards; born on 9/7/54), Ron Blair (bass; born on 9/16/52) and Stan Lynch (drums; born on 5/21/55). Howie Epstein (born on 7/21/55) replaced Blair in 1982; Blair returned in 2002, replacing Epstein. Steve Ferrone replaced Lynch in 1995. Petty appeared in the movies *FM* and *Made In Heaven*. Member of the **Traveling Wilburys**. Group inducted into the Rock and Roll Hall of Fame in 2002. Also see **Bob Dylan**, **Roger McGuinn** and **Classic Rock Tracks** section.

1)The Waiting 2)Learning To Fly 3)I Won't Back Down 4)Jammin' Me 5)You Got Lucky

DEBUT	PEAK	WKS	Mainstream Rock Track	Pop Gld	Album Title	Album Label & Number
5/2/81	❶⁶	23	1 **The Waiting**	19 ▲	Hard Promises...................	Backstreet 5160
5/16/81	5	26	2 **A Woman In Love (It's Not Me)**	79 ↓		
5/23/81	21	22	3 **Nightwatchman**	— ↓		
8/1/81	2¹	24	4 **Stop Draggin' My Heart Around**	3 ▲⁴	Bella Donna (Nicks)	Modern 139
			STEVIE NICKS (with Tom Petty and The Heartbreakers)			
11/13/82	❶³	16	5 **You Got Lucky**	20 ●	Long After Dark.............	Backstreet 5360
11/27/82+	10	13	6 **Change Of Heart**	21 ↓		
11/27/82	37	2	7 **We Stand A Chance**	— ↓		
12/4/82	15	10	8 **One Story Town**	— ↓		
12/4/82	35	1	9 **Between Two Worlds**	— ↓		
7/23/83	35	4	10 **I Will Run To You**	— ▲²	The Wild Heart (Nicks)	Modern 90084
			STEVIE NICKS (with Tom Petty and the Heartbreakers)			
3/16/85	2⁴	13	11 **Don't Come Around Here No More**	13 ▲	Southern Accents	MCA 5486
4/6/85	5	14	12 **Rebels**	74 ↓		
6/8/85	12	10	13 **Make It Better (Forget About Me)**	54 ↓		

DEBUT	PEAK	WKS	Mainstream Rock Track	Pop	Gld	Album Title	Album Label & Number
			PETTY, Tom, And The Heartbreakers — Cont'd				
12/21/85+	9	11	14 So You Want To Be A Rock & Roll Star [L]	—		*Pack Up The Plantation - Live!* . . . . MCA 8021	
			#29 Pop hit for **The Byrds** in 1967				
12/28/85+	17	11	15 Needles And Pins [L]	37		↓	
			TOM PETTY and the HEARTBREAKERS with STEVIE NICKS				
			#13 Pop hit for The Searchers in 1964; above 2 recorded at the Wiltern Theater in Los Angeles				
4/18/87	❶4	12	16 Jammin' Me	18	●	*Let Me Up (I've Had Enough)* . . . . MCA 5836	
			co-written by **Bob Dylan**				
5/9/87	6	13	17 Runaway Trains	—		↓	
5/9/87	36	9	18 Think About Me	—		↓	
8/1/87	19	6	19 All Mixed Up	—		↓	
			TOM PETTY:				
4/15/89	❶5	14	20 I Won't Back Down	12	▲5	*Full Moon Fever* . . . . MCA 6253	
			George Harrison (guitar, backing vocal)				
5/6/89	❶1	33	21 Free Fallin'	7		↓	
5/6/89	❶1	23	22 Runnin' Down A Dream	23		↓	
5/6/89	18	7	23 Feel A Whole Lot Better	—		↓	
			first recorded by **The Byrds** in 1965				
9/23/89	7	20	24 Love Is A Long Road	—		↓	
1/27/90	5	15	25 A Face In The Crowd	46		↓	
4/21/90	5	13	26 Yer So Bad	—		↓	
			TOM PETTY AND THE HEARTBREAKERS:				
6/22/91	❶6	15	27 Learning To Fly	28	▲2	*Into The Great Wide Open* . . . . MCA 10317	
7/13/91	❶2	21	28 Out In The Cold	—		↓	
9/21/91	4	22	29 Into The Great Wide Open	92		↓	
12/21/91+	4	15	30 Kings Highway	—		↓	
3/21/92	30	7	31 Makin' Some Noise	—		↓	
8/21/93	26	7	32 My Back Pages [L]	—	●	*Bob Dylan - The 30th Anniversary Concert* (various artists) . . . . Columbia 53230	
			BOB DYLAN & FRIENDS: Roger McGuinn, Tom Petty, Neil Young, Eric Clapton & George Harrison recorded on 10/16/92 at Madison Square Garden in New York City; #30 Pop hit for **The Byrds** in 1967				
11/6/93	❶2	26	33 Mary Jane's Last Dance	14	▲9	*Greatest Hits* . . . . MCA 10813	
2/5/94	19	8	34 Something In The Air	—		↓	
			TOM PETTY:				
11/5/94	❶1	23	35 You Don't Know How It Feels	13	▲3	*Wildflowers* . . . . Warner 45759	
12/10/94+	21	26	36 You Wreck Me	—		↓	
4/8/95	6	16	37 It's Good To Be King	68		↓	
7/22/95	12	12	38 A Higher Place	—		↓	
11/11/95	29	6	39 Cabin Down Below	—		↓	
			TOM PETTY & THE HEARTBREAKERS:				
12/9/95+	6	15	40 Waiting For Tonight	—		*Playback* . . . . MCA 11375	
7/27/96	6	13	41 Walls (Circus)	69	●	*She's The One (soundtrack)* . . . . Warner 46285	
10/12/96	6	17	42 Climb That Hill	—		↓	
1/4/97	20	12	43 Change The Locks	—		↓	
3/13/99	5	14	44 Free Girl Now	120	●	*Echo* . . . . Warner 47294	
4/24/99	19	12	45 Room At The Top	—		↓	
7/31/99	17	11	46 Swingin'	—		↓	
9/28/02	22	9↑	47 The Last DJ	—		*The Last DJ* . . . . Warner 47955	

PHANTOM, ROCKER & SLICK

Rock trio formed in New York City: Slim Jim Phantom (drums), Lee Rocker (vocals, bass), and Earl Slick (guitar). Phantom and Rocker were members of the **Stray Cats** and Slick was a member of **Silver Condor**.

DEBUT	PEAK	WKS	Track	Pop	Gld	Album Title	Label
10/12/85	7	11	1 Men Without Shame	—		*Phantom, Rocker & Slick* . . . . EMI America 17172	
1/25/86	33	4	2 My Mistake	—		↓	
			Keith Richards (guitar)				

PHISH

Rock group from Burlington, Vermont: Trey Anastasio (guitar), Page McConnell (keyboards), Mike Gordon (bass) and Jon Fishman (drums). All share vocals.

DEBUT	PEAK	WKS	Track	Pop	Gld	Album Title	Label
5/14/94	33	4	1 Down With Disease	—	●	*(Hoist)* . . . . Elektra 61628	
10/19/96	11	14	2 Free	—	●	*Billy Breathes* . . . . Elektra 61971	

DEBUT	PEAK	WKS	Mainstream Rock Track	Pop Gld	Album Title	Album Label & Number

PINK FLOYD ★38★
Progressive-rock group formed in England: **David Gilmour** (vocals, guitar), **Roger Waters** (vocals, bass), Rick Wright (keyboards) and **Nick Mason** (drums). Wright left in early 1982. Waters left in 1984. Band inactive from 1984-86. Gilmour, Mason and Wright regrouped in 1987. Inducted into the Rock and Roll Hall of Fame in 1996. Group name taken from Georgia bluesmen Pink Anderson and Floyd Council. Also see **Classic Rock Tracks** section.

1)Keep Talking   2)Learning To Fly   3)On The Turning Away   4)Take It Back   5)One Slip

12/12/81+	37	8	1 Money	—	▲²	A Collection Of Great Dance Songs . . . Columbia 37680
			new version of their #13 Pop hit from 1973			
4/2/83	7	18	2 Not Now John	—	▲²	The Final Cut .... Columbia 38243
4/2/83	8	10	3 Your Possible Pasts	—	↓	
4/30/83	31	10	4 The Hero's Return	—	↓	
9/5/87	❶³	12	5 Learning To Fly	70	▲⁴	A Momentary Lapse Of Reason ...... Columbia 40599
			also see #13 below			
9/26/87+	❶¹	24	6 On The Turning Away	—	↓	
9/26/87	5	17	7 One Slip	—	↓	
9/26/87	30	11	8 The Dogs Of War	—	↓	
3/5/88	36	6	9 Sorrow	—	↓	
12/3/88	24	7	10 Comfortably Numb .... [L]	—	▲³	Delicate Sound Of Thunder .... Columbia 44484
			studio version on their 1979 album The Wall			
12/10/88	34	6	11 Time .... [L]	—	↓	
			studio version on their 1973 album The Dark Side Of The Moon			
12/10/88	42	5	12 Another Brick In The Wall Part II .... [L]	—	↓	
			studio version was a #1 Pop hit in 1980			
12/17/88	45	4	13 Learning To Fly .... [L-R]	—	↓	
			live version of #5 above			
4/2/94	❶⁶	26	14 Keep Talking	—	▲³	The Division Bell .... Columbia 64200
4/16/94	4	21	15 Take It Back	73	↓	
4/16/94	16	20	16 What Do You Want From Me	—	↓	
			also see #19 below			
8/27/94	7	13	17 High Hopes	—	↓	
12/3/94+	21	10	18 Lost For Words	—	↓	
6/17/95	13	8	19 What Do You Want From Me .... [L-R]	—	▲²	Pulse .... Columbia 67065
			live version of #16 above			
4/8/00	15	7	20 Young Lust .... [L]	—		Is There Anybody Out There? - The Wall Live 1980-81 .... Columbia 62055
			studio version on their 1979 album The Wall			

PLACEBO
Punk-pop trio from England: Brian Molko (vocals, guitar), Stefan Olsdal (bass) and Steve Hewitt (drums).

| 2/13/99 | 40 | 2 | Pure Morning .... | | Without You I'm Nothing .... Hut 46531 |

PLANET P
Studio group assembled by German producer Peter Hauke. **Tony Carey** was lead singer.

4/2/83	4	15	1 Why Me?	64	Planet P .... Geffen 4000
6/4/83	24	5	2 Static	—	↓
12/1/84	25	8	3 What I See	—	Pink World .... MCA 8019
			PLANET P PROJECT		

PLANT, Robert ★10★
Born on 8/20/48 in West Bromwich, West Midlands, England. Member of groups Listen (1965) and Band Of Joy (1967). Lead singer of **Led Zeppelin** and **The Honeydrippers**. His regular band included Robbie Blunt (guitar), Jezz Woodruffe (keyboards) and Paul Martinez (bass).

1)Hurting Kind (I've Got My Eyes On You)   2)Heaven Knows   3)Tall Cool One   4)Little By Little   5)Most High

4/18/81	8	8	1 Little Sister [L]	—	Concerts For The People Of Kampuchea (various artists) .... Atlantic 7005
			ROCKPILE with Robert Plant *#5 Pop hit for Elvis Presley in 1961*		
7/10/82	3	24	2 Burning Down One Side	64	▲	Pictures At Eleven .... Swan Song 8512
7/10/82	10	16	3 Worse Than Detroit	—	↓	
7/17/82	11	14	4 Pledge Pin	74	↓	
7/17/82	19	4	5 Slow Dancer	—	↓	
10/30/82+	12	18	6 Far Post	—	(single only) .... Swan Song 19429
7/23/83	❶¹	21	7 Other Arms	—	▲	The Principle Of Moments ... Es Paranza 90101
7/23/83	6	23	8 Big Log	20	↓	
7/30/83	4	23	9 In The Mood	39	↓	
10/15/83	44	1	10 Horizontal Departure	—	↓	
5/18/85	❶²	14	11 Little By Little	36	●	Shaken 'N' Stirred .... Es Paranza 90265
6/8/85	18	13	12 Sixes And Sevens	—	↓	

DEBUT	PEAK	WKS	Mainstream Rock Track	Pop	Gld	Album Title	Album Label & Number
			PLANT, Robert — Cont'd				
2/13/88	❶⁶	12	13 Heaven Knows	—	▲³	Now And Zen	Es Paranza 90863
3/5/88	❶⁴	16	14 Tall Cool One	25		↓	
			features brief guitar riffs from **Led Zeppelin**'s "Whole Lotta Love," "Dazed And Confused," "Custard Pie," "Black Dog" and "The Ocean"; **Jimmy Page** (guitar, above 2)				
3/5/88	3	23	15 Ship Of Fools	84		↓	
6/25/88	10	13	16 Dance On My Own	—		↓	
11/12/88	46	3	17 The Way I Feel	—		↓	
12/24/88+	39	5	18 Walking Towards Paradise	—		↓	
3/17/90	❶⁶	13	19 Hurting Kind (I've Got My Eyes On You)	46	●	Manic Nirvana	Es Paranza 91336
3/31/90	6	16	20 Tie Dye On The Highway	—		↓	
4/7/90	35	4	21 Big Love	—		↓	
4/7/90	39	6	22 I Cried	—		↓	
6/9/90	8	13	23 Your Ma Said You Cried In Your Sleep Last Night	—		↓	
			#24 Pop hit for Kenny Dino in 1961				
8/18/90	47	3	24 S S S & Q	—		↓	
5/15/93	3	10	25 Calling To You	—	●	Fate Of Nations	Es Paranza 92264
6/26/93	4	20	26 29 Palms	111		↓	
10/9/93	9	9	27 I Believe	—		↓	
10/22/94	2³	14	28 Gallows Pole	—	▲	No Quarter	Atlantic 82706
12/17/94+	8	14	29 Thank You	—		↓	
4/18/98	❶²	13	30 Most High	—	●	Walking Into Clarksdale	Atlantic 83092
5/30/98	6	18	31 Shining In The Light	—		↓	
			JIMMY PAGE & ROBERT PLANT (above 4)				
6/22/02	27	11	32 Darkness, Darkness	—		Dreamland	Universal 586962
			PLIMSOULS, The				
			Rock group from Los Angeles: **Peter Case** (vocals), Eddie Munoz (guitar), Dave Pahoa (bass) and Lou Ramirez (drums).				
5/1/82	11	7	A Million Miles Away	82		(single only)	Shaky City 134
			POCO				
			Country-rock group formed in Los Angeles. Numerous personnel changes. Lineup from 1981-84: Rusty Young (vocals), Paul Cotton (guitar), Kim Bullard (keyboards), Charlie Harrison (bass; replaced by Neil Stubenhaus in 1983) and Steve Chapman (drums). Disbanded in 1984. In 1989, original members Young (pedal steel guitar), Richie Furay (rhythm guitar), Jim Messina (lead guitar), **Randy Meisner** (bass) and George Grantham (drums) reunited. Also see **Classic Rock Tracks** section.				
7/25/81	33	13	1 Widowmaker	—		Blue And Gray	MCA 5227
5/26/84	58	3	2 Days Gone By	80		Inamorata	Atlantic 80148
8/26/89	3	12	3 Call It Love	18	●	Legacy	RCA 9694
3/3/90	30	6	4 The Nature Of Love	—		↓	
			P.O.D.				
			Hard-rock group from San Diego: Paul "Sonny" Sandoval (vocals), Marcos Curiel (guitar), Mark "Traa" Daniels (bass) and Noah "Wuv" Bernardo (drums). P.O.D.: Payable On Death.				
2/5/00	31	12	1 Southtown	—	▲	The Fundamental Elements Of Southtown	Atlantic 83216
8/5/00	25	8	2 Rock The Party (Off The Hook)	—		↓	
8/25/01	4	31	3 Alive	41	▲³	Satellite	Atlantic 83475
12/22/01+	6	26	4 Youth Of The Nation	28		↓	
5/4/02	21	16	5 Boom	123		↓	
8/31/02	15	10	6 Satellite	—		↓	
			POINT BLANK				
			Rock group from Texas: Bubba Keith (vocals), Rusty Burns and Kim Davis (guitars), Mike Hamilton (keyboards), Bill Randolph (bass) and Buzzy Gruen (drums). Randolph died of a heart attack on 6/19/2001 (age 50).				
4/18/81	38	7	1 Let Me Stay With You Tonight	107		American Exce$$	MCA 5189
6/20/81	20	21	2 Nicole	39		↓	
4/24/82	27	4	3 On A Roll	—		On A Roll	MCA 5312
5/15/82	34	2	4 Great White Line	—		↓	
			POISON				
			Hard-rock group formed in Harrisburg, Pennsylvania: Bret Michaels (vocals; born on 3/15/63), C.C. DeVille (guitar; born on 5/14/62), Bobby Dall (bass; born on 11/2/58) and Rikki Rockett (drums; born on 8/8/61). Richie Kotzen (born on 3/5/60) replaced DeVille from 1992-97.				
5/7/88	19	11	1 Nothin' But A Good Time	6	▲⁵	Open Up and Say...Ahh!	Enigma 48493
8/20/88	32	7	2 Fallen Angel	12		↓	
11/12/88	11	12	3 Every Rose Has Its Thorn	❶³		↓	
3/4/89	39	4	4 Your Mama Don't Dance	10		↓	
			#4 Pop hit for **Kenny Loggins** & Jim Messina in 1973				
7/7/90	5	13	5 Unskinny Bop	3	▲³	Flesh & Blood	Capitol 918132
10/6/90	5	15	6 Something To Believe In	4		↓	
2/9/91	25	9	7 Ride The Wind	38		↓	
1/30/93	15	7	8 Stand	50	●	Native Tongue	Capitol 98961

DEBUT	PEAK	WKS	Mainstream Rock Track	Pop Gld	Album Title	Album Label & Number
	★61★		**POLICE, The**			
			Pop-rock trio formed in England: Gordon "**Sting**" Sumner (vocals, bass; born on 10/2/51), Andy Summers (guitar; born on 12/31/42) and Stewart Copeland (drums; born on 7/16/52). Sting went on to a highly successful solo career. Copeland formed Animal Logic in 1989. Group inducted into the Rock and Roll Hall of Fame in 2003. Also see **Classic Rock Tracks** section.			
			1)Every Breath You Take 2)King Of Pain 3)Every Little Thing She Does Is Magic			
3/21/81	11	7	1 Don't Stand So Close To Me	10 ▲	*Zenyatta Mondatta*	A&M 4831
			also see #11 below			
3/28/81	35	2	2 Driven To Tears	—	↓	
9/26/81	❶²	28	3 Every Little Thing She Does Is Magic	3	▲² *Ghost In The Machine*	A&M 3730
12/5/81+	7	21	4 Spirits In The Material World	11	↓	
2/6/82	29	16	5 Secret Journey	46	↓	
12/4/82	27	9	6 I Burn For You	—	*Brimstone & Treacle (soundtrack)*	A&M 4915
6/4/83	❶⁹	21	7 Every Breath You Take	❶⁸ ▲⁴	*Synchronicity*	A&M 3735
7/9/83	❶⁵	31	8 King Of Pain	3	↓	
7/9/83	9	27	9 Wrapped Around Your Finger	8	↓	
7/16/83	9	31	10 Synchronicity II	16	↓	
10/25/86	10	7	11 Don't Stand So Close To Me '86 [R]	46	▲³ *Every Breath You Take - The Singles*	A&M 3902
			new version of #1 above			
			POOR, The			
			Rock group from England: Skenie (vocals), Jullan Grynglas (guitar), Matt Whitby (bass) and James Young (drums).			
4/23/94	30	5	More Wine Waiter Please	—	*Who Cares*	550 Music 57552
			POORBOYS			
			Rock group from Claremont, California: Dennis Hill (vocals, guitar), Rik Sanchez (guitar), Joey Phillipy (bass) and Andre Bonter (drums).			
9/19/92	24	4	1 Brand New Amerika	—	*Pardon Me.*	Hollywood 60997
12/19/92+	16	16	2 Guilty	122	↓	
			POP, Iggy			
			Born James Jewel Osterberg on 4/21/47 in Muskegon, Michigan. Punk-rock pioneer. Leader of The Stooges from 1969-74. Acted in the movies *Cry Baby*, *Hardware* and *The Crow: City Of Angels*. Adopted nickname "Iggy" from his first band, The Iguanas.			
10/11/86	34	7	1 Cry For Love	—	*Blah-Blah-Blah*	A&M 5145
12/27/86+	27	12	2 Real Wild Child (Wild One)	—	↓	
			#68 Pop hit for Ivan in 1958			
7/23/88	37	5	3 Cold Metal	—	*Instinct*	A&M 5198
8/4/90	46	5	4 Home	—	*Brick By Brick.*	Virgin 91381
10/20/90+	30	16	5 Candy	28	↓	
			Kate Pierson (of **The B-52's**; female vocal)			
			PORNO FOR PYROS			
			Rock group formed by former **Jane's Addiction** members Perry Farrell (vocals) and Stephen Perkins (drums). Includes Peter DiStefano (guitar) and Martyn LeNoble (bass). LeNoble and Perkins also recorded with **Class Of '99**.			
7/10/93	25	6	Pets	67 ●	*Porno For Pyros.*	Warner 45228
			POSIES, The			
			Rock group from Seattle: Jon Auer and Ken Stringfellow (vocals, guitars), Rick Roberts (bass) and Mike Musburger (drums).			
7/3/93	17	10	Dream All Day	—	*Frosting On the Beater*	DGC 24522
			POSSUM DIXON			
			Rock group from Los Angeles: Rob Zabrecky (vocals, bass), Celso Chavez (guitar), Robert O'Sullivan (keyboards) and Richard Treuel (drums). Group named after a fugitive seen on TV's *America's Most Wanted*.			
4/30/94	37	3	Watch The Girl Destroy Me	110	*Possum Dixon*	Interscope 92291
			POUND			
			Rock group from New York City: brothers Jason (vocals) and Jerry (drums) Terwilliger, with Pat Gasperini (guitar) and Sandy Nardone (bass).			
4/24/99	16	11	Upside Down	—	*Same Old Life*	Island 524641
			POWERMAN 5000			
			Hard-rock group from Boston: Spider One (vocals), Adam 12 and M.33 (guitars), Dorian 27 (bass) and Al 3 (drums).			
7/10/99	16	26	1 When Worlds Collide	— ▲	*Tonight The Stars Revolt!*	DreamWorks 50107
12/18/99+	18	16	2 Nobody's Real	—	↓	
12/23/00	38	5	3 Ultra Mega	—	*Dracula 2000 (soundtrack)*	Columbia 61585
7/28/01	26	7	4 Bombshell	—	*Anyone For Doomsday?*	DreamWorks 50296
			POWER STATION, The			
			All-star rock group: **Robert Palmer** (vocals), **Andy Taylor** (guitar), John Taylor (bass) and Tony Thompson (drums). The Taylors were members of **Duran Duran**. Thompson was a member of Chic.			
5/4/85	19	16	1 Get It On	9 ▲	*The Power Station*	Capitol 12380
			#10 Pop hit for T. Rex in 1972			
5/4/85	34	5	2 Some Like It Hot	6	↓	
			PREFAB SPROUT			
			Pop group from England: brothers Paddy (vocals, guitar) and Martin (bass) McAloon, with Wendy Smith (vocals) and Neil Conti (drums).			
10/26/85	42	2	When Love Breaks Down	—	*Two Wheels Good*	Epic 40100

DEBUT	PEAK	WKS	Mainstream Rock Track	Pop	Gld	Album Title	Album Label & Number

PRESIDENTS OF THE UNITED STATES OF AMERICA, The
Rock trio from Seattle: Chris Ballew (vocals), Dave Dederer (guitar) and Jason Finn (drums).

9/16/95	7	20	1 Lump	21[A]	▲[3]	The Presidents Of The United States Of America .... Columbia 67291	
2/24/96	24	8	2 Peaches	29		↓	
11/23/96	24	10	3 Mach 5....................	68[A]	●	II .... Columbia 67577	

PRESSURE 4-5
Rock group from Santa Barbara, California: Adam Rich (vocals), brothers Joe (guitar) and Tom (drums) Schmidt, Mark Barry (guitar) and Lyle McKeany (bass).

11/24/01	39	2	Beat The World....................	—		Burning The Process .... DreamWorks 450325	

★58★   PRETENDERS, The
Rock group formed in England: **Chrissie Hynde** (vocals, guitar; born on 9/7/51 in Akron, Ohio), James Honeyman-Scott (guitar), Pete Farndon (bass) and Martin Chambers (drums). Honeyman-Scott died of a drug overdose on 6/16/82 (age 24); replaced by Robbie McIntosh. Farndon died of a drug overdose on 4/14/83 (age 30); replaced by Malcolm Foster. Hynde was married to Jim Kerr (of **Simple Minds**) from 1984-90. Lineup in 1994: Hynde, Chambers, Adam Seymour (guitar) and Andy Hobson (bass). Also see **Classic Rock Tracks** section.
1)Don't Get Me Wrong   2)My Baby   3)Middle Of The Road

3/21/81	5	16	1 Message Of Love	—		Extended Play .... Sire 3563	
8/22/81	12	16	2 The Adultress....................	—	●	Pretenders II................. Sire 3572	
10/16/82+	4	31	3 Back On The Chain Gang	5		The King Of Comedy (soundtrack) ..... Warner 23765	
10/23/82+	11	16	4 My City Was Gone....................	—		(single only) .... Sire 29840	
			song later used as the intro theme for radio's Rush Limbaugh Show				
12/24/83+	2[4]	15	5 Middle Of The Road	19	▲	Learning To Crawl .... Sire 23980	
2/4/84	6	14	6 Time The Avenger	—		↓	
2/18/84	8	15	7 Show Me	28		↓	
2/25/84	57	1	8 Thumbelina....................	—		↓	
10/11/86	❶[3]	13	9 Don't Get Me Wrong	10	●	Get Close .... Sire 25488	
11/8/86+	❶[2]	19	10 My Baby	64		↓	
11/29/86+	28	11	11 Room Full Of Mirrors	—		↓	
8/15/87	26	4	12 Where Has Every Body Gone	—		The Living Daylights (soundtrack) ...... Warner 25616	
5/19/90	5	11	13 Never Do That	—		packed!............................ Sire 26219	
4/30/94	13	11	14 Night In My Veins....................	71	●	Last Of The Independents .... Warner 45572	

PREVIEW
Rock group from New York City: Jon Fiore (vocals), Danny Gold (guitar), Ernie Gold (keyboards), Skip Parker (bass) and Ed Bettinelli (drums).

2/18/84	39	1	Red Lights	—		Preview........................ Geffen 2015	

PRIDE & GLORY
Rock trio formed in New York City: Zakk Wylde (vocals, guitar), James LoMenzo (bass) and Brian Tichy (drums). Wylde formerly with **Ozzy Osbourne**'s band.

6/11/94	14	15	Losin' Your Mind....................	—		Pride & Glory.................... Geffen 24703	

PRIMAL SCREAM
Rock-funk group from Glasgow, Scotland: Bobby Gillespie (vocals), Andrew Innes and Robert Young (guitars), Henry Raycock (bass) and Toby Toman (drums).

10/19/91	28	13	1 Movin' On Up....................	—		Screamadelica .... Sire 26714	
4/30/94	29	6	2 Rocks	107		Give Out But Don't Give Up .... Sire 45538	

PRIMER 55
Rock group from Memphis: Jason (vocals), Bobby Burns (guitar), Kobie Jackson (bass) and Preston Nash (drums).

10/20/01	37	1	This Life	—		(The) New Release .... Island 586183	

PRIME STH
Rock group from Sweden: Noa (vocals), Martin (guitar), Jspr (bass) and Kaz (drums).

6/2/01	27	13	I'm Stupid (Don't Worry 'Bout Me)	—		Underneath The Surface .... Giant 24774	

PRIMITIVE RADIO GODS
Group is actually solo artist Chris O'Connor.

7/20/96	32	9	Standing Outside A Broken Phone Booth With Money In My Hand	10[A]	●	Rocket............................ Ergo 67600	
			samples "How Blue Can You Get" by **B.B. King**				

PRIMUS
Rock trio from San Francisco: Les Claypool (vocals, bass), Larry LaLonde (guitar) and Tim Alexander (drums). Brian Mantia replaced Alexander in 1996.

7/15/95	23	9	1 Wynona's Big Brown Beaver	62[A]	●	Tales From The Punchbowl .... Interscope 92553	
7/15/00	2[2]	41	2 N.I.B.	—		Nativity In Black II: A Tribute To Black Sabbath (various artists) .... Divine 26095	
			PRIMUS with Ozzy Osbourne first recorded by **Black Sabbath** in 1970				

DEBUT	PEAK	WKS	Mainstream Rock Track	Pop	Gld	Album Title	Album Label & Number

PRINCE
Born Prince Roger Nelson on 6/7/58 in Minneapolis. R&B singer/songwriter/multi-instrumentalist. Starred in the movies *Purple Rain*, *Under The Cherry Moon*, *Sign 'O' The Times* and *Graffiti Bridge*. The Revolution: Wendy Melvoin (guitar), Lisa Coleman and Matt Fink (keyboards), Eric Leeds (sax), Brownmark (bass) and Bobby Z (drums).

| 4/30/83 | 17 | 5 | 1 Little Red Corvette | 6 | ▲⁴ | *1999* .... | Warner 23720 |
| 6/16/84 | 31 | 13 | 2 When Doves Cry .... | ❶⁵ | ▲¹³ | *Purple Rain (soundtrack)* .... | Warner 25110 |

PRINCE and The REVOLUTION:

8/11/84	19	11	3 Let's Go Crazy	❶²	↓		
9/22/84	18	8	4 Purple Rain .... [L]	2²	↓		
			recorded at First Avenue Nightclub in Minneapolis				
5/18/85	40	6	5 Raspberry Beret	2¹	▲²	*Around The World In A Day*	Paisley Park 25286

PRISM
Rock group from Canada: Henry Small (vocals), Lindsay Mitchell and Tom Lavin (guitars), John Hall (keyboards), Allen Harlow (bass) and Rocket Norton (drums).

1/23/82	❶¹	17	1 Don't Let Him Know	39		*Small Change*	Capitol 12184
			co-written by **Bryan Adams**				
6/26/82	55	2	2 Hole In Paradise	—	↓		
9/17/83	37	1	3 Is He Better Than Me?	—		*Beat Street*	Capitol 12266

PROCOL HARUM
Rock group formed in England: Gary Brooker (vocals, piano), **Robin Trower** (guitar), Matthew Fisher (organ), Dave Bronze (bass) and Mark Brzezicki (drums). Also see **Classic Rock Tracks** section.

| 8/10/91 | 29 | 6 | All Our Dreams Are Sold .... | — | | *The Prodigal Stranger* .... | Zoo 11011 |

PRODUCERS, The
Pop-rock group from Atlanta: Van Temple (vocals, guitar), Wayne Famous (keyboards), Kyle Henderson (bass) and Bryan Holmes (drums).

| 10/2/82 | 48 | 2 | She Sheila .... | — | | *You Make The Heat* .... | Portrait 38060 |

PSEUDO ECHO
Pop-rock group from Melbourne, Australia: Brian Canham (vocals, guitar), James Leigh (keyboards), Pierre Gigliotti (bass) and Vince Leigh (drums).

| 3/14/87 | 44 | 2 | Living In A Dream .... | 57 | | *Love An Adventure* .... | RCA Victor 5730 |

PSYCHEDELIC FURS
Techno-rock group formed in England: brothers Richard (vocals) and Tim (bass) Butler, John Ashton (guitar) and Vince Ely (drums). Phillip Calvert replaced Ely in 1983. The Butler brothers formed **Love Spit Love** in 1994.

10/9/82	30	3	1 Love My Way	44	●	*Forever Now*	Columbia 38261
5/5/84	25	12	2 The Ghost In You	59	●	*Mirror Moves*	Columbia 39278
2/21/87	11	14	3 Heartbreak Beat	26		*Midnight To Midnight*	Columbia 40466

PUDDLE OF MUDD
Hard-rock group formed in Los Angeles: Wes Scantlin (vocals, guitar), Paul Phillips (guitar), Doug Ardito (bass) and Greg Upchurch (drums).

7/7/01	3	40	1 Control	68	▲²	*Come Clean*	Flawless 493074
11/3/01+	❶¹⁰	42	2 Blurry	5	↓		
4/20/02	❶⁶	29	3 Drift & Die	61	↓		
8/10/02	❶¹	16↑	4 She Hates Me	24↑	↓		

PURSUIT OF HAPPINESS, The
Rock group from Toronto: Moe Berg (vocals, guitar), Leslie Stanwyck (vocals), Kris Abbott (guitar), John Sinclair (bass) and Dave Gilby (drums).

| 11/12/88 | 22 | 11 | I'm An Adult Now .... | — | | *Love Junk* .... | Chrysalis 41675 |

PUSHMONKEY
Rock group from Austin, Texas: Tony Park (vocals), Will Hoffman and Howie Behrens (guitars), Pat Fogarty (bass) and Darwin Keys (drums).

| 11/7/98 | 26 | 9 | Handslide .... | — | | *Pushmonkey* .... | Arista 19008 |

Q

QUARTERFLASH
Pop-rock group from Portland, Oregon: husband-and-wife Marv (guitar) and Rindy (vocals, sax) Ross, with Jack Charles (guitar), Rick DiGiallonardo (keyboards), Rich Gooch (bass) and Brian David Willis (drums). Charles and DiGiallonardo left in 1984. Group originally known as Seafood Mama.

10/31/81	❶³	24	1 Harden My Heart	3	▲	*Quarterflash*	Geffen 2003
11/21/81+	12	22	2 Find Another Fool	16	↓		
7/9/83	6	12	3 Take Me To Heart	14		*Take Another Picture*	Geffen 4011
9/21/85	41	7	4 Talk To Me	83		*Back Into Blue*	Geffen 24078

DEBUG	PEAK	WKS	Mainstream Rock Track	Pop Gld	Album Title	Album Label & Number

QUEEN

Rock group formed in England: Freddie Mercury (vocals; born on 9/5/46; died of AIDS on 11/24/91, age 45), **Brian May** (guitar; born on 7/19/47), John Deacon (bass; born on 8/19/51) and Roger Taylor (drums; born on 7/26/49). Group inducted into the Rock and Roll Hall of Fame in 2001. Also see **Classic Rock Tracks** section.

1)I Want It All 2)Headlong 3)Under Pressure

11/7/81	7	18	1 Under Pressure	29 ▲	Greatest Hits	Elektra 564
			QUEEN & DAVID BOWIE			
5/8/82	19	7	2 Body Language	11 ●	Hot Space	Elektra 60128
5/29/82	15	7	3 Put Out The Fire	— ↓		
5/29/82	40	8	4 Calling All Girls	60 ↓		
6/19/82	57	2	5 Life Is Real (Song For Lennon)	— ↓		
			tribute to **John Lennon**			
2/25/84	22	8	6 Radio Ga-Ga	16 ●	The Works	Capitol 12322
3/31/84	52	1	7 Tear It Up	— ↓		
4/7/84	57	1	8 Hammer To Fall	— ↓		
			also see #16 below			
12/14/85	19	11	9 One Vision	61	Iron Eagle (soundtrack)	Capitol 12499
5/13/89	3	11	10 I Want It All	50	The Miracle	Capitol 92357
1/26/91	3	10	11 Headlong	— ●	Innuendo	Hollywood 61020
3/16/91	17	9	12 Innuendo	— ↓		
6/8/91	28	6	13 I Can't Live With You	— ↓		
1/11/92	40	3	14 The Show Must Go On	— ↓		
4/4/92	16	10	15 Bohemian Rhapsody	2[1] ▲[2]	Wayne's World (soundtrack)	Reprise 26805
			#9 Pop hit in 1976			
5/16/92	35	6	16 Hammer To Fall [R]	— ▲[2]	Classic Queen	Hollywood 61311
			same version as #8 above			

QUEENS OF THE STONE AGE

Rock duo from Seattle: Josh Homme and Nick Oliveri.

| 6/24/00 | 21 | 11 | 1 The Lost Art Of Keeping A Secret | — | Rated R | Interscope 490683 |
| 10/19/02 | 20↑ | 6↑ | 2 No One Knows | 115↑ | Songs For The Deaf | Interscope 493425 |

★62★ QUEENSRŸCHE

Hard-rock group from Bellevue, Washington: Geoff Tate (vocals), Chris DeGarmo and Michael Wilton (guitars), Eddie Jackson (bass), and Scott Rockenfield (drums).

1)Silent Lucidity 2)Sign Of The Times 3)Real World

5/13/89	35	5	1 Eyes Of A Stranger	—	Operation:mindcrime	EMI-Manhattan 48640
8/5/89	41	5	2 I Don't Believe In Love	— ↓		
7/14/90	27	8	3 Last Time In Paris	—	The Adventures Of Ford Fairlane (soundtrack)	Elektra 60952
9/22/90	22	10	4 Empire	— ▲[3]	Empire	EMI 92806
12/8/90+	28	9	5 Best I Can	— ↓		
1/26/91	❶[1]	21	6 Silent Lucidity	9 ↓		
5/25/91	6	19	7 Jet City Woman	— ↓		
10/5/91+	7	29	8 Another Rainy Night (Without You)	— ↓		
2/15/92	16	17	9 Anybody Listening?	— ↓		
6/12/93	3	14	10 Real World	111 ▲	Last Action Hero (soundtrack)	Columbia 57127
10/22/94	8	9	11 I Am I	— ▲	Promised Land	EMI 30711
12/17/94+	6	18	12 Bridge	— ↓		
5/6/95	32	4	13 Disconnected	— ↓		
3/22/97	3	21	14 Sign Of The Times	—	Hear In The Now Frontier	EMI 56141
7/5/97	11	11	15 You	— ↓		
9/11/99	27	7	16 Breakdown	—	Q2K	Atlantic 83225

QUIET RIOT

Hard-rock group formed in Los Angeles: Kevin DuBrow (vocals), Carlos Cavazo (guitar), Rudy Sarzo (bass) and Frankie Banali (drums).

4/23/83	7	26	1 Cum On Feel The Noize	5 ▲[6]	Metal Health	Pasha 38443
			#98 Pop hit for **Slade** in 1973			
5/7/83	37	9	2 Bang Your Head (Metal Health)	31 ↓		
9/10/83	32	7	3 Slick Black Cadillac	— ↓		
2/11/84	22	7	4 Don't Wanna Let You Go	— ↓		
6/16/84	13	11	5 Mama Weer All Crazee Now	51 ▲	Condition Critical	Pasha 39516
			#76 Pop hit for **Slade** in 1973			
8/4/84	28	7	6 Sign Of The Times	— ↓		

R

RA

Rock group from New York City: Sahaj Ticotin (vocals, guitar), Ben Carroll (guitar), Sean Corcoran (bass) and Skoota Warner (drums).

| 10/26/02 | 30↑ | 5↑ | Do You Call My Name | — | From One | Republic 066093 |

DEBUT	PEAK	WKS	Mainstream Rock Track	Pop Gld	Album Title	Album Label & Number

RABIN, Trevor
Born on 1/13/54 in Johannesburg, South Africa. Rock singer/songwriter/guitarist. Joined **Yes** in 1982.

| 8/5/89 | 3 | 12 | Something To Hold On To | — | Can't Look Away............... Elektra 60781 |

RADIATORS, The
Rock group from New Orleans: Dave Malone (vocals), Camile Baudoin (guitar), Ed Volker (keyboards), Glenn Sears (percussion), Reggie Scanlan (bass) and Frank Bua (drums).

10/17/87	23	9	1 Like Dreamers Do	—	Law Of The Fish................. Epic 40888
1/16/88	20	8	2 Doctor Doctor	—	↓
3/4/89	8	10	3 Confidential	—	Zigzagging Through Ghostland .... Epic 44343

RADIOHEAD
Rock group from Oxford, England: Thom Yorke (vocals), brothers Jon (guitar) and Colin (bass) Greenwood, Ed O'Brien (guitar) and Phil Selway (drums).

| 8/14/93 | 20 | 9 | √ Creep... | 34 ▲ | Pablo Honey.................. Capitol 81409 |

RAGE AGAINST THE MACHINE
Hard-rock group formed in Los Angeles: Zack DeLa Rocha (vocals), Tom Morello (guitar), Tim Commerford (bass) and Brad Wilk (drums). DeLa Rocha left in October 2000; the others recorded with **Chris Cornell** as **Audioslave**. Morello also recorded with **Class Of '99**.

5/25/96	36	5	1 Bulls On Parade	62[A] ▲[3]	Evil Empire...................... Epic 57523
12/13/97+	35	9	2 The Ghost Of Tom Joad..................................	—	(single only) .... Epic 3455
			first recorded by **Bruce Springsteen** in 1995		
6/27/98	30	7	3 No Shelter	— ▲	Godzilla (soundtrack).............. Epic 69338
10/16/99+	11	26	4 Guerrilla Radio	69 ▲[2]	The Battle Of Los Angeles .... Epic 69630
2/26/00	16	18	5 Sleep Now In The Fire...............................	112 ↓	
8/12/00	22	11	6 Testify	— ↓	
12/2/00+	19	18	7 Renegades Of Funk	109 ▲	Renegades.................... Epic 85289
3/31/01	39	1	8 How I Could Just Kill A Man	— ↓	
			#77 Pop hit for **Cypress Hill** in 1992		

RAGING SLAB
Hard-rock group from New York City: Greg Strempka (vocals), Mark Middleton and Elyse Steinman (guitars), Alec Morton (bass) and Bob Pantella (drums).

| 5/15/93 | 18 | 8 | 1 Anywhere But Here... | — | Dynamite Monster Boogie Concert ..... Warner 45244 |
| 9/25/93 | 27 | 6 | 2 Take A Hold .... | — ↓ | |

RAINBOW
Hard-rock band led by British guitarist Ritchie Blackmore and bassist **Roger Glover**, both members of **Deep Purple**. Fluctuating lineup included vocalists Ronnie James **Dio**, Graham Bonnet (**Michael Schenker Group**) and **Joe Lynn Turner**, keyboardist **Tony Carey** and drummer Cozy Powell (**Emerson, Lake & Powell**). Group split up upon re-formation of Deep Purple in 1984. In 1990, Turner joined Deep Purple and Powell joined **Black Sabbath**. Powell died in a car crash on 4/5/98 (age 50). Also see **Classic Rock Tracks** section.

3/28/81	19	7	√ 1 I Surrender...	105	Difficult To Cure .... Polydor 6316
11/14/81	13	15	√ 2 Jealous Lover...	—	Jealous Lover .... Polydor 502
4/10/82	❶[1]	15	√ 3 Stone Cold	40	Straight Between The Eyes .... Mercury 4041
5/22/82	35	3	√ 4 Power	— ↓	
9/24/83	2[1]	18	√ 5 Street Of Dreams	60	Bent Out Of Shape............. Mercury 815305
3/10/84	53	3	6 Desperate Heart	— ↓	

RAINDOGS
Rock group from Boston: Mark Cutler (vocals), Emerson Torrey (guitar), Johnny Cunningham (fiddle), Darren Hill (bass) and James Reilly (drums).

| 4/14/90 | 44 | 3 | I'm Not Scared .... | — | Lost Souls .... Atco 91297 |

RAINMAKERS, The
Rock group from Kansas City: Bob Walkenhorst (vocals), Steve Phillips (guitar), Rich Ruth (bass) and Pat Tomek (drums).

| 11/14/87 | 31 | 9 | Snakedance .... | — | Tornado .... Mercury 832795 |

RAITT, Bonnie
Born on 11/8/49 in Burbank, California. Blues-rock singer/guitarist. Daughter of Broadway actor/singer John Raitt. Married to actor Michael O'Keefe from 1991-99. Inducted into the Rock and Roll Hall of Fame in 2000.

3/20/82	39	8	1 Keep This Heart In Mind	104	Green Light .... Warner 3630
			Jackson Browne (backing vocal)		
8/16/86	15	9	2 No Way To Treat A Lady	—	Nine Lives .... Warner 25486
			co-written by **Bryan Adams**		
3/18/89	11	10	3 Thing Called Love	— ▲[5]	Nick Of Time.................. Capitol 91268
			first recorded by **John Hiatt** in 1987		
6/24/89	49	2	4 Love Letter	— ↓	
6/22/91	12	16	5 Something To Talk About	5 ▲[7]	Luck Of The Draw.............. Capitol 96111
10/5/91	28	10	6 Slow Ride	— ↓	
3/26/94	25	9	7 Love Sneakin' Up On You	19 ▲[2]	Longing In Their Hearts .... Capitol 81427

RAMMSTEIN
Hard-rock group from Berlin, Germany: Till Lindemann (vocals), Richard Kruspe and Paul Landers (guitars), Flake Lorenz (keyboards), Oliver Riedel (bass) and Christoph Schneider (drums).

| 6/27/98 | 20 | 17 | Du Hast... | [F] — ▲ | Sehnsucht. .... Slash 539901 |
| | | | title is German for "You Hate" | | |

DEBUT	PEAK	WKS	Mainstream Rock Track	Pop	Gld	Album Title	Album Label & Number
			RANKIN, Billy				
			Born on 4/25/59 in Glasgow, Scotland. Rock singer/guitarist. Member of **Nazareth** from 1981-82.				
3/31/84	22	6	Baby Come Back........................	52		Growin' Up Too Fast..............	A&M 4977
			RATT				
			Hard-rock group formed in Los Angeles: Stephen Pearcy (vocals), Warren DeMartini and Robbin Crosby (guitars), Juan Croucier (bass) and Bobby Blotzer (drums). Pearcy joined **Arcade**. Blotzer joined **Contraband**. Pearcy, DeMartini and Blotzer reunited in 1998 with Robbie Crane (bass). Crosby died of AIDS on 6/6/2002 (age 42).				
			1)Round And Round 2)Lay It Down 3)Way Cool Jr.				
4/28/84	4	21	1 Round And Round	12	▲3	Out Of The Cellar..................	Atlantic 80143
7/28/84	27	10	2 Back For More......................	—	↓		
10/6/84	38	3	3 Wanted Man.........................	87	↓		
6/15/85	11	13	4 Lay It Down.........................	40	▲2	Invasion Of Your Privacy...........	Atlantic 81257
9/7/85	34	6	5 You're In Love......................	89			
10/25/86	36	5	6 Dance..............................	59	▲	Dancing Undercover...............	Atlantic 81683
11/19/88+	16	14	7 Way Cool Jr.........................	75	▲	Reach For The Sky................	Atlantic 81929
8/25/90	18	9	8 Lovin' You's A Dirty Job............	—	●	Detonator.........................	Atlantic 82127
1/5/91	39	6	9 Givin' Yourself Away................	—	↓		
8/28/99	36	3	10 Over The Edge......................	—		Ratt..............................	Portrait 69586
			RAVYNS, The				
			Rock group from Baltimore: Rob Fahey and David Bell (vocals, guitars), Kyf Brewer (keyboards), Lee Townsend (bass) and Tim Steele (drums). Brewer later became lead vocalist of **Company Of Wolves**.				
4/7/84	49	1	Don't Leave Me This Way.............	—		The Ravyns........................	RDM 39015
			REA, Chris				
			Born on 3/4/51 in Middlesborough, Cleveland, England. Pop-rock singer/songwriter.				
1/21/89	❶1	15	1 Working On It	73		New Light Through Old Windows.......	Geffen 24232
2/10/90	11	10	2 The Road To Hell....................	—		The Road To Hell..................	Geffen 24276
			REACHAROUND				
			Rock group from Los Angeles: Matt Caisley (vocals), Ted Hutt (guitar), Jeff Peters (bass) and Scott Capizzano (drums).				
8/10/96	33	6	Big Chair...........................	—		Who's Tommy Cooper?.............	Trauma 90067
			REAL LIFE				
			Rock group from Melbourne, Australia: David Sterry (vocals, guitar), Richard Zatorski (keyboards), Allan Johnson (bass) and Danny Simcic (drums).				
1/14/84	18	8	1 Send Me An Angel...................	29		Heart Land.......................	Curb 5459
4/14/84	46	2	2 Catch Me I'm Falling................	40	↓		

			RED HOT CHILI PEPPERS ★33★				
			Rock group formed in Los Angeles: Anthony Kiedis (vocals; born on 11/1/62), Hillel Slovak (guitar; born on 4/13/62; died of a drug overdose on 6/27/88, age 26), Michael "Flea" Balzary (bass; born on 10/16/62) and Jack Irons (drums; born on 7/18/62). John Frusciante (born on 3/5/70) replaced Slovak. Irons left in 1988 and later joined **Eleven**, then **Pearl Jam**; replaced by Chad Smith (born on 10/25/62). Frusciante left in May 1992; replaced by Zander Schloss (**Thelonious Monster**, **The Magnificent Bastards**), then by Arik Marshall, then by Jesse Tobias and finally by **Dave Navarro** in September 1993. Frusciante returned in 1998, replacing Navarro. Kiedis appeared in the movie *Point Break*. Flea and Kiedis appeared in the movie *The Chase*.				
			1)Scar Tissue 2)By The Way 3)My Friends				
12/2/89+	26	10	1 Higher Ground........................	—	●	Mother's Milk......................	EMI 92152
			#4 Pop hit for **Stevie Wonder** in 1973				
4/4/92	28	20	2 Under The Bridge	21	▲7	Blood Sugar Sex Magik............	Warner 26681
8/8/92	15	13	3 Breaking The Girl....................	—	↓		
8/21/93	7	20	4 Soul To Squeeze	22		Coneheads (soundtrack)...........	Warner 45345
9/2/95	13	12	5 Warped...........................	41A	▲2	One Hot Minute...................	Warner 45733
10/7/95	❶4	26	6 My Friends	27A			
2/3/96	12	16	7 Aeroplane.........................	49A	↓		
6/5/99	❶10	29	8 Scar Tissue	9	▲4	Californication....................	Warner 47386
10/23/99	16	14	9 Around The World..................	108	↓		
1/29/00	25	27	10 Otherside	14	↓		
7/1/00	❶2	26	11 Californication	69	↓		
6/15/02	❶7	24↑	12 By The Way	34	▲	By The Way.......................	Warner 48140
10/12/02	14↑	7↑	13 The Zephyr Song...................	49↑	↓		
			RED HOUSE, The				
			Rock group from New Jersey: Bruce Tunkel (vocals, keyboards), Tony Stives (guitar), Ron Baumann (bass) and Bob Nicol (drums).				
8/11/90	30	7	I Said A Prayer......................	—		The Red House....................	SBK 94476
			RED RIDER — see COCHRANE, Tom				

DEBUT	PEAK	WKS	Mainstream Rock Track	Pop Gld	Album Title	Album Label & Number

RED ROCKERS
Rock group from Algiers, Louisiana: John Griffith (vocals), James Singletary (guitar), Darren Hill (bass) and Jim Reilly (drums). Shawn Paddock replaced Singletary in early 1984.

5/28/83	19	9	1 China	53	Good As Gold . . . . Columbia 38629	
10/6/84	54	2	2 Eve Of Destruction	—	Schizophrenic Circus . . . . Columbia 39281	

#1 Pop hit for Barry McGuire in 1965

RED SIREN
Rock group from New York City: Kristin Massey (vocals), Robert Haas (guitar), Jon Brant (bass) and Gregg Potter (drums).

2/18/89	10	13	1 All Is Forgiven	—	All Is Forgiven . . . . Mercury 836776	
6/17/89	39	5	2 One Good Lover	—	↓	

REED, Lou
Born on 3/2/42 in Freeport, Long Island, New York. Lead singer/songwriter of the New York seminal rock band Velvet Underground. Regarded as the godfather of punk rock. Appeared in the 1980 movie *One Trick Pony*. Also see **Classic Rock Tracks** section.

8/4/84	28	11	1 I Love You, Suzanne	—	New Sensations . . . . RCA Victor 4998	
5/17/86	19	10	2 No Money Down	—	Mistrial . . . . RCA Victor 7190	
1/28/89	18	13	3 Dirty Blvd.	— ●	New York . . . . Sire 25829	
4/29/89	47	3	4 Busload Of Faith	—	↓	

REEF
Rock group from England: Gary Stringer (vocals), Kenwyn House (guitar), Jack Bessant (bass) and Domenic Greensmith (drums).

8/9/97	29	6	Place Your Hands	—	Glow . . . . Epic 67971	

RE-FLEX
Techno-rock group formed in London: Baxter (vocals, guitar), Paul Fishman (keyboards), Nigel Ross-Scott (bass) and Roland Kerridge (drums).

1/14/84	19	7	The Politics Of Dancing	24	The Politics Of Dancing . . . . Capitol 12314	

REFRESHMENTS, The
Rock group from Tempe, Arizona: Roger Clyne (vocals, guitar), Brian Blush (guitar), Buddy Edwards (bass) and P.H. Naffah (drums).

5/11/96	11	18	Banditos	—	Fizzy Fuzzy Big & Buzzy . . . . Mercury 528999	

title is Spanish for "Bandits"

R.E.M. ★13★
Rock group formed in Athens, Georgia: **Michael Stipe** (vocals; born on 1/4/60), Peter Buck (guitar; born on 12/6/56), Mike Mills (bass; born on 12/17/58) and Bill Berry (drums; born on 7/31/58). Developed huge following with college audiences in the early 1980s as one of the first "alternative rock" bands. Buck, Mills and Berry also recorded with **Warren Zevon** as the **Hindu Love Gods**. Berry retired from the group in 1997.

1)Losing My Religion 2)Orange Crush 3)Stand 4)What's The Frequency, Kenneth? 5)The One I Love

5/21/83	25	4	1 Radio Free Europe	78 ●	Murmur . . . . I.R.S. 70604	
5/26/84	43	11	2 so. Central Rain (I'm Sorry)	85 ●	Reckoning . . . . I.R.S. 70044	
9/8/84	44	1	3 Pretty Persuasion	—	↓	
7/6/85	14	11	4 Can't Get There From Here	110 ●	Fables Of The Reconstruction . . . . I.R.S. 5592	
9/7/85	22	11	5 Driver 8	—	↓	
8/9/86	5	12	6 Fall On Me	94 ●	Lifes Rich Pageant . . . . I.R.S. 5783	
11/1/86	17	10	7 Superman	—	↓	
5/9/87	39	5	8 Ages Of You	—	Dead Letter Office . . . . I.R.S. 70054	
9/5/87	2⁴	16	9 The One I Love	9 ▲	R.E.M. No. 5: Document . . . . I.R.S. 42059	
11/21/87	16	11	10 Its The End Of The World As We Know It (And I Feel Fine)	69	↓	
2/6/88	28	11	11 Finest Worksong	—	↓	
11/12/88	**❶**²	12	12 Orange Crush	— ▲²	Green . . . . Warner 25795	
12/3/88+	**❶**¹	19	13 Stand	6	↓	
			became the theme for TV's *Get A Life* starring Chris Elliott			
3/11/89	7	11	14 Turn You Inside-Out	—	↓	
5/6/89	14	9	15 Pop Song 89	86	↓	
3/9/91	**❶**³	17	16 Losing My Religion	4 ▲⁴	Out Of Time . . . . Warner 26496	
5/18/91	7	13	17 Texarkana	—	↓	
7/13/91	8	11	18 Shiny Happy People	10	↓	
			Kate Pierson (of **The B-52's**; backing vocal)			
10/12/91	43	6	19 Radio Song	—	↓	
10/3/92	2²	20	20 Drive	28 ▲⁴	Automatic For The People . . . . Warner 45138	
11/28/92+	4	13	21 Ignoreland	—	↓	
1/30/93	4	16	22 Man On The Moon	30	↓	
			tribute to Andy Kaufman			
5/8/93	28	5	23 The Sidewinder Sleeps Tonite	—	↓	

DEBUT	PEAK	WKS	Mainstream Rock Track	Pop	Gld	Album Title	Album Label & Number
			R.E.M. — Cont'd				
9/24/94	2⁵	26	24 What's The Frequency, Kenneth?	21	▲⁴	Monster	Warner 45740
12/3/94+	3	18	25 Bang And Blame	19	↓		
3/11/95	15	10	26 Star 69	74ᴬ	↓		
5/20/95	8	13	27 Strange Currencies	47	↓		
8/12/95	20	9	28 Crush With Eyeliner	113	↓		
8/31/96	15	7	29 E-Bow The Letter	49	▲	New Adventures In Hi-Fi	Warner 46320
			Patti Smith (female vocal)				
10/12/96	7	17	30 Bittersweet Me	46	↓		
1/25/97	30	5	31 The Wake-Up Bomb	—	↓		
10/24/98	30	7	32 Daysleeper	57	●	Up	Warner 47112
2/6/99	31	8	33 Lotus	—	↓		
12/25/99+	33	8	34 The Great Beyond	57		Man On The Moon (soundtrack)	Warner 47483
			REMBRANDTS, The				
			Pop-rock duo from Los Angeles: **Danny Wilde** and Phil Solem. Both were members of **Great Buildings**.				
11/10/90+	13	15	1 Just The Way It Is, Baby	14		The Rembrandts	Atco 91412
2/16/91	36	10	2 Burning Timber	—	↓		
9/26/92	24	10	3 Johnny Have You Seen Her?	54		Untitled	Atco 92200
			REMY ZERO				
			Rock group from Alabama: brothers Cinjun (vocals) and Shelby (guitar) Tate, Jeff Cain (guitar), Cedric LeMoyne (bass) and Greg Slay (drums).				
12/26/98+	25	10	Prophecy	—		Villa Elaine	DGC 25300
	★81★		**REO SPEEDWAGON**				
			Rock group from Champaign, Illinois: Kevin Cronin (vocals, guitar; born on 10/6/51), Gary Richrath (guitar; born on 10/18/49), Neal Doughty (keyboards; born on 7/29/46), Bruce Hall (bass; born on 5/3/53) and Alan Gratzer (drums; born on 11/9/48). Graham Lear replaced Gratzer in 1988. Lineup in 1990: Cronin, Doughty and Hall, joined by new members Dave Amato (guitar), Jesse Harms (keyboards) and Bryan Hitt (drums). Group appeared in the movie *FM*. Also see **Classic Rock Tracks** section.				
			1)Keep The Fire Burnin' 2)That Ain't Love 3)I Do'wanna Know				
3/21/81	6	13	1 Take It On The Run	5	▲⁹	Hi Infidelity	Epic 36844
3/21/81	9	12	2 Keep On Loving You	❶¹		↓	
3/21/81	11	26	3 Don't Let Him Go	24	↓		
3/21/81	25	3	4 Tough Guys	—	↓		
3/28/81	59	1	5 Out Of Season	—	↓		
6/19/82	2¹	16	6 Keep The Fire Burnin'	7	▲	Good Trouble	Epic 38100
7/10/82	19	10	7 Stillness Of The Night	—	↓		
8/7/82	51	2	8 Good Trouble	—	↓		
8/14/82	34	3	9 The Key	—	↓		
10/27/84	5	13	10 I Do'wanna Know	29	▲²	Wheels Are Turnin'	Epic 39593
12/8/84+	5	17	11 Can't Fight This Feeling	❶³		↓	
4/13/85	17	8	12 One Lonely Night	19	↓		
1/31/87	5	11	13 That Ain't Love	16	●	Life As We Know It	Epic 40444
4/18/87	28	8	14 Variety Tonight	60	↓		
8/11/90	6	9	15 Live It Up	—		The Earth, A Small Man, His Dog And A Chicken	Epic 45246
10/13/90	31	5	16 Love Is A Rock	65	↓		
			REPLACEMENTS, The				
			Rock group from Minneapolis: **Paul Westerberg** (vocals, guitar, piano), Slim Dunlap (guitar), Tommy Stinson (bass) and **Chris Mars** (drums). Steve Foley replaced Mars in early 1990.				
2/4/89	❶³	15	1 I'll Be You	51		Don't Tell A Soul	Sire 25831
5/20/89	43	5	2 Back To Back	—	↓		
8/5/89	37	5	3 Achin' To Be	—	↓		
			REVEILLE				
			Rock group from Harvard, Massachusetts: Drew Simollardes (vocals), Steve Miloszewski and Greg Sullivan (guitars), Carl Randolph (bass) and Justin Wilson (drums).				
3/16/02	28	9	Inside Out (Can You Feel Me Now)	—		Bleed The Sky	Elektra 62770
			RHYTHM CORPS				
			Rock group from Detroit: Michael Persh (vocals), Greg Apro (guitar), Davey Holmbo (bass) and Richie Lovsin (drums).				
6/18/88	9	17	Common Ground	—		Common Ground	Pasha 44159
			RICHARDS, Keith				
			Born on 12/18/43 in Dartford, Kent, England. Lead guitarist of **The Rolling Stones**. Married model Patti Hansen on 12/18/83.				
10/15/88	3	9	1 Take It So Hard	—	●	Talk Is Cheap	Virgin 90973
11/19/88+	18	13	2 You Don't Move Me	—	↓		
2/25/89	47	4	3 Struggle	—	↓		
10/31/92+	3	18	4 Wicked As It Seems	—		Main Offender	Virgin 86499
1/30/93	17	8	5 Eileen	—	↓		

DEBUT	PEAK	WKS	Mainstream Rock Track	Pop Gld	Album Title	Album Label & Number
			RICHIE, Lionel Born on 6/20/49 in Tuskegee, Alabama. R&B singer/songwriter/pianist. Former lead singer of the Commodores.			
2/18/84	49	1	Running With The Night	7 ▲10	Can't Slow Down	Motown 6059
			RIOT Hard-rock group formed in New York City: Rhett Forrester (vocals), Mark Reale and Rick Ventura (guitars), Kip Leming (bass) and Sandy Slavin (drums). Forrester was shot to death in Atlanta on 1/22/94 (age 37).			
9/25/82	35	3	1 Showdown	—	Restless Breed	Elektra 60134
12/17/83	44	4	2 Born In America	—	Born In America	Quality 1008
			RIVERDOGS Rock group formed in Los Angeles: Rob Lamothe (vocals), Vivian Campbell (guitar), Nick Brophy (bass) and Marc Danzeisen (drums). Campbell, formerly with **Dio** and **Whitesnake**, later joined **Def Leppard**.			
6/16/90	26	9	1 Toy Soldier	—	Riverdogs	Epic/Associated 46021
9/22/90	50	1	2 I Believe	—	↓	
			ROBERTSON, Robbie Born Jaime Robbie Robertson on 7/5/44 in Toronto. Rock singer/songwriter/guitarist. Member of The Band.			
10/17/87	2¹	15	1 Showdown At Big Sky	— ●	Robbie Robertson	Geffen 24160
			BoDeans (backing vocals)			
11/7/87+	7	15	2 Sweet Fire Of Love	—	↓	
			U2 (backing band)			
2/13/88	21	7	3 American Roulette	—	↓	
			BoDeans and Maria McKee (backing vocals)			
4/23/88	24	8	4 Somewhere Down The Crazy River..........................	—	↓	
10/5/91	15	10	5 What About Now	—	Storyville	Geffen 24303
2/8/92	32	5	6 Go Back To Your Woods................................	—	↓	
			Bruce Hornsby (piano, backing vocal)			
			ROB RULE Rock group formed in Los Angeles: Edward Anisko (vocals), David King (guitar), Robbie Allen (guitar, piano), Steven Ossana (bass) and James Bradley (drums).			
5/28/94	28	8	She Gets Too High...	—	Rob Rule....................	Mercury 522119
			ROCK AND HYDE Pop-rock duo from Vancouver: Paul Hyde (vocals) and Bob Rock (guitar, keyboards). Both formerly with **Paul Hyde & The Payolas**.			
4/11/87	6	10	Dirty Water	61	Under The Volcano	Capitol 12569
			ROCK CITY ANGELS Rock group from Memphis: Bobby Durango (vocals), Mike Barnes and Doug Banx (guitars), Andy Panik (bass), and Jackie Jukes (drums).			
10/22/88	49	1	Deep Inside My Heart......................................	—	Young Man's Blues	Geffen 24193
			ROCKETS, The Rock group from Detroit: David Gilbert (vocals), Jim McCarty and Dennis Robbins (guitars), Donnie Backus (keyboards), Bobby Neil Haralson (bass) and John Badanjek (drums). McCarty and Badanjek were members of Mitch Ryder & The Detroit Wheels. Gilbert died of cancer on 8/1/2001 (age 49). Also see **Classic Rock Tracks** section.			
8/22/81	42	3	I Can't Get Satisfied	—	Back Talk	Elektra 351
			ROCKPILE Pop-rock group formed in London: **Dave Edmunds** (vocals, guitar), **Nick Lowe** (vocals, bass), Billy Bremner (guitar) and Terry Williams (drums).			
4/18/81	8	8	Little Sister [L]	—	Concerts For The People Of Kampuchea (various artists)	Atlantic 7005
			ROCKPILE with Robert Plant #5 Pop hit for Elvis Presley in 1961			
			ROCKWELL Born Kennedy Gordy on 3/15/64 in Detroit. R&B singer. Son of Motown chairman Berry Gordy.			
2/25/84	31	5	Somebody's Watching Me..............................	2³ ●	Somebody's Watching Me	Motown 6052
			Michael Jackson (backing vocal)			
			RODGERS, Paul Born on 12/17/49 in Middlesbrough, Cleveland, England. Lead singer of Free (1969-73), **Bad Company** (1974-82), **The Firm** (1984-86) and **The Law** (1991).			
11/26/83+	15	10	1 Cut Loose	102	Cut Loose	Atlantic 80121
4/24/93	6	10	2 The Hunter	—	Muddy Water Blues - A Tribute To Muddy Waters	Victory 480013
			Slash (of **Guns N' Roses**; lead guitar)			
7/19/97	15	14	3 Soul Of Love..	—	Now	Velvel 79790
6/24/00	33	5	4 Drifters	—	Electric	CMC International 86294

DEBUT	PEAK	WKS	Mainstream Rock Track	Pop Gld	Album Title	Album Label & Number

ROLLING STONES, The ★7★

Rock group formed in London: **Mick Jagger** (vocals), **Keith Richards** and Brian Jones (guitars), Bill Wyman (bass) and Charlie Watts (drums). Group took name from a Muddy Waters song. Promoted as the bad boys in contrast to **The Beatles**. Jones drowned on 7/3/69 (age 27); replaced by Mick Taylor. **Ronnie Wood** replaced Taylor in 1975. Movie *Gimme Shelter* is a documentary of the group's performance at the 1969 Altamont concert. Wyman and Watts also formed **Willie And The Poor Boys**. Won Grammy's Lifetime Achievement Award in 1986. Inducted into the Rock and Roll Hall of Fame in 1989. Darryl Jones replaced Wyman in late 1992. Considered by many to be the world's all-time greatest rock and roll band. Also see **Classic Rock Tracks** section.

1)Start Me Up 2)Rock And A Hard Place 3)Mixed Emotions 4)Highwire 5)Almost Hear You Sigh

DEBUT	PEAK	WKS	Mainstream Rock Track	Pop Gld	Album Title	Album Label & Number
4/18/81	26	4	1 If I Was A Dancer (Dance Pt. 2)	—	*Sucking In The Seventies*	Rolling Stones 16028
8/22/81	❶¹³	32	2 Start Me Up	2³ ▲⁴	*Tattoo You*	Rolling Stones 16052
9/26/81	2³	17	3 Hang Fire	20	↓	
10/10/81	5	16	4 Little T & A	—	↓	
11/28/81+	8	14	5 Waiting On A Friend	13	↓	
6/12/82	5	12	6 Going To A Go-Go [L]	25 ▲	*"Still Life" (American Concert 1981)*	Rolling Stones 39113
			#11 Pop hit for The Miracles in 1966			
11/12/83	2¹	14	7 Undercover Of The Night	9 ▲	*Undercover*	Rolling Stones 90120
11/19/83+	4	19	8 She Was Hot	44	↓	
11/19/83	14	12	9 Too Tough	—	↓	
12/17/83	38	11	10 Too Much Blood	—	↓	
3/3/84	50	2	11 Think I'm Going Mad	—	*(single only)*	Rolling Stones 99788
3/15/86	2³	10	12 Harlem Shuffle	5 ▲	*Dirty Work*	Rolling Stones 40250
			#44 Pop hit for Bob & Earl in 1964			
4/5/86	3	16	13 One Hit (To The Body)	28	↓	
4/12/86	10	13	14 Winning Ugly	—	↓	
9/2/89	❶⁵	9	15 Mixed Emotions	5 ▲²	*Steel Wheels*	Rolling Stones 45333
9/9/89	❶⁵	19	16 Rock And A Hard Place	23	↓	
9/9/89	14	10	17 Sad Sad Sad	—	↓	
9/23/89+	8	15	18 Terrifying	—	↓	
1/20/90	❶¹	13	19 Almost Hear You Sigh	50	↓	
3/9/91	❶³	11	20 Highwire	57 ●	*Flashpoint*	Rolling Stones 47456
5/25/91	40	3	21 Sex Drive	—	↓	
7/9/94	2⁵	17	22 Love Is Strong	91 ▲²	*Voodoo Lounge*	Virgin 39782
7/23/94	2¹	19	23 You Got Me Rocking	113	↓	
10/29/94	14	14	24 Out Of Tears	60	↓	
1/7/95	30	8	25 Sparks Will Fly	—	↓	
4/1/95	20	9	26 I Go Wild	—	↓	
11/18/95	16	8	27 Like A Rolling Stone	109 ▲	*Stripped*	Virgin 41040
			#2 Pop hit for Bob Dylan in 1965			
9/20/97	3	16	28 Anybody Seen My Baby?	— ▲	*Bridges To Babylon*	Virgin 44712
11/22/97+	13	18	29 Saint Of Me	94	↓	
11/22/97	14	13	30 Flip The Switch	—	↓	
11/28/98	29	8	31 Gimme Shelter [L]	—	*No Security*	Virgin 46740
9/14/02	21	11↑	32 Don't Stop	—	*Forty Licks*	Abkco 13378

ROLLINS BAND

Born Henry Garfield on 2/13/61 in Washington DC. Hard-rock singer/poet/actor. Acted in several movies. His band: Chris Haskett (guitar), Melvin Gibbs (bass) and Sim Cain (drums).

6/25/94	40	1	Liar	109	*Weight*	Imago 21034

ROMANTICS, The

Pop-rock group from Detroit: Wally Palmar (vocals, guitar), Coz Canler (guitar), Mike Skill (bass) and Jimmy Marinos (drums). David Petratos replaced Marinos in early 1985. Also see **Classic Rock Tracks** section.

10/15/83	2³	17	1 Talking In Your Sleep	3 ●	*In Heat*	Nemperor 38880
10/22/83	49	5	2 Rock You Up	—	↓	
3/31/84	22	6	3 One In A Million	37	↓	
9/21/85	44	3	4 Test Of Time	71	*Rhythm Romance*	Nemperor 40106

ROMEO VOID

Pop-rock group from San Francisco: Debora Iyall (vocals), Peter Woods (guitar), Ben Bossi (sax), Frank Zincavage (bass) and Aaron Smith (drums).

10/16/82	27	7	1 Never Say Never	—	*Benefactor*	Columbia 38182
8/11/84	17	12	2 A Girl In Trouble (Is A Temporary Thing)	35	*Instincts*	Columbia 39155

RONSON, Mick — see HUNTER, Ian

RONSTADT, Linda

Born on 7/15/46 in Tucson, Arizona. Pop-rock-country singer. Also see **Classic Rock Tracks** section.

10/16/82	34	7	Get Closer	29 ●	*Get Closer*	Asylum 60185

ROSSDALE, Gavin

Born on 10/30/67 in London. Lead singer of **Bush**. Married **Gwen Stefani** (of **No Doubt**) on 9/14/2002.

8/31/02	24	7	Adrenaline	— ●	*XXX (soundtrack)*	Universal 156259

DEBUT	PEAK	WKS	Mainstream Rock Track	Pop Gld	Album Title	Album Label & Number

ROSSINGTON COLLINS BAND
Rock group formed in Jacksonville, Florida: Dale Krantz (vocals), Gary Rossington, Allen Collins and Barry Harwood (guitars), Billy Powell (keyboards), Leon Wilkeson (bass) and Derek Hess (drums). Rossington, Collins, Powell and Wilkeson were members of **Lynyrd Skynyrd**. Disbanded in 1982. Rossington and wife Dale, Jay Johnson (guitar), Ronnie Eades (sax), Tim Sharpton (keyboards), Tim Lindsey (bass) and Mitch Rigel (drums) recorded as **The Rossington Band** in 1988. Collins died of pneumonia on 1/23/90 (age 37). Wilkeson died on 7/27/2001 (age 49).

11/7/81	50	3	1 Gotta Get It Straight	—	*This Is The Way*	MCA 5207
5/28/88	9	11	2 Welcome Me Home	—	*Love Your Man*	MCA 42166
			THE ROSSINGTON BAND			

ROTH, David Lee ★65★
Born on 10/10/55 in Bloomington, Indiana. Lead singer of **Van Halen** from 1973-1985. Rejoined Van Halen briefly in 1996 to record two new songs.
1)Just Like Paradise 2)Damn Good 3)A Lil' Ain't Enough

1/19/85	3	10	1 California Girls	3 ▲	*Crazy From The Heat*	Warner 25222
			#3 Pop hit for The Beach Boys in 1965			
2/16/85	14	9	2 Easy Street	—	↓	
			#83 Pop hit for the Edgar Winter Group in 1974			
4/6/85	25	7	3 Just A Gigolo/I Ain't Got Nobody	12	↓	
			#1 Pop hit for Ted Lewis in 1931/#3 Pop hit for Marion Harris in 1921			
7/5/86	10	9	4 Yankee Rose	16 ▲	*Eat 'Em And Smile*	Warner 25470
7/19/86	10	11	5 Tobacco Road	—	↓	
			#14 Pop hit for The Nashville Teens in 1964			
8/30/86	12	10	6 Goin' Crazy!	66	↓	
1/16/88	❶⁴	10	7 Just Like Paradise	6 ▲	*Skyscraper*	Warner 25671
2/6/88	5	16	8 Stand Up	64	↓	
2/6/88	45	7	9 Knucklebones	—	↓	
2/13/88	2¹	12	10 Damn Good	—	↓	
1/19/91	3	10	11 A Lil' Ain't Enough	— ●	*A Little Ain't Enough*	Warner 26477
3/9/91	6	14	12 Sensible Shoes	—	↓	
6/15/91	39	5	13 Tell The Truth	—	↓	
3/5/94	12	8	14 She's My Machine	—	*Your Filthy Little Mouth*	Reprise 45391
4/25/98	11	15	15 Slam Dunk	—	*DLR Band*	Wawazat 1217
			DLR BAND			

ROXY BLUE
Hard-rock group from Memphis: Todd Poole (vocals), Sid Fletcher (guitar), Josh Weil (bass) and Scotty T (drums).

| 8/15/92 | 38 | 1 | Luv On Me | — | *Want Some?* | Geffen 24464 |

ROXY MUSIC
Art-rock group from England: Bryan Ferry (vocals, keyboards), Phil Manzanera (guitar), Andy MacKay (horns) and Paul Thompson (drums). Also see **Classic Rock Tracks** section.

7/3/82	58	1	1 More Than This	102 ▲	*Avalon*	Warner 23686
7/24/82	59	5	2 Avalon	—	↓	
5/21/83	24	5	3 Like A Hurricane	[L] —	*Musique/The High Road*	Warner 23808
			recorded at the Apollo Theatre in Glasgow, Scotland; first recorded by **Neil Young** in 1977			

ROYAL JELLY
Rock group from Los Angeles: John Edwards (vocals), Dan Steigerwald (guitar), David Seaton (bass) and Jeff Klaven (drums).

| 11/5/94 | 29 | 7 | Ceiling | — | *Royal Jelly* | Island 524015 |

RTZ
Rock group formed in Boston: Brad Delp (vocals), Barry Goudreau (guitar), Brian Maes (keyboards), Tim Archibald (bass) and David Stefanelli (drums). Delp and Goudreau were members of **Boston**. Goudreau was also with **Orion The Hunter**. RTZ: Return To Zero.

7/27/91	5	10	1 Face The Music	49	*Return To Zero*	Giant 24422
10/5/91	19	13	2 There's Another Side	—	↓	
2/8/92	38	7	3 Until Your Love Comes Back Around	26	↓	

RUFFIN, David — see HALL & OATES

RUFFNER, Mason
Born in Fort Worth, Texas. Rock singer/songwriter/guitarist.

5/16/87	11	10	1 Gypsy Blood	—	*Gypsy Blood*	CBS Associated 40601
8/8/87	42	3	2 Dancin' On Top Of The World	—	↓	
			above 2 produced by **Dave Edmunds**			

RULE, Rob — see ROB

RUNDGREN, Todd
Born on 6/22/48 in Upper Darby, Pennsylvania. Pop-rock singer/songwriter/multi-instrumentalist. Leader of Nazz and **Utopia**. Also see **Classic Rock Tracks** section.

3/21/81	18	2	1 Time Heals	107	*Healing*	Bearsville 3522
3/21/81	48	1	2 Compassion	—	↓	
5/28/83	29	3	3 Bang The Drum All Day	63	*The Ever Popular Tortured Artist Effect*	Bearsville 23732
5/27/89	15	10	4 The Want Of A Nail	—	*Nearly Human*	Warner 25881

DEBUT	PEAK	WKS	Mainstream Rock Track	Pop	Gld	Album Title	Album Label & Number

RUSH ★6★
Hard-rock trio formed in Toronto: **Geddy Lee** (vocals, bass; born on 7/29/53), **Alex Lifeson** (guitar; born on 8/27/53) and Neil Peart (drums; born on 9/12/52). Peart writes most of the group's lyrics. Also see **Bob & Doug McKenzie**, **Victor** and **Classic Rock Tracks** section.

1)Dreamline 2)Stick It Out 3)Test For Echo 4)New World Man 5)Show Don't Tell

DEBUT	PEAK	WKS	Track	Pop	Gld	Album Title	Album Label & Number
3/21/81	4	15	1 Limelight	55	▲4	Moving Pictures	Mercury 4013
3/21/81	8	21	2 Tom Sawyer	44	↓		
			also see #4 below				
11/21/81+	21	15	3 Closer To The Heart .... [L]	69	▲	Exit...Stage Left	Mercury 7001
			live version of their #76 Pop hit in 1977				
12/12/81+	42	6	4 Tom Sawyer .... [L-R]	—	↓		
			live version of #2 above				
9/11/82	❶2	21	5 New World Man	21	▲	Signals	Mercury 4063
9/25/82	8	29	6 Subdivisions	105	↓		
9/25/82	19	7	7 The Analog Kid	—	↓		
4/28/84	3	14	8 Distant Early Warning	—	▲	Grace Under Pressure	Mercury 818476
5/5/84	23	13	9 Body Electric	105	↓		
5/5/84	39	3	10 Between The Wheels	—	↓		
5/12/84	21	11	11 Red Sector A	—	↓		
10/12/85	4	14	12 The Big Money	45	▲	Power Windows	Mercury 826098
11/16/85	30	13	13 Territories	—	↓		
11/23/85+	10	14	14 Manhattan Project	—	↓		
3/8/86	21	6	15 Mystic Rhythms	—	↓		
9/5/87	3	9	16 Force Ten	—	●	Hold Your Fire	Mercury 832464
9/19/87	3	14	17 Time Stand Still	—	↓		
12/12/87+	16	10	18 Lock And Key	—	↓		
1/14/89	6	8	19 Marathon .... [L]	—	●	A Show Of Hands	Mercury 836346
3/11/89	33	5	20 Mission .... [L]	—	↓		
11/18/89+	❶1	12	21 Show Don't Tell	—	●	Presto	Atlantic 82040
1/6/90	14	12	22 Presto	—	↓		
3/3/90	15	11	23 The Pass	—	↓		
5/19/90	37	6	24 Superconductor	—	↓		
9/7/91	❶4	20	25 Dreamline	—	▲	Roll The Bones	Atlantic 82293
10/19/91+	9	22	26 Roll The Bones	—	↓		
11/30/91+	2¹	27	27 Ghost Of A Chance	—	↓		
3/28/92	13	10	28 Bravado	—	↓		
10/23/93	❶4	12	29 Stick It Out	—	●	Counterparts	Atlantic 82528
11/20/93+	2¹	22	30 Cold Fire	—	↓		
2/26/94	9	11	31 Nobody's Hero	—	↓		
5/21/94	35	3	32 Animate	—	↓		
9/7/96	❶3	13	33 Test For Echo	—	●	Test For Echo	Atlantic 82925
11/16/96+	6	16	34 Half The World	—	↓		
3/22/97	20	8	35 Driven	—	↓		
11/7/98	27	8	36 The Spirit Of Radio .... [L]	—	●	Different Stages - Live	Atlantic 83122
4/20/02	10	13	37 One Little Victory	—		Vapor Trails	Anthem 83531
7/6/02	25	9	38 Secret Touch	—	↓		

RUSSELL, Leon
Born on 4/2/41 in Lawton, Oklahoma. Rock singer/songwriter/multi-instrumentalist. Prolific session musician. Also see **Classic Rock Tracks** section.

5/16/92	47	1	No Man's Land	—		Anything Can Happen	Virgin 91821

RUST
Rock group from San Diego: John Brinton (vocals), Michael Suzick (guitar), Tim Blankenship (bass) and Pat Hogan (drums).

3/2/96	33	5	Not Today	—		Bar Chord Ritual	Atlantic 82822

RUTHERFORD, Mike
Born on 10/2/50 in Guildford, Surrey, England. Bassist of **Genesis** and leader of **Mike + The Mechanics**.

10/2/82	37	2	Maxine	—		Acting Very Strange	Atlantic 80015

RUTH RUTH
Punk-rock trio from New York City: Chris Kennedy (vocals, bass), Mike Lustig (guitar) and Dave Snyder (drums).

12/2/95+	24	11	Uninvited	—		Laughing Gallery	Ventrue 43039

DEBUT	PEAK	WKS	Mainstream Rock Track	Pop Gld	Album Title	Album Label & Number

S

SAGA
Rock group formed in Toronto: Michael Sadler (vocals), brothers Ian (guitar) and Jim (bass) Crichton, Jim Gilmour (keyboards) and Steve Negus (drums).

10/9/82	3	26	1 On The Loose	26 ●	Worlds Apart	Portrait 38246
12/25/82+	24	21	2 Wind Him Up	64	↓	
11/5/83	19	11	3 The Flyer	79	Heads Or Tales	Portrait 38999
8/31/85	24	8	4 What Do I Know?	—	Behaviour	Portrait 40145

SAIGON KICK
Hard-rock group formed in Miami: Matt Kramer (vocals), Jason Bieler (guitar), Tom DeFile (bass) and Phil Varone (drums).

8/8/92	8	20	1 Love Is On The Way	12 ●	The Lizard	Third Stone 92158
11/28/92+	15	14	2 All I Want	111	↓	

SALIVA
Hard-rock group from Memphis: **Josey Scott** (vocals), Wayne Swinny (guitar), Dave Novotny (bass) and Paul Crosby (drums). Also see **Chad Kroeger**.

3/10/01	3	32	1 Your Disease	116 ●	Every Six Seconds	Island 542959
8/18/01	15	23	2 Click Click Boom	—	↓	
1/12/02	31	8	3 After Me	—	↓	
10/5/02	12↑	8↑	4 Always	109↑	Back Into Your System	Island 063153

SAMBORA, Richie
Born on 7/11/59 in Woodbridge, New Jersey. Guitarist of **Bon Jovi**. Married actress Heather Locklear on 12/17/94.

8/31/91	13	10	1 Ballad Of Youth	63	Stranger In This Town	Mercury 848895
1/11/92	38	3	2 Stranger In This Town	—	↓	
4/4/98	39	1	3 Hard Times Come Easy	—	Undiscovered Soul	Mercury 536972

SANDLER, Adam
Born on 9/9/66 in Brooklyn, New York. Actor/comedian. Cast member of TV's *Saturday Night Live* (1990-95). Starred in several movies.

1/6/96	22	1	1 The Chanukah Song [X-C]	10^ ▲²	What The Hell Happened To Me?	Warner 46151
1/3/98	20	2	2 The Chanukah Song [X-C-R]	25^	↓	
1/2/99	28	2	3 The Chanukah Song [X-C-R]	80	↓	
12/13/97	33	1	4 The Thanksgiving Song [C]	67^ ▲	They're All Gonna Laugh At You	Warner 45393
12/12/98	29	1	5 The Thanksgiving Song [C-R]	107	↓	
12/11/99	39	1	6 The Thanksgiving Song [C-R]	109	↓	

SANTANA
Latin-rock group formed in San Francisco by Carlos Santana (born on 7/20/47 in Autlan de Navarro, Mexico). Various members over the years include Alex Ligertwood (vocals), Gregg Rolie (keyboards, vocals), **Neal Schon** (guitar), David Brown (bass) and Michael Shrieve (drums). Schon and Rolie formed **Journey**. Also see **Classic Rock Tracks** section.
1)Winning 2)Put Your Lights On 3)Smooth

4/4/81	2²	18	1 Winning	17 ▲	Zebop!	Columbia 37158
5/9/81	26	12	2 Searchin'	—	↓	
7/4/81	45	3	3 Changes	—	↓	
			first recorded by Cat Stevens in 1971			
8/28/82	13	27	4 Nowhere To Run	66 ●	Shango	Columbia 38122
8/28/82	17	11	5 Hold On	15	↓	
9/18/82	34	1	6 Night Hunting Time	—	↓	
2/16/85	15	11	7 Say It Again	46	Beyond Appearances	Columbia 39527
2/14/87	21	9	8 Veracruz	—	Freedom	Columbia 40272
7/14/90	14	9	9 Peace On Earth...Mother Earth...Third Stone From The Sun	—	Spirits Dancing In The Flesh	Columbia 46065
			"Third Stone From The Sun" was first recorded by Jimi Hendrix in 1967			
7/10/99	10	26	10 Smooth	❶¹² ▲¹⁴	Supernatural	Arista 19080
			SANTANA Featuring Rob Thomas			
9/25/99	8	27	11 Put Your Lights On	118	↓	
			SANTANA Featuring Everlast			

SARAYA
Rock group from New Jersey: Sandi Saraya (vocals), Tony Rey (guitar), Gregg Munier (keyboards), Gary Taylor (bass) and Chuck Bonfante (drums). Rey, Munier and Taylor left in 1990; Tony Bruno (guitar) and Barry Dunaway (bass) joined.

4/1/89	9	13	1 Love Has Taken Its Toll	64	Saraya	Polydor 837764
7/22/89	33	4	2 Get U Ready	—	↓	
10/14/89	26	7	3 Back To The Bullet	63	↓	
5/25/91	41	5	4 Seducer	—	When The Blackbird Sings	Polydor 849087

SATRIANI, Joe
Born on 7/15/57 in Carle Place, New York. Rock guitarist.
1)Summer Song 2)The Crush Of Love 3)Friends

2/13/88	22	8	1 Satch Boogie [I]	— ▲	Surfing With The Alien	Relativity 8193
4/9/88	37	8	2 Surfing With The Alien [I]	—	↓	
11/12/88+	6	16	3 The Crush Of Love [I]	— ●	Dreaming #11	Relativity 8265
4/22/89	17	9	4 One Big Rush [I]	—	Say Anything... (soundtrack)	WTG 45140

DEBUT	PEAK	WKS	Mainstream Rock Track	Pop	Gld	Album Title	Album Label & Number
			SATRIANI, Joe — Cont'd				
10/28/89	17	12	5 Big Bad Moon	—	●	*Flying In A Blue Dream* .... Relativity 1015
2/10/90	31	7	6 Back To Shalla-Bal .... [I]	—		↓
4/14/90	36	7	7 I Believe	—		↓
7/25/92	5	19	8 Summer Song [I]	—	●	*The Extremist* .... Relativity 1053
11/14/92	12	11	9 Friends .... [I]	—		↓
3/27/93	24	10	10 Cryin' .... [I]	—		↓
11/13/93	21	11	11 All Alone .... [I]	—	●	*Time Machine* .... Relativity 1177
			first recorded by Billie Holiday				
11/4/95	30	12	12 (You're) My World	—		*Joe Satriani* .... Relativity 1500
3/14/98	28	11	13 Ceremony .... [I]	—		*Crystal Planet* .... Epic 68018
			SAVATAGE				
			Hard-rock group from Florida: Zachary Stevens (vocals), Criss Oliva (guitar), Johnny Lee Middleton (bass) and Steve Wacholz (drums). Oliva died in a car crash on 10/17/93 (age 30).				
7/24/93	26	8	Edge Of Thorns	—		*Edge Of Thorns* .... Atlantic 82488
			SCANDAL				
			Rock group from New York City: **Patty Smyth** (vocals), Zack Smith and Keith Mack (guitars), Ivan Elias (bass) and Thommy Price (drums).				
12/18/82+	5	19	1 Goodbye To You	65	●	*Scandal* .... Columbia 38194
5/7/83	28	4	2 Love's Got A Line On You	59		↓
			SCANDAL FEATURING PATTY SMYTH:				
6/23/84	❶²	18	3 The Warrior	7	▲	*Warrior* .... Columbia 39173
9/15/84	10	14	4 Beat Of A Heart	41		↓
11/3/84	21	9	5 Hands Tied	41		↓
			SCHENKER, McAuley — see McAULEY SCHENKER GROUP				
			SCHILLING, Peter				
			Born on 1/28/56 in Stuttgart, Germany. Pop singer/songwriter.				
9/24/83	8	19	Major Tom (Coming Home)	14		*Error In The System* .... Elektra 60265
			inspired by **David Bowie**'s "Space Oddity"				
			SCHMIT, Timothy B.				
			Born on 10/30/47 in Sacramento, California. Singer/songwriter/bassist. Member of **Poco** and the **Eagles**.				
10/27/84	48	2	1 Playin' It Cool	101		*Playin' It Cool* .... Asylum 60359
9/19/87	17	8	2 Boys Night Out	25		*Timothy B* .... MCA 42049
			SCHON, Neal				
			Born on 2/27/54 in San Mateo, California. Rock singer/guitarist. Member of **Santana**, **Journey** and **Bad English**. Also see **Hagar, Schon, Aaronson & Shrieve**.				
2/19/83	42	1	No More Lies	—		*Here To Stay* .... Columbia 38428
			NEAL SCHON & JAN HAMMER				
			SCHOOL OF FISH				
			Pop-rock group from Los Angeles: Josh Clayton-Felt (vocals, guitar), Michael Ward (guitar, vocals), Dominic Nardini (bass) and M.P. (drums). Clayton-Felt died of cancer on 1/19/2000 (age 32).				
6/8/91	12	21	3 Strange Days	—		*School Of Fish* .... Capitol 94557
			SCHWARTZ, Eddie				
			Born in 1949 in Toronto. Pop singer/songwriter.				
2/13/82	40	6	No Refuge	—		*No Refuge* .... Atco 141
★48★			**SCORPIONS**				
			Hard-rock group from Germany: Klaus Meine (vocals), Rudolf Schenker and Matthias Jabs (guitars), Francis Buchholz (bass) and Herman Rarebell (drums). Ralph Rieckermann replaced Buchholz in 1992. Curt Cress replaced Rarebell in 1995. Schenker is the brother of Michael Schenker (**McAuley Schenker Group**).				
			1)No One Like You 2)Wind Of Change 3)Rock You Like A Hurricane				
4/3/82	❶¹	18	1 No One Like You	65	▲	*Blackout* .... Mercury 4039
6/19/82	47	4	2 Can't Live Without You	—		↓
3/3/84	5	19	3 Rock You Like A Hurricane	25	▲³	*Love At First Sting* .... Mercury 814981
4/14/84	14	10	4 Big City Nights	—		↓
6/23/84	56	3	5 I'm Leaving You	—		↓
6/30/84	36	11	6 Still Loving You	64		↓
4/16/88	6	12	7 Rhythm Of Love	75	▲	*Savage Amusement* .... Mercury 832963
7/2/88	12	12	8 Believe In Love	—		↓
11/18/89+	5	17	9 I Can't Explain	—	▲	*Best Of Rockers 'N' Ballads* .... Mercury 842002
			#93 Pop hit for **The Who** in 1965				
11/3/90	8	16	10 Tease Me Please Me	—	▲²	*Crazy World* .... Mercury 846908
1/19/91	13	12	11 Don't Believe Her	—		↓
4/6/91	2³	21	12 Wind Of Change	4		↓
8/31/91	8	20	13 Send Me An Angel	44		↓
1/25/92	24	8	14 Hit Between The Eyes	—		*Freejack (soundtrack)* .... Morgan Creek 20008
9/11/93	10	10	15 Alien Nation	—		*Face The Heat* .... Mercury 518258
11/27/93	15	10	16 Woman	—		↓
1/29/94	16	9	17 Under The Same Sun	—		↓

DEBUT	PEAK	WKS	Mainstream Rock Track	Pop Gld	Album Title	Album Label & Number
			SCORPIONS — Cont'd			
5/25/96	19	8	18 Wild Child	—	Pure Instinct........................	Atlantic 82913
7/10/99	26	11	19 Mysterious	—	Eye II Eye	Koch 8052
			SCOTT, Josey — see KROEGER, Chad			
			SCREAM, The			
			Rock group formed in Los Angeles: John Corabi (vocals), Bruce Bouillet (guitar), John Alderete (bass) and Walt Woodward (drums). Corabi was lead singer of **Mötley Crüe** from 1992-96.			
8/31/91	25	10	Man In The Moon................................	—	Let It Scream....................	Hollywood 60994
			SCREAMIN' CHEETAH WHEELIES, The			
			Rock group formed in Nashville: Mike Farris (vocals), Rick White and Bob Watkins (guitars), Steve Burgess (bass) and Terry Thomas (drums).			
10/23/93	9	15	1 Shakin' The Blues	—	The Screamin' Cheetah Wheelies......	Atlantic 82507
2/12/94	20	9	2 Ride The Tide	—	↓	
5/18/96	25	9	3 Hello From Venus	—	Magnolia...........................	Capricorn 534502
5/3/97	29	7	4 Magnolia	—	↓	
9/5/98	18	16	5 Boogie King	—	Big Wheel	Capricorn 558715
			SCREAMING TREES			
			Hard-rock group from Ellensburg, Washington: brothers Van (bass) and Gary Lee (guitar) Conner, with Mark Lanegan (vocals) and Barrett Martin (drums; **Mad Season**).			
12/12/92+	12	13	1 Nearly Lost You...............................	—	Sweet Oblivion	Epic 48996
7/3/93	40	1	2 Dollar Bill	—	↓	
7/6/96	9	17	3 All I Know	—	Dust	Epic 64178
			SEAL			
			Born Sealhenry Samuel on 2/19/63 in Paddington, England (Nigerian/Brazilian parents). Male singer.			
12/25/93+	10	11	Manic Depression	— ●	Stone Free: A Tribute To Jimi Hendrix	
			SEAL AND JEFF BECK		(various artists)	Reprise 45438
			first recorded by Jimi Hendrix in 1967			
			SECOND COMING			
			Rock group from Seattle: Travis John Bracht (vocals, guitar), Dudley Taft (guitar), Yanni Bacolas (bass) and James Bergstrom (drums).			
9/19/98	16	20	1 Soft	—	Second Coming	Capitol 95894
2/20/99	16	16	2 Vintage Eyes..................................	—	↓	
			SEETHER			
			Hard-rock trio from South Africa: Shaun Morgan (vocals, guitar), Dale Stewart (bass) and Nick Oshiro (drums).			
8/3/02	17	17↑	Fine Again......................................	116↑	Disclaimer	Wind-Up 13068
			SEGER, Bob, & The Silver Bullet Band ★32★			
			Born on 5/6/45 in Dearborn, Michigan; raised in Detroit. Rock singer/songwriter/guitarist. Formed own backing group, The Silver Bullet Band, in 1976: Alto Reed (horns), Robyn Robbins (keyboards), Drew Abbott (guitar), Chris Campbell (bass) and Charlie Martin (drums). Various personnel changes since then. Also see **Classic Rock Tracks** section.			
			1)Shakedown 2)Like A Rock 3)Tryin' To Live My Life Without You 4)Even Now 5)American Storm			
9/12/81	2⁴	19	1 Tryin' To Live My Life Without You [L]	5 ▲³	Nine Tonight......................	Capitol 12182
			recorded on 10/6/80 at Boston Garden; #102 Pop hit for Otis Clay in 1973			
12/25/82	29	3	2 House Behind A House	— ▲	The Distance	Capitol 12254
1/15/83	2³	19	3 Even Now	12	↓	
1/15/83	13	13	4 Roll Me Away	27	↓	
1/22/83	11	12	5 Boomtown Blues	—	↓	
			Glenn Frey (harmony vocal)			
10/13/84	5	16	6 Understanding	17 ●	Teachers (soundtrack)	Capitol 12371
3/22/86	9	8	7 Fortunate Son [L]	—	(single only)	Capitol 5532
			recorded on 3/31/83 at Cobo Hall in Detroit; #14 Pop hit for Creedence Clearwater Revival in 1969			
3/15/86	2²	10	8 American Storm	13 ▲	Like A Rock	Capitol 12398
4/19/86	❶²	13	9 Like A Rock	12	↓	
5/10/86	35	6	10 Tightrope	—	↓	
6/14/86	9	11	11 The Aftermath	—	↓	
8/23/86	8	9	12 It's You	52	↓	
11/29/86	47	3	13 Miami..	70	↓	
			Don Henley and **Timothy B. Schmit** (backing vocals)			
5/23/87	❶⁴	10	14 Shakedown	❶¹ ▲	Beverly Hills Cop II (soundtrack)	MCA 6207
6/10/89	40	4	15 Blue Monday..................................	—	Road House (soundtrack)	Arista 8576
			BOB SEGER (above 2)			
			#5 Pop hit for Fats Domino in 1957			

DEBUT	PEAK	WKS	Mainstream Rock Track	Pop	Gld	Album Title	Album Label & Number
			SEGER, Bob, & The Silver Bullet Band — Cont'd				
8/24/91	4	8	16 The Real Love	24	▲	The Fire Inside	Capitol 91134
9/21/91	6	14	17 The Fire Inside	—		↓	
11/30/91+	10	15	18 Take A Chance	—		↓	
11/4/95	22	11	19 Lock And Load	—	●	It's A Mystery	Capitol 99774
2/17/96	29	6	20 Hands In The Air	—		↓	
			SEMBELLO, Michael				
			Born on 4/17/54 in Philadelphia. Pop singer/guitarist. Prolific studio musician.				
7/30/83	34	8	Maniac	❶² ▲⁶		Flashdance (soundtrack)	Casablanca 811492
			SEMISONIC				
			Rock trio from Minneapolis: Dan Wilson (vocals, guitar), John Munson (bass) and Jacob Slichter (drums).				
1/25/97	30	4	1 F.N.T.	—		Great Divide	MCA 11414
3/21/98	13	26	✓2 Closing Time	11ᴬ	▲	Feeling Strangely Fine	MCA 11733
9/26/98	31	8	3 Singing In My Sleep	—		↓	
			SETZER, Brian				
			Born on 4/10/60 in Long Island, New York. Lead singer/guitarist of the **Stray Cats**. Played Eddie Cochran in the 1987 movie *La Bamba*. Formed own 16-piece swing orchestra in 1994.				
2/22/86	13	11	1 The Knife Feels Like Justice	—		The Knife Feels Like Justice	EMI America 17178
5/7/88	36	6	2 When The Sky Comes Tumblin' Down	—		Live Nude Guitars.	EMI-Manhattan 46963
			SEVEN CHANNELS				
			Rock group from Dallas: Kevin Kirkwood (vocals), Dallas Perry (guitar), Dalton Humphreys (bass) and Ben Holt (drums).				
8/18/01	31	10	Breathe	—		Seven Channels	Palm 2070
			SEVENDUST				
			Rock group from Atlanta: **Lajon** Witherspoon (vocals), Clint Lowery and John Connelly (guitars), Vinnie Hornsby (bass) and Morgan Rose (drums).				
1/10/98	30	11	1 Black	—	●	Sevendust	TVT 5730
5/16/98	39	1	2 Too Close To Hate	—		↓	
12/5/98	30	9	3 Bitch	—		↓	
8/14/99	14	25	4 Denial	—	●	Home	TVT 5820
2/26/00	23	17	5 Waffle	—		↓	
10/20/01	15	21	6 Praise	—	●	Animosity	TVT 5870
3/9/02	21	13	7 Live Again	—		↓	
			SEVEN MARY THREE				
			Rock group from Virginia: Jason Ross (vocals), Jason Pollock (guitar), Casey Daniel (bass) and Giti Khalsa (drums). Thomas Juliano replaced Pollock in 2000.				
9/16/95+	❶⁴	35	1 Cumbersome	39	▲	American Standard	Mammoth 92633
3/2/96	7	23	2 Water's Edge	—		↓	
8/10/96	19	10	3 My My	—		↓	
5/10/97	17	7	4 Rock Crown	—		Rock Crown	Mammoth 83018
10/25/97	35	4	5 Lucky	—		↓	
7/11/98	7	14	6 Over Your Shoulder	—		Orange Ave.	Mammoth 83114
5/5/01	7	15	7 Wait	—		The Economy Of Sound	Mammoth 65516
9/29/01	39	1	8 Sleepwalking	—		↓	
			707				
			Rock group from Detroit: Kevin Chalfant (vocals), Kevin Russell (guitar), Tod Howarth (keyboards), Phil Bryant (bass) and Jim McClarty (drums). Chalfant co-founded **The Storm** in 1991.				
5/29/82	12	14	Mega Force	62		Mega Force	Boardwalk 33253
			SEXTON, Charlie				
			Born on 8/11/68 in San Antonio, Texas. Rock singer/guitarist. Lead guitarist for **Joe Ely**'s band. Co-founder of the **Arc Angels**. Appeared in the movie *Thelma & Louise*. His brother is the leader of **Will & The Kill**.				
12/21/85+	24	13	1 Beat's So Lonely	17		Pictures For Pleasure	MCA 5629
2/4/89	22	8	2 Don't Look Back	—		Charlie Sexton	MCA 6280
5/13/95	18	8	3 Everyone Will Crawl	—		Under The Wishing Tree	MCA 11208
			CHARLIE SEXTON SEXTET				
			SEYMOUR, Phil				
			Born on 5/15/52 in Tulsa, Oklahoma. Died of cancer on 8/17/93 (age 41). Rock singer/drummer. Formerly with the **Dwight Twilley**.				
4/4/81	34	3	Precious To Me	22		Phil Seymour	Boardwalk 36996
			SHADES APART				
			Rock trio from Bridgewater, New Jersey: Mark Vecchiarelli (vocals, guitar), Kevin Lynch (bass) and Ed Brown (drums).				
5/22/99	31	8	Valentine	—		Eyewitness	Universal 53249
			SHADOW KING				
			Rock group formed in New York City: Lou Gramm (vocals; **Foreigner**), Vivian Campbell (guitar; **Def Leppard**), Bruce Turgon (bass) and Kevin Valentine (drums).				
10/5/91	22	7	I Want You	—		Shadow King	Atlantic 82324
			SHALAMAR				
			R&B vocal trio formed in Los Angeles: Jody Watley, Howard Hewett and Jeffrey Daniels.				
9/24/83	41	1	Dead Giveaway	22		The Look	Solar 60239

DEBUT	PEAK	WKS	Mainstream Rock Track	Pop	Gld	Album Title	Album Label & Number

SHAW, Tommy
Born on 9/11/53 in Montgomery, Alabama. Rock singer/guitarist. Member of **Styx** and **Damn Yankees**.

DEBUT	PEAK	WKS		Pop	Gld	Album Title	Album Label & Number
9/29/84	6	10	1 Girls With Guns	33		Girls With Guns	A&M 5020
10/12/85	18	7	2 Remo's Theme (What If)	81		What If	A&M 5097
10/24/87	41	5	3 No Such Thing	—		Ambition	Atlantic 81798
3/11/95	26	8	4 My Hallucination	—		Hallucination	Warner 45835

SHAW/BLADES

★79★ **SHEPHERD, Kenny Wayne**
Born on 6/12/77 in Shreveport, Louisiana. Blues-rock guitarist. His band: Noah Hunt (vocals), Robby Emerson (bass) and Sam Bryant (drums). Keith Christopher replaced Emerson in 1998.
1)Blue On Black 2)Slow Ride 3)Somehow, Somewhere, Someway

DEBUT	PEAK	WKS		Pop	Gld	Album Title	Album Label & Number
10/28/95	9	23	1 Deja Voodoo	—	●	Ledbetter Heights	Giant 24621
3/16/96	15	11	2 Born With A Broken Heart	—	↓		
6/29/96	23	9	3 Aberdeen	—	↓		

KENNY WAYNE SHEPHERD BAND:

DEBUT	PEAK	WKS		Pop	Gld	Album Title	Album Label & Number
9/27/97	3	25	4 Slow Ride	—	▲	Trouble Is...	Giant 24689
1/24/98	❶⁶	42	5 Blue On Black	78	↓		
7/18/98	3	22	6 Somehow, Somewhere, Someway	—	↓		
11/21/98+	10	16	7 Everything Is Broken	—	↓		
10/16/99	5	19	8 In 2 Deep	—	●	Live On	Giant 24729
1/29/00	9	17	9 Was	—	↓		
7/29/00	14	14	10 Last Goodbye	—	↓		

SHERBS
Rock group from Australia: Daryl Braithwaite (vocals), Tony Leigh (guitar), Garth Porter (keyboards), Tony Mitchell (bass) and Alan Sandow (drums).

DEBUT	PEAK	WKS		Pop	Gld	Album Title	Album Label & Number
3/21/81	14	5	1 I Have The Skill	61		The Skill	Atco 137
6/5/82	26	16	2 We Ride Tonight	—		Defying Gravity	Atco 38146

SHERIFF
Pop-rock group from Toronto: Freddy Curci (vocals), Steve DeMarchi (guitar), Arnold Lanni (keyboards), Wolf Hassel (bass) and Rob Elliott (drums). Disbanded in 1983. Hassel and Lanni formed **Frozen Ghost**. Curci and DeMarchi formed **Alias**.

DEBUT	PEAK	WKS		Pop	Gld	Album Title	Album Label & Number
10/2/82	33	2	You Remind Me	—		Sheriff	Capitol 12227

SHOCKED, Michelle
Born Michelle Johnston on 2/24/62 in Dallas. Folk singer/songwriter.

DEBUT	PEAK	WKS		Pop	Gld	Album Title	Album Label & Number
10/15/88	33	7	If Love Was A Train	—		Short Sharp Shocked	Mercury 834294

SHOOTING STAR
Rock group from Kansas City: Gary West (vocals), Van McLain (guitar, vocals), Bill Guffey (keyboards), Charles Waltz (violin), Ron Verlin (bass) and Steve Thomas (drums).

DEBUT	PEAK	WKS		Pop	Gld	Album Title	Album Label & Number
1/23/82	52	4	1 Hang On For Your Life	—		Hang On For Your Life	Epic 37407
9/25/82	37	1	2 Do You Feel Alright	—		III Wishes	Epic 38020
9/17/83	25	5	3 Straight Ahead	—		Burning	Epic 38683

SHOTGUN MESSIAH
Hard-rock group from Sweden: Tim Skold (vocals), Harry Cody (guitar), Bobby Lycon (bass) and Stixx Galore (drums).

DEBUT	PEAK	WKS		Pop	Gld	Album Title	Album Label & Number
4/11/92	46	2	Heartbreak Blvd	—		Second Coming	Relativity 1060

SILENCERS, The
Pop-rock group from Scotland: Jimme O'Neill (vocals, guitar), Cha Burns (guitar), Joe Donnelly (bass) and Martin Hanlin (drums).

DEBUT	PEAK	WKS		Pop	Gld	Album Title	Album Label & Number
8/1/87	23	10	Painted Moon	82		A Letter From St. Paul	RCA Victor 6442

SILVERCHAIR
Rock trio from Newcastle, Australia: Daniel Johns (vocals, guitar), Chris Joannou (bass) and Ben Gillies (drums).

DEBUT	PEAK	WKS		Pop	Gld	Album Title	Album Label & Number
7/8/95	❶³	26	1 Tomorrow	28ᴬ	▲²	Frogstomp	Epic 67247
11/4/95+	12	16	2 Pure Massacre	72ᴬ	↓		
3/9/96	39	1	3 Israel's Son	—	↓		
1/25/97	4	16	4 Abuse Me	44ᴬ	●	Freak Show	Epic 67905
5/3/97	25	7	5 Freak	—	↓		
3/13/99	15	13	6 Anthem For The Year 2000	—	●	Neon Ballroom	Epic 69816
7/17/99	28	9	7 Ana's Song (Open Fire)	—	↓		

SILVER CONDOR
Rock group from New York City: Joe Cerisano (vocals), Earl Slick (guitar), John Corey (keyboards), Jay Davis (bass) and Claude Pepper (drums). Slick joined **Phantom, Rocker & Slick** in 1985.

DEBUT	PEAK	WKS		Pop	Gld	Album Title	Album Label & Number
6/13/81	49	2	1 Angel Eyes	—		Silver Condor	Columbia 37163
7/4/81	26	5	2 For The Sake Of Survival	—	↓		

SIMMONS, Patrick
Born on 1/23/50 in Aberdeen, Washington; raised in San Jose, California. Rock singer/songwriter/guitarist. Member of **The Doobie Brothers**.

DEBUT	PEAK	WKS		Pop	Gld	Album Title	Album Label & Number
5/21/83	18	2	So Wrong	30		Arcade	Elektra 60225

DEBUT	PEAK	WKS	Mainstream Rock Track	Pop	Gld	Album Title	Album Label & Number

SIMON, Paul
Born on 10/13/41 in Newark, New Jersey; raised in Queens, New York. Singer/songwriter/guitarist. One-half of Simon & Garfunkel duo. Married to actress/author Carrie Fisher from 1983-85. Married **Edie Brickell** on 5/30/92. In the movies *Annie Hall* and *One-Trick Pony*. Inducted into the Rock and Roll Hall of Fame in 2001. Also see **Classic Rock Tracks** section.

DEBUT	PEAK	WKS	Track	Pop	Gld	Album	Label
9/13/86	42	4	1 You Can Call Me Al	23	▲⁵	Graceland	Warner 25447
11/15/86	38	5	2 Graceland	81		↓	
			The Everly Brothers (backing vocals)				
2/21/87	15	9	3 The Boy In The Bubble	86		↓	
10/13/90	21	10	4 The Obvious Child	92	▲²	The Rhythm Of The Saints	Warner 26098

SIMON SAYS
Rock group from Sacramento, California: Matt Franks (vocals), Zac Diebels (guitar), Mike Arrieta (bass) and Mike Johnston (drums).

7/10/99	34	7	1 Slider	—		Jump Start	Hollywood 62183
12/18/99+	23	10	2 Life Jacket	—		↓	
7/14/01	31	5	3 Blister	—		Shut Your Breath	Hollywood 162283

SIMPLE MINDS
Pop-rock group formed in Glasgow, Scotland: Jim Kerr (vocals), Charles Burchill (guitar), Michael MacNeil (keyboards), John Giblin (bass) and Mel Gaynor (drums). MacNeil and Giblin left in 1989. Kerr was briefly married to **Chrissie Hynde** (of **The Pretenders**).

2/23/85	❶³	16	✓1 Don't You (Forget About Me)	❶¹	●	The Breakfast Club (soundtrack)	A&M 5045
10/19/85	2²	15	✓2 Alive & Kicking	3	●	Once Upon A Time	A&M 5092
12/28/85+	3	13	✓3 Sanctify Yourself	14		↓	
3/22/86	9	13	✓4 All The Things She Said	28		↓	
5/13/89	37	5	5 This Is Your Land	—		Street Fighting Years	A&M 3927
			Lou Reed (additional vocal)				
3/23/91	10	13	✓6 See The Lights	40		Real Life	A&M 5352
6/29/91	42	5	7 Stand By Love	—		↓	
1/28/95	6	12	8 She's A River	52		Good News From The Next World.......	Virgin 39922
5/27/95	40	1	9 And The Band Played On	—		↓	

SINCH
Hard-rock group from New York City: Jamie Stern (vocals), Tony Lannutti (guitar), Mike Abramson (bass) and Dan McFarland (drums).

| 7/6/02 | 27 | 10 | Something More .... | — | | Sinch .... | Roadrunner 618478 |

SINOMATIC
Rock group from Youngstown, Ohio: Ken Cooper (vocals), Rick Deak and Bryan Patrick (guitars), Dave Markasky (bass) and Matt Lawrence (drums).

| 4/28/01 | 32 | 7 | Bloom .... | — | | Sinomatic........................ | Atlantic 83424 |

SISTER HAZEL
Pop-rock group formed in Gainesville, Florida: Ken Block (vocals), Ryan Newell and Andrew Copeland (guitars), Jeff Beres (bass) and Mark Trojanowski (drums).

| 12/27/97+ | 31 | 8 | Happy .... | 73ᴬ | ▲ | ...Somewhere More Familiar........ | Universal 53030 |

SKID ROW
Hard-rock group formed in New Jersey: Sebastian Bach (vocals), Dave Sabo and Scott Hill (guitars), Rachel Bolan (bass) and Rob Affuso (drums).

2/25/89	27	10	1 Youth Gone Wild	99	▲⁵	Skid Row	Atlantic 81936
6/17/89	11	17	2 18 And Life	4		↓	
10/7/89+	23	21	3 I Remember You...................................	6		↓	
6/15/91	13	11	4 Monkey Business.................................	—	▲²	Slave To The Grind	Atlantic 82278
12/14/91+	30	13	5 Wasted Time.....................................	88		↓	
4/29/95	28	6	6 Into Another....................................	—		Subhuman Race	Atlantic 82730

SKRAPE
Hard-rock group from Orlando, Florida: Billy Keeton (vocals), Mike Lynchard (guitar), Brian Milner (keyboards), Pete Sison (bass) and Will Hunt (drums).

| 2/24/01 | 29 | 9 | 1 Waste .... | — | | New Killer America.................... | RCA 67935 |
| 6/16/01 | 35 | 4 | 2 Isolated .... | — | | ↓ | |

SLADE
Hard-rock group formed in Wolverhampton, England: Noddy Holder (vocals), David Hill (guitar), Jim Lea (bass, keyboards) and Don Powell (drums). Group starred in the movie *Flame*.

2/25/84	32	9	1 My Oh My	37		Keep Your Hands Off My Power Supply	CBS Associated 39336
3/31/84	❶²	17	2 Run Runaway	20		↓	
4/20/85	13	8	3 Little Sheila....................................	86		Rogues Gallery	CBS Associated 39976

SLASH'S SNAKEPIT
Born Saul Hudson on 7/23/65 in Staffordshire, England; raised in Los Angeles. Lead guitarist of **Guns N' Roses**. His group included **Gilby Clarke** (guitar; Guns N' Roses), Eric Dover (vocals, guitar; **Imperial Drag**), Mike Inez (bass; **Alice In Chains**) and Matt Sorum (drums; Guns N' Roses).

| 2/18/95 | 21 | 9 | Beggars & Hangers-On .... | — | | It's Five O'Clock Somewhere .... | Geffen 24630 |

DEBUT	PEAK	WKS	Mainstream Rock Track	Pop Gld	Album Title	Album Label & Number

SLAUGHTER
Hard-rock group formed in Las Vegas: Mark Slaughter (vocals), Tim Kelly (guitar), Dana Strum (bass) and Blas Elias (drums). Slaughter and Strum were with the Vinnie Vincent Invasion. Kelly died in a car crash on 2/5/98 (age 35).

3/3/90	21	13	1 Up All Night	27 ▲²	Stick It To Ya	Chrysalis 21702
8/4/90	15	13	2 Fly To The Angels	19	↓	
12/1/90+	28	11	3 Spend My Life	39	↓	
4/20/91	37	7	4 Mad About You	—	↓	
7/20/91	40	4	5 Shout It Out	—	Bill & Ted's Bogus Journey (soundtrack)	Interscope 91725
5/2/92	28	6	6 The Wild Life	— ●	The Wild Life	Chrysalis 21911
7/18/92	24	8	7 Real Love	69	↓	

SLEEZE BEEZ
Hard-rock group formed in Holland: Andrew Elt (vocals), Chriz Van Jaarsveld and Don Van Spall (guitars), Ed Jongsma (bass) and Jan Koster (drums).

4/21/90	21	9	Stranger Than Paradise	—	Screwed Blued & Tattooed	Atlantic 82069

SLICK, Grace
Born Grace Wing on 10/30/39 in Chicago. Female lead singer of **Jefferson Airplane/Starship**.

3/21/81	33	2	Sea Of Love	—	Welcome To The Wrecking Ball!	RCA Victor 3851

SLIPKNOT
Hard-rock group from Des Moines, Iowa: Corey Taylor (vocals), Mick Thomson and Jim Root (guitars), Sid Wilson (DJ), Craig Jones (samples), Chris Fehn and Shawn Crahan (percussion), Paul Gray (bass) and Joey Jordison (drums). Taylor and Root also with **Stone Sour**.

1/15/00	34	7	1 Wait And Bleed	— ▲	Slipknot	Roadrunner 8655
8/25/01	30	10	2 Left Behind	— ▲	Iowa	Roadrunner 8564

★64★ SMASHING PUMPKINS, The
Rock group from Chicago: Billy Corgan (vocals, guitar; born on 3/17/67), James Iha (guitar; born on 3/26/68), D'Arcy Wretzky (bass; born on 5/1/68) and Jimmy Chamberlain (drums; born on 6/10/64). Touring keyboardist Jonathan Melvoin, brother of Wendy Melvoin (of **Prince**'s Revolution), died of a drug overdose on 7/12/96 (age 34).
1)1979 2)Bullet With Butterfly Wings 3)Tonight, Tonight

8/28/93	23	12	1 Cherub Rock	— ▲⁴	Siamese Dream	Virgin 88267
1/22/94	28	6	2 Today	69ᴬ	↓	
3/19/94	5	22	3 Disarm	48ᴬ	↓	
7/16/94	28	7	4 Rocket	—	↓	
10/21/95	4	25 ✓	5 Bullet With Butterfly Wings	22 ▲⁹	Mellon Collie And The Infinite Sadness ...	Virgin 40861
12/9/95+	❶²	26	6 1979	12	↓	
3/16/96	15	15	7 Zero	49ᴬ	↓	
6/15/96	4	16	8 Tonight, Tonight	36	↓	
10/5/96	10	16	9 Muzzle	57ᴬ	↓	
2/1/97	18	9	10 Thirty-Three	39	↓	
6/7/97	12	10	11 The End Is The Beginning Is The End	50ᴬ ▲	Batman & Robin (soundtrack)	Warner Sunset 46620
5/23/98	8	15	12 Ava Adore	42 ▲	Adore	Virgin 45879
8/29/98	33	6	13 Perfect	54	↓	
1/1/00	14	9	14 The Everlasting Gaze	113 ●	Machina/The Machines Of God	Virgin 48936
3/4/00	11	12	15 Stand Inside Your Love	—	↓	

SMASH MOUTH
Pop-rock group from San Jose: Steve Harwell (vocals), Greg Camp (guitar), Paul DeLisle (bass) and Kevin Coleman (drums).

9/13/97	13	26	Walkin' On The Sun	2¹ᴬ ▲²	Fush Yu Mang	Interscope 90142

SMITH, Patti
Born on 12/31/46 in Chicago; raised in New Jersey. Highly influential punk-rock singer. Not to be confused with Patty Smyth of Scandal. Also see **Classic Rock Tracks** section.

6/25/88	19	9	People Have The Power	—	Dream Of Life	Arista 8453

SMITHEREENS, The
Pop-rock group from Carteret, New Jersey: Pat DiNizio (vocals, guitar), Jim Babjak (guitar), Mike Mesaros (bass) and Dennis Diken (drums).
1)Only A Memory 2)A Girl Like You 3)Blues Before And After

8/30/86	14	11	1 Blood And Roses	—	Especially For You	Enigma 73208
12/6/86+	23	12	2 Behind The Wall Of Sleep	—	↓	
3/26/88	❶¹	14	3 Only A Memory	92	Green Thoughts	Capitol 48375
6/18/88	14	10	4 House We Used To Live In	—	↓	
9/3/88	34	8	5 Drown In My Own Tears	—	↓	
10/21/89	2²	21	6 A Girl Like You	38 ●	11	Enigma 91194
2/10/90	7	14	7 Blues Before And After	94	↓	
5/26/90	20	9	8 Yesterday Girl	—	↓	
9/7/91	19	7	9 Top Of The Pops	—	Blow Up	Capitol 94963
11/16/91+	28	10	10 Tell Me When Did Things Go So Wrong	—	↓	
4/23/94	17	9	11 Miles From Nowhere	—	A Date With The Smithereens	RCA 66391

DEBUT	PEAK	WKS	Mainstream Rock Track	Pop	Gld	Album Title	Album Label & Number
			SMYTH, Patty				
			Born on 6/26/57 in New York City. Lead singer of **Scandal**. Married tennis star John McEnroe in April 1997.				
2/28/87	**4**	10	1 Never Enough	61		Never Enough	Columbia 40182
5/23/87	**40**	4	2 Downtown Train	95		↓	
			first recorded by Tom Waits in 1985				
7/25/87	**26**	6	3 Isn't It Enough	—		↓	
			SNEAKER				
			Pop-rock group formed in Los Angeles: Mitch Crane (vocals, guitar), Michael Carey Schneider (vocals, keyboards), Tim Torrance (guitar), Jim King (keyboards), Michael Cottage (bass) and Mike Hughes (drums).				
12/5/81+	**25**	9	Don't Let Me In	63		Sneaker	Handshake 37631
			written by Walter Becker and **Donald Fagen (Steely Dan)**				
			SNIDER, Todd				
			Born on 10/11/66 in Portland, Oregon. Singer/songwriter/guitarist.				
12/24/94+	**31**	5	Talkin' Seattle Grunge Rock Blues	—		Songs For The Daily Planet	Margaritaville 11067
			SOCIAL DISTORTION				
			Rock group formed in Los Angeles: Mike Ness (vocals, guitar), Dennis Danell (guitar), John Maurer (bass) and Christopher Reece (drums). Danell died of a brain aneurysm on 2/29/2000 (age 38).				
4/11/92	**44**	5	1 Bad Luck	—	●	Somewhere Between Heaven And Hell	Epic 47978
9/21/96	**12**	19	2 I Was Wrong	—		White Light White Heat White Trash	550 Music 64380
2/15/97	**32**	6	3 When The Angels Sing	—		↓	
			SOFT CELL				
			Techno-pop group from London: **Marc Almond** (vocals) and David Ball (synthesizer).				
1/23/82	**12**	21	✓ Tainted Love	8		Non-Stop Erotic Cabaret	Sire 3647
			first recorded by Gloria Jones in 1964				
			SOIL				
			Hard-rock group from Chicago: Ryan McCombs (vocals), Shaun Glass and Adam Zadel (guitars), Tim King (bass) and Tom Schofield (drums).				
8/4/01	**22**	18	1 Halo	—		Scars	J Records 20022
2/9/02	**31**	8	2 Unreal	—		↓	
			SONS OF ANGELS				
			Hard-rock band group from Oslo, Norway: Solli (vocals), Staffan William-Olsson (guitar), Lars K. (keyboards), Torstein (bass) and Geir Digernes (drums).				
6/16/90	**35**	6	Cowgirl	—		Sons Of Angels	Atlantic 82101
			SON VOLT				
			Rock group formed in New Orleans: Jay Farrar (vocals), brothers Dave (guitar) and Jim (bass) Boquist, and Mike Heidorn (drums).				
2/10/96	**10**	17	Drown	—		Trace	Warner 46010
			SOUL ASYLUM				
			Rock group from Minneapolis: Dave Pirner (vocals, guitar), Dan Murphy (guitar), Karl Mueller (bass) and Grant Young (drums). Pirner appeared in the movie *Reality Bites*. Sterling Campbell (**Duran Duran**) replaced Young in 1995.				
1/2/93	**9**	14	1 Somebody To Shove		▲[2]	Grave Dancers Union	Columbia 48898
3/20/93	**4**	20	2 Black Gold	—		↓	
6/12/93	**3**	20	3 Runaway Train	5		↓	
9/25/93	**6**	12	4 Without A Trace	—		↓	
11/12/94	**24**	6	5 Can't Even Tell	—		Clerks (soundtrack)	Chaos 66660
5/27/95	**2**[4]	19	6 Misery	20	▲	Let Your Dim Light Shine	Columbia 57616
8/26/95	**11**	11	7 Just Like Anyone	—		↓	
1/20/96	**29**	6	8 Promises Broken	63		↓	
5/2/98	**23**	8	9 I Will Still Be Laughing	—		Candy From A Stranger	Columbia 67618
			SOULHAT				
			Rock group from Austin, Texas: Kevin McKinney and Bill Cassis (vocals, guitars), Brian Walsh (bass), and B.E. "Frosty" Smith (drums).				
9/17/94	**25**	8	Bonecrusher	—		Good To Be Gone	Epic 57824
			SOULMOTOR				
			Rock group from Sacramento, California: Darin Wood (vocals), Tom McClendon (guitar), Brian Wheat (bass) and Mike Vanderhule (drums).				
5/15/99	**39**	3	Guardian Angel	—		Soulmotor	CMC Int'l. 86273
	★56★		**SOUNDGARDEN**				
			Hard-rock group formed in Seattle: **Chris Cornell** (vocals), Kim Thayil (guitar), Ben Shepherd (bass) and Matt Cameron (drums). Cornell and Cameron also recorded with **Temple Of The Dog**. Group disbanded on 4/9/97.				
			1)*Black Hole Sun* 2)*Burden In My Hand* 3)*Blow Up The Outside World*				
1/11/92	**45**	6	1 Outshined	—	▲[2]	Badmotorfinger	A&M 5374
3/5/94	**3**	26	2 Spoonman	—	▲[5]	Superunknown	A&M 540198
5/14/94	**❶**[7]	26	3 Black Hole Sun	24[A]		↓	
8/27/94	**4**	26	4 Fell On Black Days	54[A]		↓	
11/5/94	**11**	19	5 My Wave	—		↓	
3/25/95	**13**	15	6 The Day I Tried To Live	—		↓	

DEBUT	PEAK	WKS	Mainstream Rock Track	Pop Gld	Album Title	Album Label & Number
			SOUNDGARDEN — Cont'd			
5/4/96	4	26	7 Pretty Noose	37[A] ▲	Down On The Upside	A&M 540526
6/15/96	❶[5]	26	8 Burden In My Hand	40[A] ↓		
10/19/96	❶[4]	26	9 Blow Up The Outside World	53[A] ↓		
3/29/97	19	15	10 Rhinosaur	— ↓		
11/8/97	13	11	11 Bleed Together	—	A-Sides	A&M 540833

SOUTHER, J.D. — see TAYLOR, James

SOUTHSIDE JOHNNY & THE JUKES
Born John Lyon on 12/4/48 in Neptune, New Jersey. Rock singer/harmonica player. Core members of The Jukes: Billy Rush (guitar), Kevin Kavanaugh (keyboards) and Alan Berger (bass).

DEBUT	PEAK	WKS	Mainstream Rock Track	Pop Gld	Album Title	Album Label & Number
8/11/84	43	7	1 New Romeo	103	In The Heat.	Mirage 90186
10/26/91	22	13	2 It's Been A Long Time	—	Better Days.	Impact 10445
			SOUTHSIDE JOHNNY & THE ASBURY JUKES written by **Little Steven**			

SPACEHOG
Rock group from Leeds, England: Royston Langdon (vocals, bass), Richard Steel and Antony Langdon (guitars), and Jonny Cragg (drums).

DEBUT	PEAK	WKS	Mainstream Rock Track	Pop Gld	Album Title	Album Label & Number
12/16/95+	❶[4]	32	1 In The Meantime	32 ●	Resident Alien	Sire 61834
7/6/96	29	5	2 Cruel To Be Kind	— ↓		
3/14/98	19	10	3 Mungo City	—	The Chinese Album	Sire 46851
3/10/01	23	10	4 I Want To Live	—	The Hogyssey	Artemis 751068

SPANDAU BALLET
Pop group formed in London: Tony Hadley (vocals), brothers Gary (guitar) and Martin (bass) Kemp, Steve Norman (sax) and John Keeble (drums). The Kemps starred in the 1990 movie *The Krays*. Gary Kemp was married to actress Sadie Frost from 1988-97.

DEBUT	PEAK	WKS	Mainstream Rock Track	Pop Gld	Album Title	Album Label & Number
10/15/83	34	4	✓1 True	4	True.	Chrysalis 41403
8/4/84	40	10	✓2 Only When You Leave	34	Parade.	Chrysalis 41473

SPANOS, Danny
Born in Detroit. Singer/songwriter/guitarist.

DEBUT	PEAK	WKS	Mainstream Rock Track	Pop Gld	Album Title	Album Label & Number
8/27/83	15	9	✓1 Hot Cherie	—	Passion In The Dark.	Epic 38805
2/16/85	42	4	2 I'd Lie To You For Your Love	—	Looks Like Trouble.	Epic 39459

SPIN DOCTORS
Rock group from New York City: Christopher Barron (vocals), Eric Schenkman (guitar), Mark White (bass) and Aaron Comess (drums).

DEBUT	PEAK	WKS	Mainstream Rock Track	Pop Gld	Album Title	Album Label & Number
6/27/92	2[4]	30	1 Little Miss Can't Be Wrong	17 ▲[5]	Pocket Full Of Kryptonite.	Epic/Assc. 47461
10/10/92	8	19	2 Jimmy Olsen's Blues	78 ↓		
1/23/93	2[7]	21	3 Two Princes	7 ↓		
5/22/93	26	6	4 What Time Is It?	— ↓		
8/14/93	28	7	5 How Could You Want Him (When You Know You Could Have Me?)	102 ↓		
6/4/94	22	6	6 Cleopatra's Cat	84 ▲	Turn It Upside Down.	Epic 52907
7/9/94	8	13	7 You Let Your Heart Go Too Fast	42 ↓		

SPINESHANK
Hard-rock group from Los Angeles: Johnny Santos (vocals), Mike Sarkisyan (guitar), Robert Garcia (bass) and Tom Decker (drums).

DEBUT	PEAK	WKS	Mainstream Rock Track	Pop Gld	Album Title	Album Label & Number
3/24/01	33	7	New Disease	—	The Height Of Callousness	Roadrunner 8563

SPIRIT
Rock group formed in Los Angeles: Randy California (vocals), **Jay Ferguson** (guitar, vocals), John Locke (keyboards), Mark Andes (bass; **Heart**) and Ed Cassidy (drums). California drowned on 1/2/97 near Molokai, Hawaii (age 45). Also see **Classic Rock Tracks** section.

DEBUT	PEAK	WKS	Mainstream Rock Track	Pop Gld	Album Title	Album Label & Number
8/18/84	54	2	I Got A Line On You	—	Spirit Of '84.	Mercury 818514
			new version of their #25 Pop hit in 1969			

SPLIT ENZ
Pop-rock group formed in Auckland, New Zealand: brothers Tim (vocals) and Neil (guitar, vocals) Finn, Eddy Rayner (keyboards), Noel Crombie (percussion), Nigel Griggs (bass) and Malcolm Green (drums). The Finns were later members of **Crowded House**.

DEBUT	PEAK	WKS	Mainstream Rock Track	Pop Gld	Album Title	Album Label & Number
5/16/81	33	9	History Never Repeats	—	Waiata.	A&M 4848

SPONGE
Rock group from Detroit: Vinnie Dombrowski (vocals), Mike Cross and Joe Mazzola (guitars), Tim Cross (bass) and Jimmy Paluzzi (drums). Charlie Grover replaced Paluzzi in early 1996.

DEBUT	PEAK	WKS	Mainstream Rock Track	Pop Gld	Album Title	Album Label & Number
11/19/94+	9	26	1 Plowed	41[A] ●	Rotting Piñata	Work 57800
6/3/95	11	14	2 Molly (Sixteen Candles)	55 ↓		
10/14/95	18	10	3 Rainin'	— ↓		
6/29/96	11	13	4 Wax Ecstatic (To Sell Angelina)	64[A]	Wax Ecstatic	Columbia 67578
11/9/96+	7	23	5 Have You Seen Mary	— ↓		

DEBUG	PEAK	WKS	Mainstream Rock Track	Pop Gld	Album Title	Album Label & Number

SPRINGFIELD, Rick
Born Richard Springthorpe on 8/23/49 in Sydney, Australia. Singer/songwriter/actor. Played "Noah Drake" on the TV soap opera *General Hospital*. Starred in the movie *Hard To Hold*.

3/21/81	10	20	1 Jessie's Girl	**❶**² ▲	Working Class Dog	RCA 3697
1/16/82	40	9	2 Love Is Alright Tonite	20	↓	
3/6/82	11	9	3 Don't Talk To Strangers	2⁴ ▲	Success Hasn't Spoiled Me Yet.	RCA 4125
3/13/82	4	12	4 Calling All Girls	—	↓	
5/14/83	23	8	5 Affair Of The Heart	9 ▲	Living In Oz	RCA 4660
8/20/83	34	4	6 Human Touch	18	↓	
3/31/84	13	8	7 Love Somebody	5 ▲	Hard To Hold (soundtrack)	RCA 4935
6/16/84	41	6	8 Don't Walk Away	26	↓	
2/27/88	45	3	9 Rock Of Life	22	Rock Of Life.	RCA 6620

SPRINGSTEEN, Bruce ★8★
Born on 9/23/49 in Freehold, New Jersey. Rock singer/songwriter/guitarist. Nicknamed "The Boss." His E-Street Band: **Little Steven** Van Zant (guitar), **Clarence Clemons** (sax), Roy Bittan (keyboards), Gary Tallent (bass) and Max Weinberg (drums). Married to model/actress Julianne Phillips from 1985-89. Married backing singer Patti Scialfa on 6/8/91. Inducted into the Rock and Roll Hall of Fame in 1999. Also see **Classic Rock Tracks** section.

1)*Dancing In The Dark* 2)*Tunnel Of Love* 3)*Trapped* 4)*Human Touch* 5)*Brilliant Disguise*

3/21/81	14	2	1 Fade Away	20 ▲³	The River	Columbia 36854
3/21/81	42	1	2 I'm A Rocker	—	↓	
3/28/81	48	2	3 Cadillac Ranch	—	↓	
4/4/81	20	1	4 Point Blank	—	↓	
4/11/81	30	1	5 Ramrod	—	↓	
3/28/81	42	1	6 Be True	—	(single only).	Columbia 11431
10/9/82	10	10	7 Atlantic City	— ▲	Nebraska	Columbia 38358
10/9/82	22	10	8 Open All Night	—	↓	
10/9/82	50	2	9 Johnny 99	—	↓	
6/2/84	27	14	10 Pink Cadillac	— ▲	(single only).	Columbia 04463
			#5 Pop hit for Natalie Cole in 1988			
5/26/84	**❶**⁶	17	11 Dancing In The Dark	2⁴ ▲¹⁵	Born In The U.S.A.	Columbia 38653
6/16/84	29	16	12 No Surrender	—	↓	
6/23/84	2²	21	13 Cover Me	7	↓	
6/23/84	8	20	14 Born In The U.S.A.	9	↓	
6/23/84	36	9	15 Bobby Jean	—	↓	
2/16/85	4	14	16 I'm On Fire	6	↓	
5/25/85	3	14	17 Glory Days	5	↓	
9/7/85	9	9	18 I'm Goin' Down	9	↓	
12/14/85+	6	9	19 My Hometown	6	↓	

BRUCE SPRINGSTEEN & THE E STREET BAND:

4/13/85	**❶**³	12	20 Trapped **[L]**	— ▲³	We Are The World (USA For Africa) . .	Columbia 40043
			recorded on 8/6/84 at the New Jersey Meadowlands			
7/6/85	32	8	21 Stand On It	—	(single only).	Columbia 04924
			#12 Country hit for Mel McDaniel in 1985			
11/22/86	4	10	22 War **[L]**	8 ▲¹³	Bruce Springsteen & The E Street Band	
			recorded on 9/30/85 at the Los Angeles Coliseum; #1 Pop hit for Edwin Starr in 1970		Live/1975-85.	Columbia 40558
11/22/86+	14	14	23 Fire **[L]**	46	↓	
			recorded on 12/16/78 at Winterland in San Francisco; #2 Pop hit for the Pointer Sisters in 1979			
12/6/86+	22	9	24 Because The Night **[L]**	—	↓	
			recorded on 12/28/80 at the Nassau Coliseum in New York; #13 Pop hit for **Patti Smith** in 1978			
12/20/86	44	6	25 Raise Your Hand **[L]**	—	↓	
			recorded on 7/7/78 at the Roxy in New York City; #79 Pop hit for Eddie Floyd in 1967			

BRUCE SPRINGSTEEN:

10/3/87	**❶**¹	8	26 Brilliant Disguise	5 ▲³	Tunnel of Love	Columbia 40999
10/17/87	**❶**⁴	17	27 Tunnel Of Love	9	↓	
10/17/87	28	13	28 Spare Parts	—	↓	
12/12/87+	2¹	17	29 One Step Up	13	↓	
2/27/88	5	12	30 All That Heaven Will Allow	—	↓	
4/16/88	45	3	31 Roulette	—	(single only).	Columbia 07726
9/17/88	16	5	32 Chimes Of Freedom **[L]**	—	Chimes Of Freedom	Columbia 44445
			recorded on 7/3/88 in Stockholm, Sweden; first recorded by **Bob Dylan** in 1964			

DEBUT	PEAK	WKS	Mainstream Rock Track	Pop	Gld	Album Title	Album Label & Number
			SPRINGSTEEN, Bruce — Cont'd				
3/21/92	❶³	10	33 Human Touch	16	▲	*Human Touch*	Columbia 53000
4/11/92	6	10	34 57 Channels (And Nothin' On)	68	↓		
4/11/92	47	2	35 All Or Nothin' At All	—	↓		
4/25/92	6	8	36 Roll Of The Dice	—	↓		
3/21/92	2¹	5	37 Better Days	flip	▲	*Lucky Town*	Columbia 53001
8/29/92	28	3	38 Leap Of Faith	—	↓		
2/12/94	25	7	39 Streets Of Philadelphia	9	▲	*Philadelphia (soundtrack)*	Epic Soundtrax 57624
3/4/95	14	8	40 Murder Incorporated	—	▲⁴	*Greatest Hits*	Columbia 67060
			recorded in 1982				
12/5/98	33	3	41 I Wanna Be With You	—	▲	*Tracks*	Columbia 69475
7/20/02	24	12	42 The Rising	52	▲²	*The Rising*	Columbia 86600
			SPRUNG MONKEY				
			Rock group from San Diego: brothers Steve (vocals), Mike (guitar) Summers, William Riley (guitar), Tony Delocht (bass) and Ernie Longoria (drums).				
12/12/98+	25	10	Super Breakdown	—		*Mr. Funny Face*	Surfdog 62151
			SPYS				
			Rock group from New York City: John Blanco (vocals), John DiGaudio (guitar), Al Greenwood (keyboards), Ed Gagliardi (bass) and Billy Milne (drums). Greenwood and Gagliardi were members of **Foreigner**.				
8/7/82	19	10	Don't Run My Life	82		*Spys*	EMI America 17073
			SQUEEZE				
			Pop-rock group formed in London by vocalists/guitarists Chris Difford and Glenn Tilbrook. Numerous personnel changes with Difford and Tilbrook the only constants. **Paul Carrack** was lead singer in 1981.				
6/6/81	39	8	1 In Quintessence	—		*East Side Story*	A&M 4854
6/20/81	8	22	2 Tempted	49	↓		
5/22/82	26	11	3 Black Coffee In Bed	103		*Sweets From A Stranger*	A&M 4899
2/19/83	40	2	4 Annie Get Your Gun	—		*Singles-45's And Under*	A&M 4922
10/5/85	39	7	5 Hits Of The Year	—		*Cosi Fan Tutti Frutti*	A&M 5085
9/5/87	22	11	6 Hourglass	15		*Babylon And On*	A&M 5161
12/19/87	50	3	7 Trust Me To Open My Mouth	—	↓		
1/23/88	37	5	8 853-5937	32	↓		
8/17/91	49	1	9 Satisfied	—		*Play*	Reprise 26644

SQUIER, Billy ★40★

Born on 5/12/50 in Wellesley Hills, Massachusetts. Hard-rock singer/songwriter/guitarist. Attended the Berklee College of Music in New York City. Member of the groups Kicks, The Sidewinders and Piper during the 1970s.

1)Everybody Wants You 2)Rock Me Tonite 3)The Stroke 4)Don't Say You Love Me 5)She Goes Down

DEBUT	PEAK	WKS	Mainstream Rock Track	Pop	Gld	Album Title	Album Label & Number
5/2/81	7	31	1 In The Dark	35	▲³	*Don't Say No*	Capitol 12146
5/16/81	3	26	2 The Stroke	17	↓		
6/20/81	31	13	3 My Kinda Lover	45	↓		
8/8/81	28	19	4 Lonely Is The Night	—	↓		
8/7/82	❶⁶	20	5 Everybody Wants You	32	▲²	*Emotions In Motion*	Capitol 12217
8/7/82	20	7	6 Emotions In Motion	68	↓		
8/7/82	46	1	7 Keep Me Satisfied	—	↓		
10/2/82	15	12	8 Learn How To Live	—	↓		
3/12/83	44	1	9 She's A Runner	75	↓		
7/7/84	❶²	15	10 Rock Me Tonite	15	▲	*Signs Of Life*	Capitol 12361
8/11/84	10	13	11 All Night Long	75	↓		
9/29/84	51	2	12 Can't Get Next To You	—	↓		
1/5/85	29	5	13 Eye On You	71	↓		
9/27/86	17	8	14 Love Is The Hero	80		*Enough Is Enough*	Capitol 12483
11/22/86	30	4	15 Shot O' Love	—	↓		
6/3/89	4	13	16 Don't Say You Love Me	58		*Hear & Now*	Capitol 48748
8/19/89	20	10	17 Tied Up	—	↓		
11/4/89	38	6	18 Don't Let Me Go	—	↓		
3/30/91	4	12	19 She Goes Down	—		*Creatures Of Habit*	Capitol 94303
6/22/91	37	6	20 Facts Of Life	—	↓		
4/17/93	15	6	21 Angry	—		*Tell The Truth*	Capitol 98690
			SR-71				
			Rock group from Baltimore: Mitch Allan (vocals, guitar), Mark Beauchemin (guitar), Jeff Reid (bass) and Dan Garvin (drums).				
9/2/00	38	2	Right Now	102	●	*Now You See Inside*	RCA 67845

DEBUT	PEAK	WKS	Mainstream Rock Track	Pop	Gld	Album Title	Album Label & Number
			STABBING WESTWARD				
			Rock group from Chicago: Christopher Hall (vocals, guitar), Walter Flakus (keyboards), Jim Sellers (bass) and Andy Kubiszewski (drums).				
2/10/96	7	21	1 What Do I Have To Do?	60[A]	●	Wither Blister Burn + Peel	Columbia 66152
7/20/96	7	26	2 Shame	69[A]	↓		
3/21/98	4	26	3 Save Yourself	—	●	Darkest Days	Columbia 69329
9/12/98	20	14	4 Sometimes It Hurts	—	↓		
1/30/99	19	11	5 Haunting Me	—	↓		
4/28/01	23	13	6 So Far Away	—		Stabbing Westward	Koch 8204
			STABILIZERS				
			Pop-rock duo from Erie, Pennsylvania: Dave Christenson (vocals) and Rich Nevens (keyboards, guitar).				
10/25/86	21	13	One Simple Thing	93		Tyranny	Columbia 40264
			STAGE DOLLS				
			Rock trio from Trondheim, Norway: Torstein Flakne (vocals), Terje Storli (bass) and Steinar Krokstad (drums).				
7/29/89	14	10	1 Love Cries	46		Stage Dolls	Chrysalis 21716
10/21/89	37	7	2 Still In Love	—	↓		
★73★			**STAIND**				
			Rock group from Boston: **Aaron Lewis** (vocals), Mike Mushok (guitar), Johnny April (bass) and Jon Wysocki (drums).				
4/3/99	24	14	1 Just Go	—	▲	Dysfunction	Flip 62356
8/7/99	10	28	2 Mudshovel	—	↓		
2/12/00	11	26	3 Home	—	↓		
4/7/01	❶[20]	42	4 It's Been Awhile	5	▲4	Break The Cycle	Flip 62626
5/19/01	11	26	5 Outside	111	↓		
8/25/01	3	26	6 Fade	62	↓		
12/22/01+	3	40	7 For You	63	↓		
5/11/02	22	14	8 Epiphany	—	↓		
			STANLEY, Michael, Band				
			Born Michael Stanley Gee on 3/25/48 in Cleveland. Rock singer/guitarist. His band: Kevin Raleigh (vocals, keyboards), Bob Pelander (keyboards), Gary Markshay (guitar), Rick Bell (sax), Mike Gismondi (bass) and Tom Dobeck (drums). Don Powers replaced Markshay in 1982.				
8/1/81	6	18	✓1 In The Heartland	—		North Coast	EMI America 17056
9/4/82	24	10	✓2 In Between The Lines	—		MSB	EMI America 17071
9/24/83	11	12	√3 My Town	39		You Can't Fight Fashion	EMI America 17100
			STARFIGHTERS				
			Rock group from New York City: Steve Burton (vocals), Pat Hambly and Steve Young (guitars), Doug Dennis (bass) and Steve Bailey (drums).				
1/30/82	28	5	Alley Cat Blues	—		Starfighters	Arista 9576
			STARR, Ringo				
			Born Richard Starkey on 7/7/40 in Liverpool, England. Drummer of **The Beatles**. Married actress Barbara Bach on 4/27/81. Also see **Classic Rock Tracks** section.				
6/13/92	43	1	Weight Of The World	—		Time Takes Time	Private M. 82097
			STARSHIP — see JEFFERSON AIRPLANE/STARSHIP				
			STATIC-X				
			Rock group from Los Angeles: Wayne Static (vocals, guitar), Koichi Fukuda (keyboards), Tony Campos (bass) and Ken Jay (drums). Fukada left in 2000; Static took over keyboards and Tripp Rex Eisen (guitar) joined.				
6/26/99	36	6	1 Bled For Days	—	▲	Wisconsin Death Trip	Warner 47271
10/9/99	20	20	2 Push It	57[8]	↓		
4/15/00	38	2	3 I'm With Stupid (He's A Loser)	—	↓		
6/9/01	36	4	4 This Is Not	—		Machine	Warner 47948
10/20/01	35	5	5 Black & White	—	↓		
3/2/02	29	8	6 Cold	—	↓		
			STEALIN HORSES				
			Rock-country group from Lexington, Kentucky: Kiya Heartwood (vocals), Mandy Meyer (guitar), John Durno (bass) and Kopana Terry (drums). Band name is an ancient Native American rite of passage in which young warriors stole horses from nearby tribes.				
6/25/88	50	1	Turnaround	—		Stealin Horses	Arista 8520
			STEEL BREEZE				
			Pop group from Sacramento, California: Ric Jacobs (vocals), Ken Goorabian and Waylin Carpenter (guitars), Rod Toner (keyboards), Vinnie Pantleoni (bass) and Barry Lowenthal (drums).				
9/25/82	9	12	You Don't Want Me Anymore	16		Steel Breeze	RCA 4424
			STEELHEART				
			Hard-rock group from Norwalk, Connecticut: Michael Matijevic (vocals), Chris Risola and Frank Dicostanzo (guitars), Jimmy Ward (bass) and John Fowler (drums).				
1/19/91	24	11	1 I'll Never Let You Go (Angel Eyes)	23		Steelheart	MCA 6368
5/25/91	34	6	2 Everybody Loves Eileen	—	↓		

DEBUT	PEAK	WKS	Mainstream Rock Track	Pop	Gld	Album Title	Album Label & Number

STEELY DAN
Pop-rock/jazz-styled group formed in Los Angeles by **Donald Fagen** and Walter Becker. Group, primarily known as a studio unit, featured Fagen and Becker with various studio musicians. Duo split from 1981-92. Inducted into the Rock and Roll Hall of Fame in 2001. Also see **Classic Rock Tracks** section.

| 3/21/81 | 13 | 7 | Time Out Of Mind .... | 22 | ▲ | Gaucho .... | MCA 6102 |

Mark Knopfler of **Dire Straits** (guitar solo); **Michael McDonald** (backing vocal)

STEGOSAURUS
Rock trio from Santa Barbara, California: Jesse Rhodes (vocals, guitar), Drew Ross (bass) and David Liker (drums).

| 5/16/98 | 37 | 5 | At The Water .... | — | | Stegosaurus .... | Reprise 46865 |

STEINMAN, Jim
Born on 11/1/47 in New York City. Songwriter/pianist/producer.

| 5/30/81 | 14 | 12 | ✓ Rock And Roll Dreams Come Through .... | 32 | | Bad For Good .... | Cleveland Int'l. 36531 |

Rory Dodd (lead vocal)

STEPHENSON, Van
Born on 11/4/53 in Hamilton, Ohio. Died of cancer on 4/8/2001 (age 47). Singer/songwriter.

| 5/12/84 | 9 | 11 | Modern Day Delilah | 22 | | Righteous Anger .... | MCA 5482 |

STEPPENWOLF
Hard-rock group formed in Los Angeles. Numerous personnel changes. Lineup in 1987: founder John Kay (vocals, guitar), Rocket Ritchotte (guitar), Michael Wilk (bass) and Ron Hurst (drums). Also see **Classic Rock Tracks** section.

| 8/29/87 | 50 | 1 | Hold On (Never Give Up, Never Give In) .... | — | | Rock & Roll Rebels .... | Qwil 1560 |

JOHN KAY & STEPPENWOLF

STEREOMUD
Hard-rock group formed in New York City: Eric Rogers (vocals), John Fattoruso and Joey Z (guitars), Corey Lowery (bass) and Dan Richardson (drums). Joey Z and Richardson were members of **Life Of Agony**.

| 4/28/01 | 8 | 20 | 1 Pain | — | | Perfect Self .... | Loud 85483 |
| 10/13/01 | 29 | 8 | 2 Steppin' Away .... | — | | ↓ | |

STEVENS, Corey
Born in Illinois. Blues-rock singer/guitarist.

| 6/21/97 | 22 | 10 | One More Time .... | — | | Road To Zen .... | Eureka 77061 |

★57★ STEWART, Rod
Born on 1/10/45 in London. Singer/songwriter. Member of the **Jeff Beck** Group from 1967-69. With Faces from 1969-75. Won Grammy's Living Legends Award in 1989. Married to actress Alana Hamilton from 1979-84. Married supermodel Rachel Hunter on 12/15/90. Inducted into the Rock and Roll Hall of Fame in 1994. Also see **Classic Rock Tracks** section.
1)Downtown Train 2)Lost In You 3)People Get Ready 4)Infatuation 5)Forever Young

4/4/81	45	1	1 Gi' Me Wings	—	▲	Foolish Behaviour	Warner 3485
10/31/81+	23	16	✓2 Young Turks	5	▲	Tonight I'm Yours	Warner 3602
12/12/81+	38	11	3 Tora, Tora, Tora (Out With The Boys)	—		↓	
1/30/82	44	3	4 Jealous	—		↓	
2/20/82	29	3	✓5 Tonight I'm Yours (Don't Hurt Me)	20		↓	
11/13/82	21	4	6 Guess I'll Always Love You .... [L]	—		Absolutely Live	Warner 23743
5/26/84	5	15	✓7 Infatuation	6	●	Camouflage	Warner 25095

Jeff Beck (guitar solo)

| 9/15/84 | 27 | 8 | ✓8 Some Guys Have All The Luck .... | 10 | | ↓ | |

#39 Pop hit for The Persuaders in 1973

| 6/15/85 | 5 | 13 | ✓9 People Get Ready | 48 | | Flash .... | Epic 39483 |

JEFF BECK and ROD STEWART
#14 Pop hit for The Impressions in 1965

| 6/7/86 | 26 | 8 | ✓10 Love Touch .... | 6 | | Rod Stewart .... | Warner 25446 |

theme from the movie *Legal Eagles* starring Robert Redford

| 9/13/86 | 45 | 3 | 11 Another Heartache .... | 52 | | ↓ | |

co-written by **Bryan Adams**

5/7/88	3	11	12 Lost In You	12	▲²	Out Of Order	Warner 25684
5/28/88	16	11	13 Dynamite	—		↓	
8/27/88	13	11	✓14 Forever Young	12		↓	
2/11/89	50	1	✓15 My Heart Can't Tell You No	4		↓	

Andy Taylor (guitar, above 4)

| 11/25/89+ | ❶² | 12 | ✓16 Downtown Train | 3 | ▲² | Storyteller/The Complete Anthology: 1964-1990 .... | Warner 25987 |

first recorded by Tom Waits in 1985

3/16/91	13	10	✓17 Rhythm Of My Heart	5	▲	Vagabond Heart	Warner 26300
5/4/91	17	7	18 Rebel Heart	—		↓	
5/15/93	16	7	19 Cut Across Shorty .... [L]	—	▲³	Unplugged...And Seated	Warner 45289

Ronnie Wood (bass guitar)

| 5/23/98 | 13 | 16 | 20 Cigarettes And Alcohol .... | — | | When We Were The New Boys .... | Warner 46792 |
| 9/19/98 | 31 | 6 | 21 Rocks .... | — | | ↓ | |

STEWART, Sandy — see NICKS, Stevie

STILLS, Stephen
Born on 1/3/45 in Dallas. Singer/songwriter/guitarist. Member of Buffalo Springfield and **Crosby, Stills & Nash**. Also see **Classic Rock Tracks** section.

| 8/11/84 | 12 | 10 | Stranger .... | 61 | | Right By You .... | Atlantic 80177 |

Graham Nash (backing vocal)

DEBUT	PEAK	WKS	Mainstream Rock Track	Pop	Gld	Album Title	Album Label & Number
			STILTSKIN				
			Rock trio from Edinburgh, Scotland: Ray Wilson (vocals), Peter Lawlor (guitar) and Ross McFarlane (drums). Wilson replaced **Phil Collins** as lead singer of **Genesis** in June 1997.				
5/6/95	37	2	**Inside**	—		The Mind's Eye	EastWest 61785
	★51★		**STING**				
			Born Gordon Sumner on 10/2/51 in Wallsend, England. Singer/songwriter/bassist. Lead singer of **The Police**. Acted in such movies as *Quadrophenia, Dune, The Bride* and *Plenty*. Married actress/producer Trudy Styler on 8/20/92. Nicknamed "Sting" because of a yellow and black jersey he liked to wear.				
			1)*All This Time* 2)*If You Love Somebody Set Them Free* 3)*Fortress Around Your Heart*				
4/10/82	28	5	1 **Roxanne** .... [L]	—		The Secret Policeman's Other Ball/	
			#32 Pop hit for **The Police** in 1979			The Music (various artists)	Island 9698
6/8/85	❶³	13	2 **If You Love Somebody Set Them Free**	3	▲³	The Dream Of The Blue Turtles	A&M 3750
7/6/85	❶²	18	3 **Fortress Around Your Heart**	8		↓	
10/5/85	19	12	4 **Love Is The Seventh Wave**	17		↓	
1/11/86	34	8	5 **Russians**	16		↓	
			samples "Romance" melody from Russian composer Sergei Prokofiev's *Lieutenant Kije Suite*				
5/17/86	14	7	6 **I Been Down So Long** .... [L]	—		Live! For Life (various artists)...........	I.R.S. 5731
			STING with **JEFF BECK** recorded at The Greek Theatre in Los Angeles				
10/10/87	20	8	7 **We'll Be Together**	7	▲²	...Nothing Like The Sun	A&M 6402
10/24/87	11	13	8 **Little Wing**	—		↓	
			first recorded by Jimi Hendrix in 1968				
11/28/87	30	9	9 **The Lazarus Heart**	—		↓	
1/16/88	2²	12	10 **Be Still My Beating Heart**	15		↓	
3/26/88	32	6	11 **Englishman In New York**	84		↓	
1/19/91	❶⁷	13	12 **All This Time**	5	▲	The Soul Cages	A&M 6405
2/9/91	7	15	13 **The Soul Cages**	—		↓	
5/18/91	32	6	14 **Why Should I Cry For You?**	—		↓	
6/13/92	20	5	15 **It's Probably Me**	—		Lethal Weapon 3 (soundtrack)	Reprise 26989
			STING with Eric Clapton				
2/13/93	5	16	16 **If I Ever Lose My Faith In You**	17	▲³	Ten Summoner's Tales	A&M 540070
6/12/93	24	9	17 **Fields Of Gold**	23		↓	
			STIR				
			Rock trio from St. Charles, Missouri: Andy Schmidt (vocals, guitar), Kevin Gagnepain (bass) and Brad Booker (drums).				
11/9/96+	8	19	1 **Looking For**	—		Stir	Aware 38398
4/5/97	21	7	2 **Stale**	—		↓	
8/23/97	23	9	3 **One Angel**	—		↓	
3/11/00	16	14	4 **New Beginning**	—		Holy Dogs	Capitol 57098
8/19/00	39	1	5 **Climbing The Walls**	—		↓	
			STONE FURY				
			Hard-rock group formed in Los Angeles: Lenny Wolf (vocals), Bruce Gowdy (guitar), Rick Wilson (bass) and Jody Cortez (drums). Wolf formed **Kingdom Come** in 1987.				
11/24/84	47	2	**Break Down The Wall**	—		Burns Like A Star	MCA 5522
			STONE ROSES, The				
			Pop-rock group from Manchester, England: Ian Brown (vocal), John Squire (guitar), Gary Mounfield (bass) and Alan Wren (drums).				
2/11/95	4	21	**Love Spreads**	—		Second Coming	Geffen 24503
			STONE SOUR				
			Rock group formed by **Slipknot** members Corey Taylor (vocals) and Jim Root (guitar), with Josh Rand (guitar), Sid Wilson (bass) and Joel Ekman (drums).				
8/31/02	4	13↑	**Bother**	56↑		Stone Sour	Roadrunner 618425
			STONE TEMPLE PILOTS ★17★				
			Rock group formed in San Diego: **Scott Weiland** (vocals; born on 10/27/67), brothers Dean (guitar; born on 8/23/61) and Robert (bass; born on 2/2/66) DeLeo, and Eric Kretz (drums; born on 6/7/66). Weiland also formed **The Magnificent Bastards**. The DeLeo brothers and Kretz also formed **Talk Show**.				
			1)*Interstate Love Song* 2)*Trippin' On A Hole In A Paper Heart* 3)*Vasoline* 4)*Plush* 5)*Lady Picture Show*				
1/2/93	23	8	1 **Sex Type Thing**	—	▲⁷	Core	Atlantic 82418
3/20/93	❶¹	31	2 **Plush**	39ᴬ		↓	
7/31/93	11	20	3 **Wicked Garden**	59ᴬ		↓	
11/13/93+	2¹	26	4 **Creep**	59ᴬ		↓	
4/23/94	3	26	5 **Big Empty**	50ᴬ	▲³	The Crow (soundtrack)	Atlantic 82519
6/11/94	❶²	26	6 **Vasoline**	38ᴬ	▲⁶	Purple	Atlantic 82607
8/20/94	❶¹⁵	33	7 **Interstate Love Song**	18ᴬ		↓	
12/24/94+	8	16	8 **Unglued**	—		↓	
3/18/95	12	10	9 **Pretty Penny**	—		↓	
3/25/95	3	17	10 **Dancing Days**	63ᴬ	●	Encomium: A Tribute To Led Zeppelin	
			first recorded by **Led Zeppelin** in 1973			(various artists)	Atlantic 82731

DEBUT	PEAK	WKS	Mainstream Rock Track	Pop	Gld	Album Title	Album Label & Number
			STONE TEMPLE PILOTS — Cont'd				
3/23/96	❶¹	16	11 Big Bang Baby	28ᴬ	▲²	Tiny Music...Songs From The Vatican Gift Shop . . . . Atlantic 82871	
5/11/96	❶⁴	26	12 Trippin' On A Hole In A Paper Heart	36ᴬ		↓	
10/26/96+	❶¹	26	13 Lady Picture Show	53ᴬ		↓	
2/15/97	9	15	14 Tumble In The Rough	—		↓	
10/2/99	5	20	15 Down	107	▲	No.4 . . . . Atlantic 83255	
1/1/00	17	10	16 Heaven & Hot Rods	—		↓	
4/22/00	4	26	17 Sour Girl	78		↓	
10/21/00	17	9	18 No Way Out	—		↓	
12/23/00	35	5	19 Break On Through	—		Stoned Immaculate – The Music Of The Doors (various artists) . . . . Elektra 62475	
			#126 Pop hit for **The Doors** in 1967				
6/16/01	4	11	20 Days Of The Week	101	●	Shangri-La Dee Da . . . . Atlantic 83449	
9/1/01	25	8	21 Hollywood Bitch	—		↓	
11/17/01	30	6	22 Revolution	11ˢ		(single only) . . . . Atlantic 85200	
			#12 Pop hit for **The Beatles** in 1968				

STORM, The
Rock group formed in San Francisco: Kevin Chalfant (vocals), Greg Rolie (vocals, keyboards), Josh Ramos (guitar), Ross Valory (bass) and Steve Smith (drums). Rolie was a member of **Santana**. Rolie, Valory and Smith were members of **Journey**. Chalfant was a member of **707**.

| 9/28/91 | 6 | 21 | 1 I've Got A Lot To Learn About Love | 26 | | The Storm . . . . Interscope 91741 | |
| 1/25/92 | 22 | 8 | 2 Show Me The Way | — | | ↓ | |

STORYVILLE
Rock group formed in Austin, Texas: Malford Milligan (vocals), David Holt and David Grissom (guitars), Chris Layton (bass) and Tommy Shannon (drums). Layton and Shannon were members of **Arc Angels** and **Stevie Ray Vaughan**'s Double Trouble.

| 7/18/98 | 28 | 10 | Born Without You | — | | Dog Years . . . . Atlantic 83111 | |

STRADLIN, Izzy, And The Ju Ju Hounds
Born Jeffrey Isbell on 4/8/62 in Lafayette, Indiana. Rock singer/guitarist. Former member of **Guns N' Roses**. The Ju Ju Hounds: Rick Richards (guitar), Jimmy Ashhurst (bass) and Charlie Quintana (drums). Richards was a member of the **Georgia Satellites**.

| 10/24/92 | 6 | 16 | 1 Shuffle It All | — | | Izzy Stradlin And The Ju Ju Hounds . . . . . Geffen 24490 | |
| 2/6/93 | 13 | 8 | 2 Somebody Knockin' | — | | ↓ | |

STRANGLERS, The
Pop-rock group formed in London: **Hugh Cornwell** (vocals, guitar), Dave Greenfield (keyboards), Jean-Jacques Burnel (bass) and Jet Black (drums).

| 4/11/87 | 47 | 2 | Always The Sun | — | | Dreamtime . . . . Epic 40607 | |

STRAY CATS
Rockabilly trio from Long Island, New York: **Brian Setzer** (vocals, guitar), Lee Rocker (bass) and Slim Jim Phantom (drums). Also see **Phantom, Rocker & Slick**.

7/17/82	4	15	✓1 Rock This Town	9	▲	Built For Speed . . . . EMI America 17070	
8/21/82	41	2	✓2 Stray Cat Strut	3		↓	
8/13/83	2¹	15	✓3 (She's) Sexy + 17	5	●	Rant n' Rave with the Stray Cats . . . EMI America 17102	
3/25/89	35	5	✓4 Bring It Back Again	—		Blast Off . . . . EMI 91401	

STREETS
Rock group formed in Atlanta: Steve Walsh (vocals, keyboards; **Kansas**), Mike Slamer (guitar), Billy Greer (bass) and Tim Gehrt (drums).

| 11/19/83+ | 6 | 12 | If Love Should Go | 87 | | 1st . . . . Atlantic 80117 | |

STYLE COUNCIL, The
Pop duo from England: Paul Weller (vocals) and Mick Talbot (keyboards).

| 5/26/84 | 52 | 3 | My Ever Changing Moods | 29 | | My Ever Changing Moods . . . . Geffen 4029 | |

STYX
Rock group from Chicago: **Dennis DeYoung** (vocals, keyboards), **Tommy Shaw** and James Young (guitars), and twin brothers Chuck (bass) and John (drums) Panozzo. Disbanded in 1984. Reunited in 1990 with guitarist **Glen Burtnick** replacing Shaw, who joined **Damn Yankees**. John Panozzo died on 7/16/96 (age 47). In Greek mythology, Styx is a river of Hades. Also see **Classic Rock Tracks** section.

3/21/81	2¹	17	1 Too Much Time On My Hands	9	▲³	Paradise Theater . . . . A&M 3719	
3/21/81	8	13	2 Rockin' The Paradise	—		↓	
3/21/81	16	9	3 The Best Of Times	3		↓	
3/21/81	22	13	4 Snowblind	—		↓	
2/12/83	3	15	5 Mr. Roboto	3	▲	Kilroy Was Here . . . . A&M 3734	
9/29/90	9	8	6 Love Is The Ritual	80	●	Edge Of The Century . . . . A&M 5327	

SUBLIME
Ska-rock trio from San Francisco: Brad Nowell (vocals, guitar), Eric Wilson (bass) and Bud Gaugh (drums). Nowell died of a drug overdose on 5/25/96 (age 28).

| 10/26/96 | 11 | 26 | What I Got | 29ᴬ | ▲ | Sublime . . . . Gasoline Alley 11413 | |

SUGAR RAY
Rock group from Los Angeles: Mark McGrath (vocals; born on 3/15/68), Craig Bullock (DJ; born on 12/17/70), Rodney Sheppard (guitar; born on 11/25/67), Murphy Karges (bass; born on 6/20/67) and Stan Frazier (drums; born on 4/23/68).

8/30/97	29	9	1 Fly	❶⁶ᴬ	▲²	Floored . . . . Lava 83006	
			SUGAR RAY Featuring Super Cat				
3/27/99	38	4	2 Every Morning	3	▲³	14:59 . . . . Lava 83151	

DEBUT	PEAK	WKS	Mainstream Rock Track	Pop	Gld	Album Title	Album Label & Number
			SUGARTOOTH				
			Rock group from Seattle: Marc Hutner (vocals, guitar), Timothy Michael Gruse (guitar), Josh Blum (bass) and Joey Castillo (drums). By 1997, Gruse left and Castillo was replaced by Dusty Watson.				
4/30/94	26	8	1 Sold My Fortune...	—		Sugartooth.........................	DGC 24628
6/21/97	38	5	2 Booty Street..	—		The Sounds Of Solid..............	DGC 25006
			SUICIDAL TENDENCIES				
			Hard-rock group from Venice, California: Mike Muir (vocals), Rocky George and Mike Clark (guitars), and Robert Trujillo (bass). Muir and Trujillo went on to form **Infectious Grooves**.				
10/31/92	28	7	1 Nobody Hears...	—		The Art Of Rebellion................	Epic 48864
2/20/93	34	5	2 I'll Hate You Better......................................	—	↓		
			SUMMER, Henry Lee				
			Born on 7/5/55 in Brazil, Indiana. Rock singer/songwriter/guitarist.				
2/13/88	❶[1]	15	1 I Wish I Had A Girl	20		Henry Lee Summer..........	CBS Associated 40895
5/7/88	9	10	2 Darlin' Danielle Don't	57	↓		
8/13/88	28	8	3 Hands On The Radio..	85	↓		
5/20/89	6	12	4 Hey Baby	18		I've Got Everything...........	CBS Associated 45124
1/18/92	47	1	5 Turn It Up...	—		Way Past Midnight..........	Epic/Associated 47059
			SUMMERCAMP				
			Rock group from Santa Barbara, California: Tim Cullen (vocals), Sean McCue (guitar), Misha Feldmann (bass) and Tony Sevener (drums).				
7/19/97	37	3	Drawer..	—		Pure Juice.......................	Maverick 46528
			SUPERTRAMP				
			Rock group formed in England: **Roger Hodgson** (vocals, guitar), Rick Davies (vocals, keyboards), John Helliwell (sax), Dougie Thomson (bass) and Bob Siebenberg (drums). Hodgson left in 1983. Also see **Classic Rock Tracks** section.				
10/30/82	7	15	1 It's Raining Again	11	●	...famous last words....	A&M 3732
11/6/82	10	17	2 Crazy	—	↓		
11/6/82	30	10	3 Waiting So Long..	—	↓		
12/4/82	32	2	4 Don't Leave Me Now.......................................	—	↓		
5/25/85	4	12	5 Cannonball	28		Brother Where You Bound..............	A&M 5014
			✓ **SURVIVOR**				
			Rock group formed in Chicago: Dave Bickler (vocals), Frankie Sullivan (guitar), Jim Peterik (keyboards), Stephan Ellis (bass) and Marc Droubay (drums). Jimi Jamison replaced Bickler in 1983. Droubay and Ellis left in early 1988.				
11/14/81+	19	16	1 Poor Man's Son...	33		Premonition.................	Scotti Brothers 37549
6/12/82	❶[5]	15	2 Eye Of The Tiger	❶[6] ▲		Eye Of The Tiger.............	Scotti Brothers 38062
			from the movie *Rocky III* starring Sylvester Stallone				
10/22/83	16	7	3 Caught In The Game..	77		Caught In The Game.........	Scotti Brothers 38791
9/15/84	❶[3]	18	4 I Can't Hold Back	13	▲	Vital Signs................	Scotti Brothers 39578
12/15/84+	8	18	5 High On You	8	↓		
11/9/85	11	13	6 Burning Heart...	2[2]	▲	Rocky IV (soundtrack).........	Scotti Brothers 40203
11/8/86	27	10	7 Is This Love..	9		When Seconds Count......	Scotti Brothers 40457
10/22/88	40	4	8 Didn't Know It Was Love...................................	61		Too Hot To Sleep...........	Scotti Brothers 44282
			SWEET, Matthew				
			Born on 10/6/64 in Lincoln, Nebraska. Singer/bassist/drummer.				
4/4/92	10	20	1 Girlfriend	—	●	Girlfriend.................	Zoo 11015
8/21/93	35	4	2 The Ugly Truth..	—		Altered Beast..............	Zoo 11050
4/8/95	13	17	3 Sick Of Myself	58	●	100% Fun..................	Zoo 11081
3/22/97	24	9	4 Where You Get Love.......................................	—		Blue Sky On Mars............	Volcano 31130
			SWINGERS				
			Rock group from New Zealand: Andrew McLennan (vocals), Phil Judd (guitar), Dwayne Hillman (bass) and Ian Gilroy (drums).				
9/18/82	45	2	Counting The Beat..	—		Counting The Beat..............	Backstreet 5328
			SWITCHED				
			Hard-rock group from Cleveland: brothers Ben (vocals) and Joe (guitar) Schigel, Brad Kochmit (guitar), Jason French (bass) and Chad Szeliga (drums).				
5/11/02	30	9	Inside...	—		Subject To Change...............	Immortal 10636
			SYSTEMATIC				
			Hard-rock group from San Francisco: Adam Ruppel (vocals, guitar), Tim Narducci (guiatr), Nick St. Dennis (bass) and Shaun Bannon (drums).				
3/31/01	22	12	Beginning Of The End......................................	—		Somewhere In Between..............	TMC 62595
			SYSTEM OF A DOWN				
			Rock group from Los Angeles: Serj Tankian (vocals), Daron Malakian (guitar), Shavo Odadjian (bass) and John Dulmayan (drums).				
11/20/99	28	11	1 Sugar...	—	▲	System Of A Down..............	American 68924
4/1/00	25	9	2 Spiders..	—	↓		
8/4/01	12	29	3 Chop Suey..	76	▲[2]	Toxicity....................	American 62240
2/2/02	10	26	4 Toxicity	70	↓		
6/22/02	❶[1]	23↑	5 Aerials	55	↓		

DEBUT	PEAK	WKS	Mainstream Rock Track	Pop	Gld	Album Title	Album Label & Number

T

TALKING HEADS
Rock group from New York City: **David Byrne** (vocals, guitar), **Jerry Harrison** (keyboards, guitar), Tina Weymouth (bass) and Chris Frantz (drums). Weymouth and Frantz married on 6/18/77; later formed the Tom Tom Club. Group inducted into the Rock and Roll Hall of Fame in 2002. Also see **Classic Rock Tracks** section.

7/23/83	6	19	1 Burning Down The House	9	▲	Speaking In Tongues	Sire 23883
6/22/85	25	8	2 Road To Nowhere	105	▲²	Little Creatures	Sire 25305
7/20/85	11	18	3 And She Was	54	↓		
10/12/85	24	10	4 Stay Up Late		↓		
8/23/86	4	14	5 Wild Wild Life	25	●	True Stories	Sire 25512
10/18/86	19	10	6 Puzzlin' Evidence	—	↓		
3/19/88	5	11	7 (Nothing But) Flowers	—	●	Naked	Sire 25654
5/21/88	39	4	8 Blind	—	↓		
2/8/92	49	3	9 Sax And Violins	—		Until The End Of The World (soundtrack). .	Warner 26707

TALK SHOW
Rock group consisting of three members of **Stone Temple Pilots**: brothers Dean (guitar) and Robert (bass) DeLeo and Eric Kretz (drums), with Dave Coutts (vocals).

| 9/6/97 | 10 | 9 | Hello Hello | — | | Talk Show . . . . | Atlantic 83040 |

TALK TALK
Pop-rock group from England: Mark Hollis (vocals), Simon Brenner (keyboards), Paul Webb (bass) and Lee Harris (drums). Brenner left in 1983.

9/11/82	26	4	1 Talk Talk	75		The Party's Over	EMI America 17083
4/14/84	23	9	2 It's My Life	31		It's My Life	EMI America 17113
2/22/86	26	9	3 Life's What You Make It	90		The Colour Of Spring	EMI America 17179

TALL STORIES
Rock group from New York City: Steve Augeri (vocals), Jack Morer (guitar), Kevin Totoian (bass) and Tom DeFaria (drums). Augeri replaced **Steve Perry** as lead singer of **Journey** in 2001.

| 11/9/91+ | 22 | 16 | Wild On The Run . . . . | — | | Tall Stories . . . . | Epic 47145 |

TANGIER
Rock group from Philadelphia: Bill Mattson (vocals), Doug Gordon and Gari Saint (guitars), Garry Nutt (bass) and Bobby Bender (drums).

| 6/17/89 | 7 | 12 | On The Line . . . . | 67 | | Four Winds . . . . | Atco 91251 |

TANTRIC
Rock group from Louisville, Kentucky: Hugo Ferreira (vocals), Todd Whitener (guitar), Jesse Vest (bass) and Matt Taul (drums). The latter three were members of **Days Of The New**.

1/6/01	❶¹	27	1 Breakdown	106	●	Tantric	Maverick 47978
6/23/01	7	26	2 Astounded	—	↓		
10/27/01	18	21	3 Mourning	—	↓		

TAPROOT
Hard-rock group from Ann Arbor, Michigan: Steve Richards (vocals), Mike DeWolf (guitar), Phil Lipscomb (bass) and Jarrod Montague (drums).

11/11/00	39	4	1 Again And Again	—		Gift	Atlantic 83341
4/7/01	34	4	2 I	—	↓		
9/21/02	13↑	10↑	3 Poem	—		Welcome	Atlantic 83561

TATTOO RODEO
Hard-rock group from Burbank, California: Dennis Churchill-Dries (vocals, bass), Rick Chadock (guitar), Michael Lord (keyboards) and Rich Wright (drums).

| 5/18/91 | 20 | 11 | Been Your Fool . . . . | — | | Rode Hard-Put Away Wet . . . . | Atlantic 82241 |

TAXXI
Rock trio from England: David Cumming (vocals, guitar), Colin Payne (keyboards) and Jeff Nead (drums).

7/24/82	39	4	1 I'm Leaving	—		States Of Emergency	Fantasy 9617
10/8/83	31	8	2 Maybe Someday	—		Foreign Tongue	Fantasy 9628
8/10/85	36	4	3 Still In Love	—		Expose	MCA 5580

TAYLOR, Andy
Born on 2/16/61 in Dolver-Hampton, England. Lead guitarist of **Duran Duran** and **The Power Station**.

| 3/7/87 | 17 | 10 | 1 I Might Lie . . . . | | | Thunder . . . . | MCA 5837 |
| 6/6/87 | 36 | 4 | 2 Don't Let Me Die Young . . . . | — | ↓ | | |

TAYLOR, B.E., Group
Pop-rock group from Pittsburgh led by vocalist Taylor. Includes former **Crack The Sky** members Rick Witkowski (guitar), Joe Macre (bass) and Joey D'Amico (drums), with Nat Kerr (keyboards).

| 8/7/82 | 54 | 1 | Never Hold Back | | | Innermission . . . . | MCA 5335 |

TAYLOR, James
Born on 3/12/48 in Boston. Singer/songwriter/guitarist. Married to Carly Simon from 1972-83. Appeared in the movie *Two Lane Blacktop*. Recipient of *Billboard*'s Century Award in 1998. Inducted into the Rock and Roll Hall of Fame in 2000. Also see **Classic Rock Tracks** section.

| 3/21/81 | 21 | 9 | 1 Stand And Fight . . . . | — | ▲ | Dad Loves His Work . . . . | Columbia 37009 |
| 3/21/81 | 21 | 5 | 2 Her Town Too . . . . | 11 | ↓ | | |

JAMES TAYLOR AND J.D. SOUTHER

DEBUT	PEAK	WKS	Mainstream Rock Track	Pop	Gld	Album Title	Album Label & Number

TEARS FOR FEARS
Pop-rock duo from England: Roland Orzabal (vocals, guitar, keyboards) and Curt Smith (vocals, bass). Adopted name from Arthur Janov's book *Prisoners Of Pain*. Assisted by Ian Stanley (keyboards) and Manny Elias (drums). Smith left in 1992.

DEBUT	PEAK	WKS	Track	Pop	Gld	Album Title	Album Label & Number
5/7/83	22	15	1 Change	73	●	*The Hurting*	Mercury 811039
3/23/85	2²	15	2 Everybody Wants To Rule The World	❶² ▲⁵		*Songs From The Big Chair*	Mercury 824300
5/25/85	6	15	3 Shout	❶³		↓	
8/10/85	7	14	4 Head Over Heels	3		↓	
9/2/89	4	12	5 Sowing The Seeds Of Love	2¹ ▲		*The Seeds Of Love*	Fontana 838730

TEDESCHI, Susan
Born on 11/7/70 in Norwell, Massachusetts. Singer/songwriter/guitarist.

| 6/19/99 | 37 | 3 | Rock Me Right .... | — | ● | *Just Won't Burn* .... | Tone-Cool 1164 |

TEMPLE OF THE DOG
Gathering of Seattle musicians in tribute to Andrew Wood, lead singer of Mother Love Bone, who died of a heroin overdose on 3/16/90 (age 24). Features Stone Gossard, Jeff Ament, **Eddie Vedder** and Mike McCready of **Pearl Jam**, with **Chris Cornell** and Matt Cameron of **Soundgarden**. Gossard and Ament were members of Mother Love Bone.

| 7/25/92 | 4 | 20 | 1 Hunger Strike | — | ▲ | *Temple Of The Dog* .... | A&M 5350 |
| 11/7/92+ | 5 | 20 | 2 Say Hello 2 Heaven | — | | ↓ | |

10,000 MANIACS
Pop group formed in Jamestown, New York: **Natalie Merchant** (vocals), Robert Buck (guitar), Dennis Drew (keyboards), Steven Gustafson (bass) and Jerome Augustyniak (drums). Merchant left in August of 1993; replaced by Mary Ramsey. Buck died of liver failure on 12/19/00 (age 42).

| 4/30/88 | 37 | 7 | 1 Like The Weather .... | 68 | ▲² | *In My Tribe* .... | Elektra 60738 |
| 5/20/89 | 20 | 11 | 2 Trouble Me .... | 44 | ▲ | *Blind Man's Zoo* .... | Elektra 60815 |

TEN YEARS AFTER
Blues-rock group from England: **Alvin Lee** (vocals, guitar), Chick Churchill (keyboards), Leo Lyons (bass) and Ric Lee (drums). Also see **Classic Rock Tracks** section.

| 8/19/89 | 23 | 8 | Let's Shake It Up .... | — | | *About Time* .... | Chrysalis 21722 |

TEPPER, Robert
Born in Bayonne, New Jersey. Rock singer/songwriter.

| 2/1/86 | 12 | 9 | No Easy Way Out .... | 22 | ▲ | *Rocky IV (Soundtrack)* .... | Scotti Brothers 40203 |

★69★ TESLA
Hard-rock group formed in Sacramento, California: Jeff Keith (vocals), Frank Hannon and Tommy Skeoch (guitars), Brian Wheat (bass) and Troy Lucketta (drums). Band named after the inventor of the alternating current generator, Nikola Tesla. Hannon was also a member of **Moon Dog Mane**.

1)Signs 2)Mama's Fool 3)What You Give

2/21/87	35	7	1 Modern Day Cowboy	—	▲	*Mechanical Resonance*	Geffen 24120
4/25/87	22	9	2 Little Suzi	91		↓	
1/9/88	46	3	3 Gettin' Better	—		↓	
1/28/89	13	11	4 Heaven's Trail (No Way Out)	—	▲²	*The Great Radio Controversy*	Geffen 24224
5/20/89	34	6	5 Hang Tough	—		↓	
9/30/89+	7	23	6 Love Song	10		↓	
2/17/90	13	13	7 The Way It Is	55		↓	
11/24/90+	2¹	17	8 Signs [L]	8	▲	*Five Man Acoustical Jam*	Geffen 24311
			#3 Pop hit for Five Man Electrical Band in 1971				
3/16/91	28	8	9 Paradise .... [L]	—		↓	
			above 2 recorded on 7/2/90 at the Trocadero in Philadelphia				
9/7/91	20	7	10 Edison's Medicine	—	▲	*Psychotic Supper*	Geffen 24424
11/16/91+	19	21	11 Call It What You Want	—		↓	
2/15/92	7	21	12 What You Give	86		↓	
6/13/92	13	14	13 Song & Emotion	—		↓	
10/17/92	35	2	14 Stir It Up	—		↓	
8/13/94	5	13	15 Mama's Fool	—	●	*Bust A Nut*	Geffen 24713
11/26/94	19	10	16 Need Your Lovin'	—		↓	
3/18/95	35	8	17 Alot To Lose	—		↓	
12/23/95+	31	6	18 Steppin' Over	—	●	*Time's Makin' Changes: The Best Of Tesla*	Geffen 24833

TESTAMENT
Hard-rock group formed in San Francisco: Chuck Billy (vocals), Eric Peterson and Glen Abelais (guitars), Greg Christian (bass) and John Tempesta (drums).

| 2/6/93 | 24 | 10 | Return To Serenity .... | — | | *The Ritual* .... | Atlantic 82392 |

TEXAS
Pop-rock group from Glasgow, Scotland: Sharleen Spiteri (vocals, guitar), Ally McErlaine (guitar), John McElhone (bass) and Stuart Kerr (drums).

| 7/29/89 | 27 | 8 | I Don't Want A Lover .... | 77 | | *Southside* .... | Mercury 838171 |

THEORY OF A DEADMAN
Rock group from Vancouver: Tyler Connolly (vocals, guitar), David Brenner (guitar), Dean Back (bass) and Tim Hart (drums).

| 8/17/02 | 8 | 15↑ | Nothing Could Come Between Us | — | | *Theory Of A Deadman* .... | Roadrunner 618442 |

DEBUT	PEAK	WKS	Mainstream Rock Track	Pop Gld	Album Title	Album Label & Number

THIN LIZZY
Rock group from Dublin, Ireland: Phil Lynott (vocals, bass), Scott Gorham and Snowy White (guitars), and Brian Downey (drums). Numerous personnel changes. **Gary Moore** was a member from 1978-79. Lynott died on 1/4/86 (age 34). Also see **Classic Rock Tracks** section.

DEBUT	PEAK	WKS	Mainstream Rock Track	Pop Gld	Album Title	Album Label & Number
2/27/82	38	6	1 Angel Of Death	—	Renegade	Warner 3622
3/20/82	24	7	2 Hollywood (Down On Your Luck)	—	↓	
3/23/91	22	6	3 Dedication	—	Dedication	Mercury 848530

THIRD DAY
Christian rock group from Marietta, Georgia: Mac Powell (vocals), Mark Lee and Brad Avery (guitars), Tai Anderson (bass) and David Carr (drums).

3/8/97	34	5	Nothing At All	—	Third Day	Reunion 41607

THIRD EYE BLIND
Rock group from San Francisco: Stephan Jenkins (vocals), Kevin Cadogan (guitar), Arion Salazar (bass) and Brad Hargreaves (drums).

5/24/97	26	13	1 Semi-Charmed Life	4 ▲6	Third Eye Blind	Elektra 62012
10/11/97	26	10	2 Graduate	—	↓	
5/2/98	36	3	3 Losing A Whole Year	—	↓	
12/18/99	35	6	4 Anything	— ▲	Blue	Elektra 62415

3RD STRIKE
Rock group from Los Angeles: Jim Korthe (vocals), Todd Deguchi and Erik Carlsson (guitars), Gabe Hammersmith (bass) and P.J. McMullan (drums).

4/6/02	23	17	1 No Light	42^S	Lost Angel	Hollywood 62344
9/28/02	40	1	2 Redemption	—	↓	

38 SPECIAL ★30★
Rock group formed in Jacksonville, Florida: Donnie Van Zant (vocals), Don Barnes and Jeff Carlisi (guitars), Larry Junstrom (bass), and Steve Brookins and Jack Grondin (drums). By 1988, Barnes and Brookins replaced by Danny Chauncey (guitar) and Max Carl (keyboards). Van Zant is the brother of **Lynyrd Skynyrd**'s Ronnie Van Zant. Also see **Van Zant**.

1)If I'd Been The One   2)Caught Up In You   3)Second Chance   4)The Sound Of Your Voice   5)Hold On Loosely

3/21/81	3	14	1 Hold On Loosely	27 ▲	Wild-Eyed Southern Boys	A&M 4835
3/21/81	30	10	2 Fantasy Girl	52	↓	
4/25/81	35	1	3 Wild-Eyed Southern Boys	—	↓	
5/1/82	❶1	15	4 Caught Up In You	10 ▲	Special Forces	A&M 4888
6/5/82	9	22	5 Chain Lightnin'	—	↓	
8/14/82	56	1	6 Back On The Track	—	↓	
9/11/82	7	8	7 You Keep Runnin' Away	38	↓	
11/12/83	❶4	15	8 If I'd Been The One	19 ▲	Tour De Force	A&M 4971
12/17/83+	4	17	9 Back Where You Belong	20	↓	
4/7/84	17	3	10 One Time For Old Times	—	↓	
9/29/84	4	10	11 Teacher Teacher	25 ●	Teachers (soundtrack)	Capitol 12371
5/3/86	4	11	12 Like No Other Night	14 ●	Strength In Numbers	A&M 5115
5/31/86	6	15	13 Somebody Like You	48	↓	
8/30/86	30	7	14 Heart's On Fire	—	↓	
6/27/87	4	11	15 Back To Paradise	41 ▲	Flashback	A&M 3910
10/8/88	5	9	16 Rock & Roll Strategy	67	Rock & Roll Strategy	A&M 5218
11/19/88+	15	11	17 Little Sheba	—	↓	
2/18/89	2²	14	18 Second Chance	6	↓	
7/8/89	43	4	19 Comin' Down Tonight	67	↓	

THIRTY EIGHT SPECIAL (above 4)

6/22/91	2¹	14	20 The Sound Of Your Voice	33	Bone Against Steel	Charisma 91640
9/21/91	30	9	21 Rebel To Rebel	—	↓	
8/9/97	33	5	22 Fade To Blue	—	Resolution	Razor & Tie 2829

30 SECONDS TO MARS
Rock group formed in Los Angeles: brothers Jared (vocals, guitar) and Shannon (drums) Leto, Solon Bixler (guitar) and Matt Wachter (bass). Jared Leto is also a popular actor (played "Jordan Catalano" on TV's *My So-Called Life*).

9/7/02	31	8	Capricorn (A Brand New Name)	—	30 Seconds To Mars	Immortal 12424

THOMAS, Mickey
Born on 12/3/49 in Cairo, Georgia. Lead singer of **Jefferson Starship/Starship** from 1979-90.

2/22/86	35	4	Stand In The Fire	—	Youngblood (soundtrack)	RCA 7172

THOMPSON, Michael, Band
Born in Long Island, New York. Rock guitarist. His band featured vocals by Moon Calhoun.

4/22/89	33	6	Can't Miss	—	How Long	Geffen 24225

DEBUT	PEAK	WKS	Mainstream Rock Track	Pop	Gld	Album Title	Album Label & Number

THOMPSON TWINS
Pop-rock trio from England: Tom Bailey (vocals, synthesizer), Alannah Currie (xylophone, percussion) and Joe Leeway (conga, synthesizer).

DEBUT	PEAK	WKS	Track	Pop	Gld	Album Title	Album Label & Number
4/2/83	36	3	1 Love On Your Side	45		Side Kicks	Arista 6607
3/10/84	9	10	2 Hold Me Now	3	▲	Into The Gap	Arista 8200
5/5/84	12	13	3 Doctor! Doctor!	11	↓		
9/8/84	51	4	4 You Take Me Up	44	↓		
9/28/85	14	11	5 Lay Your Hands On Me	6	●	Here's To Future Days	Arista 8276
2/8/86	35	4	6 King For A Day	8	↓		

★82★ THOROGOOD, George, & The Destroyers
Born on 12/31/52 in Wilmington, Delaware. Blues-rock singer/guitarist. The Destroyers: Steve Chrismar (guitar), Hank Carter (sax), Billy Blough (bass) and Jeff Simon (drums).
1)Get A Haircut 2)Born To Be Bad 3)You Talk Too Much

DEBUT	PEAK	WKS	Track	Pop	Gld	Album Title	Album Label & Number
8/14/82	32	5	1 Nobody But Me	106	●	Bad To The Bone	EMI America 17076
			#8 Pop hit for The Human Beinz in 1968				
9/18/82	27	6	2 Bad To The Bone	—	↓		
1/19/85	26	8	3 Gear Jammer	—	●	Maverick	EMI America 17145
3/16/85	13	10	4 I Drink Alone	—	↓		
6/15/85	25	10	5 Willie And The Hand Jive	63	↓		
			#9 Pop hit for Johnny Otis in 1958				
8/9/86	11	9	6 Reelin' & Rockin'	[L]	▲	Live	EMI America 17214
			recorded on 5/23/86 at the Cincinnati Gardens; #27 Pop hit for Chuck Berry in 1973				
1/23/88	4	12	7 You Talk Too Much	—	●	Born To Be Bad	EMI-Manhattan 46973
3/12/88	3	9	8 Born To Be Bad	—	↓		
6/18/88	39	3	9 Treat Her Right	—	↓		
			#2 Pop hit for Roy Head in 1965				
3/2/91	5	11	10 If You Don't Start Drinkin' (I'm Gonna Leave)	—		Boogie People	EMI 92514
5/18/91	15	8	11 Hello Little Girl	—	↓		
			written by Chuck Berry				
8/22/92	18	11	12 I'm A Steady Rollin' Man	—	▲	The Baddest Of George Thorogood And The Destroyers	EMI 97718
			written by blues legend Robert Johnson				
7/24/93	2²	11	13 Get A Haircut	124		Haircut	EMI 89529
10/2/93	12	8	14 Howlin' For My Baby	—	↓		
			written by Willie Dixon and Howlin' Wolf				
12/25/93+	24	6	15 Gone Dead Train	—	↓		
			first recorded by Crazy Horse in 1971				
4/17/99	24	9	16 I Don't Trust Nobody	—		Half A Boy/Half A Man	CMC International 86270

3
Rock trio: Robert Barry (vocals, guitar), Keith Emerson (keyboards) and Carl Palmer (drums). Also see **Emerson, Lake & Palmer**.

DEBUT	PEAK	WKS	Track	Pop	Gld	Album Title	Album Label & Number
2/20/88	9	11	Talkin' Bout	—		To The Power Of Three	Geffen 24181

★76★ 3 DOORS DOWN
Rock group from Escatawpa, Mississippi: Brad Arnold (vocals), Matt Roberts (guitar), Todd Harrell (bass) and Chris Henderson (drums).

DEBUT	PEAK	WKS	Track	Pop	Gld	Album Title	Album Label & Number
2/5/00	❶⁹	51	1 Kryptonite	3	▲⁵	The Better Life	Republic 153920
6/24/00	❶²¹	53	2 Loser	55	↓		
1/13/01	❶³	26	3 Duck And Run	110	↓		
6/16/01	10	26	4 Be Like That	24	↓		
10/5/02	3	8↑	5 When I'm Gone	67↑		Away From The Sun	Republic 064396

311
Rock-funk group from Omaha, Nebraska: Nicholas Hexum and SA Martinez (vocals), Tim Mahoney (guitar), P-Nut (bass) and Chad Sexton (drums). 311 is the police code for indecent exposure.

DEBUT	PEAK	WKS	Track	Pop	Gld	Album Title	Album Label & Number
8/24/96	19	12	1 Down	37ᴬ	▲³	311	Capricorn 42041
8/16/97	31	3	2 Transistor	—	▲	Transistor	Capricorn 536181
10/9/99	39	1	3 Come Original	119	●	Soundsystem	Capricorn 546645
7/7/01	32	7	4 You Wouldn't Believe	—	●	From Chaos	Volcano 32184

THUNDER
Hard-rock group from England: Daniel Bowes (vocals), Luke Morley (guitar), Ben Matthews (keyboards), Mark Luckhurst (bass) and Gary James (drums).

DEBUT	PEAK	WKS	Track	Pop	Gld	Album Title	Album Label & Number
4/13/91	10	15	1 Dirty Love	55		Backstreet Symphony	Geffen 24384
8/24/91	42	6	2 Until My Dying Day	—	↓		
11/30/91+	31	14	3 Love Walked In	—	↓		

TIKARAM, Tanita
Born on 12/8/69 in Munster, West Germany; raised in Basingstoke, England. Female singer/songwriter.

DEBUT	PEAK	WKS	Track	Pop	Gld	Album Title	Album Label & Number
3/25/89	47	4	Twist In My Sobriety	—		Ancient Heart	Reprise 25839

DEBUT	PEAK	WKS	Mainstream Rock Track	Pop	Gld	Album Title	Album Label & Number
			'TIL TUESDAY				
			Pop group formed in Boston: **Aimee Mann** (vocals, bass), Robert Holmes (guitar), Joey Pesce (keyboards) and Michael Hausmann (drums).				
5/4/85	14	13	1 Voices Carry	8	●	Voices Carry	Epic 39458
9/27/86	9	11	2 What About Love	26	●	Welcome Home	Epic 40314
1/10/87	37	8	3 Coming Up Close	59	↓		
			TIMBUK 3				
			Husband-and-wife duo from Austin, Texas: Patrick and Barbara MacDonald.				
9/20/86	14	10	1 The Future's So Bright, I Gotta Wear Shades	19		Greetings From Timbuk 3	I.R.S. 5739
12/27/86+	35	7	2 Life Is Hard	—	↓		
5/14/88	34	5	3 Rev. Jack & His Roamin' Cadillac Church	—		Eden Alley	I.R.S. 42124
			TIN MACHINE				
			Rock group: **David Bowie** (vocals), Reeves Gabrels (guitar), Tony Sales (bass; **Utopia, Chequered Past**) and Hunt Sales (drums; Utopia). The Sales brothers are the sons of TV comedian Soupy Sales.				
5/27/89	8	7	1 Under The God	—		Tin Machine	EMI 91990
7/29/89	47	2	2 Heaven's In Here	—	↓		
8/31/91	17	7	3 One Shot	—		Tin Machine II	Victory 511216
			TOADIES				
			Rock group from Fort Worth, Texas: Todd Lewis (vocals, guitar), Darrel Herbert (guitar), Lisa Umbarger (bass) and Mark Reznicek (drums). Clark Vogeler replaced Herbert in 2000.				
6/10/95	9	35	1 Possum Kingdom	40[A] ▲		Rubberneck	Interscope 92402
2/3/96	23	11	2 Away	—	↓		
4/7/01	34	6	3 Push The Hand	—		Hell Below / Stars Above	Interscope 490872
			TOAD THE WET SPROCKET				
			Pop-rock group from Santa Barbara, California: Glen Phillips (vocals), Todd Nichols (guitar), Dean Dinning (bass) and Randy Guss (drums). Name taken from a Monty Python skit.				
6/27/92	22	11	1 All I Want	15	▲	Fear	Columbia 47309
10/24/92	27	9	2 Walk On The Ocean	18	↓		
6/4/94	5	22	3 Fall Down	33	▲	Dulcinea	Columbia 57744
10/22/94	22	9	4 Something's Always Wrong	41	↓		
10/14/95	19	9	5 Good Intentions	23[A] ▲		Friends (soundtrack)	Reprise 46008
5/17/97	17	11	6 Come Down	51[A]		Coil	Columbia 67862
			TOMMY TUTONE				
			Rock group formed in San Francisco: Tommy Heath (vocals), Jim Keller (guitar), Jon Lyons (bass) and Victor Carberry (drums).				
11/28/81+	❶³	27	867-5309/Jenny	4		Tommy Tutone-2	Columbia 37401
			TONIC				
			Rock group from Los Angeles: Emerson Hart (vocals, guitar), Jeff Russo (guitar), Dan Rothchild (bass) and Kevin Shepard (drums). Dan Lavery replaced Rothchild in 1998.				
7/13/96	2³	29	1 Open Up Your Eyes	68[A] ▲		Lemon Parade	Polydor 531042
2/1/97	8	12	2 Casual Affair	—	↓		
4/12/97	❶⁵	37	3 If You Could Only See	11[A]	↓		
7/3/99	3	19	4 You Wanted More	103	●	American Pie (soundtrack)	Universal 53269
11/13/99	20	13	5 Knock Down Walls	—		Sugar	Universal 542069
			TONIO K.				
			Born Antonio Krikorian on 7/4/50 in California. Singer/songwriter.				
3/12/88	42	4	Without Love	—		Notes From The Lost Civilization	What? 763
	★98★		**TOOL**				
			Hard-rock group from Los Angeles: Maynard James Keenan (vocals), Adam Jones (guitar), Paul D'Amour (bass) and Danny Carey (drums). Justin Chancellor replaced D'Amour in 1995. Also see **A Perfect Circle**.				
10/9/93	13	23	1 Sober	—	▲²	Undertow	Zoo 11052
2/26/94	32	9	2 Prison Sex	—	↓		
9/28/96	17	26	3 Stinkfist	—	▲²	Aenima	Volcano 31087
2/22/97	23	18	4 H.	—	↓		
8/2/97	25	22	5 Aenima	—	↓		
11/15/97	22	18	6 Forty Six & 2	—	↓		
5/19/01	2¹³	33	7 Schism	—	▲	Lateralus	Volcano 31160
11/17/01+	14	22	8 Lateralus	—	↓		
4/20/02	10	26	9 Parabola	—	↓		
			TORA TORA				
			Hard-rock group from Memphis: Anthony Corder (vocals), Keith Douglas (guitar), Patrick Francis (bass) and John Patterson (drums).				
7/1/89	25	12	1 Walkin' Shoes	86		Surprise Attack	A&M 5261
7/25/92	39	1	2 Amnesia	—		Wild America	A&M 5371
			TORONTO				
			Rock group from Toronto: Holly Woods (vocals), Sheron Alton and Brian Allen (guitars), and Scott Kreyer (keyboards) and Jim Fox (drums).				
8/21/82	28	6	Your Daddy Don't Know	77		Get It On Credit	Network 60153

DEBUT	PEAK	WKS	Mainstream Rock Track	Pop	Gld	Album Title	Album Label & Number

TOTO
Pop-rock group formed in Los Angeles: Bobby Kimball (vocals), Steve Lukather (guitar), David Paich and Steve Porcaro (keyboards), David Hungate (bass) and Jeff Porcaro (drums). Prominent session musicians. Steve and Jeff's brother, Mike Porcaro, replaced Hungate in 1983. Jeff Porcaro died of a heart attack on 8/5/92 (age 38). Also see **Classic Rock Tracks** section.

DEBUT	PEAK	WKS			Pop	Gld	Album Title	Album Label & Number
3/21/81	40	1	1	Live For Today	—		Turn Back	Columbia 36813
4/17/82	8	14	2	Rosanna	2⁵	▲³	Toto IV	Columbia 37728
5/22/82	28	4	3	Afraid Of Love	—		↓	
6/19/82	57	3	4	Lovers In The Night	—		↓	
11/3/84	7	12	5	Stranger In Town	30	●	Isolation	Columbia 38962

TOWNSHEND, Pete
Born on 5/19/45 in London. Singer/songwriter/guitarist. Member of **The Who**. Also see **Classic Rock Tracks** section.
1)Face The Face 2)A Friend Is A Friend 3)Give Blood

DEBUT	PEAK	WKS			Pop	Gld	Album Title	Album Label & Number
5/30/81	39	5	1	Won't Get Fooled Again ... [L]	—		The Secret Policeman's Ball/The Music	
				PETE TOWNSHEND & JOHN WILLIAMS #15 Pop hit for The Who in 1971			(various artists)	Island 9630
7/3/82	15	10	2	Face Dances Part Two	105		All The Best Cowboys Have Chinese Eyes	Atco 149
7/10/82	41	5	3	Slit Skirts	—		↓	
7/24/82	30	10	4	Stardom In Action	—		↓	
11/9/85	3	14	5	Face The Face	26	●	White City - A Novel	Atco 90473
11/30/85+	5	15	6	Give Blood	—		↓	
4/5/86	32	6	7	Secondhand Love	—		↓	
9/20/86	26	6	8	Barefootin' ... [L]	—		Pete Townshend's Deep End Live!	Atco 90553
				#7 Pop hit for Robert Parker in 1966				
10/18/86	39	4	9	Life To Life	—		Playing For Keeps (soundtrack)	Atlantic 81678
6/24/89	3	10	10	A Friend Is A Friend	—		The Iron Man: The Musical By Pete Townshend	Atlantic 81996
6/5/93	19	6	11	English Boy	—		Psychoderelict	Atlantic 82494

TOY MATINEE
Pop duo formed in Los Angeles: Kevin Gilbert (vocals) and Patrick Leonard (instruments). Gilbert died of accidental asphyxiation on 5/18/96 (age 29).

DEBUT	PEAK	WKS			Pop	Gld	Album Title	Album Label & Number
9/22/90	23	11	1	Last Plane Out	—		Toy Matinee	Reprise 26235
1/19/91	23	8	2	The Ballad Of Jenny Ledge	—		↓	

TRAFFIC
Rock group formed in England. Original lineup included **Steve Winwood** (vocals, keyboards), **Dave Mason** (guitar) and **Jim Capaldi** (drums). Disbanded in 1974; Winwood and Capaldi reunited in 1994. Also see **Classic Rock Tracks** section.

DEBUT	PEAK	WKS			Pop	Gld	Album Title	Album Label & Number
5/7/94	10	8		Here Comes A Man	—		Far From Home	Virgin 39490

TRAGICALLY HIP, The
Rock group from Kingston, Ontario, Canada: Gordon Downie (vocals), Bobby Baker and Paul Langlois (guitars), Gord Sinclair (bass) and Johnny Fay (drums).

DEBUT	PEAK	WKS			Pop	Gld	Album Title	Album Label & Number
3/31/90	30	6	1	New Orleans Is Sinking	—		Up To Here	MCA 6310
4/13/91	43	4	2	Three Pistols	—		Road Apples	MCA 10173
2/20/93	16	8	3	Courage (For Hugh MacLennan)	—		Fully Completely	MCA 10700
9/26/98	39	1	4	Poets	—		Phantom Power	Sire 31025

TRAIN
Rock group from San Francisco: Patrick Monahan (vocals), Rob Hotchkiss and Jimmy Stafford (guitars), Charlie Colin (bass) and Scott Underwood (drums).

DEBUT	PEAK	WKS			Pop	Gld	Album Title	Album Label & Number
11/28/98+	12	24	1	Free	—	▲	Train	Aware 38052
5/8/99	21	14	2	Meet Virginia	20		↓	
3/17/01	19	26	3	Drops Of Jupiter (Tell Me)	5	▲²	Drops Of Jupiter	Aware 69888
3/30/02	40	1	4	She's On Fire	—		↓	

TRANS-SIBERIAN ORCHESTRA
Studio orchestra assembled by producer Paul O'Neill.

DEBUT	PEAK	WKS			Pop	Gld	Album Title	Album Label & Number
1/3/98	29	2		Christmas Eve - Sarajevo 12/24 ... [X-I]	49ᴬ	●	Christmas Eve And Other Stories	Lava 92736

TRAPT
Rock group from Los Gatos, California: Chris Brown (vocals, guitar), Simon Ormandy (guitar), Peter Charell (bass) and Aaron Montgomery (drums).

DEBUT	PEAK	WKS			Pop	Gld	Album Title	Album Label & Number
10/26/02	31	5↑		Headstrong	—		Trapt	Warner 48296

TRAVELING WILBURYS
Supergroup masquerading as a band of brothers. Spearheaded by Nelson (**George Harrison**), with Lucky (**Bob Dylan**), Otis (**Jeff Lynne** of ELO), Lefty (**Roy Orbison**) and Charlie (**Tom Petty**) Wilbury. Orbison died on 12/6/88 (age 52). For their second album, *Vol. 3*, the names have changed to Spike (Harrison), Muddy (Petty), Clayton (Lynne) and Boo (Dylan). Harrison died of cancer on 11/29/2001 (age 58).

DEBUT	PEAK	WKS			Pop	Gld	Album Title	Album Label & Number
10/22/88	2²	12	1	Handle With Care	45	▲³	Volume One	Wilbury 25796
11/19/88+	5	15	2	Last Night	—		↓	
1/14/89	41	1	3	Tweeter And The Monkey Man	—		↓	
2/4/89	2³	12	4	End Of The Line	63		↓	
4/8/89	7	8	5	Heading For The Light	—		↓	
10/27/90	2³	13	6	She's My Baby	—	▲	Vol. 3	Wilbury 26324
12/22/90+	16	11	7	Inside Out	—		↓	
3/9/91	46	4	8	Wilbury Twist	—		↓	

DEBUT	PEAK	WKS	Mainstream Rock Track	Pop	Gld	Album Title	Album Label & Number

TRAVERS, Pat
Born on 4/12/54 in Toronto. Hard-rock singer/guitarist. Also see **Classic Rock Tracks** section.

4/11/81	33	3	1 New Age Music..	—		Radio Active	Polydor 6313
4/14/84	23	5	2 Killer	—		Hot Shot	Polydor 821064

TREAT HER RIGHT
Rock group from Boston: Mark Sandman (vocals, guitar), David Champagne (guitar), Jim Fitting (harmonica) and Billy Conway (drums). Sandman died of a heart attack on 7/4/99 (age 46).

4/2/88	15	12	I Think She Likes Me.......................................	—		Treat Her Right	RCA 6884

TRICKY — see LIVE

TRIPPING DAISY
Pop-rock group from Dallas: Tim DeLaughter (vocals), Wes Berggren (guitar), Mark Pirro (bass) and Bryan Wakeland (drums). Berggren died on 10/27/99 (age 28).

7/29/95	33	6	1 I Got A Girl	53[A]		I Am An Elastic Firecracker	Island 524112
11/18/95	35	4	2 Piranha	—		↓	

★91★ TRIUMPH
Hard-rock trio formed in Toronto: Rik Emmett (vocals, guitar), Mike Levine (keyboards, bass) and Gil Moore (drums). Emmett went solo in 1988. Phil X (guitar) joined by 1992. Also see **Classic Rock Tracks** section.
1)All The Way 2)A World Of Fantasy 3)Magic Power

10/3/81	8	21	1 Magic Power..	51	●	Allied Forces	RCA 3902
10/24/81	55	4	2 Allied Forces	—		↓	
11/14/81	18	20	3 Fight The Good Fight..	—		↓	
3/27/82	50	4	4 Say Goodbye	102		↓	
1/29/83	3	19	5 A World Of Fantasy	—	●	Never Surrender	RCA 4382
2/5/83	23	14	6 Never Surrender	—		↓	
7/30/83	2[2]	10	7 All The Way	—		↓	
12/1/84+	10	11	8 Spellbound	—		Thunder Seven	MCA 5537
2/9/85	13	11	9 Follow Your Heart	88		↓	
12/7/85	49	2	10 Mind Games..	—		Stages.............................	MCA 8020
8/16/86	9	13	11 Somebody's Out There	27		The Sport Of Kings	MCA 5786
11/1/86	23	8	12 Tears In The Rain	—		↓	
11/7/87	28	10	13 Long Time Gone...	—		Surveillance.......................	MCA 42083
1/9/93	30	6	14 Child Of The City	—		Edge Of Excess	Victory 480012

TRIXTER
Hard-rock group from Paramus, New Jersey: Peter Loran (vocals), Steve Brown (guitar), P.J. Farley (bass) and Mark Scott (drums).

9/29/90	26	12	1 Give It To Me Good	65		Trixter	MCA 6389
2/9/91	33	6	2 One In A Million...	75		↓	

TROWER, Robin
Born on 3/9/45 in London. Rock guitarist. Original member of **Procol Harum**. Also see **Classic Rock Tracks** section.

3/28/81	18	8	1 Into Money	—		B.L.T.	Chrysalis 1324
4/4/81	43	1	2 Won't Let You Down	—		↓	
			JACK BRUCE/BILL LORDAN/ROBIN TROWER				
1/24/87	25	10	3 No Time	—		Passion	GNP Crescendo 2187
5/7/88	9	10	4 Tear It Up	—		Take What You Need	Atlantic 81838
3/3/90	38	5	5 Turn The Volume Up..	—		In The Line Of Fire.................	Atlantic 82080
			Davey Pattison (lead vocal, above 3)				

TRUSTCOMPANY
Rock group from Montgomery, Alabama: Kevin Palmer (vocals, guitar), James Fukai (guitar), Josh Moates (bass) and Jason Singleton (drums).

6/1/02	6	26	Downfall	91		The Lonely Position Of Neutral	Geffen 493312

TRUTH, The
Rock duo from England: Dennis Greaves and Mick Lister.

4/18/87	7	12	Weapons Of Love	65		Weapons Of Love	I.R.S. 5981

TRYNIN, Jennifer
Born on 12/27/63 in New Jersey. Singer/songwriter/guitarist.

7/29/95	40	2	Better Than Nothing	74[A]		Cockamamie.......................	Squint 45931

TSUNAMI
Rock group formed in San Francisco: Doug Denton (vocals), Tatsuya Miyazaki and Tomotaka Yamamoto (guitars), Max Load (bass) and Scott Sherman (drums). Tsunami (pronounced: soo-na-mee) is a Japanese term for a large ocean wave caused by an earthquake or volcano.

2/18/84	60	1	The Runaround	—		Tsunami..........................	Enigma 1032

TUBES, The
Pop-rock group from San Francisco: Fee Waybill (vocals), Bill Spooner and Roger Steen (guitars), Michael Cotton and Vince Welnick (keyboards), Rick Anderson (bass) and Prairie Prince (drums). Welnick joined the **Grateful Dead** in 1990.

5/30/81	7	19	✓1 Talk To Ya Later	101		The Completion Backward Principle.....	Capitol 12151
8/8/81	22	12	✓2 Don't Want To Wait Anymore..........................	35		↓	

DEBUT	PEAK	WKS	Mainstream Rock Track	Pop	Gld	Album Title	Album Label & Number
			TUBES, The — Cont'd				
4/9/83	❶5	15	3 She's A Beauty	10		Outside Inside	Capitol 12260
5/21/83	16	7	4 The Monkey Time	68		↓	
			#8 Pop hit for Major Lance in 1963				
3/9/85	25	6	5 Piece By Piece	87		Love Bomb	Capitol 12381
			written and produced by **Todd Rundgren**				
			TURNER, Joe Lynn				
			Born in New Jersey. Rock singer/guitarist. Member of **Rainbow** and **Deep Purple**.				
10/19/85	19	8	Endlessly	—		Rescue You	Elektra 60449
			TURNER, Tina				
			Born Anna Mae Bullock on 11/26/38 in Brownsville, Tennessee. R&B singer/actress. Half of Ike & Tina Turner duo. Married to Ike from 1958-76. Acted in the movies *Tommy* and *Mad Max-Beyond Thunderdome*. Her autobiography, *What's Love Got To Do With It*, was made into a movie in 1993. Ike & Tina were inducted into the Rock and Roll Hall of Fame in 1991.				
8/18/84	51	4	1 What's Love Got To Do With It	❶3	▲5	Private Dancer	Capitol 12330
9/22/84	32	9	2 Better Be Good To Me	5		↓	
11/24/84	7	25	3 It's Only Love	15	▲5	Reckless (Adams)	A&M 5013
			BRYAN ADAMS/TINA TURNER				
7/20/85	29	8	4 We Don't Need Another Hero (Thunderdome)	2[1]		Mad Max Beyond Thunderdome (soundtrack)	Capitol 12429
10/4/86	18	8	5 Back Where You Started	—	▲	Break Every Rule	Capitol 12530
			Bryan Adams (co-writer, backing vocal)				
			TUTONE, Tommy — see TOMMY				
			TWILLEY, Dwight				
			Born on 6/6/51 in Tulsa, Oklahoma. Rock singer/songwriter/pianist.				
3/20/82	14	7	1 Somebody To Love	106		Scuba Divers	EMI America 17064
2/11/84	2[1]	14	2 Girls	16		Jungle	EMI America 17107
			Tom Petty (backing vocal)				
5/12/84	44	3	3 Little Bit Of Love	77		↓	
			TWISTED SISTER				
			Hard-rock group from Long Island, New York: Dee Snider (vocals), Jay French and Eddie Ojeda (guitars), Mark Mendosa (bass) and A.J. Pero (drums). Joey Franco replaced Pero in 1987.				
6/16/84	7	18	1 We're Not Gonna Take It	21	▲3	Stay Hungry	Atlantic 80156
10/6/84	35	9	2 I Wanna Rock	68		↓	
1/5/85	19	8	3 The Price	107		↓	
12/7/85	32	8	4 Leader Of The Pack	53	●	Come Out And Play	Atlantic 81275
			#1 Pop hit for The Shangri-Las in 1964				
7/18/87	31	6	5 Hot Love	—		Love Is For Suckers	Atlantic 81772
			TWO				
			Rock group formed in Phoenix: Rob Halford (vocals; **Judas Priest**; **Fight**), John Lowery (guitar), James Woolley (keyboards), Ray Reandeau (bass) and Sid Riggs (drums).				
2/21/98	22	11	I Am A Pig	—		Voyeurs	Nothing 90155
			TYKETTO				
			Hard-rock group from Long Island, New York: Danny Vaughn (vocals), Brooke St. James (guitar), Jimi Kennedy (bass) and Michael Clayton (drums).				
5/11/91	39	4	1 Forever Young	—		Don't Come Easy	DGC 24317
8/3/91	25	7	2 Seasons	—		↓	
			TYLER, Bonnie				
			Born Gaynor Hopkins on 6/8/53 in Swansea, Wales. Female singer known for her raspy vocals.				
9/10/83	23	7	Total Eclipse Of The Heart	❶4	▲	Faster Than The Speed Of Night	Columbia 38710
			written and produced by **Jim Steinman**				
			TYPE O NEGATIVE				
			Hard-rock group from New York City: Peter Steele (vocals, bass), Kenny Hickey (guitar), Josh Silver (keyboards) and Johnny Kelly (drums).				
10/23/99	37	4	Everything Dies	—		World Coming Down	Roadrunner 8660

U

DEBUT	PEAK	WKS	Mainstream Rock Track	Pop	Gld	Album Title	Album Label & Number
			UB40				
			Reggae group formed in Birmingham, England: brothers Ali (vocals) and Robin (guitar, vocals) Campbell, Terence "Astro" Wilson (vocals), Norman Hassan (percussion), Michael Virtue (keyboards), Brian Travers (sax), Earl Falconer (bass) and James Brown (drums). Name taken from a British unemployment form.				
2/18/84	41	2	1 Red Red Wine	❶1	▲	Labour Of Love	A&M 4980
			#62 Pop hit for Neil Diamond in 1968				
8/17/85	40	5	2 I Got You Babe	28		Little Baggariddim	A&M 5090
			UB40 WITH CHRISSIE HYNDE				
			#1 Pop hit for Sonny & Cher in 1965				

DEBUT	PEAK	WKS	Mainstream Rock Track	Pop	Gld	Album Title	Album Label & Number

UFO
Hard-rock group formed in England: Phil Mogg (vocals), Paul Chapman (guitar), Neil Carter (keyboards), Pete Way (bass) and Andy Parker (drums). In 1986, Mogg fronted new lineup: Atomic Tommy M (guitar), Paul Raymond (keyboards), Paul Gray (bass) and Jim Simpson (drums).

| 3/6/82 | 23 | 8 | 1 The Writer | — | | Mechanix | Chrysalis 1360 |
| 4/19/86 | 47 | 2 | 2 This Time | — | | Misdemeanor | Chrysalis 41518 |

UGLY KID JOE
Rock group from Isla Vista, California: Whitfield Crane (vocals), Klaus Eichstadt and Dave Fortman (guitars), Cordell Crockett (bass), and Mark Davis (drums).

2/1/92	6	21	1 Everything About You	9	▲	As Ugly As They Want To Be	Stardog 868823
10/10/92	29	4	2 Neighbor	—	▲²	America's Least Wanted	Stardog 512571
2/6/93	3	14	3 Cats In The Cradle	6	↓		
			#1 Pop hit for Harry Chapin in 1974				
5/15/93	22	6	4 Busy Bee	—	↓		

ULTRAVOX
Electronic-rock group formed in England: Midge Ure (vocals, guitar), Billy Currie (keyboards), Chris Cross (bass) and Warren Cann (drums).

| 3/26/83 | 27 | 5 | 1 Reap The Wild Wind | 71 | | Quartet | Chrysalis 1394 |
| 5/12/84 | 55 | 2 | 2 One Small Day | — | | Lament | Chrysalis 41459 |

UNION
Rock group formed in Canada: Randy Bachman (vocals, guitar), Frank Ludwig (keyboards), Fred Turner (bass) and Chris Leighton (drums). Bachman and Turner were leaders of Bachman-Turner Overdrive.

| 8/1/81 | 38 | 6 | Mainstreet U.S.A. | — | | On Strike | Portrait 37368 |

UNION UNDERGROUND, The
Rock group from San Antonio: Bryan Scott (vocals, guitar), Patrick Kennison (guitar), John Moyer (bass) and Josh Memelo (drums).

7/8/00	11	26	1 Turn Me On "Mr. Deadman"	—		...An Education In Rebellion	Portrait 67778
1/6/01	13	15	2 Killing The Fly	—	↓		
5/19/01	26	10	3 Revolution Man	—	↓		
5/18/02	29	9	4 Across The Nation	—	●	WWF: Forceable Entry (various artists)	Columbia 85211

U.P.O.
Hard-rock group from Los Angeles: Shawn Albro (vocals), Chris Weber (guitar), Ben Shirley (bass) and Tommy Holt (drums).

| 4/22/00 | 6 | 26 | 1 Godless | — | | No Pleasantries | Epic 69869 |
| 11/18/00 | 25 | 12 | 2 Feel Alive | — | ↓ | | |

URE, Midge
Born James Ure on 10/10/53 in Glasgow, Scotland. Rock singer/guitarist. Member of **Ultravox**.

| 1/21/89 | 6 | 13 | Dear God | 95 | | Answers To Nothing | Chrysalis 41649 |

URGE OVERKILL
Rock trio from Chicago: Nash Kato (guitar), "Eddie" King Roeser (bass) and Blackie Onassis (drums). All share vocals.

7/31/93	10	17	1 Sister Havana	—		Saturation	Geffen 24529
12/25/93	40	2	2 Positive Bleeding	—	↓		
10/21/95	34	3	3 The Break	—		Exit The Dragon	Geffen 24818

URIAH HEEP
Hard-rock group from England. Numerous personnel changes. Lineup in 1982: Peter Goalby (vocals), Mick Box (guitar), John Sinclair (keyboards), Bob Daisley (bass) and Lee Kerslake (drums). Also see **Classic Rock Tracks** section.

| 8/14/82 | 25 | 4 | That's The Way That It Is | 106 | | Abominog | Mercury 4057 |

USA FOR AFRICA
USA: United Support of Artists. Collection of top artists formed to help starving people in Africa.

| 3/23/85 | 27 | 7 | We Are The World | ❶⁴ | ▲³ | We Are The World | Columbia 40043 |

UTOPIA
Pop-rock group: **Todd Rundgren** (vocals, guitar), Roger Powell (keyboards), Kasim Sulton (bass) and John Wilcox (drums).

| 10/23/82 | 31 | 6 | 1 Hammer In My Heart | — | | Utopia | Network 60183 |
| 2/11/84 | 30 | 5 | 2 Crybaby | — | | Oblivion | Passport 6029 |

U2 ★4★
Rock group formed in Dublin, Ireland: Paul "Bono" Hewson (vocals; born on 5/10/60), Dave "The Edge" Evans (guitar; born on 8/8/61), Adam Clayton (bass; born on 3/13/60) and Larry Mullen Jr. (drums; born on 10/30/61). Released concert tour documentary movie *Rattle And Hum* in 1988.

1)Mysterious Ways 2)Angel Of Harlem 3)With Or Without You 4)Desire 5)Even Better Than The Real Thing

4/18/81	20	11	1 I Will Follow	—	▲	Boy	Island 9646
3/12/83	2²	9	2 New Year's Day	53	▲⁴	War	Island 90067
4/16/83	7	17	3 Sunday Bloody Sunday	—	↓		
6/11/83	12	9	4 Two Hearts Beat As One	101	↓		
7/16/83	27	4	5 Surrender	—	↓		
12/10/83+	30	8	6 11 O'Clock Tick Tock	[L] —	▲³	Under A Blood Red Sky	Island 90127
			recorded on 5/6/83 in Boston				

DEBUT	PEAK	WKS	Mainstream Rock Track	Pop	Gld	Album Title	Album Label & Number
			U2 — Cont'd				
9/15/84	**2**³	21	7 Pride (In The Name Of Love)	33	▲³	*The Unforgettable Fire* . . . . Island 90231
			a tribute to Martin Luther King				
12/8/84+	**31**	9	8 Wire	—		↓
4/13/85	**45**	3	9 A Sort Of Homecoming	—		↓
6/22/85	**16**	10	10 Three Sunrises	—	▲	*Wide Awake In America* . . . . Island 90279
8/24/85	**19**	12	11 Bad	[L]	—	↓
3/21/87	**❶**⁵	13	12 With Or Without You	**❶**³	▲¹⁰	*The Joshua Tree* . . . . Island 90581
3/28/87	**2**⁴	19	13 I Still Haven't Found What I'm Looking For	**❶**²		↓
4/4/87	**11**	24	14 Where The Streets Have No Name	13		↓
4/4/87	**14**	18	15 Bullet The Blue Sky	—		↓
4/11/87+	**6**	12	16 In God's Country	44		↓
6/27/87	**11**	10	17 Spanish Eyes	—		(single only) . . . . Island 99430
9/10/88	**38**	3	18 Jesus Christ	—		*Folkways: A Vision Shared - A Tribute To Woody Guthrie And Leadbelly (various artists)* . . . . Columbia 44034
			written by Woody Guthrie				
10/1/88	**❶**⁵	11	19 Desire	3	▲⁵	*Rattle And Hum* . . . . Island 91003
10/22/88	**❶**⁶	18	20 Angel Of Harlem	14		↓
			a tribute to Billie Holiday				
10/22/88+	**2**¹	20	21 When Love Comes To Town	68		↓
			U2 WITH B.B. KING				
10/22/88+	**8**	20	22 God Part II	—		↓
			sequel to **John Lennon**'s 1970 recording "God"				
7/1/89	**13**	10	23 All I Want Is You	83		↓
8/5/89	**46**	1	24 Everlasting Love	—		(single only) . . . . Island 96550
			#13 Pop hit for Robert Knight in 1967				
11/10/90	**34**	5	25 Night And Day	—		*Red Hot + Blue (various artists)* . . . . . . Chrysalis 21799
			#1 Pop hit for Fred Astaire in 1932				
10/26/91	**2**¹	7	26 The Fly	61	▲⁸	*Achtung Baby* . . . . Island 10347
11/30/91	**❶**¹²	30	27 Mysterious Ways	9		↓
1/25/92	**2**¹	16	28 Who's Gonna Ride Your Wild Horses	35		↓
2/1/92	**5**	15	29 Until The End Of The World	—		↓
3/14/92	**❶**²	20	30 One	10		↓
7/4/92	**❶**³	17	31 Even Better Than The Real Thing	32		↓
7/10/93	**18**	3	32 Numb	61ᴬ	▲²	*Zooropa* . . . . Island 518047
7/24/93	**8**	10	33 Zooropa	—		↓
7/31/93	**12**	11	34 Stay (Faraway, So Close!)	61		↓
6/10/95	**❶**¹	19	35 Hold Me, Thrill Me, Kiss Me, Kill Me	16	▲²	*Batman Forever (soundtrack)* . . . . Atlantic 82759
1/25/97	**6**	9	36 Discothéque	10	▲	*Pop* . . . . Island 524334
3/15/97	**2**¹	18	37 Staring At The Sun	26		↓
7/5/97	**18**	8	38 Last Night On Earth	—		↓
10/24/98	**31**	6	39 Sweetest Thing	63	▲²	*The Best Of 1980-1990/The B-Sides* . . . . Island 524612
			recorded in 1987				
9/23/00	**14**	26	40 Beautiful Day	21	▲³	*All That You Can't Leave Behind* . . . . Interscope 524653
1/27/01	**19**	12	41 Walk On	118		↓
5/5/01	**21**	14	42 Elevation	116		↓
9/22/01	**35**	6	43 Stuck In A Moment You Can't Get Out Of	52		↓
9/28/02	**26**	8	44 Electrical Storm	77		*The Best Of 1990-2000* . . . . Interscope 063361

V

VAI, Steve
Born on 6/6/60 in Long Island, New York. Rock guitarist. With **Frank Zappa**'s band (1979-84), **David Lee Roth**'s band (1986-88) and **Whitesnake** (1989). Formed **Vai** in 1992 which featured vocalist Devin Townsend and fluctuating band members.

9/1/90	**38**	13	1 I Would Love To	[I]	—	●	*Passion and Warfare* . . . . Relativity 1037
10/9/93	**36**	3	2 In My Dreams With You	—		*Sex & Religion* . . . . Relativity 1132
			VAI				

VANDENBERG
Born on 1/31/54 in Holland. Hard-rock guitarist. His group: Bert Heerink (vocals), Dick Kemper (bass) and Jos Zoomer (drums). Vandenberg later joined **Whitesnake**.

| 1/15/83 | **5** | 21 | 1 Burning Heart | 39 | | *Vandenberg* . . . . Atco 90005 |
| 12/24/83 | **29** | 6 | 2 Friday Night | — | | *Heading For A Storm* . . . . Atco 90121 |

VANGELIS — see JON & VANGELIS

DEBUT	PEAK	WKS	Mainstream Rock Track	Pop	Gld	Album Title	Album Label & Number

VAN HALEN ★1★
Hard-rock group formed in Pasadena, California: **David Lee Roth** (vocals), Eddie Van Halen (guitar), Michael Anthony (bass) and Alex Van Halen (drums). The Van Halen brothers were born in Nijmegen, Holland; moved to Pasadena in 1968. **Sammy Hagar** replaced Roth as lead singer in 1985. Eddie married actress Valerie Bertinelli on 4/11/81. Hagar left in June 1996. Gary Cherone (**Extreme**) joined as lead singer in September 1996; left after one album. Roth briefly rejoined group in 1997. Also see **Classic Rock Tracks** section.

1)Jump 2)Me Wise Magic 3)Without You 4)Top Of The World 5)Runaround

DEBUT	PEAK	WKS	Mainstream Rock Track	Pop	Gld	Album Title	Album Label & Number
5/23/81	12	13	1 Mean Street	—	▲²	*Fair Warning*	Warner 3540
5/30/81	15	11	2 So This Is Love?	110	↓		
6/6/81	13	11	3 Unchained	—	↓		
6/13/81	29	6	4 Push Comes To Shove	—	↓		
2/6/82	❶²	15	5 (Oh) Pretty Woman	12	▲⁴	*Diver Down*	Warner 3677
			*#1 Pop hit for **Roy Orbison** in 1964*				
5/8/82	3	15	6 Dancing In The Street	38	↓		
			#2 Pop hit for Martha & The Vandellas in 1964				
5/8/82	17	12	7 Where Have All The Good Times Gone!	—	↓		
			first recorded by The Kinks in 1966				
5/8/82	33	10	8 Little Guitars	—	↓		
6/12/82	22	7	9 Secrets	—	↓		
6/12/82	42	3	10 The Full Bug	—	↓		
1/14/84	❶⁸	13	11 Jump	❶⁵	▲¹⁰	*1984 (MCMLXXXIV)*	Warner 23985
1/21/84	2¹	31	12 Panama	13	↓		
1/28/84	24	14	13 Hot For Teacher	56	↓		
2/4/84	2¹	21	14 I'll Wait	13	↓		
3/15/86	❶³	13	15 Why Can't This Be Love	3	▲⁵	*5150*	Warner 25394
4/5/86	6	18	16 Dreams	22	↓		
4/5/86	12	14	17 Best Of Both Worlds	—	↓		
4/19/86	4	23	18 Love Walks In	22	↓		
7/26/86	33	9	19 Summer Nights	—	↓		
5/14/88	❶³	10	20 Black And Blue	34	▲³	*OU812*	Warner 25732
6/4/88	❶¹	16	21 When It's Love	5	↓		
6/4/88	6	17	22 Feels So Good	35	↓		
6/4/88	50	3	23 Mine All Mine	—	↓		
6/18/88	2³	22	24 Finish What Ya Started	13	↓		
12/10/88	31	7	25 Cabo Wabo	—	↓		
6/8/91	❶²	11	26 Poundcake	—	▲³	*For Unlawful Carnal Knowledge*	Warner 26594
6/29/91	❶⁴	20	27 Runaround	—	↓		
6/29/91+	2⁴	46	28 Right Now	55	↓		
7/6/91	❶⁴	51	29 Top Of The World	27	↓		
2/22/92	7	17	30 The Dream Is Over	—	↓		
5/30/92	21	8	31 Man On A Mission	—	↓		
2/13/93	❶¹	9	32 Won't Get Fooled Again [L]	—	▲²	*LIVE: Right here, right now*	Warner 45198
			*#15 Pop hit for **The Who** in 1971*				
1/14/95	❶³	19	33 Don't Tell Me (What Love Can Do)	—	▲²	*Balance*	Warner 45760
2/4/95	36	5	34 The Seventh Seal	—	↓		
2/18/95	2⁴	23	35 Can't Stop Lovin' You	30	↓		
5/20/95	9	11	36 Amsterdam	—	↓		
8/5/95	27	9	37 Not Enough	97	↓		
5/4/96	❶²	19	38 Humans Being	—	●	*Twister (soundtrack)*	Warner Sunset 46254
10/19/96	❶⁶	26	39 Me Wise Magic	—	▲²	*Best Of Volume 1*	Warner 46332
11/2/96+	12	13	40 Can't Get This Stuff No More	—	↓		
3/7/98	❶⁶	12	41 Without You	—	●	*Van Halen III*	Warner 46662
5/2/98	6	13	42 Fire In The Hole	—	↓		
8/15/98	27	6	43 One I Want	—	↓		

VANNELLI, Gino
Born on 6/16/52 in Montreal. Pop singer/songwriter.

DEBUT	PEAK	WKS	Mainstream Rock Track	Pop	Gld	Album Title	Album Label & Number
6/1/85	34	8	Black Cars	42		*Black Cars*	HME 40077

VAN ZANT, Johnny, Band
Born in 1960 in Jacksonville, Florida. Rock singer. Brother of Ronnie (**Lynyrd Skynyrd**) and Donnie (**38 Special**) Van Zant. His band: Robbie Gay and Erik Lundgren (guitars), Danny Clausman (bass) and Robbie Morris (drums). Johnny and Donnie also recorded as Van Zant.

DEBUT	PEAK	WKS	Mainstream Rock Track	Pop	Gld	Album Title	Album Label & Number
6/20/81	23	7	1 (Who's) Right Or Wrong	—		*Round Two*	Polydor 6322
10/2/82	37	5	2 It's You	—		*The Last Of The Wild Ones*	Polydor 6355
3/30/85	16	10	3 I'm A Fighter	—		*Van-Zant*	Geffen 24059
6/15/85	27	5	4 You've Got To Believe In Love	102	↓		
			VAN-ZANT (above 2)				

DEBUT	PEAK	WKS	Mainstream Rock Track	Pop	Gld	Album Title	Album Label & Number

VAN ZANT, Johnny, Band — Cont'd

7/14/90	❶³	12	5 Brickyard Road	—		Brickyard Road .... Atlantic 82110
10/6/90	24	7	6 Hearts Are Gonna Roll..........	—		↓
			JOHNNY VANT ZANT (above 2)			
2/28/98	22	13	7 Rage	—		Brother To Brother .... CMC International 86236
3/17/01	33	5	8 Get What You Got Comin'	—		Van Zant II. .... CMC International 86301
			VAN ZANT (above 2)			

VAPORS, The
Pub-rock group from Guildford, Surrey, England: David Fenton (vocals), Ed Bazalgette (guitar), Steve Smith (bass) and Howard Smith (drums).

| 5/2/81 | 39 | 1 | Jimmie Jones .... | — | | Magnets .... Liberty 1090 |

VAST
Group is actually solo guitarist Jon Crosby. VAST: Visual Audio Sensory Theater.

| 10/31/98 | 38 | 4 | 1 Touched .... | — | | Visual Audio Sensory Theater .... Elektra 62173 |
| 9/2/00 | 18 | 11 | 2 Free .... | — | | Music For People .... Elektra 62511 |

★50★   VAUGHAN, Stevie Ray, and Double Trouble
Born on 10/3/54 in Dallas. Died in a helicopter crash on 8/27/90 (age 35). Blues-rock singer/guitarist. Brother of Jimmie Vaughan (of **The Fabulous Thunderbirds**). Stevie and Jimmie recorded together as **The Vaughan Brothers**. Double Trouble: Reese Wynans (keyboards), Tommy Shannon (bass) and Chris Layton (drums).
1)Crossfire 2)The Sky Is Crying 3)Telephone Song

8/13/83	20	9	1 Pride And Joy....................	—	▲²	Texas Flood .... Epic 38734
6/9/84	26	8	2 Voodoo Chile (Slight Return)	—	▲²	Couldn't Stand The Weather .... Epic 39304
			first recorded by Jimi Hendrix in 1968			
7/28/84	29	8	3 Cold Shot	—		↓
9/28/85	17	10	4 Look At Little Sister	—	▲	Soul To Soul............... Epic 40036
			first recorded by Hank Ballard in 1960			
11/23/85	17	9	5 Change It	—		↓
11/15/86	11	10	6 Superstition .... [L]	—	▲	Live Alive .... Epic 40511
			#1 Pop hit for **Stevie Wonder** in 1973			
2/14/87	19	8	7 Willie The Wimp .... [L]	—		↓
6/17/89	❶³	18	8 Crossfire	—	▲²	In Step .... Epic 45024
9/16/89	14	13	9 Tightrope	—		↓
12/16/89+	18	10	10 The House Is Rockin'...............	—		↓
4/7/90	46	3	11 Wall Of Denial	—		↓
9/29/90	7	7	12 Tick Tock	65	▲	Family Style .... Epic 46225
10/27/90+	3	19	13 Telephone Song	—		↓
2/9/91	18	11	14 Good Texan	—		↓
			THE VAUGHAN BROTHERS (above 3)			
11/9/91+	2¹	20	15 The Sky Is Crying	—	▲²	The Sky Is Crying............... Epic 47390
			recorded in 1985; written by Elmore James			
1/25/92	3	22	16 Empty Arms	—		↓
5/9/92	26	9	17 Little Wing	—		↓
			first recorded by Jimi Hendrix in 1968; above 2 recorded in 1984			
10/24/92	19	8	18 Shake For Me .... [L]	—		In The Beginning .... Epic 53168
			recorded on 4/1/80 in Austin, Texas			
11/18/95	32	5	19 Taxman	—	▲²	Greatest Hits .... Epic 66217
			first recorded by **The Beatles** in 1966			

VEDDER, Eddie
Born Edward Severson III (although he grew up with his step-father's last name of Mueller) on 12/23/64 in Evanston, Illinois; raised in San Diego. Lead singer of **Pearl Jam**. Legally changed his last name to Vedder (his mother's maiden name).

| 2/23/02 | 40 | 1 | You've Got To Hide Your Love Away .... | 117 | ● | I Am Sam (soundtrack)............... V2 27119 |
| | | | first recorded by **The Beatles** in 1965 | | | |

VEGA, Suzanne
Born on 8/12/59 in New York City. Singer/songwriter/guitarist. Married record producer Mitchell Froom (of **Gamma**) on 3/17/95.

5/23/87	15	11	1 Luka............................	3	▲	Solitude Standing .... A&M 5136
8/29/87	43	1	2 Solitude Standing	94		↓
5/12/90	47	2	3 Book Of Dreams	—		days of open Hand .... A&M 5293

VERA, Billy, & The Beaters
Born William McCord on 5/28/44 in Riverside, California; raised in Westchester County, New York. Pop singer/songwriter.

6/6/81	53	2	I Can Take Care Of Myself .... [L]	39		Billy & The Beaters .... Alfa 10001
			BILLY & THE BEATERS			
			recorded on 1/15/81 at the Roxy in Hollywood			

VERUCA SALT
Rock group from Chicago: Nina Gordon and Louise Post (vocals, guitar), with Steven Lack (bass) and Jim Shapiro (drums). Name taken from a character in the children's book Charlie and The Chocolate Factory.

2/22/97	9	26	1 Volcano Girls	59^A		Eight Arms To Hold You .... Outpost 30001
9/6/97	39	3	2 Shutterbug	—		↓
12/13/97	38	1	3 Straight	—		↓

VERVE, The
Rock group from Wigan, England: Richard Ashcroft (vocals), Nick McCabe (guitar), Simon Jones (bass) and Peter Salisbury (drums).

| 2/7/98 | 22 | 10 | ✓ Bitter Sweet Symphony .... | 12 | ▲ | Urban Hymns .... Virgin 44913 |

DEBUT	PEAK	WKS	Mainstream Rock Track	Pop	Gld	Album Title	Album Label & Number

VERVE PIPE, The
Rock group from East Lansing, Michigan: brothers Brian (vocals) and Brad (bass) Vander Ark, A.J. Dunning (guitar), Doug Corella (keyboards) and Donny Brown (drums).

4/27/96	17	11	1 Photograph	53[A] ▲		Villains	RCA 66809
9/21/96	35	3	2 Cup Of Tea	—		↓	
2/22/97	9	26	3 The Freshmen	5		↓	
7/26/97	24	9	4 Villains	—		↓	
8/14/99	38	2	5 Hero	—		The Verve Pipe	RCA 67664

VICTOR
Studio project formed by **Rush** guitarist Alex Lifeson. Features various studio musicians/vocalists.

12/30/95+	18	9	Promise	—		Victor	Atlantic 82852

VINES, The
Rock trio from Sydney, Australia: Craig Nicholls (vocals, guitar), Patrick Matthews (bass) and David Oliffe (drums).

7/6/02	27	14	Get Free	122	●	Highly Evolved	Engineroom 37527

VIRGOS MERLOT
Rock group from Birmingham, Alabama: Brett Hestla (vocals), Ted Ledbetter and Marchant (guitars), Chris Dickerson (bass) and JD Charlton (drums).

4/17/99	40	1	Gain	—		Signs Of A Vacant Soul	Atlantic 83157

VITALE, Joe
Born in Dundalk, Maryland. Rock singer/drummer.

8/1/81	47	9	Lady On The Rock	—		Plantation Harbor	Asylum 529

Joe Walsh and Don Felder (guitars)

VITO, Rick
Born on 10/13/49 in Darby, Pennsylvania. Session guitarist. Member of **Fleetwood Mac** from 1987-91.

3/7/92	36	5	Desiree	—		King Of Hearts	Modern 91789

Stevie Nicks (female vocal)

VIXEN
Female hard-rock group formed in Los Angeles: Janet Gardner (vocals, guitar), Jan Kuehnemund (guitar), Share Pedersen (bass) and Roxy Petrucci (drums). Pedersen later joined **Contraband**.

9/24/88	24	11	1 Edge Of A Broken Heart	26	●	Vixen	EMI-Manhattan 46991
1/14/89	22	9	2 Cryin'	22		↓	
7/28/90	11	12	3 How Much Love	44		Rev It Up	EMI 92923

W

WAITE, John
Born on 7/4/55 in Lancashire, England. Lead singer of The Babys and **Bad English**.

6/19/82	16	14	1 Change	54		Ignition	Chrysalis 1376
6/23/84	❶[2]	18	2 Missing You	❶[1]	●	No Brakes	EMI America 17124
8/25/84	8	15	3 Tears	37		↓	
2/9/85	28	5	4 Restless Heart	59		↓	
8/10/85	4	10	5 Every Step Of The Way	25		Mask Of Smiles	EMI America 17164
6/28/86	24	6	6 If Anybody Had A Heart	76		About Last Night... (soundtrack)	EMI America 17210
			co-produced by **Don Henley**				
6/13/87	6	11	7 These Times Are Hard For Lovers	53		Rover's Return	EMI America 17227

WAITRESSES, The
Pop-rock group from Akron, Ohio: Patty Donahue (vocals), Chris Butler (guitar), Dan Klayman (keyboards), Mars Williams (sax), Tracy Wormworth (bass) and Bill Ficca (drums; **Television**). Donahue died of cancer on 12/9/96 (age 40).

2/20/82	23	6	I Know What Boys Like	62		Wasn't Tomorrow Wonderful?	Polydor 6346

WALLFLOWERS, The
Pop-rock group formed in Los Angeles: Jakob Dylan (vocals), Michael Ward (guitar), Rami Jaffe (keyboards), Greg Richling (bass) and Mario Calire (drums). Dylan is the son of **Bob Dylan**.

6/22/96	10	26	1 6th Avenue Heartache	33[A] ▲[4]		Bringing Down The Horse	Interscope 90055
11/23/96+	❶[5]	30	2 One Headlight	2[5A]		↓	
5/17/97	3	23	3 The Difference	23[A]		↓	
10/11/97	21	12	4 Three Marlenas	51[A]		↓	
5/9/98	4	15	5 Heroes	27[A] ▲		Godzilla (soundtrack)	Epic 69338
			first recorded by **David Bowie** in 1977				
9/30/00	26	11	6 Sleepwalker	—	●	(Breach)	Interscope 490745

WALL OF VOODOO
Electronic-rock group formed in Los Angeles: **Stan Ridgway** (vocals), Marc Moreland (guitar), Chas T. Gray (bass) and Joe Nanini (drums). Moreland died of kidney failure on 3/13/2002 (age 44).

9/25/82	41	18	Mexican Radio	58		Call Of The West	I.R.S. 70026

DEBUT	PEAK	WKS	Mainstream Rock Track	Pop	Gld	Album Title	Album Label & Number

WALSH, Joe
Born on 11/20/47 in Wichita, Kansas. Rock singer/songwriter/guitarist. Member of the **Eagles**. Also see **Classic Rock Tracks** section.
1)A Life Of Illusion 2)Ordinary Average Guy 3)The Confessor

5/16/81	❶¹	14	1 A Life Of Illusion	34		There Goes The Neighborhood . . . . Asylum 523
5/30/81	36	6	2 Things	—		↓
			Timothy B. Schmit (backing vocal)			
6/6/81	35	8	3 Rivers (Of The Hidden Funk)	—		↓
9/11/82	20	7	4 Waffle Stomp	—		Fast Times At Ridgemont High (soundtrack) . . . . Full Moon 60158
7/9/83	21	6	5 Space Age Whiz Kids	52		You Bought It-You Name It . . . . Warner 23884
7/23/83	13	11	6 I Can Play That Rock & Roll	—		↓
5/11/85	8	13	7 The Confessor	—		The Confessor . . . . Warner 25281
6/20/87	8	8	8 The Radio Song	—		Got Any Gum? . . . . Warner 25606
7/25/87	14	8	9 In My Car	—		↓
			co-written by **Ringo Starr**			
5/4/91	3	13	10 Ordinary Average Guy	—		Ordinary Average Guy . . . . Pyramid 47384
7/20/91	13	9	11 All Of A Sudden	—		↓
8/22/92	10	5	12 Vote For Me	—		Songs For A Dying Planet . . . . Pyramid 48916

WANDERLUST
Rock group from Philadelphia: Scot Sax (vocals), Bob Bonfiglio (guitar), Mark Levin (bass) and Jim Cavanaugh (drums).

7/1/95	28	10	I Walked	—		Prize . . . . RCA 66575

WANG CHUNG
Pop-rock trio from London: Jack Hues (vocals, guitar, keyboards), Nick Feldman (bass, keyboards) and Darren Costin (drums). Costin left in 1985.

3/10/84	49	3	1 Don't Let Go	38		Points On The Curve . . . . Geffen 4004
3/17/84	24	15	2 Dance Hall Days	16		↓
11/2/85	21	12	3 To Live And Die In L.A.	41		To Live And Die In L.A. (soundtrack) . . . . Geffen 24081
10/11/86	25	8	4 Everybody Have Fun Tonight	2²	●	Mosaic . . . . Geffen 24115
6/3/89	31	5	5 Praying To A New God	63		The Warmer Side Of Cool . . . . Geffen 24222

WARRANT
Male hard-rock group from Los Angeles: Jani Lane (vocals), Erik Turner (guitar) and Joey Allen (guitars), Jerry Dixon (bass) and Steven Sweet (drums).

2/25/89	13	15	1 Down Boys	27	▲²	Dirty Rotten Filthy Stinking Rich . . . . . . Columbia 44383
7/1/89	3	16	2 Heaven	2²		↓
10/14/89	30	7	3 Big Talk	93		↓
1/20/90	11	11	4 Sometimes She Cries	20		↓
9/8/90	19	9	5 Cherry Pie	10	▲²	Cherry Pie . . . . Columbia 45487
12/1/90+	14	13	6 I Saw Red	10		↓
2/23/91	19	13	7 Uncle Tom's Cabin	78		↓
7/13/91	39	5	8 Blind Faith	88		↓
9/12/92	36	1	9 Machine Gun	—	●	Dog Eat Dog . . . . Columbia 52584

WATERBOYS, The
Rock group formed in London by Mike Scott (vocals, guitar; from Scotland) and Anthony Thistlethwaite (mandolin, saxophone). Numerous personnel changes. Keyboardist Karl Wallinger left in 1985 to form **World Party**.

3/4/89	48	1	World Party	—		Fisherman's Blues . . . . Chrysalis 41589

WATERS, Roger
Born George Roger Waters on 9/6/44 in Cambridgeshire, England. Former leader/bassist of **Pink Floyd**. Went solo in 1983.

5/5/84	17	10	1 5:01AM (The Pros And Cons Of Hitch Hiking)	110	●	The Pros And Cons Of Hitch Hiking . . . Columbia 39290
6/6/87	12	10	2 Radio Waves	—		Radio K.A.O.S. . . . . Columbia 40795
7/18/87	15	10	3 Sunset Strip	—		↓
8/29/92	4	9	4 What God Wants, Part I	—		Amused To Death . . . . Columbia 47127

WAX
Pop duo: Andrew Gold and Graham Gouldman (of 10cc).

4/12/86	39	3	Right Between The Eyes	43		Magnetic Heaven . . . . RCA 9546

WEEZER
Rock group from Los Angeles: Rivers Cuomo (vocals, guitar), Brian Bell (guitar), Matt Sharp (bass) and Patrick Wilson (drums). Scott Shriner replaced Sharp in 1998.

10/1/94	30	7	1 Undone-The Sweater Song	57	▲³	Weezer . . . . DGC 24629
2/4/95	34	4	2 Buddy Holly	18ᴬ		↓
6/16/01	24	15	3 Hash Pipe	106	▲	Weezer . . . . Geffen 493045

WELCH, Bob
Born on 7/31/46 in Los Angeles. Pop-rock singer/guitarist. Member of **Fleetwood Mac** from 1971-74. Also see **Classic Rock Tracks** section.

1/16/82	45	4	It's What Ya Don't Say	—		Bob Welch . . . . Capitol 4107

WHISKEYTOWN
Rock duo from Jacksonville, North Carolina: Ryan Adams (male vocals, guitar) and Caitlin Cary (female vocals, fiddle).

3/14/98	35	4	Yesterday's News	—		Strangers Almanac . . . . Outpost 30005

DEBUG	PEAK	WKS	Mainstream Rock Track	Pop	Gld	Album Title	Album Label & Number

WHITE LION
Rock group formed in Brooklyn, New York: Mike Tramp (vocals), Vito Bratta (guitar), James Lomenzo (bass) and Greg D'Angelo (drums). Lomenzo and D'Angelo left in 1991, replaced by Tommy Caradonna and Jimmy DeGrasso (of Y&T).

DEBUT	PEAK	WKS	Track	Pop	Gld	Album	Label
1/9/88	18	19	1 Wait	8	▲²	Pride	Atlantic 81768
4/23/88	25	9	2 Tell Me	58	↓		
12/24/88+	7	10	3 When The Children Cry	3	↓		
6/17/89	12	11	4 Little Fighter	52	●	Big Game	Atlantic 81969
4/20/91	24	9	5 Love Don't Come Easy	—		Mane Attraction	Atlantic 82193

WHITESNAKE
Hard-rock group formed in England. Numerous personnel changes. Lineup in 1984: David Coverdale (vocals), John Sykes and Mel Galley (guitars), Neil Murray (bass) and Cozy Powell (drums; **Emerson Lake & Powell**). Lineup in 1987: Coverdale, Sykes, Murray and Aynsley Dunbar (drums; **Jefferson Starship**). Sykes left to form **Blue Murder**. Lineup in 1989: Coverdale, **Steve Vai** and Adrian **Vandenberg** (guitars), Rudy Sarzo (bass) and Tommy Aldridge (drums).
1)Fool For Your Loving 2)The Deeper The Love 3)Here I Go Again

DEBUT	PEAK	WKS	Track	Pop	Gld	Album	Label
6/2/84	17	16	1 Slow An' Easy	—	▲²	Slide It In	Geffen 4018
8/25/84	33	9	2 Love Ain't No Stranger	—	↓		
3/21/87	18	14	3 Still Of The Night	79	▲⁸	Whitesnake	Geffen 24099
5/30/87	4	19	4 Here I Go Again	❶¹	↓		
8/29/87	13	16	5 Is This Love	2¹	↓		
11/28/87+	22	12	6 Give Me All Your Love	48	↓		
11/4/89	2⁴	13	7 Fool For Your Loving	37	▲	Slip Of The Tongue	Geffen 24249
11/18/89	32	9	8 Judgment Day	—	↓		
1/20/90	4	12	9 The Deeper The Love	28	↓		
5/5/90	15	8	10 Now You're Gone	96	↓		

WHITE TRASH
Hard-rock group from New York City: Dave Alvin (vocals), Ethan Collins (guitar), Aaron Collins (bass) and Mike Caldarella (drums).

DEBUT	PEAK	WKS	Track	Pop	Gld	Album	Label
7/6/91	39	7	Apple Pie	—		White Trash	Elektra 61053

WHITE ZOMBIE
Hard-rock group formed in New York City: **Rob Zombie** (vocals), Jay Yuenger (guitar), Sean Yseult (bass) and John Tempesta (drums). Group named after a 1932 Bela Lugosi movie.

DEBUT	PEAK	WKS	Track	Pop	Gld	Album	Label
10/2/93	26	13	1 Thunder Kiss '65	—	▲²	La Sexorcisto: Devil Music Volume One	Geffen 24460
2/5/94	39	2	2 Black Sunshine	—	↓		
4/22/95	10	26	3 More Human Than Human	53ᴬ	▲²	Astro-Creep: 2000	Geffen 24806
9/9/95	27	8	4 Electric Head Pt. 2 (The Ecstasy)	—	↓		
2/10/96	39	1	5 Super-Charger Heaven	—	↓		

WHITLEY, Chris
Born on 8/31/60 in Houston; raised in Vermont. Male singer/songwriter/guitarist.

DEBUT	PEAK	WKS	Track	Pop	Gld	Album	Label
7/27/91	28	8	1 Living With The Law	—		Living With The Law	Columbia 46966
10/19/91	36	8	2 Big Sky Country	—	↓		

★94★ WHO, The
Rock group formed in London: **Roger Daltrey** (vocals), **Pete Townshend** (guitar, vocals), **John Entwistle** (bass) and Keith Moon (drums). Moon died of a drug overdose on 9/7/78 (age 31), replaced by Kenney Jones. Disbanded in 1982; reunited several times. Jones formed **The Law** with **Paul Rodgers** in 1991. Enwistle died of a heart attack on 6/27/2002 (age 57). Group was inducted into the Rock and Roll Hall of Fame in 1990. Won Grammy's Lifetime Achievement Award in 2001. Also see **Classic Rock Tracks** section.
1)You Better You Bet 2)Athena 3)Eminence Front

DEBUT	PEAK	WKS	Track	Pop	Gld	Album	Label
3/21/81	❶⁵	15	1 You Better You Bet	18	▲	Face Dances	Warner 3516
4/4/81	6	16	2 Another Tricky Day	—	↓		
4/4/81	36	1	3 Daily Records	—	↓		
4/4/81	38	1	4 Did You Steal My Money	—	↓		
4/4/81	51	1	5 You	—	↓		
4/11/81	50	1	6 How Can You Do It Alone	—	↓		
9/4/82	3	25	7 Athena	28	●	It's Hard	Warner 23731
9/18/82	5	19	8 Eminence Front	68	↓		
9/25/82	34	4	9 Cry If You Want	—	↓		
10/2/82	38	11	10 Dangerous	—	↓		
10/2/82	39	2	11 It's Hard	—	↓		
7/8/89	9	9	12 Dig	—		The Iron Man: The Musical by Pete Townshend	Atlantic 81996
7/8/89	44	2	13 Fire	—	↓		

#2 Pop hit for The Crazy World Of Arthur Brown in 1968

DEBUT	PEAK	WKS	Track	Pop	Gld	Album	Label
11/2/91	8	13	14 Saturday Night's Alright For Fighting	—	▲	Two Rooms - Celebrating The Songs Of Elton John & Bernie Taupin (various artists)	Polydor 845750

#12 Pop hit for **Elton John** in 1973

WHY STORE, The
Rock group from Indianapolis: Chris Shaffer (vocals), Michael David Smith (guitar), Jeff Pedersen (keyboards), Greg Gardner (bass) and Charlie Bushor (drums).

DEBUT	PEAK	WKS	Track	Pop	Gld	Album	Label
7/13/96	27	11	1 Lack Of Water	—		The Why Store	Way Cool 11420
11/23/96	32	7	2 Father	—	↓		

DEBUT	PEAK	WKS	Mainstream Rock Track	Pop	Gld	Album Title	Album Label & Number
			WIDESPREAD PANIC				
			Rock group from Athens, Georgia: John Bell (vocals, guitar), Michael Houser (guitar), John Hermann (keyboards), Domingo Ortiz (percussion), Dave Schools (bass) and Todd Nance (drums). Houser died of cancer on 8/10/2002 (age 40).				
3/4/95	34	4	1 Can't Get High	—		Ain't Life Grand...................	Capricorn 42027
2/8/97	13	14	2 Hope In A Hopeless World	—		Bombs & Butterflies	Capricorn 534396
			WILCO				
			Rock group from Chicago: Jeff Tweedy (vocals, guitar), Jay Bennett (guitar), John Stirratt (bass) and Ken Coomer (drums).				
3/8/97	22	8	Outtasite (Outta Mind)	—		Being There......................	Reprise 46236
			WILDE, Danny				
			Born in Maine; raised in California. Singer/songwriter/guitarist. Member of **Great Buildings** and **The Rembrandts**.				
7/12/86	35	6	1 Isn't It Enough	—		The Boyfriend	Island 90497
1/30/88	15	11	2 Time Runs Wild	—		Any Man's Hunger.................	Geffen 24179
			WILDE, Kim				
			Born Kim Smith on 11/18/60 in Chiswick, England. Pop-rock singer. Daughter of singer Marty Wilde.				
4/24/82	29	10	1 Kids In America	25		Kim Wilde......................	EMI America 17065
5/15/82	53	2	2 Water On Glass	—		↓	
			WILDER, Webb				
			Born John Webb Wilder in Hattiesburg, Mississippi. Singer/songwriter/guitarist.				
1/25/92	16	11	Tough It Out	—		Doo Dad	Praxis 11010
			WILL AND THE KILL				
			Rock group from Austin, Texas: Will Sexton (vocals, guitar), David Grissom (guitar), Alex Napier (bass) and Jeff Boaz (drums). Sexton is the younger brother of **Charlie Sexton**.				
3/19/88	28	8	Heart Of Steel	—		Will And The Kill	MCA 42054
			WILLIAMS, John — see TOWNSHEND, Pete				
			WILLIE AND THE POOR BOYS				
			All-star rock group: Andy Fairweather Low and Mickey Gee (guitars), Geraint Watkins (keyboards), Bill Wyman (bass) and Charlie Watts (drums). Wyman and Watts are members of **The Rolling Stones**.				
5/18/85	35	7	Baby Please Don't Go	—		Willie And The Poor Boys	Passport 6047
			WILSON, Ann				
			Born on 6/19/51 in San Diego. Lead singer of **Heart**.				
12/6/86+	5	11	1 The Best Man In The World	61		The Golden Child (soundtrack)......	Capitol 12544
1/14/89	42	1	2 Surrender To Me	6		Tequila Sunrise (soundtrack)	Capitol 91185
			ANN WILSON AND ROBIN ZANDER				
			WILSON, Brian				
			Born on 6/20/42 in Hawthorne, California. Leader of The Beach Boys.				
7/30/88	40	4	Love And Mercy	—		Brian Wilson.....................	Sire 25669
			WINGER				
			Hard-rock group formed in New York City: Kip Winger (vocals, bass), Reb Beach (guitar), Paul Taylor (keyboards; left in 1992) and Rod Morgenstein (drums). Kip was a member of **Alice Cooper**'s band. Morgenstein was a member of **The Dregs**. Also see **Fiona**.				
9/24/88	27	9	1 Madalaine		▲	Winger..........................	Atlantic 81867
1/21/89	19	9	2 Seventeen	26	↓		
5/20/89	8	16	3 Headed For A Heartbreak	19	↓		
9/30/89	34	5	4 Hungry	85	↓		
7/14/90	6	15	5 Can't Get Enuff	42	▲	In The Heart Of The Young	Atlantic 82103
10/6/90	14	16	6 Miles Away	12	↓		
1/19/91	20	12	7 Easy Come Easy Go	41	↓		
5/8/93	15	15	8 Down Incognito	—		Pull............................	Atlantic 82485
			WINTER, Johnny				
			Born on 2/23/44 in Leland, Mississippi. Blues-rock singer/guitarist. Brother of Edgar Winter.				
10/29/88	43	3	1 Rain	—		The Winter Of '88	MCA 42241
8/17/91	36	6	2 Illustrated Man.....................................	—		Let Me In........................	Pointblank 91744

WINWOOD, Steve ★26★

Born on 5/12/48 in Birmingham, England. Rock singer/keyboardist/guitarist. First performed with his older brother, producer Muff Winwood, in 1961. Lead singer of Spencer Davis Group, Blind Faith and **Traffic**.

1)Higher Love 2)Roll With It 3)One And Only Man

3/21/81	2²	12	1 While You See A Chance	7	▲	Arc Of A Diver	Island 9576
3/21/81	11	11	2 Arc Of A Diver	48	↓		
8/7/82	8	25	3 Still In The Game	47		Talking Back To The Night	Island 9777
9/4/82	13	11	4 Valerie	70	↓		
			also see #11 below				

DEBUT	PEAK	WKS	Mainstream Rock Track	Pop	Gld	Album Title	Album Label & Number
			WINWOOD, Steve — Cont'd				
6/14/86	❶⁴	14	5 Higher Love	❶¹	▲³	*Back In The High Life*	Island 25448
			Chaka Khan (backing vocal)				
7/19/86	3	16	6 Split Decision	—	↓		
			Joe Walsh (guitar)				
8/9/86	33	11	7 Take It As It Comes	—	↓		
9/6/86	4	14	8 Freedom Overspill	20	↓		
			Joe Walsh (slide guitar)				
11/22/86	19	10	9 Back In The High Life Again	13	↓		
			James Taylor (backing vocal)				
2/7/87	5	14	10 The Finer Things	8	↓		
10/10/87	13	11	11 Valerie .... [R]	9	▲	*Chronicles*	Island 25660
			new version of #4 above				
1/16/88	17	9	12 Talking Back To The Night	57	↓		
6/11/88	❶⁴	11	13 Roll With It	❶⁴	▲²	*Roll With It*	Virgin 90946
7/2/88	❶²	17	14 Don't You Know What The Night Can Do?	6	↓		
7/2/88	2¹	19	15 Holding On	11	↓		
7/9/88+	22	10	16 Hearts On Fire	53	↓		
10/29/88	25	7	17 Put On Your Dancing Shoes	—	↓		
11/3/90	❶²	14	18 One And Only Man	18	●	*Refugees of the Heart*	Virgin 91405
1/5/91	10	11	19 Another Deal Goes Down	—	↓		
			WOLF, Peter Born Peter Blankfield on 3/7/46 in the Bronx, New York. Lead singer of the **J. Geils Band**. Married to actress Faye Dunaway from 1974-79. Not to be confused with the producer of the same name.				
7/14/84	6	11	1 Lights Out	12		*Lights Out*	EMI America 17121
8/18/84	26	8	2 Crazy	—	↓		
10/20/84	22	11	3 I Need You Tonight	36	↓		
2/28/87	❶¹	12	4 Come As You Are	15		*Come As You Are*	EMI America 17230
4/18/87	16	9	5 Can't Get Started	75	↓		
2/24/90	9	7	6 99 Worlds	78		*Up To No Good!*	MCA 6349
			WONDER, Stevie — see McCARTNEY, Paul				
			WOOD, Ron Born on 6/1/47 in Hillingdon, Middlesex, England. Rock singer/guitarist. Member of the **Jeff Beck** Group and **The Rolling Stones**.				
9/5/92	30	7	Show Me	—		*Slide On This*	Continuum 19210
			WORLD PARTY Group is actually singer/keyboardist Karl Wallinger (born on 10/19/57 in Prestatyn, Wales). Wallinger was also a member of The Waterboys.				
12/20/86+	5	17	1 Ship Of Fools (Save Me From Tomorrow)	27		*Private Revolution*	Chrysalis 41552
5/19/90	21	11	2 Way Down Now	—		*Goodbye Jumbo*	Ensign 21654
8/4/90	33	8	3 Put The Message In The Box	—	↓		
6/5/93	38	2	4 Is It Like Today?	—		*Bang!*	Ensign 21991
			WORLD TRADE Rock group from New York City: Billy Sherwood (vocals, bass), Bruce Gowdy (guitar), Guy Allison (keyboards) and Mark Williams (drums).				
8/26/89	33	5	The Revolution Song	—		*World Trade*	Polydor 839626
			WRABIT Rock group from Canada: Lou Nadeau (vocals), David Aplin and John Albani (guitars), Les Paulhus (keyboards), Chris Brockway (bass) and Scott Jefferson Steck (drums).				
2/13/82	17	8	Anyway Anytime	—		*Wrabit*	MCA 5268
			WRIGHT, Gary Born on 4/26/43 in Creskill, New Jersey. Singer/songwriter/keyboardist. Also see **Classic Rock Tracks** section.				
7/18/81	17	17	Really Wanna Know You	16		*The Right Place*	Warner 3511
			WYLDE, Zakk Born on 1/14/67 in Jersey City, New Jersey. Singer/guitarist. Former member of **Ozzy Osbourne**'s band and **Pride & Glory**.				
7/13/96	28	8	Between Heaven And Hell	—		*Book Of Shadows*	Geffen 24964

X

			X Rock group formed in Los Angeles: **Exene Cervenka** (vocals), Billy Zoom (guitar), **John Doe** (bass) and Don Bonebrake (drums).				
8/10/85	27	9	Burning House Of Love	—		*Ain't Love Grand*	Elektra 60430
			X-ECUTIONERS, The Rap production group from New York City: Mista Sinista, Rob Swift, Total Eclipse and Roc Raida.				
3/16/02	29	7	It's Goin' Down	85		*Built From Scratch*	Loud 86410

DEBUT	PEAK	WKS	Mainstream Rock Track	Pop	Gld	Album Title	Album Label & Number

XTC
Rock group formed in Wiltshire, England: Andy Partridge (guitar), Dave Gregory (keyboards), Colin Moulding (bass) and Terry Chambers (drums). All share vocals. Chambers left in 1986.

DEBUT	PEAK	WKS	Track	Pop	Gld	Album Title	Label & Number
3/21/81	28	3	1 Generals And Majors	104		Black Sea	Virgin 13147
4/24/82	38	3	2 Senses Working Overtime	—		English Settlement	Epic 37943
4/4/87	37	6	3 Dear God	—		Skylarking	Geffen 24117
2/25/89	15	13	4 The Mayor Of Simpleton	72		Oranges & Lemons	Geffen 24218
7/8/89	38	4	5 King For A Day	—		↓	
5/23/92	46	1	6 The Ballad Of Peter Pumpkinhead	—		Nonsuch	Geffen 24474

Y

Y&T
Hard-rock group from San Francisco: Dave Meniketti (vocals, guitar), Joey Alves (guitar), Philip Kennemore (bass) and Leonard Haze (drums). Jimmy DeGrasso replaced Haze in 1986. Stef Burns replaced Alves in 1989. Y&T: Yesterday & Today.

DEBUT	PEAK	WKS	Track	Pop	Gld	Album Title	Label & Number
9/10/83	25	5	1 Mean Streak	—		Mean Streak	A&M 4960
8/11/84	33	10	2 Don't Stop Runnin'	—		In Rock We Trust	A&M 5007
7/20/85	16	10	3 Summertime Girls	55		Open Fire	A&M 5076
11/30/85	48	2	4 All American Boy	—		Down For The Count	A&M 5101
6/20/87	41	3	5 Contagious	—		Contagious	Geffen 24142
5/26/90	31	8	6 Don't Be Afraid Of The Dark	—		Ten	Geffen 24283

YANKOVIC, "Weird Al"
Born on 10/23/59 in Lynwood, California. Novelty singer/accordionist. Specializes in song parodies. Starred in the movie *UHF*.

DEBUT	PEAK	WKS	Track	Pop	Gld	Album Title	Label & Number
3/17/84	38	2	1 Eat It **[N]**	12	▲	"Weird Al" Yankovic In 3-D	Rock 'n' Roll 39221
			parody of "Beat It" by **Michael Jackson**				
4/25/92	35	2	2 Smells Like Nirvana **[N]**	35	●	Off The Deep End	Scotti Brothers 75256
			parody of "Smells Like Teen Spirit" by **Nirvana**				

YES ★28★

Progressive-rock group formed in London. Original lineup: **Jon Anderson** (vocals), Peter Banks (guitar), Tony Kaye (keyboards), Chris Squire (bass) and Bill Bruford (drums). Numerous personnel changes. Banks later formed Flash and **After The Fire**. Group disbanded in 1980. Re-formed in 1983 with Anderson, **Trevor Rabin** (guitar), Kaye, Squire and Alan White (drums). Anderson left in 1988. Anderson, Bruford, Rick Wakeman and Steve Howe formed self-named group in early 1989. Yes reunited in 1991 with Anderson, Bruford, Wakeman, Howe, Kaye, Squire, White and Rabin. Bruford, Wakeman and Howe had left group by 1994. Lineup in 1996: Anderson, Howe, Squire, Wakeman and White. Billy Sherwood replaced Wakeman in 1997. Also see **Classic Rock Tracks** section.

1)Lift Me Up 2)Owner Of A Lonely Heart 3)Love Will Find A Way 4)Rhythm Of Love 5)Brother Of Mine

DEBUT	PEAK	WKS	Track	Pop	Gld	Album Title	Label & Number
11/12/83	❶⁴	20	1 Owner Of A Lonely Heart	❶² ▲³		90125	Atco 90125
11/12/83	32	2	2 Our Song	—		↓	
11/26/83+	6	18	3 Changes	—		↓	
12/3/83+	5	17	4 It Can Happen	51		↓	
2/11/84	3	16	5 Leave It	24		↓	
3/17/84	43	2	6 Hold On	—		↓	
11/16/85	27	8	7 Hold On **[L-R]**	—		9012Live - The Solos	Atco 90474
			live version of #6 above				
10/3/87	❶³	11	8 Love Will Find A Way	30	▲	Big Generator	Atco 90522
10/10/87	2⁶	20	9 Rhythm Of Love	40		↓	
11/14/87+	11	16	10 Shoot High Aim Low	—		↓	
2/20/88	20	9	11 Final Eyes	—		↓	
6/3/89	2²	12	12 Brother Of Mine	—	●	Anderson, Bruford, Wakeman, Howe	Arista 90126
8/12/89	24	7	13 Order Of The Universe	—		↓	
			ANDERSON, BRUFORD, WAKEMAN, HOWE (above 2)				
4/20/91	❶⁶	16	14 Lift Me Up	86	●	Union	Arista 8643
6/22/91	9	10	15 Saving My Heart	—		↓	
8/24/91	49	2	16 I Would Have Waited Forever	—		↓	
8/24/91	36	5	17 Make It Easy	—		Yesyears	Atco 91644
			recorded in 1981				
3/12/94	3	13	18 The Calling	—		Talk	Victory 480033
6/11/94	24	7	19 Walls	—		↓	
11/22/97	33	7	20 Open Your Eyes	—		Open Your Eyes	Beyond 3074

DEBUT	PEAK	WKS	Mainstream Rock Track	Pop Gld	Album Title	Album Label & Number
	★47★		**YOUNG, Neil**			
			Born on 11/12/45 in Toronto. Rock singer/songwriter/guitarist. Member of Buffalo Springfield and **Crosby, Stills, Nash & Young**. Appeared in the 1987 movie *Made In heaven*. Inducted into the Rock and Roll Hall of Fame in 1995. Also see **Classic Rock Tracks** section.			
			1)Rockin' In The Free World 2)Mansion On The Hill 3)Ten Men Workin' 4)Downtown 5)No More			
11/28/81+	22	16	1 Southern Pacific..	70	*Re-ac-tor*	Reprise 2304
1/9/82	56	2	2 Surfer Joe And Moe The Sleaze	—	↓	
			NEIL YOUNG & CRAZY HORSE (above 2)			
1/22/83	12	10	3 Little Thing Called Love	71	*Trans.*	Geffen 2018
2/5/83	14	8	4 Mr. Soul	—	↓	
2/12/83	42	1	5 We R In Control	—	↓	
7/26/86	8	10	6 Touch The Night	—	*Landing On Water*..................	Geffen 24109
9/20/86	33	6	7 Weight Of The World	—	↓	
6/20/87	14	8	8 Long Walk Home	—	*Life*	Geffen 24154
			NEIL YOUNG & CRAZY HORSE			
4/16/88	6	11	9 Ten Men Workin'	—	*This Note's For You*..............	Reprise 25719
5/28/88	19	12	10 This Note's For You	—	↓	
			NEIL YOUNG & THE BLUENOTES (above 2)			
9/23/89	2[1]	17	11 Rockin' In The Free World	—	● *Freedom*	Reprise 25899
12/23/89+	7	13	12 No More	—	↓	
3/24/90	34	6	13 Crime In The City (Sixty To Zero Part I)	—	↓	
9/15/90	3	10	14 Mansion On The Hill	—	*Ragged Glory*	Reprise 26315
12/8/90+	33	9	15 Over And Over..	—	↓	
3/23/91	49	1	16 Love To Burn	—	↓	
			NEIL YOUNG & CRAZY HORSE (above 3)			
11/14/92	7	11	17 War Of Man	—	▲[2] *Harvest Moon*	Reprise 45057
3/20/93	38	3	18 Unknown Legend	—	↓	
7/3/93	34	4	19 Long May You Run .... [L]	—	● *Unplugged*....................	Reprise 45310
			recorded on 2/7/93			
8/21/93	26	7	20 My Back Pages .... [L]	—	● *Bob Dylan - The 30th Anniversary Concert (various artists)*	Columbia 53230
			BOB DYLAN & FRIENDS: Roger McGuinn, Tom Petty, Neil Young, Eric Clapton & George Harrison			
			recorded on 10/16/92 at Madison Square Garden; #30 Pop hit for The Byrds in 1967			
8/27/94	18	9	21 Change Your Mind	—	● *Sleeps With Angels*	Reprise 45749
			NEIL YOUNG & CRAZY HORSE			
7/1/95	6	13	22 Downtown	—	● *Mirror Ball*	Reprise 45934
9/23/95	34	5	23 Peace And Love	—	↓	
7/27/96	35	5	24 Big Time..	—	*Broken Arrow*...............	Reprise 46291
			NEIL YOUNG & CRAZY HORSE			
1/5/02	32	10	25 Let's Roll	—	*Are You Passionate?*............	Reprise 48111
			YOUNG, Paul			
			Born on 1/17/56 in Bedfordshire, England. Pop-rock singer.			
3/10/84	33	7	1 Come Back And Stay.......................................	22	*No Parlez*	Columbia 38976
5/25/85	14	11	2 Everytime You Go Away	❶[1] ●	*The Secret Of Association*	Columbia 39957
			first recorded by **Daryl Hall & John Oates** in 1980			
12/6/86	43	6	3 Some People	65	*Between Two Fires*..............	Columbia 40543

Z

			ZANDER, Robin			
			Born on 1/23/53 in Rockford, Illinois. Lead singer of **Cheap Trick**.			
1/14/89	42	1	1 Surrender To Me	6	*Tequila Sunrise (soundtrack)*	Capitol 91185
			ANN WILSON AND ROBIN ZANDER			
7/3/93	13	9	2 I've Always Got You......................................	—	*Robin Zander*....................	Interscope 92204
			ZAPPA, Frank			
			Born on 12/21/40 in Baltimore; raised in California. Died of cancer on 12/4/93 (age 52). Rock music's leading satirist. Singer/songwriter/guitarist/activist. Formed The Mothers Of Invention in 1965. In the movies *200 Motels* and *Baby Snakes*. Father of Dweezil and Moon Unit Zappa. Inducted into the Rock and Roll Hall of Fame in 1995. Won Grammy's Lifetime Achievement Award in 1997. Also see **Classic Rock Tracks** section.			
6/19/82	12	8	Valley Girl	32	*Ship arriving too late to save a drowning witch*	Barking Pumpkin 38066
			featuring Zappa's daughter Moon Unit			
			ZEBRA			
			Rock trio from New Orleans: Randy Jackson (vocals, guitar), Felix Hanemann (bass) and Guy Gelso (drums).			
5/28/83	10	20	1 Who's Behind The Door?	61 ●	*Zebra*........................	Atlantic 80054
7/16/83	29	8	2 Tell Me What You Want	107	↓	
9/22/84	15	10	3 Bears	—	*No Tellin' Lies*	Atlantic 80159

DEBUT	PEAK	WKS	Mainstream Rock Track	Pop Gld	Album Title	Album Label & Number

ZEVON, Warren
Born on 1/24/47 in Chicago. Rock singer/songwriter/pianist. Also see **Hindu Love Gods** and **Classic Rock Tracks** section.

9/11/82	24	5	1 Let Nothing Come Between You	—	The Envoy	Asylum 60159
5/30/87	9	9	2 Sentimental Hygiene	—	Sentimental Hygiene	Virgin 90603
8/15/87	44	3	3 Detox Mansion	—	↓	
11/11/89	30	6	4 Run Straight Down	—	Transverse City	Virgin 91068

ZOMBIE, Rob
Born Robert Cummings on 1/12/66 in Haverhill, Massachusetts. Founder of **White Zombie**.

8/22/98	6	36	1 Dragula	116 ▲³	Hellbilly Deluxe	Geffen 25212
1/30/99	7	26	2 Living Dead Girl	—	↓	
8/7/99	26	11	3 Superbeast	—	↓	
7/29/00	25	7	4 Scum Of The Earth	— ●	Mission: Impossible 2 (soundtrack)	Hollywood 62244
10/13/01	10	17	5 Feel So Numb	— ●	The Sinister Urge	Geffen 493147
1/26/02	11	26	6 Never Gonna Stop	—	↓	
7/13/02	13	15	7 Demon Speeding	—	↓	

ZOO, The
Grouping of rock veterans spearheaded by drummer **Mick Fleetwood** with vocalists Billy Thorpe and Bekka Bramlett (the daughter of Delaney & Bonnie Bramlett), guitarist Gregg Wright, keyboardist Brett Tuggle (formerly with **David Lee Roth**) and bassist Tom Lilly. Billy Burnette was an early member. Like Burnette, Bramlett later joined **Fleetwood Mac**.

7/4/92	19	8	Shakin' The Cage	—	Shakin' The Cage	Capricorn 42004

ZZ TOP ★11★
Rock trio formed in Houston: Billy Gibbons (vocals, guitar; born on 12/16/49), Dusty Hill (vocals, bass; born on 5/19/49) and Frank Beard (drums; born on 6/11/49). Gibbons and Hill are noted for their long beards. Group appeared in the movie *Back To The Future III*. Dusty is the brother of **Rocky Hill**. Also see **Classic Rock Tracks** section.

1)My Head's In Mississippi 2)Doubleback 3)Pincushion 4)Concrete And Steel 5)Stages

8/8/81	4	17	√1 Tube Snake Boogie	103 ●	El Loco	Warner 3593
8/15/81	28	12	2 Pearl Necklace	—	↓	
4/16/83	2³	14	√3 Gimme All Your Lovin	37 ▲¹⁰	Eliminator	Warner 23774
4/16/83	18	15	4 Got Me Under Pressure	—	↓	
7/9/83	8	14	√5 Sharp Dressed Man	56	↓	
12/10/83	38	7	6 TV Dinners	—	↓	
4/14/84	3	17	7 Legs	8	↓	
10/19/85	❶²	15	8 Sleeping Bag	8 ▲⁵	Afterburner	Warner 25342
11/9/85	8	15	9 Can't Stop Rockin'	—	↓	
11/23/85+	❶²	19	√10 Stages	21	↓	
1/18/86	5	20	✓11 Rough Boy	22	↓	
2/15/86	16	9	12 Delirious	—	↓	
5/24/86	18	6	√13 Woke Up With Wood	—	↓	
7/5/86	15	12	√14 Velcro Fly	35	↓	
5/12/90	❶⁵	13	√15 Doubleback	50 ▲	Recycler	Warner 26265
10/6/90	❶⁴	9	16 Concrete And Steel	—	↓	
10/27/90	❶⁶	17	√17 My Head's In Mississippi	—	↓	
12/22/90+	2⁴	16	18 Give It Up	79	↓	
3/9/91	14	8	19 Decision Or Collision	—	↓	
4/18/92	16	3	√20 Viva Las Vegas	— ▲³	Greatest Hits	Warner 26846
			#29 Pop hit for Elvis Presley in 1964			
5/9/92	8	7	21 Gun Love	—	↓	
1/22/94	❶⁴	9	22 Pincushion	124 ▲	Antenna	RCA 66317
3/12/94	7	11	23 Breakaway	—	↓	
5/28/94	27	7	24 Girl In A T-Shirt	—	↓	
8/13/94	30	8	25 Fuzzbox Voodoo	—	↓	
2/17/96	12	11	26 She's Just Killing Me	—	From Dusk Till Dawn (soundtrack)	Epic Soundtrax 67523
9/14/96	5	12	27 What's Up With That	—	Rhythmeen	RCA 66956
11/30/96+	22	12	28 Bang Bang	—	↓	
5/3/97	35	5	29 Rhythmeen	—	↓	
10/2/99	13	11	30 Fearless Boogie	—	XXX	RCA 67850
2/5/00	31	5	31 36-22-36	—	↓	

MAINSTREAM ROCK TRACKS WRAP-UP

Top 100 Artists In Rank Order

Top 100 Artists In A-Z Order

Top Artists Achievements:

> Most Charted Tracks
> Most Top 10 Tracks
> Most #1 Tracks
> Most Weeks At The #1 Position

Top Tracks:

> All-Time
> Top 10 Tracks of Each Year

Tracks Of Longevity

> 1981-89
> 1990-99
> 2000-02

TOP 100 ARTISTS IN RANK ORDER

This section ranks the Top 100 Mainstream Rock Tracks artists from 1981-2002. Each artist's accumulated point total is shown to the right of their name. This ranking includes all titles that <u>peaked</u> from 1981-2002. A picture of each Top 40 artist is shown next to their listing in the artist section of this book.

POINT SYSTEM:

1. Each artist's charted singles are given points based on their highest charted position:

#1	=	60 points for its first week at #1, plus 5 points for each additional week at #1
#2	=	50 points for its first week at #2, plus 3 points for each additional week at #2
#3	=	40 points for its first week at #3, plus 3 points for each additional week at #3
#4-5	=	35 points
#6-10	=	30 points
#11-20	=	25 points
#21-30	=	20 points
#31-40	=	15 points
#41-50	=	10 points
#51-60	=	5 points

2. Total weeks charted are added in.

In the case of a tie, the artist listed first is determined by the following tie-breaker rules:

1) Most charted tracks
2) Most Top 20 tracks
3) Most Top 10 tracks

Special Symbols:

★ = **Hot Artist**
An artist's rank increased by at least 10 positions since the last edition of *Rock Tracks*. All new artist entries are automatically designated as "Hot Artists."

● = **Deceased Solo Artist**

■ = **Deceased Group Member**
The total number of square symbols indicates the total number of deceased members.

— = Artist did not rank in the Top 100 of the previous edition.

+ = Subject to change — still charted as of the 11/23/02 cut-off date

TOP 100 MAINSTREAM ROCK ARTISTS

Old Rank	New Rank		Points
(2)	1.	**Van Halen**	2,447
(1)	2.	**Tom Petty** (& The Heartbreakers)	2,431 +
(8)	3.	**Aerosmith**	2,166
(4)	4.	**U2**	2,160
(3)	5.	**John Cougar Mellencamp**	2,148
(6)	6.	**Rush**	1,721
(7)	7.	**The Rolling Stones** ■	1,694 +
(5)	8.	**Bruce Springsteen**	1,633
(19)	★9.	**Pearl Jam**	1,589 +
(9)	10.	**Robert Plant**	1,573
(11)	11.	**ZZ Top**	1,506
(10)	12.	**Eric Clapton**	1,473
(12)	13.	**R.E.M.**	1,420
—	★14.	**Metallica** ■	1,363
(17)	15.	**The Black Crowes**	1,343
(14)	16.	**Def Leppard** ■	1,338
(40)	★17.	**Stone Temple Pilots**	1,329
(81)	★18.	**Collective Soul**	1,244
(13)	19.	**Bryan Adams**	1,190
(47)	★20.	**Ozzy Osbourne**	1,183
—	★21.	**Creed**	1,116
(15)	22.	**Genesis**	1,106
(49)	★23.	**AC/DC** ■	1,079
(46)	★24.	**Sammy Hagar**	1,079 +
(23)	25.	**Don Henley**	1,017
(16)	26.	**Steve Winwood**	980
(18)	27.	**Huey Lewis** (& The News)	934
(21)	28.	**Yes**	928
(20)	29.	**INXS** ■	927
(22)	30.	**38 Special**	924
(65)	★31.	**Alice In Chains** ■	891
(27)	32.	**Bob Seger** (& The Silver Bullet Band)	888
—	★33.	**Red Hot Chili Peppers** ■	887 +
(24)	34.	**Pat Benatar**	878
(26)	35.	**Bon Jovi**	859
(25)	36.	**Heart**	855
(30)	37.	**Bad Company**	853
(29)	38.	**Pink Floyd**	833
(37)	39.	**Journey**	807
(28)	40.	**Billy Squier**	805
(97)	★41.	**Live**	786
(31)	42.	**Phil Collins**	781
(32)	43.	**Stevie Nicks**	780
(33)	44.	**Foreigner**	772
(34)	45.	**Eddie Money**	766
(35)	46.	**David Bowie**	759
(42)	47.	**Neil Young**	757
(41)	48.	**Scorpions**	757
(36)	49.	**The Cars** ■	753
(39)	50.	**Stevie Ray Vaughan** (& Double Trouble) ●	750
(38)	51.	**Sting**	748
—	★52.	**Bush**	722
(44)	53.	**Guns N' Roses**	709
—	★54.	**The Offspring**	695
(43)	55.	**The Fixx**	692
—	★56.	**Soundgarden**	690
(53)	57.	**Rod Stewart**	672
(45)	58.	**The Pretenders** ■ ■	672
(48)	59.	**Peter Gabriel**	662
(50)	60.	**Jefferson Airplane/Starship**	658
(51)	61.	**The Police**	645
(63)	62.	**Queensrÿche**	640
(68)	63.	**Mötley Crüe**	639
—	★64.	**The Smashing Pumpkins**	636
(57)	65.	**David Lee Roth**	634
(54)	66.	**Fleetwood Mac**	628
—	★67.	**Godsmack**	627 +
—	★68.	**Jimmy Page**	626
(55)	69.	**Tesla**	619
(52)	70.	**Asia**	618
(56)	71.	**Billy Idol**	595
(70)	72.	**Nirvana** ■	592 +
—	★73.	**Staind**	592
—	★74.	**Megadeth**	579
—	★75.	**Lenny Kravitz**	571
—	★76.	**3 Doors Down**	570 +
(58)	77.	**Loverboy** ■	565
(59)	78.	**Dire Straits**	564
—	★79.	**Kenny Wayne Shepherd**	561
—	★80.	**Foo Fighters**	558 +
(60)	81.	**REO Speedwagon**	557
(62)	82.	**George Thorogood** (& The Destroyers)	554
—	★83.	**Days Of The New**	554
(61)	84.	**Bruce Hornsby** (& The Range)	540
—	★85.	**Green Day**	534
(67)	86.	**Mick Jagger**	533
—	★87.	**Kiss** ■	532
(64)	88.	**Billy Joel**	511
—	★89.	**Goo Goo Dolls**	505
(74)	90.	**Great White**	503
—	★91.	**Nickelback**	491 +
(66)	92.	**Triumph**	491
(69)	93.	**The Moody Blues**	485
(71)	94.	**The Who** ■ ■	474
(86)	95.	**Melissa Etheridge**	469
—	★96.	**Brother Cane**	466
(73)	97.	**Jackson Browne**	464
—	★98.	**Tool**	463
(72)	99.	**Joan Jett** (& The Blackhearts)	459
(75)	100.	**The Kinks**	457

The following 22 artists were ranked in the Top 100 Artists of our *Rock Tracks (1995 edition)* book but have now dropped out of the Top 100:

The Alarm	Jeff Healey Band	The Smithereens
The Allman Brothers Band	Little Feat	Survivor
Cinderella	Men At Work	Pete Townshend
Tom Cochrane/Red Rider	Night Ranger	Traveling Wilburys
Damn Yankees	The Alan Parsons Project	Joe Walsh
Duran Duran	Queen	Whitesnake
Extreme	Joe Satriani	
George Harrison	Simple Minds	

Collective Soul

John Cougar Mellencamp

U2

TOP ARTIST ACHIEVEMENTS

MOST CHARTED TRACKS

1. Tom Petty (& The Heartbreakers) 47
2. John Cougar Mellencamp 45
3. U2 44
4. Van Halen 43
5. Bruce Springsteen 42
6. Aerosmith 40
7. Rush 38
8. Eric Clapton 34
9. R.E.M. 34
10. Pearl Jam 33
11. The Rolling Stones 32
12. Robert Plant 32
13. ZZ Top 31
14. Bryan Adams 30
15. Def Leppard 28
16. AC/DC 28
17. Ozzy Osbourne 25
18. Sammy Hagar 25
19. Neil Young 25
20. Genesis 24

MOST TOP 10 TRACKS

1. Tom Petty (& The Heartbreakers) 28
2. Van Halen 25
3. Aerosmith 23
4. John Cougar Mellencamp 23
5. Robert Plant 21
6. U2 20
7. Rush 20
8. The Rolling Stones 18
9. Bruce Springsteen 18
10. The Black Crowes 17
11. Pearl Jam 16
12. ZZ Top 16
13. Eric Clapton 16
14. Def Leppard 16
15. R.E.M. 15
16. Bryan Adams 15
17. Metallica 14
18. Stone Temple Pilots 14
19. Ozzy Osbourne 14
20. 38 Special 13

MOST #1 TRACKS

1. Van Halen 13
2. Tom Petty (& The Heartbreakers) 10
3. Aerosmith 9
4. U2 7
5. John Cougar Mellencamp 7
6. Collective Soul 7
7. Robert Plant 6
8. ZZ Top 6
9. The Black Crowes 6
10. Stone Temple Pilots 6
11. Rush 5
12. The Rolling Stones 5
13. Bruce Springsteen 5
14. Eric Clapton 5
15. Metallica 5
16. Def Leppard 5

MOST WEEKS AT THE #1 POSITION

1. Collective Soul 47
2. Van Halen 45
3. Aerosmith 38
4. Metallica 36
5. Creed 36
6. U2 34
7. 3 Doors Down 33
8. Tom Petty (& The Heartbreakers) 31
9. The Rolling Stones 27
10. The Black Crowes 26
11. Days Of The New 26
12. Stone Temple Pilots 24
13. ZZ Top 23
14. Red Hot Chili Peppers 23
15. Pearl Jam 22
16. Robert Plant 21

TOP MAINSTREAM ROCK TRACKS

ALL-TIME

Peak Year	Wks Chr	Wks T20	Wks T10	Wks @ #1	Rank	Title	Artist
00	53	50	35	21	1.	Loser	3 Doors Down
01	42	42	31	20	2.	It's Been Awhile	Staind
99	51	51	34	17	3.	Higher	Creed
97	46	44	30	16	4.	Touch, Peel And Stand	Days Of The New
99	33	33	25	15	5.	Heavy	Collective Soul
94	33	31	23	15	6.	Interstate Love Song	Stone Temple Pilots
01	48	46	38	13	7.	How You Remind Me	Nickelback
81	32	24	21	13	8.	Start Me Up	The Rolling Stones
91	30	21	16	12	9.	Mysterious Ways	U2
98	26	22	18	11	10.	Turn The Page	Metallica
92	20	18	15	11	11.	Remedy	The Black Crowes
02	42	40	28	10	12.	Blurry	Puddle Of Mudd
99	29	28	23	10	13.	Scar Tissue	Red Hot Chili Peppers
98	27	25	19	10	14.	The Down Town	Days Of The New
95	26	24	18	10	15.	Lightning Crashes	Live
00	51	50	40	9	16.	Kryptonite	3 Doors Down
01	28	28	22	9	17.	My Sacrifice	Creed
95	26	25	20	9	18.	December	Collective Soul
93	20	19	13	9	19.	Livin' On The Edge	Aerosmith
83	21	11	11	9	20.	Every Breath You Take	The Police
94	26	22	18	8	21.	Shine	Collective Soul
96	26	21	18	8	22.	Until It Sleeps	Metallica
95	26	24	17	8	23.	Better Man	Pearl Jam
93	26	20	16	8	24.	Daugher	Pearl Jam
84	13	11	10	8	25.	Jump	Van Halen
00	43	43	27	7	26.	I Disappear	Metallica
00	34	34	22	7	27.	No Leaf Clover	Metallica
02	24 +	24 +	18	7	28.	By The Way	Red Hot Chili Peppers
94	26	21	17	7	29.	Black Hole Sun	Soundgarden
91	13	10	9	7	30.	All This Time	Sting
98	42	41	26	6	31.	Blue On Black	Kenny Wayne Shepherd Band
02	29	27	23	6	32.	Drift & Die	Puddle Of Mudd
98	39	37	22	6	33.	What's This Life For	Creed
95	26	22	16	6	34.	And Fools Shine On	Brother Cane
98	23	18	14	6	35.	Given To Fly	Pearl Jam
96	26	15	14	6	36.	Me Wise Magic	Van Halen
92	20	17	13	6	37.	Hotel Illness	The Black Crowes
93	20	17	12	6	38.	Cryin'	Aerosmith
83	26	15	12	6	39.	Photograph	Def Leppard
82	20	16	11	6	40.	Everybody Wants You	Billy Squier
88	18	15	11	6	41.	Angel Of Harlem	U2
92	17	14	11	6	42.	How About That	Bad Company
94	26	13	11	6	43.	Keep Talking	Pink Floyd
93	15	13	11	6	44.	Pride And Joy	Coverdale•Page
89	14	11	11	6	45.	Pretending	Eric Clapton
82	22	14	10	6	46.	Heat Of The Moment	Asia
81	23	12	10	6	47.	The Waiting	Tom Petty & The Heartbreakers
84	17	11	10	6	48.	Dancing In The Dark	Bruce Springsteen
91	16	11	10	6	49.	Lift Me Up	Yes
91	15	11	10	6	50.	Learning To Fly	Tom Petty & The Heartbreakers

ALL-TIME

Peak Year	Wks Chr	Wks T20	Wks T10	Wks @ #1	Rank	Title	Artist
90	17	12	9	6	51.	My Head's In Mississippi	ZZ Top
86	14	11	9	6	52.	I Want To Make The World Turn Around	Steve Miller Band
90	13	10	9	6	53.	Hurting Kind (I've Got My Eyes On You)	Robert Plant
98	12	10	9	6	54.	Without You	Van Halen
88	12	9	8	6	55.	Heaven Knows	Robert Plant
97	37	36	28	5	56.	If You Could Only See	Tonic
97	30	27	21	5	57.	One Headlight	The Wallflowers
96	26	24	16	5	58.	Burden In My Hand	Soundgarden
95	26	23	15	5	59.	Name	Goo Goo Dolls
97	26	18	13	5	60.	Listen	Collective Soul
83	31	17	13	5	61.	King Of Pain	The Police
01	26	16	13	5	62.	Jaded	Aerosmith
97	26	14	12	5	63.	Falling In Love (Is Hard On The Knees)	Aerosmith
82	26	14	12	5	64.	I Love Rock 'N Roll	Joan Jett & The Blackhearts
85	17	14	12	5	65.	Silent Running (On Dangerous Ground)	Mike + The Mechanics
84	17	13	12	5	66.	The Boys Of Summer	Don Henley
83	15	13	12	5	67.	She's A Beauty	The Tubes
89	19	13	11	5	68.	Rock And A Hard Place	The Rolling Stones
97	16	13	10	5	69.	Little White Lie	Sammy Hagar
82	15	13	10	5	70.	Eye Of The Tiger	Survivor
81	15	12	10	5	71.	You Better You Bet	The Who
90	13	10	10	5	72.	Doubleback	ZZ Top
87	14	11	9	5	73.	Midnight Blue	Lou Gramm
85	14	11	9	5	74.	Lonely Ol' Night	John Cougar Mellencamp
87	13	10	9	5	75.	With Or Without You	U2
82	17	13	8	5	76.	Down Under	Men At Work
93	20	10	8	5	77.	Stand Up (Kick Love Into Motion)	Def Leppard
89	14	10	8	5	78.	I Won't Back Down	Tom Petty
88	11	9	8	5	79.	Desire	U2
87	11	8	8	5	80.	Paper In Fire	John Cougar Mellencamp
89	9	8	7	5	81.	Mixed Emotions	The Rolling Stones
84	11	8	6	5	82.	On The Dark Side	John Cafferty & The Beaver Brown Band
02	41+	40+	31	4	83.	I Stand Alone	Godsmack
00	31	29	22	4	84.	With Arms Wide Open	Creed
96	35	31	21	4	85.	Cumbersome	Seven Mary Three
96	26	23	18	4	86.	Trippin' On A Hole In A Paper Heart	Stone Temple Pilots
96	26	24	17	4	87.	The World I Know	Collective Soul
81	27	23	17	4	88.	The Voice	The Moody Blues
81	30	19	17	4	89.	Urgent	Foreigner
96	26	24	16	4	90.	Blow Up The Outside World	Soundgarden
83	25	18	16	4	91.	Separate Ways (Worlds Apart)	Journey
96	32	29	15	4	92.	In The Meantime	Spacehog
91	51	22	15	4	93.	Top Of The World	Van Halen
97	26	21	15	4	94.	Precious Declaration	Collective Soul
98	26	20	15	4	95.	I Lie In The Bed I Make	Brother Cane
95	26	20	15	4	96.	My Friends	Red Hot Chili Peppers
00	23	16	14	4	97.	Stiff Upper Lip	AC/DC
94	26	18	13	4	98.	Deuces Are Wild	Aerosmith
93	20	18	13	4	99.	Peace Pipe	Cry Of Love
91	20	17	13	4	100.	Dreamline	Rush

TOP 10 MAINSTREAM ROCK TRACKS

1981

Peak Date	Wks Chr	Wks T20	Wks T10	Wks @ Peak	Peak Pos	Rank	Title	Artist
9/05	32	24	21	13	1	1.	**Start Me Up**	*The Rolling Stones*
5/09	23	12	10	6	1	2.	**The Waiting**	*Tom Petty & The Heartbreakers*
4/04	15	12	10	5	1	3.	**You Better You Bet**	*The Who*
6/27	27	23	17	4	1	4.	**The Voice**	*The Moody Blues*
7/25	30	19	17	4	1	5.	**Urgent**	*Foreigner*
12/26	24	14	9	3	1	6.	**Harden My Heart**	*Quarterflash*
12/12	28	13	10	2	1	7.	**Every Little Thing She Does Is Magic**	*The Police*
8/22	23	13	10	2	1	8.	**Burnin' For You**	*Blue Öyster Cult*
3/21	12	9	7	2	1	9.	**I Can't Stand It**	*Eric Clapton And His Band*
6/20	14	13	10	1	1	10.	**A Life Of Illusion**	*Joe Walsh*

1982

Peak Date	Wks Chr	Wks T20	Wks T10	Wks @ Peak	Peak Pos	Rank	Title	Artist
8/28	20	16	11	6	1	1.	**Everybody Wants You**	*Billy Squier*
4/24	22	14	10	6	1	2.	**Heat Of The Moment**	*Asia*
2/06	26	14	12	5	1	3.	**I Love Rock 'N Roll**	*Joan Jett & The Blackhearts*
7/03	15	13	10	5	1	4.	**Eye Of The Tiger**	*Survivor*
11/27	17	13	8	5	1	5.	**Down Under**	*Men At Work*
1/16	25	17	13	3	1	6.	**Centerfold**	*J. Geils Band*
12/11	16	13	12	3	1	7.	**You Got Lucky**	*Tom Petty & The Heartbreakers*
10/16	21	13	11	3	1	8.	**Dirty Laundry**	*Don Henley*
4/03	27	12	9	3	1	9.	**867-5309/Jenny**	*Tommy Tutone*
8/07	14	11	9	3	1	10.	**Think I'm In Love**	*Eddie Money*

1983

Peak Date	Wks Chr	Wks T20	Wks T10	Wks @ Peak	Peak Pos	Rank	Title	Artist
6/11	21	11	11	9	1	1.	**Every Breath You Take**	*The Police*
3/19	26	15	12	6	1	2.	**Photograph**	*Def Leppard*
8/27	31	17	13	5	1	3.	**King Of Pain**	*The Police*
4/30	15	13	12	5	1	4.	**She's A Beauty**	*The Tubes*
2/19	25	18	16	4	1	5.	**Separate Ways (Worlds Apart)**	*Journey*
11/26	20	13	12	4	1	6.	**Owner Of A Lonely Heart**	*Yes*
12/24	15	12	12	4	1	7.	**If I'd Been The One**	*38 Special*
10/22	17	10	8	4	1	8.	**Love Is A Battlefield**	*Pat Benatar*
1/22	26	14	8	3	1	9.	**Hungry Like The Wolf**	*Duran Duran*
10/08	19	8	7	2	1	10.	**Suddenly Last Summer**	*The Motels*

1984

Peak Date	Wks Chr	Wks T20	Wks T10	Wks @ Peak	Peak Pos	Rank	Title	Artist
1/21	13	11	10	8	1	1.	**Jump**	*Van Halen*
6/09	17	11	10	6	1	2.	**Dancing In The Dark**	*Bruce Springsteen*
12/15	17	13	12	5	1	3.	**The Boys Of Summer**	*Don Henley*
9/22	11	8	6	5	1	4.	**On The Dark Side**	*John Cafferty & The Beaver Brown Band*
11/17	15	12	10	4	1	5.	**Run To You**	*Bryan Adams*
10/27	18	11	10	3	1	6.	**I Can't Hold Back**	*Survivor*
4/14	14	10	8	3	1	7.	**You Might Think**	*The Cars*
7/28	18	12	9	2	1	8.	**The Warrior**	*Scandal Featuring Patty Smyth*
8/04	15	10	9	2	1	9.	**Rock Me Tonite**	*Billy Squier*
8/25	18	14	8	2	1	10.	**Missing You**	*John Waite*

TOP 10 MAINSTREAM ROCK TRACKS

1985

Peak Date	Wks Chr	Wks T20	Wks T10	Wks @ Peak	Peak Pos	Rank	Title	Artist
12/28	17	14	12	5	1	1.	Silent Running (On Dangerous Ground)	Mike + The Mechanics
9/07	14	11	9	5	1	2.	Lonely Ol' Night	John Cougar Mellencamp
8/03	20	15	12	3	1	3.	Money For Nothing	Dire Straits
11/23	14	12	10	3	1	4.	Tonight She Comes	The Cars
4/20	16	11	7	3	1	5.	Don't You (Forget About Me)	Simple Minds
6/29	13	9	7	3	1	6.	If You Love Somebody Set Them Free	Sting
5/11	12	9	7	3	1	7.	Trapped	Bruce Springsteen & The E Street Band
1/26	14	9	6	3	1	8.	The Old Man Down The Road	John Fogerty
10/19	11	8	6	3	1	9.	You Belong To The City	Glenn Frey
8/24	18	13	10	2	1	10.	Fortress Around Your Heart	Sting

1986

Peak Date	Wks Chr	Wks T20	Wks T10	Wks @ Peak	Peak Pos	Rank	Title	Artist
11/29	14	11	9	6	1	1.	I Want To Make The World Turn Around	Steve Miller Band
7/19	14	11	10	4	1	2.	Higher Love	Steve Winwood
2/22	12	10	8	4	1	3.	All The Kings Horses	The Firm
8/23	18	13	9	3	1	4.	Throwing It All Away	Genesis
4/05	13	10	9	3	1	5.	Why Can't This Be Love	Van Halen
4/26	13	10	8	3	1	6.	Stick Around	Julian Lennon
11/08	13	9	7	3	1	7.	Don't Get Me Wrong	The Pretenders
6/14	11	9	7	3	1	8.	Invisible Touch	Genesis
10/11	9	7	5	3	1	9.	Amanda	Boston
2/08	19	13	11	2	1	10.	Stages	ZZ Top

1987

Peak Date	Wks Chr	Wks T20	Wks T10	Wks @ Peak	Peak Pos	Rank	Title	Artist
2/14	14	11	9	5	1	1.	Midnight Blue	Lou Gramm
4/04	13	10	9	5	1	2.	With Or Without You	U2
8/22	11	8	8	5	1	3.	Paper In Fire	John Cougar Mellencamp
11/21	17	13	12	4	1	4.	Tunnel Of Love	Bruce Springsteen
5/09	12	9	8	4	1	5.	Jammin' Me	Tom Petty & The Heartbreakers
12/19	11	8	7	4	1	6.	Say You Will	Foreigner
6/06	10	8	7	4	1	7.	Shakedown	Bob Seger
8/01	12	10	9	3	1	8.	Touch Of Grey	Grateful Dead
9/26	12	9	8	3	1	9.	Learning To Fly	Pink Floyd
7/11	11	9	8	3	1	10.	Give To Live	Sammy Hagar

1988

Peak Date	Wks Chr	Wks T20	Wks T10	Wks @ Peak	Peak Pos	Rank	Title	Artist
12/10	18	15	11	6	1	1.	Angel Of Harlem	U2
2/20	12	9	8	6	1	2.	Heaven Knows	Robert Plant
10/08	11	9	8	5	1	3.	Desire	U2
4/09	16	12	8	4	1	4.	Tall Cool One	Robert Plant
6/25	11	9	8	4	1	5.	Roll With It	Steve Winwood
8/20	11	8	8	4	1	6.	Hate To Lose Your Lovin'	Little Feat
1/23	10	8	7	4	1	7.	Just Like Paradise	David Lee Roth
7/30	12	10	8	3	1	8.	Simply Irresistible	Robert Palmer
5/14	11	9	8	3	1	9.	The Valley Road	Bruce Hornsby & The Range
6/04	10	7	7	3	1	10.	Black And Blue	Van Halen

TOP 10 MAINSTREAM ROCK TRACKS

1989

Peak Date	Wks Chr	Wks T20	Wks T10	Wks @ Peak	Peak Pos	Rank	Title	Artist
11/25	14	11	11	6	1	1.	Pretending	Eric Clapton
10/21	19	13	11	5	1	2.	Rock And A Hard Place	The Rolling Stones
4/22	14	10	8	5	1	3.	I Won't Back Down	Tom Petty
9/02	9	8	7	5	1	4.	Mixed Emotions	The Rolling Stones
2/18	14	11	9	4	1	5.	Driven Out	The Fixx
7/01	12	9	7	4	1	6.	The End Of The Innocence	Don Henley
7/29	18	11	8	3	1	7.	Crossfire	Stevie Ray Vaughan & Double Trouble
3/25	15	11	8	3	1	8.	I'll Be You	The Replacements
5/27	9	7	6	3	1	9.	The Doctor	The Doobie Brothers
10/07	11	9	8	2	1	10.	Love In An Elevator	Aerosmith

1990

Peak Date	Wks Chr	Wks T20	Wks T10	Wks @ Peak	Peak Pos	Rank	Title	Artist
12/08	17	12	9	6	1	1.	My Head's In Mississippi	ZZ Top
3/24	13	10	9	6	1	2.	Hurting Kind (I've Got My Eyes On You)	Robert Plant
5/19	13	10	10	5	1	3.	Doubleback	ZZ Top
9/15	10	9	8	4	1	4.	Suicide Blonde	INXS
10/13	9	7	6	4	1	5.	Concrete And Steel	ZZ Top
1/27	21	12	8	3	1	6.	Bad Love	Eric Clapton
8/18	12	10	8	3	1	7.	Brickyard Road	Johnny Van Zant
11/10	21	16	13	2	1	8.	Hard To Handle	The Black Crowes
6/23	14	13	11	2	1	9.	Cradle Of Love	Billy Idol
7/07	15	11	9	2	1	10.	Holy Water	Bad Company

1991

Peak Date	Wks Chr	Wks T20	Wks T10	Wks @ Peak	Peak Pos	Rank	Title	Artist
12/14	30	21	16	12	1	1.	Mysterious Ways	U2
1/19	13	10	9	7	1	2.	All This Time	Sting
5/04	16	11	10	6	1	3.	Lift Me Up	Yes
6/29	15	11	10	6	1	4.	Learning To Fly	Tom Petty & The Heartbreakers
10/26	51	22	15	4	1	5.	Top Of The World	Van Halen
9/21	20	17	13	4	1	6.	Dreamline	Rush
8/10	20	13	10	4	1	7.	Runaround	Van Halen
4/13	17	14	11	3	1	8.	Losing My Religion	R.E.M.
10/19	25	14	10	3	1	9.	Get A Let Up	John Mellencamp
3/16	11	8	7	3	1	10.	Highwire	The Rolling Stones

1992

Peak Date	Wks Chr	Wks T20	Wks T10	Wks @ Peak	Peak Pos	Rank	Title	Artist
5/02	20	18	15	11	1	1.	Remedy	The Black Crowes
11/28	20	17	13	6	1	2.	Hotel Illness	The Black Crowes
9/19	17	14	11	6	1	3.	How About That	Bad Company
8/22	23	13	10	4	1	4.	Thorn In My Pride	The Black Crowes
8/01	17	12	10	3	1	5.	Even Better Than The Real Thing	U2
3/21	10	7	6	3	1	6.	Human Touch	Bruce Springsteen
11/07	20	19	14	2	1	7.	Rest In Peace	Extreme
4/18	20	17	12	2	1	8.	One	U2
3/07	20	13	10	2	1	9.	Again Tonight	John Mellencamp
7/18	15	12	8	2	1	10.	Sting Me	The Black Crowes

TOP 10 MAINSTREAM ROCK TRACKS

1993

Peak Date	Wks Chr	Wks T20	Wks T10	Wks @ Peak	Peak Pos	Rank	Title	Artist
4/10	20	19	13	9	1	1.	Livin' On The Edge	Aerosmith
12/04	26	20	16	8	1	2.	Daughter	Pearl Jam
7/17	20	17	12	6	1	3.	Cryin'	Aerosmith
2/27	15	13	11	6	1	4.	Pride And Joy	Coverdale•Page
1/09	20	10	8	5	1	5.	Stand Up (Kick Love Into Motion)	Def Leppard
9/11	20	18	13	4	1	6.	Peace Pipe	Cry Of Love
10/23	12	9	7	4	1	7.	Stick It Out	Rush
6/12	28	28	18	2	1	8.	Are You Gonna Go My Way	Lenny Kravitz
11/20	26	22	15	2	1	9.	Mary Jane's Last Dance	Tom Petty & The Heartbreakers
7/03	20	15	12	2	1	10.	Big Gun	AC/DC

1994

Peak Date	Wks Chr	Wks T20	Wks T10	Wks @ Peak	Peak Pos	Rank	Title	Artist
9/17	33	31	23	15	1	1.	Interstate Love Song	Stone Temple Pilots
5/21	26	22	18	8	1	2.	Shine	Collective Soul
7/16	26	21	17	7	1	3.	Black Hole Sun	Soundgarden
4/09	26	13	11	6	1	4.	Keep Talking	Pink Floyd
2/26	26	18	13	4	1	5.	Deuces Are Wild	Aerosmith
1/29	9	8	7	4	1	6.	Pincushion	ZZ Top
9/03	26	25	16	2	1	7.	Vasoline	Stone Temple Pilots
3/26	26	20	15	2	1	8.	No Excuses	Alice In Chains
12/31	23	16	14	1	1	9.	You Don't Know How It Feels	Tom Petty
10/08	26	17	12	5	2	10.	What's The Frequency, Kenneth?	R.E.M.

1995

Peak Date	Wks Chr	Wks T20	Wks T10	Wks @ Peak	Peak Pos	Rank	Title	Artist
3/25	26	24	18	10	1	1.	Lightning Crashes	Live
6/03	26	25	20	9	1	2.	December	Collective Soul
1/07	26	24	17	8	1	3.	Better Man	Pearl Jam
8/12	26	22	16	6	1	4.	And Fools Shine On	Brother Cane
11/04	26	23	15	5	1	5.	Name	Goo Goo Dolls
12/09	26	20	15	4	1	6.	My Friends	Red Hot Chili Peppers
9/23	26	23	14	3	1	7.	Tomorrow	Silverchair
10/14	24	14	11	3	1	8.	Hard As A Rock	AC/DC
1/21	19	12	9	3	1	9.	Don't Tell Me (What Love Can Do)	Van Halen
8/05	19	13	11	1	1	10.	Hold Me, Thrill Me, Kiss Me, Kill Me	U2

1996

Peak Date	Wks Chr	Wks T20	Wks T10	Wks @ Peak	Peak Pos	Rank	Title	Artist
6/08	26	21	18	8	1	1.	Until It Sleeps	Metallica
10/26	26	15	14	6	1	2.	Me Wise Magic	Van Halen
8/31	26	24	16	5	1	3.	Burden In My Hand	Soundgarden
1/06	35	31	21	4	1	4.	Cumbersome	Seven Mary Three
7/27	26	23	18	4	1	5.	Trippin' On A Hole In A Paper Heart	Stone Temple Pilots
2/03	26	24	17	4	1	6.	The World I Know	Collective Soul
12/28	26	24	16	4	1	7.	Blow Up The Outside World	Soundgarden
4/06	32	29	15	4	1	8.	In The Meantime	Spacehog
12/07	33	32	20	3	1	9.	Hero Of The Day	Metallica
3/16	31	27	18	3	1	10.	Santa Monica (Watch The World Die)	Everclear

TOP 10 MAINSTREAM ROCK TRACKS

1997

Peak Date	Wks Chr	Wks T20	Wks T10	Wks @ Peak	Peak Pos	Rank	Title	Artist
10/04	46	44	30	16	1	1.	Touch, Peel And Stand	Days Of The New
6/28	37	36	28	5	1	2.	If You Could Only See	Tonic
2/01	30	27	21	5	1	3.	One Headlight	The Wallflowers
8/02	26	18	13	5	1	4.	Listen	Collective Soul
3/08	26	14	12	5	1	5.	Falling In Love (Is Hard On The Knees)	Aerosmith
5/24	16	13	10	5	1	6.	Little White Lie	Sammy Hagar
4/12	26	21	15	4	1	7.	Precious Declaration	Collective Soul
9/06	29	15	12	4	1	8.	Pink	Aerosmith
5/10	34	33	20	2	1	9.	Gone Away	The Offspring
1/18	26	20	15	1	1	10.	Lady Picture Show	Stone Temple Pilots

1998

Peak Date	Wks Chr	Wks T20	Wks T10	Wks @ Peak	Peak Pos	Rank	Title	Artist
11/28	26	22	18	11	1	1.	Turn The Page	Metallica
7/11	27	25	19	10	1	2.	The Down Town	Days Of The New
4/18	42	41	26	6	1	3.	Blue On Black	Kenny Wayne Shepherd Band
9/19	39	37	22	6	1	4.	What's This Life For	Creed
1/24	23	18	14	6	1	5.	Given To Fly	Pearl Jam
3/07	12	10	9	6	1	6.	Without You	Van Halen
6/06	26	20	15	4	1	7.	I Lie In The Bed I Make	Brother Cane
11/07	47	38	28	3	1	8.	Fly Away	Lenny Kravitz
5/09	13	11	10	2	1	9.	Most High	Jimmy Page & Robert Plant
10/31	21	15	12	1	1	10.	Psycho Circus	Kiss

1999

Peak Date	Wks Chr	Wks T20	Wks T10	Wks @ Peak	Peak Pos	Rank	Title	Artist
9/25	51	51	34	17	1	1.	Higher	Creed
2/20	33	33	25	15	1	2.	Heavy	Collective Soul
7/17	29	28	23	10	1	3.	Scar Tissue	Red Hot Chili Peppers
6/05	28	27	18	3	1	4.	Lit Up	Buckcherry
6/26	19	15	13	3	1	5.	Promises	Def Leppard
2/13	30	27	21	1	1	6.	What It's Like	Everlast
3/13	38	37	29	7	2	7.	One	Creed
10/16	26	22	20	6	2	8.	The Dolphin's Cry	Live
4/17	21	15	12	6	2	9.	Mas Tequila	Sammy Hagar and The Waboritas
11/27	30	29	24	4	2	10.	Learn To Fly	Foo Fighters

2000

Peak Date	Wks Chr	Wks T20	Wks T10	Wks @ Peak	Peak Pos	Rank	Title	Artist
9/09	53	50	35	21	1	1.	Loser	3 Doors Down
4/08	51	50	40	9	1	2.	Kryptonite	3 Doors Down
6/10	43	43	27	7	1	3.	I Disappear	Metallica
1/22	34	34	22	7	1	4.	No Leaf Clover	Metallica
7/08	31	29	22	4	1	5.	With Arms Wide Open	Creed
3/11	23	16	14	4	1	6.	Stiff Upper Lip	AC/DC
8/26	26	17	15	2	1	7.	Californication	Red Hot Chili Peppers
10/21	26	19	16	7	2	8.	Why Pt. 2	Collective Soul
4/15	27	27	21	5	2	9.	Otherside	Red Hot Chili Peppers
12/16	56	54	40	3	2	10.	Hemorrhage (In My Hands)	Fuel

TOP 10 MAINSTREAM ROCK TRACKS

2001

Peak Date	Wks Chr	Wks T20	Wks T10	Wks @ Peak	Peak Pos	Rank	Title	Artist
4/28	42	42	31	20	1	1.	It's Been Awhile	Staind
9/15	48	46	38	13	1	2.	How You Remind Me	Nickelback
12/15	28	28	22	9	1	3.	My Sacrifice	Creed
2/10	26	16	13	5	1	4.	Jaded	Aerosmith
4/07	26	24	21	3	1	5.	Duck And Run	3 Doors Down
3/17	26	20	17	2	1	6.	Outside	Aaron Lewis with Fred Durst
2/03	53	53	33	1	1	7.	Awake	Godsmack
3/31	27	24	18	1	1	8.	Breakdown	Tantric
6/02	33	33	27	13	2	9.	Schism	Tool
9/22	26	15	13	6	2	10.	Gets Me Through	Ozzy Osbourne

2002

Peak Date	Wks Chr	Wks T20	Wks T10	Wks @ Peak	Peak Pos	Rank	Title	Artist
2/16	42	40	28	10	1	1.	Blurry	Puddle Of Mudd
8/10	24 +	24 +	18	7	1	2.	By The Way	Red Hot Chili Peppers
6/29	29	27	23	6	1	3.	Drift & Die	Puddle Of Mudd
5/18	41 +	40 +	31	4	1	4.	I Stand Alone	Godsmack
11/02	7 +	6 +	6 +	4 +	1	5.	You Know You're Right	Nirvana
4/27	32	30	23	3	1	6.	Too Bad	Nickelback
10/05	19 +	17 +	14	3	1	7.	Never Again	Nickelback
6/15	24	17	14	2	1	8.	Hero	Chad Kroeger Featuring Josey Scott
9/28	23 +	21 +	18 +	1	1	9.	Aerials	System Of A Down
10/26	16 +	14 +	12 +	1	1	10.	She Hates Me	Puddle Of Mudd

3 Doors Down

Staind

Puddle Of Mudd

Albums with Most Charted *Mainstream Rock Tracks*

Each charted track is awarded points based on the artist ranking point system (see page 160)

Born In The U.S.A.....*Bruce Springsteen*
9 tracks / 467 points

Full Moon Fever...*Tom Petty*
7 tracks / 450 points

The End Of The Innocence...
Don Henley — 7 tracks / 389 points

Scarecrow...*John Cougar Mellencamp*
7 tracks / 385 points

Afterburner...*ZZ Top*
7 tracks / 366 points

Pyromania...*Def Leppard*
7 tracks / 351 points

Reckless...*Bryan Adams*
7 tracks / 335 points

Hysteria...*Def Leppard*
7 tracks / 333 points

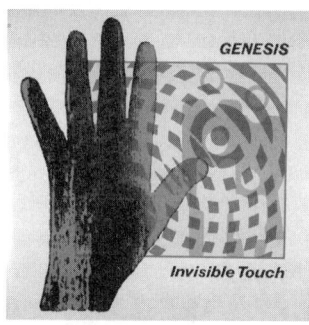

Invisible Touch...*Genesis*
7 tracks / 315 points

Genesis...*Genesis*
7 tracks / 294 points

Achtung Baby...*U2*
6 tracks / 490 points

For Unlawful Carnal Knowledge...
Van Halen — 6 tracks / 477 points

TRACKS OF LONGEVITY

1981-89

Peak Year	Peak Pos	Peak Wks	Wks Chr	Rank	Title	Artist
82	4	1	37	1.	You've Got Another Thing Comin'	Judas Priest
81	3	2	34	2.	Juke Box Hero	Foreigner
89	1	1	33	3.	Free Fallin'	Tom Petty
81	1	13	32	4.	Start Me Up	The Rolling Stones
83	6	1	32	5.	Modern Love	David Bowie
81	15	1	32	6.	Our Lips Are Sealed	Go-Go's
83	1	5	31	7.	King Of Pain	The Police
84	2	1	31	8.	Panama	Van Halen
83	4	2	31	9.	Back On The Chain Gang	The Pretenders
81	7	1	31	10.	In The Dark	Billy Squier
83	9	1	31	11.	Synchronicity II	The Police
81	1	4	30	12.	Urgent	Foreigner

1990-99

Peak Year	Peak Pos	Peak Wks	Wks Chr	Rank	Title	Artist
99	1	17	51	1.	Higher	Creed
91	1	4	51	2.	Top Of The World	Van Halen
99	5	2	48	3.	Keep Away	Godsmack
98	1	3	47	4.	Fly Away	Lenny Kravitz
97	1	16	46	5.	Touch, Peel And Stand	Days Of The New
92	2	4	46	6.	Right Now	Van Halen
97	2	10	44	7.	My Own Prison	Creed
99	7	1	44	8.	Whatever	Godsmack
98	1	6	42	9.	Blue On Black	Kenny Wayne Shepherd Band
98	1	6	39	10.	What's This Life For	Creed
99	2	7	38	11.	One	Creed
97	1	5	37	12.	If You Could Only See	Tonic

2000-02

Peak Year	Peak Pos	Peak Wks	Wks Chr	Rank	Title	Artist
00	2	3	56	1.	Hemorrhage (In My Hands)	Fuel
00	1	21	53	2.	Loser	3 Doors Down
01	1	1	53	3.	Awake	Godsmack
00	1	9	51	4.	Kryptonite	3 Doors Down
01	1	13	48	5.	How You Remind Me	Nickelback
01	5	1	46	6.	Down With The Sickness	Disturbed
02	2	7	44	7.	Wasting My Time	Default
00	4	2	44	8.	Last Resort	Papa Roach
00	1	7	43	9.	I Disappear	Metallica
01	1	20	42	10.	It's Been Awhile	Staind
02	1	10	42	11.	Blurry	Puddle Of Mudd
01	4	3	42	12.	One Step Closer	Linkin Park

#1 HITS

This section lists in chronological order, by peak date, all 312 tracks that hit the #1 position on *Billboard's* "Mainstream Rock Tracks" chart from March 21, 1981 through November 9, 2002.

For the years 1981 through 1991, *Billboard* did not publish a year-end issue. *Billboard* considered the charts listed in the last published issue of the year to be "frozen" and all chart positions remained the same for the unpublished week. This frozen chart data is included in our tabulations. Since 1992, *Billboard* has compiled a chart for the last week of the year, even though an issue is not published. This chart is only available through Member Services of Billboard.com or by mail.

DATE: Date track first peaked at the #1 position

WKS: Total weeks track held the #1 position

↕: Indicates track hit #1, dropped down, and then returned to the #1 spot

The top hit of each year is boxed out for quick reference. The top hit is determined by most weeks at the #1 position, followed by total weeks in the Top 10, Top 20, and total weeks charted.

#1 HITS

#1 HITS

1986 (cont'd)

7.	5/17	2	**Like A Rock**
			Bob Seger & The Silver Bullet Band
8.	5/31	2	**Sledgehammer** *Peter Gabriel*
9.	6/14	3	**Invisible Touch** *Genesis*
10.	7/5	2	**Secret Separation** *The Fixx*
11.	7/19	4	**Higher Love** *Steve Winwood*
12.	8/16	1	**Missionary Man** *Eurythmics*
13.	8/23	3	**Throwing It All Away** *Genesis*
14.	9/13	1	**In Your Eyes** *Peter Gabriel*
15.	9/20	2	**Take Me Home Tonight** *Eddie Money*
16.	10/4	1	**Emotion In Motion** *Ric Ocasek*
17.	10/11	3	**Amanda** *Boston*
18.	11/1	1	**Hip To Be Square** *Huey Lewis & The News*
19.	11/8	3	**Don't Get Me Wrong** *The Pretenders*
20.	11/29	6	**I Want To Make The World Turn Around**
			Steve Miller Band

DATE	WKS		1987
1.	1/10	1	**It's In The Way That You Use It**
			Eric Clapton
2.	1/17	2	**My Baby** *The Pretenders*
3.	1/31	2	**Livin' On A Prayer** *Bon Jovi*
4.	2/14	5	**Midnight Blue** *Lou Gramm*
5.	3/21	1	**I'm No Angel** *Gregg Allman Band*
6.	3/28	1	**Come As You Are** *Peter Wolf*
7.	4/4	5	**With Or Without You** *U2*
8.	5/9	4	**Jammin' Me** *Tom Petty & The Heartbreakers*
9.	6/6	4	**Shakedown** *Bob Seger*
10.	7/4	1	**Don't Mean Nothing** *Richard Marx*
11.	7/11	3	**Give To Live** *Sammy Hagar*
12.	8/1	3	**Touch Of Grey** *Grateful Dead*
13.	8/22	5	**Paper In Fire** *John Cougar Mellencamp*
14.	9/26	3	**Learning To Fly** *Pink Floyd*
15.	10/17	1	**Brilliant Disguise** *Bruce Springsteen*
16.	10/24	3	**Love Will Find A Way** *Yes*
17.	11/14	1	**Cherry Bomb** *John Cougar Mellencamp*
18.	11/21	4	**Tunnel Of Love** *Bruce Springsteen*
19.	12/19	4	**Say You Will** *Foreigner*

DATE	WKS		1988
1.	1/16	1	**On The Turning Away** *Pink Floyd*
2.	1/23	4	**Just Like Paradise** *David Lee Roth*
3.	2/20	6	**Heaven Knows** *Robert Plant*
4.	4/2	1	**I Wish I Had A Girl** *Henry Lee Summer*
5.	4/9	4	**Tall Cool One** *Robert Plant*
6.	5/7	1	**Only A Memory** *The Smithereens*
7.	5/14	3	**The Valley Road** *Bruce Hornsby & The Range*
8.	6/4	3	**Black And Blue** *Van Halen*
9.	6/25	4	**Roll With It** *Steve Winwood*
10.	7/23	1	**When It's Love** *Van Halen*
11.	7/30	3	**Simply Irresistible** *Robert Palmer*
12.	8/20	4	**Hate To Lose Your Lovin'** *Little Feat*
13.	9/17	2	**Don't You Know What The Night Can Do?** *Steve Winwood*

1988 (cont'd)

14.	10/1	1	**I'm Not Your Man**
			Tommy Conwell & The Young Rumblers
15.	10/8	5	**Desire** *U2*
16.	11/12	2	**It's Money That Matters** *Randy Newman*
17.	11/26	2	**Orange Crush** *R.E.M.*
18.	12/10	6	**Angel Of Harlem** *U2*

DATE	WKS		1989
1.	1/21	2	**Got It Made** *Crosby, Stills, Nash & Young*
2.	2/4	1	**The Love In Your Eyes** *Eddie Money*
3.	2/11	1	**Stand** *R.E.M.*
4.	2/18	4	**Driven Out** *The Fixx*
5.	3/18	1	**Working On It** *Chris Rea*
6.	3/25	3	**I'll Be You** *The Replacements*
7.	4/15	1	**Now You're In Heaven** *Julian Lennon*
8.	4/22	5	**I Won't Back Down** *Tom Petty*
9.	5/27	3	**The Doctor** *The Doobie Brothers*
10.	6/17	1	**Rooms On Fire** *Stevie Nicks*
11.	6/24	1	**Runnin' Down A Dream** *Tom Petty*
12.	7/1	4	**The End Of The Innocence** *Don Henley*
13.	7/29	3	**Crossfire**
			Stevie Ray Vaughan & Double Trouble
14.	8/19	1	**Let The Day Begin** *The Call*
15.	8/26	1	**Free Fallin'** *Tom Petty*
16.	9/2	5	**Mixed Emotions** *The Rolling Stones*
17.	10/7	2	**Love In An Elevator** *Aerosmith*
18.	10/21	5	**Rock And A Hard Place** *The Rolling Stones*
19.	11/25	6	**Pretending** *Eric Clapton*

DATE	WKS		1990
1.	1/6	1	**Show Don't Tell** *Rush*
2.	1/13	2	**Downtown Train** *Rod Stewart*
3.	1/27	3	**Bad Love** *Eric Clapton*
4.	2/17	2↕	**Black Velvet** *Alannah Myles*
5.	2/24	1	**What It Takes** *Aerosmith*
6.	3/10	1	**Almost Hear You Sigh** *The Rolling Stones*
7.	3/17	1	**Blue Sky Mine** *Midnight Oil*
8.	3/24	6	**Hurting Kind (I've Got My Eyes On You)**
			Robert Plant
9.	5/5	1	**Coming Of Age** *Damn Yankees*
10.	5/12	1	**Texas Twister** *Little Feat*
11.	5/19	5	**Doubleback** *ZZ Top*
12.	6/23	2	**Cradle Of Love** *Billy Idol*
13.	7/7	2	**Holy Water** *Bad Company*
14.	7/21	1	**Across The River**
			Bruce Hornsby & The Range
15.	7/28	2	**The Other Side** *Aerosmith*
16.	8/11	1	**Good Clean Fun** *Allman Brothers Band*
17.	8/18	3	**Brickyard Road** *Johnny Van Zant*
18.	9/8	1	**Blaze Of Glory** *Jon Bon Jovi*
19.	9/15	4	**Suicide Blonde** *INXS*
20.	10/13	4	**Concrete And Steel** *ZZ Top*
21.	11/10	2	**Hard To Handle** *The Black Crowes*
22.	11/24	2	**One And Only Man** *Steve Winwood*
23.	12/8	6	**My Head's In Mississippi** *ZZ Top*

#1 HITS

1991

	DATE	WKS		
1.	1/19	7	**All This Time**	*Sting*
2.	3/9	1	**She Talks To Angels**	*The Black Crowes*
3.	3/16	3	**Highwire**	*The Rolling Stones*
4.	4/6	1	**Silent Lucidity**	*Queensrÿche*
5.	4/13	3	**Losing My Religion**	*R.E.M.*
6.	5/4	6	**Lift Me Up**	*Yes*
7.	6/15	2	**Poundcake**	*Van Halen*
8.	6/29	6	**Learning To Fly**	
			Tom Petty & The Heartbreakers	
9.	8/10	4	**Runaround**	*Van Halen*
10.	9/7	2	**Out In The Cold**	
			Tom Petty & The Heartbreakers	
11.	9/21	4	**Dreamline**	*Rush*
12.	10/19	3↕	**Get A Leg Up**	*John Mellencamp*
13.	10/26	4↕	**Top Of The World**	*Van Halen*

> *11/23/91: Billboard begins compiling "Album Rock Tracks" chart from data provided by Broadcast Data Systems.*

	DATE	WKS		
14.	12/7	1	**Heavy Fuel**	*Dire Straits*
15.	12/14	12	**Mysterious Ways**	*U2*

1992

	DATE	WKS		
1.	3/7	2	**Again Tonight**	*John Mellencamp*
2.	3/21	3	**Human Touch**	*Bruce Springsteen*
3.	4/11	1	**Let's Get Rocked**	*Def Leppard*
4.	4/18	2	**One**	*U2*
5.	5/2	11	**Remedy**	*The Black Crowes*
6.	7/18	2	**Sting Me**	*The Black Crowes*
7.	8/1	3	**Even Better Than The Real Thing**	*U2*
8.	8/22	4	**Thorn In My Pride**	*The Black Crowes*
9.	9/19	6	**How About That**	*Bad Company*
10.	10/31	1	**Digging In The Dirt**	*Peter Gabriel*
11.	11/7	2	**Rest In Peace**	*Extreme*
12.	11/21	1	**Keep The Faith**	*Bon Jovi*
13.	11/28	6	**Hotel Illness**	*The Black Crowes*

1993

	DATE	WKS		
1.	1/9	5	**Stand Up (Kick Love Into Motion)**	
			Def Leppard	
2.	2/13	1	**Don't Tear Me Up**	*Mick Jagger*
3.	2/20	1	**Won't Get Fooled Again**	*Van Halen*
4.	2/27	6	**Pride And Joy**	*Coverdale•Page*
5.	4/10	9	**Livin' On The Edge**	*Aerosmith*
6.	6/12	2	**Are You Gonna Go My Way**	*Lenny Kravitz*
7.	6/26	1	**Plush**	*Stone Temple Pilots*
8.	7/3	2	**Big Gun**	*AC/DC*
9.	7/17	6	**Cryin'**	*Aerosmith*
10.	8/28	2	**What If I Came Knocking**	*John Mellencamp*
11.	9/11	4	**Peace Pipe**	*Cry Of Love*
12.	10/9	2	**No Rain**	*Blind Melon*
13.	10/23	4	**Stick It Out**	*Rush*
14.	11/20	2	**Mary Jane's Last Dance**	
			Tom Petty & The Heartbreakers	
15.	12/4	8	**Daughter**	*Pearl Jam*

1994

	DATE	WKS		
1.	1/29	4	**Pincushion**	*ZZ Top*
2.	2/26	4	**Deuces Are Wild**	*Aerosmith*
3.	3/26	2	**No Excuses**	*Alice In Chains*
4.	4/9	6	**Keep Talking**	*Pink Floyd*
5.	5/21	8	**Shine**	*Collective Soul*
6.	7/16	7	**Black Hole Sun**	*Soundgarden*
7.	9/3	2	**Vasoline**	*Stone Temple Pilots*
8.	9/17	15	**Interstate Love Song**	*Stone Temple Pilots*
9.	12/31	1	**You Don't Know How It Feels**	*Tom Petty*

1995

	DATE	WKS		
1.	1/7	8↕	**Better Man**	*Pearl Jam*
2.	1/21	3	**Don't Tell Me (What Love Can Do)**	
			Van Halen	
3.	3/25	10	**Lightning Crashes**	*Live*
4.	6/3	9	**December**	*Collective Soul*
5.	8/5	1	**Hold Me, Thrill Me, Kiss Me, Kill Me**	*U2*
6.	8/12	6	**And Fools Shine On**	*Brother Cane*
7.	9/23	3	**Tomorrow**	*Silverchair*
8.	10/14	3	**Hard As A Rock**	*AC/DC*
9.	11/4	5	**Name**	*Goo Goo Dolls*
10.	12/9	4	**My Friends**	*Red Hot Chili Peppers*

1996

	DATE	WKS		
1.	1/6	4	**Cumbersome**	*Seven Mary Three*
2.	2/3	4	**The World I Know**	*Collective Soul*
3.	3/2	2	**1979**	*Smashing Pumpkins*
4.	3/16	3	**Santa Monica (Watch The World Die)**	
			Everclear	
5.	4/6	4	**In The Meantime**	*Spacehog*

> *4/13/96: Billboard changes name of chart from "Album Rock Tracks" to "Mainstream Rock Tracks"*

	DATE	WKS		
6.	5/4	1	**Big Bang Baby**	*Stone Temple Pilots*
7.	5/11	2	**Where The River Flows**	*Collective Soul*
8.	5/25	2	**Humans Being**	*Van Halen*
9.	6/8	8↕	**Until It Sleeps**	*Metallica*
10.	7/27	4↕	**Trippin' On A Hole In A Paper Heart**	
			Stone Temple Pilots	
11.	8/31	5	**Burden In My Hand**	*Soundgarden*
12.	10/5	3	**Test For Echo**	*Rush*
13.	10/26	6	**Me Wise Magic**	*Van Halen*
14.	12/7	3	**Hero Of The Day**	*Metallica*
15.	12/28	4↕	**Blow Up The Outside World**	*Soundgarden*

#1 HITS

1997

	DATE	WKS	
1.	1/18	1	**Lady Picture Show** *Stone Temple Pilots*
2.	2/1	5	**One Headlight** *The Wallflowers*
3.	3/8	5	**Falling In Love (Is Hard On The Knees)** *Aerosmith*
4.	4/12	4	**Precious Declaration** *Collective Soul*
5.	5/10	2	**Gone Away** *The Offspring*
6.	5/24	5	**Little White Lie** *Sammy Hagar*
7.	6/28	5	**If You Could Only See** *Tonic*
8.	8/2	5	**Listen** *Collective Soul*
9.	9/6	4	**Pink** *Aerosmith*
10.	10/4	16	**Touch, Peel And Stand** *Days Of The New*

1998

	DATE	WKS	
1.	1/24	6	**Given To Fly** *Pearl Jam*
2.	3/7	6	**Without You** *Van Halen*
3.	4/18	6↕	**Blue On Black** *Kenny Wayne Shepherd Band*
4.	5/9	2	**Most High** *Jimmy Page & Robert Plant*
5.	6/6	4	**I Lie In The Bed I Make** *Brother Cane*
6.	7/11	10	**The Down Town** *Days Of The New*
7.	9/19	6	**What's This Life For** *Creed*
8.	10/31	1	**Psycho Circus** *Kiss*
9.	11/7	3	**Fly Away** *Lenny Kravitz*
10.	11/28	11	**Turn The Page** *Metallica*

1999

	DATE	WKS	
1.	2/13	1	**What It's Like** *Everlast*
2.	2/20	15	**Heavy** *Collective Soul*
3.	6/5	3	**Lit Up** *Buckcherry*
4.	6/26	3	**Promises** *Def Leppard*
5.	7/17	10	**Scar Tissue** *Red Hot Chili Peppers*
6.	9/25	17	**Higher** *Creed*

2000

	DATE	WKS	
1.	1/22	7	**No Leaf Clover** *Metallica*
2.	3/11	4	**Stiff Upper Lip** *AC/DC*
3.	4/8	9	**Kryptonite** *3 Doors Down*
4.	6/10	7↕	**I Disappear** *Metallica*
5.	7/8	4	**With Arms Wide Open** *Creed*
6.	8/26	2	**Californication** *Red Hot Chili Peppers*
7.	9/9	21	**Loser** *3 Doors Down*

2001

	DATE	WKS	
1.	2/3	1	**Awake** *Godsmack*
2.	2/10	5	**Jaded** *Aerosmith*
3.	3/17	2	**Outside** *Aaron Lewis with Fred Durst*
4.	3/31	1	**Breakdown** *Tantric*
5.	4/7	3	**Duck And Run** *3 Doors Down*
6.	4/28	20	**It's Been Awhile** *Staind*
7.	9/15	13	**How You Remind Me** *Nickelback*
8.	12/15	9	**My Sacrifice** *Creed*

2002

	DATE	WKS	
1.	2/16	10	**Blurry** *Puddle Of Mudd*
2.	4/27	3	**Too Bad** *Nickelback*
3.	5/18	4	**I Stand Alone** *Godsmack*
4.	6/15	2	**Hero** *Chad Kroeger Featuring Josey Scott*
5.	6/29	6	**Drift & Die** *Puddle Of Mudd*
6.	8/10	7	**By The Way** *Red Hot Chili Peppers*
7.	9/28	1	**Aerials** *System Of A Down*
8.	10/5	3	**Never Again** *Nickelback*
9.	10/26	1	**She Hates Me** *Puddle Of Mudd*
10.	11/2	4*	**You Know You're Right** *Nirvana*

*still #1 as of 11/23/02

MODERN ROCK TRACKS

Lists, alphabetically by artist name, every track that <u>debuted</u> on *Billboard's* "Modern Rock Tracks" charts from September 10, 1988, through October 26, 2002.

KEY

Here's a quick reference guide to our symbols. Refer to *RESEARCHING BILLBOARD'S ROCK TRACKS CHARTS* and *USER'S GUIDE* for complete descriptions. (The artist and titles below are NOT real.)

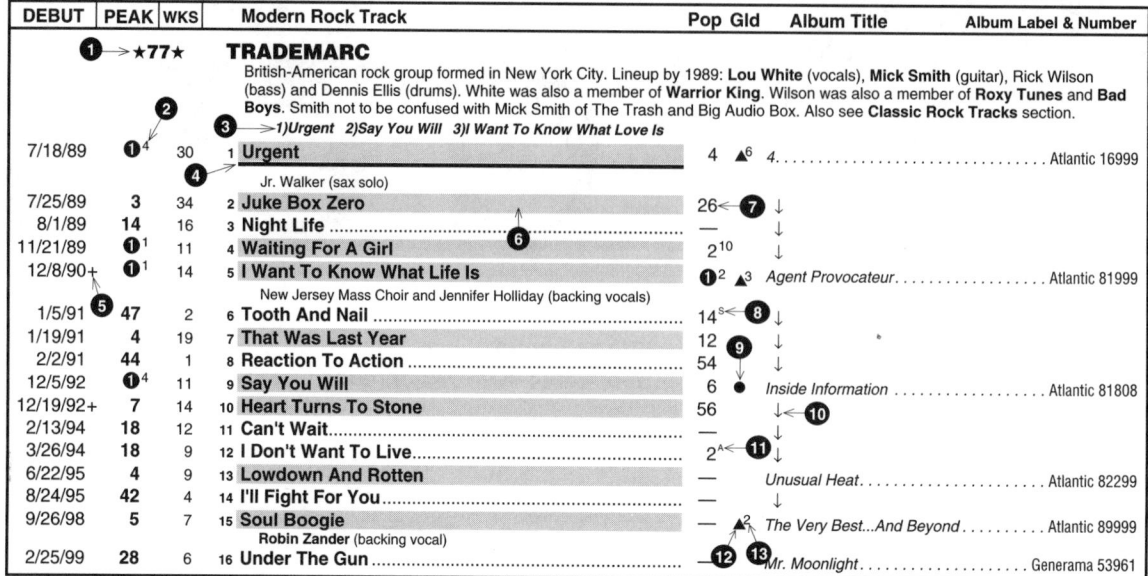

1. artist's ranking within the Top 100 artists
2. peak weeks (#1 & #2 hits only)
3. artist's top 3 or top 5 hits
4. artist's biggest hit (underlined)
5. peaked in the following year
6. Top 10 hit (shaded)
7. peak position attained on Billboard's
   Hot 100 or *Bubbling Under The Hot 100* chart
8. peak position is from Hot 100 Sales chart (S)
9. Gold seller (●) [500,000 units sold]
10. track from album listed directly above
11. peak position is from Hot 100 Airplay chart (A)
12. platinum seller (▲) [1,000,000 units sold]
13. multi-platinum (number of million units sold)

DEBUT	PEAK	WKS	Modern Rock Track	Pop Gld	Album Title	Album Label & Number

A

ABANDONED POOLS
Group is actually singer/songwriter Tommy Walter (born in Canada).

3/16/02	27	11	The Remedy..	—	Humanistic......................	Warner 48106

ACE OF BASE
Pop group from Gothenburg, Sweden: vocalists/sisters Jenny and Linn Berggren with keyboardists Jonas "Joker" Berggren (their brother) and Ulf "Buddha" Ekberg.

9/18/93	17	7	All That She Wants	2^3 ▲⁹	The Sign.........................	Arista 18740

ADEMA
Hard-rock group from Huntington Beach, California: Mark Chavez (vocals), Mike Ransom and Tim Fluckey (guitars), Dave DeRoo (bass) and Kris Kohls (drums).

7/14/01	14	25	1 Giving In	— ●	Adema	Arista 14696
12/8/01+	15	25	2 The Way You Like It	—	↓	
6/29/02	36	6	3 Freaking Out	—	↓	

ADORABLE
Pop group formed in Coventry, England: Pior Fijalkowski (vocals), Robert Dillam (guitar), Wil (bass) and Kevin Gritton (drums).

6/26/93	29	1	Sunshine Smile	—	Against Perfection	Creation 81416

AFGHAN WHIGS, The
Rock group from Cincinnati: Greg Dulli (vocals), Rick McCollum (guitar), John Curley (bass) and Steve Earle (drums). Paul Buchignani replaced Earle in 1995.

11/6/93	18	13	1 Debonair	—	Gentlemen	Elektra 61501
3/9/96	29	5	2 Honky's Ladder	—	Black Love	Elektra 61896

AFROMAN
Born Joseph Foreman in Los Angeles; later based in Hattiesburg, Mississippi. R&B singer.

8/18/01	17	8	Because I Got High	[N] 13 ●	The Good Times	Universal 014979

AGENTS OF GOOD ROOTS
Rock group from Richmond, Virginia: Andrew Winn (vocals, guitar), J.C. Kuhl (sax), Stewart Myers (bass) and Brian Jones (drums).

4/18/98	37	4	Come On	—	One By One	RCA 67590

ALARM, The
Rock group from Rhyl, Wales: Mike Peters (vocals; born on 2/25/59), Dave Sharp (guitar; born on 1/28/59), Eddie MacDonald (bass; born on 11/1/59) and Nigel Twist (drums; born on 7/18/58).

9/16/89	3	11	1 Sold Me Down The River	50	Change.......................	I.R.S. 82018
11/25/89	11	8	2 Devolution Workin' Man Blues	—	↓	
11/3/90	7	11	3 The Road	—	Standards......................	I.R.S. 13056
5/11/91	15	5	4 Raw	—	Raw	I.R.S. 13087

★60★ ALICE IN CHAINS
Male hard-rock group formed in Seattle: Layne Staley (vocals; born on 8/22/67; died of a drug overdose on 4/5/2002, age 34), **Jerry Cantrell** (guitar; born on 3/18/66), Mike Starr (bass) and Sean Kinney (drums; born on 5/27/66). Mike Inez (born on 5/14/66) replaced Starr by 1994. In 1995, Inez recorded with **Slash's Snakepit** and Staley recorded with **Mad Season** and **Class Of '99**. Scott Olson (guitar) joined in 1996.

11/28/92	30	1	1 Them Bones	— ▲⁴	Dirt	Columbia 52475
1/30/93	27	3	2 Angry Chair	—	↓	
2/12/94	3	16	3 No Excuses	48ᴬ ▲²	Jar Of Flies	Columbia 57628
12/10/94+	22	14	4 Got Me Wrong	—	Clerks (soundtrack)...............	Columbia 66660
10/28/95	18	13	5 Grind	— ▲²	Alice In Chains	Columbia 67248
1/13/96	6	18	6 Heaven Beside You	52ᴬ	↓	
6/15/96	36	6	7 Again	—	↓	
8/24/96	24	14	8 Over Now...	[L] — ▲	MTV Unplugged	Columbia 67703
6/12/99	12	12	9 Get Born Again	106 ●	Nothing Safe	Columbia 63649

ALIEN ANT FARM
Rock group from Los Angeles: Dryden Mitchell (vocals), Terry Corso (guitar), Tye Zamora (bass) and Mike Cosgrove (drums).

2/10/01	18	32	1 Movies..	— ▲	ANThology.......................	New Noize 450293
6/9/01	❶⁴	27	2 Smooth Criminal	—	↓	

#7 Pop hit for **Michael Jackson** in 1989

ALMOND, Marc
Born Peter Marc Almond on 7/9/57 in Southport, England. Half of the **Soft Cell** duo.

12/10/88+	8	12	Tears Run Rings	67	The Stars We Are.................	Capitol 91042

AMERICAN HI-FI
Male rock group from Boston: Stacy Jones (vocals), Jaime Arentzen (guitar), Drew Parsons (bass) and Brian Nolan (drums). Jones was drummer with **Letters To Cleo**.

2/3/01	5	26	1 Flavor Of The Weak	41	American Hi-Fi..................	Island 542871
7/28/01	33	6	2 Another Perfect Day	—	↓	

AMMONIA
Rock trio from Perth, Australia: Dave Johnstone (vocals, guitar), Simon Hensworth (bass) and Allan Balmont (drums).

3/30/96	29	8	Drugs...	—	Mint 400	Epic 67556

DEBUT	PEAK	WKS	Modern Rock Track	Pop	Gld	Album Title	Album Label & Number
	★95★		**AMOS, Tori**				
			Born Myra Ellen Amos on 8/22/63 in Newton, North Carolina; raised in Baltimore. Singer/songwriter/pianist.				
4/11/92	27	4	1 Silent All These Years	65	▲²	*Little Earthquakes*	Atlantic 82358
6/13/92	22	5	2 Crucify	—		↓	
1/29/94	❶²	17	3 God	72	▲²	*Under The Pink*	Atlantic 82567
5/21/94	12	12	4 Cornflake Girl	107		↓	
1/20/96	13	13	5 Caught A Lite Sneeze	60	▲	*Boys For Pele*	Atlantic 82862
4/25/98	13	15	6 Spark	49	▲	*From The Choirgirl Hotel*	Atlantic 83095
			ANDERSON, Laurie				
			Born on 6/5/47 in Chicago. Avant-garde performance artist.				
12/9/89+	7	12	Babydoll	—		*Strange Angels*	Warner 25900
			ANDREONE, Leah				
			Born on 5/24/73 in San Diego. Female singer/pianist.				
11/16/96	39	2	It's Alright, It's OK	57		*Veiled*	RCA 66897
			ANT, Adam				
			Born Stuart Goddard on 11/3/54 in London. Formed romantic-punk group **Adam And The Ants** in 1976. Three original Ants left to join **Bow Wow Wow** and Ant headed new lineup in 1980. Ant went solo in 1982. Acted in several movies and TV shows.				
3/10/90	17	7	1 Room At The Top	17		*Manners & Physique*	MCA 6315
2/25/95	7	17	2 Wonderful	39		*Wonderful*	Capitol 30335
			APARO, Angie				
			Born in Atlanta. Male singer/songwriter/guitarist.				
4/8/00	35	3	Spaceship	—		*The American*	Melisma 60000
			APOLLO FOUR FORTY				
			Techno-rock trio from England: brothers Trevor and Howard Gray (vocals, keyboards), with Noko (guitar).				
1/22/00	21	10	Stop The Rock	—		*Gettin' High On Your Own Supply*	550 Music 62238
			APPLE, Fiona				
			Born Fiona Apple Maggart on 9/13/77 in New York City. Singer/songwriter/pianist. Daughter of singer Diane McAfee and actor Brandon Maggart.				
11/30/96	34	6	1 Shadowboxer	—	▲³	*Tidal*	Clean Slate 67439
3/22/97	28	13	2 Sleep To Dream	—		↓	
7/26/97	4	26	3 Criminal	21		↓	
11/6/99	20	12	4 Fast As You Can	—	●	*When The Pawn*	Clean Slate 69195
			ARCHER, Tasmin				
			Born in 1964 in Bradford, Yorkshire, England. Female singer of Jamaican parentage.				
2/27/93	12	11	Sleeping Satellite	32		*Great Expectations*	SBK 80134
			ARMATRADING, Joan				
			Born on 12/9/50 in St. Kitts, West Indies; raised in Birmingham, England. Black singer/songwriter/guitarist.				
9/10/88	30	1	Living For You	—		*The Shouting Stage*	A&M 5211
			ARTIFICIAL JOY CLUB				
			Rock group from Ottawa, Canada: Louise "Sal" Reny (vocals), Leslie Howe and Michael Goyette (guitars), Tim Dupont (bass) and Andrew Lamarche (drums).				
6/28/97	17	14	Sick & Beautiful	—		*Melt*	Crunchy 90125
			ART OF NOISE, The				
			Techno-pop trio from England: Anne Dudley (keyboards), J.J. Jeczalik (keyboards, programmer) and Gary Langan (engineer).				
12/10/88	14	6	Kiss	31		*The Best Of The Art Of Noise*	China 837367
			THE ART OF NOISE Featuring Tom Jones #1 Pop hit for **Prince** in 1986				
			ASH, Daniel				
			Born on 7/31/57 in Northampton, England. Singer/songwriter/guitarist. Former member of **Love And Rockets**.				
1/19/91	2³	13	1 This Love	—		*Coming Down*	Beggars Banquet 3014
11/14/92+	3	13	2 Get Out Of Control	—		*Foolish Thing Desire*	Beggars Banquet 53179
			ASS PONYS				
			Rock group from Los Angeles: Chuck Cleaver (vocals, guitar), John Erhardt (guitar), Randy Cheek (bass) and David Morrison (drums).				
2/11/95	26	7	Little Bastard	—		*Electric Rock Music*	A&M 540270
			ASTLEY, Jon				
			Born in Manchester, England. Noted rock producer (**The Who**, **Eric Clapton** and **Corey Hart**).				
9/24/88	3	11	Put This Love To The Test	74		*The Compleat Angler*	Atlantic 81881
			ATHENAEUM				
			Rock group from Greensboro, North Carolina: Mark Kano (vocals), Grey Brewster (guitar), Alex McKinney (bass) and Nic Brown (drums).				
4/25/98	14	17	What I Didn't Know	58		*Radiance*	Atlantic 83071
			AT THE DRIVE-IN				
			Rock group from El Paso, Texas: Cedric Bixler (vocals), Omar Rodriguez and Jim Ward (guitars), Paul Hinojos (bass) and Tony Hajjar (drums).				
12/30/00+	26	13	One Armed Scissor	—		*Relationship Of Command*	Grand Royal 49999

DEBUT	PEAK	WKS	Modern Rock Track	Pop Gld	Album Title	Album Label & Number

AUDIOSLAVE
Group of former **Rage Against The Machine** members Tom Morello (guitar), Tim Commerford (bass) and Brad Wilk (drums), with **Chris Cornell** (vocals; **Soundgarden**).

10/12/02	9↑	7↑	Cochise	77↑	Audioslave . . . . Epic 86968

AUDIOVENT
Rock group from Calabasas, California: Jason Boyd (vocals), Ben Einziger (guitar), Paul Fried (bass) and Jamin Wilcox (drums).

6/1/02	17	15	The Energy	—	Dirty Sexy Knights In Paris . . . . Atlantic 83544

AZTEC CAMERA
Pop-rock group formed in Glasgow, Scotland: Roddy Frame (vocals, guitar), Gary Sanctuary (keyboards), Paul Powell (bass) and Frank Tontoh (drums).

| 7/14/90 | 3 | 11 | 1 The Crying Scene | — | Stray . . . . Sire 26211 |
| 9/29/90 | 12 | 6 | 2 Good Morning Britain . . . . | — | ↓ |

B

BABES IN TOYLAND
Female rock trio formed in Minneapolis: Kat Bjelland (vocals, guitar), Maureen Herman (bass) and Lori Barbero (drums).

7/29/95	37	2	Sweet '69	—	Nemesisters . . . . Reprise 45868

BAD RELIGION
Punk-rock group from Woodland Hills, California: Greg Graffin (vocals), Brett Gurewitz and Greg Hetson (guitars), Jay Bentley (bass) and Bobby Schayer (drums). Brian Baker replaced Gurewitz in 1995. Gurewitz owns the Epitaph record label.

9/10/94	29	5	1 Stranger Than Fiction	— ●	Stranger Than Fiction . . . . Atlantic 82658
11/19/94	11	13	2 21st Century (Digital Boy)	—	↓
2/25/95	27	8	3 Infected	—	↓
3/9/96	34	5	4 A Walk	—	The Gray Race . . . . Atlantic 82870
1/26/02	35	8	5 Sorrow	—	The Process Of Belief . . . . Epitaph 86635

BANGLES
Female pop-rock group from Los Angeles: Susanna Hoffs (guitar), Michael Steele (bass), sisters Vicki (guitar) and Debbi (drums) Peterson. All share vocals. Originally named The Bangs. Steele was previously in The Runaways.

10/29/88	5	13	In Your Room	5 ▲	Everything . . . . Columbia 44056

BANTON, Pato
Born Patrick Murray in Birmingham, England. Reggae singer.

9/10/94	39	3	Baby Come Back	—	Collections . . . . I.R.S. 27055

Robin & Ali Campbell (of **UB40**; guest vocals); written by **Eddy Grant**; #32 Pop hit for The Equals in 1968

BARE JR.
Rock group from Nashville: Bobby Bare Jr. (vocals), Michael Grimes (guitar), Tracy Hackney (harmonica), Dean Tomasek (bass) and Keith Brogdon (drums). Bare is the son of veteran country singer Bobby Bare.

3/6/99	40	2	You Blew Me Off	—	Boo-Tay . . . . Immortal 69353

BARENAKED LADIES
Pop-rock group from Toronto: Steven Page (vocals), Ed Robertson (vocals, guitar), Kevin Hearn (keyboards), Jim Creggan (bass) and Tyler Stewart (drums).

1/24/98	23	14	1 Brian Wilson	68 ▲	Rock Spectacle . . . . Reprise 46393
6/20/98	❶⁵	26	√ 2 One Week	❶¹ ▲⁴	Stunt . . . . Reprise 46963
11/7/98	15	15	3 It's All Been Done	44	↓
3/6/99	33	4	4 Alcohol	—	↓
9/2/00	30	16	5 Pinch Me	15 ▲	Maroon . . . . Reprise 47814

BASEMENT JAXX
Dance production duo from England: Simon Ratcliffe and Felix Buxton.

2/16/02	39	3	Where's Your Head At	43ˢ	Rooty . . . . Astralwerks 10423

BEASTIE BOYS ★86★
White rap-punk trio from New York City: Adam Horovitz, Adam Yauch and Mike Diamond. Horovitz starred in the movie *Lost Angels*; married actress Ione Skye (daughter of Donovan). Group started own Grand Royal record label.

8/26/89	18	4	1 Hey Ladies	36 ▲²	Paul's Boutique . . . . Capitol 91743

samples "Ain't It Funky" by James Brown, "Shake Your Pants" by Cameo, "Machine Gun" by Commodores, "Jungle Boogie" by Kool & The Gang, "War" by Edwin Starr and "Ballroom Blitz" by Sweet

7/4/92	22	6	2 So What 'Cha Want	93 ▲²	Check Your Head . . . . Capitol 98938
6/18/94	18	11	3 Sabotage	115 ▲²	Ill Communication . . . . Grand Royal 28599
6/13/98	4	26	4 Intergalactic	28 ▲³	Hello Nasty . . . . Grand Royal 37716

samples "Prelude C# Minor" by Les Baxter and elements of the album *Powerhouse* by The Jazz Crusaders

11/14/98	15	16	5 Body Movin'	—	↓
5/29/99	29	6	6 The Negotiation Limerick File	—	↓
10/30/99	11	15	7 Alive	—	Beastie Boys Anthology: The Sounds Of Science . . . . Grand Royal 22940

DEBUT	PEAK	WKS	Modern Rock Track	Pop Gld	Album Title	Album Label & Number

BEAUTIFUL SOUTH, The
Pop group formed in Hull, England: Paul Heaton and Dave Hemmingway (vocals), David Rotheray (guitar), Sean Welch (bass) and David Stead (drums). Female singer Briana Corrigan joined in 1991.

| 3/24/90 | 19 | 6 | 1 You Keep It All In .... | — | Welcome To The Beautiful South....... | Elektra 60917 |
| 5/2/92 | 10 | 10 | 2 We Are Each Other | — | 0898 Beautiful South .... | Elektra 61308 |

BECK ★37★
Born Beck David Campbell (later changed his last name to his mother's maiden name of Hansen) on 7/8/70 in Los Angeles. Male rock singer/songwriter/guitarist.

1)Loser 2)Where It's At 3)The New Pollution

12/25/93+	❶⁵	21	1 Loser	10	▲	Mellow Gold.......................	DGC 24634
			samples "I Walk On Guilded Splinters" by Dr. John				
7/16/94	27	2	2 Beercan..	—	↓		
6/15/96	5	20	3 Where It's At	61	▲	Odelay	DGC 24823
			samples "Get Up And Dance" by Mantronix				
9/28/96	23	13	4 Devils Haircut	94	↓		
			samples "Out Of Sight" by Them and "Soul Drums" by Pretty Purdie				
2/22/97	9	20	5 The New Pollution	78	↓		
8/2/97	15	15	6 Jack-Ass	73	↓		
			samples "It's All Over Now Baby Blue" by Them				
11/8/97+	16	17	7 Deadweight...	—		A Life Less Ordinary (soundtrack) . . .	Innerstate 540809
10/24/98	21	10	8 Tropicalia	—	●	Mutations	DGC 25309
10/23/99	21	15	9 Sexx Laws..	—	●	Midnite Vultures	DGC 490485
3/4/00	36	5	10 Mixed Bizness	—	↓		

BELEW, Adrian
Born Robert Steven Belew on 12/23/49 in Covington, Kentucky. Singer/songwriter/guitarist. Member of **King Crimson** from 1981-84.

5/27/89	5	12	1 Oh Daddy	58		Mr. Music Head	Atlantic 81959
			features vocals by his daughter Audie Belew				
5/19/90	2¹	10	2 Pretty Pink Rose	—		Young Lions......................	Atlantic 82099
			ADRIAN BELEW & DAVID BOWIE				
8/4/90	17	4	3 Men In Helicopters	—	↓		

BELLY
Pop-rock group from Newport, Rhode Island: Tanya Donelly (vocals, guitar) with brothers Thomas (guitar) and Chris (drums) Gorman. Gail Greenwood (bass) joined by mid-1993. Donelly was a member of **Throwing Muses** and **The Breeders**.

1/30/93	❶³	15	1 Feed The Tree	95	●	Star.............................	Sire 45187
5/15/93	17	6	2 Slow Dog	—	↓		
10/30/93	8	9	3 Gepetto	113	↓		
2/11/95	17	11	4 Now They'll Sleep..	103		King	Sire 45833
6/10/95	35	3	5 Super-Connected	—	↓		

BELOVED, The
Pop-rock duo from England: Jon Marsh (vocals, keyboards) and Steve Waddington (guitars).

| 2/10/90 | 6 | 12 | 1 Hello | — | | Happiness .... | Atlantic 82047 |
| 4/10/93 | 23 | 7 | 2 Sweet Harmony .... | 114 | | Conscience .... | Atlantic 82457 |

BEST KISSERS IN THE WORLD
Rock group from Seattle: Gerald Collier (vocals), Jeff Stone (guitar), Dave Swafford (bass) and Tim Arnold (drums).

| 11/6/93 | 22 | 6 | Miss Teen U.S.A. .... | — | | Been There .... | MCA 10757 |

| ★42★ | | | **BETTER THAN EZRA** | | | | |

Rock trio from New Orleans: Kevin Griffin (vocals, guitar), Tom Drummond (bass) and Cary Bonnecaze (drums). Travis McNabb replaced Bonnecaze by 1996.

3/4/95	❶⁵	26	1 Good	30	▲	Deluxe	Elektra 61784
6/24/95	4	26	2 In The Blood	48ᴬ	↓		
11/11/95	24	11	3 Rosealia	71	↓		
8/3/96	5	17	4 King Of New Orleans	62ᴬ		Friction, Baby	Elektra 61944
11/23/96+	11	26	5 Desperately Wanting	48	↓		
9/12/98	32	6	6 One More Murder	—		How Does Your Garden Grow?	Elektra 62247
11/21/98+	17	17	7 At The Stars	78	↓		
7/21/01	35	7	8 Extra Ordinary	116		Closer	Beyond 78137

DEBUT	PEAK	WKS	Modern Rock Track	Pop Gld	Album Title	Album Label & Number

★43★ B-52's, The
Pop-rock group from Athens, Georgia: Fred Schneider (vocals, keyboards; born on 7/1/51), Kate Pierson (vocals, organ; born on 4/27/48), Cindy Wilson (vocals, guitar; born on 2/28/57) and Keith Strickland (guitar; born on 10/26/53). Wilson left in 1991. Also see **Classic Rock Tracks** section.

DEBUT	PEAK	WKS	Track	Pop Gld	Album	Label
6/3/89	7	8	1 Cosmic Thing	—	▲⁴ Cosmic Thing	Reprise 25854
7/15/89	❶³	8	2 Channel Z	—	↓	
9/2/89	❶⁴	12	3 Love Shack	3	↓	
12/2/89+	6	14	4 Roam	3	↓	
6/20/92	❶⁴	9	5 Good Stuff	28 ●	Good Stuff	Reprise 26943
8/22/92	13	9	6 Tell It Like It T-I-Is	—	↓	
5/30/98	35	5	7 Debbie	—	Time Capsule - Songs For A Future Generation	Reprise 46920

tribute to **Debbie Harry**

BIBLE, The
Pop group formed in Cambridge, England: Boo Hewerdine (vocals, guitar), Neill MacColl (guitar), Tony Shepherd (keyboards) and Dave Larcombe (drums).

9/10/88	26	1	Crystal Palace	—	Eureka	Ensign 41613

★45★ BIG AUDIO DYNAMITE
Rock group from England: Mick Jones (vocals, guitar; **The Clash**), Don Letts and Dan Donovan (keyboards), Leo Williams (bass) and Greg Roberts (drums). Disbanded in 1989. Jones formed **Big Audio Dynamite II** in 1990 with Nick Hawkins (guitar), Gary Stonadge (bass) and Chris Kavanagh (drums). By 1994, group simply known as **Big Audio**.

9/10/88	❶¹	8	1 Just Play Music!	—	Tighten Up Vol. '88	Columbia 44074
9/17/88	13	8	2 Other 99	—	↓	
9/2/89	2²	10	3 James Brown	—	Megatop Phoenix	Columbia 45212
10/28/89	6	12	4 Contact	—	↓	
7/6/91	❶⁴	15	5 Rush	32 ●	The Globe	Columbia 46147

samples "Baba O'Riley" by **The Who**

10/5/91	3	10	6 The Globe	72	↓	

BIG AUDIO DYNAMITE II (above 2)

11/19/94	24	7	7 Looking For A Song	—	Higher Power	Columbia 53827

BIG AUDIO

BIG BAD VOODOO DADDY
Eclectic-jazz group from Ventura, California: Scotty Morris (vocals, guitar), Joshua Levy (piano), Jeff Harvis, Karl Hunter, Glen Marhevka and Andy Rowley (horns), Dirk Shumaker (bass) and Kurt Sodergen (drums). Group appeared as the band in the movie *Swingers*.

6/27/98	31	7	You & Me & The Bottle Makes Three Tonight (Baby)	104 ▲	Big Bad Voodoo Daddy	Coolsville 93338

BIG COUNTRY
Pop-rock group from Dunfermline, Scotland: Stuart Adamson (vocals, guitar), Bruce Watson (guitar), Tony Butler (bass) and Mark Brzezicki (drums). Adamson committed suicide on 12/16/2001 (age 43).

9/17/88	11	9	1 King Of Emotion	—	Peace In Our Time	Reprise 25787
9/4/93	17	6	2 The One I Love	—	The Buffalo Skinners	Fox 66294

BIG DIPPER
Rock group from Boston: Bill Goffrier (vocals, guitar), Gary Waleik (guitar), Steve Michener (bass) and Jeff Oliphant (drums).

5/12/90	19	6	Love Barge	—	Slam	Epic 46063

BIG HEAD TODD & THE MONSTERS
Rock trio from Boulder, Colorado: Todd Park Mohr (guitar, keyboards), Rob Squires (bass) and Brian Nevin (drums). All share vocals.

3/1/97	38	5	Resignation Superman	—	Beautiful World	Revolution 24661

BIG WRECK
Rock group from Boston: Ian Thornley (vocals), Brian Doherty (guitar), Dave Henning (bass) and Forrest Williams (drums).

2/7/98	24	9	The Oaf	—	In Loving Memory Of...	Atlantic 83032

BIRDLAND
Punk-rock group from Birmingham, England: brothers Robert (vocals) and Lee (guitar) Vincent, Sid Rogers (bass) and Gene Kale (drums).

5/11/91	12	8	Shoot You Down	—	Birdland	Radioactive 10214

BJÖRK
Born Björk Gudmundsdottir on 11/12/65 in Reykjavik, Iceland. Female singer/actress. Lead singer of **The Sugarcubes**. Played "Selma Jazkova" in the movie *Dancer In The Dark*.

7/17/93	2¹	13	1 Human Behaviour	109 ▲	Debut	Elektra 61468
1/1/94	5	14	2 Big Time Sensuality	88	↓	
4/15/95	21	9	3 Army Of Me	—	Tank Girl (soundtrack)	Elektra 61760

BLACK, Frank
Born Charles Thompson in 1965 in Long Beach, California. Rock singer/guitarist. Former leader of the **Pixies**.

3/27/93	6	8	1 Los Angeles	—	Frank Black	4 A D 61467
5/22/93	8	9	2 Hang On To Your Ego	—	↓	

first recorded by The Beach Boys in 1966

7/9/94	10	11	3 Headache	—	Teenager Of The Year	4 A D 61618

BLACK CROWES, The
Rock group from Atlanta: brothers Chris (vocals) and Rich (guitar) Robinson, Marc Ford (guitar), Eddie Harsch (keyboards), Johnny Colt (bass) and Steve Gorman (drums). Chris Robinson married actress Kate Hudson (daughter of Goldie Hawn) on 12/31/2000.

11/12/94	23	8	A Conspiracy	— ●	Amorica	American 43000

DEBUT	PEAK	WKS	Modern Rock Track	Pop	Gld	Album Title	Album Label & Number
			BLACK 47				
			Rock group from Ireland: Larry Kirwan (vocals, guitar), Geoffrey Blythe (sax), Chris Byrne (pipes), Fred Parcells (trombone), David Conrad (bass) and Thomas Hamlin (drums). Group name stands for the blackest year of the Irish potato famine (1847).				
1/23/93	27	3	Funky Ceili (Bridie's Song)	—		Black 47	SBK 80971
			BLACK GRAPE				
			Dance-rock group formed in England: Shaun Ryder (vocals), Paul Wagstaff (guitar), Mark Berry (keyboards), Paul Leveridge (bass) and Ged Lynch (drums). Ryder and Berry were members of **Happy Mondays**.				
12/2/95	31	6	In The Name Of The Father	—		It's Great When You're Straight...Yeah.	Radioactive 11224
			BLACK LAB				
			Rock group from Berkeley, California: Paul Durham (vocals), Michael Belfer (guitar), Geoff Stanfield (bass) and Bryan Head (drums).				
12/27/97+	13	17	1 Wash It Away	—		Your Body Above Me.	DGC 25127
4/25/98	28	10	2 Time Ago	75^A		↓	
			BLIND MELON				
			Male rock group formed in Los Angeles: Shannon Hoon (vocals), Rogers Stevens and Christopher Thorn (guitars), Brad Smith (bass) and Glen Graham (drums). Hoon died of a drug overdose on 10/21/95 (age 28).				
10/31/92	20	11	1 Tones Of Home	—	▲⁴	Blind Melon.	Capitol 96585
7/24/93	❶³	16	2 No Rain	20		↓	
1/22/94	20	14	3 Tones Of Home .... [R]	—		↓	
			same version as #1 above				
8/12/95	8	11	4 Galaxie	54^A		Soup.	Capitol 28732
			BLINDSIDE				
			Rock group from Stockholm, Sweden: Christian Lindskog (vocals), Simon Grenehed (guitar), Tomas Naslund (bass) and Marcus Dahlstrom (drums).				
10/26/02	36	4	Pitiful	—		Silence	Elektra 62675

			BLINK-182 ★14★				
			Rock trio from San Diego: Tom Delonge (vocals, guitar), Mark Hoppus (vocals, bass) and Scott Raynor (drums). Travis Barker replaced Raynor in late 1998. Delonge and Barker also formed **Box Car Racer**.				
10/11/97+	11	28	✓ Dammit (Growing Up)	61^A	▲	Dude Ranch	MCA 11624
5/8/99	2¹¹	30	✓ 2 What's My Age Again?	58	▲⁵	Enema Of The State	MCA 11950
10/16/99	❶⁸	27	✓ 3 All The Small Things	6		↓	
3/18/00	2⁷	26	4 Adam's Song	101		↓	
9/30/00	2²	22	✓ 5 Man Overboard	117	●	The Mark, Tom, And Travis Show (The Enema Strikes Back!)	MCA 112379
5/19/01	2⁴	26	✓ 6 The Rock Show	71	▲²	Take Off Your Pants And Jacket	MCA 112627
9/22/01	7	26	✓ 7 Stay Together For The Kids	116		↓	
2/2/02	6	25	✓ 8 First Date	106		↓	
			BLOODHOUND GANG				
			Rock group from Philadelphia: Jimmy Pop Ali (vocals), Lupus (guitar), Q-Ball (DJ), Evil Jared (bass) and Spanky G (drums).				
12/14/96+	18	10	1 Fire Water Burn	—	●	One Fierce Beer Coaster	Geffen 25124
3/4/00	6	15	2 The Bad Touch	52	▲	Hooray For Boobies.	Republic 490455
			BLUE AEROPLANES, The				
			Pop-rock group formed in Bristol, England: brothers Gerard (vocals) and John (drums) Langley, Rodney Allen, Alex Lee and Angelo Bruschini (guitars), and Andy McCreeth (bass).				
10/5/91	13	7	Yr Own World	—		Beatsongs.	Ensign 21856
			BLUE NILE, The				
			Melodic-pop trio from Glasgow, Scotland: Paul Buchanan (vocals, guitar), Robert Bell (bass) and Paul Moore (keyboards).				
2/3/90	10	11	The Downtown Lights	—		Hats	A&M 5284
			BLUE RODEO				
			Folk-rock group from Toronto: Jim Cuddy (vocals, guitar), Greg Keelor (guitar), Bob Wiseman (keyboards), Bazil Donovan (bass) and Cleave Anderson (drums). Group appeared as Meryl Streep's backing band in the 1990 movie *Postcards From The Edge*.				
2/16/91	19	5	Til I Am Myself Again	—		Casino.	EastWest 91601
			BLUES TRAVELER				
			Blues-rock group from New York City: John Popper (vocals, harmonica), Chan Kinchla (guitar), Bobby Sheehan (bass) and Brendan Hill (drums). Sheehan died of a drug overdose on 8/20/99 (age 31).				
4/1/95	14	26	1 Run-Around	8	▲⁶	four	A&M 540265
10/7/95	13	20	2 Hook	23		↓	
7/13/96	17	13	3 But Anyway .... [L]	36^A	▲	Live From The Fall	A&M 540515
6/21/97	30	6	4 Carolina Blues	—	▲	Straight On Till Morning	A&M 540750
8/30/97	25	10	5 Most Precarious	74^A		↓	

DEBUT	PEAK	WKS	Modern Rock Track	Pop Gld	Album Title	Album Label & Number

BLUR
Techno-rock group from London: Damon Albarn (vocals), Graham Coxon (guitar), Alex James (bass) and Dave Rowntree (drums).

9/14/91	**5**	19	1 **There's No Other Way**	82	Leisure	Food 97880
12/11/93	**27**	6	2 **Chemical World**	—	Modern Life Is Rubbish	Food 89442
6/4/94	**4**	13	3 **Girls & Boys**	59	Parklife	Food 29194
4/12/97	**6**	26	4 **Song 2**	55ᴬ ●	Blur	Food 42876

BoDEANS
Folk-rock group from Waukesha, Wisconsin: Kurt Neumann and Sam Llanas (vocals, guitars), Michael Ramos (keyboards), Bob Griffin (bass) and Guy Hoffman (drums).

| 7/15/89 | **15** | 7 | **You Don't Get Much** . . . . | — | home . . . . | Slash 25876 |

BOINGO — see OINGO BOINGO

BONHAM, Tracy
Born on 3/16/67 in Eugene, Oregon. Female singer/songwriter/guitarist.

| 4/6/96 | **❶**³ | 21 | ✓1 **Mother Mother** | 32ᴬ ● | The Burdens Of Being Upright . . . . | Island 524187 |
| 8/17/96 | **23** | 9 | 2 **The One** . . . . | — | ↓ | |

BOOK OF LOVE
Dance-pop group from New York City: Susan Ottaviano (vocals), Ted Ottaviano and Lauren Roselli (keyboards), and Jade Lee (percussion). The Ottavianos are not related.

| 2/16/91 | **21** | 5 | **Alice Everyday** . . . . | — | Candy Carol . . . . | Sire 26389 |

BOOM CRASH OPERA
Pop-rock group from Melbourne, Australia: Dale Ryder (vocals), Pete Farnan (guitar), Greg O'Connor (keyboards), Richard Pleasance (bass) and Peter Maslin (drums).

| 6/23/90 | **8** | 9 | **Onion Skin** | — | These Here Are Crazy Times . . . . | Giant 26160 |

BOO RADLEYS, The
Rock group from Liverpool, England: Simon "Sice" Rowbottom (vocals), Martin Carr (guitar), Tim Brown (bass) and Rob Cieka (drums). Group named after a character in Harper Lee's novel *To Kill A Mockingbird.*

| 10/2/93 | **30** | 2 | 1 **Lazarus** . . . . | — | Giant Steps . . . . | Creation 53794 |
| 1/22/94 | **30** | 1 | 2 **Barney (...And Me)** . . . . | — | ↓ | |

BOWIE, David
Born David Jones on 1/8/47 in London. Pop-rock singer/actor. Acted in several movies. Starred in *The Elephant Man* on Broadway. Formed **Tin Machine** in 1988. Married Somalian actress/supermodel Iman on 4/24/92. Inducted into the Rock and Roll Hall of Fame in 1996. Also see **Classic Rock Tracks** section.

| 5/19/90 | **2**¹ | 10 | 1 **Pretty Pink Rose** | — | Young Lions . . . . | Atlantic 82099 |

ADRIAN BELEW & DAVID BOWIE

8/1/92	**11**	6	2 **Real Cool World**	—	Cool World (soundtrack)	Warner 45009
4/3/93	**4**	8	3 **Jump They Say**	—	Black Tie White Noise	Savage 50212
9/16/95	**20**	7	✓4 **The Hearts Filthy Lesson**	92	Outside	Virgin 40711
12/13/97+	**29**	8	5 **I'm Afraid Of Americans**	66	Earthling	Virgin 42627

BOWLING FOR SOUP
Punk-rock group from Wichita Falls, Texas: Jaret Reddick (vocals, guitar), Chris Burney (guitar), Erik Chandler (bass) and Gary Wiseman (drums).

| 9/21/02 | **38** | 6 | **Girl All The Bad Guys Want** . . . . | — | Drunk Enough To Dance . . . . | Silvertone 41819 |

BOX CAR RACER
Rock group from San Diego: Tom Delonge (vocals, guitar), David Kennedy (guitar), Anthony Celestino (bass) and Travis Barker (drums). Delonge and Barker are also members of **Blink-182**.

| 5/18/02 | **8** | 16 | 1 **I Feel So** . . . . | 120 | Box Car Racer . . . . | MCA 112894 |
| 10/26/02 | **32**↑ | 5↑ | 2 **There Is** . . . . | — | ↓ | |

BOY GEORGE
Born George O'Dowd on 6/14/61 in Bexleyheath, England. Former lead singer of **Culture Club**.

| 3/13/93 | **13** | 7 | **The Crying Game** . . . . | 15 | The Crying Game (soundtrack) . . . . | SBK 89024 |

produced by the **Pet Shop Boys**; #87 Pop hit for Brenda Lee in 1965

BRAGG, Billy
Born Steven William Bragg on 12/20/57 in Barking, Essex, England. Rock singer/songwriter.

10/22/88	**20**	1	1 **Waiting For The Great Leap Forwards**	—	Workers Playtime	Elektra 60824
11/26/88	**16**	2	2 **She's Got A New Spell**	—	↓	
9/7/91	**2**²	11	3 **Sexuality**	—	Don't Try This At Home	Elektra 61121
11/16/91	**16**	9	4 **You Woke Up My Neighbourhood**	—	↓	

BREEDERS, The
Rock group from Dayton, Ohio: twin sisters/guitarists/vocalists Kim and Kelley Deal, bassist Josephine Wiggs (native of Bedfordshire, England) and drummer Jim MacPherson. Kim was a member of the **Pixies**. Tanya Donelly (**Throwing Muses**, **Belly**) was an early member.

9/11/93	**2**²	29	1 **Cannonball**	44 ▲	Last Splash	4 A D 61508
12/4/93	**28**	4	2 **Divine Hammer**	104	↓	
7/9/94	**12**	8	3 **Saints**	109	↓	

DEBUT	PEAK	WKS	Modern Rock Track	Pop	Gld	Album Title	Album Label & Number

BRICKELL, Edie, & New Bohemians
Born on 3/10/66 in Oak Cliff, Texas. Female singer/songwriter. New Bohemians consisted of Kenny Withrow (guitar), Brad Houser (bass) and John Bush (drums). Joining the band by 1990 were Wes Burt-Martin (guitar) and Matt Chamberlain (drums). Brickell married **Paul Simon** on 5/30/92.

DEBUT	PEAK	WKS	Modern Rock Track	Pop	Gld	Album Title	Album Label & Number
9/10/88	4	21	What I Am	7	$\blacktriangle^2$	Shooting Rubberbands At The Stars	Geffen 24192
1/21/89	14	9	2 Little Miss S.	—		↓	
2/10/90	21	4	3 A Hard Rain's A Gonna Fall	—		Born On The Fourth Of July (soundtrack)	MCA 6340
			first recorded by **Bob Dylan** in 1963				
11/10/90	17	10	4 Mama Help Me	—		Ghost Of A Dog	Geffen 24304

BROOKS, Meredith
Born on 6/12/66 in Oregon City, Oregon. Female rock singer/guitarist.

| 4/12/97 | 4 | 21 | Bitch | 2^4 | ▲ | Blurring The Edges | Capitol 36919 |

BT
Born Brian Transeau on 10/4/70 in Washington DC. Electronic keyboardist/producer.

| 7/15/00 | 16 | 11 | Never Gonna Come Back Down | — | | Movement In Still Life | Nettwerk 30154 |

BUCKCHERRY
Rock group from Los Angeles: Joshua Todd (vocals), Keith Nelson and Yogi (guitars), Jon Brightman (bass) and Devon Glenn (drums).

| 5/15/99 | 33 | 5 | 1 Lit Up | — | ● | Buckcherry | DreamWorks 50044 |
| 8/7/99 | 24 | 12 | 2 For The Movies | — | | ↓ | |

BUCKLEY, Jeff
Born on 11/17/66 in Los Angeles. Drowned in Memphis on 5/29/97 (age 30). Singer/songwriter/guitarist. Son of folk music legend Tim Buckley.

| 3/25/95 | 19 | 13 | Last Goodbye | — | | Grace | Columbia 57528 |

BUCK-O-NINE
Ska-rock group from San Diego: Jon Pebsworth (vocals), Jonas Kleiner (guitar), Anthony Curry (trumpet), Dan Albert (trombone), Craig Yarnold (sax), Scott Kennerly (bass) and Steve Bauer (drums).

| 8/9/97 | 32 | 8 | My Town | — | | Twenty-Eight Teeth | TVT 5760 |

BUCK PETS, The
Rock group from Dallas: Andy Thompson (vocals), Chris Savage (guitar), Ian Beach (bass) and Tony Alba (drums).

| 2/9/91 | 25 | 2 | Libertine | — | | Mercurotones | Island 846867 |

BUFFALO, Grant Lee — see GRANT

BUFFALO TOM
Rock trio from Boston: Bill Janovitz (vocals, guitar), Chris Colbourn (bass) and Tom Maginnis (drums).

| 9/18/93 | 7 | 10 | Sodajerk | — | | [big red letter day] | Beggars Banquet 92292 |

BUSH ★7★
Rock group from London: **Gavin Rossdale** (vocals, guitar; born on 10/30/67), Nigel Pulsford (guitar; born on 4/11/63), Dave Parsons (bass; born on 7/2/65) and Robin Goodridge (drums; born on 9/10/66). Rossdale married Gwen Stefani (lead singer of **No Doubt**) on 9/14/2002.

1)Swallowed 2)The Chemicals Between Us 3)Glycerine

12/10/94+	2^2	26	1 Everything Zen	40^A	$\blacktriangle^6$	Sixteen Stone	Trauma 92531
4/8/95	4	23	2 Little Things	46^A		↓	
7/22/95	❶²	26	3 Comedown	30		↓	
11/11/95	❶²	23	4 Glycerine	28		↓	
2/24/96	4	26	5 Machinehead	43		↓	
11/2/96	❶⁷	20	6 Swallowed	27^A	$\blacktriangle^3$	Razorblade Suitcase	Trauma 90091
12/28/96+	3	26	7 Greedy Fly	41^A		↓	
4/26/97	23	10	8 Cold Contagious	—		↓	
10/25/97	5	23	9 Mouth	63^A		An American Werewolf In Paris (soundtrack)	Hollywood 62131
9/25/99	❶⁵	26	10 The Chemicals Between Us	67	▲	The Science Of Things	Trauma 490483
1/22/00	4	17	11 Letting The Cables Sleep	113		↓	
6/17/00	38	2	12 Warm Machine	—		↓	
9/15/01	11	13	13 The People That We Love	114		Golden State	Atlantic 83488
			originally titled "Speed Kills" (title changed due to the 9/11 terrorist attacks)				
1/5/02	38	3	14 Headful Of Ghosts	—		↓	

★98★ **BUSH, Kate**
Born on 7/30/58 in Bexleyheath, Kent, England. Singer/songwriter.

10/28/89	❶⁴	15	1 Love And Anger	—	●	The Sensual World	Columbia 44164
1/20/90	6	8	2 The Sensual World	—		↓	
11/9/91	11	10	3 Rocket Man (I Think It's Going To Be A Long, Long Time)	—	▲	Two Rooms - Celebrating The Songs Of Elton John & Bernie Taupin (various artists)	Polydor 845750
			#6 Pop hit for **Elton John** in 1972				
10/2/93	10	7	4 Eat The Music	—		The Red Shoes	Columbia 53737
11/20/93	7	11	5 Rubberband Girl	88		↓	

DEBUT	PEAK	WKS	Modern Rock Track	Pop Gld	Album Title	Album Label & Number

BUTTHOLE SURFERS
Rock group from San Antonio, Texas: Gibby Haynes (vocals), Paul Leary (guitar), Jeff Pinkus (bass) and King Coffey (drums).

DEBUT	PEAK	WKS	Modern Rock Track	Pop Gld	Album Title	Album Label & Number
5/22/93	24	2	1 Who Was In My Room Last Night?	—	Independent Worm Saloon	Capitol 98798
5/18/96	❶³	26	2 Pepper	26ᴬ ●	Electriclarryland	Capitol 29842
8/18/01	24	10	3 The Shame Of Life		Weird Revolution	Surfdog 162269

BYRNE, David
Born on 5/14/52 in Dumbarton, Scotland; raised in Baltimore. Lead singer of the **Talking Heads**. Composed scores for several movies and plays. Formed own Luaka Bop record label.

10/21/89	11	7	1 Make Believe Mambo	—	Rei Momo	Luaka Bop 25990
12/9/89	8	6	2 Dirty Old Town	—	↓	
3/7/92	3	11	3 She's Mad	—	Uh-Oh	Luaka Bop 26799
6/4/94	24	4	4 Angels	—	David Byrne	Luaka Bop 45558

C

CADELL, Meryn
Born in New York City; raised in Waterloo, Canada. Female singer/songwriter.

5/30/92	24	3	The Sweater		Angel Food For Thought	Sire 26877

CAKE ★53★
Rock group from Sacramento, California: John McCrea (vocals, guitar), Greg Brown (guitar), Vince DiFiore (trumpet), Victor Damiani (bass) and Todd Roper (drums). Brown left in 1987. Gabriel Nelson replaced Damiani in early 1998.

4/22/95	31	7	1 Rock 'N' Roll Lifestyle		Motorcade Of Generosity	Capricorn 42035
10/5/96	4	25	✓2 The Distance	35ᴬ ▲	Fashion Nugget	Capricorn 532867
2/15/97	28	8	3 I Will Survive	—	↓	
			#1 Pop hit for Gloria Gaynor in 1979			
9/26/98	❶³	33	4 Never There	78 ▲	Prolonging The Magic	Capricorn 538092
2/20/99	16	14	5 Sheep Go To Heaven	—	↓	
7/17/99	28	10	6 Let Me Go	—	↓	
6/30/01	7	20	7 Short Skirt/Long Jacket	119	Comfort Eagle	Columbia 62132

CALE, John
Born on 3/9/40 in Crynant, West Glamorgan, Wales. Singer/songwriter/producer. Member of the Velvet Underground.

5/12/90	13	7	1 Nobody But You	—	Songs For Drella	Sire 26140
			LOU REED/JOHN CALE			
10/27/90	11	10	2 Been There Done That	—	Wrong Way Up	Opal 26421
			BRIAN ENO/JOHN CALE			

CALL, The
Rock group from California: Michael Been (vocals, guitar), Tom Ferrier (guitar), Jim Goodman (keyboards) and Scott Musick (drums).

6/24/89	5	12	1 Let The Day Begin	51	Let The Day Begin	MCA 6303
10/13/90	25	4	2 What's Happened To You	—	Red Moon	MCA 10033
			Bono (of **U2**; backing vocal)			

CALLING, The
Rock group from Los Angeles: Alex Band (vocals), Aaron Kamin and Sean Woolstenhulme (guitars), Billy Mohler (bass) and Nate Wood (drums).

6/23/01	14	14	Wherever You Will Go	5 ●	Camino Palmero	RCA 67585

CAMOUFLAGE
Dance trio from Germany: Marcus Meyn (vocals), Heiko Maile (keyboards) and Oliver Kreyssig (backing vocals; left in 1990).

10/22/88	3	15	1 The Great Commandment	59	Voices & Images	Atlantic 81886
2/11/89	26	5	2 That Smiling Face	—	↓	
10/14/89	23	3	3 Love Is A Shield	—	Methods Of Silence	Atlantic 82002
6/1/91	18	5	4 Heaven (I Want You)	—	Meanwhile	Atlantic 82212

CAMPER VAN BEETHOVEN
Rock group from Santa Cruz, California: David Lowery (vocals, guitar), Greg Lisher (guitar), Morgan Fichter (violin), Victor Krummenacher (bass) and Chris Pedersen (drums). Lowery later formed **Cracker**.

9/16/89	❶³	12	Pictures Of Matchstick Men	—	Key Lime Pie	Virgin 91289
			#12 Pop hit for Status Quo in 1968			

CANDLEBOX
Rock group from Seattle: Kevin Martin (vocals), Peter Klett (guitar), Bardi Martin (bass) and Scott Mercado (drums). Dave Krusen replaced Mercado in 1997.

7/23/94	7	25	✓1 Far Behind	18 ▲³	Candlebox	Maverick 45313
11/19/94	23	8	2 Cover Me	—	↓	
9/16/95	12	8	3 Simple Lessons	60ᴬ ●	Lucy	Maverick 45962
8/22/98	32	4	4 It's Alright	—	Happy Pills	Maverick 46975

CANDYFLIP
Duo from England: Danny Spencer (vocals) and Ric Peet (keyboards).

8/4/90	11	6	1 Strawberry Fields Forever	—	Madstock...	Atlantic 82264
			#8 Pop hit for The Beatles in 1967			
8/3/91	19	6	2 Redhills Road	—	↓	

DEBUT	PEAK	WKS	Modern Rock Track	Pop	Gld	Album Title	Album Label & Number

CANDY SKINS, The
Psychedelic-pop group formed in Oxford, England: brothers Nick (vocals) and Mark (guitar) Cope, Nick Burton (guitar) and John Halliday (drums). Karl Shale (bass) joined in 1992. The Cope brothers are the sons of TV actor/comedian Kenneth Cope.

| 6/29/91 | 9 | 10 | 1 Submarine Song | — | | Space I'm In | DGC 24370 |
| 2/13/93 | 12 | 8 | 2 Wembley | — | | Fun? | DGC 24494 |

CANTRELL, Jerry
Born on 3/18/66 in Tacoma, Washington. Lead guitarist of **Alice In Chains**.

| 3/7/98 | 15 | 15 | Cut You In | — | | Boggy Depot | Columbia 68147 |

CARDIGANS, The
Pop-rock group from Malmo, Sweden: Nina Persson (vocals), Peter Svensson (guitar), Lars-Olof Johansson (keyboards), Magnus Sveningsson (bass) and Bengt Lagersburg (drums).

| 12/28/96+ | 9 | 17 | 1 Lovefool | 2[8A] ▲ | | First Band On The Moon | Stockholm 533117 |
| 11/28/98+ | 16 | 26 | 2 My Favourite Game | — | | Gran Turismo | Stockholm 559081 |

CARTER U.S.M.
Duo from England: Jim "Jim Bob" Morrison (vocals) and Les "Fruit Bat" Carter (guitar). U.S.M.: Unstoppable Sex Machine.

9/14/91	29	1	1 Sheriff Fatman	—		101 Damnations	Chrysalis 21881
8/29/92	26	2	2 The Only Living Boy In New Cross	—		1992 The Love Album	Chrysalis 21946
			CARTER				

CASE, Peter
Born on 4/5/54 in Buffalo. Lead singer of **The Plimsouls**.

| 4/4/92 | 16 | 8 | Dream About You | — | | Six-Pack Of Love | Geffen 24466 |

CATERWAUL
Rock group formed in Los Angeles: Betsy Martin (vocals), Mark Schafer (guitar), Fred Cross (bass) and Kevin Pinnt (drums).

| 4/29/89 | 25 | 8 | The Sheep's A Wolf | — | | Pin And Web | I.R.S. 42281 |

CATHERINE WHEEL
Rock group from England: Rob Dickinson (vocals), Brian Futter (guitar), Dave Hawes (bass) and Neil Sims (drums). Dickinson is the cousin of **Bruce Dickinson** (of **Iron Maiden**).

6/6/92	9	11	1 Black Metallic	—		Ferment	Fontana 512510
9/5/92	20	5	2 I Want To Touch You	—		↓	
8/7/93	5	13	3 Crank	—		Chrome	Fontana 518039
5/27/95	15	10	4 Waydown	—		Happy Days	Mercury 526850
8/19/95	22	8	5 Judy Staring At The Sun	—		↓	
5/20/00	37	3	6 Sparks Are Gonna Fly	—		Wishville	Columbia 69515

CAUSE & EFFECT
Pop duo formed in California: Sean Rowley (keyboards) and Robert Rowe (vocals, guitar). Rowley died of asthma-related cardiac arrest on 11/12/92 (age 23).

| 6/18/94 | 12 | 8 | It's Over Now (It's Alright) | 67 | | Trip | Zoo 11056 |

CAVEDOGS, The
Rock trio from Boston: Todd Spahr (vocals, guitar), Brian Stevens (bass) and Mark Rivers (drums).

| 8/25/90 | 17 | 8 | Leave Me Alone | — | | Joyrides For Shut-Ins | Enigma 73571 |

CAVIAR
Rock group from Chicago: Blake Smith (vocals, guitar), Dave Suh (guitar), Mike Willison (bass) and Jason Batchko (drums).

| 9/30/00 | 28 | 7 | Tangerine Speedo | — | | Caviar | Island 542917 |

CERVENKA, Exene
Born Christine Cervenka on 2/1/56 in Chicago. Lead singer of **X** (with former husband **John Doe**).

| 9/16/89 | 17 | 6 | He's Got A She | — | | Old Wives' Tales | Rhino 70913 |

CHALK FARM
Rock group from Los Angeles: Michael Duff (vocals, guitar), Trace Ritter (guitar), Orlando Sims (bass) and Toby Scarbrough (drums).

| 10/26/96 | 36 | 5 | Lie On Lie | — | | Notwithstanding | Columbia 67613 |

CHAPMAN, Tracy
Born on 3/20/64 in Cleveland. Folk-R&B singer/songwriter/guitarist. Won the 1988 Best New Artist Grammy Award.

| 9/10/88 | 24 | 1 | 1 Talkin' Bout A Revolution | 75 | ▲[4] | Tracy Chapman | Elektra 60774 |
| 10/14/89 | 7 | 9 | 2 Crossroads | 90 | ▲ | Crossroads | Elektra 60888 |

CHAPTERHOUSE
Rock group formed in England: Andrew Sheffiff and Stephen Patman (vocals, guitars), Simon Rowe (guitar), Russell Barrett (bass) and Ashley Bates (drums).

6/29/91	7	9	1 Pearl	—		Whirlpool	Dedicated 3006
1/11/92	21	4	2 Mesmerise	—		↓	
2/26/94	29	1	3 We Are The Beautiful	—		Blood Music	Arista 18742

CHARLATANS UK, The ★75★
Rock group from Northwich, England: Tim Burgess (vocals), Jon Baker (guitar), Rob Collins (organ), Martin Blunt (bass) and Jon Brookes (drums). Mark Collins (guitar) replaced Baker in 1993. Simply known as **The Charlatans** by 1994. Rob Collins died in a car crash on 7/23/96 (age 32).

8/18/90	5	11	1 The Only One I Know	—		Some Friendly	Beggars Banquet 2411
10/27/90	4	16	2 Then	—		↓	
2/2/91	18	2	3 White Shirt	—		↓	
2/23/91	25	3	4 Sproston Green	—		↓	

DEBUT	PEAK	WKS	Modern Rock Track	Pop Gld	Album Title	Album Label & Number
			CHARLATANS UK, The — Cont'd			
3/21/92	❶¹	16	5 Weirdo	—	*Between 10th & 11th* . . . . Beggars Banquet 61108
6/20/92	13	8	6 I Don't Want To See The Sights	—	↓
3/19/94	6	9	7 Can't Get Out Of Bed	—	*Up To Our Hips* . . . . Beggars Banquet 92352
			THE CHARLATANS			
			CHEMICAL BROTHERS, The			
			Techno-dance DJ duo from England: Tom Rowlands and Ed Simons.			
6/21/97	40	1	1 Block Rockin' Beats	[I] 105 ●	*Dig Your Own Hole* . . . . Astralwerks 6180
			samples "Gucci Again" by Schooly D			
6/12/99	29	8	2 Let Forever Be	[I] —	*Surrender* . . . . Freestyle Dust 47610
			CHERRY, Eagle-Eye			
			Born on 5/7/69 in Stockholm, Sweden. Son of trumpeter Don Cherry. Half-brother of **Neneh Cherry**.			
7/25/98	8	26	Save Tonight	5 ▲	*Desireless* . . . . Work 69434
			CHERRY, Neneh			
			Born on 8/10/64 in Stockholm, Sweden; raised in New York City. Female R&B singer. Stepdaughter of jazz trumpeter Don Cherry. Half-sister of **Eagle-Eye Cherry**.			
11/7/92+	2¹	14	Trout	—	*Homebrew* . . . . Virgin 86516
			NENEH CHERRY Featuring Michael Stipe			
			CHERRY POPPIN' DADDIES			
			Eclectic-jazz group from Eugene, Oregon: Steve Perry (vocals, guitar), Jason Moss (guitar), Dana Heitman, Sean Falnnery and Ian Early (horns), Darren Cassidy (bass) and Tim Donahue (drums).			
3/7/98	15	25	Zoot Suit Riot	41ᴬ ▲²	*Zoot Suit Riot* . . . . Mojo 53081
			CHEVELLE			
			Rock trio from Chicago: brothers Pete (vocals, guitar), Joe (bass) and Sam (drums) Loeffler.			
7/27/02	8↑	18↑	The Red	101↑	*Wonder What's Next* . . . . Epic 86157
			CHILDS, Toni			
			Born on 7/20/60 in Orange, California. Female singer.			
9/10/88	17	4	Don't Walk Away	72 ●	*Union* . . . . A&M 5175
			CHILLS, The			
			Rock group formed in Dunedin, New Zealand: Martin Phillipps (vocals, guitar), Andrew Todd (keyboards), Justin Harwood (bass) and James Stephenson (drums).			
4/14/90	17	7	Heavenly Pop Hit	—	*Submarine Bells* . . . . Slash 26130
			CHRISTMAS			
			Rock trio from Boston: brothers Michael (vocals, guitar) and Nicholas (bass) Cudahy, with Elizabeth Cox (vocals, drums).			
2/25/89	26	3	Stupid Kids	—	*Ultraprophets Of Thee Psykick Revolution*. I.R.S. 42273
			CHUMBAWAMBA			
			Post-punk group from Leeds, England: Alice Nutter, Lou Watts, Danbert Nubacon, Paul Greco, Jude Abbott, Dunstan Bruce, Neil Ferguson and Harry Hamer.			
9/20/97	❶⁷	25	Tubthumping	6 ▲³	*Tubthumper* . . . . Republic 53099
			CHURCH, The			
			Folk-rock group from Canberra, Australia: Steve Kilbey (vocals, bass), Peter Koppes and Marty Willson-Piper (guitars), and Richard Ploog (drums). Jay Dee Daugherty replaced Ploog in 1991.			
3/3/90	❶¹	15	1 Metropolis	—	*Gold Afternoon Fix* . . . . Arista 8579
6/30/90	27	2	2 You're Still Beautiful	—	↓
2/29/92	3	10	3 Ripple	—	*Priest = Aura* . . . . Arista 18683
			CITIZEN KING			
			Rock group from Milwaukee: Matt Sims (vocals, bass), Kristian Riley (guitar), Malcolm Michiles (DJ), Dave Cooley (keyboards) and DJ Brooks (drums).			
3/6/99	3	26	Better Days (And The Bottom Drops Out)	25	*Mobile Estates* . . . . Warner 47023
			CIV			
			Punk-rock group from New York City: Anthony Civocelli (vocals), Charlie Garriga (guitar), Arthur Smilios (bass) and Sam Sigeler (drums).			
9/23/95	21	8	Can't Wait One Minute More	—	*Set Your Goals* . . . . Lava 92603
			CLAIL, Gary, & The On-U Sound System			
			Born in Ireland; raised in Bristol, England. Techno-rave artist. The On-U Sound System consisted of over 30 musicians.			
8/10/91	10	9	Human Nature (On The Mix)	—	*The Emotional Hooligan* . . . . Perfecto 61007
			CLASS OF '99			
			All-star rock group: Layne Staley (vocals; **Alice In Chains**), Tom Morello (guitar; **Rage Against The Machine**), Matt Serletic (keyboards), Martyn LeNoble (bass; **Porno For Pyros**) and Stephen Perkins (drums; Porno For Pyros).			
1/2/99	34	5	Another Brick In The Wall (Part 2)	—	*The Faculty* (soundtrack) . . . . Columbia 69762
			#1 Pop hit for **Pink Floyd** in 1980			
			CLEGG, Johnny, & Savuka			
			Born on 7/13/53 in Rochdale, Lancashire, England; raised in South Africa. Singer/guitarist/dancer. Savuka: Steve Mavuso (keyboards), Keith Hutchinson (sax), Solly Letwaba (bass) and Dundu Zulu and Derek De Beer (drums).			
5/12/90	27	3	Cruel, Crazy, Beautiful World	—	*Cruel, Crazy, Beautiful World* . . . . Capitol 93446
			CLIFFS OF DOONEEN			
			Rock group from Boston: Eric Sean Murphy (vocals), Martin Crotty (guitars), Ira Nulton (bass) and Lex Lianos (drums).			
1/4/92	10	7	Through An Open Window		*The Dog Went East, And God Went West* . . . . Critique 15404

DEBUT	PEAK	WKS	Modern Rock Track	Pop	Gld	Album Title	Album Label & Number
			COCKBURN, Bruce				
			Born on 5/27/45 in Ottawa, Canada. Pop-rock singer/songwriter.				
2/11/89	20	8	1 If A Tree Falls	—		*Big Circumstance* . . . . Gold Castle 71320
11/23/91	22	6	2 A Dream Like Mine	—		*Nothing But A Burning Light* . . . . Columbia 47983
			COCTEAU TWINS				
			Pop trio from Grangemouth, Scotland: Elizabeth Fraser (vocals), Robin Guthrie (guitar) and Simon Raymonde (bass). Guthrie and Fraser also recorded in 1984 as This Mortal Coil. Name Cocteau Twins is taken from a **Simple Minds** song.				
10/8/88	2²	11	1 Carolyn's Fingers	—		*Blue Bell Knoll* . . . . Capitol 90892
9/15/90	4	11	2 Iceblink Luck	—		*Heaven or Las Vegas* . . . . Capitol 93669
11/24/90+	9	11	3 Heaven or Las Vegas	—		↓
			COLD				
			Rock group from Jacksonville, Florida: Scooter Ward (vocals, guitar), Kelley Hayes (guitar), Jeremy Marshall (bass) and Sam McCandless (drums).				
2/24/01	13	17	No One	—		*13 Ways To Bleed On Stage* . . . . Geffen 490726
			COLDPLAY				
			Rock group from Edinburgh, Scotland: Chris Martin (vocals), Jon Buckland (guitar), Guy Berryman (bass) and Will Champion (drums).				
12/2/00+	6	26	⌐ Yellow	48	▲	*Parachutes* . . . . Nettwerk 30162
5/19/01	26	8	∨2 Shiver	—		↓
10/27/01	28	17	√3 Trouble	115		↓
7/20/02	17	15	✓ 4 In My Place	117	●	*A Rush Of Blood To The Head* . . . . Capitol 40504
			COLE, Lloyd				
			Born on 1/31/61 in Buxton, Derbyshire, England; raised in Glasgow, Scotland. The Commotions: Neil Clark (guitar), Blair Cowan (keyboards), Lawrence Donegan (bass) and Steven Irvine (drums).				
10/8/88	13	9	1 My Bag	—		*Mainstream* . . . . Capitol 90893
			LLOYD COLE & THE COMMOTIONS				
4/21/90	5	11	2 Downtown	—		*Lloyd Cole* . . . . Capitol 92751
9/7/91	7	11	3 She's A Girl And I'm A Man	—		*Don't Get Weird On Me, Babe* . . . . Capitol 96077
12/14/91+	6	9	4 Tell Your Sister	—		↓
			COLE, Paula				
			Born on 4/5/68 in Rockport, Masschusetts. Female singer/songwriter. Won the 1997 Best New Artist Grammy Award.				
4/19/97	32	7	Where Have All The Cowboys Gone?	8	▲²	*This Fire* . . . . Imago 46424
			COLLAPSIS				
			Rock group from Chapel Hill, North Carolina: Ryan Pickett (vocals, guitar), Mike Garrigan (guitar), Chris Holloway (bass) and Scott Carle (drums).				
4/1/00	28	5	Automatic	—		*Dirty Wake* . . . . Cherry 153792
			COLLECTIVE SOUL ★34★				
			Rock group from Stockbridge, Georgia: brothers Ed (vocals; born on 8/3/63) and Dean (guitar; born on 10/10/72) Roland with Ross Childress (guitar; born on 9/8/70), Will Turpin (bass; born on 2/8/71) and Shane Evans (drums; born on 4/26/70).				
			1)December 2)Shine 3)Heavy				
5/7/94	4	18	1 Shine	11	▲²	*Hints Allegations And Things Left Unsaid* Atlantic 82596
2/4/95	14	11	2 Gel	49ᴬ		*The Jerky Boys (soundtrack)* . . . . Select 82708
4/29/95	2¹	24	3 December	20	▲³	*Collective Soul* . . . . Atlantic 82745
11/18/95+	6	24	4 The World I Know	19		↓
2/15/97	6	15	5 Precious Declaration	65	▲	*Disciplined Breakdown* . . . . Atlantic 82984
5/31/97	17	16	6 Listen	72		↓
2/7/98	39	1	7 She Said	—	●	*Scream 2 (soundtrack)* . . . . Capitol 21911
1/23/99	5	26	8 Heavy	73	▲	*Dosage* . . . . Atlantic 83162
4/3/99	36	3	9 Run	76		↓
7/10/99	32	7	10 No More, No Less	123		↓
9/30/00	19	17	11 Why Pt.2	111	●	*Blender* . . . . Atlantic 83400
			COLLINS, Edwyn				
			Born on 8/23/59 in Edinburgh, Scotland. Pop-rock singer/songwriter.				
8/26/95	7	16	A Girl Like You	32	●	*Empire Records (soundtrack)* . . . . A&M 540384
			COLVIN, Shawn				
			Born Shanna Colvin on 1/10/58 in Vermillion, South Dakota. Female folk singer. Backing vocalist for **Suzanne Vega**.				
1/20/90	23	3	1 Steady On	—		*Steady On* . . . . Columbia 45209
12/5/92+	25	7	2 Round Of Blues	—		*Fat City* . . . . Columbia 47122
			COMPULSION				
			Rock group from Ireland: Joseph Mary (vocals), Garret Lee (guitar), Sid Rainey (bass) and Jan Alkema (drums).				
11/19/94	37	2	Delivery	—		*Comforter* . . . . Interscope 92456

DEBUT	PEAK	WKS	Modern Rock Track	Pop Gld	Album Title	Album Label & Number

★68★ CONCRETE BLONDE
Rock group from Los Angeles: Johnette Napolitano (vocals, bass), James Andrew Mankey (guitar) and Harry Rushakoff (drums). Paul Thompson replaced Rushakoff in early 1990; Rushakoff returned in late 1991, replacing Thompson. Group originally known as Dream 6, renamed by **Michael Stipe** of **R.E.M.**

DEBUT	PEAK	WKS	Track	Pop Gld	Album Title	Album Label & Number
5/13/89	15	9	1 God Is A Bullet	—	Free	I.R.S. 82001
6/9/90	❶⁴	14	2 Joey	19 ●	Bloodletting	I.R.S. 82037
11/24/90	23	4	3 Caroline		↓	
9/22/90	20	4	4 Everybody Knows	—	Pump Up The Volume (soundtrack)	MCA 8039
2/22/92	2¹	9	5 Ghost Of Texas Ladies' Man	—	Walking In London	I.R.S. 13137
4/18/92	8	11	6 Someday?	—	↓	
10/30/93	16	8	7 Heal It Up	—	Mexican Moon	Capitol 81129

CONNELLS, The
Rock group from Raleigh, North Carolina: brothers Mike (guitar) and David (bass) Connell with Doug MacMillan (vocals), George Huntley (guitar) and Peele Wimberley (drums). Steve Potak (keyboards) joined by 1993.

DEBUT	PEAK	WKS	Track	Pop Gld	Album Title	Album Label & Number
4/8/89	7	9	1 Something to Say	—	Fun & Games	TVT 2550
11/10/90	3	12	2 Stone Cold Yesterday	—	One Simple Word	TVT 2580
2/9/91	24	2	3 Get A Gun	—	↓	
10/2/93	9	10	4 Slackjawed	—	Ring	TVT 2590

COPE, Julian
Born on 10/21/57 in Bargoed, Wales; raised in Tamworth, England. Former lead singer/songwriter/bassist of British group the Teardrop Explodes.

DEBUT	PEAK	WKS	Track	Pop Gld	Album Title	Album Label & Number
11/12/88+	❶¹	14	1 Charlotte Anne	—	My Nation Underground	Island 91025
1/28/89	10	8	2 5 O'Clock World	—	↓	
			#4 Pop hit for The Vogues in 1966			
5/4/91	4	8	3 Beautiful Love	—	Peggy Suicide	Island 848388
7/6/91	25	4	4 East Easy Rider	—	↓	

CORNELL, Chris
Born on 7/20/64 in Seattle. Lead singer of **Soundgarden** and **Audioslave**.

DEBUT	PEAK	WKS	Track	Pop Gld	Album Title	Album Label & Number
1/31/98	12	14	1 Sunshower	— ●	Great Expectations (soundtrack)	Atlantic 83058
8/28/99	7	17	2 Can't Change Me	102	Euphoria Morning	A&M 490412

CORNERSHOP
Rock group formed in London: Tjinder Singh (vocals), Ben Ayers (guitar), Anthony Saffrey (sitar), Peter Bengry (percussion) and Nick Simms (drums).

DEBUT	PEAK	WKS	Track	Pop Gld	Album Title	Album Label & Number
11/15/97+	16	21	Brimful Of Asha	—	When I Was Born For The 7th Time	Luaka Bop 46576

CORNWELL, Hugh
Born on 8/28/49 in London. Singer/songwriter/guitarist. Member of **The Stranglers**.

DEBUT	PEAK	WKS	Track	Pop Gld	Album Title	Album Label & Number
9/17/88	11	11	Another Kind Of Love	—	Wolf	Virgin 90947

★94★ COSTELLO, Elvis
Born Declan McManus on 8/25/54 in Paddington, London, England. Leading eclectic rock singer. Changed name to Elvis Costello in 1976; Costello is his mother's maiden name. In 1977, formed backing band The Attractions: Steve "Nieve" Nason (keyboards), Bruce Thomas (bass) and Peter Thomas (drums). Married Cait O'Riordan, former bassist with **The Pogues**, on 5/16/86. Appeared in the 1987 movie *Straight To Hell*. Inducted into the Rock and Roll Hall of Fame in 2003. Also see **Classic Rock Tracks** section.

DEBUT	PEAK	WKS	Track	Pop Gld	Album Title	Album Label & Number
2/11/89	❶²	12	1 Veronica	19 ●	Spike	Warner 25848
			Paul McCartney (co-writer, bass guitar)			
4/8/89	4	13	2 ...This Town...	—	↓	
			Roger McGuinn (guitar); Paul McCartney (bass guitar)			
5/11/91	❶⁴	10	3 The Other Side Of Summer	—	Mighty Like A Rose	Warner 26575
3/5/94	6	9	4 13 Steps Lead Down	115	Brutal Youth	Warner 45535

COUNTING CROWS ★39★
Rock group from San Francisco: Adam Duritz (vocals; born on 8/1/64), David Bryson (guitar), Charlie Gillingham (piano), Matt Malley (bass) and Steve Bowman (drums). Ben Mize replaced Bowman in 1994. Dan Vickrey (guitar) joined in 1996.

DEBUT	PEAK	WKS	Track	Pop Gld	Album Title	Album Label & Number
11/27/93+	2³	23	1 Mr. Jones	5ᴬ ▲⁷	August And Everything After	DGC 24528
4/16/94	7	14	2 Round Here	31ᴬ	↓	
7/23/94	❶¹	19	3 Einstein On The Beach (For An Eggman)	45ᴬ	DGC Rarities Vol. 1 (various artists)	DGC 24704
10/12/96	3	13	4 Angels Of The Silences	45ᴬ ▲²	Recovering The Satellites	DGC 24975
12/21/96+	5	19	5 A Long December	6ᴬ	↓	
5/3/97	26	9	6 Daylight Fading	51ᴬ	↓	
8/30/97	34	6	7 Have You Seen Me Lately?	—	↓	
10/16/99	17	19	8 Hanginaround	28 ▲	This Desert Life	DGC 490415

COURSE OF NATURE
Rock trio from Enterprise, Alabama: Mark Wilkerson (vocals, guitar), John Milldrum (bass) and Rickey Shelton (drums).

DEBUT	PEAK	WKS	Track	Pop Gld	Album Title	Album Label & Number
2/2/02	22	12	Caught In The Sun	—	Superkala	Lava 83526

DEBUT	PEAK	WKS	Modern Rock Track	Pop	Gld	Album Title	Album Label & Number
			COWBOY JUNKIES				
			Country-punk group from Toronto: siblings Margo (vocals), Michael (guitar) and Peter (drums) Timmins, with Alan Anton (bass).				
12/17/88+	5	17	1 Sweet Jane	—	▲	*The Trinity Session*	RCA 8568
			first recorded by **Lou Reed** in 1974; also see #5 below				
3/17/90	11	9	2 Sun Comes Up, It's Tuesday Morning	—		*The Caution Horses*	RCA 2058
3/7/92	25	6	3 Murder, Tonight, In The Trailer Park	—		*Black Eyed Man*	RCA 61049
12/25/93	28	6	4 Anniversary Song	—		*Pale Sun, Crescent Moon*	RCA 66344
10/8/94	9	17	5 Sweet Jane [R]	52^	●	*Natural Born Killers (soundtrack)*	Nothing 92460
			edited version of #1 above, with dialog dubbed in from the movie *Natural Born Killers* starring Woody Harrelson and Juliette Lewis				
3/23/96	20	12	6 A Common Disaster	75^		*Lay It Down*	Geffen 24952
			COWBOY MOUTH				
			Rock group from New Orleans: John Thomas Griffith (vocals), Paul Sanchez (guitar), Rob Savoy (bass) and Fred LeBlanc (drums).				
5/17/97	33	8	1 Jenny Says	—		*Are You With Me?*	MCA 11447
10/24/98	35	4	2 Whatcha Gonna Do?	—		*Mercyland*	MCA 11847
	★72★		**CRACKER**				
			Rock group from Redlands, California: David Lowery (vocals; **Camper Van Beethoven**), John Hickman (guitar) and Dave Faragher (bass). Faragher left in 1995. Bob Rupe (bass) and Charlie Quintana (drums) joined in 1996.				
3/21/92	❶²	14	1 Teen Angst (What The World Needs Now)	—		*Cracker*	Virgin 91816
6/13/92	13	8	2 Happy Birthday To Me	—		↓	
9/11/93	3	20	3 Low	64	●	*Kerosene Hat*	Virgin 39012
1/22/94	6	14	4 Get Off This	102		↓	
9/3/94	25	9	5 Euro-Trash Girl	—		↓	
3/30/96	13	7	6 I Hate My Generation	67^		*The Golden Age*	Virgin 41498
6/29/96	32	5	7 Nothing To Believe In	—		↓	
			CRAMPS, The				
			Rock group formed in New York City: Erick "Lux Interior" Purkhiser (vocals), Christine "Poison Ivy" Wallace (guitar), Candy Del Marr (bass) and Nicholas "Nick Knox" Stephanoff (drums).				
3/10/90	10	8	Bikini Girls With Machine Guns	—		*Stay Sick!*	Enigma 73543

			CRANBERRIES, The ★32★				
			Pop-rock group from Limerick, Ireland: Dolores O'Riordan (vocals; born on 9/6/71), brothers Noel (guitar; born on 12/25/71) and Mike (bass; born on 4/29/73) Hogan, and Fergal Lawler (drums; born on 3/4/71).				
5/29/93	15	25	1 Dreams	42	▲⁵	*Everybody Else Is Doing It, So Why Can't We?*	Island 514156
9/4/93	4	26	2 Linger	8		↓	
10/1/94	❶⁶	23	3 Zombie	22^	▲⁷	*No Need To Argue*	Island 524050
1/7/95	11	19	4 Ode To My Family	39^		↓	
5/20/95	14	12	5 Ridiculous Thoughts	—		↓	
4/13/96	❶⁴	14	6 Salvation	21^	▲²	*To The Faithful Departed*	Island 524234
7/6/96	8	14	7 Free To Decide	48		↓	
3/27/99	12	10	8 Promises	—	●	*Bury The Hatchet*	Island 524611
			CRASH TEST DUMMIES				
			Pop-rock group from Winnipeg, Canada: brothers Brad (vocals) and Dan (bass) Roberts, with Ellen Reid (keyboards), Benjamin Darvill (harmonica) and Mitch Dorge (drums).				
1/22/94	❶¹	17	1 Mmm Mmm Mmm Mmm	4	▲²	*God Shuffled His Feet*	Arista 16531
6/11/94	13	9	2 Afternoons & Coffeespoons	66		↓	
			CRAZY TOWN				
			Rock-rap group from Los Angeles: Seth "Shifty Shellshock" Binzer and Bret "Epic" Mazur (vocals), DJ AM (DJ), Craig Tyler and Anthony Valli (guitars), Doug Miller (bass) and James Bradley (drums).				
11/18/00+	❶²	26	Butterfly	❶²	▲	*The Gift Of Game*	Columbia 63654
			samples "Pretty Little Ditty" by the **Red Hot Chili Peppers**				
			CREATURES, The				
			Duo from England: Siouxsie Sioux (vocals) and her husband, Peter "Budgie" Clark (percussion). Both are members of **Siouxsie And The Banshees**.				
11/25/89+	4	14	1 Standing There	—		*Boomerang*	Geffen 24275
3/3/90	12	7	2 Fury Eyes	—		↓	

DEBUT	PEAK	WKS	Modern Rock Track	Pop Gld	Album Title	Album Label & Number

CREED ★20★
Rock group from Tallahassee, Florida: Scott Stapp (vocals; born on 8/8/73), Mark Tremonti (guitar; born on 2/18/75), Brian Marshall (bass; born on 4/24/73) and Scott Phillips (drums; born on 2/22/73).

1)Higher 2)With Arms Wide Open 3)One

DEBUT	PEAK	WKS	Modern Rock Track	Pop Gld	Album Title	Album Label & Number
11/29/97+	7	28	1 My Own Prison	54[A] ▲[6]	My Own Prison	Wind-Up 13049
6/27/98	10	26	2 What's This Life For	—	↓	
12/26/98+	2[2]	31	3 One	70	↓	
9/11/99	❶[3]	27	4 Higher	7	▲[10] Human Clay	Wind-Up 13053
1/22/00	15	16	5 What If	102	↓	
4/8/00	2[4]	26	6 With Arms Wide Open	❶[1]	↓	
10/14/00	37	4	7 Are You Ready?	125	↓	
10/27/01+	2[1]	26	8 My Sacrifice	4	▲[5] Weathered	Wind-Up 13075
2/9/02	27	7	9 Bullets	—	↓	
5/11/02	17	24	10 One Last Breath	6	↓	

CRENSHAW, Marshall
Born on 11/11/53 in Detroit. Rockabilly singer/guitarist. Played **John Lennon** in the road show of *Beatlemania* in 1976. Appeared in the movie *Peggy Sue Got Married* and portrayed Buddy Holly in the 1987 movie *La Bamba*.

| 6/15/91 | 17 | 5 | Better Back Off | — | Life's Too Short .... | Paradox 10223 |

★64★ CROW, Sheryl
Born on 2/11/62 in Kennett, Missouri. Pop-rock singer/songwriter/guitarist. Worked as backing singer for **Michael Jackson**, **Don Henley**, **George Harrison** and others. Won the 1994 Best New Artist Grammy Award.

2/12/94	8	13	1 Leaving Las Vegas	60	▲[7] Tuesday Night Music Club	A&M 540126
7/23/94	4	19	2 All I Wanna Do	2[6]	↓	
1/21/95	10	14	3 Strong Enough	5	↓	
7/15/95	38	3	4 Can't Cry Anymore	36	↓	
8/31/96	6	22	5 If It Makes You Happy	10	▲[3] Sheryl Crow	A&M 540587
1/4/97	17	16	6 Everyday Is A Winding Road	11	↓	
6/7/97	25	9	7 A Change Would Do You Good	19[A]	↓	
9/12/98	26	11	8 My Favorite Mistake	20	▲ The Globe Sessions	A&M 540959

CROWDED HOUSE
Pop group from New Zealand: Neil Finn (vocals, guitar, piano), Nick Seymour (bass) and Paul Hester (drums). Finn and Hester were members of **Split Enz**. Neil's brother, Tim Finn (also of Split Enz), joined band in 1991; left in 1993, replaced by Mark Hart. Hester left band in April 1994. Group disbanded in June 1996.

9/10/88	29	1	1 Better Be Home Soon	42	Temple Of Low Men	Capitol 48763
6/15/91	2[1]	11	2 Chocolate Cake	—	Woodface	Capitol 93559
8/17/91	5	10	3 It's Only Natural		↓	
12/25/93+	8	13	4 Locked Out	120	Together Alone	Capitol 27048
4/16/94	26	3	5 Distant Sun	113	↓	

CRUISE, Julee
Born on 12/1/56 in Creston, Iowa. Singer/actress.

| 6/2/90 | 11 | 7 | Falling | — | Floating Into The Night .... | Warner 25859 |

CRUSH
Rock group formed in New York City: Fred Schreck (vocals), John Valentine Carruthers (guitar), John Micco (bass) and Paul Ferguson (drums).

| 5/15/93 | 26 | 2 | The Rain | — | Crush .... | EastWest 4992 |

CRYSTAL METHOD, The
Electronic-dance duo from Los Angeles: Ken Jordan and Scott Kirkland.

8/16/97	29	10	1 (Can't You) Trip Like I Do	— ●	Spawn (soundtrack)	Immortal 68494
			FILTER & THE CRYSTAL METHOD			
7/14/01	22	10	2 Name Of The Game	—	Tweekend	Geffen 493063

CULT, The
Rock group from England. Nucleus of evercharging lineup included Ian Astbury (vocals; real name: Ian Lindsay), Billy Duffy (guitar), Jamie Stewart (bass) and Les Warner (drums). Warner left in 1988; replaced by Matt Sorum (**Guns N' Roses**). Stewart left in 1990.

4/15/89	2[1]	12	1 Fire Woman	46	▲ Sonic Temple	Sire 25871
7/15/89	21	2	2 Sun King	—	↓	
9/21/91	4	8	3 Wild Hearted Son	—	Ceremony	Sire 26673
11/23/91	21	3	4 Heart Of Soul	—	↓	
10/8/94	26	8	5 Coming Down (Drug Tongue)	—	The Cult	Sire 45673
5/19/01	19	9	6 Rise	125	Beyond Good And Evil	Lava 83440

DEBUT	PEAK	WKS	Modern Rock Track	Pop	Gld	Album Title	Album Label & Number

CURE, The ★10★
Techno-rock group from England: Robert Smith (vocals, guitar; born on 4/21/59), Porl Thompson (guitar), Laurence "Lol" Tolhurst (keyboards), Simon Gallup (bass) and Boris Williams (drums). Numerous personnel changes with Smith the only constant.

1)Fascination Street   2)Friday I'm In Love   3)High

4/22/89	❶⁷	16	1 **Fascination Street**	46	▲	Disintegration .... Elektra 60855
7/1/89	2³	17	✓2 **Love Song**	2¹	↓	
11/18/89	23	8	✓3 Lullaby	74	↓	
4/21/90	19	7	4 Pictures Of You	71	↓	
9/22/90	❶³	17	✓5 Never Enough	72	▲	Mixed Up. .... Elektra 60978
10/20/90	6	9	6 Hello I Love You	—		Rubaiyat - Elektra's 40th Anniversary
			#1 Pop hit for **The Doors** in 1968			(various artists). .... Elektra 60940
3/28/92	❶⁴	11	✓7 **High**	42	▲	Wish .... Fiction 61309
5/9/92	❶⁴	14	✓8 **Friday I'm In Love**	18	▲	↓
8/8/92	2¹	10	✓9 A Letter To Elise	—		↓
11/27/93+	2¹	16	10 Purple Haze	66^	●	Stone Free: A Tribute To Jimi Hendrix
			#65 Pop hit for Jimi Hendrix in 1967			(various artists) .... Reprise 45438
4/20/96	15	6	11 The 13th	44	●	Wild Mood Swings .... Fiction 61744
6/1/96	14	12	✓12 Mint Car......................	58		↓
10/18/97	8	16	✓13 Wrong Number	64^		Galore - The Singles 1987-1997....... Fiction 62117
2/5/00	10	11	14 Maybe Someday			Bloodflowers .... Fiction 62236

CURRY, Mark
Born in Sacramento, California. Singer/songwriter/guitarist.

| 10/3/92 | 20 | 4 | Sorry About The Weather............................. | — | | It's Only Time. .... Virgin 86290 |

CURVE
Pop-rock group from England: Toni Halliday (vocals), Debbie Smith and Alex Mitchell (guitars), Dean Garcia (bass) and Monti (drums).

11/9/91	12	8	1 Coast Is Clear	—		Frozen........................ Charisma 96293
3/28/92	17	6	2 Fait Accompli	—		Doppelganger .... Anxious 92108
5/30/92	23	5	3 Horror Head	—		↓

CUSTOM
Born Duane Lavold in New York City. Singer/songwriter.

| 12/29/01+ | 20 | 17 | Hey Mister .... | — | | Fast...................... Artist Direct 1016 |

CYPRESS HILL
Rap trio from Los Angeles: Senen "Sen Dog" Reyes, Louis "B-Real" Freese and Lawrence "Mixmaster Muggs" Muggerud.

| 4/8/00 | 18 | 24 | (Rock) Superstar.................................. | — | ▲ | Skull & Bones .... Columbia 69990 |

D

dada
Pop trio from Los Angeles: Joie Calio (vocals, bass), Michael Gurley (guitar) and Phil Leavitt (drums).

11/7/92	5	12	1 Dizz Knee Land	102		Puzzle........................... I.R.S. 13141
3/20/93	24	4	2 Dim	—		↓
9/24/94	27	8	3 All I Am..................................	—		American Highway Flower .... I.R.S. 27986

DAMBUILDERS, The
Pop-rock group from Boston: Eric Masunaga (vocals, guitar), Joan Wasser (violin), Dave Derby (bass) and Kevin March (drums).

| 7/30/94 | 13 | 10 | Shrine.................................. | — | | Encendedor..................... EastWest 92356 |

DANDELION
Rock group from Philadelphia: brothers Kevin (vocals, guitar) and Mike (bass) Morpurgo, Carl Hinds (guitar) and Dante Cimino (drums).

| 8/5/95 | 14 | 9 | Weird-Out.................................. | 74^ | | Dyslexicon..................... Ruffhouse 64194 |

DANDY WARHOLS, The
Rock group from Portland, Oregon: Courtney Taylor (vocals), Peter Holmstrom (guitar), Zia McCabe (bass) and Eric Hedford (drums).

| 8/16/97 | 31 | 7 | 1 Not If You Were The Last Junkie On Earth................. | — | | ...The Dandy Warhols Come Down ..... Capitol 36505 |
| 8/19/00 | 28 | 6 | 2 Bohemian Like You.................................. | — | | Thirteen Tales From Urban Bohemia.... Capitol 57787 |

DANGER, Harvey — see HARVEY DANGER

DANGERMAN
Rock duo from New York City: Chris Scianni (vocals, guitar, bass) and Dave Borla (drums).

| 3/20/99 | 20 | 10 | Let's Make A Deal.................................. | — | | Dangerman .... 550 Music 69774 |

DEBUT	PEAK	WKS	Modern Rock Track	Pop Gld	Album Title	Album Label & Number
			DANZIG Born Glenn Danzig on 6/23/59 in Lodi, New Jersey. Hard-rock singer/songwriter. His group: John Christ (guitar), Eerie Von (bass) and Chuck Biscuits (drums).			
2/18/95	40	1	Cantspeak..	—	Danzig 4 .... American 45647	
			D'ARBY, Terence Trent Born on 3/15/62 in New York City. R&B-pop singer.			
5/8/93	5	12	She Kissed Me	—	Terence Trent D'Arby's Symphony Or Damn..................... Columbia 53616	
			DARLING BUDS, The Pop group from Caerlon, Wales: Andrea Lewis (vocals), Harley Farr (guitar), Chris McDonagh (bass) and Bloss (drums). Jimmy Hughes replaced Bloss in early 1992.			
7/15/89	27	4	1 Let's Go Round There..	—	Pop Said... .... Columbia 45208	
9/29/90	5	10	2 Crystal Clear	—	Crawdaddy .... Columbia 46816	
12/22/90+	13	8	3 It Makes No Difference	—	↓	
10/10/92	22	6	4 Please Yourself	—	Erotica .... Chaos 52913	
			DASHBOARD CONFESSIONAL Rock trio from Boca Raton, Florida: Christopher Carraba (vocals, guitar), Dan Bonebrake (bass) and Mike Marsh (drums).			
4/6/02	22	11	Screaming Infidelities	—	The Places You Have Come To Fear The Most...................... Vagrant 354	
			DAVID J Born David J. Haskins on 4/24/57 in Northampton, England. Singer/bassist. Member of **Love And Rockets**.			
7/14/90	❶¹	11	I'll Be Your Chauffeur	—	Songs From Another Season.... Beggars Banquet 2261	
			DAX, Danielle Born in Southend, Essex, England. Singer/songwriter.			
12/10/88+	19	8	1 Cat-House..	—	Dark Adapted Eye .... Sire 25818	
12/8/90+	5	10	2 Tomorrow Never Knows	—	Blast The Human Flower .... Sire 26126	
			DAYS OF THE NEW Rock group from Louisville, Kentucky: Travis Meeks (vocals), Todd Whitener (guitar), Jesse Vest (bass) and Matt Taul (drums). Whitener, Vest and Taul left in 1999 to form **Tantric**; Meeks continued group name as a solo project.			
9/27/97+	6	28	1 Touch, Peel And Stand	57^ ▲	Days Of The New .... Outpost 30004	
2/28/98	22	16	2 Shelf In The Room	—	↓	
7/18/98	19	15	3 The Down Town	—	↓	
8/14/99	10	13	4 Enemy	110	Days Of The New .... Outpost 30037	
			DEACON BLUE Pop group from Glasgow, Scotland: Ricky Ross and Lorraine McIntosh (vocals), Graeme Kelling (guitar), James Prime (keyboards), Ewen Vernal (bass) and Douglas Vipond (drums). Band name taken from **Steely Dan's** 1978 pop hit "Deacon Blues."			
7/17/93	27	3	Your Town	—	Whatever You Say, Say Nothing........ Chaos 53755	
			DEAD CAN DANCE Duo of Brendan Perry (lives in Ireland) and Lisa Gerrard (lives in Australia's Snow River Mountains).			
11/13/93	8	11	The Ubiquitous Mr Lovegrove	—	Into The Labyrinth .... 4 A D 45384	
			DEAD MILKMEN, The Punk-rock group from Philadelphia: Rodney "Anonymous" Linderman (vocals), Anthony "Jasper Thread" Genaro (guitar), David "Lord Maniac" Schulthise (bass) and Dean "Clean" Sabatino (drums).			
1/7/89	11	10	Punk Rock Girl	—	Beelzebubba .... Enigma 73151	
			DEEP BLUE SOMETHING Pop-rock group from Dallas: brothers Todd (vocals, bass) and Toby (guitar) Pipes, Kirk Tatom (guitar) and John Kirtland (drums).			
9/23/95	30	12	✓ Breakfast At Tiffany's	5 ●	Home........................... RainMaker 92608	
			DEEP FOREST French keyboardist Michel Sanchez and Brussels-based producer Dan Lacksman.			
7/17/93	14	9	Sweet Lullaby	78 ●	Deep Forest .... Epic 53747	
			DEFAULT Rock group from Vancouver: Dallas Smith (vocals), Jeremy Hora (guitar), Dave Benedict (bass) and Dan Craig (drums).			
9/29/01+	3	37	1 Wasting My Time	13 ●	The Fallout .... TVT 2310	
5/11/02	14	22	2 Deny	—	↓	
			DEFTONES Rock group from Sacramento, California: Chino Moreno (vocals), Stephen Carpenter (guitar), Chi Cheng (bass) and Abe Cunningham (drums).			
5/27/00	3	26	1 Change (In The House Of Flies)	105 ●	White Pony .... Maverick 47667	
11/4/00	27	8	2 Back To School	—	↓	
1/27/01	16	11	3 Digital Bath	—	↓	
			DEL AMITRI Pop-rock group from Glasgow, Scotland: Justin Currie (vocals, bass), David Cummings and Iain Harvie (guitars), and Brian McDermott (drums).			
3/10/90	13	10	1 Kiss This Thing Goodbye....................................	35	Waking Hours .... A&M 5287	
6/27/92	11	9	2 Always The Last To Know...................................	30	Change Everything .... A&M 5385	
			DEL FUEGOS, The Rock group from Boston: Dan Zanes (vocals, guitar), Adam Roth (guitar), Tom Lloyd (bass) and Joe Donnelly (drums).			
11/18/89	22	3	Move With Me Sister	—	Smoking In The Fields.............. RCA 9860	

DEBUT	PEAK	WKS	Modern Rock Track	Pop	Gld	Album Title	Album Label & Number

DEPECHE MODE ★13★
All-synthesized rock group formed in Basildon, England: singer David Gahan and synthesizer players **Martin L. Gore**, Vince Clarke and Andy Fletcher. Clarke left in 1982 (formed Yaz, then **Erasure**), replaced by Alan Wilder (left in 1995). Group name is French for fast fashion.

1)I Feel You 2)Enjoy The Silence 3)Policy Of Truth

DEBUT	PEAK	WKS	Modern Rock Track	Pop	Gld	Album Title	Album Label & Number
4/15/89	13	9	1 Everything Counts .... [L]	—	●	101 .... Sire 25853
			recorded on 6/18/88 at the Rose Bowl in Pasadena			
1/13/90	13	6	2 Dangerous	—		(single only) .... Sire 19941
10/7/89	3	13	3 Personal Jesus	28	▲³	Violator .... Sire 26081
3/10/90	❶³	12	4 Enjoy The Silence	8		↓
4/28/90	❶¹	16	5 Policy Of Truth	15		↓
8/11/90	21	3	6 Halo	—		↓
9/22/90	17	4	7 World In My Eyes	52		↓
2/27/93	❶⁵	11	8 I Feel You	37	●	Songs Of Faith And Devotion .... Sire 45243
4/24/93	❶¹	15	9 Walking In My Shoes	69		↓
8/28/93	23	5	10 Condemnation	—		↓
1/18/97	11	9	11 Barrel Of A Gun...................	47	●	Ultra .... Mute 46522
4/12/97	4	22	12 It's No Good	38		↓
10/3/98	36	4	13 Only When I Lose Myself..............	61		The Singles 86-98 .... Mute 47110
4/14/01	12	17	14 Dream On..........................	85	●	Exciter .... Mute 47960

DEVO
Robotic-rock group from Akron, Ohio: brothers Mark (synthesizers) and Bob (vocals, guitar) Mothersbaugh, brothers Jerry (bass) and Bob (guitar) Casale, and ALan Myers (drums). Also see **Classic Rock Tracks** section.

7/21/90	7	9	Post Post-Modern Man	—		smoothnoodlemaps .... Enigma 73526

DEXTER FREEBISH
Rock group from Austin, Texas: Rob Kyle (vocals), Scott Roming and Charles Martin (guitars), Chris Lowe (bass) and Rob Schilz (drums).

8/26/00	25	19	Leaving Town	—		A Life Of Saturdays .... Capitol 20464

DIFFUSER
Rock group from Long Island, New York: Tom Costanza (vocals, guitar), Tony Cangelosi (guitar), Larry Sullivan (bass) and Billy Alemaghides (drums).

12/30/00+	26	11	Karma..........................	—		Injury Loves Melody............. Hollywood 162246

DIG
Rock group from San Diego: Scott Hackwith (vocals, guitar), Jon Morris and Johnny Cornwell (guitars), Phil Friedmann (bass) and Anthony Smedile (drums).

2/5/94	19	8	Believe	—		Dig .... Radioactive 10916

DINK
Rock group from Akron, Ohio: Rob Lightbody (vocals), Sean Carlin and Jer Herring (guitars), Jeff Finn (bass) and Jan Eddy Van Der Kuil (drums).

1/7/95	35	6	Green Mind	118		Dink .... Capitol 7243

DINOSAUR JR.
Rock trio from Amherst, Massachusetts: Joseph Mascis (vocals, guitar), Mike Johnson (guitar) and Patrick Murphy (drums). George Berz replaced Murphy in late 1993.

4/6/91	22	6	1 The Wagon.....................	—		Green Mind........................ Sire 26479
2/6/93	3	14	2 Start Choppin	—		Where You Been .... Sire 45108
8/27/94	4	20	3 Feel The Pain	62ᴬ		Without A Sound.................... Sire 45719

DIRE STRAITS
Rock group formed in London: Mark Knopfler (vocals, guitar), Guy Fletcher and Phil Palmer (guitars), Paul Franklin (pedal steel), Alan Clark (keyboards), Chris White (sax), Danny Cummings (percussion), John Illsley (bass) and Chris Whitten (drums). Also see **Classic Rock Tracks** section.

9/28/91	25	3	1 Calling Elvis......................	—	▲	On Every Street .... Warner 26680
12/7/91	22	2	2 Heavy Fuel	—		↓

DISHWALLA
Pop-rock group from Santa Barbara, California: J.R. Richards (vocals), Rodney Browning (guitar), Scot Alexander (bass) and George Pendergast (drums). Jim Wood (keyboards) added in 1997.

4/6/96	❶¹	26	1 Counting Blue Cars	15	●	Pet Your Friends.................... A&M 540319
8/1/98	20	11	2 Once In A While....................	—		And You Think You Know What Life's About............. A&M 540948

DISTURBED
Hard-rock group from Chicago: **David Draiman** (vocals), Dan Donegan (guitar), Steve "Fuzz" Kmak (bass) and Mike Wengren (drums).

6/24/00	10	26	1 Stupify	112	▲²	The Sickness .... Giant 24738
12/23/00+	18	24	2 Voices	—		↓
6/23/01	8	28	3 Down With The Sickness	104		↓
8/17/02	3	15↑	4 Prayer	58↑		Believe........................ Reprise 48320

DEBUT	PEAK	WKS	Modern Rock Track	Pop	Gld	Album Title	Album Label & Number
			DIVINYLS Rock duo from Australia: Christina Amphlett (vocals) and Mark McEntee (guitar).				
2/9/91	2²	11	1 I Touch Myself	4	●	Divinyls	Virgin 91397
4/27/91	19	9	2 Make Out Alright	—		↓	
			D.N.A. Remix duo from Bristol, England: Neal Slateford and Nick Bett.				
9/1/90	7	10	Tom's Diner	5		(single only)	A&M 1529
			D.N.A. Featuring SUZANNE VEGA special mix of Vega's original acapella recording which appeared on her 1987 *Solitude Standing* album				
			DR. ALBAN Born Alban Nwapa in Nigeria; later based in Stockholm, Sweden. Dance DJ.				
5/1/93	28	1	It's My Life	88		It's My Life	Arista 18720
			DOE, John Born John Nommensen on 2/25/53 in Decatur, Illinois. Founded the band **X** with his former wife **Exene Cervenka**. Appeared in several movies. Took name from the Frank Capra movie *Meet John Doe*.				
6/16/90	19	7	Let's Be Mad	—		Meet John Doe	DGC 24291
			DOG'S EYE VIEW Rock group from New York City: Peter Stuart (vocals, guitar), Oren Bloedow (guitar), John Abbey (bass) and Alan Bezozi (drums).				
2/17/96	19	14	Everything Falls Apart	14ᴬ		Happy Nowhere	Columbia 66882
			DOLBY, Thomas Born Thomas Morgan Robertson on 10/14/58 in Cairo, Egypt (of British parentage). Singer/keyboardist.				
11/21/92+	9	12	Eastern Bloc	—		Astronauts & Heretics	Giant 24478
			DOVETAIL JOINT Rock group from Chicago: Chuck Gladfelter (vocals), Robert Byrne (guitar), Jon Kooker (bass) and Joe Dapier (drums).				
2/20/99	17	13	Level On The Inside	—		001	Columbia 69451
			DRAMARAMA Rock group formed in Los Angeles: John Easdale (vocals), Peter Wood and Mr. E Boy (guitars), Chris Carter (bass) and Jesse (drums; left in 1991).				
11/18/89	13	11	1 Last Cigarette	—		Stuck In Wonderamaland	Chameleon 74822
10/12/91+	6	15	2 Haven't Got A Clue	—		Vinyl	Chameleon 61242
1/25/92	10	8	3 What Are We Gonna Do?	—		↓	
7/3/93	10	8	4 Work For Food	—		Hi-Fi Sci-Fi	Chameleon 61489
			DREAM WARRIORS Hip-hop duo from Toronto: "King Lou" Robinson (born in Jamaica) and Frank "Capitol Q" Alert (born in Trinidad).				
5/11/91	24	5	My Definition Of A Boombastic Jazz Style	—		And Now The Legacy Begins	4th & Broadway 444037
			DRIVIN' N' CRYIN' Rock group from Atlanta: Kevn Kinney (vocals), Buren Fowler (guitar), Tim Nielsen (bass) and Jeff Sullivan (drums).				
2/2/91	15	7	Fly Me Courageous	—	●	Fly Me Courageous	Island 848000
			DROGE, Pete Born on 3/11/69 in Portland, Oregon. Rock singer/songwriter/guitarist.				
12/17/94	40	1	If You Don't Love Me (I'll Kill Myself)	119		Necktie Second	American 45620
			DROWNING POOL Hard-rock group from Dallas: Dave Williams (vocals), C.J. Pierce (guitar), Stevie Benton (bass) and Mike Luce (drums). Williams died of a drug overdose on 8/13/2002 (age 30).				
7/28/01	12	16	1 Bodies	119	▲	Sinner	Wind-Up 13065
12/15/01+	36	6	2 Sinner	—		↓	
4/20/02	37	4	3 Tear Away	—		↓	
			DURAN DURAN Pop-rock group from Birmingham, England: Simon LeBon (vocals), Nick Rhodes (keyboards) and John Taylor (bass). Warren Cuccurullo (guitar; **Missing Persons**) and Sterling Campbell (drums; **Soul Asylum**) joined in 1990. Campbell later joined **Soul Asylum**.				
10/29/88	13	7	1 I Don't Want Your Love	4	●	Big Thing	Capitol 90958
1/28/89	24	6	2 All She Wants Is	22		↓	
8/25/90	13	6	3 Violence Of Summer (Love's Taking Over)	64		Liberty	Capitol 94292
			DURANDURAN (above 3)				
12/26/92+	2¹	13	4 Ordinary World	3	▲	Duran Duran	Capitol 98876
3/27/93	12	10	5 Come Undone	7		↓	
6/5/93	30	1	6 Too Much Information	45		↓	
			DURST, Fred — see LEWIS, Aaron				
			DUST FOR LIFE Rock group from Memphis: Chris Gavin (vocals, guitar), Jason Hughes (guitar), David Rhea (bass) and Rick Shelton (drums).				
11/11/00+	22	14	Step Into The Light	—		Dust For Life	Wind-Up 13060
			DYLANS, The Rock group formed in Sheffield, Yorkshire, England: Colin Gregory (vocals), Jim Rodger (guitar), Quentin Jennings (keyboards), Garry Jones (bass) and Andy Cook (drums).				
11/23/91	10	11	Planet Love	—		The Dylans	Beggars Banquet 61054

DEBUT	PEAK	WKS	Modern Rock Track	Pop	Gld	Album Title	Album Label & Number

DYNAMITE HACK
Rock group from Austin, Texas: Mark Morris (vocals, guitar), Mike Vlahakis (guitar), Chad Robinson (bass) and Chase Scott (drums). Group name taken from a line in the movie *Caddyshack*.

| 5/6/00 | 12 | 16 | Boyz-N-The-Hood | — | | *Superfast* | Woppitzer 157884 |

E

E
Born Mark Everett on 4/9/63 in Richmond, Virginia. Singer/songwriter. Later formed the **Eels**.

| 3/21/92 | 8 | 10 | Hello Cruel World | — | | *A Man Called (E)* | Polydor 511570 |

EARSHOT
Rock group from Los Angeles: Will Martin (vocals), Scott Kohler and Mike Callahan (guitars), and Dieter Hartmann (drums).

| 4/6/02 | 20 | 23 | Get Away | — | | *Letting Go* | Warner 47961 |

EASTERHOUSE
Rock duo from Manchester, England: brothers Andy (vocals) and Ivor (guitar) Perry.

| 2/11/89 | 7 | 11 | Come Out Fighting | 82 | | *Waiting For The Redbird* | Columbia 44467 |

ECHO & THE BUNNYMEN
Rock group from Liverpool, England: **Ian McCulloch** (vocals), Will Sergent (guitar), Les Pattinson (bass) and Pete DeFreitas (drums). DeFreitas died in a motorcycle accident on 6/14/89 (age 27). McCulloch went solo in 1988, replaced by Noel Burke. Lineup in 1990: Burke (vocals), Sergent (guitar), Jake Brockman (mellotron), Pattinson (bass) and Damon Reece (drums). McCulloch and Sergeant also collaborated in **Electrafixion**.

12/1/90+	8	10	1 Enlighten Me	—		*Reverberation*	Sire 26388
2/16/91	23	3	2 Gone, Gone, Gone	—		↓	
6/21/97	26	10	3 I Want To Be There (When You Come)	—		*Evergreen*	London 828905

ECONOLINE CRUSH
Rock group from Vancouver: Trevor Hurst (vocals), Robbie Morfitt and Ziggy (guitars), Don Binns (bass) and Nico Quintal (drums).

| 5/22/99 | 28 | 11 | All That You Are (X3) | — | | *The Devil You Know* | Restless 72960 |

EDELWEISS
Trio of remixers from Austria: Martin Gletschermayer, Walter Werzowa and Matthias Schweger.

| 5/20/89 | 24 | 5 | Bring Me Edelweiss | — | | *(single only)* | Atlantic 88911 |

Maria Mathis (vocal); same melody as "SOS" by Abba (#15 Pop hit in 1975).

EELS
Rock trio formed in Los Angeles: Mark Everett (vocals, guitar; **E**), Tommy Walter (bass) and Butch Norton (drums).

| 8/17/96 | ❶² | 25 | 1 Novocaine For The Soul | 39ᴬ | | *Beautiful Freak* | DreamWorks 50001 |
| 11/14/98 | 40 | 4 | 2 Last Stop: This Town | — | | *Electro-Shock Blues* | DreamWorks 50052 |

808 STATE
Techno-dance group from England: Martin Price (vocals), Graham Massey (programmer), and Darren Partington & Andy Barker (DJs). Formed at Price's Manchester record shop, Eastern Bloc. 808 refers to the Roland 808 Drum Machine.

| 1/23/93 | 13 | 9 | 1 One In Ten | — | | *Gorgeous* | Tommy Boy 1067 |

UB40 (guest vocals)

| 3/13/93 | 21 | 6 | 2 Moses | — | | ↓ | |

8STOPS7
Rock group from Los Angeles: Evan Sula-Goff (vocals, guitar), Seth Watson (guitar), Adam Powell (bass) and Alex Viveros (drums).

| 4/22/00 | 35 | 7 | 1 Satisfied | — | | *In Moderation* | Reprise 47387 |
| 7/22/00 | 25 | 9 | 2 Question Everything | — | | ↓ | |

ELASTICA
Rock group from London: Justine Frischmann (vocals), Donna Matthews (guitar), Annie Holland (bass) and Justin Welch (drums).

3/4/95	2³	25	1 Connection	53	●	*Elastica*	DGC 24728
7/8/95	10	13	2 Stutter	67		↓	
12/9/95	33	3	3 Car Song	—		↓	

ELECTRAFIXION
Collaboration between **Ian McCulloch**, Johnny Marr and Will Sergeant. McCulloch and Sergeant were with **Echo & The Bunnymen**. Marr was with **The The** and **Electronic**.

| 2/18/95 | 38 | 1 | Zephyr | — | | *(single only)* | Spacejunk 61793 |

ELECTRONIC
Dance duo from Manchester, England: Bernard Sumner (of **New Order**) and Johnny Marr (of **The The** and **Electrafixion**).

1/20/90	4	11	1 Getting Away With It	38		*Electronic*	Warner 26387
4/27/91	❶²	16	2 Get The Message	—		↓	
7/13/91	6	10	3 Tighten Up	—		↓	
9/28/91	27	2	4 Feel Every Beat	—		↓	
7/25/92	9	9	5 Disappointed	—		*Cool World (soundtrack)*	Warner 45009

DEBUT	PEAK	WKS	Modern Rock Track	Pop Gld	Album Title	Album Label & Number

ELEVENTH DREAM DAY
Pop-rock group from Chicago: husband-and-wife Rick Rizzo (guitar) and Janet Bean (drums), with Baird Figi (guitar) and Doug McCombs (bass).

DEBUT	PEAK	WKS	Track	Pop	Gld	Album Title	Label & Number
1/20/90	26	2	1 Testify	—		Beet	Atlantic 82053
3/23/91	27	3	2 Rose Of Jericho	—		Lived To Tell	Atlantic 82179

ELWOOD
Born Prince Elwood Strickland in North Carolina. Male singer/songwriter/guitarist.

6/24/00	33	6	Sundown	—		The Parlance Of Our Time	Palm 2047
			#1 Pop hit for Gordon Lightfoot in 1974				

EMF
Techno-funk group from Forest of Dean, Gloucestershire, England: James Atkin (vocals), Ian Dench (guitar), Derry Brownson (keyboards, percussion), Zac Foley (bass) and Mark Decloedt (drums). Foley died of a drug overdose on 1/3/2002 (age 31).

2/16/91	3	12	✓1 Unbelievable	❶¹ ▲		Schubert Dip	EMI 96238
4/27/91	10	9	2 I Believe	—	↓		
7/27/91	26	2	3 Children	—	↓		
9/14/91	27	2	4 Lies	18	↓		
12/12/92	27	2	5 They're Here	—		Stigma	EMI 80348

EMINEM
Born Marshall Mathers on 10/17/72 in Kansas City; raised in Detroit. White male rapper.

3/20/99	37	4	1 My Name Is	36	▲⁴	The Slim Shady LP	Aftermath 90287
6/3/00	19	9	2 The Real Slim Shady	4	▲⁸	The Marshall Mathers LP	Aftermath 490629
6/1/02	15	12	3 Without Me	2⁵	▲⁶	The Eminem Show	Aftermath 493290
10/19/02	16↑	6↑	4 Lose Yourself	❶³↑		8 Mile (soundtrack)↑	Shady 493508

EMOTIONAL FISH, An
Rock group formed in Dublin, Ireland: Gerard Whelan (vocals), David Frew (guitar), Enda Wyatt (bass) and Martin Murphy (drums).

10/13/90	4	16	1 Celebrate	—		An Emotional Fish	Atlantic 82150
2/2/91	18	8	2 Grey Matter	—	↓		
6/19/93	15	7	3 Rain	—		Junk Puppets	Atlantic 82473

ENIGMA
Born Michael Cretu on 5/18/57 in Bucharest, Romania. Producer. Moved to Germany in 1975. Worked with **Vangelis** and **The Art Of Noise**. Featured vocalist is Cretu's wife, Sandra.

2/9/91	6	9	1 Sadeness Part 1 [F]	5	▲⁴	MCMXC A.D.	Charisma 91642
2/26/94	2⁵	15	2 Return To Innocence	4	▲²	Enigma 2: The Cross of Changes	Charisma 39236

ENO, Brian
Born on 5/15/48 in Woodbridge, Suffolk, England. Rock producer/keyboardist. Founding member of **Roxy Music**. Production work for **David Bowie**, **Devo**, **Ultravox** and **Talking Heads**.

10/27/90	11	10	Been There Done That	—		Wrong Way Up	Opal 26421
			BRIAN ENO/JOHN CALE				

ENYA
Born Eithne Ni Brennan on 5/17/61 in Gweedore, County Donegal, Ireland. Female singer.

1/7/89	6	12	1 Orinoco Flow (Sail Away)	24	▲⁴	Watermark	Geffen 24233
12/7/91+	3	14	2 Caribbean Blue	79	▲⁵	Shepherd Moons	Reprise 26775

ERASURE ★90★
Dance duo formed in England: Andy Bell (vocals) and Vince Clarke (instruments). Clarke was a member of **Depeche Mode** and **Yaz**.

9/10/88	22	2	1 Chains Of Love	12	▲	The Innocents	Sire 25730
11/26/88+	15	10	2 A Little Respect	14	↓		
3/4/89	19	9	3 Stop!	97		Crackers International	Sire 25904
10/14/89	11	9	4 Drama!	—		Wild!	Sire 26026
7/13/91	4	12	5 Chorus (Fishes In The Sea)	83		Chorus	Sire 26668
10/19/91	6	12	6 Love To Hate You	—	↓		
4/30/94	8	11	7 Always	20		I Say I Say I Say	Mute 61633

ESCAPE CLUB, The
Rock group formed in London: Trevor Steel (vocals), John Holliday (guitar), Johnnie Christo (bass) and Milan Zekavica (drums).

9/10/88	3	6	✓ Wild, Wild West	❶¹ ●		Wild Wild West	Atlantic 81871

ETHERIDGE, Melissa
Born on 5/29/61 in Leavenworth, Kansas. Singer/songwriter/guitarist.

9/30/89	18	4	1 No Souvenirs	95	▲	Brave And Crazy	Island 91285
10/28/95	32	6	2 Your Little Secret	47ᴬ	▲²	Your Little Secret	Island 524154

EURYTHMICS
Pop-rock duo: **Annie Lennox** (vocals, keyboards) and David A. Stewart (guitar). Lennox was born on 12/25/54 in Aberdeen, Scotland. Stewart was born on 9/9/52 in Sunderland, England. Both had been in The Tourists from 1977-80. Stewart married Siobhan Fahey of **Bananarama** on 8/1/87.

11/11/89	12	8	Don't Ask Me Why	40		We Too Are One	Arista 8606

DEBUT	PEAK	WKS	Modern Rock Track	Pop Gld	Album Title	Album Label & Number

EVERCLEAR ★22★
Rock trio formed in Portland, Oregon: Art Alexakis (vocals, guitar; born on 4/12/62), Craig Montoya (bass; born on 9/14/70) and Greg Eklund (drums; born on 4/18/70).

1)Everything To Everyone 2)I Will Buy You A New Life 3)Wonderful

6/24/95	34	5	1 Heroin Girl	—	▲	Sparkle And Fade................. Capitol 30929
11/11/95+	5	29	2 **Santa Monica (Watch The World Die)**	29^	↓	
5/4/96	13	10	3 **Heartspark Dollarsign**.................	85	↓	
9/13/97	❶¹	29	4 **Everything To Everyone**	43^	▲	So Much For The Afterglow .... Capitol 36503
2/7/98	3	27	5 **I Will Buy You A New Life**	33^	↓	
7/25/98	4	27	6 **Father Of Mine**	46^	↓	
1/23/99	12	13	7 **One Hit Wonder**	—	↓	
6/3/00	3	20	8 **Wonderful**	11	▲	Songs From An American Movie Vol. One: Learning How To Smile.................. Capitol 97061
9/16/00	15	9	9 **AM Radio**	101		
11/18/00	12	13	10 **When It All Goes Wrong Again**	121		Songs From An American Movie Vol. Two: Good Time For A Bad Attitude .... Capitol 95873
3/24/01	34	5	11 **Out Of My Depth**	—		↓

EVERLAST ★73★
Born Erik Schrody on 8/18/69 in Valley Stream, New York. Singer/songwriter/guitarist/actor. Former member of rap group House Of Pain. Played "Rhodes" in the movie *Judgment Night*.

10/10/98	❶⁹	34	1 **What It's Like**	13	▲²	Whitey Ford Sings The Blues .... Tommy Boy 1236
4/3/99	7	21	2 **Ends**	109		↓
10/2/99	17	21	3 **Put Your Lights On**	118	▲¹⁴	Supernatural (Santana) .... Arista 19080
			SANTANA Featuring Everlast			
9/23/00	15	15	4 **Black Jesus**	—	●	Eat At Whitey's .... Tommy Boy 1411
1/13/01	24	9	5 **I Can't Move**	—		↓

EVERYTHING
Ska-rock group from Sperryville, Virginia: Craig Honeycutt (vocals, guitar), Rich Bradley, Wolfe Quinn and Steve Van Dam (horns), David Slankard (bass) and Nate Brown (drums).

| 7/4/98 | 12 | 15 | **Hooch**........................ | 69 | | Super Natural .... Blackbird 38003 |

EVERYTHING BUT THE GIRL
Pop duo formed in London: Tracey Thorn (vocals) and Ben Watt (instruments). Group name taken from a furniture store on England's Hull University campus.

| 3/24/90 | 26 | 4 | **Driving**........................ | — | | The Language Of Life .... Atlantic 82057 |

EVE 6 ★58★
Rock trio from Los Angeles: Jon Siebels (vocals, guitar), Max Collins (bass) and Tony Fagenson (drums).

5/2/98	❶⁴	41	1 **Inside Out**	28	▲	Eve 6 .... RCA 67617
12/12/98+	6	21	2 **Leech**	—		↓
5/8/99	23	9	3 **Open Road Song**	—		↓
6/17/00	3	20	4 **Promise**	108	●	Horrorscope .... RCA 67713
11/11/00	19	13	5 **On The Roof Again**	—		↓
3/31/01	33	10	✓6 **Here's To The Night**	30		↓

EVE'S PLUM
Rock group from New York City: Colleen Fitzpatrick (vocals), brothers Michael (guitar) and Ben (drums) Kotch, and Theo Mack (bass). Fitzpatrick later recorded as Vitamin C. Group's name derived from actress Eve Plumb ("Jan" on TV's *The Brady Bunch*).

| 4/2/94 | 30 | 1 | **I Want It All** .... | — | | Envy .... 550 Music 53070 |

F

FABULON
Born Kevin MacBeth in Miami. Rock singer/keyboardist.

| 8/21/93 | 24 | 3 | **In A Mood** .... | — | | All Girls Are Pretty Volume I .... Chrysalis 21999 |

FACE TO FACE
Punk-rock group from Los Angeles: Trevor Keith (vocals), Chard Yaro (guitar), Scott Shiflett (bass) and Rob Kurth (drums).

| 3/18/95 | 39 | 2 | **Disconnected** .... | — | | Big Choice .... Victory 38348 |

FAILURE
Rock group from Los Angeles: Ken Andrews (vocals), Troy Van Leeuwen (guitar), Greg Edwards (bass) and Kellii Scott (drums).

| 12/7/96+ | 23 | 9 | **Stuck On You** .... | — | | Fantastic Planet .... Slash 46269 |

FAIRGROUND ATTRACTION
Pop group from England: Eddi Reader (female vocals), Mark Nevin (guitar), Simon Edwards (bass) and Roy Dodds (drums).

| 12/3/88 | 23 | 6 | **Perfect**........................ | 80 | | The First Of A Million Kisses .... RCA 8596 |

DEBUT	PEAK	WKS	Modern Rock Track	Pop Gld	Album Title	Album Label & Number

FAITH NO MORE
Rock group from San Francisco: Michael "Vlad Dracula" Patton (vocals), Jim Martin (guitar), Roddy Bottum (keyboards), Billy Gould (bass) and Mike Bordin (drums).

| 6/13/92 | ❶¹ | 12 | 1 MidLife Crisis | — ● | Angel Dust | Slash 26785 |
| 8/29/92 | 11 | 10 | 2 A Small Victory | — ↓ | | |

FARM, The
Rock group from Liverpool, England: Peter Hooton (vocals), Steve Grimes and Keith Mullin (guitars), Ben Leach (keyboards), Carl Hunter (bass) and Roy Boulter (drums).

4/27/91	7	9	1 All Together Now	—	Spartacus	Sire 26600
6/29/91	15	10	2 Groovy Train	41 ↓		
1/9/93	30	2	3 Love See No Colour	—	Love See No Colour	Sire 26959
7/2/94	30	1	4 Messiah	—	Hullabaloo	Sire 45588

FASTBALL
Rock trio from Austin, Texas: Miles Zuniga (vocals, guitar), Tony Scalzo (vocals, bass) and Joey Shuffield (drums).

| 2/21/98 | ❶⁷ | 26 | 1 The Way | 5ᴬ ▲ | All The Pain Money Can Buy | Hollywood 62130 |
| 8/15/98 | 13 | 15 | 2 Fire Escape | 86 ↓ | | |

FATBOY SLIM
Born Norman Cook on 7/31/63 in Brighton, Sussex, England. Techno-house instrumentalist.

1/17/98	28	7	1 Going Out Of My Head	—	Better Living Through Chemistry	Astralwerks 6203
8/29/98	39	2	2 The Rockafeller Skank	76 ▲	You've Come A Long Way, Baby	Skint 66247
1/30/99	2⁷	26	3 Praise You	36 ↓		
			samples "Take Yo Praise" by Camille Yarborough			
6/2/01	33	5	4 Weapon Of Choice	—	Halfway Between The Gutter And The Stars	Skint 50460

FAT LADY SINGS, The
Rock group from Dublin, Ireland: Nick Kelly (vocals), Tim Bradshaw (guitar), Dermot Lynch (bass) and Robert Hamilton (drums).

| 7/20/91 | 20 | 6 | Man Scared | — | Twist | Atlantic 82211 |

FEAR FACTORY
Hard-rock group from Los Angeles: Burton Bell (vocals), Dino Cazares (guitar), Christian Olde Wolbers (bass) and Raymond Herrera (drums).

| 6/5/99 | 38 | 7 | Cars | — ● | Obsolete | Roadrunner 8752 |
| | | | #9 Pop hit for Gary Numan in 1980 | | | |

FEEDER
Rock trio from England: Grant Nicholas (vocals), Taka Hirose (bass) and Jon Lee (drums).

| 6/27/98 | 24 | 12 | High | — | Polythene | Echo/Elektra 62085 |

FEELIES, The
Rock group from Hoboken, New Jersey: Glenn Mercer (vocals), Bill Million (guitar), Dave Weckerman (percussion), Brenda Sauter (bass) and Stanley Demeski (drums).

| 10/15/88 | 6 | 10 | 1 Away | — | Only Life | A&M 5214 |
| 4/6/91 | 13 | 7 | 2 Sooner Or Later | — | Time For A Witness | A&M 5344 |

FENIX*TX
Punk-rock group from Houston: Willie Salazar (vocals, guitar), Damon De La Paz (guitar), Adam Lewis (bass) and Donnie Vomit (drums).

| 4/29/00 | 21 | 14 | All My Fault | — | Fenix*TX | MCA 12013 |

FERRY, Bryan
Born on 9/26/45 in County Durham, England. Lead singer of **Roxy Music**.

| 10/29/94 | 37 | 3 | Mamouna | — | Mamouna | Virgin 39838 |

FETCHIN BONES
Rock group from Los Angeles: Hope Nicholls (vocals), Aaron Pitkin and Errol Stewart (guitars), Danna Pentes (bass) and Clay Richardson (drums).

| 8/12/89 | 19 | 5 | Love Crushing | — | Monster | Capitol 90661 |

FIALKA, Karel
Born in Bengal, India (of Czech and Scottish parentage); raised in England. Male singer/saxophonist.

| 2/11/89 | 29 | 2 | Hey Matthew | — | Human Animal | I.R.S. 42252 |

FIGURES ON A BEACH
Techno-rock group from Boston: Anthony Kaczynski (vocals), John Rolski (guitar), Christopher Ewen (keyboards), Percy Tell (bass) and Michael Smith (drums).

| 8/19/89 | 14 | 6 | Accidentally 4th St. (Gloria) | — | Figures On A Beach | Sire 25804 |

FILTER ★87★
Industrial rock duo from Cleveland: Richard Patrick (vocals, guitar, bass) and Brian Liesegang (keyboards, drums). Both worked with Trent Reznor in **Nine Inch Nails**.

4/29/95	10	20	1 Hey Man Nice Shot	76 ▲	Short Bus	Reprise 45864
8/16/97	29	10	2 (Can't You) Trip Like I Do	— ●	Spawn (soundtrack)	Immortal 68494
			FILTER & THE CRYSTAL METHOD			
7/31/99	17	13	3 Welcome To The Fold	— ▲	Title Of Record	Reprise 47388
10/16/99+	3	26	4 Take A Picture	12 ↓		
4/1/00	18	10	5 The Best Things	— ↓		
7/13/02	11	10	6 Where Do We Go From Here	94	theAmalgamut	Reprise 47963

DEBUT	PEAK	WKS	Modern Rock Track	Pop Gld	Album Title	Album Label & Number

FINE YOUNG CANNIBALS
Pop-rock trio formed in Birmingham, England: Roland Gift (vocals), Andy Cox (guitar) and David Steele (bass). Cox and Steele were with English Beat. Group name taken from the 1960 movie *All The Fine Young Cannibals*. Group appeared in the movie *Tin Men*. Gift acted in the movies *Sammy And Rosie Get Laid* and *Scandal*.

1/28/89	5	15	1 She Drives Me Crazy	❶[1] ▲[2]	*The Raw & The Cooked*	I.R.S. 6273
3/25/89	2[1]	19	2 Good Thing	❶[1]	↓	
8/12/89	9	7	3 Don't Look Back	11	↓	

fIREHOSE
Rock trio formed in California: Ed Crawford (vocals, guitar), **Mike Watt** (bass) and George Hurley (drums).

4/15/89	26	2	Time With You	—	*"fROMOHIO"*	SST 235

FIRE TOWN
Rock trio from Madison, Wisconsin: Doug Erickson (vocals, guitar), Phil Davis (vocals, guitar) and Butch Vig (drums). Vig and Erickson later formed **Garbage**.

3/18/89	18	6	The Good Life	—	*The Good Life*	Atlantic 81945

FISHBONE
Funk-rock group from Los Angeles: Angelo Moore (vocals, sax), Kendall Jones and Charlie Down (guitars), Christopher Dowd (keyboards), Walter Kirby (trumpet), John Fisher (bass) and Phillip Fisher (drums).

4/13/91	7	10	1 Sunless Saturday	—	*The Reality Of My Surroundings*	Columbia 46142
6/22/91	14	6	2 Everyday Sunshine	—	↓	

FIVE THIRTY
Rock trio from London: Paul Bassett (vocals, guitar), Tara Milton (bass) and Phil Hopper (drums).

10/12/91	14	7	13th Disciple	—	*Bed*	Atco 91757

FIXX, The
Techno-pop group formed in London: Cy Curnin (vocals), Jamie West-Oram (guitar), Rupert Greenall (keyboards), Dan Brown (bass) and Adam Woods (drums).

1/28/89	11	11	1 Driven Out	55	*Calm Animals*	RCA 8566
2/23/91	10	7	2 How Much Is Enough	35	*Ink*	MCA 10205

FLAMING LIPS, The
Rock group from Oklahoma City: Wayne Coyne (vocals), Ron Jones (guitar), Michael Ivins (bass) and Steven Drozd (drums).

12/10/94+	9	14	She Don't Use Jelly	55	*Transmissions From The Satellite Heart*	Warner 45334

FLESH FOR LULU
Punk-rock group from England: Nick Marsh (vocals), Rocco Barker (guitar), Derek Greening (keyboards), Mike Steed (bass) and Hans Perrson (drums).

9/23/89	15	6	1 Decline And Fall	—	*Plastic Fantastic*	Beggars Banquet 90232
11/11/89	9	10	2 Time And Space	—	↓	

FLICKERSTICK
Rock group from Dallas: brothers Brandin (vocals, guitar) and Fletcher (bass) Lea, with Rex James Ewing (guitar), Cory Kreig (keyboards) and Dominic Weir (drums).

11/3/01	27	8	Beautiful	—	*Welcoming Home The Astronauts*	Epic 86132

FLYS, The
Rock group from Los Angeles: brothers Adam and Joshua Paskowitz (vocals), Peter Perdichizzi (guitar), James Book (bass) and Nick Lucero (drums).

8/22/98	5	29	1 Got You (Where I Want You)	104	*Disturbing Behavior (soundtrack)*	Trauma 74007
4/3/99	32	5	2 She's So Huge	—	*Holiday Man*	Delicious Vinyl 74006

FOLDS, Ben, Five
Born on 9/12/66 in Winston-Salem, North Carolina. Singer/songwriter/pianist. His trio included Robert Sledge (bass) and Darren Jessee (drums).

3/29/97	22	12	1 Battle Of Who Could Care Less	— ▲	*Whatever And Ever Amen*	550 Music 67762
11/22/97+	6	26	2 Brick	19[A]	↓	
5/9/98	23	9	3 Song For The Dumped	—	↓	
4/24/99	17	11	4 Army	—	*The Unauthorized Biography Of Reinhold Messner*	550 Music 69808
8/11/01	28	11	5 Rockin' The Suburbs . . . . BEN FOLDS	—	*Rockin' The Suburbs*	Epic 61610

FOLK IMPLOSION
Rock duo from San Francisco: Lou Barlow (vocals, bass) and John Davis (guitar, drums).

10/21/95	4	26	Natural One	29	*Kids (soundtrack)*	London 828640

FOO FIGHTERS ★12★
Rock group formed in Seattle: **Dave Grohl** (vocals, guitar; born on 1/14/69), Pat Smear (guitar; born on 8/5/59), Nate Mendel (bass; born on 12/2/68) and William Goldsmith (drums; born on 7/4/72). Taylor Hawkins (born on 2/10/68) replaced Goldsmith in 1997. Franz Stahl (born on 10/30/61) replaced Smear in 1998. Grohl was drummer for **Nirvana**. Group name taken from the fiery UFO-like apparitions seen by U.S. Pilots during World War II.

1)Learn To Fly   2)All My Life   3)This Is A Call

7/8/95	2[2]	15	⋁1 This Is A Call	35[A] ▲	*Foo Fighters*	Roswell 34027
9/23/95	8	22	2 I'll Stick Around	51[A]	↓	
1/27/96	3	23	⋁3 Big Me	13[A]	↓	

DEBUT	PEAK	WKS	Modern Rock Track	Pop	Gld	Album Title	Album Label & Number
			FOO FIGHTERS — Cont'd				
5/3/97	9	15	4 Monkey Wrench	58ᴬ	▲	*The Colour And The Shape* .... Roswell 55832	
8/2/97	3	28	5 Everlong	42ᴬ		↓	
1/17/98	6	26	6 My Hero	59ᴬ		↓	
6/6/98	12	15	7 Walking After You	—		↓	
10/2/99	❶¹	26	8 Learn To Fly	19	▲	*There Is Nothing Left To Lose*........ Roswell 67892	
2/12/00	25	7	9 Stacked Actors	—		↓	
4/1/00	8	18	10 Breakout	—		↓	
9/9/00	17	10	11 Next Year	—		↓	
12/22/01+	14	13	12 The One.......................	121		*Orange County (soundtrack)*........ Columbia 85933	
9/14/02	❶¹↑	11↑	13 All My Life	51↑		*One By One* .... Roswell 68008	

FOREST FOR THE TREES
Group is actually solo singer/songwriter/producer Carl Stephenson (co-writer of **Beck**'s "Loser").

8/30/97	18	11	Dream	72		*Forest For The Trees*.......... DreamWorks 50002	

FOR SQUIRRELS
Rock group from Gainesville, Florida: John Francis Vigliatura (vocals), Travis Michael Tooke (guitar), William Richard White (bass) and Thomas Jacob Griego (drums). Vigliatura (age 20) and White (age 22) were killed in a car crash on 9/8/95. Tooke and Griego went on to form Subrosa.

12/9/95+	15	14	Mighty K.C.	70ᴬ		*Example* .... 550 Music 67150	

K.C.: Kurt Cobain (of **Nirvana**)

FOUNTAINS OF WAYNE
Pop-rock duo from New York: Chris Collingwood (vocals, guitar) and Adam Schlesinger (keyboards, drums).

11/30/96+	14	13	1 Radiation Vibe	71ᴬ		*Fountains Of Wayne* .... Atlantic 92725	
5/8/99	34	4	2 Denise	—		*Utopia Parkway*................... Scratchie 83177	

4 NON BLONDES
Pop-rock group from San Francisco: Linda Perry (vocals), Roger Rocha (guitar), Christa Hillhouse (bass) and Dawn Richardson (drums).

3/13/93	29	1	What's Up.......................	14	▲	*Bigger, Better, Faster, More!*....... Interscope 92112	

4 OF US, The
Rock group from Newry, Ireland: brothers Brendan (vocals), Paul (keyboards) and Declan (drums) Murphy, with John McCandless (bass).

5/5/90	22	4	Drag My Bad Name Down	77		*Songs For The Tempted*.......... Columbia 46025	

FRAZIER CHORUS
Pop trio from Brighton, England: Tim Freeman (vocals), Kate Holmes (woodwinds) and Chris Taplin (bass).

3/30/91	17	6	Cloud 8.......................	—		*Ray* .... Charisma 91641	

FRENTE!
Pop-rock group from Melbourne, Australia: Angie Hart (vocals), Simon Austin (guitar), Tim O'Connor (bass) and Mark Picton (drums). Band name is Spanish for "Front."

4/9/94	10	10	1 Bizarre Love Triangle	49		*Marvin The Album* .... Mammoth 92390	
7/2/94	9	9	2 Labour Of Love	106		↓	

FRONT 242
Industrial dance group from Brussels, Belgium: vocalists Jean-Luc De Meyer and Richard Jonckheere with instrumentalists Daniel Bressanutti and Patrick Codenys.

12/8/90	18	9	Tragedy For You	—		*Tyranny For You* .... Epic 46998	

FUEL ★33★
Rock group from Harrisburg, Pennsylvania: Brett Scallions (vocals; born on 12/21/71), Carl Bell (guitar; born on 1/9/68), Jeff Abercrombie (bass; born on 1/8/69) and Kevin Miller (drums; born on 9/6/70).

3/14/98	2¹	31	1 Shimmer	42	▲	*Sunburn*....................... 550 Music 68554	
10/3/98	17	23	2 Bittersweet.......................	—		↓	
5/15/99	26	9	3 Jesus Or A Gun	—		↓	
11/20/99	31	9	4 Sunburn	—		↓	
8/26/00	❶¹²	40	5 Hemorrhage (In My Hands)	30	▲²	*Something Like Human*.......... 550 Music 69436	
2/3/01	4	20	6 Innocent	113		↓	
6/16/01	12	18	7 Bad Day.......................	64		↓	
11/24/01	25	10	8 Last Time	—		↓	

FUN LOVIN' CRIMINALS
Eclectic hip-hop trio from New York City: Huey Morgan (vocals, guitar), Brian Leiser (bass, keyboards) and Steve Borgovini (drums).

9/7/96	14	17	Scooby Snacks	73ᴬ		*Come Find Yourself* .... EMI 35703	

samples "Moment Of Fear" by Tones on Tail

DEBUT	PEAK	WKS	Modern Rock Track	Pop Gld	Album Title	Album Label & Number

FURY IN THE SLAUGHTERHOUSE
Pop-rock group from Hannover, Germany: Kai Uwe Wingenfelder (vocals), Thorsten Wingenfelder and Christof Stein (guitars), Gero Drenk (keyboards), Hannes Schafer (bass) and Rainer Schumann (drums).

| 2/19/94 | 13 | 10 | Every Generation Got Its Own Disease .... | — | Mono | RCA 66352 |

FUZZBOX
Female group from Birmingham, England: sisters Jo (guitar) and Maggie (bass) Dunne, with Vickie Perks (vocals) and Tina O'Neill (drums).

| 9/30/89 | 16 | 7 | Self! .... | — | Big Bang! | Geffen 24185 |

G

GABRIEL, Peter
Born on 2/13/50 in London. Pop-rock singer/songwriter. Lead singer of **Genesis** from 1966-75. Also see **Youssou N'Dour**, **Peace Together** and **Classic Rock Tracks** section.

9/12/92	❶²	14	1 Digging In The Dirt	52 ▲	Us	Geffen 24473
11/7/92	❶⁵	16	2 Steam	32 ↓		
2/6/93	18	8	3 Kiss That Frog	— ↓		
1/29/94	22	8	4 Lovetown	— ▲	Philadelphia (soundtrack)	Epic Soundtrax 57624

GANG OF FOUR
Rock duo formed in Leeds, England: Jon King (vocals) and Andy Gill (guitar).

| 5/18/91 | 14 | 7 | Don't Fix What Ain't Broke .... | — | Mall | Polydor 849124 |

GARBAGE ★29★
Rock group formed in Madison, Wisconsin: Shirley Manson (vocals, guitar; native of Edinburgh, Scotland), Doug Erikson (guitar, bass, keyboards), Steve Marker (guitar, samples) and Butch Vig (drums). Vig and Erickson were members of **Fire Town**. Vig produced albums for **Nirvana**, **Soul Asylum**, **Sonic Youth** and **Smashing Pumpkins**.

6/17/95	26	9	1 Vow...	97	Garbage	Almo Sounds 80004
9/23/95	12	15	2 Queer..	57ᴬ ↓		
1/27/96	16	19	3 Only Happy When It Rains	55 ↓		
6/8/96	2¹	25	4 Stupid Girl	24 ▲² ↓		
11/30/96+	❶⁴	22	5 #1 Crush	29ᴬ ▲³	Romeo & Juliet (soundtrack)	Capitol 37715
4/11/98	5	21	6 Push It	52 ▲	Version 2.0	Almo Sounds 80018
7/18/98	6	26	7 I Think I'm Paranoid	70ᴬ ↓		
10/31/98+	11	26	8 Special	52 ↓		
5/1/99	23	15	9 When I Grow Up	— ↓		

GEGGY TAH
Rock trio from Los Angeles: singers/multi-instrumentalists Tommy Jordan and Greg Kurstin, with drummer Daren Hahn.

| 8/31/96 | 16 | 14 | Whoever You Are .... | 67ᴬ | Sacred Cow | Luaka Bop 46113 |

GELDOF, Bob
Born on 10/5/54 in Dublin, Ireland. Leader of The Boomtown Rats. Played "Pink" in the **Pink Floyd** movie *The Wall*. Organized British superstar benefit group **Band Aid** and earned a Nobel Peace Prize nomination.

| 9/15/90 | 24 | 6 | Love Or Something .... | — | The Vegetarians Of Love | Atlantic 82041 |

GENE LOVES JEZEBEL
Techno-rock group formed in England: Jay Aston (vocals), James Stevenson (guitar), Peter Rizzo (bass) and Chris Bell (drums).

| 6/30/90 | ❶² | 12 | 1 Jealous | 68 | Kiss Of Life | Geffen 24260 |
| 11/28/92 | 18 | 9 | 2 Josephina .... | — | Heavenly Bodies | Savage 50210 |

GENERAL PUBLIC
Pop duo from Birmingham, England: **Dave Wakeling** (vocals, guitar) and **Ranking Roger** (vocals, keyboards).

4/2/94	6	10	1 I'll Take You There	22	Threesome (soundtrack)	Epic Soundtrax 57881
			#1 Pop hit for The Staple Singers in 1972			
4/29/95	40	1	2 Rainy Days	93	Rub It Better	Epic 64270

GIN BLOSSOMS ★89★
Pop-rock group from Tempe, Arizona: Robin Wilson (vocals), Jesse Valenzuela and Scott Johnson (guitars), Bill Leen (bass) and Phillip Rhodes (drums). Early guitarist Doug Hopkins died of a self-inflicted bullet wound on 12/5/93 (age 32).

10/30/93+	❶¹	23	1 Found Out About You	25 ▲⁴	New Miserable Experience	A&M 5403
4/30/94	13	14	2 Until I Fall Away	21ᴬ ↓		
10/8/94	39	1	3 Allison Road	24ᴬ ↓		
8/5/95	5	14	4 Til I Hear It From You	11 ●	Empire Records (soundtrack)	A&M 540384
2/10/96	8	12	5 Follow You Down	9 ▲	Congratulations I'm Sorry	A&M 540469
5/18/96	21	7	6 Day Job	— ↓		

DEBUT	PEAK	WKS	Modern Rock Track	Pop Gld	Album Title	Album Label & Number

GO-BETWEENS, The
Rock group from Australia: Robert Forster (vocals), Grant McLennan (guitar), Amanda Brown (violin), John Willsteed (bass) and Lindy Morrison (drums).

12/24/88+	16	7	**Was There Anything I Could Do?**	—	*16 Lovers Lane* .... Beggars Banquet 91230

GODFATHERS, The
Rock group formed in London: brothers Peter (vocals) and Chris (bass) Coyne, Mike Gibson and Kris Dollimore (guitars), and George Mazur (drums). Chris Burrows replaced Dollimore in 1990.

5/13/89	8	8	1 **She Gives Me Love**	—	*More Songs About Love & Hate* .... Epic 45023
3/9/91	6	9	2 **Unreal World**	—	*Unreal World* .... Epic 46026

GOD LIVES UNDERWATER
Techno-rock duo from Los Angeles: David Reilly and Jeff Turzo.

3/14/98	17	15	**From Your Mouth**	—	*Life In The So-Called Space Age* .... A&M 540871

GODS CHILD
Rock group from New York City: Chris Seefried (vocals, guitar), Gary DeRosa (keyboards), Craig Ruda (bass) and Alex Alexander (drums).

9/10/94	25	3	**Everybodys 1**	—	*Everybody* .... Qwest 45632

GODSMACK ★54★
Hard-rock group formed in Boston: Salvatore "Sully" Erna (vocals; born on 2/7/68), Tony Rombola (guitar; born on 11/24/64), Robbie Merrill (bass; born on 6/13/63) and Tommy Stewart (drums; born on 5/26/66).

4/10/99	19	26	1 **Whatever**	116 ▲⁴	*Godsmack* .... Republic 53190
10/23/99	31	12	2 **Keep Away**	—	↓
2/19/00	6	26	3 **Voodoo**	102	↓
8/5/00	32	6	4 **Bad Religion**	—	↓
10/21/00+	12	28	5 **Awake**	101 ▲²	*Awake* .... Republic 159688
4/14/01	28	23	6 **Greed**	123	↓
9/29/01	28	8	7 **Bad Magick**	—	↓
2/16/02	20	26	8 **I Stand Alone**	102 ●	*The Scorpion King (soundtrack)* ..... Universal 017115

GO-GO'S
Female rock group formed in Los Angeles: Belinda Carlisle (vocals), Jane Wiedlin (guitar), Charlotte Caffey (guitar), Kathy Valentine (bass) and Gina Schock (drums). Disbanded in 1984. Reunions in 1990, 1994 and 2001.

11/5/94	21	8	**The Whole World Lost Its Head**	108	*Return To The Valley Of The Go-Go's* .... I.R.S. 29694

GOLDEN PALOMINOS, The
Group is actually drummer Anton Fier (born on 6/20/56 in Cleveland) with revolving studio musicians.

10/5/91	14	9	**Alive And Living Now**	—	*Drunk With Passion* .... Charisma 91745
			Michael Stipe (of R.E.M.; lead vocal)		

GOLDFINGER
Rock group from Santa Monica, California: John Feldman (vocals, guitar), Charlie Paulson (guitar), Simon Williams (bass) and Darrin Pfeiffer (drums). Kelly LeMieux replaced Williams in 1999.

4/13/96	5	21	1 **Here In Your Bedroom**	47ᴬ	*Goldfinger* .... Mojo 53007
9/20/97	14	11	2 **This Lonely Place**	—	*Hang-Ups* .... Mojo 53079
6/22/02	37	4	3 **Open Your Eyes**	—	*Open Your Eyes* .... Mojo 41806

GOOD, Matthew, Band
Born in Vancouver. Rock singer/guitarist. His band: Dave Genn (keyboards), Rich Priske (bass) and Ian Browne (drums).

1/6/01	34	10	**Hello Time Bomb**	—	*Beautiful Midnight* .... Atlantic 83423

GOOD CHARLOTTE
Rock group from New York City: Joel (vocals), Benji and Billy (guitars), Paul (bass) and Aaron (drums).

9/23/00	23	19	1 **Little Things**	—	*Good Charlotte* .... Daylight 61452
9/14/02	11	11↑	2 **Lifestyles Of The Rich And Famous**	111↑ ●	*The Young And The Hopeless* .... Daylight 86486

GOO GOO DOLLS ★17★
Rock trio from Buffalo, New York: Johnny Rzeznik (vocals, guitar; born on 12/5/65), Robby Takac (bass; born on 9/30/64) and George Tutuska (drums; born on 2/27/65). Mike Malinin (born on 10/10/67) replaced Tutuska in 1995.

1)Iris 2)Name 3)Slide

1/12/91	24	3	1 **There You Are**	—	*Hold Me Up* .... Metal Blade 26259
3/6/93	5	10	2 **We Are The Normal**	—	*Superstar Car Wash* .... Metal Blade 45206
4/15/95	36	3	3 **Only One**	— ▲²	*A Boy Named Goo* .... Warner 45750
8/12/95	❶⁴	26	4 **Name**	5	↓
12/30/95+	9	17	5 **Naked**	47ᴬ	↓
6/29/96	25	9	6 **Long Way Down**	—	↓
7/26/97	20	10	7 **Lazy Eye**	— ▲	*Batman & Robin (soundtrack)* .... Warner Sunset 46620
4/11/98	❶⁵	26	8 **Iris**	❶¹⁸ᴬ ▲⁵	*City Of Angels (soundtrack)* ..... Warner Sunset 46867

DEBUT	PEAK	WKS	Modern Rock Track	Pop	Gld	Album Title	Album Label & Number
			GOO GOO DOLLS — Cont'd				
9/19/98	❶²	26	↙9 Slide	8	▲²	Dizzy Up The Girl	Warner 47058
3/6/99	9	14	↙10 Dizzy	108	↓		
6/26/99	13	16	↙11 Black Balloon	16	↓		
5/13/00	38	6	↙12 Broadway	24	↓		
3/30/02	21	10	↙13 Here Is Gone	18	●	Gutterflower	Warner 48206
			GORE, Martin L.				
			Born on 7/23/61 in Basildon, England. Member of **Depeche Mode**.				
8/19/89	18	7	Compulsion	—		Counterfeit e.p.	Sire 25980
			GORILLAZ				
			Animated hip-hop group created by Jamie Hewlett and Dan Nakamura: 2-D (vocals, keyboards), Noodle (guitar), Murdoc (bass) and Russel (drums).				
7/7/01	3	26	1 Clint Eastwood	57	▲	Gorillaz	Parlophone 33748
11/17/01	23	12	2 19-2000	—	↓		
			GRANT LEE BUFFALO				
			Rock trio from Los Angeles: Grant Lee Phillips (vocals, guitar), Paul Kimble (bass) and Joey Peters (drums).				
9/17/94	14	10	1 Mockingbirds	—		Mighty Joe Moon	Slash 45714
6/13/98	11	13	2 Truly, Truly			Jubilee	Slash 46879
			GRAPES OF WRATH, The				
			Folk-rock group from Kelowna, British Columbia, Canada: brothers Tom (bass) and Chris (drums) Hooper, with Kevin Kane (vocals, guitar) and Vincent Jones (piano).				
10/5/91	27	3	I Am Here	—		These Days	Capitol 96431
			GRAVITY KILLS				
			Techno-rock group from Jefferson City, Missouri: Jeff Scheel (vocals), Matt Dudenhoeffer (guitar), Douglas Firley (keyboards) and Kurt Kerns (bass, drums).				
3/2/96	24	24	Guilty	86		Gravity Kills	TVT 5910
			GRAY, David				
			Born in 1968 in Manchester, England; raised in Solva, Wales. Rock singer/songwriter/guitarist.				
12/2/00+	25	13	✓Babylon	57	▲	White Ladder	ATO 69351
			GREBENSHIKOV, Boris				
			Born on 11/27/53 in Leningrad. Rock singer/songwriter/guitarist.				
7/8/89	7	10	Radio Silence	—		Radio Silence	Columbia 44364
			produced by Dave Stewart (of **Eurythmics**)				
			GREEN DAY ★5★				
			Punk-rock trio formed in Berkeley, California: Billie Joe Armstrong (vocals, guitar; born on 2/17/72), Mike "Dirnt" Pritchard (bass; born on 5/4/72) and Frank "Tre Cool" Wright (drums; born on 12/9/72).				
			1)When I Come Around 2)Basket Case 3)Minority				
3/19/94	❶¹	22	1 Long View	36ᴬ	▲¹⁰	Dookie	Reprise 45529
7/16/94	❶⁵	23	2 Basket Case	26ᴬ	↓		
9/24/94	7	18	3 Welcome To Paradise	56ᴬ	↓		
12/3/94+	❶⁷	26	4 When I Come Around	6ᴬ	↓		
4/15/95	5	17	5 She	41ᴬ	↓		
7/29/95	❶¹	12	6 J.A.R. (Jason Andrew Relva)	22ᴬ		Angus (soundtrack)	Reprise 45960
10/7/95	3	12	7 Geek Stink Breath	27ᴬ	▲²	Insomniac	Reprise 46046
12/23/95+	3	25	8 Brain Stew/Jaded	35ᴬ	↓		
6/15/96	21	9	9 Walking Contradiction	70ᴬ	↓		
9/13/97	5	24	10 Hitchin' A Ride	59ᴬ	▲²	Nimrod	Reprise 46794
11/29/97+	2¹³	26	11 Good Riddance (Time Of Your Life)	11ᴬ	↓		
4/25/98	16	13	12 Redundant	—	↓		
10/17/98	31	6	13 Nice Guys Finish Last	—	↓		
9/9/00	❶⁵	23	14 Minority	101	●	Warning:	Reprise 47613
12/2/00+	3	19	15 Warning	114	↓		
3/31/01	26	8	16 Waiting	—	↓		
			GREENWHEEL				
			Rock group from St. Louis: Ryan Jordan (vocals), Andrew Dwiggins and Marc Wanninger (guitars), Brandon Armstrong (bass) and Douglas Randall (drums).				
9/21/02	37	3	Breathe	—		Soma Holiday	10 Inch 586661
			GUADALCANAL DIARY				
			Rock group formed in Marietta, Georgia: Murray Attaway (vocals), Jeff Walls (guitar), Rhett Crowe (bass) and John Poe (drums). Group named after a 1943 war movie.				
3/11/89	7	10	Always Saturday	—		Flip-Flop	Elektra 60848

DEBUT	PEAK	WKS	Modern Rock Track	Pop Gld	Album Title	Album Label & Number

GUSTER
Rock trio from Boston: Adam Gardner (vocals, guitar), Ryan Miller (guitar) and Brian Rosenworcel (drums).

| 6/20/98 | 35 | 5 | Airport Song | — | *Goldfly* | Hybrid 20006 |

H

HANDSOME DEVIL
Rock group from Orange County, California: Danny Walker (vocals, guitar), Billie Stevens (guitar), Darren Roberts (bass) and Keith Morgan (drums).

| 9/1/01 | 22 | 9 | Makin' Money | — | *Love And Kisses From The Underground* | RCA 68055 |

HAPPYHEAD
Pop-rock trio formed in London: Carl Marsh (vocals, guitar), Steve Gretham (bass) and Jim Kimberly (drums).

| 3/14/92 | 7 | 9 | Fabulous | — | *Give Happyhead* | EastWest 92114 |

HAPPY MONDAYS
Dance-rock group formed in Manchester, England: brothers Shaun (vocals) and Paul (bass) Ryder, Mark Day (guitar), Paul Davis (keyboards), Mark Berry (percussion) and Gary Whelan (drums). Shaun Ryder and Berry later formed **Black Grape**.

7/14/90	9	11	1 Step On	—	*Pills 'N' Thrills And Bellyaches*	Elektra 60986
12/1/90+	❶[1]	12	2 Kinky Afro	—	↓	
3/23/91	23	3	3 Bob's Yer Uncle	—	↓	
9/19/92	21	7	4 Stinkin Thinkin	—	*Yes, Please!*	Elektra 61391

HARDING, John Wesley
Born Wesley Harding Stace on 10/22/65 in Hastings, England. Singer/songwriter. *John Wesley Harding* was the title of a 1968 **Bob Dylan** album.

2/10/90	17	10	1 The Devil In Me	—	*Here Comes The Groom*	Sire 26087
3/16/91	8	7	2 The Person You Are	—	*The Name Above The Title*	Sire 26481
5/11/91	29	2	3 The People's Drug	—	↓	

HARRISON, Jerry: Casual Gods
Born on 2/21/49 in Milwaukee. Rock keyboardist/producer. Member of **Talking Heads**. The Casual Gods are 13 backing musicians.

| 5/19/90 | 13 | 8 | Flying Under Radar | — | *Walk On Water* | Sire 25943 |

HARRY, Deborah
Born on 7/1/45 in Miami; raised in Hawthorne, New Jersey. Lead singer of **Blondie**. Acted in several movies.

9/10/88	14	4	1 Liar, Liar	—	*Married To The Mob (soundtrack)*	Reprise 25763
			DEBBIE HARRY #12 Pop hit for The Castaways in 1965			
9/30/89	2[2]	11	2 I Want That Man	—	*Def, Dumb & Blonde*	Sire 25938
12/16/89+	12	6	3 Kiss It Better	—	↓	

HARVEY, PJ
Born Polly Jean Harvey on 10/9/69 in Yeovil, England. Female singer/guitarist. Had own trio, also named PJ Harvey, which included bassist Stephen Vaughan and drummer Rob Ellis.

7/25/92	9	10	1 Sheela-Na-Gig	—	*Dry*	Indigo 555001
2/25/95	2[3]	14	2 Down By The Water	48[A]	*To Bring You My Love*	Island 524085
9/26/98	33	3	3 A Perfect Day Elise	—	*Is This Desire?*	Island 524563

HARVEY DANGER
Rock group from Seattle: Sean Nelson (vocals), Jeff Lin (guitar), Aaron Huffman (bass) and Evan Sult (drums).

4/11/98	3	28	1 Flagpole Sitta	38[A] ●	*Where Have All The Merrymakers Gone?*	Slash 556000
3/20/99	29	5	2 Save It For Later	—	*200 Cigarettes (soundtrack)*	Mercury 538738
9/2/00	27	9	3 Sad Sweetheart Of Rodeo	—	*King James Version*	London 31143

HATFIELD, Juliana, Three
Born on 7/2/67 in Wiscasset, Maine. Female rock singer/guitarist. Group also included bassist Dean Fisher and drummer Todd Philips.

8/7/93	❶[1]	12	1 My Sister	112	*Become What You Are*	Atlantic 92278
3/25/95	5	12	2 Universal Heart-Beat	84	*Only Everything*	Mammoth 92540
			JULIANA HATFIELD			

HAVANA 3 A.M.
Rock group formed in England: Nigel Dixon (vocals, guitar), Gary Myrick (guitar), Paul Simonon (bass) and Travis Williams (drums). Simonon was a member of **The Clash**.

| 2/16/91 | 6 | 11 | Reach The Rock | — | *Havana 3 A.M.* | I.R.S. 13069 |

HAZA, Ofra
Born on 11/19/57 in Tel Aviv, Israel. Died of AIDS on 2/23/2000 (age 42). Female singer/songwriter/actress.

| 12/3/88 | 18 | 9 | Im Nin'alu | — | *Shaday* | Sire 25816 |

HEART THROBS, The
Rock group from Reading, England: sisters Rose (vocals) and Rachel (bass) Carlotti, Alan Barclay (guitar), Stephen Ward (keyboards) and Mark Side (drums).

| 8/11/90 | 2[3] | 11 | 1 Dreamtime | — | *Cleopatra Grip* | Elektra 60961 |
| 10/27/90 | 21 | 4 | 2 She's In A Trance | — | ↓ | |

DEBUT	PEAK	WKS	Modern Rock Track	Pop	Gld	Album Title	Album Label & Number

(HED)PLANET EARTH
Rap-rock group from Huntington Beach, California: Jahred Shaine (vocals), DJ Product (DJ), Wesstyle and Chizad (guitars), Mawk (bass) and B.C. (drums).

| 9/16/00 | 27 | 11 | Bartender (I Just Want Your Company) | — | | Broke | Volcano 41710 |

HELMET
Rock group from New York: Page Hamilton (vocals, guitar), Peter Mengede (guitar), Henry Bogdan (bass) and John Stanier (drums).

| 10/10/92 | 29 | 1 | Unsung | — | ● | Meantime | Interscope 92162 |

HEYWARD, Nick
Born on 5/20/61 in Beckenham, Kent, England. Pop-rock singer/guitarist. Member of **Haircut One Hundred** (1981-83).

| 12/4/93+ | 4 | 16 | Kite | 107 | | From Monday To Sunday | Epic 57755 |

HIATT, John
Born on 8/20/52 in Indianapolis. Singer/songwriter/guitarist. Member of **Little Village**.

| 10/1/88 | 22 | 4 | 1 Slow Turning | — | | Slow Turning | A&M 5206 |
| 7/7/90 | 24 | 5 | 2 Child Of The Wild Blue Yonder | — | | Stolen Moments | A&M 5310 |

HIGH, The
Rock group from Manchester, England: John Matthews (vocals), Andy Couzens (guitar), Simon Davies (bass) and Chris Goodwin (drums).

| 12/22/90+ | 19 | 7 | Up & Down | — | | Somewhere Soon | London 828224 |

HIMMELMAN, Peter
Born in St. Louis Park, Minnesota. Singer/songwriter.

| 6/1/91 | 18 | 6 | Woman With The Strength Of 10,000 Men | — | | From Strength To Strength | Epic 47073 |

HINDU LOVE GODS
One-time gathering: **Warren Zevon** (vocals) with **R.E.M.** members: Peter Buck (guitar), Mike Mills (bass) and Bill Berry (drums).

| 10/27/90 | 23 | 7 | Raspberry Beret | — | | Hindu Love Gods | Giant 24406 |

#2 Pop hit for **Prince** in 1985

HITCHCOCK, Robyn, & The Egyptians
Born on 3/3/52 in London. Male rock singer/guitarist. The Egyptians: Andy Metcalfe (bass) and Morris Windsor (drums).

3/18/89	2³	11	1 Madonna Of The Wasps	—		Queen Elvis	A&M 5241
8/24/91	●⁵	11	2 So You Think You're In Love	—		Perspex Island	A&M 5368
11/23/91	29	2	3 Oceanside	—		↓	
			Peter Buck (of **R.E.M.**; guitar, above 2)				
1/25/92	23	2	4 Ultra Unbelievable Love	—		↓	
3/13/93	19	7	5 Driving Aloud (Radio Storm)	—		Respect	A&M 540064

HIVES, The
Rock group from Fagersta, Sweden: brothers Pete (vocals) and Niklas (guitar) Almqvist, Vigilante Carlstroem (guitars), Dr. Matt Destruction (bass) and Chris Dangerous (drums).

| 5/25/02 | 6 | 25 | Hate To Say I Told You So | 86 | | Veni Vidi Vicious | Epitaph 48327 |

HOLE
★41★

Rock group formed in Los Angeles: Courtney Love (vocals, guitar), Eric Erlandson (guitar), Kristen Pfaff (bass) and Patty Schemel (drums). Love acted in several movies; married to Kurt Cobain (of **Nirvana**) from 2/24/92 until his death on 4/8/94. Pfaff was found dead in her bathtub on 6/16/94 (age 27); replaced by Melissa Auf Der Maur.

4/23/94	13	10	1 Miss World	—	▲	Live Through This	DGC 24631
10/15/94	4	17	2 Doll Parts	58		↓	
2/11/95	29	10	3 Violet	—		↓	
2/11/95	36	4	4 Asking For It	—		↓	
8/19/95	32	5	5 Softer, Softest	—		↓	
7/27/96	31	9	6 Gold Dust Woman	—	▲	The Crow - City Of Angels (soundtrack)	Miramax 20476
			first recorded by **Fleetwood Mac** in 1977				
9/5/98	●⁴	26	7 Celebrity Skin	85	▲	Celebrity Skin	DGC 25164
12/12/98+	3	20	8 Malibu	81		↓	
4/17/99	13	14	9 Awful	—		↓	

HOLLOW MEN, The
Rock group formed in Manchester, England: David Ashmore (vocals), Brian Roberts and Choque (guitars), Howard Taylor (bass) and Johnny Cragg (drums).

| 2/16/91 | 16 | 7 | November Comes | — | | Cresta | Arista 8666 |

HOOBASTANK
Rock group from Agoura Hills, California: Doug Robb (vocals), Dan Estrin (guitar), Markku Lappalainen (bass) and Chris Hesse (drums).

10/27/01+	3	36	1 Crawling In The Dark	68	▲	Hoobastank	Island 586435
4/27/02	2⁵	28	2 Running Away	44		↓	
10/12/02	27↑	7↑	3 Remember Me	—		↓	

HOODOO GURUS
Pop-rock group from Sydney, Australia: Dave Faulkner (vocals), Brad Shepherd (guitar), Rick Grossman (bass) and Mark Kingsmill (drums).

| 7/22/89 | ●³ | 13 | 1 Come Anytime | — | | Magnum Cum Louder | RCA 9781 |
| 4/6/91 | 3 | 9 | 2 Miss Freelove '69 | — | | Kinky | RCA 3009 |

DEBUT	PEAK	WKS	Modern Rock Track	Pop Gld	Album Title	Album Label & Number
			HOOTIE & THE BLOWFISH			
			Pop-rock group formed in South Carolina: Darius Rucker (vocals), Mark Bryan (guitar), Dean Felber (bass) and Jim Sonefeld (drums). Won the 1995 Best New Artist Grammy Award.			
5/6/95	34	6	1 Let Her Cry...	9	▲[16] *Cracked Rear View* . . . . Atlantic 82613	
7/1/95	22	11	2 Only Wanna Be With You	6	↓	
4/27/96	33	2	3 Old Man & Me (When I Get To Heaven).............	13	▲[3] *Fairweather Johnson* . . . . Atlantic 82886	
			HOTHOUSE FLOWERS			
			Folk-rock group from Dublin, Ireland: Liam O'Maonlai (vocals), Fiachna O'Braonain (guitar), Peter O'Toole (bass) and Jerry Fehily (drums).			
9/10/88	7	9	1 Don't Go	—	*people* . . . . London 828101	
10/22/88	12	13	2 I'm Sorry	—	↓	
6/2/90	2[1]	14	3 Give It Up	—	*Home* . . . . London 828197	
3/20/93	14	7	4 Thing Of Beauty	—	*Songs From The Rain* . . . . London 828350	
			HOUSE, A			
			Rock group from Dublin, Ireland: David Couse (vocals), Fergal Bunbury (guitar), Martin Healy (bass) and Dermot Wylie (drums).			
12/10/88+	9	10	Call Me Blue	—	*On Our Big Fat Merry-Go-Round* . . . . Sire 25821	
			HOUSE OF FREAKS			
			Rock duo from Richmond, Virginia: singer/guitarist Bryan Harvey and drummer Johnny Hott.			
4/29/89	23	6	1 Sun Gone Down	—	*Tantilla* . . . . Rhino 70846	
7/15/89	27	4	2 When The Hammer Came Down	—	↓	
9/28/91	11	8	3 Rocking Chair	—	*Cakewalk* . . . . Giant 24417	
			HOUSE OF LOVE, The			
			Pop-rock group from England: Guy Chadwick (vocals, guitar), Simon Walker (guitar), Chris Groothuizen (bass) and Pete Evans (drums).			
9/10/88	8	10	1 Christine	—	*The House Of Love* . . . . Relativity 8245	
3/3/90	2[1]	14	2 I Don't Know Why I Love You	—	*The House Of Love* . . . . Fontana 842293	
6/29/91	5	11	3 Marble	—	*A Spy In The House Of Love* . . . . Fontana 848671	
8/29/92	9	12	4 You Don't Understand	—	*Babe Rainbow* . . . . Fontana 512549	
			HOWLIN' MAGGIE			
			Rock group from Columbus, Ohio: Harold "Happy" Chichester (vocals), Andy Harrison (guitar), James Rico (bass) and Jerome Dillon (drums).			
5/25/96	37	2	Alcohol...	—	*Honeysuckle Strange* . . . . Columbia 67421	
			HUFFAMOOSE			
			Rock group from Philadelphia: Craig Elkins (vocals), Kevin Hanson (guitar), Jim Stager (bass) and Erik Johnson (drums).			
2/14/98	34	6	Wait	—	*We've Been Had Again* . . . . Interscope 90076	
			HUM			
			Rock group from Champaign, Illinois: Matt Talbott (vocals), Tim Lash (guitar), Jeff Dimpsey (bass) and Bryan St. Pere (drums).			
6/3/95	11	16	1 Stars...	72[A]	*You'd Prefer An Astronaut* . . . . RCA 66577	
2/14/98	37	3	2 Comin' Home	—	*Downward Is Heavenward* . . . . RCA 67446	
			HUMAN LEAGUE, The			
			Electro-pop trio from Sheffield, Yorkshire, England: lead singer/synthesist Philip Oakey, with female vocalists Joanne Catherall and Susanne Sulley.			
9/29/90	17	7	Heart Like A Wheel	32	*Romantic?* . . . . Virgin 5316	
			HUNTERS & COLLECTORS			
			Rock group from Melbourne, Australia: Mark Seymour (vocals, guitar), Barry Palmer (guitar), Jeremy Smith, Michael Waters and Jack Howard (horns), John Archer (bass) and Doug Falconer (drums).			
9/10/88	6	12	1 Back On The Breadline	—	*Fate* . . . . I.R.S. 42110	
5/5/90	5	11	2 When The River Runs Dry	—	*Ghost Nation* . . . . Atlantic 82096	
			HYNDE, Chrissie — see UB40			

I

DEBUT	PEAK	WKS	Modern Rock Track	Pop Gld	Album Title	Album Label & Number
			ICICLE WORKS			
			Rock trio from Liverpool, England: Robert Ian McNabb (vocals, guitar), Chris Layhe (bass) and Chris Sharrock (drums).			
9/10/88	13	2	High Time...	—	*Blind* . . . . Beggars B. 8424	
			IDOL, Billy			
			Born William Broad on 11/30/55 in Stanmore, Middlesex, England. Rock singer. Leader of punk group Generation X from 1977-81. Appeared in the movie *The Wedding Singer*.			
5/5/90	7	10	1 Cradle Of Love	2[1] ▲	*Charmed Life* . . . . Chrysalis 21735	
6/19/93	23	5	2 Shock To The System	105	*Cyberpunk* . . . . Chrysalis 26000	
			IMBRUGLIA, Natalie			
			Born on 2/4/75 in Sydney, Australia. Female singer/songwriter.			
2/14/98	12	22	1 Torn	❶[11A] ▲[2]	*Left Of The Middle* . . . . RCA 67634	
7/4/98	26	8	2 Wishing I Was There	25[A]	↓	
			IMPERIAL DRAG			
			Rock group from San Francisco: Eric Dover (vocals, guitar; **Slash's Snakepit**), Roger Manning (keyboards; **Jellyfish**), Joseph Karnes (bass) and Eric Skadis (drums).			
5/25/96	30	5	Boy Or A Girl	—	*Imperial Drag* . . . . Work 67378	

DEBUT	PEAK	WKS	Modern Rock Track	Pop Gld	Album Title	Album Label & Number

INCUBUS ★25★
Hard-rock group from Calabasas, California: Brandon Boyd (vocals), Mike Einziger (guitar), Chris Kilmore (DJ), Alex Katunich (bass) and Jose Pasillas (drums).

11/13/99+	3	42	1 **Pardon Me**	102	▲² *Make Yourself* .... Immortal 63652
7/1/00	2¹	26	2 **Stellar**	107	↓
12/2/00+	❶⁸	39	3 **Drive**	9	↓
8/25/01	2⁶	37	4 **Wish You Were Here**	60	▲² *Morning View.* .... Immortal 85227
12/22/01+	9	23	5 **Nice To Know You**	105	↓
5/4/02	3	26	6 **Warning**	104	↓

INDIGO GIRLS
Folk-rock duo from Decatur, Georgia: singers/songwriters/guitarists Amy Ray (born on 4/12/64) and Emily Sailers (born on 7/22/63).

6/17/89	26	1	✓1 **Closer To Fine**	52	▲² *Indigo Girls* .... Epic 45044
10/20/90	12	5	2 **Hammer And A Nail**	—	● *Nomads-Indians-Saints* .... Epic 46820
			Mary-Chapin Carpenter (backing vocal)		
5/16/92	10	10	✓3 **Galileo**	89	▲ *Rites Of Passage* .... Epic 48865
			Jackson Browne and **David Crosby** (backing vocals)		
9/3/94	28	5	4 **Least Complicated**	—	▲ *Swamp Ophelia* .... Epic 57621

INDIO
Born Gordon Peterson in Toronto. Singer/songwriter/guitarist.

| 7/8/89 | 10 | 11 | **Hard Sun** | — | *Big Harvest* .... A&M 5257 |

INFORMATION SOCIETY
Techno-dance group from Minneapolis: Kurt Valaquen and Paul Robb (vocals), Amanda Kramer (keyboards) and Jack Cassidy (bass).

| 9/10/88 | 10 | 3 | ✓1 **What's On Your Mind (Pure Energy)** | 3 | ● *Information Society* .... Tommy Boy 25691 |
| 12/17/88 | 15 | 8 | 2 **Walking Away** .... | 9 | ↓ |

INJECTED
Rock group from Atlanta: Danny Grady (vocals, guitar), Jade Lemmons (guitar), Steve Slovisky (bass) and Chris Wojtal (drums).

| 2/2/02 | 22 | 11 | **Faithless** .... | — | *Burn It Black* .... Island 548878 |

INNOCENCE MISSION, The
Rock group from Lancaster, Pennsylvania: Karen Peris (vocals), her husband Don Peris (guitar), with Mike Bitts (bass) and Steve Brown (drums).

| 10/14/89 | 22 | 5 | 1 **Black Sheep Wall** .... | — | *The Innocence Mission* .... A&M 5274 |
| 9/9/95 | 33 | 4 | 2 **Bright As Yellow** .... | 117 | ● *Empire Records (soundtrack)* .... A&M 540384 |

INSPIRAL CARPETS
Post-punk group from Manchester, England: Tom Hingley (vocals), Graham Lambert (guitar), Clint Boon (keyboards), Martyn Walsh (bass) and Craig Gill (drums).

11/17/90	27	4	1 **Commercial Rain**	—	*Life* .... Mute 60987
2/2/91	22	4	2 **This Is How It Feels**	—	↓
5/25/91	15	7	3 **Caravan**	—	*The Beast Inside* .... Mute 61089
12/5/92+	8	13	4 **Two Worlds Collide**	—	*Revenge Of The Goldfish* .... Mute 61397

IN TUA NUA
Rock group from Dublin, Ireland: Leslie Dowdall (vocals), Martin Clancy and Jack Dublin (guitars), Lovely Previn (violin), Brian O'Briain (sax), Matt Spalding (bass) and Paul Byrne (drums).

| 9/10/88 | 17 | 4 | **All I Wanted** .... | — | *The Long Acre* .... Virgin 90948 |

INXS ★24★
Rock group from Sydney, Australia: Michael Hutchence (vocals), Kirk Pengilly (guitar, saxophone), Garry Beers (bass) and brothers Tim (guitar), Andy (keyboards, guitar) and Jon (drums) Farriss. Hutchence starred in the movies *Dogs In Space* and *Frankenstein Unbound*; formed the group **Max Q**. Jon Farriss married actress Leslie Bega (TV's *Head Of The Class*) on 2/14/92. Hutchence committed suicide on 11/22/97 (age 37).

1)Suicide Blonde 2)Not Enough Time 3)Heaven Sent

9/10/88	28	1	1 **Never Tear Us Apart**	7	▲⁶ *Kick* .... Atlantic 81796
9/8/90	❶¹	10	2 **Suicide Blonde**	9	▲² *X* .... Atlantic 82140
11/3/90	10	14	3 **Disappear**	8	↓
2/2/91	6	9	4 **Bitter Tears**	46	↓
11/9/91	4	10	5 **Shining Star**	—	▲ *Live Baby Live* .... Atlantic 82294

DEBUG	PEAK	WKS	Modern Rock Track	Pop	Gld	Album Title	Album Label & Number
			INXS — Cont'd				
7/11/92	2¹	6	6 Heaven Sent	—	▲	Welcome To Wherever You Are	Atlantic 82394
8/15/92	2⁵	12	7 Not Enough Time	28		↓	
11/7/92	5	10	8 Taste It	101		↓	
1/16/93	10	10	9 Beautiful Girl	46		↓	
10/16/93	6	7	10 The Gift	—		Full Moon, Dirty Hearts	Atlantic 82541
12/11/93	25	2	11 Time	—		↓	
3/29/97	13	12	12 Elegantly Wasted	27ᴬ		Elegantly Wasted	Mercury 534531

ISAAK, Chris
Born on 6/26/56 in Stockton, California. Singer/songwriter/guitarist/actor. Acted in several movies; starred in own TV show.

DEBUG	PEAK	WKS	Modern Rock Track	Pop	Gld	Album Title	Album Label & Number
7/8/89	18	7	1 Don't Make Me Dream About You............	—	▲²	Heart Shaped World	Reprise 25837
1/5/91	2¹	11	2 Wicked Game	6		↓	
4/24/93	7	8	3 Can't Do A Thing (To Stop Me)	105	●	San Francisco Days	Reprise 45116
7/22/95	34	2	4 Somebody's Crying	45	▲	Forever Blue	Reprise 45845
12/23/95+	32	6	5 Go Walking Down There....................	102		↓	

J

JACK RUBIES, The
Pop group from London: Ian Wright (vocals), SD Ineson (guitar), Steve Brockway (bass), Lawrence Giltnane (percussion) and Peter Maxted (drums). Named after the man who shot Lee Harvey Oswald, the assassin of President John F. Kennedy.

DEBUG	PEAK	WKS	Modern Rock Track	Pop	Gld	Album Title	Album Label & Number
11/26/88	18	8	Be With You....................	—		Fascinatin' Vacation	TVT 2560

JACKSON, Joe
Born on 8/11/55 in Burton-on-Trent, Staffordshire, England. Singer/songwriter/pianist. Also see **Classic Rock Tracks** section.

DEBUG	PEAK	WKS	Modern Rock Track	Pop	Gld	Album Title	Album Label & Number
4/29/89	4	9	1 Nineteen Forever	—		Blaze Of Glory	A&M 5249
5/4/91	2³	10	2 Obvious Song	—		Laughter & Lust	Virgin 91628
7/13/91	20	2	3 Oh Well....................	—		↓	
			#55 Pop hit for **Fleetwood Mac** in 1970				

JACKSON, Luscious — see LUSCIOUS

JAMES
Rock group from Manchester, England: Tim Booth (vocals), James Gott (guitar), Mark Hunter (keyboards), Saul Davies (violin), Andy Diagram (trumpet), Jim Glennie (bass) and David Baynton-Power (drums).

DEBUG	PEAK	WKS	Modern Rock Track	Pop	Gld	Album Title	Album Label & Number
8/3/91	9	9	1 Sit Down	—		James	Fontana 848658
3/7/92	5	15	2 Born Of Frustration	—		Seven	Fontana 510932
10/16/93	3	28	3 Laid	61	●	Laid	Fontana 514943
5/21/94	19	10	4 Say Something	105		↓	

JAMIROQUAI
Group is actually singer/songwriter Jason Kay (born on 12/30/69 in Stretford, Manchester, England).

DEBUG	PEAK	WKS	Modern Rock Track	Pop	Gld	Album Title	Album Label & Number
5/10/97	38	4	Virtual Insanity	—	▲	Traveling Without Moving	Work 67903

★56★ JANE'S ADDICTION
Rock group from Los Angeles: Perry Farrell (vocals), **Dave Navarro** (guitar), Eric Avery (bass) and Stephen Perkins (drums). Farrell and Perkins later formed **Porno For Pyros**. Navarro joined **Red Hot Chili Peppers**.

DEBUG	PEAK	WKS	Modern Rock Track	Pop	Gld	Album Title	Album Label & Number
10/8/88	6	7	1 Jane Says	—	▲	Nothing's Shocking	Warner 25727
			also see #7 below				
8/11/90	❶²	9	2 Stop!	—	▲²	Ritual de lo Habitual.............	Warner 25993
9/29/90	❶⁴	17	3 Been Caught Stealing	—		↓	
1/26/91	15	6	4 Classic Girl	—		↓	
5/25/91	13	6	5 Ripple	—		Deadicated (various)	Arista 8669
			first recorded by the **Grateful Dead** in 1970				
11/8/97	22	6	6 So What!	—	●	Kettle Whistle	Warner 46752
12/13/97+	25	18	7 Jane Says .... [L-R]	—		↓	
			live version of #1 above				

JARS OF CLAY
Christian pop group formed in Illinois: Dan Haseltine (vocals), Steve Mason and Matt Odmark (guitars), and Charlie Lowell (keyboards).

DEBUG	PEAK	WKS	Modern Rock Track	Pop	Gld	Album Title	Album Label & Number
3/2/96	12	17	1 Flood	37	▲²	Jars Of Clay....................	Essential 5573
10/25/97	38	2	2 Crazy Times	—	▲	Much Afraid	Essential 41612

JAYHAWKS, The
Rock group from Minneapolis: Mark Olson (vocals), Gary Louris (guitar), Marc Perlman (bass) and Ken Callahan (drums).

DEBUG	PEAK	WKS	Modern Rock Track	Pop	Gld	Album Title	Album Label & Number
12/19/92	29	3	Waiting For The Sun	—		Hollywood Town Hall.	Def American 26829

JELLYFISH
Rock group from San Francisco: Andy Sturmer (vocals, drums), Jason Falkner (guitar), and brothers Chris (bass) and Roger (keyboards) Manning. Falkner and Chris Manning left by 1993; bassist Tim Smith joined. Roger Manning joined **Imperial Drag**.

DEBUG	PEAK	WKS	Modern Rock Track	Pop	Gld	Album Title	Album Label & Number
9/1/90	19	7	1 The King Is Half-Undressed	—		Bellybutton	Charisma 91400
12/22/90+	11	10	2 That Is Why....................	—		↓	
2/20/93	9	9	3 The Ghost At Number One	—		Spilt Milk	Charisma 86459

DEBUT	PEAK	WKS	Modern Rock Track	Pop Gld	Album Title	Album Label & Number

★66★ JESUS & MARY CHAIN, The
Pop-rock group from Glasgow, Scotland: brothers William and Jim Reid (vocals, guitar), Douglas Hart (bass) and Murray Dalgish (drums). Numerous personnel changes with the Reid brothers the only constants.

DEBUT	PEAK	WKS	Track	Pop	Album	Label
11/11/89+	**❶**²	11	1 Blues From A Gun	—	Automatic...................... Warner 26015
1/20/90	2⁴	14	2 Head On	—	↓
2/22/92	22	2	3 Sugar Ray	—	Freejack (soundtrack)........ Morgan Creek 20008
4/25/92	3	15	4 Far Gone And Out	—	Honey's Dead................ Def American 26830
8/8/92	13	6	5 Almost Gold	—	↓
8/13/94	4	16	6 Sometimes Always	96	Stoned & Dethroned............ American 45573

Hope Sandoval of **Mazzy Star** (female vocal)

★77★ JESUS JONES
Pop-rock group formed in London: Mike Edwards (vocals, guitar), Jerry DeBorg (guitar), Iain Baker (keyboards), Al Jaworski (bass) and Simon Matthews (drums).

1/19/91	**❶**⁵	14	✓1 Right Here, Right Now	2¹ ▲	Doubt....................... Food 95715
3/23/91	6	13	2 International Bright Young Thing	—	↓
8/3/91	26	3	3 Real, Real, Real	4	↓
1/16/93	**❶**⁶	11	4 The Devil You Know	—	Perverse................... Food 80647
3/27/93	12	8	5 The Right Decision	—	↓

JETT, Joan, & The Blackhearts
Born Joan Larkin on 9/22/60 in Philadelphia. Rock singer/guitarist.

8/24/91	7	8	Backlash	—	Notorious...................... Blackheart 47488

JEWEL
Born Jewel Kilcher on 5/23/74 in Payson, Utah; raised in Homer, Alaska. Singer/songwriter/guitarist. Wrote own book of poetry. Played "Sue Lee Shelley" in the movie *Ride With The Devil*.

5/4/96	14	21	1 Who Will Save Your Soul	11 ▲¹¹	Pieces Of You.................. Atlantic 82700
3/15/97	26	10	2 You Were Meant For Me	2²	↓

JIMMIE'S CHICKEN SHACK
Rock group from Bowie, Maryland: James Davies (vocals), David Dowling (guitar), Che Lemon (bass) and Mike Sipple (drums).

9/4/99	12	21	Do Right	—	Bring Your Own Stereo............ Rocket 546382

JIMMY EAT WORLD
Rock group from Mesa, Arizona: Jim Adkins (vocals), Tom Linton (guitar), Rick Burch (bass) and Zach Lind (drums).

7/14/01	18	15	1 Bleed American	— ▲	Bleed American.............. DreamWorks 450334
11/10/01+	**❶**⁴	36	2 The Middle	5	↓
6/1/02	2³	26	3 Sweetness	75	↓
10/26/02	23↑	5↑	4 A Praise Chorus	—	↓

JOHNSON, Jack
Born in Hawaii. Singer/songwriter/guitarist.

3/9/02	22	26	Flake	73 ●	Brushfire Fairytales.............. Enjoy 860994

JOHNSTON, Freedy
Born in 1961 in Kinsley, Kansas. Male rock singer/songwriter.

9/24/94	28	9	Bad Reputation	54	This Perfect World.............. Elektra 61655

JONES, Howard
Born on 2/23/55 in Southampton, Hampshire, England. Pop singer/songwriter/keyboardist.

4/1/89	19	7	1 Everlasting Love	12	Cross That Line.............. Elektra 60794
7/29/89	24	5	2 The Prisoner	30	↓

JONES, Rickie Lee
Born on 11/8/54 in Chicago. Female singer/songwriter. Won the 1979 Best New Artist Grammy Award. Also see **Classic Rock Tracks** section.

10/21/89	23	5	Satellites	—	Flying Cowboys.................. Geffen 24246

JONES, Tom — see ART OF NOISE, The

JOPLIN, Josh, Group
Born in Lancaster, Pennsylvania. Singer/songwriter/guitarist. His group: Deb Davis (guitar), Allen Broyles (keyboards), Geoff Melkonian (bass) and Eric Taylor (drums).

2/10/01	40	2	Camera One	—	Useful Music.................. Artemis 751058

JOYDROP
Rock group from Toronto: Tara Slone (vocals), Thomas Payne (guitar), Tom McKay (bass) and Tony Rabalao (drums).

7/24/99	20	12	Beautiful	—	Metasexual.................. Tommy Boy 1237

JUDE
Born Michael Jude Christodal on 10/16/67 in Boston. Male singer/songwriter.

3/20/99	28	7	Rick James	—	No One Is Really Beautiful........ Maverick 47087

JUDYBATS, The
Rock group formed in Knoxville, Tennessee: Jeff Heiskell (vocals), Johnny Sughrue and Ed Winters (guitars), Peggy Hambright (keyboards; left in late 1992), Timothy Stutz (bass) and Terry Casper (drums; left in late 1991). Paul Noe replaced Stutz and Dave Jenkins (drums) joined in early 1993.

2/23/91	9	11	1 Native Son	—	Native Son.................... Sire 26459
2/29/92	21	5	2 Saturday	—	Down In The Shacks Where The Satellite Dishes Grow.................... Sire 26801
4/3/93	7	9	3 Being Simple	—	Pain Makes You Beautiful.......... Sire 45155

DEBUT	PEAK	WKS	Modern Rock Track	Pop Gld	Album Title	Album Label & Number

K

KATYDIDS
Pop group formed in San Diego: Susie Hug (vocals), Adam Seymour and Dan James (guitars), Dave Hunter (bass) and Shane Young (drums).

| 7/14/90 | 17 | 8 | Heavy Weather Traffic | — | Katydids | Reprise 26146 |

KELLY, Paul, and The Messengers
Born 1/12/55 in Adelaide, Australia. Rock singer/songwriter/guitarist. The Messengers: Steve Connolly (guitar), Peter Bull (keyboards), Jon Schofield (bass) and Michael Barclay (drums).

| 9/10/88 | 16 | 1 | Dumb Things | — | Under The Sun | A&M 5207 |

KHALEEL
Born Robert Khaleel on 6/7/65 in the Bronx, New York. Male singer/songwriter.

| 1/16/99 | 36 | 2 | No Mercy | — | People Watching | Hollywood 62110 |

KID ROCK
Born Robert Ritchie on 1/17/71 in Dearborn, Michigan. Hip-hop/rock singer.

4/10/99	10	26	1 Bawitdaba	104	▲10 Devil Without A Cause	Lava 83119
8/28/99	5	24	2 Cowboy	82	↓	
12/25/99+	13	19	3 Only God Knows Why	19	↓	
5/20/00	33	9	4 American Bad Ass	—	▲2 The History Of Rock	Lava 83314
11/10/01	21	7	5 Forever	—	▲ Cocky	Lava 83482

KING, B.B. — see U2

KING MISSILE
Rock group formed in New York City: John Hall (vocals), Dave Rick (guitar), Chris Xefos (bass) and Roger Murdock (drums).

| 1/30/93 | 25 | 5 | Detachable Penis | — | Happy Hour | Atlantic 82459 |

KITCHENS OF DISTINCTION
Pop-rock trio formed in London: Patrick Fitzgerald (vocals, bass), Julian Swales (guitar) and Dan Goodwin (drums).

2/9/91	12	11	1 Drive That Fast	—	Strange Free World	A&M 5340
4/13/91	18	5	2 Quick As Rainbows	—	↓	
8/22/92	15	8	3 Smiling	—	The Death Of Cool	A&M 5402
10/24/92	28	2	4 4 Men	—	↓	

KLF, The
Dance duo formed in England: Bill Drummond and Jim Cauty. KLF: Kopyright Liberation Front. Previously recorded as The Timelords.

10/1/88	17	6	1 Doctorin' The Tardis	66	(single only)	TVT 4025
			THE TIMELORDS			
2/8/92	21	3	2 Justified & Ancient	11	● The White Room	Arista 8657
			THE KLF (Featuring Tammy Wynette)			

KORN
★57★

Techno-rock group from Huntington Beach, California: Jonathan Davis (vocals), Brian Welch and James Munkey (guitars), Reggie Fieldy Arvizu (bass) and David Silveria (drums).

8/22/98	17	26	1 Got The Life	—	▲5 Follow The Leader	Immortal 69001
2/20/99	6	27	2 Freak On A Leash	106	↓	
11/13/99+	7	24	3 Falling Away From Me	108	▲2 Issues	Immortal 63710
2/19/00	7	26	4 Make Me Bad	114	↓	
7/22/00	23	8	5 Somebody Someone	—	↓	
3/30/02	4	22	6 Here To Stay	72	▲ Untouchables	Immortal 61488
7/6/02	11	21↑	7 Thoughtless	108	↓	

KOTTONMOUTH KINGS
Rap-rock group from Los Angeles: Saint, D-Loc, Bobby B, Pakelika and Daddy X.

| 8/21/99 | 28 | 9 | 1 Bump | — | Royal Highness | Capitol 23857 |
| 7/8/00 | 37 | 5 | 2 Peace Not Greed | — | High Society | Suburban Noize 21480 |

KRAVITZ, Lenny   ★23★
Born on 5/26/64 in New York City. Singer/songwriter/guitarist. Married to actress Lisa Bonet (played "Denise Huxtable" on TV's *The Cosby Show*) from 1989-91. Son of actress Roxie Roker (played "Helen Willis" on TV's *The Jeffersons*).

1)Fly Away 2)Are You Gonna Go My Way 3)Let Love Rule

10/28/89	5	15	1 Let Love Rule	89	● Let Love Rule	Virgin 91290
2/24/90	25	4	2 I Build This Garden For Us	—	↓	
4/6/91	8	8	3 Always On The Run	—	▲ Mama Said	Virgin 91610
3/20/93	2²	15	4 Are You Gonna Go My Way	—	▲2 Are You Gonna Go My Way	Virgin 86984
6/5/93	10	18	5 Believe	60	↓	

DEBUT	PEAK	WKS	Modern Rock Track	Pop	Gld	Album Title	Album Label & Number
			KRAVITZ, Lenny — Cont'd				
9/2/95	10	8	6 Rock And Roll Is Dead	75	●	Circus.	Virgin 40696
5/16/98	39	4	7 If You Can't Say No	—	▲²	5	Virgin 45605
9/5/98	❶²	32	8 Fly Away	12		↓	
5/29/99	7	24	9 American Woman	49	▲	Austin Powers - The Spy Who Shagged	
			#1 Pop hit for The Guess Who in 1970			Me (soundtrack)	Maverick 47348
10/21/00+	23	26	10 Again	4	▲³	Greatest Hits	Virgin 50316
9/22/01	13	13	11 Dig In	31	▲	Lenny	Virgin 11233
3/2/02	38	2	12 Stillness Of Heart	118		↓	
			KROEGER, Chad				
			Born on 11/15/74 in Hanna, Alberta, Canada. Lead singer of **Nickelback**.				
5/4/02	❶³	21	Hero	3	▲	Spider-Man (soundtrack)	Columbia 86402
			K'S CHOICE				
			Rock group from Belgium: Sarah Bettens (vocals), her brother Gert Bettens (vocals, keyboards), Jan Van Sichem (guitar) and Bart Van Der Zeeuw (drums).				
3/29/97	5	26	1 Not An Addict	56^A		Paradise In Me	550 Music 67720
8/15/98	28	6	2 Everything For Free	—		Cocoon Crash	550 Music 69366
			KULA SHAKER				
			Rock group from London: Crispian Mills (vocals, guitar), Jay Darlington (keyboards), Alonza Bevan (bass) and Paul Winter-Hart (drums). Mills is the son of actress/singer Hayley Mills.				
11/2/96	10	14	1 Tattva	63^A		K	Columbia 67822
3/1/97	25	7	2 Hey Dude	—		↓	
			KWELLER, Ben				
			Born in Greenville, Texas. Singer/songwriter/guitarist.				
7/27/02	29	7	Wasted & Ready	—		Sha Sha	ATO 68114

L

DEBUT	PEAK	WKS	Modern Rock Track	Pop	Gld	Album Title	Album Label & Number
			LAING, Shona				
			Born in 1955 in New Zealand. Female singer/songwriter/guitarist.				
9/10/88	14	8	(Glad I'm) Not A Kennedy	—		South	TVT 2470
			LAJON				
			Born Lajon Witherspoon in Atlanta. Lead singer of **Sevendust**.				
12/9/00+	15	13	Angel's Son	—		Strait Up (various artists)	Immortal 50365
			LA'S, The				
			Rock group from Liverpool, England: brothers Lee (vocals) and Neil (drums) Mavers, Peter Camell (guitar) and John Power (bass). Group name is slang for lads.				
4/13/91	2¹	13	1 There She Goes	49		The La's	London 828202
7/13/91	12	8	2 Timeless Melody	—		↓	
	★81★		**LEMONHEADS, The**				
			Rock group formed in Boston by Evan Dando (vocals, guitar; born on 3/4/67). Numerous personnel changes with Dando the only constant.				
6/20/92	5	11	1 It's A Shame About Ray	—	●	It's A Shame About Ray	Atlantic 82460
11/14/92	8	13	✓2 Mrs. Robinson	118		↓	
			#1 Pop hit for Simon & Garfunkel in 1968				
10/23/93	❶⁹	16	✓3 Into Your Arms	67	●	Come On Feel The Lemonheads	Atlantic 82537
1/29/94	15	9	4 The Great Big NO	—		↓	
10/12/96	15	12	5 If I Could Talk I'd Tell You	—		Car Button Cloth	Atlantic 92726
			LEN				
			Rock group from Toronto: Marc Costanzo (vocals), his sister Sharon Costanzo, D. Rock, DJ Moves, Planet Pea and Drunkness Monster.				
5/29/99	5	25	Steal My Sunshine	9	●	You Can't Stop The Bum Rush	Work 69528
			samples "More More More" by the Andrea True Connection				
			LENNON, Julian				
			Born on 4/8/63 in Liverpool, England. Singer/songwriter/keyboardist. Son of Cynthia and **John Lennon**.				
5/6/89	27	2	Now You're In Heaven	93		Mr. Jordan	Atlantic 81928
			LENNOX, Annie				
			Born on 12/25/54 in Aberdeen, Scotland. Lead singer of the **Eurythmics**. Recipient of *Billboard*'s Century Award in 2002.				
5/9/92	12	11	✓1 Why	34	▲²	Diva	Arista 18704
8/15/92	7	7	✓2 Walking On Broken Glass	14		↓	
12/26/92+	24	5	✓3 Love Song For A Vampire	—		Bram Stoker's Dracula (soundtrack) . . .	Columbia 53165
			LESS THAN JAKE				
			Rock trio from Gainesville, Florida: Chris DeMakes (vocals, guitar), Roger Manganelli (bass) and Vinnie Fiorello (drums).				
12/26/98	39	2	History Of A Boring Town	—		Hello Rockview	Capitol 57663
			LET'S ACTIVE				
			Pop-rock trio formed in North Carolina: Mitch Easter (vocals, guitar), Faye Hunter (bass) and Sara Romweber (drums).				
9/24/88	17	5	Every Dog Has His Day	—		Every Dog Has His Day	I.R.S. 42151

DEBUT	PEAK	WKS	Modern Rock Track	Pop	Gld	Album Title	Album Label & Number

LETTERS TO CLEO
Pop-rock group from Boston: Kay Hanley (vocals), Michael Eisenstein and Greg McKenna (guitars), Scott Riebling (bass) and Stacy Jones (drums). Jones later became lead singer with **American Hi-Fi**.

1/21/95	10	19	1 **Here & Now**	56		Aurora Gory Alice	Giant 24598
8/5/95	17	11	2 Awake	88		Wholesale Meats And Fish	Giant 24613

LEVELLERS
Post-punk group formed in Brighton, England: Mark Chadwick (vocals), Simon Friend (guitar), Jon Sevink (violin), Jeremy Cunningham (bass) and Charlie Heather (drums).

6/13/92	11	8	One Way	—		Levelling The Land	China 61325

LEWIS, Aaron
Born on 4/13/72 in Boston. Rock singer. Lead singer of **Staind**.

11/25/00+	2⁶	25	**Outside** [L]	56		The Family Values Tour 1999	
			AARON LEWIS from Staind (with Fred Durst)			(various artists)	Flawless 490641

LIFEHOUSE
Rock trio from Malibu, California: Jason Wade (vocals, guitar), Sergio Andrade (bass) and Rick Woolstenhulme (drums).

10/28/00+	❶³	35	1 **Hanging By A Moment**	2⁴ ▲²		No Name Face	DreamWorks 50231
5/26/01	21	12	2 Sick Cycle Carousel			↓	
8/10/02	25	9	3 Spin	84↑		Stanley Climbfall	DreamWorks 50377

LIGHTNING SEEDS, The
Group is actually singer/producer Ian Broudie (born on 8/4/58 in Liverpool, England).

4/7/90	8	10	1 **Pure**	31		Cloudcuckooland	MCA 6404
6/9/90	9	11	2 All I Want	—		↓	
2/1/92	2¹	12	3 **The Life Of Riley**	98		Sense	MCA 10388
4/18/92	19	4	4 Blowing Bubbles	—		↓	
9/24/94	38	3	5 Lucky You	—		Jollification	Trauma 71008

LILAC TIME, The
Rock group from England: brothers Stephen (vocals) and Nick (guitar) Duffy, with Michael Giri (bass) and Micky Harris (drums).

2/24/90	28	2	1 American Eyes	—		Lilac Time	Fontana 836744
10/6/90	22	6	2 All For Love And Love For All	—		& Love For All	Fontana 846190

LIMP BIZKIT ★28★
Hard-rock/hip-hop group from Jacksonville, Florida: **Fred Durst** (vocals; born on 8/20/71), Wes Borland (guitar; born on 2/8/75), Sam Rivers (bass; born in 1979) and John Otto (drums; born in 1978). Also see **Aaron Lewis**.

1/23/99	28	12	1 Faith	—	▲²	Three Dollar Bill, Y'all$	Flip 90124
			#1 Pop hit for George Michael in 1987				
6/12/99	3	26	2 **Nookie**	80	▲⁷	Significant Other	Flip 90335
10/9/99	❶¹	29	3 **Re-Arranged**	88		↓	
3/11/00	14	26	4 Break Stuff	123		↓	
4/29/00	8	22	5 Take A Look Around	115	▲	Mission: Impossible 2 (soundtrack) . . .	Hollywood 62244
9/23/00	4	26	6 **Rollin' (Urban Assault Vehicle)**	65	▲⁵	Chocolate Starfish And The Hot Dog	
						Flavored Water	Flip 490759
9/23/00	18	9	7 My Generation	—		↓	
2/24/01	3	26	8 **My Way**	75		↓	
1/8/00	31	7	9 Crushed	—	▲	End Of Days (soundtrack)	Geffen 490508

LINKIN PARK ★50★
Rap-rock group from Los Angeles: Chester Bennington (vocals), Mike Shinoda (rap vocals), Joseph Hahn (DJ), Brad Delson (guitar), Darren "Phoenix" Farrell (bass) and Rob Bourdon (drums).

10/7/00+	5	33	1 **One Step Closer**	75	▲⁸	Hybrid Theory	Warner 47755
3/31/01	5	34	2 **Crawling**	79		↓	
8/25/01	❶⁵	44	3 **In The End**	2¹		↓	
3/16/02	32	18	4 Papercut	—		↓	
7/6/02	40	1	5 Runaway	—		↓	
8/10/02	29	10	6 Points Of Authority	—	▲	Reanimation	Warner 48326

LIT ★48★
Rock group from Los Angeles: brothers A.J. (vocals) and Jeremy (bass) Popoff, Kevin Blades (bass) and Allen Shellenberger (drums).

2/13/99	❶¹¹	36	1 **My Own Worst Enemy**	51	▲	A Place In The Sun	RCA 67775
8/14/99	11	15	2 Zip-Lock	—		↓	
12/18/99+	3	26	3 **Miserable**	117		↓	
6/17/00	22	9	4 Over My Head	—		Titan A.E. (soundtrack)	Java 25275
9/8/01	10	12	5 Lipstick And Bruises	—		Atomic	RCA 68086
12/22/01+	23	9	6 Addicted	—		↓	

DEBUT	PEAK	WKS	Modern Rock Track	Pop	Gld	Album Title	Album Label & Number

LIVE ★9★

Rock group formed in York, Pennsylvania: Edward Kowalczyk (vocals; born on 7/16/71), Chad Taylor (guitar; born on 11/24/70), Patrick Dahlheimer (bass; born on 5/30/71) and Chad Gracey (drums; born on 7/23/71).

1)Lightning Crashes 2)Selling The Drama 3)Lakini's Juice

DEBUT	PEAK	WKS	Modern Rock Track	Pop	Gld	Album Title	Album Label & Number
1/25/92	9	9	1 Operation Spirit (The Tyranny Of Tradition)	—	●	*Mental Jewelry*	Radioactive 10346
5/2/92	24	6	2 Pain Lies On The Riverside	—		↓	
4/9/94	❶[3]	19	3 Selling The Drama	43	▲[8]	*Throwing Copper*	Radioactive 10997
8/20/94	6	26	4 I Alone	38[A]		↓	
1/28/95	❶[9]	25	5 Lightning Crashes	12[A]		↓	
5/6/95	4	26	6 All Over You	33[A]		↓	
7/29/95	15	12	7 White, Discussion	71[A]		↓	
2/1/97	❶[1]	18	8 Lakini's Juice	35[A]	▲	*Secret Samadhi*	Radioactive 11590
4/26/97	13	9	9 Freaks	73[A]		↓	
6/14/97	3	21	10 Turn My Head	45[A]		↓	
10/25/97	18	12	11 Rattlesnake	—		↓	
9/4/99	3	26	12 The Dolphin's Cry	78	▲	*The Distance To Here*	Radioactive 11966
2/12/00	14	11	13 Run To The Water	—		↓	
8/12/00	31	4	14 They Stood Up For Love	—		↓	
8/11/01	18	9	15 Simple Creed	—		*V.*	Radioactive 12485
			LIVE Featuring Tricky				
10/13/01	30	4	16 Overcome	—		↓	

LIVING COLOUR

Black rock group from New York City: Corey Glover (vocals), Vernon Reid (guitar), Muzz Skillings (bass) and William Calhoun (drums). Doug Wimbish replaced Skillings in early 1992. Glover played "Francis" in the movie *Platoon*.

DEBUT	PEAK	WKS	Modern Rock Track	Pop	Gld	Album Title	Album Label & Number
9/8/90	3	11	1 Type	—	●	*Time's Up*	Epic 46202
12/1/90	25	2	2 Elvis Is Dead	—		↓	
2/2/91	8	9	3 Love Rears Its Ugly Head	—		↓	
7/27/91	12	7	4 Talkin' Loud And Sayin' Nothing	—		*Biscuits*	Epic 47988
			#27 Pop hit for James Brown in 1972				
2/27/93	4	11	5 Leave It Alone	—		*Stain*	Epic 52780
5/15/93	17	8	6 Nothingness	—		↓	

LIVING END, The

Rock trio from Melbourne, Australia: Chris Cheney (vocals, guitar), Scott Owen (bass) and Travis Demsey (drums).

DEBUT	PEAK	WKS	Modern Rock Track	Pop	Gld	Album Title	Album Label & Number
2/6/99	23	13	1 Prisoner Of Society	—		*The Living End.*	Reprise 47128
4/14/01	33	4	2 Roll On	—		*Roll On.*	Reprise 48063

LOCAL H

Rock duo from Zion, Illinois: Scott Lucas (vocals, guitar, bass) and Joe Daniels (drums).

DEBUT	PEAK	WKS	Modern Rock Track	Pop	Gld	Album Title	Album Label & Number
9/28/96	5	26	1 Bound For The Floor	46[A]		*As Good As Dead*	Island 524202
7/19/97	38	2	2 Eddie Vedder	—		↓	
8/29/98	20	13	3 All The Kids Are Right	—		*Pack Up The Cats*	Island 524549

LOEB, Lisa, & Nine Stories

Born on 3/11/68 in Bethesda, Maryland; raised in Dallas. Female singer/songwriter/guitarist. Nine Stories consisted of Tim Bright (guitar), Joe Quigley (bass) and Jonathan Feinberg (drums).

DEBUT	PEAK	WKS	Modern Rock Track	Pop	Gld	Album Title	Album Label & Number
6/18/94	7	14	✓1 Stay (I Missed You)	❶[3]	▲[2]	*Reality Bites (soundtrack)*	RCA 66364
9/16/95	20	11	✓2 Do You Sleep?	18	●	*Tails*	Geffen 24734

LO FIDELITY ALLSTARS

Rock group from Brighton, Sussex, England: Dave Randall (vocals), Martin Whiteman (keyboards), Andy Dickinson (bass) and Johnny Machin (drums).

DEBUT	PEAK	WKS	Modern Rock Track	Pop	Gld	Album Title	Album Label & Number
4/17/99	6	26	Battle Flag	117		*How To Operate With A Blown Mind.*	Skint 69654
			LO FIDELITY ALLSTARS Featuring Pigeonhead				

LONG BEACH DUB ALLSTARS

Rock-reggae group from Long Beach, California: Opie Ortiz (vocals), Ras-1 (guitar), Jack Maness (keyboards), Marshall Goodman (percussion), Tim Wu (sax), Eric Wilson (bass) and Bud Gaugh (drums). Wilson and Gaugh were members of **Sublime**.

DEBUT	PEAK	WKS	Modern Rock Track	Pop	Gld	Album Title	Album Label & Number
8/18/01	28	6	Sunny Hours	—		*Wonders Of The World*	DreamWorks 450295

LONGPIGS

Rock group from Sheffield, Yorkshire, England: Crispin Hunt (vocals, guitar), Richard Hawley (guitar), Simon Stafford (bass) and Dee Boyle (drums).

DEBUT	PEAK	WKS	Modern Rock Track	Pop	Gld	Album Title	Album Label & Number
10/11/97	17	12	On And On	106		*The Sun Is Often Out*	Mother 531542

DEBUT	PEAK	WKS	Modern Rock Track	Pop Gld	Album Title	Album Label & Number
			LOS LOBOS			
			Latin rock group formed in East Los Angeles: David Hildago (vocals), Cesar Rosas (guitar), Steve Berlin (sax), Conrad Lozano (bass) and Louie Perez (drums).			
9/1/90	16	9	1 Down On The Riverbed	—	The Neighborhood	Slash 26131
6/8/91	24	2	2 Bertha	—	Deadicated (various artists)	Arista 8669
			first recorded by the **Grateful Dead** in 1971			
7/4/92	24	4	3 Reva's House	—	Kiko	Slash 26786
			LOSTPROPHETS			
			Rock group formed in Wales: Ian Watkins (vocals), Mike Lewis and Lee Gaze (guitars), Stuart Richardson (bass) and Mike Chiplin (drums).			
3/9/02	33	6	Shinobi vs. Dragon Ninja	—	The Fake Sound Of Progress	Columbia 85955
			LOUD LUCY			
			Rock trio from Chicago: Christian Lane (vocals, guitar), Tom Furar (bass) and Mark Doyle (drums).			
12/30/95+	31	8	Ticking	—	Breathe	DGC 24733
			LOVE, G., & Special Sauce			
			Born Garrett Sutton on 10/3/72 in Philadelphia. Blues singer/guitarist. Special Sauce: Jim Prescott (bass) and Jeff Clemens (drums).			
11/22/97	30	9	1 Stepping Stones	—	Yeah, It's That Easy	Okeh 67784
8/28/99	39	3	2 Rodeo Clowns	—	Philadelphonic	Okeh 69746
			LOVE AND ROCKETS			
			Pop-rock trio formed in England: **Daniel Ash** (vocals, guitar), **David J** (bass) and Kevin Haskins (drums).			
2/25/89	20	8	1 Motorcycle	— ●	Love And Rockets	Beggars Banquet 9715
5/6/89	❶5	16	2 So Alive	3	↓	
9/2/89	29	1	3 Rock And Roll Babylon	—	↓	
9/16/89	19	5	4 No Big Deal	82	↓	
3/16/96	10	10	5 Sweet Lover Hangover	66[A]	Sweet F.A.	American 43058
			LOVE SPIT LOVE			
			Rock group featuring brothers/former **Psychedelic Furs** Richard (vocals) and Tim (bass) Butler, with Richard Fortus (guitar) and Frank Ferrer (drums).			
7/30/94	3	15	1 Am I Wrong	83	Love Spit Love	Imago 21030
12/3/94	31	5	2 Change In The Weather	—	↓	
9/13/97	33	6	3 Long Long Time	—	Trysome Eatone	Maverick 46560
12/20/97	39	2	4 Fall On Tears	—	↓	
			L7			
			Female punk-rock group from Los Angeles: Suzi Gardner (guitar, vocals), Donita Sparks (guitar, vocals), Jennifer Finch (bass, vocals) and Dee Plakas (drums).			
5/23/92	8	13	1 Pretend We're Dead	—	Bricks Are Heavy	Slash 26784
8/13/94	20	6	2 Andres	—	Hungry For Stink	Slash 45624
			LUCAS			
			Born Lucas Secon in 1970 in Copenhagen, Denmark. Male rapper/producer.			
10/1/94	22	7	Lucas With The Lid Off	29	Lucacentric	Big Beat 92467
			Junior Dangerous (ragga vocal)			
			LUCKY BOYS CONFUSION			
			Ska-rock group from Chicago: Kaustubh Pandav (vocals), Adam Krier and Joe Sell (guitars), Jason Shultejann (bass) and Ryan Fergus (drums).			
4/21/01	34	8	Fred Astaire	—	Throwing The Game	Elektra 62641
			LUSCIOUS JACKSON			
			Female pop-rock group from New York City: Jill Cunniff (vocals, bass), Gabrielle Glaser (vocals, guitar), Vivian Trimble (keyboards) and Kate Schellenbach (drums). Trimble left in 1998. Group named after the former pro basketball player.			
11/5/94	39	1	1 Citysong	—	Natural Ingredients	Grand Royal 28356
			samples "On And On" by Gladys Knight & The Pips			
11/2/96+	18	26	2 Naked Eye	36	Fever In Fever Out	Grand Royal 35534
6/19/99	28	10	3 Ladyfingers	—	Electric Honey	Grand Royal 96084
			LUSH			
			Rock group from London: Miki Berenyi (vocals, guitar), Emma Anderson (guitar), Steve Ribbon (bass) and Chris Acland (drums). Philip King replaced Ribbon in 1991. Acland committed suicide on 10/17/96 (age 30).			
12/15/90+	4	9	1 Sweetness And Light	—	Gala	4 A D 26463
3/2/91	14	8	2 De-Luxe	—	↓	
12/21/91+	22	7	3 Nothing Natural	—	Spooky	4 A D 26798
2/8/92	9	12	4 For Love	—	↓	
4/20/96	18	9	5 Ladykillers	—	Lovelife	4 A D 46170

DEBUT	PEAK	WKS	Modern Rock Track	Pop Gld	Album Title	Album Label & Number

M

MacCOLL, Kirsty
Born 10/10/59 in Croydon, Surrey, England. Died in a boating accident in Mexico on 12/18/2000 (age 41). Singer/songwriter/guitarist. Married to noted record producer Steve Lillywhite from 1984-94.

7/6/91	4	12	1 Walking Down Madison	—	Electric Landlady................ Charisma 91688
10/23/93	20	7	2 Can't Stop Killing You	—	Titanic Days .... I.R.S. 27214
2/5/94	26	3	3 Angel	—	↓

MACHINES OF LOVING GRACE
Rock group from New York City: Scott Benzel (vocals), Stuart Kupers (guitar, bass), Mike Fisher (keyboards) and Brad Kemp (drums). Named after a poem by Richard Brautigan.

| 10/9/93 | 13 | 15 | Butterfly Wings | — | Concentration .... Mammoth 92282 |

MAD SEASON
All-star rock project: Layne Staley (vocals, guitar; **Alice In Chains**), Mike McCready (guitar; **Pearl Jam**), John Baker Saunders (bass) and Barrett Martin (drums; **Screaming Trees**). Band name is an English term for the time of year when psilocybin mushrooms are in full bloom. Staley died of a drug overdose on 4/5/2002 (age 34).

| 4/1/95 | 9 | 18 | River Of Deceit | — ● | Above .... Columbia 67057 |

MAGNAPOP
Rock group from Athens, Georgia: Linda Hopper (vocals), Ruthie Morris (guitar), Shannon Mulvaney (bass) and David McNair (drums).

| 9/10/94 | 25 | 7 | 1 Slowly, Slowly .... | — | Hot Boxing .... Priority 53909 |
| 6/22/96 | 28 | 9 | 2 Open The Door .... | — | Rubbing Doesn't Help .... Priority 53992 |

MAGNIFICENT BASTARDS, The
All-star rock project: **Scott Weiland** (vocals; **Stone Temple Pilots**), Zander Schloss (**Thelonious Monster**, **Red Hot Chili Peppers**), and Jeff Nolan (guitars), and Bob Thomson (bass).

| 4/29/95 | 12 | 10 | Mockingbird Girl .... | 66[A] | Tank Girl (soundtrack) .... Elektra 61760 |

MANN, Aimee
Born on 8/9/60 in Richmond, Virginia. Former lead singer of **'Til Tuesday**. Married **Michael Penn** on 12/29/97.

| 5/29/93 | 16 | 8 | 1 I Should've Known .... | — | Whatever...................... Imago 21017 |
| 11/5/94+ | 24 | 13 | 2 That's Just What You Are........................... | 93 | Melrose Place (soundtrack) .... Giant 24577 |

MANSON, Marilyn
Born Brian Warner on 1/5/69 in Canton, Ohio. Hard-rock singer/songwriter. Noted for his controversial stage performances. His band includes: Scott "Daisy Berkowitz" Putesky (guitar), Steve "Madonna Wayne Gacy" Bier (keyboards), Jeordi "Twiggy Ramirez" White (bass) and Ken "Ginger Fish" Wilson (drums).

5/4/96	26	7	1 Sweet Dreams (Are Made Of This)	— ▲	Smells Like Children .... Nothing 92641
			#1 Pop hit for **Eurythmics** in 1983		
10/5/96	26	16	2 The Beautiful People	— ▲	Antichrist Superstar.............. Nothing 90086
8/29/98	15	21	3 The Dope Show	122 ▲	Mechanical Animals .... Nothing 90273
1/30/99	36	5	4 I Don't Like The Drugs (But The Drugs Like Me).............	—	↓
4/17/99	30	7	5 Rock Is Dead	—	↓
11/4/00	24	11	6 Disposable Teens	—	Holy Wood (In The Shadow Of The Valley Of Death)...................... Nothing 490790
12/8/01+	33	8	7 Tainted Love...........................	—	Not Another Teen Movie (soundtrack). . Maverick 48250
			#8 Pop hit for **Soft Cell** in 1982		

MANSUN
Rock group from Manchester, England: Paul Draper (vocals), Dominic Chad (guitar), Stove King (bass) and Andie Rathbone (drums).

| 7/5/97 | 25 | 9 | Wide Open Space........................... | — | Attack Of The Grey Lantern .... Epic 67935 |

★97★ MARCY PLAYGROUND
Rock trio from New York City: John Wozniak (vocals, guitar), Dylan Keefe (bass) and Dan Reiser (drums).

11/1/97	❶[15]	34	1 Sex and Candy	8 ▲	Marcy Playground .... Capitol 53569
5/9/98	8	21	2 Saint Joe On The School Bus	—	↓
10/30/99	25	9	3 It's Saturday...........................	—	Shapeshifter...................... Capitol 23142

MARLEY, Bob
Born on 2/6/45 in Rhoden Hall, Jamaica. Died of cancer on 5/11/81 (age 36). The most popular reggae singer/songwriter of all-time. Father of **Ziggy Marley & The Melody Makers**. Inducted into the Rock and Roll Hall of Fame in 1994. Won Grammy's Lifetime Achievement Award in 2001.

| 11/21/92 | 11 | 9 | Iron Lion Zion .... | — ▲[2] | Songs Of Freedom............... Tuff Gong 512280 |
| | | | previously unreleased recording | | |

MARLEY, Ziggy, And The Melody Makers
Family reggae group from Kingston, Jamaica. Children of **Bob Marley**: David "Ziggy" (vocals, guitar), Stephen, Sharon and Cedella Marley.

9/10/88	5	4	1 Tumblin' Down	— ▲	Conscious Party.................. Virgin 90878
8/5/89	2[1]	10	2 Look Who's Dancing	— ●	One Bright Day .... Virgin 91256
6/22/91	6	7	3 Kozmik	—	Jahmekya .... Virgin 91626
7/3/93	16	9	4 Brothers And Sisters	—	Joy And Blues .... Virgin 87961

MARS, Chris
Born on 4/26/61 in Minneapolis. Drummer of **The Replacements** from 1980-90.

| 5/16/92 | 9 | 8 | Popular Creeps | — | Horseshoes And Hand Grenades...... Smash 513198 |

DEBUT	PEAK	WKS	Modern Rock Track	Pop Gld	Album Title	Album Label & Number

MARVELOUS 3
Rock trio from Atlanta: Butch Walker (vocals, guitar), Jayce Fincher (bass) and Slug (drums).

1/9/99	5	20	Freak Of The Week	112	Hey! Album . . . . HiFi 62375

MARY'S DANISH
Pop-rock group from Los Angeles: Gretchen Seager and Julie Ritter (vocals), David King and Louis Gutierrez (guitars), Chris Wagner (bass) and James Bradley (drums).

7/22/89	7	10	1 Don't Crash The Car Tonight	—	There Goes The Wondertruck. . . . . . . Chameleon 74803
8/10/91	14	9	2 Julie's Blanket (pigsheadsnakeface)	—	Circa . . . . Morgan Creek 20003
9/26/92	20	8	3 Leave It Alone.	—	American Standard. . . . . Morgan Creek 20016

MASSIVE ATTACK
Techno group from Bristol, England: Robert Delnaja, Gary Marshall and Andy Vowles.

9/14/91	28	2	Safe From Harm	—	Blue Lines . . . . Virgin 91685

★96★ MATCHBOX 20
Pop-rock group from Orlando, Florida: **Rob Thomas** (vocals), Kyle Cook and Adam Gaynor (guitars), Brian Yale (bass) and Paul Doucette (drums).

5/3/97	❶[1]	26	1 Push	5[A] ▲[12]	Yourself Or Someone Like You . . . . Lava 92721
10/18/97	3	26	2 3 AM	3[A] ↓	
4/4/98	13	25	3 Real World	38 ↓	
4/29/00	16	18	4 Bent	❶[1] ▲[4]	Mad Season . . . . Lava 83339
			MATCHBOX TWENTY		

MATERIAL ISSUE
Pop trio from Chicago: Jim Ellison (vocals, guitar), Ted Ansani (bass) and Mike Zelenko (drums). Ellison committed suicide on 6/20/96 (age 31).

2/16/91	3	11	1 Valerie Loves Me	—	International Pop Overthrow . . . . Mercury 848155
4/27/91	6	11	2 Diane	—	↓
5/23/92	6	11	3 What Girls Want	—	Destination Universe. . . . . Mercury 512333
4/9/94	20	7	4 Kim The Waitress	—	Freak City Soundtrack . . . . Mercury 518894

MATTHEWS, Dave, Band ★18★
Born on 1/9/67 in Johannesburg, South Africa; raised in New York City. Rock singer/guitarist. His band: Leroi Moore (sax), Boyd Tinsley (violin), Stefan Lessard (bass) and Carter Beauford (drums).

1)Don't Drink The Water 2)I Did It 3)Too Much

2/18/95	11	23	1 What Would You Say	22[A] ▲[6]	Under The Table And Dreaming . . . . RCA 66449
7/1/95	18	19	2 Ants Marching	21[A] ↓	
12/16/95+	18	12	3 Satellite	55[A] ↓	
4/13/96	5	15	4 Too Much	39[A] ▲[7]	Crash . . . . RCA 66904
7/20/96	19	14	5 So Much To Say	48[A] ↓	
11/30/96+	7	26	6 Crash Into Me	19[A] ↓	
5/31/97	18	15	7 Tripping Billies	— ↓	
4/11/98	4	16	8 Don't Drink The Water	50[A] ▲[3]	Before These Crowded Streets . . . . RCA 67660
7/11/98	8	16	9 Stay (Wasting Time)	44[A] ↓	
10/31/98+	11	29	10 Crush.	75 ↓	
1/20/01	5	14	11 I Did It	71 ▲[3]	Everyday . . . . RCA 67988
4/21/01	10	25	12 The Space Between	22 ↓	
11/17/01	38	4	13 Everyday	101 ↓	
6/1/02	20	17	14 Where Are You Going	39 ▲[2]	Busted Stuff . . . . RCA 68117

MAX Q
Rock duo formed in Melbourne, Australia: Michael Hutchence (of **INXS**) and Ian Olsen. Max Q is the name of Olsen's dog. Hutchence committed suicide on 11/22/97 (age 37).

9/2/89	6	10	Way Of The World	—	Max Q . . . . Atlantic 82014

MAZZY STAR
Pop-rock duo from California: songwriter/guitarist David Roback and vocalist Hope Sandoval. Also see **The Jesus & Mary Chain**.

8/11/90	29	3	1 Blue Flower.	—	She Hangs Brightly . . . . Rough Trade 80077
8/13/94	3	18	2 Fade Into You	44	So Tonight That I Might See. . . . . Capitol 98253
12/3/94+	19	12	3 Halah		She Hangs Brightly. . . . . Capitol 96508

MC 900 FT. JESUS
Experimental electronic artist Mark Griffin (born in Dallas). Name refers to a vision by evangelist Oral Roberts.

7/23/94	25	8	If I Only Had A Brain	—	One Step Ahead Of The Spider . . . . . . American 45560

McCULLOCH, Ian
Born on 5/5/59 in Liverpool, England. Lead singer of **Echo & The Bunnymen** and **Electrafixion**.

10/28/89	❶[4]	15	1 Proud To Fall	—	Candleland . . . . Sire 26012
2/3/90	10	7	2 Faith And Healing	—	↓
12/7/91+	13	8	3 Hey That's No Way To Say Goodbye . . . . first recorded by Leonard Cohen in 1968	—	I'm Your Fan: The Songs Of Leonard Cohen (various artists) . . . . Atlantic 82349
2/22/92	6	10	4 Honeydrip	—	Mysterio . . . . Sire 26684
4/25/92	9	9	5 Lover Lover Lover	❶	↓

DEBUT	PEAK	WKS	Modern Rock Track	Pop	Gld	Album Title	Album Label & Number
			McKEE, Maria				
			Born on 8/17/64 in Los Angeles. Former lead singer of **Lone Justice**.				
8/12/89	29	1	I've Forgotten What It Was In You (That Put The Need In Me)	—		Maria McKee .... Geffen 24229	
			McKENNITT, Loreena				
			Born in 1957 in Morden, Manitoba, Canada. Female singer/harpist.				
12/27/97+	17	15	The Mummers' Dance	18		The Book Of Secrets .... Warner 46719	
	★80★		**McLACHLAN, Sarah**				
			Born on 1/28/68 in Halifax, Nova Scotia, Canada. Singer/songwriter/guitarist.				
2/15/92	4	15	1 Into The Fire	—	●	Solace .... Arista 18631	
3/26/94	4	15	2 Possession	73	▲³	Fumbling Towards Ecstasy ...... Arista 18725	
9/10/94	16	14	3 Good Enough	77	↓		
2/4/95	29	11	4 Hold On	—	↓		
7/5/97	3	26	5 Building A Mystery	13	▲⁴	Surfacing .... Arista 18970	
11/8/97	14	20	6 Sweet Surrender	28	↓		
			MEAT PUPPETS				
			Rock trio from Phoenix: brothers Curt (vocals, guitar) and Cris (bass) Kirkwood with Derrick Bostrom (drums).				
8/10/91	13	8	1 Sam	—		Forbidden Places .... London 828254	
2/19/94	11	24	2 Backwater	47	●	Too High To Die .... London 828484	
9/30/95	23	6	3 Scum	—		No Joke! .... London 828665	
			MERCHANT, Natalie				
			Born on 10/26/63 in Jamestown, New York. Lead singer of **10,000 Maniacs** from 1981-93.				
11/13/93	9	14	1 Photograph	—		Born To Choose (various artists) ...... Rykodisc 10256	
			R.E.M. with Natalie Merchant				
6/17/95	12	23	2 Carnival	10	▲⁴	Tigerlily .... Elektra 61745	
10/21/95	16	20	3 Wonder	20	↓		
5/16/98	32	9	4 Kind & Generous	18ᴬ	▲	Ophelia .... Elektra 62196	
			MESSIAH				
			Techno-dance duo from England: Ali Ghani and Mark Davies.				
11/28/92	17	10	Temple Of Dreams	117		21st Century Jesus .... Warner 45168	
			METALLICA				
			Hard-rock group formed in Los Angeles: James Hetfield (vocals, guitar; born on 8/3/63), Kirk Hammett (guitar; born on 11/18/62), Cliff Burton (bass; born on 2/10/62; died in a bus crash on 9/27/86, age 24) and Lars Ulrich (drums; born on 12/26/63). Original guitarist Dave Mustaine left in 1982 to form **Megadeth**. Jason Newstad (born on 3/4/63) replaced Burton.				
6/8/96	27	7	1 Until It Sleeps	10	▲⁴	Load .... Elektra 61923	
1/2/99	39	2	2 Turn The Page	102	▲⁵	Garage Inc. .... Elektra 62299	
			first recorded by **Bob Seger** in 1973				
12/11/99+	18	20	3 No Leaf Clover [L]	74	▲⁴	S&M .... Elektra 62504	
			with the San Francisco Symphony Orchestra; recorded on 4/21/99 at the Berkeley Community Theater				
5/6/00	11	24	4 I Disappear	76	▲	Mission: Impossible 2 (soundtrack) ... Hollywood 62244	
	★44★		**MIDNIGHT OIL**				
			Rock group formed in Sydney, Australia: Peter Garrett (vocals), Martin Rotsey (guitar), James Moginie (keyboards), Dwayne Hillman (bass) and Rob Hirst (drums).				
10/29/88	16	3	1 Dreamworld	—	▲	Diesel And Dust .... Columbia 40967	
2/17/90	❶¹	11	2 Blue Sky Mine	47	●	Blue Sky Mining .... Columbia 45398	
3/31/90	❶¹	13	3 Forgotten Years	—	↓		
6/30/90	3	10	4 King Of The Mountain	—	↓		
5/30/92	20	5	5 Sometimes [L]	—		Scream In Blue Live .... Columbia 52731	
4/3/93	10	7	6 Drums Of Heaven	—		Earth And Sun And Moon ...... Columbia 53793	
4/17/93	4	13	7 Truganini	—	↓		
7/24/93	9	11	8 Outbreak Of Love	108	↓		
			MIGHTY LEMON DROPS, The				
			Pop group from Wolverhampton, England: Paul Marsh (vocals), David Newton (guitar), Marcus Williams (bass) and Keith Rowley (drums).				
10/7/89	5	11	1 Into The Heart Of Love	—		Laughter .... Sire 26017	
1/6/90	8	9	2 Where Do We Go From Heaven?	—	↓		
6/8/91	28	3	3 Unkind	—		Sound...Goodbye To Your Standards ..... Sire 26512	
			MIGHTY MIGHTY BOSSTONES, The				
			Ska-rock group from Boston: Dickey Barrett (vocals), Nate Albert (guitar), Ben Carr (dancer), Kevin Lenear, Tim Burton and Dennis Brockenborough (horns), Joe Gittleman (bass) and Joe Sirois (drums). Lawrence Katz replaced Albert and Roman Fleysher replaced Lenear in 1999.				
7/24/93	19	5	1 Someday I Suppose	—		Don't Know How To Party .... Mercury 514836	
3/8/97	❶¹	29	2 The Impression That I Get	23ᴬ	▲	Let's Face It .... Mercury 534472	
8/9/97	7	20	3 The Rascal King	68ᴬ	↓		
12/13/97+	22	11	4 Royal Oil	—	↓		
4/8/00	11	13	5 So Sad To Say	—		Pay Attention .... Big Rig 542451	

DEBUT	PEAK	WKS	Modern Rock Track	Pop Gld	Album Title	Album Label & Number
			MILLA			
			Born Milla Jovovich on 12/17/75 in Kiev, Ukraine; raised in Sacramento, California. Female actress/model. Starred in several movies.			
4/30/94	21	7	Gentleman Who Fell	—	*The Divine Comedy*	SBK 27984
			MILLTOWN BROTHERS			
			Pop-rock group from Colne, Lancashire, England: Matt Nelson (vocals), Simon Nelson (guitar), Barney James (keyboards), James Fraser (bass) and Nian Brindle (drums).			
6/15/91	10	9	Which Way Should I Jump?	—	*Slinky*	A&M 5346
			MINISTRY			
			An assemblage of musicians spearheaded by Chicago-based producers/performers Alain Jourgensen and Paul Barker. Formed by Jourgensen in 1981. Barker joined Ministry in 1986. Varying personnel are members of The Tribe, an affiliation of musicians from various groups.			
12/16/89+	23	9	1 Burning Inside	— ●	*The Mind Is A Terrible Thing To Taste*	Sire 26004
11/30/91+	19	7	2 Jesus Built My Hotrod	— ▲	*Psalm 69.*	Sire 26727
8/8/92	11	8	3 N.W.O.	—	↓	
			N.W.O.: New World Order			
			MIRACLE LEGION			
			Pop-rock group from Connecticut: Mark Mulcahey (vocals), Ray Neal (guitar), Dave McCaffrey (bass) and Scott Boutier (drums).			
3/28/92	28	3	Snacks and Candy	—	*Drenched*	Morgan Creek 20006
			MISSION U.K., The			
			Rock group formed in Leeds, England: Wayne Hussey (vocals, guitar), Simon Hinkler (guitar), Craig Adams (bass) and Mick Brown (drums). Hussey and Adams were members of **The Sisters Of Mercy**.			
2/10/90	6	14	1 Deliverance	—	*Carved In Sand.*	Mercury 842251
4/28/90	23	5	2 Butterfly On A Wheel	—	↓	
12/15/90+	7	9	3 Hands Across The Ocean	—	*Grains Of Sand.*	Mercury 846937
			MR. MIRAINGA			
			Rock-salsa group formed in California: Craig Poturalski (vocals), Steve Garcia (guitar), Steve "Hedge" Gunderson (bass) and Greg "Drt" Jones (drums).			
11/25/95	25	9	Burnin' Rubber	122	*Ace Ventura: When Nature Calls* (soundtrack)	MCA Soundtrax 11374
			MOBY			
			Born Richard Hall on 9/11/65 in Harlem, New York; raised in Darien, Connecticut.			
7/24/99	26	11	1 Bodyrock	— ▲²	*Play*	V2 27049
1/22/00	24	11	2 Natural Blues	75ˢ	↓	
			samples "Trouble So Hard" by Vera Hall			
5/13/00	18	16	3 Porcelain	—	↓	
11/4/00+	3	31	4 South Side	14	↓	
			MOBY Featuring Gwen Stefani			
4/20/02	22	8	5 We Are All Made Of Stars	— ●	*18*	V2 27127
			MOCK TURTLES, The			
			Rock group from Manchester, England: Martin Coogan (vocals, guitar), Martin Glyn Murray (guitar), Joanne Gent (keyboards), Andrew Stewardson (bass) and Steve Cowen (drums).			
8/31/91	19	4	Can You Dig It?	—	*Turtle Soup*	Relativity 1058
			MONACO			
			Rock duo from England: Peter Hook (of **New Order**) and David Potts.			
7/12/97	24	10	What Do You Want From Me?	61ᴬ	*Music For Pleasure*	Polydor 537629
			MONO			
			Dance duo from England: Siobahn DeMare (female vocals) and Martin Virgo (instruments).			
2/28/98	28	9	Life In Mono	70	*Formica Blues*	Echo 536676
			MONSTER MAGNET			
			Hard-rock group from Red Bank, New Jersey: David Wyndorf (vocals), Ed Mundell (guitar), Joe Calandra (bass) and Joe Kleinman (drums).			
5/20/95	26	7	1 Negasonic Teenage Warhead	—	*Dopes To Infinity*	A&M 540315
8/8/98	29	12	2 Space Lord	— ●	*Powertrip.*	A&M 540908
			MOODSWINGS			
			Techno-dance duo from London: J.F.T. "Fred" Hood and Grant Showbiz.			
9/12/92	6	12	Spiritual High (State Of Independence) Part II	—	*Moodfood.*	Arista 18619
			Chrissie Hynde (guest vocal)			
			MOORE, Abra			
			Born on 6/8/69 in San Diego; raised in Puni, Hawaii. Female singer/songwriter/guitarist.			
5/24/97	27	10	Four Leaf Clover	63	*Strangest Places*	Arista Austin 18839
			MOORE, Mae			
			Born in Vancouver. Female singer/songwriter/guitarist.			
12/11/93+	25	10	Bohemia	—	*Bohemia*	Tristar 57373

DEBUT	PEAK	WKS	Modern Rock Track	Pop Gld	Album Title	Album Label & Number

MORISSETTE, Alanis ★26★
Born on 6/1/74 in Ottawa, Ontario, Canada. Female singer/songwriter. At age 12, acted on the Nickelodeon cable-TV kids series *You Can't Do That On Television.* Started musical career as a dance singer.

6/17/95	**❶**⁵	19	1 **You Oughta Know**	13ᴬ ▲¹⁶	*Jagged Little Pill*	Maverick 45901
8/26/95	**❶**¹	23	2 **Hand In My Pocket**	15ᴬ	↓	
10/28/95	**14**	16	3 **All I Really Want**	65ᴬ	↓	
1/6/96	**❶**³	21	4 **Ironic**	4	↓	
5/18/96	**7**	16	5 **You Learn**	6	↓	
9/28/96	**25**	11	6 **Head Over Feet**	3ᴬ	↓	
4/4/98	**26**	16	7 **Uninvited**	4ᴬ ▲⁵	*City Of Angels (soundtrack)*	Warner Sunset 46867
10/10/98	**12**	9	8 **Thank U**	17 ▲³	*Supposed Former Infatuation Junkie.* . .	Maverick 47094
12/5/98+	**16**	13	9 **Joining You**	—	↓	

MORRISSEY ★16★
Born Stephen Morrissey on 5/22/59 in Davyhulme, Lancashire, England. Former lead singer/songwriter of The Smiths.

1)The More You Ignore Me, The Closer I Get   2)Tomorrow   3)Piccadilly Palare

3/18/89	**3**	9	1 **The Last Of The Famous International Playboys**	— ●	*Bona Drag*	Sire 26221
7/1/89	**11**	7	2 **Interesting Drug**	—	↓	
12/23/89+	**2**¹	9	3 **Ouija Board, Ouija Board**	—	↓	
5/19/90	**6**	9	4 **November Spawned A Monster**	—	↓	
11/24/90+	**2**²	10	5 **Piccadilly Palare**	—	↓	
3/16/91	**2**²	9	6 **Our Frank**	—	*Kill Uncle.*	Sire 26514
5/18/91	**10**	9	7 **Sing Your Life**	—	↓	
5/30/92	**2**²	9	8 **We Hate It When Our Friends Become Successful**	—	*Your Arsenal.*	Sire 26994
7/25/92	**❶**⁶	14	9 **Tomorrow**	—	↓	
10/3/92	**13**	8	10 **Glamorous Glue**	—	↓	
3/19/94	**❶**⁷	12	11 **The More You Ignore Me, The Closer I Get**	46	*Vauxhall And I*	Sire 45451

MOULD, Bob
Born on 10/12/60 in Malone, New York. Singer/songwriter/guitarist. Member of Hüsker Dü and Sugar.

5/20/89	**4**	13	1 **See A Little Light**	—	*Workbook.*	Virgin 91240
8/25/90	**10**	10	2 **It's Too Late**	—	*Black Sheets Of Rain.*	Virgin 91395

MOYET, Alison
Born Genevieve Alison-Jane Moyet on 6/18/61 in Basildon, Essex, England. Female singer.

12/14/91	**29**	3	**It Won't Be Long**	—	*Hoodoo*	Columbia 47841

MUDHONEY
Rock group formed in Seattle: Mark Arm (vocals), Steve Turner (guitar), Matt Lukin (bass) and Dan Peters (drums).

11/7/92	**23**	6	**Suck You Dry**	—	*Piece Of Cake*	Reprise 45090

MULLINS, Shawn
Born on 3/8/68 in Atlanta. Male singer/songwriter/guitarist.

9/5/98	**9**	22	**Lullaby**	7 ●	*Soul's Core*	Columbia 69637

MUNDY
Born Edmund Enright in 1976 in Birr, Offaly, Ireland. Male singer/songwriter/guitarist.

3/1/97	**37**	2	**To You I Bestow**	—	*Jelly Legs*	Epic 67894

MURMURS, The
Female rock duo from New York City: singers/guitarists Heather Grody and Leisha Hailey.

11/26/94	**23**	9	**You Suck**	89	*The Murmurs*	MCA 11086

MURPHY, Peter ★91★
Born on 7/11/57 in Northampton, England. Singer/songwriter.

11/4/89	**18**	5	1 **The Line Between The Devil's Teeth (And That Which Cannot Be Repeat)**	—	*Deep*	Beggars Banquet 9877
1/20/90	**❶**⁷	18	2 **Cuts You Up**	55	↓	
7/7/90	**21**	5	3 **A Strange Kind Of Love**	—	↓	

DEBUT	PEAK	WKS	Modern Rock Track	Pop Gld	Album Title	Album Label & Number
			MURPHY, Peter — Cont'd			
4/11/92	2¹	12	4 The Sweetest Drop	—	Holy Smoke	Beggars Banquet 66007
6/27/92	18	5	5 You're So Close	—	↓	
			MXPX			
			Christian punk-rock trio from Bremerton, Washington: Mike Herrera (vocals, bass), Tom Wisniewski (guitar) and Yuri Ruley (drums).			
7/15/00	24	8	Responsibility	—	The Ever Passing Moment	A&M 490656
			MY BLOODY VALENTINE			
			Rock group from Dublin, Ireland: Bilinda Butcher (vocals, guitar), Kevin Shields (vocals, guitar), Debbie Googe (bass) and Colm O'Ciosoig (drums). Group named after a 1981 horror movie.			
2/1/92	27	2	Only Shallow	—	Loveless	Sire 26759
			MY FRIEND STEVE			
			Rock group from Gainesville, Florida: Steven Burry (vocals), Eric Steinberg (guitar), Patrick Koch (keyboards), David McMahon (bass) and Eric Gardner (drums).			
4/24/99	38	3	Charmed	—	Hope & Wait.	Mammoth 980191
			MY LIFE WITH THE THRILL KILL KULT			
			Rock group from Chicago. Assembled by Mr. Groovie Mann (vocals) and Mr. Buzz McCoy (keyboards).			
7/13/91+	17	11	Sex On Wheelz	—	Sexplosion!	Wax Trax 7163

N

			NADA SURF			
			Rock trio from Los Angeles: Matthew Caws (vocals, guitar), Daniel Lorca (bass) and Ira Elliot (drums).			
7/6/96	11	13	Popular	51ᴬ	High/Low.	Elektra 61913
			NAVARRO, Dave			
			Born on 6/6/67 in Santa Monica, California. Rock singer/guitarist. Former member of **Jane's Addiction** and **Red Hot Chili Peppers**.			
6/9/01	12	11	1 Rexall	—	Trust No One	Capitol 32802
9/29/01	24	7	2 Hungry	—	↓	
			N'DOUR, Youssou			
			Born on 10/1/59 in Dakar, Senegal, Africa. Popular singer in his native language of Wolof.			
8/19/89	9	6	Shakin' The Tree	—	The Lion.	Virgin 91253
			Peter Gabriel (co-lead vocal)			
			NED'S ATOMIC DUSTBIN			
			Rock group from England: Jonathan Penney (vocals), Garath Pring (guitar), Alexander Griffin (bass), Matthew Cheslin (bass) and Daniel Worton (drums).			
7/20/91	11	11	1 Happy	—	God Fodder.	Columbia 47929
10/19/91	24	6	2 Grey Cell Green	—	↓	
10/24/92+	❶¹	17	3 Not Sleeping Around	—	Are You Normal?	Columbia 53154
1/30/93	13	8	4 Walking Through Syrup	—	↓	
7/31/93	26	1	5 Saturday Night	—	So I Married An Axe	
			#1 Pop hit for the Bay City Rollers in 1976		Murderer (soundtrack).	Chaos 57303
			N*E*R*D			
			Male rap/production trio from Virginia Beach: Shay, Chad Hugo and Pharrell Williams. Also known as The Neptunes.			
8/3/02	36	5	Rock Star	—	In Search Of...	Virgin 11521
			NERF HERDER			
			Rock trio from Santa Barbara, California: Parry Gripp (vocals, guitar), Charlie Dennis (bass) and Steve Sherlock (drums). Group named after a line in the movie The Empire Strikes Back.			
1/4/97	34	4	Van Halen.	—	Nerf Herder	Arista 18954
			NESS, Mike			
			Born on 4/3/62 in Stoneham, Massachusetts. Lead singer of **Social Distortion**.			
5/8/99	28	8	Don't Think Twice	—	Cheating At Solitaire	Time Bomb 43524
			NEVE			
			Rock group from Los Angeles: John Stephens (vocals), Mike Raphael (guitar), Tommy Gruber (bass) and Brian Burwell (drums).			
3/13/99	30	5	It's Over Now	—	The Faculty (soundtrack)	Columbia 69762
			NEW FAST AUTOMATIC DAFFODILS			
			Pop-rock group from Manchester, England: Andy Spearpont (vocals), Dolan Hewison (guitar), Icarus Wilson-Wright (percussion), Justin Crawford (bass) and Perry Saunders (drums).			
2/20/93	30	4	Stockholm.	—	Body Exit Mind	Mute/Elektra 61398
			NEW FOUND GLORY			
			Rock group from Coral Springs, Florida: Jordan Pundik (vocals), Chad Gilbert and Steve Klein (guitars), Ian Grushka (bass) and Cyrus Bolooki (drums).			
2/17/01	15	16	1 Hit Or Miss	—	New Found Glory	Drive-Thru 112338
6/22/02	5	23↑	2 My Friends Over You	85	Sticks And Stones	Drive-Thru 112916

DEBUT	PEAK	WKS	Modern Rock Track	Pop	Gld	Album Title	Album Label & Number
	★69★		**NEW ORDER**				

Techno-dance group formed in Manchester, England: Bernard Sumner (vocals, guitar), Gillian Gilbert (keyboards), Peter Hook (bass) and Stephen Morris (drums). Sumner was also a member of **Electronic**. Hook was also a member of **Monaco** and **Revenge**. Morris and Gilbert also recorded as **The Other Two**.

DEBUT	PEAK	WKS	Modern Rock Track	Pop	Gld	Album Title	Album Label & Number
1/7/89	3	13	1 **Fine Time**	—	●	Technique	Qwest 25845
3/18/89	6	13	2 **Round & Round**	64	↓		
7/7/90	5	8	3 **World In Motion**	—		(single only)	Qwest 21582
4/17/93	❶⁶	18	4 **Regret**	28	●	Republic	Qwest 45250
7/17/93	30	1	5 **Ruined In A Day**	—	↓		
7/31/93	5	10	6 **World** (The Price Of Love)	92	↓		

NEW RADICALS

Group is actually solo rock singer/musician Gregg Alexander.

DEBUT	PEAK	WKS	Modern Rock Track	Pop	Gld	Album Title	Album Label & Number
10/31/98+	8	23	**You Get What You Give**	36	▲	Maybe You've Been Brainwashed Too	MCA 11858
	★59★		**NICKELBACK**				

Rock group from Vancouver: brothers **Chad Kroeger** (vocals) and Mike Kroeger (bass), with Ryan Peake (guitar) and Ryan Vikedal (drums).

DEBUT	PEAK	WKS	Modern Rock Track	Pop	Gld	Album Title	Album Label & Number
7/1/00	21	16	1 **Leader Of Men**	—	●	The State	Roadrunner 8586
11/25/00+	21	15	2 **Breathe**				
8/4/01	❶¹³	38	3 **How You Remind Me**	❶⁴	▲⁴	Silver Side Up	Roadrunner 618485
12/15/01+	6	27	4 **Too Bad**	42	↓		
8/3/02	24	13	5 **Never Again**	124	↓		

NINEDAYS

Rock group from New York City: John Hampson (vocals, guitar), Brian Desveaux (vocals, guitar), Jeremy Dean (keyboards), Nick Dimichino (bass) and Vincent Tattanelli (drums).

DEBUT	PEAK	WKS	Modern Rock Track	Pop	Gld	Album Title	Album Label & Number
4/15/00	10	19	**Absolutely (Story Of A Girl)**	6	●	The Madding Crowd	550 Music 63634

NINE INCH NAILS ★38★

Group is actually industrial rock musician Trent Reznor (born on 5/17/65 in Mercer, Pennsylvania). Richard Patrick and Brian Liesegang (both of **Filter**) provided instrumentation on several of the albums below.

1)Hurt 2)Closer 3)The Perfect Drug

DEBUT	PEAK	WKS	Modern Rock Track	Pop	Gld	Album Title	Album Label & Number
12/16/89+	16	12	1 **Down In It**	—	▲²	Pretty Hate Machine	TVT 2610
3/31/90	28	1	2 **Head Like A Hole**	109	↓		
10/3/92	13	9	3 **Happiness In Slavery**	—	▲	Broken	Nothing 92213
2/20/93	25	1	4 **Wish**	—	↓		
5/7/94	11	25	5 **Closer**	41	▲⁴	The Downward Spiral	Nothing 92346
12/24/94+	20	9	6 **Piggy**	—	↓		
4/22/95	8	14	7 **Hurt**	54ᴬ	↓		
2/1/97	11	14	8 **The Perfect Drug**	46	●	Lost Highway (soundtrack)	Nothing 90090
8/7/99	39	3	9 **Starfuckers, Inc.**	—	▲²	The Fragile	Nothing 490473
9/18/99	11	14	10 **We're In This Together**	—	↓		
12/4/99+	11	18	11 **Into The Void**	—	↓		
5/26/01	18	9	12 **Deep**	—	●	Lara Croft: Tomb Raider (soundtrack)	Elektra 62665

NIRVANA ★19★

Grunge-rock trio from Aberdeen, Washington: Kurt Cobain (vocals, guitar; born on 2/20/67), Krist Novoselic (bass; born on 5/16/65) and **Dave Grohl** (drums; born on 1/14/69). Cobain married Courtney Love (lead singer of **Hole**) on 2/24/92. Cobain died of a self-inflicted gunshot wound on 4/8/94 (age 27). Grohl formed **Foo Fighters** in 1995.

1)You Know You're Right 2)Heart-Shaped Box 3)All Apologies

DEBUT	PEAK	WKS	Modern Rock Track	Pop	Gld	Album Title	Album Label & Number
9/21/91	❶¹	20	1 **Smells Like Teen Spirit**	6	▲¹⁰	Nevermind	DGC 24425
1/18/92	3	18	2 **Come As You Are**	32	↓		
1/18/92	25	2	3 **On A Plain**	—	↓		
2/8/92	25	3	4 **Lithium**	64	↓		
1/23/93	19	4	5 **Sliver**	—	▲	Incesticide	DGC 24504
9/18/93	❶³	14	6 **Heart-Shaped Box**	—	▲⁵	In Utero	DGC 24607
12/4/93+	❶²	21	7 **All Apologies**	45ᴬ	↓		
10/15/94	❶¹	19	8 **About A Girl** [L]	22ᴬ	▲⁵	MTV Unplugged In New York	DGC 24727
1/7/95	6	21	9 **The Man Who Sold The World** [L]	39ᴬ	↓		
			first recorded by **David Bowie** in 1970				
9/28/96	13	12	10 **Aneurysm** [L]	63ᴬ		From The Muddy Banks Of The Wishkah	DGC 25105
			recorded on 12/28/91 at the Del Mar Fairgrounds in California				
10/12/02	❶⁴	7↑	11 **You Know You're Right**	45↑		Nirvana	DGC 493507
			recorded on 1/30/94				

DEBUT	PEAK	WKS	Modern Rock Track	Pop	Gld	Album Title	Album Label & Number

NITZER EBB
Industrial-rock duo from Chelmsford, Essex, England: Douglas McCarthy and Bon Harris.

2/25/89	25	2	1 Control Im Here	—		*Belief*	Geffen 24213
4/28/90	28	2	2 Lightning Man	—		*Showtime*	Geffen 24284
9/7/91	21	5	3 Family Man	—		*Ebbhead*	Geffen 24456
11/30/91	27	2	4 I Give To You	—	↓		

NIXON, Mojo, & Skid Roper
Novelty-rock duo. Nixon (vocals, guitar) was born Neill Kirby McMillan on 8/2/57 in Chapel Hill, North Carolina. Roper (washboard, bass) was born Richard Banke on 10/19/54 in National City, California. Split in early 1990. Nixon appeared in the 1989 movie *Great Balls Of Fire*.

5/6/89	16	4	1 Debbie Gibson Is Pregnant With My Two Headed Love Child	[N] —		*Root Hog Or Die*	Enigma 73335
9/29/90	20	4	2 Don Henley Must Die	[N] —		*Otis*	Enigma 73529
			MOJO NIXON				

NIXONS, The
Rock group from Dallas: Zac Maloy (vocals, guitar), Jesse Davis (guitar), Ricky Brooks (bass) and John Humphrey (drums).

| 3/16/96 | 11 | 20 | Sister | 48[A] | | *Foma* | MCA 11209 |

NO DOUBT ★40★
Ska-rock group from Orange County, California: **Gwen Stefani** (vocals; born on 10/3/69), Tom Dumont (guitar; born on 1/11/68), Tony Kanal (bass; born on 8/27/70) and Adrian Young (drums; born on 8/26/69). Stefani married **Gavin Rossdale** (lead singer of **Bush**) on 9/14/2002.

11/18/95+	10	26	1 Just A Girl	23	▲10	*Tragic Kingdom*	Trauma 92580
4/27/96	5	26	2 Spiderwebs	18[A]	↓		
10/19/96	2[5]	23	3 Don't Speak	❶16[A]	↓		
2/8/97	17	10	4 Excuse Me Mr.	—	↓		
3/13/99	7	22	5 New	123		*Go (soundtrack)*	Work 69851
2/5/00	2[3]	18	6 Ex-Girlfriend	111	▲	*Return Of Saturn*	Trauma 490441
5/13/00	14	14	7 Simple Kind Of Life	38	↓		

NORTHSIDE
Rock group from Manchester, England: Warren Dermody (vocals), Tim Walsh (guitar), Cliff Ogier (bass) and Paul Walsh (drums).

| 8/31/91 | 5 | 11 | Take 5 | — | | *Chicken Rhythms* | Geffen 24412 |

NOVA, Heather
Born on 7/6/68 on an island in the Bermuda Sound. Raised on a 40-foot sailboat in the Caribbean. Later settled in London. Singer/songwriter.

| 9/2/95 | 13 | 14 | Walk This World | 63[A] | | *Oyster* | Big Cat 67113 |

OASIS ★15★
Rock group from Manchester, England: brothers Liam (vocals; born on 9/12/72) and Noel (guitar; born on 5/29/67) Gallagher, Paul Arthurs (guitar), Paul McGuigan (bass) and Tony McCarroll (drums). Alan White replaced McCarroll in 1995.

1)Wonderwall 2)Champagne Supernova 3)Live Forever

10/1/94	11	16	1 Supersonic	—	▲	*Definitely Maybe*	Epic 66431
1/7/95	2[2]	24	2 Live Forever	39[A]	↓		
6/3/95	36	4	3 Rock 'n' Roll Star	—	↓		
10/7/95	24	6	4 Morning Glory	—	▲4	*(What's The Story) Morning Glory?*	Epic 67351
11/25/95	❶10	25	5 Wonderwall	8	↓		
2/24/96	❶5	19	6 Champagne Supernova	20[A]	↓		
6/22/96	10	14	7 Don't Look Back In Anger	55	↓		
7/19/97	4	16	8 D' You Know What I Mean?	49[A]	▲	*Be Here Now*	Epic 68530
9/27/97	5	18	9 Don't Go Away	35[A]	↓		
1/24/98	15	9	10 All Around The World	—	↓		
10/31/98	24	9	11 Acquiesce	—		*The Masterplan*	Epic 69647
1/29/00	14	11	12 Go Let It Out	—		*Standing On The Shoulder Of Giants*	Epic 63586

Modern Rock

DEBUT	PEAK	WKS	Modern Rock Track	Pop	Gld	Album Title	Album Label & Number

OCASEK, Ric
Born Richard Otcasek on 3/23/49 in Baltimore. Lead singer/guitarist/songwriter of **The Cars**. Appeared in the 1987 movie *Made In Heaven*. Married supermodel/actress Paulina Porizkova on 8/23/89. His son Christopher Otcasek is leader of **Glamour Camp**.

DEBUT	PEAK	WKS	Modern Rock Track	Pop	Gld	Album Title	Album Label & Number
7/6/91	19	5	Rockaway	—		*Fireball Zone*	Reprise 26552

★83★ **OCEAN BLUE, The**
Pop-rock group formed in Hershey, Pennsylvania: Dave Schelzel (vocals, guitar), Steve Lau (keyboards), Bobby Mittan (bass) and Rob Minnig (drums).

DEBUT	PEAK	WKS	Modern Rock Track	Pop	Gld	Album Title	Album Label & Number
8/19/89	2³	13	1 Between Something And Nothing	—		*The Ocean Blue*	Sire 25906
12/2/89	10	10	2 Drifting, Falling	—		↓	
9/28/91	16	6	3 Cerulean	—		*Cerulean*	Sire 26550
11/16/91+	3	13	4 Ballerina Out Of Control	—		↓	
2/15/92	27	2	5 Mercury	—		↓	
8/28/93	3	12	6 Sublime	121		*Beneath The Rhythm And Sound*	Sire 45369

O'CONNOR, Sinéad
Born on 12/12/66 in Glenageary, Ireland. Female singer/songwriter. Also see **Peace Together**.

DEBUT	PEAK	WKS	Modern Rock Track	Pop	Gld	Album Title	Album Label & Number
9/17/88	17	3	1 Jump In The River	—		*Married To The Mob (soundtrack)*	Reprise 25763
2/10/90	❶¹	13	2 Nothing Compares 2 U	❶⁴	▲²	*I Do Not Want What I Haven't Got*	Ensign 21759
			written by **Prince**				
4/7/90	❶¹	15	3 The Emperor's New Clothes	60		↓	
9/12/92	20	6	4 Success Has Made A Failure Of Our Home	—		*Am I Not Your Girl?*	Ensign 21952
4/2/94	24	2	5 You Made Me The Thief Of Your Heart	—		*In The Name Of The Father (soundtrack)*	Island 518841

OFFSPRING, The ★11★
Punk-rock group from Anaheim, California: Brian "Dexter" Holland (vocals; born on 12/29/66), Kevin "Noodles" Wasserman (guitar; born on 2/4/63), Greg Kriesel (bass; born on 1/20/65) and Ron Welty (drums; born on 1/1/71).

1)Come Out And Play 2)Original Prankster 3)Pretty Fly (For A White Guy)

DEBUT	PEAK	WKS	Modern Rock Track	Pop	Gld	Album Title	Album Label & Number
5/28/94	❶²	26	1 Come Out And Play	38ᴬ	▲⁶	*Smash*	Epitaph 86432
8/13/94	4	25	2 Self Esteem	45ᴬ		↓	
11/26/94+	6	20	3 Gotta Get Away	58ᴬ		↓	
4/15/95	22	10	4 Kick Him When He's Down	—	●	*Ignition*	Epitaph 86424
6/17/95	16	10	5 Smash It Up	47ᴬ	▲²	*Batman Forever (soundtrack)*	Atlantic 82759
1/18/97	13	8	6 All I Want	65ᴬ	▲	*Ixnay On The Hombre*	Columbia 67810
3/8/97	4	24	7 Gone Away	50ᴬ		↓	
10/4/97	24	10	8 I Choose	—		↓	
10/17/98	3	26	9 Pretty Fly (For A White Guy)	53	▲⁴	*Americana*	Columbia 69661
			intro samples "Rock Of Ages" by **Def Leppard**				
1/30/99	4	26	10 Why Don't You Get A Job?	74		↓	
5/29/99	6	26	11 The Kids Aren't Alright	105		↓	
10/23/99	11	15	12 She's Got Issues	—		↓	
5/13/00	27	9	13 Totalimmortal	—		*Me, Myself & Irene (soundtrack)*	Elektra 62512
10/21/00	2²	17	14 Original Prankster	70	▲	*Conspiracy Of One*	Columbia 61419
1/6/01	10	16	15 Want You Bad	—		↓	
12/1/01+	8	18	16 Defy You	77		*Orange County (soundtrack)*	Columbia 85933

OINGO BOINGO
Rock group formed in Los Angeles: Danny Elfman (vocals), Steve Bartek (guitar), John Avila (bass) and Johnny Hernandez (drums). Group appeared in the 1986 movie *Back To School*. Elfman also scored several movies.

DEBUT	PEAK	WKS	Modern Rock Track	Pop	Gld	Album Title	Album Label & Number
10/22/88	14	6	1 Winning Side	—		*Boingo Alive*	MCA 8030
3/3/90	15	6	2 When The Lights Go Out	—		*Dark At The End Of The Tunnel*	MCA 6365
6/11/94	23	6	3 Hey!	—		*Boingo*	Giant 24555
			BOINGO				

OK GO
Pop-rock group from Chicago: Damian Kulash (vocals), Andrew Duncan (guitar), Tim Nordwind (bass) and Dan Konopka (drums).

DEBUT	PEAK	WKS	Modern Rock Track	Pop	Gld	Album Title	Album Label & Number
9/7/02	21	12↑	Get Over It	—		*Ok Go*	Capitol 33724

OLEANDER
Pop-rock group from Sacramento, California: Thomas Flowers (vocals), Ric Ivaniesevich (guitar), Doug Eldridge (bass) and Fred Nelson (drums).

DEBUT	PEAK	WKS	Modern Rock Track	Pop	Gld	Album Title	Album Label & Number
5/29/99	13	25	1 Why I'm Here	107	●	*February Son*	Republic 53242
12/4/99	37	4	2 I Walk Alone	—		↓	
2/17/01	19	12	3 Are You There?	—		*Unwind*	Republic 013377

ONE DOVE
Pop-rock trio from Glasgow, Scotland: Dorothy Allison, Ian Carmichael and Jim McKinven.

DEBUT	PEAK	WKS	Modern Rock Track	Pop	Gld	Album Title	Album Label & Number
12/18/93+	14	10	White Love	—		*Morning Dove White*	ffrr 351042

DEBUT	PEAK	WKS	Modern Rock Track	Pop Gld	Album Title	Album Label & Number
			OPM			
			Rock trio from Los Angeles: Matthew Lo (vocals, guitar), John Necro (bass) and Geoff Turney (drums).			
8/5/00	18	9	**Heaven Is A Halfpipe (If I Die)**	—	*Menace To Sobriety*	Atlantic 83369
			O-POSITIVE			
			Rock group from Boston: Dave Herlihy (vocal), Dave Martin (guitar), Alan Petitti (keyboards), David Ingham (bass) and Alex Lob (drums).			
6/2/90	22	4	**Back Of My Mind**	—	*Toy Boat*	Epic 46018
			OPUS III			
			Pop-rock group from England: vocalist Kirsty Hawkshaw with trio of producers/musicians Kevin Dodds, Ian Munro and Nigel Walton.			
8/15/92	30	2	**It's A Fine Day**	—	*Mind Fruit*	EastWest 92160
			ORBIT			
			Rock trio from Boston: Jeff Lowe Robbins (vocals, guitar), Wally Gagel (bass) and Paul Buckley (drums).			
4/19/97	32	6	**Medicine**	—	*Libido Speedway*	A&M 540652
			ORCHESTRAL MANOEUVRES IN THE DARK			
			Electro-pop trio formed in England: singer/keyboardist Andrew McCluskey, multi-instrumentalist Martin Cooper and drummer Malcolm Holmes.			
8/3/91	19	5	1 **Pandora's Box (It's A Long, Long Way)**	—	*Sugar Tax*	Virgin 91715
6/12/93	5	10	2 **Stand Above Me**	111	*Liberator*	Virgin 88225
			ORGY			
			Electronic rock group from Los Angeles: Jay Gordon (vocals), Ryan Shuck (guitar), Amir Derakh (keyboards), Paige Hailey (bass) and Bobby Hewitt (drums).			
12/5/98+	4	31	1 **Blue Monday**	56 ▲	*Candyass*	Elementree 46923
7/3/99	18	13	2 **Stitches**	— ↓		
9/9/00	6	21	3 **Fiction (Dreams In Digital)**	— ●	*Vapor Transmission*	Elementree 47832
3/3/01	26	6	4 **Opticon**	— ↓		
			ORIGIN, The			
			Pop-rock group from La Jolla, California: Michael Andrews (vocals), Daniel Silverman (keyboards), Topper Rimel (bass) and Rony Abada (drums).			
6/9/90	19	9	1 **Growing Old**	—	*The Origin*	Virgin 91353
2/15/92	17	9	2 **Bonfires Burning**	—	*Bend*	Virgin 91740
			ORTON, Beth			
			Born on 12/14/70 in Norwich, Norfolk, England. Female singer/songwriter.			
4/24/99	32	7	**Stolen Car**	—	*Central Reservation*	Heavenly 19038
			OSBORNE, Joan			
			Born on 7/8/62 in Anchorage, Kentucky. Singer/songwriter/guitarist.			
9/30/95	7	24	**One Of Us**	4 ▲³	*Relish*	Blue Gorilla 526699
			OTHER TWO, The			
			Duo from England: **New Order** members Gillian Gilbert (vocals, keyboards, guitar) and Stephen Morris (programs, percussion).			
2/12/94	30	2	**Selfish**	—	*The Other Two And You*	Qwest 45140
	★47★		**OUR LADY PEACE**			
			Rock group from Toronto: Raine Maida (vocals), Mike Turner (guitar), Chris Eacrett (bass) and Jeremy Taggart (drums). Duncan Coutts replaced Eacrett in 1996.			
3/18/95	10	14	1 **Starseed**	—	*Naveed*	Relativity 1507
8/2/97	11	20	2 **Superman's Dead**	74ᴬ ●	*Clumsy*	Columbia 67940
12/6/97+	5	26	3 **Clumsy**	59ᴬ ↓		
5/23/98	31	11	4 **4 AM**	— ↓	*Happiness...Is Not A Fish That You Can Catch*	Columbia 63707
8/28/99	13	14	5 **One Man Army**	—		
2/5/00	20	14	6 **Is Anybody Home?**	— ↓		
2/10/01	27	12	7 **Life**	—	*Spiritual Machines*	Columbia 85368
4/20/02	7	22	8 **Somewhere Out There**	44 ●	*Gravity*	Columbia 86585
9/7/02	20	12↑	9 **Innocent**	— ↓		
			OURS			
			Group is actually solo singer/songwriter/guitarist Jimmy Gnecco (from New Jersey).			
5/26/01	31	5	**Sometimes**	—	*Distorted Lullabies*	DreamWorks 50036

P

DEBUT	PEAK	WKS	Modern Rock Track	Pop Gld	Album Title	Album Label & Number
			PALMER, Robert			
			Born Alan Palmer on 1/19/49 in Batley, Yorkshire, England; raised on the Mediterranean island of Malta. Lead singer of **The Power Station**. Also see **Classic Rock Tracks** section.			
3/17/90	14	8	1 **Life In Detail**	— ▲³	*Pretty Woman (soundtrack)*	EMI 93492
1/26/91	24	2	2 **I'll Be Your Baby Tonight**	—	*Don't Explain*	EMI 93935
			first recorded by **Bob Dylan** on the 1968 album *John Wesley Harding*			

DEBUT	PEAK	WKS	Modern Rock Track	Pop	Gld	Album Title	Album Label & Number

★76★ PAPA ROACH
Rock group from Vacaville, California: Coby Dick (vocals), Jerry Horton (guitar), Tobin Esperance (bass) and Dave Buckner (drums).

DEBUT	PEAK	WKS	Track	Pop	Gld	Album	Label
4/22/00	❶[7]	37	1 Last Resort	57	▲[3]	Infest	DreamWorks 50223
10/7/00	9	20	2 Broken Home	—	↓		
3/3/01	16	15	3 Between Angels And Insects	—	↓		
5/25/02	5	22	4 She Loves Me Not	76	●	Lovehatetragedy	DreamWorks 50381
10/19/02	33	5	5 Time And Time Again	—	↓		

PAPA VEGAS
Rock group from Grand Rapids, Michigan: Joel Ferguson (vocals), Pete Dunning (guitar), Mick Force (bass) and Scott Stefanski (drums).

4/24/99	20	9	Bombshell	—		Hello Vertigo	RCA 67644

PARKER, Graham
Born on 11/18/50 in London. Pop-rock singer/songwriter/guitarist.

9/10/88	27	1	1 Don't Let It Break You Down	—		The Mona Lisa's Sister	RCA 8316
11/11/89	18	9	2 Big Man On Paper	—		Human Soul	RCA 9876

PAVEMENT
Rock group formed in Stockton, California: Stephen Malkmus (vocals, guitar), Scott Kannberg (guitar), Bob Nastanovich (percussion), Mark Ibold (bass) and Steve West (drums).

3/26/94	10	12	Cut Your Hair	—		Crooked Rain, Crooked Rain	Matador/Atl. 92343

PEACE TOGETHER
Group formed to benefit youths in Northern Ireland. Formed by Robert Hamilton (from Dublin) and Alistair McMordie (from Belfast). Main vocals by **Peter Gabriel**, **Sinéad O'Connor** and Feargal Sharkey.

8/28/93	28	2	Be Still	—		Peace Together (various artists)	Island 518063

PEARL JAM ★4★
Rock group formed in Seattle: **Eddie Vedder** (vocals; born on 12/23/64), Stone Gossard (guitar; born on 7/20/66), Mike McCready (guitar; born on 4/5/66), Jeff Ament (bass; born on 3/10/63) and Dave Krusen (drums; born on 3/10/66). Dave Abbruzzese (born on 5/17/68) replaced Krusen in 1993. Gossard and Ament were members of Mother Love Bone. All except Krusen recorded with **Temple Of The Dog**. Band acted in the movie *Singles* as Matt Dillon's band, Citizen Dick. Abruzzese left band in August 1994. Drummer Jack Irons (of the **Red Hot Chili Peppers**; born on 7/18/62) joined in late 1994. McCready also put together **Mad Season** in 1994. Matt Cameron (born on 11/28/62) replaced Irons in 1999.

1)Daughter 2)Who You Are 3)Better Man 4)Last Kiss 5)Given To Fly

DEBUT	PEAK	WKS	Track	Pop	Gld	Album	Label
1/25/92	18	8	1 Alive	107	▲[11]	Ten.	Epic/Associated 47857
5/16/92	21	6	2 Even Flow	108	↓		
8/15/92	5	11	3 Jeremy	79	↓		
12/26/92+	20	9	4 Black	—	↓		
8/7/93	8	10	5 Crazy Mary	—		Sweet Relief: A Benefit For Victoria Williams (various artists)	Thirsty Ear 57134
10/16/93	8	7	6 Go	—	▲[7]	Vs.	Epic/Associated 53136
10/30/93+	❶[1]	19	7 Daughter	97	↓		
2/26/94	17	9	8 Elderly Woman Behind The Counter In A Small Town	—	↓		
			also see #25 below				
7/9/94	26	3	9 Yellow Ledbetter	flip		(single only)	Epic 77935
11/19/94	11	3	10 Spin The Black Circle	58	▲[5]	Vitalogy	Epic 66900
11/19/94	16	4	11 Tremor Christ	18	↓		
12/3/94+	2[4]	26	12 Better Man	13[A]	↓		
12/10/94+	13	26	13 Corduroy	53[A]	↓		
4/8/95	38	3	14 Not For You	102	↓		
7/8/94	31	6	15 Immortality	102	↓		
12/9/95	3	20	16 I Got Id	7	●	(single only)	Epic 78199
3/9/96	31	4	17 Leaving Here	—		Home Alive - The Art Of Self Defense (various artists)	Epic 67486
			#76 Pop hit for Eddie Holland in 1964				
8/10/96	❶[1]	11	18 Who You Are	31	▲	No Code.	Epic 67500
10/5/96	9	16	19 Hail, Hail	69[A]	↓		
1/4/97	31	6	20 Off He Goes	—	↓		
1/3/98	3	25	21 Given To Fly	21	▲	Yield.	Epic 68164
2/28/98	6	26	22 Wishlist	47	↓		
8/1/98	13	11	23 In Hiding	—	↓		
10/10/98	33	4	24 Do The Evolution	—	↓		
11/28/98	26	10	25 Elderly Woman Behind The Counter In A Small Town . . . . . . [L-R]	—	●	Live On Two Legs	Epic 69752
			live version of #8 above				
5/1/99	2[3]	22	26 Last Kiss	2[1]		No Boundaries - A Benefit For The Kosovar Refugees (various artists)	Epic 63653
			#2 Pop hit for J. Frank Wilson and The Cavaliers in 1964				
4/29/00	10	9	27 Nothing As It Seems	49	●	Binaural	Epic 63665
7/8/00	26	7	28 Light Years	42[S]	↓		
10/5/02	6	8↑	29 I Am Mine	43		Riot Act.	Epic 86825

DEBUT	PEAK	WKS	Modern Rock Track	Pop	Gld	Album Title	Album Label & Number
			PENN, Michael				
			Born on 8/1/58 in New York City. Pop-rock singer/songwriter. Brother of actors Sean and Christopher Penn. Son of actor/director Leo Penn and actress Eileen Ryan. Married **Aimee Mann** on 12/29/97.				
11/18/89+	4	17	1 **No Myth**	13		March	RCA 9692
3/10/90	10	13	2 **This & That**	53		↓	
8/4/90	20	5	3 **Brave New World**	—		↓	
9/5/92	5	13	4 **Seen The Doctor**	—		Free-For-All	RCA 61113
12/19/92+	14	10	5 **Long Way Down (Look What The Cat Drug In)**	—		↓	
			PENNYWISE				
			Hard-rock group from Hermosa Beach, California: Jim Lindberg (vocals), Fletcher Dragge (guitar), Randy Bradbury (bass) and Byron McMackin (drums).				
7/31/99	36	4	1 **Alien**	—		Straight Ahead	Epitaph 86553
8/4/01	38	2	2 **F**k Authority**	—		Land Of The Free?	Epitaph 86600
			PERE UBU				
			Rock group from Cleveland: David Thomas (vocals), Jim Jones (guitar), Allen Ravenstine (keyboards), Scott Krause (percussion), Tony Maimone (bass) and Chris Cutler (drums).				
6/17/89	6	9	**Waiting For Mary**	—		Cloudland	Fontana 838237
			PERFECT CIRCLE, A				
			Rock duo from Hollywood: Maynard James Keenan (vocals) and Billy Howerdel (guitar). Keenan is also lead singer of **Tool**.				
4/29/00	5	26	1 **Judith**	105	▲	Mer De Noms	Virgin 49253
9/16/00	12	26	2 **3 Libras**	—		↓	
2/17/01	17	14	3 **The Hollow**	—		↓	
			PET SHOP BOYS				
			Pop duo formed in England: Neil Tennant (vocals) and Chris Lowe (keyboards).				
10/22/88	22	5	1 **Domino Dancing**	18	●	Introspective	EMI-Manhattan 90868
9/22/90	17	7	2 **So Hard**	62		Behavior	EMI 94310
8/21/93	10	9	3 **Can You Forgive Her?**	109	●	Very	EMI 89721
			PETTY, Tom				
			Born on 10/20/50 in Gainesville, Florida. Singer/songwriter/guitarist. Inducted into the Rock and Roll Hall of Fame in 2002. Also see **Classic Rock Tracks** section.				
5/13/89	29	2	**I Won't Back Down**	12	▲5	Full Moon Fever	MCA 6253
			George Harrison (guitar, backing vocal)				
			PHAIR, Liz				
			Born on 4/17/67 in New Haven, Connecticut. Rock singer/songwriter.				
9/17/94	6	19	1 **Supernova**	78	●	Whip-Smart	Matador 92429
1/28/95	24	7	2 **Whip-Smart**	—		↓	
			PHANTOM PLANET				
			Rock group from Los Angeles: Alex Greenwald (vocals), Jacques Brautbaur and Darren Robinson (guitars), Sam Farrar (bass) and Jason Schwartzman (drums). Farrar is the son of prolific songwriter John Farrar. Schwartzman is the son of actress Talia Shire; he starred in the movie *Rushmore*.				
3/30/02	35	5	**California**	—		The Guest	Daylight 62066
			PHILLIPS, Sam				
			Born Leslie Phillips on 1/28/62 in Glendale, California. Female singer/songwriter/actress. Married record producer T-Bone Burnett in 1989. Played "Katya" in the movie *Die Hard With A Vengeance*.				
4/22/89	22	1	**Holding on to the Earth**	—		The Indescribable Wow	Virgin 90919
			PHISH				
			Rock group from Burlington, Vermont: Trey Anastasio (guitar), Page McConnell (keyboards), Mike Gordon (bass) and Jon Fishman (drums). All share vocals.				
11/2/96	24	11	**Free**	—	●	Billy Breathes	Elektra 61971
			PHUNK JUNKEEZ				
			Punk-funk group from Arizona: Soulman and K-Tel Disco (vocals), Jeff O'Rourke (guitar), Jumbo Jim (bass) and Disko Danny Dynomite (drums).				
4/29/95	38	1	**I Love It Loud**	—		Injected	Trauma 92556
			PIL — see PUBLIC IMAGE LTD.				
	★84★		**PIXIES**				
			Pop-rock group formed in Boston: **Frank Black** (vocals), Joey Santiago (guitar), Kim Deal (bass) and David Lovering (drums). Deal was also a member of **The Breeders**.				
4/22/89	5	11	1 **Monkey Gone To Heaven**	—	●	Doolittle	Elektra 60856
6/24/89	3	14	2 **Here Comes Your Man**	—		↓	
8/11/90	4	9	3 **Velouria**	—		Bossanova	Elektra 60963
10/20/90	11	14	4 **Dig For Fire**	—		↓	
10/19/91	6	9	5 **Letter To Memphis**	—		Trompe Le Monde	Elektra 61118
1/4/92	6	6	6 **Head On**	—		↓	
			PLACEBO				
			Punk-pop trio from England: Brian Molko (vocals, guitar), Stefan Olsdal (bass) and Steve Hewitt (drums).				
10/31/98	19	19	**Pure Morning**	—		Without You I'm Nothing	Hut 46531

DEBUT	PEAK	WKS	Modern Rock Track	Pop Gld	Album Title	Album Label & Number

PLAN B
Techno-rock group from Berlin: Johnny Haeussler (vocals, guitar), Hans Hackenberger (guitar, vocals), Fritz (bass) and Andreas Perzborn (drums, samples).

| 9/4/93 | 28 | 4 | Life's A Beat .... — | | Cyber Chords And Sushi Stories .... Imago 21031 |

PM DAWN
Rap duo from Jersey City: brothers Attrell "Prince Be" and Jarrett Cordes.

| 9/16/95 | 39 | 3 | Downtown Venus .... 48 | | Jesus Wept .... Gee Street 524147 |
| | | | samples "Hush" by **Deep Purple** | | | |

★61★ **P.O.D.**
Hard-rock group from San Diego: Paul "Sonny" Sandoval (vocals), Marcos Curiel (guitar), Mark "Traa" Daniels (bass) and Noah "Wuv" Bernardo (drums). P.O.D.: Payable On Death.

3/18/00	28	8	1 Southtown .... — ▲		The Fundamental Elements Of
					Southtown .... Atlantic 83216
8/19/00	27	6	2 Rock The Party (Off The Hook) .... —		↓
12/16/00	38	3	3 School Of Hard Knocks .... —		Little Nicky (soundtrack) ...... Maverick 47856
9/8/01	2⁴	26	4 Alive	41 ▲³	Satellite .... Atlantic 83475
12/15/01+	❶²	26	5 Youth Of The Nation	28	↓
4/27/02	13	17	6 Boom 123		↓
8/31/02	21	7	7 Satellite .... —		↓

POE
Born Annie Danielewski in New York City. Female singer/songwriter.

12/16/95	27	9	1 Trigger Happy Jack .... 106 ●		Hello .... Modern 92605
7/20/96	7	17	2 Angry Johnny	60ᴬ	↓
11/30/96+	13	14	3 Hello 65ᴬ		↓
3/17/01	13	16	4 Hey Pretty .... —		Haunted .... FEI 83362

POGUES, The
Punk-folk group formed in London: Shane MacGowan (vocals), Philip Chevron (guitar), Terry Woods (mandolin), Spider Stacy (tin whistle), James Fearnley (accordion), Jem Finer (banjo), Darryl Hunt (bass) and Andrew Ranken (drums). Original bassist Cait O'Riordan married **Elvis Costello** on 5/16/86. MacGowan left band in mid-1991. Joe Strummer (formerly with **The Clash**) joined as lead singer from late 1991-93, then Stacy took over lead vocals.

2/18/89	17	7	1 Yeah Yeah Yeah Yeah Yeah .... —		Lost Angels (soundtrack) .... A&M 3926
1/5/91	23	5	2 The Sunny Side Of The Street .... —		Hell's Ditch .... Island 422846
11/6/93	11	12	3 Tuesday Morning .... —		Waiting For Herb .... Chameleon 61598

POP, Iggy
Born James Jewel Osterberg on 4/21/47 in Muskegon, Michigan. Punk-rock pioneer. Leader of The Stooges from 1969-74. Acted in the movies *Cry Baby*, *Hardware* and *The Crow: City Of Angels*. Adopted nickname "Iggy" from his first band, The Iguanas.

11/25/89	16	4	1 Livin' On The Edge Of The Night .... —		Black Rain (soundtrack) .... Virgin 91292
7/21/90	2¹	10	2 Home .... —		Brick By Brick .... Virgin 91381
9/22/90	5	17	3 Candy	28	↓
			Kate Pierson (of **The B-52's**; female vocal)			
10/9/93	25	3	4 Wild America .... —		American Caesar .... Virgin 39002

POPINJAYS, The
Pop-rock trio from London: Wendy Robinson (vocals), Polly Hancock (guitar) and Ben Kesteven (bass).

| 5/25/91 | 17 | 5 | Vote Elvis .... — | | Vote Elvis .... Alpha International 73021 |

POP WILL EAT ITSELF
Psychedelic-rap-rock group from Stourbridge, England: Clint Mansell and Graham Crabb (vocals), Adam Mole (guitar) and Richard March (bass).

| 9/24/88 | 30 | 1 | 1 Def Con One .... — | | Def Con One .... Chapter 22 12001 |
| 2/9/91 | 11 | 11 | 2 X Y & Zee .... — | | Cure For Sanity .... RCA 2485 |

PORNO FOR PYROS
Rock group formed by former **Jane's Addiction** members Perry Farrell (vocals) and Stephen Perkins (drums). Includes Peter DiStefano (guitar) and Martyn LeNoble (bass). LeNoble and Perkins also recorded with **Class Of '99**.

4/10/93	3	10	1 Cursed Female	— ●	Porno For Pyros .... Warner 45228
5/22/93	❶⁵	14	2 Pets	67	↓
5/25/96	8	19	3 Tahitian Moon	46ᴬ	Good God's Urge .... Warner 46126
2/22/97	23	7	4 Hard Charger .... — ▲		Private Parts (soundtrack) .... Warner 46477

PORTISHEAD
Duo from Bristol, England: multi-instrumentalist Geoff Barrow and vocalist Beth Gibbons. Duo named after a coastal shipping town near Bristol.

| 12/17/94+ | 5 | 17 | Sour Times (Nobody Loves Me) | 53 ● | Dummy .... London 828553 |

POSIES, The
Rock group from Seattle: Jon Auer and Ken Stringfellow (vocals, guitars), Rick Roberts (bass) and Mike Musburger (drums).

| 10/20/90 | 17 | 7 | 1 Golden Blunders .... — | | Dear 23 .... DGC 24305 |
| 5/22/93 | 4 | 14 | 2 Dream All Day .... — | | Frosting On The Beater .... DGC 24522 |

POSSUM DIXON
Rock group from Los Angeles: Rob Zabrecky (vocals, bass), Celso Chavez (guitar), Robert O'Sullivan (keyboards) and Richard Treuel (drums). Group named after a fugitive seen on TV's *America's Most Wanted*.

| 1/29/94 | 9 | 11 | Watch The Girl Destroy Me | 110 | Possum Dixon .... Interscope 92291 |

DEBUT	PEAK	WKS	Modern Rock Track	Pop Gld	Album Title	Album Label & Number

POWDERFINGER
Rock group from Brisbane, Australia: Bernard Fanning (vocals), Darren Middleton and Ian Haug (guitars), John Collins (bass) and Jon Coghill (drums).

| 3/10/01 | 23 | 10 | My Happiness | — | *Odyssey Number Five* | Republic 549092 |

POWERMAN 5000
Hard-rock group from Boston: Spider One (vocals), Adam 12 and M.33 (guitars), Dorian 27 (bass) and Al 3 (drums).

| 7/17/99 | 18 | 22 | 1 When Worlds Collide | — ▲ | *Tonight The Stars Revolt!* | DreamWorks 50107 |
| 12/18/99+ | 23 | 13 | 2 Nobody's Real | ↓ | | |

PRESIDENTS OF THE UNITED STATES OF AMERICA, The
Rock trio from Seattle: Chris Ballew (vocals), Dave Dederer (guitar) and Jason Finn (drums).

8/19/95	**❶**[1]	26	1 Lump	21[A] ▲[3]	*The Presidents Of The United States Of America*	Columbia 67291
11/25/95	13	10	2 Kitty	67[A] ↓		
2/3/96	8	12	3 Peaches	29 ↓		
11/9/96	11	11	4 Mach 5	68[A] ●	*II*	Columbia 67577

PRETENDERS, The
Rock group formed in England: **Chrissie Hynde** (vocals, guitar; born on 9/7/51 in Akron, Ohio), James Honeyman-Scott (guitar), Pete Farndon (bass) and Martin Chambers (drums). Honeyman-Scott died of a drug overdose on 6/16/82 (age 24); replaced by Robbie McIntosh. Farndon died of a drug overdose on 4/14/83 (age 30); replaced by Malcolm Foster. Hynde was married to Jim Kerr (of **Simple Minds**) from 1984-90. Lineup in 1994: Hynde, Chambers, Adam Seymour (guitar) and Andy Hobson (bass). Also see **Classic Rock Tracks** section.

11/12/88	21	2	1 1969	—	*(single only)*	Polydor 887816
5/19/90	4	11	2 Never Do That	—	*packed!*	Sire 26219
7/21/90	18	5	3 Hold A Candle To This	— ↓		
9/1/90	23	3	4 Sense Of Purpose	— ↓		
4/30/94	2[2]	13	5 Night In My Veins	71 ●	*Last Of The Independents*	Warner 45572
8/13/94	21	7	6 I'll Stand By You	16 ↓		

PRIMAL SCREAM
Rock-funk group from Glasgow, Scotland: Bobby Gillespie (vocals), Andrew Innes and Robert Young (guitars), Henry Raycock (bass) and Toby Toman (drums).

11/10/90	19	4	1 Loaded	—	*Come Together*	Sire 26384
12/22/90+	13	9	2 Come Together	— ↓		
10/12/91	2[1]	16	3 Movin' On Up	—	*Screamadelica*	Sire 26714
4/9/94	16	7	4 Rocks	107	*Give Out But Don't Give Up*	Sire 45538

PRIME STH
Rock group from Sweden: Noa (vocals), Martin (guitar), Jspr (bass) and Kaz (drums).

| 6/9/01 | 27 | 11 | I'm Stupid (Don't Worry 'Bout Me) | — | *Underneath The Surface* | Giant 24774 |

PRIMITIVE RADIO GODS
Group is actually solo artist Chris O'Connor.

| 6/8/96 | **❶**[6] | 21 | Standing Outside A Broken Phone Booth With Money In My Hand | 10[A] ● | *Rocket* | Ergo 67600 |

samples "How Blue Can You Get" by **B.B. King**

PRIMITIVES, The
Pop-rock group from Coventry, England: Tracy Tracey (vocals), Paul Court (guitar), Steve Dullaghan (bass) and Tig Williams (drums).

| 9/10/88 | 3 | 6 | 1 Crash | — | *Lovely* | RCA 8443 |

also see #5 below

11/19/88	8	10	2 Way Behind Me	— ↓		
9/23/89	9	10	3 Sick Of It	—	*Pure*	RCA 9934
12/2/89	12	9	4 Secrets	— ↓		
2/18/95	33	6	5 Crash - The '95 Mix [R]	— ●	*Dumb And Dumber (soundtrack)*	RCA 66523

remix of #1 above

PRIMUS
Rock trio from San Francisco: Les Claypool (vocals, bass), Larry LaLonde (guitar) and Tim Alexander (drums).

| 7/13/91 | 23 | 3 | 1 Jerry Was A Race Car Driver | — ● | *Sailing The Seas Of Cheese* | Interscope 91659 |
| 2/15/92 | 30 | 1 | 2 Making Plans For Nigel | — | *Miscellaneous Debris* | Interscope 96208 |

first recorded by **XTC** in 1980

| 5/1/93 | 9 | 10 | 3 My Name Is Mud | — ▲ | *Pork Soda* | Interscope 92257 |
| 6/10/95 | 12 | 12 | 4 Wynona's Big Brown Beaver | 62[A] ● | *Tales From The Punchbowl* | Interscope 92553 |

PRINCE
Born Prince Roger Nelson on 6/7/58 in Minneapolis. Influential R&B singer/songwriter/multi-instrumentalist.

| 7/1/89 | 18 | 7 | Batdance | **❶**[1] ▲[2] | *Batman (soundtrack)* | Warner 25936 |

PROCLAIMERS, The
Pop duo from Edinburgh, Scotland: identical twin brothers Craig and Charlie Reid (born on 3/5/62).

| 3/18/89 | 21 | 6 | 1 I'm Gonna Be (500 Miles) | — ● | *Sunshine On Leith* | Chrysalis 41668 |
| 6/12/93 | 8 | 15 | 2 I'm Gonna Be (500 Miles) [R] | 3 | *Benny & Joon (soundtrack)* | Milan 35644 |

above 2 are the same version

DEBUT	PEAK	WKS	Modern Rock Track	Pop	Gld	Album Title	Album Label & Number

PRODIGY
Techno-dance group from England: Maxim Reality and Keith Flint (vocals), Liam Howlett (instruments) and Leeroy Thronhill (dancer).

2/8/97	24	9	1 Firestarter	30	▲²	The Fat Of The Land	Maverick 46606

samples "SOS" by **The Breeders** and "Close (To The Edit)" by **Art Of Noise**

| 7/12/97 | 18 | 23 | 2 Breathe | — | | ↓ | |

★67★ PSYCHEDELIC FURS
Techno-rock group formed in England: brothers Richard (vocals) and Tim (bass) Butler, John Ashton (guitar), and Philip Calvert (drums). The Butler brothers formed **Love Spit Love** in 1994.

9/10/88	❶³	9	1 All That Money Wants	—		All Of This And Nothing	Columbia 44377
11/4/89	8	9	2 Should God Forget	—		Book Of Days	Columbia 45412
12/2/89+	❶³	13	3 House			↓	
7/20/91	❶²	13	4 Until She Comes	—		World Outside	Columbia 47303
10/19/91	13	6	5 Don't Be A Girl	—		↓	

★88★ PUBLIC IMAGE LTD.
Punk-rock group formed by lead singer Johnny "Rotten" Lydon (of the Sex Pistols). Featured an ever-changing lineup with Lydon the only constant.

| 4/22/89 | 16 | 5 | 1 Warrior | — | | Slaves Of New York (soundtrack) | Virgin 91229 |

PIL

6/3/89	❶¹	13	2 Disappointed	—		9	Virgin 91062
9/9/89	15	5	3 Happy	—		↓	
10/20/90	2²	14	4 Don't Ask Me	—		The Greatest Hits So Far	Virgin 91581
2/29/92	11	9	5 Covered	—		That What Is Not	Virgin 91815
5/9/92	29	2	6 Acid Drops	—		↓	

PIL (above 2)

★52★ PUDDLE OF MUDD
Hard-rock group formed in Los Angeles: Wes Scantlin (vocals, guitar), Paul Phillips (guitar), Doug Ardito (bass) and Greg Upchurch (drums).

7/7/01	3	29	1 Control	68	▲²	Come Clean	Flawless 493074
11/3/01+	❶⁹	34	2 Blurry	5		↓	
4/13/02	3	26	3 Drift & Die	61		↓	
8/17/02	2³	15↑	4 She Hates Me	24↑		↓	

PURE
Pop-rock group from Vancouver: Jordy Birch (vocals), Todd Simko (guitar), Mark Henning (keyboards), Dave Hadley (bass) and Leigh Grant (drums).

| 2/27/93 | 22 | 6 | Blast | — | | Pureafunalia | Reprise 45038 |

PURSUIT OF HAPPINESS, The
Rock group from Toronto: Moe Berg (vocals, guitar), Leslie Stanwyck (vocals), Kris Abbott (guitar), John Sinclair (bass) and Dave Gilby (drums).

| 11/19/88+ | 6 | 14 | I'm An Adult Now | — | | Love Junk | Chrysalis 41675 |

Q

QUARASHI
Rap-rock group from Iceland: Sölvi Blondal, Hössi Olafsson, Steini Fjelsted and Omar Swarez.

| 3/30/02 | 27 | 11 | Stick 'Em Up | — | | Jinx | Time Bomb 86179 |

QUAYE, Finley
Born on 3/25/74 in Edinburgh, Scotland. Male singer/songwriter.

| 2/7/98 | 26 | 11 | Sunday Shining | — | | Maverick A Strike | 550 Music 68506 |

QUEENS OF THE STONE AGE
Rock duo from Seattle: Josh Homme and Nick Oliveri.

| 9/2/00 | 36 | 6 | 1 The Lost Art Of Keeping A Secret | — | | Rated R | Interscope 490683 |
| 10/12/02 | 11↑ | 7↑ | 2 No One Knows | 115↑ | | Songs For The Deaf | Interscope 493425 |

R

RADFORD
Rock group from Los Angeles: Jonny Mead (vocals, guitar), Chris Hower (guitar), Bobby Stefano (bass) and Kane McGee (drums).

| 4/15/00 | 32 | 4 | Don't Stop | — | | Radford | RCA 67776 |

★51★ RADIOHEAD
Rock quintet from Oxford, England: Thom Yorke (vocals), brothers Jonny (guitar) and Colin (bass) Greenwood, Ed O'Brien (guitar) and Phil Selway (drums).

4/17/93	2¹	17	1 Creep	34	▲	Pablo Honey	Capitol 81409
10/16/93	23	3	2 Stop Whispering	—		↓	
5/6/95	11	11	3 Fake Plastic Trees	65^	▲	The Bends	Capitol 29626
11/4/95	37	3	4 Just	—		↓	
12/23/95+	18	13	5 High And Dry	78		↓	

DEBUT	PEAK	WKS	Modern Rock Track	Pop Gld	Album Title	Album Label & Number
			RADIOHEAD — Cont'd			
8/16/97	29	8	6 Let Down..	— ▲	*OK Computer*..........................	Capitol 55229
11/15/97+	14	26	7 Karma Police..	69[A]	↓	
10/7/00	10	18	8 Optimistic	— ▲	*Kid A*................................	Capitol 27753
5/19/01	27	8	9 I Might Be Wrong	— ●	*Amnesiac*.............................	Capitol 27642
★65★			**RAGE AGAINST THE MACHINE**			

Hard-rock group formed in Los Angeles: Zack DeLa Rocha (vocals), Tom Morello (guitar), Tim Commerford (bass) and Brad Wilk (drums). DeLa Rocha left in October 2000; the others recorded with **Chris Cornell** as **Audioslave**. Morello also recorded with **Class Of '99.**

DEBUT	PEAK	WKS	Modern Rock Track	Pop Gld	Album Title	Album Label & Number
4/20/96	11	16	1 Bulls On Parade	62[A] ▲3	*Evil Empire*	Epic 57523
12/20/97+	34	7	2 The Ghost Of Tom Joad	—	*(single only)*	Epic 3455
			first recorded by **Bruce Springsteen** in 1995			
6/27/98	33	10	3 No Shelter	— ▲	*Godzilla (soundtrack)*	Epic 69338
10/16/99+	6	26	4 Guerrilla Radio	69 ▲2	*The Battle Of Los Angeles*	Epic 69630
2/26/00	8	24	5 Sleep Now In The Fire	112	↓	
8/12/00	16	16	6 Testify	—	↓	
11/25/00	9	26	7 Renegades Of Funk	109 ▲	*Renegades*	Epic 85289
3/31/01	37	2	8 How I Could Just Kill A Man	—	↓	
			#77 Pop hit for **Cypress Hill** in 1992			
			RAILWAY CHILDREN, The			

Pop-rock group from Manchester, England: Gary Newby (vocals), Brian Bateman (guitar), Stephen Hull (bass) and Guy Keegan (drums).

DEBUT	PEAK	WKS	Modern Rock Track	Pop Gld	Album Title	Album Label & Number
7/21/90	❶1	10	Every Beat Of The Heart	—	*Native Place*........................	Virgin 91385
			RAINDOGS			

Rock group from Boston: Mark Cutler (vocals), Emerson Torrey (guitar), Johnny Cunningham (fiddle), Darren Hill (bass) and James Reilly (drums).

DEBUT	PEAK	WKS	Modern Rock Track	Pop Gld	Album Title	Album Label & Number
2/24/90	23	5	I'm Not Scared	—	*Lost Souls*	Atco 91297
			RAMONES			

Punk group formed in New York City. All members have taken Ramone as their last name. Lineup since 1989: Joey (Jeffrey Hyman; vocals), Johnny (John Cummings; guitar), Dee Dee (Douglas Colvin; bass) and Marky (Marc Bell; drums). Dee Dee left band in August 1989 and C.J. "Ramone" was added. Group appeared in the 1979 movie *Rock 'n' Roll High School*. Joey Ramone died of cancer on 4/15/2001 (age 49). Dee Dee Ramone died of a drug overdose on 6/5/2002 (age 49). Group inducted into the Rock and Roll Hall of Fame in 2002. Also see **Classic Rock Tracks** section.

DEBUT	PEAK	WKS	Modern Rock Track	Pop Gld	Album Title	Album Label & Number
5/13/89	4	10	1 Pet Sematary	—	*Brain Drain*	Sire 25905
9/5/92	6	12	2 Poison Heart	—	*Mondo Bizarro*	Radioactive 10615
7/15/95	30	6	3 I Don't Want To Grow Up..	—	*Adios Amigos*........................	Radioactive 11273
			first recorded by Tom Waits in 1992			
			RANCID			

Punk-rock group from Berkeley, California: Tim Armstrong (vocals, guitar), Lars Frederiksen (vocals, guitar), Matt Freeman (bass) and Brett Reed (drums).

DEBUT	PEAK	WKS	Modern Rock Track	Pop Gld	Album Title	Album Label & Number
9/17/94+	21	15	1 Salvation	— ●	*Let's Go*	Epitaph 86434
12/24/94+	27	8	2 Roots Radical	—	↓	
8/26/95	8	17	3 Time Bomb	48[A] ●	*...And Out Come The Wolves*	Epitaph 86444
12/16/95+	13	15	4 Ruby Soho	63[A]	↓	
			RANKING ROGER			

Born Roger Charley on 2/21/61 in Birmingham, England. Lead vocalist of English Beat and **General Public**.

DEBUT	PEAK	WKS	Modern Rock Track	Pop Gld	Album Title	Album Label & Number
9/10/88	23	1	So Excited	—	*Radical Departure*	I.R.S. 42197
			RATCAT			

Rock trio from Sydney, Australia: Simon Day (vocals, guitar), Amr Zaid (bass) and Andrew Polin (drums).

DEBUT	PEAK	WKS	Modern Rock Track	Pop Gld	Album Title	Album Label & Number
10/26/91	27	3	That Ain't Bad..	—	*Tingles*.............................	Roo-Art 868573
			RAVE-UPS, The			

Rock group formed in Los Angeles: Jimmer Podrasky (vocals, guitar), Terry Wilson (guitar), Tom Blatnik (bass) and Tim Jimenez (drums). Group appeared in the 1986 movie *Pretty In Pink*.

DEBUT	PEAK	WKS	Modern Rock Track	Pop Gld	Album Title	Album Label & Number
2/3/90	12	11	Respectfully King Of Rain	—	*Chance*..............................	Epic 45255
			REACHAROUND			

Rock group from Los Angeles: Matt Caisley (vocals), Ted Hutt (guitar), Jeff Peters (bass) and Scott Capizzano (drums).

DEBUT	PEAK	WKS	Modern Rock Track	Pop Gld	Album Title	Album Label & Number
8/3/96	28	9	Big Chair	—	*Who's Tommy Cooper?*..............	Trauma 90067
			REAL LIFE			

Rock group from Melbourne, Australia: David Sterry (vocals, guitar), Steve Williams (keyboards), Allan Johnson (bass) and Danny Simcic (drums).

DEBUT	PEAK	WKS	Modern Rock Track	Pop Gld	Album Title	Album Label & Number
7/21/90	15	9	God Tonight...	—	*Lifetime*	Curb 77271
			REAL PEOPLE, The			

Pop group from Liverpool, England: brothers Tony (bass, vocals) and Chris (guitar, vocals) Griffiths, Sean Simpson (guitar), and Tony Elson (drums).

DEBUT	PEAK	WKS	Modern Rock Track	Pop Gld	Album Title	Album Label & Number
2/1/92	11	8	Window Pane...	—	*The Real People*	Relativity 1080
			REDD KROSS			

Pop-rock trio from Los Angeles: brothers Jeff (vocals, guitar) and Steve (bass) McDonald, with Robert Hecker (guitar).

DEBUT	PEAK	WKS	Modern Rock Track	Pop Gld	Album Title	Album Label & Number
11/10/90	16	6	Annie's Gone	—	*Third Eye*	Atlantic 82148

DEBUT	PEAK	WKS	Modern Rock Track	Pop	Gld	Album Title	Album Label & Number

RED HOT CHILI PEPPERS ★3★

Rock group formed in Los Angeles: Anthony Kiedis (vocals; born on 11/1/62), Hillel Slovak (guitar; born on 4/13/62; died of a drug overdose on 6/27/88, age 26), Michael "Flea" Balzary (bass; born on 10/16/62) and Jack Irons (drums; born on 7/18/62). John Frusciante (born on 3/5/70) replaced Slovak. Irons left in 1988 and later joined **Eleven**, then **Pearl Jam**; replaced by Chad Smith (born on 10/25/62). Frusciante left in May 1992; replaced by Zander Schloss (**Thelonious Monster**, **The Magnificent Bastards**), then by Arik Marshall, then by Jesse Tobias and finally by **Dave Navarro** in September 1993. Frusciante returned in 1998, replacing Navarro. Kiedis appeared in the movie *Point Break*. Flea and Kiedis appeared in the movie *The Chase*.

1)Scar Tissue 2)By The Way 3)Otherside 4)Soul To Squeeze 5)My Friends

DEBUT	PEAK	WKS	Modern Rock Track	Pop	Gld	Album Title	Album Label & Number
9/2/89	6	10	1 Knock Me Down	—	●	Mother's Milk	EMI 92152
10/28/89	11	14	2 Higher Ground	—	↓		
			#4 Pop hit for Stevie Wonder in 1973				
4/7/90	10	8	3 Show Me Your Soul	—	▲3	Pretty Woman (soundtrack)	EMI 93492
9/21/91	❶2	17	4 Give It Away	73	▲7	Blood Sugar Sex Magik	Warner 26681
12/14/91+	15	9	5 Suck My Kiss	—	↓		
2/15/92	6	17	6 Under The Bridge	21			
8/8/92	19	9	7 Breaking The Girl	—	↓		
11/21/92	7	10	8 Behind The Sun	124		What Hits!?	EMI 94762
8/7/93	❶5	13	9 Soul To Squeeze	22		Coneheads (soundtrack)	Warner 45345
9/2/95	7	9	10 Warped	41^A	▲2	One Hot Minute	Warner 45733
9/30/95	❶4	23	11 My Friends	27^A		↓	
1/27/96	8	17	12 Aeroplane	49^A		↓	
11/16/96	14	14	13 Love Rollercoaster	40^A	●	Beavis & Butt-Head Do America (soundtrack)	Geffen 25002
			#1 Pop hit for the Ohio Players in 1976				
6/5/99	❶16	26	14 Scar Tissue	9	▲4	Californication	Warner 47386
9/25/99	7	23	15 Around The World	108		↓	
1/1/00	❶13	27	16 Otherside	14		↓	
6/17/00	❶1	26	17 Californication	69		↓	
3/24/01	37	2	18 Parallel Universe	—		↓	
6/15/02	❶14	24↑	19 By The Way	34	▲	By The Way	Warner 48140
8/24/02	6↑	14↑	20 The Zephyr Song	49↑		↓	

REED, Lou

Born on 3/2/42 in Freeport, Long Island, New York. Lead singer/songwriter of the New York seminal rock band Velvet Underground. Regarded as the father of punk rock. Appeared in the 1980 movie *One Trick Pony*. Also see **Classic Rock Tracks** section.

DEBUT	PEAK	WKS	Modern Rock Track	Pop	Gld	Album Title	Album Label & Number
1/21/89	❶4	13	1 Dirty Blvd.	—	●	New York	Sire 25829
4/29/89	11	5	2 Busload Of Faith	—	↓		
5/12/90	13	7	3 Nobody But You	—		Songs For Drella	Sire 26140
			LOU REED/JOHN CALE				
1/18/92	❶3	10	4 What's Good	—		Magic And Loss	Sire 26662

REEL BIG FISH

Ska-punk group from Huntington Beach, California: Aaron Barrett (vocals, guitar), Scott Klopfenstein (vocals, trumpet), Tavis Werts (trumpet), Grant Barry and Dan Regan (trombones), Matt Wong (bass) and Andrew Gonzales (drums).

DEBUT	PEAK	WKS	Modern Rock Track	Pop	Gld	Album Title	Album Label & Number
5/24/97	10	26	Sell Out	69^A	●	Turn The Radio Off	Mojo 53013

REFRESHMENTS, The

Rock group from Tempe, Arizona: Roger Clyne (vocals, guitar), Brian Blush (guitar), Buddy Edwards (bass) and P.H. Naffah (drums).

DEBUT	PEAK	WKS	Modern Rock Track	Pop	Gld	Album Title	Album Label & Number
4/27/96	14	21	1 Banditos	71^A		Fizzy Fuzzy Big & Buzzy	Mercury 528999
			title is Spanish for "Bandits"				
9/28/96	38	1	2 Down Together			↓	

REHAB

Hip-hop duo from Atlanta: Brooks and Danny Boone.

DEBUT	PEAK	WKS	Modern Rock Track	Pop	Gld	Album Title	Album Label & Number
4/14/01	20	13	It Don't Matter	—		Southern Discomfort	Epic 63648

R.E.M. ★2★

Rock group formed in Athens, Georgia: **Michael Stipe** (vocals; born on 1/4/60), Peter Buck (guitar; born on 12/6/56), Mike Mills (bass; born on 12/17/58) and Bill Berry (drums; born on 7/31/58). Developed huge following with college audiences in the early 1980s as one of the first "alternative rock" bands. Buck, Mills and Berry also recorded with **Warren Zevon** as the **Hindu Love Gods**. Berry retired from the group in 1997.

1)Losing My Religion 2)Orange Crush 3)What's The Frequency, Kenneth? 4)Drive 5)Bang And Blame

DEBUT	PEAK	WKS	Modern Rock Track	Pop	Gld	Album Title	Album Label & Number
11/19/88	❶8	12	1 Orange Crush	—	▲2	Green	Warner 25795
12/3/88	16	8	2 Pop Song 89	86	↓		
12/10/88+	❶2	17	3 Stand	6	↓		
			became the theme for TV's Get A Life starring Chris Elliott				
3/18/89	10	8	4 Turn You Inside-Out	—	↓		

DEBUT	PEAK	WKS	Modern Rock Track	Pop	Gld	Album Title	Album Label & Number
			R.E.M. — Cont'd				
3/9/91	❶⁸	11	5 Losing My Religion	4	▲⁴	Out Of Time . . . . Warner 26496
5/18/91	4	8	6 Texarkana	—		↓
6/29/91	3	12	7 Shiny Happy People	10		↓
			Kate Pierson of The B-52's (backing vocal)				
1/18/92	11	4	8 First We Take Manhattan	—		I'm Your Fan: The Songs Of Leonard Cohen (various artists) . . . . Atlantic 82349
			first recorded by Jennifer Warnes in 1987				
10/3/92	❶⁵	11	9 Drive	28	▲⁴	Automatic For The People . . . . Warner 45138
11/21/92	5	9	10 Ignoreland	—		↓
1/16/93	2¹	11	11 Man On The Moon	30		↓
			tribute to Andy Kaufman				
5/1/93	24	3	12 The Sidewinder Sleeps Tonite	—		↓
10/16/93	21	2	13 Everybody Hurts	29		↓
11/13/93	9	14	14 Photograph	—		Born To Choose (various artists) . . . . . Rykodisc 10256
			R.E.M. with Natalie Merchant				
9/24/94	❶⁵	19	15 What's The Frequency, Kenneth?	21	▲⁴	Monster . . . . Warner 45740
11/26/94	❶³	15	16 Bang And Blame	19		↓
2/18/95	8	10	17 Star 69	74ᴬ		↓
4/29/95	14	11	18 Strange Currencies	47		↓
8/12/95	33	5	19 Crush With Eyeliner	113		↓
8/31/96	2¹	9	20 E-Bow The Letter	49	▲	New Adventures In Hi-Fi . . . . Warner 46320
			Patti Smith (female vocal)				
10/12/96	6	16	21 Bittersweet Me	46		↓
10/17/98	18	10	22 Daysleeper	57	●	Up . . . . Warner 47112
2/6/99	31	6	23 Lotus	—		↓
11/20/99+	11	17	24 The Great Beyond	57		Man On The Moon (soundtrack) . . . . . . Warner 47483
4/28/01	22	9	25 Imitation Of Life	83	●	Reveal . . . . Warner 47946
			REMBRANDTS, The				
			Pop-rock duo from Los Angeles: Danny Wilde and Phil Solem. Both were members of Great Buildings.				
10/10/92	17	6	1 Johnny Have You Seen Her?	54		Untitled . . . . Atco 92200
6/10/95	23	5	2 I'll Be There For You	17	▲	Friends (soundtrack) . . . . Reprise 46008
			REMY ZERO				
			Rock group from Alabama: brothers Cinjun (vocals) and Shelby (guitar) Tate, Jeff Cain (guitar), Cedric LeMoyne (bass) and Greg Slay (drums).				
11/28/98+	27	12	1 Prophecy	—		Villa Elaine . . . . DGC 25300
10/20/01	27	12	2 Save Me	—		The Golden Hum . . . . Elektra 62678
			RENEGADE SOUNDWAVE				
			Techno-dance trio from England: Karl Bonnie (vocals), Gary Asqwith and Danny Briochett.				
2/17/90	11	8	Biting My Nails	—		Soundclash . . . . Enigma/Mute 75422
			RENTALS, The				
			Pop-rock group from Los Angeles: Matt Sharp (vocals, bass), Cherielynn Westrich (vocals), Petra Haden (violin), Rod Cervera (guitar), Tom Gaimley (synthesizer) and Pat Wilson (drums). Sharp and Wilson are also members of Weezer.				
10/21/95	7	12	Friends Of P.	82		Return Of The Rentals . . . . Maverick 46093
	★63★		**REPLACEMENTS, The**				
			Rock group from Minneapolis: Paul Westerberg (vocals, guitar, piano), Slim Dunlap (guitar), Tommy Stinson (bass) and Chris Mars (drums). Steve Foley replaced Mars in early 1990.				
11/26/88+	11	8	1 Cruella De Ville	—		Stay Awake: Various Interpretations Of Music from Vintage Disney Films (various artists) . . . A&M 3918
			written for the animated Disney movie 101 Dalmations				
2/4/89	❶¹	14	2 I'll Be You	51		Don't Tell A Soul . . . . Sire 25831
6/10/89	28	1	3 Back To Back	—		↓
8/19/89	22	4	4 Achin' To Be	—		↓
9/29/90	❶⁴	10	5 Merry Go Round	—		All Shook Down . . . . Sire 26298
12/15/90+	15	7	6 Someone Take The Wheel	—		↓
1/26/91	4	10	7 When It Began	—		↓
			REPUBLICA				
			Rock group from London: Saffron (female vocals), Johnny Male (guitar), Tim Dorney and Andy Todd (keyboards) and Dave Barbarossa (drums).				
7/27/96	7	21	1 Ready To Go	56		Republica . . . . Deconstruction 66899
2/1/97	39	1	2 Drop Dead Gorgeous	93		↓
			REVENGE				
			Rock trio from Manchester, England: Peter Hook (vocals, bass; New Order), Dave Hicks (guitar) and Chris Jones (keyboards).				
6/2/90	8	11	Pineapple Face	—		One True Passion . . . . Capitol 94053
			REVEREND HORTON HEAT				
			Rock trio from Corpus Christi, Texas: Jim "Reverend" Horton Heath (vocals, guitar), Jimbo Wallace (bass) and Scott Churilla (drums).				
10/8/94	40	1	One Time For Me	—		Liquor In The Front . . . . Sub Pop 92364
			RIDDLIN' KIDS				
			Punk-rock group from Austin, Texas: Clint Baker (vocals, guitar), Dustin Stroud (guitar), Mark Johnson (bass) and Dave Keel (drums).				
6/29/02	35	6	I Feel Fine	—		Hurry Up And Wait . . . . Aware 85118

DEBUT	PEAK	WKS	Modern Rock Track	Pop Gld	Album Title	Album Label & Number

RIDE
Rock group from England: Mark Gardener (vocals), Andrew Bell (guitar), Steve Queralt (bass) and Loz Colbert (drums).

2/9/91	24	5	1 Taste	—	Nowhere	Sire 26462
3/14/92	20	7	2 Leave Them All Behind	—	Going Blank Again	Sire 26836
5/16/92	12	8	3 Twisterella	—	↓	

RIDGWAY, Stan
Born in 1954 in Los Angeles. Lead singer of **Wall Of Voodoo** from 1977-83.

5/13/89	8	9	1 Goin' Southbound	—	Mosquitos	Geffen 24216
8/12/89	13	3	2 Calling Out To Carol	—	↓	
6/22/91	13	6	3 I Wanna Be A Boss	—	Partyball	Geffen 24385

RIGHT SAID FRED
Pop trio from England: brothers Richard (vocals) and Fred (guitar) Fairbrass, with Rob Manzoli (guitar).

1/11/92	28	2	I'm Too Sexy	❶³ ●	Up	Charisma 92107

RIVERSIDE
Pop-rock group from Philadelphia: brothers Keith (vocals, guitar) and Glenn (bass, vocals) Kochan, Ken Dai (guitar) and John Liney (drums).

10/31/92	26	6	Waterfall	—	One	Sire 45012

ROBERTSON, Robbie
Born Jaime Robbie Robertson on 7/5/44 in Toronto. Rock singer/songwriter/guitarist. Member of The Band.

10/19/91	28	5	What About Now	—	Storyville	Geffen 24303

ROLLING STONES, The
Rock group formed in London: **Mick Jagger** (vocals), **Keith Richards** and **Ronnie Wood** (guitars), Bill Wyman (bass) and Charlie Watts (drums). Won Grammy's Lifetime Achievement Award in 1986. Inducted into the Rock and Roll Hall of Fame in 1989. Considered by many to be the world's all-time greatest rock and roll band. Also see **Classic Rock Tracks** section.

9/16/89	22	5	1 Mixed Emotions	5 ▲²	Steel Wheels	Rolling Stones 45333
3/23/91	28	1	2 Highwire	57 ●	Flashpoint	Rolling Stones 47456

ROLLINS BAND
Born Henry Garfield on 2/13/61 in Washington DC. Hard-rock singer/poet/actor. Acted in several movies. His band: Chris Haskett (guitar), Melvin Gibbs (bass) and Sim Cain (drums).

3/28/92	25	4	1 Low Self Opinion	—	The End Of Silence	Imago 21006
5/7/94	26	4	2 Liar	109	Weight	Imago 21034

ROSSDALE, Gavin
Born on 10/30/67 in London. Lead singer of **Bush**. Married **Gwen Stefani** (of **No Doubt**) on 9/14/2002.

8/24/02	20	7	Adrenaline	— ●	XXX (soundtrack)	Universal 156259

ROTHBERG, Patti
Born in 1973 in Scarsdale, New York. Female singer/songwriter/guitarist.

5/25/96	25	16	Inside	71ᴬ	Between The 1 And The 9	EMI 36834

ROYAL CRESCENT MOB
Pop-rock group from Columbus, Ohio: David Ellison (vocals), B (guitar), Harold Chichester (bass) and Carlton Smith (drums).

6/17/89	27	3	Hungry	—	Spin The World	Sire 25914

RUBY
Pop-rock duo: vocalist Lesley Rankine (from England) and producer Mark Walk (from Seattle).

2/10/96	22	10	Tiny Meat	—	Salt Peter	Creation 67458

RUSTY
Rock group from Canada: Ken MacNeil (vocals), Scott McCullough (guitar), Jim Moore (bass) and Mitch Perkins (drums).

8/5/95	26	6	Wake Me	—	Fluke	Tag 92573

RUTH RUTH
Punk-rock trio from New York City: Chris Kennedy (vocals, bass), Mike Lustig (guitar) and Dave Snyder (drums).

10/21/95	24	8	Uninvited	—	Laughing Gallery	Ventrue 43039

S

SAINT ETIENNE
Pop trio from London: Moira Lambert (vocals), Bob Stanley and Peter Wiggs.

1/18/92	11	9	Only Love Can Break Your Heart	97	Foxbase Alpha	Warner 26793

#33 Pop hit for **Neil Young** in 1970

SAINTS, The
Punk-rock trio from Brisbane, Australia: Chris Bailey (vocals, guitar), Kym Bradshaw (bass) and Ivor Hay (drums).

1/7/89	11	7	1 Grain Of Sand	—	Prodigal Son	TVT 2121
2/4/89	19	5	2 Music Goes Round My Head	—	↓	

SALIVA
Hard-rock group from Memphis: **Josey Scott** (vocals), Wayne Swinny (guitar), Dave Vovotny (bass) and Paul Crosby (drums). Also see **Chad Kroeger**.

3/17/01	7	26	1 Your Disease	116 ●	Every Six Seconds	Island 542959
9/1/01	25	20	2 Click Click Boom	—	↓	
10/5/02	7↑	8↑	3 Always	109↑	Back Into Your System	Island 063153

DEBUT	PEAK	WKS	Modern Rock Track	Pop	Gld	Album Title	Album Label & Number

SALT
Rock trio from Stockholm, Sweden: Nina Ramsby (vocals, guitar), Daniel Ewerman (bass) and Jim Tegman (drums).

| 2/3/96 | 21 | 10 | Bluster .... | — | | Auscultate .... | Island 524198 |

SANDLER, Adam
Born on 9/9/66 in Brooklyn, New York. Actor/comedian. Cast member of TV's *Saturday Night Live* (1990-95). Starred in several movies.

1/6/96	29	1	1 The Chanukah Song	[X-C]	10[A] ▲2	*What The Hell Happened To Me?*	Warner 46151
1/3/98	25	2	2 The Chanukah Song	[X-C-R]	25[A]	↓	
1/2/99	34	2	3 The Chanukah Song	[X-C-R]	80	↓	

SANTANA
Latin-rock group formed in San Francisco by Carlos Santana (born on 7/20/47 in Autlan de Navarro, Mexico). Also see **Classic Rock Tracks** section.

10/2/99	17	21	1 Put Your Lights On	118	▲14	*Supernatural*	Arista 19080
			SANTANA Featuring Everlast				
11/13/99	24	12	2 Smooth	❶12		↓	
			SANTANA Featuring Rob Thomas				

SAVE FERRIS
Ska-rock group from California: Monique Powell (vocals), Brian Mashburn (vocals, guitar), Eric Zamora, T-Bone Willy and Jose Castellanos (horns), Bill Uechi (bass) and Marc Harismendy (drums).

10/4/97	26	7	1 Come On Eileen	104		*It Means Everything*	Starpool 68183
			#1 Pop hit for **Dexys Midnight Runners** in 1983				
1/24/98	32	8	2 Goodbye	—		↓	

SCAPEGOAT WAX
Born Martin James in New York City. Singer/songwriter.

| 7/14/01 | 38 | 3 | Aisle 10 .... | — | | *Okeeblow* .... | Grand Royal 10130 |

SCHOOL OF FISH
Pop-rock group from Los Angeles: Josh Clayton-Felt (vocals, guitar), Michael Ward (guitar, vocals), Dominic Nardini (bass) and M.P. (drums). Clayton-Felt died of cancer on 1/19/2000 (age 32).

| 4/6/91 | 6 | 8 | 1 3 Strange Days | — | | *School Of Fish* .... | Capitol 94557 |
| 2/13/93 | 5 | 11 | 2 Take Me Anywhere | — | | *Human Cannonball* .... | Capitol 98930 |

SCOTT, Josey — see KROEGER, Chad

SCREAMING TREES
Hard-rock group from Ellensburg, Washington: brothers Van (bass) and Gary Lee (guitar) Conner, with Mark Lanegan (vocals) and Barrett Martin (drums; **Mad Season**).

2/23/91	23	7	1 Bed Of Roses	—		*Uncle Anesthesia*	Epic 46800
9/5/92	5	19	2 Nearly Lost You	—		*Sweet Oblivion*	Epic 48996
1/9/93	28	2	3 Dollar Bill	—		↓	
6/29/96	9	13	4 All I Know	62[A]		*Dust*	Epic 64178

SCREAMING TRIBESMEN, The
Pop-rock group from Brisbane, Australia: Mick Medew (vocals, guitar), Chris "Klondike" Masuak (guitar), Bob Wackley (bass) and Warwick Fraser (drums).

| 9/17/88 | 7 | 12 | I've Got A Feeling | — | | *Bones & Flowers* .... | Rykodisc 10077 |

SCRUFFY THE CAT
Rock group from Boston: Charlie Chesterman (vocals), Stephen Fredette (guitar), Burns Stanfield (keyboards), Mac Stanfield (bass) and Randall Gibson (drums).

| 12/10/88+ | 23 | 6 | Moons Of Jupiter .... | — | | *Moons Of Jupiter* .... | Relativity 8237 |

SEAL
Born Sealhenry Samuel on 2/19/63 in Paddington, England (Nigerian/Brazilian parents). Male singer.

6/15/91	5	13	1 Crazy	7	▲	*Seal*	Sire 26627
6/11/94	3	17	2 Prayer For The Dying	21	▲4	*Seal*	ZTT 45415
8/12/95	35	2	3 Kiss From A Rose	❶1	▲2	*Batman Forever (soundtrack)*	Atlantic 82759

SEAWEED
Rock group from Tacoma, Washington: Aaron Stauffer (vocals), Wade Neal and Clint Werner (guitars), John Atkins (bass) and Bob Bulgrien (drums).

| 10/14/95 | 38 | 1 | Start With .... | — | | *Spanaway* .... | Hollywood 62009 |

SEBADOH
Rock trio from Boston: Lou Barlow (vocals, guitar), Jason Lowenstein (bass) and Bob Fay (drums).

| 9/7/96 | 23 | 8 | Ocean .... | — | | *Harmacy* .... | Sub Pop 370 |

SEERS, The
Rock group from New York City: Spider McCallum (vocals), Leigh Wildman (guitar), Kat Day (harmonica), Jason Kidd (bass) and Age Blackmore (drums).

| 5/4/91 | 16 | 7 | Psych Out .... | — | | *Psych Out* .... | Cherry Red 1043 |

SEETHER
Hard-rock trio from South Africa: Shaun Morgan (vocals, guitar), Dale Stewart (bass) and Nick Oshiro (drums).

| 8/10/02 | 12↑ | 16↑ | Fine Again .... | 116↑ | | *Disclaimer* .... | Wind-Up 13068 |

DEBUT	PEAK	WKS	Modern Rock Track	Pop	Gld	Album Title	Album Label & Number
			SEMISONIC				
			Rock trio from Minneapolis: Dan Wilson (vocals, guitar), John Munson (bass) and Jacob Slichter (drums).				
3/14/98	❶⁵	26	√ 1 **Closing Time**	11ᴬ	▲	*Feeling Strangely Fine*	MCA 11733
9/5/98	11	13	2 **Singing In My Sleep**	—		↓	
2/6/99	21	8	3 **Secret Smile**	—		↓	
2/10/01	39	1	4 **Chemistry**	—		*All About Chemistry*	MCA 112355
			SETZER, Brian				
			Born on 4/10/60 in Long Island, New York. Lead singer/guitarist of the **Stray Cats**. Played Eddie Cochran in the 1987 movie *La Bamba*. Formed own 16-piece swing orchestra in 1994.				
7/25/98	15	16	**Jump Jive An' Wail**	23ᴬ	▲²	*The Dirty Boogie*	Interscope 90183
			THE BRIAN SETZER ORCHESTRA				
			first recorded by Louis Prima in 1956				
			SEVENDUST				
			Rock group from Atlanta: **Lajon** Witherspoon (vocals), Clint Lowery and John Connelly (guitars), Vinnie Hornsby (bass) and Morgan Rose (drums).				
9/25/99	26	14	1 **Denial**	—	●	*Home*	TVT 5820
4/15/00	33	3	2 **Waffle**	—		↓	
10/27/01	23	16	3 **Praise**	—	●	*Animosity*	TVT 5870
3/30/02	36	6	4 **Live Again**	—		↓	
			SEVEN MARY THREE				
			Rock group from Virginia: Jason Ross (vocals), Jason Pollock (guitar), Casey Daniel (bass) and Giti Khalsa (drums).				
10/28/95+	7	26	1 **Cumbersome**	39	▲	*American Standard*	Mammoth 92633
6/1/96	37	3	2 **Water's Edge**	—		↓	
9/27/97	19	18	3 **Lucky**	—		*Rock Crown*	Mammoth 83018
7/18/98	16	12	4 **Over Your Shoulder**	—		*Orange Ave.*	Mammoth 83114
5/12/01	21	10	5 **Wait**	—		*The Economy Of Sound*	Mammoth 65516
			SHAGGY				
			Born Orville Richard Burrell on 10/22/68 in Kingston, Jamaica. Reggae singer.				
8/14/93	14	6	**Oh Carolina**	59		*Pure Pleasure*	Virgin 87953
			samples "Peter Gunn" by Henry Mancini				
			SHAKESPEAR'S SISTER				
			Female vocal duo: Siobhan Fahey and Marcella Detroit. Fahey was a member of **Bananarama**. Married David A. Stewart (of **Eurythmics**). Detroit was born Marcy Levy in Detroit.				
2/22/92	22	3	1 **Goodbye Cruel World**	—	●	*Hormonally Yours*	London 828266
8/22/92	25	2	2 **Stay**	4		↓	
			SHAMEN, The				
			Techno-rave dance group from Aberdeen, Scotland: brothers Derek and Keith McKenzie, Richard West, Colin Angus, Will Sinnott and Peter Stephenson. Sinnott drowned on 5/23/90 (age 31).				
10/19/91	4	14	**Move Any Mountain (Progen 91)**	38		*En-Tact.*	Epic 48722
			SHELLEYAN ORPHAN				
			Pop duo from Bournemouth, England: Jemaur Tayle (vocals, guitar) and Caroline Crawley (vocals, clarinet).				
9/30/89	23	4	**Shatter**	—		*Century Flower*	Columbia 45198
			SHOCKED, Michelle				
			Born Michelle Johnston on 2/24/62 in Dallas. Folk singer/songwriter.				
9/17/88	16	4	1 **Anchorage**	66		*Short Sharp Shocked*	Mercury 834294
10/22/88	20	6	2 **If Love Was A Train**	—		↓	
12/23/89+	19	7	3 **On The Greener Side**	—		*Captain Swing*	Mercury 838878
			SHOOTYZ GROOVE				
			Rock group from New York City: Sense Live and Season Love (vocals), Donny (guitar), Paul Freaky (bass) and Dose Big (drums).				
7/31/99	40	1	**L Train**	—		*High Definition*	Kinetic 47359
			SHOWOFF				
			Rock group from Chicago: brothers Chris (vocals) and Dave (bass) Envy, Graham Jordan (guitar) and Dan Castady (drums).				
8/14/99	36	4	**Falling Star**	—		*Showoff*	Maverick 47380
			SHRIEKBACK				
			Pop-rock trio formed in London: Barry Andrews (vocals, bass), Mike Cozzi (guitar) and Martyn Barker (drums).				
9/10/88	6	5	1 **Intoxication**	—		*Go Bang!*	Island 90949
9/17/88	19	2	2 **Shark Walk**	—		↓	
			SIDEWINDERS				
			Rock group from Arizona: Dave Slutes (vocals, guitar), Rich Hopkins (guitar), Mark Perrodin (bass) and Andrea Curtis (drums). Bruce Halper replaced Curtis in early 1990.				
4/15/89	18	6	1 **Witchdoctor**	—		*Witchdoctor*	Mammoth 9663
6/2/90	23	6	2 **We Don't Do That Anymore**	—		*Auntie Ramos' Pool Hall*	Mammoth 2068
			SILENCERS, The				
			Pop-rock group from Scotland: Jimme O'Neill (vocals, guitar), Cha Burns (guitar), Joe Donnelly (bass) and Martin Hanlin (drums).				
1/27/90	14	8	**Razor Blades Of Love**	—		*A Blues For Buddha*	RCA 9960

DEBUT	PEAK	WKS	Modern Rock Track	Pop Gld	Album Title	Album Label & Number
	★78★		**SILVERCHAIR**			
			Rock trio from Newcastle, Australia: Daniel Johns (vocals, guitar), Chris Joannou (bass) and Ben Gillies (drums).			
6/24/95	❶³	26	1 Tomorrow	28ᴬ ▲²	*Frogstomp*	Epic 67247
11/11/95	17	12	2 Pure Massacre	72ᴬ	↓	
1/25/97	4	16	3 Abuse Me	44ᴬ ●	*Freak Show*	Epic 67905
4/26/97	29	7	4 Freak	—	↓	
3/13/99	12	13	5 Anthem For The Year 2000	— ●	*Neon Ballroom*	Epic 69816
7/3/99	12	13	6 Ana's Song (Open Fire)	—	↓	
			SIMON, Paul			
			Born on 10/13/41 in Newark, New Jersey; raised in Queens, New York. Singer/songwriter/guitarist. One-half of Simon & Garfunkel duo. Married to actress/author Carrie Fisher from 1983-85. Married **Edie Brickell** on 5/30/92. Inducted into the Rock and Roll Hall of Fame in 2001. Also see **Classic Rock Tracks** section.			
11/10/90	24	7	The Obvious Child	92 ▲²	*The Rhythm Of The Saints*	Warner 26098
	★93★		**SIMPLE MINDS**			
			Pop-rock group formed in Glasgow, Scotland: Jim Kerr (vocals), Charles Burchill (guitar), Michael MacNeil (keyboards), John Giblin (bass) and Mel Gaynor (drums). MacNeila and Giblin left in 1989. Kerr was briefly married to **Chrissie Hynde** (of **The Pretenders**).			
4/1/89	17	4	✔1 Mandela Day	—	*Street Fighting Years*	A&M 3927
			tribute to Nelson Mandela			
5/20/89	12	5	2 This Is Your Land	—	↓	
			Lou Reed (additional vocal)			
6/24/89	14	6	3 Take A Step Back	—	↓	
3/23/91	❶²	13	✔4 See The Lights	40	*Real Life*	A&M 5352
6/22/91	4	5	5 Stand By Love	—	↓	
1/21/95	10	12	6 She's A River	52	*Good News From The Next World*	Virgin 39922
	★46★		**SIOUXSIE AND THE BANSHEES**			
			Avant-punk group formed by singer Siouxsie Sioux (Susan Dallion) and bassist Steve Severin (Steve Havoc). Fluctuating personnel around nucleus of group: Sioux, Severin and Peter "Budgie" Clark (drums). Husband-and-wife, Sioux and Budgie, also recorded as **The Creatures**.			
9/10/88	❶²	14	1 Peek-A-Boo	53	*Peepshow*	Geffen 24205
10/1/88	2¹	19	2 The Killing Jar	—	↓	
5/25/91	❶⁵	15	3 Kiss Them For Me	23	*Superstition*	Geffen 24387
9/21/91	13	6	4 Shadowtime	—	↓	
1/4/92	12	7	5 Fear (Of The Unknown)	—	↓	
7/11/92	7	7	6 Face To Face	—	*Batman Returns (soundtrack)*	Warner 26972
2/18/95	21	7	7 O Baby	125	*The Rapture*	Geffen 24630
			SISTER HAZEL			
			Pop-rock group formed in Gainesville, Florida: Ken Block (vocals), Ryan Newell and Andrew Copeland (guitars), Jeff Beres (bass) and Mark Trojanowski (drums).			
10/4/97	39	3	1 All For You	11 ▲	*...Somewhere More Familiar*	Universal 53030
2/7/98	37	2	2 Happy	73ᴬ	↓	
			SISTERS OF MERCY, The			
			Rock duo formed in Leeds, England: Andrew Taylor (vocals) and Patricia Morrison (bass). Morrison left in early 1990; expanded to a quintet which included Tony James, Tim Bricheno and Andreas Bruhn (guitars), and Doktor Avalanche (drums).			
11/17/90	❶⁵	13	1 More	—	*Vision Thing*	Elektra 61017
3/2/91	17	8	2 Detonation Boulevard	—	↓	
			SLOAN			
			Rock group from Halifax, Novia Scotia, Canada: Jay Ferguson (vocals), Patrick Pentland (guitar), Chris Murphy (bass) and Andrew Scott (drums).			
2/27/93	25	4	Underwhelmed	—	*Smeared*	DGC 24498
			SMASHING PUMPKINS, The ★6★			
			Rock group from Chicago: Billy Corgan (vocals, guitar; born on 3/17/67), James Iha (guitar; born on 3/26/68), D'Arcy Wretzky (bass; born on 5/1/68) and Jimmy Chamberlin (drums; born on 6/10/64). Touring keyboardist Jonathan Melvoin, brother of Wendy Melvoin (of **Prince**'s Revolution), died of a drug overdose on 7/12/96 (age 34).			
			1)1979 2)Bullet With Butterfly Wings 3)Stand Inside Your Love			
11/9/91	27	3	1 Rhinoceros	— ▲	*Gish*	Caroline 1705
10/17/92	24	4	2 Drown	— ▲	*Singles (soundtrack)*	Epic 52476
7/24/93	7	14	3 Cherub Rock	— ▲⁴	*Siamese Dream*	Virgin 88267
9/11/93+	8	26	4 Disarm	48ᴬ	↓	
10/30/93	4	23	5 Today	69ᴬ	↓	
10/15/94	3	17	6 Landslide	30ᴬ ▲	*Pisces Iscariot*	Virgin 39834
			first recorded by **Fleetwood Mac** in 1975			

DEBUT	PEAK	WKS	Modern Rock Track	Pop	Gld	Album Title	Album Label & Number
			SMASHING PUMPKINS, The — Cont'd				
10/21/95	2⁶	22	7 Bullet With Butterfly Wings	22	▲⁹	Mellon Collie And The Infinite Sadness . . . Virgin 40861	
11/25/95+	❶¹	26	8 1979	12		↓	
2/17/96	9	19	9 Zero	49ᴬ		↓	
6/1/96	5	22	10 Tonight, Tonight	36		↓	
9/14/96	8	17	11 Muzzle	57ᴬ		↓	
12/7/96+	2¹	21	12 Thirty-Three	39		↓	
3/22/97	8	18	13 Eye	49ᴬ	●	Lost Highway (soundtrack) . . . . Nothing 90090	
6/7/97	4	12	14 The End Is The Beginning Is The End	50ᴬ	▲	Batman & Robin (soundtrack) . . . . Warner Sunset 46620	
5/23/98	3	24	15 Ava Adore	42	▲	Adore . . . . Virgin 45879	
6/27/98	3	26	16 Perfect	54		↓	
12/25/99+	4	11	17 The Everlasting Gaze	113	●	Machina/The Machines Of God . . . . Virgin 48936	
2/26/00	2³	16	18 Stand Inside Your Love	106		↓	
	★79★		**SMASH MOUTH**				
			Pop-rock group from San Jose: Steve Harwell (vocals), Greg Camp (guitar), Paul DeLisle (bass) and Kevin Coleman (drums).				
7/19/97	❶⁵	32	1 Walkin' On The Sun	2¹ᴬ	▲²	Fush Yu Mang . . . . Interscope 90142	
1/31/98	28	6	2 Why Can't We Be Friends	—		↓	
			#6 Pop hit for War in 1975				
8/8/98	30	7	3 Can't Get Enough Of You Baby	27ᴬ	●	Can't Hardly Wait (soundtrack) . . . . Elektra 62201	
			#56 Pop hit for ? & The Mysterians in 1967				
5/8/99	2³	26	4 All Star	4	▲³	Astro Lounge . . . . Interscope 90316	
10/16/99	26	18	5 Then The Morning Comes	11		↓	
			SMITH, Patti				
			Born on 12/31/46 in Chicago; raised in New Jersey. Highly influential punk-rock singer. Not to be confused with Patty Smyth of Scandal. Also see **Classic Rock Tracks** section.				
9/10/88	6	7	Up There Down There	—		Dream Of Life . . . . Arista 8453	
			SMITHEREENS, The				
			Pop-rock group from Carteret, New Jersey: Pat DiNizio (vocals, guitar), Jim Babjak (guitar), Mike Mesaros (bass) and Dennis Diken (drums).				
10/21/89	3	13	1 A Girl Like You	38	●	11 . . . . Enigma 91194	
1/20/90	18	4	2 Blues Before And After	94		↓	
2/3/90	16	8	3 Yesterday Girl	—		↓	
9/7/91	2¹	8	4 Top Of The Pops	—		Blow Up . . . . Capitol 94963	
11/2/91	11	13	5 Tell Me When Did Things Go So Wrong	—		↓	
			SMOKING POPES				
			Rock group from Crystal Lake, Illinois: brothers Josh (vocals), Eli (guitar) and Matt (bass) Caterer, with Mike Felumlee (drums).				
7/15/95	35	3	Need You Around	—		Born To Quit . . . . Capitol 33831	
			SNAKE RIVER CONSPIRACY				
			Rock duo: Tobey Torres (female vocals) and Jason Slater (instruments).				
7/8/00	38	5	How Soon Is Now?	—		Sonic Jihad . . . . Reprise 47383	
			SNEAKER PIMPS				
			Rock trio from Manchester, England: Kelli Drayton (vocals), Chris Comer (guitar) and Liam Howe (keyboards).				
4/26/97	7	26	6 Underground	45		Becoming X . . . . Virgin 42587	
			SOBULE, Jill				
			Born on 1/16/59 in Denver. Singer/songwriter/guitarist.				
5/20/95	20	8	I Kissed A Girl	67		Jill Sobule . . . . Lava 82741	
	★71★		**SOCIAL DISTORTION**				
			Rock group formed in Los Angeles: Mike Ness (vocals, guitar), Dennis Danell (guitar), John Maurer (bass) and Christopher Reece (drums). Danell died of a brain aneurysm on 2/29/2000 (age 38).				
3/24/90	11	9	1 Let It Be Me	—	●	Social Distortion . . . . Epic 46055	
5/26/90	13	11	2 Ball And Chain	—		↓	
9/8/90	25	4	3 Ring Of Fire	—		↓	
			#17 Pop hit for Johnny Cash in 1963				
2/1/92	2⁴	12	4 Bad Luck	—	●	Somewhere Between Heaven And Hell . . . . Epic 47978	
5/2/92	11	7	5 Cold Feelings	—		↓	
6/27/92	14	6	6 When She Begins	—		↓	
9/14/96	4	22	7 I Was Wrong	54ᴬ		White Light White Heat White Trash . . 550 Music 64380	
2/1/97	33	6	8 When The Angels Sing	—		↓	
			SOHO				
			Dance trio formed in London: identical twin sisters Jackie and Pauline Cuff (vocals), with Tim Brinkhurst (guitar).				
9/8/90	11	9	Hippychick	14	●	Goddess . . . . Savage 91585	
			samples "How Soon Is Now" by The Smiths				
			SOLUTION A.D.				
			Rock group from Pennsylvania: Toby Costa (vocals, guitar), Mike Hoover (guitar), Kevin Leggieri (bass) and M.J. Law (drums).				
6/8/96	33	6	Fearless	—		Happily Ever After . . . . Atlantic 92708	

DEBUT	PEAK	WKS	Modern Rock Track	Pop Gld	Album Title	Album Label & Number

SOMETHING CORPORATE
Rock group from Anaheim, California: Andrew McMahon (vocals, piano), Josh Partington (guitar), Clutch (bass) and Brian Ireland (drums).

| 2/23/02 | 29 | 8 | If You C Jordan | — | Leaving Through The Window | Drive-Thru 112887 |

SOMETHING HAPPENS
Pop-rock group from Dublin, Ireland: Tom Dunne (vocals), Ray Harman (guitar), Alan Byrne (bass) and Eamonn Ryan (drums).

| 6/16/90 | 14 | 9 | Hello, Hello, Hello, Hello, Hello, (Petrol) | — | Stuck Together With God's Glue | Charisma 91365 |

SONIC YOUTH
Rock group formed in New York City: Thurston Moore and Lee Ranaldo (guitars), Kim Gordon (bass) and Steve Shelley (drums). All share vocals. Moore and Gordon married in 1983.

12/24/88+	20	9	1 Teen Age Riot	—	Daydream Nation	Enigma 75403
6/30/90	7	12	2 Kool Thing	—	Goo	DGC 24297
7/18/92	4	13	3 100%	—	Dirty	DGC 24493
5/28/94	13	8	4 Bull In The Heather	—	Experimental Jet Set, Trash And No Star	DGC 24632
9/17/94	26	7	5 Superstar	—	If I Were A Carpenter (various artists)	A&M 540258

#2 Pop hit for the Carpenters in 1971

SON VOLT
Rock group formed in New Orleans: Jay Farrar (vocals), brothers Dave (guitar) and Jim (bass) Boquist and Mike Heidorn (drums).

| 1/27/96 | 25 | 10 | Drown | — | Trace | Warner 46010 |

SOUL ASYLUM ★30★
Rock group from Minneapolis: Dave Pirner (vocals, guitar), Dan Murphy (guitar), Karl Mueller (bass) and Grant Young (drums). Pirner appeared in the movie *Reality Bites*. Sterling Campbell (**Duran Duran**) replaced Young in 1995.

1)Misery 2)Somebody To Shove 3)Black Gold

9/8/90	15	7	1 Spinnin'	—	And The Horse They Rode In On	A&M 5318
12/8/90	26	2	2 Easy Street	—	↓	
10/10/92	❶¹	16	3 Somebody To Shove	— ▲²	Grave Dancers Union	Columbia 48898
1/23/93	6	11	4 Black Gold	—	↓	
5/15/93	13	17	5 Runaway Train	5	↓	
10/2/93	27	4	6 Without A Trace	—	↓	
7/31/93	20	7	7 Summer Of Drugs	—	Sweet Relief: A Benefit For Victoria Williams (various artists)	Thirsty Ear 57134
11/20/93	10	9	8 Sexual Healing	—	No Alternative (various artists)	Arista 18737

#3 Pop hit for Marvin Gaye in 1983

10/29/94	16	6	9 Can't Even Tell	—	Clerks (soundtrack)	Chaos 66660
5/20/95	❶³	13	10 Misery	20 ▲	Let Your Dim Light Shine	Columbia 57616
9/9/95	19	7	11 Just Like Anyone	—	↓	
5/2/98	24	8	12 I Will Still Be Laughing	—	Candy From A Stranger	Columbia 67618

SOUL COUGHING
Rock group from New York City: Mike Doughty (vocals, guitar), Mark Antoni (keyboards), Sebastian Steinberg (bass) and Yuval Gabay (drums).

9/14/96	37	5	1 Soundtrack To Mary	—	Irresistible Bliss	Slash 46175
12/21/96+	27	12	2 Super Bon Bon	—	↓	
9/19/98	8	25	3 Circles	124	El Oso	Slash/Warner 46800

SOUNDGARDEN ★36★
Hard-rock group formed in Seattle: Chris Cornell (vocals), Kim Thayil (guitar), Ben Shepherd (bass) and Matt Cameron (drums). Cornell and Cameron also recorded with **Temple Of The Dog**.

3/12/94	9	10	1 Spoonman	— ▲⁵	Superunknown	A&M 540198
4/23/94	2¹	24	2 Black Hole Sun	24ᴬ	↓	
8/20/94	13	26	3 Fell On Black Days	54ᴬ	↓	
10/22/94	18	9	4 My Wave	—	↓	
4/1/95	25	7	5 The Day I Tried To Live	—	↓	
5/11/96	2¹	16	6 Pretty Noose	37ᴬ ▲	Down On The Upside	A&M 540526
6/29/96	2²	26	7 Burden In My Hand	40ᴬ	↓	
10/26/96	8	21	8 Blow Up The Outside World	53ᴬ	↓	
11/15/97	32	6	9 Bleed Together	—	A-Sides	A&M 540833

DEBUT	PEAK	WKS	Modern Rock Track	Pop	Gld	Album Title	Album Label & Number
			SOUP DRAGONS, The				
			Pop-rock group from Glasgow, Scotland: Sean Dickinson (vocals), Jim McCulloch (guitar), Sushil Dade (bass) and Paul Quinn (drums).				
8/25/90	2²	14	1 I'm Free	79		Lovegod	Big Life 842985
			first recorded by **The Rolling Stones** in 1965				
4/25/92	3	12	2 Divine Thing	35		Hotwired	Big Life 13178
7/11/92	14	9	3 Pleasure	69		↓	
			SPACE				
			Rock group from Liverpool, England: Tommy Scott (vocals, bass), Jamie Murphy (guitar), Franny Griffith (keyboards) and Andy Parle (drums).				
2/8/97	15	13	Female Of The Species	71^		Spiders	Universal 53028
			SPACEHOG				
			Rock group from Leeds, England: Royston Langdon (vocals, bass), Richard Steel and Antony Langdon (guitars), and Jonny Cragg (drums).				
12/9/95+	2³	26	1 In The Meantime	32	●	Resident Alien	Sire 61834
3/7/98	21	9	2 Mungo City	—		The Chinese Album	Sire 46851
			SPACE MONKEYS				
			Rock group from Manchester, England: Richard McNevin-Duff (vocals, guitar), Tony Pipes (keyboards), Dom Morrison (bass) and Chas Morrison (drums).				
11/8/97	20	14	Sugar Cane	58		The Daddy Of Them All	Chingón 90153
			samples "Bring The Noise" by Public Enemy				
			SPARKLEHORSE				
			Group is actually solo singer/songwriter/guitarist Mark Linkous (from Bremo Bluff, Virginia).				
4/20/96	35	4	Someday I Will Treat You Good	—		Vivadixiesubmarinetransmissionplot	Capitol 32816
			SPECIALS, The				
			Ska-rock group from Coventry, England: Neville Staple (vocals), Roddy Byers and Lynval Golding (guitars), Adam Birch and Jonathan Reed (horns), Mark Adams (keyboards), Horace Panter (bass) and Harrington Bembridge (drums).				
3/28/98	29	9	It's You	—		Guilty 'Til Proved Innocent!	Way Cool Music 11735
			SPIN DOCTORS				
			Rock group from New York City: Christopher Barron (vocals), Eric Schenkman (guitar), Mark White (bass) and Aaron Comess (drums).				
6/4/94	22	5	1 Cleopatra's Cat	84	▲	Turn It Upside Down	Epic 52907
7/30/94	20	7	2 You Let Your Heart Go Too Fast	42		↓	
			SPLENDER				
			Rock group from New York City: Wayne Boone (vocals), Jonathan Svec (guitar), James Cruz (bass) and Mike Slutsky (drums).				
6/12/99	24	18	Yeah, Whatever	—		Halfway Down The Sky	Columbia 69144
			SPONGE				
			Rock group from Detroit: Vinnie Dombrowski (vocals), Mike Cross and Joe Mazzola (guitars), Tim Cross (bass) and Jimmy Paluzzi (drums). Charlie Grover replaced Paluzzi in early 1996.				
2/4/95	5	23	1 Plowed	41^	●	Rotting Piñata	Work 57800
5/13/95	3	26	2 Molly (Sixteen Candles)	55		↓	
11/4/95	34	4	3 Rainin'	—		↓	
6/22/96	15	13	4 Wax Ecstatic (To Sell Angelina)	64^		Wax Ecstatic	Columbia 67578
			SPRUNG MONKEY				
			Rock group from San Diego: brothers Steve (vocals), Mike (guitar) Summers, William Riley (guitar), Tony Delocht (bass) and Ernie Longoria (drums).				
5/30/98	13	19	Get 'Em Outta Here	—		Mr. Funny Face	Surfdog 62151
			SQUEEZE				
			Pop-rock group formed in London by vocalists/guitarists Chris Difford and Glenn Tilbrook. Numerous personnel changes with Difford and Tilbrook the only constants.				
9/30/89	7	9	1 If It's Love	—		frank	A&M 5278
8/3/91	3	11	2 Satisfied	—		Play	Reprise 26644
10/26/91	14	6	3 Crying In My Sleep	—		↓	
9/18/93	9	8	4 Everything In The World	—		Some Fantastic Place	A&M 540140
			SQUIRREL NUT ZIPPERS				
			Eclectic-jazz group from Chapel Hill, North Carolina: Jim Mathus (vocals, guitar, trombone), Katharine Whalen (vocals, banjo), Ken Mosher (guitar, sax), Tom Maxwell (sax, clarinet), Je Widenhouse (trumpet), Don Raleigh (bass) and Chris Phillips (drums). Group name taken from a brand of candy.				
4/12/97	13	19	Hell	72^	▲	Hot	Mammoth 0137
			SR-71				
			Rock group from Baltimore: Mitch Allan (vocals, guitar), Mark Beauchemin (guitar), Jeff Reid (bass) and Dan Garvin (drums).				
5/27/00	2¹	27	1 Right Now	102	●	Now You See Inside	RCA 67845
12/2/00+	22	10	2 Politically Correct	—		↓	
10/12/02	18↑	7↑	3 Tomorrow	—		Tomorrow	RCA 68130

DEBUT	PEAK	WKS	Modern Rock Track	Pop Gld	Album Title	Album Label & Number

STABBING WESTWARD
Rock group from Chicago: Christopher Hall (vocals, guitar), Walter Flakus (keyboards), Jim Sellers (bass) and Andy Kubiszewski (drums).

2/3/96	11	19	1 What Do I Have To Do?	60[A] ●	Wither Blister Burn + Peel	Columbia 66152
8/3/96	14	16	2 Shame	69[A] ↓		
3/28/98	20	26	3 Save Yourself	— ●	Darkest Days	Columbia 69329
10/17/98	39	3	4 Sometimes It Hurts	— ↓		
2/27/99	34	4	5 Haunting Me	— ↓		
5/5/01	21	10	6 So Far Away	—	Stabbing Westward	Koch 8204

STAIND ★31★
Rock group from Boston: **Aaron Lewis** (vocals; born on 4/13/72), Mike Mushok (guitar; born on 4/10/74), Johnny April (bass; born on 3/27/71) and Jon Wysocki (drums; born on 1/17/71).

9/4/99	14	26	1 Mudshovel	— ▲	Dysfunction	Flip 62356
3/4/00	17	20	2 Home	— ↓		
4/7/01	❶[16]	29	3 It's Been Awhile	5 ▲[4]	Break The Cycle	Flip 62626
5/12/01	16	26	4 Outside	111 ↓		
9/1/01	4	26	5 Fade	62 ↓		
12/29/01+	3	32	6 For You	63 ↓		
5/25/02	28	17	7 Epiphany	— ↓		

STAKKA BO
Dance-rap duo from Sweden: Johan "Stakka Bo" Renck and Oscar Franzen.

5/21/94	20	7	Here We Go	109	Supermarket	Polydor 521089

STARCLUB
Pop-rock group from England: Owen Vyse (vocals, guitar), Steve French (guitar), Julian Taylor (bass) and Alan White (drums).

1/16/93	10	8	Hard To Get	119	Starclub	Island 514320

STARSAILOR
Rock group from Chorley, England: James Walsh (vocals, guitar), Barry Westhead (keyboards), James Stelfox (bass) and Ben Byrne (drums).

1/26/02	28	9	Good Souls	—	Love Is Here	Capitol 36448

STATIC-X
Rock group from Los Angeles: Wayne Static (vocals, guitar), Koichi Fukada (keyboards), Tony Campos (bass) and Ken Jay (drums). Fukada left in 2000; Static took over keyboards and Tripp Rex Eisen (guitar) joined.

11/27/99	36	8	Push It	57[S] ▲	Wisconsin Death Trip	Warner 47271

STEFANI, Gwen — see MOBY

STEREO MC'S
Dance trio from London: Rob Birch, Nick Hallam and Owen Rossiter.

1/30/93	5	13	1 Connected	20	Connected	Gee Street 514061
5/8/93	19	6	2 Step It Up	58 ↓		

STEREOMUD
Hard-rock group formed in New York City: Eric Rogers (vocals), John Fattoruso and Joey Z (guitars), Corey Lowery (bass) and Dan Richardson (drums). Joey Z and Richardson were members of **Life Of Agony**.

6/30/01	34	5	Pain	—	Perfect Self	Loud 85483

STING
Born Gordon Sumner on 10/2/51 in Wallsend, England. Singer/songwriter/bassist. Lead singer of **The Police**. Acted in such movies as *Quadrophenia*, *Dune*, *The Bride* and *Plenty*. Married actress/producer Trudie Styler on 8/20/92. Nicknamed "Sting" because of a yellow and black jersey he liked to wear.

1/19/91	❶[2]	11	1 All This Time	5 ▲	The Soul Cages	A&M 6405
3/16/91	9	8	2 The Soul Cages			
2/13/93	4	14	3 If I Ever Lose My Faith In You	17 ▲[3]	Ten Summoner's Tales	A&M 540070
5/15/93	12	9	4 Fields Of Gold	23 ↓		

STIPE, Michael — see CHERRY, Neneh

STIR
Rock trio from St. Charles, Missouri: Andy Schmidt (vocals, guitar), Kevin Gagnepain (bass) and Brad Booker (drums).

3/18/00	18	11	1 New Beginning	—	Holy Dogs	Capitol 57098
8/19/00	39	1	2 Climbing The Walls	— ↓		

DEBUT	PEAK	WKS	Modern Rock Track	Pop	Gld	Album Title	Album Label & Number

STONE ROSES, The
Pop-rock group from Manchester, England: Ian Brown (vocal), John Squire (guitar), Gary Mounfield (bass) and Alan Wren (drums).

DEBUT	PEAK	WKS					
8/26/89	9	9	1 She Bangs The Drums	—		The Stone Roses . . . . Silvertone 1184	
12/9/89+	18	11	2 I Wanna Be Adored	—		↓	
3/24/90	5	14	3 Fools Gold	—		↓	
8/18/90	9	9	4 One Love	—		(single only) . . . . Silvertone 1399	
12/24/94+	2¹	21	5 Love Spreads	55^A		Second Coming . . . . Geffen 24503	

STONE SOUR
Rock group formed by **Slipknot** members Corey Taylor (vocals) and Jim Root (guitar), with Josh Rand (guitar), Sid Wilson (bass) and Joel Eckman (drums).

DEBUT	PEAK	WKS					
9/7/02	4↑	12↑	Bother	56↑		Stone Sour . . . . Roadrunner 618425	

STONE TEMPLE PILOTS ★8★
Rock group formed in San Diego: **Scott Weiland** (vocals; born on 10/27/67), brothers Dean (guitar; born on 8/23/61) and Robert (bass; born on 2/2/66) DeLeo, and Eric Kretz (drums; born on 6/7/66). Weiland also formed **The Magnificent Bastards**. The DeLeo brothers also formed **Talk Show**.

1)Big Bang Baby   2)Interstate Love Song   3)Vasoline

DEBUT	PEAK	WKS					
4/10/93	9	18	1 Plush	39^A	▲7	Core . . . . Atlantic 82418	
8/14/93	21	9	2 Wicked Garden	—		↓	
12/25/93+	12	13	3 Creep	59^A		↓	
5/28/94	7	13	4 Big Empty	50^A	▲3	The Crow (soundtrack) . . . . Atlantic 82519	
6/18/94	2²	23	5 Vasoline	38^A	▲6	Purple . . . . Atlantic 82607	
8/20/94	2²	26	6 Interstate Love Song	18^A		↓	
12/31/94+	16	11	7 Unglued	—		↓	
4/1/95	11	11	8 Dancing Days	63^A	●	Encomium: A Tribute To	
			first recorded by **Led Zeppelin** in 1973			Led Zeppelin (various artists) . . . . Atlantic 82731	
3/23/96	2⁴	15	9 Big Bang Baby	28^A	▲2	Tiny Music...Songs From The Vatican Gift	
						Shop . . . . Atlantic 82871	
5/18/96	3	26	10 Trippin' On A Hole In A Paper Heart	36^A		↓	
10/26/96	6	22	11 Lady Picture Show	53^A		↓	
3/15/97	36	4	12 Tumble In The Rough	—		↓	
10/2/99	9	11	13 Down	107	▲	No.4 . . . . Atlantic 83255	
1/1/00	30	7	14 Heaven & Hot Rods	—		↓	
4/22/00	3	26	15 Sour Girl	78		↓	
10/21/00	24	7	16 No Way Out	—		↓	
6/16/01	5	11	17 Days Of The Week	101	●	Shangri-La Dee Da . . . . Atlantic 83449	
9/8/01	29	6	18 Hollywood Bitch	—		↓	

STRANGLERS, The
Pop-rock group formed in London: **Hugh Cornwell** (vocals, guitar), Dave Greenfield (keyboards), Jean-Jacques Burnel (bass) and Jet Black (drums).

DEBUT	PEAK	WKS					
6/16/90	5	10	Sweet Smell Of Success	—		10 . . . . Epic 46120	

STRAW, Syd
Born Susan Straw Harris in Hollywood. Female singer/songwriter/actress.

DEBUT	PEAK	WKS					
7/29/89	16	7	Future 40's (String Of Pearls)	—		Surprise . . . . Virgin 91266	
			Michael Stipe of **R.E.M.** (co-writer, backing vocal)				

STRESS
Black rock trio from London: Wayne Binitie (vocals), Mitch Ogugua (bass) and Ian Mussington (drums).

DEBUT	PEAK	WKS					
6/15/91	7	7	Flowers In The Rain	—		Stress . . . . Reprise 26519	

STROKE 9
Rock group from San Francisco: Luke Esterkyn (vocals), John McDermott (guitar), Greg Gueldner (bass) and Eric Stock (drums).

DEBUT	PEAK	WKS					
10/9/99+	6	27	1 Little Black Backpack	104	●	Nasty Little Thoughts . . . . Cherry 53157	
4/22/00	27	11	2 Letters	—		↓	
8/4/01	36	6	3 Kick Some Ass	—		Stroke 9 . . . . Cherry 53257	

STROKES, The
Rock group formed in New York City: Julian Casablancas (vocals), Albert Hammond Jr. (son of prolific songwriter Albert Hammond) and Nick Valensi (guitars), Nikolai Fraiture (bass) and Fab Moretti (drums).

DEBUT	PEAK	WKS					
11/10/01+	5	26	1 Last Nite	108	●	Is This It . . . . RCA 68101	
5/11/02	27	11	2 Hard To Explain	27^S		↓	
9/14/02	17	11↑	3 Someday	—		↓	

SUBLIME ★82★
Ska-rock trio from San Francisco: Brad Nowell (vocals, guitar), Eric Wilson (bass) and Bud Gaugh (drums). Nowell died of a drug overdose on 5/25/96 (age 28).

DEBUT	PEAK	WKS					
8/24/96	❶³	27	1 What I Got	29^A	▲	Sublime . . . . Gasoline Alley 11413	
1/18/97	3	26	2 Santeria	43^A		↓	
6/14/97	3	26	3 Wrong Way	47^A		↓	
10/4/97	28	10	4 Doin' Time	87		↓	

DEBUT	PEAK	WKS	Modern Rock Track	Pop Gld	Album Title	Album Label & Number
			SUEDE Rock group from London: Brett Anderson (vocals), Bernard Butler (guitar, piano), Matt Osman (bass) and Simon Gilbert (drums).			
5/1/93	7	11	Metal Mickey	—	*Suede*	Columbia 53792
			SUGAR Rock trio formed in Athens, Georgia: Bob Mould (vocals, guitar), David Barbe (bass) and Malcolm Travis (drums).			
8/29/92	5	13	1 Helpless	—	*Copper Blue*	Rykodisc 10239
9/3/94	14	11	2 Your Favorite Thing	120	*File Under: Easy Listening*	Rykodisc 10300
			SUGARCUBES, The Rock group from Reykjavik, Iceland: **Björk** Gudmundsottir (vocals), Einar Orn Benediktsson (vocals, trumpet), Thor Eldon Jonsson (guitar), Margret Ornolfsdottir (keyboards), Bragi Olafsson (bass) and Siggi Baldursson (drums). Group began as an artist's collective called Kukl (an Icelandic term for witches). Björk and Thor were married for a time. Thor and Margret married in 1989.			
9/10/88	10	10	1 Motorcrash	—	*Life's Too Good*	Elektra 60801
9/23/89	2²	10	2 Regina	—	*Here Today, Tomorrow Next Week!*	Elektra 60860
2/8/92	❶⁵	14	3 Hit	—	*Stick Around For Joy*	Elektra 61123
4/18/92	16	7	4 Walkabout	—	↓	
			SUGARCULT Rock group from Santa Barbara, California: Tim Pagnotta (vocals, guitar), Marko 72 (guitar), Airin (bass) and Ben Davis (drums).			
4/27/02	40	1	1 Bouncing Off The Walls	—	*Start Static*	Ultimatum 076673
9/28/02	30	9↑	2 Pretty Girl (The Way)	—	↓	
★49★			**SUGAR RAY** Rock group from Los Angeles: Mark McGrath (vocals; born on 3/15/68), Craig Bullock (DJ; born on 12/17/70), Rodney Sheppard (guitar; born on 11/25/67), Murphy Karges (bass; born on 6/20/67) and Stan Frazier (drums; born on 4/23/68).			
6/28/97	❶⁸	30	1 Fly	❶⁶ᴬ ▲²	*Floored*	Lava 83006
			SUGAR RAY Featuring Super Cat			
12/27/97+	35	6	2 RPM	—	↓	
12/12/98+	❶⁶	26	3 Every Morning	3 ▲³	*14:59*	Lava 83151
4/24/99	5	12	4 Falls Apart	29	↓	
6/19/99	7	21	5 Someday	7	↓	
			SUICIDAL TENDENCIES Hard-rock group from Venice, California: Mike Muir (vocals), Rocky George and Mike Clark (guitars), and Robert Trujillo (bass). Muir and Trujillo went on to form **Infectious Grooves**.			
8/1/92	21	6	I Wasn't Made To Feel This/Asleep At The Wheel	—	*The Art Of Rebellion*	Epic 48864
			SUICIDE MACHINES, The Rock group from Detroit: Jason Navarro (vocals), Dan Lukacinsky (guitar), Royce Nunley (bass) and Derek Grant (drums). Ryan Vandeberghe replaced Grant in 1999.			
1/4/97	31	7	1 No Face	—	*Destruction By Definition*	Hollywood 62048
1/29/00	22	12	2 Sometimes I Don't Mind	—	*The Suicide Machines*	Hollywood 62189
			SUM 41 Punk-rock group from New York City: Deryck Whibley (vocals, guitar), Dave Baksh (guitar), Cone McCaslin (bass) and Steve Jocz (drums).			
8/19/00	32	5	1 Makes No Difference	—	*Half Hour Of Power*	Island 542419
4/28/01	❶¹	28	2 Fat Lip	66 ▲	*All Killer No Filler*	Island 548662
10/13/01	10	17	3 In Too Deep	—	↓	
2/2/02	24	8	4 Motivation	28ˢ	↓	
			SUMMERCAMP Rock group from Santa Barbara, California: Tim Cullen (vocals), Sean McCue (guitar), Misha Feldman (bass) and Tony Sevener (drums).			
5/31/97	21	10	Drawer	—	*Pure Juice*	Maverick 46528
			SUN 60 Rock duo from Los Angeles: singer/songwriters Joan Jones and David Russo.			
7/17/93	29	2	Mary Xmess	—	*Only*	Epic 53447
			Dave Navarro (lead guitar)			
			SUNDAYS, The Pop-rock group from London: Harriet Wheeler (vocals), David Gavurin (guitar), Paul Brindley (bass) and Patrick Hannan (drums).			
4/21/90	❶¹	16	1 Here's Where The Story Ends	— ●	*Reading, Writing And Arithmetic*	DGC 24277
10/17/92	2²	14	2 Love	— ●	*Blind*	DGC 24479
1/23/93	11	7	3 Goodbye	—	↓	
9/6/97	10	22	4 Summertime	—	*Static & Silence*	DGC 25131
			SUNSCREEM Techno-pop group from England: Lucia Holm (vocals), Darren Woodford (guitar), Paul Carnell (keyboards), Rob Fricker (bass) and Sean Wright (drums).			
12/5/92+	3	14	Love U More	36	*03 (lower the 3)*	Columbia 53449
			SUPER CAT — see SUGAR RAY			
			SUPERDRAG Rock group from Knoxville, Tennessee: John Davis (vocals), Brandon Fisher (guitar), Tom Pappas (bass) and Don Coffey (drums).			
7/6/96	17	12	Sucked Out	72ᴬ	*Regretfully Yours*	Elektra 61900

DEBUT	PEAK	WKS	Modern Rock Track	Pop	Gld	Album Title	Album Label & Number

SUPERGRASS
Rock trio from England: Gaz Coombes (vocals, guitar), Mick Quinn (bass) and Danny Goffey (drums).

| 6/21/97 | 35 | 4 | Cheapskate | — | | *In It For The Money* | Capitol 55228 |

SUPREME LOVE GODS
Pop-rock group from England: Thomas Dew (vocals), Tommy Joy (guitar), John Wilson (bass) and Eric Dansby (drums).

| 11/14/92 | 16 | 12 | Souled Out | — | | *Supreme Love Gods* | Def Amer. 45073 |

SWANS, The
Pop-rock trio from New York City: Jarobe (female vocals), Michael Gira and Norman Westberg (guitars).

| 6/3/89 | 28 | 4 | Saved | — | | *The Burning World* | Uni 601 |

★92★ SWEET, Matthew
Born on 10/6/64 in Lincoln, Nebraska. Singer/bassist/drummer.

12/21/91+	23	4	1 Divine Intervention	—	●	*Girlfriend*	Zoo 11015
1/18/92	4	10	2 Girlfriend	—		↓	
7/3/93	3	11	3 The Ugly Truth	—		*Altered Beast*	Zoo 11050
3/11/95	2¹	24	4 Sick Of Myself	58	●	*100% Fun*	Zoo 11081
8/12/95	34	4	5 We're The Same	113		↓	
3/15/97	14	14	6 Where You Get Love			*Blue Sky On Mars*	Volcano 31130

★99★ SYSTEM OF A DOWN
Rock group from Los Angeles: Serj Tankian (vocals), Daron Malakian (guitar), Shavo Odadjian (bass) and John Dulmayan (drums).

11/27/99+	31	9	1 Sugar	—	▲	*System Of A Down*	American 68924
4/15/00	38	1	2 Spiders	—		↓	
8/4/01	7	35	3 Chop Suey	76	▲²	*Toxicity*	American 62240
1/26/02	3	26	4 Toxicity	70		↓	
6/15/02	❶³	24↑	5 Aerials	55		↓	

T

TALKING HEADS
Rock group from New York City: David Byrne (vocals, guitar), Jerry Harrison (keyboards, guitar), Tina Weymouth (bass) and Chris Frantz (drums). Weymouth and Frantz married on 6/18/77; later formed the Tom Tom Club. Group inducted into the Rock and Roll Hall of Fame in 2002. Also see **Classic Rock Tracks** section.

| 12/21/91+ | ❶¹ | 12 | 1 Sax And Violins | — | | *Until The End Of The World (soundtrack)* | Warner 26707 |
| 10/17/92 | 11 | 8 | 2 Lifetime Piling Up | — | | *Popular Favorites 1976-1992: Sand In The Vasoline* | Sire 26760 |

TALK SHOW
Rock group consisting of three members of **Stone Temple Pilots**: brothers Dean (guitar) and Robert (bass) DeLeo and Eric Kretz (drums), with Dave Coutts (vocals).

| 9/6/97 | 16 | 8 | Hello Hello | — | | *Talk Show* | Atlantic 83040 |

TANTRIC
Rock group from Louisville, Kentucky: Hugo Ferreira (vocals), Todd Whitener (guitar), Jesse Vest (bass) and Matt Taul (drums). The latter three were members of **Days Of The New**.

3/10/01	4	26	1 Breakdown	106	●	*Tantric*	Maverick 47978
8/25/01	30	8	2 Astounded	—		↓	
12/1/01+	22	14	3 Mourning	—		↓	

TAPROOT
Hard-rock group from Ann Arbor, Michigan: Steve Richards (vocals), Mike DeWolf (guitar), Phil Lipscomb (bass) and Jarrod Montague (drums).

| 10/12/02 | 19↑ | 7↑ | Poem | — | | *Welcome* | Atlantic 83561 |

TAXIRIDE
Rock group from Australia: Tim Watson and Tim Wild (guitars), Dan Hall (bass) and Jason Singh (drums). All share lead vocals.

| 5/22/99 | 36 | 5 | Get Set | — | | *Imaginate* | Sire 31056 |

TEARS FOR FEARS
Pop-rock duo from England: Roland Orzabal (vocals, guitar, keyboards) and Curt Smith (vocals, bass). Adopted name from Arthur Janov's book *Prisoners Of Pain*. Assisted by Ian Stanley (keyboards) and Manny Elias (drums). Smith left in 1992.

9/2/89	❶¹	11	1 Sowing The Seeds Of Love	2¹	▲	*The Seeds Of Love*	Fontana 838730
12/9/89	27	6	2 Woman In Chains	36		↓	
			Oleta Adams (female vocal); **Phil Collins** (drums)				
2/29/92	10	9	3 Laid So Low (Tears Roll Down)	—	▲	*Tears Roll Down (Greatest Hits 82-92)*	Fontana 510939
6/5/93	❶³	17	4 Break It Down Again	25	●	*Elemental*	Mercury 514875

TEENAGE FANCLUB
Pop-rock group from Glasgow, Scotland: Norman Blake (vocals, guitar), Ray McGinley (guitar), Gerry Love (bass) and Brendan O'Hare (drums).

11/30/91+	4	13	1 Star Sign	—		*Bandwagonesque*	DGC 24461
2/15/92	12	8	2 The Concept	—		↓	
5/9/92	19	4	3 What You Do To Me	—		↓	
11/27/93	19	9	4 Hang On	—		*Thirteen*	DGC 24533

DEBUT	PEAK	WKS	Modern Rock Track	Pop	Gld	Album Title	Album Label & Number

TELEVISION
Punk-rock group from New York City: Tom Verlaine (vocals, guitar), Richard Lloyd (guitar), Fred Smith (bass) and Billy Ficca (drums).

| 10/31/92 | 27 | 2 | Call Mr. Lee | — | | Television | Capitol 98396 |

TEMPLE OF THE DOG
Gathering of Seattle musicians in tribute to Andrew Wood, lead singer of Mother Love Bone, who died of a heroin overdose on 3/16/90 (age 24). Features Stone Gossard, Jeff Ament, Eddie Vedder and Mike McCready of **Pearl Jam**, with Chris Cornell and Matt Cameron of **Soundgarden**. Gossard and Ament were members of Mother Love Bone.

| 7/18/92 | 7 | 12 | Hunger Strike | — | ▲ | Temple Of The Dog | A&M 5350 |

★55★ **10,000 MANIACS**
Pop group formed in Jamestown, New York: **Natalie Merchant** (vocals), Robert Buck (guitar), Dennis Drew (keyboards), Steven Gustafson (bass) and Jerome Augustyniak (drums). Merchant left in August of 1993; replaced by Mary Ramsey. Buck died of liver failure on 12/19/2000 (age 42).

9/10/88	9	4	1 What's The Matter Here?	80	▲²	In My Tribe	Elektra 60738
5/27/89	3	11	2 Trouble Me	44	▲	Blind Man's Zoo	Elektra 60815
7/29/89	12	9	3 Eat For Two	—	↓		
9/26/92	❶²	15	4 These Are Days	66	▲²	Our Time In Eden	Elektra 61385
12/5/92+	5	19	5 Candy Everybody Wants	67	↓		
2/20/93	22	3	6 Everyday Is Like Sunday	—		(single only)	Elektra 66342
			first recorded by **Morrissey** in 1988				
10/23/93	7	15	7 Because The Night [L]	11	▲³	MTV Unplugged	Elektra 61569
			#13 Pop hit for **Patti Smith** in 1978				

TEXAS
Pop-rock group from Glasgow, Scotland: Sharleen Spiteri (vocals, guitar), Ally McErlaine (guitar), John McElhone (bass) and Stuart Kerr (drums).

| 8/5/89 | 11 | 9 | 1 I Don't Want A Lover | 77 | | Southside | Mercury 838171 |
| 11/2/91 | 14 | 7 | 2 In My Heart | — | | Mothers Heaven | Mercury 848578 |

THAT DOG
Rock group from Los Angeles: sisters Rachel (bass) and Petra (violin) Haden, Anna Waronker (vocals, guitar) and Tony Maxwell (drums).

| 5/31/97 | 27 | 7 | Never Say Never | — | | Retreat From The Sun | DGC 25115 |

THAT PETROL EMOTION
Pop group from Ireland: Steve Mack (vocals), Damian O'Neill and Reamann O'Gormain (guitars), John Marchini (bass) and Ciaran McLaughlin (drums).

| 4/21/90 | 9 | 10 | Hey Venus | — | | Chemicrazy | Virgin 91354 |

★85★ **THE, The**
Rock group formed in London by songwriter Matt Johnson. Changing lineup features contributing musicians headed and produced by Johnson. Guitarist Johnny Marr, earlier with The Smiths, is also a member of **Electronic** and **Electrafixion**.

6/3/89	13	8	1 The Beat(en) Generation	—		Mind Bomb	Epic 45241
8/12/89	15	6	2 Gravitate To Me	—	↓		
10/7/89	16	7	3 Kingdom Of Rain	—	↓		
2/10/90	7	7	4 Jealous Of Youth	—		(single only)	Epic 73151
1/23/93	2³	12	5 Dogs Of Lust	—		Dusk	Epic 53164
4/17/93	14	8	6 Love Is Stronger Than Death	—	↓		
2/4/95	24	8	7 I Saw The Light	—		Hanky Panky	550 Music 66908
			written by Hank Williams in 1948				

THELONIOUS MONSTER
Rock group formed in Los Angeles: Bob Forrest (vocals), Dix Denney (guitar), Chris Handsome (bass) and Pete Weiss (drums).

| 4/8/89 | 29 | 1 | So What If I Did | — | | Stormy Weather | Relativity 88561 |
| | | | produced by **John Doe** | | | | |

THERAPY?
Punk-rock trio from Belfast, Ireland: Andy Cairns (vocals, guitar), Michael McKeegan (bass) and Fyfe Ewing (drums).

| 10/9/93 | 16 | 7 | Screamager | — | | Hats Off To The Insane | A&M 540139 |

THEY EAT THEIR OWN
Pop-rock group formed in Los Angeles: Laura B. (vocals), Kevin Dixon and Shark Darkwater (guitars), J.D. Dotson (bass) and Juno Brown (drums).

| 1/19/91 | 10 | 8 | Like A Drug | — | | They Eat Their Own | Relativity 1042 |

THEY MIGHT BE GIANTS
Novelty-rock duo from Boston: John Flansburgh (guitar) and John Linnell (accordian). Group named after a 1971 George C. Scott movie.

11/5/88	11	9	1 Ana Ng	—		Lincoln	Bar/None 72600
1/27/90	3	11	2 Birdhouse In Your Soul	—	●	Flood	Elektra 60907
4/14/90	22	7	3 Twisting	—	↓		
3/14/92	24	8	4 The Statue Got Me High	—		Apollo 18	Elektra 61257
9/3/94	19	8	5 Snail Shell	—		John Henry	Elektra 61654

DEBUT	PEAK	WKS	Modern Rock Track	Pop Gld	Album Title	Album Label & Number

THIRD EYE BLIND ★35★
Rock group from San Francisco: Stephan Jenkins (vocals; born on 9/27/64), Kevin Codogan (guitar), Arion Salazar (bass; born on 8/9/70) and Brad Hargreaves (drums; born on 7/30/72).

3/29/97	❶⁸	31	1 Semi-Charmed Life	4	▲⁶ *Third Eye Blind* . . . . Elektra 62012
8/9/97	14	16	2 Graduate	—	↓
11/8/97+	5	26	3 How's It Going To Be	9	↓
3/21/98	13	14	4 Losing A Whole Year	—	↓
7/25/98	9	26	5 Jumper	5	↓
11/20/99	11	8	6 Anything	—	▲ *Blue* . . . . Elektra 62415
1/1/00	4	21	7 Never Let You Go	14	↓
5/6/00	21	10	8 10 Days Late	—	↓
8/26/00	39	2	9 Deep Inside Of You	—	↓

3RD STRIKE
Rock group from Los Angeles: Jim Korthe (vocals), Todd Deguchi and Erik Carlsson (guitars), Gabe Hammersmith (bass) and P.J. McMullan (drums).

6/15/02	36	4	No Light	42ˢ	*Lost Angel* . . . . Hollywood 62344

THIS PICTURE
Rock group from Bath, England: Symon Bye (vocals), Austen Rowley (bass), brothers Robert (guitar) and Duncan (drums) Forrester.

10/12/91	10	13	1 Naked Rain	—	*A Violent Impression* . . . . Dedicated 3010
2/8/92	24	2	2 Breathe Deeply Now	—	*Breathe Deeply Now* . . . . Dedicated 62177

THOMAS, Rob — see SANTANA

THOMPSON, Richard
Born on 4/3/49 in London. Singer/songwriter/guitarist. Formed Fairport Convention in 1969. Went solo in 1971. Married singer Linda Peters from 1972-82.

11/12/88	30	1	1 Turning Of The Tide	—	*Amnesia* . . . . Capitol 48845
7/6/91	15	8	2 I Feel So Good	—	*Rumor And Sigh* . . . . Capitol 95713

THOMPSON TWINS
Pop-rock duo from England: Tom Bailey (vocals, synthesizer) and Alannah Currie (xylophone, percussion).

9/30/89	16	6	1 Sugar Daddy	28	*Big Trash* . . . . Warner 25921
9/7/91	23	5	2 Come Inside	—	*Queer* . . . . Warner 26631

THRASHING DOVES
Pop-rock group from London: brothers Ken (vocals) and Brian (guitar) Foreman, with Ian Button (bass) and Kevin Sargent (drums).

3/4/89	14	9	Angel Visit	—	*Trouble In The Home* . . . . A&M 5235

★70★ 3 DOORS DOWN
Rock group from Escatawpa, Mississippi: Brad Arnold (vocals), Matt Roberts (guitar), Todd Harrell (bass) and Chris Henderson (drums).

3/25/00	❶¹¹	33	1 Kryptonite	3	▲⁵ *The Better Life* . . . . Republic 153920
8/5/00	2¹	32	2 Loser	55	↓
1/27/01	11	26	3 Duck And Run	110	↓
6/23/01	22	12	4 Be Like That	24	↓
10/12/02	14	7↑	5 When I'm Gone	67↑	*Away From The Sun* . . . . Republic 064396

311 ★21★
Rock-funk group from Omaha, Nebraska: Nicholas Hexum and SA Martinez (vocals), Tim Mahoney (guitar), P-Nut (bass) and Chad Sexton (drums). 311 is the police code for indecent exposure.

1)Down 2)All Mixed Up 3)Come Original

4/10/93	27	3	1 Do You Right	—	● *Music* . . . . Capricorn 42008
10/28/95	29	7	2 Don't Stay Home	—	▲³ *311* . . . . Capricorn 42041
2/24/96+	4	26	3 All Mixed Up	36ᴬ	↓
7/6/96	❶⁴	26	4 Down	37ᴬ	↓
7/5/97	14	10	5 Transistor	—	▲ *Transistor* . . . . Capricorn 536181
9/6/97	21	10	6 Prisoner	—	↓
12/13/97+	21	23	7 Beautiful Disaster	—	↓
9/11/99	6	19	8 Come Original	119	● *Soundsystem* . . . . Capricorn 546645
1/29/00	17	16	9 Flowing	—	↓
6/16/01	7	15	10 You Wouldn't Believe	120	● *From Chaos* . . . . Volcano 32184
10/6/01	15	19	11 I'll Be Here Awhile	—	↓
3/9/02	13	30	12 Amber	103	↓

DEBUT	PEAK	WKS	Modern Rock Track	Pop Gld	Album Title	Album Label & Number
			3 LB. THRILL Rock group from Basking Ridge, New Jersey: Matt Brown (vocals), Jeff Jensen (guitar), Bill Becker (bass) and Pete McDade (drums).			
2/17/96	35	6	Diana	—	Vulture.......................	550 Music 67395
			THROWING MUSES Pop-rock group from Boston: Kristin Hersh (vocals, guitar), Tanya Donelly (vocals, guita), Leslie Langston (bass) and David Narcizo (drums). Langston left by October 1989, replaced by David Abong. By 1992, reduced to a duo of Hersh and Narcizo. Donnelly (an early member of **The Breeders**) later formed **Belly**.			
2/18/89	8	11	1 Dizzy	—	Hunkpapa........................	Sire 25855
3/30/91	11	8	2 Counting Backwards	—	The Real Ramona	Sire 26489
1/7/95	20	13	3 Bright Yellow Gun	120	University	Sire 45796
			TIKARAM, Tanita Born on 12/8/69 in Munster, West Germany; raised in Basingstoke, England. Female singer/songwriter.			
4/1/89	25	4	✓Twist In My Sobriety	—	Ancient Heart.....................	Reprise 25839
			'TIL TUESDAY Pop group formed in Boston: **Aimee Mann** (vocals, bass), Robert Holmes (guitar), Michael Montes (keyboards) and Michael Hausmann (drums).			
12/17/88	30	3	✓ (Believed You Were) **Lucky**	95	Everything's Different Now.............	Epic 44041
			TIMELORDS, The — see KLF, The			
			TIN MACHINE Rock group: **David Bowie** (vocals), Reeves Gabrels (guitar), Tony Sales (bass; **Utopia**, **Chequered Past**) and Hunt Sales (drums, Utopia), The Sales brothers are the sons of TV comedian Soupy Sales.			
6/3/89	4	9	1 Under The God	—	Tin Machine	EMI 91990
8/5/89	12	4	2 Heaven's In Here	—	↓	
8/31/91	3	9	3 One Shot	—	Tin Machine II..................	Victory 511216
11/2/91	21	8	4 Baby Universal	—	↓	
			TIN STAR Rock trio from London: David Tomlinson (vocals), Tim Bricheno (guitar) and Tim Gordine (bass).			
2/6/99	10	13	Head	—	The Thrill Kisser	V2 27039
			TOADIES Rock group from Fort Worth, Texas: Todd Lewis (vocals, guitar), Darrel Herbert (guitar), Lisa Umbarger (bass) and Mark Reznicek (drums).			
9/2/95	4	26	1 Possum Kingdom	40ᴬ ▲	Rubberneck...............	Interscope 92402
2/3/96	28	8	2 Away	—	↓	
★74★			**TOAD THE WET SPROCKET** Pop-rock group from Santa Barbara, California: Glen Phillips (vocals), Todd Nichols (guitar), Dean Dinning (bass) and Randy Guss (drums). Name taken from a Monty Python skit.			
9/9/89	24	4	1 One Little Girl	—	Bread And Circus	Columbia 45326
3/31/90	27	4	✓2 Come Back Down	—	Pale........................	Columbia 46060
7/11/92	22	7	✓3 All I Want	15 ▲	Fear	Columbia 47309
5/21/94	❶⁶	19	✓4 Fall Down	33 ▲	Dulcinea	Columbia 57744
9/10/94	9	13	✓5 Something's Always Wrong	41	↓	
10/14/95	20	11	6 Good Intentions	23ᴬ ▲	Friends (soundtrack)	Reprise 46008
5/3/97	13	13	7 Come Down	51ᴬ	Coil	Columbia 67862
			TOM TOM CLUB Studio project formed by husband-and wife Chris Frantz and Tina Weymouth. Both were members of **Talking Heads**.			
4/29/89	10	11	1 Suboceana	—	Boom Boom Chi Boom Boom...........	Sire 25888
6/6/92	15	7	2 Sunshine And Ecstacy	—	Dark Sneak Love Action.............	Sire 26951
			TONIC Rock group from Los Angeles: Emerson Hart (vocals), Jeff Russo (guitar), Dan Rothchild (bass) and Kevin Shepard (drums). Dan Lavery replaced Rothchild in 1998.			
10/19/96	22	22	1 Open Up Your Eyes	68ᴬ ▲	Lemon Parade..................	Polydor 531042
3/29/97	3	26	2 If You Could Only See	11ᴬ	↓	
7/3/99	10	20	3 You Wanted More	103 ●	American Pie (soundtrack)	Universal 53269
			TOOL Hard-rock group from Los Angeles: Maynard James Keenan (vocals), Adam Jones (guitar), Justin Chancellor (bass) and Danny Carey (drums). Also see **A Perfect Circle**.			
10/5/96	19	19	1 Stinkfist..................................	— ▲²	Aenima	Volcano 31087
5/19/01	2¹	29	2 Schism	67 ▲	Lateralus	Volcano 31160
11/17/01+	18	18	3 Lateralus	—	↓	
4/27/02	31	7	4 Parabola	—	↓	
			TOO MUCH JOY Pop-rock group from Scarsdale, New York: Tim Quirk (vocals), Jay Blumenfield (guitar), Sandy Smallens (bass) and Tommy Vinton (drums).			
4/27/91	17	7	1 Crush Story	—	Cereal Killers.................	Giant 24410
9/12/92	11	8	2 Donna Everywhere	—	Mutiny....................	Giant 24467

DEBUT	PEAK	WKS	Modern Rock Track	Pop	Gld	Album Title	Album Label & Number
			TOP Rock trio from England: Paul, Alan and Joe.				
11/30/91+	17	9	Number One Dominator	—		*Emotion Lotion*	Island 510096
			TRAGICALLY HIP, The Rock group from Kingston, Ontario, Canada: Gordon Downie (vocals), Bobby Baker and Paul Langlois (guitars), Gord Sinclair (bass) and Johnny Fay (drums).				
2/13/93	16	9	Courage (For Hugh MacLennan)	—		*Fully Completely*	MCA 10700
			TRAIN Rock group from San Francisco: Patrick Monahan (vocals), Rob Hotchkiss and Jimmy Stafford (guitars), Charlie Colin (bass) and Scott Underwood (drums).				
6/5/99	25	16	1 Meet Virginia	20	▲	*Train*	Aware 38052
3/3/01	11	26	2 Drops Of Jupiter (Tell Me)	5	▲²	*Drops Of Jupiter*	Aware 69888
			TRANSVISION VAMP Pop-rock group from England: Wendy James (vocals), Nick Sayer (guitar), Tex Axile (keyboards), Dave Parsons (bass) and Pol Burton (drums).				
9/17/88	9	5	1 Tell That Girl To Shut Up first recorded by Holly & The Italians in 1981	87		*Pop Art*	Uni 5
8/17/91	14	10	2 (I Just Wanna) B With U	—		*Little Magnets Versus The Bubble Of Babble*	MCA 10331
			TRASH CAN SINATRAS, The Pop-rock group from Irvine, Scotland: brothers John (guitar) and Stephen (drums) Douglas, Frank Reader (vocals), Paul Livingston (guitar) and George McDaid (bass). David Hughes replaced McDaid in 1992.				
11/17/90	8	11	1 Only Tongue Can Tell	—		*Cake*	Go! Discs 828201
2/9/91	12	6	2 Obscurity Knocks	—		↓	
5/29/93	11	9	3 Hayfever	—		*I've Seen Everything*	Go! Discs 828412
			TRAVIS Rock group from Glasgow, Scotland: Fran Healy (vocals), Andy Dunlop (guitar), Dougie Payne (bass) and Neil Primrose (drums).				
6/10/00	35	4	1 Why Does It Always Rain On Me?	—		*The Man Who...*	Independiente 62151
6/2/01	37	3	2 Sing	—		*The Invisible Band*	Independiente 85788
			TRICKY Born Adrian Thaws in 1964 in Bristol, England. Male techno-dance artist.				
6/30/01	35	5	1 Evolution Revolution Love TRICKY Featuring Ed Kowalczyk & Hawkman	—		*Blowback*	Hollywood 162285
8/11/01	18	9	2 Simple Creed LIVE Featuring Tricky	—		*V.*	Radioactive 12485
			TRIK TURNER Rock-rap group from Phoenix: David Bowers and Doug Moore (vocals), Danny Marquez (DJ), Tracy "Tre" Thorstad (guitar), Steve Faulkner (bass) and Sean Garden (drums).				
1/26/02	7	18	1 Friends & Family	123		*Trik Turner*	RCA 68073
7/20/02	35	3	2 Sacrifice	—		↓	
			TRIPPING DAISY Pop-rock group from Dallas: Tim DeLaughter (vocals), Wes Berggren (guitar), Mark Pirro (bass) and Bryan Wakeland (drums). Berggren died on 10/27/99 (age 28).				
10/30/93	24	2	1 My Umbrella	—		*Bill*	Island 555002
6/24/95	6	15	2 I Got A Girl	53ᴬ		*I Am An Elastic Firecracker*	Island 524112
11/11/95	32	6	3 Piranha	—		↓	
			TRUSTCOMPANY Rock group from Montgomery, Alabama: Kevin Palmer (vocals, guitar), James Fukai (guitar), Josh Moates (bass) and Jason Singleton (drums).				
6/15/02	6	24↑	Downfall	91		*The Lonely Position Of Neutral*	Geffen 493312
			TRYNIN, Jennifer Born on 12/27/63 in New Jersey. Singer/songwriter/guitarist.				
6/24/95	15	10	Better Than Nothing	74ᴬ		*Cockamamie*	Squint 45931
			25TH OF MAY, The Techno-dance group from Liverpool, England: Steve Swindelli (vocals), Eddie G. (guitar), NC Cope (bass) and Jimmy Jazz (drums).				
9/5/92	28	3	It's All Right	—		*Lenin & McCarthy*	Arista 18712

U

DEBUT	PEAK	WKS	Modern Rock Track	Pop	Gld	Album Title	Album Label & Number
			UB40 Reggae group formed in Birmingham, England: brothers Ali (vocals) and Robin (guitar) Campbell, Terence "Astro" Wilson (vocals), Norman Hassan (percussion), Michael Virtue (keyboards), Brian Travers (sax), Earl Falconer (bass), James Brown (drums). Name taken from a British unemployment form. Also see **Pato Banton** and **808 State**.				
9/10/88	4	8	1 Breakfast In Bed UB40 with Chrissie Hynde	—		*UB40*	A&M 5213
1/27/90	6	8	2 Here I Am (Come And Take Me) #10 Pop hit for Al Green in 1973	7	▲	*Labour Of Love II*	Virgin 91324
5/1/93	11	14	3 Can't Help Falling In Love #2 Pop hit for Elvis Presley in 1962	❶⁷	●	*Sliver (soundtrack)*	Virgin 88064
8/28/93	14	8	4 Higher Ground	45	▲	*Promises And Lies*	Virgin 88229

DEBUT	PEAK	WKS	Modern Rock Track	Pop Gld	Album Title	Album Label & Number

ULTRA VIVID SCENE
Group iks actually solo singer/songwriter/guitarist Kurt Ralske (born in 1967 in New York City).

6/2/90	25	2	1 Staring At The Sun	—	Joy 1967-1990	4 A D 46227
8/18/90	19	3	2 It Happens Every Time	—	↓	
10/6/90	14	6	3 Special One	—	↓	
2/13/93	27	3	4 Blood And Thunder	—	Rev	4 A D 53133

UNDERWORLD
Rock group from England: Karl Hyde (vocals, guitar), Alfie Thomas (guitar), Rick Smith (keyboards), Baz Allen (bass) and Pascal Console (drums).

9/2/89	14	6	Stand Up	67	Change The Weather	Sire 25945

UNTOUCHABLES, The
Funk group from Los Angeles: Jerry Miller and Chuck Askerneese (vocals), Clyde Grimes (guitar), Brewster (keyboards), Derek Breakfield (bass) and Willie McNeil (drums).

3/25/89	28	1	Agent Double O Soul	—	Agent Double O Soul	Restless 72342

#21 Pop hit for Edwin Starr in 1965

UNWRITTEN LAW
Pop-rock group from Poway, California: Scott Russo (vocals), Rob Brewer (guitar), Steve Morris (bass) and Wade Youman (drums).

8/28/99	28	8	1 Cailin	—	Unwritten Law	Interscope 90189
2/2/02	❶⁴	26	2 Seein' Red	105	Elva	Interscope 493139
7/27/02	14	11	3 Up All Night	63ˢ	↓	

URE, Midge
Born James Ure on 10/10/53 in Glasgow, Scotland. Rock singer/guitarist. Member of **Ultravox**.

1/21/89	4	12	1 Dear God	95	Answers To Nothing	Chrysalis 41649
4/29/89	26	2	2 Answers To Nothing	—	↓	
1/18/92	12	7	3 Cold, Cold Heart	—	Pure	RCA 61010

URGE, The
Ska-rock group from St. Louis: Steve Ewing (vocals), Jerry Jost (guitar), Bill Reiter, Matt Kwiatkowski and Todd Painter (horns), Karl Grable (bass) and John Pessoni (drums).

4/11/98	10	19	Jump Right In	—	Master Of Styles	Immortal 69152

THE URGE Featuring Nick Hexum

URGE OVERKILL
Rock trio from Chicago: Nash Kato (guitar), "Eddie" King Roeser (bass) and Blackie Onassis (drums). All share vocals.

7/10/93	6	15	1 Sister Havana	—	Saturation	Geffen 24529
3/26/94	23	4	2 Positive Bleeding	—	↓	
11/12/94	11	11	3 Girl, You'll Be A Woman Soon	59 ▲³	Pulp Fiction (soundtrack)	MCA 11103

#10 Pop hit for Neil Diamond in 1967

USED, The
Rock group from Orem, Utah: Bert McCracken (vocals), Quinn Allman (guitar), Jeph Howard (bass) and Branden Steineckert (drums).

9/28/02	24↑	9↑	The Taste Of Ink	—	The Used	Reprise 48287

US3
Jazz/rap collaboration by London producers Mel Simpson (keyboards) and Geoff Wilkinson (samples). Samples of recordings on the Blue Note jazz record label serve as the backdrop for new rap solos and jazz playing by some of Britain's top players.

11/13/93	29	4	Cantaloop	9 ▲	Hand On The Torch	Blue Note 80883

UTAH SAINTS
Techno-rave duo from England: Jez Willis and Tim Garbutt.

8/8/92	7	9	Something Good	98	Something Good	London 869843

samples "Cloudbusting" by **Kate Bush**

U2 ★1★
Rock group formed in Dublin, Ireland: Paul "Bono" Hewson (vocals; born on 5/10/60), Dave "The Edge" Evans (guitar; born on 8/8/61), Adam Clayton (bass; born on 3/13/60) and Larry Mullen Jr. (drums; born on 10/30/61). Released concert tour documentary movie *Rattle And Hum* in 1988.

1)Mysterious Ways   2)Desire   3)Hold Me, Thrill Me, Kiss Me, Kill Me   4)Discothéque   5)Staring At The Sun

9/17/88	9	4	1 Jesus Christ	—	Folkways: A Vision Shared - A Tribute To Woody Guthrie And Leadbelly (various artists)	Columbia 44034
			written by Woody Guthrie			
10/8/88	❶⁵	11	2 Desire	3 ▲⁵	Rattle And Hum	Island 91003
11/5/88	3	17	3 Angel Of Harlem	14	↓	
			a tribute to Billie Holiday			
11/19/88	10	13	4 When Love Comes To Town	68	↓	
			U2 WITH B.B. KING			
3/11/89	28	3	5 God Part II	—	↓	
			sequel to **John Lennon**'s 1970 recording "God"			
4/15/89	14	7	6 Dancing Barefoot	—	(single only)	Island 99225
7/8/89	11	8	7 Everlasting Love	—	(single only)	Island 96550

#13 Pop hit for Robert Knight in 1967

DEBUT	PEAK	WKS	Modern Rock Track	Pop	Gld	Album Title	Album Label & Number
			U2 — Cont'd				
11/10/90	2³	13	8 **Night And Day**	—		Red Hot + Blue (various artists)	Chrysalis 21799
			#1 Pop hit for Fred Astaire in 1932				
10/26/91	❶²	12	9 **The Fly**	61	▲⁸	Achtung Baby	Island 10347
11/23/91	❶⁹	13	✓10 **Mysterious Ways**	9		↓	
1/4/92	❶¹	23	✓11 **One**	10		↓	
2/1/92	4	8	12 **Until The End Of The World**	—		↓	
7/4/92	5	13	✓13 **Even Better Than The Real Thing**	32		↓	
10/24/92	7	9	14 **Who's Gonna Ride Your Wild Horses**	35		↓	
7/10/93	2¹	12	✓15 **Numb**	61ᴬ	▲²	Zooropa	Island 518047
8/7/93	13	8	16 **Zooropa**			↓	
10/2/93	3	9	17 **Lemon**	71ᴬ		↓	
12/4/93+	15	14	18 **Stay (Faraway, So Close!)**	61		↓	
6/10/95	❶⁴	15	✓19 **Hold Me, Thrill Me, Kiss Me, Kill Me**	16	▲²	Batman Forever (soundtrack)	Atlantic 82759
1/25/97	❶⁴	10	✓20 **Discothéque**	10	▲	Pop	Island 524334
3/15/97	❶³	16	✓21 **Staring At The Sun**	26		↓	
6/28/97	11	10	22 **Last Night On Earth**	57		↓	
11/1/97	31	4	23 **Please**	103		↓	
10/17/98	9	24	✓24 **Sweetest Thing**	63	▲²	The Best Of 1980-1990/The B-Sides	Island 524612
			recorded in 1987				
2/26/00	20	6	25 **The Ground Beneath Her Feet**	—		The Million Dollar Hotel (soundtrack)	Interscope 542395
9/23/00	5	26	✓26 **Beautiful Day**	21	▲³	All That You Can't Leave Behind	Interscope 524653
1/6/01	10	15	✓27 **Walk On**	118		↓	
4/28/01	8	15	✓28 **Elevation**	116		↓	
9/15/01	35	8	✓29 **Stuck In A Moment You Can't Get Out Of**	52		↓	
9/21/02	14	6	✓30 **Electrical Storm**	77		The Best Of 1990-2000	Interscope 063361

V

VAST
Group is actually solo guitarist Jon Crosby. VAST: Visual Audio Sensory Theater.

DEBUT	PEAK	WKS	Modern Rock Track	Pop	Gld	Album Title	Album Label & Number
1/9/99	31	8	1 **Touched**	—		Visual Audio Sensory Theater	Elektra 62173
8/26/00	12	13	2 **Free**	—		Music For People	Elektra 62511
2/24/01	34	5	3 **I Don't Have Anything**	—		↓	

VEDDER, Eddie
Born Edward Severson III (although he grew up with his step-father's last name of Mueller) on 12/23/64 in Evanston, Illinois; raised in San Diego. Lead singer of **Pearl Jam**. Legally changed his last name to Vedder (his mother's last name).

DEBUT	PEAK	WKS	Modern Rock Track	Pop	Gld	Album Title	Album Label & Number
1/5/02	30	10	**You've Got To Hide Your Love Away**	117	●	I Am Sam (soundtrack)	V2 27119
			first recorded by **The Beatles** in 1965				

VEGA, Suzanne
Born on 8/12/59 in New York City. Singer/songwriter/guitarist. Married record producer Mitchell Froom (of **Gamma**) on 3/17/95.

DEBUT	PEAK	WKS	Modern Rock Track	Pop	Gld	Album Title	Album Label & Number
4/21/90	8	9	1 **Book Of Dreams**	—		days of open Hand	A&M 5293
9/1/90	7	10	2 **Tom's Diner**	5		(single only)	A&M 1529
			D.N.A. Featuring SUZANNE VEGA				
			special mix of Vega's original acapella recording which appeared on her 1987 Solitude Standing album				
9/5/92	❶¹	12	3 **Blood Makes Noise**	—	●	99.9 F°	A&M 540005
11/28/92+	13	13	4 **99.9 F°**	—		↓	

VERTICAL HORIZON
Rock group from Boston: Matt Scfannell (vocals), Keith Kane (guitar), Sean Hurley (bass) and Ed Toth (drums).

DEBUT	PEAK	WKS	Modern Rock Track	Pop	Gld	Album Title	Album Label & Number
7/10/99	21	10	1 **We Are**	—	▲²	Everything You Want	RCA 67818
12/4/99+	5	26	2 **Everything You Want**	3		↓	
7/8/00	15	13	3 **You're A God**	23		↓	

VERUCA SALT
Rock group from Chicago: Nina Gordon and Louise Post (vocals, guitar). with Steven Lack (bass) and Jim Shapiro (drums). Name taken from a character in the children's book Charlie and The Chocolate Factory.

DEBUT	PEAK	WKS	Modern Rock Track	Pop	Gld	Album Title	Album Label & Number
9/10/94	8	22	1 **Seether**	53ᴬ	●	American Thighs	Minty Fresh 7
1/28/95	20	8	2 **Number One Blind**			↓	
2/8/97	8	26	3 **Volcano Girls**	59ᴬ		Eight Arms To Hold You	Outpost 30001

VERVE, The
Rock group from Wigan, England: Richard Ashcroft (vocals), Nick McCabe (guitar), Simon Jones (bass) and Peter Salisbury (drums).

DEBUT	PEAK	WKS	Modern Rock Track	Pop	Gld	Album Title	Album Label & Number
10/11/97+	4	29	1 **Bitter Sweet Symphony**	12	▲	Urban Hymns	Virgin 44913
5/2/98	16	12	2 **Lucky Man**	—		↓	

DEBUT	PEAK	WKS	Modern Rock Track	Pop Gld	Album Title	Album Label & Number
			VERVE PIPE, The			
			Rock group from East Lansing, Michigan: brothers Brian (vocals) and Brad (bass) Vander Ark, A.J. Dunning (guitar), Doug Corella (keyboards) and Donny Brown (drums).			
3/30/96	6	18	1 Photograph	53ᴬ ▲	*Villains*	RCA 66809
2/15/97	❶³	26	2 The Freshmen	5	↓	
8/9/97	22	9	3 Villains	—	↓	
7/10/99	17	11	4 Hero	—	*The Verve Pipe*	RCA 67664
			VIBROLUSH			
			Rock group from New York City: Phil Vassil (vocals, guitar), James Mazler (guitar), B (bass) and Tobias Ralph (drums).			
8/12/00	36	6	Touch And Go	—	*Touch And Go*	V2 27074
			VINES, The			
			Rock trio from Sydney, Australia: Craig Nicholls (vocals, guitar), Patrick Matthews (bass) and David Oliffe (drums).			
6/15/02	7	20	Get Free	122 ●	*Highly Evolved*	Engineroom 37527
			VIOLENT FEMMES			
			Punk-folk trio from Milwaukee: Gordon Gano (vocals, guitar), Brian Ritchie (bass) and Victor DeLorenzo (drums). Guy Hoffman replaced DeLorenzo in 1992.			
2/4/89	4	13	1 Nightmares	—	*3*	Slash 25819
4/13/91	2¹	13	2 American Music	—	*Why Do Birds Sing?*	Slash 26476
5/14/94	12	9	3 Breakin' Up	—	*New Times*	Elektra 61553
			VOICE OF THE BEEHIVE			
			Pop group formed in London by California-born sisters Melissa (vocals) and Tracey (vocals, guitar) Belland. British personnel included Mike Jones (guitar), Martin Brett (bass) and former **Madness** member Dan Woodgate (drums). The Bellands are the daughters of Bruce Belland, member of '50s vocal group The Four Preps.			
11/5/88	11	10	1 I Say Nothing	—	*Let It Bee*	London 828100
8/31/91	8	10	2 Monsters And Angels	74	*Honey Lingers*	London 828253

W

DEBUT	PEAK	WKS	Modern Rock Track	Pop Gld	Album Title	Album Label & Number
			WAILING SOULS			
			Reggae group led by vocalists Lloyd "Bread" McDonald and Winston "Pipe" Matthews.			
11/6/93	28	3	Wild Wild Life	— ●	*Cool Runnings* (soundtrack)	Chaos 57553
			#25 Pop hit for **Talking Heads** in 1986			
			WAKELING, Dave			
			Born in Birmingham, England. Lead singer of English Beat and **General Public**.			
4/20/91	12	8	I Want More	—	*No Warning*	I.R.S. 13085
	★62★		**WALLFLOWERS, The**			
			Pop-rock group formed in Los Angeles: Jakob Dylan (vocals), Michael Ward (guitar), Rami Jaffe (keyboards), Greg Richling (bass) and Mario Calire (drums). Dylan is the son of **Bob Dylan**.			
8/3/96	8	19	1 6th Avenue Heartache	33ᴬ ▲⁴	*Bringing Down The Horse*	Interscope 90055
12/14/96+	❶⁵	26	2 One Headlight	2⁵ᴬ	↓	
5/17/97	5	22	3 The Difference	23ᴬ	↓	
10/11/97	17	12	4 Three Marlenas	51ᴬ	↓	
5/9/98	9	12	5 Heroes	27ᴬ ▲	*Godzilla* (soundtrack)	Epic 69338
			first recorded by **David Bowie** in 1977			
9/30/00	31	10	6 Sleepwalker	— ●	*(Breach)*	Interscope 490745
			WANG CHUNG			
			Pop-rock duo from London: Jack Hues (vocals, guitar, keyboards) and Nick Feldman (bass, keyboards).			
6/24/89	22	4	Praying To A New God	63	*The Warmer Side Of Cool*	Geffen 24222
			WAS (NOT WAS)			
			R&B-pop group from Detroit. Fronted by composer/bassist Don Fagenson ("Don Was") and lyricist/flutist David Weiss ("David Was"). Includes vocalists Sweet Pea Atkinson and Sir Harry Bowens. Group appeared in the movie *The Freshman*.			
11/19/88	30	1	Walk The Dinosaur	7	*What Up, Dog?*	Chrysalis 41664
			WATERBOYS, The			
			Rock group formed in London by Mike Scott (vocals, guitar; from Scotland) and Anthony Thistlethwaite (mandolin, saxophone). Numerous personnel changes. Keyboardist Karl Wallinger left in 1985 to form **World Party**.			
12/10/88+	3	14	1 Fisherman's Blues	—	*Fisherman's Blues*	Chrysalis 41589
2/11/89	19	6	2 World Party	—	↓	
11/3/90	15	9	3 A Life Of Sundays	—	*Room To Roam*	Chrysalis 21768
5/22/93	10	8	4 The Return Of Pan	—	*Dream Harder*	Geffen 24476
			WATT, Mike			
			Born on 12/20/57 in Portsmouth, Virginia. Hard-rock singer/bassist.			
3/11/95	21	8	Against The 70's	—	*Ball-Hog Or Tugboat?*	Columbia 67086
			WAX			
			Rock group formed in Los Angeles: Joe Sib (vocals), Soda (guitar), Burdie Cutlass (bass) and Loomis (drums).			
3/25/95	28	8	California	—	*13 Unlucky Numbers*	Interscope 92544

DEBUT	PEAK	WKS	Modern Rock Track	Pop	Gld	Album Title	Album Label & Number

WEEN
Rock duo from Lambertville, New Jersey: Mickey Melchiondo ("Dean Ween") and Aaron Freeman ("Gene Ween").

DEBUT	PEAK	WKS	Track	Pop	Gld	Album	Label
3/20/93	21	3	1 Push th' Little Daisies	—		Pure Guava	Elektra 61428
12/10/94	32	5	2 Voodoo Lady	—		Chocolate And Cheese	Elektra 61639

WEEZER ★27★
Rock group from Los Angeles: Rivers Cuomo (vocals, guitar; born on 6/13/70), Brian Bell (guitar; born on 12/9/68), Matt Sharp (bass; born on 9/20/69) and Patrick Wilson (drums; born on 2/1/69). Scott Shriner (born on 7/11/65) replaced Sharp in 1998. Sharp and Wilson also formed **The Rentals**.

1)Hash Pipe 2)Buddy Holly 3)Undone-The Sweater Song

DEBUT	PEAK	WKS	Track	Pop	Gld	Album	Label
7/23/94	6	18	1 Undone-The Sweater Song	57	▲³	Weezer	DGC 24629
11/5/94	2¹	22	2 Buddy Holly	18ᴬ	↓		
6/10/95	7	24	3 Say It Ain't So	51ᴬ	↓		
9/21/96	19	10	4 El Scorcho	—	●	Pinkerton	DGC 25007
1/11/97	32	6	5 The Good Life	—	↓		
4/28/01	2⁸	26	6 Hash Pipe	106	▲	Weezer	Geffen 493045
7/21/01	11	20	7 Island In The Sun	111	↓		
11/10/01	17	12	8 Photograph	—	↓		
3/23/02	8	15	9 Dope Nose	—	↓		
7/13/02	15	12	10 Keep Fishin'	—	↓		

WEILAND, Scott
Born on 10/27/67 in Santa Cruz, California. Lead singer of **Stone Temple Pilots**.

DEBUT	PEAK	WKS	Track	Pop	Gld	Album	Label
1/10/98	39	1	1 Lady, Your Roof Brings Me Down	—	●	Great Expectations (soundtrack)	Atlantic 83058
3/28/98	36	3	2 Barbarella	—		12 Bar Blues	Atlantic 83084

WELLER, Paul
Born on 5/25/58 in Woking, Surrey, England. Leader of **The Jam** and **The Style Council**.

DEBUT	PEAK	WKS	Track	Pop	Gld	Album	Label
10/17/92	10	10	Uh Huh Oh Yeh	—		Paul Weller	Go! Discs 828343

WESTERBERG, Paul
Born on 12/31/60 in Minneapolis. Rock singer/guitarist. Member of **The Replacements**.

DEBUT	PEAK	WKS	Track	Pop	Gld	Album	Label
8/1/92	4	12	1 Dyslexic Heart	—	▲	Singles (soundtrack)	Epic 52476
6/19/93	4	11	2 World Class Fad	—		14 Songs	Sire 45255
4/27/96	21	10	3 Love Untold	—		Eventually	Reprise 46176

WHALE
Grunge/hip-hop trio from Sweden: Henrik Schyffert, Cia Berg and Gordon Cyrus.

DEBUT	PEAK	WKS	Track	Pop	Gld	Album	Label
5/7/94	24	4	Hobo Humpin Slobo Babe	102		(single only)	EastWest 98281

WHEATUS
Rock group from Long Island, New York: brothers Brendan (vocals, guitar) and Peter (drums) Brown, with Phil Jimenez (guitar) and Rich Leigey (bass).

DEBUT	PEAK	WKS	Track	Pop	Gld	Album	Label
7/22/00	7	24	Teenage Dirtbag	124		Wheatus	Columbia 62146

WHITE STRIPES, The
Rock duo from Detroit: Jack White (vocals, guitar) and Meg White (drums).

DEBUT	PEAK	WKS	Track	Pop	Gld	Album	Label
3/23/02	12	21	1 Fell In Love With A Girl	121		White Blood Cells	Third Man 27124
8/10/02	19	16↑	2 Dead Leaves And The Dirty Ground	—	↓		

WHITE TOWN
Born Jyoti Mishra on 7/30/66 in Rourkela, India; raised in England. Male singer/multi-instrumentalist.

DEBUT	PEAK	WKS	Track	Pop	Gld	Album	Label
2/22/97	5	22	Your Woman	23		Women In Technology	Chrysalis/EMI 56129

WHITE ZOMBIE
Hard-rock group formed in New York City: **Rob Zombie** (vocals), Jay Yuenger (guitar), Sean Yseult (bass) and John Tempesta (drums). Group named after a 1932 Bela Lugosi movie.

DEBUT	PEAK	WKS	Track	Pop	Gld	Album	Label
4/22/95	7	20	More Human Than Human	53ᴬ	▲²	Astro-Creep: 2000	Geffen 24806

WHY STORE, The
Rock group from Indianapolis: Chris Shaffer (vocals), Michael David Smith (guitar), Jeff Pederson (keyboards), Greg Gardner (bass) and Charlie Bushor (drums).

DEBUT	PEAK	WKS	Track	Pop	Gld	Album	Label
8/24/96	37	3	Lack Of Water	—		The Why Store	Way Cool 11420

WILCO
Rock group from Chicago: Jeff Tweedy (vocals, guitar), Jay Bennett (guitar), John Stirratt (bass) and Ken Coomer (drums).

DEBUT	PEAK	WKS	Track	Pop	Gld	Album	Label
3/15/97	39	1	Outtasite (Outta Mind)	—		Being There	Reprise 46236

WINTER HOURS
Rock group from Lyndhurst, New Jersey: Joseph Marques (vocals), Michael Carlucci and Bob Perry (guitars), Bob Messing (bass) and Dave Scheff (drums).

DEBUT	PEAK	WKS	Track	Pop	Gld	Album	Label
8/26/89	12	7	Smoke Rings	—		Winter Hours	Chrysalis 21682

WIRE
Rock group from London: Colin Newman (vocals, guitar), Bruce Gilbert (guitar), Graham Lewis (bass) and Mark Field (drums).

DEBUT	PEAK	WKS	Track	Pop	Gld	Album	Label
5/20/89	2¹	12	1 Eardrum Buzz	—		It's Beginning To And Back Again	Enigma 73516
8/19/89	24	2	2 In Vivo	—	↓		

DEBUT	PEAK	WKS	Modern Rock Track	Pop Gld	Album Title	Album Label & Number
			WIRE TRAIN Rock group formed in San Francisco: Kevin Hunter (vocals), Jeff Trott (guitar), Anders Rundblad (bass) and Brian MacLeod (drums).			
6/6/92	23	7	Stone Me	—	*No Soul No Strain*	MCA 10604
			WOBBLE('S), Jah, Invaders Of The Heart Rock trio formed in England: Jah Wobble (bass, vocals), Justin Adams (guitar) and Mark Ferda (keyboards, drums). Wobble was bassist of **Public Image Ltd.**			
3/28/92	10	9	1 Visions Of You	—	*Rising Above Bedlam*	Atlantic 82386
			Sinead O'Connor (backing vocal)			
7/2/94	22	6	2 The Sun Does Rise	—	*Take Me To God*	Island 524000
			Dolores O'Riordan of **The Cranberries** (lead vocal)			
			WOLFGANG PRESS, The Techno-dance trio from England: Mick Allen (vocals), Andrew Gray (guitar) and Mark Cox (keyboards).			
7/4/92	2[1]	9	1 A Girl Like You	—	*Queer*	4 A D 26908
2/18/95	33	6	2 Going South	—	*Funky Little Demons*	4 A D 45738
			WONDER STUFF, The Pop-rock group formed in Wolverhampton, England: Miles Hunt (vocals, guitar), Malcolm Treece (guitar, vocals), Rob Jones (bass) and Martin Gilks (drums). Paul Clifford replaced Jones in 1990. Martin Bell (fiddle) joined in early 1991. Jones died of a heroin overdose on 7/30/93 (age 29).			
3/4/89	17	7	1 Give, Give, Give Me More, More, More	—	*The Eight-Legged Groove Machine.*	Polydor 837802
1/6/90	11	8	2 Don't Let Me Down, Gently..	—	*Hup*	Polydor 841187
1/6/90	26	2	3 Radio Ass Kiss	—	↓	
7/13/91	8	11	4 Caught In My Shadow	—	*Never Loved Elvis*	Polydor 847252
2/22/92	27	2	5 Welcome To The Cheap Seats..	—	↓	
10/9/93	17	8	6 On The Ropes	—	*Construction For The Modern Idiot*	Polydor 519894
			WORLD PARTY Group is actually singer/keyboardist Karl Wallinger (born on 10/19/57 in Prestatyn, Wales). Wallinger was also a member of **The Waterboys.**			
5/5/90	❶[5]	13	1 Way Down Now	—	*Goodbye Jumbo*	Ensign 21654
7/28/90	8	9	2 Put The Message In The Box	—	↓	
4/3/93	5	13	3 Is It Like Today?	—	*Bang!*	Ensign 21991
			WYNETTE, Tammy — see KLF, The			
			WYNN, Steve Born on 2/21/60 in Santa Monica, California. Rock singer/songwriter.			
5/26/90	10	8	1 Tears Won't Help	—	*Kerosene Man*	Rhino 70969
5/23/92	30	2	2 Drag	—	*Dazzling Display*	RNA 70283

X

DEBUT	PEAK	WKS	Modern Rock Track	Pop Gld	Album Title	Album Label & Number
			X Rock group formed in Los Angeles: **Exene Cervenka** (vocals), Billy Zoom (guitar), **John Doe** (bass) and Don Bonebrake (drums).			
5/15/93	15	9	1 Country At War..	—	*Hey Zeus!*	Big Life 519261
8/14/93	26	3	2 New Life	—	↓	
			X-ECUTIONERS, The Rap production group from New York City: Mista Sinista, Rob Swift, Total Eclipse and Roc Raida.			
2/2/02	13	16	It's Goin' Down	85	*Built From Scratch.*	Loud 86410
	★100★		**XTC** Rock trio formed in Wiltshire, England: Andy Partridge (guitar), Dave Gregory (keyboards) and Colin Moulding (bass). All share vocals.			
2/25/89	❶[5]	14	1 The Mayor Of Simpleton	72	*Oranges & Lemons*	Geffen 24218
5/27/89	11	13	2 King For A Day	—	↓	
5/2/92	❶[2]	12	3 The Ballad Of Peter Pumpkinhead	—	*Nonsuch*	Geffen 24474
7/25/92	18	6	4 Dear Madam Barnum	—	↓	
			XYMOX Pop trio from Amsterdam, Holland: Ronny Moorings (vocals, guitar, keyboards), Pieter Nooten (keyboards) and Anka Wolbert (bass, vocals, keyboards).			
5/6/89	16	10	1 Obsession..	—	*Twist Of Shadows*	Wing 839233
4/13/91	16	8	2 Phoenix Of My Heart..	—	*Phoenix*	Wing 848516
			contains an interpolation of "Wild Thing" by The Troggs			

DEBUT	PEAK	WKS	Modern Rock Track	Pop	Gld	Album Title	Album Label & Number

Y

YORN, Pete
Born in Montville, New Jersey. Singer/songwriter/guitarist.

DEBUT	PEAK	WKS	Modern Rock Track	Pop	Gld	Album Title	Album Label & Number
10/27/01	28	8	1 For Nancy ('Cos It Already Is)	—	●	*Music For The Morning After*	Columbia 62216
3/23/02	36	3	2 Strange Condition	—	↓		

YOUNG FRESH FELLOWS
Rock group from Seattle: Scott McCaughey (vocals), Kurt Bloch (guitar), Jim Sangster (bass) and Tad Hutchinson (drums).

1/13/90	29	2	Carrot Head	—		*This One's For The Ladies*	Frontier 1034

Z

ZEBRAHEAD
Rock-rap group from Los Angeles: Justin Mauriello (vocals), Ali Tabatabee (rap vocals), Greg Bergdorf (guitar), Ben Osmundson (bass) and Ed Udhus (drums).

11/28/98+	32	10	Get Back	—		*Waste Of Mind*	Columbia 69155

ZOMBIE, Rob
Born Robert Cummings on 1/12/66 in Haverhill, Massachusetts. Founder of **White Zombie**.

10/10/98	27	26	1 Dragula	116	▲³	*Hellbilly Deluxe*	Geffen 25212
3/6/99	22	21	2 Living Dead Girl	—	↓		
10/20/01	18	15	3 Feel So Numb	—	●	*The Sinister Urge*	Geffen 493147
2/23/02	23	13	4 Never Gonna Stop	—	↓		

MODERN ROCK TRACKS WRAP-UP

Top 100 Artists In Rank Order

Top 100 Artists In A-Z Order

Top Artists Achievements:

> Most Charted Tracks
> Most Top 10 Tracks
> Most #1 Tracks
> Most Weeks At The #1 Position

Top Tracks:

> All-Time
> Top 10 Tracks of Each Year

Tracks Of Longevity

> 1988-89
> 1990-99
> 2000-02

TOP 100 ARTISTS IN RANK ORDER

This section ranks the Top 100 Modern Rock Tracks artists from 1988-2002. Each artist's accumulated point total is shown to the right of their name. This ranking includes all titles that <u>peaked</u> from 1988-2002. A picture of each Top 40 artist is shown next to their listing in the artist section of this book.

POINT SYSTEM:

1. Each artist's charted singles are given points based on their highest charted position:

#1	=	60 points for its first week at #1, plus 5 points for each additional week at #1
#2	=	50 points for its first week at #2, plus 3 points for each additional week at #2
#3	=	40 points for its first week at #3, plus 3 points for each additional week at #3
#4-5	=	35 points
#6-10	=	30 points
#11-20	=	25 points
#21-30	=	20 points
#31-40	=	15 points

2. Total weeks charted are added in.

In the case of a tie, the artist listed first is determined by the following tie-breaker rules:

1) Most charted tracks
2) Most Top 20 tracks
3) Most Top 10 tracks

Special Symbols:

★ = **Hot Artist**
> An artist's rank increased by at least 10 positions since the last edition of *Rock Tracks*. All new artist entries are automatically designated as "Hot Artists."

■ = **Deceased Group Member**
> The total number of square symbols indicates the total number of deceased members.

— = Artist did not rank in the Top 100 of the previous edition.

+ = Subject to change — still charted as of the 11/23/02 cut-off date

TOP 100 MODERN ROCK ARTISTS

Old Rank	New Rank	Artist	Points
(1)	1.	U2	1,582
(10)	2.	Red Hot Chili Peppers ■	1,327 +
(2)	3.	R.E.M.	1,287
(5)	4.	Pearl Jam	1,219 +
(9)	5.	Green Day	1,045
(28)	★6.	The Smashing Pumpkins	1,020
(57)	★7.	Bush	872
(13)	8.	Stone Temple Pilots	838
(11)	9.	Live	837
(3)	10.	The Cure	821
(30)	★11.	The Offspring	807
—	★12.	Foo Fighters	733 +
(6)	13.	Depeche Mode	677
—	★14.	Blink-182	650
—	★15.	Oasis	639
(4)	16.	Morrissey	639
(84)	★17.	Goo Goo Dolls	631
(7)	18.	Nirvana ■	631 +
—	★19.	Dave Matthews Band	630
—	★20.	Creed	592
—	★21.	311	554
—	★22.	Everclear	539
(52)	★23.	Lenny Kravitz	537
(8)	24.	INXS ■	530
—	★25.	Incubus	522
(88)	★26.	Alanis Morissette	499
(86)	★27.	Weezer	491
—	★28.	Limp Bizkit	491
—	★29.	Garbage	483
(12)	30.	Soul Asylum	482
—	★31.	Staind	481
(24)	32.	The Cranberries	468
—	★33.	Fuel	465
(96)	★34.	Collective Soul	462
—	★35.	Third Eye Blind	459
(53)	★36.	Soundgarden	443
—	★37.	Beck	428
(39)	38.	Nine Inch Nails	414
(65)	★39.	Counting Crows	403
—	★40.	No Doubt	402
—	★41.	Hole ■	386
(97)	★42.	Better Than Ezra	386
(17)	43.	The B-52's ■	385
(14)	44.	Midnight Oil	378
(15)	45.	Big Audio Dynamite	376
—	★46.	Our Lady Peace	375 +
(16)	47.	Siouxsie & The Banshees	370
—	★48.	Lit	358
—	★49.	Sugar Ray	355
—	★50.	Korn	349 +
—	★51.	Puddle Of Mudd	349 +
—	★52.	Linkin Park	340
—	★53.	3 Doors Down	340 +
—	★54.	Radiohead	337
—	★55.	Cake	332
—	★56.	Godsmack	330
(18)	57.	10,000 Maniacs ■	330
(31)	58.	Jane's Addiction	329
—	★59.	Eve 6	319
—	★60.	Nickelback	319
—	★61.	Alice In Chains ■	318
—	★62.	P.O.D.	317
—	★63.	The Wallflowers	316
(19)	64.	The Replacements	314
—	★65.	Sheryl Crow	312
—	★66.	Rage Against The Machine	312
(20)	67.	The Jesus & Mary Chain	311
(21)	68.	Psychedelic Furs	310
(22)	69.	Concrete Blonde	309
(23)	70.	New Order	308
(50)	71.	Social Distortion ■	306
(38)	72.	Cracker	300
—	★73.	Everlast	300
(56)	74.	Toad The Wet Sprocket	296
(25)	75.	The Charlatans UK	295
—	★76.	Papa Roach	294
(26)	77.	Jesus Jones	289
—	★78.	Silverchair	287
—	★79.	Smash Mouth	285
(90)	★80.	Sarah McLachlan	281
(43)	81.	The Lemonheads	276
—	★82.	Sublime	274
(27)	83.	The Ocean Blue	270
(29)	84.	Pixies	267
—	★85.	System Of A Down	265 +
(32)	86.	The The	262
—	★87.	Beastie Boys	259
—	★88.	Jimmy Eat World	258 +
—	★89.	Filter	257
(33)	90.	Public Image Ltd.	256
(73)	91.	Gin Blossoms ■	256
(34)	92.	Erasure	255
(35)	93.	Peter Murphy	255
(59)	94.	Matthew Sweet	252
(36)	95.	Simple Minds	250
(37)	96.	Elvis Costello	249
(92)	97.	Tori Amos	246
—	★98.	Matchbox Twenty	245
—	★99.	Marcy Playground	244
(40)	100.	Kate Bush	241

Alice In Chains	61	Hole	41	P.O.D.	62
Amos, Tori	97	Incubus	25	Psychedelic Furs	68
Beastie Boys	87	INXS	24	Public Image Ltd.	90
Beck	37	Jane's Addiction	58	Puddle Of Mudd	51
Better Than Ezra	42	Jesus & Mary Chain, The	67	Radiohead	54
B-52's, The	43	Jesus Jones	77	Rage Against The Machine	66
Big Audio Dynamite	45	Jimmy Eat World	88	Red Hot Chili Peppers	2
Blink-182	14	Korn	50	R.E.M.	3
Bush	7	Kravitz, Lenny	23	Replacements, The	64
Bush, Kate	100	Lemonheads, The	81	Silverchair	78
Cake	55	Limp Bizkit	28	Simple Minds	95
Charlatans UK, The	75	Linkin Park	52	Siouxsie & The Banshees	47
Collective Soul	34	Lit	48	Smashing Pumpkins, The	6
Concrete Blonde	69	Live	9	Smash Mouth	79
Costello, Elvis	96	Marcy Playground	99	Social Distortion	71
Counting Crows	39	Matchbox Twenty	98	Soul Asylum	30
Cracker	72	Matthews, Dave, Band	19	Soundgarden	36
Cranberries, The	32	McLachlan, Sarah	80	Staind	31
Creed	20	Midnight Oil	44	Stone Temple Pilots	8
Crow, Sheryl	65	Morissette, Alanis	26	Sublime	82
Cure, The	10	Morrissey	16	Sugar Ray	49
Depeche Mode	13	Murphy, Peter	93	Sweet, Matthew	94
Erasure	92	New Order	70	System Of A Down	85
Everclear	22	Nickelback	60	10,000 Maniacs	57
Everlast	73	Nine Inch Nails	38	The, The	86
Eve 6	59	Nirvana	18	Third Eye Blind	35
Filter	89	No Doubt	40	3 Doors Down	53
Foo Fighters	12	Oasis	15	311	21
Fuel	33	Ocean Blue, The	83	Toad The Wet Sprocket	74
Garbage	29	Offspring, The	11	U2	1
Gin Blossoms	91	Our Lady Peace	46	Wallflowers, The	63
Godsmack	56	Papa Roach	76	Weezer	27
Goo Goo Dolls	17	Pearl Jam	4		
Green Day	5	Pixies	84		

The following 44 artists were ranked in the Top 100 Artists of our *Rock Tracks (1995 edition)* book but have now dropped out of the Top 100:

Belly	House Of Love	Lou Reed
Blind Melon	James	The Smithereens
Catherine Wheel	The Lightning Seeds	Sonic Youth
Lloyd Cole & The Commotions	Living Colour	Squeeze
Julian Cope	Love & Rockets	Sting
Cowboy Junkies	Ziggy Marley & The Melody Makers	The Stone Roses
Crowded House	Material Issue	The Sugarcubes
The Cult	Ian McCulloch	The Sundays
Duran Duran	Ned's Atomic Dustbin	Tears For Fears
Electronic	Sinéad O'Connor	They Might Be Giants
EMF	Michael Penn	Suzanne Vega
Peter Gabriel	Iggy Pop	The Wonder Stuff
Happy Mondays	The Pretenders	World Party
Robyn Hitchcock & The Egyptians	Primal Scream	XTC
Hothouse Flowers	The Primitives	

Pearl Jam

The Smashing Pumpklins

Green Day

TOP ARTIST ACHIEVEMENTS

MOST CHARTED TRACKS

1. U2...30
2. Pearl Jam 29
3. R.E.M. 25
4. Red Hot Chili Peppers.....................20
5. The Smashing Pumpkins 18
6. Stone Temple Pilots 18
7. Green Day 16
8. Live 16
9. The Offspring 16
10. Bush 14
11. The Cure..14
12. Depeche Mode....................................14
13. Dave Matthews Band 14
14. Foo Fighters 13
15. Goo Goo Dolls 13
16. Oasis 12
17. 311 12
18. Lenny Kravitz 12
19. INXS 12
20. Soul Asylum 12
21. Nine Inch Nails....................................12
22. Morrissey 11
23. Nirvana 11
24. Everclear 11
25. Collective Soul 11

MOST TOP 10 TRACKS

1. U2...20
2. The Smashing Pumpkins 16
3. R.E.M. 15
4. Red Hot Chili Peppers.....................14
5. Pearl Jam 13
6. Green Day 12
7. Bush 10
8. Stone Temple Pilots..........................10
9. The Cure..10
10. The Offspring 10
11. Morrissey 9
12. INXS 9
13. Live 8
14. Foo Fighters 8
15. Blink-182 7
16. Nirvana 7
17. Lenny Kravitz 7
18. Depeche Mode......................................6
19. Oasis 6
20. Goo Goo Dolls 6
21. Dave Matthews Band 6
22. Creed 6
23. Incubus 6
24. Midnight Oil..6

MOST #1 TRACKS

1. U2...7
2. Red Hot Chili Peppers.......................7
3. R.E.M. 6
4. Green Day 5
5. Nirvana 5
6. Bush 4
7. The Cure..4
8. Depeche Mode......................................4
9. Live 3
10. Goo Goo Dolls 3
11. Alanis Morissette 3
12. The B-52's 3
13. Psychedelic Furs 3

MOST WEEKS AT THE #1 POSITION

1. Red Hot Chili Peppers.....................55
2. R.E.M. 31
3. U2...28
4. Green Day 19
5. The Cure..18
6. Bush 16
7. Staind 16
8. Oasis 15
9. Marcy Playground 15
10. Sugar Ray 14
11. Live 13
12. Morrissey 13
13. Nickelback 13

TOP MODERN ROCK TRACKS

ALL-TIME

Peak Year	Wks Chr	Wks T20	Wks T10	Wks @ #1	Rank	Title	Artist
01	29	29	24	16	1.	It's Been Awhile	Staind
99	26	25	21	16	2.	Scar Tissue	Red Hot Chili Peppers
97	34	32	24	15	3.	Sex and Candy	Marcy Playground
02	24 +	24 +	21	14	4.	By The Way	Red Hot Chili Peppers
01	38	36	24	13	5.	How You Remind Me	Nickelback
00	27	24	20	13	6.	Otherwise	Red Hot Chili Peppers
00	40	39	29	12	7.	Hemorrhage (In My Hands)	Fuel
99	36	34	27	11	8.	My Own Worst Enemy	Lit
00	33	31	24	11	9.	Kryptonite	3 Doors Down
95	25	17	14	10	10.	Wonderwall	Oasis
02	34	32	26	9	11.	Blurry	Puddle Of Mudd
98	34	30	24	9	12.	What It's Like	Everlast
95	25	18	15	9	13.	Lightning Crashes	Live
93	16	15	13	9	14.	Into Your Arms	The Lemonheads
91	13	12	12	9	15.	Mysterious Ways	U2
01	39	37	29	8	16.	Drive	Incubus
99	27	25	22	8	17.	All The Small Things	Blink 182
97	31	30	20	8	18.	Semi-Charmed Life	Third Eye Blind
97	30	28	18	8	19.	Fly	Sugar Ray Featuring Super Cat
91	11	11	10	8	20.	Losing My Religion	R.E.M.
88	12	10	10	8	21.	Orange Crush	R.E.M.
00	37	31	23	7	22.	Last Resort	Papa Roach
98	26	24	19	7	23.	The Way	Fastball
95	26	21	17	7	24.	When I Come Around	Green Day
97	25	18	14	7	25.	Tubthumping	Chumbawamba
90	18	17	14	7	26.	Cuts You Up	Peter Murphy
96	20	14	13	7	27.	Swallowed	Bush
89	16	15	11	7	28.	Fascination Street	The Cure
94	12	11	11	7	29.	The More You Ignore Me, The Closer I Get	Morrissey
99	26	21	19	6	30.	Every Morning	Sugar Ray
94	23	17	16	6	31.	Zombie	The Cranberries
93	18	16	15	6	32.	Regret	New Order
96	21	15	12	6	33.	Standing Outside A Broken Phone Booth With Money In My Hand	Primitive Radio Gods
94	19	15	12	6	34.	Fall Down	Toad The Wet Sprocket
93	11	10	10	6	35.	The Devil You Know	Jesus Jones
92	14	12	9	6	36.	Tomorrow	Morrissey
01	44	40	27	5	37.	In The End	Linkin Park
98	26	24	22	5	38.	Closing Time	Semisonic
97	32	31	21	5	39.	Walkin' On The Sun	Smash Mouth
99	26	23	19	5	40.	The Chemicals Between Us	Bush
98	26	22	19	5	41.	Iris	Goo Goo Dolls
98	26	19	16	5	42.	One Week	Barenaked Ladies
95	26	18	16	5	43.	Good	Better Than Ezra
97	26	22	14	5	44.	One Headlight	The Wallflowers
89	16	15	14	5	45.	So Alive	Love & Rockets
94	21	16	13	5	46.	Loser	Beck
95	19	15	13	5	47.	You Oughta Know	Alanis Morissette
91	15	14	13	5	48.	Kiss Them For Me	Siouxsie And The Banshees
94	23	16	12	5	49.	Basket Case	Green Day
93	14	14	11	5	50.	Pets	Porno For Pyros

ALL-TIME

Peak Year	Wks Chr	Wks T20	Wks T10	Wks @ #1	Rank	Title	Artist
89	14	14	11	5	51.	The Mayor Of Simpleton	XTC
90	13	13	11	5	52.	More	Sisters Of Mercy
93	13	12	11	5	53.	Soul To Squeeze	Red Hot Chili Peppers
00	23	14	10	5	54.	Minority	Green Day
96	19	14	10	5	55.	Champagne Supernova	Oasis
92	16	13	10	5	56.	Steam	Peter Gabriel
91	14	12	10	5	57.	Right Here, Right Now	Jesus Jones
93	11	11	10	5	58.	I Feel You	Depeche Mode
88	11	11	10	5	59.	Desire	U2
92	14	13	9	5	60.	Hit	The Sugarcubes
94	19	12	9	5	61.	What's The Frequency, Kenneth?	R.E.M.
90	13	11	9	5	62.	Way Down Now	World Party
91	11	10	9	5	63.	So You Think You're In Love	Robyn Hitchcock and the Egyptians
92	11	10	9	5	64.	Drive	R.E.M.
98	41	37	25	4	65.	Inside Out	Eve 6
02	36	31	20	4	66.	The Middle	Jimmy Eat World
98	26	23	17	4	67.	Celebrity Skin	Hole
01	27	22	16	4	68.	Smooth Criminal	Alien Ant Farm
95	23	17	15	4	69.	My Friends	Red Hot Chili Peppers
95	26	19	13	4	70.	Name	Goo Goo Dolls
96	26	18	13	4	71.	Down	311
90	17	15	13	4	72.	Been Caught Stealing	Jane's Addiction
02	26	20	12	4	73.	Seein' Red	Unwritten Law
97	22	16	12	4	74.	#1 Crush	Garbage
89	15	14	12	4	75.	Love And Anger	Kate Bush
89	15	14	12	4	76.	Proud To Fall	Ian McCulloch
91	15	14	12	4	77.	Rush	Big Audio Dynamite II
92	14	13	11	4	78.	Friday I'm In Love	The Cure
89	13	13	10	4	78.	Dirty Blvd.	Lou Reed
95	15	12	10	4	80.	Hold Me, Thrill Me, Kiss Me, Kill Me	U2
96	14	12	10	4	81.	Salvation	The Cranberries
90	14	11	9	4	82.	Joey	Concrete Blonde
92	11	11	8	4	83.	High	The Cure
89	12	9	8	4	84.	Love Shack	The B-52's
90	10	9	8	4	85.	Merry Go Round	The Replacements
91	10	9	8	4	86.	The Other Side Of Summer	Elvis Costello
92	9	8	8	4	87.	Good Stuff	The B-52's
97	10	8	7	4	88.	Discothéque	U2
01	35	33	26	3	89.	Hanging By A Moment	Lifehouse
98	33	32	21	3	90.	Never There	Cake
99	27	27	20	3	91.	Higher	Creed
02	24+	22+	18+	3	92.	Aerials	System Of A Down
96	27	23	17	3	93.	What I Got	Sublime
96	26	22	16	3	94.	Pepper	Butthole Surfers
97	26	19	14	3	95.	The Freshmen	The Verve Pipe
94	19	16	14	3	96.	Selling The Drama	Live
95	26	19	13	3	97.	Tomorrow	Silverchair
96	21	15	13	3	98.	Ironic	Alanis Morissette
93	14	13	12	3	99.	Heart-Shaped Box	Nirvana
96	21	15	11	3	100.	Mother Mother	Tracy Bonham

TOP 10 MODERN ROCK TRACKS

1988

Peak Date	Wks Chr	Wks T20	Wks T10	Wks @ Peak	Peak Pos	Rank	Title	Artist
11/26	12	10	10	8	1	1.	Orange Crush	R.E.M.
10/22	11	11	10	5	1	2.	Desire	U2
10/01	9	9	9	3	1	3.	All That Money Wants	Psychedelic Furs
9/10	14	13	10	2	1	4.	Peek-A-Boo	Siouxsie & The Banshees
9/17	8	7	6	1	1	5.	Just Play Music!	Big Audio Dynamite
11/05	11	9	8	2	2	6.	Carolyn's Fingers	Cocteau Twins
11/19	19	16	12	1	2	7.	The Killing Jar	Siouxsie & The Banshees
12/24	17	14	9	4	3	8.	Angel Of Harlem	U2
12/03	15	14	14	2	3	9.	The Great Commandment	Camouflage
11/05	11	10	8	2	3	10.	Put This Love To The Test	Jon Astley

1989

Peak Date	Wks Chr	Wks T20	Wks T10	Wks @ Peak	Peak Pos	Rank	Title	Artist
5/06	16	15	11	7	1	1.	Fascination	The Cure
6/24	16	15	14	5	1	2.	So Alive	Love & Rockets
4/01	14	14	11	5	1	3.	The Mayor Of Simpleton	XTC
12/09	15	14	12	4	1	4.	Love And Anger	Kate Bush
11/11	15	14	12	4	1	5.	Proud To Fall	Ian McCulloch
2/11	13	13	10	4	1	6.	Dirty Blvd.	Lou Reed
9/16	12	9	8	4	1	7.	Love Shack	The B-52's
8/26	13	11	9	3	1	8.	Come Anytime	Hoodoo Gurus
10/21	12	10	8	3	1	9.	Pictures Of Matchstick Men	Camper Van Beethoven
8/05	8	7	5	3	1	10.	Channel Z	The B-52's

1990

Peak Date	Wks Chr	Wks T20	Wks T10	Wks @ Peak	Peak Pos	Rank	Title	Artist
2/10	18	17	14	7	1	1.	Cuts You Up	Peter Murphy
12/15	13	13	11	5	1	2.	More	Sisters Of Mercy
6/09	13	11	9	5	1	3.	Way Down Now	World Party
10/27	17	15	13	4	1	4.	Been Caught Stealing	Jane's Addiction
7/14	14	11	9	4	1	5.	Joey	Concrete Blonde
10/13	10	9	8	4	1	6.	Merry Go Round	The Replacements
9/29	17	13	9	3	1	7.	Never Enough	The Cure
4/21	12	11	9	3	1	8.	Enjoy The Silence	Depeche Mode
1/20	13	10	9	3	1	9.	House	Psychedelic Furs
1/06	11	11	9	2	1	10.	Blues From A Gun	The Jesus & Mary Chain

1991

Peak Date	Wks Chr	Wks T20	Wks T10	Wks @ Peak	Peak Pos	Rank	Title	Artist
11/30	13	12	12	9	1	1.	Mysterious Ways	U2
3/16	11	11	10	8	1	2.	Losing My Religion	R.E.M.
7/06	15	14	13	5	1	3.	Kiss Them For Me	Siouxsie And The Banshees
2/09	14	12	10	5	1	4.	Right Here, Right Now	Jesus Jones
9/21	11	10	9	5	1	5.	So You Think You're In Love	Robyn Hitchcock and the Egyptians
8/10	15	14	12	4	1	6.	Rush	Big Audio Dynamite II
5/25	10	9	8	4	1	7.	The Other Side Of Summer	Elvis Costello
9/07	13	12	11	2	1	8.	Until She Comes	The Psychedelic Furs
10/26	17	16	9	2	1	9.	Give It Away	Red Hot Chili Peppers
6/22	16	13	9	2	1	10.	Get The Message	Electronic

TOP 10 MODERN ROCK TRACKS

1992

Peak Date	Wks Chr	Wks T20	Wks T10	Wks @ Peak	Peak Pos	Rank	Title	Artist
8/15	14	12	9	6	1	1.	Tomorrow	Morrissey
12/12	16	13	10	5	1	2.	Steam	Peter Gabriel
2/29	14	13	9	5	1	3.	Hit	The Sugarcubes
10/17	11	10	9	5	1	4.	Drive	R.E.M.
6/13	14	13	11	4	1	5.	Friday I'm In Love	The Cure
4/11	11	11	8	4	1	6.	High	The Cure
7/11	9	8	8	4	1	7.	Good Stuff	The B-52's
2/08	10	9	8	3	1	8.	What's Good	Lou Reed
11/21	15	12	10	2	1	9.	These Are Days	10,000 Maniacs
9/26	14	12	10	2	1	10.	Digging In The Dirt	Peter Gabriel

1993

Peak Date	Wks Chr	Wks T20	Wks T10	Wks @ Peak	Peak Pos	Rank	Title	Artist
11/06	16	15	13	9	1	1.	Into Your Arms	The Lemonheads
5/01	18	16	15	6	1	2.	Regret	New Order
1/23	11	10	10	6	1	3.	The Devil You Know	Jesus Jones
6/19	14	14	11	5	1	4.	Pets	Porno For Pyros
8/14	13	12	11	5	1	5.	Soul To Squeeze	Red Hot Chili Peppers
3/27	11	11	10	5	1	6.	I Feel You	Depeche Mode
10/16	14	13	12	3	1	7.	Heart-Shaped Box	Nirvana
7/24	17	15	11	3	1	8.	Break It Down Again	Tears For Fears
9/18	16	14	11	3	1	9.	No Rain	Blind Melon
3/06	15	13	11	3	1	10.	Feed The Tree	Belly

1994

Peak Date	Wks Chr	Wks T20	Wks T10	Wks @ Peak	Peak Pos	Rank	Title	Artist
4/02	12	11	11	7	1	1.	The More You Ignore Me, The Closer I Get	Morrissey
10/29	23	17	16	6	1	2.	Zombie	The Cranberries
6/18	19	15	12	6	1	3.	Fall Down	Toad The Wet Sprocket
2/05	21	16	13	5	1	4.	Loser	Beck
8/20	23	16	12	5	1	5.	Basket Case	Green Day
9/24	19	12	9	5	1	6.	What's The Frequency, Kenneth?	R.E.M.
5/21	19	16	14	3	1	7.	Selling The Drama	Live
12/17	15	13	11	3	1	8.	Bang And Blame	R.E.M.
1/22	21	18	14	2	1	9.	All Apologies	Nirvana
3/19	17	16	13	2	1	10.	God	Tori Amos

1995

Peak Date	Wks Chr	Wks T20	Wks T10	Wks @ Peak	Peak Pos	Rank	Title	Artist
12/30	25	17	14	10	1	1.	Wonderwall	Oasis
2/25	25	18	15	9	1	2.	Lightning Crashes	Live
1/07	26	21	17	7	1	3.	When I Come Around	Green Day
4/29	26	18	16	5	1	4.	Good	Better Than Ezra
7/22	19	15	13	5	1	5.	You Oughta Know	Alanis Morissette
11/18	23	17	15	4	1	6.	My Friends	Red Hot Chili Peppers
10/07	26	19	13	4	1	7.	Name	Goo Goo Dolls
6/24	15	12	10	4	1	8.	Hold Me, Thrill Me, Kiss Me, Kill Me	U2
9/02	26	19	13	3	1	9.	Tomorrow	Silverchair
6/03	13	10	9	3	1	10.	Misery	Soul Asylum

TOP 10 MODERN ROCK TRACKS

1996

Peak Date	Wks Chr	Wks T20	Wks T10	Wks @ Peak	Peak Pos	Rank	Title	Artist
11/16	20	14	13	7	1	1.	Swallowed	Bush
7/27	21	15	12	6	1	2.	Standing Outside A Broken Phone Booth With Money In My Hand	Primitive Radio Gods
4/06	19	14	10	5	1	3.	Champagne Supernova	Oasis
9/14	26	18	13	4	1	4.	Down	311
5/11	14	12	10	4	1	5.	Salvation	The Cranberries
10/26	27	23	17	3	1	6.	What I Got	Sublime
7/06	26	22	16	3	1	7.	Pepper	Butthole Surfers
3/16	21	15	13	3	1	8.	Ironic	Alanis Morissette
6/08	21	15	11	3	1	9.	Mother Mother	Tracy Bonham
10/12	25	16	12	2	1	10.	Novocaine For The Soul	Eels

1997

Peak Date	Wks Chr	Wks T20	Wks T10	Wks @ Peak	Peak Pos	Rank	Title	Artist
12/27	34	32	24	15	1	1.	Sex and Candy	Marcy Playground
5/24	31	30	20	8	1	2.	Semi-Charmed Life	Third Eye Blind
8/02	30	28	18	8	1	3.	Fly	Sugar Ray Featuring Super Cat
11/01	25	18	14	7	1	4.	Tubthumping	Chumbawamba
9/27	32	31	21	5	1	5.	Walkin' On The Sun	Smash Mouth
3/08	26	22	14	5	1	6.	One Headlight	The Wallflowers
1/04	22	16	12	4	1	7.	#1 Crush	Garbage
2/01	10	8	7	4	1	8.	Discothéque	U2
5/03	26	19	14	3	1	9.	The Freshmen	The Verve Pipe
4/12	16	14	11	3	1	10.	Staring At The Sun	U2

1998

Peak Date	Wks Chr	Wks T20	Wks T10	Wks @ Peak	Peak Pos	Rank	Title	Artist
12/26	34	30	24	9	1	1.	What It's Like	Everlast
4/11	26	24	19	7	1	2.	The Way	Fastball
5/30	26	24	22	5	1	3.	Closing Time	Semisonic
7/04	26	22	19	5	1	4.	Iris	Goo Goo Dolls
8/22	26	19	16	5	1	5.	One Week	Barenaked Ladies
8/08	41	37	25	4	1	6.	Inside Out	Eve 6
10/10	26	23	17	4	1	7.	Celebrity Skin	Hole
12/05	33	32	21	3	1	8.	Never There	Cake
11/21	32	29	23	2	1	9.	Fly Away	Lenny Kravitz
10/31	26	25	20	2	1	10.	Slide	The Goo Goo Dolls

1999

Peak Date	Wks Chr	Wks T20	Wks T10	Wks @ Peak	Peak Pos	Rank	Title	Artist
6/26	26	25	21	16	1	1.	Scar Tissue	Red Hot Chili Peppers
4/10	36	34	27	11	1	2.	My Own Worst Enemy	Lit
12/25	27	25	22	8	1	3.	All The Small Things	Blink 182
2/20	26	21	19	6	1	4.	Every Morning	Sugar Ray
10/23	26	23	19	5	1	5.	The Chemicals Between Us	Bush
10/16	27	27	20	3	1	6.	Higher	Creed
11/06	26	24	20	1	1	7.	Learn To Fly	Foo Fighters
12/18	29	28	23	1	1	8.	Re-Arranged	Limp Bizkit
7/24	30	29	22	11	2	9.	What's My Age Again?	Blink 182
4/17	26	21	15	7	2	10.	Praise You	Fatboy Slim

TOP 10 MODERN ROCK TRACKS

2000

Peak Date	Wks Chr	Wks T20	Wks T10	Wks @ Peak	Peak Pos	Rank	Title	Artist
2/19	27	24	20	13	1	1.	Otherside	Red Hot Chili Peppers
11/04	40	39	29	12	1	2.	Hemorrhage (In My Hands)	Fuel
5/20	33	31	24	11	1	3.	Kryptonite	3 Doors Down
8/05	37	31	23	7	1	4.	Last Resort	Papa Roach
9/30	23	14	10	5	1	5.	Minority	Green Day
8/12	26	17	12	1	1	6.	Californication	Red Hot Chili Peppers
4/29	26	20	14	7	2	7.	Adam's Song	Blink 182
6/17	26	22	12	4	2	8.	With Arms Wide Open	Creed
3/18	18	12	19	3	2	9.	Ex-Girlfriend	No Doubt
4/08	16	12	9	3	2	10.	Stand Inside Your Love	The Smashing Pumpkins

2001

Peak Date	Wks Chr	Wks T20	Wks T10	Wks @ Peak	Peak Pos	Rank	Title	Artist
4/28	29	29	24	16	1	1.	It's Been Awhile	Staind
9/22	38	36	24	13	1	2.	How You Remind Me	Nickelback
3/03	39	37	29	8	1	3.	Drive	Incubus
12/22	44	40	27	5	1	4.	In The End	Linkin Park
8/25	27	22	16	4	1	5.	Smooth Criminal	Alien Ant Farm
1/27	35	33	26	3	1	6.	Hanging By A Moment	Lifehouse
2/17	26	21	17	2	1	7.	Butterfly	Crazy Town
8/18	28	23	15	1	1	8.	Fat Lip	Sum 41
5/19	26	23	19	8	2	9.	Hash Pipe	Weezer
10/06	37	36	25	6	2	10.	Wish You Were Here	Incubus

2002

Peak Date	Wks Chr	Wks T20	Wks T10	Wks @ Peak	Peak Pos	Rank	Title	Artist
6/29	24 +	24 +	21	14	1	1.	By The Way	Red Hot Chili Peppers
1/26	34	32	26	9	1	2.	Blurry	Puddle Of Mudd
4/13	36	31	20	4	1	3.	The Middle	Jimmy Eat World
5/11	26	20	12	4	1	4.	Seein' Red	Unwritten Law
10/26	7 +	6 +	6 +	4	1	5.	You Know You're Right	Nirvana
10/05	24 +	22 +	18 +	3	1	6.	Aerials	System Of A Down
6/08	21	14	11	3	1	7.	Hero	Chad Kroeger Featuring Josey Scott
3/30	26	21	15	2	1	8.	Youth Of The Nation	P.O.D.
7/20	28	26	18	5	2	9.	Running Away	Hoobastank
8/24	26	19	16	3	2	10.	Sweetness	Jimmy Eat World

Jimmy Eat World

Nickelback

Fuel

Albums with Most Charted *Modern Rock Tracks*

Each charted track is awarded points based on the artist ranking point system (see page 262)

Achtung Baby...*U2*
6 tracks / 403 points

Mellon Collie And The Infinite Sadness...
The Smashing Pumpkins — 6 tracks / 397 points

Jagged Little Pill...*Alanis Morissette*
6 tracks / 391 points

Vitalogy...*Pearl Jam*
6 tracks / 232 points

Californication...*Red Hot Chili Peppers*
5 tracks / 464 points

Dookie...*Green Day*
5 tracks / 401 points

Break The Cycle...*Staind*
5 tracks / 385 points

Sixteen Stone...*Bush*
5 tracks / 377 points

Throwing Copper...*Live*
5 tracks / 368 points

Third Eye Blind...*Third Eye Blind*
5 tracks / 323 points

Hybrid Theory...*Linkin Park*
5 tracks / 310 points

Monster...*R.E.M.*
5 tracks / 280 points

TRACKS OF LONGEVITY

1988-89

Peak Year	Peak Pos	Peak Wks	Wks Chr	Rank	Title	Artist
88	4	1	21	1.	What I Am	Edie Brickell & New Bohemians
88	2	1	19	2.	The Killing Jar	Siouxsie & The Banshees
89	2	1	19	3.	Good Thing	Fine Young Cannibals
89	1	2	17	4.	Stand	R.E.M.
89	2	3	17	5.	Love Song	The Cure
88	3	4	17	6.	Angel Of Harlem	U2
89	5	2	17	7.	Sweet Jane	Cowboy Junkies
89	1	7	16	8.	Fascination Street	The Cure
89	1	5	16	9.	So Alive	Love & Rockets
89	1	4	15	10.	Proud To Fall	Ian McCulloch
89	1	4	15	11.	Love And Anger	Kate Bush
88	3	2	15	12.	The Great Commandment	Camouflage

1990-99

Peak Year	Peak Pos	Peak Wks	Wks Chr	Rank	Title	Artist
98	1	4	41	1.	Inside Out	Eve 6
99	1	11	36	2.	My Own Worst Enemy	Lit
97	1	15	34	3.	Sex and Candy	Marcy Playground
98	1	9	34	4.	What It's Like	Everlast
98	1	3	33	5.	Never There	Cake
97	1	5	32	6.	Walkin' On The Sun	Smash Mouth
98	1	2	32	7.	Fly Away	Lenny Kravitz
97	1	8	31	8.	Semi-Charmed Life	Third Eye Blind
99	2	2	31	9.	One	Creed
98	2	1	31	10.	Shimmer	Fuel
99	4	1	31	11.	Blue Monday	Orgy
97	1	8	30	12.	Fly	Sugar Ray Featuring Super Cat

2000-02

Peak Year	Peak Pos	Peak Wks	Wks Chr	Rank	Title	Artist
01	1	5	44	1.	In The End	Linkin Park
00	3	3	42	2.	Pardon Me	Incubus
00	1	12	40	3.	Hemorrhage (In My Hands)	Fuel
01	1	8	39	4.	Drive	Incubus
01	1	13	38	5.	How You Remind Me	Nickelback
00	1	7	37	6.	Last Resort	Papa Roach
01	2	6	37	7.	Wish You Were Here	Incubus
02	3	1	37	8.	Wasting My Time	Default
02	1	4	36	9.	The Middle	Jimmy Eat World
02	3	1	36	10.	Crawling In The Dark	Hoobastank
01	1	3	35	11.	Hanging By A Moment	Lifehouse
01	7	5	35	12.	Chop Suey	System Of A Down

#1 HITS

This section lists in chronological order, by peak date, all 188 tracks that hit the #1 position on *Billboard's* "Modern Rock Tracks" chart from September 10, 1988 through November 9, 2002.

For the years 1981 through 1991, *Billboard* did not publish a year-end issue. *Billboard* considered the charts listed in the last published issue of the year to be "frozen" and all chart positions remained the same for the unpublished week. This frozen chart data is included in our tabulations. Since 1992, *Billboard* has <u>compiled</u> a chart for the last week of the year, even though an issue is <u>not</u> <u>published</u>. This chart is only available through Member Services of Billboard.com or by mail.

> **DATE:** Date track first peaked at the #1 position
>
> **WKS:** Total weeks track held the #1 position
>
> ↕: Indicates track hit #1, dropped down, and then returned to the #1 spot

> The <u>top</u> hit of each year is boxed out for quick reference. The top hit is determined by most weeks at the #1 position, followed by total weeks in the Top 10, Top 20, and total weeks charted.

#1 HITS

1988

	DATE	WKS		
1.	9/10	2↕	**Peek-A-Boo**	*Siouxsie & The Banshees*
2.	9/17	1	**Just Play Music!**	*Big Audio Dynamite*
3.	10/1	3	**All That Money Wants**	*Psychedelic Furs*
4.	10/22	5	**Desire**	*U2*
5.	11/26	8	**Orange Crush**	*R.E.M.*

1989

	DATE	WKS		
1.	1/21	1	**Charlotte Anne**	*Julian Cope*
2.	1/28	2	**Stand**	*R.E.M.*
3.	2/11	4	**Dirty Blvd.**	*Lou Reed*
4.	3/11	1	**I'll Be You**	*The Replacements*
5.	3/18	2	**Veronica**	*Elvis Costello*
6.	4/1	5	**The Mayor Of Simpleton**	*XTC*
7.	5/6	7	**Fascination Street**	*The Cure*
8.	6/24	5	**So Alive**	*Love & Rockets*
9.	7/29	1	**Disappointed**	*Public Image Ltd.*
10.	8/5	3	**Channel Z**	*The B-52's*
11.	8/26	3	**Come Anytime**	*Hoodoo Gurus*
12.	9/16	4	**Love Shack**	*The B-52's*
13.	10/14	1	**Sowing The Seeds Of Love** *Tears For Fears*	
14.	10/21	3	**Pictures Of Matchstick Men** *Camper Van Beethoven*	
15.	11/11	4	**Proud To Fall**	*Ian McCulloch*
16.	12/9	4	**Love And Anger**	*Kate Bush*

1990

	DATE	WKS		
1.	1/6	2	**Blues From A Gun**	*The Jesus & Mary Chain*
2.	1/20	3	**House**	*Psychedelic Furs*
3.	2/10	7	**Cuts You Up**	*Peter Murphy*
4.	3/31	1	**Nothing Compares 2 U**	*Sinéad O'Connor*
5.	4/7	1	**Blue Sky Mine**	*Midnight Oil*
6.	4/14	1	**Metropolis**	*The Church*
7.	4/21	3	**Enjoy The Silence**	*Depeche Mode*
8.	5/12	1	**The Emperor's New Clothes** *Sinéad O'Connor*	
9.	5/19	1	**Forgotten Years**	*Midnight Oil*
10.	5/26	1	**Here's Where The Story Ends** *The Sundays*	
11.	6/2	1	**Policy Of Truth**	*Depeche Mode*
12.	6/9	5	**Way Down Now**	*World Party*
13.	7/14	4	**Joey**	*Concrete Blonde*
14.	8/11	2↕	**Jealous**	*Gene Loves Jezebel*
15.	8/18	1	**I'll Be Your Chauffeur**	*David J*
16.	9/1	2↕	**Stop!**	*Jane's Addiction*
17.	9/8	1	**Every Beat Of The Heart** *The Railway Children*	
18.	9/22	1	**Suicide Blonde**	*INXS*
19.	9/29	3↕	**Never Enough**	*The Cure*
20.	10/13	4↕	**Merry Go Round**	*The Replacements*
21.	10/27	4↕	**Been Caught Stealing**	*Jane's Addiction*
22.	12/15	5	**More**	*Sisters Of Mercy*

1991

	DATE	WKS		
1.	1/19	1	**Kinky Afro**	*Happy Mondays*
2.	1/26	2	**All This Time**	*Sting*
3.	2/9	5	**Right Here, Right Now**	*Jesus Jones*
4.	3/16	8	**Losing My Religion**	*R.E.M.*
5.	5/11	2	**See The Lights**	*Simple Minds*
6.	5/25	4	**The Other Side Of Summer**	*Elvis Costello*
7.	6/22	2	**Get The Message**	*Electronic*
8.	7/6	5	**Kiss Them For Me** *Siouxsie And The Banshees*	
9.	8/10	4	**Rush**	*Big Audio Dynamite II*
10.	9/7	2	**Until She Comes**	*The Psychedelic Furs*
11.	9/21	5	**So You Think You're In Love** *Robyn Hitchcock and the Egyptians*	
12.	10/26	2	**Give It Away**	*Red Hot Chili Peppers*
13.	11/9	2	**The Fly**	*U2*
14.	11/23	1	**Smells Like Teen Spirit**	*Nirvana*
15.	11/30	9	**Mysterious Ways**	*U2*

1992

	DATE	WKS		
1.	2/1	1	**Sax And Violins**	*Talking Heads*
2.	2/8	3	**What's Good**	*Lou Reed*
3.	2/29	5	**Hit**	*The Sugarcubes*
4.	4/4	1	**One**	*U2*
5.	4/11	4	**High**	*The Cure*
6.	5/9	2	**Teen Angst (What The World Needs Now)** *Cracker*	
7.	5/23	1	**Weirdo**	*The Charlatans UK*
8.	5/30	2	**The Ballad Of Peter Pumpkinhead**	*XTC*
9.	6/13	4	**Friday I'm In Love**	*The Cure*
10.	7/11	4	**Good Stuff**	*The B-52's*
11.	8/8	1	**MidLife Crisis**	*Faith No More*
12.	8/15	6	**Tomorrow**	*Morrissey*
13.	9/26	2	**Digging In The Dirt**	*Peter Gabriel*
14.	10/10	1	**Blood Makes Noise**	*Suzanne Vega*
15.	10/17	5	**Drive**	*R.E.M.*
16.	11/21	2	**These Are Days**	*10,000 Maniacs*
17.	12/5	1	**Somebody To Shove**	*Soul Asylum*
18.	12/12	5	**Steam**	*Peter Gabriel*

1993

	DATE	WKS		
1.	1/16	1	**Not Sleeping Around**	*Ned's Atomic Dustbin*
2.	1/23	6	**The Devil You Know**	*Jesus Jones*
3.	3/6	3	**Feed The Tree**	*Belly*
4.	3/27	1	**I Feel You**	*Depeche Mode*
5.	5/1	6↕	**Regret**	*New Order*
6.	5/15	1	**Walking In My Shoes**	*Depeche Mode*

6/12/93: Billboard begins compiling "Modern Rock Tracks" chart from data provided by Broadcast Data Systems.

	DATE	WKS		
7.	6/19	5	**Pets**	*Porno For Pyros*
8.	7/24	3	**Break It Down Again**	*Tears For Fears*
9.	8/14	5↕	**Soul To Squeeze**	*Red Hot Chili Peppers*
10.	9/11	1	**My Sister**	*The Juliana Hatfield Three*
11.	9/18	3↕	**No Rain**	*Blind Melon*
12.	10/16	3	**Heart-Shaped Box**	*Nirvana*
13.	11/6	9	**Into Your Arms**	*The Lemonheads*

#1 HITS

1994

	DATE	WKS		
1.	1/8	1	**Daughter**	*Pearl Jam*
2.	1/15	1	**Found Out About You**	*Gin Blossoms*
3.	1/22	2	**All Apologies**	*Nirvana*
4.	2/5	5	**Loser**	*Beck*
5.	3/12	1	**Mmm Mmm Mmm Mmm**	
			Crash Test Dummies	
6.	3/19	2	**God**	*Tori Amos*
7.	4/2	7	**The More You Ignore Me, The Closer I Get** *Morrissey*	
8.	5/21	3	**Selling The Drama**	*Live*
9.	6/11	1	**Long View**	*Green Day*
10.	6/18	6	**Fall Down**	*Toad The Wet Sprocket*
11.	7/30	2	**Come Out And Play**	*Offspring*
12.	8/13	1	**Einstein On The Beach (For An Eggman)**	
			Counting Crows	
13.	8/20	5	**Basket Case**	*Green Day*
14.	9/24	5	**What's The Frequency, Kenneth?**	*R.E.M.*
15.	10/29	6	**Zombie**	*The Cranberries*
16.	12/10	1	**About A Girl**	*Nirvana*
17.	12/17	3	**Bang And Blame**	*R.E.M.*

1995

	DATE	WKS		
1.	1/7	7	**When I Come Around**	*Green Day*
2.	2/25	9	**Lightning Crashes**	*Live*
3.	4/29	5	**Good**	*Better Than Ezra*
4.	6/3	3	**Misery**	*Soul Asylum*
5.	6/24	4	**Hold Me, Thrill Me, Kiss Me, Kill Me**	*U2*
6.	7/22	5	**You Oughta Know**	*Alanis Morissette*
7.	8/26	1	**J.A.R. (Jason Andrew Relva)**	*Green Day*
8.	9/2	3	**Tomorrow**	*Silverchair*
9.	9/23	2	**Comedown**	*Bush*
10.	10/7	4↕	**Name**	*Goo Goo Dolls*
11.	10/14	1	**Hand In My Pocket**	*Alanis Morissette*
12.	10/21	1	**Lump**	
			Presidents Of The United States Of America	
13.	11/18	4	**My Friends**	*Red Hot Chili Peppers*
14.	12/16	2	**Glycerine**	*Bush*
15.	12/30	10↕	**Wonderwall**	*Oasis*

1996

	DATE	WKS		
1.	3/2	1	**1979**	*Smashing Pumpkins*
2.	3/16	3	**Ironic**	*Alanis Morissette*
3.	4/6	5	**Champagne Supernova**	*Oasis*
4.	5/11	4	**Salvation**	*The Cranberries*
5.	6/8	3	**Mother Mother**	*Tracy Bonham*
6.	6/29	1	**Counting Blue Cars**	*Dishwalla*
7.	7/6	3	**Pepper**	*Butthole Surfers*
8.	7/27	6	**Standing Outside A Broken Phone Booth With Money In My Hand**	
			Primitive Radio Gods	

1996 (cont'd)

9.	9/7	1	**Who You Are**	*Pearl Jam*
10.	9/14	4	**Down**	*311*
11.	10/12	2	**Novocaine For The Soul**	*Eels*
12.	10/26	3	**What I Got**	*Sublime*
13.	11/16	7	**Swallowed**	*Bush*

1997

	DATE	WKS		
1.	1/4	4	**#1 Crush**	*Garbage*
2.	2/1	4	**Discothéque**	*U2*
3.	3/1	1	**Lakini's Juice**	*Live*
4.	3/8	5	**One Headlight**	*The Wallflowers*
5.	4/12	3	**Staring At The Sun**	*U2*
6.	5/3	3	**The Freshmen**	*The Verve Pipe*
7.	5/24	8↕	**Semi-Charmed Life**	*Third Eye Blind*
8.	6/28	1	**The Impression That I Get**	
			The Mighty Mighty Bosstones	
9.	7/26	1	**Push**	*Matchbox 20*
10.	8/2	8	**Fly**	*Sugar Ray Featuring Super Cat*
11.	9/27	5	**Walkin' On The Sun**	*Smash Mouth*
12.	11/1	7	**Tubthumping**	*Chumbawamba*
13.	12/20	1	**Everything To Everyone**	*Everclear*
14.	12/27	15	**Sex and Candy**	*Marcy Playground*

1998

	DATE	WKS		
1.	4/11	7	**The Way**	*Fastball*
2.	5/30	5	**Closing Time**	*Semisonic*
3.	7/4	5	**Iris**	*Goo Goo Dolls*
4.	8/8	4↕	**Inside Out**	*Eve 6*
5.	8/22	5↕	**One Week**	*Barenaked Ladies*
6.	10/10	4↕	**Celebrity Skin**	*Hole*
7.	10/31	2↕	**Slide**	*The Goo Goo Dolls*
8.	11/21	2	**Fly Away**	*Lenny Kravitz*
9.	12/5	3	**Never There**	*Cake*
10.	12/26	9↕	**What It's Like**	*Everlast*

1999

	DATE	WKS		
1.	2/20	6↕	**Every Morning**	*Sugar Ray*
2.	4/10	11	**My Own Worst Enemy**	*Lit*
3.	6/26	16	**Scar Tissue**	*Red Hot Chili Peppers*
4.	10/16	3↕	**Higher**	*Creed*
5.	10/23	5↕	**The Chemicals Between Us**	*Bush*
6.	11/6	1	**Learn To Fly**	*Foo Fighters*
7.	12/18	1	**Re-Arranged**	*Limp Bizkit*
8.	12/25	8	**All The Small Things**	*Blink 182*

#1 HITS

DATE	WKS	**2000**
1.	2/19	13	**Otherside** *Red Hot Chili Peppers*
2.	5/20	11	**Kryptonite** *3 Doors Down*
3.	8/5	7↕	**Last Resort** *Papa Roach*
4.	8/12	1	**Californication** *Red Hot Chili Peppers*
5.	9/30	5	**Minority** *Green Day*
6.	11/4	12	**Hemorrhage (In My Hands)** *Fuel*

DATE	WKS	**2001**
1.	1/27	3	**Hanging By A Moment** *Lifehouse*
2.	2/17	2	**Butterfly** *Crazy Town*
3.	3/3	8	**Drive** *Incubus*
4.	4/28	16	**It's Been Awhile** *Staind*
5.	8/18	1	**Fat Lip** *Sum 41*
6.	8/25	4	**Smooth Criminal** *Alien Ant Farm*
7.	9/22	13	**How You Remind Me** *Nickelback*
8.	12/22	5	**In The End** *Linkin Park*

DATE	WKS	**2002**
1.	1/26	9	**Blurry** *Puddle Of Mudd*
2.	3/30	2	**Youth Of The Nation** *P.O.D.*
3.	4/13	4	**The Middle** *Jimmy Eat World*
4.	5/11	4	**Seein' Red** *Unwritten Law*
5.	6/8	3	**Hero** *Chad Kroeger Featuring Josey Scott*
6.	6/29	14	**By The Way** *Red Hot Chili Peppers*
7.	10/5	3	**Aerials** *System Of A Down*
8.	10/26	4	**You Know You're Right** *Nirvana*

SONG TITLE SECTION

This section contains an all-inclusive, alphabetical listing of every track title that appears in the "Mainstream Rock Tracks" and "Modern Rock Tracks" artist sections. The artist's name is listed next to each track title along with the highest position attained and the year the track peaked on the chart. An 'A' shown in front of a peak position indicates a "Mainstream Rock Tracks" hit and an 'M' indicates a "Modern Rock Tracks" hit. For example, 'A-21/89' indicates the track title peaked at position 21 on the "Mainstream Rock Tracks" chart in 1989. If a track by an artist hits both charts, the track is shown once, with the chart information from both charts shown beneath the track in order of highest peak position.

A song with more than one charted version is listed once, with the artists' names listed below in chronological order. Many songs that have the same title, but are different tunes, are listed separately, with the most popular title listed first. This will make it easy to determine which songs are the same composition, the number of charted versions of a particular song, and which of these were the most popular.

Cross references have been used throughout to aid in finding a title.

Please keep the following in mind when searching for titles:

Titles such as "N.W.O." and "S S S & Q" will be found at the beginning of their respective letters; however, titles such as "C-I-T-Y" and "F.I.N.E." which are spellings of words, are listed with their regular spellings.

Two-word titles which have the <u>exact</u> same spelling as one-word titles are listed together alphabetically. ("High Wire" is listed directly before "Highwire.")

Titles which are identical, except for an apostrophized word in one of the titles, are shown together. ("Comin' Home" appears immediately above "Coming Home.")

Titles which have only a very slight discrepancy are shown together. ("Last Night" appears immediately above "Last Nite" and "It's Alright" appears immediately above "It's All Right.")

A

M-15/00 **AM Radio** *Everclear*

A-4/81 **Abacab** *Genesis*

A-23/96 **Aberdeen**
Kenny Wayne Shepherd

About A Girl *Nirvana*
M-1/94 A-3/94

A-34/99 **Above** *Finger Eleven*

A-4/82 **Abracadabra** *Steve Miller Band*

A-9/86 **Absolute Beginners**
David Bowie

M-10/00 **Absolutely (Story Of A Girl)**
Nine Days

Abuse Me *Silverchair*
A-4/97 M-4/97

M-14/89 **Accidentally 4th St. (Gloria)**
Figures On A Beach

Achin' To Be *Replacements*
M-22/89 A-37/89

M-29/92 **Acid Drops** *PIL*

M-24/98 **Acquiesce** *Oasis*

A-29/02 **Across The Nation**
Union Underground

A-1/90 **Across The River**
Bruce Hornsby

A-24/89 **Acting This Way**
Robert Cray Band

A-42/83 **Action! Not Words** *Def Leppard*

M-2/00 **Adam's Song** *Blink 182*

A-7/82 **Addicted** *Le Roux*

M-23/02 **Addicted** *Lit*

A-1/86 **Addicted To Love**
Robert Palmer

A-39/89 **Addicted To That Rush** *Mr. Big*

Adrenaline *Gavin Rossdale*
M-20/02 A-24/02

A-15/02 **Adriana** *Headstrong*

A-23/84 **Adult Education**
Daryl Hall & John Oates

A-12/81 **Adultress, The** *Pretenders*

A-25/97 **Aenima** *Tool*

Aerials *System Of A Down*
M-1/02 A-1/02

Aeroplane
Red Hot Chili Peppers
M-8/96 A-12/96

A-23/83 **Affair Of The Heart**
Rick Springfield

A-10/97 **Afraid** *Mötley Crüe*

A-28/82 **Afraid Of Love** *Toto*

A-31/02 **After Me** *Saliva*

A-4/88 **After Midnight** *Eric Clapton*

A-30/83 **After The Fall** *Journey*

A-3/85 **After The Fire** *Roger Daltrey*

A-39/90 **After The Rain** *Nelson*

A-9/86 **Aftermath, The** *Bob Seger*

M-13/94 **Afternoons & Coffeespoons**
Crash Test Dummies

Again *Alice In Chains*
A-8/96 M-36/96

M-23/01 **Again** *Lenny Kravitz*

A-36/02 **Again** *Jeremiah Freed*

A-39/00 **Again And Again** *Taproot*

A-1/92 **Again Tonight**
John Mellencamp

A-1/84 **Against All Odds (Take A Look
At Me Now)** *Phil Collins*

M-21/95 **Against The 70's** *Mike Watt*

M-28/89 **Agent Double O Soul**
Untouchables

A-39/87 **Ages Of You** *R.E.M.*

A-19/81 **Ah! Leah!** *Donnie Iris*

A-44/81 **Ain't Even Done With The Night**
John Cougar

A-32/83 **Ain't Going Down** *Eric Clapton*

A-8/93 **Ain't It Fun** *Guns N' Roses*

A-10/92 **Ain't It Heavy** *Melissa Etheridge*

A-15/96 **Ain't My Bitch** *Metallica*

A-17/87 **Ain't So Easy** *David & David*

M-35/98 **Airport Song** *Guster*

M-38/01 **Aisle 10** *Scapegoat Wax*

A-19/95 **Albatross**
Corrosion Of Conformity

Alcohol *Howlin' Maggie*
A-25/96 M-37/96

M-33/99 **Alcohol** *Barenaked Ladies*

M-21/91 **Alice Everyday** *Book Of Love*

A-18/81 **Alien** *Atlanta Rhythm Section*

M-36/99 **Alien** *Pennywise*

A-10/93 **Alien Nation** *Scorpions*

Alive *P.O.D.*
M-2/01 A-4/01

M-11/99 **Alive** *Beastie Boys*

Alive *Pearl Jam*
A-16/92 M-18/92

A-2/85 **Alive & Kicking** *Simple Minds*

M-14/91 **Alive And Living Now**
Golden Palominos

A-21/93 **All Alone** *Joe Satriani*

A-48/85 **All American Boy** *Y&T*

A-24/94 **All American Girl**
Melissa Etheridge

All Apologies *Nirvana*
M-1/94 A-4/94

M-15/98 **All Around The World** *Oasis*

A-2/88 **All Fired Up** *Pat Benatar*

M-22/90 **All For Love And Love For All**
Lilac Time

A-22/90 **All For You** *David Baerwald*

M-39/97 **All For You** *Sister Hazel*

M-27/94 **All I Am** *Dada*

All I Know *Screaming Trees*
A-9/96 M-9/96

A-6/86 **All I Need Is A Miracle**
Mike + The Mechanics

M-14/95 **All I Really Want**
Alanis Morissette

All I Wanna Do *Sheryl Crow*
M-4/94 A-35/94

A-2/90 **All I Wanna Do Is Make Love To
You** *Heart*

M-9/90 **All I Want** *Lightning Seeds*

All I Want *Offspring*
M-13/97 A-18/97

A-15/93 **All I Want** *Saigon Kick*

All I Want
Toad The Wet Sprocket
A-22/92 M-22/92

A-13/89 **All I Want Is You** *U2*

A-10/86 **All I Wanted** *Kansas*

M-17/88 **All I Wanted** *In Tua Nua*

A-49/87 **All In My Mind** *Love & Rockets*

A-10/89 **All Is Forgiven** *Red Siren*

A-16/90 **All Lips N' Hips** *Electric Boys*

A-10/84 **All Lovers Are Deranged**
David Gilmour

M-4/97 **All Mixed Up** *311*

A-19/87 **All Mixed Up** *Tom Petty*

M-21/00 **All My Fault** *Fenix*TX*

All My Life *Foo Fighters*
M-1/02 A-10/02

A-10/84 **All Night Long** *Billy Squier*

A-13/91 **All Of A Sudden** *Joe Walsh*

A-25/83 **All Of The Good Ones Are
Taken** *Ian Hunter*

A-47/92 **All Or Nothin' At All**
Bruce Springsteen

A-29/91 **All Our Dreams Are Sold**
Procol Harum

A-17/90 **All Over But The Cryin'**
Georgia Satellites

A-29/81 **All Over Town** *April Wine*

All Over You *Live*
A-2/95 M-4/95

M-24/89 **All She Wants Is** *Duran Duran*

A-1/85 **All She Wants To Do Is Dance**
Don Henley

A-25/92 **All She Wrote** *Firehouse*

M-2/99 **All Star** *Smash Mouth*

A-5/88 **All That Heaven Will Allow**
Bruce Springsteen

M-1/88 **All That Money Wants**
Psychedelic Furs

M-17/93 **All That She Wants**
Ace Of Base

All That You Are (X3)
Econoline Crush
A-18/99 M-28/99

All The Kids Are Right *Local H*
A-19/98 M-20/98

A-1/86 **All The Kings Horses** *Firm*

A-14/86 **All The Love** *Outfield*

M-1/99 **All The Small Things** *Blink 182*

A-9/86 **All The Things She Said**
Simple Minds

A-24/91 **All The Time In The World**
Junkyard

A-2/83 **All The Way** *Triumph*

A-12/91 **All The Way From Memphis**
Contraband

All This Time *Sting*
A-1/91 M-1/91

A-6/81 **All Those Years Ago**
George Harrison

A-38/84 **All Through The Night**
Cyndi Lauper

M-7/91 **All Together Now** *Farm*

A-11/85 **All You Zombies** *Hooters*

A-28/82 **Allentown** *Billy Joel*

A-28/82 **Alley Cat Blues** *Starfighters*

A-55/81 **Allied Forces** *Triumph*

Allison Road *Gin Blossoms*
A-20/94 M-39/94

M-13/92 **Almost Gold**
Jesus And Mary Chain

A-1/90 **Almost Hear You Sigh**
Rolling Stones

A-8/97 **Almost Honest** *Megadeth*

A-18/81 **Almost Saturday Night**
Dave Edmunds

A-3/87 **Alone** *Heart*

A-20/85 **Alone Again** *Dokken*

A-50/81 **Alone Again Or** *Damned*

A-10/85 **Along Comes A Woman**
Chicago

A-35/95 **Alot To Lose** *Tesla*

M-8/94 **Always** *Erasure*

Always *Saliva*
M-7↑/02 A-12↑/02

Always On The Run
Lenny Kravitz
M-8/91 A-40/91

M-7/89 **Always Saturday**
Guadalcanal Diary

A-20/83 **Always Something There To
Remind Me** *Naked Eyes*

Always The Last To Know
Del Amitri
M-11/92 A-18/92
A-47/87 **Always The Sun** *Stranglers*
A-10/93 **Am I Ever Gonna Change**
Extreme
M-3/94 **Am I Wrong** *Love Spit Love*
A-1/86 **Amanda** *Boston*
A-3/93 **Amazing** *Aerosmith*
M-13/02 **Amber** *311*
A-8/87 **America** *KBC Band*
American Bad Ass *Kid Rock*
A-20/00 M-33/00
A-40/02 **American Cliche** *Filter*
A-4/88 **American Dream**
Crosby, Stills, Nash & Young
M-28/90 **American Eyes** *Lilac Time*
A-38/94 **American Life In The**
Summertime *Francis Dunnery*
M-2/91 **American Music**
Violent Femmes
A-24/89 **American Music**
Ian Hunter/Mick Ronson
A-21/88 **American Roulette**
Robbie Robertson
A-2/86 **American Storm** *Bob Seger*
American Woman
Krokus
A-53/82
Lenny Kravitz
A-3/99 M-7/99
A-39/92 **Amnesia** *Tora Tora*
A-9/95 **Amsterdam** *Van Halen*
M-11/88 **Ana Ng** *They Might Be Giants*
Ana's Song (Open Fire)
Silverchair
M-12/99 A-28/99
A-19/82 **Analog Kid** *Rush*
M-16/88 **Anchorage** *Michelle Shocked*
A-1/95 **And Fools Shine On**
Brother Cane
A-11/85 **And She Was** *Talking Heads*
A-40/95 **And The Band Played On**
Simple Minds
A-3/85 **And We Danced** *Hooters*
M-20/94 **Andres** *L7*
Aneurysm *Nirvana*
A-11/96 M-13/96
A-2/88 **Angel** *Aerosmith*
M-26/94 **Angel** *Kirsty MacColl*
A-24/89 **Angel Eyes** *Jeff Healey Band*
A-49/81 **Angel Eyes** *Silver Condor*
(also see: I'll Never Let You Go)
A-38/82 **Angel Of Death** *Thin Lizzy*
Angel Of Harlem *U2*
A-1/88 M-3/88
A-57/81 **Angel Of The Morning**
Juice Newton
A-18/89 **Angel Song** *Great White*
M-14/89 **Angel Visit** *Thrashing Doves*
A-42/90 **Angel With A Dirty Face**
Lou Gramm
A-4/00 **Angel's Eye** *Aerosmith*
Angel's Son *Lajon*
A-11/01 M-15/01
A-20/96 **Angeline Is Coming Home**
Badlees
M-24/94 **Angels** *David Byrne*
A-34/90 **Angels, The** *Melissa Etheridge*
Angels Of The Silences
Counting Crows
M-3/96 A-4/96

A-10/02 **Anger Rising** *Jerry Cantrell*
A-15/93 **Angry** *Billy Squier*
A-44/86 **Angry** *Paul McCartney*
A-18/93 **Angry Again** *Megadeth*
Angry Chair *Alice In Chains*
M-27/93 A-34/93
M-7/96 **Angry Johnny** *Poe*
A-5/87 **Animal** *Def Leppard*
A-21/94 **Animal** *Pearl Jam*
A-35/94 **Animate** *Rush*
A-40/83 **Annie Get Your Gun** *Squeeze*
M-16/90 **Annie's Gone** *Redd Kross*
M-28/93 **Anniversary Song**
Cowboy Junkies
Another Brick In The Wall
Pink Floyd
A-42/88
Class Of '99
A-18/99 M-34/99
A-47/89 **Another Chance**
Georgia Satellites
A-22/93 **Another Day** *Dream Theater*
A-33/87 **Another Day** *Bryan Adams*
A-7/89 **Another Day In Paradise**
Phil Collins
A-10/91 **Another Deal Goes Down**
Steve Winwood
A-45/86 **Another Heartache** *Rod Stewart*
M-11/88 **Another Kind Of Love**
Hugh Cornwell
M-33/01 **Another Perfect Day**
American Hi-Fi
A-7/92 **Another Rainy Night (Without**
You) *Queensrÿche*
A-6/81 **Another Tricky Day** *Who*
M-26/89 **Answers To Nothing** *Midge Ure*
Anthem For The Year 2000
Silverchair
M-12/99 A-15/99
A-14/81 **Antmusic** *Adam & The Ants*
Ants Marching
Dave Matthews Band
A-18/95 M-18/95
A-16/92 **Anybody Listening?**
Queensrÿche
A-3/97 **Anybody Seen My Baby?**
Rolling Stones
Anything *Third Eye Blind*
M-11/99 A-35/99
A-43/92 **Anything At All** *Mitch Malloy*
A-3/87 **Anything Goes**
Gregg Allman Band
A-40/86 **Anything She Does** *Genesis*
A-5/90 **Anytime**
McAuley Schenker Group
A-17/82 **Anyway Anytime** *Wrabit*
A-18/93 **Anywhere But Here**
Raging Slab
A-39/91 **Apple Pie** *White Trash*
A-11/81 **Arc Of A Diver** *Steve Winwood*
A-1/84 **Are We Ourselves?** *Fixx*
Are You Gonna Go My Way
Lenny Kravitz
A-1/93 M-2/93
Are You Ready? *Creed*
A-4/00 M-37/00
A-16/91 **Are You Ready** *AC/DC*
Are You There? *Oleander*
A-6/01 M-19/01
A-3/88 **Armageddon It** *Def Leppard*
M-17/99 **Army** *Ben Folds Five*
M-21/95 **Army Of Me** *Björk*

Around The World
Red Hot Chili Peppers
M-7/99 A-16/99
A-23/83 **Art In America** *Art In America*
A-13/81 **Arthur's Theme (Best That You**
Can Do) *Christopher Cross*
A-15/89 **As Long As You Follow**
Fleetwood Mac
A-23/98 **Ashes To Ashes** *Faith No More*
A-3/84 **Ask The Lonely** *Journey*
M-36/95 **Asking For It** *Hole*
Asleep At The Wheel ..see: I
Wasn't Made To Feel This
Astounded *Tantric*
A-7/01 M-30/01
A-12/88 **Astronomy** *Blue Öyster Cult*
M-17/99 **At The Stars** *Better Than Ezra*
A-37/98 **At The Water** *Stegosaurus*
A-3/82 **Athena** *Who*
A-10/82 **Atlantic City** *Bruce Springsteen*
A-30/99 **Attention Please**
Caroline's Spine
A-15/84 **Authority Song**
John Cougar Mellencamp
M-28/00 **Automatic** *Collapsis*
Ava Adore *Smashing Pumpkins*
M-3/98 A-8/98
A-59/82 **Avalon** *Roxy Music*
Awake *Godsmack*
A-1/01 M-12/01
M-17/95 **Awake** *Letters To Cleo*
M-6/88 **Away** *Feelies*
Away *Toadies*
A-23/96 M-28/96
M-13/99 **Awful** *Hole*

B

A-22/84 **Baby Come Back** *Billy Rankin*
M-39/94 **Baby Come Back** *Pato Banton*
A-4/93 **Baby Come On Home**
Led Zeppelin
A-3/90 **Baby, It's Tonight** *Jude Cole*
A-35/85 **Baby Please Don't Go**
Willie & The Poor Boys
M-21/91 **Baby Universal** *Tin Machine*
A-35/82 **Baby's On Fire** *Sammy Hagar*
M-7/90 **Babydoll** *Laurie Anderson*
M-25/01 **Babylon** *David Gray*
A-27/84 **Back For More** *Ratt*
A-51/81 **Back In Black** *AC/DC*
A-19/86 **Back In The High Life Again**
Steve Winwood
A-45/87 **Back In The U.S.S.R.** *Billy Joel*
A-3/85 **Back In Time** *Huey Lewis*
A-32/90 **Back 'N Blue** *Cheap Trick*
M-22/90 **Back Of My Mind** *O-Positive*
A-3/97 **Back On Earth** *Ozzy Osbourne*
M-6/88 **Back On The Breadline**
Hunters & Collectors
A-4/83 **Back On The Chain Gang**
Pretenders
A-34/88 **Back On The Streets**
John Norum
A-56/82 **Back On The Track** *38 Special*
Back To Back *Replacements*
M-28/89 A-43/89
A-4/87 **Back To Paradise** *38 Special*
Back To School *Deftones*
M-27/00 A-35/00

A-31/90	**Back To Shalla-Bal** *Joe Satriani*	
A-31/90	**Back To Square One** *Ernie Isley*	
A-26/89	**Back To The Bullet** *Saraya*	
A-22/88	**Back To The Cave** *Lita Ford*	
A-20/89	**Back To The Wall** *Steve Earle*	
A-38/98	**Back To You** *Bryan Adams*	
A-14/84	**Back Where I Started** *Box Of Frogs*	
A-29/94	**Back Where It All Begins** *Allman Brothers Band*	
A-4/84	**Back Where You Belong** *38 Special*	
A-18/86	**Back Where You Started** *Tina Turner*	
	Backlash *Joan Jett* M-7/91 A-40/91	
A-48/84	**Backstabber** *Hyts*	
	Backwater *Meat Puppets* A-2/94 M-11/94	
A-19/85	**Bad** *U2*	
A-14/87	**Bad Attitude** *Deep Purple*	
A-22/86	**Bad Attitude** *Honeymoon Suite*	
A-37/94	**Bad Attitude Shuffle** *Cinderella*	
	Bad Day *Fuel* M-12/01 A-14/01	
A-34/83	**Bad Girls** *Don Felder*	
A-40/00	**Bad Little Doggie** *Gov't Mule*	
A-1/90	**Bad Love** *Eric Clapton*	
	Bad Luck *Social Distortion* M-2/92 A-44/92	
A-40/93	**Bad Luck Blue Eyes Goodbye** *Black Crowes*	
	Bad Magick *Godsmack* A-12/01 M-28/01	
A-20/89	**Bad Man** *Bad Company*	
A-3/88	**Bad Medicine** *Bon Jovi*	
A-42/91	**Bad Rain** *Allman Brothers Band*	
	Bad Religion *Godsmack* A-8/00 M-32/00	
M-28/94	**Bad Reputation** *Freedy Johnston*	
A-31/91	**Bad Reputation** *Damn Yankees*	
A-48/81	**Bad Reputation** *Joan Jett*	
A-2/94	**Bad Thing** *Cry Of Love*	
A-38/85	**Bad Times** *Michael McDonald*	
A-27/82	**Bad To The Bone** *George Thorogood*	
M-6/00	**Bad Touch** *Bloodhound Gang*	
A-29/01	**Bag Of Tricks** *Isle Of Q*	
A-34/98	**Baker Street** *Foo Fighters*	
M-13/90	**Ball And Chain** *Social Distortion*	
A-14/82	**Ball & Chain** *Elton John*	
A-25/90	**Ballad of Jayne** *L.A. Guns*	
A-23/91	**Ballad Of Jenny Ledge** *Toy Matinee*	
	Ballad Of Peter Pumpkinhead *XTC* M-1/92 A-46/92	
A-13/91	**Ballad Of Youth** *Richie Sambora*	
A-25/96	**Ballbreaker** *AC/DC*	
M-3/92	**Ballerina Out Of Control** *Ocean Blue*	
A-22/82	**Ballroom Dancing** *Paul McCartney*	
A-21/84	**Balls To The Wall** *Accept*	
A-28/86	**Band Of The Hand (Hell Time, Man!)** *Bob Dylan with "The Heartbreakers"*	
	Banditos *Refreshments* A-11/96 M-14/96	
A-41/89	**Bang** *Gorky Park*	

	Bang And Blame *R.E.M.* M-1/94 A-3/95	
A-22/97	**Bang Bang** *ZZ Top*	
A-38/87	**Bang Bang** *David Bowie*	
A-39/90	**Bang Bang** *Danger Danger*	
A-29/83	**Bang The Drum All Day** *Todd Rundgren*	
A-37/83	**Bang Your Head (Metal Health)** *Quiet Riot*	
A-40/87	**Bangin' On My Heart** *Outfield*	
M-36/98	**Barbarella** *Scott Weiland*	
A-26/86	**Barefootin'** *Pete Townshend*	
A-12/84	**Bark At The Moon** *Ozzy Osbourne*	
M-30/94	**Barney (...And Me)** *Boo Radleys*	
M-11/97	**Barrel Of A Gun** *Depeche Mode*	
	Bartender (I Just Want Your Company) *(HED)Planet Earth* A-23/00 M-27/00	
A-33/00	**Basic Breakdown** *Apartment 26*	
	Basket Case *Green Day* M-1/94 A-9/94	
M-18/89	**Batdance** *Prince*	
A-9/97	**Baton Rouge** *Nixons*	
M-6/99	**Battle Flag** *Lo Fidelity Allstars*	
M-22/97	**Battle Of Who Could Care Less** *Ben Folds Five*	
A-22/93	**Battle Rages On** *Deep Purple*	
A-11/87	**Battleship Chains** *Georgia Satellites*	
	Bawitdaba *Kid Rock* M-10/99 A-11/99	
A-3/83	**Be Good Johnny** *Men At Work*	
A-2/86	**Be Good To Yourself** *Journey*	
	Be Like That *3 Doors Down* A-10/01 M-22/01	
A-33/82	**Be My Lady** *Jefferson Starship*	
A-29/98	**Be Quiet And Drive (Far Away)** *Deftones*	
M-28/93	**Be Still** *Peace Together*	
A-2/88	**Be Still My Beating Heart** *Sting*	
A-42/81	**Be True** *Bruce Springsteen*	
M-18/88	**Be With You** *Jack Rubies* *(also see: I Just Wanna)*	
A-15/84	**Bears** *Zebra*	
A-50/82	**Beastie** *Jethro Tull*	
A-14/83	**Beat It** *Michael Jackson* *(also see: Eat It)*	
A-10/84	**Beat Of A Heart** *Scandal*	
A-39/01	**Beat The World** *Pressure 4-5*	
A-24/86	**Beat's So Lonely** *Charlie Sexton*	
M-13/89	**Beat(en) Generation** *The*	
M-20/99	**Beautiful** *Joydrop*	
M-27/01	**Beautiful** *Flickerstick*	
	Beautiful Day *U2* M-5/00 A-14/00	
M-21/98	**Beautiful Disaster** *311*	
M-10/93	**Beautiful Girl** *INXS*	
M-4/91	**Beautiful Love** *Julian Cope*	
	Beautiful People *Marilyn Manson* M-26/96 A-29/96	
A-37/97	**Beauty** *Mötley Crüe*	
M-17/01	**Because I Got High** *Afroman*	
	Because The Night	
A-22/87	*Bruce Springsteen*	
M-7/93	*10,000 Maniacs*	
	(Because of Me) ..see: Right Next Door	
A-4/87	**Bed Of Lies** *Cruzados*	
M-23/91	**Bed Of Roses** *Screaming Trees*	

A-25/93	**Bed Of Roses** *Bon Jovi*	
A-6/88	**Beds Are Burning** *Midnight Oil*	
	Been Caught Stealing *Jane's Addiction* M-1/90 A-29/90	
M-11/90	**Been There Done That** *Brian Eno/John Cale*	
A-20/91	**Been Your Fool** *Tattoo Rodeo*	
M-27/94	**Beercan** *Beck*	
A-9/90	**Before You Accuse Me** *Eric Clapton*	
A-21/95	**Beggars & Hangers-On** *Slash's Snakepit*	
A-38/91	**Beggars & Thieves** *Beggars & Thieves*	
A-22/01	**Beginning Of The End** *Systematic*	
A-58/81	**Behind The Lines** *Phil Collins*	
M-7/92	**Behind The Sun** *Red Hot Chili Peppers*	
A-23/87	**Behind The Wall Of Sleep** *Smithereens*	
M-7/93	**Being Simple** *Judybats*	
	Believe *Lenny Kravitz* M-10/93 A-15/93	
	Believe *Dig* M-19/94 A-34/94	
A-12/88	**Believe In Love** *Scorpions*	
A-39/02	**Believe Me** *Mesh Stl*	
M-30/88	**(Believed You Were) Lucky** *'Til Tuesday*	
	Bent *Matchbox Twenty* M-16/00 A-24/00	
	Bertha *Los Lobos* M-24/91 A-37/91	
A-28/91	**Best I Can** *Queensrÿche*	
A-5/87	**Best Man In The World** *Ann Wilson*	
A-12/86	**Best Of Both Worlds** *Van Halen*	
A-16/81	**Best Of Times** *Styx*	
A-9/90	**Best Of What I Got** *Bad English*	
	(Best That You Can Do) ..see: Arthur's Theme	
	Best Things *Filter* M-18/00 A-31/00	
A-5/81	**Bette Davis Eyes** *Kim Carnes*	
M-17/91	**Better Back Off** *Marshall Crenshaw*	
A-32/84	**Better Be Good To Me** *Tina Turner*	
	Better Be Home Soon *Crowded House* A-18/88 M-29/88	
A-2/92	**Better Days** *Bruce Springsteen*	
A-19/90	**Better Days** *Gun*	
M-3/99	**Better Days (And The Bottom Drops Out)** *Citizen King*	
	Better Man *Pearl Jam* A-1/95 M-2/95	
	Better Than Nothing *Jennifer Trynin* M-15/95 A-40/95	
A-7/98	**Better Than You** *Metallica*	
A-12/81	**Better Things** *Kinks*	
A-41/89	**(Between A) Rock And A Hard Place** *Cutting Crew*	
	Between Angels And Insects *Papa Roach* M-16/01 A-27/01	
A-28/96	**Between Heaven And Hell** *Zakk Wylde*	
M-2/89	**Between Something And Nothing** *Ocean Blue*	
A-39/84	**Between The Wheels** *Rush*	

A-35/82 **Between Two Worlds**
 Tom Petty
A-17/89 **Big Bad Moon** *Joe Satriani*
A-26/81 **Big Balls** *AC/DC*
 Big Bang Baby
 Stone Temple Pilots
 A-1/96 M-2/96
 Big Chair *Reacharound*
 M-28/96 A-33/96
A-14/84 **Big City Nights** *Scorpions*
A-17/83 **Big Crash** *Eddie Money*
 Big Empty *Stone Temple Pilots*
 A-3/94 M-7/94
A-20/92 **Big Goodbye** *Great White*
A-1/93 **Big Gun** *AC/DC*
A-9/88 **Big League**
 Tom Cochrane & Red Rider
A-22/91 **Big Lie** *Rik Emmett*
A-6/83 **Big Log** *Robert Plant*
A-2/87 **Big Love** *Fleetwood Mac*
A-35/90 **Big Love** *Robert Plant*
M-18/89 **Big Man On Paper**
 Graham Parker
 Big Me *Foo Fighters*
 M-3/96 A-18/96
A-4/85 **Big Money** *Rush*
A-36/91 **Big Sky Country** *Chris Whitley*
A-30/89 **Big Talk** *Warrant*
A-3/87 **Big Time** *Peter Gabriel*
A-35/96 **Big Time**
 Neil Young & Crazy Horse
M-5/94 **Big Time Sensuality** *Björk*
M-10/90 **Bikini Girls With Machine Guns**
 Cramps
A-33/83 **Billy's Got A Gun** *Def Leppard*
M-3/90 **Birdhouse In Your Soul**
 They Might Be Giants
 (Birds Fly) ..see: Whisper To A Scream
A-38/88 **Birth, School, Work, Death**
 Godfathers
A-35/90 **Birthday** *Paul McCartney*
M-4/97 **Bitch** *Meredith Brooks*
A-30/98 **Bitch** *Sevendust*
M-11/90 **Biting My Nails**
 Renegade Soundwave
A-22/98 **Bitter Pill** *Mötley Crüe*
 Bitter Sweet Symphony *Verve*
 M-4/98 A-22/98
 Bitter Tears *INXS*
 A-4/91 M-6/91
A-14/93 **Bittersweet**
 Big Head Todd & The Monsters
 Bittersweet *Fuel*
 A-15/99 M-17/98
 Bittersweet Me *R.E.M.*
 M-6/96 A-7/96
M-10/94 **Bizarre Love Triangle** *Frente!*
 Black *Pearl Jam*
 A-3/93 M-20/93
A-30/98 **Black** *Sevendust*
A-1/88 **Black And Blue** *Van Halen*
 (also see: Back 'N Blue)
A-35/01 **Black & White** *Static-X*
 Black Balloon *Goo Goo Dolls*
 M-13/99 A-28/99
A-34/85 **Black Cars** *Gino Vannelli*
A-26/82 **Black Coffee In Bed** *Squeeze*
A-17/92 **Black Flag** *King's X*
 Black Gold *Soul Asylum*
 A-4/93 M-6/93
 Black Hole Sun *Soundgarden*
 A-1/94 M-2/94

 Black Jesus *Everlast*
 M-15/00 A-30/00
A-38/93 **Black Lodge** *Anthrax*
M-9/92 **Black Metallic** *Catherine Wheel*
A-13/91 **Black Money** *Vinnie James*
A-44/92 **Black Moon**
 Emerson, Lake & Palmer
A-4/93 **Black On Black II** *Heart*
M-22/89 **Black Sheep Wall**
 Innocence Mission
A-39/94 **Black Sunshine** *White Zombie*
A-1/90 **Black Velvet** *Alannah Myles*
A-34/91 **Black, White And Blood Red**
 BoDeans
A-6/96 **Blackberry** *Black Crowes*
A-11/97 **Blame** *Collective Soul*
M-22/93 **Blast** *Pure*
A-1/90 **Blaze Of Glory** *Jon Bon Jovi*
A-36/99 **Bled For Days** *Static-X*
M-18/01 **Bleed American**
 Jimmy Eat World
 Bleed Together *Soundgarden*
 A-13/97 M-32/97
A-32/01 **Bleeder** *Nothingface*
A-6/97 **Bleeding Me** *Metallica*
A-39/88 **Blind** *Talking Heads*
A-39/91 **Blind Faith** *Warrant*
A-3/94 **Blind Man** *Aerosmith*
A-31/01 **Blister** *Simon Says*
M-40/97 **Block Rockin' Beats**
 Chemical Brothers
A-38/85 **Blondes In Black Cars**
 Autograph
A-14/86 **Blood And Roses** *Smithereens*
M-27/93 **Blood And Thunder**
 Ultra Vivid Scene
M-1/92 **Blood Makes Noise**
 Suzanne Vega
A-14/91 **Blood On The Bricks** *Aldo Nova*
A-31/82 **Bloody Reunion** *Molly Hatchet*
A-32/01 **Bloom** *Sinomatic*
 Blow Up The Outside World
 Soundgarden
 A-1/96 M-8/96
A-24/81 **Blow Wind Blow** *Eric Clapton*
M-19/92 **Blowing Bubbles**
 Lightning Seeds
A-39/93 **Blue Eyes** *Steve Miller Band*
M-29/90 **Blue Flower** *Mazzy Star*
A-2/84 **Blue Jean** *David Bowie*
A-35/84 **Blue Light** *David Gilmour*
 Blue Monday *Orgy*
 M-4/99 A-18/99
A-40/89 **Blue Monday** *Bob Seger*
A-1/98 **Blue On Black**
 Kenny Wayne Shepherd Band
 Blue Sky Mine *Midnight Oil*
 M-1/90 A-1/90
A-32/83 **Blue World** *Moody Blues*
A-32/97 **Blueboy** *John Fogerty*
 Blues Before And After
 Smithereens
 A-7/90 M-18/90
M-1/90 **Blues From A Gun**
 Jesus & Mary Chain
 Blurry *Puddle Of Mudd*
 A-1/02 M-1/02
M-21/96 **Bluster** *Salt*
M-23/91 **Bob's Yer Uncle**
 Happy Mondays
A-36/84 **Bobby Jean** *Bruce Springsteen*
 Bodies *Drowning Pool*
 A-6/01 M-12/01

A-23/84 **Body Electric** *Rush*
A-19/82 **Body Language** *Queen*
M-15/98 **Body Movin'** *Beastie Boys*
M-26/99 **Bodyrock** *Moby*
A-22/87 **Bogged Down In Love With**
 You *Charlie Daniels Band*
M-25/94 **Bohemia** *Mae Moore*
M-28/00 **Bohemian Like You**
 Dandy Warhols
A-16/92 **Bohemian Rhapsody** *Queen*
A-30/01 **Boiler** *Limp Bizkit*
M-20/99 **Bombshell** *Papa Vegas*
A-26/01 **Bombshell** *Powerman 5000*
A-25/94 **Bonecrusher** *Soulhat*
M-17/92 **Bonfires Burning** *Origin*
A-18/98 **Boogie King**
 Screamin' Cheetah Wheelies
 Book Of Dreams *Suzanne Vega*
 M-8/90 A-47/90
 Boom *P.O.D.*
 M-13/02 A-21/02
A-29/98 **Boom Boom**
 Big Head Todd & The Monsters
 With John Lee Hooker
A-11/83 **Boomtown Blues** *Bob Seger*
A-38/97 **Booty Street** *Sugartooth*
A-44/83 **Born In America** *Riot*
A-8/84 **Born In The U.S.A.**
 Bruce Springsteen
M-5/92 **Born Of Frustration** *James*
A-3/88 **Born To Be Bad**
 George Thorogood
A-7/88 **Born To Be My Baby** *Bon Jovi*
A-37/93 **Born To Run** *Lynyrd Skynyrd*
A-15/96 **Born With A Broken Heart**
 Kenny Wayne Shepherd
A-28/98 **Born Without You** *Storyville*
A-11/97 **Both Sides Now** *Sammy Hagar*
A-24/93 **Both Sides Of The Story**
 Phil Collins
 Bother *Stone Sour*
 M-4↑/02 A-4/02
M-40/02 **Bouncing Off The Walls**
 Sugarcult
 Bound For The Floor *Local H*
 M-5/96 A-10/96
A-13/94 **Box Of Miracles**
 Barefoot Servants
A-15/87 **Boy In The Bubble** *Paul Simon*
A-17/86 **Boy Inside The Man**
 Tom Cochrane & Red Rider
M-30/96 **Boy Or A Girl** *Imperial Drag*
 Boys Are Back In Town
A-48/89 *Bon Jovi*
A-40/99 *Everclear*
A-3/90 **Boys Cry Tough** *Bad Company*
A-15/87 **Boys' Night Out** *Sammy Hagar*
A-17/87 **Boys Night Out**
 Timothy B. Schmit
A-1/84 **Boys Of Summer** *Don Henley*
A-41/86 **Boystown** *Rob Jungklas*
M-12/00 **Boyz-N-The-Hood**
 Dynamite Hack
 Brain Stew/Jaded *Green Day*
 M-3/96 A-8/96
A-24/92 **Brand New Amerika** *Poorboys*
 (Brand New Name) ..see:
 Capricorn
A-13/92 **Bravado** *Rush*
 Brave New World *Michael Penn*
 M-20/90 A-26/90
A-6/00 **Breadline** *Megadeth*
A-25/95 **Breadmaker** *Brother Cane*

A-34/95	**Break, The** *Urge Overkill*	
A-47/84	**Break Down The Wall**	
	Stone Fury	
M-1/93	**Break It Down Again**	
	Tears For Fears	
A-35/00	**Break On Through**	
	Stone Temple Pilots	
	Break Stuff *Limp Bizkit*	
	M-14/00 A-19/00	
A-46/81	**Break The Rules Tonite (Out Of School)** *Kim Carnes*	
A-7/94	**Breakaway** *ZZ Top*	
A-19/85	**Breakaway** *Cars*	
	(also see: Crack The Sky)	
	Breakdown *Tantric*	
	A-1/01 M-4/01	
A-27/99	**Breakdown** *Queensrÿche*	
M-30/95	**Breakfast At Tiffany's**	
	Deep Blue Something	
M-4/88	**Breakfast In Bed**	
	UB40 with Chrissie Hynde	
M-12/94	**Breakin' Up** *Violent Femmes*	
A-12/81	**Breaking All The Rules**	
	Peter Frampton	
A-36/81	**Breaking Down Barriers**	
	Elton John	
A-32/83	**Breaking The Chains** *Dokken*	
	Breaking The Girl	
	Red Hot Chili Peppers	
	A-15/92 M-19/92	
	Breakout *Foo Fighters*	
	M-8/00 A-11/00	
A-5/81	**Breakup Song (They Don't Write 'Em)** *Greg Kihn Band*	
	Breathe *Nickelback*	
	A-10/00 M-21/01	
A-12/94	**Breathe** *Collective Soul*	
M-18/97	**Breathe** *Prodigy*	
A-31/01	**Breathe** *Seven Channels*	
M-37/02	**Breathe** *Greenwheel*	
M-24/92	**Breathe Deeply Now**	
	This Picture	
M-23/98	**Brian Wilson** *Barenaked Ladies*	
M-6/98	**Brick** *Ben Folds Five*	
A-1/90	**Brickyard Road**	
	Johnny Van Zant	
A-6/95	**Bridge** *Queensrÿche*	
	(Bridie's Song) ..see: Funky Ceili	
M-33/95	**Bright As Yellow**	
	Innocence Mission	
M-20/95	**Bright Yellow Gun**	
	Throwing Muses	
A-1/87	**Brilliant Disguise**	
	Bruce Springsteen	
M-16/98	**Brimful Of Asha** *Cornershop*	
A-35/89	**Bring It Back Again** *Stray Cats*	
A-33/97	**Bring It On** *Lynyrd Skynyrd*	
M-24/89	**Bring Me Edelweiss** *Edelweiss*	
A-10/88	**Bring Me Some Water**	
	Melissa Etheridge	
A-47/90	**Bringing Me Down** *Bonham*	
M-38/00	**Broadway** *Goo Goo Dolls*	
A-9/93	**Broken Hearted Savior**	
	Big Head Todd & The Monsters	
	Broken Home *Papa Roach*	
	M-9/00 A-18/00	
A-39/88	**Broken Land** *Adventures*	
A-4/85	**Broken Wings** *Mr. Mister*	
A-37/90	**Brother, Don't You Walk Away**	
	Hooters	
A-2/89	**Brother Of Mine** *Anderson, Bruford, Wakeman, Howe*	

M-16/93	**Brothers And Sisters**	
	Ziggy Marley	
	Buddy Holly *Weezer*	
	M-2/94 A-34/95	
A-8/92	**Bug, The** *Dire Straits*	
A-15/91	**Build A Fire** *Drivin' N' Cryin'*	
A-27/91	**Build Me Up** *Huey Lewis*	
M-3/97	**Building A Mystery**	
	Sarah McLachlan	
A-13/86	**Built For The Future** *Fixx*	
M-13/94	**Bull In The Heather** *Sonic Youth*	
A-14/87	**Bullet The Blue Sky** *U2*	
A-32/02	**Bullet (What Did You Sell Your Soul For?)** *Injected*	
	Bullet With Butterfly Wings	
	Smashing Pumpkins	
	M-2/95 A-4/95	
	Bullets *Creed*	
	A-11/02 M-27/02	
	Bulls On Parade	
	Rage Against The Machine	
	M-11/96 A-36/96	
M-28/99	**Bump** *Kottonmouth Kings*	
	Burden In My Hand	
	Soundgarden	
	A-1/96 M-2/96	
A-1/81	**Burnin' For You**	
	Blue Öyster Cult	
M-25/95	**Burnin' Rubber** *Mr. Mirainga*	
A-46/81	**Burning Bones** *Krokus*	
A-3/82	**Burning Down One Side**	
	Robert Plant	
A-6/83	**Burning Down The House**	
	Talking Heads	
A-5/83	**Burning Heart** *Vandenberg*	
A-11/85	**Burning Heart** *Survivor*	
A-27/85	**Burning House Of Love** *X*	
A-47/84	**Burning In Love**	
	Honeymoon Suite	
M-23/90	**Burning Inside** *Ministry*	
A-20/87	**Burning Like A Flame** *Dokken*	
A-33/97	**Burning My Soul**	
	Dream Theater	
A-36/91	**Burning Timber** *Rembrandts*	
	Busload Of Faith *Lou Reed*	
	M-11/89 A-47/89	
A-22/93	**Busy Bee** *Ugly Kid Joe*	
	But Anyway *Blues Traveler*	
	M-17/96 A-19/96	
	Butterfly *Crazy Town*	
	M-1/01 A-21/01	
M-23/90	**Butterfly On A Wheel**	
	Mission U.K.	
M-13/93	**Butterfly Wings**	
	Machines Of Loving Grace	
A-36/94	**Buying My Way Into Heaven**	
	Sammy Hagar	
	By The Way	
	Red Hot Chili Peppers	
	M-1/02 A-1/02	

C

A-29/95	**Cabin Down Below** *Tom Petty*	
A-31/88	**Cabo Wabo** *Van Halen*	
A-48/81	**Cadillac Ranch**	
	Bruce Springsteen	
A-16/84	**Cage Of Freedom** *Jon Anderson*	
M-28/99	**Cailin** *Unwritten Law*	
M-28/95	**California** *Wax*	

M-35/02	**California** *Phantom Planet*	
A-3/85	**California Girls** *David Lee Roth*	
	Californication	
	Red Hot Chili Peppers	
	A-1/00 M-1/00	
A-3/89	**Call It Love** *Poco*	
A-4/91	**Call It Rock N' Roll** *Great White*	
A-19/92	**Call It What You Want** *Tesla*	
M-9/89	**Call Me Blue** *House*	
M-27/92	**Call Mr. Lee** *Television*	
A-14/87	**Call Of The Wild** *Deep Purple*	
A-26/90	**Call Of The Wild**	
	Company Of Wolves	
A-3/85	**Call To The Heart** *Giuffria*	
A-3/94	**Calling, The** *Yes*	
A-4/82	**Calling All Girls** *Rick Springfield*	
A-40/82	**Calling All Girls** *Queen*	
A-22/86	**Calling America**	
	Electric Light Orchestra	
A-42/89	**Calling America**	
	Tom Cochrane & Red Rider	
	Calling Elvis *Dire Straits*	
	A-3/91 M-25/91	
M-13/89	**Calling Out To Carol**	
	Stan Ridgway	
A-3/93	**Calling To You** *Robert Plant*	
M-40/01	**Camera One** *Josh Joplin Group*	
A-47/88	**Can I Play With Madness**	
	Iron Maiden	
M-19/91	**Can You Dig It?** *Mock Turtles*	
M-10/93	**Can You Forgive Her?**	
	Pet Shop Boys	
	Can't Change Me *Chris Cornell*	
	A-5/99 M-7/99	
M-38/95	**Can't Cry Anymore** *Sheryl Crow*	
M-7/93	**Can't Do A Thing (To Stop Me)**	
	Chris Isaak	
	Can't Even Tell *Soul Asylum*	
	M-16/94 A-24/94	
A-5/85	**Can't Fight This Feeling**	
	REO Speedwagon	
A-16/82	**Can't Find Love**	
	Jefferson Starship	
A-10/90	**Can't Find My Way Home**	
	House Of Lords	
M-30/98	**Can't Get Enough Of You Baby**	
	Smash Mouth	
A-6/90	**Can't Get Enuff** *Winger*	
A-34/95	**Can't Get High**	
	Widespread Panic	
A-49/82	**Can't Get Loose** *Sammy Hagar*	
A-51/84	**Can't Get Next To You**	
	Billy Squier	
M-6/94	**Can't Get Out Of Bed**	
	Charlatans	
A-3/88	**Can't Get Over You**	
	Gregg Allman Band	
A-16/87	**Can't Get Started** *Peter Wolf*	
A-14/85	**Can't Get There From Here**	
	R.E.M.	
A-12/97	**Can't Get This Stuff No More**	
	Van Halen	
A-34/93	**Can't Have Your Cake**	
	Vince Neil	
M-11/93	**Can't Help Falling In Love**	
	UB40	
A-25/87	**Can't Keep Running**	
	Gregg Allman Band	
A-47/82	**Can't Live Without You**	
	Scorpions	
A-20/90	**(Can't Live Without Your) Love And Affection** *Nelson*	
A-33/89	**Can't Miss**	
	Michael Thompson Band	

	Can't Speak ..see: Cantspeak
A-4/90	**Can't Stop Fallin' Into Love**
	Cheap Trick
M-20/93	**Can't Stop Killing You**
	Kirsty MacColl
A-2/95	**Can't Stop Lovin' You**
	Van Halen
A-8/85	**Can't Stop Rockin'** *ZZ Top*
A-2/91	**Can't Stop This Thing We**
	Started *Bryan Adams*
A-33/97	**Can't Tame The Lion** *Journey*
A-18/88	**Can't Wait** *Foreigner*
M-21/95	**Can't Wait One Minute More**
	CIV
M-29/97	**(Can't You) Trip Like I Do**
	Filter & The Crystal Method
A-7/87	**Can'tcha Say (You Believe In**
	Me)/Still In Love *Boston*
	Candy *Iggy Pop*
	M-5/90 A-30/91
M-5/93	**Candy Everybody Wants**
	10,000 Maniacs
	Cannonball *Breeders*
	M-2/93 A-32/94
A-4/85	**Cannonball** *Supertramp*
M-29/93	**Cantaloop** *US3*
M-40/95	**Cantspeak** *Danzig*
A-31/02	**Capricorn (A Brand New Name)**
	30 Seconds To Mars
M-33/95	**Car Song** *Elastica*
M-15/91	**Caravan** *Inspiral Carpets*
A-24/01	**Careful With That Mic...** *Clutch*
M-3/92	**Caribbean Blue** *Enya*
M-12/95	**Carnival** *Natalie Merchant*
	Carolina Blues *Blues Traveler*
	A-4/97 M-30/97
M-23/90	**Caroline** *Concrete Blonde*
M-2/88	**Carolyn's Fingers**
	Cocteau Twins
A-35/87	**Carrie** *Europe*
M-29/90	**Carrot Head**
	Young Fresh Fellows
	Cars *Fear Factory*
	A-16/99 M-38/99
A-31/84	**Castaway** *Mi-Sex*
A-8/97	**Casual Affair** *Tonic*
M-19/89	**Cat-House** *Danielle Dax*
	Cat People (Putting Out Fire)
	David Bowie
	A-9/82
	A-11/83
A-40/99	**Cat Scratch Fever** *Pantera*
A-46/84	**Catch Me I'm Falling** *Real Life*
A-23/81	**Catch Me If You Can**
	Eric Clapton
A-24/84	**Catch My Fall** *Billy Idol*
A-3/93	**Cats In The Cradle** *Ugly Kid Joe*
M-13/96	**Caught A Lite Sneeze**
	Tori Amos
M-8/91	**Caught In My Shadow**
	Wonder Stuff
A-16/83	**Caught In The Game** *Survivor*
	Caught In The Sun
	Course Of Nature
	A-9/02 M-22/02
A-1/82	**Caught Up In You** *38 Special*
A-29/94	**Ceiling** *Royal Jelly*
M-4/90	**Celebrate** *Emotional Fish*
	Celebrity Skin *Hole*
	M-1/98 A-4/98
A-31/98	**Cement** *Feeder*
A-4/85	**Centerfield** *John Fogerty*
A-1/82	**Centerfold** *J. Geils Band*

A-12/88	**Century's End** *Donald Fagen*
A-28/98	**Ceremony** *Joe Satriani*
M-16/91	**Cerulean** *Ocean Blue*
A-30/97	**Chain, The** *Fleetwood Mac*
A-9/82	**Chain Lightnin'** *38 Special*
A-17/90	**Chain Of Fools** *Little Caesar*
A-16/92	**Chained** *Giant*
M-22/88	**Chains Of Love** *Erasure*
	Champagne Supernova *Oasis*
	M-1/96 A-8/96
A-16/82	**Change** *John Waite*
A-18/93	**Change** *Candlebox*
A-22/83	**Change** *Tears For Fears*
	Change (In The House Of Flies)
	Deftones
	M-3/00 A-9/00
A-3/86	**Change In The Weather**
	John Fogerty
M-31/94	**Change In The Weather**
	Love Spit Love
A-17/85	**Change It** *Stevie Ray Vaughan*
A-32/92	**Change Of A Season** *Bonham*
A-10/83	**Change Of Heart** *Tom Petty*
A-20/97	**Change The Locks** *Tom Petty*
M-25/97	**Change Would Do You Good**
	Sheryl Crow
A-18/94	**Change Your Mind**
	Neil Young & Crazy Horse
A-6/84	**Changes** *Yes*
A-9/93	**Changes** *Ozzy Osbourne*
A-45/81	**Changes** *Santana*
M-1/89	**Channel Z** *B-52's*
	Chanukah Song *Adam Sandler*
	A-22/96 M-29/96
	A-20/98 M-25/98
	A-28/99 M-34/99
A-24/96	**Charlie Brown's Parents**
	Dishwalla
M-1/89	**Charlotte Anne** *Julian Cope*
M-38/99	**Charmed** *My Friend Steve*
A-54/82	**Chasing Shadows** *Kansas*
A-9/89	**Chasing You Into The Light**
	Jackson Browne
M-35/97	**Cheapskate** *Supergrass*
A-3/88	**Check It Out**
	John Cougar Mellencamp
A-37/01	**Check Ya** *From Zero*
A-29/00	**Check Your Head** *Buckcherry*
A-7/89	**Cheer Down** *George Harrison*
M-27/93	**Chemical World** *Blur*
	Chemicals Between Us *Bush*
	M-1/99 A-3/99
M-39/01	**Chemistry** *Semisonic*
A-1/87	**Cherry Bomb**
	John Cougar Mellencamp
A-19/90	**Cherry Pie** *Warrant*
	Cherub Rock
	Smashing Pumpkins
	M-7/93 A-23/93
A-30/93	**Child Of The City** *Triumph*
	Child Of The Wild Blue Yonder
	John Hiatt
	A-17/90 M-24/90
M-26/91	**Children** *EMF*
	Children Of The Grave ..see:
	Iron Man
A-16/88	**Chimes Of Freedom**
	Bruce Springsteen
A-19/83	**China** *Red Rockers*
A-3/83	**China Girl** *David Bowie*
A-13/89	**Chip Away The Stone**
	Aerosmith

M-2/91	**Chocolate Cake**
	Crowded House
	Chop Suey *System Of A Down*
	M-7/01 A-12/01
M-4/91	**Chorus (Fishes In The Sea)**
	Erasure
M-8/88	**Christine** *House Of Love*
A-29/98	**Christmas Eve - Sarajevo 12/24**
	Trans-Siberian Orchestra
A-31/86	**Christmas Time** *Bryan Adams*
A-22/89	**Chrome Plated Heart**
	Melissa Etheridge
A-8/92	**Church Of Logic, Sin, & Love**
	Men
A-17/83	**Church Of The Poison Mind**
	Culture Club
A-13/98	**Cigarettes And Alcohol**
	Rod Stewart
A-21/93	**Circle**
	Big Head Todd & The Monsters
A-32/89	**Circle** *Edie Brickell*
M-8/98	**Circles** *Soul Coughing*
A-31/02	**Circles** *Incubus*
A-9/85	**C-I-T-Y** *John Cafferty*
A-15/82	**City's Burning** *Heart*
M-39/94	**Citysong** *Luscious Jackson*
A-4/90	**Civil War** *Guns N' Roses*
M-15/91	**Classic Girl** *Jane's Addiction*
A-19/95	**Clean My Wounds**
	Corrosion Of Conformity
A-40/97	**Cleopatra** *Chris Duarte Group*
	Cleopatra's Cat *Spin Doctors*
	A-22/94 M-22/94
	Click Click Boom *Saliva*
	A-15/01 M-25/01
A-5/90	**Cliffs Of Dover** *Eric Johnson*
A-6/96	**Climb That Hill** *Tom Petty*
	Climbing The Walls *Stir*
	A-39/00 M-39/00
M-3/01	**Clint Eastwood** *Gorillaz*
A-25/89	**Close My Eyes Forever**
	Lita Ford (with Ozzy Osbourne)
	Closer *Nine Inch Nails*
	M-11/94 A-35/94
A-19/85	**Closer** *Firm*
	Closer To Fine *Indigo Girls*
	M-26/89 A-48/89
A-46/92	**Closer To Me** *Outfield*
A-38/90	**Closer To The Flame**
	Dave Edmunds
A-21/82	**Closer To The Heart** *Rush*
	Closing Time *Semisonic*
	M-1/98 A-13/98
M-17/91	**Cloud 8** *Frazier Chorus*
A-9/88	**Cloud 9** *George Harrison*
	Clumsy *Our Lady Peace*
	M-5/98 A-13/98
M-12/91	**Coast Is Clear** *Curve*
	Cochise *Audioslave*
	A-6↑/02 M-9↑/02
A-29/02	**Cold** *Static-X*
M-12/92	**Cold, Cold Heart** *Midge Ure*
	Cold Contagious *Bush*
	A-18/97 M-23/97
A-22/92	**Cold Day In Hell** *Gary Moore*
M-11/92	**Cold Feelings** *Social Distortion*
A-29/86	**Cold Fever** *Models*
A-2/94	**Cold Fire** *Rush*
A-37/88	**Cold Metal** *Iggy Pop*
A-29/84	**Cold Shot** *Stevie Ray Vaughan*
A-5/90	**Come Again** *Damn Yankees*
M-1/89	**Come Anytime** *Hoodoo Gurus*

A-24/84	**Dance Hall Days** *Wang Chung*
A-21/94	**Dance Naked** *John Mellencamp*
A-10/88	**Dance On My Own** *Robert Plant*
A-9/86	**Dancin' In The Ruins** *Blue Öyster Cult*
A-42/87	**Dancin' On Top Of The World** *Mason Ruffner*
M-14/89	**Dancing Barefoot** *U2*
	Dancing Days *Stone Temple Pilots* A-3/95 M-11/95
A-1/84	**Dancing In The Dark** *Bruce Springsteen*
	Dancing In The Street
A-3/82	*Van Halen*
A-3/85	*Mick Jagger/David Bowie*
A-7/86	**Danger Zone** *Kenny Loggins*
A-2/91	**Dangerous** *Doobie Brothers*
M-13/90	**Dangerous** *Depeche Mode*
A-23/85	**Dangerous** *Loverboy*
A-38/82	**Dangerous** *Who*
A-31/85	**Dangerous Moments** *Martin Briley*
A-27/87	**Dark Light** *Beat Farmers*
A-27/02	**Darkness, Darkness** *Robert Plant*
A-4/82	**Darlene** *Led Zeppelin*
A-9/88	**Darlin' Danielle Don't** *Henry Lee Summer*
A-19/87	**Darling It Hurts** *Paul Kelly*
	Daughter *Pearl Jam* A-1/93 M-1/94
A-22/00	**Day After Day** *Def Leppard*
A-3/86	**Day By Day** *Hooters*
	Day I Tried To Live *Soundgarden* A-13/95 M-25/95
A-3/87	**Day-In Day-Out** *David Bowie*
A-9/94	**Day In The Sun** *Peter Frampton*
	Day Job *Gin Blossoms* M-21/96 A-29/96
A-24/83	**Daylight** *Asia*
	Daylight Fading *Counting Crows* A-24/97 M-26/97
A-30/85	**Days Are Numbers (The Traveller)** *Alan Parsons Project*
A-58/84	**Days Gone By** *Poco*
A-2/90	**Days Like These** *Asia*
A-6/92	**Days Of Light** *Roger Daltrey*
	Days Of The Week *Stone Temple Pilots* A-4/01 M-5/01
	Daysleeper *R.E.M.* M-18/98 A-30/98
A-38/99	**Dead Again** *Buckcherry*
A-41/93	**Dead Giveaway** *Shalamar*
A-11/88	**Dead Heart** *Midnight Oil*
M-19/02	**Dead Leaves And The Dirty Ground** *White Stripes*
M-16/98	**Deadweight** *Beck*
	Dear God *XTC* A-37/87 *Midge Ure* M-4/89 A-6/89
M-18/92	**Dear Madam Barnum** *XTC*
A-32/01	**Death Blooms** *Mudvayne*
M-35/98	**Debbie** *B-52's*
M-16/89	**Debbie Gibson Is Pregnant With My Two Headed Love Child** *Mojo Nixon & Skid Roper*

M-18/93	**Debonair** *Afghan Wigs*
A-45/90	**Decadence Dance** *Extreme*
	December *Collective Soul* A-1/95 M-2/95
A-14/91	**Decision Or Collision** *ZZ Top*
M-15/89	**Decline And Fall** *Flesh For Lulu*
A-22/91	**Dedication** *Thin Lizzy*
	Deep *Nine Inch Nails* M-18/01 A-37/01
A-20/85	**Deep Cuts The Knife** *Helix*
A-49/88	**Deep Inside My Heart** *Rock City Angels*
M-39/00	**Deep Inside Of You** *Third Eye Blind*
A-3/84	**Deeper And Deeper** *Fixx*
A-4/90	**Deeper The Love** *Whitesnake*
M-30/88	**Def Con One** *Pop Will Eat Itself*
A-11/88	**Defenders Of The Flag** *Bruce Hornsby*
	Defy You *Offspring* M-8/02 A-8/02
A-9/95	**Deja Voodoo** *Kenny Wayne Shepherd*
A-52/81	**Deja Vu (Da Voodoo's In You)** *Les Dudek*
A-16/86	**Delirious** *ZZ Top*
	Deliverance *Mission U.K.* M-6/90 A-27/90
M-37/94	**Delivery** *Compulsion*
M-14/91	**De-Luxe** *Lush*
A-13/02	**Demon Speeding** *Rob Zombie*
	Denial *Sevendust* A-14/99 M-26/99
M-34/99	**Denise** *Fountains Of Wayne*
	Deny *Default* A-7/02 M-14/02
	Der Kommissar
A-4/83	*After The Fire*
A-22/83	*Falco*
A-38/99	**Descent** *Fear Factory*
A-16/91	**Desert Moon** *Great White*
A-31/84	**Desert Moon** *Dennis DeYoung*
A-12/93	**Desert Song** *Def Leppard*
	Desire *U2* A-1/88 M-1/88
A-36/92	**Desiree** *Rick Vito*
A-21/88	**Desolation Angel** *John Brannen*
A-53/84	**Desperate Heart** *Rainbow*
	Desperately Wanting *Better Than Ezra* A-10/97 M-11/97
A-24/82	**Destination Unknown** *Missing Persons*
A-3/81	**Destroyer** *Kinks*
M-25/93	**Detachable Penis** *King Missile*
M-17/91	**Detonation Boulevard** *Sisters Of Mercy*
A-44/87	**Detox Mansion** *Warren Zevon*
A-24/86	**Detroit Diesel** *Alvin Lee*
A-15/94	**Deuce** *Lenny Kravitz*
A-1/94	**Deuces Are Wild** *Aerosmith*
M-17/90	**Devil In Me** *John Wesley Harding*
A-2/88	**Devil Inside** *INXS*
M-1/93	**Devil You Know** *Jesus Jones*
A-44/82	**Devil's Deck** *Coney Hatch*
A-4/87	**Devil's Radio** *George Harrison*
M-23/96	**Devils Haircut** *Beck*
	Devolution Workin' Man Blues *Alarm* A-9/90 M-11/89
A-20/84	**Diamond Field** *Pat Benatar*

A-21/85	**Diana** *Bryan Adams*
M-35/96	**Diana** *3 Lb. Thrill*
M-6/91	**Diane** *Material Issue*
A-36/98	**Dickeye** *Jerry Cantrell*
A-48/91	**Did Ya** *Kinks*
A-38/81	**Did You Steal My Money** *Who*
A-40/88	**Didn't Know It Was Love** *Survivor*
A-26/99	**Die, Die My Darling** *Metallica*
	Died In Your Arms ..see: (I Just)
	Difference, The *Wallflowers* A-3/97 M-5/97
A-9/89	**Dig** *Who*
A-33/01	**Dig** *Mudvayne*
M-11/90	**Dig For Fire** *Pixies*
	Dig In *Lenny Kravitz* A-11/01 M-13/01
	Digging In The Dirt *Peter Gabriel* A-1/92 M-1/92
	Digital Bath *Deftones* M-16/01 A-38/01
A-22/88	**Dignity** *Deacon Blue*
M-24/93	**Dim** *Dada*
A-37/81	**Dire Wolf** *Grateful Dead*
	Dirty Blvd. *Lou Reed* M-1/89 A-18/89
	Dirty Deeds Done Dirt Cheap
A-4/81	*AC/DC*
A-23/90	*Joan Jett*
A-6/97	**Dirty Eyes** *AC/DC*
A-1/82	**Dirty Laundry** *Don Henley*
A-35/93	**Dirty Little Mind** *Jackyl*
A-10/91	**Dirty Love** *Thunder*
M-8/89	**Dirty Old Town** *David Byrne*
A-6/87	**Dirty Water** *Rock & Hyde*
	Disappear *INXS* A-6/91 M-10/90
	(Disappeared Ones) ..see: Los Desaparecidos
M-1/89	**Disappointed** *Public Image Ltd.*
M-9/92	**Disappointed** *Electronic*
	Disarm *Smashing Pumpkins* A-5/94 M-8/94
A-32/95	**Disconnected** *Queensrÿche*
M-39/95	**Disconnected** *Face To Face*
	Discothéque *U2* M-1/97 A-6/97
	Disneyland ..see: Dizz Knee Land
	Disposable Teens *Marilyn Manson* A-22/00 M-24/00
A-3/94	**Dissident** *Pearl Jam*
	Distance, The *Cake* M-4/96 A-38/96
A-49/90	**Distance, The** *Company Of Wolves*
A-3/84	**Distant Early Warning** *Rush*
M-26/94	**Distant Sun** *Crowded House*
M-28/93	**Divine Hammer** *Breeders*
M-23/92	**Divine Intervention** *Matthew Sweet*
M-3/92	**Divine Thing** *Soup Dragons*
A-30/81	**Dixie Highway** *Journey*
	Dizz Knee Land *Dada* M-5/92 A-27/92
M-8/89	**Dizzy** *Throwing Muses*
	Dizzy *Goo Goo Dolls* M-9/99 A-13/99
A-4/84	**Do It Again** *Kinks*
A-41/85	**Do Me Right** *Giuffria*

M-30/92 **Drag** *Steve Wynn*
M-22/90 **Drag My Bad Name Down**
4 Of Us
A-47/86 **Drag You Down** *Cysterz*
Dragula *Rob Zombie*
A-6/98 M-27/98
M-11/89 **Drama!** *Erasure*
Drawer *Summercamp*
M-21/97 A-37/97
M-18/97 **Dream** *Forest For The Trees*
M-16/92 **Dream About You** *Peter Case*
Dream All Day *Posies*
M-4/93 A-17/93
A-7/92 **Dream Is Over** *Van Halen*
M-22/91 **Dream Like Mine**
Bruce Cockburn
M-12/01 **Dream On** *Depeche Mode*
A-34/90 **Dream On** *Britny Fox*
A-23/92 **Dream Until Tomorrow**
Lynch Mob
A-22/87 **Dream Warriors** *Dokken*
A-10/02 **Dreamer** *Ozzy Osbourne*
A-1/91 **Dreamline** *Rush*
A-6/86 **Dreams** *Van Halen*
M-15/93 **Dreams** *Cranberries*
A-32/88 **Dreams** *BoDeans*
A-38/89 **Dreams In The Dark** *Badlands*
M-2/90 **Dreamtime** *Heart Throbs*
A-11/86 **Dreamtime** *Daryl Hall*
Dreamworld *Midnight Oil*
M-16/88 A-37/88
Drift & Die *Puddle Of Mudd*
A-1/02 M-3/02
A-33/00 **Drifters** *Paul Rodgers*
M-10/89 **Drifting, Falling** *Ocean Blue*
A-41/91 **Drinking Again** *Neverland*
Drive *R.E.M.*
M-1/92 A-2/92
Drive *Incubus*
M-1/01 A-8/01
A-3/84 **Drive** *Cars*
A-3/89 **Drive My Car** *David Crosby*
M-12/91 **Drive That Fast**
Kitchens Of Distinction
A-20/97 **Driven** *Rush*
A-9/93 **Driven By You** *Brian May*
Driven Out *Fixx*
A-1/89 M-11/89
A-35/81 **Driven To Tears** *Police*
A-22/85 **Driver 8** *R.E.M.*
A-9/85 **Drivin' With Your Eyes Closed**
Don Henley
M-26/90 **Driving** *Everything But The Girl*
M-19/93 **Driving Aloud (Radio Storm)**
Robyn Hitchcock
A-25/92 **Driving The Last Spike** *Genesis*
A-38/88 **Driving Wheels** *Jimmy Barnes*
M-39/97 **Drop Dead Gorgeous** *Republica*
A-30/90 **Drop The Gun**
Kings Of The Sun
A-33/83 **Drop The Pilot**
Joan Armatrading
A-33/98 **Dropping Anchor**
Jimmie's Chicken Shack
Drops Of Jupiter (Tell Me) *Train*
M-11/01 A-19/01
Drown *Son Volt*
A-10/96 M-25/96
M-24/92 **Drown** *Smashing Pumpkins*
A-33/97 **Drown In Me**
Jason Bonham Band
A-34/88 **Drown In My Own Tears**
Smithereens

A-21/95 **Drowning** *Hootie & The Blowfish*
A-27/96 **Drowning In A Daydream**
Corrosion Of Conformity
M-29/96 **Drugs** *Ammonia*
M-10/93 **Drums Of Heaven** *Midnight Oil*
A-20/98 **Du Hast** *Rammstein*
Duck And Run *3 Doors Down*
A-1/01 M-11/01
A-4/87 **Dude (Looks Like A Lady)**
Aerosmith
Dumb Things *Paul Kelly*
M-16/88 A-49/88
A-16/88 **Dynamite** *Rod Stewart*
M-4/92 **Dyslexic Heart** *Paul Westerberg*

E

E-Bow The Letter *R.E.M.*
M-2/96 A-15/96
A-22/87 **Eagles Fly** *Sammy Hagar*
M-2/89 **Eardrum Buzz** *Wire*
A-40/88 **Early In The Morning**
Robert Palmer
M-25/91 **East Easy Rider** *Julian Cope*
M-9/93 **Eastern Bloc** *Thomas Dolby*
A-20/91 **Easy Come Easy Go** *Winger*
A-32/83 **Easy Livin'** *Fastway*
A-5/85 **Easy Lover**
Philip Bailey with Phil Collins
A-14/85 **Easy Street** *David Lee Roth*
M-26/90 **Easy Street** *Soul Asylum*
M-12/89 **Eat For Two** *10,000 Maniacs*
A-38/84 **Eat It** *"Weird Al" Yankovic*
M-10/93 **Eat The Music** *Kate Bush*
A-5/93 **Eat The Rich** *Aerosmith*
A-33/83 **Eat The Rich** *Krokus*
A-34/82 **Ebony And Ivory**
Paul McCartney
(with Stevie Wonder)
(Ecstasy, The) .. see: Electric Head
M-38/97 **Eddie Vedder** *Local H*
A-37/01 **Eden (Turn The Page)**
Mayfield Four
A-24/88 **Edge Of A Broken Heart** *Vixen*
A-37/86 **Edge Of Forever**
Dream Academy
Edge Of Seventeen (Just Like The White Winged Dove)
A-4/81 *Stevie Nicks*
A-26/82 *Stevie Nicks*
A-12/81 **Edge Of Sundown**
Danny Joe Brown
A-26/93 **Edge Of Thorns** *Savatage*
A-17/89 **Edie (Ciao Baby)** *Cult*
A-20/91 **Edison's Medicine** *Tesla*
A-37/88 **853-5937** *Squeeze*
A-1/82 **867-5309/Jenny** *Tommy Tutone*
A-11/89 **18 And Life** *Skid Row*
A-17/93 **Eileen** *Keith Richards*
M-1/94 **Einstein On The Beach (For An Eggman)** *Counting Crows*
M-19/96 **El Scorcho** *Weezer*
Elderly Woman Behind The Counter In A Small Town
Pearl Jam
M-17/94 A-23/94
A-21/98 M-26/98
A-22/92 **Elected** *Def Leppard*
A-12/83 **Electric Avenue** *Eddy Grant*
A-10/88 **Electric Blue** *Icehouse*

A-38/82 **Electric Eye** *Judas Priest*
A-27/95 **Electric Head (The Ecstasy)**
White Zombie
Electrical Storm *U2*
M-14/02 A-26/02
A-2/82 **Electricland** *Bad Company*
Elegantly Wasted *INXS*
M-13/97 A-37/97
Elevation *U2*
M-8/01 A-21/01
A-30/84 **11 O'Clock Tick Tock** *U2*
M-25/90 **Elvis Is Dead** *Living Colour*
A-5/82 **Eminence Front** *Who*
A-22/83 **Emotion** *DFX2*
A-1/86 **Emotion In Motion** *Ric Ocasek*
A-20/82 **Emotions In Motion** *Billy Squier*
Emperor's New Clothes
Sinéad O'Connor
M-1/90 A-40/90
A-22/90 **Empire** *Queensrÿche*
A-3/92 **Empty Arms**
Stevie Ray Vaughan
A-12/83 **Enchanted** *Stevie Nicks*
End Is The Beginning Is The End *Smashing Pumpkins*
M-4/97 A-12/97
A-1/89 **End Of The Innocence**
Don Henley
A-2/89 **End Of The Line**
Traveling Wilburys
A-2/91 **End Of The Line**
Allman Brothers Band
A-24/01 **End Of The World** *Cold*
A-10/87 **Endless Nights** *Eddie Money*
A-41/88 **Endless Summer Nights**
Richard Marx
A-19/85 **Endlessly** *Joe Lynn Turner*
Ends *Everlast*
M-7/99 A-13/99
Enemy *Days Of The New*
A-2/99 M-10/99
Energy, The *Audiovent*
A-9/02 M-17/02
A-19/93 **English Boy** *Pete Townshend*
A-32/88 **Englishman In New York** *Sting*
M-1/90 **Enjoy The Silence**
Depeche Mode
M-8/91 **Enlighten Me**
Echo And The Bunnymen
A-9/82 **Enough Is Enough** *April Wine*
A-34/99 **Enter My Mind** *Drain STH*
A-10/91 **Enter Sandman** *Metallica*
A-25/90 **Epic** *Faith No More*
Epiphany *Staind*
A-22/02 M-28/02
A-16/94 **Estranged** *Guns N' Roses*
M-25/94 **Euro-Trash Girl** *Cracker*
A-37/82 **Europa And The Pirate Twins**
Thomas Dolby
A-54/84 **Eve Of Destruction**
Red Rockers
Even Better Than The Real Thing *U2*
A-1/92 M-5/92
Even Flow *Pearl Jam*
A-3/92 M-21/92
A-2/83 **Even Now** *Bob Seger*
Everlasting Gaze
Smashing Pumpkins
M-4/00 A-14/00
Everlasting Love *U2*
M-11/89 A-46/89
Everlasting Love *Howard Jones*
M-19/89 A-49/89

A-3/83	Fight Fire With Fire *Kansas*
A-8/88	Fight (No Matter How Long) *Bunburys*
A-18/81	Fight The Good Fight *Triumph*
A-8/90	Figure Of Eight *Paul McCartney*
A-18/87	Final Countdown *Europe*
A-20/88	Final Eyes *Yes*
A-41/84	Finally Found A Home *Huey Lewis*
A-12/82	Find Another Fool *Quarterflash*
A-3/81	Find Your Way Back *Jefferson Starship*
	Fine Again *Seether*
	M-12↑/02 A-17/02
A-1/84	Fine Fine Day *Tony Carey*
A-43/84	Fine, Fine Line *Andy Fraser*
A-14/90	F.I.N.E. (Fucked-up, Insecure, Neurotic, Emotional) *Aerosmith*
M-3/89	Fine Time *New Order*
A-5/87	Finer Things *Steve Winwood*
A-28/88	Finest Worksong *R.E.M.*
A-2/88	Finish What Ya Started *Van Halen*
A-14/87	Fire *Bruce Springsteen*
A-44/89	Fire *Who*
A-44/90	Fire *Front*
A-2/81	Fire And Ice *Pat Benatar*
	Fire Escape *Fastball*
	M-13/98 A-25/98
A-20/91	Fire In The Basement *Deep Purple*
A-6/98	Fire In The Hole *Van Halen*
A-6/91	Fire Inside *Bob Seger*
A-50/90	Fire On The Cross *Bruce Hornsby*
A-15/85	Fire Still Burns *Russ Ballard*
	Fire Water Burn *Bloodhound Gang*
	M-18/97 A-28/97
	Fire Woman *Cult*
	M-2/89 A-4/89
A-59/81	Fireflies *Fleetwood Mac*
M-24/97	Firestarter *Prodigy*
M-6/02	First Date *Blink-182*
A-21/84	First Day Of Summer *Tony Carey*
A-46/89	First Love *Marchello*
A-38/83	First Time For Everything *Coney Hatch*
A-32/00	First Trip To The Moon *Nixons*
M-11/92	First We Take Manhattan *R.E.M.*
M-3/89	Fisherman's Blues *Waterboys* (Fishes In The Sea) ..see: Chorus
A-15/82	Fits Ya Good *Bryan Adams*
M-10/89	5 O'Clock World *Julian Cope*
A-17/84	5.01 AM. (The Pros and Cons of Hitch Hiking) *Roger Waters*
A-20/89	500 Miles *Hooters* (also see: I'm Gonna Be)
	Flagpole Sitta *Harvey Danger*
	M-3/98 A-33/98
M-22/02	Flake *Jack Johnson*
A-3/88	Flame, The *Cheap Trick*
A-30/82	Flamethrower *J. Geils Band*
A-38/95	Flat Top *Goo Goo Dolls*
M-5/01	Flavor Of The Weak *American Hi-Fi*
A-8/84	Flesh For Fantasy *Billy Idol*
A-26/83	Flick Of The Switch *AC/DC*
A-8/83	Flight Of Icarus *Iron Maiden*
A-14/97	Flip The Switch *Rolling Stones*

	Flood *Jars Of Clay*
	M-12/96 A-16/96
	Flowers ..see: (Nothing But)
M-7/91	Flowers In The Rain *Stress*
M-17/00	Flowing *311*
	Fly, The *U2*
	M-1/91 A-2/91
	Fly *Sugar Ray*
	M-1/97 A-29/97
A-11/99	Fly *Loudmouth*
	Fly Away *Lenny Kravitz*
	A-1/98 M-1/98
A-9/81	Fly Away *Blackfoot*
A-27/90	Fly High Michelle *Enuff Z'Nuff*
	Fly Me Courageous *Drivin' N' Cryin'*
	M-15/91 A-19/91
A-15/90	Fly To The Angels *Slaughter*
A-19/83	Flyer, The *Saga*
A-2/82	Flying High Again *Ozzy Osbourne*
A-36/81	Flying Lip Lock *Ted Nugent*
	Flying Under Radar *Jerry Harrison*
	M-13/90 A-42/90
A-23/87	Follow You *Glen Burtnick*
	Follow You Down *Gin Blossoms*
	A-6/96 M-8/96
A-13/85	Follow Your Heart *Triumph*
A-2/89	Fool For Your Loving *Whitesnake*
A-42/87	Fool In Love *Farrenheit*
A-9/83	Foolin' *Def Leppard*
A-8/89	Foolish Heart *Grateful Dead*
A-27/83	Fools Game *Michael Bolton*
M-5/90	Fools Gold *Stone Roses*
A-2/84	Footloose *Kenny Loggins*
A-7/83	For A Rocker *Jackson Browne*
A-3/86	For America *Jackson Browne*
M-9/92	For Love *Lush*
M-28/01	For Nancy ('Cos It Already Is) *Pete Yorn*
A-44/82	For Openers (Welcome Home) *Ambrosia*
A-30/89	For The Love Of Money *BulletBoys*
	For The Movies *Buckcherry*
	M-24/99 A-25/99
A-26/81	For The Sake Of Survival *Silver Condor*
A-4/82	For Those About To Rock (We Salute You) *AC/DC*
	For You *Staind*
	A-3/02 M-3/02
A-13/90	For You *Outfield*
A-15/81	For You *Manfred Mann*
A-3/87	Force Ten *Rush*
A-11/90	Forecast (Calls For Pain) *Robert Cray Band*
A-30/92	Foreclosure Of A Dream *Megadeth*
A-17/90	Forever *Kiss*
	Forever *Kid Rock*
	A-18/01 M-21/01
A-39/83	Forever *Little Steven*
A-1/85	Forever Man *Eric Clapton*
A-13/87	Forever Young *Rod Stewart*
A-39/91	Forever Young *Tyketto*
A-36/89	Forget About Love *Eddie Money*
A-2/89	Forget Me Not *Bad English*
	Forgotten Years *Midnight Oil*
	M-1/90 A-11/90

A-25/02	Forsaken *David Draiman*
A-1/85	Fortress Around Your Heart *Sting*
A-9/86	Fortunate Son *Bob Seger*
A-22/97	Forty Six & 2 *Tool*
	Found Out About You *Gin Blossoms*
	M-1/94 A-5/94
	4 AM *Our Lady Peace*
	M-31/98 A-38/98
A-13/85	Four In The Morning (I Can't Take Any More) *Night Ranger*
M-27/97	Four Leaf Clover *Abra Moore*
M-28/92	4 Men *Kitchens Of Distinction*
	Freak *Silverchair*
	A-25/97 M-29/97
	Freak Of The Week *Marvelous 3*
	M-5/99 A-23/99
	Freak On A Leash *Korn*
	M-6/99 A-10/99
	Freaking Out *Adema*
	A-25/02 M-36/02
	Freaks *Live*
	A-5/97 M-13/97
M-34/01	Fred Astaire *Lucky Boys Confusion*
	Free *Phish*
	A-11/96 M-24/96
	Free *Vast*
	M-12/00 A-18/00
A-12/99	Free *Train*
A-8/95	Free As A Bird *Beatles*
A-1/89	Free Fallin' *Tom Petty*
A-5/99	Free Girl Now *Tom Petty*
M-8/96	Free To Decide *Cranberries*
A-38/02	Freechild *Must*
A-4/86	Freedom Overspill *Steve Winwood*
A-8/82	Freeze-Frame *J. Geils Band*
A-30/83	French Song *Joan Jett*
	Freshmen, The *Verve Pipe*
	M-1/97 A-9/97
	Friday I'm In Love *Cure*
	M-1/92 A-21/92
A-29/83	Friday Night *Vandenberg*
A-3/89	Friend Is A Friend *Pete Townshend*
A-12/92	Friends *Joe Satriani*
M-7/02	Friends & Family *Trik Turner*
A-33/81	Friends Of Mr. Cairo *Jon & Vangelis*
M-7/95	Friends Of P. *Rentals*
A-36/97	Fritz's Corner *Local H*
A-46/81	From A Whisper To A Scream *Elvis Costello*
A-28/82	From Small Things (Big Things One Day Come) *Dave Edmunds*
A-49/89	From The Greenhouse *Crack The Sky*
M-17/98	From Your Mouth *God Lives Underwater*
M-38/01	F**k Authority *Pennywise*
A-6/98	Fuel *Metallica*
A-42/82	Full Bug *Van Halen*
A-16/90	Full Circle *Jeff Healey Band*
M-27/93	Funky Ceili (Bridie's Song) *Black 47*
M-12/90	Fury Eyes *Creatures*
M-16/89	Future 40's (String Of Pearls) *Syd Straw*
A-14/86	Future's So Bright, I Gotta Wear Shades *Timbuk 3*
A-30/94	Fuzzbox Voodoo *ZZ Top*

G

A-40/99 **Gain** *Virgos Merlot*
Galaxie *Blind Melon*
　　　M-8/95　A-25/95
M-10/92 **Galileo** *Indigo Girls*
A-2/94 **Gallows Pole**
　　　Jimmy Page & Robert Plant
A-34/02 **Game, The** *Disturbed*
A-16/96 **Garden Of Allah** *Don Henley*
A-26/85 **Gear Jammer**
　　　George Thorogood
Geek Stink Breath *Green Day*
　　　M-3/95　A-9/95
Gel *Collective Soul*
　　　A-2/95　M-14/95
A-13/81 **Gemini Dream** *Moody Blues*
A-28/81 **Generals And Majors** *XTC*
A-32/83 **Genetic Engineering** *Orchestral Manoeuvres In The Dark*
M-21/94 **Gentleman Who Fell** *Milla*
M-8/93 **Gepetto** *Belly*
M-13/98 **Get 'Em Outta Here**
　　　Sprung Monkey
M-24/91 **Get A Gun** *Connells*
A-2/93 **Get A Haircut**
　　　George Thorogood
A-34/96 **Get A Job** *Hog*
A-1/91 **Get A Leg Up** *John Mellencamp*
Get Away *Earshot*
　　　A-6/02　M-20/02
M-32/99 **Get Back** *Zebrahead*
Get Born Again *Alice In Chains*
　　　A-4/99　M-12/99
A-34/82 **Get Closer** *Linda Ronstadt*
Get Free *Vines*
　　　M-7/02　A-27/02
A-4/88 **Get It On** *Kingdom Come*
A-19/85 **Get It On** *Power Station*
Get Off This *Cracker*
　　　M-6/94　A-18/94
M-3/93 **Get Out Of Control** *Daniel Ash*
A-4/94 **Get Over It** *Eagles*
M-21/02 **Get Over It** *Ok Go*
M-36/99 **Get Set** *Taxiride*
A-23/88 **Get Started, Start A Fire**
　　　Graham Parker
A-34/91 **Get The Funk Out** *Extreme*
M-1/91 **Get The Message** *Electronic*
A-33/89 **Get U Ready** *Saraya*
A-46/82 **Get Up And Go** *Go-Go's*
A-33/01 **Get What You Got Comin'**
　　　Van Zant
A-2/01 **Gets Me Through**
　　　Ozzy Osbourne
A-20/85 **Gets Us All In The End**
　　　Jeff Beck
A-46/88 **Gettin' Better** *Tesla*
M-4/90 **Getting Away With It** *Electronic*
A-34/87 **Gettysburg** *Brandos*
M-9/93 **Ghost At Number One** *Jellyfish*
A-25/84 **Ghost In You** *Psychedelic Furs*
A-2/92 **Ghost Of A Chance** *Rush*
M-2/92 **Ghost Of Texas Ladies' Man**
　　　Concrete Blonde
Ghost Of Tom Joad
　　　Rage Against The Machine
　　　M-34/98　A-35/98
A-8/87 **Ghost On The Beach** *Insiders*
A-15/81 **(Ghost) Riders In The Sky**
　　　Outlaws
A-32/88 **Ghost Town** *Cheap Trick*

A-38/84 **Ghostbusters** *Ray Parker Jr.*
A-45/81 **Gi' Me Wings** *Rod Stewart*
M-6/93 **Gift, The** *INXS*
A-2/83 **Gimme All Your Lovin** *ZZ Top*
A-29/98 **Gimme Shelter** *Rolling Stones*
A-21/90 **Gimme Your Good Lovin'**
　　　Diving For Pearls
A-40/87 **Gimme Your Love**
　　　McAuley Schenker Group
M-38/02 **Girl All The Bad Guys Want**
　　　Bowling For Soup
A-9/86 **Girl Can't Help It** *Journey*
A-4/97 **Girl I Love She Got Long Black Wavy Hair** *Led Zeppelin*
A-27/94 **Girl In A T-Shirt** *ZZ Top*
A-17/84 **Girl In Trouble (Is A Temporary Thing)** *Romeo Void*
Girl Like You *Smithereens*
　　　A-2/89　M-3/89
M-2/92 **Girl Like You** *Wolfgang Press*
M-7/95 **Girl Like You** *Edwyn Collins*
A-26/91 **Girl Money** *Kix*
A-57/81 **Girl Most Likely**
　　　Greg Kihn Band
M-11/94 **Girl, You'll Be A Woman Soon**
　　　Urge Overkill
Girlfriend *Matthew Sweet*
　　　M-4/92　A-10/92
A-2/84 **Girls** *Dwight Twilley*
M-4/94 **Girls & Boys** *Blur*
A-20/87 **Girls, Girls, Girls** *Mötley Crüe*
A-16/84 **Girls Just Want To Have Fun**
　　　Cyndi Lauper
A-25/02 **Girls Of Summer** *Aerosmith*
A-19/83 **Girls On Film** *Duran Duran*
A-6/84 **Girls With Guns** *Tommy Shaw*
A-29/84 **Give** *Missing Persons*
A-5/86 **Give Blood** *Pete Townshend*
M-17/89 **Give, Give, Give Me More, More, More** *Wonder Stuff*
M-1/91 **Give It Away**
　　　Red Hot Chili Peppers
A-26/90 **Give It To Me Good** *Trixter*
Give It Up *Hothouse Flowers*
　　　M-2/90　A-29/90
A-2/91 **Give It Up** *ZZ Top*
Give Me ..see: Gimme
A-22/88 **Give Me All Your Love**
　　　Whitesnake
Give Me Wings ..see: Gi' Me Wings
A-1/87 **Give To Live** *Sammy Hagar*
Given To Fly *Pearl Jam*
　　　A-1/98　M-3/98
A-39/91 **Givin' Yourself Away** *Ratt*
Giving In *Adema*
　　　M-14/01　A-16/01
M-14/88 **(Glad I'm) Not A Kennedy**
　　　Shona Laing
M-13/92 **Glamorous Glue** *Morrissey*
A-26/89 **Glamour Boys** *Living Colour*
M-3/91 **Globe, The**
　　　Big Audio Dynamite II
Gloria
A-18/83　*Doors*
A-36/93　*Van Morrison*
　　　(also see: Accidentally 4th St.)
A-39/94 **Glorified G** *Pearl Jam*
A-3/85 **Glory Days** *Bruce Springsteen*
Glycerine *Bush*
　　　M-1/95　A-4/96
Go *Pearl Jam*
　　　A-3/93　M-8/93

A-7/85 **Go** *Asia*
A-32/92 **Go Back To Your Woods**
　　　Robbie Robertson
A-24/99 **Go Faster** *Black Crowes*
A-12/85 **Go For Soda** *Kim Mitchell*
A-4/84 **Go Insane** *Lindsey Buckingham*
M-14/00 **Go Let It Out** *Oasis*
M-32/96 **Go Walking Down There**
　　　Chris Isaak
M-1/94 **God** *Tori Amos*
God *U2*
　　　A-8/89　M-28/89
A-24/01 **God Gave Me Everything**
　　　Mick Jagger
A-21/91 **God Gave Rock And Roll To You II** *Kiss*
God Is A Bullet
　　　Concrete Blonde
　　　M-15/89　A-49/89
M-15/90 **God Tonight** *Real Life*
A-6/00 **Godless** *U.P.O.*
A-12/86 **Goin' Crazy!** *David Lee Roth*
M-8/89 **Goin' Southbound**
　　　Stan Ridgway
M-28/98 **Going Out Of My Head**
　　　Fatboy Slim
M-33/95 **Going South** *Wolfgang Press*
A-5/82 **Going To A Go-Go**
　　　Rolling Stones
A-49/88 **Gold** *Pete Bardens*
M-31/96 **Gold Dust Woman** *Hole*
A-16/87 **Golden Ball And Chain**
　　　Jason & The Scorchers
M-17/90 **Golden Blunders** *Posies*
A-55/81 **Golden Down** *Willie Nile*
Gone Away *Offspring*
　　　A-1/97　M-4/97
A-28/02 **Gone Away** *Cold*
A-24/94 **Gone Dead Train**
　　　George Thorogood
M-23/91 **Gone, Gone, Gone**
　　　Echo And The Bunnymen
　　　(also see: My Girl)
A-31/84 **Gone Too Far** *Dan Fogelberg*
Good *Better Than Ezra*
　　　M-1/95　A-3/95
A-1/90 **Good Clean Fun**
　　　Allman Brothers Band
M-16/94 **Good Enough** *Sarah McLachlan*
A-3/96 **Good Friday** *Black Crowes*
A-28/85 **Good Friends** *Joni Mitchell*
Good Intentions
　　　Toad The Wet Sprocket
　　　A-19/95　M-20/95
M-18/89 **Good Life** *Fire Town*
M-32/97 **Good Life** *Weezer*
A-6/93 **Good Lovin's Hard To Find**
　　　Lynyrd Skynyrd
M-12/90 **Good Morning Britain**
　　　Aztec Camera
Good Riddance (Time Of Your Life) *Green Day*
　　　M-2/98　A-7/98
M-28/02 **Good Souls** *Starsailor*
M-1/92 **Good Stuff** *B-52's*
A-18/91 **Good Texan** *Vaughan Brothers*
Good Thing
　　　Fine Young Cannibals
　　　M-2/89　A-39/89
A-3/87 **Good Times**
　　　INXS & Jimmy Barnes
A-51/82 **Good Trouble**
　　　REO Speedwagon
A-50/89 **Good Work** *BoDeans*

M-11/90 **Hippychick** *Soho*
A-33/81 **History Never Repeats**
Split Enz
M-39/98 **History Of A Boring Town**
Less Than Jake
M-1/92 **Hit** *Sugarcubes*
A-24/92 **Hit Between The Eyes**
Scorpions
M-15/01 **Hit Or Miss** *New Found Glory*
A-28/97 **Hit The Ground Running**
Jonny Lang
Hitchin' A Ride *Green Day*
M-5/97 A-9/97
A-39/85 **Hits Of The Year** *Squeeze*
A-53/81 **Hitsville U.K.** *Clash*
M-24/94 **Hobo Humpin Slobo Babe**
Whale
A-5/93 **Hocus Pocus** *Gary Hoey*
M-18/90 **Hold A Candle To This**
Pretenders
A-3/82 **Hold Me** *Fleetwood Mac*
A-41/87 **Hold Me** *Colin James Hay*
A-5/02 **Hold Me Down** *Tommy Lee*
A-9/84 **Hold Me Now** *Thompson Twins*
Hold Me, Thrill Me, Kiss Me, Kill Me *U2*
A-1/95 M-1/95
A-4/94 **Hold My Hand**
Hootie & The Blowfish
A-17/82 **Hold On** *Santana*
Hold On *Yes*
A-43/84
A-27/85
M-29/95 **Hold On** *Sarah McLachlan*
A-42/81 **Hold On** *Badfinger*
A-3/81 **Hold On Loosely** *38 Special*
A-50/87 **Hold On (Never Give Up, Never Give In)**
John Kay & Steppenwolf
A-2/81 **Hold On Tight** *ELO*
A-50/84 **Hold On To 18** *Black 'n Blue*
A-2/88 **Holding On** *Steve Winwood*
M-22/89 **Holding on to the Earth**
Sam Phillips
A-27/89 **Holding On To You**
Peter Frampton
A-2/91 **Hole Hearted** *Extreme*
A-4/97 **Hole In My Soul** *Aerosmith*
A-55/82 **Hole In Paradise** *Prism*
Hollow, The *Perfect Circle*
A-14/01 M-17/01
Hollywood Bitch
Stone Temple Pilots
A-25/01 M-29/01
A-24/82 **Hollywood (Down On Your Luck)** *Thin Lizzy*
A-40/83 **Holy Diver** *Dio*
A-39/00 **Holy Man** *One Minute Silence*
A-25/87 **Holy War** *Jon Butcher*
A-1/90 **Holy Water** *Bad Company*
Home *Iggy Pop*
M-2/90 A-46/90
Home *Staind*
A-11/00 M-17/00
A-35/98 **Home** *Econoline Crush*
A-24/84 **Home By The Sea** *Genesis*
A-45/91 **Home For Better Days** *Dillinger*
Home Sweet Home
A-38/85 *Mötley Crüe*
A-41/94 *Mötley Crüe ('91)*
A-20/93 **Honest To God** *Brad Gillis*
M-6/92 **Honeydrip** *Ian McCulloch*
M-29/96 **Honky's Ladder** *Afghan Whigs*

M-12/98 **Hooch** *Everything*
Hook *Blues Traveler*
M-13/95 A-15/95
A-49/89 **Hooks In You** *Marillion*
A-10/94 **Hooligan's Holiday** *Mötley Crüe*
A-13/97 **Hope In A Hopeless World**
Widespread Panic
(Hopelessly In Love) ..see:
Party's Over
A-44/83 **Horizontal Departure**
Robert Plant
M-23/92 **Horror Head** *Curve*
A-45/92 **Hot And Bothered** *Cinderella*
Hot Cherie
A-15/83 *Danny Spanos*
A-25/92 *Hardline*
A-24/84 **Hot For Teacher** *Van Halen*
A-2/83 **Hot Girls In Love** *Loverboy*
A-31/82 **Hot In The City** *Billy Idol*
A-31/87 **Hot Love** *Twisted Sister*
A-1/92 **Hotel Illness** *Black Crowes*
A-22/87 **Hourglass** *Squeeze*
M-1/90 **House** *Psychedelic Furs*
A-29/82 **House Behind A House**
Bob Seger
A-18/90 **House Is Rockin'**
Stevie Ray Vaughan
A-7/90 **House Of Broken Love**
Great White
A-39/90 **House Of Fire** *Alice Cooper*
A-23/90 **House Of Pain** *Faster Pussycat*
A-14/88 **House We Used To Live In**
Smithereens
A-1/92 **How About That** *Bad Company*
A-8/90 **How Bad Do You Want It?**
Don Henley
A-1/83 **How Can I Refuse** *Heart*
A-50/81 **How Can You Do It Alone** *Who*
A-28/93 **How Could You Want Him (When You Know You Could Have Me?)** *Spin Doctors*
A-21/89 **How Do I Get Close** *Kinks*
A-22/87 **How Do You Spell Love**
Fabulous Thunderbirds
A-15/93 **How Does It Feel** *Ian Moore*
How I Could Just Kill A Man
Rage Against The Machine
M-37/01 A-39/01
A-34/91 **How Long Can A Man Be Strong** *Jeff Healey Band*
How Much Is Enough *Fixx*
M-10/91 A-11/91
A-50/84 **How Much Is Too Much?**
Chequered Past
A-11/90 **How Much Love** *Vixen*
M-38/00 **How Soon Is Now?**
Snake River Conspiracy
How You Remind Me
Nickelback
A-1/01 M-1/01
M-5/98 **How's It Going To Be**
Third Eye Blind
A-12/93 **Howlin' For My Baby**
George Thorogood
M-2/93 **Human Behaviour** *Björk*
M-10/91 **Human Nature (On The Mix)**
Gary Clail
A-11/83 **Human Race** *Red Rider*
A-1/92 **Human Touch**
Bruce Springsteen
A-34/83 **Human Touch** *Rick Springfield*
A-2/93 **Human Wheels**
John Mellencamp
A-1/96 **Humans Being** *Van Halen*

Hunger Strike
Temple Of The Dog
A-4/92 M-7/92
A-14/90 **Hungry** *Lita Ford*
Hungry *Dave Navarro*
M-24/01 A-38/01
M-27/89 **Hungry** *Royal Crescent Mob*
A-34/89 **Hungry** *Winger*
A-30/85 **Hungry For Heaven** *Dio*
A-1/83 **Hungry Like The Wolf**
Duran Duran
A-6/93 **Hunter, The** *Paul Rodgers*
A-14/86 **Hunter, The** *GTR*
A-25/86 **Hunter, The** *Dokken*
A-36/84 **Hunters Of The Night** *Mr. Mister*
M-8/95 **Hurt** *Nine Inch Nails*
A-1/90 **Hurting Kind (I've Got My Eyes On You)** *Robert Plant*
A-1/82 **Hurts So Good** *John Cougar*
A-19/97 **Hush** *Kula Shaker*
A-44/88 **Hush** *Deep Purple*
A-21/86 **Hyperactive** *Robert Palmer*
A-39/84 **Hyperactive** *Thomas Dolby*
A-9/88 **Hysteria** *Def Leppard*

I

A-17/82 **I.G.Y. (What A Beautiful World)**
Donald Fagen
A-34/01 **I** *Taproot*
A-26/87 **I Ain't Ever Satisfied**
Steve Earle
I Ain't Got Nobody ..see: Just A Gigolo
I Alone *Live*
A-6/94 M-6/94
A-22/98 **I Am A Pig** *Two*
M-27/91 **I Am Here** *Grapes Of Wrath*
A-8/94 **I Am I** *Queensrÿche*
I Am Mine *Pearl Jam*
M-6/02 A-7/02
A-31/99 **I Am The Bullgod** *Kid Rock*
A-14/86 **I Been Down So Long**
Sting with Jeff Beck
A-9/93 **I Believe** *Robert Plant*
M-10/91 **I Believe** *EMF*
A-36/90 **I Believe** *Joe Satriani*
A-38/99 **I Believe** *Moon Dog Mane*
A-43/84 **I Believe** *Steve Perry*
A-50/90 **I Believe** *Riverdogs*
M-25/90 **I Build This Garden For Us**
Lenny Kravitz
A-27/82 **I Burn For You** *Police*
A-13/83 **I Can Play That Rock & Roll**
Joe Walsh
A-53/81 **I Can Take Care Of Myself**
Billy & The Beaters
A-2/92 **I Can't Dance** *Genesis*
A-9/84 **I Can't Drive 55** *Sammy Hagar*
A-5/90 **I Can't Explain** *Scorpions*
A-42/81 **I Can't Get Satisfied** *Rockets*
A-28/82 **I Can't Go For That (No Can Do)**
Daryl Hall & John Oates
A-47/81 **I Can't Hear You** *Donnie Iris*
A-1/84 **I Can't Hold Back** *Survivor*
A-28/91 **I Can't Live With You** *Queen*
M-24/01 **I Can't Move** *Everlast*
A-1/81 **I Can't Stand It** *Eric Clapton*
A-6/86 **I Can't Wait** *Stevie Nicks*
I Choose *Offspring*
A-5/97 M-24/97

M-15/01 **I'll Be Here Awhile** *311*
A-5/89 **I'll Be There For You** *Bon Jovi*
M-23/95 **I'll Be There For You**
Rembrandts
I'll Be You *Replacements*
A-1/89   M-1/89
M-24/91 **I'll Be Your Baby Tonight**
Robert Palmer
M-1/90 **I'll Be Your Chauffeur** *David J*
A-16/82 **I'll Drink To You** *Duke Jupiter*
A-2/82 **I'll Fall In Love Again**
Sammy Hagar
A-42/91 **I'll Fight For You** *Foreigner*
A-34/93 **I'll Hate You Better**
Suicidal Tendencies
A-58/84 **I'll Keep Holding On**
Jim Capaldi
A-24/91 **I'll Never Let You Go (Angel Eyes)** *Steelheart*
A-7/90 **I'll See You In My Dreams** *Giant*
A-29/93 **I'll Sleep When I'm Dead**
Bon Jovi
M-21/94 **I'll Stand By You** *Pretenders*
I'll Stick Around *Foo Fighters*
M-8/95   A-12/95
M-6/94 **I'll Take You There**
General Public
A-2/84 **I'll Wait** *Van Halen*
A-13/89 **I'm A Believer** *Giant*
A-16/85 **I'm A Fighter** *Van-Zant*
A-42/81 **I'm A Rocker** *Bruce Springsteen*
A-18/92 **I'm A Steady Rollin' Man**
George Thorogood
M-29/98 **I'm Afraid Of Americans**
David Bowie
A-18/93 **I'm Alive** *Jackson Browne*
I'm An Adult Now
Pursuit Of Happiness
M-6/89   A-22/88
M-2/90 **I'm Free** *Soup Dragons*
A-42/84 **I'm Free (Heaven Helps The Man)** *Kenny Loggins*
A-9/85 **I'm Goin' Down**
Bruce Springsteen
I'm Gonna Be (500 Miles)
Proclaimers
M-21/89
M-8/93
A-39/82 **I'm Leaving** *Taxxi*
A-56/84 **I'm Leaving You** *Scorpions*
A-54/81 **I'm Losing You** *John Lennon*
A-25/84 **I'm Moving On** *Eddie Money*
A-1/87 **I'm No Angel**
Gregg Allman Band
A-37/99 **I'm Not Running Anymore**
John Mellencamp
I'm Not Scared *Raindogs*
M-23/90   A-44/90
A-29/86 **I'm Not The One** *Cars*
A-1/88 **I'm Not Your Man**
Tommy Conwell
A-4/85 **I'm On Fire** *Bruce Springsteen*
A-33/88 **I'm On To You** *Hurricane*
A-26/83 **I'm Ready** *Bryan Adams*
A-15/90 **I'm Seventeen** *Tommy Conwell*
I'm Sorry *Hothouse Flowers*
M-12/88   A-23/89
(also see: so. Central Rain)
A-34/84 **I'm Stepping Out** *John Lennon*
A-12/88 **I'm Still Searching** *Glass Tiger*
A-34/83 **I'm Still Standing** *Elton John*
I'm Stupid (Don't Worry 'Bout Me) *Prime Sth*
M-27/01   A-27/01

A-10/93 **I'm The Only One**
Melissa Etheridge
M-28/92 **I'm Too Sexy** *Right Said Fred*
A-5/94 **I'm Tore Down** *Eric Clapton*
A-38/00 **I'm With Stupid (He's A Loser)**
Static-X
A-13/93 **I've Always Got You**
Robin Zander
A-50/87 **I've Been In Love Before**
Cutting Crew
M-29/89 **I've Forgotten What It Was In You (That Put The Need In Me)** *Maria McKee*
M-7/88 **I've Got A Feeling**
Screaming Tribesmen
A-6/91 **I've Got A Lot To Learn About Love** *Storm*
A-24/83 **I've Got A Rock N' Roll Heart**
Eric Clapton
(I've Got My Eyes On You)
..see: Hurting Kind
A-43/84 **I've Got You** *Kind*
M-4/90 **Iceblink Luck** *Cocteau Twins*
A-28/81 **Icehouse** *Icehouse*
M-20/89 **If A Tree Falls** *Bruce Cockburn*
A-24/86 **If Anybody Had A Heart**
John Waite
A-44/90 **If Anybody Had A Heart**
Crosby, Stills & Nash
A-8/83 **If Anyone Falls** *Stevie Nicks*
A-8/90 **If Dirt Were Dollars** *Don Henley*
M-15/96 **If I Could Talk I'd Tell You**
Lemonheads
If I Ever Lose My Faith In You
Sting
M-4/93   A-5/93
A-16/85 **If I Had A Rocket Launcher**
Bruce Cockburn
M-25/94 **If I Only Had A Brain**
MC 900 Ft. Jesus
A-37/91 **If I Say** *Kingofthehill*
A-26/81 **If I Was A Dancer (Dance)**
Rolling Stones
A-1/83 **If I'd Been The One** *38 Special*
If It Makes You Happy
Sheryl Crow
M-6/96   A-37/96
M-7/89 **If It's Love** *Squeeze*
A-6/84 **If Love Should Go** *Streets*
If Love Was A Train
Michelle Shocked
M-20/88   A-33/88
A-3/84 **If This Is It** *Huey Lewis*
A-9/89 **If We Never Meet Again**
Tommy Conwell
M-29/02 **If You C Jordan**
Something Corporate
M-39/98 **If You Can't Say No**
Lenny Kravitz
If You Could Only See *Tonic*
A-1/97   M-3/97
If You Don't Love Me (I'll Kill Myself) *Pete Droge*
A-28/95   M-40/94
A-5/91 **If You Don't Start Drinkin' (I'm Gonna Leave)**
George Thorogood
A-1/85 **If You Love Somebody Set Them Free** *Sting*
A-2/91 **If You Needed Somebody**
Bad Company
A-26/82 **If You See Kay** *April Wine*
A-11/82 **If You Want My Love**
Cheap Trick

A-17/92 **If You're Gonna Love Me**
Sass Jordan
Ignoreland *R.E.M.*
A-4/93   M-5/92
A-21/84 **Illegal Alien** *Genesis*
A-36/91 **Illustrated Man** *Johnny Winter*
M-18/88 **Im Nin'alu** *Ofra Haza*
A-20/86 **Imagine** *John Lennon*
M-22/01 **Imitation Of Life** *R.E.M.*
Immortality *Pearl Jam*
A-10/95   M-31/95
M-1/97 **Impression That I Get**
Mighty Mighty Bosstones
A-5/99 **In 2 Deep**
Kenny Wayne Shepherd Band
A-3/83 **In A Big Country** *Big Country*
A-37/94 **In A Daydream**
Freddy Jones Band
M-24/93 **In A Mood** *Fabulon*
A-37/85 **In And Out Of Love** *Bon Jovi*
A-24/82 **In Between The Lines**
Michael Stanley Band
A-5/93 **In Bloom** *Nirvana*
A-41/87 **In Dreams** *Pete Bardens*
A-6/88 **In God's Country** *U2*
A-32/92 **In Heaven** *McQueen Street*
In Hiding *Pearl Jam*
M-13/98   A-14/98
A-30/85 **In Jeopardy** *Roger Hodgson*
A-14/87 **In My Car** *Joe Walsh*
A-24/86 **In My Dreams** *Dokken*
A-36/93 **In My Dreams With You** *Vai*
M-14/91 **In My Heart** *Texas*
M-17/02 **In My Place** *Coldplay*
A-39/81 **In Quintessence** *Squeeze*
A-2/81 **In The Air Tonight** *Phil Collins*
In The Blood *Better Than Ezra*
M-4/95   A-6/95
A-7/81 **In The Dark** *Billy Squier*
In The End *Linkin Park*
M-1/01   A-3/01
A-6/81 **In The Heartland**
Michael Stanley Band
In The Meantime *Spacehog*
A-1/96   M-2/96
A-4/83 **In The Mood** *Robert Plant*
M-31/95 **In The Name Of The Father**
Black Grape
A-15/86 **In The Shape Of A Heart**
Jackson Browne
A-32/93 **In These Arms** *Bon Jovi*
M-10/01 **In Too Deep** *Sum 41*
A-34/86 **In Too Deep** *Genesis*
M-24/89 **In Vivo** *Wire*
A-35/91 **In Your Arms** *Little Caesar*
A-1/86 **In Your Eyes** *Peter Gabriel*
M-5/88 **In Your Room** *Bangles*
A-24/87 **Incommunicado** *Marillion*
A-9/82 **Industrial Disease** *Dire Straits*
A-5/84 **Infatuation** *Rod Stewart*
Infected *Bad Religion*
M-27/95   A-33/95
A-28/85 **Injured In The Game Of Love**
Donnie Iris
Innocent *Fuel*
M-4/01   A-10/01
Innocent *Our Lady Peace*
M-20/02   A-35/02
A-30/91 **Innocent, The** *Drivin' N' Cryin'*
A-11/90 **Innocent Days** *Giant*
A-14/86 **Innocent Eyes** *Graham Nash*
A-17/91 **Innuendo** *Queen*

M-10/98	**Jump Right In**	A-23/82	**Keeping Our Love Alive**	

M-10/98 **Jump Right In**
Urge Featuring Nick Hexum
A-12/88 **Jump Start** *Jethro Tull*
M-4/93 **Jump They Say** *David Bowie*
M-9/98 **Jumper** *Third Eye Blind*
A-36/86 **Jumpin' Jack Flash**
Aretha Franklin
A-8/97 **Jungle** *Kiss*
A-17/86 **Jungle Boy** *John Eddie*
A-35/94 **Junior** *John Mellencamp*
M-37/95 **Just** *Radiohead*
A-25/85 **Just A Gigolo/I Ain't Got
Nobody** *David Lee Roth*
M-10/96 **Just A Girl** *No Doubt*
A-10/83 **Just A Job To Do** *Genesis*
A-41/90 **Just A Little Light**
Grateful Dead
A-33/92 **Just A Loser** *Robert Cray Band*
A-13/97 **Just Another Day**
John Mellencamp
A-1/85 **Just Another Night** *Mick Jagger*
A-4/89 **Just Between You And Me**
Lou Gramm
A-11/81 **Just Between You And Me**
April Wine
A-7/90 **Just Came Back** *Colin James*
A-24/99 **Just Go** *Staind*
A-27/85 **Just Got Lucky** *Dokken*
A-25/00 **Just Got Wicked** *Cold*
Just Like Anyone *Soul Asylum*
A-11/95 M-19/95
A-15/81 **Just Like Me** *Pat Benatar*
A-1/88 **Just Like Paradise**
David Lee Roth
A-47/87 **Just Like You** *Martha Davis*
M-1/88 **Just Play Music!**
Big Audio Dynamite
A-10/01 **Just Push Play** *Aerosmith*
A-18/92 **Just Take My Heart** *Mr. Big*
A-13/91 **Just The Way It Is, Baby**
Rembrandts
A-16/89 **Just Wanna Hold** *Mick Jones*
A-28/86 **Justice And Independence '85**
John Cougar Mellencamp
M-21/92 **Justified & Ancient**
KLF (Feat. Tammy Wynette)

K

A-47/88 **Karla With A K** *Hooters*
Karma *Diffuser*
A-20/01 M-26/01
M-14/98 **Karma Police** *Radiohead*
A-14/85 **Kayleigh** *Marillion*
Keep Away *Godsmack*
A-5/99 M-31/99
A-14/83 **(Keep Feeling) Fascination**
Human League
M-15/02 **Keep Fishin'** *Weezer*
A-46/82 **Keep Me Satisfied** *Billy Squier*
A-21/90 **Keep On Loving Me Baby**
Colin James
A-9/81 **Keep On Loving You**
REO Speedwagon
A-1/94 **Keep Talking** *Pink Floyd*
A-1/92 **Keep The Faith** *Bon Jovi*
A-2/82 **Keep The Fire Burnin'**
REO Speedwagon
A-39/82 **Keep This Heart In Mind**
Bonnie Raitt
A-2/86 **Keep Your Hands To Yourself**
Georgia Satellites

A-23/82 **Keeping Our Love Alive**
Henry Paul Band
A-10/91 **Keeping The Faith**
Lynyrd Skynyrd
A-34/82 **Key, The** *REO Speedwagon*
A-10/96 **Key West Intermezzo (I Saw
You First)** *John Mellencamp*
A-33/88 **Kick** *INXS*
M-22/95 **Kick Him When He's Down**
Offspring
M-36/01 **Kick Some Ass** *Stroke 9*
A-32/87 **Kick The Wall**
Jimmy Davis & Junction
A-3/98 **Kicking My Heart Around**
Black Crowes
A-18/89 **Kickstart My Heart** *Mötley Crüe*
A-39/89 **Kid Ego** *Extreme*
A-42/81 **Kid Is Hot Tonite** *Loverboy*
Kids Aren't Alright *Offspring*
M-6/99 A-11/99
A-29/82 **Kids In America** *Kim Wilde*
A-42/85 **Kids Wanna Rock** *Bryan Adams*
A-21/00 **Kill The King** *Megadeth*
A-23/84 **Killer** *Pat Travers*
M-2/88 **Killing Jar**
Siouxsie & The Banshees
A-13/01 **Killing The Fly**
Union Underground
M-20/94 **Kim The Waitress**
Material Issue
M-32/98 **Kind & Generous**
Natalie Merchant
A-37/86 **Kind Words** *Joan Armatrading*
King For A Day *XTC*
M-11/89 A-38/89
A-35/86 **King For A Day**
Thompson Twins
M-19/90 **King Is Half-Undressed**
Jellyfish
A-6/97 **King Nothing** *Metallica*
A-6/90 **King Of Dreams** *Deep Purple*
King Of Emotion *Big Country*
M-11/88 A-20/88
King Of New Orleans
Better Than Ezra
M-5/96 A-7/96
A-38/93 **King Of Nothing**
Ghost Of An American Airman
A-1/83 **King Of Pain** *Police*
A-2/91 **King Of The Hill** *Roger McGuinn*
King Of The Mountain
Midnight Oil
M-3/90 A-20/90
M-16/89 **Kingdom Of Rain** *The*
A-4/92 **Kings Highway** *Tom Petty*
M-1/91 **Kinky Afro** *Happy Mondays*
M-14/88 **Kiss** *Art Of Noise Ft. Tom Jones*
A-40/88 **Kiss And Tell** *Bryan Ferry*
M-35/95 **Kiss From A Rose** *Seal*
**Kiss Him Goodbye ..see: Na Na
Hey Hey**
M-12/90 **Kiss It Better** *Deborah Harry*
A-40/88 **Kiss Me Deadly** *Lita Ford*
A-16/91 **Kiss My Love Goodbye**
L.A. Guns
A-34/82 **Kiss Of Life** *Peter Gabriel*
A-54/81 **Kiss On My List**
Daryl Hall & John Oates
Kiss That Frog *Peter Gabriel*
A-18/93 M-18/93
A-24/86 **Kiss The Dirt (Falling Down The
Mountain)** *INXS*
M-1/91 **Kiss Them For Me**
Siouxsie And The Banshees

Kiss This Thing Goodbye
Del Amitri
M-13/90 A-17/90
A-6/89 **Kissing Willie** *Jethro Tull*
M-4/94 **Kite** *Nick Heyward*
M-13/95 **Kitty** *Presidents Of The United
States Of America*
A-13/86 **Knife Feels Like Justice**
Brian Setzer
A-20/99 **Knock Down Walls** *Tonic*
M-6/89 **Knock Me Down**
Red Hot Chili Peppers
A-18/90 **Knockin' On Heaven's Door**
Guns N' Roses
A-7/85 **Knocking At Your Back Door**
Deep Purple
A-45/88 **Knucklebones** *David Lee Roth*
M-7/90 **Kool Thing** *Sonic Youth*
M-6/91 **Kozmik** *Ziggy Marley*
Kryptonite *3 Doors Down*
A-1/00 M-1/00
A-1/86 **Kyrie** *Mr. Mister*

L

M-40/99 **L Train** *Shootyz Groove*
A-18/90 **L.A. Woman** *Billy Idol*
A-11/87 **La Bamba** *Los Lobos*
M-9/94 **Labour Of Love** *Frente!*
Lack Of Water *Why Store*
A-27/96 M-37/96
A-46/82 **Lady Luck** *Molly Hatchet*
A-30/86 **Lady Nina** *Marillion*
A-47/81 **Lady On The Rock** *Joe Vitale*
Lady Picture Show
Stone Temple Pilots
A-1/97 M-6/96
A-47/87 **Lady Red Light** *Great White*
M-39/98 **Lady, Your Roof Brings Me
Down** *Scott Weiland*
M-28/99 **Ladyfingers** *Luscious Jackson*
M-18/96 **Ladykillers** *Lush*
M-3/93 **Laid** *James*
M-10/92 **Laid So Low (Tears Roll Down)**
Tears For Fears
A-22/95 **Lake Of Fire** *Nirvana*
Lakini's Juice *Live*
M-1/97 A-2/97
A-47/81 **Land Of A Thousand Dances**
Ted Nugent
A-11/86 **Land Of Confusion** *Genesis*
M-3/94 **Landslide** *Smashing Pumpkins*
A-8/84 **Language Of Love**
Dan Fogelberg
A-30/84 **Lap Of Luxury** *Jethro Tull*
A-12/92 **Last Chance** *John Mellencamp*
M-13/89 **Last Cigarette** *Dramarama*
A-14/97 **Last Cup Of Sorrow**
Faith No More
A-22/02 **Last DJ** *Tom Petty*
A-29/86 **Last Domino** *Genesis*
A-14/00 **Last Goodbye**
Kenny Wayne Shepherd
M-19/95 **Last Goodbye** *Jeff Buckley*
A-10/84 **Last In Line** *Dio*
Last Kiss *Pearl Jam*
M-2/99 A-5/99
A-18/89 **Last Mile** *Cinderella*
A-5/95 **Last Night** *Traveling Wilburys*
M-5/02 **Last Nite** *Strokes*
Last Night On Earth *U2*

A-14/87	**Little Lies** *Fleetwood Mac*	
A-2/92	**Little Miss Can't Be Wrong**	
	Spin Doctors	
A-22/86	**Little Miss Dangerous**	
	Ted Nugent	
	Little Miss S. *Edie Brickell*	
	M-14/89 A-38/89	
A-17/83	**Little Red Corvette** *Prince*	
A-40/86	**Little Red House** *Glen Burtnick*	
M-15/89	**Little Respect** *Erasure*	
A-18/83	**Little Robbers** *Motels*	
A-29/00	**Little Scene** *Isle Of Q*	
A-15/89	**Little Sheba** *Thirty Eight Special*	
A-13/85	**Little Sheila** *Slade*	
A-8/81	**Little Sister**	
	Rockpile with Robert Plant	
A-22/87	**Little Suzi** *Tesla*	
A-5/81	**Little T & A** *Rolling Stones*	
A-12/83	**Little Thing Called Love**	
	Neil Young	
	Little Things *Bush*	
	M-4/95 A-6/95	
M-23/00	**Little Things** *Good Charlotte*	
A-38/83	**Little Too Late** *Pat Benatar*	
A-1/97	**Little White Lie** *Sammy Hagar*	
	Little Wing	
A-11/87	*Sting*	
A-26/92	*Stevie Ray Vaughan*	
	Live Again *Sevendust*	
	A-21/02 M-36/02	
A-20/91	**Live And Let Die**	
	Guns N' Roses	
A-40/81	**Live For Today** *Toto*	
	Live Forever *Oasis*	
	M-2/95 A-10/95	
A-21/86	**Live In Peace** *Firm*	
A-6/90	**Live It Up** *REO Speedwagon*	
A-7/90	**Live It Up** *Crosby, Stills & Nash*	
A-15/81	**Live Now-Pay Later** *Foghat*	
A-6/97	**Live Through This (Fifteen Stories)** *Mighty Joe Plum*	
A-35/97	**Live Tomorrow** *Chalk Farm*	
A-33/86	**Lives In The Balance**	
	Jackson Browne	
A-6/82	**Livin' In The Limelight**	
	Peter Cetera	
A-1/87	**Livin' On A Prayer** *Bon Jovi*	
A-1/93	**Livin' On The Edge** *Aerosmith*	
M-16/89	**Livin' On The Edge Of The Night** *Iggy Pop*	
	Living Dead Girl *Rob Zombie*	
	A-7/99 M-22/99	
M-30/88	**Living For You**	
	Joan Armatrading	
A-6/92	**Living In A Dream** *Arc Angels*	
A-44/87	**Living In A Dream** *Pseudo Echo*	
A-37/89	**Living In Sin** *Bon Jovi*	
A-24/85	**Living On A Thin Line** *Kinks*	
A-27/88	**Living Out Of Touch**	
	Kingdom Come	
A-28/91	**Living With The Law**	
	Chris Whitley	
A-5/89	**Living Years**	
	Mike + The Mechanics	
M-19/90	**Loaded** *Primal Scream*	
A-16/88	**Lock And Key** *Rush*	
A-22/95	**Lock And Load** *Bob Seger*	
A-15/97	**Locked & Loaded** *Jackyl*	
A-25/86	**Locked In** *Judas Priest*	
M-8/94	**Locked Out** *Crowded House*	
A-39/91	**Lone Star** *Stuart Hamm*	
A-17/90	**Lone Wolf** *Havana Black*	
A-9/85	**Lonely At The Top** *Mick Jagger*	

A-43/85	**Lonely In Love** *Giuffria*	
A-28/81	**Lonely Is The Night** *Billy Squier*	
A-3/82	**Lonely Nights** *Bryan Adams*	
A-1/85	**Lonely Ol' Night**	
	John Cougar Mellencamp	
A-15/02	**Lonely Road Of Faith** *Kid Rock*	
A-8/97	**Long Day** *Matchbox 20*	
	Long December	
	Counting Crows	
	M-5/97 A-9/97	
M-33/97	**Long Long Time** *Love Spit Love*	
A-34/93	**Long May You Run** *Neil Young*	
A-22/82	**Long Stick Goes Boom** *Krokus*	
A-28/87	**Long Time Gone** *Triumph*	
A-19/88	**Long Time Till I Get Over You**	
	Little Feat	
	Long View *Green Day*	
	M-1/94 A-13/94	
A-14/87	**Long Walk Home**	
	Neil Young & Crazy Horse	
	Long Way Down *Goo Goo Dolls*	
	A-7/96 M-25/96	
M-14/93	**Long Way Down (Look What The Cat Drug In)**	
	Michael Penn	
A-11/89	**Long Way To Go** *Stevie Nicks*	
A-33/88	**Long Way To Love** *Britny Fox*	
A-17/85	**Look At Little Sister**	
	Stevie Ray Vaughan	
A-20/86	**Look At That, Look At That**	
	Fabulous Thunderbirds	
A-5/86	**Look Away** *Big Country*	
A-28/82	**Look In Your Eye** *Hughes/Thrall*	
A-32/82	**Look Of Love** *ABC*	
A-5/88	**Look Out Any Window**	
	Bruce Hornsby	
	(Look What The Cat Drug In)	
	..see: Long Way Down	
M-2/89	**Look Who's Dancing**	
	Ziggy Marley	
A-8/97	**Looking For** *Stir*	
M-24/94	**Looking For A Song** *Big Audio*	
A-4/83	**Looking For A Stranger**	
	Pat Benatar	
A-12/84	**Looks That Kill** *Mötley Crüe*	
M-6/93	**Los Angeles** *Frank Black*	
A-27/84	**Los Desaparecidos (The Disappeared Ones)**	
	Little Steven	
M-16↑/02	**Lose Yourself** *Eminem*	
	Loser *3 Doors Down*	
	A-1/00 M-2/00	
	Loser *Beck*	
	M-1/94 A-39/94	
A-14/94	**Losin' Your Mind** *Pride & Glory*	
	Losing A Whole Year	
	Third Eye Blind	
	M-13/98 A-36/98	
	Losing My Religion *R.E.M.*	
	A-1/91 M-1/91	
A-37/87	**Lost And Found** *Kinks*	
	Lost Art Of Keeping A Secret	
	Queens Of The Stone Age	
	A-21/00 M-36/00	
A-21/95	**Lost For Words** *Pink Floyd*	
A-45/81	**Lost In The Sun** *Dan Fogelberg*	
A-3/88	**Lost In You** *Rod Stewart*	
	Lot To Lose ..see: Alot To Lose	
	Lotus *R.E.M.*	
	A-31/99 M-31/99	
M-2/92	**Love** *Sundays*	
A-33/84	**Love Ain't No Stranger**	
	Whitesnake	

	Love And Affection ..see: (Can't Live Without Your)	
M-1/89	**Love And Anger** *Kate Bush*	
A-5/92	**Love And Happiness**	
	John Mellencamp	
A-40/88	**Love And Mercy** *Brian Wilson*	
A-50/86	**Love And Rock And Roll**	
	Greg Kihn	
M-19/90	**Love Barge** *Big Dipper*	
A-3/88	**Love Bites** *Def Leppard*	
A-22/90	**Love Can Make You Blind**	
	Every Mother's Nightmare	
A-13/88	**Love Changes Everything**	
	Honeymoon Suite	
A-14/89	**Love Cries** *Stage Dolls*	
M-19/89	**Love Crushing** *Fetchin Bones*	
A-24/91	**Love Don't Come Easy**	
	White Lion	
A-33/90	**Love Don't Come Easy** *Alarm*	
A-50/89	**Love Don't Lie** *House Of Lords*	
A-9/89	**Love Has Taken Its Toll** *Saraya*	
A-1/89	**Love In An Elevator** *Aerosmith*	
A-1/89	**Love In Your Eyes** *Eddie Money*	
A-19/90	**Love Is** *Alannah Myles*	
A-1/83	**Love Is A Battlefield**	
	Pat Benatar	
A-7/89	**Love Is A Long Road** *Tom Petty*	
A-31/90	**Love Is A Rock**	
	REO Speedwagon	
M-23/89	**Love Is A Shield** *Camouflage*	
A-7/92	**Love Is Alive** *Joe Cocker*	
A-40/82	**Love Is Alright Tonite**	
	Rick Springfield	
A-7/90	**Love Is Dangerous**	
	Fleetwood Mac	
A-9/82	**Love Is Like A Rock** *Donnie Iris*	
A-49/88	**Love Is Not A Game**	
	McAuley Schenker Group	
A-8/92	**Love Is On The Way**	
	Saigon Kick	
A-2/94	**Love Is Strong** *Rolling Stones*	
M-14/93	**Love Is Stronger Than Death**	
	The	
A-17/86	**Love Is The Hero** *Billy Squier*	
A-9/90	**Love Is The Ritual** *Styx*	
A-19/85	**Love Is The Seventh Wave**	
	Sting	
A-19/82	**Love Leads To Madness**	
	Nazareth	
A-49/89	**Love Letter** *Bonnie Raitt*	
A-41/83	**Love Me Again** *John Hall Band*	
A-27/90	**Love Me Two Times** *Aerosmith*	
A-30/82	**Love My Way** *Psychedelic Furs*	
	Love On Me ..see: Luv On Me	
A-36/83	**Love On Your Side**	
	Thompson Twins	
M-24/90	**Love Or Something** *Bob Geldof*	
A-18/82	**Love Plus One**	
	Haircut One Hundred	
	Love Rears Its Ugly Head	
	Living Colour	
	A-8/91 A-28/91	
A-15/87	**Love Removal Machine** *Cult*	
M-14/96	**Love Rollercoaster**	
	Red Hot Chili Peppers	
M-30/90	**Love See No Colour** *Farm*	
M-1/89	**Love Shack** *B-52's*	
A-25/94	**Love Sneakin' Up On You**	
	Bonnie Raitt	
A-13/84	**Love Somebody**	
	Rick Springfield	
	Love Song *Cure*	
	M-2/89 A-30/89	
A-7/90	**Love Song** *Tesla*	

M-24/93	**Love Song For A Vampire** *Annie Lennox*	
	Love Spreads *Stone Roses* M-2/95 A-4/95	
A-14/90	**Love That Never Dies** *Byrds*	
A-49/91	**Love To Burn** *Neil Young & Crazy Horse*	
M-6/91	**Love To Hate You** *Erasure*	
A-26/86	**Love Touch** *Rod Stewart*	
M-3/93	**Love U More** *Sunscreem*	
M-21/96	**Love Untold** *Paul Westerberg*	
A-31/92	**Love Walked In** *Thunder*	
A-4/86	**Love Walks In** *Van Halen*	
A-1/87	**Love Will Find A Way** *Yes*	
A-24/84	**Love Will Show Us How** *Christine McVie*	
	Love You ..see: Love U	
A-31/91	**Love's A Loaded Gun** *Alice Cooper*	
A-28/83	**Love's Got A Line On You** *Scandal*	
M-9/97	**Lovefool** *Cardigans*	
M-9/92	**Lover Lover Lover** *Ian McCulloch*	
A-56/84	**Lovers In A Dangerous Time** *Bruce Cockburn*	
A-57/82	**Lovers In The Night** *Toto*	
M-22/94	**Lovetown** *Peter Gabriel*	
A-3/85	**Lovin' Every Minute Of It** *Loverboy*	
A-18/90	**Lovin' You's A Dirty Job** *Ratt*	
	Low *Cracker* M-3/93 A-5/94	
A-15/94	**Low Rider** *Gary Hoey*	
M-25/92	**Low Self Opinion** *Rollins Band*	
A-4/91	**Lowdown And Dirty** *Foreigner*	
M-22/94	**Lucas With The Lid Off** *Lucas*	
	Lucky *Seven Mary Three* M-19/97 A-35/97	
A-24/85	**Lucky** *Greg Kihn* (also see: Believed You Were)	
A-5/85	**Lucky In Love** *Mick Jagger*	
M-16/98	**Lucky Man** *Verve*	
A-36/82	**Lucky Ones** *Loverboy*	
M-38/94	**Lucky You** *Lightning Seeds*	
A-35/98	**Lucy** *Caramel*	
A-15/87	**Luka** *Suzanne Vega*	
M-9/98	**Lullaby** *Shawn Mullins*	
M-23/89	**Lullaby** *Cure*	
A-24/92	**Lumberjack, The** *Jackyl*	
	Lump *Presidents Of The United States Of America* M-1/95 A-7/95	
A-11/81	**Lunatic Fringe** *Red Rider*	
A-38/92	**Luv On Me** *Roxy Blue*	
A-30/82	**Lyin' In A Bed Of Fire** *Little Steven*	
A-4/86	**Lying** *Peter Frampton*	

M

	Mach 5 *Presidents Of The United States Of America* M-11/96 A-24/96	
A-12/98	**Machete** *Brother Cane*	
A-36/92	**Machine Gun** *Warrant*	
	Machinehead *Bush* A-4/96 M-4/96	
A-37/91	**Mad About You** *Slaughter*	
A-27/88	**Madalaine** *Winger*	

A-54/81	**Madman** *Tom Johnston*
M-2/89	**Madonna Of The Wasps** *Robyn Hitchcock*
A-1/84	**Magic** *Cars*
A-8/81	**Magic Power** *Triumph*
A-10/88	**Magic Touch** *Mike Oldfield*
A-42/88	**Magic Touch** *Aerosmith*
A-28/85	**Magical** *John Parr*
A-29/97	**Magnolia** *Screamin' Cheetah Wheelies*
A-34/00	**Mainline** *Jesse James Dupree*
A-38/81	**Mainstreet U.S.A.** *Union*
A-8/83	**Major Tom (Coming Home)** *Peter Schilling*
M-11/89	**Make Believe Mambo** *David Byrne*
A-12/85	**Make It Better (Forget About Me)** *Tom Petty*
A-36/91	**Make It Easy** *Yes*
A-41/87	**Make It Mean Something** *Rob Jungklas*
A-21/01	**Make It Right** *Econoline Crush*
A-3/92	**Make Love Like A Man** *Def Leppard*
	Make Me Bad *Korn* M-7/00 A-9/00
M-19/91	**Make Out Alright** *Divinyls*
A-11/92	**Make You A Believer** *Sass Jordan*
M-32/00	**Makes No Difference** *Sum 41*
M-22/01	**Makin' Money** *Handsome Devil*
A-30/92	**Makin' Some Noise** *Tom Petty*
M-30/92	**Making Plans For Nigel** *Primus*
	Malibu *Hole* M-3/99 A-16/99
A-5/83	**Mama** *Genesis*
	Mama Help Me *Edie Brickell* M-17/90 A-26/90
A-2/92	**Mama, I'm Coming Home** *Ozzy Osbourne*
A-13/84	**Mama Weer All Crazee Now** *Quiet Riot*
A-5/94	**Mama's Fool** *Tesla*
M-37/94	**Mamouna** *Bryan Ferry*
	(Man In Motion) ..see: St. Elmo's Fire
	Man In The Box *Alice In Chains* A-18/91 A-39/00
A-25/91	**Man In The Moon** *Scream*
A-21/92	**Man On A Mission** *Van Halen*
A-14/82	**Man On The Corner** *Genesis*
	Man On The Moon *R.E.M.* M-2/93 A-4/93
M-2/00	**Man Overboard** *Blink-182*
M-20/91	**Man Scared** *Fat Lady Sings*
	Man Who Sold The World *Nirvana* M-6/95 A-12/95
A-38/85	**Man With The Horn** *Phil Collins*
M-17/89	**Mandela Day** *Simple Minds*
A-2/87	**Mandolin Rain** *Bruce Hornsby*
A-18/82	**Maneater** *Daryl Hall & John Oates*
A-10/86	**Manhattan Project** *Rush*
A-34/81	**Maniac** *Michael Sembello*
A-10/94	**Manic Depression** *Seal & Jeff Beck*
A-43/86	**Manic Monday** *Bangles*
A-13/97	**Mann's Chinese** *Naked*
A-3/90	**Mansion On The Hill** *Neil Young & Crazy Horse*
A-6/89	**Marathon** *Rush*

M-5/91	**Marble** *House Of Love*
A-3/97	**Marching To Mars** *Sammy Hagar*
A-8/89	**Martha Say** *John Cougar Mellencamp*
A-38/82	**Martyrs And Madmen** *Roger Daltrey*
A-29/92	**Mary In The Mystery World** *Electric Gipsy*
A-1/93	**Mary Jane's Last Dance** *Tom Petty*
M-29/93	**Mary Xmess** *Sun 60*
A-2/99	**Mas Tequila** *Sammy Hagar & the Waboritas*
A-20/84	**Mask, The** *Roger Glover*
A-14/86	**Matter Of Trust** *Billy Joel*
A-37/82	**Maxine** *Mike Rutherford*
A-48/81	**Maybe It's You** *Great Buildings*
A-36/94	**Maybe Love Will Change Your Mind** *Stevie Nicks*
M-10/00	**Maybe Someday** *Cure*
A-31/83	**Maybe Someday** *Taxxi*
A-26/01	**Maybe Tomorrow** *Mesh Stl*
	Mayor Of Simpleton *XTC* M-1/89 A-15/89
A-32/90	**Me & Elvis** *Human Radio*
A-47/82	**Me And The Boys** *Dave Edmunds*
A-1/96	**Me Wise Magic** *Van Halen*
A-25/83	**Mean Streak** *Y&T*
A-12/81	**Mean Street** *Van Halen*
A-11/81	**Meanwhile** *Moody Blues*
	Medicine *Orbit* A-29/97 M-32/97
A-43/91	**Medicine Man** *Aldo Nova*
	Meet Virginia *Train* A-21/99 M-25/99
A-12/82	**Mega Force** *707*
A-22/00	**Meltdown** *AC/DC*
A-3/97	**Memory Remains** *Metallica*
M-17/90	**Men In Helicopters** *Adrian Belew*
A-7/85	**Men Without Shame** *Phantom, Rocker & Slick*
M-27/92	**Mercury** *Ocean Blue*
A-34/81	**Mercury Blues** *David Lindley*
M-1/90	**Merry Go Round** *Replacements*
	Merry Xmas ..see: Mary Xmess
M-21/92	**Mesmerise** *Chapterhouse*
A-5/81	**Message Of Love** *Pretenders*
A-18/96	**Message Of Love** *Journey*
M-30/94	**Messiah** *Farm*
M-7/93	**Metal Mickey** *Metal Mikey*
A-42/85	**Method Of Modern Love** *Daryl Hall/John Oates*
	Metropolis *Church* M-1/90 A-11/90
A-41/82	**Mexican Radio** *Wall Of Voodoo*
A-47/86	**Miami** *Bob Seger*
A-29/85	**Miami Vice Theme** *Jan Hammer*
	Middle, The *Jimmy Eat World* M-1/02 A-39/02
A-2/84	**Middle Of The Road** *Pretenders*
	MidLife Crisis *Faith No More* M-1/92 A-32/92
A-1/87	**Midnight Blue** *Lou Gramm*
A-10/84	**Midnite Maniac** *Krokus*
A-38/89	**Might As Well Be Free** *Jon Butcher*
M-15/96	**Mighty K.C.** *For Squirrels*
A-14/90	**Miles Away** *Winger*
A-17/94	**Miles From Nowhere** *Smithereens*

A-11/82 **Million Miles Away** *Plimsouls*
A-39/94 **Milquetoast** *Helmet*
A-49/85 **Mind Games** *Triumph*
A-50/88 **Mine All Mine** *Van Halen*
Minority *Green Day*
M-1/00 A-15/00
M-14/96 **Mint Car** *Cure*
A-14/86 **Minutes To Memories**
John Cougar Mellencamp
A-20/90 **Miracle** *Jon Bon Jovi*
A-22/83 **Mirror Man** *Human League*
A-26/90 **Mirror Mirror** *Don Dokken*
Miserable *Lit*
M-3/00 A-29/00
Misery *Soul Asylum*
M-1/95 A-2/95
M-3/91 **Miss Freelove '69**
Hoodoo Gurus
M-22/93 **Miss Teen U.S.A.**
Best Kissers In The World
M-13/94 **Miss World** *Hole*
A-9/87 **Miss You** *Eric Clapton*
A-38/91 **Miss You In A Heartbeat** *Law*
A-1/84 **Missing You** *John Waite*
A-30/82 **Missing You** *Dan Fogelberg*
A-37/84 **Missing You** *Hagar, Schon,*
Aaronson, Shrieve
A-33/89 **Mission** *Rush*
A-23/82 **Mission Of Mercy** *Motels*
A-1/86 **Missionary Man** *Eurythmics*
A-27/89 **Mista Bone** *Great White*
Mister ..see: Mr.
Mister Bone ..see: Mista Bone
A-24/94 **Misunderstood** *Mötley Crüe*
M-36/00 **Mixed Bizness** *Beck*
Mixed Emotions *Rolling Stones*
A-1/89 M-22/89
Mmm Mmm Mmm Mmm
Crash Test Dummies
M-1/94 A-25/94
Mockingbird Girl
Magnificent Bastards
M-12/95 A-27/95
M-14/94 **Mockingbirds** *Grant Lee Buffalo*
A-35/87 **Modern Day Cowboy** *Tesla*
A-9/84 **Modern Day Delilah**
Van Stephenson
A-41/85 **Modern Girl** *Meat Loaf*
A-6/83 **Modern Love** *David Bowie*
A-34/86 **Modern Woman** *Billy Joel*
Molly (Sixteen Candles)
Sponge
M-3/95 A-11/95
A-37/82 **Money** *Pink Floyd*
A-37/85 **Money Changes Everything**
Cyndi Lauper
A-1/85 **Money For Nothing** *Dire Straits*
A-3/91 **Moneytalks** *AC/DC*
A-13/91 **Monkey Business** *Skid Row*
M-5/89 **Monkey Gone To Heaven**
Pixies
A-17/90 **Monkey On My Back** *Aerosmith*
A-12/83 **Monkey On Your Back**
Aldo Nova
A-16/83 **Monkey Time** *Tubes*
Monkey Wrench *Foo Fighters*
A-9/97 M-9/97
A-24/98 **Monster Side** *Addict*
M-8/91 **Monsters And Angels**
Voice Of The Beehive
A-27/87 **Mony Mony "Live"** *Billy Idol*
M-23/89 **Moons Of Jupiter**
Scruffy The Cat
M-1/90 **More** *Sisters Of Mercy*

More Human Than Human
White Zombie
M-7/95 A-10/95
A-44/91 **More Than Ever** *Nelson*
A-58/82 **More Than This** *Roxy Music*
A-12/91 **More Than Words** *Extreme*
A-41/91 **More Things Change** *Cinderella*
A-30/94 **More Wine Waiter Please** *Poor*
M-1/94 **More You Ignore Me, The**
Closer I Get *Morrissey*
A-10/84 **More You Live, The More You**
Love *Flock Of Seagulls*
A-55/84 **Morning Dew** *Blackfoot*
M-24/95 **Morning Glory** *Oasis*
M-21/93 **Moses** *808 State*
A-1/98 **Most High**
Jimmy Page & Robert Plant
Most Precarious *Blues Traveler*
M-25/97 A-27/97
A-17/94 **Mother** *Danzig*
Mother Earth ..see: Peace On
Earth
Mother Mother *Tracy Bonham*
M-1/96 A-18/96
A-17/91 **Mother's Eyes** *Enuff Z'Nuff*
A-23/94 **Motherless Child** *Eric Clapton*
M-24/02 **Motivation** *Sum 41*
A-22/01 **Moto Psycho** *Megadeth*
M-10/88 **Motorcrash** *Sugarcubes*
M-20/89 **Motorcycle** *Love & Rockets*
A-15/85 **Motorcycle Girl** *Cruzados*
Mourning *Tantric*
A-18/01 M-22/02
Mouth *Bush*
M-5/97 A-28/98
M-4/91 **Move Any Mountain (Progen**
91) *Shamen*
Move With Me Sister
Del Fuegos
M-22/89 A-32/89
Movies *Alien Ant Farm*
M-18/01 A-38/02
Movin' On Up *Primal Scream*
M-2/91 A-28/91
A-30/91 **Moving On** *Gary Moore*
A-50/90 **Mr. Cab Driver** *Lenny Kravitz*
Mr. Jones *Counting Crows*
A-2/94 M-2/94
A-3/93 **Mister Please** *Damn Yankees*
A-3/83 **Mr. Roboto** *Styx*
A-14/83 **Mr. Soul** *Neil Young*
A-34/92 **Mr. Tinkertrain** *Ozzy Osbourne*
A-36/93 **Mrs. Rita** *Gin Blossoms*
M-8/92 **Mrs. Robinson** *Lemonheads*
A-18/95 **Muddy Jesus** *Ian Moore*
Mudshovel *Staind*
A-10/99 M-14/99
M-17/98 **Mummers' Dance**
Loreena McKennitt
Mungo City *Spacehog*
A-19/98 M-21/98
A-13/84 **Murder** *David Gilmour*
A-14/95 **Murder Incorporated**
Bruce Springsteen
A-17/95 **Murder Of One** *Counting Crows*
M-25/92 **Murder, Tonight, In The Trailer**
Park *Cowboy Junkies*
M-19/89 **Music Goes Round My Head**
Saints
A-40/81 **Musta Notta Gotta Lotta**
Joe Ely
Muzzle *Smashing Pumpkins*
M-8/96 A-10/96

A-1/87 **My Baby** *Pretenders*
A-32/81 **My Baby** *Cold Chisel*
A-26/93 **My Back Pages**
Bob Dylan/Roger McGuinn/
Tom Petty/Neil Young/
Eric Clapton/George Harrison
M-13/88 **My Bag** *Lloyd Cole*
A-12/89 **My Brave Face** *Paul McCartney*
A-11/83 **My City Was Gone** *Pretenders*
A-24/91 **My Definition Of A Boombastic**
Jazz Style *Dream Warriors*
A-52/84 **My Ever Changing Moods**
Style Council
A-26/98 **My Father's Eyes** *Eric Clapton*
A-20/00 **My Favorite Headache**
Geddy Lee
M-26/98 **My Favorite Mistake**
Sheryl Crow
M-16/99 **My Favourite Game** *Cardigans*
My Friends
Red Hot Chili Peppers
A-1/95 M-1/95
M-5/02 **My Friends Over You**
New Found Glory
My Generation *Limp Bizkit*
M-18/00 A-33/00
My Girl ..see: Nite At The Apollo
A-16/81 **My Girl (Gone, Gone, Gone)**
Chilliwack
A-26/95 **My Hallucination** *Shaw/Blades*
M-23/01 **My Happiness** *Powderfinger*
A-1/90 **My Head's In Mississippi**
ZZ Top
A-50/89 **My Heart Can't Tell You No**
Rod Stewart
My Hero *Foo Fighters*
M-6/98 A-8/98
A-6/86 **My Hometown**
Bruce Springsteen
A-31/81 **My Kinda Lover** *Billy Squier*
A-33/86 **My Mistake**
Phantom, Rocker & Slick
A-19/96 **My My** *Seven Mary Three*
M-37/99 **My Name Is** *Eminem*
M-9/93 **My Name Is Mud** *Primus*
A-32/84 **My Oh My** *Slade*
My Own Prison *Creed*
A-2/97 M-7/98
My Own Worst Enemy *Lit*
M-1/99 A-6/99
A-34/89 **My Paradise** *Outfield*
My Sacrifice *Creed*
A-1/01 M-2/02
M-1/93 **My Sister** *Juliana Hatfield Three*
A-6/98 **My Song** *Jerry Cantrell*
A-11/83 **My Town** *Michael Stanley Band*
M-32/97 **My Town** *Buck-O-Nine*
M-24/93 **My Umbrella** *Tripping Daisy*
My Wave *Soundgarden*
A-11/94 M-18/94
My Way *Limp Bizkit*
M-3/01 A-4/01
(My World) ..see: You're
A-26/99 **Mysterious** *Scorpions*
Mysterious Ways *U2*
A-1/91 M-1/91
A-20/84 **Mystery** *Dio*
A-21/86 **Mystic Rhythms** *Rush*
A-17/89 **Mystify** *INXS*

N

A-2/00 **N.I.B.**
    Primus with Ozzy Osbourne
M-11/92 **N.W.O.** *Ministry*
A-26/83 **Na Na Hey Hey Kiss Him Goodbye** *Bananarama*
    Naked *Goo Goo Dolls*
    A-8/96 M-9/96
M-18/97 **Naked Eye** *Luscious Jackson*
M-10/91 **Naked Rain** *This Picture*
    Name *Goo Goo Dolls*
    A-1/95 M-1/95
A-43/87 **Name Names** *Del Fuegos*
M-22/01 **Name Of The Game**
    Crystal Method
M-9/91 **Native Son** *Judybats*
M-24/00 **Natural Blues** *Moby*
    Natural One *Folk Implosion*
    M-4/95 A-20/96
A-32/93 **Natural Thing** *Journey*
A-30/90 **Nature Of Love** *Poco*
A-6/85 **Naughty Naughty** *John Parr*
    Nearly Lost You
    Screaming Trees
    M-5/92 A-12/93
A-3/89 **Need A Little Taste Of Love**
    Doobie Brothers
M-35/95 **Need You Around**
    Smoking Popes
A-12/87 **Need You Tonight** *INXS*
A-19/94 **Need Your Lovin'** *Tesla*
A-17/86 **Needles And Pins**
    Tom Petty with Stevie Nicks
    Negasonic Teenage Warhead
    Monster Magnet
    A-19/95 M-26/95
M-29/99 **Negotiation Limerick File**
    Beastie Boys
A-29/92 **Neighbor** *Ugly Kid Joe*
A-37/84 **Neighborhood Bully** *Bob Dylan*
A-40/84 **Neighborhood Threat**
    David Bowie
A-2/85 **Never** *Heart*
    Never Again *Nickelback*
    A-1/02 M-24/02
A-45/88 **Never Be The Same**
    Crowded House
    Never Do That *Pretenders*
    M-4/90 A-5/90
    Never Enough *Cure*
    M-1/90 A-33/90
A-4/87 **Never Enough** *Patty Smyth*
    (also see: Surefire)
M-16/00 **Never Gonna Come Back Down**
    BT
    Never Gonna Stop *Rob Zombie*
    A-11/02 M-23/02
A-45/89 **Never Had A Lot To Lose**
    Cheap Trick
A-38/82 **Never Had It Better**
    Franke & The Knockouts
A-54/82 **Never Hold Back**
    B.E. Taylor Group
A-15/87 **Never Let Me Down**
    David Bowie
M-4/00 **Never Let You Go**
    Third Eye Blind
A-11/87 **Never Say Goodbye** *Bon Jovi*
A-27/82 **Never Say Never** *Romeo Void*
M-27/97 **Never Say Never** *That Dog*
A-8/85 **Never Surrender** *Corey Hart*
A-23/83 **Never Surrender** *Triumph*

Never Tear Us Apart *INXS*
    A-5/88 M-28/88
    Never There *Cake*
    M-1/98 A-40/99
M-7/99 **New** *No Doubt*
A-33/81 **New Age Music** *Pat Travers*
    New Beginning *Stir*
    A-16/00 M-18/00
A-33/01 **New Disease** *Spineshank*
A-7/84 **New Girl Now** *Honeymoon Suite*
M-26/93 **New Life** *X*
A-4/84 **New Moon On Monday**
    Duran Duran
A-30/90 **New Orleans Is Sinking**
    Tragically Hip
M-9/97 **New Pollution** *Beck*
A-43/84 **New Romeo**
    Southside Johnny & The Jukes
A-8/88 **New Sensation** *INXS*
A-58/84 **New Song** *Howard Jones*
A-35/89 **New Thing** *Enuff Z'Nuff*
A-1/82 **New World Man** *Rush*
A-2/83 **New Year's Day** *U2*
A-24/90 **New York Minute** *Don Henley*
A-39/01 **Next Homecoming**
    Collective Soul
    (Next To Me) ..see: Ya Ya
M-17/00 **Next Year** *Foo Fighters*
M-31/98 **Nice Guys Finish Last**
    Green Day
    Nice To Know You *Incubus*
    A-9/02 M-9/02
A-20/81 **Nicole** *Point Blank*
    Night ..also see: Nite
A-34/83 **Night, The** *Animals*
    Night And Day *U2*
    M-2/90 A-34/90
A-34/82 **Night Hunting Time** *Santana*
    Night In My Veins *Pretenders*
    M-2/94 A-13/94
A-14/81 **Night Life** *Foreigner*
A-18/86 **Night Moves** *Marilyn Martin*
A-4/90 **Night On The Town**
    Bruce Hornsby
A-9/81 **Night Owls** *Little River Band*
A-49/88 **Night Patrol** *Robert Cray Band*
A-32/84 **Nightbird** *Stevie Nicks*
    (with Sandy Stewart)
M-4/89 **Nightmares** *Violent Femmes*
A-26/89 **Nightrain** *Guns N' Roses*
A-39/88 **Nighttime For Generals**
    Crosby, Stills, Nash & Young
A-21/81 **Nightwatchman** *Tom Petty*
A-37/97 **Nine Lives** *Aerosmith*
    Nineteen Forever *Joe Jackson*
    M-4/89 A-16/89
M-23/01 **19-2000** *Gorillaz*
A-5/81 **96 Tears** *Garland Jeffreys*
A-23/84 **99 Luftballons** *Nena*
A-23/93 **99 Ways To Die** *Megadeth*
A-9/90 **99 Worlds** *Peter Wolf*
M-13/93 **99.9 F** *Suzanne Vega*
M-21/88 **1969** *Pretenders*
    1979 *Smashing Pumpkins*
    A-1/96 M-1/96
A-43/85 **Nite At The Apollo Live! The Way You Do The Things You Do/**
    My Girl *Hall & Oates/*
    David Ruffin/Eddie Kendrick
A-4/90 **No Alibis** *Eric Clapton*
M-19/89 **No Big Deal** *Love & Rockets*

    (No Can Do) ..see: I Can't Go For That
A-60/82 **No Control** *Eddie Money*
A-12/86 **No Easy Way Out**
    Robert Tepper
    No Excuses *Alice In Chains*
    A-1/94 M-3/94
M-31/97 **No Face** *Suicide Machines*
    No Leaf Clover
    Metallica with Michael Kamen
    A-1/00 M-18/00
    No Light *3rd Strike*
    A-23/02 M-36/02
A-4/85 **No Lookin' Back**
    Michael McDonald
A-18/93 **No Man's Land** *Billy Joel*
A-47/92 **No Man's Land** *Leon Russell*
M-36/99 **No Mercy** *Khaleel*
A-19/86 **No Money Down** *Lou Reed*
A-7/90 **No More** *Neil Young*
A-42/83 **No More Lies**
    Neal Schon & Jan Hammer
A-16/84 **No More Lonely Nights**
    Paul McCartney
    No More, No Less
    Collective Soul
    A-10/99 M-32/99
A-10/91 **No More Tears** *Ozzy Osbourne*
A-25/84 **No More Words** *Berlin*
    No Myth *Michael Penn*
    M-4/90 A-5/90
A-18/88 **No New Tale To Tell**
    Love & Rockets
    No One *Cold*
    M-13/01 A-17/01
A-20/86 **No One Is To Blame**
    Howard Jones
    No One Knows
    Queens Of The Stone Age
    M-11↑/02 A-20↑/02
A-1/82 **No One Like You** *Scorpions*
A-7/94 **No One To Run With**
    Allman Brothers Band
A-9/86 **No Promises** *Icehouse*
A-37/89 **No Questions Asked**
    Fleetwood Mac
    No Rain *Blind Melon*
    A-1/93 M-1/93
A-40/82 **No Refuge** *Eddie Schwartz*
A-7/92 **No Regrets** *Tom Cochrane*
A-2/81 **No Reply At All** *Genesis*
A-41/86 **No Second Prize** *Jimmy Barnes*
    No Shelter
    Rage Against The Machine
    A-30/98 M-33/98
A-4/88 **No Smoke Without A Fire**
    Bad Company
A-3/91 **No Son Of Mine** *Genesis*
    No Souvenirs *Melissa Etheridge*
    A-9/89 M-18/89
A-41/87 **No Such Thing** *Tommy Shaw*
A-29/84 **No Surrender**
    Bruce Springsteen
A-34/99 **No Tears Left**
    Crosby, Stills, Nash & Young
A-25/87 **No Time** *Robin Trower*
A-1/84 **No Way Out** *Jefferson Starship*
    No Way Out
    Stone Temple Pilots
    A-17/00 M-24/00
    (also see: Heaven's Trail)
A-15/86 **No Way To Treat A Lady**
    Bonnie Raitt

A-32/82 **Nobody But Me**
George Thorogood

M-13/90 **Nobody But You**
Lou Reed/John Cale

A-9/87 **Nobody But You Baby**
Steve Miller Band

A-28/92 **Nobody Hears**
Suicidal Tendencies

A-39/98 **Nobody Knows** Addict

(Nobody Loves Me) ..see: Sour Times

A-16/91 **Nobody Said It Was Easy**
Four Horsemen

A-2/84 **Nobody Told Me** John Lennon

A-25/87 **Nobody's Fool** Cinderella

A-30/88 **Nobody's Fool** Kenny Loggins

A-9/94 **Nobody's Hero** Rush

A-20/85 **Nobody's Home** Deep Purple

A-3/88 **Nobody's Perfect**
Mike + The Mechanics

Nobody's Real Powerman 5000
A-18/00 M-23/00

A-44/91 **None Of It Matters**
Blackeyed Susan

A-35/92 **Nonstop To Nowhere**
Faster Pussycat

Nookie Limp Bizkit
M-3/99 A-6/99

Not A Kennedy ..see: (Glad I'm)

A-24/02 **Not Afraid** Earshot

M-5/97 **Not An Addict** K's Choice

A-27/95 **Not Enough** Van Halen

A-17/85 **Not Enough Love In The World**
Don Henley

Not Enough Time INXS
M-2/92 A-13/92

A-21↑/02 **Not Falling** Mudvayne

Not For You Pearl Jam
A-12/95 M-38/95

M-31/97 **Not If You Were The Last Junkie On Earth**
Dandy Warhols

A-6/88 **Not Just Another Girl**
Ivan Neville

A-7/83 **Not Now John** Pink Floyd

M-1/93 **Not Sleeping Around**
Ned's Atomic Dustbin

A-33/96 **Not Today** Rust

A-6/86 **Nothin' At All** Heart

A-19/88 **Nothin' But A Good Time**
Poison

A-29/93 **Nothin' To Lose** Arcade

A-12/89 **Nothin' You Can Do About It**
Richard Marx

A-23/94 **Nothing** Ian Moore

Nothing As It Seems Pearl Jam
A-3/00 M-10/00

A-34/97 **Nothing At All** Third Day

A-5/88 **(Nothing But) Flowers**
Talking Heads

Nothing Compares 2 U
Sinéad O'Connor
M-1/90 A-23/90

A-8/02 **Nothing Could Come Between Us** Theory Of A Deadman

A-11/92 **Nothing Else Matters** Metallica

A-19/83 **Nothing Ever Changes**
Stevie Nicks

M-22/92 **Nothing Natural** Lush

Nothing To Believe In Cracker
M-32/96 A-40/96

A-23/00 **Nothing To Prove**
Caroline's Spine

A-16/87 **Nothing's Gonna Stop Us Now**
Starship

M-17/93 **Nothingness** Living Colour

A-8/87 **Notorious** Loverboy

M-16/91 **November Comes** Hollow Men

A-15/92 **November Rain** Guns N' Roses

M-6/90 **November Spawned A Monster**
Morrissey

M-1/96 **Novocaine For The Soul** Eels

A-26/02 **Now** Def Leppard

A-3/92 **Now More Than Ever**
John Mellencamp

A-28/01 **Now Or Never** Dope

A-22/99 **Now That You're Gone**
Indigenous

M-17/95 **Now They'll Sleep** Belly

A-23/00 **Now You Know**
Full Devil Jacket

A-15/90 **Now You're Gone** Whitesnake

Now You're In Heaven
Julian Lennon
A-1/89 M-27/89

A-13/82 **Nowhere To Run** Santana

A-34/82 **Nuclear Attack** Greg Lake

Numb U2
M-2/93 A-18/93

M-20/95 **Number One Blind** Veruca Salt

M-1/97 **#1 Crush** Garbage

M-17/92 **Number One Dominator** Top

O

M-21/95 **O Baby**
Siouxsie & The Banshees

Oaf, The Big Wreck
A-9/98 M-24/98

M-12/91 **Obscurity Knocks**
Trash Can Sinatras

M-16/89 **Obsession** Xymox

Obvious Child Paul Simon
A-21/90 M-24/90

Obvious Song Joe Jackson
M-2/91 A-28/91

M-23/96 **Ocean** Sebadoh

M-29/91 **Oceanside** Robyn Hitchcock

M-11/95 **Ode To My Family** Cranberries

Off He Goes Pearl Jam
M-31/97 A-34/97

M-14/93 **Oh Carolina** Shaggy

M-5/89 **Oh Daddy** Adrian Belew

A-26/99 **Oh My God** Guns N' Roses

A-1/82 **(Oh) Pretty Woman** Van Halen

A-15/90 **Oh Pretty Woman** Gary Moore

A-1/84 **Oh Sherrie** Steve Perry

Oh Well Joe Jackson
M-20/91 A-25/91

A-24/01 **Old Enough** Nickelback

Old Man & Me (When I Get To Heaven)
Hootie & The Blowfish
A-6/96 M-33/96

A-1/85 **Old Man Down The Road**
John Fogerty

A-23/93 **Old Rose Motel** Great White

A-59/82 **Olympia** Jon Anderson

M-25/92 **On A Plain** Nirvana

A-27/82 **On A Roll** Point Blank

M-17/97 **On And On** Longpigs

A-1/84 **On The Dark Side** John Cafferty

M-19/90 **On The Greener Side**
Michelle Shocked

A-7/89 **On The Line** Tangier

A-3/82 **On The Loose** Saga

M-19/00 **On The Roof Again** Eve 6

M-17/93 **On The Ropes** Wonder Stuff

A-1/88 **On The Turning Away**
Pink Floyd

A-6/87 **On The Western Skyline**
Bruce Hornsby

A-6/89 **Once Bitten Twice Shy**
Great White

Once In A While Dishwalla
A-17/98 M-20/98

One U2
A-1/92 M-1/92

One Creed
A-2/99 M-2/99

One, The Foo Fighters
M-14/02 A-20/02

M-23/96 **One, The** Tracy Bonham

A-46/89 **One** Metallica

A-1/90 **One And Only Man**
Steve Winwood

A-23/97 **One Angel** Stir

M-26/01 **One Armed Scissor**
At The Drive-In

A-17/89 **One Big Rush** Joe Satriani

A-10/89 **One Clear Moment** Little Feat

A-29/87 **One For The Mockingbird**
Cutting Crew

A-39/89 **One Good Lover** Red Siren

A-20/88 **One Good Reason** Paul Carrack

One Headlight Wallflowers
A-1/97 M-1/97

A-3/86 **One Hit (To The Body)**
Rolling Stones

M-12/99 **One Hit Wonder** Everclear

M-4/92 **100%** Sonic Youth

A-13/93 **One I Am** Dan Baird

A-2/87 **One I Love** R.E.M.

One I Love Big Country
M-17/93 A-34/93

A-27/98 **One I Want** Van Halen

A-22/84 **One In A Million** Romantics

A-22/85 **One In A Million**
Eddie & The Tide

A-27/84 **One In A Million**
Christine McVie

A-33/91 **One In A Million** Trixter

M-13/93 **One In Ten** 808 State

One Last Breath Creed
A-5/02 M-17/02

M-24/89 **One Little Girl**
Toad The Wet Sprocket

A-10/02 **One Little Victory** Rush

A-17/85 **One Lonely Night**
REO Speedwagon

M-9/90 **One Love** Stone Roses

One Man Army Our Lady Peace
M-13/99 A-16/99

A-19/96 **One More Astronaut**
I Mother Earth

M-32/98 **One More Murder**
Better Than Ezra

A-4/85 **One More Night** Phil Collins

A-22/97 **One More Time** Corey Stevens

A-9/89 **One Night** Bad Company

A-7/85 **One Night Love Affair**
Bryan Adams

A-35/82 **One Night Stand** Janis Joplin

A-38/02 **One Of A Kind** Breaking Point

A-17/83 **One Of Our Submarines**
Thomas Dolby

One Of Us Joan Osborne
M-7/95 A-26/96

	One Shot *Tin Machine*	M-23/99	**Open Road Song** *Eve 6*	A-24/87	**Over The Hills And Far Away**
	M-3/91 A-17/91	M-28/96	**Open The Door** *Magnapop*		*Gary Moore*
A-21/86	**One Simple Thing** *Stabilizers*		**Open Up Your Eyes** *Tonic*	A-38/82	**Over The Mountain**
A-5/87	**One Slip** *Pink Floyd*		A-2/96 M-22/96		*Ozzy Osbourne*
A-55/84	**One Small Day** *Ultravox*	A-24/00	**Open Your Eyes** *Guano Apes*		**Over Your Shoulder**
	One Step Closer *Linkin Park*	A-27/82	**Open Your Eyes**		*Seven Mary Three*
	A-4/01 M-5/01		*Lords Of The New Church*		A-7/98 M-16/98
A-2/88	**One Step Up** *Bruce Springsteen*	A-33/97	**Open Your Eyes** *Yes*	M-30/01	**Overcome** *Live*
A-15/82	**One Story Town** *Tom Petty*	M-37/02	**Open Your Eyes** *Goldfinger*	A-3/83	**Overkill** *Men At Work*
A-2/83	**One Thing** *INXS*	M-9/92	**Operation Spirit (The Tyranny**	A-1/83	**Owner Of A Lonely Heart** *Yes*
A-24/02	**One Thing** *Gravity Kills*		**Of Tradition)** *Live*	A-14/82	**Ozone Baby** *Led Zeppelin*
A-2/83	**One Thing Leads To Another**	M-26/01	**Opticon** *Orgy*		
	Fixx	M-10/00	**Optimistic** *Radiohead*		
M-40/94	**One Time For Me**		**Orange Crush** *R.E.M.*		
	Reverend Horton Heat		A-1/88 M-1/88		
A-17/84	**One Time For Old Times**	A-24/89	**Order Of The Universe**		
	38 Special		*Anderson, Bruford, Wakeman,*		**Pain** *Stereomud*
A-19/85	**One Vision** *Queen*		*Howe*		A-8/01 M-34/01
M-11/92	**One Way** *Levellers*	A-3/91	**Ordinary Average Guy**	M-24/92	**Pain Lies On The Riverside**
M-1/98	**One Week** *Barenaked Ladies*		*Joe Walsh*		*Live*
A-46/92	**One Word** *Baby Animals*	M-2/93	**Ordinary World** *Duran Duran*	A-29/92	**Painless** *Baby Animals*
A-8/85	**One World** *Dire Straits*		**Original Prankster** *Offspring*	A-23/87	**Painted Moon** *Silencers*
A-41/81	**One's Too Many**		M-2/00 A-7/01	A-26/00	**Painted On My Heart** *Cult*
	Fabulous Thunderbirds	A-43/84	**Original Sin** *INXS*	A-16/00	**Painted Perfect** *One Way Ride*
M-8/90	**Onion Skin** *Boom Crash Opera*	M-6/89	**Orinoco Flow (Sail Away)** *Enya*	A-33/89	**Painting By Numbers**
A-26/93	**Only** *Anthrax*	A-1/83	**Other Arms** *Robert Plant*		*James McMurtry*
A-7/99	**Only A Fool** *Black Crowes*	A-37/90	**Other Kind** *Steve Earle*	A-2/84	**Panama** *Van Halen*
A-1/88	**Only A Memory** *Smithereens*	M-13/88	**Other 99** *Big Audio Dynamite*	M-19/91	**Pandora's Box (It's A Long,**
A-40/95	**Only Dreaming**		**Otherside**		**Long Way)** *Orchestral*
	Maids Of Gravity		*Red Hot Chili Peppers*		*Manoeuvres In The Dark*
A-44/84	**Only Flame In Town**		M-1/00 A-2/00	A-26/92	**Paper Doll** *Fleetwood Mac*
	Elvis Costello	A-1/90	**Other Side** *Aerosmith*	A-1/87	**Paper In Fire**
	Only God Knows Why *Kid Rock*	A-11/86	**Other Side Of Life** *Moody Blues*		*John Cougar Mellencamp*
	A-5/00 M-13/00		**Other Side Of Summer**	A-11/99	**Paper Sun** *Def Leppard*
M-16/96	**Only Happy When It Rains**		*Elvis Costello*	A-18/89	**Paper Thin** *John Hiatt*
	Garbage		M-1/91 A-40/91	M-32/02	**Papercut** *Linkin Park*
M-26/92	**Only Living Boy In New Cross**	M-2/90	**Ouija Board, Ouija Board**	A-2/82	**Paperlate** *Genesis*
	Carter		*Morrissey*		**Parabola** *Tool*
A-28/85	**Only Lonely** *Bon Jovi*	M-2/91	**Our Frank** *Morrissey*		A-10/02 M-31/02
A-16/87	**Only Love** *BoDeans*	A-9/83	**Our House** *Madness*	A-28/91	**Paradise** *Tesla*
M-11/92	**Only Love Can Break Your**	A-15/81	**Our Lips Are Sealed** *Go-Go's*	A-14/89	**Paradise City** *Guns N' Roses*
	Heart *Saint Etienne*	A-22/85	**Our Love** *Krokus*	M-37/01	**Parallel Universe**
A-19/90	**Only My Heart Talkin'**	A-32/83	**Our Song** *Yes*		*Red Hot Chili Peppers*
	Alice Cooper	A-1/91	**Out In The Cold** *Tom Petty*	A-31/93	**Paralyzed** *Eric Gales Band*
A-13/88	**Only One** *Jimmy Page*	A-22/86	**Out Of Mind Out Of Sight**	A-25/83	**Paranoid** *Ozzy Osbourne*
	Only One *Goo Goo Dolls*		*Models*		**Pardon Me** *Incubus*
	A-21/95 M-36/95	M-34/01	**Out Of My Depth** *Everclear*		M-3/00 A-7/00
A-44/83	**Only One** *Bryan Adams*	A-55/84	**Out Of My Hands** *Face To Face*	A-28/98	**Park Avenue** *Girls Against Boys*
	Only One I Know *Charlatans UK*	A-59/81	**Out Of Season**	A-10/88	**Part Of The Machine** *Jethro Tull*
	M-5/90 A-37/91		*REO Speedwagon*	A-9/91	**Part Of You, Part Of Me**
M-27/92	**Only Shallow**	A-14/94	**Out Of Tears** *Rolling Stones*		*Glenn Frey*
	My Bloody Valentine	A-18/84	**Out Of Touch**	A-48/90	**Party Starts Now!!**
A-22/82	**Only Solutions** *Journey*		*Daryl Hall/John Oates*		*Manitoba's Wild Kingdom*
A-6/82	**Only The Lonely** *Motels*	A-10/82	**Out Of Work** *Gary U.S. Bonds*	A-2/81	**Party's Over (Hopelessly In**
A-3/85	**Only The Young** *Journey*	A-40/90	**Out With The Boys** *Lord Tracy*		**Love)** *Journey*
A-8/82	**Only Time Will Tell** *Asia*		*(also see: Tora, Tora, Tora)*	A-5/82	**Partytown** *Glenn Frey*
M-8/90	**Only Tongue Can Tell**	M-9/93	**Outbreak Of Love** *Midnight Oil*	A-15/90	**Pass, The** *Rush*
	Trash Can Sinatras	A-45/92	**Outshined** *Soundgarden*	A-7/89	**Patience** *Guns N' Roses*
	Only Wanna Be With You		**Outside**	A-36/86	**Patio Lanterns** *Kim Mitchell*
	Hootie & The Blowfish		*Aaron Lewis with Fred Durst*	A-33/96	**Pavilion** *Eric Johnson*
	A-2/95 M-22/95		A-1/01 M-2/01	A-33/01	**Payback** *Flaw*
M-36/98	**Only When I Lose Myself**		*Staind*	A-17/91	**Payin' The Cost To Be The**
	Depeche Mode		A-11/01 M-16/01		**Boss** *Pat Benatar*
A-40/84	**Only When You Leave**		**Outtasite (Outta Mind)** *Wilco*	A-34/95	**Peace And Love** *Neil Young*
	Spandau Ballet		A-22/97 M-39/97	A-2/90	**Peace In Our Time**
A-22/85	**Ooh Ooh Song** *Pat Benatar*	A-33/91	**Over And Over**		*Eddie Money*
A-6/88	**Open All Night**		*Neil Young & Crazy Horse*	M-37/00	**Peace Not Greed**
	Georgia Satellites	M-22/00	**Over My Head** *Lit*		*Kottonmouth Kings*
A-22/82	**Open All Night**		**Over Now** *Alice In Chains*	A-14/90	**Peace On Earth...Mother**
	Bruce Springsteen		A-4/96 M-24/96		**Earth...Third Stone From The**
A-35/82	**Open Arms** *Journey*	A-24/93	**Over Now** *Coverdale-Page*		**Sun** *Santana*
	(Open Fire) ..see: Ana's Song	A-36/99	**Over The Edge** *Ratt*	A-1/93	**Peace Pipe** *Cry Of Love*
A-11/89	**Open Letter (To A Landlord)**			A-38/01	**Peaceful World**
	Living Colour				*John Mellencamp*

	Peaches
	Presidents Of The United State
	s Of America
	M-8/96 A-24/96
M-7/91	**Pearl** *Chapterhouse*
A-28/81	**Pearl Necklace** *ZZ Top*
M-1/88	**Peek-A-Boo**
	Siouxsie & The Banshees
A-5/85	**People Get Ready**
	Jeff Beck & Rod Stewart
A-19/88	**People Have The Power**
	Patti Smith
	People That We Love *Bush*
	A-10/01 M-11/01
A-50/81	**People Who Died**
	Jim Carroll Band
M-29/91	**People's Drug**
	John Wesley Harding
	Pepper *Butthole Surfers*
	M-1/96 A-19/96
	Perfect *Smashing Pumpkins*
	M-3/98 A-33/98
M-23/88	**Perfect** *Fairground Attraction*
M-33/98	**Perfect Day Elise** *PJ Harvey*
	Perfect Drug *Nine Inch Nails*
	M-11/97 A-21/97
A-54/84	**Perfect Lover** *Kansas*
A-12/84	**Perfect Strangers** *Deep Purple*
A-5/88	**Perfect World** *Huey Lewis*
A-16/93	**Perfectly Good Guitar**
	John Hiatt
A-3/95	**Perry Mason** *Ozzy Osbourne*
M-8/91	**Person You Are**
	John Wesley Harding
M-3/89	**Personal Jesus** *Depeche Mode*
M-4/89	**Pet Sematary** *Ramones*
	Peter Pumpkinhead ..see:
	Ballad Of
	Pets *Porno For Pyros*
	M-1/93 A-25/93
M-16/91	**Phoenix Of My Heart** *Xymox*
A-1/83	**Photograph** *Def Leppard*
	Photograph *Verve Pipe*
	M-6/96 A-17/96
M-9/93	**Photograph**
	R.E.M. with Natalie Merchant
M-17/01	**Photograph** *Weezer*
A-19/81	**Physical (You're So)**
	Adam & The Ants
M-2/91	**Piccadilly Palare** *Morrissey*
M-1/89	**Pictures Of Matchstick Men**
	Camper Van Beethoven
M-19/90	**Pictures Of You** *Cure*
A-25/85	**Piece By Piece** *Tubes*
M-20/95	**Piggy** *Nine Inch Nails*
	(pigsheadsnakeface) ..see:
	Julie's Blanket
M-30/00	**Pinch Me** *Barenaked Ladies*
A-1/94	**Pincushion** *ZZ Top*
M-8/90	**Pineapple Face** *Revenge*
A-1/97	**Pink** *Aerosmith*
A-27/84	**Pink Cadillac** *Bruce Springsteen*
A-3/84	**Pink Houses**
	John Cougar Mellencamp
	Piranha *Tripping Daisy*
	M-32/95 A-35/95
A-40/81	**Pirates (So Long Lonely**
	Avenue) *Rickie Lee Jones*
	Pitiful *Blindside*
	A-18/02 M-36/02
A-29/97	**Place Your Hands** *Reef*
A-24/89	**Planes** *Jefferson Airplane*
A-21/94	**Planet Caravan** *Pantera*
M-10/91	**Planet Love** *Dylans*

A-28/84	**Play Guitar**
	John Cougar Mellencamp
A-4/82	**Play The Game Tonight** *Kansas*
A-48/84	**Playin' It Cool**
	Timothy B. Schmit
A-15/81	**Playing To Win** *LRB*
A-37/00	**Playing With Fire**
	Shannon Curfman
M-31/97	**Please** *U2*
M-22/92	**Please Yourself** *Darling Buds*
M-14/92	**Pleasure** *Soup Dragons*
A-12/85	**Pleasure And Pain** *Divinyls*
A-11/82	**Pledge Pin** *Robert Plant*
	Plowed *Sponge*
	M-5/95 A-9/95
	Plush *Stone Temple Pilots*
	A-1/93 M-9/93
	Poem *Taproot*
	A-13↑/02 M-19↑/02
A-39/98	**Poets** *Tragically Hip*
A-20/81	**Point Blank** *Bruce Springsteen*
A-40/00	**Point #1** *Chevelle*
M-29/02	**Points Of Authority** *Linkin Park*
A-15/89	**Poison** *Alice Cooper*
M-6/92	**Poison Heart** *Ramones*
A-21/81	**Police On My Back** *Clash*
M-1/90	**Policy Of Truth** *Depeche Mode*
M-22/01	**Politically Correct** *SR-71*
A-19/84	**Politics Of Dancing** *Re-Flex*
A-19/02	**Polyamorous**
	Breaking Benjamin
A-21/89	**Poor Little Girl** *George Harrison*
A-19/82	**Poor Man's Son** *Survivor*
A-18/82	**Poor Tom** *Led Zeppelin*
A-2/89	**Pop Singer**
	John Cougar Mellencamp
	Pop Song 89 *R.E.M.*
	A-14/89 M-16/88
M-11/96	**Popular** *Nada Surf*
M-9/92	**Popular Creeps** *Chris Mars*
M-18/00	**Porcelain** *Moby*
	Positive Bleeding *Urge Overkill*
	M-23/94 A-40/93
M-4/94	**Possession** *Sarah McLachlan*
	Possum Kingdom *Toadies*
	M-4/95 A-9/95
M-7/90	**Post Post-Modern Man** *Devo*
A-44/82	**Pound Is Sinking**
	Paul McCartney
A-1/91	**Poundcake** *Van Halen*
A-25/88	**Pour Some Sugar On Me**
	Def Leppard
A-35/82	**Power** *Rainbow*
A-38/87	**Power** *Kansas*
A-1/85	**Power Of Love** *Huey Lewis*
A-13/83	**Power (Strength In Numbers)**
	Red Rider
A-19/91	**Power Windows** *Billy Falcon*
A-3/88	**Powerful Stuff**
	Fabulous Thunderbirds
A-20/98	**Powertrip** *Monster Magnet*
	Praise *Sevendust*
	A-15/01 M-23/01
M-23↑/02	**Praise Chorus** *Jimmy Eat World*
M-2/99	**Praise You** *Fatboy Slim*
	Prayer *Disturbed*
	A-3/02 M-3/02
M-3/94	**Prayer For The Dying** *Seal*
	Praying To A New God
	Wang Chung
	M-22/89 A-31/89
A-26/99	**Preacher Man** *Lynyrd Skynyrd*

	Precious Declaration
	Collective Soul
	A-1/97 M-6/97
A-23/89	**Precious Stone** *Fixx*
A-34/81	**Precious To Me** *Phil Seymour*
A-19/98	**Premonition** *John Fogerty*
A-16/88	**Presence Of Love** *Alarm*
A-8/82	**Pressure** *Billy Joel*
A-14/90	**Presto** *Rush*
M-8/92	**Pretend We're Dead** *L7*
A-46/91	**Pretender** *Cry Wolf*
A-1/89	**Pretending** *Eric Clapton*
	Pretty Fly (For A White Guy)
	Offspring
	M-3/98 A-5/99
M-31/02	**Pretty Girl (The Way)** *Sugarcult*
	Pretty Noose *Soundgarden*
	M-2/96 A-4/96
A-12/95	**Pretty Penny**
	Stone Temple Pilots
A-44/84	**Pretty Persuasion** *R.E.M.*
	Pretty Pink Rose
	Adrian Belew & David Bowie
	M-2/90 A-24/90
A-35/92	**Pretty Tied Up** *Guns N' Roses*
	Pretty Woman ..see: Oh, Pretty
	Woman
A-17/91	**Pretzel Logic** *Donald Fagen &*
	Michael McDonald
A-19/85	**Price, The** *Twisted Sister*
A-30/90	**Price Of Love** *Bad English*
A-42/90	**Pride** *Living Colour*
A-1/93	**Pride And Joy** *Coverdale·Page*
A-20/83	**Pride And Joy**
	Stevie Ray Vaughan
A-2/84	**Pride (In The Name Of Love)**
	U2
A-21/91	**Primal Scream** *Mötley Crüe*
A-3/84	**Prime Time**
	Alan Parsons Project
A-31/87	**Primitive Love Rites**
	Mondo Rock
A-26/88	**Prison Blues** *Jimmy Page*
A-32/94	**Prison Sex** *Tool*
M-21/97	**Prisoner** *311*
M-24/89	**Prisoner, The** *Howard Jones*
A-37/88	**Prisoner** *Dokken*
M-23/99	**Prisoner Of Society** *Living End*
A-33/81	**Private Eyes**
	Daryl Hall & John Oates
A-35/91	**Prodigal Blues** *Billy Idol*
	Promise *Eve 6*
	M-3/00 A-25/00
A-18/96	**Promise** *Victor*
A-1/99	**Promises** *Def Leppard*
M-12/99	**Promises** *Cranberries*
A-29/96	**Promises Broken** *Soul Asylum*
A-16/81	**Promises In The Dark**
	Pat Benatar
	Prophecy *Remy Zero*
	A-25/99 M-27/99
	(Pros and Cons of Hitch Hiking)
	..see: 5.01 AM.
M-1/89	**Proud To Fall** *Ian McCulloch*
M-16/91	**Psych Out** *Seers*
A-1/98	**Psycho Circus** *Kiss*
A-3/98	**Psycho Man** *Black Sabbath*
A-54/82	**Psychobabble**
	Alan Parsons Project
A-10/93	**Pull Me Under** *Dream Theater*
M-11/99	**Punk Rock Girl** *Dead Milkmen*
M-8/90	**Pure** *Lightning Seeds*

A-28/01 **Riders On The Storm** *Creed*

M-14/95 **Ridiculous Thoughts**
Cranberries

A-9/01 **Ridin'** *Buckcherry*

A-26/00 **Riding With The King**
BB. King & Eric Clapton

A-11/86 **Right And Wrong** *Joe Jackson*

A-33/82 **Right Away** *Kansas*

A-39/86 **Right Between The Eyes** *Wax*

M-12/93 **Right Decision** *Jesus Jones*

Right Here, Right Now
Jesus Jones
M-1/91   A-7/91

A-27/87 **Right Next Door (Because of Me)** *Robert Cray Band*

Right Now *SR-71*
M-2/00   A-38/00

A-2/92 **Right Now** *Van Halen*

Right Or Wrong ..see: (Who's)

A-10/82 **Right The First Time** *Gamma*

A-8/91 **Righteous** *Eric Johnson*

M-25/90 **Ring Of Fire** *Social Distortion*

A-5/83 **Rio** *Duran Duran*

A-47/89 **Rip And Tear** *L.A. Guns*

M-3/92 **Ripple** *Church*

Ripple
A-50/81   *Grateful Dead*
M-13/91   *Jane's Addiction*

Rise *Cult*
A-3/01   M-19/01

A-40/90 **Rise To It** *Kiss*

A-24/02 **Rising, The** *Bruce Springsteen*

A-18/81 **Rita Mae** *Eric Clapton*

River Of Deceit *Mad Season*
A-2/95   M-9/95

A-19/91 **River Of Love** *Lynch Mob*

A-35/81 **Rivers (Of The Hidden Funk)**
Joe Walsh

Road, The *Alarm*
M-7/90   A-16/90

A-14/88 **Road, The** *Kinks*

A-11/90 **Road To Hell** *Chris Rea*

A-3/92 **Road To Nowhere**
Ozzy Osbourne

A-25/85 **Road To Nowhere**
Talking Heads

Roadhouse Blues
A-24/82   *Blue Öyster Cult*
A-29/89   *Jeff Healey Band*

A-46/87 **Roadrunner** *Joan Jett*

M-6/90 **Roam** *B-52's*

A-25/81 **R.O.C.K.** *Garland Jeffreys*

A-1/89 **Rock And A Hard Place**
Rolling Stones
(also see: Between A)

Rock And Roll ..also see: Rock 'N' Roll

A-13/96 **Rock And Roll All Nite** *Kiss*

M-29/89 **Rock And Roll Babylon**
Love & Rockets

A-34/81 **Rock And Roll Doctor**
Little Feat

Rock And Roll Dreams Come Through
A-14/81   *Jim Steinman*
A-25/94   *Meat Loaf*

A-5/85 **Rock And Roll Girls**
John Fogerty

Rock And Roll Is Dead
Lenny Kravitz
A-4/95   M-10/95

A-5/88 **Rock & Roll Strategy**
Thirty Eight Special

A-11/88 **Rock Bottom** *Dickey Betts Band*

A-17/97 **Rock Crown** *Seven Mary Three*

Rock In America ..see: (You Can Still)

A-6/85 **R.O.C.K. In The U.S.A.**
John Cougar Mellencamp

Rock Is Dead *Marilyn Manson*
A-28/99   M-30/99

A-24/94 **Rock It** *Steve Miller Band*

A-9/87 **Rock Me** *Great White*
(also see: Young Thing, Wild Dreams)

A-37/99 **Rock Me Right**
Susan Tedeschi

A-1/84 **Rock Me Tonite** *Billy Squier*

A-55/84 **Rock My Nights Away**
Michael Schenker Group

A-26/85 **Rock 'N' Roll Children** *Dio*

A-37/86 **Rock 'N' Roll Cities** *Kinks*

A-19/83 **Rock 'N' Roll Is King** *ELO*

M-31/95 **Rock 'N' Roll Lifestyle** *Cake*

A-23/82 **Rock 'N' Roll Party In The Streets** *Axe*

A-40/84 **Rock 'N' Roll Rebel**
Ozzy Osbourne

M-36/95 **Rock 'n' Roll Star** *Oasis*

A-1/83 **Rock Of Ages** *Def Leppard*

A-45/88 **Rock Of Life** *Rick Springfield*

M-2/01 **Rock Show** *Blink-182*

M-36/02 **Rock Star** *N*E*R*D*

M-18/00 **(Rock) Superstar** *Cypress Hill*

A-6/82 **Rock The Casbah** *Clash*

A-22/87 **Rock The Night** *Europe*

Rock The Party (Off The Hook)
P.O.D.
A-25/00   M-27/00

A-10/89 **Rock This Place**
Fabulous Thunderbirds

A-4/82 **Rock This Town** *Stray Cats*

A-32/84 **Rock You** *Helix*

A-5/84 **Rock You Like A Hurricane**
Scorpions

A-49/83 **Rock You Up** *Romantics*

M-39/98 **Rockafeller Skank** *Fatboy Slim*

Rockaway *Ric Ocasek*
A-11/91   M-19/91

A-5/89 **Rocket** *Def Leppard*

A-28/94 **Rocket** *Smashing Pumpkins*

M-11/91 **Rocket Man** *Kate Bush*

A-9/91 **Rocket O' Love** *Knack*

A-8/84 **Rockin' At Midnight**
Honeydrippers

A-2/89 **Rockin' In The Free World**
Neil Young

A-38/92 **Rockin' Is Ma' Business**
Four Horsemen

A-8/81 **Rockin' The Paradise** *Styx*

M-28/01 **Rockin' The Suburbs**
Ben Folds Five

M-11/91 **Rocking Chair** *House Of Freaks*

A-44/88 **Rocking Pneumonia And The Boogie Woogie Flu** *Aerosmith*

Rocks *Primal Scream*
M-16/94   A-29/94

A-31/98 **Rocks** *Rod Stewart*

M-39/99 **Rodeo Clowns**
G. Love & Special Sauce

A-13/83 **Roll Me Away** *Bob Seger*

A-6/92 **Roll Of The Dice**
Bruce Springsteen

M-33/01 **Roll On** *Living End*

A-9/92 **Roll The Bones** *Rush*

A-1/88 **Roll With It** *Steve Winwood*

A-12/91 **Rollin' On** *Doobie Brothers*

A-8/99 **Rollin' Stoned** *Great White*

Rollin' (Urban Assault Vehicle)
Limp Bizkit
M-4/00   A-10/00

A-39/84 **Romancing The Stone**
Eddy Grant

M-17/90 **Room At The Top** *Adam Ant*

A-19/99 **Room At The Top** *Tom Petty*

A-28/87 **Room Full Of Mirrors**
Pretenders

A-27/82 **Room Of Our Own** *Billy Joel*

A-1/89 **Rooms On Fire** *Stevie Nicks*

A-7/93 **Rooster** *Alice In Chains*

M-27/95 **Roots Radical** *Rancid*

A-7/88 **Rooty Toot Toot**
John Cougar Mellencamp

(Rosa Lee) ..see: Set Me Free

A-8/82 **Rosanna** *Toto*

M-27/91 **Rose Of Jericho**
Eleventh Dream Day

M-24/95 **Rosealia** *Better Than Ezra*

A-5/86 **Rough Boy** *ZZ Top*

A-28/89 **Rough Night In Jericho**
Dreams So Real

A-45/88 **Roulette** *Bruce Springsteen*

A-4/84 **Round And Round** *Ratt*

M-6/89 **Round & round** *New Order*

A-44/88 **Round And Round**
Frozen Ghost

Round Here *Counting Crows*
M-7/94   A-11/94

M-25/93 **Round Of Blues** *Shawn Colvin*

A-28/82 **Roxanne** *Sting*

M-22/98 **Royal Oil**
Mighty Mighty Bosstones

M-7/93 **Rubberband Girl** *Kate Bush*

M-13/96 **Ruby Soho** *Rancid*

M-30/93 **Ruined In A Day** *New Order*

A-4/86 **Rumbleseat**
John Cougar Mellencamp

A-26/84 **Rumours In The Air**
Night Ranger

A-21/87 **Run** *Eric Clapton*

M-36/99 **Run** *Collective Soul*

Run-Around *Blues Traveler*
A-13/95   M-14/95

A-1/91 **Runaround** *Van Halen*

A-60/84 **Runaround, The** *Tsunami*

A-1/84 **Run Runaway** *Slade*

A-40/90 **Run So Far** *Eric Clapton*

A-30/89 **Run Straight Down**
Warren Zevon

A-33/89 **Run To Paradise** *Choirboys*

Run To The Water *Live*
M-14/00   A-17/00

A-1/84 **Run To You** *Bryan Adams*

A-5/84 **Runaway** *Bon Jovi*

A-9/91 **Runaway** *Damn Yankees*

Runaway *Linkin Park*
A-37/02   M-40/02

Runaway Train *Soul Asylum*
A-3/93   M-13/93

A-10/92 **Runaway Train**
Elton John & Eric Clapton

A-6/87 **Runaway Trains** *Tom Petty*

A-3/84 **Runner** *Manfred Mann*

A-1/89 **Runnin' Down A Dream**
Tom Petty

Running Away *Hoobastank*
M-2/02   A-9/02

A-15/93 **Running On Faith** *Eric Clapton*

A-34/85 **Running Up That Hill** *Kate Bush*

A-49/84	**Running With The Night** *Lionel Richie*	M-29/99	**Save It For Later** *Harvey Danger*	A-25/02	**Secret Touch** *Rush*
		A-3/90	**Save Me** *Fleetwood Mac*	A-34/93	**Secret World** *Peter Gabriel*

Code	Title
A-49/84	**Running With The Night** *Lionel Richie*
	Rush *Big Audio Dynamite II*
	M-1/91 A-40/91
A-34/86	**Russians** *Sting*
A-14/86	**Ruthless People** *Mick Jagger*

S

Code	Title
	(S.O.S.) ..see: Same Ol' Situation
A-47/90	**S S S & Q** *Robert Plant*
M-18/94	**Sabotage** *Beastie Boys*
M-35/02	**Sacrifice** *Trik Turner*
A-15/93	**Sad But True** *Metallica*
A-14/89	**Sad Sad Sad** *Rolling Stones*
A-24/84	**Sad Songs (Say So Much)** *Elton John*
M-27/00	**Sad Sweetheart Of Rodeo** *Harvey Danger*
M-6/91	**Sadeness** *Enigma*
M-28/91	**Safe From Harm** *Massive Attack*
A-21/01	**Safe In New York City** *AC/DC*
A-21/83	**Safety Dance** *Men Without Hats*
A-9/94	**Sail Away** *Great White*
	(also see: Orinoco Flow)
	Saint ..also see: St.
	Saint Joe On The School Bus *Marcy Playground*
	M-8/98 A-30/98
A-13/98	**Saint Of Me** *Rolling Stones*
M-12/94	**Saints** *Breeders*
A-15/83	**Salt In My Tears** *Martin Briley*
	Salvation *Cranberries*
	M-1/96 A-25/96
M-21/95	**Salvation** *Rancid*
A-40/00	**Salvation** *Little Steven*
M-13/91	**Sam** *Meat Puppets*
A-34/90	**Same Ol' Situation (S.O.S.)** *Mötley Crüe*
A-3/86	**Sanctify Yourself** *Simple Minds*
A-38/98	**Santa Claus And His Old Lady** *Cheech & Chong*
	Santa Monica (Watch The World Die) *Everclear*
	A-1/96 M-5/96
M-3/97	**Santeria** *Sublime*
A-12/86	**Sara** *Starship*
A-22/88	**Satch Boogie** *Joe Satriani*
A-13/87	**Satellite** *Hooters*
	Satellite *P.O.D.*
	A-15/02 M-21/02
	Satellite *Dave Matthews Band*
	M-18/96 A-36/96
A-7/00	**Satellite Blues** *AC/DC*
M-23/89	**Satellites** *Rickie Lee Jones*
A-4/85	**Satisfaction Guaranteed** *Firm*
	Satisfied *Squeeze*
	M-3/91 A-49/91
A-5/89	**Satisfied** *Richard Marx*
	Satisfied *8Stops7*
	A-26/00 M-35/00
A-13/84	**Satisfied Man** *Molly Hatchet*
A-30/84	**Satisfy Me** *Billy Satellite*
M-21/92	**Saturday** *Judybats*
M-26/93	**Saturday Night** *Ned's Atomic Dustbin*
A-8/91	**Saturday Night's Alright For Fighting** *Who*
A-27/81	**Sausalito Summernight** *Diesel*

Code	Title
M-29/99	**Save It For Later** *Harvey Danger*
A-3/90	**Save Me** *Fleetwood Mac*
M-27/01	**Save Me** *Remy Zero*
M-8/98	**Save Tonight** *Eagle Eye Cherry*
A-9/88	**Save Your Love** *Great White*
A-49/81	**Save Your Love** *Jefferson Starship*
	Save Yourself *Stabbing Westward*
	A-4/98 M-20/98
M-28/89	**Saved** *Swans*
A-16/91	**Saved By Love** *Rik Emmett*
A-9/83	**Saved By Zero** *Fixx*
A-9/91	**Saving My Heart** *Yes*
	Sax And Violins *Talking Heads*
	M-1/92 A-49/92
A-39/97	**Say Goodbye** *Cheap Trick*
A-50/82	**Say Goodbye** *Triumph*
A-11/81	**Say Goodbye To Hollywood** *Billy Joel*
A-5/93	**Say Hello 2 Heaven** *Temple Of The Dog*
A-15/85	**Say It Again** *Santana*
M-7/95	**Say It Ain't So** *Weezer*
A-41/82	**Say It Ain't So, Joe** *Roger Daltrey*
A-18/83	**Say It Isn't So** *Daryl Hall & John Oates*
A-18/85	**Say It Isn't So** *Outfield*
A-22/91	**Say It With Love** *Moody Blues*
A-24/83	**Say Say Say** *Paul McCartney & Michael Jackson*
M-19/94	**Say Something** *James*
A-14/83	**Say What You Will** *Fastway*
A-1/87	**Say You Will** *Foreigner*
A-39/87	**Say You Will** *Mick Jagger*
A-3/85	**Say You're Wrong** *Julian Lennon*
A-38/82	**Scandinavian Skies** *Billy Joel*
	Scar Tissue *Red Hot Chili Peppers*
	A-1/99 M-1/99
A-46/89	**Scared** *Dangerous Toys*
	Schism *Tool*
	A-2/01 M-2/01
M-38/00	**School Of Hard Knocks** *P.O.D.*
M-14/96	**Scooby Snacks** *Fun Lovin' Criminals*
M-16/93	**Screamager** *Therapy?*
A-21/83	**Screaming In The Night** *Krokus*
M-22/02	**Screaming Infidelities** *Dashboard Confessional*
	Scum *Meat Puppets*
	A-20/95 M-23/95
A-25/00	**Scum Of The Earth** *Rob Zombie*
A-11/84	**Sea Of Love** *Honeydrippers*
A-33/81	**Sea Of Love** *Grace Slick*
A-27/91	**Sea Of Sorrow** *Alice In Chains*
A-26/81	**Searchin'** *Santana*
A-25/91	**Seasons** *Tyketto*
A-2/89	**Second Chance** *Thirty Eight Special*
	(Second Wind) ..see: You're Only Human
A-32/86	**Secondhand Love** *Pete Townshend*
A-29/82	**Secret Journey** *Police*
A-12/87	**Secret Of My Success** *Night Ranger*
A-19/98	**Secret Place** *Megadeth*
A-1/86	**Secret Separation** *Fixx*
M-21/99	**Secret Smile** *Semisonic*

Code	Title
A-25/02	**Secret Touch** *Rush*
A-34/93	**Secret World** *Peter Gabriel*
M-12/89	**Secrets** *Primitives*
A-22/82	**Secrets** *Van Halen*
A-41/91	**Seducer** *Saraya*
M-4/89	**See A Little Light** *Bob Mould*
A-33/89	**See The Light** *Jeff Healey Band*
	See The Lights *Simple Minds*
	M-1/91 A-10/91
A-20/85	**See What Love Can Do** *Eric Clapton*
A-5/96	**See You On The Other Side** *Ozzy Osbourne*
A-39/01	**Seed** *Dust For Life*
M-1/02	**Seein' Red** *Unwritten Law*
A-18/89	**Seeing Is Believing** *Mike + The Mechanics*
A-2/91	**Seeing Things** *Black Crowes*
	Seen The Doctor *Michael Penn*
	M-5/92 A-33/92
M-8/94	**Seether** *Veruca Salt*
M-16/89	**Self!** *Fuzzbox*
	Self Esteem *Offspring*
	M-4/94 A-7/94
M-30/94	**Selfish** *Other Two*
M-10/97	**Sell Out** *Reel Big Fish*
A-17/99	**Selling My Soul** *Black Sabbath*
	Selling The Drama *Live*
	M-1/94 A-4/94
	Semi-Charmed Life *Third Eye Blind*
	M-1/97 A-26/97
A-8/91	**Send Me An Angel** *Scorpions*
A-18/84	**Send Me An Angel** *Real Life*
A-53/81	**Send Me An Angel** *Robin Lane*
A-7/89	**Send Me Somebody** *Jon Butcher*
M-23/90	**Sense Of Purpose** *Pretenders*
A-38/82	**Senses Working Overtime** *XTC*
A-6/91	**Sensible Shoes** *David Lee Roth*
M-6/90	**Sensual World** *Kate Bush*
A-6/92	**Sent By Angels** *Arc Angels*
A-9/87	**Sentimental Hygiene** *Warren Zevon*
A-3/85	**Sentimental Street** *Night Ranger*
A-1/83	**Separate Ways (Worlds Apart)** *Journey*
A-34/84	**Serious Business** *John Cougar Mellencamp*
A-10/00	**Serious JuJu** *Sammy Hagar*
A-19/88	**Serpentine** *Kings Of The Sun*
A-21/87	**Set Me Free (Rosa Lee)** *Los Lobos*
A-33/91	**Set Me In Motion** *Bruce Hornsby*
A-15/90	**7 O'Clock** *London Quireboys*
A-12/90	**Seven Turns** *Allman Brothers Band*
A-2/87	**Seven Wonders** *Fleetwood Mac*
A-19/89	**Seventeen** *Winger*
A-36/95	**Seventh Seal** *Van Halen*
	Sex and Candy *Marcy Playground*
	M-1/97 A-4/98
A-5/85	**Sex As A Weapon** *Pat Benatar*
A-40/91	**Sex Drive** *Rolling Stones*
A-10/83	**Sex (I'm A...)** *Berlin*
M-17/92	**Sex On Wheelz** *My Life With The Thrill Kill Kult*
A-23/93	**Sex Type Thing** *Stone Temple Pilots*
M-10/93	**Sexual Healing** *Soul Asylum*

M-2/91 **Sexuality** *Billy Bragg*
M-21/99 **Sexx Laws** *Beck*
Sexy + 17 ..see: (She's)
A-23/85 **Shades Of '45** *Gary O'*
M-34/96 **Shadowboxer** *Fiona Apple*
A-3/82 **Shadows Of The Night**
Pat Benatar
M-13/91 **Shadowtime**
Siouxsie & The Banshees
A-22/99 **Shag** *Sammy Hagar*
A-19/92 **Shake For Me**
Stevie Ray Vaughan
A-2/82 **Shake It Up** *Cars*
A-9/89 **Shake It Up** *Bad Company*
A-41/86 **Shake Me** *Cinderella*
A-14/91 **Shake Me Up** *Little Feat*
A-3/93 **Shake My Tree** *Coverdale·Page*
A-1/87 **Shakedown** *Bob Seger*
A-9/82 **Shakin'** *Eddie Money*
A-29/99 **Shakin' And A Bakin'**
Honky Toast
A-4/87 **Shakin' Shakin' Shakes**
Los Lobos
A-9/93 **Shakin' The Blues**
Screamin' Cheetah Wheelies
A-19/92 **Shakin' The Cage** *Zoo*
M-9/89 **Shakin' The Tree**
Youssou N'Dour
Shame *Stabbing Westward*
A-7/96 M-14/96
A-10/85 **Shame** *Motels*
M-24/01 **Shame Of Life** *Butthole Surfers*
A-13/93 **Shape I'm In** *Arc Angels*
M-19/88 **Shark Walk** *Shriekback*
A-8/83 **Sharp Dressed Man** *ZZ Top*
M-23/89 **Shatter** *Shelleyan Orphan*
She *Green Day*
M-5/95 A-18/95
M-9/89 **She Bangs The Drums**
Stone Roses
A-6/83 **She Blinded Me With Science**
Thomas Dolby
A-27/84 **She Bop** *Cyndi Lauper*
A-42/89 **She Did It** *Glamour Camp*
A-44/84 **She Don't Know Me** *Bon Jovi*
A-13/87 **She Don't Look Back**
Dan Fogelberg
M-9/95 **She Don't Use Jelly**
Flaming Lips
M-5/89 **She Drives Me Crazy**
Fine Young Cannibals
A-28/94 **She Gets Too High** *Rob Rule*
M-8/89 **She Gives Me Love** *Godfathers*
A-4/91 **She Goes Down** *Billy Squier*
A-8/93 **She Got Me (When She Got Her Dress On)** *Masters Of Reality*
She Hates Me *Puddle Of Mudd*
A-1/02 M-2/02
M-5/93 **She Kissed Me**
Terence Trent D'Arby
A-47/82 **She Looks A Lot Like You**
Clocks
She Loves Me Not *Papa Roach*
A-3/02 M-5/02
A-17/92 **She Runs Hot** *Little Village*
She Said *Collective Soul*
A-16/98 M-39/98
A-48/82 **She Sheila** *Producers*
A-39/96 **She Shines** *Gren*
A-5/92 **She Takes My Breath Away**
Eddie Money
A-1/91 **She Talks To Angels**
Black Crowes
A-39/83 **She Wants You** *Breaks*

A-4/84 **She Was Hot** *Rolling Stones*
A-1/83 **She's A Beauty** *Tubes*
M-7/91 **She's A Girl And I'm A Man**
Lloyd Cole
A-26/89 **She's A Mystery To Me**
Roy Orbison
She's A River *Simple Minds*
A-6/95 M-10/95
A-44/83 **She's A Runner** *Billy Squier*
A-19/98 **She's Gone** *Eric Clapton*
M-16/88 **She's Got A New Spell**
Billy Bragg
She's Got Issues *Offspring*
M-11/99 A-19/99
M-21/90 **She's In A Trance** *Heart Throbs*
A-12/96 **She's Just Killing Me** *ZZ Top*
M-3/92 **She's Mad** *David Byrne*
A-15/84 **She's Mine** *Steve Perry*
A-2/90 **She's My Baby**
Traveling Wilburys
A-12/94 **She's My Machine**
David Lee Roth
A-40/02 **She's On Fire** *Train*
A-2/83 **(She's) Sexy + 17** *Stray Cats*
M-32/99 **She's So Huge** *Flys*
A-11/85 **She's Waiting** *Eric Clapton*
M-9/92 **Sheela-Na-Gig** *PJ Harvey*
M-16/99 **Sheep Go To Heaven** *Cake*
M-25/89 **Sheep's A Wolf** *Caterwaul*
A-39/81 **Sheila** *Greg Kihn Band*
A-20/86 **Shela** *Aerosmith*
Shelf In The Room
Days Of The New
A-3/98 M-22/98
A-26/86 **Shelter** *Lone Justice*
A-5/90 **Shelter Me** *Cinderella*
A-11/86 **Shelter Me** *Joe Cocker*
M-29/91 **Sheriff Fatman** *Carter U.S.M.*
Shimmer *Fuel*
M-2/98 A-11/98
Shine *Collective Soul*
A-1/94 M-4/94
A-6/98 **Shining In The Light**
Jimmy Page & Robert Plant
Shining Star *INXS*
M-4/91 A-14/91
M-33/02 **Shinobi Vs. Dragon Ninja**
Lostprophets
Shiny Happy People *R.E.M.*
M-3/91 A-8/91
A-3/88 **Ship Of Fools** *Robert Plant*
A-5/87 **Ship Of Fools (Save Me From Tomorrow)** *World Party*
M-26/01 **Shiver** *Coldplay*
Shock The Monkey
A-1/82 Peter Gabriel
A-26/99 Coal Chamberr Featuring
Ozzy Osbourne
Shock To The System *Billy Idol*
A-7/93 M-23/93
A-11/88 **Shoot High Aim Low** *Yes*
A-60/81 **Shoot To Thrill** *AC/DC*
M-12/91 **Shoot You Down** *Birdland*
A-21/89 **Shooting From My Heart**
Big Bam Boo
A-16/83 **Shooting Shark**
Blue Öyster Cult
M-7/01 **Short Skirt/Long Jacket** *Cake*
A-10/86 **Shot In The Dark**
Ozzy Osbourne
A-30/86 **Shot O' Love** *Billy Squier*
A-38/81 **Shot Of Love** *Bob Dylan*
A-21/91 **Shot Of Poison** *Lita Ford*

M-8/89 **Should God Forget**
Psychedelic Furs
A-4/87 **Should I See** *Frozen Ghost*
A-13/82 **Should I Stay Or Should I Go**
Clash
A-7/87 **Should've Known Better**
Richard Marx
A-42/82 **Shoulder Of The Road**
Johnny & His Distractions
A-6/85 **Shout** *Tears For Fears*
A-43/83 **Shout** *Grand Prix*
A-30/83 **Shout At The Devil** *Mötley Crüe*
A-40/91 **Shout It Out** *Slaughter*
A-1/90 **Show Don't Tell** *Rush*
A-8/84 **Show Me** *Pretenders*
A-30/92 **Show Me** *Ron Wood*
A-22/92 **Show Me The Way** *Storm*
M-10/90 **Show Me Your Soul**
Red Hot Chili Peppers
A-40/92 **Show Must Go On** *Queen*
A-35/82 **Showdown** *Riot*
A-2/87 **Showdown At Big Sky**
Robbie Robertson
M-13/94 **Shrine** *Dambuilders*
A-6/92 **Shuffle It All** *Izzy Stradlin*
A-39/97 **Shutterbug** *Veruca Salt*
M-17/97 **Sick & Beautiful**
Artificial Joy Club
Sick Cycle Carousel *Lifehouse*
M-21/01 A-38/01
M-9/89 **Sick Of It** *Primitives*
Sick Of Myself *Matthew Sweet*
M-2/95 A-13/95
Sidewinder Sleeps Tonite
R.E.M.
M-24/93 A-28/93
A-20/84 **Sign Of Fire** *Fixx*
A-19/81 **Sign Of The Gypsy Queen**
April Wine
A-9/91 **Sign Of The Storm**
Eric Gales Band
A-3/97 **Sign Of The Times**
Queensrÿche
A-28/84 **Sign Of The Times** *Quiet Riot*
A-2/91 **Signs** *Tesla*
A-20/93 **Silence Is Broken**
Damn Yankees
M-27/92 **Silent All These Years**
Tori Amos
A-1/91 **Silent Lucidity** *Queensrÿche*
A-24/86 **Silent Night** *Bon Jovi*
A-1/85 **Silent Running (On Dangerous Ground)**
Mike + The Mechanics
A-15/00 **Silver Future** *Monster Magnet*
A-22/91 **Silver Thunderbird** *Marc Cohn*
A-60/81 **Silverado** *Marshall Tucker Band*
A-5/88 **Silvio** *Bob Dylan*
A-6/89 **Similar Features**
Melissa Etheridge
A-24/99 **Simon Says** *Drain S.T.H.*
Simple Creed *Live*
A-11/01 M-18/01
M-14/00 **Simple Kind Of Life** *No Doubt*
Simple Lessons *Candlebox*
A-5/95 M-12/95
A-47/89 **Simple Man** *Junkyard*
A-1/88 **Simply Irresistible**
Robert Palmer
A-24/82 **Since You're Gone** *Cars*
A-11/87 **Since You've Been Gone**
Outfield
M-37/01 **Sing** *Travis*
A-39/83 **Sing Me Away** *Night Ranger*

311

	Something's Always Wrong *Toad The Wet Sprocket* M-9/94 A-22/94	A-21/83	**Space Age Whiz Kids** *Joe Walsh*	A-3/87	**Standing On Higher Ground** *Alan Parsons Project*
M-20/92	**Sometimes** *Midnight Oil*	M-10/01	**Space Between** *Dave Matthews Band*		**Standing Outside A Broken Phone Booth With Money In My Hand** *Primitive Radio Gods*
M-31/01	**Sometimes** *Ours*		**Space Lord** *Monster Magnet*		
M-4/94	**Sometimes Always** *Jesus & Mary Chain*		A-3/98 M-29/98		M-1/96 A-32/96
M-22/00	**Sometimes I Don't Mind** *Suicide Machines*	A-39/93	**Spaceman** *4 Non Blondes*	M-4/90	**Standing There** *Creatures*
		M-35/00	**Spaceship** *Angie Aparo*	M-4/92	**Star Sign** *Teenage Fanclub*
	Sometimes It Hurts *Stabbing Westward* A-20/98 M-39/98	A-11/87	**Spanish Eyes** *U2*		**Star 69** *R.E.M.*
		A-28/87	**Spare Parts** *Bruce Springsteen*		M-8/95 A-15/95
A-7/91	**Sometimes It's A Bitch** *Stevie Nicks*	M-13/98	**Spark** *Tori Amos*	A-30/82	**Stardom In Action** *Pete Townshend*
		M-37/00	**Sparks Are Gonna Fly** *Catherine Wheel*		
A-7/93	**Sometimes Salvation** *Black Crowes*	A-30/95	**Sparks Will Fly** *Rolling Stones*	M-39/99	**Starfuckers, Inc.** *Nine Inch Nails*
A-11/90	**Sometimes She Cries** *Warrant*	M-11/99	**Special** *Garbage*		**Staring At The Sun** *U2*
A-24/88	**Somewhere Down The Crazy River** *Robbie Robertson*	M-14/90	**Special One** *Ultra Vivid Scene*		M-1/97 A-2/97
		A-38/94	**Speed** *Billy Idol*	M-25/90	**Staring At The Sun** *Ultra Vivid Scene*
	Somewhere Out There *Our Lady Peace* M-7/02 A-26/02	A-10/85	**Spellbound** *Triumph*		
		A-28/91	**Spend My Life** *Slaughter*		**Stars** *Hum*
A-47/88	**Song & Dance** *John Cafferty*		**Spiders** *System Of A Down*		M-11/95 A-28/95
A-13/92	**Song & Emotion** *Tesla*		A-25/00 M-38/00	A-39/86	**Stars** *Hear 'n Aid*
	(Song For Lennon) ..see: Life Is Real	M-5/96	**Spiderwebs** *No Doubt*		**Starseed** *Our Lady Peace*
		A-31/85	**Spies Like Us** *Paul McCartney*		A-7/95 M-10/95
M-23/98	**Song For The Dumped** *Ben Folds Five*		**Spin** *Lifehouse*	M-3/93	**Start Choppin** *Dinosaur Jr.*
			M-25/02 A-34/02	A-1/81	**Start Me Up** *Rolling Stones*
	Song 2 *Blur* M-6/97 A-25/97		**Spin The Black Circle** *Pearl Jam* M-11/94 A-16/94	A-6/92	**Start The Car** *Jude Cole*
				M-38/95	**Start With** *Seaweed*
M-13/91	**Sooner Or Later** *Feelies*			A-26/83	**State Of Confusion** *Kinks*
A-34/02	**Sore Throat** *Color Red*	M-15/90	**Spinnin'** *Soul Asylum*	A-42/84	**State Of Shock** *Jackson 5*
M-35/00	**Sorrow** *Bad Religion*	A-37/94	**Spinning Around Over You** *Lenny Kravitz*	A-26/89	**Statesboro Blues** *Allman Brothers Band*
A-36/88	**Sorrow** *Pink Floyd*				
M-20/92	**Sorry About The Weather** *Mark Curry*	A-27/98	**Spirit Of Radio** *Rush*	A-24/83	**Static** *Planet P*
		A-29/86	**Spirit Of '76** *Alarm*	M-24/92	**Statue Got Me High** *They Might Be Giants*
A-50/84	**Sorry Me, Sorry You** *Jefferson Starship*	A-7/82	**Spirits In The Material World** *Police*		
				M-25/92	**Stay** *Shakespear's Sister*
A-45/85	**Sort Of Homecoming** *U2*	M-6/92	**Spiritual High (State Of Independence)** *Moodswings*		**Stay (Faraway, So Close!)** *U2* A-12/93 M-15/94
	Soul Cages *Sting* A-7/91 M-9/91				
		A-3/86	**Split Decision** *Steve Winwood*	M-7/94	**Stay (I Missed You)** *Lisa Loeb & Nine Stories*
A-5/92	**Soul Doctor** *Foreigner*		**Spoonman** *Soundgarden*		
A-15/97	**Soul Of Love** *Paul Rodgers*		A-3/94 M-9/94	A-6/86	**Stay The Night** *Benjamin Orr*
A-12/01	**Soul Singing** *Black Crowes*	M-25/91	**Sproston Green** *Charlatans UK*	A-7/84	**Stay The Night** *Chicago*
	Soul To Squeeze *Red Hot Chili Peppers* M-1/93 A-7/93	A-23/02	**Squash That Fly** *Fu Manchu*	M-7/01	**Stay Together For The Kids** *Blink-182*
		A-2/85	**St. Elmo's Fire (Man In Motion)** *John Parr*		
M-16/92	**Souled Out** *Supreme Love Gods*			A-24/85	**Stay Up Late** *Talking Heads*
A-17/88	**Sound Alarm** *Michael Anderson*		**Stacked Actors** *Foo Fighters*		**Stay (Wasting Time)** *Dave Matthews Band* M-8/98 A-35/98
A-2/91	**Sound Of Your Voice** *38 Special*		A-9/00 M-25/00		
		A-1/86	**Stages** *ZZ Top*		
M-37/96	**Soundtrack To Mary** *Soul Coughing*	A-21/97	**Stale** *Stir*	A-31/83	**Stayed Awake All Night** *Krokus*
			Stand *R.E.M.*	M-23/90	**Steady On** *Shawn Colvin*
	Sour Girl *Stone Temple Pilots* M-3/00 A-4/00		A-1/89 M-1/89	M-5/99	**Steal My Sunshine** *Len*
		A-15/93	**Stand** *Poison*		**Steam** *Peter Gabriel*
M-5/95	**Sour Times (Nobody Loves Me)** *Portishead*	M-5/93	**Stand Above Me** *Orchestral Manoeuvres In The Dark*		M-1/92 A-2/92
				A-10/87	**Steel Monkey** *Jethro Tull*
A-43/84	**so. Central Rain (I'm Sorry)** *R.E.M.*	A-21/81	**Stand And Fight** *James Taylor*		**Stellar** *Incubus*
		A-2/83	**Stand Back** *Stevie Nicks*		M-2/00 A-17/00
A-30/89	**South Of The Border** *Doobie Brothers*	A-8/87	**Stand Back** *Fabulous Thunderbirds*		**Step Into The Light** *Dust For Life* A-16/01 M-22/01
M-3/01	**South Side** *Moby*	A-13/88	**Stand Beside Me** *Kansas*		
A-39/82	**Southern Cross** *Crosby, Stills & Nash*		**Stand By Love** *Simple Minds* M-4/91 A-42/91	M-19/93	**Step It Up** *Stereo MC's*
				M-9/90	**Step On** *Happy Mondays*
A-22/82	**Southern Pacific** *Neil Young & Crazy Horse*	A-35/86	**Stand In The Fire** *Mickey Thomas*	A-29/01	**Steppin' Away** *Stereomud*
				A-7/82	**Steppin' Out** *Joe Jackson*
	Southtown *P.O.D.* M-28/00 A-31/00		**Stand Inside Your Love** *Smashing Pumpkins* M-2/00 A-11/00	A-31/96	**Steppin' Over** *Tesla*
				M-30/97	**Stepping Stones** *G. Love & Special Sauce*
	Sowing The Seeds Of Love *Tears For Fears* M-1/89 A-4/89	A-32/85	**Stand On It** *Bruce Springsteen*		
		A-35/89	**Stand On It** *Jeff Beck with Terry Bozzio & Tony Hymas*	A-5/86	**Stereotomy** *Alan Parsons Project*
A-59/82	**Space Age Love Song** *Flock Of Seagulls*			A-1/86	**Stick Around** *Julian Lennon*
		A-7/82	**Stand Or Fall** *Fixx*	M-27/02	**Stick 'Em Up** *Quarashi*
		A-5/88	**Stand Up** *David Lee Roth*	A-56/84	**Stick It** *Great White*
		M-14/89	**Stand Up** *Underworld*	A-1/93	**Stick It Out** *Rush*
		A-1/93	**Stand Up (Kick Love Into Motion)** *Def Leppard*	A-43/82	**Stick It Where The Sun Don't Shine** *Nick Lowe*
				A-1/00	**Stiff Upper Lip** *AC/DC*

A-39/00 **Still After You** *Earth To Andy*
A-9/90 **Still Got The Blues** *Gary Moore*
A-36/85 **Still In Love** *Taxxi*
A-37/89 **Still In Love** *Stage Dolls*
(also see: Can'tcha Say You
Believe
In Me)
A-2/82 **Still In Saigon**
Charlie Daniels Band
A-8/82 **Still In The Game**
Steve Winwood
A-36/84 **Still Loving You** *Scorpions*
A-18/87 **Still Of The Night** *Whitesnake*
A-8/98 **Still Rainin'** *Jonny Lang*
A-47/82 **Still They Ride** *Journey*
M-38/02 **Stillness Of Heart** *Lenny Kravitz*
A-19/82 **Stillness Of The Night**
REO Speedwagon
A-1/92 **Sting Me** *Black Crowes*
Stinkfist *Tool*
A-17/96 M-19/96
M-21/92 **Stinkin Thinkin** *Happy Mondays*
A-35/92 **Stir It Up** *Tesla*
Stitches *Orgy*
M-18/99 A-38/99
M-30/93 **Stockholm**
New Fast Automatic Daffodils
M-32/99 **Stolen Car** *Beth Orton*
A-39/01 **Stomp** *Craving Theo*
A-1/82 **Stone Cold** *Rainbow*
A-32/94 **Stone Cold Hearted** *Bloodline*
M-3/90 **Stone Cold Yesterday** *Connells*
A-4/92 **Stone Free** *Eric Clapton*
A-13/81 **Stone In Love** *Journey*
A-26/85 **Stone In Your Heart**
Molly Hatchet
M-23/92 **Stone Me** *Wire Train*
A-40/95 **Stone The Crow** *Down*
M-1/90 **Stop!** *Jane's Addiction*
M-19/89 **Stop!** *Erasure*
A-31/85 **Stop** *Jon Butcher Axis*
A-2/81 **Stop Draggin' My Heart Around**
Stevie Nicks (with Tom Petty)
M-21/00 **Stop The Rock**
Apollo Four Forty
A-9/93 **Stop The World** *Extreme*
A-50/89 **Stop The World** *Big Big Sun*
M-23/93 **Stop Whispering** *Radiohead*
(Story Of A Girl) ..see:
Absolutely
A-37/92 **Story Of The Blues** *Gary Moore*
A-38/97 **Straight** *Veruca Salt*
A-25/83 **Straight Ahead** *Shooting Star*
A-36/82 **Straight Back** *Fleetwood Mac*
A-11/81 **Straight From The Heart**
Allman Brothers Band
A-32/83 **Straight From The Heart**
Bryan Adams
A-9/91 **Straight To Your Heart**
Bad English
A-25/90 **Stranded** *Heart*
M-36/02 **Strange Condition** *Pete Yorn*
Strange Currencies *R.E.M.*
A-8/95 M-14/95
A-9/83 **Strange Dreams** *Frank Marino*
M-21/90 **Strange Kind Of Love**
Peter Murphy
A-12/84 **Stranger** *Stephen Stills*
A-17/81 **Stranger** *Jefferson Starship*
A-38/92 **Stranger In This Town**
Richie Sambora
A-7/84 **Stranger In Town** *Toto*
A-9/91 **Stranger Stranger**
Bad Company

M-29/94 **Stranger Than Fiction**
Bad Religion
A-21/90 **Stranger Than Paradise**
Sleeze Beez
A-4/87 **Strap Me In** *Cars*
M-11/90 **Strawberry Fields Forever**
Candy Flip
A-41/82 **Stray Cat Strut** *Stray Cats*
A-2/83 **Street Of Dreams** *Rainbow*
A-25/94 **Streets Of Philadelphia**
Bruce Springsteen
A-12/86 **Strength** *Alarm*
A-23/83 **Strike Zone** *Loverboy*
(String Of Pearls) ..see: Future
40's
A-3/81 **Stroke, The** *Billy Squier*
M-10/95 **Strong Enough** *Sheryl Crow*
A-47/89 **Struggle** *Keith Richards*
A-17/84 **Strung Out** *Steve Perry*
Stuck In A Moment You Can't
Get Out Of *U2*
M-35/01 A-35/01
A-39/95 **Stuck In The Middle With You**
Jeff Healey Band
Stuck On You *Failure*
M-23/97 A-31/97
A-2/86 **Stuck With You** *Huey Lewis*
Stupid Girl *Garbage*
M-2/96 A-39/96
M-26/89 **Stupid Kids** *Christmas*
Stupify *Disturbed*
M-10/00 A-12/00
M-10/95 **Stutter** *Elastica*
A-8/82 **Subdivisions** *Rush*
M-3/93 **Sublime** *Ocean Blue*
M-9/91 **Submarine Song** *Candy Skins*
M-10/89 **Suboceana** *Tom Tom Club*
M-20/92 **Success Has Made A Failure Of**
Our Home *Sinéad O'Connor*
M-15/92 **Suck My Kiss**
Red Hot Chili Peppers
M-23/92 **Suck You Dry** *Mudhoney*
M-17/96 **Sucked Out** *Superdrag*
A-42/83 **Sucker For A Pretty Face**
Eric Martin Band
A-1/83 **Suddenly Last Summer** *Motels*
Sugar *System Of A Down*
A-28/99 M-31/00
M-20/97 **Sugar Cane** *Space Monkeys*
A-22/97 **Sugarcane** *Cry Of Love*
M-16/89 **Sugar Daddy** *Thompson Twins*
M-22/92 **Sugar Ray**
Jesus And Mary Chain
Suicide Blonde *INXS*
A-1/90 M-1/90
A-23/98 **Sullivan** *Caroline's Spine*
A-33/86 **Summer Nights** *Van Halen*
M-20/93 **Summer Of Drugs** *Soul Asylum*
A-40/84 **Summer Of '69** *Bryan Adams*
A-5/92 **Summer Song** *Joe Satriani*
M-10/97 **Summertime** *Sundays*
A-24/82 **Summertime Blues** *Joan Jett*
A-16/85 **Summertime Girls** *Y&T*
A-41/85 **Sun City**
Artists United Against Apartheid
M-11/90 **Sun Comes Up, It's Tuesday**
Morning *Cowboy Junkies*
M-22/94 **Sun Does Rise** *Jah Wobble's*
Invaders Of The Heart
M-23/89 **Sun Gone Down**
House Of Freaks
Sun King *Cult*
A-18/89 M-21/89

M-31/99 **Sunburn** *Fuel*
A-7/83 **Sunday Bloody Sunday** *U2*
M-26/98 **Sunday Shining** *Finley Quaye*
M-33/00 **Sundown** *Elwood*
A-15/84 **Sunglasses At Night**
Corey Hart
M-7/91 **Sunless Saturday** *Fishbone*
M-28/01 **Sunny Hours**
Long Beach Dub Allstars
M-23/91 **Sunny Side Of The Street**
Pogues
A-7/85 **Sunset Grill** *Don Henley*
A-15/87 **Sunset Strip** *Roger Waters*
A-23/01 **Sunshine** *Aerosmith*
M-15/92 **Sunshine And Ecstasy**
Tom Tom Club
A-37/84 **Sunshine In The Shade** *Fixx*
M-29/93 **Sunshine Smile** *Adorable*
Sunshower *Chris Cornell*
A-8/98 M-12/98
M-27/97 **Super Bon Bon** *Soul Coughing*
A-25/99 **Super Breakdown**
Sprung Monkey
A-39/96 **Super-Charger Heaven**
White Zombie
M-35/95 **Super-Connected** *Belly*
A-26/99 **Superbeast** *Rob Zombie*
A-37/90 **Superconductor** *Rush*
A-17/86 **Superman** *R.E.M.*
A-21/01 **Superman Inside** *Eric Clapton*
Superman's Dead
Our Lady Peace
M-11/97 A-14/97
M-6/94 **Supernova** *Liz Phair*
Supersonic *Oasis*
M-11/94 A-38/94
M-26/94 **Superstar** *Sonic Youth*
(also see: Rock)
A-11/86 **Superstition**
Stevie Ray Vaughan
A-9/88 **Superstitious** *Europe*
A-18/98 **Surefire (Never Enough)**
Econoline Crush
A-56/82 **Surfer Joe And Moe The Sleaze**
Neil Young & Crazy Horse
A-37/88 **Surfing With The Alien**
Joe Satriani
A-27/83 **Surrender** *U2*
A-42/89 **Surrender To Me**
Ann Wilson & Robin Zander
A-10/85 **Sussudio** *Phil Collins*
A-11/86 **Suzanne** *Journey*
Swallowed *Bush*
M-1/96 A-2/96
A-14/86 **Swallowed By The Cracks**
David & David
A-16/88 **Swamp Music** *Lynyrd Skynyrd*
M-24/92 **Sweater, The** *Meryn Cadell*
A-27/93 **Sweating Bullets** *Megadeth*
A-7/88 **Sweet Child O' Mine**
Guns N' Roses
A-17/01 **Sweet Daze** *Pete.*
Sweet Dreams (Are Made Of
This)
Eurythmics
A-16/83
Marilyn Manson
M-26/96 A-31/96
A-36/91 **Sweet Emotion** *Aerosmith*
A-7/88 **Sweet Fire Of Love**
Robbie Robertson
M-23/93 **Sweet Harmony** *Beloved*
A-52/81 **Sweet Home Alabama**
Charlie Daniels Band

	Sweet Jane *Cowboy Junkies*	

Sweet Jane *Cowboy Junkies*
M-5/89 A-50/89
M-9/94

M-10/96 **Sweet Lover Hangover**
Love & Rockets

M-14/93 **Sweet Lullaby** *Deep Forest*

A-31/81 **Sweet Merilee** *Donnie Iris*

A-26/87 **Sweet Sixteen** *Billy Idol*

M-37/95 **Sweet '69** *Babes In Toyland*

M-5/90 **Sweet Smell Of Success**
Stranglers

A-14/90 **Sweet Soul Sister** *Cult*

M-14/97 **Sweet Surrender**
Sarah McLachlan

A-34/93 **Sweet Thing** *Mick Jagger*

A-33/96 **Sweet Thistle Pie** *Cracker*

M-2/92 **Sweetest Drop** *Peter Murphy*

Sweetest Thing *U2*
M-9/98 A-31/98

A-27/81 **Sweetheart**
Franke & The Knockouts

M-2/02 **Sweetness** *Jimmy Eat World*

M-4/91 **Sweetness And Light** *Lush*

A-17/99 **Swingin'** *Tom Petty*

A-27/89 **Sword And Stone** *Paul Dean*

A-10/94 **Sympathy For The Devil**
Guns N' Roses

A-29/92 **Symphony Of Destruction**
Megadeth

A-9/83 **Synchronicity II** *Police*

T

A-38/83 **TV Dinners** *ZZ Top*

M-8/96 **Tahitian Moon** *Porno For Pyros*

A-39/96 **T.A.I.L.** *Into Another*

Tainted Love
Soft Cell
A-12/82
Marilyn Manson
A-30/02 M-33/02

A-10/92 **Take A Chance** *Bob Seger*

A-27/93 **Take A Hold** *Raging Slab*

Take A Look Around
Limp Bizkit
M-8/00 A-15/00

**(Take A Look At Me Now) ..see:
Against All Odds**

Take A Picture *Filter*
M-3/00 A-4/00

M-14/89 **Take A Step Back** *Simple Minds*

M-5/91 **Take 5** *Northside*

A-32/81 **Take It Anyway You Want It**
Pat Benatar

A-33/86 **Take It As It Comes**
Steve Winwood

A-39/82 **Take It Away** *Paul McCartney*

A-4/94 **Take It Back** *Pink Floyd*

A-6/81 **Take It On The Run**
REO Speedwagon

A-3/88 **Take It So Hard** *Keith Richards*

M-5/93 **Take Me Anywhere**
School Of Fish

A-11/83 **Take Me Away** *Blue Öyster Cult*

A-21/83 **Take Me Back** *Bryan Adams*

A-15/93 **Take Me For A Little While**
Coverdale-Page

A-12/86 **Take Me Home** *Phil Collins*

A-46/87 **Take Me Home** *Roger Daltrey*

A-1/86 **Take Me Home Tonight**
Eddie Money

A-6/83 **Take Me To Heart** *Quarterflash*

A-23/82 **Take Me To The Top** *Loverboy*

A-7/82 **Take Off** *Bob & Doug McKenzie*

A-36/82 **Take The L.** *Motels*

A-29/93 **Take The Time** *Dream Theater*

A-37/92 **Takin' Me Down** *Hardline*

A-41/84 **Taking It All Too Hard** *Genesis*

A-41/82 **Talk Dirty** *John Entwistle*

A-26/82 **Talk Talk** *Talk Talk*

A-1/85 **Talk To Me** *Stevie Nicks*

A-12/85 **Talk To Me** *Fiona*

A-41/85 **Talk To Me** *Quarterflash*

A-7/81 **Talk To Ya Later** *Tubes*

A-9/88 **Talkin' Bout** *3*

Talkin' Bout A Revolution
Tracy Chapman
A-22/88 M-24/88

M-12/91 **Talkin' Loud And Sayin'
Nothing** *Living Colour*

A-31/95 **Talkin' Seattle Grunge Rock
Blues** *Todd Snider*

A-17/88 **Talking Back To The Night**
Steve Winwood

A-2/83 **Talking In Your Sleep**
Romantics

A-1/88 **Tall Cool One** *Robert Plant*

A-24/90 **Tall, Dark Handsome Stranger**
Heart

A-37/98 **Tangerine** *Life Of Agony*

M-28/00 **Tangerine Speedo** *Caviar*

A-13/92 **Tangled In The Web** *Lynch Mob*

A-28/87 **Tango In The Night**
Fleetwood Mac

M-24/91 **Taste** *Ride*

M-5/92 **Taste It** *INXS*

A-3/98 **Taste Of India** *Aerosmith*

M-24↑/02 **Taste Of Ink** *Used*

A-42/82 **Tattoo** *Novo Combo*

A-32/99 **Tattooed Bruise** *Doubledrive*

A-42/90 **Tattooed Millionaire**
Bruce Dickinson

M-10/96 **Tattva** *Kula Shaker*

A-32/95 **Taxman** *Stevie Ray Vaughan*

A-4/84 **Teacher Teacher** *38 Special*

Tear Away *Drowning Pool*
A-18/02 M-37/02

A-42/92 **Tear Down The Walls** *Kix*

A-9/88 **Tear It Up** *Robin Trower*

A-52/84 **Tear It Up** *Queen*

A-51/81 **Teardrops** *George Harrison*

A-5/87 **Tearing Us Apart** *Eric Clapton*

A-8/84 **Tears** *John Waite*

A-20/85 **Tears Are Falling** *Kiss*

A-9/92 **Tears In Heaven** *Eric Clapton*

A-23/86 **Tears In The Rain** *Triumph*

A-36/94 **Tears Of The Dragon**
Bruck Dickinson

M-8/89 **Tears Run Rings** *Marc Almond*

M-10/90 **Tears Won't Help** *Steve Wynn*

A-8/90 **Tease Me Please Me** *Scorpions*

A-35/99 **Teaser** *Mötley Crüe*

M-20/89 **Teen Age Riot** *Sonic Youth*

**Teen Angst (What The World
Needs Now)** *Cracker*
M-1/92 A-27/92

M-7/00 **Teenage Dirtbag** *Wheatus*

A-32/83 **Telegraph** *Orchestral
Manoeuvres In The Dark*

A-15/88 **Telephone Box**
Ian Gillan & Roger Glover

A-3/91 **Telephone Song**
Vaughan Brothers

A-17/83 **Tell Her About It** *Billy Joel*

M-13/92 **Tell It Like It T-I-Is** *B-52's*

A-25/88 **Tell Me** *White Lion*

A-27/84 **Tell Me** *Fastway*
(also see: Drops Of Jupiter)

A-29/83 **Tell Me What You Want** *Zebra*

**Tell Me When Did Things Go So
Wrong** *Smithereens*
M-11/91 A-28/92

M-9/88 **Tell That Girl To Shut Up**
Transvision Vamp

A-39/91 **Tell The Truth** *David Lee Roth*

M-6/92 **Tell Your Sister** *Lloyd Cole*

M-17/92 **Temple Of Dreams** *Messiah*

A-25/99 **Temple Of Your Dreams**
Monster Magnet

A-52/82 **Temporary Beauty**
Graham Parker

A-49/91 **Temptation** *Box*

A-8/81 **Tempted** *Squeeze*

M-21/00 **10 Days Late** *Third Eye Blind*

A-6/88 **Ten Men Workin'**
Neil Young & The Bluenotes

A-13/98 **10,000 Horses** *Candlebox*

A-33/00 **Ten Years Gone** *Jimmy Page &
The Black Crowes*

A-18/83 **Tender Is The Night**
Jackson Browne

A-10/84 **Tender Years** *John Cafferty*

A-39/85 **Tenderness** *General Public*

A-8/90 **Terrifying** *Rolling Stones*

A-30/85 **Territories** *Rush*

A-1/96 **Test For Echo** *Rush*

A-44/85 **Test Of Time** *Romantics*

A-5/82 **Testify** *Greg Kihn Band*

Testify
Rage Against The Machine
M-16/00 A-22/00

M-26/90 **Testify** *Eleventh Dream Day*

Texarkana *R.E.M.*
M-4/91 A-7/91

A-1/90 **Texas Twister** *Little Feat*

M-12/98 **Thank U** *Alanis Morissette*

A-8/95 **Thank You**
Jimmy Page & Robert Plant

A-27/87 **Thank You Girl** *John Hiatt*

Thanksgiving Song
Adam Sandler
A-33/97
A-29/98
A-39/99

M-27/91 **That Ain't Bad** *Ratcat*

A-5/87 **That Ain't Love**
REO Speedwagon

A-6/93 **That Don't Satisfy Me**
Brother Cane

A-25/89 **That Girl**
Crosby, Stills, Nash & Young

M-11/91 **That Is Why** *Jellyfish*

M-26/89 **That Smiling Face** *Camouflage*

A-32/98 **That Song** *Big Wreck*

A-14/86 **That Voice Again** *Peter Gabriel*

A-35/84 **That Was Then But This Is Now**
ABC

A-4/85 **That Was Yesterday** *Foreigner*

A-2/84 **That's All!** *Genesis*

A-17/87 **That's Freedom** *Tom Kimmel*

M-24/95 **That's Just What You Are**
Aimee Mann

A-35/93 **That's Love** *April Wine*

A-18/90 **That's Not Her Style** *Billy Joel*

A-28/88 **That's The Way I Wanna Rock
N Roll** *AC/DC*

A-25/82 **That's The Way That It Is**
Uriah Heep

A-17/90 **Too Late To Say Goodbye**
Richard Marx
A-48/82 **Too Many Losers**
Bobby & The Midnites
A-2/93 **Too Many Ways To Fall**
Arc Angels
Too Much *Dave Matthews Band*
M-5/96 A-9/96
A-3/88 **Too Much Ain't Enough Love**
Jimmy Barnes
A-38/83 **Too Much Blood** *Rolling Stones*
M-30/93 **Too Much Information**
Duran Duran
A-46/82 **Too Much Love To Hide**
Crosby, Stills & Nash
A-2/81 **Too Much Time On My Hands**
Styx
A-23/83 **Too Shy** *Kajagoogoo*
A-14/83 **Too Tough** *Rolling Stones*
A-17/84 **Too Young To Fall In Love**
Mötley Crüe
A-47/85 **Tooth And Nail** *Foreigner*
Top Of The Pops *Smithereens*
M-2/91 A-19/91
A-15/84 **Top Of The Rock** *Hagar, Schon,
Aaronson, Shrieve*
A-1/91 **Top Of The World** *Van Halen*
A-38/82 **Tora, Tora, Tora (Out With The
Boys)** *Rod Stewart*
A-19/85 **Tore Down A La Rimbaud**
Van Morrison
A-3/98 **Torn** *Creed*
M-12/98 **Torn** *Natalie Imbruglia*
A-23/83 **Total Eclipse Of The Heart**
Bonnie Tyler
Totalimmortal *Offspring*
M-27/00 A-36/00
A-2/86 **Touch & Go**
Emerson, Lake & Powell
M-36/00 **Touch And Go** *Vibrolush*
A-29/90 **Touch Of Evil** *Judas Priest*
A-1/87 **Touch Of Grey** *Grateful Dead*
Touch, Peel And Stand
Days Of The New
A-1/97 M-6/98
A-13/92 **Touch The Hand** *Bryan Adams*
A-8/86 **Touch The Night** *Neil Young*
Touched *Vast*
M-31/99 A-38/98
A-1/85 **Tough All Over** *John Cafferty*
Tough Enough ..see: Tuff Enuff
A-25/81 **Tough Guys** *REO Speedwagon*
A-16/92 **Tough It Out** *Webb Wilder*
A-26/82 **Tough World** *Donnie Iris*
A-30/97 **Tourniquet** *Marilyn Manson*
A-31/95 **Tout Le Monde** *Megadeth*
A-31/82 **Town Called Malice** *Jam*
Toxicity *System Of A Down*
M-3/02 A-10/02
A-26/90 **Toy Soldier** *Riverdogs*
A-7/91 **Trademark** *Eric Johnson*
M-18/90 **Tragedy For You** *Front 242*
A-29/87 **Trail Of Broken Treaties**
Little Steven
A-29/94 **Train Of Consequences**
Megadeth
Transistor *311*
M-14/97 A-31/97
A-1/85 **Trapped** *Bruce Springsteen*
A-22/97 **Travelin' Man** *Lynyrd Skynyrd*
(Traveller, The) ..see: Days Are
Numbers

A-7/90 **Travelling Riverside Blues**
Led Zeppelin
A-39/88 **Treat Her Right**
George Thorogood
A-31/81 **Treat Me Right** *Pat Benatar*
A-35/99 **Tremble For My Beloved**
Collective Soul
Tremor Christ *Pearl Jam*
M-16/94 A-16/94
A-24/97 **Trials** *Cool For August*
M-27/95 **Trigger Happy Jack** *Poe*
A-21/97 **Trip Free Life** *Hazies*
**Trippin' On A Hole In A Paper
Heart** *Stone Temple Pilots*
A-1/96 M-3/96
M-18/97 **Tripping Billies**
Dave Matthews Band
A-28/83 **Trooper, The** *Iron Maiden*
M-21/98 **Tropicalia** *Beck*
A-12/81 **Trouble** *Lindsey Buckingham*
M-28/01 **Trouble** *Coldplay*
A-11/85 **Trouble In Paradise** *Huey Lewis*
Trouble Me *10,000 Maniacs*
M-3/89 A-20/89
M-2/93 **Trout** *Neneh Cherry Featuring
Michael Stipe*
A-12/87 **Truck Drivin' Man**
Lynyrd Skynyrd
A-34/83 **True** *Spandau Ballet*
A-42/87 **True** *Concrete Blonde*
A-23/90 **True Blue Love** *Lou Gramm*
A-20/83 **True Colors** *Asia*
A-27/99 **True Friends** *Shannon Curfman*
A-15/88 **True Love** *Glenn Frey*
A-9/86 **True To You** *Ric Ocasek*
Truganini *Midnight Oil*
M-4/93 A-10/93
M-11/98 **Truly, Truly** *Grant Lee Buffalo*
A-5/97 **Trust** *Megadeth*
A-50/87 **Trust Me To Open My Mouth**
Squeeze
A-2/81 **Tryin' To Live My Life Without
You** *Bob Seger*
A-4/81 **Tube Snake Boogie** *ZZ Top*
M-1/97 **Tubthumping** *Chumbawamba*
A-29/96 **Tucker's Town**
Hootie & The Blowfish
M-11/93 **Tuesday Morning** *Pogues*
A-4/86 **Tuff Enuff**
Fabulous Thunderbirds
Tumble In The Rough
Stone Temple Pilots
A-9/97 M-36/97
Tumblin' Down *Ziggy Marley*
M-5/88 A-43/88
A-1/87 **Tunnel Of Love**
Bruce Springsteen
A-44/86 **Turbo Lover** *Judas Priest*
A-36/99 **Turn It Up** *Moon Dog Mane*
A-47/92 **Turn It Up** *Henry Lee Summer*
A-11/93 **Turn It Up Or Turn It Off**
Drivin' N' Cryin'
A-6/81 **Turn Me Loose** *Loverboy*
A-11/00 **Turn Me On "Mr. Deadman"**
Union Underground
Turn My Head *Live*
A-3/97 M-3/97
Turn The Page *Metallica*
A-1/98 M-39/99
A-38/90 **Turn The Volume Up**
Robin Trower
A-24/82 **Turn Up The Night**
Black Sabbath

A-17/85 **Turn Up The Radio** *Autograph*
Turn You Inside-Out *R.E.M.*
A-7/89 M-10/89
A-50/88 **Turnaround** *Stealin Horses*
M-30/88 **Turning Of The Tide**
Richard Thompson
A-41/89 **Tweeter And The Monkey Man**
Traveling Wilburys
M-11/94 **21st Century (Digital Boy)**
Bad Religion
A-4/93 **29 Palms** *Robert Plant*
A-38/81 **22,000 Days** *Moody Blues*
A-11/90 **Twice As Hard** *Black Crowes*
A-1/83 **Twilight Zone** *Golden Earring*
Twist In My Sobriety
Tanita Tikaram
M-25/89 A-47/89
A-7/91 **Twist Of The Knife**
Fabulous Thunderbirds
M-12/92 **Twisterella** *Ride*
M-22/90 **Twisting** *They Might Be Giants*
A-12/83 **Twisting By The Pool**
Dire Straits
A-12/83 **Two Hearts Beat As One** *U2*
A-25/84 **2 Minutes To Midnight**
Iron Maiden
A-2/93 **Two Princes** *Spin Doctors*
A-5/84 **Two Sides Of Love**
Sammy Hagar
A-15/93 **Two Steps Behind** *Def Leppard*
A-27/84 **Two Tribes**
Frankie Goes To Hollywood
M-8/93 **Two Worlds Collide**
Inspiral Carpets
A-11/88 **Two Wrongs** *Joe Cocker*
Type *Living Colour*
M-3/90 A-5/90
(Tyranny Of Tradition) ..see:
Operation Spirit

U

M-8/93 **Ubiquitous Mr Lovegrove**
Dead Can Dance
Ugly Truth *Matthew Sweet*
M-3/93 A-35/93
M-10/92 **Uh Huh Oh Yeh** *Paul Weller*
A-38/00 **Ultra Mega** *Powerman 5000*
M-23/92 **Ultra Unbelievable Love**
Robyn Hitchcock
M-3/91 **Unbelievable** *Emf*
A-21/90 **Unbelievable** *Bob Dylan*
A-11/87 **Unchain My Heart** *Joe Cocker*
A-13/81 **Unchained** *Van Halen*
A-19/91 **Uncle Tom's Cabin** *Warrant*
A-10/85 **Under A Raging Moon**
Roger Daltrey
A-35/99 **Under It All**
New American Shame
A-7/81 **Under Pressure**
Queen & David Bowie
A-19/86 **Under The Boardwalk**
John Cougar Mellencamp
Under The Bridge
Red Hot Chili Peppers
A-2/92 M-6/92
Under The God *Tin Machine*
M-4/89 A-8/89
A-28/95 **Under The Gun** *Foreigner*
A-2/88 **Under The Milky Way** *Church*
A-16/94 **Under The Same Sun** *Scorpions*

A-33/83	**Undercover Lover** *Art In America*	A-10/96	**Vanishing Cream** *Hunger*	A-30/94	**Waiting In The Wings** *BBM*
A-2/83	**Undercover Of The Night** *Rolling Stones*	A-28/87	**Variety Tonight** *REO Speedwagon*	A-8/82	**Waiting On A Friend** *Rolling Stones*
A-18/86	**Underground** *David Bowie*		**Vasoline** *Stone Temple Pilots*	A-30/82	**Waiting So Long** *Supertramp*
A-20/83	**Underground** *Men At Work*		A-1/94 M-2/94	M-26/95	**Wake Me** *Rusty*
A-35/85	**Underground** *Angel City*	A-15/86	**Velcro Fly** *ZZ Top*	A-30/97	**Wake-Up Bomb** *R.E.M.*
A-5/84	**Understanding** *Bob Seger*	M-4/90	**Velouria** *Pixies*	A-19/85	**Wake Up (Next To You)** *Graham Parker & The Shot*
A-19/95	**Understanding** *Candlebox*	A-34/01	**Vent** *Collective Soul*		
M-25/93	**Underwhelmed** *Sloan*	A-21/87	**Veracruz** *Santana*		**Walk, A** *Bad Religion*
	Undone-The Sweater Song *Weezer*		**Veronica** *Elvis Costello*		M-34/96 A-38/96
	M-6/94 A-30/94		M-1/89 A-10/89	A-16/98	**Walk Away** *Cool For August*
A-10/92	**Unforgiven, The** *Metallica*	A-23/82	**Victim, The** *Pat Benatar*	A-34/02	**Walk Away** *Epidemic*
A-2/98	**Unforgiven II** *Metallica*	A-10/87	**Victim Of Love** *Bryan Adams*	A-38/02	**Walk Away** *Mad At Gravity*
	Unglued *Stone Temple Pilots*	A-39/82	**Victim Of Love** *Cars*	A-48/89	**Walk Away** *Dokken*
	A-8/95 M-16/95	A-42/85	**View To A Kill** *Duran Duran*	A-6/85	**Walk Of Life** *Dire Straits*
	Uninvited *Ruth Ruth*		**Villains** *Verve Pipe*		**Walk On** *U2*
	M-24/95 A-24/96		M-22/97 A-24/97		M-10/01 A-19/01
M-26/98	**Uninvited** *Alanis Morissette*	A-16/99	**Vintage Eyes** *Second Coming*	A-10/87	**Walk On Fire** *Little America*
A-2/84	**Union Of The Snake** *Duran Duran*	M-13/90	**Violence Of Summer (Love's Taking Over)** *Duran Duran*	A-14/94	**Walk On Medley** *Boston*
M-5/95	**Universal Heart-Beat** *Juliana Hatfield*	M-29/95	**Violet** *Hole*	A-27/92	**Walk On The Ocean** *Toad The Wet Sprocket*
M-28/91	**Unkind** *Mighty Lemon Drops*	A-19/84	**Violet And Blue** *Stevie Nicks*	A-2/88	**Walk On Water** *Eddie Money*
A-38/93	**Unknown Legend** *Neil Young*	M-38/97	**Virtual Insanity** *Jamiroquai*	A-16/95	**Walk On Water** *Aerosmith*
A-31/02	**Unreal** *Soil*	M-10/92	**Visions Of You** *Jah Wobble's Invaders Of The Heart*	A-28/96	**Walk On Water** *Ozzy Osbourne*
M-6/91	**Unreal World** *Godfathers*	A-16/92	**Viva Las Vegas** *ZZ Top*	M-30/88	**Walk The Dinosaur** *Was (Not Was)*
A-5/90	**Unskinny Bop** *Poison*	A-1/81	**Voice, The** *Moody Blues*	M-13/95	**Walk This World** *Heather Nova*
	Unsung *Helmet*	A-30/96	**Voice Of Eujena** *Brother Cane*	A-14/91	**Walk Through Fire** *Bad Company*
	M-29/92 A-32/92	A-15/84	**Voices** *Russ Ballard*	M-16/92	**Walkabout** *Sugarcubes*
	Until ..also see: Til		**Voices** *Disturbed*		**Walkin' On The Sun** *Smash Mouth*
	Until I Fall Away *Gin Blossoms*		A-16/01 M-18/01		M-1/97 A-13/97
	M-13/94 A-40/94	A-14/85	**Voices Carry** *'Til Tuesday*	A-25/89	**Walkin' Shoes** *Tora Tora*
	Until It Sleeps *Metallica*	A-2/89	**Voices Of Babylon** *Outfield*	M-12/98	**Walking After You** *Foo Fighters*
	A-1/96 M-27/96		**Volcano Girls** *Veruca Salt*	M-15/88	**Walking Away** *Information Society*
A-42/91	**Until My Dying Day** *Thunder*		M-8/97 A-9/97		
M-1/91	**Until She Comes** *Psychedelic Furs*		**Voodoo** *Godsmack*		**Walking Contradiction** *Green Day*
	Until The End Of The World *U2*		A-5/00 M-6/00		M-21/96 A-25/96
	M-4/92 A-5/92	A-46/82	**Voodoo** *Black Sabbath*	M-4/91	**Walking Down Madison** *Kirsty MacColl*
A-38/92	**Until Your Love Comes Back Around** *RTZ*	A-26/84	**Voodoo Chile (Slight Return)** *Stevie Ray Vaughan*	A-14/97	**Walking In A Hurricane** *John Fogerty*
A-48/86	**Untouchable One** *Tom Cochrane & Red Rider*	M-32/94	**Voodoo Lady** *Ween*	A-12/83	**Walking In L.A.** *Missing Persons*
M-14/02	**Up All Night** *Unwritten Law*	M-30/88	**Voodoo Thing** *Colin James*	A-7/91	**Walking In Memphis** *Marc Cohn*
A-21/90	**Up All Night** *Slaughter*	M-17/91	**Vote Elvis** *Popinjays*	M-1/93	**Walking In My Shoes** *Depeche Mode*
M-19/91	**Up & Down** *High*	A-10/92	**Vote For Me** *Joe Walsh*	A-4/84	**Walking In My Sleep** *Roger Daltrey*
A-43/82	**Up Periscope** *Novo Combo*	M-26/95	**Vow** *Garbage*	A-16/84	**Walking On A Thin Line** *Huey Lewis*
A-36/84	**Up The Creek** *Cheap Trick*	A-18/85	**Vox Humana** *Kenny Loggins*	M-7/92	**Walking On Broken Glass** *Annie Lennox*
M-6/88	**Up There Down There** *Patti Smith*			A-21/85	**Walking On Sunshine** *Katrina & The Waves*
A-16/99	**Upside Down** *Pound*		# W	M-13/93	**Walking Through Syrup** *Ned's Atomic Dustbin*
A-22/83	**Uptown Girl** *Billy Joel*			A-39/89	**Walking Towards Paradise** *Robert Plant*
A-1/81	**Urgent** *Foreigner*		**Waffle** *Sevendust*	A-47/88	**Walking With The Kid** *Huey Lewis*
A-15/98	**Use The Man** *Megadeth*		A-23/00 M-33/00	A-22/90	**Walks Like A Woman** *Baton Rouge*
A-25/87	**Usual, The** *Bob Dylan*	A-20/82	**Waffle Stomp** *Joe Walsh*	A-34/91	**Wall I Must Climb** *Michael McDermott*
		M-22/91	**Wagon, The** *Dinosaur Jr.*	A-46/90	**Wall Of Denial** *Stevie Ray Vaughan*
	# V		**Wait** *Seven Mary Three*	A-37/02	**Wall Of Shame** *Course Of Nature*
			A-7/01 M-21/01	A-24/94	**Walls** *Yes*
A-13/82	**Vacation** *Go-Go's*	A-18/88	**Wait** *White Lion*	A-17/83	**Walls Came Down** *Call*
A-31/99	**Valentine** *Shades Apart*	M-34/98	**Wait** *Huffamoose*	A-6/96	**Walls (Circus)** *Tom Petty*
A-37/91	**Valentine** *Nils Lofgren*	A-34/00	**Wait And Bleed** *Slipknot*	A-23/99	**Wander This World** *Jonny Lang*
	Valerie *Steve Winwood*	A-9/89	**Wait For You** *Bonham*		
	A-13/82	A-40/88	**Wait On Love** *Michael Bolton*		
	A-13/87	A-1/81	**Waiting, The** *Tom Petty*		
M-3/91	**Valerie Loves Me** *Material Issue*	M-26/01	**Waiting** *Green Day*		
A-12/82	**Valley Girl** *Frank Zappa*	A-1/81	**Waiting For A Girl Like You** *Foreigner*		
A-1/88	**Valley Road** *Bruce Hornsby*	M-6/89	**Waiting For Mary** *Pere Ubu*		
A-2/84	**Valotte** *Julian Lennon*	M-20/88	**Waiting For The Great Leap Forwards** *Billy Bragg*		
M-34/97	**Van Halen** *Nerf Herder*		**Waiting For The Sun** *Jayhawks*		
			M-29/92 A-20/93		
		A-6/96	**Waiting For Tonight** *Tom Petty*		

A-35/87 **Wanderer, The**
Dave Edmunds Band

A-41/88 **Waning Moon**
Peter Himmelman

A-15/89 **Want Of A Nail** *Todd Rundgren*

Want You Bad *Offspring*
M-10/01 A-23/01

A-13/86 **Wanted Dead Or Alive** *Bon Jovi*

A-38/84 **Wanted Man** *Ratt*

A-4/86 **War** *Bruce Springsteen*

A-13/83 **War Games**
Crosby, Stills & Nash

A-7/92 **War Of Man** *Neil Young*

Warm Machine *Bush*
A-16/00 M-38/00

Warning *Green Day*
M-3/01 A-24/01

Warning *Incubus*
M-3/02 A-27/02

Warped *Red Hot Chili Peppers*
M-7/95 A-13/95

A-1/84 **Warrior, The** *Scandal*

M-16/89 **Warrior** *PIL*

A-9/00 **Was**
Kenny Wayne Shepherd Band

M-16/89 **Was There Anything I Could Do?** *Go-Betweens*

Wash It Away *Black Lab*
A-6/98 M-13/98

A-29/01 **Waste** *Skrape*

A-37/01 **Wasted** *Beautiful Creatures*

M-29/02 **Wasted & Ready** *Ben Kweller*

A-9/82 **Wasted On The Way**
Crosby, Stills & Nash

A-30/92 **Wasted Time** *Skid Row*

Wasting My Time *Default*
A-2/02 M-3/02

A-4/88 **Wasting My Time** *Jimmy Page*

A-35/00 **Wasting Time** *Kid Rock*
(also see: Stay)

Watch The Girl Destroy Me
Possum Dixon
M-9/94 A-37/94

A-21/91 **Watch Yourself** *Eric Clapton*

A-25/81 **Watching The Wheels**
John Lennon

A-53/82 **Water On Glass** *Kim Wilde*

Water's Edge
Seven Mary Three
A-7/96 M-37/96

M-26/92 **Waterfall** *Riverside*

Wax Ecstatic (To Sell Angelina)
Sponge
A-11/96 M-15/96

Way, The *Fastball*
M-1/98 A-25/98

M-8/88 **Way Behind Me** *Primitives*

A-16/89 **Way Cool Jr.** *Ratt*

Way Down Now *World Party*
M-1/90 A-21/90

A-46/88 **Way I Feel** *Robert Plant*

A-3/86 **Way It Is** *Bruce Hornsby*

A-13/90 **Way It Is** *Tesla*

M-6/89 **Way Of The World** *Max Q*

Way You Do The Things You Do
..see: Nite At The Apollo

Way You Like It *Adema*
M-15/02 A-21/02

Waydown *Catherine Wheel*
M-15/95 A-24/95

A-29/85 **Ways To Be Wicked**
Lone Justice

A-35/94 **We All Fall Down** *Blue Murder*

M-21/99 **We Are** *Vertical Horizon*

M-22/02 **We Are All Made Of Stars** *Moby*

M-10/92 **We Are Each Other**
Beautiful South

We Are In Control ..see: We R In Control

M-29/94 **We Are The Beautiful**
Chapterhouse

M-5/93 **We Are The Normal**
Goo Goo Dolls

A-27/85 **We Are The World**
USA For Africa

A-38/87 **We Are What We Are**
Other Ones

A-3/84 **We Belong** *Pat Benatar*

A-1/85 **We Built This City** *Starship*

A-51/81 **We Can Get Together** *Icehouse*

A-6/89 **We Didn't Start The Fire**
Billy Joel

M-23/90 **We Don't Do That Anymore**
Sidewinders

A-28/94 **We Don't Exist** *Meat Puppets*

A-29/85 **We Don't Need Another Hero (Thunderdome)** *Tina Turner*

A-43/90 **We Got Married** *Paul McCartney*

A-7/82 **We Got The Beat** *Go-Go's*

A-28/82 **We Gotta Get Out Of This Place/Don't Bring Me Down/It's My Life** *David Johansen*

M-2/92 **We Hate It When Our Friends Become Successful**
Morrissey

A-42/83 **We R In Control** *Neil Young*

A-26/82 **We Ride Tonight** *Sherbs*

A-18/86 **We Should Be Sleeping**
Eddie Money

A-37/82 **We Stand A Chance** *Tom Petty*

A-20/87 **We'll Be Together** *Sting*

A-31/98 **We're An American Band**
Jackyl

We're In This Together
Nine Inch Nails
M-11/99 A-21/99

A-7/84 **We're Not Gonna Take It**
Twisted Sister

A-2/86 **We're Ready** *Boston*

M-34/95 **We're The Same**
Matthew Sweet

A-10/00 **Weapon & The Wound**
Days Of The New

M-33/01 **Weapon Of Choice** *Fatboy Slim*

A-7/87 **Weapons Of Love** *Truth*

A-36/85 **(Wearing Down) Like A Wheel**
Elliot Easton

A-27/97 **Weeds** *Life Of Agony*

A-33/86 **Weight Of The World**
Neil Young

A-43/92 **Weight Of The World**
Ringo Starr

Weird-Out *Dandelion*
M-14/95 A-36/95

M-1/92 **Weirdo** *Charlatans UK*

A-30/97 **Welcome** *Outhouse*

A-9/88 **Welcome Me Home**
Rossington Band

M-7/94 **Welcome To Paradise**
Green Day

A-8/86 **Welcome To The Boomtown**
David & David

M-27/92 **Welcome To The Cheap Seats**
Wonder Stuff

Welcome To The Fold *Filter*
A-8/99 M-17/99

A-37/88 **Welcome To The Jungle**
Guns N' Roses

M-12/93 **Wembley** *Candy Skins*

A-37/86 **West End Girls** *Pet Shop Boys*

A-40/87 **West L.A. Fadeaway**
Grateful Dead

A-24/01 **What A Day** *Nonpoint*

A-3/85 **What About Love?** *Heart*

A-9/86 **What About Love** *'Til Tuesday*

What About Now
Robbie Robertson
A-15/91 M-28/91

M-10/92 **What Are We Gonna Do?**
Dramarama

A-44/90 **What Are You Doing With A Fool Like Me** *Joe Cocker*

A-28/02 **What Comes Around** *Ill Niño*

A-20/82 **What Do All The People Know**
Monroes

What Do I Have To Do?
Stabbing Westward
A-7/96 M-11/96

A-24/85 **What Do I Know?** *Saga*

What Do You Want From Me
Pink Floyd
A-16/94
A-13/95

M-24/97 **What Do You Want From Me?**
Monaco

A-38/86 **What Does It Take**
Honeymoon Suite

M-6/92 **What Girls Want** *Material Issue*

A-4/92 **What God Wants** *Roger Waters*

What I Am *Edie Brickell*
M-4/88 A-9/88

M-14/98 **What I Didn't Know** *Athenaeum*

What I Got *Sublime*
M-1/96 A-11/96

A-25/84 **What I See** *Planet P Project*

What If *Creed*
A-3/00 M-15/00
(also see: Remo's Theme)

A-1/93 **What If I Came Knocking**
John Mellencamp

A-13/00 **What Is And What Should Never Be** *Jimmy Page & The Black Crowes*

A-20/84 **What Is Love?** *Howard Jones*

A-1/90 **What It Takes** *Aerosmith*

What It's Like *Everlast*
M-1/98 A-1/99

A-4/98 **What Kind Of Love Are You On**
Aerosmith

A-26/88 **What Love Can Be**
Kingdom Come

A-19/93 **What The Hell Have I**
Alice In Chains

(What The World Needs Now) ..see: Teen Angst

A-26/93 **What Time Is It?** *Spin Doctors*

What Would You Say
Dave Matthews Band
A-5/95 M-11/95

M-19/92 **What You Do To Me**
Teenage Fanclub

A-7/92 **What You Give** *Tesla*

A-3/86 **What You Need** *INXS*

M-1/92 **What's Good** *Lou Reed*

What's Happened To You *Call*
M-25/90 A-39/90

A-51/84 **What's Love Got To Do With It**
Tina Turner

What's My Age Again?
Blink 182
M-2/99 A-19/99

M-10/88 **What's On Your Mind (Pure Energy)** *Information Society*

CLASSIC ROCK TRACKS

We are pleased to introduce this brand new Classic Rock Tracks section. It features classic rock artists and tracks beginning with The Beatles invasion of 1964 up to the debut of *Billboard's* Rock Tracks chart in 1981. The term "classic" indicates that these songs are still played regularly on today's classic rock stations throughout the U.S. Please do not consider this to be the definitive list of the best rock songs of all time. Obviously opinions vary widely in regards to "classic rock" hits, but we think this is a great overall guide.

This section is organized alphabetically by artist. Each artist's classic tracks (from 1964-1980) are listed below their name in alphabetical order. The peak year of the album from which the track is taken is shown in brackets after the title.

Please e-mail additional nationwide classic rock tracks that you would like considered for future editions to books@recordresearch.com.

AC/DC
Highway To Hell [79]
T.N.T. [76]
Whole Lotta Rosie [77]
You Shook Me All Night Long [80]

ACE
How Long [75]

AEROSMITH
Back In The Saddle [76]
Come Together [78]
Draw The Line [77]
Dream On [73]
Kings And Queens [77]
Last Child [76]
Mama Kin [73]
Remember (Walking In The Sand)
[79]
Same Old Song And Dance [74]
Sweet Emotion [75]
Train Kept A Rollin' [74]
Walk This Way [75]

ALLMAN, Gregg
Midnight Rider [73]

ALLMAN BROTHERS BAND, The
Ain't Wastin' Time No More [72]
Blue Sky [72]
Crazy Love [79]
Dreams [70]
In Memory Of Elizabeth Reed [70]
Jessica [73]
Melissa [72]
One Way Out [72]
Ramblin' Man [73]
Revival (Love Is Everywhere) [70]
Statesboro Blues [71]
Whipping Post [70]

AMBOY DUKES, The
Journey To The Center Of The Mind
[68]

AMERICA
Horse With No Name [72]
Sandman [72]
Sister Golden Hair [75]
Tin Man [74]
Ventura Highway [72]

ANIMALS, The
Don't Bring Me Down [66]
Don't Let Me Be Misunderstood [65]
House Of The Rising Sun [64]
It's My Life [66]
Monterey [68]
San Franciscan Nights [67]
See See Rider [66]
Sky Pilot [68]
We Gotta Get Out Of This Place [65]

APRIL WINE
I Like To Rock [80]
Roller [79]
You Could Have Been A Lady [72]

ARGENT
Hold You Head Up [72]

ATLANTA RHYTHM SECTION
Champagne Jam [78]
Doraville [74]
I'm Not Gonna Let It Bother Me
Tonight [78]
Imaginary Lover [78]
So In To You [77]
Spooky [79]

AVERAGE WHITE BAND
Pick Up The Pieces [74]

BABYS, The
Back On My Feet Again [80]
Every Time I Think Of You [79]
Isn't It Time [77]

BACHMAN-TURNER OVERDRIVE
Blue Collar [73]
Hey You [75]
Let It Ride [74]
Roll On Down The Highway [74]
Takin' Care Of Business [74]
You Ain't Seen Nothin' Yet [74]

BAD COMPANY
Bad Company [74]
Burnin' Sky [77]
Can't Get Enough [74]
Feel Like Makin' Love [75]
Good Lovin' Gone Bad [75]
Movin' On [74]
Ready For Love [74]
Rock 'N' Roll Fantasy [79]
Run With The Pack [76]
Shooting Star [75]
Silver, Blue & Gold [76]
Young Blood [76]

BADFINGER
Baby Blue [72]
Come And Get It [70]
Day After Day [72]
No Matter What [70]

BAND, The
Ain't Got No Home [73]
Chest Fever [68]
Don't Do It [72]
Life Is A Carnival [71]
Night They Drove Old Dixie Down
[69]
Ophelia [76]
Rag Mama Rag [69]
Shape I'm In [70]
This Wheel's On Fire [68]

BAND, The — Cont'd
Time To Kill [70]
Up On Cripple Creek [69]
Weight, The [68]

BEATLES, The
Across The Universe [70]
All My Loving [64]
All You Need Is Love [67]
And I Love Her [64]
Baby You're A Rich Man [67]
Back In The U.S.S.R. [68]
Ballad Of John And Yoko [69]
Birthday [68]
Blackbird [68]
Can't Buy Me Love [64]
Come Together [69]
Day In The Life [67]
Day Tripper [66]
Dear Prudence [68]
Do You Want To Know A Secret [64]
Don't Let Me Down [69]
Drive My Car [66]
Eight Days A Week [65]
Eleanor Rigby [66]
Fool On The Hill [67]
From Me To You [64]
Get Back [69]
Glass Onion [68]
Golden Slumbers/Carry That
Weight/The End/Her Majesty [69]
Good Day Sunshine [66]
Got To Get You Into My Life [66]
Hard Day's Night [64]
Hello Goodbye [67]
Help! [65]
Helter Skelter [68]
Here Comes The Sun [69]
Hey Jude [68]
I Am The Walrus [67]
I Feel Fine [64]
I Saw Her Standing There [64]
I Should Have Known Better [64]
I Want To Hold Your Hand [64]
I'm A Loser [65]
In My Life [65]
Lady Madonna [68]
Let It Be [70]
Long And Winding Road [70]
Love Me Do [64]
Lovely Rita [67]
Lucy In The Sky With Diamonds [67]
Magical Mystery Tour [67]
Maxwell's Silver Hammer [67]
Michelle [65]
No Reply [65]
Norwegian Wood (This Bird Has
Flown) [65]
Nowhere Man [66]
Ob-La-Di, Ob-La-Da [68]
Octopus's Garden [69]
Oh! Darling [69]

BEATLES, The — Cont'd
Old Brown Shoe [69]
Paperback Writer [66]
Penny Lane [67]
Please Please Me [64]
Revolution [68]
Rock And Roll Music [64]
Rocky Raccoon [68]
Roll Over Beethoven [64]
Sgt. Pepper's Lonely Hearts Club
   Band/With A Little Help From My
   Friends [67]
She Came In Through The
   Bathroom Window [69]
She Loves You [64]
Something [69]
Strawberry Fields Forever [67]
Taxman [66]
Ticket To Ride [65]
Twist And Shout [64]
We Can Work It Out [65]
When I'm Sixty-Four [67]
While My Guitar Gently Weeps [68]
Yellow Submarine [66]
Yesterday [65]
You're Going To Lose That Girl [65]
You've Got To Hide Your Love Away
   [65]

BENATAR, Pat
Heartbreaker [79]
Hell Is For Children [80]
Hit Me With Your Best Shot [80]
I Need A Lover [79]
We Live For Love [79]
You Better Run [80]

B-52's, The
Private Idaho [80]
Rock Lobster [79]

BIG BROTHER & THE HOLDING COMPANY
Ball And Chain [68]
Down On Me [67]
Piece Of My Heart [68]

BISHOP, Elvin
Fooled Around And Fell In Love [76]

BLACKFOOT
Highway Song [79]
Train, Train [79]

BLACK OAK ARKANSAS
Jim Dandy [73]

BLACK SABBATH
Black Sabbath [70]
Children Of The Grave [71]
Iron Man [71]
N.I.B. [70]
Paranoid [71]
War Pigs [71]

BLIND FAITH
Can't Find My Way Home [69]

BLOOD, SWEAT & TEARS
And When I Die [69]
Go Down Gamblin' [71]
Hi-De-Ho [70]
Lucretia Mac Evil [70]
Spinning Wheel [69]
You've Made Me So Very Happy
   [69]

BLUE CHEER
Summertime Blues [68]

BLUE OYSTER CULT
(Don't Fear) The Reaper [76]
Godzilla [77]
In Thee [79]

BLUES BROTHERS
Hey Bartender [79]
Rubber Biscuit [79]
Soul Man [79]

BLUES IMAGE
Ride Captain Ride [70]

BLUES MAGOOS
(We Ain't Got) Nothin' Yet [67]

BOOMTOWN RATS, The
I Don't Like Mondays [80]

BOSTON
Don't Look Back [78]
Feelin' Satisfied [78]
Hitch A Ride [76]
Let Me Take You Home Tonight [76]
Long Time [76]
Man I'll Never Be [78]
More Than A Feeling [76]
Peace Of Mind [76]
Rock & Roll Band [76]
Smokin' [76]
Something About You [76]

BOWIE, David
Ashes To Ashes [80]
Changes [72]
Diamond Dogs [74]
Fame [75]
Fashion [80]
Golden Years [76]
Heroes [77]
Jean Genie [73]
Rebel Rebel [74]
Space Oddity [73]
Starman [72]
Suffragette City [72]
TVC 15 [76]
Young Americans [75]
Ziggy Stardust [72]

BROWNE, Jackson
Boulevard [80]
Doctor My Eyes [72]
Here Come Those Tears Again [76]
Hold On Hold Out [80]
Late For The Sky [74]
Load-Out/Stay [78]
Pretender, The [76]
Redneck Friend [72]
Rock Me On The Water [72]
Running On Empty [78]
That Girl Could Sing [80]
You Love The Thunder [78]

BROWNSVILLE STATION
Smokin' In The Boy's Room [73]

BUBBLE PUPPY, The
Hot Smoke & Sasafrass [69]

BUFFALO SPRINGFIELD, The
Bluebird [67]
For What It's Worth (Stop, Hey
   What's That Sound) [67]
Mr. Soul [67]
Rock 'N' Roll Woman [67]

BUFFETT, Jimmy
Cheeseburger In Paradise [78]
Margaritaville [77]

BURDON, Eric, & War
Spill The Wine [70]

BYRDS, The
All I Really Want To Do [65]
Eight Miles High [66]
Mr. Spaceman [66]
Mr. Tambourine Man [65]
My Back Pages [67]
So You Want To Be A Rock 'N' Roll
   Star [67]
Turn! Turn! Turn! (To Everything
   There Is A Season) [65]

CANNED HEAT
Going Up The Country [69]
Let's Work Together [70]
On The Road Again [68]

CARS, The
Bye Bye Love [78]
Dangerous Type [79]
Good Times Roll [78]
It's All I Can Do [79]
Just What I Needed [78]
Let's Go [79]
Moving In Stereo [78]
My Best Friend's Girl [78]
Touch And Go [80]
You're All I've Got Tonight [78]

CHAPIN, Harry
Cat's In The Cradle [74]
Taxi [72]

CHEAP TRICK
Ain't That A Shame [79]
Dream Police [79]
I Want You To Want Me [79]
Surrender [78]
Voices [79]

CHEECH & CHONG
Basketball Jones [73]
Black Lassie [74]
Dave [71]
Earache My Eye [74]
Sister Mary Elephant [72]
Three Little Pigs [74]

CHICAGO
Beginnings [69]
Does Anybody Really Know What
   Time It Is? [69]
I'm A Man [69]
Make Me Smile [70]
Questions 67 & 68 [69]
Saturday In The Park [72]
25 Or 6 To 4 [70]

CLAPTON, Eric
After Midnight [70]
Bell Bottom Blues [70]
Blues Power [70]
Cocaine [77]
Hello Old Friend [76]
I Shot The Sheriff [74]
Lay Down Sally [77]
Layla [70]
Let It Rain [70]
Promises [78]
Tulsa Time [78]
Watch Out For Lucy [78]
Willie And The Hand Jive [74]
Wonderful Tonight [77]

CLASH, The
Train In Vain (Stand By Me) [80]

CLIMAX BLUES BAND
Couldn't Get It Right [77]

COCKER, Joe
Cry Me A River [70]
Delta Lady [69]
Feeling Alright [69]
High Time We Went [71]
Letter, The [70]
She Came In Through The
   Bathroom Window [69]
With A Little Help From My Friends
   [69]
You Are So Beautiful [75]

COMMANDER CODY AND HIS LOST PLANET AIRMEN
Hot Rod Lincoln [72]

COOPER, Alice
Be My Lover [72]
Billion Dollar Babies [73]
Clones (We're All) [80]
Eighteen [71]
Elected [72]
Hello Hurray [73]
No More Mr. Nice Guy [73]
School's Out [72]
Under My Wheels [72]
Welcome To My Nightmare [75]

COSTELLO, Elvis
Accidents Will Happen [79]
Allison [77]
I Can't Stand Up For Falling Down
   [80]
Oliver's Army [79]
Pump It Up [78]
Radio, Radio [78]
Watching The Detectives [77]
(What's So Funny 'Bout) Peace,
   Love And Understanding [79]

COUNTRY JOE AND THE FISH
I-Feel-Like-I'm-Fixin'-To-Die-Rag
   [67]
Not So Sweet Martha Lorraine [67]
Rock And Soul Music [68]

CREAM
Badge [69]
Crossroads [68]
I Feel Free [67]
Spoonful [68]
Strange Brew [67]
Sunshine Of Your Love [67]
White Room [68]

CREEDENCE CLEARWATER REVIVAL
Bad Moon Rising [69]
Born On The Bayou [69]
Down On The Corner [69]
Fortunate Son [69]
Green River [69]
Have You Ever Seen The Rain [71]
Hey Tonight [71]
I Heard It Through The Grapevine
   [70]
I Put A Spell On You [68]
Lodi [69]
Long As I Can See The Light [70]
Lookin' Out My Back Door [70]
Proud Mary [69]
Run Through The Jungle [70]
Someday Never Comes [72]
Suzie Q. [68]
Sweet Hitch-Hiker [71]
Travelin' Band [70]
Up Around The Bend [70]
Who'll Stop The Rain [70]

CROCE, Jim
Bad, Bad Leroy Brown [73]
You Don't Mess Around With Jim
   [72]

CROSBY, STILLS, NASH & YOUNG
Almost Cut My Hair [70]
Carry On [70]
Dark Star [77]
Fair Game [77]
Helplessly Hoping [69]
Just A Song Before I Go [77]
Marrakesh Express [69]
Ohio [70]
Our House [70]
Suite: Judy Blue Eyes [69]
Teach Your Children [70]
Wooden Ships [69]
Woodstock [70]

CROSS, Christopher
Ride Like The Wind [80]

CROW
Evil Woman Don't Play Your Games
   With Me [69]

DANIELS, Charlie, Band
Devil Went Down To Georgia [79]
Long Haired Country Boy [75]
South's Gonna Do It [75]

DAVIS, Spencer, Group
Gimme Some Lovin' [67]
I'm A Man [67]

DEEP PURPLE
Black Night [70]
Highway Star [72]
Hush [68]
Kentucky Woman [68]
Might Just Take Your Life [74]
River Deep-Mountain High [69]
Smoke On The Water [72]
Space Truckin' [72]
Strange Kind Of Woman [71]
Woman From Tokyo [73]

DELANEY & BONNIE & FRIENDS
Comin' Home [70]
Never Ending Song Of Love [71]
Only You Know And I Know [71]

DERRINGER, Rick
Rock And Roll, Hoochie Koo [74]

DEVO
Whip It [80]

DIRE STRAITS
Sultans Of Swing [79]

DR. HOOK & THE MEDICINE SHOW
The Cover Of "Rolling Stone" [73]

DR. JOHN
Right Place Wrong Time [73]

DONOVAN
Atlantis [69]
Hurdy Gurdy Man [68]
Mellow Yellow [66]
Sunshine Superman [66]

DOOBIE BROTHERS, The
Another Park, Another Sunday [74]
Black Water [74]
China Grove [73]
Dependin' On You [79]
Eyes Of Silver [74]
It Keeps You Runnin' [76]
Jesus Is Just Alright [72]
Listen To The Music [72]
Long Train Runnin' [73]
Minute By Minute [79]
One Step Closer [80]
Real Love [80]
Rockin' Down The Highway [72]
South City Midnight Lady [73]
Sweet Maxine [75]
Take Me In Your Arms (Rock Me) [75]
Takin' It To The Streets [76]
What A Fool Believes [79]
You Belong To Me [77]

DOORS, The
Alabama Song (Whiskey Bar) [67]
Back Door Man [67]
Break On Through (To The Other Side) [67]
Crystal Ship [67]
End, The [67]
Five To One [68]
Hello, I Love You [68]
L.A. Woman [71]
Light My Fire [67]
Love Her Madly [71]
Love Me Two Times [67]
Moonlight Drive [67]
People Are Strange [67]
Riders On The Storm [71]
Roadhouse Blues [70]
Strange Days [67]
Tell All The People [69]
Touch Me [69]
Unknown Soldier [68]
When The Music's Over [67]
Wishful Sinful [69]

DYLAN, Bob
All Along The Watchtower [68]
Ballad Of A Thin Man [65]
Blowin' In The Wind [63]
Can You Please Crawl Out Your Window? [66]
Don't Think Twice, It's All Right [63]
Fool Such As I [73]
Forever Young [74]

DYLAN, Bob — Cont'd
Gotta Serve Somebody [79]
Hurricane [76]
I Threw It All Away [69]
I Want You [66]
Isis [76]
It Ain't Me Babe [64]
It's All Over Now, Baby Blue [65]
Just Like A Woman [66]
Knockin' On Heaven's Door [73]
Lay Lady Lay [69]
Leopard-Skin Pill-Box Hat [67]
Like A Rolling Stone [65]
Maggie's Farm [65]
Most Likely You Go Your Way (And I'll Go Mine) [74]
Mozambique [76]
Mr. Tambourine Man [65]
My Back Pages [64]
On A Night Like This [74]
Positively 4th Street [65]
Rainy Day Women #12 & 35 [66]
Subterranean Homesick Blues [65]
Tangled Up In Blue [75]
Times They Are A-Changin' [64]
Watching The River Flow [71]
You Angel You [74]

EAGLES
After The Thrill Is Gone [75]
Already Gone [74]
Best Of My Love [74]
Desperado [73]
Doolin-Dalton [73]
Heartache Tonight [79]
Hotel California [77]
I Can't Tell You Why [79]
In The City [79]
James Dean [74]
Life In The Fast Lane [77]
Long Run [79]
Lyin' Eyes [75]
New Kid In Town [77]
One Of These Nights [75]
Outlaw Man [73]
Peaceful Easy Feeling [72]
Please Come Home For Christmas [78]
Sad Café [79]
Seven Bridges Road [80]
Take It Easy [72]
Take It To The Limit [75]
Tequila Sunrise [73]
Those Shoes [79]
Victim Of Love [77]
Wasted Time [77]
Witchy Woman [72]

EASYBEATS, The
Friday On My Mind [67]

EDMUNDS, Dave
I Hear You Knocking [71]

ELECTRIC LIGHT ORCHESTRA
All Over The World [80]
Can't Get It Out Of My Head [74]
Confusion [79]
Do Ya [76]
Don't Bring Me Down [79]
Evil Woman [75]
Fire On High [75]
I'm Alive [80]
Last Train To London [79]
Livin' Thing [76]
Mr. Blue Sky [77]
Roll Over Beethoven [73]
Shine A Little Love [79]
Showdown [73]
Strange Magic [75]
Sweet Talkin' Woman [77]
Telephone Line [76]
Turn To Stone [77]

ELECTRIC PRUNES, The
I Had Too Much To Dream (Last Night) [67]

EMERSON, LAKE & PALMER
Fanfare For The Common Man [77]
From The Beginning [72]
Hoedown [72]
Karn Evil 9 [73]
Lucky Man [71]

ESSEX, David
Rock On [74]

FEVER TREE
San Francisco Girls (Return Of The Native) [68]

FIVE MAN ELECTRICAL BAND
Signs [71]

FLEETWOOD MAC
Albatross [69]
Black Magic Woman [69]
Chain, The [77]
Don't Stop [77]
Dreams [77]
Go Your Own Way [77]
Gold Dust Woman [77]
Hypnotized [73]
I Don't Want To Know [77]
Landslide [75]
Monday Morning [75]
Never Going Back Again [77]
Oh Well [70]
Over My Head [75]
Rhiannon (Will You Ever Win) [75]
Sara [79]
Say You Love Me [75]
Second Hand News [77]
Silver Springs [77]
Think About Me [79]

FLEETWOOD MAC — Cont'd
Tusk *[79]*
You Make Loving Fun *[77]*

FOCUS
Hocus Pocus *[73]*

FOGELBERG, Dan
Part Of The Plan *[75]*

FOGERTY, John
Almost Saturday Night *[75]*
Rockin' All Over The World *[75]*

FOGHAT
Drivin' Wheel *[76]*
Fool For The City *[75]*
I Just Want To Make Love To You *[72]*
Slow Ride *[75]*
Stone Blue *[78]*
Third Time Lucky (First Time I Was A Fool) *[79]*

FORBERT, Steve
Romeo's Tune *[80]*

FOREIGNER
Blue Morning, Blue Day *[78]*
Cold As Ice *[77]*
Dirty White Boy *[79]*
Double Vision *[78]*
Feels Like The First Time *[77]*
Head Games *[79]*
Hot Blooded *[78]*
Long, Long Way From Home *[77]*

FRAMPTON, Peter
Baby, I Love Your Way *[76]*
Do You Feel Like We Do *[76]*
I Can't Stand It No More *[79]*
I'm In You *[77]*
Show Me The Way *[76]*

FREE
All Right Now *[70]*

FREHLEY, Ace
New York Groove *[78]*

FRIJID PINK
House Of The Rising Sun *[70]*

GABRIEL, Peter
Games Without Frontiers *[80]*
Solsbury Hill *[77]*

GEILS, J., Band
Come Back *[80]*
Give It To Me *[73]*
Looking For A Love *[71]*
Love Stinks *[80]*
Must Of Got Lost *[74]*
One Last Kiss *[78]*

GENESIS
Follow You Follow Me *[78]*
Lamb Lies Down On Broadway *[75]*
Misunderstanding *[80]*
Turn It On Again *[80]*

GLITTER, Gary
Rock And Roll Part 2 *[72]*

GOLDEN EARRING
Radar Love *[74]*

GRAND FUNK RAILROAD
Bad Time *[75]*
Closer To Home/I'm Your Captain *[70]*
Footstompin' Music *[71]*
Loco-Motion, The *[74]*
Rock 'N Roll Soul *[72]*
Shinin' On *[74]*
Some Kind Of Wonderful *[75]*
Walk Like A Man *[73]*
We're An American Band *[73]*

GRATEFUL DEAD
Alabama Getaway *[80]*
Bertha *[71]*
Casey Jones *[70]*
Dark Star *[70]*
Franklin's Tower *[75]*
Music Never Stopped *[75]*
One More Saturday Night *[72]*
Playing In The Band *[71]*
Ripple *[70]*
Shakedown Street *[78]*
St. Stephen *[69]*
Sugar Magnolia *[70]*
Terrapin Station *[77]*
Truckin' *[70]*
Turn On Your Love Light *[70]*
Uncle John's Band *[70]*

GREENBAUM, Norman
Spirit In The Sky *[70]*

GUESS WHO, The
Albert Flasher *[71]*
American Woman *[70]*
Clap For The Wolfman *[74]*
Dancin' Fool *[75]*
Hand Me Down World *[70]*
Laughing *[69]*
No Sugar Tonight/New Mother Nature *[70]*
No Time *[69]*
Share The Land *[70]*
Star Baby *[74]*
These Eyes *[69]*
Undun *[69]*

HARRISON, George
Bangla-Desh *[71]*
Blow Away *[79]*
Crackerbox Palace *[76]*
Dark Horse *[74]*
Ding Dong; Ding Dong *[74]*
Give Me Love (Give Me Peace On Earth) *[73]*
Isn't It A Pity *[70]*
My Sweet Lord *[70]*
This Song *[76]*
What Is Life *[71]*
You *[75]*

HEAD EAST
Never Been Any Reason *[75]*
Since You've Been Gone *[78]*

HEART
Barracuda *[77]*
Crazy On You *[76]*
Dog & Butterfly *[78]*
Dreamboat Annie *[76]*
Even It Up *[80]*
Heartless *[78]*
Kick It Out *[77]*
Little Queen *[77]*
Magic Man *[76]*
Straight On *[78]*
Tell It Like It Is *[80]*

HENDRIX, Jimi
All Along The Watchtower *[68]*
Angel *[71]*
Are You Experienced? *[67]*
Burning Of The Midnight Lamp *[68]*
Crosstown Traffic *[68]*
Dolly Dagger *[71]*
Fire *[67]*
Foxey Lady *[67]*
Freedom *[71]*
Hey Joe *[67]*
If 6 Was 9 *[68]*
Little Wing *[68]*
Manic Depression *[67]*
Purple Haze *[67]*
Red House *[69]*
Star Spangled Banner *[71]*
Stone Free *[69]*
Third Stone From The Sun *[67]*
Up From The Skies *[68]*
Voodoo Child (Slight Return) *[68]*
Wind Cries Mary *[67]*

HOLLIES, The
Long Cool Woman (In A Black Dress) *[72]*

HUMBLE PIE
Hot 'N' Nasty *[72]*
I Don't Need No Doctor *[71]*
Stone Cold Fever *[71]*
30 Days In The Hole *[72]*

IDES OF MARCH, The
Vehicle [70]

IRON BUTTERFLY
In-A-Gadda-Da-Vida [68]

IT'S A BEAUTIFUL DAY
White Bird [69]

JACKSON, Joe
Is She Really Going Out With Him? [79]

JAMES GANG
Funk #49 [70]
Walk Away [71]

JEFFERSON AIRPLANE/ STARSHIP
Count On Me [78]
Crown Of Creation [68]
Greasy Heart [68]
Jane [79]
Miracles [75]
Plastic Fantastic Lover [67]
Play On Love [75]
Pretty As You Feel [71]
Ride The Tiger [74]
Runaway [78]
Somebody To Love [67]
Volunteers [69]
White Rabbit [67]
With Your Love [76]

JETHRO TULL
Aqualung [71]
Bouree [69]
Bungle In The Jungle [74]
Cross-Eyed Mary [71]
Hymn 43 [71]
Living In The Past [72]
Locomotive Breath [71]
Minstrel In The Gallery [75]
New Day Yesterday [69]
Skating Away On The Thin Ice Of A New Day [74]
Teacher [70]
Thick As A Brick [72]
Too Old To Rock 'N' Roll: Too Young To Die [76]

JOEL, Billy
All For Leyna [80]
Ballad Of Billy The Kid [74]
Big Shot [78]
Captain Jack [74]
Close To The Borderline [80]
Don't Ask Me Why [80]
Entertainer, The [74]
Honesty [78]
It's Still Rock And Roll To Me [80]
Just The Way You Are [77]
Movin' Out (Anthony's Song) [77]
My Life [78]
New York State Of Mind [76]

JOEL, Billy — Cont'd
Only The Good Die Young [77]
Piano Man [74]
Rosalinda's Eyes [78]
Scenes From An Italian Restaurant [77]
She's Always A Woman [77]
Sometimes A Fantasy [80]
Stranger, The [77]
You May Be Right [80]

JOHN, Elton
Bennie And The Jets [73]
Bitch Is Back [74]
Border Song [70]
Burn Down The Mission [71]
Candle In The Wind [73]
Crocodile Rock [73]
Daniel [73]
Don't Let The Sun Go Down On Me [74]
Funeral For A Friend/Love Lies Bleeding [73]
Goodbye Yellow Brick Road [73]
Grey Seal [73]
Grow Some Funk Of Your Own [75]
Harmony [73]
Hercules [72]
Honky Cat [72]
Island Girl [75]
Levon [71]
Lucy In The Sky With Diamonds [74]
Madman Across The Water [71]
Mona Lisas And Mad Hatters [72]
Philadelphia Freedom [75]
Pinball Wizard [75]
Rocket Man [72]
Saturday Night's Alright For Fighting [73]
Someone Saved My Life Tonight [75]
Step Into Christmas [73]
Take Me To The Pilot [70]
Tiny Dancer [71]
Your Song [70]

JOHNSTON, Tom
Savannah Nights [79]

JONES, Rickie Lee
Chuck E.'s In Love [79]

JOPLIN, Janis
Cry Baby [71]
Get It While You Can [71]
Kozmic Blues [69]
Me And Bobby McGee [71]
Mercedes Benz [71]
Move Over [71]
Try (Just A Little Bit Harder) [69]

JOURNEY
Any Way You Want It [80]
Anytime [78]
Just The Same Way [79]

JOURNEY — Cont'd
Lights [78]
Lovin', Touchin', Squeezin' [79]
Walks Like A Lady [80]
Wheel In The Sky [78]

JUDAS PRIEST
Breaking The Law [80]
Living After Midnight [80]

KANSAS
Carry On Wayward Son [76]
Dust In The Wind [77]
Hold On [80]
People Of The South Wind [79]
Point Of Know Return [77]
Portrait (He Knew) [77]

KING, Carole
I Feel The Earth Move [71]
It's Too Late [71]
So Far Away [71]

KING CRIMSON
Court Of The Crimson King [69]

KINGS, The
This Beat Goes On/Switchin' To Glide [80]

KINKS, The
All Day And All Of The Night [65]
Apeman [70]
Celluloid Heroes [72]
Father Christmas [77]
Lola [70]
Low Budget [79]
Rock 'N' Roll Fantasy [78]
Sleepwalker [77]
Sunny Afternoon [66]
Tired Of Waiting For You [65]
Victoria [70]
Well Respected Man [66]
(Wish I Could Fly Like) Superman [79]
You Really Got Me [64]

KISS
Beth [76]
Calling Dr. Love [76]
Christine Sixteen [77]
Cold Gin [74]
Detroit Rock City [76]
Deuce [74]
Hard Luck Woman [76]
Hotter Than Hell [74]
I Was Made For Lovin' You [79]
Love Gun [77]
Nothin' To Lose [74]
Rock And Roll All Nite [75]
Rocket Ride [78]
Shout It Out Loud [76]
Strutter [74]
Sure Know Something [79]

KNACK, The
Baby Talks Dirty [80]
Frustrated [79]
Good Girls Don't [79]
My Sharona [79]

LED ZEPPELIN
All My Love [79]
Babe I'm Gonna Leave You [69]
Black Dog [71]
Communication Breakdown [69]
Crunge, The [73]
D'yer Mak'er [73]
Dancing Days [73]
Dazed And Confused [69]
Fool In The Rain [79]
Gallows Pole [70]
Going To California [71]
Good Times Bad Times [69]
Heartbreaker [69]
Hot Dog [79]
Houses Of The Holy [75]
How Many More Times [69]
I Can't Quit You Baby [69]
Immigrant Song [70]
In The Evening [79]
Kashmir [75]
Living Loving Maid (She's Just A
    Woman) [69]
Misty Mountain Hop [71]
Nobody's Fault But Mine [76]
Ocean, The [73]
Over The Hills And Far Away [73]
Rain Song [73]
Ramble On [69]
Rock And Roll [71]
Since I've Been Loving You [70]
Song Remains The Same [73]
Stairway To Heaven [71]
Thank You [69]
Trampled Under Foot [75]
What Is And What Should Never Be
    [69]
When The Levee Breaks [71]
Whole Lotta Love [69]

LENNON, John
Beautiful Boy (Darling Boy) [80]
Cold Turkey [70]
Give Peace A Chance [69]
God [70]
Happy Xmas (War Is Over) [71]
Imagine [71]
Instant Karma (We All Shine On)
    [70]
(Just Like) Starting Over [80]
Mind Games [73]
Mother [70]
#9 Dream [74]
Power To The People [71]

LENNON, John — Cont'd
Stand By Me [75]
Whatever Gets You Thru The Night
    [74]
Woman Is The Nigger Of The World
    [72]

LIGHTFOOT, Gordon
Carefree Highway [74]
If You Could Read My Mind [70]
Sundown [74]
Wreck Of The Edmund Fitzgerald
    [76]

LIGHTHOUSE
One Fine Morning [71]

LOGGINS & MESSINA
Danny's Song [72]
My Music [73]
Your Mama Don't Dance [72]

LOVE
Alone Again Or [68]
My Little Red Book [66]
7 And 7 Is [66]

LOWE, Nick
Cruel To Be Kind [79]

LYNYRD SKYNYRD
Call Me The Breeze [74]
Don't Ask Me No Questions [74]
Double Trouble [76]
Free Bird [73]
Gimme Back My Bullets [76]
Gimme Three Steps [73]
I Ain't The One [73]
Saturday Night Special [75]
Sweet Home Alabama [74]
That Smell [77]
What's Your Name [77]
Workin' For MCA [74]
You Got That Right [77]

MANFRED MANN
Blinded By The Light [76]
Do Wah Diddy Diddy [64]
Mighty Quinn (Quinn The Eskimo)
    [68]
Spirit In The Night [75]

MARSHALL TUCKER BAND, The
Can't You See [73]
Fire On The Mountain [75]
Heard It In A Love Song [77]

MASON, Dave
Let It Go, Let It Flow [77]
Only You Know And I Know [70]
So High (Rock Me Baby And Roll
    Me Away) [77]
We Just Disagree [77]

MAYALL, John
Don't Waste My Time [70]
Room To Move [69]

McCARTNEY, Paul
Another Day [71]
Arrow Through Me [79]
Band On The Run [74]
Bip Bop [71]
Coming Up [80]
Getting Closer [79]
Goodnight Tonight [79]
Helen Wheels [74]
Hi, Hi, Hi [73]
I've Had Enough [78]
Jet [74]
Junior's Farm [74]
Let 'Em In [76]
Letting Go [75]
Listen To What The Man Said [75]
Live And Let Die [73]
London Town [78]
Maybe I'm Amazed [70]
My Love [73]
Nineteen Hundred And Eighty Five
    [74]
Silly Love Songs [76]
Uncle Albert/Admiral Halsey [71]
Venus And Mars/Rock Show [75]
With A Little Luck [78]

McCLINTON, Delbert
Giving It Up For Your Love [80]

MC5
Kick Out The Jams [69]

McGUINN, CLARK & HILLMAN
Don't You Write Her Off [79]

McLEAN, Don
American Pie [72]

MEAT LOAF
Bat Out Of Hell [77]
Paradise By The Dashboard Light
    [77]
Two Out Three Ain't Bad [77]
You Took The Words Right Out Of
    My Mouth [77]

MEISNER, Randy
Deep Inside My Heart [80]

MELLENCAMP, John Cougar
I Need A Lover [79]
This Time [80]

MICHAELS, Lee
Do You Know What I Mean [71]

MILLER, Steve, Band
Dance, Dance, Dance [76]
Fly Like An Eagle [76]
Gangster Of Love [68]
Going To The Country [70]
Jet Airliner [77]
Joker, The [73]

MILLER, Steve, Band — Cont'd
Jungle Love [77]
Living In The U.S.A. [68]
Rock'n Me [76]
Space Cowboy [69]
Swingtown [77]
Take The Money And Run [76]
Your Cash Ain't Nothin' But Trash [73]

MITCHELL, Joni
Big Yellow Taxi [70]
Free Man In Paris [74]
Help Me [74]

MOBY GRAPE
Hey Grandma [67]
Omaha [67]

MOLLY HATCHET
Flirtin' With Disaster [79]

MONEY, Eddie
Baby Hold On [78]
Gimme Some Water [79]
Maybe I'm A Fool [79]
Two Tickets To Paradise [78]

MOODY BLUES, The
Driftwood [78]
Eyes Of A Child [70]
Go Now! [65]
I'm Just A Singer (In A Rock And Roll Band) [72]
Isn't Life Strange [72]
Legend Of A Mind [68]
Never Comes The Day [69]
Nights In White Satin [68]
Question [70]
Ride My See-Saw [68]
Steppin' In A Slide Zone [78]
Story In Your Eyes [71]
Tuesday Afternoon (Forever Afternoon) [68]

MORRISON, Van
Blue Money [71]
Brown Eyed Girl [67]
Call Me Up In Dreamland [71]
Come Running [70]
Crazy Love [70]
Domino [71]
Into The Mystic [70]
Jackie Wilson Said (I'm In Heaven When You Smile) [72]
Moondance [70]
Redwood Tree [72]
Tupelo Honey [71]
Wavelength [78]
Wild Night [71]

MOTT THE HOOPLE
All The Young Dudes [72]

MOUNTAIN
Mississippi Queen [70]

NASH, Graham
Chicago [71]

NAZARETH
Hair Of The Dog [75]
Love Hurts [75]
This Flight Tonight [74]

NEWMAN, Randy
Political Science [72]
Sail Away [72]
Short People [77]

NITTY GRITTY DIRT BAND
Mr. Bojangles [71]

NUGENT, Ted
Cat Scratch Fever [77]
Dog Eat Dog [76]
Free-For-All [76]
Hey Baby [75]
Home Bound [77]
Need You Bad [78]
Wang Dang Sweet Poontang [77]
Wango Tango [80]
Yank Me, Crank Me [78]

ORLEANS
Dance With Me [75]

OUTLAWS
Green Grass & High Tides [75]
There Goes Another Love Song [75]

OZARK MOUNTAIN DAREDEVILS
If You Wanna Get To Heaven [74]
Jackie Blue [75]

PALMER, Robert
Bad Case Of Loving You (Doctor, Doctor) [79]
Can We Still Be Friends [79]
Every Kinda People [78]

PARSONS, Alan, Project
Breakdown [77]
Damned If I Do [79]
Don't Let It Show [77]
Games People Play [80]
I Robot [77]
I Wouldn't Want To Be Like You [77]
Raven, The [76]
(System Of) Doctor Tarr And Professor Feather [76]
What Goes Up [78]

PETTY, Tom, And The Heartbreakers
American Girl [77]
Breakdown [77]
Don't Do Me Like That [79]
Even The Losers [79]
Here Comes My Girl [79]
I Need To Know [78]

PETTY, Tom, And The Heartbreakers — Cont'd
Listen To Her Heart [78]
Refugee [79]

PINK FLOYD
Another Brick In The Wall [80]
Brain Damage/Eclipse [73]
Comfortably Numb [80]
Great Gig In The Sky [73]
Have A Cigar [75]
Hey You [80]
Money [73]
One Of These Days [71]
Run Like Hell [80]
See Emily Play [67]
Shine On You Crazy Diamond [75]
Speak To Me/Breathe [73]
Time [73]
Us And Them [73]
Welcome To The Machine [75]
Wish You Were Here [75]
Young Lust [80]

POCO
Crazy Love [79]
Heart Of The Night [79]

POLICE, The
De Do Do Do, De Da Da Da [80]
Message In A Bottle [79]
Roxanne [79]

PRETENDERS, The
Brass In Pocket (I'm Special) [80]
Stop Your Sobbing [80]

PROCOL HARUM
Conquistador [72]
Whiter Shade Of Pale [67]

PURE PRAIRIE LEAGUE
Amie [75]

QUEEN
Another One Bites The Dust [80]
Bicycle Race [78]
Bohemian Rhapsody [76]
Crazy Little Thing Called Love [80]
Don't Stop Me Now [78]
Don't Try Suicide [80]
Fat Bottomed Girls [78]
Killer Queen [75]
Play The Game [80]
Somebody To Love [77]
Tie Your Mother Down [77]
We Will Rock You/We Are The Champions [77]
You're My Best Friend [76]

? (QUESTION MARK) & THE MYSTERIANS
96 Tears [66]

QUICKSILVER MESSENGER SERVICE
Fresh Air [70]

RAFFERTY, Gerry
Baker Street [78]
Home And Dry [78]
Right Down The Line [78]

RAINBOW
Since You Been Gone [79]

RAM JAM
Black Betty [77]

RAMONES
Do You Remember Rock 'N' Roll
Radio [80]
Do You Wanna Dance [78]
I Wanna Be Sedated [78]
Rock 'N' Roll High School [80]
Rockaway Beach [78]
Sheena Is A Punk Rocker [77]

RARE EARTH
Get Ready [70]
I Just Want To Celebrate [71]

RASPBERRIES
Go All The Way [72]
I Wanna Be With You [73]

REED, Lou
Coney Island Baby [76]
Sally Can't Dance [74]
Satellite Of Love [73]
Street Hassle [78]
Sweet Jane [74]
Walk On The Wild Side [73]
White Light/White Heat [74]

REO SPEEDWAGON
Ridin' The Storm Out [74]
Roll With The Changes [78]
Time For Me To Fly [78]

ROCKETS
Oh Well [79]

ROLLING STONES, The
Ain't Too Proud To Beg [74]
Angie [73]
As Tears Go By [66]
Beast Of Burden [78]
Bitch [71]
Brown Sugar [71]
Dandelion [67]
Doo Doo Doo Doo Doo
(Heartbreaker) [73]
Emotional Rescue [80]
Far Away Eyes [78]
Fool To Cry [76]
Get Off Of My Cloud [65]
Gimme Shelter [69]
Happy [72]
Have You Seen Your Mother, Baby,
Standing In The Shadow? [66]
Heart Of Stone [65]

ROLLING STONES, The — Cont'd
Honky Tonk Women [69]
(I Can't Get No) Satisfaction [65]
It's All Over Now [64]
It's Only Rock 'N Roll (But I Like It)
[74]
Jumpin' Jack Flash [68]
Lady Jane [66]
Last Time [65]
Let's Spend The Night Together [67]
Miss You [78]
Mothers Little Helper [66]
19th Nervous Breakdown [66]
Not Fade Away [64]
Paint It, Black [66]
Ruby Tuesday [67]
Shattered [78]
She's A Rainbow [68]
She's So Cold [80]
Street Fighting Man [68]
Sympathy For The Devil [68]
Tell Me (You're Coming Back) [64]
Time Is On My Side [64]
Tumbling Dice [72]
Under My Thumb [66]
Wild Horses [71]
You Can't Always Get What You
Want [69]

ROMANTICS, The
What I Like About You [80]

RONSTADT, Linda
How Do I Make You [80]
Poor Poor Pitiful Me [77]
Tumbling Dice [77]
You're No Good [75]

ROXY MUSIC
Love Is The Drug [76]

RUNDGREN, Todd
Can We Still Be Friends [78]
Good Vibrations [76]
Hello It's Me [73]
I Saw The Light [72]
We Gotta Get You A Woman [71]

RUSH
Closer To The Heart [77]
Fly By Night [75]
Freewill [80]
Spirit Of Radio [80]

RUSSELL, Leon
Tight Rope [72]

RYDER, Mitch, And The Detroit Wheels
Devil With A Blue Dress On & Good
Golly Miss Molly [66]
Jenny Take A Ride! [66]
Sock It To Me-Baby! [67]

SANFORD/TOWNSEND BAND, The
Smoke From A Distant Fire [77]

SANTANA
Black Magic Woman/Gypsy Queen
[70]
Everybody's Everything [71]
Evil Ways [69]
Jingo [69]
Let It Shine [76]
No One To Depend On [71]
One Chain (Don't Make No Prison)
[78]
Oye Como Va [70]
She's Not There [77]
Stormy [78]
You Know That I Love You [79]

SCAGGS, Boz
Breakdown Dead Ahead [80]
Georgia [76]
It's Over [76]
JoJo [80]
Lido Shuffle [76]
Lowdown [76]
Miss Sun [80]

SEALS & CROFTS
Diamond Girl [73]
Summer Breeze [72]

SEEDS, The
Pushin' Too Hard [67]

SEGER, Bob
Against The Wind [80]
Beautiful Loser [75]
Betty Lou's Getting' Out Tonight [80]
Feel Like A Number [78]
Fire Down Below [77]
Fire Lake [80]
Get Out Of Denver [76]
Her Strut [80]
Hollywood Nights [78]
Horizontal Bop [80]
Katmandu [75]
Mainstreet [77]
Night Moves [77]
Old Time Rock & Roll [78]
Ramblin' Gamblin' Man [69]
Rock And Roll Never Forgets [77]
Still The Same [78]
Travelin' Man [75]
Turn The Page [76]
We've Got Tonite [78]
You'll Accomp'ny Me [80]

SEX PISTOLS
Anarchy In The U.K. [77]
God Save The Queen [77]
Pretty Vacant [77]

SHADOWS OF KNIGHT, The
Gloria [66]

SIMON, Carly
You're So Vain [73]

SIMON, Paul
American Tune [73]
50 Ways To Leave Your Lover [75]
Kodachrome [73]
Late In The Evening [80]
Loves Me Like A Rock [73]
Me And Julio Down By The Schoolyard [72]
Mother And Child Reunion [72]
Slip Slidin' Away [77]
Still Crazy After All These Years [75]

SIMON & GARFUNKEL
America [68]
Boxer, The [69]
Bridge Over Troubled Water [70]
Cecilia [70]
Hazy Shade Of Winter [66]
Homeward Bound [66]
I Am A Rock [66]
Mrs. Robinson [68]
My Little Town [75]
Sounds Of Silence [66]

SMALL FACES
Itchycoo Park [68]

SMITH, Patti, Group
Because The Night [78]

SNIFF 'N' THE TEARS
Driver's Seat [79]

SPIRIT
I Got A Line On You [69]
Nature's Way [71]

SPRINGSTEEN, Bruce
Badlands [78]
Blinded By The Light [73]
Born To Run [75]
Darkness On The Edge Of Town [78]
For You [73]
4th Of July, Asbury Park (Sandy) [73]
Hungry Heart [80]
Jungleland [75]
Prove It All Night [78]
Rosalita (Come Out Tonight) [73]
Spirit In The Night [73]
Tenth Avenue Freeze-Out [75]
Thunder Road [75]

STARR, Ringo
Back Off Boogaloo [72]
It Don't Come Easy [71]
No No Song [75]
Oh My My [73]
Photograph [73]
You're Sixteen [73]

STATUS QUO, The
Pictures Of Matchstick Men [68]

STEALER'S WHEEL
Stuck In The Middle With You [73]

STEELY DAN
Aja [77]
Any Major Dude Will Tell You [74]
Babylon Sisters [80]
Black Cow [77]
Black Friday [75]
Bodhisattva [73]
Deacon Blues [77]
Dirty Work [72]
Do It Again [72]
FM (No Static At All) [78]
Fez, The [76]
Hey Nineteen [80]
Josie [77]
Kid Charlemagne [76]
My Old School [73]
Peg [77]
Pretzel Logic [74]
Reeling In The Years [72]
Rikki Don't Lose That Number [74]

STEPPENWOLF
Born To Be Wild [68]
Hey Lawdy Mama [70]
Magic Carpet Ride [68]
Monster [70]
Pusher, The [68]
Rock Me [69]

STEVENS, Cat
Another Saturday Night [74]
Moon Shadow [71]
Morning Has Broken [71]
Oh Very Young [74]
Peace Train [71]
Wild World [71]

STEWART, Al
Year Of The Cat [77]

STEWART, John
Gold [79]
Lost Her In The Sun [79]
Midnight Wind [79]

STEWART, Rod
Ain't Love A Bitch [79]
Angel [72]
Cut Across Shorty [70]
Da Ya Think I'm Sexy? [79]
Every Picture Tells A Story [71]
First Cut Is The Deepest [76]
Handbags And Gladrags [69]
Hot Legs [77]
(I Know) I'm Losing You [71]
I Was Only Joking [77]
Killing Of Georgie [76]
Maggie May [71]
Mine For Me [74]
Passion [80]
Reason To Believe [71]
Sailing [75]

STEWART, Rod — Cont'd
Stay With Me [72]
This Old Heart Of Mine [75]
Tonight's The Night (Gonna Be Alright) [76]
You Wear It Well [72]
You're In My Heart (The Final Acclaim) [77]

STILLS, Stephen
Change Partners [71]
Love The One You're With [70]
Sit Yourself Down [70]

STRAWBERRY ALARM CLOCK
Incense And Peppermints [67]

STYX
Babe [79]
Blue Collar Man (Long Nights) [78]
Come Sail Away [77]
Crystal Ball [76]
Fooling Yourself (The Angry Young Man) [77]
Grand Illusion [77]
Lady [75]
Lorelei [76]
Mademoiselle [76]
Renegade [78]
Sing For The Day [78]
Suite Madame Blue [76]
Why Me [79]

SUGARLOAF
Green-Eyed Lady [70]

SUPERTRAMP
Bloody Well Right [75]
Breakfast In America [79]
Dreamer [75]
Give A Little Bit [77]
Goodbye Stranger [79]
Logical Song [79]
Rudy [75]
School [75]
Take The Long Way Home [79]

SWEET
Ballroom Blitz [75]
Fox On The Run [75]

TALKING HEADS
Life During Wartime [79]
Once In A Lifetime [80]
Psycho Killer [77]
Take Me To The River [78]

TAYLOR, James
Fire And Rain [70]
Handy Man [77]
How Sweet It Is (To Be Loved By You) [75]
Shower The People [76]
You've Got A Friend [71]
Your Smiling Face [77]

10cc
I'm Not In Love *[75]*
Things We Do For Love *[77]*

TEN YEARS AFTER
I'd Love To Change The World *[71]*

THEM
Gloria *[65]*
Here Comes The Night *[65]*
Mystic Eyes *[65]*

THIN LIZZY
Boys Are Back In Town *[76]*

THREE DOG NIGHT
Celebrate *[69]*
Easy To Be Hard *[69]*
Eli's Coming *[69]*
Joy To The World *[71]*
Liar *[71]*
Mama Told Me (Not To Come) *[70]*
Never Been To Spain *[71]*
Old Fashioned Love Song *[71]*
One *[69]*
Shambala *[73]*
Try A Little Tenderness *[69]*

THUNDERCLAP NEWMAN
Something In The Air *[69]*

TOTO
Hold The Line *[78]*
I'll Supply The Love *[78]*
99 *[79]*

TOWNSHEND, Pete
Let My Love Open The Door *[80]*
Rough Boys *[80]*

TRAFFIC
Dear Mr. Fantasy *[68]*
Empty Pages *[70]*
Feelin' Alright? *[68]*
Forty Thousand Headmen *[68]*
Freedom Rider *[70]*
Hole In My Shoe *[68]*
John Barleycorn *[70]*
Low Spark of High Heeled Boys *[71]*
Paper Sun *[68]*
Rock & Roll Stew *[71]*
You Can All Join In *[68]*

TRAVERS, Pat, Band
Boom Boom (Out Go The Lights) *[79]*

T. REX
Bang A Gong (Get It Out) *[72]*

TRIUMPH
Hold On *[79]*
I Can Survive *[80]*
I Live For The Weekend *[80]*
Lay It On The Line *[79]*
Rock & Roll Machine *[78]*

TROGGS, The
Wild Thing *[66]*

TROWER, Robin
Bridge Of Sighs *[74]*
Caledonia *[76]*
Day Of The Eagle *[74]*
Little Bit Of Sympathy *[74]*
Too Rolling Stoned *[74]*
Victims Of The Fury *[80]*

URIAH HEEP
Easy Livin *[72]*
Stealin' *[73]*

VAN HALEN
Ain't Talkin' ' Bout Love *[78]*
And The Cradle Will Rock... *[80]*
Beautiful Girls *[79]*
Dance The Night Away *[79]*
Ice Cream Man *[78]*
Jamie's Cryin' *[78]*
Runnin' With The Devil *[78]*
You Really Got Me *[78]*

VANILLA FUDGE
You Keep Me Hangin' On *[67]*

WALSH, Joe
All Night Long *[80]*
Life's Been Good *[78]*
Meadows *[73]*
Rocky Mountain Way *[73]*

WAR
Cisco Kid *[73]*
Low Rider *[75]*

WELCH, Bob
Ebony Eyes *[77]*
Precious Love *[79]*
Sentimental Lady *[77]*

WET WILLIE
Keep On Smilin' *[74]*

WHO, The
Baba O'Riley *[71]*
Bargain *[71]*
Behind Blue Eyes *[71]*
Boris The Spider *[67]*
Call Me Lightning *[68]*
5:15 *[73]*
Goin' Mobile *[71]*
Happy Jack *[67]*
I Can See For Miles *[67]*
I Can't Explain *[65]*
I'm Free *[69]*
Join Together *[72]*
Kids Are Alright *[71]*
Long Live Rock *[79]*
Love, Reign, O'er Me *[73]*
Magic Bus *[68]*
My Generation *[66]*
My Wife *[6]*
Pictures Of Lily *[67]*

WHO, The — Cont'd
Pinball Wizard *[69]*
Real Me *[73]*
Relay, The *[73]*
See Me, Feel Me *[70]*
Seeker, The *[70]*
Squeeze Box *[75]*
Substitute *[66]*
Summertime Blues *[70]*
We're Not Gonna Take It *[69]*
Who Are You *[78]*
Won't Get Fooled Again *[71]*

WINTER, Edgar, Group
Frankenstein *[73]*
Free Ride *[73]*

WRIGHT, Gary
Dream Weaver *[76]*
Love Is Alive *[76]*

YARDBIRDS, The
For Your Love *[65]*
Heart Full Of Soul *[65]*
I'm A Man *[65]*
Little Games *[67]*
Over Under Sideways Down *[66]*
Shapes Of Things *[66]*

YES
America *[72]*
And You And I *[72]*
Close To The Edge *[72]*
Every Little Thing *[69]*
Going For The One *[77]*
Long Distance Runaround *[72]*
Roundabout *[72]*
Starship Trooper *[71]*
Your Move/All Good People *[71]*
Yours Is No Disgrace *[71]*

YOUNG, Neil
After The Gold Rush *[70]*
Cinnamon Girl *[69]*
Comes A Time *[78]*
Cowgirl In The Sand *[69]*
Down By The River *[69]*
Four Strong Winds *[78]*
Heart Of Gold *[72]*
Like A Hurricane *[77]*
Needle And The Damage Done *[72]*
Old Man *[72]*
Only Love Can Break Your Heart *[70]*
Rust Never Sleeps (Hey Hey, My My) *[79]*
Southern Man *[70]*
Walk On *[74]*
When You Dance I Can Really Love *[70]*

YOUNGBLOODS, The
Get Together *[67]*

ZAPPA, Frank
Cosmik Debris *[74]*
Dancin' Fool *[79]*
Don't Eat The Yellow Snow *[74]*
Joe's Garage *[79]*
Montana *[73]*
My Guitar Wants To Kill Your Mama *[70]*
Peaches En Regalia *[69]*
Transylvania Boogie *[70]*

ZEVON, Warren
Certain Girl *[80]*
Excitable Boy *[78]*
Lawyers, Guns And Money *[78]*
Werewolves Of London *[78]*

ZOMBIES, The
She's Not There *[64]*
Tell Her No *[65]*
Time Of The Season *[69]*

ZZ TOP
Arrested For Driving While Blind *[77]*
Cheap Sunglasses *[80]*
Francene *[72]*
Heard It On The X *[75]*
I Thank You *[80]*
I'm Bad, I'm Nationwide *[80]*
It's Only Love *[77]*
La Grange *[73]*
Tush *[75]*
Waitin' For The Bus/Jesus Just Left Chicago *[72]*

THE RECORD RESEARCH COLLECTION

TOP POP SINGLES 1955-1999 .... 960 pages. $79.95 Hardcover / $69.95 Softcover.
POP ANNUAL 1955-1999 .... 912 pages. $79.95 Hardcover / $69.95 Softcover.
HIT LIST 1955-1999 .... 304 pages. Spiral-bound softcover. $39.95.
POP HITS SINGLES & ALBUMS 1940-1954 .... 576 pages. Hardcover. $69.95.
POP MEMORIES 1890-1954 .... 660 pages. Hardcover. $59.95.
TOP POP ALBUMS 1955-2001 .... 1,208 pages. Hardcover. $99.95.
ALBUM CUTS 1955-2001 .... 720 pages. Hardcover. $44.95.
BILLBOARD HOT 100 CHARTS/THE NINETIES 1990-1999 .... 552 pages. Deluxe Hardcover. $79.95.
BILLBOARD HOT 100 CHARTS/THE EIGHTIES 1980-1989 .... 552 pages. Deluxe Hardcover. $79.95.
BILLBOARD HOT 100 CHARTS/THE SEVENTIES 1970-1979 .... 560 pages. Deluxe Hardcover. $79.95.
BILLBOARD HOT 100 CHARTS/THE SIXTIES 1960-1969 .... 568 pages. Deluxe Hardcover. $79.95.
BILLBOARD POP SINGLES CHARTS 1955-1959 .... 496 pages. Deluxe Hardcover. $59.95.
BILLBOARD POP ALBUM CHARTS 1965-1969 .... 496 pages. Deluxe Hardcover. $59.95.
TOP ADULT CONTEMPORARY 1961-2001 .... 352 pages. Hardcover. $44.95.
TOP COUNTRY SINGLES 1944-2001 .... 608 pages. Hardcover. $69.95.
COUNTRY ANNUAL 1944-1997 .... 704 pages. Hardcover. $64.95.
TOP COUNTRY ALBUMS 1964-1997 .... 304 pages. Hardcover. $49.95.
A CENTURY OF POP MUSIC 1990-1999 .... 256 pages. Softcover. $39.95.
TOP R&B SINGLES 1942-1999 .... 688 pages. Hardcover. $69.95.
TOP R&B ALBUMS 1965-1998 .... 360 pages. Hardcover. $49.95.
ROCK TRACKS 2002 Edition .... 336 pages. Hardcover. $49.95.
BUBBLING UNDER SINGLES AND ALBUMS 1998 Edition .... 416 pages. Softcover. $49.95.
BILLBOARD TOP 10 SINGLES CHARTS 1955-2000 .... 712 pages. Hardcover. $49.95.
BILLBOARD TOP 10 ALBUM CHARTS 1963-1998 .... 536 pages. Hardcover. $39.95.
BILLBOARD SINGLES REVIEWS 1958 .... 280 pages. Softcover. $29.95.
BILLBOARD TOP 1000 x 5 1996 Edition .... 288 pages. Softcover. $29.95.
DAILY #1 HITS 1940-1992 .... 392 pages. Spiral-bound softcover. $24.95.
MUSIC YEARBOOKS 2001/2000/1999 .... Various page lengths. Softcover. $39.95 each.
MUSIC YEARBOOKS 1998/1997/1996/1995 .... Various page lengths. Softcover. $34.95 each.
MUSIC YEARBOOKS 1994/1993/1992/1991/1990 .... Various page lengths. Softcover. $29.95 each.

Ordering Information:

Shipping/Handling Extra — If you do not order through our online Web site (see below), please contact us for shipping rates.

Order By:

☎ **U.S. Toll-Free:** **1-800-827-9810**
(orders only please – Mon-Fri 8 AM-12 PM, 1 PM-5 PM CST)

Foreign Orders: 1-262-251-5408

Questions?: 1-262-251-5408 or **E-mail:** books@recordresearch.com

🖥 **Online at our Web site:** www.recordresearch.com

📄 **Fax** (24 hours): 1-262-251-9452

📫 **Mail:** Record Research Inc.
P.O. Box 200
Menomonee Falls, WI 53052-0200   U.S.A.